THE REVELATION RAINBOW

THE BOOK COVER

God is not a man that he should lie (Nu 23:19). No, God is a Spirit, and "Those who worship Him will worship in Spirit and in TRUTH" (Jn 4:24). Yes, our book cover has some very graphic depictions of God on the THRONE in the center of the universe. The Godhead is surrounded by the attesting celestial beings and sensations that we earthlings have learned to understand or perceive only by seeing with our enlightened eyes. IT IS UNDERSTOOD, THAT NO FLESH CAN SEE GOD'S GLORY (1Co 1:29). LIKEWISE, FLESH AND BLOOD CANNOT INHERIT THE KINGDOM OF GOD (1Co 15:50).

When I ask talented young lady Brittany Martin to do an artistic conception of what she read about God on the throne and the covenant rainbow over His head, she drew what she read in John's vision (Rev 4:3). The rainbow spanning the presence of divinity is not depicted as our seven-colored rainbow that always has red on top, which we take to represent the cleansing blood of Christ for the sins of the world. In John's vision, the rainbow had the glow of an emerald, a greenish-yellow color.

Larry Lee asked if he should represent the rainbow with seven colors, like we see it from Earth. I told Larry to use the seven-colored rainbow because this is how the rainbow appears to us on the underside of heaven, beneath God's throne. Of course, we know the scientific-meteorological explanations for why the rainbow appears as it does to the human eye. God is the God of LAW. God ordains all spiritual laws, physical laws, and laws of human morality. We see seven-colored rainbows when sunlight is refracted, reflected, and dispersed in water droplets after a rainstorm. Prisms provide us the same seven- colored spectrum. God gave the rainbow as a reminder of His covenant with us: The law of the God of physics will always exist, as long as the Earth and heavens exist. We are reminded of His covenant every time we see the rainbow (Ge 9:17). But unlike the earthly rainbow, the rainbow surrounding the Heavenly Throne must be an emblem of His eternal, heavenly NEW COVENANT. Just as God is true to the end of His earthly covenant, He will be faithful and true to His Eternal Covenant of Christ.

The reason the rainbow above the heavens is like the glow of an emerald is because no rainstorms are there, and the light that causes a rainbow is not the Sun, for THE SON OF GOD IS THE LIGHT OF HEAVEN.

Both Larry and Brittany gave spiritual diligence and technical excellence to their art works. They must have met the requirements of Alexander Campbell, who was one of the first theological reformers who insisted that a man or woman could not accurately interpret Scripture unless they understood the laws of Hermeneutics. Campbell insisted that unless a person understood metaphors, similes, parables, synecdoche's, allegories, alliterations, personifications, parallelisms, types, antitypes, and other such expressions of divine vocabulary, especially in regard to apocalyptic literature (as we shall see in this book), they were unqualified to expound on the Scriptures with authority (Mt 7:29; Tit 2:15).

When we read the first chapters of Ezekiel and Revelation, we see glimpses of the glory of the Godhead, but we can only understand them in terms of human experiences with sights and sounds like the following: the "glowing furnace of fire," "hair like wool," a "sound as the rushing of mighty waters," a "vision like lightening," and "a voice as a trumpet." To Ezekiel and John, the things of the vision in human terms "seemed to be."

They "seemed to be" because "Christ dwells in unapproachable light, immortality, and majesty" (1Tit 6:16). Therefore, while human language, expressions, and familiarity with earthly sights and sounds aid us with visualizing in our spiritual minds just how awesome and majestic the eternal world of the Godhead must be, these human capacities fail to adequately reveal in pictorial language what the real Godhead is. Therefore, we must pray that our enlightened minds and eyes will be awakened by these inferior literary snapshots and by this pictorial language.

Thus, in our prayerful desire to extrapolate the great truths and message from the symbolic language and photos of The Apocalypse, we commend Larry Lee and Brittany Martin for enhancing our understanding of The Apocalypse.

Sincerely thankful,

Charles Walter Doughty

Other Books by Charles Walter Doughty

After Death-What?

Aids-Cause, Curse, Cure

Always be Prepared - Debates with Sabbatarian's, Jehovah Witnesses, and Charismatics

Biblical Anthropology

Christian Management

Christian Perfection

Death in the Pot

Perfectionism Debate

Conscience, Conviction & Control of the Holy Spirit

New Birth Process

My Most Intimate friend on Earth

Your Complex Nature

The Spirit's Work in Evangelism

The End (CDs and Outlines-Antichrist, Magog, Armageddon, 666, Millennialism, Tribulation)

Commentary on Hebrews

How Christ Plants a New Testament Church in Your Living Room

Crucified in Sodom

God Forbid that I Should Sin and Not Pray

Hermeneutics

Judgment Day Will Come This Sunday

Motivation-Congregational Management

Christian Management

Shine With Joy

Sidney Rigdon University

365 Days of Anxious Free Living

The Eternal King and His Kingdom

The Eternal Kingdom versus Pre-millennialism

The Greatest Mystery Story Ever Told

The Prospect of Prostate Cancer

The Reign of Christ-Here or Hereafter?

The Whole Counsel of God

We Must Remember our Deliverance

Why Am I Going to Hell?

Why Christians Have Happy Marriages

To Russia with Love

A Letter to Dr. Agnostheos,

The Divine Potential within Every Person

On My Way to Heaven in 2011

Soul Winning

God's Christmas Tree

Trashing the Bible

Angels, Demons, Satan

Debate on Calvinism.

CD SETS - 50 lectures on the Apocalypse, 12 Lectures on "Overcomers in 1st, 2nd, 3rd John", Trusting the Lord of the Harvest, End Times-Six Sermons, and Revelation Rainbow

THE REVELATION RAINBOW

By:

Charles Walter Doughty

Professor of Christian Kingdom College

Published by

Christian Kingdom College

Copyright 2016 A.D. by Charles Walter Doughty

All rights reserved. No part of this publication may be reproduced or transmitted in any form or by any means electronic or mechanical, including photocopy, recording, or any information storage and retrieval system now known or to be invented without permission in writing from the publisher, except by a reviewer who wishes to quote brief passages in connection with a review written for inclusion in a magazine, newspaper, website, broadcast, or by a teacher who wishes to use brief passages in connection with his class.

The author requests that a significant portion of royalties received go toward the training by the local congregation of evangelists, pastors, teachers, and disciples. This training shall focus upon the importance of The New Covenant Kingdom of Christ, and the establishing of New Covenant Christian congregations throughout the world. According to the Apostles Doctrine, this work is to be done by local congregations and not a para-congregation institution that is lacking an eldership given by Christ to protect His sheep from doctrinal apostasy and cultural-political-ecclesiastical corruption. History has proven that no matter how sincere their intentions, a board of directors can never insure the doctrinal stability or spiritual purity of an institution in succeeding generations, even if they call it a Bible College.

The appointed elders of each and any New Covenant congregation that establishes a Bible College education in their congregation may be eligible for financial assistance from the trust fund generated by the sale of this book. Our humble prayer is that this work will generate a vast amount of stewardship for the training of evangelist and pastors for full-time service; and likewise teachers or any Christian disciple who desires such college level Bible training.

Published by Dog Ear Publishing
4011 Vincennes Rd
Indianapolis, IN 46268
www.dogearpublishing.net

ISBN: 978-1-4575-4670-9

This book is printed on acid-free paper.

Printed in the United States of America

DEDICATION

Of the Big Three, Abraham, Isaac and Jacob, the historical Bible record of the Patriarch Isaac is the shortest, but Isaac lived the longest –180 years. When Isaac first beheld Rebecca, he was overwhelmed with love, affection, and devotion to this remarkable lady, "And he married her, and Isaac loved Rebecca and he took her home and she comforted Isaac after his Mother's death" (Ge 24:67).

But no man has reason to love his wife more than I have to love Dorothy Claire Elliott Doughty. As Isaac loved Rebecca at first sight, so (54 years ago) I loved "Dotty" the first time I saw her walking down the steps from the Girl's Dormitory to the dining hall for breakfast that Lord's Day morning at Kentucky Christian College. Dave Milliard said, "She sure is pretty isn't she?" I said, "Yes indeed!" Then Brother Milliard added, "A lot of other guys think she is pretty too." In that moment of reflection, I added in silent contemplation, "Yes, but I am going to get her!"

I believe firmly that God still plans marriages. God had a plan for my life as a soul winner and minister of Christ, and He knew I could not do it without the aid, influence, and help-mate assistance of such a darling, devoted Christian wife as Dotty. Yesterday she baked a pie and delivered it to a family I have been discipling. The mother of the husband in this family had just died. He was grieving with his wife and father. I have been teaching them, but a loving gesture, a cherry pie, and a beautiful countenance of a Christian lady like my dear companion of over 50 years goes a long, long way.

I have immersed hundreds of lost souls into Christ as a result of the Christian hospitality exhibited unconditionally, without any expectation of return by my Spirit-filled wife. And it is not a surprise that her children do the same. Thirty years ago, I wrote a love song for my wife. She has never seen it. The first time she will is when she reads the Dedication to this book, a lifetime project. My humble prayer is that if my Lord tarries, millions of others will read this book, and when they read this Dedication, they will realize that next to God so loving this world that He gave His ONLY begotten Son, He so loved husbands (like you and me) that He gave us the most exquisitely beautiful and valuable temple treasure that can be bestowed upon any man in this world – a Godly Woman.

By accepting the risk of belaboring this subject of dedicating this commentary to the wife so dear to my heart, I have condensed The Dedication by alerting the reader to three very pertinent factors.

1) John was in Spirit when he wrote The Apocalypse. In Spirit we understand things unseen. Of all earthly physical and spiritual relationships, marriage has the maximum potential of spiritual fulfillment.

2) The Apocalypse gives us a vision of Heaven and Earth as ONE. It even goes further in revealing the activity of things beneath the earth- The Abyss. The visions of The Bride of Christ and the Marriage of the Lamb portray to the spiritual mind that even though our marriages are temporary earthly institutions, they rise above all other earthly institutions as prototypes and examples (however weak and frail we seem at times) of the amazingly beautiful relationship we all have with Christ on His eternal throne.

3) We cannot look into the face of our Bride and not look up to heaven without being profoundly reminded of the words of James, "Every good and perfect gift comes down from the Father of Lights, in whom there is no shadow of changing" (Jas 1:17). Christ has given many gifts to His congregation, and each of them equips us to better follow and serve Him on our way to Heaven in eternity. It is more and more obvious that the most important part of His equipping us in our sojourn on Earth to the end of life (or at His return) is the provision of a spiritually compatible wife. She is a very unique gift in a lifetime that excels them all. Thus I speak, "Heaven made but ONE like you for me!"

I do not know how long I will live (I will never catch up with Isaac.), but I do know that the reason Isaac lived so long is because he was comforted and supported by such a Godly helpmate, companion, and friend as Rebecca. Like Isaac, I only want to live to advance the cause of our Eternal Messiah and King on Earth. Like Isaac, I want to leave behind a legacy of what the Lord has done in my life, and what He can do with any Christian man to whom He has given the heavenly blessing of a beloved wife.

HEAVEN MADE BUT ONE LIKE YOU FOR ME

FIRST STANZA

"I'll always love you. You mean the world to me
No one else can take my heart, so convincingly"
From eternity, the Lord had you in mind
And when He made your Soul-He matched it up with mine"

(Chorus)

"When you're around me, you make me feel secure
And though I love you, it makes me want to love you more"
If I should lose you, no one could take your place
Cause Heaven made but ONE like you for me"

SECOND STANZA

"In this world below, we have our trials you know
One by one they come and go just like the billows roll"
But you stood by me, so calm and silently,
Yes, heaven gave but ONE like you for me"

(Chorus)

"When you're around me, you make me feel secure
And though I love you, it makes me want to love you more"
If I should lose you, no one could take your place
Cause heaven made but ONE like you for me".

So I dedicate this lifetime of work to the woman who stood by me in a lifetime of service to the Master, the ONE and only girl of my life and dreams, Dotty Doughty[1]

Charles Walter Doughty

ACKNOWLEDGEMENTS

DOUG HARDMAN, BRIAN DICKEN WITH THE ELDERS OF THE CONGREGATION OF CHRIST AT MOUNTAIN VIEW- KERNSTOWN, VIRGINIA

There was a time in my busy career when compiling hundreds of pages of Christian Literature would have been unthinkable. But once again, in His providence, the Lord sent extremely capable servants of Gospel Exposition like Evangelists Doug and Brian to our pulpit and bonded the hearts of Pastors Dave Wright, Steve Davey, Christopher Straley, Wayne Keiter, and emeritus Robert Pifer to spread the Gospel to The Lost through every means of discipleship, including the spoken word on cassettes and the printed word you are now reading. We also remember our Pastors, James McFarland, Vernon Barton, Robert Rexrode, and Tom Armel, who have gone to their reward before us. We extend a special thanks to Pastor Kevin Brewster for designing the rainbow charts. Thousands of precious souls are being reached every year because of the unselfish dedication of these soldiers of the cross. Each man seeks to know and use his own personal spiritual gifts for the expedience and benefit of the Body of Christ here and throughout the world. All royalties from this book will be placed in the hands of The Eldership to advance the Kingdom of Christ from shore to shore through Gospel literature, internet lectureships, and electronic media.

RICK BONIFIELD

I thank Rick for capturing my class on The Revelation on his laptop; for his assistance with computer design, format, diagrams, and drawings; and finally, for his contributions to the doctrinal content, especially those dealings with the Christological controversy of "Christ in the flesh." While Rick was studying for the Ministry of our Lord Jesus Christ at Christian Kingdom College (C.K.C.), I soon realized that God had blessed Rick with many spiritual gifts for serving The Kingdom. When I began lecturing on The Revelation at The Lake Mount Church of Christ in New Waterford, Ohio in 1967, I lectured from very limited notes, so I began to transcribe the notes that students like June Feezel submitted for extra credit. Since then, Brother Bonifield has recorded the lectures on his laptop. In addition to Rick's spiritual talents mentioned above, he also has an excellent grasp of theological terms along with a unique comprehension of the overall message of

God's Word from classes taught by Professors Hardman, Jeff Wickert, John Doughty, and Dick Chambers. Rick is a Godsend.

DEBRA CUSSEN, MAXINE SHIFFLETT, AND DIANE WRIGHT

These secretaries gave an amazing amount of their time and energy to this project. "Debbie" taught Computer Class at our Mountain View Christian academy. She brought her expertise to this Revelation Project from an earlier, unfinished work I wrote on End Time Theology entitled "Trashing the Bible." Rick Bonifield used much of the editorial content from "Trashing…" in the book you are now reading. God bless these women for humbly using their gifts to advance the cause of King Jesus.

RACHEL HAMMAN

Rachel is a God Send. In addition to her responsibilities as being church secretary to the congregation, Rachel took time to duplicate sections of this book so students of our C.K.C. could follow the classroom lectures. Rachel is a strong woman of faith who uses her office to help coordinate efforts to evangelize The Lost. She has her own discipleship ministry and orchestrates our book mission ministry to send the New Covenant Gospel to the world. Nobody is supposed to be indispensable, but Rachel is a willing worker for the Lord and echoes the words, "Here am I Lord, use me."

LAURA SMITH

Laura was a student at our Harrisonburg C.K.C. Branch. She is an extremely gifted artist and possesses the talent for placing Apocalyptic Visions into artwork, like the artwork in this book. I know of no other person quite so dedicated to using and offering her talents for the glorification of her risen King and Lord.

BRITTANY S. MARTIN AND LARRY LEE

Brittany did the drawing, and Pastor Lee contributed his computer science skills to make this book possible. When I spoke at The Sterling Park Christian Congregation, where Larry Lee and Leon Owens serve as Elders-Pastors, I announced that I was looking for a front page drawing of The Throne of Christ with the circling rainbow. Brittany and Pastor Lee volunteered. Again, this to me was a providential Godsend. Bless these Brethren at Sterling Park and their Minister John Martin.

CHAD BEAHR

Chad was instrumental in helping to compile the first draft of this book. Chad and his family attend our annual end of August, "Winning at Winchester Rally." His expertise, assistance, and advice are deeply appreciated. Chad is not only a professional printer; he is a very conscientious servant of our Lord and Master. May the Lord continue to use Chad's work to the glory of Heaven.

GERALD WAKEFIELD

Gerald did the yeoman's share of editing this book. Although we come from vastly different backgrounds, challenges, and occupations, Gerald Wakefield is in many ways a contemporary of mine. As a follower of Christ and devout Bible believer, Gerald began his journey into eternity about the same time your author did (early 1950s). After retiring with 20 years in the Air Force (a Vietnam veteran), Gerald worked another 20 years at insurance company headquarters and for the College of Information Science and Technology at the University of Nebraska – Omaha. As a firm believer in Providence, I believe that God foresaw in this present-day and age the need for an up-to-date exegetical work on The Apocalypse. All this time, He was preparing Gerald to assist me with the editing. Gerald read the book and told me, "If anything happens to you, I want you to know that I am committed to getting this book published."

DONOVAN (MARK) QUIMBY

Mark worked for nine months on the final editing of this book. He retired from the Army with more than 22 years of service before becoming a Certified Public Accountant and working 19 years in government and quasi-government agency auditing positions. Mark has a love for the Lord that continues to grow with each of life's challenges. His contribution towards the final editing of this book and the innumerable hours of fastidious review of the manuscript has enhanced the value of this work immensely. Donovan (Mark) Quimby will never be forgotten in the minds of all who helped to produce this book.

PINE GROVE CHURCH OF CHRIST (Bluewell, WV)

Evangelist Gary Lamie, Elders Jack Johnson and Darrell Powers, and the brethren at Pine Grove have made significant contributions to the publishing of this book.

CHURCH OF CHRIST AT ATHENS, WV

Evangelist Kenny Hylton, Elders Randy Bailey and Jim French, and the congregation in Athens have supported this work immensely. It was the flagship congregation in advancing (under the leadership of Doug Hardman) the historic 1987 debate between Evangelist Charles Doughty and Dr. Karl Fezer (Head of the Biology Department – Concord University), "Creation is Superior to Evolution in Explaining the Origin of the Universe." They have been a friend to Christian Kingdom evangelism and apologetics ever since.

STACY B. LLOYD, III

Gail Boyd is Brother Lloyd's nurse. Gail witnessed to him of the saving grace of Jesus Christ. She invited him to attend the assembly with her. Gail thought Stacey would be interested in new Covenant Christianity. When she took him to a super market, she put a disk of one of my sermons in the car radio player, and Stacey listened while Gail shopped. He said afterward, "I would like to meet this man."

This soul winning incident so paralleled the saga of Naaman the Leper and his servant lady (2 Kings, Chapter 5) that we would be remiss in not drawing attention to it. The Israelite girl had been taken captive in war between Syria and Israel and was a servant to Naaman's wife. Naaman was a mighty commander of military valor but was greatly ashamed and distressed because of his leprosy. The servant lady knew the power of YHWH and she told Naaman's wife, "If only your husband could contact the prophet of Israel, he could heal your husband" (2Ki 5:3).

The whole Chapter deals with what the Prophet Elisha told Naaman to do, and getting Naaman to humble himself and do what he was told. Naaman stumbled over the same thing that many stumble over today; that being the simplicity of Gospel obedience. The Prophet told him to immerse himself seven times in the River Jordan (1Ki 5:14). This was not an easy task for a man like Naaman who told people where to go and they went, told them what to do, and they did it. The bottom line: Naaman was telling Elisha what he should do to heal himself of his leprosy. This same problem exists today when people are told what to do to have forgiveness of sin (Ac 2:38). Most people give their own ideas as to how to get to heaven. But praise God, at last Naaman relented. He immersed himself seven times, and he was clean.

Stacey is 78 years old and uses a walker. Gail led him to our office and the first thing we read from Scripture was the saga of Naaman, the servant girl and the prophet Elisha. We told Stacey that being born again after living to the age of 78 was an even greater blessing and healing than the healing of Naaman's physical disease. We then explained what those who are lost "must do" (Ac 2:35-37) in the covenant of salvation, and what the Godhead promised to do in the covenant of salvation (Acts 2:38-42). We then explained the little book (New Testament) and how Stacey could be "added" to the New Covenant Congregation of Christ (Ac 2:42-47).

Stacey said, "I will do it." Because Stacey needed his walker, we knew we would need some assistance. At that very moment, Mark and Gerald were working on the final editing of this book. We told Stacey that they would assist us just as four men assisted the paralyzed man in Luke 5:19. Jesus was preaching in a crowded house. Because the paralyzed man was being carried on a stretcher, he could not enter the house through the crowd. His four friends devised a plan whereby they carried the man up the steps to the roof of the house. They then tore up the tile and by securing the stretcher with four ropes on the four points of the stretcher, they let the paralyzed man down right into the presence of The Teacher. Jesus was so taken by this act of faith that he forgave his sins and healed him of his paralysis.

Within minutes, Gerald and Mark were helping Stacey into the water. When Stacey arose being filled with the spirit of joy and peace, forgiven by the Blood of The Lamb, and added to the Kingdom of Christ, the most wonderful smile came over his uplifted face. He kissed my check and thanked us all for assisting him.

Afterward, Stacey inquired as to why we were all together on that day. After we told him we were wrapping up some of the final editing of this book, his face filled with delight. He told us that books were part of a life-long passion. When we later went to visit him, we discovered he had one of the largest private libraries in the country. Although Stacey's library was filled with thousands of volumes, it centered specially on a collection of old Bibles. Stacey also expressed his great fascination with this Commentary on The Apocalypse.

When we returned to our editing of this book, we could not help but remember the servant, Nurse Gail Boyd, who like the servant in Naaman's house brought the infirm man to The Prophet. We could not forget the immersion of Stacey

Lloyd. In fact, as long as we have a God given memory, we will always associate this book with the immersion of Stacey Lloyd and his nurse.

MARYLAND AVENUE CHURCH OF CHRIST

We conducted Christian Kingdom College classes at this host church. We greatly appreciate the contributions that the students provided for this work.

TODD McKEEHAN

I met the parents of Todd McKeehan during an evangelistic meeting in Florida. In the discussion, they mentioned the name of their son, Todd, and I recall that he was the ATF agent who was shot on the roof of the Branch Davidian Compound in Waco, TX on February 28, 1993. I had been lecturing on how false interpretations of the Apocalypse could lead to very fanatical and dangerous views of the Revelation of Christ. I also spoke of how men like David Koresh can interpret this divine book to fulfill their own selfish needs.

I told Tony and Jane McKeehan that I would remember their son in this work. Todd paid the ultimate price in defending the people of Waco and the Nation by laying down his life. A bridge on US Highway 19E between Elizabethton and Johnson City, TN has been named in Todd's honor. Tony was a leader in the Christian Church, and Todd was an outstanding Christian man. We want to honor him also.

CHARLES F. WILLIAMS

Chuck is our Son-in-Law, and trusted adviser to Dottie and I as our Financial Administrator. Chuck has a servant's heart. He has provided investment opportunities to thousands of people through his Financial Services vocation. It is very humbling to us to have such expertise as has been rendered by Brother Williams who has taken the Administrative Stewardship of this book.

Chuck's wise and prudent negotiations and marketing skills in connection with several publishing houses have proven invaluable to the completion of this process, to say the least. Subsequently, it is our prayer that our loving Savior will likewise, supply grace, peace and abundance of life to Chuck, his wife; Cynthia and his house henceforth and always ... immeasurably!

TABLE OF CONTENTS

DEDICATION x

ACKNOWLEDGEMENTS xiii

FORWARD xxii

PREFACE xxvi

THE REVELATION RAINBOW..1

    Rainbow Charts 19

    The parallels within each cycle of Revelation 20

SUMMARY OF THE ADDENDA..26

INTRODUCTION 31

    John's Book of Revelation..31

    The Views of Eschatology and Revelation 47

    Historicist View..48

    Futurist View 49

    Post-Millennial View 64

    Preterist View 64

    A-Millennialist View 70

    The Philosophical School of History View 70

    Recapitulationalist View...71

    Remnant Restoration View of Eschatology 72

CYCLE 1 - THE SEVEN CONGREGATIONS................................77

    Revelation Chapter One...77

Revelation Chapter Two 110

Revelation Chapter Three 145

Revelation Chapter Four 173

CYCLE 2 – THE SEVEN SEALS 183

Revelation Chapter Five 183

Revelation Chapter Six 202

Revelation Chapter Seven 220

CYCLE 3 – THE SEVEN TRUMPETS 230

Revelation Chapter Eight 230

Revelation Chapter Nine 242

Revelation Chapter Ten 267

Revelation Chapter Eleven 272

CYCLE 4 – THE SEVEN PERSONAGES 292

Revelation Chapter Twelve 296

Revelation Chapter Thirteen 340

Revelation Chapter Fourteen 367

CYCLE 5 – THE SEVEN BOWLS OF WRATH 382

Revelation Chapter Fifteen 382

Revelation Chapter Sixteen 389

CYCLE 6 – THE SEVEN JUDGMENTS 404

Revelation Chapter Seventeen 404

Revelation Chapter Eighteen 441

Revelation Chapter Nineteen 446

CYCLE 7 – THE SEVEN EVENTS 459

Revelation Chapter Twenty 459

Revelation Chapter Twenty-one 504

Revelation Chapter Twenty-Two 516

ADDENDA 526

Addendum A – Steps of Departure...526

Addendum B – Twenty-one Similarities between Daniel
and Ezekiel..568

Addendum C – Fulfilled prophecies of 70 A.D. 600

Addendum D – Chronological Order of the Destruction
of Jerusalem by Dan Dyke..605

Addendum E – George Peter Holford's "Destruction of Jerusalem" 607

Addendum F – Extra Evidential Resources 630

Addendum G – The Biggest Fear of a Pre-Millennialist 638

Addendum H – THE END! 653

Addendum I – Satan's Powerful Persuasive...744

Addendum J – The Eccentrics Who Base Their Hope of Eternal
Life on Made-Up Visions Rather than Divine Revelation 769

Addendum K – "WHAT IS ZION?" 773

WORKS READ..818

INDEX..827

ENDNOTES...838

FORWARD

Allow me first to identify my affiliation with the author of this work. Charles W. Doughty, "Chuck" as I have known him the past 40 years is a lifetime friend. I always find him positive and very spiritual so when I am in his presence, he always lifts my spirits immensely.

He and President Doug Hardman at Christian Kingdom College engaged my service in teaching several classes in Virginia, and I am currently teaching C.K.C. extension courses at the Lake Mount Church of Christ, New Waterford, OH. Interestingly enough, presently, I have chosen from the College Curriculum the Three Semester Course on the Book of Revelation. I have settled on using Chuck's approach, "The Cyclical View," for my controlling purpose.

I have taught Revelation in the past but always got bogged down around the Fifth Chapter. In the past (realizing The Futurist view was nonsense), I used the Historicist approach taken from Johnson's *Peoples New Testament* and *Halley's Handbook of The Bible*. Both employed the continuous running historical approach which is quite applicable in the Old Testament but aside from the Roman Apostasy, dubious "date guessing" in post New Testament history. Since I was not convinced of the historical accuracy, I abandoned my teaching several times. Lord willing and with this new exegetical insight, I will have finished the entire Book of Revelation for the first time in 40 years. We cannot help but be impressed with the quality of this work, its thoroughness, and unimaginable research. The wise man said, "Beyond this, my son, be warned: the writing of many books is endless and excessive devotion to books is wearying to the body" (Ecc 12:12). Chuck writes on subjects that most scholars ignore, and after years of producing books, tracts, articles, sermons, and syllabuses, Chuck has to show the evidences of wear and tear.

Although Chuck tells me his final dream in Christian journalism is to publish the 1,000-page encyclopedia of religious thought regarding The End Times Controversy, the book you now hold may be Chuck's crowning achievement. I have read dozens of commentaries on Revelation, and all have some good insight, but this work is in a league of its own. It is the turning point in how Revelation will be studied in the future. It is the clearest view of The Seven Cycles of Revelation available today, and in my opinion is most certainly the most plausible and most exhaustive work of its kind ever done.

Why am I so eager to recommend this work to the world? The word "credibility" comes to my mind. Most other commentaries are inconsistent and contradictory to the Book of Revelation and plain scripture found in the rest of The Bible. I called my friend Art Marcum who is a student of the Cyclical View of Revelation. He cited the Late Greek Professor Dr. Donald Nash who used Hendriksen's *More Than Conquerors* at Kentucky Christian College. Art now owns Dr. Nash's personal copy of Hendriksen's book with his personal notes in the margin. I also consulted Rick Mathena who uses the Hendriksen approach. Rick is past Greek Professor at Bluefield College of Evangelism, and he conducts seminars across the country. Professor Doughty tells me that Hendriksen can be trusted up to the 13th Chapter, but in addition to his Cyclical View, Hendriksen is also an avowed School of Philosophy student, and therefore, fails to see the historical connection of the Greek-Roman apostasy and the clash between their seed and the woman's seed in the Post-Apostolic departure from Apostolic Faith.

All of this led me to contact Chuck. I knew his approach over the years, but I still was not a ready listener. He trusted me with a rough draft of his manuscript. Even though it was unfinished, it then had 354 pages of what I consider to be painstaking accurate insight into this famous but little known book. Chuck's draft was the game changer for me. I am a Johnny-come-lately, but I am now running with this newly discovered cyclical unveiling. A few years ago a full-fledged Preterist walked into my life. Denying that Jesus will return, he believed that Jesus came in 70 A.D. I ask him why he communes at the table on the Lord's Day where we are to "Remember His death until He comes again." He did not answer. I acquired a book from an Elder friend of mine entitled *The Book of Revelation* by Foy E. Wallace Jr. Wallace was considered in some circles a great writer, but after reading this book, I found the author to be coming off the wall but not yet "crash landed." Chuck openly and honestly deals with Preterism and will take this teaching off the wall and put it where it belongs.

Chuck also deals with Futurism in a very pragmatic manner. He deals with plain scripture (Ro 9); he insists that Christ's Congregation is New Testament Israel; and he proposes there is no such thing as New Testament Jewish supremacy and literal Israelism.

In the early 70's, following my immersion into Christ, a Deacon placed Hal Lindsey's *Late Great Planet Earth* in my hand. I was taught Dispensational Pre-Millennialism (pre-tribulation). Contrary to our Lord's warning in Matthew 24:36,

Lindsey and his endless allies to the present (with ad nauseam literature "Left Behind") set the date for our Lord's return. My friend David Vaughn Elliot very successfully refuted these heretical assertions in his book *Nobody Left Behind!* Most of the preachers around my homestead in S.W. Pennsylvania graduated from Johnson Bible College where this eschatological theory was taught. The large Southland Christian Church now embraces this Pre-Millennialism theory. By virtue of numbers, a great number of people are being affected by this unscriptural view of Jewish supremacy.

The following is a quote from Chuck's book,

> "Dispensational Pre-Millennialism maintains that the millennium will begin on earth after the second coming. This doctrine teaches that when Christ came in the flesh, He intended to set up an earthly kingdom for the Jews. However, since they rejected Him, He instituted His congregation instead. They now look to the unknown future for a definite establishment of an earthly kingdom at the second (technically third or more) coming of Christ."

This pretty much sums up radical Futurism. But The END comes when Christ comes (1Co 15:24), and it will be the END of all things including Pre-Millennialism.

For all of his great contributions to New Testament Christianity, Alexander Campbell's Post-Millennialism was part of his downfall. Granted, he felt justified in embracing this view because the Restoration Movement was "turning America upside down," and Campbell thought the revival of New Testament Christianity would bring about Christ's reign on Earth, but the world of Campbell is today's world. If you think "the church" is creating a better world and the social good of society will usher in a millennium, just read or view the news headlines and take a good look at the world we live in. We are thrilled to read every morsel of 500 pages of this book. We are taken with the scholarship, experience, straightforwardness, and remarkable love the author has for TRUTH and the Bride of Christ. He is always ready to answer any reasonable question and defend the Faith once for all delivered to the Saints.

Without the slightest hesitation, I recommend this volume to any serious student of The WORD. Brother Doughty will encourage you to receive the blessing of this book, "Blessed is he who reads and those who hear the words of this prophecy, and heed the things which are written in it, for the time is NEAR!" (Rev 1:3).

> By God's grace, I am,
> C. Richard Chambers,
> Evangelist (Saint Dick)

PREFACE

At last, after 50 years of research, this Part A of my work on The Apocalypse is completed. I pray the Lord will allow me enough time to finish Part B before He calls me home. The Part B is a comprehensive collection of the many views of eschatology and was first circulated in sections under the title "The Millennial Controversy."

As we distributed different sections of the book in our classes at C.K.C., student Mike Wilcock suggested I call it "Trashing the Bible." He arrived at this conclusion after hearing the various theories of End Time Theology. The rules of hermeneutical context have been violated so much that their conclusions are absurd and contradictory. Instead of edifying our understanding of end time theology, these rules actually "trashed" the Scriptures.

Part B is completed. The difficulty lies in the book's length; it is over 1,000 pages long and currently exists in rough draft. When I was faced with the decision to publish Part B, I realized it would take months to prepare for publication. Also, should Part B be three volumes or one? Thus, I am burdened with the prayerful decision of how, where, and when this book will be made available to readers. These same readers have asked for an Apocalyptic alternative to the standard, repetitive interpretation of The Revelation, a Revelation written 2,000 years ago for a readership interested in what is going to happen in the Middle East tomorrow.

Therefore, I decided to temporarily set aside this monumental struggle to publish over 1,000 pages of eschatological insights, and instead focus on this book, a shorter volume of verse-by-verse commentary on The Revelation.

President Hardman has assigned me several theological topics to teach at C.K.C., but by and large, my students have found more interest and expressed more gratitude for the exegetical insights of this marvelous Revelation of Jesus Christ – The Apocalypse.

I begin each session with these six words, "LET'S GET READY FOR THE APOCALYPSE!" The students then burst into a hearty "AMEN", and a round of applause. May you find the same delight in what the Lord has written, and what I humbly and faithfully attempt to put in lecture form, for classroom study and print.

Since I started my Eschatological career as a Pre-Millennialist, and then became fascinated with Preterism and Historicism, I learned how embarrassing it can be to try to defend end time theories that sometimes crash on the rock of Divine Revelation. Although there is some truth in all such theories, I am more determined than ever not to allow my human theories and presuppositions to contradict Divine Revelation.

I have prayed diligently over every sentence written in this book. I do not claim to have all the answers to this fabulous Revelation. I realize there may still be some more stumps in the field, but I have spent 50 years studying this field and have marked carefully where the stumps are not.

> Submitted to my readers,
> Heartbroken because of Calvary
> Jubilant because of the Ascension
> Charles Walter Doughty

THE REVELATION RAINBOW

THE REVELATION RAINBOW

The book includes many historical 'firsts' concerning Revelation research. It is the first exegetical study of Revelation on the following:

1. "The Rest of the Dead" (Rev 20:5, 6)
2. Revelation Rainbow – Seven sections within seven sections
3. The Hadean World Abyss as viewed apocalyptically
4. Beholding the Lamb on the Throne
5. The parallel study between Daniel and Ezekiel, the end of Judaism, and organized opposition against the messiah
6. Comparative study of the four major "Ends"
7. The heavenly existence at the pre- and post-apocalyptic manifestation of Christ

Thus, this commentary also gives you some of the first answers to some of The Revelation's hermeneutical difficulties. Answers are addressed for the following firsts:

- To explain, in Revelation 20:4, 5, what "the rest of the dead live not until after the 1,000 years were finished" means.

- To analyze the seven parallel sections of Revelation in the light of "The Revelation Rainbow" (Rev 4:3, 10:1) with seven theological subjects within each section.

- To associate the Hadean Spiritual world with Satan, his abyss, and the parallelisms between Revelation 12 and 20.

- To explain the reasons why the lord gave us this apocalypse and to show how important it is to behold the Lamb on His Throne of Glory.

- To evaluate and examine the prophecies of Daniel and Ezekiel in ways that show they are both dealing with Gog of Magog, which is the Anti-Messiah from the North.

- To compare the following four major threats to the existence of the Kingdom of Christ: the Abomination of Desolation of Daniel, Abomination of Desolation of 70 A.D., the great Apostasy of the mystery of iniquity, and the last conflict between good and evil at Christ's Coming – Armageddon.

- To show the destiny of God's children throughout the ages, what kind of eternal existence they will experience with Christ before He comes again, and their experience with God and the Lamb on the Throne after Christ comes again.

Samuel spoke of the Days in which restitution would be made. God held His council over until this occurred (Ac 3:19-24). This book is the first to give a clear understanding of what Jesus and the Apostles meant when they said that their ministry and Apostolic writings made restitution and restoration for all things. God promised through the prophets that this truth could be believed, taught, and understood throughout all the ages.

THERE ARE THREE ASPECTS OF REVELATION

1. Things that have been fulfilled

2. Things that are being fulfilled

3. Things that are to be fulfilled

THERE ARE THREE WAYS TO VIEW REVELATION

1. Telescopic View of Revelation – a long-range panorama off in the distance. The details are difficult to recognize.

2. Microscopic View of Revelation – the detail is recognized.

3. Stethoscopic View of Revelation – applying hidden apocalyptic truths to our regenerated minds, "Let him who has ears, hear what the spirit is saying" (Rev 2:17).

In each view, we can see the fulfillment of contemporary history in every generation. The miraculous thing is that Revelation adjusts and fits all historical ages. Whereas all others books become obsolete, this Book never will. Revelation is a harmonious book. No one but God could write a book that is so perfectly coded, harmonious, and complete. The following are important concepts of Revelation:

THE VISION OF REVELATION

1. It gives hope to the believer.

2. It gives consternation to the enemies of God. "Anguish and wrath" to those that pierced him. Reverential mourning and encouragement to those about to give up hope.

3. It gives Godly mourning to the hopeless (non-Christians).

THE SEVEN DOCTRINES OF REVELATION

1. Monotheism

2. Christ is the exalted and glorified Lord.

3. The Holy Spirit is the prophetic voice of God.

4. Local assemblies make up the universal fellowship of God (Christ).

5. Salvation is liberation from sin and allegiance to Christ.

6. Angelology because angels are divine messengers sent from God to do His will.

7. Eschatology or end times is composed of the resurrection, judgment, and undetermined definiteness of Christ's certain reign and Second Coming.

THE SEVEN RULES OF INTERPRETATION

1. Apostle Paul wrote primarily to encourage the Congregation of his day and those who maintain faithful to that Congregation throughout history. We must know the history of Paul's day.

2. When we find an event or person to which the prophecy is applicable, that event or person may be considered fulfilled for its time but not fulfilled for all time.

3. The Revelation is a divine picture book of spiritual descriptions and a pictorial presentation of certain forces that underlie the historical development of the Congregation and its conflict with evil.

4. Since it is a book of symbols and pictures, their meanings are to be sought in their usage of the day. The Revelation was written in the prophetic figures used in the Old Testament and the apocalyptic literature of Daniel, Ezekiel, Zechariah, and Isaiah.

5. In interpreting a vision, its significance must be grasped as a whole without being sidetracked by too much detail, unless the text addresses detail such as the "heads" being "mountains."

6. The Book of Revelation addresses the spiritual imagination through vivid word pictures.

7. A chronology (sometimes undistinguishable) exists between the beginning and ending of the bridge from the Jerusalem Congregation to her destiny at the end of the world and the Whore from Rome, and her disgraceful ending. There is also a reference to the short-term history of the rise and fall of the European Kingdoms. However, the series of figures (mostly in reference to how strong the Whore seems to be and how weak the Bride of Christ seems to be) are dealing with these two, completely opposite religious institutions.

BIBLICAL INTERPRETATIONS

1. Anachronism means to look at events (past, present, and future) as one. This is a representation of something existing or occurring at other periods of time.

2. Synecdoche – "Receiving together with" – This figure of speech uses a part or individual whole to represent a whole or class of something else, or the reverse of it. An example would be bread for food or army for soldier. Paul said, "When you come together, this is not to eat the Lord's Supper" (1Co 11:20). The disciples were partaking of the Lord's Supper (vs. 21), but Paul said they were not. The Disciples had to receive both what Paul said and what he meant.

3. Metonymy – The use of the name of one thing for that of another associated with it. For example, unleavened bread is Christ's body; "fruit of the vine" is His blood.

4. Hermeneutics – The science of Biblical interpretation by comparing Scripture with Scripture, observing the time of the writing, to whom written, the context, and original meaning of every word of the text.

5. Numerology – In the Bible, the following numbers are more than statistics. They have religious, hidden, and prophetic meanings.

One = God's Number

Two = Division

Three = God (Father, Son, Holy Spirit) or Family (Father, Mother, Child).

Four = Earth. It is the signature of the Creator (i.e. North, South, East, and West.).

Five = The number of grace, with responsibility or service. There are many scriptures that deal with this number, but Jesus took five loaves to feed thousands. We are given five toes, five fingers (each hand) and five senses to serve and give grace to others.

Six = Man's number (666). This number represents both one and many man-made organizational systems that take the place of and oppose the spread of New Covenant Christianity. In part, this number represents a succession of religious despots who caused Christians to suffer horrendous persecution and slaughter in John's day. In general, it addresses Christians who have suffered under heretical doctrines down through the ages. Early scholarship always associates 666 with the Roman Empire. The number 666 has many numerical computations associated with "The Man" (2Th 2) of the late 1st and 2nd Centuries. One thing that comprehensive scholarship has in common with 666 is its association with the Roman Empire Beast (the fourth kingdom), its favorable comparison to Pagan Rome, and its successor Papal Rome.

Seven = God's divine number of fullness and totality. Seven is a perfect, absolute number, and at the end, there is always judgment.

There are seven Biblical mysteries. A mystery is not itself a revelation, for it was given to the Apostles. But a mystery does not declare itself. The Spirit discloses a mystery to the obedient hearer when proclaimed.

1. God's Incarnation – 1 Timothy 3:16; 1 Corinthians 2:7

2. Salvation of both Jew and Gentile by God's Grace – Ephesians 3:2, 3

3. The Sudden Apostasy and iniquity of the primitive faith – 2 Thessalonians 2:7

4. Christ's resurrection as the first fruits of those at His coming – 1 Corinthians 15:51

5. Christ's marriage to His bride – Ephesians 5:31; Matthew 25:6

6. God's eternal program of redeeming and justifying humanity – 1 Corinthians 1:14-2:9

7. Regeneration – Colossians 1:26; Titus 3:5

Ten = Completeness.

Twelve = Government.

40 = Trial.

Properly using these interpretative tools will be a tremendous help to our understanding of this spiritual Revelation.

As we move through the apocalyptic world, I recommend strongly that we occasionally return to this Introduction and review the information regarding this Book. It is important for us to remain completely objective when reading this book. This requires that we remove any presuppositions and previous interpretations concerning the Book of Revelation. Only a Covenant Christian, who is obeying the Gospel, can fully comprehend the spiritual writing of this book (Ac 2:38; 1Co 2:9ff).

God, as the Holy Spirit, originally divided Revelation into seven chapters or seven cycles; this division is different from the 22 Chapters that man invented. **CYCLES** are a complete round or series of occurrences that repeat or are repeated. An analogy to the cycles of Revelation is the Water Cycle.

1. Water storage in the ocean
2. Evaporation
3. Condensation.
4. Water storage in the atmosphere
5. Precipitation
6. Infiltration
7. Discharge of water

    Revelation cycle 1 – The Seven Congregations

    Revelation cycle 2 – The Seven Seals

    Revelation cycle 3 – The Seven Trumpets

    Revelation cycle 4 – The Seven Personages

    Revelation cycle 5 – The Seven Bowls

    Revelation cycle 6 – The Seven Judgments

    Revelation cycle 7 – The Seven Events

As the Book of Revelation comes to the end of the 6th cycle, God places the burden upon us to determine the cyclical events of the 7th cycle. God expects us to understood and learn from the previous cycles in order to determine spiritually the parallel sections of the 7th cycle. God refers us back to the previous judgments (Rev 21:9) from the comprehensive views of the 2nd, 3rd, 5th, and 6th cycles and provides sufficient evidence for us to understand the meaning of the end and final events.

GOD'S OLD TESTAMENT RAINBOW COVENANT

In the Old Testament, the first mentioned principle of the rainbow is in connection with God's Covenant over all nations after The Flood. Modern-day advocates of the justification of sodomy (in 21st Century America) have taken the rainbow as the symbol of their evil lifestyle. Such contempt for the Holy God, and the victory that deluded souls celebrate for "getting by" with despising His righteous judgments does not come as a surprise to those who understand God's will, His mercy and longsuffering (Ro 2:4). God permits flagrant perversions and blasphemies of His Word and counsel to the human race. The only unforgiveable sin is "Blasphemy of The Holy Spirit," and he who commits this sin is liable for eternal judgment (Mk 3:29). "Perversion" is in keeping with God's accurate, penetrating evaluation of sodomite behavior. Because of God's predestined foreknowledge, He knew that such an addiction to "same sex" would lead perverts of God's gift of natural sexual relations to willfully hold back, "suppress," truth (in favor) of their love of iniquity and unrighteousness (Ro 1:18). Subsequently, God abandoned them to degrading lust. Even their women traded natural sexual relations for perverted sex relations (Ro 1:26).

The word "pervert" does not simply mean to "change," it means to "twist." For now, God allows those who pervert the true meaning of God's "Rainbow" to "get by" with their folly. Some may laugh at this success; others consider it a very serious ill-omened assault upon God's Holy Throne. Among the children of God in this world, there is an emerging fear and reverence for what the Lord of this Universe is about to do after His justice has been so impugned, and accordingly, His austere court scorned and ridiculed.

Although it can be explained scientifically (light shining through water droplets), we still cannot help but feel an awesome feeling of reverence for our Creator God when we see the development of a gigantic Rainbow, arching the sky with colors (red, orange, yellow, green, blue, indigo, violet), all of which are compatible with the Laws of physics that were designed by the Creator of the entire Universe.

There are at least six dogmatic injunctions given in connection with God's Rainbow Covenant.

1) The command to eat the flesh of animals, drained of their blood (Ge 9:2-3)

2) Forbidding murder (9:4)

3) Establish courts of law to curtail murder, terror and violence (9:5, 6).

4) Have a reverential respect for the image of God in humankind (9:6).

5) The progeny commandment to foster marriage, family relationships and begat children (9:7).

6) A promise from the Creator God to never again intervene with a world-wide flood (8:21,9:11), but there would be international "climate changes" from the days of Noah until the end, at which time Scripture teaches the world will be utterly destroyed "burned up" by fire (Pe 3:5-11).

Several suggestions have been given as to the meaning of the rainbow colors (www.biblenews1.com: Colors), but none of them have as good a Biblical connotation as the color red that always appears on top. We who live on Earth below can look up and see at the top of our rainbow, "The blood of Jesus cleanses us from all sin" (1Jn1:7).

The difficulty of finding the seven cycles and seven themes lies in the fact that Stephen Langton in 1244-1248 A.D., who did a great work of organizing the Bible by chapters and verses, did not understand how the Holy Spirit organized the Apocalypse into parallel sections. Some scholars say there are five sections, but as we shall see, it seems almost certain that the Lord allowed the spiritually discerning scholar of God's Word to see this Divine Revelation, synchronized miraculously into seven complete cycles.... the perfect number seven being God's number. We are, however, beholden for a lifetime to Langton's Scriptural, book-chapter-verse arrangement. Thus, while we allow for the natural division of this majestic revelation into the seven cycles, we are compelled to use the book-chapter-verse divisions within each cycle.

Although Tyconius (370-390 A.D.) is one of the first scholars on record to see the idea of recapitulation being incumbent in Revelation, it was not until 1889 that William Milligan wrote his, *Reason and Revelation* that a slight, but scholarly attempt was made to disclose the underlying spiritual, recapitulatory themes of the Apocalypse. Since H.B. Sweete in 1906, Albertus Pieters (1937), Ray Summers (1951), and others (Leon Morris, Michael Wilcock), there seems to have been a growing trend among scholars to unlock the meaning of the symbols and meaning of The Apocalypse. This trend culminated in the famous work of William Hendriksen *More Than Conquerors* in 1934 AD. An excellent work on the history of *End Time Theology* (and the scholars who influenced it through history) is done in Dr. J. Paul Tanner's book, *History of Interpretation* (paultanner.org).

It was out of the study of Hendriksen's work in Dr. Donald Nash's Class on Revelation (Kentucky Christian College – 1963, A.D.) that I began to prayerfully piece together the cycles of the recapitulation "School of Philosophy" understanding of The Apocalypse. This book combines what I consider to be the best of the views taught by Historicists, Preterists, and Recapitulationist (sometimes called "The Idealistic View").

THE SEVEN THEMES WITHIN EACH OF THE SEVEN CYCLES

In many ways, The Revelation to John is like the meditations that filled the heart of David as he wrote The Psalms. We notice the interludes correspond to David's "Selah", or pausing and lifting up his devotional thoughts toward the Lord, "I will lift up my head unto thee, who sits enthroned in heaven" (Ps 123:1). This is called a "Psalm of Ascents." It is one of 14 such Psalms (120-134), otherwise called "Songs of Degrees," or Progressive Psalms. The whole theme is predicated upon the pilgrimage the children of God would take as they progressed from the beginning of their trek to the end of their journey at the top of the Holy Mountain, where they could, "Lift up their hands in the sanctuary and praise the Lord" (134:2).

From the Isle of Patmos, the Apostle John would have lifted up his heart, soul, mind, eyes of his understanding and his whole being to the presence of the Heavenly Sanctuary and the ONE on the Throne. David lifted his head and eyes, and just as David's spiritual, peripheral view was far greater than human vision, so John had a breathtaking, spectacular view into eternity. Thus, John had his "selah" moments, or interludes as the curtains of perception opened and new scenes in heaven and earth were introduced to his spiritually enlightened mind.

As mentioned previously, I believe there are seven cycles, but Michael Wilcock believes there are eight (He calls them "scenes."). He admits The Revelation divides itself naturally into seven cycles "scenes', but he believes the book closes with the Eighth Scene of things to come. He argues that just as after the seven days of the week, Jesus arose on the eight day and entered an eternal pause that follows the seventh (He 4:9-11). thus, the eighth "scene" of Heaven is that of "New Beginnings" (www.wordandspirit.co.uk).

In the 4,000 years of Old Testament History (even though there were 360 days on the Hebrew Calendar), there is no eighth day because the week reverted to the First Day of the week, which by the way, was the day our Lord created "The evening and the morning, day and night" (Ge 1:5). In the New Testament it is upon the First Day of the week which our Lord Jesus appeared alive forevermore (Mt 20:1; Mk 16:1, 2, 9; Lk 24:1; Jn 20:1, 19; Ac 20:7; 1 Cor 16:2; Re 1:10), and the first day of the week is actually called the eighth "okto" day in John 20:26. Scholars of numerology associate eight with resurrection or a new beginning (www.google.com: Symbolic Meaning of the Number Eight). For instance, eight souls of Noah's family were saved by virtue of the Ark being lifted to safety by the very same waters that destroyed the world.

It all boils down to how God deigns to the human comprehension of time on earth, and our knowledge of the fact that heaven is above any human contemplation of time. Although it transcends our human understanding of time, yet God (being God and acting like God) rested on the Seventh Day, and that rest never ceased. God's rest was still available to those who sought it in the days of Joshua (Heb 3:17-19) and David (Ps 95:7, 11) and Paul (Heb 4:11). Therefore, that day of rest long ago is actually an eternal day (Heb 4:4, 5). Thus, the Sabbath was made for man, not for God (Mk 2:27). Although the Godhead condescends to meet us in our 24-hour day "lock ins," the Godhead is not bound, restricted, or confined to time as is the human race. Thus, I am not completely persuaded that the glorious City of Heaven in Revelation 21 and 22 is an eighth, eternal pause that follows seven past cycles.

Conversely, in my spirit's mind, someway, somehow I have this commitment to discover the interludes that the Godhead placed in this elite, divine masterpiece of literature called The Apocalypse. I have never read a scholarly work on this heavenly masterpiece of literature that has not considered the fact that there are some interludes, but the scholars disagree with how many there are, and where they are placed in The Apocalypse.

Confessedly, the hardest part of this book is finding the interludes. I am convinced there are seven interludes. The number seven appears 49 times in Revelation. This is, of course a miracle of divine multiplication of seven times seven which John by human genius could never have been aware of until he read the finished copy himself.[2] Further, we have discovered seven extremely vital subjects that are unavoidable if we are to have an accurate insight into the jurisdictive providence and rule of Christ from His Throne of Righteousness.

Dr. Donald Nash emphasized, repeatedly, in his Kentucky Christian College lectures that this Revelation deals basically with two themes: 1) The righteous will be rewarded eternally, and 2) The unrighteous will be punished eternally. The Apocalypse is a serious book dealing with serious topics. This Book presupposes that you already understand God's mercy, grace, love and longsuffering. This Book deals with the sobering themes that Christ's Kingdom will suffer much tribulation on Earth. There will be persecution, loss, punishment and death without mercy. This book deals with martyrdom, the patience of the saints, and Heaven's anger against those people and nations that oppose Christ's glorious but militant Kingdom. While there is victory for individual Christians, victory for the Kingdom down through the ages seems to be unattainable at times. Unless we look to the throne, we will despair and faint under the crushing blows of Babylon and the world.

Far from the lighter themes of love, joy, and brotherhood fraternity that we see in other New Testament Scriptures, which encourage us to live victorious lives in Christ, in The Apocalypse, we contemplate victory in the midst of ostensible, insurmountable odds. In the light of these sobering facts, we expect to see Christ in His reign in the midst of our tribulation. Yes, we are in tribulation, but His Throne is fixed and unmovable. His Throne represents to us that the victory has already been won.

What should impress us is that in each of the seven cycles, there emerges seven thought provoking themes. We did not select these themes at random, and they could not simply be coincidental. I am convinced that our Lord put these seven themes in each cycle to encourage His congregation to be faithful until the end. We consider the seven themes:

1) The redemption of His Bride Whom He loves and gave Himself for.

2) Temporal warnings to those who abuse The Bride of Christ, along with earthly judgments that are discerned by the spiritually minded.

3) Evangelism is thwarted in every generation. Satan's arsenal is filled with anti-evangelism weapons, and his prime targets are to cripple or kill soldiers of evangelism. It is unbelievable, but rather than attempt to destroy evangelism from without, he does it from within the "church." Satan accomplishes this primarily by working through members who hate evangelism and evangelistic preaching, through those who agree with evangelism but do not support it, though those who agree with evangelism but expect only the "experts" to do it, and though those who wholeheartedly support and encourage evangelism in personal life and assistance.

4) Christ's reigns on earth through His Christian Kingdom, Covenant Congregations.

5) God justice is vindicated. This is a very important theme in the Book of Revelation. There have been many times in history where the kingdoms of this world came very close to destroying the Kingdom of Christ. The enemy with all his power and propaganda (political, religious, philosophical, academic, military) is far too powerful for the humble children of Christ to withstand. So we see, throughout history, the thunderbolts of Heaven are released at the right time, and strike down upon the Earth those who oppose the Kingdom of Christ, in such a way that unless they are immobilized, they could eliminate Christianity from the world. Of course, the world hates justice and will always find fault with God. The Book of Revelation is very vigilant in its defense of the integrity of God's righteous judgments.

6) Of course, Christ is King of Kings, Lord of Lords, and the humble Lamb of God will reveal Himself as the Lion of Judgment. So we are not surprised to see the reoccurring theme of Christ's coming and the last and final conflict between righteousness and unrighteousness settled once and for all.

7) Eternal rewards and punishments. This theme is extremely important because it reinforces what we have known all along, and that is it pays to be a Christian and serve the Lord, but it does not pay to live a life without hope in the risen Christ. The final reward of the righteous

will be eternal joy that is unspeakable and full of glory. The final punishment for those who have not come under the Covenant blood of Christ's righteousness will be eternal, unbearable punishment, forever.

These seven themes stand out in each of the seven cycles, and we cannot ignore them. They are like seven colors of light in the spectrum of the everlasting covenant of the Godhead. We have taken each of the colored arcs (red, orange, yellow, green, blue, indigo, and violet) and inserted each one at the introduction of each of the seven cycles. Within each arc, we have given the Scriptures where the seven themes are found: 1) Redemption 2) Temporal warnings to repent and temporal judgments 3) Evangelism thwarted 4) The congregational reign of Christ 5) God's justice is vindicated 6) The Second Coming and last conflict of good and evil, and 7) Rewards for the righteous, and punishment for the wicked. It will be an uplifting experience for you to highlight in the Bible each of these rainbow themes.

The cycles of Revelation are also like a *play* in which "*interludes*" occur and scenes are introduced. **Interludes** are "short dramatic episodes, periods, or spaces introduced between the acts of a play or movie."

There may be seven recesses or interludes in Revelation:

1. Revelation 4:1-11

2. Revelation 7:1-17

3. Revelation 8:1-5,

4. Revelation 11:19

5. Revelation 14:1-5

6. Revelation 17:1,2

7. Revelation 19:1-10

In addition to the cycles that comprise the water cycle, there is a rain cycle that occurs in linear time with thunderstorms, lightening, and rain. Revelation is like the water cycle. Each of its cycles advances in linear time and includes storms, lightening, and rain, with each element of the rain cycle becoming more severe as the water cycles progress. As the cycle circulates, snapshots of history occur within each of the seven cycles.

A cement truck provides another illustration of how we should visualize the cycles in Revelation. As the truck drives down the road of history, the cement mixer spins in cycles. In apocalyptic literature, as linear time continues, the spinning of the cement mixer becomes more severe. This spinning reaches its crescendo just before the entire load is emptied.

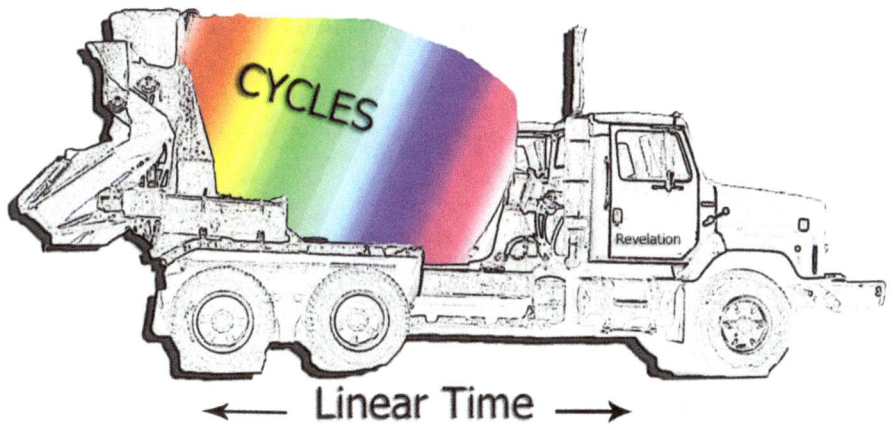

The next page depicts "The Revelation Rainbow." This chart should significantly help us to understand the cycles occurring within the Book of Revelation. Each color of the seven-colored rainbow will be introduced at the beginning of each cycle chapter.

Each color represents a different cycle. Each radiation from the center represents a parallel subject addressed in each cycle.

The Revelation cycle shows historical events, just like lightning flashes within different scenes, with each follow-on cycle possessing more severity than the last.

When an Interlude is introduced, sometimes it falls within a specific cycle. For instance, the Interlude between Cycle 1 (the seven congregations), that brings Cycle 1 to an end, covers Chapters 4 and 5, but the actual Cycle 2 (the seven seals) does not begin until Chapter 6. Thus, in our color chart and in our Chapter headings, the Interlude and the Cycle are Chapter 4 through 7. However, as we mentioned, Chapters 4 and 5 is an Interlude, and Chapters 6 through 8:1 is the actual second Cycle with that Interlude included. The difficulty is with Stephen Langton, who in1244-1248 A.D. did a great work organizing the Bible by chapters and verses, but now we realize that like many coming out of The Dark Ages, Langton would not have known how the Holy Spirit organized the Apocalypse into seven parallel sections or cycles. Therefore, instead of 22 chapters there are actually 7 cycles.

Rainbow Charts

The charts on the following pages should help you to understand "The Rainbow" division of the book of Revelation.

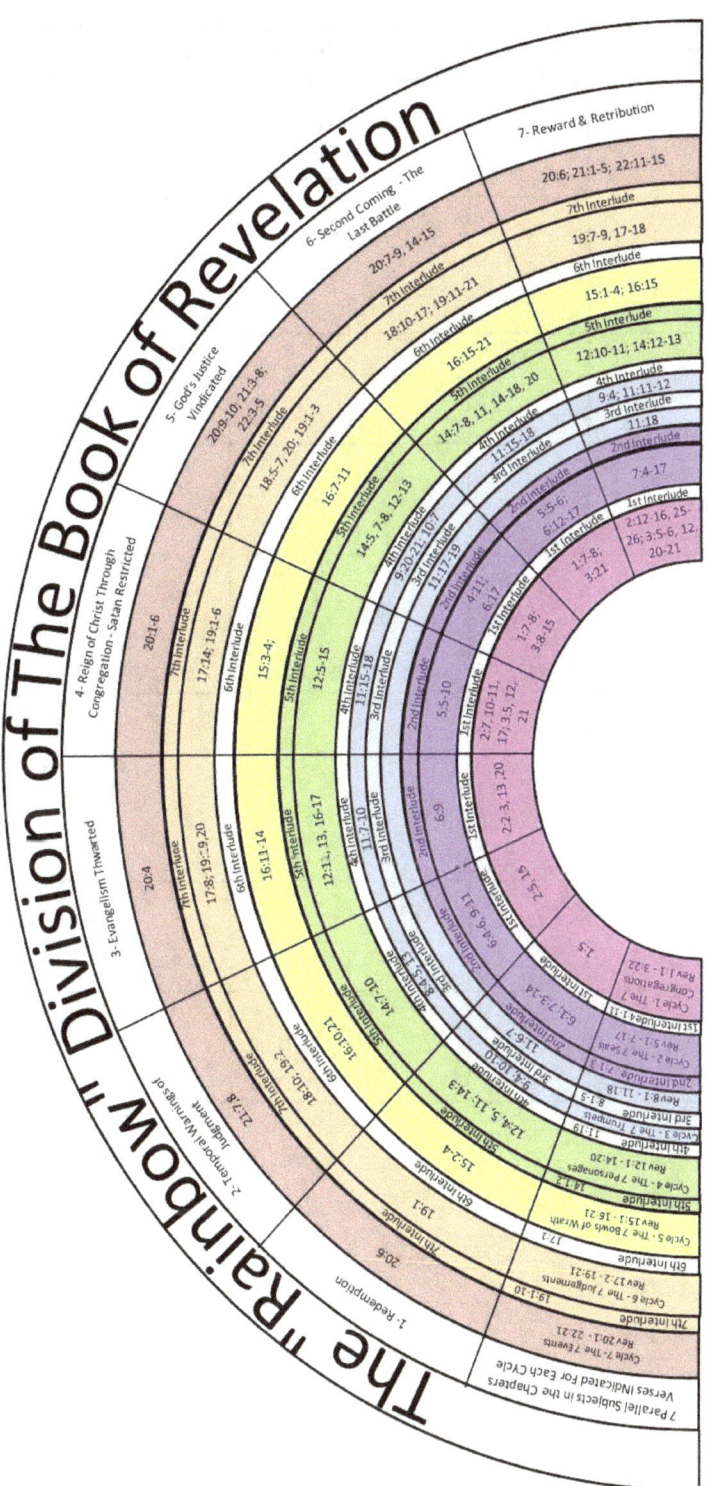

The Book of Revelation	Redemption	Temporal Warnings of Judgment	Evangelism Thwarted	Reign of Christ Through Congregation, Satan Restricted	God's Justice Vindicated	Second Coming, The Last battle	Rewards & Retribution
Seven Congregations' Chapters 1-3	1:5	2:5, 16	2:2-3, 13, 20	2:7, 10-11, 17; 3:5, 12, 21	1:7-8; 3:8-15	1:7-8; 3:21	2:12-16, 25-26; 3:5-6, 12, 20-21
Seven Seals Chapters 4-7	6:1; 7:3-14	6:4-6, 9-11	6:9	5:5-10	4:11; 6:17	5:5-6; 6:12-17	7:4-17
Seven Trumpets Chapters 8-11	9:4; 10:10; 11:6-7	8:4-5, 13	11:7-10	11:15-18	9:20-21; 10:7; 11:17-19	11:15-18	9-4; 11:11-12; 11:18
Seven Personages Chapters 12-14 **THE**	12:4, 5, 11; 14:3	14:7-10 **TRINITY**	12:11, 13, 16-17 **OF EVIL**	12:5-15 Undiluted Judgment **SATAN'S**	14:5, 7-8, 12-13 **TRINITY**	14:7-8, 11, 14-18, 20	12:10-11; 14:12-13
Seven Bowls (vials) Chapters 15-16	15:2-4 **VIALS OF**	16:10-21 **WRATH**	16:11-14 Lying Blasphemy Miracles **FROM THE**	15:3-4 **ASPECT**	16:7-11 **OF**	16:15-21 **FINALITY**	15:1-4; 16:15 **COMPLETION**
Seven Judgments Chapters 17-19	19:1	18:10; 19:2	17:8; 19:19-20	17:14; 19:1-6	18:5-7, 20; 19:1-3	18:10-17 (Babylon); 19:11-21 (The World)	19:7-9, 17-18
Seven Events Chapters 20-22	20:6	21:7-8	20:4	20:1-6	20:9-10; 21:3-8; 22:3-5	20:7-9; 14-15	20:6; 21:1-5; 22:11-15

The original writing of Revelation was divided into seven chapters (cycles), with seven parallel sections, and the seven major teachings expounded in this Revelation.

Structure of Revelation:

Below are the seven cycles of Revelation, each in a different color. These cycles recapitulate the first Advent of Christ to His Second Coming from seven different points of view. There are also seven parallel sections in Revelation. Like the cycles going through time, from light purple to red – the judgments become more severe as the picture of Revelation becomes more complete. Scholars are indebted to William Milligan's work, *Reason and Revelation,* and William Hendrickson's work, *More Than Conquerors,* for embellishing the concepts of the seven sections in Revelation.

The Cycles of Revelation:

SEVEN CONGREGATIONS – CHRIST IN THE CONGREGATION (CHAPTERS 2, 3)

1. Ephesus – 2:1-7
2. Smyrna – 2:8-11
3. Pergamum – 2:12-17
4. Thyatira – 2:18-29
5. Sardis – 3:1-6
6. Philadelphia – 3:7-13
7. Laodicea – 3:14-22

SEVEN SEALS – CHRIST IN THE COSMOS (CHAPTERS 6:1-8:1)

1. White Horse – 6:1,2
2. Red Horse – 6:3,4
3. Black Horse – 6:5,6

4. Pale Horse – 6:7,8
5. Souls under Altar – 6:9-11
6. Climatic Events – 6:12-17
7. Silence (judgment) – 8:1

SEVEN TRUMPETS – CHRIST IN CONDEMNATION (CHAPTERS 8:2-11:19)

1. Hail fire, blood – 8:7
2. Mountains – 8:8,9
3. Falling Star – 8:10,11
4. Darkness – 8:12
5. Horsemen from bottomless Pit – 9:1-11
6. Four Angels – 9:13-21
7. Great Voices – 11:15-19

SEVEN PERSONAGES – WOMAN AND DRAGON – CHRIST IN CONFLICT (CHAPTER 12-14)

1. Radiant Woman – 12:1,2
2. Dragon – 12:3,4
3. Man Child – 12:5
4. Michael – 12:7
5. Great Beast – 13:1-10
6. Little Beast – 13:1-18
7. Babylon (Harlot) 14:8

SEVEN BOWLS – GOD'S ANSWER – CHRIST IN CALAMITY (CHAPTERS 15, 16)

1. Earth – 16:2
2. Sea to Blood – 16:3
3. Rivers to blood – 16:4-7
4. Sun Afflicted – 16:8,9
5. Darkness – 16:9,10
6. River Euphrates dried – 16:12
7. Declaration form heaven – 16:17-21

SEVEN JUDGMENTS – CHRIST IN CONQUEST (CHAPTERS 17-19)

1. Harlot Judged – 17:1-7
2. Great beast – 17:8-18
3. Babylon – 18:2
4. Nations – 18:3
5. Merchants – 18:15
6. Kings of Earth – 19:19
7. False Prophets – 19:20

SEVEN EVENTS – CHRIST IN CONSUMMATION (CHAPTERS 20-22)

1. Binding of Satan – 20:1,3
2. Reigning of Saints – 20:4-6
3. Release of Satan – 20:7
4. Deceiving of Nations – 20:8

5. Great war – 20:8

6. Defeat of Satan – 20:9,10

7. Judgment and Introduction of Heaven and Hell – 20:11-15, 21:1-22:21

NOTES:

    a) The Seven Congregations are actually churches then in existence. Their spiritual condition is "the things that are" of John's outline in 1:19, but the Seven Congregations could represent the spiritual condition of various congregations at various times throughout the Christian dispensation.

    b) Chapters 4 and 5 introduce the Seven Seals.

    c) There is an obvious interlude of the 144,000 and the great multitude that appears between the sixth and seventh seals and provides a picture of the safety for the Old Testament Saints who were destined to be taken to their Heavenly reward through the ascension of Christ to Mount Zion. We have a mention of an intervening period (lengthy intermission) of the four Angels of Death (9:15), of The Angel of The Little Book (10:5, 6), and the measured Congregation with the Two Witnesses (11:1, 2), appearing between the sixth and the seventh trumpets (9:15-11:13). The last three trumpets are called three woes.

    d) Chapters 21 and 22 are an epilogue picturing the eternity to be revealed for the saints at Christ's Second Coming.

The parallels within each cycle of Revelation

1. Redemption

2. Temporal Judgments and Warnings

3. Evangelism Thwarted

4. Reign of Christ through the Congregation with Subsequent Binding of Satan

5. God's Justice Vindicated

6. The Second Coming and the Last Battle

7. Rewards and Retribution

SUMMARY OF THE ADDENDA

You will find additional information in the Addenda to expand your knowledge of the following subjects:

Addendum A: Steps of Departure

One of the most incredible contradictions in the world is the discrepancy students of history see when they read The New Testament and then compare and contrast some of the "Christian" creeds, catechisms, denominational "Confessions of Faith," and doctrinal statements of the thousands of church hierarchies and sects that are identified as being "Christian." After The Apostles died, the "Church" fell into the hands of unscrupulous "wolves." Such unprincipled, deceitful "Lords of Christ's flock" led those of the New Testament Witness into the "wilderness" of oppression, censorship, and death. Because there were so many "false witnesses," much of what passes for Christianity today is not at all what Christ and His apostles established before 70 A.D. Addendum A addresses some of the key heresies of this departure from The Faith, the date they were introduced, and the way they contradict the pure New Testament.

Addendum B: Twenty-one Similarities between Daniel and Ezekiel

This section alone is worth the price of the book. We have yet to find a Commentary that gives a theological assessment of the obvious comparison of Daniel's Prophecy of the Anti-Messiah from the North and Ezekiel's warning of Gog of Magog's threat to the Covenant People. When we open the Prophecies of Daniel and Ezekiel, we discover interesting and elaborate similarities of names, nations, locations, personalities, and methods of warfare predicted by these two contemporary prophets.

Addendum C: Fulfilled Prophesies of 70 A.D.

It is not an understatement to state that more than a hundred specific and general New Testament Biblical Prophecies focus on the Destruction of Jerusalem (Abomination of Desolation) in 70 A.D. If you add to this list of the Old Testament (Leviticus-Deuteronomy and The Major and Minor Prophets), we could find approximately 1,000 such verses. No one is fit to write a book concerning Biblical Prophecy who does not have a working knowledge of what occurred in 70 A.D.

Addendum D: Chronological Order of the Destruction of Jerusalem by Dan Dyke

Addendum E: George Peter Holford's Destruction of Jerusalem

George Peter Holford, a lawyer and political leader in England, wrote the book, *Destruction of Jerusalem*, in 1805. Notwithstanding the overwhelming evidence of Christ's Divinity in both the Old and New Testaments, Holford believed that the greatest proof that Jesus Christ was the Only Begotten Son of God was his prediction of the details of the historical panorama and ultimate results of the Abomination of Desolation in 70 A.D. The writing style, spelling, and punctuation of 1805 are difficult for modern readers to understand, but with the help of Debbie Cussen, who without disturbing the original content of the message, translated it into a more readable version.

Addendum F: Extra Evidential Resources

I provide a verse-by-verse break down of Jesus' farewell message to the Jewish Nation. The amazing prognostications of Divine Truth that fell from our Savior's lips and the remarkable details that would find their fulfillment in unparalleled earthshaking events in Jerusalem 40 years later are examined in detail. The students of Christian Kingdom College have testified that these little known facts that the Devil has tried to conceal are some of the most breathtakingly influential and vital truths of Scripture.

This Addendum verifies what is stated elsewhere in your book.

Addendum F provides incontrovertible evidence that Christ will return in final wrath and judgment to destroy the world. What is the divine, prophetic evidence? What is this evidence of Christ's return in judgment that would prove decisive in a modern-day court of law? In a court of law, presided over by rational, logical, sane-thinking judges, at least one of the following three arguments would lead to a conclusive judgment: 1) Testimony evidence, 2) Documentary evidence, and 3) Physical evidence.

If we examine the truths that emerge from the Abomination of Desolation, 70 A.D., we discover the following:

1) Christ gave divine TESTIMONY that just as The Temple and Jerusalem would be "Abominated" and "Desolated," so the next event in divine providence would be the destruction of the WHOLE world when He returns.

2) Christ proclaimed that The New Testament Witness would be completed before The Abomination came to pass. He said, "Let the reader of DOCUMENTARY EVIDENCE understand," (Lk 21:20, 21), and this document is available for us to read today before the END comes.

3) Backhoe and spade after spade have uncovered the PHYSICAL EVIDENCE of the invasion, siege, and total Abomination-Desolation of Jerusalem, even down to the inscription of The Roman Tenth Legion left behind in the ruins.

If we were in a modern-day court of law, we would be convicted by any ONE of the THREE judicial arguments that Christ was RIGHT on 70 A.D., and He will be RIGHT on His prediction of THE END. However, in almost unbelievable precision, our Lord met the judicial criterion that would lead to a final verdict on ALL THREE OF THE ABOVE ARGUMENTS. That verdict is that Christ came in judgment in 70 A.D., and He is coming again. No wonder, in the context of 70 A.D., Luke spoke to all of us down to the present, "Be alert at all times...lest that day come upon you as a snare" (Lk 19:36-38).

Scripture after Scripture tell us to be ready for Christ's coming at our death or at the final END of all things. The reader will bow before The King in amazement at the final truth and verdict that if He is right on, "dead center," in His prophetic accuracy of THE END in 70 A.D., He will also fulfill His prophecy to come for us, soon, in any generation in which we are alive when He does come.

Addendum G: The Biggest Fear of a Pre-Millennialist

In the hope that we will be delivered from the malady of basing serious Biblical conclusions on nothing but hearsay, this addendum addresses both the FEAR and the CURE of Pre-Millennialism. If we think this addendum is unduly judgmental, we must remember that this doctrinal disease affected me in my formidable years of theological studies at Kentucky Christian

College. No person can engage in the arduous ministry of deliverance and experience the joy of seeing a person delivered from doctrinal bondage like a person who has been delivered from such darkness himself.

Addendum H: The End!

I quote hundreds of Scripture dealing with the words, "The End," but challenge you to consider what "end" the Lord is leading us to think about. Briefly, we already know about the end of Noah's world, the end of the Old Testament, the end of the Old Testament economy, and, certainly, the end of the world. Thus, I go into detail to ensure we are interpreting Scripture in their proper "end time" context.

Addendum I: Satan's Powerful Persuasive

This addendum is about the tactics and techniques employed by Satan to infiltrate a country, institution, or an organization through word change agencies, class and racial warfare, and humanistic, socialistic philosophies. These changes are calculated to demoralize and weaken the spiritual, Godly values that make a country strong and its people free and independent.

Addendum J: The Eccentrics Who Base Their Hope of Eternal Life on Made-Up Visions Rather than Divine Revelation

This addendum addresses publications like those of Tim LaHaye and others who have in the past and who probably will in the future continue to undermine the Old Testament prophecies that predict the reign of Christ-Messiah, and the unmistakable New Testament fulfillment of such prophecies proving beyond all doubt that Christ is presently seated on the right hand of the Throne of God's majesty and glory.

The study of the apocalypse of Jesus is the unfolding of ongoing historical events in any historical age. We are lifted above all of the uncertainties, perplexities, including the gloom and doom found in history, to focus upon the Throne of Jesus Christ. The encouragement lies in the fact that no matter when people read this Revelation, and no matter where they are in history or reside nationally, they can be confident that He is in control; it is "His Story."

Addendum K: What is Zionism?

This addendum addresses the following six questions: 1) What is Zion Eternal? 2) What was Zion in the Old Testament? 3) Was Old Testament pure Israel taken to Heaven? 4) The Spiritual Zion on Earth. 5) What is the Zion "Heavenly Jerusalem"? 6) What is secular, political Zion?

We set out to prove that the overriding theme of the City of Zion or the City of Salem is an eternal heavenly abode where Jesus Christ is The Melchesidek or the Prince of Peace and King of Righteousness.

INTRODUCTION

Before we begin this journey into John's book called Revelation, let us enhance our background and knowledge of Revelation, its author, and the various views prevalent in the world today regarding its interpretation. You just completed reading a brief description of my view – *The Revelation Rainbow*, and a short summary of each addendum.

John's Book of Revelation

The Writing of Revelation

The Book of Revelation is the most misunderstood book in the entire Bible. From scholars of the New Testament to the Bible novice, God's word has been misrepresented, negated, and adulterated to the point of mass confusion. This book is *the* Book of Revelation, not the plural Revelation(s). This would be the same as referring to America as, "*The United States of Americas.*" This simple scrutiny is the first step in revealing whether one is a student of God's word and has an elementary knowledge concerning the Book of Revelation. To understand it, we must use a proper hermeneutical approach to the Scripture by understanding when Revelation was written, why it was written, to whom it was written, and what the culture was like during that time. We must attempt to know the meaning of apocalypse before we can interpret it.

Apocalypse means to unveil.[3] Only a spiritual mind can grasp the hidden meanings of this book. In the study of Revelation, we can easily become frustrated and confused. However, take heart! The Apostle John said, "I was in the Spirit on the Lord's Day" (Rev 1:10). The student of this writing must be a spiritual child of God in order to see the spiritual meanings in this book.

The Revelation was written under Roman domination and Caesar worship. There was great Christian persecution as well as an idolatrous society. Christians were being forced to give up occupations, to worship Caesar, to deny Christ, and to sink into pagan society to keep their families alive. The early readers of Revelation would need this book to charge them to repentance, to give them the insight of faithfulness, and to prepare them for the persecutions they would continue to endure. We readers of Revelation must take it as a completely continuous story that depicts the power of Satan at work against the power of God. Ours is a war of the earthly throne versus the heavenly throne. We will fail to properly understand this book if context is removed and "scripture jumping" takes place. This study of Revelation will adhere to proper hermeneutics as well as provide the proper foundation for correct interpretation.

Who Wrote the Book of Revelation?

There is some debate over who wrote the Book of Revelation. This book states John wrote the Revelation (Rev 1:1). However, a question remains, "By which John?" Obviously, this John was banished to the Island of Patmos (Rev 1:9). Also, we know this John was Jewish due to the numerous Old Testament quotations and the reference to the Temple in Jerusalem (Rev 11). The traditional view, from the early 2nd century A.D., is that the John of Revelation is the same man who wrote the Gospel of John, as well as 1 John, 2 John, and 3 John. Justin Martyr[4] (100-165 A.D.), Irenaeus[5] (early 2nd Century-c. 202 A.D.), and Tertullian[6] (160-225 A.D.) all believed that John, the Apostle, wrote Revelation. Clement of Alexandria (c. 150-c. 215 A.D.) understood that it was John, the Apostle, who returned from the Island of Patmos.[7]

However, early church historian, Eusebius (263-339 A.D.), challenged this common view because he sought to diminish the authority of Revelation. Eusebius claimed John, the Apostle, could not have possibly written Revelation because the author did not claim to be the beloved Apostle; the style of Revelation is markedly dissimilar to that of John's Gospel; and there was a second early Christian leader named John, *John the Elder*.[8] Eusebius' criticisms cause the authority of the Book of Revelation to be disputed, and consequently, weakened. As a result, some eastern churches denied that the Revelation was canonical (should be included in the Bible). The only evidence for this belief in the existence of *John the Elder* is a quote from Papias (A.D. 130) found in Eusebius' history.[9]

Neither Papias nor Eusebius claim that a second John wrote Revelation. The Papias quote says nothing about Revelation, and Eusebius only gave *John the Elder* as an alternative to the Apostle. The author of Revelation never called himself *the Elder*, but the Apostle John referred to himself as *the Elder* in 2 John 1 and 3 John 1. Despite the different literary styles of the Gospel of John and Revelation, solid similarities exist between the two writings. Christ is known as the Shepherd in both books (Jn 10:11; Rev 7:17); He is known as the Lamb (Jn 1:29; Rev 5:6); and He is known as the Word (Jn 1:1; Rev 19:13). The denial of John' authorship of the Book of Revelation by some scholars based on a simple observation of writing style is foolish. Apocalyptic writing style, by its very nature, is completely different from any writing style found anywhere in the New Testament! The inspiration is not in the man anyway…it is in the Holy Spirit!

John wrote this apocalyptic vision during the reign of the Roman emperor Nero (Discussed in Chapter 2). For his activities as a Christian, John was banished to the island of Patmos, which is a small island off the coast of modern-day Turkey in the Aegean Sea (Rev 1:9). This was a great time of persecution for Christians holding to the Lordship of Christ. They were faced with martyrdom (Rev 2:13, 6:9), and this martyrdom was just the beginning (Rev 2:10, 3:10). Christians needed this book! Jesus would not tell John to write these things to the Christian community unless, owning to the extremities of their persecution, it would be an encouragement to them.

How discouraging life would have been for the early, persecuted Christians if the Lord were writing Revelation, as the Pre-Millennialists (to be addressed later) believe, only to those living in the far off "no one knows when" future. This Pre-Millenialist view is absurd. Remember, understanding the context of Revelation is key in understanding the book. John wrote this epistle for two reasons:

1. To give hope that Jesus is coming! Through the trials, through the persecutions, through the difficult times, Christians know that Jesus is on His Throne, and He is coming again! It is an encouragement to believe that Jesus is the Son of Man (Mk 14:61, 62), and He will return to this Earth one day to "take" those in His kingdom home. This is comfort for saints in any age, right up to the present.

2. To bless those who are looking for His return. He is coming in the clouds, with a shout, a voice, and a trumpet! Contrary to the Futurist view (to be addressed later), this is not a secret coming!

The Date of Revelation

People ask this question, "Could the Book of Revelation and the Bible be written and circulated throughout the known world of that time?" This question has been debated for centuries. Scholar after scholar has attempted to prove when the Apostle John wrote Revelation. Many modern day scholars believe Revelation was written as late as 95 A.D., or even as late as the mid-4th Century. Opposing these late dates are many sources of information that point overwhelmingly to an earlier date. Revelation could easily have been written prior to 70 A.D. (The meaning of A.D. stems from the Latin "anno-year" and "domini-Lord, Master or Sovereign Ruler.") Personally, we advise Christians to always insert A.D. after the date when they sign official documents (even checks). I do this, and one of his bank tellers came to hear me preach. She said, "I wondered why you always put A.D. on the date of your check? I looked it up and found out what it meant and decided to come and hear you preach."

One should not debunk and discredit the abilities of the ancient world to accomplish what needed to be done. When the Roman Empire was under Caesar Augustus, Caesar issued a decree that a census be taken of the entire Roman world (Lk 2:1, 2), thus improving the effectiveness of collecting taxes throughout the Roman Empire. In addition, on a smaller scale, the capacity existed to issue a metropolitan edict of slaughtering every male child two years of age and under as is indicated in Matthew 2:16. Ancient accomplishments like these make it extremely possible for the Book of Revelation to be circulated very quickly throughout the Roman world and beyond. We must give the Holy Spirit of God some credit. There are several reasons why an accurate writing date of pre-70 A.D. is more acceptable than 90 A.D. The Catholic idea of a mid-4th Century writing of the book is an embarrassment to both Catholics and Protestants.

Why is the Date for the Book of Revelation So Important?

There are several reasons why dating the Book of Revelation is crucial to Christianity.

    A.   Consider the source of the late date. Many religious leaders want to usurp the validity of the Scriptures. Church lords who want control over their followers want a date that extends after 70 A.D., when all Scripture should have been recognized, so they can insert their own apostolic lordship without having to be challenged by Apostolic Scriptures. John mentions such a man, Diotrephes (3Jn 9-11), who loved preeminence. Adolph Harnack said Diotrephes was the first to aspire to a bogus office of monarchial bishop. At the turn of the 2nd Century, the celebrated Gnostic, Cerinthus, was also an early aspirant for apostolic usurpation. He was profoundly anti-Christ believing that divinity was given to Jesus at His immersion and departed Him at His crucifixion.[10]

Although the "church" views Ignatius of Antioch as a super-saint because he was martyred, this man was advocating the Monarchial Bishop as early as the end of the 1st Century. This became the "Doctrine of Apostolic Succession." This doctrine advocates a single Bishop over local elders and over many "churches." This power-grab doctrine also led to Apostolic Succession meaning that they trace their right of office to the Apostles and have the same authority.

Thus, a post-70 A.D. writing of any of the New Testament Books leads such thinkers to deduce that the Old Testament priesthood was still in effect. We would then expect to see Christian leaders acting in the same fashion as Aaron, the High Priest, and the ordinary Levitical Priests. We must not budge on the unequivocal injunction of Christ annulling Old Law by His being the ONLY person to fulfill it (Mt 5:17), and thereby "nailed to the cross, and cancelled the ordinances that were against us" (Col 2:14). No amount of scriptural wiggling, or leap-frog theology can prove we are in any way under the Law of Moses when we consider that Christ made the Old Law "Obsolete, it waxed old and was ready to fade away" (Heb 8:13). The final "passing away" or death blow of The Law was when the temple and Holy City of Jerusalem was destroyed, and after 70 A.D., there would be no further revelation to God's heritage other than what was written in the 27 New Covenant books of the New Testament.

Paul, speaking prophetically, said, "They will be abolished"; tongues, Paul said, will cease; and as for (supernatural) knowledge; it will be abolished (1Co 13:8). The same Greek word translated, "abolished," is used for both prophecies and knowledge. This abolishment would take place in point of time, which from reading Second Corinthians, Chapter 3, we take to be the completion of the New Testament writings. When we study the context, "that which is *perfect* is come" (1Co 13:10), we can appreciate that the Corinthian Christians would have understood more perfectly through their reading of the perfect New Testament than what they had previously in the inferior temporary gifts of supernatural, instantaneous gifts of prophecy, tongues, and knowledge. Paul's assessment, "We know in part and prophesy in part" (1Co 13:9) makes it clear that the "perfect" Paul is addressing is the complete New Testament and not just part of it. If The New Testament was not "perfect" and complete, then those of the latter day (after 70 A.D.) needed modern-day soothsayers who would claim divine revelation. The precedent would be set for false prophets to claim divine inspiration, in both speech and writing, to steer the deluded "church" down through the ages.

Recognizing the completion of all Scripture after 70 A.D. gives church lords room for tradition, human opinion, and denominational creeds to pre-empt Scriptures that they say came at a later date. Those who claim to have the ability to produce sign gifts, like those given by Christ to the Apostles, also desire a later date. "Sign gifts" were given to the Apostles and those associated with them by the "laying on of hands" (Ac 6:6, 8:17 with 1Co 12:29, 30). The Apostle Paul was compelled to give his credentialed right of apostleship consisting of "sign gifts" (1Co 9:1-3; 2Co 12:12, 13). Today, Christians are not expected to look for such signs (Mt 12:39) because signs are now confirmed through the Apostolic Word (Mk 16:17, 18, with Heb 2:1-3).

Hundreds of modern-day "Christian" leaders claim that Peter, James, John, and Paul were wrong to condemn sins in the 1st Century, which are now tolerated in the 21st Century. In this sense, the Scriptural authority continues to be subordinated to the interpretation of today's "know more than the Spirit-inspired Scripture" false prophets. Peter's statement, "No Scripture is of private interpretation" (2Pe 1:20) refers to the interpreter's own preconceived idea of what he wants the verse to say. Peter's verse also requires Scripture to be interpreted in the light of other Scripture on the subject. It is critically important for us to understand that we are accountable to God for how we teach His Word (Jas 3:1)!

Sign gifters conclude that the first Christian congregation needed sign-gifts because they did not have the completed Scriptures. This thinking allows them to extend the time required for completing the Scripture as far into the future as they want. Even today, some religious groups claim God's Word has not been completed. We must examine the evidence and come to the most logical conclusion.

B. If the book was not finished before 70 A.D., then Christ lied. Jesus prayed, "I have given them Thy word" (Jn 17:14). Jesus continued,

"Thy word is Truth" (17:17). Jesus is talking about the Apostolic Word (17:20), and the fact that the world would believe in Him through reading God's Word in the future. Nothing reveals the omniscience of Jesus more than this prayer. Jesus also says in Matthew, "Let the reader understand," speaking of the abomination of desolation in 70 A.D. (Mt 24:15; Mk 13:14). They would not have been reading something that had not been written. Jesus said this Gospel would be preached to the world as a testimony before the end (abomination of desolation) came (Mt 24:14; Mk 13:9-11; Lk 21:10-13). Verse 20 of this context says, "When you see Jerusalem surrounded," so we know it was before 70 A.D. when this witness was recorded. Thus, Jesus did not tell the truth if this witness was not completed in His designated time frame.

It is highly possible that some of the Apostles were in Jerusalem in 70 A.D., and the sight of Christ's prophecies being fulfilled would have been a great encouragement to them and their followers.

If the Apostles and their fellow Christians escaped (which they did) after the retreat of Cestus Gallus (September, 66 A.D.), or when the siege was relaxed, "cut short," (Mt 24:22) with the recall of Titus to Rome to succeed Emperor Nero (68 A.D.), they would have been with thousands of Christians who were fleeing the city of doom. The Apostles were spared the horrors of the "Visitation" of Christ (Lk 19: 41-44). Jesus was speaking to His disciples when He said, "When you see Jerusalem surrounded with armies" (Lk 21:20). Thus, the Apostles saw the beginning of the siege, but fled before witnessing the greatest tribulation since the beginning of time (Mt 24:21; Mk 13:19). The tribulation of 70 A.D. was greater than the Global Flood because it was a long drawn-out siege of pain, suffering, and prolonged death. The flood came and took them away quickly (Mt 24:39).

C. Remember, the Old Testament was completely taken away in 70 A.D. God's New Testament included the Revelation when it was published by the Holy Spirit. It is not characteristic of God, the Lord and provider, to take away the Old Covenant without establishing the New in its place (Heb 8:5-7, 13). By characteristic, we mean representative of His holiness and consistent righteousness in dealing with

His covenant people. Adonai "Lord" refers to the Master making provision for His servants to safely and effectively perform their duties. If there were a lapse of even ONE year after 70 A.D. when His servants did not have a complete NEW TESTAMENT, then the Godhead would have failed Their duty as Lord, Master, and YHWH-Jireh, which means "The Lord Will Provide!"

D. Daniel said the Prince would establish the covenant in the middle of the week (See the abomination of desolation in Da 9:25-27.). A late date would break down the order of events if the New Covenant was not complete before 70 A.D. The "desolation" comes after the Messiah makes His sacrifice for sins and thereby establishes His New Covenant with the human race. The Messiah-Christ was recognized as "Lord-Adonai, and Christ-Messiah" at Pentecost (30 A.D.), 40 years prior to the Abomination of Desolation (Ac 2:36). (See the time line in Addendum H.) Peter was given divine revelation of the pending disaster that would befall his generation of Jews when he concluded his sermon, "Save yourselves from this perverse 'morally twisted' generation" (Ac 2:40). His generation and their children would have Christ's blood on their hands (Mt 27:23).

E. The Holy Spirit was the vehicle for the New Covenant to be established. The Greek-Roman apostates love to use the word "canonization" to suggest that "the church" (not the Holy Spirit) gave us the 27 Books of the New Testament. The early congregations (Pre-70 A.D.) had all Spirit inspired Scripture (2Ti 3:16). Peter could read Paul's Epistles (2Pe 3:15, 16), and this Gospel went to the whole world (Col 1:6). Remember, the Gospel was also letters, and the Letter to The Colossians was written in approximately 62 A.D. Jude, the Brother of James wrote in verse 17 of his Book, "But Brethren, remember you the words which were spoke before of the Apostles of our Lord Jesus Christ." Among the collection of inspired New Testament Books, the Book of Jude was written very late. In the above verse, Jude's use of the "words spoken by the Apostles" could only be remembered if the Apostles had written them in the remote past. Jude begins his letter by referencing the remote past when the "Faith was once delivered to the saints" (Jude 3). The FAITH was old enough for certain men to creep in unawares and through the doctrine "Of turning the grace of God into lasciviousness, and deny the only Lord God and our Lord Jesus Christ," establish a foothold among the Apostolic Congregations. These verses afford reliable evidence that the inspired Jude (a brother to James), and an avid reader of other Apostle's doctrine (knowing what "Grace" was, and what "Grace was NOT) took his place with those in the Kingdom of Christ who had access to the writings of the Apostles many years before 70 A.D.

Christians must insist that the Holy Spirit was capable of completing the entire New Testament before 95 A.D., or we must admit He is inferior to Caesar Augustus and modern-day scholars. Remember Caesar Augustus was able, without the aid of the Holy Spirit, to circulate a decree (official pronouncement) that the whole world was to be taxed (Lk 2:1, 2).

F. Our accepting a late date would be an insult to the Apostles because they were the deliverers and executors of the New Covenant (2Co 3:5, 6; Ac 6:2). John was part of the collegium of Apostles.

G. If the Apostles did not complete the New Testament by 70 A.D., they did not fulfill Christ's command to "teach all things" (Mt 28:18-20). John's writing of Revelation in 95 A.D. would have completely divorced him from the disciples who were members of the first Apostolic Congregation. They would have died without the perfect and complete New Testament "Covenant."

H. The Apostles had to be an Apostolic Collegium (2Co 3:1-6). Paul's use of the plural "we" throughout 2 Corinthians 3 refers to the other Apostles. When he said we are competent witnesses of the New Covenant (vs. 6), he did not say, "We are competent witnesses at the present time, with the exception of the Apostle John." Most Bible scholars admit the other Apostles died before 70 A.D. They admit their writings were completed before 70 A.D. They knew that Peter and John would die martyr's deaths (Mk 10:38, 39), yet some scholars have John living and writing four more books a quarter of a century after the other Apostles finished their testimony. Christ did not set up the Apostleship to be executed by only one Apostle. If John wrote Revelation in 95 A.D., he would have been the only Apostle for more than 20 years.

I. If Revelation was not finished before 70 A.D., then Jesus did not prepare Christians, for whom He died, for the persecution recorded in Revelation. Instead, He would have reacted to it. This cannot be possible. Jesus is proactive, not reactive. In contrast with false apostles, the true Apostles would still be living. Jesus said the Ephesian Congregation, and other congregations as well, "tried" certain false teachers who claimed to be apostles (Rev 2:2). The criteria for such a trial was very simple (Ac 1:23-26). Paul, out of due season, was the only Apostle added later, and he too had criteria to meet (1Co 9:21, 15:8; 2Co 12:12; 1Ti 2:7). God would not add another apostle to this list (Eph 2:20; Rev 21:14). One so-called successor to the apostles is ONE too many.

J. John was told to "write this down" (Rev 1:1, 21:5), and "it is written" (Rev 22:18). We must conclude that one of the purposes of Revelation was for the immediate encouragement of the Congregation.

K. Jesus said the Gospel would be preached to the whole world as a "Testimony" prior to the Abomination of Desolation (Mt 24:14). (See the evidence of the word "Testimony-martyr" in the commentary on Revelation 1:2 of this book.)

L. After the Apostles began their "deaconate" work in The Word (Ac 6:2), the Apostles did not just preach the Word, they wrote it. Realizing their duty as executers of this New Testament (2Co 3:1-6), the Apostles were very competent. Paul said they were competent witnesses of this holy, sacrosanct New Testament. The New Testament was completed and declared to the world (Col 1:5, 6) in the Apostles' lifetimes and that included the Apostle John's lifetime. Both the Books of Hebrews and The Revelation address the power and influence the Jews had in banking, commerce, industry, and trade. They used this power to boycott and discriminate against Christians. However, this power was severely diminished after 70 A.D. with the destruction of Jerusalem. For Christ to warn Christians against the once powerful, but now ruined Judaist system, would be tantamount to beating a dead horse.

M. John was an eyewitness to the current affairs in a concourse of Jerusalem and the city's famous sheep gate (Jn 5:2). After 70 A.D., there was no such scenery.

In the final years of Nero's persecution (pre-68 A.D.), the Apostle John wrote the Book of Revelation. The internal and external evidence for this date is firmly attested by well-known scholars and early Church writings.

Spiritual Christians should reject the *canonization* of the New Covenant documents. Even though the Holy Spirit led the apostolic administration in the writing of the 27 letters, there is no certainty as to the exact date or time in Scripture. To be sure, it seems more logical and accurate to conclude that all New Covenant books were completed before the fall of Jerusalem in 70 A.D. This was also, in essence, the historic end of Old Testament Judaism.

Most of Christ's prophecies of the Olivet Discourse were fulfilled in the events surrounding the fall of Jerusalem (Mt 24:1-28); although, some of His prophesies lie in the future.

In spite of the fact that the late date of 95 A.D. is popular, this date is embarrassingly inaccurate. It is flawed with historical inconsistency. The following information gives a sampling of the external and internal evidence that supports the late, and then more likely, early date under Nero's reign.

The Single Evidence for a Late Date

The main reason for belief in the late date rests upon one debatable statement of Irenaeus, the Bishop of Lyons (130-200 A.D.), in his writing "Against Heresies." Around 174 A.D., he wrote,

> "We will not, however, incur the risk of pronouncing positively as to the name of Antichrist; for if it were necessary that his name should be distinctly revealed in this present time, it would have been announced by him who beheld the Revelation. For that was seen no very long time since, but almost in our day, towards the end of Domitian's reign."[11]

First, the uninspired Irenaeus refers to ONE antichrist, but John, an inspired Apostle, said there were many antichrists (1Jn 2:18). Second, it is highly controversial as to what Irenaeus actually said. Irenaeus' testimony is considered the supporting evidence for the late date, but uncertainties exist concerning this quote. First, the Greek language of Irenaeus can be understood to refer to John's being seen on Patmos, not to his writing of Revelation. Secondly, it is possible that Irenaeus has been misunderstood. It has been stated that the name Domitianou, which was a name for Nero, was mistaken by later writers for Domitian.

Scholar Robert Young stated,

> "It was written in Patmos about A.D.68, whither John had been banished by Domitius Nero, as stated in the title of the Syriac version of the Book; and with this concurs the express statement of Irenaeus (A.D.175), who says it happened in the reign of Domitianou, i.e., Domitius (Nero). Sulpicius Severus, Orosius, &c., stupidly mistaking Domitianou for Domitianikos, supposed Irenaeus to refer to Domitian, 95 A.D., and most succeeding writers have fallen into the same blunder. The internal testimony is wholly in favor of the earlier date."[12]

Steve Gregg adds

> "Since the text is admittedly 'uncertain' in many places, and the quotation in question is known only from a Latin translation of the original, we must not place too high a degree of certainty upon our preferred reading of the statement of Irenaeus."[13]

He also concluded,

> "Earlier in the passage, Irenaeus refers to 'all the...ancient copies' of Revelation. This presupposes that the book had been around a good long while before this statement was written. If there were 'ancient copies,' was not the original more ancient still? Yet, in Irenaeus' estimation, the time of Domitian's reign was not considered to have been very ancient history, for he speaks of it as "almost in our day.' How could Irenaeus speak of ancient copies of a work the original of which has been written 'almost' in his own time?"[14]

Internal Evidence Examined for an Early Date

Internal evidence from the Book of Revelation points to its being written during Nero's reign. The following points are evidences from The Book of Revelation confirming the early date of its writing. It is important to be able to memorize the majority of these instances.

1) No historic support for a severe persecution of the congregation under Domitian during 90-99 A.D. exists that compares to Nero's persecutions in 54-68 A.D. Domitian neither fed Christians to lions nor burned them at the stake or on light poles.[15]

2) According to the epistles to the congregations, the Judaizers were persecuting the Christians (Rev 2:9, 3:9). This assigns The Revelation to the pre-A.D. 70 timeframe because the Jewish persecution of the body dissolved at 70 A.D.

3) The Jewish Temple and Jerusalem were apparently still standing in Revelation, Chapter 11. John is sent to apocalyptically measure the city and temple. It would not be possible for John to speak of these as still standing after 70 A.D., when they were destroyed. In addition, if John is referring to some rebuilt temple in the far distant future, while writing in 95 A.D., his complete silence about the destruction of the temple and city in 70 A.D. is deafening. The destruction of Jerusalem is perhaps the greatest disaster in antiquity, as well as the greatest disaster in Israel's history. To imagine John's overlooking the apocalyptic destruction of Jerusalem and the Temple while discussing both as still standing is impossible. Rather, John is prophesying their impending doom just two or three years before they were made utterly desolate.

4) We assume that if there were "false apostles" according to Revelation 2:2, there were true Apostles to counter this falsehood. According to tradition, all the Apostles were dead before 70 A.D., and John was the only Apostle of the original 12 alive at that time.

5) In numerology, Caesar Nero's name, in Hebrew (Gematria) and in Greek (Koine), adds up to 666. Since The Revelation was written about events occurring in the near future, no other person whose name fits this numerology can be found within that time period. None can be found in the near future of 96 A.D.

6) Almost all scholars believe Revelation is inextricably linked directly to the Olivet Discourse. Since the best commentaries on the Olivet Discourse demonstrate that it is speaking of the events leading up to 70 A.D., Revelation is also speaking of these events.

7) The sixth king in Revelation 17:3, 4 is the one that persecutes the saints. Josephus and Tacitus listed the following Roman emperors: (1) Julius, (2) Augustus, (3) Tiberius, (4) Caligula, (5) Claudius, and then (6) Nero.[16] Nero was the first and only Roman Caesar of the Julian line to persecute Christians. Nero's death ended the Julian dynasty.

The emperor ruling after Nero was Galba; he reigned a short time. After Galba's reign (June 68 to January 69 A.D.) and Otho's three-month rise and fall (January-April 69 A.D.), the Flavian Dynasty (July 69 A.D. - 96 A.D.) replaced the Caesarian Line (Julio-Claudian).

If the sixth king was indeed Nero, he would be the one that "*now is*" according to the prophecy. This would date the writing of Revelation before 68 A.D. when Nero died of assisted suicide. Nero also persecuted Christians for 42 months, which is a prophetic expression found in Revelation 11:2.

8) The Vision of Revelation 17:3-11 uses the present tense, "That is." Seven Kings are mentioned, Julius Caesar, Augustus, Tiberius, Caligula, Claudius. The sixth "who is," as John writes (Nero 68 A.D.), is followed by the seventh, "who is not yet come, and when he does come, but for a short time." This Galba reigned from June 68 A.D. to January A.D. 69, the shortest reign.

9) Nero persecuted Christians for 3 ½ years (Rev 13:5), from November 64 A.D. to June 68 A.D., his year of death.

10) The Jewish temple present in typology (Rev 11:1, 2) is standing in figure. That is, according to the figurative interpretation of Revelation, The Temple was still standing for the purpose of measuring it by New Testament spiritual standards.

Evidence Examined – Early Church Fathers

1) Clement (150-215 A.D.) said, "For the teaching of our Lord at His advent, beginning with Augustus and Tiberius, was completed in the middle of the times of Tiberius. And that of the apostles, embracing the ministry of Paul, end with Nero."[17]

2) Tertullian (160-220 A.D.) places John's banishment in conjunction with Peter's and Paul's martyrdom (67, 68 A.D.).

3) Epiphanies (315-403 A.D.) twice states Revelation was written under "Claudius [Nero] Caesar."[18]

4) The Muratorian Canon (170 A.D.) notes, "The blessed Apostle Paul, following the rule of his predecessor John, writes to no more than seven churches by name." "John too, indeed, in the Apocalypse, although he writes to only seven churches, yet addresses all."[19] Therefore, John's Revelation was circulated to the seven congregations in his lifetime and not during the reign of Domitian.

5) The Syriac Vulgate Bible (6th Century) states, "The Apocalypse of St. John, written in Patmos, whither John was sent by Nero Caesar."[20]

6) Arethas (6th Century) "Arethas in the 6th Century, applies the sixth seal to the destruction of Jerusalem (70 A.D.), adding that the Apocalypse was written before that event."[21]

(On Rev 6:12) "Some refer this to the siege of Jerusalem by Vespasian."

(On Rev 7:1) "Here, then, were manifestly shown to the Evangelist what things were to befall the Jews in their war against the Romans, in the way of avenging the sufferings inflicted upon Christ."

(On Rev 7:4) "When the Evangelist received these oracles, the destruction in which the Jews were involved was not yet inflicted by the Romans."

It really is not incumbent upon me to provide the above quotes from the Post-Apostolic Fathers about when they thought The Revelation was written. Although the above quotes are provided, it is only to show that there is just as much information from the Post-Apostolic Fathers on a pre-70 A.D. Revelation as there is afterwards. In reality, the only action necessary to prove the early dates is to read the New Testament books.

Why do the Post-Apostolic scholars and some present-day scholars want a late date for The Apocalypse? Is it not a selfish quest for power, not the least that of Apostolic Power? They know these scholars cannot prove the late date for other New Testament books, and since John's letters are more general and apocalyptic than historic, they are the only letters modern scholars can use to justify their acceptance of a dishonest late date. It is indisputable that from a cursory reading of the history of the Acts of the Apostles and historical references in The New Testament Epistles that all of the epistles including John's (John 5:2) were written before 70 A.D.

If we permit a little folly here, we might revisit the question, "When did John write The Revelation?" The student answers, "In 96 A.D." Then you enquire, "What is the evidence?" The student answers, "My last professor said it was 96 A.D." Then we ask his last professor the same question and he replies, "My last professor said it was 96 A.D." If you ask the professor when the Book of Matthew, Mark, and Luke were written, he would say "About 63-65 A.D." We continue, "How about 1st and 2nd Thessalonians and he answers "About 52-53 A.D." Thus, we continue, "What about the Corinthian Letters, Romans, Philippians, Colossians, Philemon, Ephesians, 1st and 2nd Peter, Hebrews, Timothy, Titus, and Philemon, and the answer is the same, "Approximately 62-68 A.D." The student is correct, and we know it is true because of the history of the New Testament and the ease of date setting in connection with the apostolic establishment of these congregations in the historical cities.

But the wonder of ironies is when we ask, "When did John write?" Some historians answer, "About 96 A.D." Some scholars also make the outrageous claim that John did not write his epistles until 98 A.D. Suppose we have 27 men standing before us and each man represents the birth of a Book of The New Testament. We want to know when their books were born so we ask them the question, "When was your New Covenant Testimony born on Earth?" The first 23 answer us in various orders of historic dates from 53 to 68 A.D. We may ask, "How do you know these birth dates are accurate?" and the 23 men say, "From the study of the Book of Acts, the Bible tells us so!" Then we ask the 24th (the Gospel of John), 25th (1st John), 26th (2nd John), and the 27th man (3rd John), "When was your testimony born on Earth?" and they say, "We guess about 96 or 98 A.D." Then we ask them the question, "Why were the 23 other men so much younger than you are?" Each of the 24th through 27th men replied, "The books of the other 23 men have legitimate, historical birth certificates and our books do not." They could not answer the question accurately because they have been victimized by latter day misapplications of inaccurate dating of the writing of their books,

There is a reason the millennial mythologists want a late date, or any date after 70 A.D. They want to minimize the events of 70 A.D. so they can use prophesies of Christ to fit into their futurist, eschatological scheme. Are they aware they are making Christ a lying prophet? They take the events predicted previously in 70

A.D., which would happen within at least a 40- year time block, and force these events into an end-time period, which at the time of this writing is 2,000 years later, and still has not happened. If we consider what Jesus said in Matthew 24 and Luke 21, and then read what the Millennial mythologists are saying, we would conclude that Jesus did not know what He was talking about. No other conclusion but a pre-70 A.D. writing for the Book of Revelation and all New Testament books should be accepted. The dating is critical because it provides context to The Revelation and gives meaning to those to whom it was written. Without the correct context, Revelation will be greatly misunderstood.

The Views of Eschatology and Revelation

The following views of eschatology (the study of last events or end times) and Revelation expressed in this section will be most meaningful to you who have previously studied the Book of Revelation. All recognized views are presented, and while I appreciate the eschatological scholarship dealing with this subject, new ideas have been identified that will benefit you.

When we read this Prophecy, we must see Christ in His exalted position on the right hand of the Throne of Majesty. If Revelation teaches anything, it teaches the universal reign of The Messiah on the right hand of God the Father, who is on His Throne.

It is essential to have some knowledge of the following: 1) Apocalyptic literature, 2) A great apostasy from the original Congregation of Christ, which was based upon the foundational New Covenant teachings of the Apostles, 3) Beastology, 4) Numerology, 5) Satan's strategy to remove the exalted Christ from His Throne (We recommend a reading of the Christological Controversy of the first three centuries A.D.), 6) A cursory understanding of the history of the rise of Orthodoxism in the East and Catholicism in the West, and 7) Finally, but not least, we MUST be Born Again of water and Spirit.

Unless we possess the Spirit of Christ, we will take the sublime revelations of Heaven and descend to the manifest absurdities of Earth. Being in the Spirit is most essential because John "Was in Spirit" when he received the Revelation, and Jesus said repeatedly, "He who has an ear, let him hear what the Spirit says to the congregations" (Rev 2:7, 11, 3:22).

Historicist View

Definition: The Book of Revelation was designed to forecast a general view of the whole period of congregational history from when John wrote until the end of time.

Doctrine: The Historicist view teaches a panorama, a series of pictures, which delineate the successive steps and outstanding features of the Congregation's struggle toward final victory. Most early Restorationists (to be addressed later) belong to the Historicist School (Including Campbell, a wishful Post-Millennialist – also to be addressed later). For people alive before Christ, the Historicist school would have been the only eschatological school. However, with the establishment of the Kingdom of God, this strict Historical view ended. God no longer has one nation (Israel) around which history revolves. In today's world, any nation can oppose the Kingdom of Christ on Earth. On the other hand, any nation can have citizens who are members of the Congregation of Christ.

Congregation of Christ – Christian Congregation scholar, H.S. Halley, author of *Halley's Handbook of the Bible*, believed this Historicist view. There are certain historical events in Revelation, like the following, which will not go away: the birth of the man-child, the birth of the Congregation, the rise of empires, including Rome and The Roman Catholic apostasy and the end of the world. Whether we like it or not, all schools of eschatological thought have to be Historicists from time to time. It is a paradox that the Futurist school (to be addressed later) finds Biblical fulfillment in modern-day history. Futurists are the worst eschatological school in their insane desire to examine history for fulfilling signs. The problem with pursuing fulfilling signs in history is that it is always yesterday's or today's history. No matter when we live in history, the Revelation also addresses that time.

The Historicist view of Revelation attempts to relate the events described in Revelation to historical events. The diversified views of various historicists indicate that there is no standard historical view of relating history to the symbols found in The Revelation. Overall, it appears that Revelation addresses historicity (linear time) as evidenced from the dramatic picture of the ongoing Congregation of Christ and Her breathtaking conflict with Political Rome (Rev 13), the ongoing struggle with Papal Rome (13:3) and her many children and worldly friends, and Babylonian habits and tactics.

Historicists have a good hermeneutical law of interpretation. They teach that all apocalyptic prophecy is about the rise and fall of historical nations. Just as Daniel's prophecy deals with Babylon, Persia, Greece, and Rome, (Da 2:38-43) so they expect Revelation to deal with nations down through the ages. We can agree with this interpretation, as far as the Old Testament is concerned. However, this "rise and fall of nations" interpretation cannot fit into the New Testament scheme of things. In the Old Testament, God had only one nation, which was physical Israel, through which He chose to reveal His will. Now, spiritual Israel is in all nations. Revelation shows the remnant congregation is in all nations, in all peoples and tongues (Rev 7: 9). So rather than revealing some particular nation in opposition to Old Israel, any nation at any given time in history can now be in opposition to the New Israel, which is the Congregation of Christ. We can correctly state that the Historicist keeps running out of time when the next generation comes with new history. Historicists must revamp their historical schedule. History eventually overtakes their predictions based on historical events when Christ does not come in their day.

Futurist View

Definition: Applying the Book of Revelation to the *distant Future.*

Doctrine: This view teaches that everything after Revelation 3 is future. They believe in Jewish supremacy, and their only concerns are about the future history of a literal Israel. They believe carnal Israel will again occupy Palestine; the Temple will be physically rebuilt; and the Holy City trodden down for 1,260 days by Gentiles. They still desire, as Jesus' disciples desired, Israel as it was in the days of Solomon (Ac 1:6). Futurists holding this view do not understand the Israel of Romans, Chapter 9. They do not know what Jesus meant when He said, "Destroy the temple and I will raise it up again in three days." They are still searching for The Ark, unmindful of the fact it has already been found (Rev 11:19). They are still searching for a red heifer to sacrifice, unaware that the very ashes of its sacrifice no longer work (Heb 9:13). According to Futurist doctrine, everything Christ did in the past was practically a failure. He failed to establish His Kingdom. He failed to sit on David's Throne. Therefore, Pre-Millennialists (to be addressed) look to the long lost future. This looking to the future continues today, over 2,000 years after Christ's crucifixion and resurrection. Like the hybridized Jew, they keep looking for the *real* Messiah to come and grant long awaited Jewish supremacy over the nations. Those of the Islamic faith will never accept this theological view. The following, in general, are the beliefs the Futurist entertain concerning Christ's return:

1. The Gospel will be preached to all nations.

2. A great apostasy

3. Wars, famines, earthquakes

4. *The* Great Tribulation

5. *The* rapture

6. Appearance of *the* Antichrist

7. The return of Christ will be followed by a period of peace before the end of the world (*the* millennium).

8. Christ will become King.

9. His reign, rather than being established by individual conversion, will come about suddenly with overwhelming power.

10. The Jews are converted and are very prominent at this time. If there are no authentic Jews of Judean ancestry, God will create another Jewish nation.

11. Nature will share the millennial blessings and become extremely productive. Lions will lie down with lambs; children will play with snakes; and the leopard will lie down with a young goat.

12. Evil is held in check by "the rod of iron reign."

13. The dead believers will intermingle in glorified bodies with Earth's inhabitants.

14. After *the* 1,000 years, the non-Christian dead are resurrected.

15. Since all the passages that address Heaven are applied to the "millennial reign," no one knows when or if anyone goes to Heaven or Hell.

Darbyite Futurist (Pre-Tribulation Pre-Millennialism)

Plymouth Brethren preacher, John N. Darby, taught that Jesus came to establish a visible rule on Earth. However, after the Jews rejected Jesus and His plan, the Kingdom was postponed until the Second Coming. Meanwhile, Jesus establishes a church, which is not a fulfillment of Old Testament prophecies, but a temporary measure to buy time until the rapture occurs. All believers will be caught up in *the secret rapture*, which occurs before the tribulation. Cyrus Scofield's Bible holds this view.[22] This thinking is also called Dispensationalism.

Dispensationalists believe the Kingdom of God will not come until Jesus returns. They do not believe the Bible is composed of two distinct covenants, the Old Covenant and the New Covenant. Yet, this distinction is made hundreds of times and is known from a random sampling of just a few inspired verses found throughout *the* New Testament. After reading the Bible as a single drama with two acts, Dispensationalist John Bright concludes,

> "Had we to give that book The Bible a title, we might with justice call it 'The Book of The Coming Kingdom of God.'"[23]

The inference here is that the Kingdom of God did not come in the Old; neither did it come in the New Testament. For that matter, all we can know from the one book is that the Kingdom of God may come someday. Interesting, the Pre-Millennials use the signs that preceded the 70 A.D. event and apply them to their end-time views. Let us examine the following verses REGARDING "signs" and arrive at our own conclusions (Mt 24:5-10, 15-20, 22, 25). Matthew 24 also includes Christ's prophecy that the Gospel would be preached to the world before the 70 A.D. destruction of Jerusalem. Nevertheless, this prophecy was fulfilled in the 1st Century (Ro 1:5, 8, 10:18, 16:26; Ac 17:6; Col 1:6).

Since Margaret Macdonald in 1820 A.D., and up to the present, soothsayers have been busy collecting random, prophetic Bible verses and arbitrarily arranging them to fit an historical scheme that always begins during the time when the soothsayer is living.

Dispensational Pre-Millennialism (Pre-Tribulation)

Dispensational Pre-Millennialism maintains that the millennium will begin on Earth, after Christ's Second Coming. This doctrine teaches that when Christ came in the flesh, He intended to set up His earthly kingdom for the Jews. However, since they rejected Him, He instituted His congregation instead. They now look to the unknown future for a definite establishment of an earthly kingdom at the Second, technically Third, Coming of Christ.

The above-mentioned events are referred to as a two-stage Coming of Christ. The first stage is Christ coming invisibly. This is known as the *rapture*. The dead Christians are raised first (first resurrection) and the Christians then living on Earth are changed. Both groups are taken to Heaven to live with Christ for a seven-year wedding feast. All of this occurs in secret. Meanwhile, for those people remaining on Earth, these seven years are dramatic. Evil men now control the world; they institute a period known to Futurists as *the great tribulation*. The Jews will restore their Old Testament greatness but experience some tribulation. During the tribulation, the Antichrist revives the Roman Empire and makes a covenant of peace with the Jews for 3 ½ years. After 3 ½ years, the covenant is broken with the Jews, and the Antichrist destroys them in the final Battle of Armageddon.

After these events, Christ visibly appears, in this second stage of His Second Coming, with the saints that He had raptured previously. Now, Satan will be bound by a chain in a sealed pit. The Jews who are alive will enjoy physical blessings on Earth for a period during this millennium. The Jewish saints and Christians will live on the planet Earth with Christ for a physical 1,000-year reign. Christ's Throne will be established on Earth, and the Old Testament temple will be rebuilt. When the millennium ends, Satan leads a rebellion, and Christ returns yet again, only this time with judgment.

The Great Tribulationists (Post-Tribulation)

The Great Tribulationists reject this Dispensationalism. While they hold a Future view of Revelation, they teach that all believers pass through *the great tribulation* before the rapture occurs. At the rapture, Christ will establish a Kingdom in Jerusalem, build the City of God, and rule the nations with an iron rod for a 1,000-year reign. After Christ's reign, He will return again in judgment.

The Secret Rapture: The Origination

Dave MacPherson spent a huge part of his life researching where the idea of a secret rapture originated. The connection of the word "rapture" with Christ's coming is a total misnomer. The word the Holy Spirit chose in association with the taking up of His people in both body and soul is *harpadzo*, "to seize, grasp firmly, catch away, take by force" (1Th 4:17). The word *harpadzo* is even used to describe a wolf raping a lamb. Harpadzo is derived from harpax and means "rapacious." It is used in association with extortionist (Lk 18:11) and "ravening wolves" (Mt 7:15; Ac 20:29). It means to seize, snatch, and plunder or catch away. Obviously, Christ wants His people to know that He is not going to let loose of them once He takes hold in view of eternity.

Another problem facing the rapture cult is that 1 Thessalonians 4:17 addresses both the body and soul-spirit being caught up in the rapture. The word rapture in its English context can only refer to soul ecstasy. This is why no honest, intelligent, reputable translator of Scripture has ever used the word "rapture" to translate the Thessalonians 4:17 *harpadzo*.

Anyone who could get a two-stage rapture coming out of 1 Thessalonians 4:14-17 by interpreting the preposition "for" as one coming for His saints and the preposition "with" as another coming with His saints could build the Empire State Building out of a doughnut hole. It is not only bad theology; it is horrible grammar.

MacPherson certainly put forth proper efforts to track the counterfeit origin of the theological word "rapture." On page 7 of *The Incredible Cover-Up*, he began with an early Brethren scholar, Samuel P. Tregelles, who wrote,

"I am not aware that there was any definite teaching that there would be a secret rapture of the Church at a secret coming, until this was given forth as an 'utterance' in Mr. Irving's Church from what was there received as being the voice of the Spirit. But whether anyone ever asserted such a thing or not, it was from that supposed revelation that the modern doctrine and the modern phraseology respecting it arose. It came not from Holy Scripture, but from that which falsely pretended to be the Spirit of God, while not owning the true doctrines of our Lord's incarnation in the same flesh and blood as His brethren, but without taint of sin."[24]

Tregelles said the secret *rapture* began with an *utterance* around the year 1832, and that Edward Irving, the person guilty of the *utterance,* did not believe that Christ was God in the flesh. This is an antichrist doctrine (1Jn 4:2). Irving was excommunicated for his views that Christ was not incarnated in a flesh body like our body. We know that Christ had to have a flesh body to be human, and Christ had to be human to be sinless.

Edward Irving founded the Catholic Apostolic Church in England.

> "In D.H. Kromminga's, 'The Millennium in the Church,' he says Pre-tribulationism may have other sources than Darby.' It is quite clear when we turn our attention to the Catholic Apostolic Church, which came into being about the same time. In 1830, members of a Presbyterian family near Glasgow began to speak in tongues. These prophecies made it plain that the return of our Lord depended upon proper spiritual preparation of His church, which included the restoration of the apostolate."[25]

A prophetic writer, J. Barton Payne who authored, *The Imminent Appearing of Christ*, wrote,

"For soon after 1830 a woman, while speaking in tongues announced the revelation that the true church would be caught up (raptured) to heaven before the tribulation and before Christ's return to earth. Irving was deposed from the ministry and died in 1834, but not before his 'Pre-tribulationism' had been introduced at the Powerscourt meetings."[26]

In *Kept from the Hour*, by Gerald B. Stanton (1956), he wrote,

"Pre-tribulationism has been variously attributed to the writings of Edward Irving, to the utterances of a woman-prophet in a trance, to the writings of Darby and his associates, to a godly clergyman named Tweedy, and ultimately to the Devil himself!"[27]

William B. Neatby's *A History of the Plymouth Brethren* (1901) drew the following conclusion:

"Brethrenism is the study of unfulfilled prophecy, and of the expectation of the immediate return of the Savior. If anyone had told the first Brethren that three quarters of a century might elapse and the church still is on earth, the answer would probably have been a smile, partly of pity, partly of disapproval, wholly of incredulity. Yet, so it proved. It is impossible not to respect hopes so congenial to an ardent devotion; yet it is clear now that Brethrenism took shape under the influence of a delusion, and that the delusion was a decisive element in all its distinctive features."[28]

Remember, Neatby wrote in 1901 and said, "*The Brethren were deceived.*" Neatby's honest and expert evaluation of a denomination based on delusions resembles closely the origin of Seventh Day Adventism and the delusions of Ellen G. White. It is a reminder of the origin of Mormonism as documented in Alexander Campbell's writing, *Delusions*" Joe Smith's spurious book of Mormon, his philandering, and his Elmer Gantry-like tactics to steal property, money, and wives in the name of his new religion is well documented in Fawn Brodie's *No One Knows My History*. Additional evidence confirming this apostasy from the true Christian faith can be found in monthly periodicals by Christian Apologists Jerald and Sandra Tanner, in Cowdery, Davis & Vanick's book, *Who Really Wrote the Book of Mormon*, and my work, *Sydney Rigdon University*. It is also a reminder of the delusions of Mary Baker Eddy in Christian Science.

LeRoy E. Froom produced his massive work, *The Prophetic Faith of Our Fathers* (1950), which included this insight:

"The 'utterances' appeared, first in Scotland and then in London, in 1831, and were revived as the gift of prophecy. During Irving's first tour of Scotland prayer had healed some young women. Later when supernatural manifestations began to appear, they claimed to have the gift of tongues. A favorable report from a delegation of Irving's congregation led to the organization of meetings to seek the restoration of the gifts. Despair of the world's conversion by ordinary methods of evangelism, and the expectation of supernatural manifestations as a prelude to Christ's second advent, laid the foundation for acceptance."[29]

Harold H. Rowdon's, in his *The Origins of the Brethren* (1967) stated,

> "It was later alleged-and strenuously denied-that one of the distinctive Brethren ideas regarding the Second Advent was of Irvingite origin (remember, the Brethren defrocked him for false teaching.) We must examine the Irvingite background to the Brethren view that, prior to the open return of Christ in judgment, He will return secretly in order to remove His people from a doomed world."

As early as September 1830, a distinction was drawn in an article in "The Morning Watch" (an Irvingite journal) between the *epiphany* and the *advent* or *Parousia* of Christ.[30]

F. Roy Coad wrote in *A History of the Brethren Movement* (1968),

"Within a few weeks Bulteel was taken up violently by the rising craze for the 'gifts' of healing and tongues' so soon to be identified with the Irvingite movement. Wigram and Darby, at Newton's suggestion, had already investigated these 'gifts' in the course of visits paid to their first place of occurrence at Row in Scotland, and had rejected them."

"Darby used the third Powerscourt conference in September 1833 to continue to attack apostasy in the church. In a sense this was the first assembly of the new sect. It was also the first occasion of disagreement between Darby and Newton. Darby introduced the ideas of a secret rapture and of a parenthesis in prophetic fulfillment between the 69th and 70th week of Daniel. These two concepts were the basis for what is known as Dispensationalism. Newton commented on Darby's interpretation of Daniel's 70 weeks, 'the secret rapture was bad enough, but this was worse.'"[31]

Darby went to his grave denying that the *rapture* idea originated with a clairvoyant woman prophetess, but McPherson's forensic evidence is overwhelming to the contrary.

Iain H. Murray's, *The Puritan Hope*, (1971) shed much light,

"All the salient features of Darby's scheme are to be found in Irving. At Albury and in Irving's London congregation a curious belief, practically unknown in earlier church history, had arisen, namely, that Christ's appearance before the millennium is to be in two stages, the first a 'secret rapture', removing the church before 'a great tribulation' smites the earth, the second the coming with His saints to set up His Kingdom. This idea came into full prominence in Darby. ' I deny that saints before Christ's first coming, or after His second, are part of the church', with breathtaking dogmatism Darby swept away what had been previously axiomatic in Christian Theology…" Murray says, "The link between Irving and Brethren prophetic beliefs seems to have been missed by most writers."[32]

Who is this Irving? Who is this dark horse the Brethren Movement would rather shun? Who is the defrocked preacher who is to the Brethren what Sydney Rigdon is to the Mormons? MacPherson gives us a background of his life. In summary, Irving was an ordained Presbyterian Minister who read Manuel de Lacunza's *The Coming of Messiah in Glory and Majesty* (1812). He translated it from Spanish into English in 1826. Lacunza, who wrote under the pen name Juan Josafat Ben-Ezra, believed in a future antichrist. This antichrist would not be an individual, however, but a corrupted Catholic priesthood.

Because the weight of Protestant scholarship fell, full-force on the fact that Rome was Religious Babylon, Lacunza was a product of the Roman zeal to encourage their priests to produce a work on Revelation that would get the prophetic heat of Babylon off them. But, the idea of answering Protestants with apocalyptic Scripture actually began in 1580. To the 16th Century, Rome saw no need to use the Bible as an apologetic to prove the legitimacy of their existence. Why use the Bible when they had government backed armies, the sword, the rack, the dungeon, and the power of boycott? But now things changed drastically. Millions of people began reading their Bibles. Luther encouraged his followers to fight the "Whore of Babylon" with Scripture because violence only feeds the beast. The Roman Church rebounded.

Maybe Catholic scholars can understand Scripture, and especially The Apocalypse? So, the Roman Catholics belatedly attempted a Catholic Reformation against Protestantism with a Counter Reformation (Councils of Trent: 1545-1547, 1551-1552, 1562-1563), which only strengthened previous Catholic doctrine. The Catholic use of apocalyptic Scripture started with Spanish Jesuit Francisco Ribera in 1580. The idea was to save Catholicism from the obvious attacks of people who had a prophetic-historical understanding of Papal Rome's rise like a phoenix from Pagan Rome's ashes.

Ribera Rescues Roman Catholicism: Jesuit scholarship came to Rome's rescue. In 1590, a Jesuit Francisco Ribera published a 500-page commentary on the apocalypse. The difference between the former, Ribera (1590, 1591) and the latter Lacunza (1812) is that Ribera thought an "antichrist" was an individual, but Lacunza thought it was a corrupted Catholic priesthood. Ribera seized the idea that an antichrist would appear in the last days and bring a 3½ year period of tribulation that would be centered on the Jews in Palestine.

Catholic historian G.S. Hitchcock wrote,

> "The Futurist School, founded by the Jesuit Ribera in 1591, looks for Antichrist, Babylon, and a rebuilt temple in Jerusalem, at the end of the Christian dispensation."[33]

For three centuries, Ribera's theology made no headway with Protestants. They refuted it in numerous publications, until the 19th Century, when it finally penetrated Protestantism. Ribera's theology was especially accepted in England, where it was incorporated into a more complex theology called Dispensationalism. Today, men like Oral Roberts, Pat Robertson, Billy Graham, Hal Lindsey, John Hagee, and Tim LaHaye all accept Ribera's Catholic supporting eschatology. This theology is contrary to Reformation theology, whether or not they realize its origin.

Despite its questionable beginnings, Futurism reigns over much of evangelical Protestantism. Most Futurists, with their maps of impending Middle East wars in one hand and their Hal Lindsey-type books in the other, see themselves on the cutting edge of last-day events. In reality, they are following the non-Biblical version of a Jesuit who died without hope almost four centuries ago.

Although much was written, the basic underlying pre-conceived idea behind both Ribera and Lacunza was to make the Revelation orient only to the *future,* regardless of one's historical standpoint, be it in the 16th Century or the 26th. The Papacy never thought anyone would ever take this theory seriously, but then along came Edward Irving. The Roman papacy could now smile and enjoy relief from the horrible embarrassments they had suffered previously from the theological Reformers. Catholicism had a champion in Irving. No wonder he called his cult the *Catholic Apostolic Church.*

Irving thought the last days were beginning with the restoration of the Apostolic Gifts. Although Irving never spoke in tongues or prophesied, he is called *the Father of Modern Pentecostalism.*

Irving was put on trial by the Presbytery on April 26, 1832 and found guilty. He had violated Presbyterian order by allowing a disruption of services with unauthorized utterances. They ordered him removed from the church. On May 6, the Trustees locked Irving and his disciples out of the building. They began meeting at Gray's Inn Road, where the Catholic Apostolic Church was born. Irving was finally deposed from the Presbyterian ministry altogether on Christological heresy.

We are placing our eternal soul at risk if, as Tregelles noted in *The Christian Annotator* (1855), "*not owning the true doctrine of our Lord's incarnation.*" If the Son of God is not fully God and fully man, and the Holy Spirit made Him sinless, then any person in a flesh body with the Holy Spirit could become the sinless, Son of God.

John Nelson Darby, born November 18, 1800 was an ordained Anglican Priest. He was thrown from a horse and during his recovery, he recounted that he meditated in the Bible and discovered the *rapture*. Dave MacPherson, mentioned previously, stated that a careful search of Darby's writings proves that his story is not true.

Darby, like Irving, was a former Post-Millennialist. They both switched to the Pre-Millennialist school. Irving did this because of Lacunza's book. According to a pamphlet, "Reflections upon The Prophetic Inquiry" (1829), William Kelly documented that Darby made no mention of the secret rapture. Finally, in 1830, Darby confessed that he had discovered that the rapture would precede the Day of the Lord. In that same year, he told his friend Benjamin Newton that a Mr. T. Tweedy, who was a Brethren from Ireland, cleared up the exegetical difficulties from 1Thessalonians 4:14-17.[34]

Brethren Church historian Harold Rowan states that according to Newton, the Brethren were teaching a two-stage coming as late as 1831. Darby was enthused with the doctrine at the 1833 Powerscourt session, but according to historian Sandeen, had doubts about his ideas of a secret rapture as late as 1843 or 1845.[35]

MacPherson took vital information about the idea of rapture from *Rev*. Robert Norton, who wrote *The Restoration of Apostles and Prophets in the Catholic Apostolic Church* (1861). This is what Norton witnessed in The Scottish Revival.

> "Marvelous light was shed upon Scripture, and especially upon the doctrine of the second advent, by the revived spirit of prophecy. In the following account by Miss M. M., of an evening during which the Holy Ghost rested upon her for several successive hours, in mingled prophecy and vision, we have an instance, for here we FIRST see the distinction between that final stage of the Lord's coming, when every eye shall see Him, and His prior appearing in glory to them that look for Him"[36]

The whole Macdonald family was involved.

> "Margaret's brother's James and George, 'whose mouths were open to confess and glorify the Lord when the power of the Spirit was most upon them, such heavenliness and awe-inspiring solemnity in their whole appearance and manner,' such deep toned inimitable music in their voices, such ecstatic rapture (at least a proper use of the word), in their eye, yea such a supernatural brightness stamped upon their countenances, as stamped upon their utterances a seal of divinity, the impression of which is quite incommunicable."[37]

The event that led up to the Scottish Revival is the report that Margaret became deathly sick. She was later healed by the laying on of hands and received the gift of prophecy.[38] The Miss M. M'D received the gift of tongues.[39] In reading MacPherson's reporting, the reader will notice that only Margaret MacDonald's name is repeatedly abbreviated. It is as if the writers do not want people to know the identity of the person behind the *rapture*.

The MacDonald's were acquainted with Edward Irving and George MacDonald. It is written on May 8, 1832 that the things taking place in Irving's London Church were presumptuous and "the work in him is all a delusion."[40] Both Irving and Darby were first hand observers of this wild, ecstatic Scottish revival, and yet, they distanced themselves as far from it as possible. The following is Darby's own account.

> "There was a pretended interpretation (of tongues). Two brothers and their sister Margaret Macdonald were the chief person who spoke, with a Gaelic maidservant, in the tongues, and a J. M'D spoke for a quarter of an hour then sang a hymn and sat down and requested an interpreter. His sister got up and professed to give the interpretation, but it was a string of texts on overcoming, and a hymn, and one if not more of the texts were quoted wrongly."

MacPherson says it is incredible that Darby could remember such small details after 23 years, and yet be silent on the central theme of the manifestations – Margaret's Pre-Tribulation rapture teaching. When Darby wrote (1853) of the experience that he had witnessed 23 years earlier, he knew the parties were dead or dispersed. He had preserved an understandably special interest in the unassuming Scottish lassie from which he had borrowed a key ingredient for his Dispensational system. Darby borrowed from her, modified her views, and then popularized them under his name without giving her credit. In his *Roots of Fundamentalism*, p. 20, Sandeen stated that Darby was intolerant of other prophetic teachers and did his part to draw attention away from the real origin of his special teaching.[41]

The Secret Rapture - The Truth:

The word RAPTURE is an unscriptural millennial mantra. Therefore, if we ask, "What is the difference between the 'alleged rapture' and Christ's Second Coming," there is no answer. We use the word "mantra" because a Scottish girl went into a trance and had a vision of a two-stage coming of Christ, and Edward Irving found out about it.

Without MacPherson's investigation into where and when the word "rapture" entered historical end time speculations, we would be greatly confused as to how ONE word can influence a cult of millions of people. Paul said, "We speak not in words taught by human wisdom, but in those taught by The Spirit-combining spiritual thoughts with spiritual words (1Co 2:13). It is true that koine Greek words have various synonyms, and a few modern Lexicographers try to force "rapture" into Scripture, but prior to Margaret Macdonald, the word "rapture" was never used in theological discussions.

Even more important than finding the origin of the word *rapture* in theology is the discovery that there is no such thing as *rapture*. The wheat and tares will grow together unto the end, but the tares will be gathered first (Mt 13:30). It does not say that the (righteous) wheat will be *raptured* and the (wicked) tares left behind for seven years or so of tribulation. Likewise, it is absurd for those of the Pre-Tribulation Pre-Millennial mindset to place 1,000 years in the middle of verse 30. To paraphrase (Mt 13:30), Jesus did not say, "Gather first the righteous and then gather the wicked later."

Therefore, when a Scottish girl went into a trance, Edward Irving found out about it. Darby learned it either firsthand from the girl or from Irving. During one of Darby's five visits to America, he told the story about the Scottish girl's trance to one, Cyrus Scofield. Now, you know the rest of the story.

Little did this Scottish Lassie ever realize that when she experienced her vision (from either the Devil, or she just made it up), she was providing Christian fiction for books about a "Great Snatch," sermons entitled "Missing", and movies called "Left Behind"! We would think it a real embarrassment to sell tons of books, make tons of money, make tons of tapes and movies, and do tons of talking about a subject that is unheard of and unknown in Scripture. But apparently there is no such embarrassment. No such transliteration has appeared. Nevertheless, God continues to allow great delusions to people who do not love or obey the truth.

No evidence exists anywhere for the word *rapture* in Scriptural translations. Sometimes God does not intend Scriptural expressions to be pretty or poetical, and this is one of them. Christ's coming to seize His Saints out of this wicked world is serious business. Since the tares, "the children of the wicked one," will be taken first (Mt 13: 30, 40), and they grow together with the wheat (children of God) unto the end, it is obvious that the righteous will see the casting of the wicked into the fire (vs. 40). Christ and His angels will gather out of His Kingdom and cast the wicked into the furnace. First, there will be weeping and gnashing of teeth (vs. 42), and afterward, the righteous shall shine forth with His glory. Maybe God wants the righteous to see this so they too can understand what could have happened to them had they spurned the Covenant of Grace.

This scene is indicative of Christ's great wrath toward those whom He showered mercy. It proceeds the great day of wrath and judgment. The word *rapture* defined by Funk & Wagnall (*Standard Desk Dictionary*) writes, "the state of being rapt, transported, ecstatic joy, ecstasy or excitement." This does no justice to the scene of the final day. I believe that the hardest job that Christ will have since the cross of Calvary will be to judge sinners who could have been saved and then condemn them into Hell fire.

The last memory of this final earth to hold sway over the minds of Christians will be the weeping, wailing, and gnashing of teeth of those "tares" that were taken. Remember, 1 Thessalonians 4:16 is talking about those dead in Christ rising before those who are alive in Christ rise when He comes. It does not say one thing about the dead in Christ being taken before the sinner. The two groups in the Thessalonians text are both Christians. Many Pre-Millennial preachers know this and hope that their gullible disciples will not read it. Once this true meaning in Thessalonians is understood, the complete Pre-Millennial scheme falls apart.

The teaching of Matthew 13:40 is about two different groups, the righteous and the unrighteous. This is contrary to the Pre-Millennial mythology that the unrighteous are taken first.

One Taken-the Other Left: Who is Behind the Left "Behind?" What about Luke 17:34 that states, "One shall be taken, the other left?" Of course, this may shake the faith of those who love to read the "Left Behind" series, or attend the "Left Behind" movies. However, the word "behind" is not in this or any other Scripture. The word is simply "left." To translate it "left behind" is to add to Scripture. The meaning "left behind" is not even remotely implied in the text.

First, there is nothing in the text that has anything to do with one person being raptured and another being left behind for a seven-year, or 3½ year tribulation.

Pre-Millennialists fail in their homework on the word "taken." The word *paralambano* means "to take to or with." It can mean to take into a good or bad relationship. *Paralambano* is used to describe the soldiers scourging Jesus (Mt 27:27) with the scorpion whip (not a good thing) and their taking Him to be crucified (Jn 19:16), which is certainly not a good thing. Even so, the context of Matthew 24:40, 41 is also to be taken into a bad relationship. The Pre-Millennialists do not bother with reading context, and if they had read the preceding (vs. 39), they would have understood, "And they (the wicked) knew not until the flood came and took them all away."

The word for "took" is *airo*. The English word *air* is derived from it. *Airo* means to lift, or take up or away, to raise (Strong 142). In 1 Corinthians 5:2, it is of divine judgment that would have been exercised by "taking away" from the congregation the incestuous delinquent (See Vines 1129.). In this context, this is a bad word, not a good one, as Pre-Millennialists want us to believe.

In the Great Judgment, Christians will see their friends, neighbors, loved ones, and fellow citizens taken away for judgment. This would be as horrible as seeing the police handcuff and take your best friend into instant trial and damnation. Yet, Pre-Millennialists do absolutely no research at all on the word "taken." Granted, the word can be used in a good sense, in light of Matthew 24:39, Jesus gave the context of being "taken" in a bad sense.

Pre-Millennialists do the same thing with the word "left." They love to employ the expression "left behind," but the word is *apheimi,* which means to send from. Vine defines *apheimi (p.* 665) as "send forth, let go or forgive, to leave, leave alone, forsake or neglect." Vine tells his reader to "see *forgive* for a further understanding of the word." The Pre-Millennialist gives the impression that those *left* are the bad people who are *left behind.* However, if the Holy Spirit wanted the reader to think that way, He would have used the Greek word *apoleipo,* which does mean, "to leave *apo* 'from, or behind.'" However, the word *apheimi* simply means that those left will be sent forth from the scene of the slaughter and destruction.

Therefore, a *left behind* interpretation of Scripture is totally unwarranted by the Holy Spirit. Yet, the Devil pays a soothsayer a lot of money to twist these verses to mean the exact opposite of what they mean. Dishonesty can pay, at least for a while!

Vaughn Elliot wrote a little book entitled *I Want to Be Left Behind!* Vaughn saw the discrepancy in the popular interpretation of Matthew 24:39 and wrote his book with a title to try and arrest the attention of those who want to be in the wrong group when Christ comes.

Post-Millennial View

Doctrine: Post-Millennialism is a system of eschatology that states the Messianic Kingdom was founded on Earth during Christ's earthly ministry, through the redemptive labors of the Lord, Jesus Christ. This founding fulfilled the Old Testament prophetic expectation. The fundamental nature of that Kingdom is essentially redemptive and spiritual, not political and corporeal. Bahnsen, in his work *House Divided*, presents very strong and convincing opposition to the Pre-Millennial cult. One captivating footnote from Bahnsen's book concerned the rapture cult craze that Christ's rapture was very near. Thousands of rapture books were sent to Jerusalem to be stored and read after the rapture took place. In fact, the boxes of books were emptied, and the paper was used to make cigarettes.[42]

Post-Millennialism teaches that the Kingdom will exercise a transformational socio-cultural influence in history as more people become converted to Christ. There will be a gradual development of the Kingdom on Earth over time. Christ reigns now over the Earth, and He directs His Spirit-filled people. Post-Millennialism confidently anticipates the time when the church will overcome the world. During that time (millennium), the overwhelming majority of the nations will be Christianized. Righteousness will abound; all wars will cease; and prosperity and safety will flourish. After this extended period of Gospel prosperity (Some Post-Millennials do not believe it is a literal 1,000 years.). Christ will return personally, visibly, and bodily (accompanied by a literal resurrection and to introduce a general judgment). He will take His blood-bought people into the eternal form of His Kingdom.

Preterist View

Doctrine: There are two main divisions in Preterism.

<u>Fundamental</u>: This view holds everything in Scripture was fulfilled at the destruction of Jerusalem in 70 A.D. It teaches that the description of the New Heaven in Revelation is associated with the 70 A.D. events. Revelation is only a picture of Early Church conflicts, which have already been fulfilled; thus, Fundamental

Preterists deny the future predictability of the New Testament after 70 A.D.

Liberal: This view supports both pre- and post-70 A.D. events recorded in the Bible, but not for events later than 476 A.D. (when Rome fell). Paradoxically, this view of the true Preterist doctrine does not recognize in Matthew 24, Mark 13, and Luke 20 and 21 anything concerning Christ's Second Coming.

Questionable philosophies: The danger of Preterism is that Biblical Christians do not have a complete Biblical view of the end time (See Addendum H – The End!). According to the Preterist view, all Biblical revelation ends either in 70 or 476 A.D. This violates the promise that what was lost in the past (Ge 2), will be gained in the future (Rev 22). Preterism not only confuses the Second Coming of Christ with the visitation of Christ during the destruction of Jerusalem, but it breaks down the hermeneutical approach to the Scriptures and fails to understand the time and judgment of the Gentiles (Lk 21:24), which occurs long after the destruction of Jerusalem.

While the liberal division of Preterism can be commended for the wisdom of understanding the Scriptural importance of 70 and 476 A.D., its failure to properly present the Second Coming in these prophecies weakens the overall content that the Prophet Jesus intended. This view, of course, does not aid its pursuit of prophetic honesty, and the evangelistic appeal or warning of the prophecy is lost. Because of the absence for the urgency of the Second Coming of Christ, neither the Preterit nor Pre-Millennial view has a real New Covenant soul-winning-conversion conscience. Preterists are not as numerous as they would be if they would just fit Preterism into its proper historical perspective and preach earnestly that what happened to the Jews in 70 A.D. will happen to us Gentiles if we do not repent before we meet the Lord. Pre-Millennial preaching creates such controversy and confusion that people are more afraid of a so-called rapture than they are being prepared to meet the Lord either in death or in His ONCE and FINAL coming (whichever comes first).

Biblical evidence: The Preterist view has difficulty understanding the difference between the *signs of His coming* and the *day of His coming*. There are several "ends" discussed in the Bible (See Addendum H.). Two ends in particular are the *end of Judaism* and the end *of the world*. These are known as dual prophesies, which are prophesies of two related events in the same context.

Every honest Bible scholar realizes that in the Matthew, Mark, and Luke accounts of Jesus' Olivet discourse (regarding the end of the Jewish temple and end of the age), Jesus is addressing the 70 A.D. Abomination of Desolation. What Preterists miss is that all three Gospels not only speak of the end of the Jewish world but also the end of the world (this present age). It is very obvious that in the following Gospel accounts, Jesus addressed the end of the world.

Matthew's Account

> "But of that day and hour no one knows, no, not even the angels of heaven, but my Father only. But as the days of Noah were, so shall also will the coming of the Son of man be. For as in the days before the flood, they were eating and drinking, marrying and giving in marriage, until the day that Noah entered into the ark, and did not know until the flood came and took them all away, so shall also will the coming of the Son of man be. Then two men will be in the field: one will be taken, and the other left. Two women will be grinding at the mill: one will be taken, and the other left. Watch therefore, for you do not know what hour your Lord is coming. But know this, if the master of the house had known what hour the thief would come, he would have watched and not allowed his house to be broken into. Therefore, you also be ready, for the Son of man is coming at an hour you do not expect" (Mt 24:36-44).

Mark's Account

> "Take heed, watch and pray; for you do not know when the time is. It is like a man going to a far country, which left his house and gave authority to his servants, and to each his work, and commanded the doorkeeper to watch. Watch therefore, for you do not know when the master of the house is coming — in the evening, at midnight, at the crowing of the rooster, or in the morning —lest, coming suddenly, he finds you sleeping. And what I say to you, I say to all: Watch!" (Mk 13: 33-37)

As we can clearly see from the warning, "What I say to you, I say to all: Watch!" can be applied to both the Jewish nation facing 70 A.D. judgment and billions of Jewish and Gentile souls after 70 A.D. These billions of souls are those who will have lived and died in each successive generation after 70 A.D. and in the end, with the whole world's living and dead, facing the Last Judgment.

Luke's Account

"But take heed to yourselves, lest your hearts be weighed down with carousing, drunkenness, and cares of this life, and that Day come on you unexpectedly. For it will come as a snare on all those who dwell on the face of the whole earth. Watch therefore, and pray always that you may be counted worthy to escape all these things that will come to pass, and to stand before the Son of Man" (Lk 21:34-36).

Approximately 250 New Testament verses refer to either the post-70 A.D. history or the actual war of Rome against the Jews in 70 A.D. We will also find the significance of other 70 A.D. references in the Old Testament, such as Deuteronomy 28:50-68.

Matthew: 3:7,11, 12; 5:18; 8:11, 12, 16-24; 12:32-34, 42-45 13:15; 15:14; 19:30; 21:19, 40-45; 22:7,13; 23:31,33-38; 24:2-28; 32-35; 27:25, 42-43

Mark: 3:29, 30; 4:12; 7:6-13; 11:13, 14, 17-21; 13:1-13; 13:20.

Luke: 2:34; 3:7,9; 6:49; 7:31, 32; 10:11-15; 11:31,49; 12:11,47; 13:3- 9, 28, 34; 14:16,24; 17:23,30-37; 19:12,40; 20:14,46; 21:6,21,28; 23:28

John: 11:47, 48; 12:37

Acts: 2:40; 3:20; 5:28; 13:41, 46

Romans: 2:4, 9; 4:15; 9:15, 22; 13:11

Galatians: 4:9, 24

Philippians: 4:5

1 Thessalonians: 2:14

Hebrews: 6:8; 10:37; 12:25; 13:15

James: 4:13; 5:1

1 Peter: 4:7

Revelation: 22:7, 12, 20

There are also hundreds of references to 70 A.D. in the Old Testament for us to discover for ourselves.

Improper hermeneutics: Does the evidence support the conclusion?

Preterists reason that Jesus' saying, "the time is near" (Rev 1:3), and "things which will take place hereafter" (1:19) support their view of a pre-70 A.D. fulfillment of the Book of Revelation. However, Jesus begins the Book of Revelation saying, "things, which must shortly take place" (1:1), and John closed the Book with "even so, come quickly, Lord Jesus." In the sense of His visitation of judgment on The Jewish nation, Jesus did come. James said, "The Judge is at the door" (Jas 5:9). This had to refer to 70 A.D. There is no honest way any interpreter of Scripture can deduce from Revelation 21 and 22 any vision other than that of eternal bliss in Heaven. Truly, Jesus did say to the early Congregation, "the time is near," but He also spoke of the grand, climactic event which "will take place hereafter."

Just as the Futurist view robs God's children of the prophetic past, so too does the Preterist view rob God's children of the prophetic warnings of ongoing persecution. It also robs us of the prophetic New Testament verses that make no sense unless they are understood in a post-70 A.D. context dealing with our Heavenly reward. Revelation was written to comfort the Saints of the 1st and 2nd Centuries, as well as Christians throughout the ages. The Preterist time-period must be understood in the context of cyclical time (to be discussed further in this Section). Several aspects of the Preterist teachings simply do not support the proper application of hermeneutics. The Preterist view forces an interpretation on Scripture and causes us to miss the beauty and hope of that unfulfilled New Testament Prophecy. If evidence does not support the theory that we are testing, those propositions supporting the theory must be discarded instead of forcing them into a false interpretation.

Preterism is so far of a "swing of the pendulum" against Futurism that it causes a Preterist to miss the true Biblical teachings of the Biblical prophecies. Preterist scholars cannot see Religious Rome in the Book of Revelation, the compilation of Daniel's Beast in Revelation 13, or the little horn rising out of Rome that, according to Daniel, corresponds exactly with the head that was wounded. Nonetheless, some Preterist scholars can see Religious Rome as the "Man of Iniquity" in 2 Thessalonians 2:3, but fail to see the link to Revelation 18:8-16. The only difference is that the Thessalonians enemy is the "man of iniquity," whereas the Revelation enemy is the "Woman of Iniquity." The simple solution to the difference is the fact that the iniquitous men and women get married. This is an excellent example of being guilty of *supposing or assuming something beforehand and taking it for granted in advance.*

Guilty of presupposition: The outcome of the fundamental Preterist View is due largely to an overreaction to the fundamental Futurist view. Many Biblical scholars succumb to this overreaction. Unfortunately, they approach God's word with a mindset of "No fulfilled Prophecy after 70 A.D. (Fundamental) or A.D. 476 (Liberal)." In examining the Biblical evidence further, we see that Daniel's "little horn" corresponds exactly to the Thessalonians "Man of iniquity." If the little horn of Daniel is found compatible with the symbols of the healed head, which is the whore and Babylon, then why cut the horn off in 476 A.D. That horn would grow unto the end and make it very difficult to make a factual case that the end was in 476 A.D. The idea of the "end" is better suited to fit the *end of time*, for "Christ slays him with the breath of his mouth." Preterism is an adequate approach to eschatology, but it can be an overreaction to the Futurist view, if it forces everything into the 70 or 476 A.D. mold.

Unloving father: Another issue vital to this discussion is whether God kept His promise to warn His people (Dt 18:9-22). Hundreds of times, God inspired the writers to write, "It shall come to pass." Jesus said, "I have told you before it comes to pass" (Jn 14:29). 2 Thessalonians 2:5 records Paul telling them "these things" before it happened. Christians would have been greatly confused if the Lord had not warned them that being a Christian could lead them to persecution, deprivation, and death. Pagan Rome slaughtered thousands of Christians, and the blood of martyrs was the seed of the Congregation. Then, when the absolute, imperial power shifted from Pagan to Papal Rome, the total amount of Christians that died is listed by some scholars as being more than a million, and by others "Innumerable." David A. Plaisted quotes various scholars that estimate 50 million, 68 million, 100 million and 150 million. Roman Catholic scholars typically give smaller numbers, but do not document where their information comes from.[43] Without begging the issue, from what your author has read over the years from many apocalyptic scholars, the absolute truth remains that millions of Christians were martyred by the Roman Church. Consequently, we conclude that if the Lord had not warned his people of such a wholesale slaughter, He would not have been fair in His candid, yet instructive message to prepare His suffering congregation to face such evil forces with courage and victorious persuasion.

The Revelation mentions the worse crime against New Covenant Christianity. This crime is far worse than martyrdom, torture, boycott, or starvation. The most heinous crime against New Covenant Christianity is the flood of false doctrine that comes from the serpent's mouth through secular laws and human religious dogmas. It would neither be fair nor be characteristic of the loving Father and gracious Lord to not warn His children in each generation of the coming rise of Rome and her children. The Preterist view misses this.

A-Millennialist View

A-Millennialism maintains that the millennium began at the Resurrection and Ascension of Christ and will end shortly before Christ's Second Coming. At this moment, while Satan is bound by the Gospel of an apocalyptic 1,000-year reign, he cannot prevent the Congregation of Christ from spreading the Gospel of Christ to all the nations.

This view holds that Christians now enjoy spiritual blessings in Christ. This reign will continue until the last Gentile, who is to be saved, is saved. Those in Christ during the millennium enjoy a state of paradise with Christ as they sit on their thrones in Heaven. All Christians reign as priests and Kings with God. This 1,000-year period is a symbol for a long period until the end of the world. The millennium will end with God's allowing Satan's release for a little while, and finally, with Satan being punished by Christ's judgment.

The Philosophical School of History View

Doctrine: This view teaches that The Revelation can be applied in each period throughout church history. This view does not attach one particular symbol to one particular historical event as, for example, the locusts of Revelation 9:3 being Muslim hordes. However, we admire the skill and historical discernment of Historicists as they identify in history, nations, and events and connect these with current events in church history. This work is not altogether in vain, but the Philosophical School is correct to say that Historicists keep running out of time, and when the next generation comes with new history, they must revamp their historical schedule. History eventually wears out the Historical view when Christ does not come when each generation of Historicists live.

Under the Christian persecution, symbols are given in Revelation. The School of Philosophy interprets any anti-Christian government or religion at any given time throughout history, as a fulfillment of that symbol. For instance, the lamb that spoke like a dragon could have been the heathen religions of Rome who pretended to *join* the Christian Congregation in the 2nd Century, but it could also refer to the Shinto religion of Japan in the 20th Century, or Washington's cultural religion today in America.

Recapitulationalist View

Doctrine: Closely associated with School of Philosophy is the Recapitulation View of Parallelisms in Revelation. Apparently, this idea first originated with Robert Milligan. The conservative William Hendrickson popularized Recapitulationalism in his book *More Than Conquerors*. Holders of this view believe spiritual warfare exists between the Church and the world, between good and evil, from Pentecost until the end of time. The Beast from the Sea stands for political opposition against the Church in any given age. The Beast of the Land is corrupt religion in any given age. The Harlot is the compromised Church. Scholars have taken great interest in combining the best of Historicism (The battle to the end between the true Church and the Whore-Romanism and her children.) and the Philosophy of History approach (The true Church faces recurrent enemies in each historical age.).

Thus, Revelation is historical because it has a beginning (the Seven Churches, the Risen Lord, the Man-Child, the Espoused Bride), and it has an ending (the Golden City and commencement from time to eternity). Yet, the book is also cyclical in its obvious parallelisms. It is easy to see both linear-chronological times in Revelation, and at the same time, see recapitulations. John is on Earth in the midst of war, famine, death, persecution, martyrdom, and opposition to the Kingdom of God, and this goes on in linear time. Yet, John's visions lift him into the heavenly realm where he sees things outside of time. These visions are snapshots, such as the Lamb on the Throne, the Heavenly Court and witnesses, the angels, the martyrs under the altar, and the souls that were beheaded. In the end, of course, he sees the Holy City.

Accordingly, linear time revolves through timeless eternity like the hands of a grandfather clock revolve in a stationary cabinet. James 3:6 provides a great illustration of this from a contrary viewpoint. He says that the evil tongue sets on fire the cycle, or turning of nature, of those born *genomai* in each revolving cycle of life from one generation to the other. Yet, the cycle of each evil-speaking generation revolves so close to eternal Hell-fire that each generation is spun off into the red-hot flames. The generation that recycles into the next sphere of earthly activity has its evil tongues set ablaze by the same Hell-fire. Thus, we can see the cycle of the wicked world revolving so closely to the eternal fire that we can experience the heat in a person's blasting gossip, slander, or backbiting. In this sense, history does repeat itself when the familiar spirits of the parents affect their offspring.

Actually, it is a wonder the scholars did not see the seven cycles sooner because Revelation naturally divides itself into seven parallel sections. These sections are woven throughout the book, and for that matter, throughout the time of the Congregation's existence in this hostile world. Therefore, in any give age, Christians can expect to see Revelation being fulfilled. Earth was affected by the powers depicted under the symbolism of the horsemen, seals, trumpets, good or evil supernatural creatures in the days of the Caesars, and the Czars, as much as it is affected by the same today. The heavenly institutions in John's vision are permanent but the generations and nations that have come into being and spun off into eternity keep springing up like flowers in the springtime, destined to die in winter. In a country like America, for instance, the people can foolishly elect rulers as evil as Nero. But in America, the ruler's ability to impose the rule of social-benevolent demons upon the country's population is determined more or less upon the quota of true believers, indwelt by the Holy Spirit, who influence the general population.

Remnant Restoration View of Eschatology

Doctrine: There are a surprising number of Congregation of Christ and Christian Congregation scholars who are beginning to use the word *remnant* to describe the primitive Apostolic Congregation of Christ that is found in any age.

One cannot really pigeon hole this Eschatological view. This view is Historicist in that it teaches the Roman Church, which is an extension of Pagan Rome, and the Congregation of Christ are revealed in continuous history from Jerusalem and Rome unto the end. The true Bride comes from Jerusalem. The Whore comes from Babylon, which is really the seven-hilled city of Rome. The true Bride will never be universally known until the Whore is exposed. Since the Whore masquerades as the Bride of Christ, the world will never know the identity of the true Congregation.

However, the Remnant knows who the Bride is, and they are waiting for her to be revealed in totality. The remnant is described as those who did not embrace the

Greek-Babylonian-Roman apostasy. They are also considered to be those who emerged from The Dark Ages (a part of The Middle Ages) as still embracing the pure Bride of Christ. Some scholars take the remnant as being the number of true Christians who have been espoused to Christ down through the ages. This divine acknowledgement of the faithful will occur when all of them "As His Bride" are presented to the Lamb and the Father for the eternal marriage feast. The Whore, whom everyone thought was the true Bride, will be burnt with fire. Only at the end of the world will the distinction between the two be manifest. Our understanding of this requires knowledge of history, especially the history of the rise and fall of old Rome and the rise of Papal Rome upon her ashes.

The Remnant Restoration also contains viewpoints similar to those found in the School of Philosophy. Even though the Remnant position contains a continuous history of the Congregation and Papal Rome, it also teaches cyclical history. However, rather than selecting one nation or empire, it holds political, religious, or intellectual antichrist activities from any age as being threats to primitive Christianity. God no longer has one nation in physical Israel. The Kingdom of Christ is scattered throughout all the nations of the Earth and has been for 2,000 years. Therefore, it is foolish to look at one nation such as Austria-Hungary, France, Germany, Russia, China, or any other as one of the Revelation Beasts or Antichrist. This is true for Christians who have been and are in all of these countries. Any antichrist in general, in any age, is understood under the imagery of Beastology in Revelation. Time in Revelation is both cyclical and chronological. The Remnant position also shares the Preterist view concerning what happened in 70 A.D. because the same calamity that befell the Jews can happen to any violator of the New Testament Covenant (Ro 11:18-21).

In addition, this Remnant view is Post-Millennial because the Remnant view recognizes Christ on the throne but rejects a literal 1,000-year reign on Earth with Christ in a physical Jerusalem. It only recognizes a spiritual reign of Christ over the Earth. Even though some of its members are still on Earth, Christ's reign is still a spirit-filled, soul-winning reign. The view is also Post-Millennial in the sense that it teaches the Gospel changes the world, makes the nations prove the glories of Christ's righteousness, and proves the wonders of God's love.

The Remnant view denies the Post-Millennial assumption that because the different books of the Bible were combined into one book, Christians should consult the Old Testament when considering rule, faith, and practice. The Remnant view accepts the Old Testament as inspired of God but accepts what the Apostle Paul taught, "These things happened to them as examples, and they are written for our admonition, upon whom the ends of the world have come" (1Co 10:11).

When Paul speaks of "These things happened," Paul gives a condensed history of Israel in the first ten verses. When that history is examined, we discover very few of them pleased God. For example, only two people of all the Ten Tribes who left Egypt in the Exodus entered into the Promised Land. Later, Israelites killed the prophets and experienced captivity several times, under Assyria, Babylon, Persia, Greece, Syria, and Rome. Those things were not necessarily written for the Israelites at that time, but as examples for New Testament Christians.

Additionally, Paul wrote so plainly in the books of Romans, Galatians, Ephesians, and Hebrews that Christians are not under the Law. Remnantists are New Covenant Christians only. No other options exist in God's plan!

This Remnant view contains aspects of A-Millennialism, but only in the sense that it denies the Pre-Millennial view of things. Since the Remnant view accepts 1,000, apocalyptic years of Christ's spiritual reign, it must accept with reservation the Latin millennial label for 1,000. However, this view is self-evident. "Do not put a 'Pre', 'Post', or 'A' on it."

The Remnant view is not Pre-Millennial or Dispensational. It totally rejects a future, complicated scheme of things. The future existing when Christ spoke prior to the 70 A.D. desolation is past history for Christians. The future Apostasy, that was future when Paul spoke, is now past history as well. The victory of the Gospel over Babylon, associated with the weakening of Papal Babylon through the Iron-Rod-Reign of the Gospel, is behind us; it is past. This victory is indicated by the Evangelistic witnesses standing up (Rev 11:11) and a powerful Remnant Reformation causing the nations of the world to hate the Whore (17:16, 17), "For God put in their hearts to fulfill His will, to agree and give their kingdom to the beast, until the words of God shall be fulfilled" (17:17).

It is true that the powerful Protestant movement to break the shackles of Eastern and Western Catholicism would have been future to those living prior to the 15th Century. However, the same thing is true today. Christians live with a future hope just as they live their lives to encourage others to break the shackles of the Whore and all the Whore's children living today. These challenges were completely unknown to Peter, James, John, and Paul in the 1st Century.

If we are disgusted with the modern-day soothsaying Futurist, who looks daily in the newspaper and listens to the latest news about happenings in the in Middle East, let us remember that the Apocalypse focuses solely on the war between the Woman and her Gospel seed against the Whore and her lies. This is not a physical war between two or more nations; this is not a war involving planes, tanks, missiles, antiaircraft gunners, and atomic bombs; and this is an even greater war involving the far greater stakes of eternal life and death. This war is the good fight of the faith, and it goes on in every day and age.

The war of contending for the faith is past, present, and future. It is possible that the best days for fighting against the Whore and her children lie in the future. Only in this sense can we call them *Futurists*. Only in this sense can we interpret in The Revelation a future for the steadfast Disciples of Christ who will overcome the Beast and the world through New Covenant Christianity.

As we can expect, the one great future event is Christ's returning in great victory and power to reward His waiting covenant people and to punish the wicked overshadows all future events. This event is seen in each of the seven parallel sections of Revelation. Meanwhile, the Remnant view insists on continuing to contend for the New Covenant faith. It charges Christians to be active, to rebuke the works of darkness, to evangelize the world, and to prayerfully encourage according to the New Testament world view how everything from eco-politics to private enterprise to foreign policy should be influenced by Christian virtue and judgment.

The Apocalypse needs to be approached with a proper hermeneutical mindset. We must remove all presuppositions from our minds. This book needs to be examined with an open Spirit to God's truth and a closed Spirit to false doctrine.

> "Reverential caution must be taken when we attach a completely, literal times sensitive meaning to an apocalyptic symbol, for in doing so we destroy the God-intended purpose of the symbol."
>
> -Charles Walter Doughty

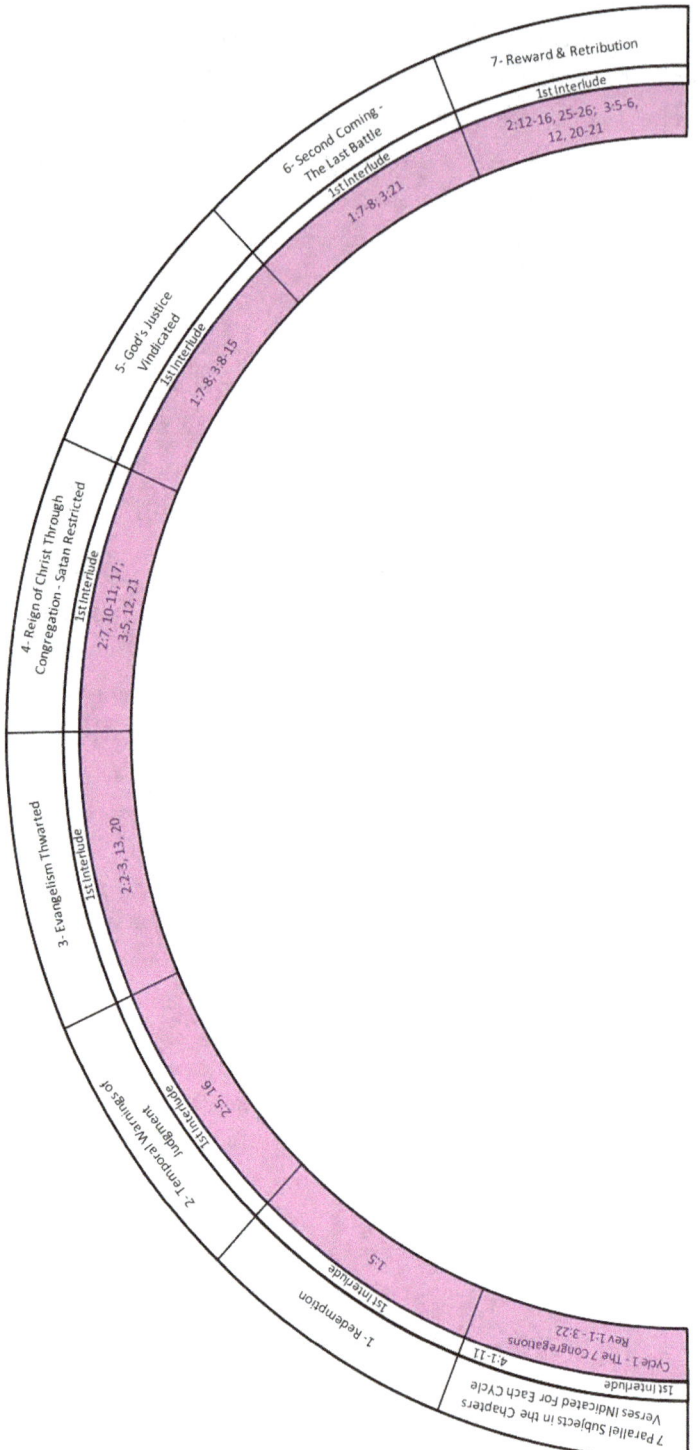

CYCLE 1 - THE SEVEN CONGREGATIONS

Christ in the congregation

Revelation Chapter One

Revelation 1:1: *The Revelation of Jesus Christ, which God gave unto him, to shew unto his servants' things which must **shortly come to pass; a**nd he sent and signified it by his angel to his servant John:*

This is the Revelation of Christ, recorded by the Apostle John. Jesus Christ is the author and editor of this book. John is simply recording the things that he saw and bore record (verse 2). John is writing this book to "show the servants of the things that must shortly take place." Did God give this vision of hope, encouragement, and truth to John only for Christians to enjoy a thousand or so years later? That would not make sense! Any Christian throughout the ages could gather strength and encouragement from this Book. However, this Revelation was given to persecuted Christians for their immediate needs.

This Revelation was given specially to persecuted Christians throughout history to the end time. This first verse obliterates the philosophy that Revelation is only talking about its being fulfilled in the distant future. The events mentioned in Revelation were coming to pass shortly, not thousands of years later. Jesus says at the end of Revelation that He is coming quickly (Rev 22:20). The word "come" (erchomai) can mean to appear or accompany. Was John wrong by saying, "Even so come Lord Jesus?" How soon would Jesus come in order to answer John's prayer? Jesus was coming quickly!

Our physical death and expiration from this world is the last stop before the Second Coming of Christ. The word "quickly" means without delay, soon, or suddenly. It is significant that Christ did come in 70 A.D. (Mt 22:7, 24:3-27; Lk 19:27, 40-44, 20:16, and 21: 20). In his Greek lexicon, Joseph Thayer cites the many references to Christ's Second Coming, but he observes that one word for His coming "parausia" (which means to come along side, or be present with) is associated with Christ's presence with Roman General Titus as he advanced upon and destroyed Jerusalem. If we look up the word "coming" in Thayer's work, we are also reminded of the kindred word, "visitation," that is used with the "Destruction of Jerusalem." Whether the Day of His Visitation is associated with the subpoena to judgment because of the Jewish rejection of Christ, or the actual "Abomination of Desolation," these two events amount to the same thing. Some people easily confuse these events with the Second Coming of Christ at the end of our world, but it also refers to the Abomination of Desolation and the coming of Christ at the end of the Jewish World, by which Christ brought to an end the Temple worship, Mosaic Law, animal sacrifices, the Levitical Priesthood, and the Israel that existed in the Old Testament.

Jesus spoke of the end of our present world in Matthew 24:28 when he said, "Immediately after those days." Those were the last days of the Jewish world. The next event on God's calendar is Christ's Second Coming. Remember, Revelation was written from God's perspective, which is outside of time.

WE ARE STUDYING AN APOCALYPTIC BOOK

The Greek word for Revelation is *"apokalupsis,"* and it means to unveil or discover a concealed or hidden thing. Remember, this Greek word is not plural, "Revelations," but is one solid revelation from God given to His faithful Apostle John by Jesus Christ.

Apocalyptic literature is unlike any other New Testament writing. Parallels to this writing are found in the Old Testament in Daniel, Ezekiel (See Addendum B), parts of Isaiah, and Zechariah. We would be foolish to attempt to interpret this vision in harmony with historic or poetic styles. This writing is not a parable or a large metaphor. It is an apocalyptic writing and must be interpreted as such. Scholars not familiar with apocalyptic figures, terms, and literary style will make a total mess of the Revelation message.

Revelation 1:2: Who bear record of the word of God, and of the testimony of Jesus Christ, and of all things that he saw.

The Word of God is from God the Father, and the testimony of Christ is the New Testament. John is getting prepared to write things that he saw personally. He had already given an eyewitness account concerning the ministry of Christ (Gospel of John and 1, 2, 3 John), and now John is beginning his apocalyptic vision of what he *heard, saw, and felt*. This spiritual experience was far more than surreal. It would have been the most factual experience John ever had. This letter is called an epistolary (letter) in the aorist tense (past tense). This means that John was writing to us, his readers, as though he, himself, were looking us in the eye and speaking to us in Spirit.

The word witness or testimony comes from the Greek *martus*. Vine, p. 1248, defines it as one who can or does aver what he has seen or heard or knows. Kittel defines it pp. 564, 565 as bearing judicial witness to the facts. Although the English "martyr" implies a dying for the faith, the original word meant to bear witness in life or death.

This word "testimony" or "witness" gives additional proof of the pre-70 A.D. writing of Revelation. Jesus prophesied that the Gospel would be preached as a testimony before The Abomination of Desolation (Mt 24:14; Mk 13:10; Lk 24:14). Witness or testimony is found in the singular and plural 18 times in Revelation. It is found 173 times in the New Testament and is used by the Apostle John 83 times in his five writings. John uses these words more than any of the other inspired apostolic writers. Furthermore, John begins and ends Revelation with "Testimony" and "Testifies" (Rev 1:2, 22:20).

No judicial testimony can exist only by word of mouth. For the Word of God to be preached as a witness to all nations, it must be bound in a legal document. Jesus did not say that the Word would simply be preached. It would also be a witness, *a judicial evidential proof*, to all nations before the end. To be a witness was to possess a covenant appointment to establish Christ's Kingdom and to write the covenant documents.

When Paul said he was *appointed* a preacher in 1Timothy 2:7 and 2 Timothy 1:11, he used the Greek word *tithimi* which is the same root word, *diatithima*, used by Jesus in Luke 22:29. Christ authorized the Apostles to organize His Covenant Kingdom. Jesus gave the Covenant appointment to His Apostles, just as God gave His Covenant appointment to Jesus. Paul is stressing the same fact in the Timothy text. "I lie not," he says, "I too am covenantal appointed" to the preaching and teaching work of an Apostle of Jesus. Paul's 14 epistles make him the most prolific editor of the Holy Spirit's Testimony. We must understand the word "witness" or "testimony." We will see this word 18 times as we read through the Book of Revelation.

The Holy Spirit is a legal witness

Christians refer to the New Testament writings as Apostolic, but The Holy Spirit is the real New Testament *ghostwriter*.

> "But the Holy Spirit also witnessed to us (martur, gave legal, judicial evidence to us), for after He said before, this is the (New) Covenant I will make with them..." (Heb 10:15, 16).

In reality, as believers read the New Testament, they are hearing the testimony of the Holy Spirit. In fact, commentators like John Calvin taught that the real "cannonizer" of the New Testament is the Holy Spirit who dwells in the believer.

> "...It is the Spirit who bears witness, for the Spirit is truth" (1Jn 5:6).

> "There are three that bear witness in Heaven, the father, the Word and the Spirit, and these three are one" (1Jn 5:7).

Again, the word *martur* means judicial evidence, record, testimony, witness, and evidence. The New Testament document is a Holy Spirit inspired testimony (*martur*). The New Testament is the word (*logos*) that was preached to all nations as a testimony before 70 A.D. All Christians from all generations should concur with the Apostles that when we share the New Testament Word, our sharing is like proclaiming a testimony in a courtroom consisting of spectators from Heaven, Earth, and Hell.

> "... I have fully (to its entire completion) preached the Gospel of Christ from Jerusalem and around about to Illyricum..." (Ro 15:19).

> "Faith comes by hearing, and hearing the word of God. But I say, 'have they not heard?' Yes, indeed! For their sound has gone out to all the earth, and their words to the end of the world" (Ro 10:17, 18).

All of this happened before 70 A.D. The Testimony-Witness of the Word of the New Covenant had been preached and recorded in the whole world. Otherwise, how could the people in Rome be reading these verses that give ample evidence to this fact?

> "...The truth of the gospel, which has come to you, as it has also in ALL the world..." (Col 1:5b.6a).

> ".... The hope of the Gospel, which you heard, which was preached to every rational created being under heaven, of which I Paul, became a minister" (Col 1:23b).

All of this happened before 70 A.D. How could the people in Colossi be reading these verses that give ample evidence to the fact that the Testimony-Witness of the New Testament Covenant Word was preached in the entire world if it had not been recorded?

There are some that might object to this saying, "Their Gospel was only delivered to the known world, not the entire world." This objection limits the omnipotence of God. If the 1st Century Congregation failed to deliver the Word unto the whole world, then God's power is lacking. However, this is not true. God can accomplish what seems to be impossible. He is God! He breathed the physical elements and laws of nature into existence when He created the world. Surely, God could enable His messengers to carry this Word into the whole world.

If we read scholarly accounts of the lives of the Apostles, vast amounts of historical evidence inform us that the Apostles and their disciples took the Gospel to countries considered "far off" in those days, including Great Britain, Spain, France, and European, Asian, and African nations.

Archeological and historical evidence exists that all pagan and heathen nations have a vestige of Christianity in corrupted form. I have written, in my works on Biblical Anthropology, about traces of Christianity in the Deli Lama Heathen worship, the Voodoo worship in Africa, and the Indian worship in South America. As we shall see, even the people of Asia turned away from the pure Gospel. God through His Spirit and the laws of the Pax Romano Empire kept back the rise of religious iniquity long enough to allow for writing the New Testament and evangelizing the world. God accomplished His purpose for us. How we recognize the world of that day and what we do with it today is our own choice. The heathen world rejected His message and more than likely murdered His messengers.

A Deaconate Minister

Notice that Paul uses the word *minister* to describe his Apostleship. It is *deaconate*, or the same word used to describe the other Apostles who had a *deaconate* of the Word of the New Testament in Acts 6:4. Deaconate is usually a general word when used to describe Christ's servants. However, when associated with the Apostles and the New Covenant Word of Christ, it is defined as a very special ministry. We should appreciate that the Apostles were faithful to this ministry and completed it in their lifetimes. On the other hand, there are Ecclesiastical Romanist, Judiazers, and Millennialists who do not rejoice in the completion of New Testament Scriptures before 70 A.D. The recorded historical fact of their completion before 70 A.D. disproves their arrogant claims to self-authority and makes them speculators and soothsayers.

Laying all speculation aside, the fact remains that the resurrection Gospel had legal witnesses. Legal witnesses are abundantly supported by numerous New Testament verses (Lk 24:48; Jn 5:37,15:27; Ac 1:8, 22, 4:33, 5:32, 10:39, 41, 14:3, 22:15,18, 23:11; 2Th 1:18).

Remember, when The New Testament uses *Gospel*, it means more than just Matthew, Mark, Luke and John. Noted earlier, Paul's *deaconate* witness to the Gospel of Christ (including all of his Epistles) is also considered the Gospel. The Bible emphasizes that what all of the Apostles had seen and witnessed was recorded (1Jn 1:2). The Written Word also mentions the evangelistic witnesses who were beheaded or slain for the Word of Christ (Rev 11:3, 20:4). The Apostles were preaching the Great Commission of Matthew 28:18, Luke 24:45-49, and Mark 16. Mark 16 included all things Christ commanded them from Pentecost 30 A.D. to the end in 70 A.D. Christians today carry on this apostolic truth! However, eyewitnesses to the work of the original Apostles are no longer alive. Therefore, Christians of God's Word cannot give judicial documents inspired by the Holy Spirit for they have not been judicially ordained by Jesus Christ to write a third, fourth, or additional covenants. John is in fact writing before 70 A.D. He is giving the people of God a factual document to be established as God's Holy Word.

In Revelation 1:2, as stated previously, the word *martur* is translated as both *witness* and *testimony*, and it refers to the last book of the New Covenant revelation. Far from being written in 90 A.D. or later, as the canonizing critics would have us believe, Jesus said this testimony would be complete before the Abomination of Desolation of 70 A.D.

Paul told Timothy not to be ashamed of the Lord's testimony (1Ti 1:8). This refers not only to the Old Testament but also to the New Testament writings from which Timothy was educated as a child. The Lord was in Heaven, but He spoke His testimony through the inspired writings of the Apostles.

Moulton, on p. 96 of his Analytical Greek Lexicon, states that *martur* means a judicial witness to a circumstance or to testify a doctrine. It is the declaration of something as a fact or a doctrine (Jn 1:19, 32). Paul does not make a distinction between speaking or writing in 2 Thessalonians 2:2. The Hebrew letter also associates "testimony" with the New Covenant Scripture (Heb 10:15, 16).

Paul's Gospel was a declaration of God's testimony (1Cor 2:1). Paul uses the word *diatheamai* (Vine, p. 70) testimony as it would have been used in a judicial courtroom setting. He affirms that his ministry was a testimony to the ransom of Christ, given in due time (the period of history in which Paul gave both oral and written testimony before A.D. 70), and he affirms with solemn truth that he was appointed a preacher and apostle in this matter (1Ti 2:7). John affirms the same.

Revelation 1:3: Blessed is he that readeth, and they that hear the words of this prophecy, and keep those things which are written therein: for the time is at hand.

Once again, what a blessing to read Revelation! Jesus referenced Revelation 1:3 before in Matthew 24:15 concerning the destruction of Jerusalem. Christ gives His followers a judicial document that cannot be changed. If it is going to be established as Scriptural truth, then it must be written down! Many denominational churches do not want judicial truth. The Charismatic Gospel Churches (inclined to excessive emotionalism) want constant and current revelation from God to teach people. Some scholars in the Roman and Greek Churches probably wish the New Covenant had never been written. This is spiritual suicide! We say this because such an attitude is an unrealistic denial of the very basic fundamental, historically written document that provided the true faith, from which they deducted their false documents. Their authority rests with their clergy of priests, bishops, archbishops, cardinals, and popes.

Of course, they need the New Testament writing to give partial credence to their outlandish claims. They teach that their divine authority continues to come through the mouth of men rather than through God's eternal word!

John is writing this Revelation to the assemblies of Christ because the time of great tribulation was upon them. This was written for all Christians, but it was specifically written to the pre-70 A.D. Christians because of the extreme hardships they were enduring under Roman and Jewish persecution. The most bogus religious claim made by modern-day leaders is that of a continuous or modern-day revelation. Any revelation after the one you hold in your hand is too late!

Revelation 1:4: John to the seven churches which are in Asia: Grace be unto you, and peace, from him which is, and which was, and which is to come; and from the seven spirits which are before his throne;

When Revelation was written, more than seven congregations existed in the Roman province of Asia, which was in Eastern Asia Minor (Asia Minor is modern Turkey.). When John is writing to the seven congregations, he is really writing to all Christians. In numerology, the number seven represents completion. John is giving His written vision to all Christians who were preparing to embark upon a troublous time for New Testament Christianity. However, in order for us to properly understand this vision, we must understand the proper context of the Scripture. We must place ourselves in the time and place of this writing, as well as the time and place of the people to whom this letter was written. No doubt, the Evangelist proclaimed this letter within each congregation. People living in John's day would have understood this letter best because they understood the language, culture, writing style, interpretation, and its application to them.

However, this peace and grace that John writes about is the reflection of God's smile in the hearts of Christians. God is the essence of peace, comfort, and friendship. Christ always brings peace from God the Father through the Holy Spirit.

God names Himself as "which is, which was, and which is to come." He also states that this Revelation is from the Seven Spirits before *His* throne. Once again, numerology is present in this apocalyptic writing. The seven Spirits of God show His completion as God (Isa 11:2). It also shows the perfect seven-fold Spirit as the active energy in the delivery of this Revelation.

Revelation 1:5-8: And from Jesus Christ, who is the faithful witness, and the first begotten of the dead, and the prince of the kings of the earth. Unto him that loved us, and washed us from our sins in his own blood, and hath made us kings and priests unto God and his Father; to him be glory and dominion forever and ever. Amen. Behold, he cometh with clouds; and every eye shall see him, and they also which pierced him: and all kindred of the earth shall wail because of him. Even so, Amen. I am Alpha and Omega, the beginning and the ending, saith the Lord, which is, and which was, and which is to come, the Almighty.

John keeps saying "us, us, and us." Certain teachers hold the opinion that the Apostle John is to be venerated as a special saint in the Congregation of Christ. However, John levels with his fellow Christians. The Bible says that all Christians are in the Kingdom of God because of the love of His Son.

There are Seven Important Facts of Christ

1. Jesus is a faithful witness (He 3:6).

2. He is the first-born of the dead, *protokos*, because He goes before death, never to die again (1Th 4:14; 1Co 15).

3. Jesus loves Christians, in the present tense (1Ti 6:16, 17).

4. He is trustworthy Mediator (Ro 8:35).

5. He has made Christians Kings and Priests (Eph 5:26; Heb 10:22).

6. To him belongs the glory, praise, and dominion forever and ever, Amen! (1Ti 6:15, 16).

7. He will come again (Rev 1:5-9).

Christians serve an amazing Savior! He is faithful to them (Heb 3:6); He is risen for them (1Co 15); He is reigning for them (1Ti 6:16, 17); He loves them (Ro 8:35); He washed them (Eph 5:26; Heb10: 22); He saved them (Ac 2:38); and He has crowned them (1Pe 2:9)! He is the seven-fold perfect Savior.

Once again, John reiterates the words of Christ (Mt 24:30, 25:31) that He will be coming on the clouds. Every eye shall see Him coming, even those who pierced Him (Lk 21:28). When Christ comes, those who are dead will be united with an imperishable body. Both those in Christ and out of Christ will see Him as He is! All the earth's people will see Him (Mt 24:30, 31) and will be gathered unto Him.

Verse 8 is unique. Previously, in verse 4, God the Father calls Himself that "Which is, which was, and which is to come." How interesting that Christ calls Himself the very same thing in verse 8. He not only equates Himself with God the Father, but He also says, "I am the Alpha (beginning), the Omega (end), and the Almighty." This verse contradicts the Jehovah Witnesses doctrine that Jesus is a created angel, or the Mormon religion that says Jesus was just another god. It contradicts the doctrine of the Gnostics and Muslims that teach Jesus was but a mere man.

The Lord gives a twofold blessing to those who read this book:

1. It is hope for the One who is *saying* He is coming! The reader must believe that Jesus is the Son of Man (Mk 14:61, 62) and that He is coming again!

2. What a blessing for those who are *looking* for Him to come. He is coming in the clouds. He is coming with a shout, a voice, and a trumpet! Does this sound like the coming of a secret rapture? Readers must be prepared and ready for their Master to return suddenly, visibly, and in finality, to world history.

Revelation 1:9: I, John, who also am your brother, and companion in tribulation, and in the kingdom and patience of Jesus Christ, was in the isle that is called Patmos, for the word of God, and for the testimony of Jesus Christ.

John is a fellow brother in the Lord who is no greater or lesser than any other Christian who has been immersed into Christ Jesus. All are saints under one King, Jesus Christ (Eph 2:19, 4:12; Php 4:21).

Christians are in the kingdom of *tribulation*, but there is a day when Jesus will return and triumph over all. As John was writing, he had been banished to this Island for being a Christian. Tertullian said this of John,

> "The Apostle John was first plunged, unhurt, into boiling oil, and thence remitted to his island-exile!"[44]

John was in *great tribulation*. There are three great truths in the words tribulation, trial, and triumph. Some say Christians are going to have *the great tribulation* when some falsely believe the Antichrist comes in the distant future. However, Christians already experience tribulation through everyday life! The Bible says, "Through much tribulation one enters into the Kingdom of God" (Ac 14:22). Anytime the Apostles quoted the testimony, they were persecuted, martyred, and made a spectacle. These men were preaching and teaching under great tribulation! Those who teach a future great tribulation actually hate the New Testament teachings of Christ.

Many religious groups have one thing in common. They hate those who are bound to God through the anointed Christ in the Holy Spirit (Ps 2:1-12). They shut up the Kingdom of Heaven by teaching an earthly carnal reign of Christ on Earth. They forgo the tribulation for the testing of Covenant Christians by predicting a future bogus tribulation. This is to no avail.

Because Christians come into contact with tribulation every day, the New Testament declares that they suffer with Jesus as they serve Him. We can think of just a few of the problems Paul encountered.

> 2 Timothy 4: 14: Alexander the coppersmith did great harm to me.
>
> At my first defense, no one came to my assistance, but everyone deserted me (4:16). So I was rescued from the lion's mouth (4:17).
>
> 2 Timothy 3:12: In fact, everyone who wants to live a godly life in Christ Jesus will be persecuted.
>
> Philippians 3:10, 11: I want to know Christ and the power of His resurrection and the fellowship of sharing in His sufferings, becoming like Him in his death, and so, somehow, to attain to the resurrection from the dead.

Revelation 1:10: I was in the Spirit on the Lord's Day, and heard behind me a great voice, as of a trumpet,

John was in the Spirit on the Lord's Day, and he hears the voice as of a trumpet. A trumpet would be used to make one aware that war was upon them or to signal trouble (Joel 2:1), or to assemble and prepare the people for an offensive attack (Jdg 6:4; 1Sa 13:3; Ne 4:18-20), or indicates judgment (Mt 24:31; 1Th 4:16). The voice of the trumpet aroused John so he turned his attention to the important matters at hand.

John's being in the spirit is significant because he is ready, prepared, and paying attention to God's presence. John is a spiritual man ready to do spiritual things. How many Christians get up and drag themselves to the assembly of the called-out ones? How many Christians are so sluggish and depressed they fail to be in the Spirit and experience spiritual worship with God? God must experience great disappointment when Christians complain about His blood, sacrifice, mercy, and grace. The Lord's Day is a memorial worship service of the greatest Man to have ever lived, the greatest God to ever be proclaimed!

Now, concerning the "First Day of the week," three commentators have said this:

Dean Alfred[45]

> "It's astounding that anyone would give this as a future tense day, it had to be a certain day of the week."

William Hendrickson[46]

> "It has to be the Lord's Day, when they broke Bread. To interpret it differently, other than as the First day of the week to break bread, would be just silly."

Albertus Pieters[47]

> "On the Lord's Day, is commonly, and rightly understood as the First day of the week, our Sunday. The day our Lord chose to remember Him through the institution of the Lord's Supper."

We can meditate on the IMPORTANCE of connecting the Lord's Day to the First Day of the Week (Mt 28; Mk 16:2; Lk 24:1; Jn 20:1,19, 26; Ac 20:7; 1Co 16:2). We can only express sorrow and grieve for Seven Day Adventists and some Baptists who are held in bondage to the Day of the Law of Moses. A spirit-filled disciple of Christ holds every day as being equal (Ro 14:5), and worshiping on Saturday is no different than The First Day of the Week, but it is evil to allow ourselves to be deceived into calling The First Day of the Week assembly "The mark of the beast." This Imperial Day "Resurrection Day" was a day for partaking The Communion together with Christ and gathering collections for specific purposes. This day differs from others in that separate meetings could be held during the week for smaller groups (Ac 2:36), but from New Testament history, we learn the whole communion of the Body came together on The First Day of the Week (1Co 10:16, 11:20).

The Lord's Day is the First Day of the Week, the Day of The Lord is the last day of our existing cosmos, or the end of this present world (Ac 17:3; 1Co 1:8; 2Pt 3:10; Rev 6:17, 16:14).

Christians are *not bound* to keep the Sabbath day.

1. The law of the Sabbath was given in the Law of Moses, and unless repeated in the New Testament, it is not binding upon Christians.

This is because Christians are not under the Law. The Bible declares the saints, "delivered from the Law" (Ro 7:6); it also says, "Christ is the end of the law for righteousness to everyone that believeth" (Ro 10:4). It continues, "Wherefore the law was the schoolmaster to bring us unto Christ, that we might be justified by faith. But after that, faith is come, we are no longer under a schoolmaster" (Gal 3:24, 25).

2. The New Testament repeats nine of Ten Commandments (Mt 22:40; Mk10:19; Lk 18.20; Ro 7:7), but does not repeat the one that says, "Remember the Sabbath Day, to keep it holy" (Ex 20:8).

3. When the Gentile congregation was confronted with the "law-keepers" from Jerusalem, Acts 15 tells us that a council was called. It was decided at the meeting that four things out of the law should be brought into the gentile congregation. They were commanded to abstain from (1) meats offered to idols, (2) blood, (3) things strangled, and (4) fornication. The Apostles said nothing at all about Sabbath keeping. If the Gentile Christians observed these regulations, they would do well and no greater burden would be laid upon them (Ac15:28, 29). If the seventh day Sabbath were to be observed as well, it would have been mentioned in this council meeting. However, since Pentecost, no such command has been placed upon the Gentiles. Would not this assembly meeting have been a good time to command Sabbath keeping for the Gentiles? But it was not.

4. The seventh day Sabbath was given in the Law found in the Old Covenant. However, Jeremiah 31:31 prophesied of a New Covenant to come unlike the first one given by Moses. This is the New Covenant (Heb 8:8-13).

5. A strict observance of the Sabbath, like Exodus 16:29, is not kept by anyone today. Consider the following similar commandments:

   a. "And on the Sabbath day take two lambs… this is the burnt offering of every Sabbath, beside the continual burnt offering…" (Nu 28:9, 10).

   b. A "Sabbath day's journey" could be no longer than about $3/5^{th}$ of a mile (Ac 1:12-15).

c. "...whosoever doeth any work on the Sabbath day, he shall surely be put to death" (Ex 31:14).

d. "Ye shall kindle no fire throughout your habitations upon the Sabbath day" (Ex 35:3). A sabbatarian could not live in Alaska or any Arctic Region.

e. While Israel was yet in the wilderness, they found a man gathering sticks on the Sabbath day, and the LORD commanded him to be stoned to death (Nu 15:32-36).

6. The Sabbath day was to be a sign between God and the Nation of Israel (Ex 31:17). One of the reasons why they were to keep it was to "Remember that thou were a servant in the land of Egypt, and that the LORD thy God brought thee out thence through a mighty hand and by a stretched arm: therefore, the LORD thy God commanded thee to keep the Sabbath day" (Dt 5:15). It is gross religious hypocrisy to remotely suggest that anyone anywhere in the world today is keeping the Sabbath day holy. How could one not be tempted to congratulate those meeting in a Seven Day Adventist denomination for having made a successful exodus from the nation of Egypt?

7. The Bible says, "Let no Man judge you in meat, or in drink, or in respect of a holy day, or of the new moon, or of the Sabbath days. These were just a shadow of the things to come" (Col 2:16, 17). Likewise, what are Christians to think of a person's rationality when he worships shadows?

8. Jesus said that man was not made for the Sabbath, but the Sabbath was made for man (Mk 2:27). This was the argument that Jesus made to justify the many things that He did that were contrary to popular opinion and tradition on the Sabbath Day.

9. The New Testament tells us that we should not be enslaved (Gal 4:10, 11) and shackled with a yoke of slavery by trying to keep such works of the law (Gal 5:1). The Holy Spirit said of the Ten Commandments, "The letter written on stone is death" (2Co 3:4-11). While Judaism was a religion of "ends" (thou shalt not commit adultery), Christianity is a religion of "means" (Do not even look to covet sexually outside of marriage.).

Why the Lord's Day is the first day of the week ("Sunday") and not Saturday?

1. Sunday was the day Jesus rose from the dead (Mk 16:9; Lk 24:1, 12, 21).

2. Jesus made his first appearances to the collective group of disciples after His resurrection on the first day of the week (Jn 20: 26).

3. The Holy Spirit came on a Sunday, the first day of the week (Ac 2:1-13). Pentecost came "On the morrow after the Seventh Sabbath after the Sabbath Passover" (Lev 23:15; Dt 16:9).

4. The congregation was established on a Sunday, the first day of the week (Ac 2:1).

5. The early congregation met on Sunday, the first day of the week, to "break bread" (Ac 20:7).

6. They were to "lay by in store" on that day (1Co 16:2).

7. Early writers acknowledged the first day of the week to be the Lord's Day. Although extra biblical sources are not needed to authenticate God's word, the following two are interesting:

    a. Ignatius – to the Magnesians, Chapter 9, written about 110-115 A.D. "… Let every friend of Christ keep the Lord's Day as a festival, the resurrection-day, the queen and chief of all…the eighth day, on which our life, both sprang up again…" (http://www.earlychristianwritings.com/text/ignatius-magnesians-longer.html (See Jn 20:19, 21, 26.). The expression "eight days later" is used in the original Greek.)

    b. Justin Martyr – "And on the day called Sunday, all who live in cities or in the country gather together to one place, and the memoirs of the Apostles or the writings of the prophets are read, as long as time permits… (Ante-Nicene Fathers, p. 63).

Revelation 1:11: Saying, I am Alpha and Omega, the first and the last: and, what thou seest, write in a book, and send it unto the seven congregations which are in

Asia; unto Ephesus, and unto Smyrna, and unto Pergamos, and unto Thyatira, and unto Sardis, and unto Philadelphia, and unto Laodicea.

God wanted John to write it in a book! Once again, God writes a judicial contract. The reason God did not leave His authority and eternal truth in the minds of men was because without a judicial covenant contract, His truth would become corrupted. The most efficient and reliable method for relaying truth is to write it down! Greek and Roman apostates corrupted the original Apostolic Congregation through man-made creeds and writings. Written documents contain the power of good and evil!

Revelation 1:12: And I turned to see the voice that spake with me. And being turned, I saw seven golden candlesticks;

How can a person see a voice? How can a voice walk? It was Jesus Christ, who is the Word of God. Just as Christ was the word walking and communicating in the garden so is Christ the visible Word of God (Ge 3:8-10).

Bible translators translate the Greek word "luchnia" interchangeably with either "lampstands" or "candle sticks." The first translation, "lamp stands," is probably the most accurate. The seven golden lamp stands are the seven congregations that are commanded to spread the Word of God. Christians will be held accountable by the truth they teach people. Unless the Word dwells within us, both Christians and those being taught will be led astray. Satan communicates through clairvoyant and charismatic expressions. Christ communicates through New Testament, Apostolic truth (2Co 3:5-16).

The first three Chapters of Revelation begin with the assemblies of Christ. Jesus does this because judgment starts first with the House of God and then to the world (1Pe 4:7-19). However, judgment for Christians is completely different than for those who are outside of Christ (1Co 11:31, 32). For the Christian, judgment is not only day-to-day; it is also at the Lord's Table where each Christian judges himself (11:31, 32).

The seven lamp stands are the control centers of operation for the spread of the Gospel voice to the world. Christians are His voice. Christians are His messengers! How can a person have faith? How can people hear without a messenger with this message? (Ro 10:14)

Revelation 1:13: And in the midst of the candlesticks one like unto a son of man, clothed with a garment down to the foot, and girt about at the breasts with a golden girdle.

Jesus was speaking through the assemblies to the world. Christ does not function without the bride, the Assembly (His Church). This truth built His Congregation, and in turn, His Congregation teaches His truth.

His royal apparel is that of truth and righteousness. He is girded with the apparel of royal armor, protecting and leading His people.

Revelation 1:14, 15: And his head and his hair were white as white wool, [white] as snow; and his eyes were as a flame of fire; - and his feet like unto burnished brass, as if it had been refined in a furnace; and his voice as the voice of many waters.

His head reveals the wisdom of the Ancient of Days. His eyes are penetrating orbs of discretion. His bronze feet stand for judgment. The wheels are like the fires of judgment that burn and grind. They glow like the furnace-fire. His voice is of the sound of waters; it is powerful and mighty (Ps 29:3).

There has been debate concerning the post-ascended Body of Christ. Some claim that Christ remains in his body of flesh in Heaven. This idea would be more false than the Zoroastrian doctrine (held also by Muslims) that the afterlife is a physical paradise that is no different than this world of lustful eyes and flesh and the pride of life. Some teach that Christ has eternal flesh. The undeniable fact is that upon Christ's ascension to the Throne of His glory, Christ changed to His former glory. He changed to the glory He enjoyed in association with The Godhead before the world began (Jn 17:5). A research of the Biblical word "glory" reveals the innermost desire of every created human soul. Christ's glory is infinitely greater than the glory of the Earth and flesh.

Moses said, "Show me Thy glory" (Ex 33:18). It was a rare, awesome and privileged Old Testament vision to see God's glory (Ex 16:7-10, 40:34, 35), but New Covenant Christians behold more than the divine aurora that surrounded God and the mere words that described His glory (2Co 3:10, 18, 4:15, 17; Eph 3:13, 16; Col 1:27, 3:4; Heb 13:21; Jas 2:1). Christians behold the face of Christ in the New Covenant glass and are changed from glory (Old Testament) to glory (New Testament) as by The Spirit of The Lord. Our sinful nature (character) is changed into a nature that is dominated largely by the divine, not human (2Pt 1:4). This glorious transformation within us is working through us and will work into an eternal encumbrance of glory (1Pe 4:13; 2Co 4:17). "Glory" is the essence and character of something, and we hold this treasure in our earthen vessels (flesh bodies-2Co 4:7). There is nothing wrong with the quest of glory's greatness as long as the person is meek and humble. But the most disappointed human being on Earth is that person who does not understand that this quest for glory's greatness is actually inbred from birth, or an innate longing for God, the Creator's glory.

"CHRIST HAS COME IN THE FLESH"

Some religious groups teach that if a person denies the continuation of Christ in the flesh, that person is of the spirit of the Antichrist! They cite the phrase, "has come in the flesh" (1Jn 4:2, 3). They claim that because the word "come" is in the perfect tense, this must mean the interpretation should really read, "Has come and still remains in the flesh." This is absurd. This is not only a misapplication of the perfect tense, but it is also a false interpretation and blasphemous mistake. We cannot possibly subscribe to the Gnostic philosophy that Jesus resides in a post-resurrection body of flesh. Such theology is sheer non-sense and manifest absurdity in light of this vision. The appearance of Jesus in the resurrection, a body of flesh and bone, was to demonstrate His power over all flesh (Jn 17:3).

> THE RESURECTED BODY OF CHRIST WAS AN UNBELIEVABLE DEMONSTRATION OF GOD'S POWER OVER DEATH, THE GRAVE, AND HADES, BUT HIS ASCENSION TO THE THRONE, WHEN HE ENTERED HIS GLORY IN A GLORIFIED BODY, IS INDISCRIBABLE IN HUMAN TERMS.

A mature child of God is familiar with the expression "glory." Although glory is something we can experience in our spiritually regenerated mind, we can never satisfactorily explain and define what God's "glory" really is. The glorified body of Christ on the Throne (as related in Revelation 1) may be understood in Spirit, but it is inexplicable in human words.

John, being inspired by the Holy Spirit, wrote this passage because he was confronting the Gnostic doctrine that Jesus was a supernatural visitant that seemed to be human and that Jesus did not die for the sins of the world.

The Gospels concerning Christ no doubt showed His humanity through suffering (Lk 12:50), emotional pain (Jn 11:35, 38), hunger (Mt 4:2), weariness (Jn 4:6), and thirst (Jn 19:28). In fact, the writer of Hebrews draws a direct parallel to the humanity of Christ with His ability to assist Christians in their struggles in this life (Heb 2:17, 18, 4:15, 16).

Unfortunately, those who believe in the eternal flesh of Christ failed to harmonize 1 Corinthians 15:35-41,

> "But someone may ask, 'How are the dead raised? With what kind of body will they come?' How foolish! What you sow does not come to life unless it dies. When you sow, you do not plant the body that will be, but just a seed, perhaps of wheat or of something else. But God gives it a body as he has determined, and to each kind of seed he gives its own body. All flesh is not the same: Men have one kind of flesh, animals have another, birds another, and fish another. There are also heavenly bodies and there are earthly bodies; but the splendor of the heavenly bodies is one kind, and the splendor of the earthly bodies is another. The sun has one kind of splendor, the moon another and the stars another; and star differs from star in splendor".

We understand that the post-resurrected Body of Christ possessed some of the characteristics of our bodies, but it differed in several ways. John's writing of Revelation seals the deal concerning Christ and His state in Heaven.

Scholars have researched what Christian bodies will be like at the resurrection. Christians of Paul's day wanted to know this answer as well. After proclaiming this as foolishness, Paul tells them that your body must die (cease to live) in order for it to live. This is God's decision. He will give bodies as He desires. In a parallel to the difference between human bodies and heavenly bodies, Paul says that not all flesh is the same flesh. A difference exists among the flesh of a human, a dog, a fish, and a bird. In the same manner, there are also celestial bodies and terrestrial bodies.

There are *epouranios* bodies. These are the bodies that relate to the sky; they are located in the celestial or heavenly sky. This is the same word used to describe the type of city called God's city, the heavenly Jerusalem (Heb 12:22). A celestial body is literally from God.

There are also *epigeios* bodies. These are bodies that relate to the Earth; they are human. This is the same word used to describe the temporary "earthly house, tabernacle" (2Co 4:17-5:11). The word "temporary" in this passage is πρόσκαιρος (*proskairos*) which means to last only for a short while, such as enjoying sin (Heb 11:25), and the lasting of faith when people do not allow it to take root (Mt 13:21; Mk 4:17).

Some people might propose that, "The difference between the heavenly and earthly bodies is not one of essence, but location." However, further investigation disproves this claim. Further Biblical investigation reveals that the eternal, after existence of both the saved and lost, defies what we presently know as location. It is "after existence" not "life after death" because for the lost, there is no life, but everlasting death. For the saved, it is life after life. A prayerful contemplation of the Scripture on this subject causes us to acknowledge that this existence is timeless, spaceless, matterless, and can therefore, not be confined to what may be called "location." Paul said, "Eye has not seen, ear has not heard and neither has it entered the heart of man" (1Co 2:9) in regard to what God has prepared for those who love Him. John said, "We do not know what we shall be, but when He comes, we shall be like Him" (1Jn 3:2). Christ's glorified body is not confined to "location."

Paul uses the word "soulish man" (1Co 2:14). It is translated "natural man," but it is "psuchikos," which differs from the higher "spiritual" man. James Strong (5591) says the soulish man is the person who yields in everything to the soul's human reasonings, without thinking there is a need for help from above. Of course, a soulish human being who has lived in a cosmic universe consisting of oxygen, fire, water, vegetation, animal flesh, and chemical elements has great difficulty comprehending an existence where none of this is seen or known. However, in the pre-cosmic universe, none of these "elements of location" existed. That pre-Adamic world was completely spiritual. God is spirit, the Godhead is spirit, and the angels were spirit-creatures. The tragic and psychological fatal flaw of the human race is neglect of the spiritual. Yes, indeed, God placed us in a world of air, water, fire, time, space, energy, and the subsequent laws of physics that govern us with tyrannical power and force. But He also placed a spirit within us. This present world is a proving test ground to determine, in the sight of Godhead Almighty, whether or not we are going to walk according to flesh or spirit in this world. Every human being is a human spirit, and if in our human spirit, we obey the leading of the Holy Spirit, we will be delivered from both the curse of this present world and spiritual darkness.

In 2 Corinthians, Paul goes onto say, "We know that after this earthly house of the tabernacle body is destroyed, we have a building from God, a house made without hands, eternal in the heavens" (2Co 5:1). The word destroyed in this passage is καταλύω, which means to tear down, destroy completely (Mt 21:40-41). Interestingly, this is the same word used to describe the destruction of Jerusalem and the tearing down of the physical nation of Israel through rejection of Christ's claim to be King. Just as God brought a New Testament Israel in place of Old Testament Israel, He will grant a new body in place of the old one.

Paul continues to write in 1 Corinthians 15:40, "There are also heavenly bodies and there are earthly bodies; but the splendor of the heavenly bodies is one kind, and the splendor of the earthly bodies is another."

Paul says that the heavenly bodies are different from the earthly bodies. As previously proved, this difference is not in location, but in essence. The essence of the earthly body is flesh, blood, limited, earthly, physical, perishing, and being temporary. But the essence of the heavenly body is quite different. We should note: to assume that the post-resurrected body of Christ is the same as the glorified Christ would be incorrect.

We can collect evidence from the harmony of the Gospels after Christ's resurrection. The following are a list of recorded facts concerning the body of Jesus. In His post-resurrected body, Jesus

Had not yet ascended to the Father to sit at his right hand –

> John 20:17: Jesus said, "Do not hold on to me, for I have not yet returned to the Father. Go instead to my brothers and tell them, 'I am returning to my Father and your Father, to my God and to your God'."

Was able to walk –

> Luke 24:13-17: Now that same day two of them were going to a village called Emmaus, about seven miles from Jerusalem. They were talking with each other about everything that had happened. As they talked and discussed these things with each other, Jesus himself came up and walked along with them; but they were kept from recognizing him. He asked them, "What are you discussing together as you walk along?"

Was able to be touched –

> Matthew 28:8-10: So the women hurried away from the tomb, afraid yet filled with joy, and ran to tell his disciples. Suddenly Jesus met them. "Greetings," he said. They came to him, clasped his feet and worshiped him. Then Jesus said to them, "Do not be afraid. Go and tell my brothers to go to Galilee; there they will see me."

Was able to appear in a different form –

> Mark 16:12, 13: Afterward Jesus appeared in a different form to two of them while they were walking in the country. These returned and reported it to the rest; but they did not believe them either.

Was able to appear in many places, to many people, at once –

> 1 Corinthians 15:6-8: After that, he appeared to more than five hundred of the brothers at the same time, most of whom are still living, though some have fallen asleep. Then he appeared to James, then to all the apostles, and last of all he appeared to me also, as to one abnormally born.

Was able to disappear - φαντος (*aphantos* –to literally become invisible) –

> Luke 24:31, 32: Then their eyes were opened and they recognized him, and he disappeared from their sight. They asked each other, "Were not our hearts burning within us while he talked with us on the road and opened the Scriptures to us?"

Was able to appear without physical transportation or being limited to the physical elements –

> John 20:19, 20: On the evening of that first day of the week, when the disciples were together, with the doors locked for fear of the Jews, Jesus came and stood among them and said, "Peace be with you!" After he said this, he showed them his hands and side. The disciples were overjoyed when they saw the Lord.

Was not completely physical, with the ability to appear to human sensory perception as if He was a spirit –

Luke 24:36-41: While they were still talking about this, Jesus himself stood among them and said to them, "Peace be with you." They were startled and frightened, thinking they saw a ghost. He said to them, "Why are you troubled, and why do doubts rise in your minds? Look at my hands and my feet. It is I myself! Touch me and see; a ghost does not have flesh and bones, as you see I have." When he had said this, he showed them his hands and feet. And while they still did not believe it because of joy and amazement, he asked them, "Do you have anything here to eat?"

Appeared as an ordinary man in the flesh –

John 20:26, 27: A week later his disciples were in the house again, and Thomas was with them. Though the doors were locked, Jesus came and stood among them and said, "Peace be with you!" Then he said to Thomas, "Put your finger here; see my hands. Reach out your hand and put it into my side. Stop doubting and believe."

Had the capability of eating food, or at least accommodating the idea of eating –

Luke 24:41-43: And while they still did not believe it because of joy and amazement, he asked them, "Do you have anything here to eat?" They gave him a piece of broiled fish, and he took it and ate it in their presence.

John 21:11-14: Simon Peter climbed aboard and dragged the net ashore. It was full of large fish, 153, but even with so many the net was not torn. Jesus said to them, "Come and have breakfast." None of the disciples dared ask him, "Who are you?" They knew it was the Lord. Jesus came, took the bread and gave it to them, and did the same with the fish. This was now the third time Jesus appeared to his disciples after he was raised from the dead.

Was able to continue to perform miracles –

John 20:30, 31: Jesus did many other miraculous signs in the presence of his disciples, which are not recorded in this book. But these are written that you may believe that Jesus is the Christ, the Son of God, and that by believing you may have life in his name.

Went to heaven in a glorified body, perfectly fit to sit on a Throne of Glory (Mt 25:31) and be surrounded by glory (Lk 24:26). This glory fills the whole universe and is humanly unspeakable –

> Ephesians 1:12: In order that we, who were the first to hope in Christ, might be for the praise of His glory. (See also Eph 1:14, 17, 18, and 23).

Was able to continue His work with the disciples from His Throne in Heaven –

> Mark 16:19, 20: So then the Lord, after he had spoken to them, was received up into heaven, and sat down at the right hand of God. They went out, and preached everywhere, the Lord working with them, and confirming the word by the signs that followed. Amen.

> Luke 24:50-53: When he had led them out to the vicinity of Bethany, he lifted up his hands and blessed them. While he was blessing them, he left them and was taken up into heaven. Then they worshiped him and returned to Jerusalem with great joy. And they stayed continually at the temple, praising God.

> Acts 1:7-9: He said to them: "It is not for you to know the times or dates the Father has set by his own authority. But you will receive power when the Holy Spirit comes on you; and you will be my witnesses in Jerusalem, and in all Judea and Samaria, and to the ends of the earth." After he said this, he was taken up before their very eyes, and a cloud hid him from their sight.

Through the Apostolic New Testament, Jesus continues to speak from Heaven through their writings:

> "That the world may believe through their Word" (Jn 17:20).

> "Through this Man (ascended man) is preached to you the forgiveness of sin" (Ac 13:38).

The Apostles considered Jesus as speaking from Heaven through their inspired message and testimony:

> "It was confirmed to us by those who heard Him" (Heb 2:3).

> "We have come to Jesus, the mediator of the New Covenant, and to the sprinkled blood that speaks better things than that of Abel" (Heb 12: 24).

> "We shall not escape if we turn away from Him who speaks from heaven" (Heb 12: 25).

CHRISTIAN DISCIPLES ARE GREATLY DECEIVED WHEN THEY CONTINUOSLY SEEK OUT 'CHURCHES' THAT OFFER A STEADY DIET OF CHARACTER BUILDING AND EMOTIONAL HEALING SERVICES BUT OMIT THE ESSENTIAL SUBSTANCE OF LISTENING TO CHRIST'S NEW COVENANT.

NO MATTER HOW EXCITING THE SINGING MAY BE, NO MATTER HOW EMOTIONALLY CHARGED THE WORSHIP SERVICE MAY BE, AND NO MATTER HOW DEEPLY THE SERVICE TOUCHES OUR DAMAGED EMOTIONS, THERE CAN NEVER BE A TRUE INWARD HEAVEN-PRODUCED REGENERATION OF HEART AND MIND WITHOUT THE PREACHING AND OBEYING OF CHRIST'S NEW COVENANT.

THERE IS A VAST DIFFERENCE BETWEEN THE FANTASY OF MODERN CHURCHANITY "WORD SMITHS" WHO CAST THE APOSTLE'S DOCTRINE IN A DIFFERENT LIGHT TO SATISFY MODERN CULTURE RATHER THAN THE FACTS OF CHRIST'S ETERNAL COVENANT THAT PAVES THE WAY FOR THE HOLY SPIRIT TO GENERATE REPENTANCE, CONVICTION, AND OBEDIENCE.

THE UPLIFTED, EXALTED NEW COVEANT MESSIAH-CHRIST IS OUR ONLY CENTER AND HOPE OF MAXIMUM ALLEGIANCE.

There is no way we can truly explain how these New Covenant facts produce an awakening of life and hope within our regenerated spirit and mind. Granted, a temporary experience or emotional release may occur when modern cultural "churchanity" offers us a "gospel" that is devoid of New Covenant substance, but this is but a religious fling with no lasting value. A religious fling consists of soul power for soulish people, but it will not provide a catalyst for a deep spiritual transformation and a lifetime of regenerated life. People also revel in Biblical "head knowledge" that lacks a deep relationship to Christ in Spirit. This too, is soulish.

No doubt there was a change in the essence of the post-resurrected Body of Christ. He was able to randomly appear, disappear, change His appearance, defy the physical elements and restrictions, and appear as a spirit. While at the same time, His body could be touched, felt, eat, and maintain the same appearance as having been nailed to the cross. It is evident Jesus still had the holes in His hands and the gash in His side. However, did Jesus also have holes in His head and stripes on His body as well? This is not clear. It is also obvious that His body was able to maintain these characteristics without the human necessity of blood, for "life is in the blood" (Lev 17:11, 14). In spite of the fact that this resurrected body was powerful beyond belief, we can only ascribe praise to the incomprehensible wisdom and power of God that a glorified Body of Christ (which is the Congregation through the ages and fills the whole universe) is far greater than a resurrected human body. Lazarus had a resurrected body, but it was not a glorified body.

CHRIST ENTERED HIS GLORY IN A GLORIFIED BODY

We assume that Jesus ascended to the throne in His resurrected body, immediately without any change. However, John gave a different description of the appearance of Christ in Revelation 1:12-14. The description is apocalyptic and therefore beyond human literalism, but what John saw in vision was all that his human mind and senses could tolerate. He was actually visualizing the glorious sight of the glorious, glorified Christ. We can only assume just what the vision of Christ entails, but Christ's presence on the Throne of His glory is in a glorified body that is also The Temple of Heaven (Rev 21:22). Try to discern that millions of redeemed Christians are gathered in a collective state in His glorified body.

Some attempt to carnalize the Christ by quoting Acts 1:9-11; however, Luke's account in Acts actually says,

> After he said this, he was taken up before their very eyes, and a cloud hid him from their sight. They were looking intently up into the sky as he was going, when suddenly two men dressed in white stood beside them. "Men of Galilee," they said, "why do you stand here looking into the sky? This same Jesus, who has been taken from you into heaven, will come back in the same way you have seen him go into heaven" (Ac 1:9-11).

This text teaches that Christ will return in the same way He ascended into Heaven. This text does not speak of Christ's returning as the same essence, but in the same manner. This is how His return will take place. It would be a far stretch to indicate anything else.

This Scripture from Acts 1 is necessary to answer the question, "How are the dead raised? With what kind of body will they come?" (1Co15: 35) Concerning the heavenly body, Paul says, "There are also heavenly bodies and there are earthly bodies; but the splendor of the heavenly bodies is one kind, and the splendor of the earthly bodies is another." The text says, "The heavenly bodies are different (ἀλλοιόω – *alloio*), and different (ἀλλοιόω *alloio*) of the earthly." This word "different" means to change in appearance. This same word is used to describe the change in Christ's appearance, in what He looked like (Lk 9:29). Paul likens it to that of the heavenly bodies in the second heaven (universe). All of them are in heaven, but each has a different "glory" or appearance. The sun, moon, and stars look different in their own way (1Co 15: 41). Paul is developing an answer to describe the difference between the earthly body of the present and the heavenly body at the resurrection. He makes the following parallels in the following texts: (Parallel chart by Rick Bonifield)

Scripture	Earthly Body	Heavenly Body
1 Corinthians 15:42	Corruption = perishable, destruction, decay, rot.	Incorruptibility – immortality, imperishable, unceasing, a continuous state.
15:42	Dishonor = disgrace, shame, unclean.	Glory – splendor, brightness, amazing might, greatness, heavenly.
15:43	Weak = incapacity, limitation, illness, timidity.	Power = ability, mighty, ruler, supernatural.
15:44	Natural = physical, worldly.	Spiritual = from the spirit, not physical, supernatural powers.
15:45, 46	Adam = Natural, all die, figure.	Christ – Spiritual, all alive, fulfillment
15:47	Made of dust, earth.	Out of heaven, heavenly.
15:48, 49	Man's current image.	Man's future image.

Paul continues to say, "I declare to you, brothers, that flesh and blood cannot inherit the kingdom of God, nor does the perishable inherit the imperishable" (1Co 15: 50).

The physical bodies that Christians possess cannot inherit the Kingdom of God because our bodies must undergo a change. Like the Body of Christ, we must become spiritual. To say that Christ remains in the body in which He came and to cite 1 John 4: 2 as proof is exegetical recklessness. This passage of Scripture rules out the interpretation that the body of Christ has remained in the flesh of His pre-resurrected body and post-resurrected body. If Jesus remained in His earthly body, He could not have ascended into Heaven. However, His body is different. Just as a man's spirit could not unite with the Spirit of Christ in a corruptible state, the bodies of Christians must be perfected in order to inherit the incorruptible Heaven. It is a simple parallel.

The mystery that Paul states in 1 Corinthians 15:51, 52 is that not all Christians will undergo death, but at Christ's coming, their bodies will be transformed into an incorruptible state. At the trumpet sound, the dead bodies, not spirits, will be changed. It is an absolute mandate for the corrupted bodies to be transformed into an incorruptible state for entrance into the Heavenly Kingdom. Death will officially be defeated when Christ comes, but until then, Christ must reign at the right hand of the Father (1Co 15:24-27, 54).

Why does the Scripture go into so much detail about what Christ was like before He ascended, or what Christians will be like at His Second Coming, and much more?

John wrote this, "Dear friends, now we are children of God, and what we will be has not yet been made known. But we know that when he appears, we shall be like him, for we shall see him as he is. Everyone who has this hope in him purifies himself, just as he is pure" (1Jn 3:2, 3).

What shall Christians be like? If they are like Christ in spirit, attitude, relationship to the Father, and view of the Father then what more can be changed? The only logical conclusion is the body. As children of God, their hope rests in being Christ-like and with Christ. The New Testament has declared what God thinks of them. They are His kings, priests, sons, heirs, judges, righteous, holy ones, and much more. Why would John say, "Not yet manifested what we shall be (in eternal future)?" This is a great mystery. There are none who can describe the essence of Christ's Body. It is spiritual. The Apostle John was not sure what this essence would be. However, one truth is eternal, "if He be manifested, like Him we shall be, for we shall see Him as He is."

Christians should strive to be like Christ. John continued,

> "We know that we live in him and he in us, because he has given us of his Spirit. And we have seen and testify that the Father has sent his Son to be the Savior of the world. If anyone acknowledges that Jesus is the Son of God, God lives in him and he in God. And so we know and rely on the love God has for us. God is love. Whoever lives in love lives in God, and God in him. In this way, love is made complete among us so that we will have confidence on the Day of Judgment, because in this world we are like him" (1Jn 4:13-17).

Focusing on being like Christ in lifestyle (not glorified body) is what gives Christians encouragement. In fact, being Christ-like will give them confidence on the Day of Judgment. Although we do not know what we shall be when we are made manifest, as long as we continue to live like Him, we shall be like Him for we shall see Him as He is.

We do not know what the body will be like at the resurrection, only that it is imperishable. We know that the body will not consist of the flesh and blood like we currently have because we would not be able to enter into God's Kingdom (1Co 15:50). We also know that we will not consist of the flesh and blood that we currently have because we all will be changed (1Co 15:51). All of these characteristics reflect the current post-resurrected, heavenly, eternal Body of Christ.

We are convinced that after the Old Covenant was dedicated with the Covenant Blood, Moses, Aaron, Nadab, Abihu, and 70 elders beheld mystically what we know spiritually to be the eternal Body of Christ (Ex 24:10, 11). In this vision:

1) Christ is called the God of Israel.

2) The universe was "Under His feet" (Yes, "His" is in the Hebrew text.).

3) The sub-universe was "under" Him, as if it were a pavement of sapphire (indigo stone).

4) To the observers, it appeared to be the "body of heaven in His clearness" (Yes, words, "body" and "His clearness" are in the Hebrew text.).

5) Some translators who have had a great problem with this text try to depict the vision as being simply a spectacular view of Heaven, but

Moses, Aaron, Nadab, Abihu and the 70 elders would never accept this interpretation. In their minds, they see the God of Israel (Ex 24:11). Since no man can see God the Father and live, it is quite obvious that in this vision they saw the body of God's Son. Oh what a marvelous vision to behold His Eternal Body and, especially, to be a part of His Body, His ecclesia. We have this vision now in spirit and at His coming; we shall see Him more brightly in our resurrected body. It will even supersede the vision John is having here in Revelation 1.

6) The Scribes of the King James Version are correct to cross-reference John 1:18 with Exodus 24:11.

We may divide the mystery of the incarnation into seven aspects (See 1Ti 3:16.).

1) The pre-cosmic Jesus who was equal to and ONE with the Godhead. His body was prefigured in Exodus 24:10, 11 and continues through His ecclesia presently and will go on eternally through the shared, communal fellowship of His Body which is the sacred Temple (Rev 21, 22; Jn 4:23, 24).

2) The incarnation when God became flesh.

3) The life of Christ from a babe to the understanding of WHO He was and WHO the Father was.

4) The 3½ years of sacrificial service from His immersion unto His death and as the incarnated part of the Godhead, purchased the ecclesia with His own, humanly shed blood (Ac 20:28).

5) His appearances to the disciples in a resurrected body in order to demonstrate that a body can be resurrected and live after death.

6) His ascension into Heaven in a glorified body in order to prove that God can fashion a body to be qualified to spend eternity in His presence.

7) His eternal reign continues in a glorified body where, before the presence of Holy God the Father, He becomes an advocate for the saints on Earth. This mediation of Christ continues now, until His coming and into eternity.

Christ overcame sin when he lived in a fleshy, human body (Ro 8:3). Christ was put to death in a physical body, but made alive in The Spirit (1Pe 3:18). Christ faced sin in the flesh and suffered in the flesh, but after He died, He finished His fight against mans' sin and lives no longer in the flesh (1Pe 4:1, 2). The Gnostics denied this. The Christians believed this.

One thing is very clear; the Glory of God is not in the physical. It never has been, nor will it ever be. Therefore, "No flesh can glory in God's presence" (1Co 1:29). We must be in the spirit to have a proper relationship with God. Therefore, we must be born again of the water and spirit (Jn 3:5, 6). There is a distinction between flesh and spirit. The conclusion to this thought is that the "flesh profits nothing" because it is imperfect (Jn 6:63). Jesus condemned those who follow the flesh (Jn 8:15).

Obviously, the Pre-Millennial doctrine is of the flesh, which includes blood that gives life to the body (Lev 17:11). The life of Christ is in the spirit. Christ would never return to Palestine and reign over flesh and blood human beings, in a flesh and blood body for a 1,000 flesh and blood years. We no longer know Christ in the flesh that He once lived in (2Co 5:16). We shall never again know Christ in the flesh He once lived in.

The Pre-Millennial doctrine demands the appearance of the same human, carnal, flesh and blood Jesus as ascended in Ac 1:11. They think His body will be no different than the ones we now live in (Lev 17:11). They say that just as He ascended in a physical, flesh and blood body, He will return in the same. But they are wrong. Jesus ascended in a glorified, bloodless body. There is a difference between Acts 1:11 and Revelation 1:7. Acts 1:11 addresses the manner in which Christ ascended, and in the same manner, He shall descend from Heaven. But Revelation 1:7 is describing His coming in glory and majesty when every eye of every person who has ever lived will be fixed upon Him. Jesus did not ascend in a flesh and blood body to sit upon the Throne of Glory. Neither will He return in a flesh and blood body. Flesh and blood is confined to space and time. His body of glory and majesty transcends space and time.

Therefore, flesh and blood cannot inherit the Kingdom of God (1Co 15:50). Christ's sole purpose for appearing in His body after the resurrection was to confirm His Word. This is the case with any sign or wonder (Mk 16:16-20; Heb 2:1-4). It is also definitely confirmed that Jesus does not remain in His physical state, for John described Him as reentering the previous glory of God (Jn 17:5; Rev 2:8, 19:12; Da 7:9, 10, 13).

Revelation 1:16-18: *And he had in his right hand seven stars: and out of his mouth preceded a sharp two-edged sword: and his countenance was as the sun shineth in his strength. And when I saw him, I fell at his feet as one dead. And he laid his right hand upon me, saying, Fear not; I am the first and the last, I am the Living One; I was dead, and behold I am alive forever and ever! And I hold the keys of death and Hades.*

The seven stars represent the messengers of the local assemblies. He is speaking the Word of God, a sharp two-edged sword of truth (Heb 4:12), throughout the assembly. This was the Son of the Almighty God, and He gives four reasons why we should not to be afraid to proclaim the Gospel.

1. Jesus is the first and last, He is God almighty. His deity reigns and nothing compares to Him. In worshipping Him, Christians know the omniscient God. They can know the future and be assured of the truth.

2. He is the living one who was dead. He is life inherent; He has life in Him; and He is life. Jesus loves enough to take on death for the world. Christians do not fear death.

3. Jesus is alive forever, and Christians are reigning with Him. They have a future reward, not a future punishment! There is hope in this truth.

4. He exists for Christians. He has the keys of death and Hades. When He resurrected, "some" in the graves (according to Mt 27:51ff,) were resurrected, and their bodies were seen in Jerusalem. He did this as a demonstration so that people could see with their eyes what He had promised with His lips. There is a resurrection! Jesus has authority, power over death, and He built His Congregation upon Himself. He is the immovable rock and chief cornerstone! What a comforting thought to be in the hands of the Master of the Universe.

    The Evangelist is the messenger of the congregation. With these four encouraging thoughts burning in his heart, the evangel can proclaim the Gospel of Christ fearlessly.

Revelation 1:19, 20: Write therefore the things which thou sawest, and the things which are, and the things which shall come to pass hereafter; The mystery of the seven stars that you saw in my right hand and of the seven golden lampstands is this: The seven stars are the angels of the seven churches, and the seven lampstands are the seven churches.

Jesus wanted John to get this out in print! How interesting that the word book, *biblos*, begins the New Testament and ends the New Testament (Mt 1:1; Re 22:19). The Greek word *biblos* is noted throughout Scripture. People should want to read the book, hear the book, look into the book, live by the book, and teach the book. We should know this book because the world will be judged by it (Rev 20:12). Denominational people and cults attempt to justify hidden motives by removing the word, "bible," from the bible. However, the word *biblos* is translated bible. In my debate with Sabbatarians in Ocean City, Delaware, in order to justify Ellen G. White's doctrines, the spokeswoman of the group said that White's writings were superior to The Bible, and the word "Bible" was not even in the Bible. However, the word "Biblos" is the original word for Bible and is found as the first word of the Greek in Matthew 1:1 and at the end of the New Testament in Revelation 21:27 and 22:20.

There was a time when Christians in the congregations of Christ were known as a "People of the Book" because they took God's word seriously. We should want our names written in the Lamb's Book, *biblos*, of Life. If evangels proclaim the "Biblia," they will have their names personally engraved by Jesus in the "Lamb's Biblia."

John was writing to New Covenant Christians because they were getting ready to endure the most difficult time of their lives, but if they knew "who was, is, and is to come," they could endure with their minds fixed upon, "The Lamb on the Throne." The Book of Revelation gave encouragement to the persecuted congregation because they knew it. Are Christians today considered "People of the book?" Do you know this Book? Great encouragement is Christ's reward for those who value their time enough to know it.

Christ in the congregation – The seven congregations (Chapters 2 and 3)

1. Ephesus – 2:1-7

2. Smyrna – 2:8-11

3. Pergamos – 2:12-17
4. Thyatira – 2:18-29
5. Sardis – 3:1-6
6. Philadelphia – 3:7-13
7. Laodicea – 3:14-22

Revelation Chapter Two

Revelation 2:1: Unto the angel of the congregation in Ephesus write: These things saith he that holdeth the seven stars in his right hand, he that walketh in the midst of the seven golden candlesticks:

"The Seven Stars in his right hand" are the angels or messengers of the congregation (Rev 1:20). Christ holds the evangel in His hands. Some scholars think every congregation has a guardian angel, as if a created angel is standing guard over the "church" building. Both Roman and Greek Catholics teach their "churches" to pray to angels, a practice forbidden by God (Col 2:18). But the angels of the seven congregations are receiving instructions to communicate to the congregations. Angel simply means "to bring tidings, a messenger." James Strong (32) actually connects the word to Revelation 1:20.

Angel "messengers" are either created, supernatural beings (good or evil), or they are human messengers with good or evil messages. In the case of the seven congregations, they cannot be created supernatural angels because they represent the very important ministry of delivering the message from Christ to the members of the congregations. The evangelist is a gift from Christ to His congregation (Eph 4:11). Christ communicated His message to John through ONE supernatural angel, probably Michael (Rev 1:1, 6, 16). The messengers to the seven congregations were not created, supernatural angels; they are men. God has ordained that Gospel preachers should preach and live from the Gospel (1Co 9:14).

Incidents exist where angels were profoundly involved in assisting the Gospel, but God's program is that when the disciples were scattered abroad, they went "everywhere" declaring the Gospel (Ac 8:4). As we shall see, there is a patron angel of the everlasting Gospel (Rev 14:6), and angels are very interested in this power of God unto salvation (1Pe 1:12).

Angels assisted Phillip in his preaching to the eunuch (Ac 8:26) and to Peter in his preaching to Cornelius and The Jews (Ac 10:3, 22, 11:13, 12:7). Christians will judge angels (1Co 6:3), and not the reverse. The primitive congregation had a more intimate relationship with angels than we do today. This is because, in the absence of the Written New Testament, the early congregation needed sign-gifts to assist them and that included visible angels. After the completion of the New Testament Word (Heb 2:1-4), the glory of the engrafted Word in us surpasses that of a visitation of heavenly creatures. The more earnestly we heed the Word, the more aware we are of the ministering Spirits around us (Heb 1:14). God's angels are all around us today and like Christ, "they are loved and unseen" (1Pe 1:8).

This powerful truth should encourage all who teach, preach, or disciple in the New Testament word. In order to accentuate the Testimony, the evangel places a constant emphasis on Biblical truth. Christ led the evangel "To ordain elders in every city and set in order things that are lacking in the assembly" (Tit 1:3). The Holy Spirit installs the Elder as an overseer (Bishop) of the flock of Christ (Ac 20:28). Christ personally takes hold of an evangelist, and as he follows the Lord, He secures His life and work. The Elders in turn ordain the evangel (1Ti 4:14), not so much as a holy calling, but to expediently make necessary their mutual servant's accountability to the flock. Somewhere in the evangel's life, Christ laid His invisible hands upon him and called him to this holy charge.

The Assembly depends on Christ for their source of knowledge, strength, and comfort. Paul exclaimed that Christ is over all, and He is the lifeline. It is humbling to think that Christ places such stress upon the local congregation's evangel so he will remain true to this divine order (Gal 1:11, 12; Eph 1:22; Col 2:10).

Christ said in Matthew 28:28, "All Authority in heaven and on earth has been given to me. Therefore, as you are going into all the world making disciples, baptize them in the name of the Father, Son, and Holy Spirit teaching them to observe all things I have command you." The same truth is prevalent today. The messengers of the congregations, the evangelists, are teaching the commandments of Christ to the congregations. The preacher may easily be tempted to bow to the whims of the people and desist from apostolic truth, but the invisible presence of Christ encourages him, and he will not quit!

Christ is an Awesome, Invisible Presence

As Adam and Eve heard the voice of the Lord walking in the garden, so the evangel and the congregation should hear Christ's voice "walking in the midst." "Walking in the midst of the seven golden sticks," means that Christ, who is the light-giver, dwells in the midst of the light-bearers. As light-bearers, each Assembly should cause its light (Gospel) to radiate to the lost people of the world who are perishing in their sin (1Ti 3:15; Mt 5:14-16; Php 2:15).

Christ dwells in each congregation separately, and He deals with each separately, as well. Each congregation is responsible to do its *own* work as pastors oversee their congregations. The most awesome responsibility is given to the evangelist, who as Christ's messenger must address the congregation when they assemble. God gave various messengers to the assemblies to equip the saints for the work of the ministry (Eph 4:11). We are to build only upon the one foundation (1Co 3:10; Eph 2:20), which the Apostles and Prophets laid with Christ Himself, that being the chief cornerstone (Eph 2:21).

The title *Apostolic Father* belongs to only 12 men, plus one born out of due season (1Co 15:8), who were selected by Christ to fulfill the role of His apostleship. Apostle means *one who is sent*. These Apostles were ordained and sent out by Christ Himself. Several denominations proclaim to follow *modern-day Apostles*. One question needs to be asked, "Which Apostles do you follow according to Revelation 21:14?" The eternal foundational ministry of Christ's Kingdom is already established and is a permanent structure. The Word clearly states that the foundation of Heaven is built upon Christ's 12 Apostles. In numerology, the number "12" represents government. "As the one born out of due time" (1Co 15:8), Paul's writings were also included with those of the other Apostles. Like other Apostles, signs, miracles, and wonders confirmed Paul's ministry (2Co 12:11, 12). It is impossible for Christ's Apostles to exist today. When anyone claims to be an apostle, certain qualifications must be met.

Peter describes the following qualifications in Acts 1:20-26. A person:

1. Must have been with the Apostles from the beginning until the end.

2. Must have been with the Apostles at Jesus' Immersion.

3. Must have been with the Apostles to witness the resurrection of Christ.

4. Must be selected by Christ (They prayed to Jesus and cast lots upon the one whom Christ selected.).

5. Paul met these qualifications by being personally taught from Heaven by Christ (1Co 11: 26). Paul, having written 14 Epistles, is definitely included in this government of Christ (See my introduction to "Commentary on Hebrews.").

We must understand that to be an apostle of Christ, a person must be sent out by Christ Himself. Modern-day apostles claim apostleship of Christ, but Christ never selected them when He was on Earth! The unique case was the Apostle Paul. Paul was not there from the beginning, but he did receive supernatural revelation from Christ in Arabia for three years (Gal 1:16-18). He also proved himself as an Apostle of Christ (2Co 12:12). Modern-day apostles must be measured with the same measuring rod as Paul. They must first meet the qualifications that Peter listed in Acts 1 and perform the signs of an apostle as Paul did. Failure to do so immediately disqualifies modern-day apostles from their proclaimed position. Apostolic succession is scripturally indefensible and untenable.

Because the Apostles and Prophets (Eph 2: 20) have laid the Congregation's foundation, the evangelist and pastors can now build upon that foundation with New Testament truth. Evangelist comes from the word *euangelos,* which in the Greek means *messenger of the good news.* The Pastors have synonymous names like shepherd, overseer, and bishop. Unfortunately, nearly all congregations have done away with the role of the evangelist and replaced them with *pastors* of the congregation (For more information, see Jeff Wickert's Church Polity book, *Restoring the Foundation.*).

Unlike the responsibilities of the evangel, Biblical pastors oversee the flock, as a father would take care of his children. *Pastors* in the congregation are always referred to in the plural. There is no mention of ministry teams, ruling elders, a head shepherd, president, or pastor of a congregation. Paul said to Timothy, "Appoint *elders* (plural) in every city…" (Tit 1:5). The Greek word is *presbuteros.* The parsing of this word is *adjective, accusative, plural, and masculine.* Never was an *elder,* in the singular, ruling over a congregation in the New Testament.

Evangelists are responsible for upholding and maintaining New Testament government in the congregation. It is not unscriptural to have a preaching pastor. There is a problem, however, when a preaching pastor may want to annul the Christ-given ministry of an evangelist. Not only this, but congregations can become complicit and force this scenario because the elders often want the pastor to do their work. In turn, the people love him when he does their work. Satan is victorious when the "pastor" becomes so bogged down with administrative duties that he cannot implement the necessary outreach to the lost.

Also, while women were very active as servants in the early congregation, biblically, there was no such thing as an ordained female evangelist, elder, or deacon.

Clement, in his First Epistle to the Corinthians, written late in the 1st Century, always speaks of the pastorate in the plural as *bishops*, serving along with the deacons.[48] Half a decade later, in the early 2nd Century, Polycarp continued to refer to a plurality of elders as *presbyters*.[49]

However, Ignatius of Antioch referred to elevated bishops. The Latin phrase, "The Catholic Church," is found for the first time in the letter of St. Ignatius to the Smyrnaeans, written about 110 A.D. Ignatius wrote, "Wheresoever the bishop shall appear, there let the people be, even as where Jesus may be, there is the universal Church."[50]

This is the beginning of the labyrinth-like, hierarchical reign of the monarchial bishop, in which the bishop's authority is the same as Christ's authority. This system first began making distinctions between the collegiums of presbyters or bishops and a monarchial bishop. This then led to the heresy against "the priesthood of all believers" because it created a special priesthood of selected individuals. It is conceded, even by Catholic scholars, that "a Christian Special Priesthood" was nothing but a resurrection of Judaism and the aligning of those with the most ecclesiastical influence with Sanhedrin-type power. The grab for apostolic succession was not far behind. This led to a resurrection of a power structure similar to the hierarchy of Judaism. Just as Judaism's power structure led to Sanhedrin-type power, so the "husterion" (latter time) departure (turn of the 2nd Century) from the Apostolic Faith led to monarchial elder-bishop power, with Apostolic Succession not far behind. Church organization resembled a tangled web a spider weaves over the first few centuries after the Apostles died, in order to capture innocent, deluded souls who were denied the real Gospel.

This labyrinth scenario, from Ignatious of Antioch (approximately 100 A.D.) to Pope John in 533 A.D., took approximately 400 years to play out. Ignatius wrote,

> "Since therefore I have, in the persons before mentioned, beheld the whole multitude of you in faith and love, I exhort you to study to do all things with a divine harmony, while your *bishop presides in the place of god*, and your presbyters in the place of the assembly of the apostles, along with your deacons, who are most dear to me, and are entrusted with the ministry of Jesus Christ, who was with the Father before the beginning of time, and in the end was revealed. Do ye all then, imitating the same divine conduct, pay respect to one another, and let no one look upon his neighbor after the flesh, but do ye continually love each other in Jesus Christ. Let nothing exist among you that may divide you; but be ye united with your *bishop*, and those that preside over you, as a type and evidence of your immortality"[51]

> "Revere God and the bishop…Honour thou God indeed, as the Author and Lord of all things, but the bishop as the high-priest, who bears the image of God-of- God. Inasmuch as he is a ruler, and of Christ, in his capacity of a priest… [there is no] one in the Church greater than the bishop, who ministers as a priest to God for the salvation of the whole world…He who presumes to do anything without the bishop, thus both destroying the [Church's] unity, and throwing its order into confusion? For the priesthood is the very highest point of all good things among men… Let the laity be subject to the deacons; the deacons to the presbyters; the presbyters to the bishop; the bishop to Christ, even as He is to the Father."[52]

> "So neither do ye anything without the bishop and presbyters."[53]

> "Even as the bishop is the representative of the Father of all things, and the presbyters are the Sanhedrin of God."[54]

> "For, since ye are subject to the bishop as to Jesus Christ, ye appear to me to live not after the manner of men, but according to Jesus Christ, who died for us, in order, by believing in His death, ye may escape from death. It is therefore necessary that, as ye indeed do, so without the bishop ye should do nothing, but should also be subject to the presbytery, as to the apostle of Jesus Christ, who is our hope, in whom, if we live, we shall [at last] be found."[55]

This apostasy of monarchial bishops would never have occurred if the ministry of the evangel to the local congregations had not been eliminated. I will devote considerable space to the death of the witnesses (Rev 11:7, 8) in our commentary on the seven churches. There is a correlation between the witnesses, "martyrs," and those who have the testimony, "martyrs" (Rev 12:11, 18). When we look at this apocalyptic deduction, we see the emphasis of eliminating not only the evangelistic witness but all witnesses who evangelize for Christ.

Indisputably, in Ephesians 4:11, Jesus gave to His congregation apostles, prophets, pastors, and teachers, but He also gave the gift of evangelists. The question is, "Where are they now?" As we have already noticed, there is hardly any reference made to the work given to evangelists (Ac 21:8; 2Ti 4:5) after the 2nd Century. Nearly four centuries after the position of evangel was eliminated, there was nothing to stand in the way or to oppose what Emperor Justinian said of Bishop John II (533 A.D.).

> "Therefore, We have exerted Ourselves to unite all the priests of the East and subject them to the See of Your Holiness, and hence the questions which have at present arisen, although they are manifest and free from doubt, and according to the doctrines of your Apostolic See, are constantly firmly observed and preached by all priests, We have still considered it necessary that they should be brought to the attention of Your Holiness. For we do not suffer anything which has reference to the state of the Church, even though what causes difficulty may be clear and free from doubt, to be discussed without being brought to the notice of Your Holiness, because you are the head of all the Holy Churches, for We shall exert Ourselves in every way (as has already been stated), to increase the honor and authority of your See."[56]

When your Author reads these quotes, he is thoroughly convinced that through the craft and guile of men like Ignatius, the New Covenant Evangelist (Eph 4:11) was partially terminated. Ignatius' elevating one Bishop over the church was his deliberate attempt to destroy the Christ-given gift of the evangel to His Ecclesia. There are some church historians who are convinced that Ignatius' writings are spurious and forgeries. The constant refrain that sounds through his writings is that one bishop heads the local congregation. Of course, this eventually led to one bishop being constituted as head of the universal "church."

All things considered, in the New Testament, evangelists like Timothy and Titus occupied the place of an oracle to the people of a congregation. After Ignatius, we do not read about evangelists again, but we do read much history about "A Head Bishop." Much of Ignatius' writings did not appear until the 6th Century. By that time, the poisonous seeds of the monarchial bishop had been sown; Catholicism was in full bloom; and most of the evangels had died in total obscurity. Whether Ignatius wrote such monarchial Bishop propaganda or not is now moot.

It is a long way from the evangel of Revelation, Chapter 2, to the monarchial bishop of 533 A.D. However, it is a longer way from 2000 A.D. back to Revelation, Chapter 2. The evangelist's role is surely being replaced by *a one pastor system*. However, The Restoration Movement has brought back God's true congregational government. The role of the evangelists has been restored, although with much rejection and hatred. The qualifications of an evangelist are listed in Timothy's 1st and 2nd Epistles, along with Titus. Timothy is responsible for establishing congregational order and for appointing elders for service. The Evangelist is called to rebuke, reprove, exhort, prescribe, teach, give attendance to the public reading of Scripture, study the word, and exercise the gifts that were bestowed upon them. Timothy is to teach the elders to visit the widows, orphans, sick, and shut-ins (2Ti 3:15; Jas 5: 14, 15).

THE MINISTRY OF THE GOSPEL EVANGEL IN PROPHECY

The prophecies of Zechariah and Revelation mention the role of the evangelist in the Congregation of Christ. Zechariah mentions two olive trees (Zec 4:3), but what are they? These olive trees are men of God who are receiving God's oil. These two men are anointed by God and owned by God (Zec 4:14). The one thing that evangelists have in common with the Apostles is that they are both witnesses to the New Testament testimony (Rev 11:3, 4, 7). Because these witnesses were killed, they ceased to set the congregations in order. These killings left room for *elevated bishops, archbishops, cardinals*, and *popes*. It opened the pathway for false doctrine to pollute the Kingdom of Christ for over 1,000 years.

What Joshua and Zerubabbel were to the temple of old (Zec 3:8, 4:7-10) is a prototype of what the evangel "witnesses" are to the New Testament spiritual temple. The two olive trees in Zechariah are like the two anointed witnesses of Revelation, and they stand before the Lord of all the Earth. We know that Jesus Christ is the anointed of God, the Son of oil. (Heb 1:9) The New Testament also declares that the Holy Spirit is the anointed oil. Most scholars believe that the two olive trees are Joshua and Zerubabbel, but the text only mentions Zerubabbel (Zec 4:1-6). It is highly doubtful that a mere man can provide the oil needed to stir the kings (Cyrus or Darius) to aid God's people.

Joshua, the High Priest previously mentioned (Zec 3:1), is pictured and dressed in rags of unrighteousness. This is not a good description of the man who can supply the pure oil of the Spirit to the downcast servants of God. Since there are two "anointed ones" who stand before the Lord of all the Earth, it would really be making too much of two mortal men who lived and died in the land of ancient Judea. On the other hand, with the direction of the Holy Spirit and the power of God, the Lord God was willing to do great things with humble accomplices such as Joshua and Zerubabbel. We shall see later in Revelation, Chapter 11, the demanding prophetic work of the two evangels under great duress and persecution.

The Evangelists of the Congregations are the Stars in the Right Hand of Jesus.

In Revelation 1, Christ is in the midst of the seven lamps or candlestick holders. The lamps are the congregations of the first born from the dead, Jesus Christ. As previously noted, they are not giving light to Christ; He is giving light to them. He has the power to light up the lamp or remove it. Obviously, the lamps have wicks that can be trimmed by the lamp owner. The ten virgins were responsible for the maintenance of their lamps. Unlike the Calvinist interpretation, Christ does not control the lamp and give "perseverance to the saints." If He had, He would never have warned the Christians if they did not repent and return to their first love. He would have removed their lamp. Christians are in charge of filling and trimming their lamps according to the parable of the ten virgins of Matthew 25. Christ encourages, helps, comforts, assures, blesses, defends, and protects those who are His; however, *He will not persevere for Christians* nor will He trim their lamps. It is definitely a New Covenant relationship, where the Covenant Maker has made a responsible commitment to Christians, and Christians have a commitment to Him.

In Vine's Dictionary (p. 648), he says there is no mention of a candle in the original manuscript (Old or New Testament). The Bible does not refer to what one calls a candle or candlestick, and the translators who do are in error when they mention them. The New American Standard is correct when it translates Christ's words.

> "As for the mystery of the seven stars which you saw in my right hand, and the seven lamp stands, the seven stars are the *messengers* of the seven congregations, and the seven golden lamp stands are the seven congregations" (Rev 1:20).

It is difficult for us to determine from the text whether Christ is the stand upon which all seven lamps rest, or they are seven individual lamp stands surrounding His presence. In any event, we can know for sure that Christ is providing the source (oil) for light. John 13-16 tells us that Christ is corporately *one* with the Holy Spirit, and He is *one* with His Congregations. Each congregation is autonomous because they have a collective will to serve or not to serve. They also have the right to be or not to be one with the source of energy. The unity of the Godhead, the unity of the witnesses, and the congregation produce the vision of the picture. Thus, as Zechariah mentions the three persons of the Godhead (the two anointed Ones and the Lord of all the earth) so Revelation corroborates the same truth. It is difficult to ascertain whether verse (Zec 4:14) refers to the Godhead, the compound unity of the two witnesses and their relationship to the Godhead, or both.

> "John, To the seven churches in the province of Asia: Grace and peace to you from him who is, and who was, and who is to come, and from the seven spirits before his throne, and from Jesus Christ, who is the faithful witness, the firstborn from the dead, and the ruler of the kings of the earth" (Rev 1:4, 5).

Christ is the oil-anointed *Messiah,* and Christians receive from His fullness (Jn 1:16; Eph 4:13). The Holy Spirit is the *unction anointing* that they have received; although, John relates this anointing to the apostolic understanding (1Jn 2:20-27). John connects "anointing" with the apostolic word.

When we hear certain charismatic preachers speaking continuously of anointing, and yet, they do not support their doctrinal statements by citing the Word of Truth, we wonder whether their "anointing" is true. Emotional fervor and entrancing entertainment is not anointing. There was a time when evangelists were known for being orators of the Word of God. They won people to Christ through personal evangelism. Today, we entertain people in our "church" without ever really giving them birth through the Word.

Christ and the Holy Spirit stand before the *Throne* of the Lord God of all the Earth, ready to go forth and do His great work.

With this in mind, another apocalyptic vision,

> "'And I will give power to my two witnesses, and they will prophesy for 1,260 days, clothed in sackcloth.' These are the two olive trees and the two lamp stands that stand before the Lord of the earth. If anyone tries to harm them, fire comes from their mouths and devours their enemies. This is how anyone who wants to harm them must die" (Rev 11:3-5).

At first glance, there appears to be a contradiction concerning the lamp stands and the olive trees. It might seem that the witnesses were the olive trees. However, upon closer observation, we can see that it does not say two olive trees *only*, but verse 4 links them to the lamp stands as well. The verse does not say the witnesses are only olive trees nor does it say they are only lamp stands, but both! Consequently, the lamp is made of different parts yet molded into one piece. Likewise, Christ is *one* conjugal unity with His congregation and with His servant witnesses. Just as Christ and the Holy Spirit stand before God's Throne, so the two witnesses (of New Covenant Christianity) and lamp stands (The Congregations) stand before the Lord. An interesting note is that there are 66 parts (knobs, flowers, and buds) on the original tabernacle lamp stand, and there are 66 books of the Bible (Ex 25:31-40).

Additional typology is given in the vine and branches (Jn 15:1-5). The whole vine is presented as one single unit. One is the giver and the other is the receiver, but they are still one. The vine gives the life sap to the branch, and the branch receives it, but they are still connected. The olive tree gives the oil and the lamp stands receive it, but they are still one. If the mistake were made to make the witnesses the olive trees only, then they would need to receive oil from Christ and the Holy Spirit. However, if they are both the trees and the lamp stands, then they are one with both the giver of the oil and the receiver of the oil (the congregations). Just as it took Zerubabbel and his successors a long time to rebuild the temple (Da 9:25), so it would take a long time to finish preaching the everlasting Gospel of the true temple of Spiritual Israel. These witnesses were killed by sacerdotalism. Sacerdotalism continues to kill the witnesses today. Different methods are employed, but the desired effect is to silence them.

If we return to Revelation 1:20, the truth that Christ holds the seven stars in His right hand will be seen. These seven stars are still the *Angelos* or messengers given by Christ to the Congregation, His Assembly for all time (Eph 4:11). Because Christ gave the messengers, and He holds them in His right hand, He must be responsible for them. They are one with Him. This verse gives much comfort to today's evangelists. Revelation 1 refers to all true New Testament evangelists in general, whereas Revelation 11 refers to the evangelist-prophet in particular.

This text in Revelation 11 mentions two witnesses. We can find that working in pairs of two is Christ's method for soul winning. No evangelist should work by himself. The 200-year old idea of having a one-man pastor is not only unscriptural; it is also impractical. This impossible burden that local congregations place upon modern-day ministers creates situations that lead to deplorable consequences, like *burnouts*, nervous breakdowns, and even apostasy and immorality.

Spiritually, having one mouth and one body, these evangelists are one with each other (Rev 11:9). Revelation 11:8 states, literally, "Their dead corpse (singular) will lie in the public square." The word for corpse is *ptoma*, which means fallen or downfall. Unfortunately, Bible translators attempt to correct the Holy Spirit of God by making corpse plural.[57] If it is in the singular, leave it that way in the translation. If it does not satisfy our grammatical curiosity – too bad! This is apocalyptic language and is intended to teach the spiritual mind of the people.

As previously noted, the oil, lamp stand, and evangel messenger are one with Christ and the Congregation. Likewise, the two witnesses are one with each other. When one goes down the other goes down with him. We will see things written the way God sees them, and not like a man sees them. Not even the Apostle Paul would work by himself. He had companions like Timothy, Barnabas, Silas, and Luke. This was in keeping with His master's plan, which sent them out two by two (Mt 11:2, 18:19; Mk 6:7). Paul also arranged for his fellow workers to go in pairs. The two are actually *one* voice. Even though one of the two might be the dominant one, the partner has no problem deferring to him, as Aaron deferred to Moses, Elisha to Elijah, and Barnabas to Paul.

The Congregation at Ephesus (2:1-7)

Revelation 2:2-6: "I know thy works, and thy toil and patience, and that thou canst not bear evil men, and didst try them that call themselves apostles, and they are not, and didst find them false; and thou hast patience and didst bear for my *name's sake, and hast not grown weary. Yet I hold this against you: You have forsaken your first love. Remember the height from which you have fallen! Repent and do the things you did at first. If you do not repent, I will come to you and remove your lamp stand from its place. But you have this in your favor: You hate the practices of the Nicolaitans, which I also hate."*

The Apostle Paul tested the foundation of the Ephesian congregation in 53 A.D. His first visit was brief. At the closing of his second journey (Ac 18:18-21), he trusted this assembly to Priscilla and Aquila to accomplish the work God had set before them (Ac 18:18-21). They then awaited Paul's return (Ac 19:1-6). This congregation is noted for burning false doctrinal books worth approximately $50,000 in 2005 dollars.

The city of Ephesus existed on the Cayster River. It was the pride of the Roman Provence, Asia, with business and with great commercial importance. Ephesus was also a city of the greatest political importance. It was what was known as a *free* city. The Romans had granted it the right of self-government within limits.

Ephesus was founded as early as the 10th Century B.C. and flourished during the Roman Empire (www.wikipedia.ed: Ephesus). Ephesus was also a city of the greatest religious importance. Its greatest glory, the Temple of Diana (Ac 19:26, 27), was one of the Seven Wonders of the World. The Temple's image was so old that none knew when it had come, and some said that it had fallen from Heaven itself (Ac 19:35). The image was a black, squat, repulsive figure, covered with many breasts (the symbol of fertility), and held a club in one hand and a trident in the other. The Ephesus of 53 A.D. had an image that to millions of people was the most sacred thing in the world.

EPHESUS, THE BIGGEST SITE OF APOSTASY IN HISTORY

Paul prophesied to the elders at Ephesus, "Savage wolves would come in among you, not sparing the flock" (Ac 20:29). Ironically, in three centuries at the site where the Ephesians destroyed the veneration of mother Diana, they replaced it with the veneration of Mary at the Council of Ephesus in 431 A.D. The Word of God addresses the Virgin Mary as the most blessed woman of all time. However, to venerate her as "the mother of God" is no different than the worship of Diana.

The people of this congregation were on death row. As John was banished to the Island of Patmos, they were receiving and getting ready to receive nearly unbearable persecution. This Revelation, written to this congregation, applies to all ages and assemblies. The Evangelist is commanded to deliver these things to the congregation. When "eu" is put before angel "euangelos," it means "Messenger of good news." However, this message was a message of discipline. It is not good news, but news to take "corrective action."

Jesus told them that He knows everything, and He is *not* pleased with them. They were trying to live to their own glory. Christ holds them in His hands. Is He pleased? Some were calling themselves apostles, but they were not. God had only 12 Apostles to lay the foundation. Be alert to what Paul said in Acts 20:29 about ferocious wolves coming among the flock, the Ecclesia, and the Council of Ephesus in 431 A.D. when paganism was almost fully developed in the Church. This congregation had already lost their first love and was teaching false doctrine. They were getting into the health and wealth Gospel while forgetting the salvation and grace of Jesus Christ (Col 2:19).

Jesus proclaimed his hatred for the deeds of the Nicolaitians. Nicolaitian is a compound word from Nico (put down) and laos (people). The foundation for Greek-Roman Catholicism started with this teaching. This first apostasy began with elevating the bishop and clergy above the congregation, while putting all others down in order to prove their supremacy. The rise of Greek-Catholicism's first "monarchial bishop" apostasy was very instrumental in undermining the New Covenant Congregation's local congregation kingdom government of evangelists and collegium of elders.

Throughout this apocalyptic study, we have focused on the long war between the religious autocracies on Earth and the Lord and His Messiah in Heaven (Ps 2:1-9). From Earth's standpoint, there were times when the victories in this war seemed almost too close to call. While The Apocalypse gives us a very, realistic view of how powerful the Lord's enemies are, it promises victory time and time again to those Christians who overcome.

A VERY IMPORTANT, BUT LITTLE KNOWN SUBJECT

We know one thing for certain; the devil's warriors are very clever. Here in Ephesus, we are introduced to their method of warfare. This is very simple. Change the leadership to your own liking, and you can change the government for your personal control. So in the first couple of centuries, we do not see a drastic change in the Gospel, the plan of salvation, the practice of immersion, or ordinance of

The Lord's Supper. But we do see drastic tampering and radical changes in the way the congregations were governed. The reason we do not read of diocese, consistories', synods, district or monarchial bishops in the 1st Century congregations is because they were all locally governed, with evangelist, pastors, deacons, teachers and disciplers.

The Devil knew he could not change the Gospel message, the supremacy of Christ, the holiness of the local congregations, the plan of salvation, the practice of immersion, the memorial feast of the Lord's Supper, and a hundred other New Testament doctrines unless he changed the government.

Let us illustrate with a modern-day political example. We might compare the government of the 1st Century congregation to the government created by our American Forefathers. The New Testament's message of "individual freedom from sin" was to the 1st Century congregation what our Constitution, with its Bill of Rights, and the Declaration of Independence message of "individual freedom from tyranny" was to our American Forefathers. For these sacrosanct documents to work in our system of Covenant Christianity, we must have a reverential respect for them. We Americans must be taught not only the precepts, but also the logic that motivated our Founding Fathers to write them.

Suppose, through fraud, deceit, and cunning, we are duped into electing a person who usurps the Office of the President. Our new leader really wants to transfer the power of this country to a foreign country. He desires to destroy our political landscape and heritage and to subjugate us to the laws and governing system of another nation. How would he do this?

Such power-grabs have been accomplished throughout the ages by hundreds of tyrants who wished to destroy a nation's political infrastructure. First, the tyrant's philosophy must come from outside the established norms of the targeted nation. That is, he must have the backing of other sources, be they inside or outside the nation. This backing provides him the strength, resources, support, and finances necessary to undermine his new country. Next, he must attempt to destroy the sacred charters of the country. When he puts "his" people in the right positions and judgeships, he can begin economic, social class, and race warfare against his new country. Through propaganda networks, he seeks to emphasize freedom rather than the law. He knows, however, that the freedom he promises will last only until he has absolute control of the nation. When he feels these things are in place, a president could transform a nation in a short time.

Let us apply this scenario to the collapse of local New Covenant Christian governments with Christ as the HEAD and evangelists, pastors, deacons, teachers, and disciplers as His servants (Eph 4:11-14). The Devil catered to those who wanted bishops to exert monarchal rule over the elders of the local congregations. He placed in the hearts of those vying for supremacy of the new Christian Faith, the desire to seek power and recognition. The greatest hindrance to overthrowing New Covenant Christian governments was the Christ-appointed evangelists who were testifying in the New Covenant Scripture only. Those bishops wanting monarchal rule needed the Christ-appointed evangelists eliminated…gone!

As the Elevated Bishopric grew, the zeal for New Testament preaching began to wane. The New Testament was laid aside in favor of the writings of the Bishops. This led to the formation of human, man-made creeds and confessions. Just like the libertine "progressives" want to destroy our charters in America, the ruling bishops wanted to replace the sacred New Testament charter of The Faith with their creeds. As orthodox and papal, clerical supremacy prevailed, they were able to push the original faith of the Apostles into the wilderness of obscurity.

Oh, both the governmental and New Testament documents were still in print, but no one seemed to care whether or not they existed. They were like dead documents. Later, as the supreme heads of the different ecclesia (church) took their places of authority, they had the power to punish or execute all dissenters. As with political apostasy, governments do not start executing those who do not parrot the party line until they have complete control over them, so it is true of religious apostasy.

Under Christ's divine system, a congregation's ruling elder could not manipulate and change the function of the Christ-appointment structure and government of His Kingdom. But as the Bishoprics continued to grow, the Kingdom structure of the Christ-appointment government changed from a Christ-centered authority to a clergy-laity centered autocracy.

The origin of the word clergy meant "to cast lots." This word is found in Acts 1:26 in which the Apostles cast lots for a replacement of Judas. An interesting truth about this passage of Scripture is the context of Acts 2:45, "They had everything in common." How could the Apostles have a higher rank than the recent converts if they had everything in common? The word layman or laywoman was never used by any of the Apostles. Even the Apostle Peter considered himself a lively stone among the other lively stones in Christ's spiritual house (1Pe 2:5). The only distinguishing characteristic to set the Apostles apart from the rest of the eternal congregation was that they wrote The New Testament Scripture once for all, for all time (2Co 14:36). The Disciples recognized this fact with great reverence (Ac 5:13).

As mentioned previously, the Ephesian Congregation had an orthodox conviction in their hatred of the deeds of the Nicolaitians. Their "hate" is a strong word, but the Ephesian Christians hated nicolaitianism.

I believe this abomination of the word *cleros* was nothing other than a desperate power-grab. The Catholic Church replaced the priesthood of the common Christian with a select clergy few *"chosen by God."* It was not until 1793 A.D. when James O'Kelly and The Restoration Movement renounced the apostasy and returned to New Covenant Christianity and the Biblical congregation polity. The Restoration Movement decided to call themselves just Christians, in Manheim, NC. They also accepted the New Testament as their only authority and rule of faith. These were the infant steps that lead to a further restoration of the people to New Testament Christianity, with immersion into Christ and the reinstitution of the Lord's Supper.

The change in church government was at the heart of the first steps to apostasy. How incredible that Satan knew the first step that led into apostasy was to change the Christ-centered government of the New Testament congregation. Should it be surprising that this is the last and hardest principle for modern-day evangelist to restore?

Paul warned the Elders at Ephesus that "From among them" would raise unscrupulous wolves who will lead disciples to themselves. At the same Council of Ephesus in 431 A.D., leading bishops from around the world assembled in Ephesus to attempt to convince Emperor Theodosius that their interpretation of the "Theotokos Controversy" was the correct one. Here the "Mary Mother of God" doctrine won the day with Theodosius and one of the first "church" buildings was erected, "Church of Mary." Of course the worshipful place of Mary is foreign to the New Testament, but another rather subtle evil entered the "church." After this Council of Ephesus, some leading bishops gained much influence with the Emperor and the "universal church." This council was a great impetus toward the rise of the monarchial bishop. It would take only another century for the rise of the leading bishop to be called "Pope." It is so easy to forget that what was being called "Catholic" at the time included what, after the 11th Century, would be called Greek Orthodox or Russian Orthodox, etc.

The works of labor and perseverance in the Lord by the congregation at Ephesus was recognized (Jas 2:14-26; Php 2:12). They had great patience with one another (Ac 2:42; 1Cor 15:58) and despised the evil practices and those bearing evil (2Th 3:6; Ro 16:17; 2 Jn 9-11; 1Co 5:1-6). They were concerned with doctrine, so they tested the legitimacy of the self-proclaimed apostles. If the leaders of the Ephesian congregation had such conviction in 431 A.D., no Council of Ephesus would have occurred in 431. This is where the doctrine of Apostolic Succession gained its foothold in the religious world. After all, the Pope is nothing but the end result of such a false doctrine. Doctrine is important (Gal 1:6-9; 2 Co 11:13; Mt 15:9).

The Ephesian congregation was "orthodox" in a good way. They had an orthodox conviction of their hatred for the deeds of the Nicolaitians, which also led to the rise of monarchal bishops who created Orthodox denominations.

Even though "The Woman," (Bride of Christ) emerged from Dark Age obscurity by the late 18th Century, we still wrestle with the idea of whether New Testament Christianity will survive the advent of the 21st Century and whether "The Son of Man will find THE FAITH" if He comes in our life time (Lk 18:8). "Cultural-Churchanity" in many ways is just as powerful today as was the religious, secular, and political power of the ecclesiastical bishopric that drove the true New Testament faith into the wilderness of obscurity. We wonder if those who profess New Testament Christianity are spiritually enlightened enough and Biblically strong enough to resist the temptation to surrender to the opiate of religious, cultural, and political correctness that is entering every segment of life from churchanity, to education, sports, entertainment, and speech.

One of the most powerful pens of the hundreds of writers about The Restoration "Remnant" Movement belonged in the hand of L. Edsil Dale. When we were struggling with the one-man-pastor church polity system in the 1960s, Professor Dale broke out of the mold with crystal clear clarity in addressing the Nicolaitan (clergy-laity) Apostasy (Rev 2:6, 14, 15). This "One-Man-Pastor-Priest-Serve-All" polity was inherited primarily from the Greek-Roman hierarchal system that greatly prevailed during the 1,260-year historical period called the "Dark Ages." From secular man's historic prospective, the Dark Ages lasted from approximately 476 to 800 A.D., and according to other estimates, from 476 to Isaac Newton[58] (late 17th Century) but many religious scholars contend that the apocalyptic number 1,260 days is representative of 1,260 years from 533 A.D. (the first Pope John) to 1793 (www.google: Republican Methodist). Other religious scholars take the Dark Ages end date to refer to the French Revolution in 1792.

James O'Kelly had problems with the mode of baptism and the Unitarian controversy, but he pioneered some New Testament restoration views of Christ being the head of the Church, local autonomy, the Bible being the only authority, and the divine Name of Christ. O'Kelly's associate, Rice Haggard, was a powerful force in leading people of former denominations and creeds to call themselves "Christians" only. Reportedly, the Republican Methodist Church (Flavana, NC) broke away from the Methodist denomination on December 25, 1793. Later, on August 18, 1794, Haggard took the floor before interested brethren at the Old Lebanon Meeting House and motioned, "I move that we all, hence force, be known as 'Christians' forever."

Although far from being a return to the New Testament in "Faith and Practice," many Restoration Fathers from the past viewed the daring attempts of O'Kelly-Haggard to restore New Testament doctrines as "land-mark" events of providence to bring the Congregation out of a 1,260-year wilderness of obscurity.

Even into the 20th Century, autonomous New Testament congregations had problems in understanding New Testament policy. L. Edsil Dale provided excellent Biblical Hermeneutics regarding local congregational polity based on the Ephesians 4 model. Dale used Scriptural outline charts, graphs, and diagrams to communicate concise thoughts regarding the New Testament model for establishing a congregation with Christ-appointed servants who will obey and carry on our Lord's ministry over the long term. Now deceased, Dale was a very true-to-Scripture scholar, par-excellent.[59]

However, whatever positives the Ephesians had in their Christian walk, the Ephesians had left their first love! Christ commanded them to "do the first works" that they had when they first committed their loving obedience to Him. The same problems exist in modern-day congregations. Newlywed Christians seem to have such zeal and passion for their savior, only to fall into complacency and dead works. The Ephesians had fallen (Gal 5:4), and Christ was calling them to repentance. He threatened them with the removal of their lampstand, which was their light support. Without the lampstand, it is impossible for them to have a candlestick. Without Christ's love, it is impossible for us to be the Light of the World.

Revelation 2:7: He that hath an ear, let him hear what the Spirit saith unto the churches; to him that overcometh will I give to eat of the tree of life, which is in the midst of the paradise of God.

This verse addresses the responsibility of human will to "hear" and "overcome." It is human nature to think that because of God's providential rule, we are exempt from engaging in the rigorous work of human service in response to divine commands. We must realize that such obedience is so essential to God's divine sovereign program. We must emphasize that this promise is based upon the fact that we want to overcome. While this verse is not specific as to what we are to "overcome," Paul states that there are at least 17 emotional and physical threats that confront the human race at all times (Ro 8:35-38). Through Christ's love, we can overcome all troubling issues that affect us. Read those 17 threats and discover for yourself how you can be an "overcomer." God's sovereignty does not exclude loving, volitional, human effort… Rather, God's sovereignty demands it.

A tribute is due here to God's overall program which began in Eden's paradise and ends in God's Paradise. This proves to us that we have the entire Bible Revelation for man and that it is now complete. We are fascinated, elated, and comforted by the thought that what began in the paradise in the past with "The Tree of Death" has now reached the climax and the divine privilege of all God's children eating from the "The Tree of Life" in Heaven. Notice that unlike the tree in the paradise of Eden, God's tree is called "The Tree of Life" and not "The Tree of the Knowledge of Good and Evil." We started in the paradise of Eden, and we shall end in the paradise of God. The Paradise of God has always existed in eternity. Can you imagine the joy, unspeakable and full of glory that will fill our hearts when it is manifested for the Ecclesia to enjoy? Halleluiah!

The Congregation at Smyrna (2:8-11)

Revelation 2:8-11: "To the angel of the church in Smyrna write: These are the words of him who is the First and the Last, who died and came to life again. I know your afflictions and your poverty—yet you are rich! I know the slander of

> those who say they are Jews and are not, but are a synagogue of Satan. Do not be afraid of what you are about to suffer. I tell you, the devil will put some of you in prison to test you, and you will suffer persecution for ten days. Be faithful, even to the point of death, and I will give you the crown of life. He who has an ear, let him hear what the Spirit says to the churches. He who overcomes will not be hurt at all by the second death.

This letter to the congregation at Smyrna was the shortest. Smyrna was a great trade city that specialized in rich trade wines. It stood on a deep gulf about 35 miles north of Ephesus. The Lydians destroyed Smyrna in 627 B.C. Alexander the Great's general, Lysimachus, rebuilt this city. Smyrna had political power, and its people were offering donations for public displays. Smyrna was an important city and had chosen the right side in all civil wars.

There were several Roman Civil wars, especially during the Late Republic. Not the least of which were those between Julius Caesar versus Pompey (48 B.C.) and Octavia versus Marc Anthony (32 B.C.). In an intense debate with Octavia during the Olympic Games, Mark Anthony eloquently and vigorously defended the "Liberators of Rome" against the "Dictators of Rome." He forbade Caesar's ivory statue, golden chair, and wreath to be carried in the part of the parade known as The Procession of The Gods. But though Anthony's rhetoric and persuasion was unanswerable, he was actually defeated by a strange act of nature. During the first day of the Parade, a meteoric star appeared and then vanished when the parade was over. It was rumored that this was Caesar's Star, thus indicating Caesar's Godhead. The conclusion, "Caesar is the Son of God," was based on the assumed premise "God has a Son." This was approximately 40 years (Before Christ) who is indeed The Son of God. Thus, fiction is sometimes the forerunner of FACT.[60]

Smyrna was outstandingly beautiful. It claimed to be the *glory of Asia*. The city had erected several temples to idols, like those to Cybele and Baachus (god of wine) (See www.biblestudyweb.org: The Church at Smyrna, A Study of Revelation 2:8-11.). This was a city of culture and arts. Smyrna had an exquisitely beautiful public stadium which was the largest in the world, a public library, Odeon House of Music, and was the birthplace of the poet and author Homer. Temples lavished the hills with numerous gods. The people of Smyrna also claimed to be the first in Caesar worship.

Smyrna looked with contempt upon the poor and humble Christians and despised them as being insignificant. Polycarp was burned at the stake here in 155 A.D. Nowhere was life more dangerous for a Christian. To become a Christian in this city would be almost instant death. Smyrna had characteristics that placed the lives of Christians in constant and continued peril.

1. Smyrna was one of the great centers of Caesar worship.

2. When Caesar Julius Tiberius ruled, Caesar worship became compulsory. "We have no king but Caesar."

3. Annually, Roman citizens were required to burn a pinch of incense on the altar to the Godhead of Caesar.

4. A certificate was provided to those who worshipped Caesar.

5. Smyrna was populated with self-proclaimed Jews who hated Christians!

Jesus claims to be "the First." He is the self-existent being who is the origin of all things (Jn 1:1, 8:58; Col 1:15-17), and He should be first with man (Mt 6:33). He also claims to be "the Last." The universe is upheld because of the power of His Word (Heb 1:3). These statements regarding the attributes of Jesus (the true Godhead) are set in the context of the ridiculous homage paid to emperors and political leaders like Caesar.

Jesus is that "Which was dead and is alive." He has been through what they were experiencing (Heb 4:15). His death, burial, and resurrection are fundamental facts of the Gospel (1Co 15:1-4; Ro 1:4) for He died for the sins of the world (Ro 5:8). This gives Him the ability to sympathize with the world and encourage those of the world to overcome their sin.

Once again, Jesus said, "I know" (Rev 2:9). The reader can be assured that Christ possesses a complete and perfect knowledge of everyone's life. He knows their needs and character. We have no chance of deceiving Him about our personal lives *or* the accomplishments of any of our congregations. He knew the works of Smyrna. God says that all will be judged according to the actions completed here on Earth (Rev 22:12).

Jesus knew of their tribulation, and "Them which say they are Jews, and are not, but are the synagogue of Satan" (Rev 2:9). They call themselves Jews, but they are not. People want to call themselves Jews, but in reality, they are nothing but a synagogue of Satan (Ro 9:4). In Romans 9, Paul is dealing with the people who were teaching Judaism supremacy. The Jews were saying, "Why isn't God making us rulers of the world and over the Gentiles?" They were saying the Word of God had failed. They wanted to be the great nation, but it was not so. Paul said in Romans 9:6 that the Word of God has not failed because those who call themselves Israel are *not* Israel and *neither* are they all God's children. The word Jew means praise of Yahweh God, while the word Israel means prince of Elohim. Neither Jew nor Israel was originally intended to be national titles; they originated from the naming of two individuals, Jacob and then later Judah. That is how Paul used the word Jew to describe every Christian. A Christian is a true Jew because he is circumcised in the heart, and he praises the Lord Jesus, *Yeshua*. The word Yehudah means *praised* or *praises the Lord*. Any Christian man or woman in the world who praises God through the Holy Spirit is a Jew in God's eyes. In the Greek text, Paul uses the Hebrew word for Jew, *ioudias*. However, he also uses the Greek word "*epainos*" to describe spirit-filled Christians who praise God, not man (Ro 2:28, 29).

This word "tribulation" (2:9) means to press, to be pressured, or afflicted. Is this a reference to *the great tribulation?* Such fragmentized theology is never taught in the Bible. *All Christians will experience tribulation if they live how God would have them live* (Php 3:10). Paul says Christians should glory in tribulations (Ro 5:3), and the Word tells Christians what tribulation does (Ro 5:3, 4; Jas 1:3, 4; 1Pe 1:6, 7, 4:16).

These Christians are in "Poverty." Physical poverty was not a new concept for Christians. The Macedonian congregations were poor (2Co 8:1-5). One probable reason for their poverty is, "Having their property taken" (Heb 10:34). Political intrigue and Jewish connivers were robbing these Christians. Yet, Jesus says, "But Thou art Rich." They were rich in spiritual things.

Furthermore, these imposter Jews were guilty of blasphemy. Those who "called themselves Jews" had the ear of those in high places. (Please note, this is not modern-day "anti-Semitism" since there is no longer a pure Semitic descendant of Noah's Son Shem on Earth.) If we are prejudiced or reveal loathing toward any nationality, we are greatly violating God's will "Who made of one blood (from

Adam) all nations of men to dwell on Earth" (Ac 17:6). Children of God will never tolerate genocide, and those who call themselves "Jews" have the divine right of our God to live as a people and as a Nation anywhere, at any time on Earth. In the best interest of Biblical scholarship, we insist that after Christ's death and atonement for all nations and generations of people, God does not have ONE particular nation He calls a "Favorite, Chosen Nation," unless it is Christ's "Select people of all nations" (Hag 2:7; Rev 7:9).

"Abraham's children according to the flesh" (Mt 3:9; Jn 8:58; Ro 9:7) were no longer God's people (Rev 2:9; Ro 2:28, 29). They claimed to be God's people, but they were the Devil's people (Rev 2:9). Many today can do the same thing (2Co 11:13-15). Although many friends call themselves Jews today, they readily admit they are of Gentile origin. In admitting freely that there are no Jews today, many Pre-Millennialists beg the question when they say that Christ's coming will establish Jewish supremacy and create a Jewish nation. This is neither a realistic nor a biblical belief.

John wrote, "Do not fear what you are about to suffer." Their sufferings were going to get worse! The 10 days of suffering is symbolic of a complete tribulation and oppression. It is not a literal 10 days for in numerology the number 10 signifies "completion." This tribulation always exists and is encountered by all Christians at all times. The Preterist doctrine declares the 10 days as a full-term for being a Christian, yet a short time compared to eternity. Then again, Historicism teaches the 10 days are 10 Roman emperors from Nero to Diocletian. However, it seems more fitting to associate this representation with the tribulation all Christians experience during his or her lifetime, "…so that we ourselves boast of you among the churches of God for your patience and faith in your persecutions and tribulations that you endure, … (2Th 1:4). Christians are called to overcome tribulations in this life in order to receive the **crown** of life in the next (Rev 2:10, 3:11).

SPECIAL TEACHING ON THE CROWNS OF THE NEW TESTAMENT

1) The incorruptible crown of immortality (1Co 9:25).

2) The crown of joy and exaltation (1Th 2:19).

3) The crown of glory that does not fade (1Pe 1:4, 5:4).

4) The crown of righteousness (2Ti 4:8).

5) The crown of life (Jas 1:12; Rev 2:10).)

6) The crown of victory (Rev 2:10) or evangelistic service (Rev 6:2).

7) The crown of affection for a Christian Brother or Sister (Php 4:1).

It is notable that Peter refers to the amaranthos crown (1 Pe 1:4, 5:4), which means it is incorruptible or unfading. This is another promise of immortality for those who overcome. Paul uses another word for incorruptible, "apthartos" (1Co 9:25), which denotes a life that is not affected by entropy, as expressed in the 2nd Law of Thermodynamics.

The ancient Greeks used the long-lasting Amaranth flower to symbolize immortality. The Hawaiian Amaranthaceae flower is noted for retaining freshness. The Apostles used this symbol of the crown of life "eternal inheritance" that will not eventually wither away like earthly flowers. But the most immortal symbol of life on Earth must eventually die. It is refreshing to see a newly cut flower in a vase, but this also teaches us that life will come to an end just as the blossoms wither and die. Tulips are probably the greatest symbol of mortality. The flower comes to life quickly but dies just as fast.

At this juncture, let us ask two different questions. The first question, "What shall be done with all seven of the crowns mentioned above?" The answer – we shall cast them all before the Throne of Christ, for to Him alone, "Belongs all honor and glory" (Rev 4:10). The second question, "What is the greatest theft in the history of the world?" We may answer, "The lives, possessions, and legacies of millions that were taken during World War II, The Great Gardner Heist, Art Theft, or the Great Train Robberies of 1903 and 1963," but such answers, as accurate and poignant as they may appear, fall infinitely short of the Greatest Heist in History. What is it? It is the ominous and momentous warning, "Let no one take your crown!" (Rev 4:10)

They were promised a crown of life, and they "Shall not be hurt by the Second Death" (Rev 2:11, 20:14, 15). The Second Death is when one is cast into the Lake of Fire. Hebrews 9:27 states that after death comes judgment! However, for the Christian, judgment takes place day-to-day, week-to- week (1Co 11:31).

Modern-day cults teach the doctrine of annihilationism. This means when a person dies they are annihilated and do not suffer eternally. If this second death hurts, how can something hurt someone if they are annihilated? The Jehovah's Witnesses use Ecclesiastes 9:4-12 to prove that the dead know nothing at all, and therefore, annihilationism is a Biblical fact. However, when we examine the entire Book of Ecclesiastes, we find this is not the case. Ecclesiastes 1:3 is the first of 29 times Solomon is writing about things that are happening under the sun. This Ecclesiastes passage is not talking about a dead person ceasing to exist in the next world but the fact that they have no knowledge relevant to current everyday life existence.

These Christians at Smyrna were being accused of dividing families and partaking of sex orgies (love feasts). Philosophers who actively oppose Christ said Christians were cannibals because they partook of Jesus' flesh and blood. The Christians refused to worship Caesar because they would be forced to call Him, Augustus, a title that means "reverend." They were being slandered at every opportunity. Nevertheless, Christ charges them to remain faithful, to overcome, and to love Him.

The Congregation at Pergamum (2:12-17)

Revelation 2:12-17: "To the angel of the church in Pergamum write: These are the words of him who has the sharp, double-edged sword. I know where you live—where Satan has his throne. Yet you remain true to my name. You did not renounce your faith in me, even in the days of Antipas, my faithful witness, who was put to death in your city—where Satan lives. Nevertheless, I have a few things against you: You have people there who hold to the teaching of Balaam, who taught Balak to entice the Israelites to sin by eating food sacrificed to idols and by committing sexual immorality. Likewise, you also have those who hold to the teaching of the Nicolaitans. Repent therefore! Otherwise, I will soon come to you and will fight against them with the sword of my mouth. He who has an ear, let him hear what the Spirit says to the churches. To him who overcomes, I will give some of the hidden manna. I will also give him a white stone with a new name written on it, known only to him who receives it.

The previous two congregations were in seacoast cities whereas Pergamum is inland. It was a capital city and previously the capital of the Attalid Kingdom. Rome had made it the capital city of its Asia province until 130 A.D. When John wrote this letter, it had been a capital for nearly 100 years. Pergamum is the farthest north of the seven congregations, is the oldest city of the Asia province, and has always glorified itself as being the last outpost of Greek civilization. It was also the center of Caesar worship. This luxurious city had the second largest library in the world with 200,000 volumes, the largest after the library in Alexandria, Egypt. It built the Temple of Aesculapius, a healing god, who was worshipped in the form of a serpent. Tame snakes were kept in the temple. Those who were suffering were allowed to spend the night in the darkness of the temple. If a snake touched the sick, this was held to be the touch of the god himself.

Once again, Jesus said, "I know thy works" and "where thou dwellest, even where Satan's (the Devil's) seat is." The Lord knows the surroundings and the wickedness that Christians are confronted with daily. They were in Pergamum; they had to go on living there; they could not escape; and life had set them where Satan's seat was. Pergamum was where they must live, and Pergamum was where they must show they were Christians.

Where Satan's seat is, "Satan's throne is." This is more than just a physical throne but an idea that was perfectly understood by citizens in Pergamum. Satan was the genius behind this throne. While he is a ruler in the darkness of this world, he also puts it in the hearts and egos of men and women seeking Satan's glory. So he put it in the hearts of his priests and worshipers to transfer a seat of special authority from ancient Babylon to Pergamum. Since the priests and much of the anti-Christian population were enamored with the pomp and exquisitely beautiful ceremonies of the ancient Babylonian religion, they welcomed the introduction and resurrection of this old religion in their town. Thus, Pergamum was a place where the anti-Christ forces of Satan were the most authoritative and most powerful. (For a modern-day example, consider America adopting Islam and killing off those Christians who would not submit to Islam.) The followers of this adopted religion murdered Antipas because he would not bow down to Caesar.

The ancient Babylonian chief priest had carried the title of "Pontifex Maximus" and that title had been transferred to Pergamum. Then, because Pergamum honored Rome, Pergamum's political-religious authority decided to transfer this authority on to Rome. Pergamum was a transition city between Babylon and Rome. This is why Rome is labeled the Babylonian whore. These historical facts give an acute insight into the doctrinal warfare that Christ expected these Christians to fight in order to survive a holocaust of anti-Christ beliefs. Yet, we are told that in modern-day Christianity, forget doctrine, "just preach love." Thus, Christian doctrine is compromised by those who masquerade as Christians and use Christ's authority. These usurpers do this under the banner of love and place sentimentalism over the supremacy of doctrine, even to the point of degrading doctrine. If we recall, the Christian Congregation at Smyrna would scorn this view (Rev 2:9, 10). It is to be noted that "Satan's seat" remains in the New Babylon. (See Addendum A, "Steps of Departure.")

Jesus said, "Thou holdest fast my name." They had not denied their confession of Christ (Mt 10:32, 33). The word "Christ" means messiah or anointed king. The name "Christian" was divinely given "chrematizo" and originated at Antioch. God gave Christ's followers the new name "Christian" in prophecy (Isa 56:5, 62:2). After this, "Christian" was proudly worn by both Jew and Gentile (Ac 11:26; 1Pe 4:16). Prior to the title of "Christian," Christ's followers were called "disciples" (Ac 6:1, 2, 19, 9:38). They were still called "disciples" afterwards, and we still use the word "disciples" to this day. Christ told the Smyrna Christians, previously, to "hold Fast" (Rev 2:10 with 1Co 15:58) because of great persecution. Christians must endure to the end to be saved! They had to cling to the name of Jesus.

Unfortunately, in today's world, the name "Christian" no longer holds the meaning of a person necessarily truly dedicated to Christ, Jesus. Anyone who attends church, however infrequently, can be labeled a Christian. Being called a "disciple," however, conveys a much stronger meaning. Nonbelievers would call a "disciple" a Jesus freak. How unfortunate all this has become. Notwithstanding our modern failure to fully appreciate the name "Christian," this name is still very dear to the Heart of God who gave it.

THE GREATEST SHIP WRECK IN HISTORY

"THE SHIP WRECK OF FAITH" (1Ti 1:19; 2Ti 2:18)

THE DARK AGES

The apostasy from New Covenant Apostolic authority was a "ship wreck of faith" that plunged the world into spiritual and moral darkness. It was not just the prevention of scientific enlightenment that marked the Dark Ages; the darkest aspect of The Age was Biblical and spiritual illiteracy. The average student of this overall Age of history is more knowledgeable of the scientific ignorance that shrouded

The European world, but the DARKNESS of New Testament apostasy was even worse. We tend to forget the fact that when Biblical Scholarship is discouraged, it leads to a spiritual vacuum in every other discipline of life. When scholars are found wanting in spiritual values, they cannot make good judgments in other areas of life.

Babylon feared Biblical scholarship because, as we heard, Dr. Henry Morris referenced that Hermeneutics is the queen of all scientific enquiry. We also read William Grassie's work on *Hermeneutics in Science and Religion* and learned that the greatest boon to scientific advancement is a reverence for God and His Word.[61]

Because the Roman Church discouraged the want of penetrating insight into Scripture, it also robbed the world of scientific enlightenment and advancement. When Galileo, Copernicus, Lorenzo Valla, and other "Humanist" were defrocked and discredited by Religious Babylon, it was not because they were good scientists, but because they threatened the "Babel Ignorance" of Babylon with hard, fast scientific truths that if unchecked would lead to hard, fast truths in Theology as well.

Although various scholars debate about when this Dark Age period began, it appears reasonable to mark the date of March 533 A.D. with the Codex of Emperor Justinian stating (among many other things) that The Bishop of Rome would head both the Eastern and Western branches of the "church" (www.moellerhaus.com). As previously mentioned, 1,260 years later, in 1793, New Testament readers began calling themselves, simply "Christian." This is the traditional view the early proponents of the Restoration Movement espoused. The renaissance of Biblical enlightenment took longer than the renaissance of scientific enlightenment, and just as scientific advancement continues, so should theological advancement continue.

While 1793 did not mark the end of religious ignorance, that year was instrumental in leading to a more perfect renaissance, "enlightenment," of the religious world because it answered much religious confusion. Not everyone could agree with the Menno Simons-Ammann, Luther, Calvin, Zwingli, or Wesley connections so they decided they would leave the denominational titles and creeds behind, return to the Scriptures, and call themselves simply "Christians."

Various theories exist as to when the Dark Ages of scientific investigation started and came to a close. We agree with Theodore Mommsen who believes it was a period of intellectual darkness from the 6th to the 14th Centuries. Merriam Webster's Dictionary also offers this explanation.62 But we see a close correlation between scientific and social liberation and Biblical Reformation. For instance, although they have profited greatly by the European Scientific Renaissance, Asia and The Middle East have never had a protestant-like or acceptable Biblical reformation to this day.

Concerning the Scientific Revolution, Francis Bacon is credited with beginning the scientific revolution in 1620 with his *Novum Organum,* (www.wikipedia: Novum Organum), and this revolution reached its peak under the God-given breakthroughs made by Sir Isaac Newton in the 17th Century. Bacon was thoroughly indoctrinated with the various views of Christianity in his day, and Newton was also an ardent student of The Bible, especially "Historical Prophecy," as we are addressing in this Commentary. We might say that it took the Religious Reformers to break the Roman shackles that bound them in order for the scientific thinkers of the Renaissance to break the shackles of the Dark Age aversion to science held by Rome's church tyrants.

Satan's Seat

Caesar worship was even more powerful in Pergamum then say a personality cult worship of a president of the U.S.A., an entertainer, or religious cult leader is today. Pergamum became so bad that anyone who refused this political-culturally accepted obeisance would be black balled, censored, imprisoned or murdered.

Christianity and its Connection with Liberation from the Dark Ages

Pergamum needed to understand that Jesus' name is divine (Mt 1:21, 28:19; Jn 14:13). For approximately 1,700 years during the Dark Ages, the name Christian was not used. It reappeared in 1793 with Rice Haggard and James O'Kelly.63 The unfortunate denial of Christ's name throughout the Dark Ages was the denial of the divine name Jesus and the divinely appointed name Christian (Ac 11:26). As Antiochus Epiphanes raged against Old Testament Covenant (Da 11:28-32 where "covenant" is referred to five times.), the 21st Century is marked with a savage persecution of Christians worldwide, and among some of the elite oligarchs in politics, education, industry, and entertainment, there is an odious hatred of the Covenant Name, "Christian."

Christ edified the Pergamum congregation by saying, "You have not denied my faith." The faith in Christ is precious and worth keeping! There is only one faith (Ep 4:5), and Christians should contend for it (Jude 3). These Christians were murdered and slaughtered for their faith in Christ, and in the days when Christians were killed, they still held fast to Jesus (Rev 2:13). Antipas was an example of faithfulness unto death.

On the other hand, these Christians were acting like Balaam for "He taught Balak to cast a stumbling block before the children of Israel" (Rev 2: 14). It is treacherous to sin and involve others with our sin. Balaam means "not of the people or a foreigner." Balaam's father was from Beor or Edom (Nu 31:8). In Numbers 25, we discover why Balaam was killed. Balak, King of Moab, paid Balaam to curse the Israelites, but God told Balaam not to curse them. This upset Balak so he asked Balaam what he could do to destroy the Israelites. Balaam told Barak to cause the Israelite leaders to sin. He got the leaders to sin by arranging for the Israelite men to have an orgy with the Moabite women (Nu 31:8, 16). Just as money was paid to Balaam to teach Israel that they could sin and get by because they were God's chosen people, Christians today are also commercialized into sinning! Something worse than falling into the sin trap ourselves is to teach others to sin (Jas 3:1) and to become a stumbling block to others' relationships with God (2Co 6:1-4; Heb 10:29).

Balaam taught two things,

1. To eat things sacrificed to idols (1Co 8:8-13)

2. To commit fornication (1Co 5:11, 6:9-19; Gal 5:19; Eph 5:5; Col 3:5, 6; 1Th 4:5-7).

These teachings were blasphemous and treacherous to the Assembly of the Saints. The easiest way to cause Christian people to stumble is to lay sexual immorality, alcohol, and drugs at their feet. Today, Satan knows that he cannot stop the Word of God from being preached. The authority of the Word of God binds him. However, in these last days, his chief means of bringing Christian men and women down is through sexual promiscuity, sexual immorality, and sexual infidelity. What is astounding being how Christians still think that they are Christians, saved by grace, and can continue in willful, self-justifying sin (Ro 6:1, 2; Jude 4).

When Satan causes Christians to turn away from God, he replaces their priestly position in Christ by offering them the pleasures of the world. Christ said *repent* (1Co 5:1-8), and those who *overcome* get the following:

1. The tree of life (Rev 2:7)
2. The crown of life and saved from the second death (2:10, 11)
3. A white stone (2:17)
4. Authority (2:26)
5. White garments (3:5)
6. To be a pillar in the Temple of God (3:12)
7. Seated on the Throne (3:21)

Some teachers explain the last command of Christ to his disciples is the Great Commission. However, here, it is "Repent!" The last command to us is "Repent!"

They would receive the hidden manna, which is Jesus Christ! (Jn 6:51). Their reward would involve a new name that is spoken of seven times in the Book of Revelation.

1. 2:17
2. 3:12
3. 12:13
4. 14:1
5. 14:19
6. 21:27
7. 22:4

The Congregation of Thyatira (2:18-29)

Revelation 2:18-29: "To the angel of the church in Thyatira write: These are the words of the Son of God, whose eyes are like blazing fire and whose feet are like burnished bronze. I know your deeds, your love and faith, your service and perseverance, and that you are now doing more than you did at first. Nevertheless, I have this against you: You tolerate that woman Jezebel, who calls herself a prophetess. By her teaching she misleads my servants into sexual immorality and the eating of food sacrificed to idols. I have given her time to repent of her immorality, but she is unwilling. So I will cast her on a bed of suffering, and I will make those who commit adultery with her suffer intensely, unless they repent of her ways. I will strike her children dead. Then all the churches will know that I am he who searches hearts and minds, and I will repay each of you according to your deeds. Now I say to the rest of you in Thyatira, to you who do not hold to her teaching and have not learned Satan's so-called deep secrets (I will not impose any other burden on you): Only hold on to what you have until I come. To him who overcomes and does my will to the end, I will give authority over the nations – 'He will rule them with an iron scepter; he will dash them to pieces like pottery' – just as I have received authority from my Father. I will also give him the morning star. He who has an ear, let him hear what the Spirit says to the churches.

It is odd that the longest of the letters to the seven congregations was written to the assembly in the smallest and least important of the seven towns. The name Thyatira emerged in history in 290 B.C. as the name of a military center. Thyatira's supreme importance was its being the gateway to Pergamum, the Capital City of Asia (as discussed earlier). It was the first established Macedonian city; it was prosperous and industrious. Trade-guilds (unions) were a way of life, and every guild had its own patron god. One Thyatiran industry consisted of making very expensive dye. The roads that passed through its valley brought much of the trade of the known world to its door. The danger that threatened the Congregation at Thyatira resulted from the existence of the powerful trade guilds. No merchant or trader could hope to prosper and to make money unless he was a member of his trade guild. A working man who refused to join his trade guild would be in much the same position as he would be today, if he refused to join his trade union.

Why should Christians refuse to join one of these trade guilds? Surely, being a patron of a trade organization was not a sin in itself. However, the social activities of these trade guilds were intimately bound up with the worship of the heathen gods. They had common meals together that would begin and end with a cup of wine poured out as a libation and an offering to the gods. Such a meal would almost certainly follow a sacrifice. At these social activities, drunkenness and fornication were the accepted practices. A very real dilemma faced the Thyatiran Christians; they either decided to make money in the context of immorality or to serve Jesus Christ. In addition, it seemed this woman, Jezebel, was teaching Christians it was all right to be a member of these trade guilds. Once again, it was also the center of special religious importance, including Caesar Worship.

The fact that Jesus' eyes were like blazing fire means "justice." He can look at certain things with intolerable justice. With Christ, justice always overrides friendship and affection. Jesus' feet were like burnished brass bringing judgment. Justice always overrides friendship!

Jesus is "The Son of God." As this Son, He possesses certain essential divine components. Jesus is:

1. The gift of God (Jn 3:16)

2. God's spokesman (Heb 1:1, 2)

3. The way to the Father (Jn 14:6)

4. Man's Savior (Mt 1:21)

His "Eyes like flames of fire" means he sees with complete, comprehensible, penetration, and wisdom (Heb 4:13). His feet are like thoroughly refined brass for He is strong, durable, and able to tread under foot all evil His eyes discover.

The Ecclesia was commended on certain accomplishments. Therefore, Jesus says, "I know thy works." They possessed charity or love. Love is the fountain from which flows true activities (Gal 5:6; 1Co 13). Service is a great work of benevolence. Service is a faith of fidelity and faithfulness. A Christian's patience perseveres under all circumstances (1Co 15:58; Heb 10:36). Many Christians had a growth in works because they desired "The last more than the first" (1Pe 2:2; 2Co 4:16).

Thyatira was just the opposite of Ephesus. In Ephesus, there was zeal for doctrine and hard work, but not much love. In Thyatira, there is activity of faith and love, but insufficient zeal for doctrine and discipline. A sinner is tolerated with the character like Jezebel of the Old Testament, the wife of Ahab. They should have withdrawn from her (1Co 5:1-13; 2Th 3:6). Jezebel called herself a prophetess, but she was a false teacher. She taught it was right to:

1. Commit fornication

2. To eat things sacrificed to Idols

This doctrine was the "depths of Satan" (Rev 2:24). His doctrine is very simple, "Since you are saved by grace, you can do whatever you please. If you like it, do it, and grace will cause God to keep forgiving you." However, even though divine grace was extended (2:21), they had little time to repent.

Tribulation comes for discipline and judgment because it is meant to bring those who fall away back to Christ. Jesus posed this threat (Rev 2:22, 23) that tribulation can come at any time for the believer and the unbeliever. However, they would get whatever their heart desired. Satan is a master of leading Christians to misconstrue God's toleration of sin with His acceptance and condoning of sin. If we tolerate sin, then Christ takes matters into His own hands.

Jesus says, "I will cast her into a bed," which means afflict or punish. He will also punish those who follow her false teaching (Mt 15:14). He also says, "I will kill her children with death." Her followers will be destroyed! Once again, Christ reiterates the holding of all those accountable for their actions by saying, "I will give unto every one of you according to your works" (2Co 5:10). If God's grace and longsuffering do not work, His last step before giving people up, is a massive dose of tribulation.

Jesus shows an end in sight! God knows Satan's secrets, and He promises to give a reward to those who do not fall for them. He gives "The rest," or to those who had not gone along with Jezebel's teaching, He promises, "I will put upon you no other burden." These Christians had the wisdom to label the occultist poison as Jezebel's esoteric doctrine. The doctrines of Jezebel are still taught today. They replace the Spirit of Christ with self-will (Col 2:18-23). Jezebel teaches a doctrine that she claims has depth to it. So these feeble-minded Christians thought that she offered something *deeper* than what the true Christian faith had to offer. This is why Jesus said sarcastically, "You do not know the depths." There is no depth to any doctrine outside of Jesus Christ, King in His Kingdom. He ends with this, "Hold fast until I come" with a two-fold promise in verses 26-28.

1. "I'll give you the morning star." It is a humbling truth that the King of Kings would give this great recognition to his servants. The morning star rules this known universe.

2. "I'll give you authority." Christ is giving Christians authority over towns, cities, and nations. This is a great missionary message!

Revelation Chapter Three

The Congregation at Sardis (3:1-6)

Revelation 3:1-6: "To the angel of the church in Sardis write: These are the words of him who holds the seven spirits of God and the seven stars. I know your deeds; you have a reputation of being alive, but you are dead. Wake up! Strengthen what remains and is about to die, for I have not found your deeds complete in the sight of my God. Remember, therefore, what you have received and heard; obey it, and repent. But if you do not wake up, I will come like a thief, and you will not know at what time I will come to you. Yet you have a few people in Sardis who have not soiled their clothes. They will walk with me, dressed in white, for they are worthy. He who overcomes will, like them, be dressed in white. I will never blot out his name from the book of life, but will acknowledge his name before my Father and his angels. He who has an ear, let him hear what the Spirit says to the churches.

Sardis, in the locale of Lydia, was located 30 miles southeast of Thyatira and is one of the oldest cities in the Roman province of Asia, which is part of modern-day Turkey. Sardis was a wealthy trading center on the routes between the Aegean Sea and the interior of Asia Minor. King Croesus, the first king known to make gold coins, founded Sardis in 700 B.C. He was obsessed with his wealth and fame. Sardis was where the minting of money originated. It was built on top of a mountain with its position regarded as being well-nigh impregnable. Its position seemed to defy assault.

Cyrus, the King of Persia, captured Sardis in 546 B.C. He promised to give a special reward for any man who could discover a method to scale this unscalable cliff. One Persian soldier saw a Lydian soldier on the battlement accidentally drop his helmet over the battlement, down the cliff. He watched the Lydian soldier pick his way down the cliffs, get his helmet, and climb back. He marked the path in his memory. That night he led a picked band of troops up the cliffs and took

Sardis. The same thing happened about 200 years later when Alexander the Great conquered Sardis in 218 B.C. Ultimately, an earthquake destroyed Sardis in 17 A.D. How ironic that the city was destroyed the second time because the leaders forgot history. After being rebuild, Sardis was destroyed a third time because they forgot God.

Sardis was a great commercial center and extremely wealthy with its international gold standard. It was a great center of the wool industry. Despite their wealth, the people of Sardis were notoriously, spiritually foolhardy. They had grown flabby and had plunged into immoral despair. The fate of the congregation at Sardis was the same. They were at peace, but it was the peace of the dead. These Christians were arrogant, proud, and dead, but did not even know it. Christians should work out their salvation with just as much faithfulness at the point of their death as they do during their productive lives. They must beware of those who encourage laziness by saying, "People are not saved by works." Christians must understand Christ's intent when He mentions works. The key word of this letter is *"watch"* (Rev 3:2, 3). This encourages work and faithfulness. These people should have known from history that disaster comes many times, especially when we feel most secure and at ease.

Herodotus, the ancient Greek historian called "the father of history" (www.wikipedia.ed: Herodotus), reported things concerning Solon, who was a wise Greek philosopher who addressed the lackadaisical attitude of the citizens of Sardis. He said they were procrastinators and stupid. Solon said, "Call no man happy until he is dead."[64] Christians in the Body of Christ should call no man a Christian until he is dead, because no one ever knows what will happen to them during their life. If they happen to fall away, the faithful ones should not condemn them but restore them with love and exhortation (1Co 11:30; Gal 6:1; Heb 10:25, 26). Death could come at any moment. No one wants to bury a fallen-away Christian. If Christians realize there is redeeming love in "chosen death," the result is true abundant life now and forever. By "chosen death," Christians are choosing what Paul said, "Reckon yourself to be dead and alive to Christ" (Ro 6:11).

Jesus is described as He that, "Hath the seven Spirits of God." He possessed the Spirit without measure (Jn 3:34) and in complete fashion. The seven spirits do not represent *seven different spirits* of God, but the completeness and unity of God's Holy Spirit. He also, "Hath the Seven stars." These stars are the messengers of the congregation (Rev 1:20) for they are under His authority!

This Congregation at Sardis had a reputation. Jesus said, "Thou has a name that thou livest." Let us understand, then, that what men think of a congregation is not necessarily what the Lord thinks of it. Their status was possibly composed of a large membership with material wealth, prominent people, and who were sound in doctrine. However, Sardis was a dead Church in the Lord's sight (Rev 3:1). This is a deathblow to congregations who have the wrong methodology and philosophy to *grow a congregation*. Why are the assemblies growing or not growing today? Is it because of the music, the building, or the Word of God? A congregation is dead when it worships its own past, when it lives on its memories instead of finding its challenges in its hopes for the future. A church is dead when it is more concerned with material than with spiritual things, or when love for one another is gone. Their works before God were *not* perfect! (Rev 3:2) (Strong 4137 – "perfect" means to fill up or finish things). They did not finish or complete the tasks that Christ commanded His body to do.

Jesus also gives admonition to Sardis (Rev 3:2, 3). Christian works are always commended. The works that are condemned are works of self-righteousness and works of the law. However, faith and works should complement each other. Christians should never rely on past works (3:3).

God strikes suddenly. Christians should live as though Jesus is coming today. It would be terrible to meet the face of Jesus and not be prepared. Jesus says there is something in them left that needs to be awakened! For some Christians, there is just enough life in them even though they are almost dead. These people were physically strong, but they were spiritually dead. If Christians will turn to Jesus and live the way He commands, they will be filled in every way. He is the perfect God!

There are seven aspects of Jesus that makes Him complete:

1. He has wisdom. Wisdom is applied understanding (Rev 3:1).

2. He has understanding (3:1).

3. He counsels (3:2).

4. He has strength (3:3).

5. He has knowledge (3:4).

6. He has fear of the Lord (3:5).

7. He has decisiveness. He does not judge after the sight of his eyes or the hearing of his ears (3:5, 6). For further reading see Rev 19:11; Jn 17:4, 8:16; Ps 75:2, 96:10, and 98:9; and Isa 11:3, 4.

Jesus commands them to "Be watchful." The two points that man must be most watchful of are his weakest point and his strongest point. This means that they must always be ready! He also says, "Strengthen the things which remain that are ready to die." Some were very weak and sickly, ready to die (1Co 11:30). They needed to stir up their gifts and fan their spark into a fiery flame (2Ti 1:6). Strong members have a responsibility to the weak members (Gal 6:1). "Remember, therefore, how thou hast received and heard." In other words, "Remember your past state and get back to it." He says, "Hold fast," which is a condition of success in every field of endeavor.

Sardis was a congregation with a remnant (Rev 3:4). Their garment is the righteousness of Christ. Few are found in white garments for most have defiled and dirtied their garments. As a whole, Sardis had defiled their garments. It could be that we are the only ones remaining pure (doctrinally) in family and relationships. Understand that if Christians stay pure, they will be rewarded on Judgment Day and have no need to fear. There are always a few people, a remnant, who still believe in New Covenant Christianity. A congregation needs faith, hope, love, and sincerity to remain true to Christ. However, even more importantly, it needs to hold to the one true faith of Jesus Christ (Eph 4:5, 6; 2Ti 3:14-17). Jesus commands Christians to walk in white garments *all* the time and *not* the soiled garments of sin. This congregation was worshipping the past and concerning themselves about material things. As the true Bride of Christ, the brotherhood needs to finish what God has ordained for them to do and to persevere with one another in love and good works (Ro 2:7).

Jesus continues to say, "There are a few names even in Sardis which have not defiled their garments." These people are not identified because only God knows who they are. Unfortunately, "few" is true in too many places. The faithful *few* are the ones keeping the assembly going. They are the *few* who have been able to keep themselves unspotted (Jas 1:2). However, those few shall "Walk with me in white" (Rev 3:4, 5). God knows everyone's name and the minutest details of their service. He does not need gifts but desires the right attitude of the gift-giver. God will never blot a name from the Book of Life if faithfulness is shown.

The Bible refers to several different books throughout Scripture.

- A. The Old Testament refers to the Book of Natural Life (Ps 69:28; Ex 32:32; Ps 139:16).

- B. Malachi 3:16 is the Book of Remembrance. This is a book of life with all deeds, righteous and unrighteous, recorded.

- C. The New Testament it is the Lamb's Book of Life, thus speaking of eternal life and the roster of believers (Php 4:3; Rev 3:5; 22:19; 13:8; 21:27). In Acts 2:47 and 13:48, the word "added and ordained," means to be inscribed on a ledger. This is the same application concerning the Lamb's Book of Life.

Jesus says, "I will not blot out his name of the book of life" (Rev 3:5) for this would be condemnation to eternal hell (Rev 20:15). The heart cutting truth about this congregation is that the majority was on their way to hell. On the other hand, the Spirit-praising fact is Jesus said, "I will confess his name before My Father, and before his angels" (3:5). Jesus will do this for those who remain faithful unto Him.

Jesus leaves them with this threat "I will come like a thief in the night." Is it not interesting that the only thing these Christians in Sardis had to do was look at their history? This city experienced a sudden invasion by Cyrus and Alexander, a sudden invasion by an earthquake, and now the next event is a sudden coming of Jesus. How many times must a fool be warned before his attention is gained? Christians are to always be watchful and ready for the Lord and Savior to come unto us. This teaching can transform our life into a state of readiness and obedience.

The Congregation at Philadelphia (3:7-13)

Revelation 3:7-13: "To the angel of the church in Philadelphia write: These are the words of him who is holy and true, who holds the key of David. What he opens no one can shut, and what he shuts no one can open. I know your deeds. See, I have placed before you an open door that no one can shut. I know that you have little strength, yet you have kept my word and have not denied my name. I will make those who are of the synagogue of Satan, who claim to be Jews though they are not, but are liars—I will make them come and fall down at your feet and *acknowledge that I have loved you. Since you have kept my command to endure patiently, I will also keep you from the hour of trial that is going to come upon the whole world to test those who live on the earth. I am coming soon. Hold on to what you have, so that no one will take your crown. Him who overcomes I will make a pillar in the temple of my God. Never again will he leave it. I will write on him the name of my God and the name of the city of my God, the new Jerusalem, which is coming down out of heaven from my God; and I will also write on him my new name. He who has an ear, let him hear what the Spirit says to the churches.*

Philadelphia was 28 miles southeast of Sardis. Compared to other cities, it was not an ancient city. Eumenes II, King of Pergamum, founded Philadelphia in 189 B.C. Attalus' endearing relationship to his brother Eumenes earned them the title *brotherly love*. He was called Philadelphos, and the city was named, "Philadelphia," after him. It stood at the place where the borders of three countries, Mysia, Lydia, and Phrygia, met. Philadelphia's location made it the gateway to the east. It commanded one of the greatest highways in the world, which led from Europe to the eastern countries. They had Bacchus on their currency so a false deity was worshipped. It was the center for the spreading of the Greek language to the east. Today, Philadelphia's pillars remain.

Philadelphia was on the edge of a great volcanic area. In one way, this brought prosperity because the volcanic ash created a great plain with one of the most fertile areas in the world. It was a great grape-growing area with rich hot springs. These springs made it a center where the infirm came to bathe. However, this prosperity brought danger. This region was subject to frightening earthquakes that caused the abandonment of the city (Rev 3:12). It was also a famous center of heathen worship with many temples to pagan Gods. A customary practice for men who served the state well was to erect pillars with their names inscribed upon them (Rev 3:12).

Christians should want the same honor pronounced upon them by God for their service. We cannot help but experience a queasy feeling of disappointment when we read of people making huge donations and bequeathing large portions of their inheritance to the state and secular causes, while withholding their talents, resources, and wealth from their service to Christ.

The way of salvation is the door He opens that no one can shut. Jesus is the highest authority in Heaven (Mt 28:18). God gave David authority; Christ received

David's prophecy (Mt 16:18) and gave it to Peter (Mt 28:18ff; Ac 2:38). In Matthew 16:18, Jesus says, "I will give you the keys." Why is the key singular in Revelation and plural in the Matthew passage? The keys in Matthew 16:18 are the same keys given to congregations to open the way of salvation to the lost. Everyone who opens the New Covenant Gospel is opening Heaven's door to a lost sinner. Jesus gives this key to everyone who takes the responsibility of evangelism to the lost. These keys are what binds on Earth and in Heaven and looses on Earth and in Heaven (Mt 18:18; Rev 5:5). Christ's having the "key" in the singular means that He has all authority.

Every Christian has "keys" in the plural, which indicates designated and delegated authority. It is an awesome responsibility for Christians to use the keys as Peter did on the day of Pentecost. Likewise, even greater accountability lies upon those who know how to use these keys but refuse to do so. Whether these keys are used will determine the destiny of thousands of souls that are now suspended in the balance.

The Congregation is the fulfillment of the promise of the Davidic Kingdom. Christ is the head and authority in the Congregation. The Bible describes Jesus of Nazareth and his lineage in King David. What Peter preached on Pentecost can be preached by all and in every generation. Christ is the door and the only way!

1. He is "Holy," separated from all evil. He is called "The Holy One" (Ac 2:27) and "Who is holy?" (Heb 7:26)

2. He is "True" which means genuine and real (Jn 14:6).

3. He is holy and true in contrast with the wicked and non-genuine (Heb 1:9).

4. He "Has the Key of David" (Isa 22:22).

    a. David's steward kept the key of the House of David.

    b. It was His responsibility to grant or deny access to the King.

    c. The key is the symbol of all authority.

    d. Today Christ has that authority (Mt 28:18).

e. He is reigning *now* on the Throne promised to David (1Co 15:23-25; Ac 2:29-35).

Jesus is "He who opens and no man can shut," with the key of David. This means that power and authority belong exclusively to Christ even when He shares it with individuals and His earthly congregation. However, Christians must recognize His authority alone (Eph 1:22, 23; Ac 2:30, 31).

The door of evangelism in Revelation 3:8 (2Co 2:12) is the great door opened (Col 4:3), even to the Gentiles (Ac 14:27). The door is always opened for soul winning, and not even Satan has the power to shut it or remove the authority in the name of Jesus. For modern-day church growth "experts," who think Christ's name is no longer important, they need to recognize that the name of Christ is the highest name in the universe (Php 2:9, 10; Ac 4:12). There is no way we can preach the Gospel without highly exalting the name of Jesus Christ.

The name of God is also important to this discussion. Christ's name is mentioned in verse eight, "You have not denied my name," and when Christ delivers up the kingdom to God the Father, the name of God is greatly exalted. We find this exaltation four times in Revelation 3:12, "temple of my God, city of my God, name of my God and from my God." When altars were erected under the Old Covenant, God had expressly commanded that His name be inscribed on them (Dt 12:5, 11, 21, 14:23, 24, 16:2, 6, 11, 25, 26:2). In business, change is necessary for survival. However, no one is at liberty to change the old Jerusalem Gospel. Despite a modern marketing of the "church," when a modern-day "church merchant" substitutes the name of Christ or Christian on their marquee with a widespread human designation, we can be sure that God is not the slightest bit impressed. How easy it is for some people to say that Jesus is the way, the truth, and the life, and really not believe it.

The "open door" is a symbol of the great opportunity before the Congregation in Philadelphia to preach the Gospel (1Co 16:9; 2Co 2:12; Col 4:3). Before them was a door of usefulness in the Kingdom of Christ. When Jesus said, "No man can shut the door," he is referring to the spread of the Gospel that even Satan cannot prevent (Rev 20:3-5). However, Christ can take the Gospel away from people who despise or do not appreciate it. Christ can open this door, AND God can shut this door. God forbid that this should happen to anyone.

We can have an open door to opportunity.

1. The door of self-improvement in Bible study and fellowship
2. The door of opportunity to convert others
3. The door of prayer
4. The door to use time, talent, treasure, and tithe

Philadelphia was a congregation with "little power (strength)" (Rev 3:8). It was small and without abundant resources. Nevertheless, they were great in the Lord's sight. God can perform wonders with little things (1Co 1:25-29; 1Sa 17:49; Zec 4:10). When we understand that "the battle is the Lord's" (1Sa 17:47), we can grasp true victory.

Jesus says, "You have kept my word!" They patiently endured during opposition and persecution (Rev 3:10), and they "Had not denied my name" (Mt 10:32, 33).

The enemies of God are to be exposed and punished (Rev 3:9). Millions of people persecute the true Bride of Christ using the argument that they do not think God loves them, or God has forsaken them. However, Christ says, "I am going to punish them and show them that I love you" (Rev 3:9). Christians should be humble about service. Christians prove to the world and lead the world in knowing that God loves, within His Covenant, by the way His disciples serve, live, and obey (1Jn 2:5; Jn 8:31, 14:23, 15:20).

It is very dear and tender to the ear to hear Jesus say, "I will show your enemies that I love you." What else must a Christian need to hear? They simply cry out, "Dear Jesus, show them that you love me."

Jesus promises them divine protection (Rev 3:10). We should understand that our best is not enough without divine protection. God keeps those who keep the Word. He helps and keeps His children from doing wrong when it is beyond their power (1Co 3:6, 7). Above all things, the struggling and persecuted child of God needs to know that He is coming again! (Rev 3:11)

Jesus continues, "I will make him who overcomes a pillar in the temple of God" (Ps 27:4). The word *nike* comes from a Greek word that means to "overcome";

this means "victory." What is being emphasized here, in this context, is the permanence of the true spiritual temple of God. Biblical Zionism also means something permanent and stable. Political Zionism will never happen. Spiritual Zionism will continue forever (Rev 14:1). Why do people have to call themselves "Jews?" Is there something to gain from this when it is common knowledge that all are from gentile extraction? Even today there are people who derive a false security from the wishful thinking that a Political Zion can be established on Earth. Obviously, people then thought there was something to gain, and people today still think there is something to gain. The conclusion is left to our imagination. The fact is that the Jewish people (many in name only) of Philadelphia were a viable force, and they still are.

Josephus (www.wikipedia: Josephus, who was present at the Roman Feast of the Celebration of the Vanquishing Jew-71 A.D.) writes that from 70 A.D. the Jews were scattered, and many of them taken back to Egypt in ships (Dt 28:68). In the 2nd Century, the Cultural Jewish population was being formed (See Addendums C, D, E, and F.). This Jewish Abomination of Desolation did not just affect Jews in Jerusalem; it affected them on a worldwide scale (See www.wikipedia: The Jewish Diaspora.). Authentic Judaism was desolated and Rome was correct in its assessment of using the word "vanquished," rather than the word "desolate." Judaism since then is non-authentic, cultural Judaism in name only. Gentile-Jews have since become a worldwide, heterogeneous population. While not being of the Jewish bloodline, many Gentile-Jews possess the same "entrepreneurial determinism" (akin to what is now called The Protestant Work Ethic) of the true Jew of the Old Testament. They also possess the same opposing spirit of Judaism that Christ and His Apostles encountered before 70 A.D.

After the Roman siege and mass-suicide at Masada (73 A.D.), Judaism's resistance to any outside threat was reduced to minus zero. Judaism lost its Temple, its national records, its resistance armies, the Law of Moses, the High Priest and Priesthood, its language (replaced with Yiddish of the Ashkenazi Jews in the 19th Century), its BOOK (replaced with the Talmud in 200 A.D., including the Mishnah in 217 A.D., and Gemara in 500 A.D). After 73 A.D., there is nothing in the world that even faintly resembles the once proud nations of either Judah or Israel. The nation that was abandoned by its God as "a dry tree" (Lk 23:31) lost all hope and resolve to carry on. However, secular cultural Judaism arose from the ashes of Masada, along with the idea of Jewish nationalism. This nationalism became Zionism, which is the Jewish political movement that developed from the late 19th Century and continues today. (See Addendum K for a comprehensive, historical view of political Zionism.)

Arthur Koestler in his, *The Thirteenth Tribe*, documents in detail the efforts of Gentile-Jews, "Ashkenazi or Sephardim," through the process of self-identification (ethno-genesis) to resurrect the idea of a Jewish Population. The Ashkenazi Jews who suffered the horrible, deplorable Holocaust of Hitler's Third Reich were Ashkenazi Jews of Khazar descent (www.wikipedia: Khazars). Anti-Khazar-Jew prejudice and ethnic hate is inexcusable for a Christian. If these modern Jews gain supremacy, it is only because of their determination and work ethic. Nations are more blessed because of their presence.

Modern Israel is to be commended for its national pride and résistance to those who would destroy it. It is true that God did not found this modern-day nation (Israel was created by the U.N. in 1948.), but we support Israel because it shares our democratic ideals and values. Of course, we would be naive idealist to expect that modern-day Israel will come to grips with the fact that 70 A.D. was God's final retribution on a Nation that, for the most part, hated and despised Him. The only way this heterogeneous mix of many races called "Israel" can return their love to God is by loving and accepting His Son's reconciliation for all humankind. When this happens, there will be hope for a reconciliation of Jews and Arabs.

Paul addresses this subject in Romans 9-11. Sometimes we get in trouble; we error, when we do not examine a Biblical subject in its complete context. Paul introduces the subject of who Israel is in Romans 9:6-8, and he makes it clear that the children of Abraham's flesh are no longer the Children of God. At the end of the context in Romans 11:26, 27, he says, "All Israel will be saved." Paul continues to quote Isaiah 59:20, 21 to show how all Israel is saved and how their salvation is now through their obedience in New Covenant Christianity, "For this is my covenant with them when I take away their sins" (Ro 11:27).

Because God always had in mind a priestly, kingly nation of Israel, which means "Prince with God," comprised of both Jews and Gentiles (1Pe 2:4-10), Peter says that the very rock upon which both Jew and Gentile should put their trust is the rock that crushed physical Israel (1Pe 2:6-8). In conclusion, the context of Romans, Chapter 9-11, is written about a physical Israel that existed when Paul wrote this epistle to Rome, but theirs was a terminal generation so Paul calls them "vessels fitted for destruction"

(Ro 9:22). The Gentiles are as important in God's eyes as the Jews are (Ro 9:24-27). Paul's reference to the abomination of desolation affirms that within less than two years, the physical nation of Israel would be desolate (Ro 9:28, 29). Only a remnant of genealogical Israel became Christians and escaped this desolation. Modern-day Arab nations and Muslims simply do not know these facts because evangelicals do not preach this very critical teaching. God expected us to read, understand, and teach the following four things concerning Romans 9-11:

1. True Israel is Jew, Arab, and all Gentiles who accept Christ in New Testament persuasion.

2. Physical Israel existed as a nation when Paul wrote.

3. Physical Israel did not exist approximately three years after Paul wrote Romans, and the pressure was on the disciples to convert as many Israelites (Jews) as possible before the Abomination of Desolation. This meant that Christian disciples were to show much love and evangelistic fervor to them.

4. According to Paul's definition of Israel, it consists of only "The Children of promise" (Ro 9:8), which are Jews, Arabs, and all Gentiles. When the select ones of all nations are viewed from Heaven as the redeemed throng of Christ in the New Covenant relationship, they are considered to be God's saved Israel (Ro 11:26, 27).

<u>What a tremendous difference this would make if this divine exposition from Romans was taught in the Middle East.</u>

It is incredible that the Prince of Peace could give reconciliation and peace to all human-kind regardless of the hostilities and barriers that formally existed among all nations, including the ancient nations of Judah and Israel, and Arabs, and all Gentiles (Ac 2:8-12). What Christ is giving to Christians is a quality of life one cannot inherently possess. No Christian has a right to God's mercy or forgiveness. However, He shares it openly and lovingly. All this is obtained only in the name of Jesus (1Pe 4:14-16). The name of Christ is on God's every marquee! (Eph 3:15)

God is described in many different ways (Rev 3:12, 13). He is:

1) Elohim – in the beginning – creator. He is in covenant with the entire universe (Ge 1:1).

2) Yahweh – He is a personal creator of the human race in covenant with his people (Ge 2:4).

3) El Shaddai – "Almighty." The sufficiency of almighty God (Ge 17:1).

4) Adonai – The Lord and Master (Ge 15:2).

5) Yahweh Jireh – One who provides before the need is realized (Ge 22:8, 14).

6) Yahweh Rophe – The healer of nations (Ex 15:26; Ps 6:2).

7) Yahweh Nissi – Banner of victory (Ex 17:17).

8) Yahweh M'Kaddesh – The sanctifier (Lev 20:7).

9) Yahweh Shalom – The peace (Jdg 6:24).

10) El Roi – The God who sees (Ge 16:13, 14).

11) Yahweh Tsidkenu – The righteousness (Jer 23:5, 6).

12) Yahweh Rohi – The shepherd (Isa 40:11).

13) El Elyon – God Almighty in the highest (Ge 14:19, 20). *

- Of all the names of God, Satan covets to be God Almighty in the highest (Eze 28:2ff; Isa 14:14). Allah is a corruption of El Elohim. The other names do not mean much to these colossal tyrants.

Christ's *new name* is identified with the "New Jerusalem" or the Assembly of the living God (Old and New Testament). They are accepted as one redeemed throng. Christ will claim the faithful and give His new name before God the Father. A name known by him that no one else knows.

The Congregation of Laodicea (3:14-22)

Revelation 3:14-22: To the angel of the church in Laodicea write: These are the words of the Amen, the faithful and true witness, the ruler of God's creation. I know your deeds, that you are neither cold nor hot. I wish you were either one or the other! So, because you are lukewarm—neither hot nor cold—I am about to spit you out of my mouth. You say, 'I am rich; I have acquired wealth and do not need a thing.' But you do not realize that you are wretched, pitiful, poor, blind and naked. I counsel you to buy from me gold refined in the fire, so you can become rich; and white clothes to wear, so you can cover your shameful nakedness; and salve to put on your eyes, so you can see. Those whom I love I rebuke and discipline. So be earnest, and repent. Here I am! I stand at the door and knock. If anyone hears my voice and opens the door, I will come in and eat with him, and he with me. To him who overcomes, I will give the right to sit with me on my throne, just as I overcame and sat down with my Father on his throne. He who has an ear, let him hear what the Spirit says to the churches.

Laodicea is 40-43 miles southeast of Philadelphia. Laodicea means *justice of the people*. Cicero, the Roman Philosopher, held his court here. It was one of three towns that lay within sight of each other in the valley of the River Lycus. The two companion towns were Kierapolis and Colosse (Col 4:13, 16). In 133 B.C., Laodicea became part of the Roman Empire, and Jupiter became the prominent idol. Laodicea and the surrounding districts contained a very large number of Jews. The history given here substantiates the fact that the Laodicean Jews were a viable force in numbers, power, and position at the time of John's writing. This is proof positive the Abomination of Desolation of Judaism (70 A.D.) had not yet occurred.

This is just another of the many evidences of a pre-70 A.D. writing. These Jews were useful citizens and brought money and trade to every city where they settled. Laodicea was notably wealthy because it was the center of Asia Minor's banking. It was so wealthy that when it was laid waste in 60 A.D. by an earthquake, this city refused all help. It preferred to use its own resources to rebuild itself. This self-sufficient attitude was present within Laodicea's three congregations of Christ (Rev 3:17). A considerable part of its wealth also came from the cloth and the clothing industry, consisting of black glossy wool. Above all, it was famous for the ophthalmic industry (Rev 3:18) and had a famous medical school that produced a treatment for eye ailments.

"These things say the Amen, the faithful and true witness, the beginning of the creation of God." Jehovah Witnesses use this verse to teach that since Jesus is the beginning of creation, they think He is a created being, man, or angel. However, the beginning in the Greek is *arche*, which means Christ is the spark to the creation. Jesus is the cause of creation. This word would be better translated as the source or origin (Heb 1:10-12; Jn 1:1-3; Col 1:16, 17). In an attempt to justify

Jesus being a created being, the Jehovah's Witnesses also misinterpret the word firstborn in Colossians 1:15, 18. They have a glaring discrepancy in their accepted interpretation of Greek words. The word *firstborn* is *protokos,* which means that Jesus is the *first in rank among all creation as its creator.* The "amen" means Christ is the true one whose words are final. He is a "Faithful and true Witness." This portrays three eternal truths:

1. He would not misrepresent the truth.

2. His testimony would not be biased.

3. He speaks based on His being the source of truth, not just knowing the truth.

Jesus said, "You are neither hot nor cold" (Rev 3:15). The city's water supply originated from hot springs six miles away at Denizli. In the process of traveling through the aqueduct to Laodicea, the water became tepid, being neither hot nor cold. Christ rebuked these Christians for being *luke*warm. This absolute rebuke has echoed throughout the history of the Christ's Congregation. Jesus wants Christians to take sides (Rev 3:16; Jdg 5:28). True Christianity allows Christ to work through Christians and develop their spiritual life. To pray without ceasing and to make Christ our constant companion is the essence of a Christian lifestyle. Christians choose to allow Christ to use their faithfulness and discipline. They must choose whether they will let Christ rule their lives.

Laodiceans were very complacent. Referring to their spiritual tepidness Christ says, "I am going to spew you out of my mouth." Vomit is actually a better translation. "You're making me vomit, and you think you have need of nothing." They are not infidels or atheist. They do not deny Christ or His atonement, *but* they have lost intimate touch with Christ! These branches are withering away. Previously, they had preached the Gospel, but now they are a castaway. Christ would rather that a person be an atheist who rejects Him than be a lukewarm Christian. Jesus said, "I want you to be hot or cold!" They were listless and indifferent, inactive, and unconcerned.

The greatest hindrances to New Covenant Christianity are *Christians* who are like the Laodiceans. They know the truth and understand their duty to obey Christ, and yet they refuse to promote The Kingdom. Such lukewarm Christians lack passion and zeal for redemption. The Laodicean congregations have a high opinion of themselves

(Rev 3:17). Because of their medical schools, banks, the eye salve, and the textile industry, they regarded material prosperity as a token of divine pleasure. They even tried to validate their spirituality by their prosperity! The truth is that the Laodicean congregations were blind to its real condition.

Jesus uses antithetic parallelism to describe the Laodiceans. Jesus uses a play on words, "You are wretched and miserable." They are really an object of pity because of their self-complacency. Who is more to be pitied than individuals who imagine that they are fine Christians, yet Christ is ashamed of them? They are actually "poor" paupers for they had no treasures in Heaven (Mt 16:19, 20). They were "blind" to their obligation to Christ and their responsibility to themselves and to one another.

Without certain Christian graces, followers today are blind! (2Pe 1:5-9) They had failed to wear their spiritual garments (Col 3:12-14). Christ encourages them to buy of Him with gold refined in fire (faith). Isaiah said, "Why do you spend money on that which perishes?" He also said, "Come and drink cool, clear, fresh water" (Isa 55:1, 2). Christ rebukes and tells them to repent and be zealous. The reader needs to understand that the reference to Christ's "knocking at the door" is not an evangelistic Calvinistic invitation to the sinner to become a Christian. The "knocking at the door" is an invitation to one who is already a Christian (Rev 3:20). The Greek word for faith is "pisteuo" which means "persuasion from evidence given."

While Jesus stands at the door and knocks (Lk 6:47; 9:48; Jn 15:16; Rev 22:17), Christians should be inviting sinners to Christ for His Congregation is always inviting, the Spirit is always calling, and Jesus is always choosing. When we are added to the Congregation and Kingdom, our names are added to the Book of Life (Php 4:3; Ac 2:47). There is rejoicing in Heaven when one repents and their name is added. The three steps that Jesus takes to keep Christians on the right track without breaking their will is loving them, reproving them, and treating them with corrective discipline (Rev 3:19). God has a marvelous predestined plan to save this world in Christ (Ro 8:28-30). People are affected by this predestined plan only if they personally choose to accept it.

Christ admonishes the Laodiceans. He wants them to realize His blessings, that they are enriched and clothed in Him, and that their vision may be restored. He wants His Kingdom to "Be Zealous" for Him! Real religion cannot exist without enthusiasm. The Congregation at Laodicea had lost its enthusiasm for Christ (Rev 2:4), but Christ wants Christians to be boiling for Him! (3:15, 16). This kind of zeal is contagious (2Cor 9:2), and it produces good works (Gal 4:18; Col 3:23).

Because the Laodiceans lacked zeal, Christ calls them to "repent!" Repentance is what stands between an erring Christian and our Savior's forgiveness. He says, "I stand at the door and knock" making a touching plea for the repentance of his followers. He threatens them that if they do not repent, God will turn them away from His grace (Heb 3:12; Gal 5:4; Jn 15:16). However, to those who overcome, there is a promised reward that is honor above all honors. Faithful believers will sit on God's very throne with Christ. Those believers will sit at the place of the highest honor! Sitting next to Christ!

It is spiritually breathtaking and intellectually staggering to think that Christ wants to invite others to dine with Him. However, this is exactly what He is saying in verse 20. The Greek word for dine or eat is *deipnon*, which is the chief meal of the day. The word *deipnon* is used when Christ celebrates His marriage to His spiritual bride (Rev 19:9) and is also used for the Lord's Supper (1Co 11:20). But there is more. In addition, *deipnon* is used for the supper in Revelation 19:17, which is the feast of all the ungodly. What a dynamic revelation that every person in the universe is invited to a religious supper. Some will partake of the Lord's Supper at His Communion Table on the First Day of (each) week (Ac 20:7) and dine with Him eternally in the next world (Rev 19:9). Others will become a supper themselves for carrion fowl, which like buzzard's feast on their carcasses (Rev. 19:17). Partaking of a divine supper or being supper for flesh-eating buzzards is the greatest choice a person will ever make. Of course, the vultures devouring human flesh is an apocalyptic representation of how horrible it is to die outside of the grace of our Lord, Jesus Christ.

How interesting to note that those who are married to the Lamb of God are invited to "The marriage supper of the Lamb" (Rev 19:9), while on the other hand, the flesh-eating vultures are eating the human carcasses of those that rejected Christ, in what the Scriptures call "the supper of the great God" (Rev 19:17).

Jesus will have supper with us at the table – personally. This text gives a deep-seated emotional reflection upon how privileged we are to have a personal invitation from

Jesus Christ to sit at the Lord's Table with Him in His Kingdom every first day of the week. Jesus prophesied, "I will not eat it again until it finds fulfillment in the Kingdom of God" (Lk 22:16; 1Co 11:20; Ac 20:7).

It is ungratefulness to the nth degree for Christians to refuse to dine with Him at the Lord's Table weekly. Yes, we fellowship with Him daily, but this includes a special fellowship every week.

WE ARE NOW GETTING READY TO ENVISION THE LAMB UPON HIS ETERNAL THRONE.

It was never God's desire to establish an earthly throne. In fact, God has always been their recognized King from Heaven. It was not until the sin of covetousness became so prevalent in the Israelites' hearts that God finally relented and gave them what they wanted. They rejected Him as their king and replaced Him with a man.

> "Now it came to pass when Samuel was old that he made his sons judges over Israel. The name of his firstborn was Joel, and the name of his second, Abijah; they were judges in Beersheba. But his sons did not walk in his ways; they turned aside after dishonest gain, took bribes, and perverted justice. Then all the elders of Israel gathered together and came to Samuel at Ramah, and said to him, 'Look, you are old, and your sons do not walk in your ways. Now make us a king to judge us like all the nations.' But the thing displeased Samuel when they said, 'Give us a king to judge us.' So Samuel prayed to the Lord. And the Lord said to Samuel, 'Heed the voice of the people in all that they say to you; for they have not rejected you, but they have rejected Me, that I should not reign over them. According to all the works which they have done since the day that I brought them up out of Egypt, even to this day — with which they have forsaken Me and served other gods — so they are doing to you also. Now therefore, heed their voice. However, you shall solemnly forewarn them, and show them the behavior of the king who will reign over them'" (1Sa 8:1-9).

They chose to reject God! They rejected Him with their lifestyle when God brought them out of Egypt, and now they are rejecting Him with their lips. They do not want God as their king. This is the same mindset of a Pre-Millennialist. They do not want God to be their king. As the Israelites rejected the throne of God, so the Pre-Millennialist have rejected the Throne of Christ. God commanded Samuel to make the Israelites aware of the severity of their choice to reject God,

> "And he said, 'This will be the behavior of the king who will reign over you: He will take your sons and appoint them for his own chariots and to be his horsemen, and some will run before his chariots. He will appoint captains over his thousands and captains over his fifties, will set some to plow his ground and reap his harvest, and some to make his weapons of war and equipment for his chariots. He will take your daughters to be perfumers, cooks, and bakers. And he will take the best of your fields, your vineyards, and your olive groves, and give them to his servants. He will take a tenth of your grain and your vintage, and give it to his officers and servants. And he will take your male servants, your female servants, your finest young men, and your donkeys, and put them to his work. He will take a tenth of your sheep. And you will be his servants. And you will cry out in that day because of your king whom you have chosen for yourselves, and the Lord will not hear you in that day'" (1Sa 8:11-18).

One would expect after hearing the consequences of rejecting God as their king that they would most assuredly repent! But, unbelievably, they did not. Their hearts were hard, and they could rationalize the truth. In fact, this earthly throne is an apostasy! Every aspect of an earthly king would be negative for them. Yet, they still chose a man over God, the Earth over Heaven, and the flesh over the Spirit.

No matter how much doctrine and truth Pre-Millennialists receive, their hearts are often so hard that they refuse to accept the truth. The cost of rejecting Jesus is significantly more harmful today. Some people want to be their own savior, want social acceptance, want physical satisfaction, want to resist the truth, and they want to reign on Earth. The Pre-Millennial doctrine is so fascinated with the Earth that they refuse to accept Christ in Heaven. They have rejected Him, His throne, and His purpose.

The Israelites did not care about the consequence, but they did care about getting their way, getting what they wanted. Samuel records,

> "Nevertheless the people refused to obey the voice of Samuel; and they said, 'No, but we will have a king over us, that we also may be like all the nations, and that our king may judge us and go out before us and fight our battles.' And Samuel heard all the words of the people, and he repeated them in the hearing of the Lord. So the Lord said to Samuel, 'Heed their voice, and make them a king'" (1Sa 8:19-22a).

When the Israelites rejected their Heavenly King for an earthly king, this was one of the saddest days in history. They knew the truth about God being their King, yet they wanted another. God did not force them to accept His Kingship. God was willing to accept their rejection. But the Israelites were going to experience God's rejection. We should be aware that once a nation or a person decides to reject God as King, they must forever live with the consequences. God will accept a person's rebellion against Christ; God will punish them because this choice is sinful. The Israelites committed a sin by asking for an earthly king!

> "But when you saw that Nahash king of the Ammonites was moving against you, you said to me, 'No, we want a king to rule over us' - even though the Lord your God was your king. Now here is the king you have chosen, the one you asked for; see, the Lord has set a king over you. If you fear the Lord and serve and obey him and do not rebel against his commands, and if both you and the king who reigns over you follow the Lord your God – good! But if you do not obey the Lord, and if you rebel against his commands, his hand will be against you, as it was against your fathers. "Now then, stand still and see this great thing the Lord is about to do before your eyes! Is it not wheat harvest now? I will call upon the Lord to send thunder and rain. And you will realize what an evil thing you did in the eyes of the Lord when you asked for a king" (1Sa 12:12-17).

The earthly throne would never function like the Heavenly one. It was only a representation of the true and rightful King. The Israelites understood this concept.

> "Of all my sons (for the Lord has given me many sons), He has chosen my son Solomon to sit on the throne of the kingdom of the Lord over Israel" (1Ch 28:5).

> "Then Solomon sat on the throne of the LORD as king instead of David his father; and he prospered, and all Israel obeyed him" (1Ch 29:23).

> "Blessed be the Lord your God who delighted in you, setting you on His throne to be king for the Lord your God! Because your God has loved Israel, to establish them forever, therefore He made you king over them, to do justice and righteousness" (2Ch 9:8).

> "So now you intend to resist the kingdom of the Lord through the sons of David, being a great multitude and having with you the golden calves which Jeroboam made for gods for you" (2Ch 13:8).

This Kingdom would one day be established, forever. God prophesied to David concerning this eternal Kingdom,

> "When your days are fulfilled that you must go to be with your fathers, that I will set up one of your descendants after you, who will be of your sons; and I will establish his kingdom. He shall build for Me a house, and I will establish his throne forever. I will be his father and he shall be My son; and I will not take My loving-kindness away from him, as I took it from him who was before you. But I will settle him in My house and in My kingdom forever, and his throne shall be established forever" (1Ch 17:11-14).

Interestingly, God made a prophecy to the earthly throne that one day He would establish it forever. However, He made a promise *to* the earthly throne, not *of* the earthly throne.

> "He shall build a house for My name, and I will establish the throne of his kingdom forever. I will be a father to him and he will be a son to Me; when he commits iniquity, I will correct him with the rod of men and the strokes of the sons of men, but My loving-kindness shall not depart from him, as I took it away from Saul, whom I removed from before you. Your house and your kingdom shall endure before Me forever; your throne shall be established forever" (2Sa 7:13-16).

> "There will be no end to the increase of His government or of peace, on the throne of David and over his kingdom, to establish it and to uphold it with justice and righteousness From then on and forevermore. The zeal of the Lord of hosts will accomplish this" (Isa 9:7).

> "A throne will even be established in loving-kindness, and a judge will sit on it in faithfulness in the tent of David; Moreover, he will seek justice and be prompt in righteousness…" (Isa 16:5).

Jesus is Both King of Peace and Priest of God (Heb 7:1, 2)

> "I have made a covenant with My chosen; I have sworn to David My servant, I will establish your seed forever and build up your throne to all generations" (Ps 89:3, 4).

David's earthly throne was destroyed. The Apostle Peter tells us that David had a Lord in Acts 2:34. His Lord was Jesus Christ. David foresaw the resurrection of

Christ in prophecy. He also saw Christ's ascension to Heaven. And he saw Christ seated on the throne that was promised to him (Ac 2:29-33). Christ was the seed of David after the flesh but His Throne was Heavenly. It is in this sense that the Throne is forever.

To assume that God would re-establish an earthly throne after it was already destroyed could only come from a pre-supposition. Pre-Millennial doctrine states that Christ will rule upon this Earth on David's throne sometime in the future. There is, however, a very major problem. It is impossible for this to happen because Christ's reigning on Earth is not Scriptural. God promised that it would never happen! The Lord prophesied through Jeremiah,

> "Is this man Coniah a despised, shattered jar? Or is he an undesirable vessel? Why have he and his descendants been hurled out and cast into a land that they had not known? O land, land, land, Hear the word of the LORD! "Thus says the LORD, 'Write this man down childless, a man who will not prosper in his days; for no man of his descendants will prosper, sitting on the throne of David or ruling again in Judah'" (Jer 22:28-30).

Christ is a descendent of Coniah.

> "After the deportation to Babylon: Jeconiah became the father of Shealtiel, and Shealtiel the father of Zerubbabel" (Mt 1:12).

Notice that Jeremiah prophesied that no descendent of Jeconiah (Coniah) can ever sit on David's throne. How could this be possible? How can Christ reign upon David's throne if God said it would never happen again? Jesus Christ is a literal descendant of Coniah, which proves David's throne is forever in Heaven. Christ is now reigning from this Throne:

> "Brethren, I may confidently say to you regarding the patriarch David that he both died and was buried, and his tomb is with us to this day. And so, because he was a prophet and knew that God had sworn to him with an oath to seat one of his descendants on his throne, he looked ahead and spoke of the resurrection of the Christ, that He was neither abandoned to Hades, nor did His flesh suffer decay. This Jesus God raised up again, to which we are all witnesses. Therefore, having been exalted to the right hand of God, and having received from the Father the promise of the Holy Spirit, He has poured forth this which you both see and hear. For it was not David

who ascended into heaven, but he himself says: 'The Lord said to my Lord, Sit at My right hand, until I make Your enemies a footstool for Your feet.' Therefore, let all the house of Israel know for certain that God has made Him both Lord and Christ—this Jesus whom you crucified" (Ac 2:29-36).

If Christ is on the Throne then He is King. A logical conclusion will lead us to that fact that Christ has a Kingdom! If Christ is on the Throne as King, reigning over a Kingdom, it would be contradictory to teach that He has not yet established his Kingdom or that He will establish it in the future. Pre-Millennialists reject this Biblical doctrine. They have failed to see that God was so angered by the disobedient paganism of the kings that sat on God's Throne, that He removed the throne from the Earth and returned His Throne to Heaven.

> "It is your destruction, O Israel that you are against Me, against your help. Where now is your king that he may save you in all your cities, and your judges of whom you requested, "Give me a king and princes"? I gave you a king in My anger and took him away in My wrath" (Hos 13:9-11).

This was God's Throne to give, and it was God's Throne to take away. Israel always recognized that this throne was just as much God's Throne as the human king's throne. Just as David shared in God's Throne, so too Christ and God co-reign together.

> "For this you know with certainty, that no immoral or impure person or covetous man, who is an idolater, has an inheritance in the kingdom of Christ and God" (Eph 5:5).

> "He who overcomes, I will grant to him to sit down with Me on My throne, as I also overcame and sat down with My Father on His throne" (Rev 3:21).

The Pre-Millennialists teach that Christ is High Priest, but not King. To make this statement is a self-defeating claim! Christ cannot be High Priest without being King, and He cannot be King without being High Priest! This is confirmed through Zechariah's proclamation,

> "Then say to him, 'Thus says the LORD of hosts, "Behold, a man whose name is Branch, for He will branch out from where He is; and He will build the temple of the LORD. Yes, it is He who will build the temple of the LORD, and He who will bear the honor and sit and rule on His throne.

Thus, He will be a priest on His throne, and the counsel of peace will be between the two offices'" (Zec 6:12, 13).

As a Priest on His Throne, Christ built His Temple. The Bible speaks about this Temple,

> "Do you not know that you are a temple of God and that the Spirit of God dwells in you? If any man destroys the temple of God, God will destroy him, for the temple of God is holy, and that is what you are" (1Co 3:16, 17).

In the Book of Hebrews, where Christ is proclaimed High Priest numerous times, God makes a truth claim concerning God the Son,

> "But of the Son He says, "Your throne, O God, is forever and ever, and the righteous scepter is the scepter of His kingdom" (Heb 1:8; Ps 110).

Christ's Throne is a Throne that reigns forever, and He reigns as a priest forever! (Heb 5:6). For the Priestly Christ to reign from His Throne on Earth would not only nullify His priesthood, but according to the Law, He would be disqualified because He is a descendant of Jeconiah, not Levi.

> "If he were on earth, he would not be a priest, for there are already men who offer the gifts prescribed by the law" (Heb 8:4).

If the Priest has a temple, then the King has a Kingdom! Christ will reign from this throne until the end.

> "For it was not David who ascended into heaven, but he himself says: 'The Lord said to my Lord, "Sit at My right hand, until I make Your enemies a footstool for Your feet."' Therefore let all the house of Israel know for certain that God has made Him both Lord and Christ—this Jesus whom you crucified" (Ac 2:34-36).

> "For He must reign until He has put all His enemies under His feet. The last enemy that will be abolished is death" (1Co 15:25, 26).

> "And He is the radiance of His glory and the exact representation of His nature, and upholds all things by the word of His power. When He had made purification of sins, He sat down at the right hand of the Majesty on

> high ... But of the Son He says, "Your throne, O God, is forever and ever, And the righteous scepter is the scepter of His kingdom" ... But to which of the angels has He ever said, "Sit at My right hand, Until I make Your enemies A footstool for Your feet" (Heb 1:3, 8, 13).
>
> "Every priest stands daily ministering and offering time after time the same sacrifices, which can never take away sins; but He, having offered one sacrifice for sins for all time, sat down at the right hand of God, waiting from that time onward until his enemies be made a footstool for his feet" (Heb 10:11-13).
>
> "'He who overcomes, I will grant to him to sit down with Me on My throne, as I also overcame and sat down with My Father on His throne" (Rev 3:21).

After the judgment and punishment of the wicked, Christ will present the Kingdom of his bride to the Father.

> "For as in Adam all die, so also in Christ all will be made alive. But each in his own order: Christ the first fruits, after that those who are Christ's at His coming, then comes the end, when He hands over the kingdom to the God and Father, when He has abolished all rule and all authority and power. For He must reign until He has put all His enemies under His feet. The last enemy that will be abolished is death. For He has put all things in subjection under His feet. But when He says, "All things are put in subjection," it is evident that He is exempted who put all things in subjection to Him. When all things are subjected to Him, then the Son Himself also will be subjected to the One who subjected all things to Him, so that God may be all in all" (1Co 15:22-28).

It is not at the Second Coming when Christ will establish His Kingdom, but when He will give it away! He presents it to the Father as complete, whole, and, without spot. This is exactly opposite of all Pre-Millennial doctrine. By this time, the Pre-Millennials will be too late. They will try to justify to God why they taught their false doctrine. This will lead to their begging for mercy. They might think, "Maybe God will at least reward me for trying to do well and trying to accomplish wonderful things in His name." This will not be the case. They will hear, "Depart from me, you who are cursed, into the eternal fire prepared for the devil and his angels" (Mt 24:41).

The fact that Christ will present His Kingdom to the Father at the Second Coming; not establish His Kingdom, proves that Christ is reigning as King of His current Kingdom. The Scriptures state,

> "And so, because he was a prophet and knew that GOD HAD SWORN TO HIM WITH AN OATH TO SEAT one OF HIS DESCENDANTS ON HIS THRONE, he looked ahead and spoke of the resurrection of the Christ" (Ac 2:30, 31).

The Jews continued to seek an earthly King (Jn 6:15; Ac 1:6). When Christ refused, they were angered. In fact, they decided to once again reject God as their King! The Bible records, "They shouted, 'Take him away! Take him away! Crucify him!' 'Shall I crucify your king?' Pilate asked. 'We have no king but Caesar,' the chief priests answered." It is interesting to note that this king brought horrendous troubles upon them, such as the world has never seen. Christ warned them of this coming wrath (Mt 23:39-24:28), but they still chose to reject Him. Christ was sent to save them, but they rejected Him.

The Bible declares,

> Jesus said to them: "Have you never read in the Scriptures: 'The stone the builders rejected has become the capstone; the Lord has done this, and it is marvelous in our eyes'? Therefore, I tell you that the kingdom of God will be taken away from you and given to a people who will produce its fruit. He who falls on this stone will be broken to pieces, but he on whom it falls will be crushed" (Mt 21:42-44).

> "There is a judge for the one who rejects me and does not accept my words; that very word which I spoke will condemn him at the last day. For I did not speak of my own accord, but the Father who sent me commanded me what to say and how to say it. I know that his command leads to eternal life. So whatever I say is just what the Father has told me to say" (Jn 12:48-50).

The Pre-Millennalists reject the words of Jesus, "'my kingdom is not of this world. If it were, my servants would fight to prevent my arrest by the Jews. But now my kingdom is from another place.' 'You are a king, then!' said Pilate. Jesus answered, 'You are right in saying I am a king. In fact, for this reason I was born, and for this I came into the world, to testify to the truth. Everyone on the side of truth listens to me'" (Jn 18:36, 37).

To reject Christ and His word is to accept condemnation and punishment. Paul says,

> "The wrath of God is being revealed from heaven against all the godlessness and wickedness of men who suppress the truth by their wickedness, since what may be known about God is plain to them, because God has made it plain to them. For since the creation of the world God's invisible qualities — his eternal power and divine nature — have been clearly seen, being understood from what has been made, so that men are without excuse. For although they knew God, they neither glorified him as God nor gave thanks to him, but their thinking became futile and their foolish hearts were darkened. Although they claimed to be wise, they became fools and exchanged the glory of the immortal God for images made to look like mortal man and birds and animals and reptiles. Therefore, God gave them over in the sinful desires of their hearts to sexual impurity for the degrading of their bodies with one another. They exchanged the truth of God for a lie, and worshiped and served created things rather than the Creator — who is forever praised. Amen" (Ro 1:18-25).

This is the consequence for rejecting Christ as King. Any worship other than worshipping God in spirit and truth is not acceptable. There is no excuse for denying that Christ is sitting on David's throne and reigning from Heaven. The Scriptures are clear. Even when Pre-Millennialists are shown truth and the consequences of their actions, they still reject Christ. This was the same verdict for the Israelites. However, the punishment for rejecting God's Son as King and Messiah is more severe. Paul says,

> "But because of your stubbornness and your unrepentant heart, you are storing up wrath against yourself for the day of God's wrath, when his righteous judgment will be revealed. God "will give to each person according to what he has done." To those who by persistence in doing good seek glory, honor and immortality, he will give eternal life. But for those who are self-seeking and who reject the truth and follow evil, there will be wrath and anger" (Ro 2:5-8).

We are encouraged by the Spirit of God to rivet our eyes upon the eternal, Heavenly Throne of Christ. The Throne resides in Heaven with the true, eternal King of Kings and Lord of Lords (1Ti 1:17, 6:15). To reject the King who Christ claimed to be is to result in our dying in their sins (Jn 8:24).

THE CONSEQUENCIES OF DYING IN SINS (Jn 8:24)

The following hindrances prevent us from entering the apocalyptic world of discernment:

1. Preconceived ideas gotten from sub-novice ideas of what The Spirit is saying to Christ's congregations.

2. Not being born again of the water "immersion" and Spirit of John 3:5 (Jn 3:23 with Ac 8:37). How can we trust people to teach us if they are not born again?

3. Unforgiven sin in the interpreter's life.

4. A failure to give rapt attention to views that may contradict our traditional views.

5. A failure to pray earnestly that Christ would open this revelation to our minds.

6. A failure to understand New Covenant Christianity as Christ's last Will and Testament to the human race.

7. Beginning every session in devotional petitions for Spiritual illumination (Heb 6:4, 10:32) and an earnest quest for discernment (Mt 16:3; 1Co 2:14), lest our enlightenment turn to darkness.

8. Hostility toward people or circumstances.

9. Suspicions of God's providential hand.

10. Being led of soulish-naturalism.

11. Too much pride and spiritual short-sightedness to actually believe such an apocalyptic world exists.

12. Possessing a death wish in order to avoid contemplating such a world.

13. Not having a deep, abiding presence of Christ (1Pe 4:14, 5:1; Php 3:3-20; Col 3:3, 4; Gal 2:20).

14. Not bearing the reproach or evangelistic witness of the Gospel of Christ (Rev 1:9).

15. Being a stranger to fervent, intercessory prayer.

16. Failing to live in the Spirit (Ro 8:4-16; Gal 5:25).

Remember, John was in Spirit (and tribulation) when he wrote this book (Rev 1:9, 10). In such a state, we can see the invisible beyond the veil of flesh. I was greatly deceived in my understanding of this book as a young theological student at Kentucky Christian College. I credit Dr. Donald Nash's extreme patience and Godly wisdom in dealing with the brash, impudent, amateurish, futuristic ideas that I exhibited in my first semester Revelation class.

Revelation Chapter Four

INTERLUDE

We have just completed the first cycle of the Rainbow consisting of Chapters 1-3. The second cycle of the Rainbow consists of Chapters 5:1 -7:17. Now, we will examine Chapter 4 as an interlude. The concept of interludes goes back to Psalms 3, 24, 46, 68 (and other Psalms) where there is a pause called "Selah." Sometimes this pause is associated with the idea of "Lifting up," which means to pause and lift oneself up to God in praise (www.wikipedia: Selah).

The numerology in Revelation is highly significant in our understanding of its teachings. Following is an interlude or snapshot of God on His Throne. This interlude teaches that in the midst of the cycles, God remains in control.

Remember, interludes are short dramatic episodes, periods, or spaces introduced between the acts of a play or movie. They *are not* chapter divisions. Interludes occur sporadically throughout the Revelation.

This interlude shows that the One sitting on the Throne governs all things in the universe. God is in control. John gives a new vision to the congregations. This Throne is not a carnal throne because it is a Throne called righteousness (Ps 80:1). This Throne has no physical limitations. This Throne is far greater because this is the Throne God uses to rule over all the Earth. This Throne is the center of all power, glory, authority, and honor. Four different views exist about the centrality of the universe of what signifies the sovereign rule of everything visible or invisible.

1. Geocentric – The Earth is the center of the universe.
2. Heliocentric – The Sun is the center of the universe.
3. Sagittarius-centric – Constellations are the center of the universe.
4. Coelocentric/theocentric – The Throne of Heaven is the center of the universe.

Once again, in order to understand apocalyptical language, we must open our minds to the Spirit and allow the acuity of John's vision from God's Holy Word to unveil itself to us. This hidden world of God can be found in the Scriptures and revealed by the Holy Spirit before being integrated with our spirit (1Co 2:9, 10).

The Throne has never left God's paradise. It was man's desire to reject God's Throne in Heaven and to replace it with a carnal throne. The Pre-Millennial doctrine advocates an earthly kingdom with an earthly throne. Their doctrine denies the spiritual reign of Christ from Heaven while looking forward to a future reign on Earth. Like the disobedient Israelites of the past, Pre-Millennialists are actually rejecting God as their king. They are seeking an earthly throne to reign over everyone else. This carnal mindset has prevailed for 4,000 years. This mindset began with the Israelites and will end with the Pre-Millennialists.

Revelation 4:1: After this I looked, and there before me was a door standing open in heaven. And the voice I had first heard speaking to me like a trumpet said, "Come up here, and I will show you what must take place after this."

This is a panoramic view of the world, past, present, and future, that has been synchronized by God. Jesus says, "I will show you what must take place. God told Abraham in the book of Genesis, "Shall I hide from Abraham what I am about to do?" (18:17) God makes this statement now because He has shared with His people all knowledge relating to this Book. Christians know a judgment is coming, but the time and season of this event is unknown. As stated earlier, the servant needs to be aware at all times concerning His coming.

Revelation 4:2: At once I was in the Spirit, and there before me was a throne in heaven with someone sitting on it.

Futurists say this is the rapture of the Congregation. However, this is not talking about the future. This verse is talking about John's being in the Spirit and not about the Congregation being raptured into Heaven. Jesus says, "Come up here." How can John get into this world? John was in the Spirit! John was not in the world of the flesh where we experience our hearing, tasting, smelling, feeling, and seeing. Physical senses will not get us into the apocalyptic world. God wants Christians to hear Him from Heaven, repent of their sin, and enter into the Spirit. This is the only way we can enter into God's dominion.

Revelation 4:3: And the one who sat there had the appearance of jasper and carnelian. A rainbow, resembling an emerald, encircled the throne.

This is a beautiful, imaginative image of God. He is behind everything that happens. Colors are used in this verse because no one can look on God and live. Precious iridescent jewels and their colors are given in an attempt to convey the absolute holiness of the Godhead. God's form is not described; only His appearance is described.

- Jasper – dazzling white; probably like a diamond = purity
- Sardius – bloody red – judgments
- Emerald – iridescent, crystal green = the storm is over = God's faithfulness
- There was a rainbow because the Book of Revelation is like a rainbow. God is complete in seven fold, uplifted perfection like a rainbow.

Revelation 4:4: Surrounding the throne were twenty-four other thrones, and seated on them were twenty-four elders. They were dressed in white and had crowns of gold on their heads.

The 24 thrones with 24 elders signify all the redeemed in both the Old Testament and the New Testament. The 24 elders (as a representative number) signify the divinely appointed government of the Lord. The prophecy of Isaiah 24:23 is fulfilled by what was said at Pentecost concerning the ascended Lord to Mount Zion

(Heb 12:22-14). When we read Acts 2:4 with 2:36, we see where God fulfilled Isaiah's prophecy by revealing to the 3,000 souls at The Pentecost Feast in Jerusalem that His Son was the risen Messianic Lord and King who was promised through the prophet David. In Ephesians 4:11, Christ the Messiah gave evangelists, pastors, and teachers to His congregation. Isaiah said the Law (New Testament) would go forth from Jerusalem and Mount Zion (Heaven) (Isa 2:3). This is a latter-day prophecy (Isa 2:2), which applied to the establishment of the New Covenant (Ac 2:17). Since the Law is going to leave Jerusalem in 30 A.D. (when Peter preached), it cannot be the Old Law.

This Law, "Law of the Spirit," written in the heart (Ro 8:2; Heb 10:16) would constitute the last Covenant the Godhead would give to the human race. Christ, therefore, reigns with His Pastors-Elders from Mount Zion. Some scholars mistakenly translate elders in Isaiah 24:23 as "ancients." There is absolutely no excuse for such an embarrassing error in translation. The word "ancient" is a completely different word than the traditional Hebrew word for elder (See Strong's 6931.). It is a shame that such translations are so discomfiting to the average reader that they are forced to look them up in a Hebrew Lexicon. We are not addressing a scholarship error regarding synonyms. We are looking at two altogether different words "elders" and "ancients." Thank God some translators got it right, "And His glory shall be before His Elders" (Isa 24:23).

Mathew 19:28 shows the New Testament is superior to the Old Testament because the 12 Apostles will judge the world. Those being judged include the 12 tribes of Israel. Twelve is the number of government. Hendriksen in his book, *More than Conquerors*, writes that the 24 Elders represent the combined authority of the Old and New Testament revelation. The woman in Revelation 12:1 has a garland of 12 stars on her head. The final revelation given to us comes through the 12 Apostles.

Through the representative number of 12 Apostles is laid the comprehensive foundation (Eph 2:19-22). Christ "deputized" or assigned His glory to His apostles when He breathed on them (Jn 20:22). He "appointed" (Lk 22:29) them a Kingdom. The word "diathethemai" (1303) translated "appoint" or "confer" is never used in quite the same context as we would understand "to appoint or confer." It is more profound than these words can convey. It comes from the word construction "To dispose or make a testator," Strong's (1242). It is a deposition, especially a devisory will, covenant, testament. Jesus Christ appointed His apostles as executors of His Will, Testament, or New Covenant Kingdom.

While the heads of the 12 Old Testament tribes are gone, yet they took their place in prophetic government necessary to hold Christ's Messianic Line over until He came to the Earth, "the fullness of time." Thus, they are given honorable mention alongside the final Apostolic Messianic Kingdom Authority (represented by "The Twelve Apostles"). This accounts for the delegated "stephanos" golden crowns on the heads of The Twenty-Four.

The 24 Elders had white robes. The "white robes" mean they overcame (Gal 3:27). The only way they entered into Heaven is by their white garments, which are to be as pure and as perfect as God is. All of them are clothed, which means they are in robes of righteousness. It is the Lord who clothes us and not we ourselves.

This court of 24 Elders reveals that God's judicial, providential government is established for all time, past and future. The Book of Daniel does not mention 24 Elders because Israel did not have 24 tribes. Christians have a complete book, the New Testament, for the Apostles laid the New Testament foundation upon which our eternal foundation is based in these last days (Rev 21:14).

Revelation 4:5: From the throne came flashes of lightning, rumblings and peals of thunder. Before the throne, seven lamps were blazing. These are the seven Spirits of God.

Thunder and lightning precede the storm. The Book of Revelation thunders like a storm! The end is coming! The seven lamps and seven spirits are the complete Spirit of God. Isaiah shows the seven-fold Spirit of God (Isa 11:1, 2), which are: 1) the Spirit of the Lord, 2) wisdom, 3) understanding, 4) counsel, 5) might, 6) knowledge, and 7) the fear of the Lord. This is the completeness of the Godhead (Ps 110; 80:17). Revelation shows the Godhead in 4:1; 4:5; 5:6, as complete. This complete Spirit gave seven gifts to the congregation to represent their completed establishment (Ro 12:6-8). Count them.

1. Prophecy
2. Serve
3. Teach
4. Encourage

5. Contribute
6. Leadership
7. Mercy

Revelation 4:6: Also before the throne there was what looked like a sea of glass, clear as crystal. In the center, around the throne, were four living creatures, and they were covered with eyes, in front and in back.

The Sea of Glass means peacefulness and calmness. In the midst of the storm, there is calmness. There is no use for us to panic about life's adversaries because God's peace is in the midst of every storm. The Bible tells us there are three Heavenly beings: Angels, Cherubim, and Seraphim. As we understand and define these three types, the four creatures mentioned in this verse align most closely with Cherubim (plural cherub). We have many reasons to believe these "four living creatures" are the same as the Cherubim mentioned 18 times in the Book of Ezekiel (See my book, *Angels and Demons*.). They are intelligent creatures; they may be even more intelligent than angels. They are unfamiliar with sin (Ps 80:1; 99:1; Ge 3:24). A cherub is a very innocent-looking adult who appears almost childlike.

God gave us a creature example of an everlasting creature that can retain childlike innocence forever. It is assumed that all of us get frustrated in the battles of this evil world and because we are surrounded by wickedness, at times we want to throw away this imputed innocence given us by Christ and His Spirit. But the Cherubim have eyes to see all, and they are aware of the evil beneath the Throne and yet maintain their child-like trust and purity. They exemplify what would designate the perfect character of a child of God.

Another creature that God created is a Seraph. They are winged, serpent-looking, manlike creatures of the highest order of created beings in the universe. God uses these creatures to help His people.

Revelation 4: 7: The first living creature was like a lion, the second was like an ox, the third had a face like a man, the fourth was like a flying eagle.

Our previous definition of innocent Cherub may be confusing when we read of their lion-like, ox-like, man-like, and eagle-like characteristics, but some scholars say that these creatures are immortal in innocence and mortal in knowledge.

Likewise, they are as innocent and pure as a little child in attitude, but they are terrifying in justice. What is consistent to God in righteousness, holiness, and justice seems paradoxical to man. But God's consistency should make good men fear.

The first living creature was like a lion; this represents strength. The second is like an ox; this represents nobility. The third has the face like a man; this represents intelligence. Finally, the fourth face, like a flying eagle portrays the serenity of peace.

Revelation 4:8: Each of the four living creatures had six wings and was covered with eyes all around, even under his wings. Day and night they never stop saying: "Holy, holy, holy is the Lord God Almighty, who was, and is, and is to come."

The number "four" represents the number of Earth and the "six wings" the "number of man." These creatures exist for God's pleasure. "Holy, Holy, Holy" stands for the Father, Son, and Holy Spirit. Day and night, they never stopped praising God because He reigns on His Throne, forever.

Revelation 4:9: Whenever the living creatures give glory, honor and thanks to him who sits on the throne and who lives forever and ever.

The creatures give glory and honor to God for He is sovereign and eternal. The "lives forever" stated above is that which belongs exclusively to God, "from everlasting to everlasting, thou art God" (Ps 90:2b). Life inherent means God is life, not just alive. He is not just alive; He is living. Life is His quality (Ps 47:8, 9). No man can pay God enough for life.

Revelation 4:10, 11: The twenty-four elders fall down before him who sits on the throne, and worship him who lives forever and ever. They lay their crowns before the throne and say: "You are worthy, our Lord and God, to receive glory and honor and power, for you created all things, and by your will they were created and have their being."

The Elders fall prostrate and lay their crowns before the throne. They are submitting to the almighty God. There are two kinds of crowns:

1. Stephanos – (used in verse 10) This is a victor's crown and is given to those who work and overcome. The Elders lay their crowns at the base of God's Throne.

2. Diadem – This is a crown of inheritance because one is a child of God; this is Jesus' crown. The diadem was called a filet, which is a piece of silk tied around the head. Jesus will have seven diadems on his head when He comes.

Once more, notice the numerology in verse 11. God is worthy, receiving glory, honor, and power on the created Earth. The number four represents the Earth. God created all things and nothing has been made without him (Heb 1:2; Col 1:16; Jn 1:1).

LET US BRING BACK THE LOST CONGREGATIONS OF ASIA

"I sat where they sat" (Ez. 3:15)

This Commentary is written from the perspective that your author is sitting in the seven Congregations of Asia and listening to the Evangels sent by Christ to speak to them. Except for the congregation at Laodicea Christ found some things for which He could commend the six other congregations. It would be good for every preacher and congregation to take a mental trip back to those Asian congregations and hear and do today those things that Christ commended, and at the same time discourage and eschew the things that Christ condemned and hated.

This means we would have to go back beyond the rise of the Greek and Roman ecclesiastical hierarchies in the Third Century, the rise of Mohammedanism in the Seventh Century, the Protestant reformation of the Sixteenth Century and the contradicting doctrines of The Nineteen Century Cults, and anchor our spiritual minds on the rock of what Christ said a congregation should do to honor Him, and considered with horror and fear at what happens when we dishonor Him by turning to doctrines of Nicolaitanes, Jezebel, Judaism and worldly philosophies.

I know that Christ allowed every one of those congregations to be destroyed with the bloody sword of Mohammedanism, and their former meeting places have been reduced to ruin and rubble, but I desire to bring back what those New Covenant congregations could have been, TODAY, if only they had heeded and obeyed King Jesus.

I challenge the Evangelists and Pastors of every congregation of Christ in the world today to sincerely and prayerfully examine each and every commandment given by the Lord to His Body, the assembly of The Seven Congregation and call their Brethren to prayer and holy fasting before the Risen Lord.

Further, let these servant leaders examine in detail (with a thorough background and history of the evil and evil doers) the damnable doctrines Christ warned would cause those seven congregations to wind up in total darkness. May our "churches" today, sincerely grasp the tragic truth of how such evil doctrines put down the roots for noxious weeds. Snuffing out the Apostolic Truths of the 1st Century, the poison spread into the 2nd Century and by the 7th Century there was hardly a trace of New Testament Christianity left in what was once a cradle of New Covenant Christianity. The false doctrines that poisoned those congregations, still poisons all who come under their influence

.

When I lecture on the subject I simply make a simple Debit-Credit balance sheet. To the left I put what Christ condemned. To the right I put what He commended and his commanded solution to the matter.

EXAMPLE

DEBUT	CREDIT
Damnable teachings of Jezebel	Do not permit her to teach, warn her disciples of Her Hellfire

In our DEBUT column, we place the rudimentary false doctrines that the Risen Christ taught would corrupted Primitive Christianity. These doctrines are actually given to us in abbreviates form. For instance, the doctrine of Nicolaitanes is the underlying basis for the whole Greek-Roman ecclesiastical, hierarchal system of governing the Lord's people by a pyramid political system based on the model of the Roman Empire.

Yes, in each generation there will be worldly admiration for the worldly conquests of such worldly religious government, but in our CREDIT column we are duty-bound to put "Christ the Head of All Things", and the once and final answer to the reason for His Body on earth, along with the purpose, existence and destiny of the human race.

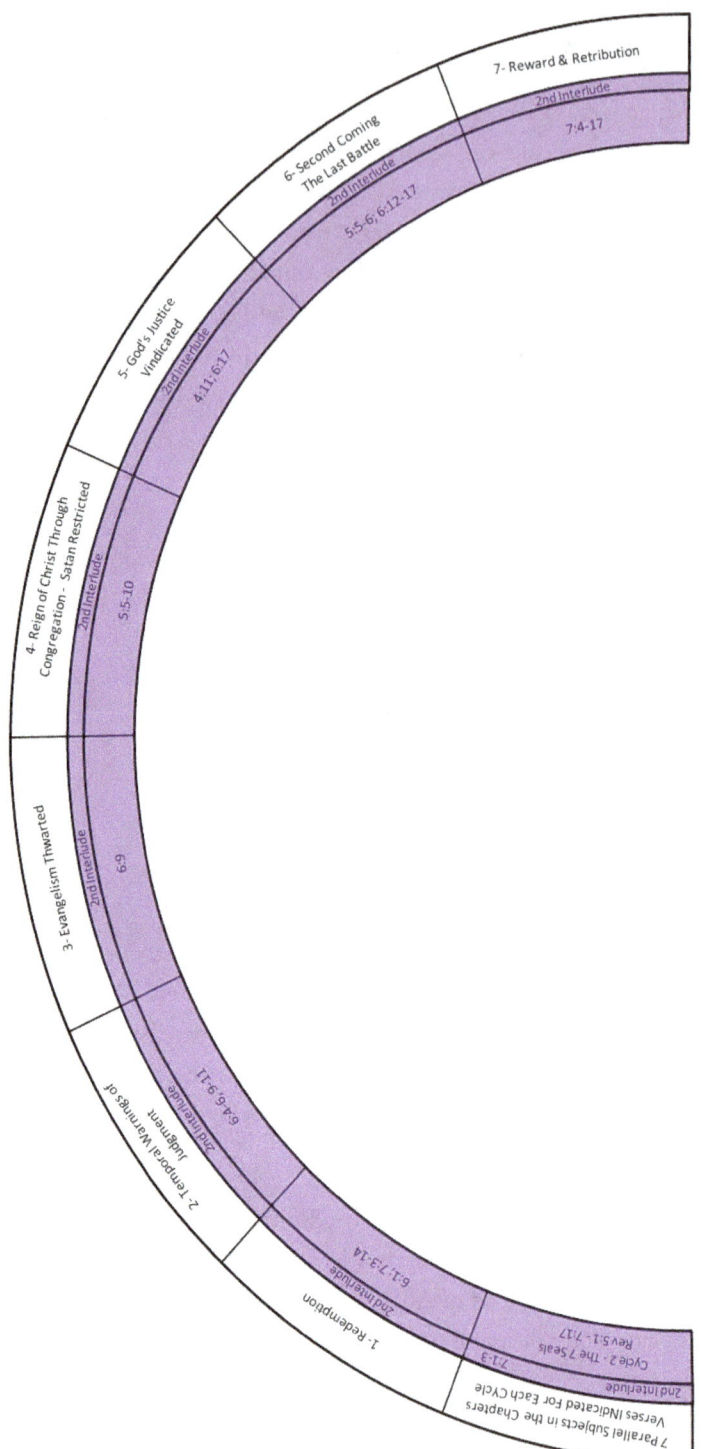

CYCLE 2 – THE SEVEN SEALS

Christ in the Cosmos

The following passages of Scripture depict the second cycle of Revelation. Within these seven seals, we shall notice parallel passages of Scripture as in the first cycle. Understand that after the interlude, the events start again. We need to understand that in teaching cycles, each cycle does not repeat verbatim what is in the other cycles. At times the aspect changes, the events change, and the severity of the events change. Within these changes are the unchanging parallel events that continue to happen throughout time. Notice the severity of the seals and their judgment upon the Earth compared to the unbearable severity of the bowls in Chapters 16 and 17.

Revelation Chapter Five

The Scroll and the Lamb

Revelation 5:1: Then I saw in the right hand of him who sat on the throne a scroll with writing on both sides and sealed with seven seals.

Let us go to the Book of Daniel to obtain a complete understanding of this verse. God the Father is sitting on the Throne (Da 7:9, 10), with one before His Throne (Da 7:13, 14). The Bible mentions different thrones and kingdoms. The Throne of the Ancient of Days (Da 7:13) is a prophetic parallel to this vision. Daniel 7:13 is a prophetic vision of the "Son of Man" (Lamb of God), who by virtue of His merited righteousness takes the Book of Universal Judgment, "the Book," from the hand of The Holy God the Father. The Throne of God the Father is central to these visions, but the contemplative counsel of the Most High God the Father requires and desires the coregent reign of God the Son on behalf of the doomed human race.

Daniel deals with "Beastology" (Nations). In Daniel's interpretation of visions, he is historical and deals with four different nations:

1. Lion is Babylon
2. Bear is Persia

3. Leopard is Greece

4. Horrible monster (dinosaur) is Rome.

These interpretations are not arbitrary conclusions, but absolute historical facts (Da 8:20-22). It is important that Daniel's prophecies involve a continuous, unbroken line of historical kingdoms without a parenthetical break as the Pre-Millennialists claim.

Daniel mentions "thrones" in the plural (Da 7:9). These thrones are in contrast to the dominion of the horn of pagan Rome and her offspring (7:8). There is a drastic difference and a stark contrast between legitimate divine thrones and the usurping dominion of the horns. Christ is King over all kingdoms, secular or religious, as the case may be.

"But the judgment shall sit" (Da 7:26) is an expression used in Daniel to show that the Christ of the Godhead, even in the Old Testament, is above all things and in control of all things. This Daniel verse reinforces the prevailing absolute truth of the Apocalyptic, Spiritual Reign of Christ, and His parliament (Rev 4:4, 5:6, 7, 11:16, 20:3, 4). There is only one true Throne where the Ancient of Days has taken His seat (God the Father & God the Son). The picture of the Godhead being on the Throne means His reign is everlasting. All other thrones upon the Earth are stationary and limited, whereas God's dominion knows no bounds. The wheels on His Throne mean He is omnipresent. God can be anywhere He wants to be at any point in time (Da 7:9).

The thousands (of) thousands mentioned in Da 7:10 really mean 10,000's of 10,000's. This verse signifies that judgment is getting ready to happen. Judgment is always ready to take place, from the Pharaoh, Caesar, Napoleon, Mohammad, Hitler, Stalin, or any other human being playing the fool. They can fall at any time.

The horn of Daniel is pagan Rome who took away the previous animal's dominion. Daniel was fascinated with the fourth beast, which lasted approximately 1,247 years (approximately 771 B.C. (www.wikipedia: The Founding of Rome) to 476 A.D. (www.wikipedia: Ancient Rome). An interesting side note is that the City of Roman was founded by Romulus (746 B.C.) and ended with Romulus Augustulus (who died after 476 A.D.). The name, Romulus, in Latin has a gematria of 666. The important Roman theologian of the 3rd Century, Hippolytus

(200 A.D.) read Daniel and mused, "Thou Art Right Daniel, The Iron Kingdom Reigns."[65] The Ancient of Days is God the Father (Rev 5:1); the Son of Man is Jesus Christ, "The Lamb," standing before His Throne (Rev 5:6, 7). In these prophetic visions, there is always a place beside God's Throne (Ps 2:1-7, 110:1, 2, and 4). The hidden man of infinity (Da 7:13) is always next to God's Throne, and He (Jesus) always looked like a man. Daniel predicted His ascension. To Him was given dominion, glory, and a Kingdom so that all the peoples, nations, and languages should serve him. The picture in Revelation 5:1 shows that the Godhead is in complete control! (See Eze 1:25-ff with 8:2, and 9:1, 2).

The differences between Daniel's and John's writings encompass chronology and aspect. There is no chronology in Revelation, Chapter 5, whereas Daniel is writing a historical narrative. We also must understand that Daniel is writing in aspect of prophecy (type), and John is writing in fulfillment (anti-type). Up to the 4th kingdom, there was a chronological parade of national "beasts." After Rome, the one beast, (little horn of Daniel and whore of Babylon) exists until the end of time.

Revelation 5:2: And I saw a mighty angel proclaiming in a loud voice, "Who is worthy to break the seals and open the scroll?"

This is the Lamb's "Book of Life," and it determines whether we are saved or lost. This book contains privileged information! Who is worthy enough to open it? The scroll can be defined as God's full contemplative counsel regarding Christ as the anointed, worthy King and His Kingdom in eternity, past, present, and future. This scroll affects the destiny of all creatures in Heaven, on the Earth, and under the Earth, as well as all nations through time and after time.

Revelation 5:3: But no one in heaven or on earth or under the earth could open the scroll or even look inside it.

At times, Revelation gives us a view of things that have already happened, but presents them as though they have not happened yet. At the time of John's writing, the sensational events affecting the Earth and all of its inhabitants, past, present, and future, were given as having already taken place. John is telling the story from a past perspective while looking into the future. These departed spirits in Heaven (dead) and those on the Earth (alive) could not open the scroll or look upon it.

Revelation 5:4: I wept and wept because no one was found who was worthy to open the scroll or look inside.

John wept. He was very disappointed because there was no one worthy to open, look into, and even attempt to read the Book. The angels cannot open the Book because they did not sacrifice for the world; they did not take on a physical body. No created being could ever be a perfect blood atonement worthy of opening this scroll for no created beings ever attempted to make themselves worthy to do so.

THE BOOK OF THE SEVEN SEALS CONTAINS SEVEN OF THE MOST POWERFUL COSMIC, WORLD INFLUENCING DYNAMICS EVER KNOWN THROUGHOUT TIME, SPACE, AND ETERNITY.

We can read the above text in advance and focus upon the following seven themes of the Book that only Christ can disclose. While these visions are invisible and imperceptible in time and run throughout The Old (as seen by Zachariah) and, now, New Testament chronology, we, through Christ, are given the vision of the invisible which causes the eyes of our perceptive minds to see the vision fulfilled in history in a noticeable way (Heb 11:27). The seven themes issue forth, and the Earth and the nations feel their impact but do not perceive how these intrusions into the world of natural affairs should lead them to God.

1) The conquest of the White Horse (The pure Gospel of Christ – 6:2, 3). The spirit-filled teacher and evangelist of The New Covenant Word go into the world unnoticeably. Yet, the Gospel affects much of humanity, angels, demons, and nations.

For instance, because of our Bible Science Association with Christian Kingdom College, in 1990-91 A.D., Allen Borden with Abilene Christian University invited us to lecture in Universities on Bible-Science in Moscow and St. Petersburg, Russia. We also spoke at the Universities of Kharkov and Kiev, in Ukraine.

Before we traveled to Russia, we wrote a four-page letter to Premier Gorbachev explaining the reason we were coming to Russia. We explained our position as citizens of Christ's eternal Kingdom of Heaven. We stated that we bring to any nation the spirit of freedom and loyalty to God and Country and that we supported Gorbachev fully in his perestroika reforms.

While preparing to board the train in Moscow, we encountered armed opposition from the Russian Mafia, but by the grace of God, they retreated. We cannot take valuable space here to explain how my son, John Doughty, faced down armed Mafia thugs who tried to rob us. John pointed his camera at them and told them that photos and print are mightier than the sword. The thugs backed off.

Later, while riding the train, the conductor told me to come to the front of the engine room. The engine room was a long way from where I was sitting so I picked my way from passenger car to passenger car. I was nearly frostbitten by the time I arrived because the space between the cars was not enclosed. Upon my arrival at the engine room, the engineer said, "We expect a bribe for your transportation." I told him I work for the Lord, and the Lord's people gave me enough funds to make this trip, along with several others on this mission. I added, "I cannot give you God's money!"

He replied, "If you do not cough up some money, we will put you off the train, next stop!" I told him, "If you do that I will bow down right here and now, and tell God on you!" A strange look came over this big man's face. All he said was "Get back to your state room and do not show your face in the aisle way until we arrive at our destination."

Why does the author write these things? It is to reveal that no one on Earth can stop the momentum of The White Horse. John immersed our travel agent, Svetlana Nikitina. A few years later, he married her. Today they have nine children, all of whom are Gospel testimonies. He then immersed Victor and Irene Nikitina. Victor was a MIG Pilot in the Russian Air Force. He knew of the persecution, torture and execution of some of the hundreds of thousands of Christians who were murdered because of their Faith. At one of our Mission Rallies, He wept softly when he recalled how he condoned the horrible slaughter of those who are now his Christian brothers and sisters.

We immersed two KGB agents, one of whom had come to our hotel room to enlist us in The Black Market agenda. I pulled out a chart on evangelism, hung it on the wall and taught him The Gospel for roughly four hours. I immersed him the next morning in a swimming pool along with several others, and he became a leader in the newly planted congregation in his town. The next year we received news that he was their song leader.

Again, space prevents my recording the many events that occurred in two years of Russian Evangelism. We planted five congregations and saw the mighty impact that the Gospel made on Russia. The whole story of evangelism to Russia is not just about our mission. Many other evangelists can be included in the incredible panorama of events that took place in Sochi, Russia, where the 2014 Winter Olympics took place.

The Russian citizens and the Vladimir Putin we saw on The Screen was not the haughty Khrushchev of 1958, or the cold, timid, frightened citizens we saw in 1991 A.D. Say what you want, and think what you want, but we experienced the difference The Gospel of Christ made to those whom Christ touched. For 70 years, the Communist Arm and Sickle tried to prevent the spread of the Gospel, but Gorbachev in effect said, "Let the White Horse Come!" He came! He saw! He conquered! No one can stop the spread of the Pure Gospel. For all the cold war rhetoric with Russia, one undeniable fact prevails – the Gospel of Jesus Christ is taught openly in Russia today. At the same time, we also spread the Gospel to Ukraine. As we write this commentary, we are mindful of the hundreds of souls converted to King Jesus in both countries. May the peace of the Prince of Peace work its way into the hearts of the leaders of both nations.

2) All world wars (The Red Horse) whether in Heaven, Earth, under the Earth, angelic or human are affected and impacted by the contents of the Book in the Hand of The Lamb (Rev 6:4).

3) In this Scroll, the Black Horse is the history of all famine, scarcity, hard times, and economic depression throughout the ages (6:6).

4) The Pale Horse depicts physical deaths, and the spirits of the deceased descending into Hades, resulting from certain catastrophic judgments sent upon a fourth of the Earth's population, at any given time in history. Although unknown to us, these earthly catastrophes are already recorded in The Book (6:7, 8). Presumably, we are given a universal obituary of only the deaths of lost souls whose destiny is the Hadean World.

5) The Book opens a scene under Heaven's altar and has a record of Christian Martyrs down through the ages. There are millions of them (6:9-11). Today Muslims and even some Hindus would drink the blood of someone who is called "Christian."

6) The Book (Sixth Seal) records the time of the end of this universe. The lost human race is completely "beside themselves" in fear, consternation, and horror at what they will all simultaneously encounter as they realize the Day of Reckoning has finally come. Having appraised their unavoidable clash with The God, "Whose Son they murdered," they prefer the worst of deaths rather than face God's judgment (6:12, 17).

7) The Book (silence in Heaven under the Seventh Seal) records an awestricken human race on the eve of eternal judgment. Silence fills the universal atmosphere, as every person must face the Holy God they only knew as perfect in love, mercy, long suffering, and kindness, but NOW, THE GOD requires ONLY total justice and retribution. Words fail to convey the horror of this moment. It is inexplicable! (Rev 8:1)

We read this section with sense-staggering reverence. We contemplate that in this Book, through the seven chapters of omniscient records of the destinies of angels, demons, humankind, and nations, is given a history of every conceivable force that can affect them, from the preaching of the New Covenant to the end when all shall stand before His Throne.

In between life's two extremes, from preaching the New Testament to the world-enthralling eternal judgment, are the seven-fold judgments that affect the wicked directly and the righteous indirectly. The first four judgments, i.e., the White Horse, the Red Horse, the Black Horse, and the Pale Horse, affect all humankind in every generation. The wicked do not have the mind to perceive these judgments, and as a result, are taken by surprise when they happen. The reason the wicked just do not get it is because the Apocalypse (Revelation) of these things is only unveiled to the regenerated, spirit-minded. Like Elijah (2Ki 6:17), we pray the Lord will open the eyes, and we will be given that MIND (1Co 2:16; Php 2:5-11).

The last three judgments are the unseen martyrs in Heaven, the apprehension and contemplation of the end of the universe, and the final Judgment Day; these are completely ignored by most people. Some people question why the sixth and seventh horses are both associated with final judgment. The answer to this question is found in common judicial procedures. There is as much fear of facing an austere judge before the sentencing as there is after the sentence is pronounced, and the death sentence is executed.

THIS SEVEN-FOLD SCROLL CONTAINS THE COMPLETE RECORDS AND TEMPORARY JUDGMENTS OF ALL CIVILIZATIONS UNDER HEAVEN.

This scroll in God's hand is like the scrolls used by the ancients for keeping records and communicating knowledge. We get our word "paper" from "papyri." The papyri plant yielded a thin bark-like substance that could be stretched and pressed into paper. For longer manuscripts, it was rolled up onto a smooth rod. If a scroll had more than one chapter, another rod was inserted to separate the chapters. The rods were called "captions," hence chapters. They were also called "seals." Consequently, the author or reader of the manuscript could scroll out (or roll out) the specific chapter he wanted without unrolling the whole scroll. This is the historical imagery behind the Seven-Sealed Scroll that Christ took from God the Father and, then, opened each seal, one-by-one. There is an old saying, "IT'S IN THE BOOK!" INDEED!

It is true, but hard to believe, that even our idle or profane words are recorded in this book (Mt 12:36). What was considered to be incredible with God 50 years ago now is as easy to comprehend as dialing up a person's cell phone in Outer Mongolia today. We are not surprised that God can have a record of every word that comes from our mouths. This fact alone should be enough to prevent us from cursing.

This difference between Christ and us is that while we may know the destination of our phone conversions, Christ knows the secrets of every heart (Jn 2:24; Mk 2:8, 7:23; Ro 2:16). Secrets that have been kept from friends, as intimate as those between husband and wife, will be shouted from the housetops of Judgment (Lk 12:3). None of us should want this to happen. Christ knows all about our iniquities should bring us to Him for salvation and cause us to turn to Him. It is not just what our sins did to Him; it is what our sins WILL DO TO US!

REVELATION 5:2, 3 MENTIONS ONE BOOK WHICH IS A SEVEN-FOLD-SCROLL, BUT DANIEL 7:10 MENTIONS 'BOOKS' IN THE PLURAL.

The eternal books mentioned in Daniel 7:10 are probably the same as those that will be opened in the End (Rev 20:12). There are at least the following three books: the Seven-Fold-Scroll, the Bible, and the Lamb's Book of Life. In this Revelation passage, "The books were opened. And then another Book was opened which is the Book of Life." Our minds are taxed here as we try to draw steadfast conclusions, but this passage suggests that the Seven-Fold-Scroll (record of all human thoughts and deeds, including those of the Old Testament (Mal 3:16)), will be used in the Last Judgment Day. Daniel mentions "Books" because he was writing in the dark, dismal age of the Old Testament when the histories of men and nations, demons, and angels were being chronicled. To humankind, God's predestined plan for the human race throughout the ages had not yet been revealed (Eph 3:9; Col 1:26). But now, "The Perfect Word has come" (1Co 13:10; Ro 16:25) and that which was known in part is now complete in ONE Book – The New Testament.

What about the Lamb's Book of Life? The Lamb's Book (Rev 21:27) stands between the other two books (The Bible consisting of an Old Testament, which condemns us, with the New Testament, which gives us hope, and the Book of Our Life and Our Deeds) for two very important reasons. First, because of the covering of the Lamb's Blood, the Lamb's Book cancels out the condemnation the human race deserves because the other two books pronounce them guilty, and therefore, condemned before Holy God. Secondly, because of the want of the Lamb's blood to cover sin, The Lamb's Book reinforces the validity of the judgment of those condemned. Because they are not redeemed by the Lamb's blood, their names are not recorded in this Book.

These books have confounded learned scholars down through the ages, and there are no hard and fast conclusions. Certainly, God wants us to examine the Truth of these books. The following paragraphs are my best, most prayerful, summary of an understanding of these books.

Book Number One is probably The Seven-Fold Scroll of Jesus, the Universal Judge of all humankind who lived in eternity before Adam to the end of time. Book Number One is a composite of the Old Testament history of all past universal affairs or the Book of Remembrance or Record of Deeds (Mal 3:16) and the disclosure of all things throughout all history. Even though Book Number One starts with the Gospel Horse, we remember that the Gospel judges all mankind, even Old Testament humanity (Ro 2:16). It would include all past, present, and future events and deeds of all who have ever lived. If Book Number One is the only book to be opened, "we are of all men most miserable" (1Co 15:19) and condemned.

Book Number Two might be The Bible (The Old and New Testament). If The Old Testament is the only book we face in judgment, then we all stand condemned. There is no hope. Remember the Old Testament condemns us. The New Testament saves us. The Bible records the comprehensive works from the "seed plot" in Genesis, and the development of early civilizations up until the Messiah's coming. The Bible may not be opened as much as it should be in today's world, but IT WILL BE OPENED IN JUDGMENT DAY FOR ALL HUMANITY TO SEE AND KNOW!

The most important Book of all is "The Lamb's Book of Life" which stands between the other two books. If our name is written there, the other two books have no law of condemnation that can incriminate us.

There is however, an inseparable connection between the New Testament and the Lamb's Book of Life. We mentioned the Bible as Book Number Two, but there are two parts of this Bible. If we have obeyed New Testament commandments and walk in New Testament congregational life, we are added to Christ's Assembly (Ac 2:42, 47). Granted, the word "added" has a meaning of Christ's adding a soul to His Kingdom (not joining a "church"[66]). The word "add" (prostithemi) means literally "to put to what already exists." When truly immersed, one is "put to" the ledger of the names in The Book of Life. What a wonderful thought!

Jesus said, "My (New Testament) words will judge you in the last day" (Jn 12:48). Thus, the New Testament is a double-edged sword. It can cut one way unto life (Ac 2:36) or cut another way to death (Pr 18:21; Ac 5:33). Since the New Testament Book is the Covenant of the Lamb's Blood, these two books cannot be separated because they embrace in essence, one in the same content.

Humanly speaking, we tread here very cautiously on the thin ice of understanding God's divine revelation in regard to the "three books." We mentioned the whole Bible (both Old and New Testaments) as the Second Book, and then we compared the New Testament of our Lord Jesus Christ as part and parcel of the Third Book (The Lamb's Book of Life). We confess that while we may fall short of understanding the three (or more) books, our consolation is that we do know the author of the Lamb's Book of Life. We can be sure this will be made known in that Great Judgment Day.

Revelation 5: 5, 6: Then one of the elders said to me, "Do not weep! See, the Lion of the tribe of Judah, the Root of David, has triumphed. He is able to open the scroll and its seven seals." Then I saw a Lamb, looking as if it had been slain, standing in the center of the throne, encircled by the four living creatures and the elders. He had seven horns and seven eyes, which are the seven Spirits of God sent out into all the earth.

An elder speaks, not an angel. An elder has authority and could identify more clearly with John. He could do this because he had lived on Earth and knew what John was going through. He gave him comfort, for the Lion, the Root of David, who is Jesus Christ, has overcome to open the Book and its seven seals. It is interesting that John was told to look for a lion and yet he saw a lamb! Lions have no regard towards their prey whether it is a child or man. It has no regard for justice or judgment. If we know Christ as a Lamb, He will never be known as a Lion! This recognition depends upon our personal relationship with Jesus. This Book gives the portrayal of the Christ being the Lamb of God. Those who read the Old Testament prophets looked for a coming Messiah to rule with power and force on Earth. However, the Messiah is reigning presently before the Throne of God in the manner of a sacrificial lamb to prevent eternal judgment and wrath to those on Earth, which is an insult to power-hungry religious glory-seekers. These pompous, vain earthly rulers parallel the power-hungry rulers who also have come and gone, and have killed followers of The Lamb, but the Lamb still reigns.

IT IS OF THE UTMOST SIGNIFICANCE THAT WE SEE THE REMARKABLE COMPARISON BETWEEN DANIEL 7:13 IN PROPHECY AND REVELATION 5: 7, 8 IN FULFILLMENT.

Daniel predicted that in the days of the Fourth Kingdom (Rome), Heaven would celebrate the coronation of the King of Kings, "The King of Heaven and Earth." The Jews did not conceive of a "Father in Heaven" since they were not cognizant of the fact that He had a Son. This God whom we know as "Father" was called the "Ancient of days" (Da 7:13). Even though we are perfectly positive that "The ONE like the Son of Man" was "The Son of God," such a revelation had not yet been given to the Old Testament saints. In my book, *Crucified in Sodom*, we analyze those Old Testament verses that reveal the pre-incarnation presence of Christ in Creation, and His appearing to Abraham, Moses (on many occasions), Jacob (who wrestled with Him), David, Daniel (even His contemporary, Nebuchadnezzar), and several of the Prophets.

Daniel foresaw the sensational event of Christ's ascending triumphantly into the heavens. He foresaw Him as "The Lamb having been slain" in prophecy, coming before the Father, "The Ancient of Days," to receive this eternal Kingdom. This breathtaking, heavenly hallelujah celebration of Christ's coronation was fulfilled in Revelation 5: 6, 7. To be sure, Christ was always, eternally past King of Heaven, but now that He has overcome the world of men and nations, He has merited the right to be King of Heaven and Earth. Thus, in the expression, "The lamb having been slain," Christ shed His blood and gave His perfect life as proof that He earned the right to reign over and judge all humankind, all who had ever lived on Earth. An awesome God, crowned with the same glory as "The Ancient of Days," Christ could have been content to sit on the Throne of Heavenly Regency and leave it at that. But in His great love, He chose to reign over the vast numbers of lost, hopeless human beings. That love would cost Him what God required of animal sacrifices in the Old Testament. He could not be the King from God, unless He was "The Lamb of God" for man. We marvel at the significance of this title, "Lamb, having been slain."

It is also very interesting that this extremely, remarkable appearance of Christ before the Throne of God, the Father, (to receive Heaven's Mandate to rule) finds its way into Christ's teachings in Luke 19:11, 12. There is no doubt the wealthy, noble man, "child of the king," who ascended into Heaven to receive a Kingdom is Jesus Christ. He ascended to "receive" the Kingdom and then "return" (vs.12). He was "made King" and then "returned" (vs. 15). Now this is so logical that a third grader can figure it out, yet the Pre-Millennial scholar "just does not get it." His reign here is the same reign of Acts 2:30 and Revelation 20:2-5.

Upon His ascension, Christ received a Kingdom from the Father, "Ancient of Days," and when He returns to this world, it will not be to receive another kingdom, but to demand an accounting from those who should have accepted His Kingdom and brought forth the stewardship of talents in seeking this Kingdom above all. They may love the Lord, but I simply cannot find justification or sympathy for Bible scholars who think that Christ is going to return to set up an earthly Kingdom. As we have said repeatedly, the reign of The Messiah in Revelation 20 cannot contradict the reign of Christ in Daniel 7 or Acts 2.

When we are asked, "What drives you to be so involved in evangelism in order to seek lost souls, to set local congregations in order, to call the nation of America to fall before the Christ of Heaven, and to repent and turn from their wicked ways," we can only give the answer from Luke 19:11-27. Verse 27 states, "As for these enemies of mine who did not want me to reign over them, bring them before me and execute them." Some translations imply that Christ was affirming, "I DO NOT WANT TO SEE THEM AGAIN!" Yes, Jesus said, "Kill them!" Some translators say, "Slaughter them."

We remember that it was the Roman General Titus who slaughtered these Jews. This deadbeat nation was behind on rent; they did not give a percentage of the enormous profits; and they refused to give God credit for anything. They stole from God, took His multiplied blessings, and refused to render any stewardship. They did not just sin against God seventy-times seven, but from Daniels prophecy of 70 weeks, they sinned against God 490 years. Why would I want to render the best of my service and life to my King? If I responded in this fashion to my loving Savior (as did His people prior to 70 A.D.), eternal vengeance in Hell is too good for me. I know there is an eternal Hell. I do not want to go there!

In Europe, there once existed in history a legal codex called "The Divine Rights of Kings." What we see here by comparing Daniel 7:12, 13 with Luke 19:11-13 and Revelation 5:6-8 is "THE DIVINE RIGHT OF THE KING!"

The purpose of Jesus' going to the Father in Daniel 7:14 is to receive His Kingdom. The prophet John, by inspired revelation, gave insight to the fulfillment of Daniel's prophecy in 49 verses from Revelation 5:1 to Revelation 8:1, including an interlude in Chapter 7. The prophet John gave prophetic fulfillment of what Daniel said in such amazing detail that we suppose that Daniel himself would have been astonished at the magnitude and enormity of the prophetic fulfillment (1Pe 1:10; 2Pe 3:2). In this specific instance, the purpose in Revelation was for Him to receive the Book of Eternal Destines from beginning to end. Daniel was not given the revelation of Christ receiving this Book of Seven-Fold Seals (judgments) in Revelation 5:1, 9, 6:1, 8:1, but, he simply says, in effect, that the Son of Man came before the Ancient of Days and to Him was given dominion and glory and an everlasting Kingdom (Da 7:13, 14). The reason Daniel could not be fully informed was because the Kingdom of Christ had not yet been established on Earth. Daniel knew that

God had a book (Da 12:1), he but was not aware that the Lamb of God had a Book of Life. All the names of the faithful down through the ages are now written in another book called "The Lambs Book" (Rev 20:15).

FUTURE-PASSIVE OMNISCIENCE OF GOD

Christians have difficulty understanding the Apostle John's writing style. Yet, we use such future-passive tense every day, such as, "I will be paid next week." We need to know John is writing from what is known as the *future-passive omniscience of God*. In exegeting the theological implications concerning Christ's visions, we will examine this writing style in the light of Scripture.

Jesus began his ministry with *vision statements* concerning the Kingdom of Heaven. He said, "The Kingdom of heaven is at hand" (Mt 4:17); "Theirs is the Kingdom of Heaven" (5:3, 5, 10); "The least in the Kingdom of Heaven" (5:19); "Enter the Kingdom of Heaven" (5:20); and "The Kingdom of Heaven is like" (Seven times in Mt 13:24, 31, 33, 44, 45, 47, 52). The Kingdom of Heaven is mentioned more than 30 times in Matthew alone. The reason why Matthew uses "Kingdom of Heaven" rather than "Kingdom of God" is that his primary goal was to reach the Jews who thought Jesus would establish an earthly kingdom.

The Kingdom of God and the Kingdom of Heaven are the same. The Kingdom is also called the Kingdom of Christ. He alone gives the "keys to the Kingdom" (Mt 16:19). Only fools could miss the Kingdom of Christ as taught in Luke 23:32, John 18:36, Ephesians 5:5, Colossians 1:13, and Hebrews 1:8. The Kingdom of God and the Kingdom of Heaven are used interchangeably in Matthew 4:17, 12:28, 19:23, 24, 21:43 and 22:2. Nothing is more indicative of the sameness of The Kingdom of God and the Kingdom of Heaven than the fact that the "Mysteries of the Kingdom of Heaven" in Matthew 13:11 are called the "Mysteries of the Kingdom of God" in Luke 8:10.

One of the most fascinating expressions Jesus ever uttered is found in Matthew 16:19:

> "And I will give you the keys of the kingdom of heaven, and whatever you bind on earth will be bound in heaven, and whatever you loose on earth will be loosed in heaven."

The Greek translation is, "Whatever you loose on earth shall already have been loosed in heaven." This is called the "*future passive tense.*" The only other time this particular Greek future-passive construction is found is in Matthew 18:18:

> "Assuredly, I say to you, whatever you bind on earth will be bound in heaven, and whatever you loose on earth will be loosed in heaven."

The Congregation of Christ is connected with this future-passive expression in both instances. The word "bound" means to "incarcerate" for punishment. This is from "deo," which means "to tie up, wind, or secure with bonds." The word "loose" (luo) means to "break up, destroy, dissolve, unloose, melt, or put off."[67] When these words are taken together, they mean to release from punishment or destroy whatever it is that binds us.

Apocalyptic Future-Passive

The apocalyptic picture that John portrays here is Christ being recognized before the Heavenly Throne. This picture shows His right to be at the right hand of God the Father. The interesting aspect of this Scripture passage is that Christ has always been on His Throne. He is the Prince of Heaven, King of Angels, and the Word of God. However, from earth's viewpoint, He was not recognized until He came to Earth and triumphed over Satan, sin, death, and the grave. When we move from the historical Gospel that announced His victory over the world (for all authority was given Him in Heaven and Earth – Mt 28:18-20), we enter with Christ into His Apocalyptic Kingdom, through the new birth (Jn 3:5). Then, we join with the heavenly Cherubim, Seraphim, millions-upon-millions of angels and the Godhead in praise, adoration, and recognition of the Lamb of God before the Throne. In addition, we will join the 24 Elders who represent the Congregation of Christ on Earth.

Thus, the Elders and those who have lived in time will be celebrating what was designed in God's eternally predestined Council of Heaven. What the ancestors of all nations thought God may have worked out in their lifetime, and what modern Christians think He is working out in this lifetime, has in reality, already been worked out or completed in the contemplative Council of Eternity, past and future. Because of this, Christ's receiving of the Book of the Seven-Fold Seals from the Hand of the Father is one of the most dramatic and enlightening scenes of the Apocalypse (Da 7:14, 15; Rev 5:7). There are several explanations concerning what was written in that Book of the Seven-Fold Seals, but since all nations and all celestial human beings are called upon to celebrate the Lamb's loosing of the seals of that Book, it obviously contained the eternal destinies of all men and nations of all time.

Since Christ's will has "been done on earth as it is in heaven" (Mt 6:10), and since the Kingdom of Heaven (Congregation of Christ) has been established on Earth though the apostolic teachings and writings, (1Co 3:10; Eph 3:10; Col 1:6, 2:10; Php 2:10; Rev 21:14), we are left dumbfounded with astonishment that God's absolute standard from eternity past has already been established. Granted, the multitudes have not attained this standard, and since it is invisible, it works like a heartbeat, but when we press our hand to our thoracic cavity, we can feel it. Truth is like flowing water that encountered resistance in the past, but it still flowed faithful, and it will find its way out in succeeding generations. Therefore, when we read the Old Testament, should we be surprised? Psalm 119:160 says, "Thy word is true from the beginning."

Other Old Testament Scripture passages prove this point. The Book of Isaiah is filled with the following verses about God's eternity past point of view.

> "Have ye not known? Have ye not heard? Hath it not been told you from the beginning? Have ye not understood from the foundations of the earth?" (Isa 40: 21)

> "Who hath wrought and done it, calling the generations from the beginning? I the Lord, the first, and with the last; I am he" (Isa 41: 4).

> "Who hath declared from the beginning, that we may know? And before time, that we may say, He is righteous? Yea, there is none that showeth, yea, there is none that declareth, yea, there is none that heareth your words" (Isa 41: 26).

> "Declaring the end from the beginning, and from ancient times the things that are not yet done, saying, My counsel shall stand, and I will do all my pleasure" (Isa 46: 10).

> "I have declared the former things from the beginning; and they went forth out of my mouth, and I showed them; I did them suddenly, and they came to pass" (Isa 48: 3).

> "I have even from the beginning declared it to thee; before it came to pass I shewed it thee" (Isa 48: 5).

And Ecclesiastes 3:11 says,

> "He has made everything beautiful in its time. Also He has put eternity in their hearts, except that no one can find out the work that God does from beginning to end."

Time-shackled human beings start from the beginning and work toward the end. As Christians become more mature, they increasingly are able to work from the end back toward the beginning. Most Christians are not strangers to persecution but are strangers to God's means of vindicating the truth for which we suffer. This is because God's means of vindication is invisibly built into the process of suffering for righteousness sake. Even when Christians are delivered, they often fail to allow God to take the logical steps He must take in retribution. Man cannot interfere with divine retribution. For example, God opened the earth, and it swallowed up Israel's worst enemies, rebellious anarchists of their own community. Then fire descended from Heaven and consumed 250 blaspheming, sacrilegious enemies (Nu 16:31-35). The nation of Israel and friends of Moses were actually more frightened at what God may do to defend and aid them than they were of being slaughtered by their enemies (Nu 16:41-47).

We pray for our deliverance, the deliverance of our families, friends, our nation, and our civil institutions from the incursion and infiltration of demonic influences, but sometimes we do not agree with God's methods of deliverance. This is a real problem because it puts us in the same class as the most implacable of God's enemies. The problem we face in this scenario is especially exacerbated by our ignorance of God's character of absolute holiness and justice.

The *Book* that Christ is worthy to receive should bring us comfort and assurance. He has received this Book that represents everything Christians are taught to know about God's providence. Nothing can be more descriptive of God's *predestined–future–passive* omniscience and counsel than this scene in Revelation, Chapter 5.

Revelation 5: 7, 8: He came and took the scroll from the right hand of him who sat on the throne. And when he had taken it, the four living creatures and the twenty-four elders fell down before the Lamb. Each one had a harp and they were holding golden bowls full of incense, which are the prayers of the saints.

The incense going up to God from the golden bowls is the saints' (Christians') prayers. The seven days of prayer before Pentecost (Mk 16:19) correspond to the coronation event in Heaven (Rev 5:7, 8). When Christ was instructing the disciples, He was acting as a *prophet*, but now He is also speaking through the Word to His followers as a *king*. He was recognized as King when He ascended (Mk 16:19; Eph 4:8; Ac 1:6-8, 2: 22, 23, 36). Quite possibly, after Christ's ascension, the events of Revelation, Chapter 5, were in concurrence with the seven-day period of Pentecost on Earth (Ac 1:12-14, 2:1).

Christ is now in Heaven, and He takes the scroll for He is worthy. He is worthy to take this Book because He must be recognized first as King in Heaven, then on Earth. Now He can reign with His saints (Ac 2:47; 2Ti 2:12). Many people do not teach that Jesus is King today because they cannot witness or testify to Christ's kingship without the Holy Spirit (Ac 1:8).

A king becomes entitled to a kingdom through one or more of the following four methods:

A. Inheritance – Jesus is the prince, the son of a king (Isa 9:6ff).

B. Mandated – God, the Father gave Jesus all authority and power (Mt 28:18-20).

C. Unanimous/Universal Acclaim – Jesus received God's approval to receive this position because Christ proved Himself in life, death, resurrection, and ascension (Ac 2:22-24).

D. Force – Jesus has taken His kingdom from Satan and triumphed over death (Heb 2:8-15).

Christ became King because He proved Himself worthy of this kingship in the eyes of God. Christ's coronation as King of Heaven and Earth was a main reason why He came into this world (Jn 18:37).

Revelation 5: 9, 10: And they sang a new song: "You are worthy to take the scroll and to open its seals, because you were slain, and with your blood you purchased men for God from every tribe and language and people and nation. You have made them to be a kingdom and priests to serve our God, and they will reign on the earth."

This is the National Anthem or Enthronement Ceremony. It is a song of conversion and deliverance. This is a complete spiritual reign:

    A.   Reigning with the prayers of the saints being offered first, seven days before the Day of Pentecost (Rev 8: 3).

    B.   Reigning with a new song (which is the Gospel) (Rev 14: 3).

    C.   Reigning through the praise of the saints (Rev 8: 4).

Revelation 5:11: Then I looked and heard the voice of many angels, numbering thousands upon thousands, and ten thousand times ten thousand. They encircled the throne and the living creatures and the elders.

We can express this verse numerically as follows: 10,000 x 10,000, 1,000 upon 1,000s of Angels. Have ever such a vast number of personalities been together in history?

Revelation 5:12: In a loud voice they sang: "Worthy is the Lamb, who was slain, to receive power and wealth and wisdom and strength and honor and glory and praise!"

In numerology, seven would represent Heaven's perfection. There are seven ways Jesus is worthy. The angels sang this Song twice, once for Heaven, and once for Earth. Whatsoever He loosed and bound in Heaven, He loosed and bound on Earth.

1. Worthy of Power – 1Co 1:24

2. Worthy of Riches – 2Co 8:9; Da 7:13

3. Worthy of Wisdom – 1Co 1:24

4. Worthy of Strength – Lk 11:21, 22

5. Worthy of Honor and Power – 1Ti 6:16

6. Worthy of Glory – Eph 1:16

7. Worthy of Praise (Blessing) – Ro 15:29

Revelation 5:13, 14: Then I heard every creature in heaven and on earth and under the earth and on the sea, and all that is in them, singing: "To him who sits on the throne and to the Lamb be praise and honor and glory and power, forever and ever!" The four living creatures said, "Amen," and the elders fell down and worshiped.

The four blessings to God represent all the Earth giving Him praise. Remember, in numerology four is the number of Earth. Thus, the four blessings are: 1) praise, 2) honor, 3) glory, and 4) power.

Revelation Chapter Six

Revelation 6:1, 2: I watched as the Lamb opened the first of the seven seals. Then I heard one of the four living creatures say in a voice like thunder, "Come!" I looked, and there before me was a white horse! Its rider held a bow, and he was given a crown, and he rode out as a conqueror bent on conquest.

We are introduced to apocalyptic horses in Zechariah 1:8-11, 6:1-9. In Zechariah, the Red Horse comes first. The Red Horse is War; this represents the absence of the Gospel in the Old Testament. In the New Testament Revelation, the White Horse is mentioned first because God will have His wrath satisfied by the Gospel of Redemption before the final day of wrath arrives. Many commentators believe the rider on the white horse is Jesus, but other reliable commentators believe this horse is evangelism. We can see Christ reigning through the White Horse. What a disservice to Jesus to *NOT* spread the Gospel (Ps 110:1-2; Eph 1:21-23; Heb 1:3; 2:8, 9; Lk 19:12; Da 7:9-14). Christ has authority, and He is preaching, judging, rewarding, and condemning the world through preaching (Jn 12:48; Zec 1:8, 6:3; Ps 45:14).

Riding a White Horse represents authority, power, and righteousness. In Revelation 19:12, Christ rides a White Horse but the spirit of the sword is proceeding from His mouth. However, in Revelation 6:2, the rider has a conquering bow. This verse also says the Gospel rider "was given a crown." This crown is not of inherent royalty; it is bestowed upon the one who wears it. The Gospel rider on the White Horse is victorious, but most likely not Christ because of his *"stephanos"* crown. This is an earned crown of victory. This crown was not bequeathed by royalty but was awarded to a victor in an Olympic contest. This identifies with the saints casting their crowns before the Christ who earned their victory (Rev 4:10). On the other hand, in Revelation 19:12, Christ wears multiple "*diadem*" crowns of royalty. How could Christ go forth to conquer if He has already conquered death, hell, sin, Satan and the grave? Because these tasks have been delegated to His followers, Christ does not wear a stephanos crown, but His followers do.

The rider on the White Horse has the ability to conquer. Paul says that Christians are conquers (Ro 8:27, 12:21), and John says that Christians are overcomers (Rev 2:7). The congregations at Smyrna (2:11), Pergamum (2:17), Thyatira (2:26), Sardis (3:5), Philadelphia (3:12), and Laodicea (3:21); all have overcomers. The White Horse and its rider are victorious, conquering, and overcoming because of their direct relationship to the Gospel. This White Horse is conquering to conquer!

The White Horse is always used in the positive light. We can best understand the White Horse as a representative of the spreading of the Gospel of the Kingdom. Of the four horses, the White Horse is the only horse we recognize as being good. The other three horses stand for war, pestilence, and death.

FIRST SEAL (6:1-2)	FIRST TRUMPET (8:7)	FIRST BOWL (16:1-2)
The First Seal is the White Horse spreading the Gospel throughout the Earth. The Saints are praying. Because of the preaching of the Saints, God is judging the Earth with His Word.	The First Trumpet is a partial judgment – 1/3 of the Earth is affected. This includes the Earth, sea, and those that dwell on the Earth (people & animals).	The First Bowl is the Angel pouring the bowl out upon the Earth; this results in God's Judgment. Once again, because of the prayers of the Saints, God gives His Judgment with His warning! Now is the time for a complete judgment of God upon the Earth.

Our evangelistic life and service is governed from Heaven. If we constantly seek to be enabled by Christ and His Spirit, the opened seal of this book in Heaven means our lives (in the final analysis) are governed from Heaven whether we know it, or like it or not. We may ask the question, "Are these seals open to our hearts, minds, and imagination?"

The whole point of the seals is for Christians to make an appeal for the truth by the Holy Spirit and *not* by any other means. One question we might ask ourselves, "What is my attitude towards these cycles?" These cycles are meant for Christians to recognize Christ's Reign and God's Judgments. The soulish, carnal person can neither see nor understand the warnings and judgments of God. When Christians fail to understand this principle, the cycles of Revelation have no value. They will just be seen through the eyes of the soul rather than the eyes of the Spirit.

Revelation 6: 3-8: When the Lamb opened the second seal, I heard the second living creature say, "Come!" Then another horse came out, a fiery red one. Its rider was given power to take peace from the earth and to make men slay each other. To him was given a large sword. When the Lamb opened the third seal, I heard the third living creature say, "Come!" I looked, and there before me was a black horse! Its rider was holding a pair of scales in his hand. Then I heard what sounded like a voice among the four living creatures, saying, "A quart of wheat for a day's wages and wine!" When the Lamb opened the fourth seal, I heard the voice of the fourth living creature say, "Come!" I looked, and there before me was a pale horse! Its rider was named Death, and Hades was following close behind him. They were given power over a fourth of the earth to kill by sword, famine and plague, and by the wild beasts of the earth.

Remember, whether it be the Seals (and horsemen), the Trumpets or, as we shall see later, the Crucibles of Wrath, the first four seals, trumpets, and crucibles (bowls) have a more severe impact in ascending, progressive order, and the last three increase in their intensity of consequences upon the ungodly world. At this point, we shall again review the first Four Horsemen of the Apocalypse.

1. **THE WHITE HORSE** is purity and the spread of the Gospel. As previously stated, this White Horse is not Christ Himself; it represents the spread of Evangelism. The world will be judged through the preaching of the Gospel. The White Horse cannot be Christ because the Lamb is breaking the seals and calling for the White Horse to go out. We know the White Horse of Revelation 19:11-13 is the coming of Christ because the rider is called "The Word" of God. The Gospel sword has two edges, life and death.

BECAUSE THE GOSPEL SWORD BRINGS LIFE AND ANNOUNCES DEATH, IT IS GOOD FOR US TO REMEMBER THAT THOSE WHO BEAR THE MESSAGE ARE LIKE SOLDIERS OF CHRIST (2 Ti 2:3).

The "White Horse" symbolism would have been well understood by the people the Roman Empire. Since we are interpreting this White Horse as being the spread of the Gospel, and our King is releasing this horse for such active duty, it is indicative of such a good King to share the honor of His Kingdom with His subjects. There is no greater honor on Earth than to spread the Gospel of Jesus Christ to the world.

After winning a war, the Roman Emperor would call for a victory celebration day. A triumphal arch was built at the entrance of the city's main thoroughfare. The victorious army was paraded before the cheering crowds. There was a public recognition of the soldiers' battlefield valor and the spoils of war were divided among the soldiers.

At the rear of the parade, thousands of the enemy captives were paraded to the place of their execution. Mixed in with the captive solders were foreign citizens who were brought from the war zones to be exhibited as a sorry spectacle of defeat and a symbolic expression or tribute to the conquering emperor.

But the most significant feature that marked this memorable "victory march" occasion was the aroma of incense that filled the atmosphere. Thousands of incense poles line the streets, and the fragrance could be smelled from miles away. It is at here that the Apostle Paul stops and draws the analogy of the Gospel of life and death. It was the smell of life and victory to the conquerors, but the incense of death to the vanquished.

> "Now thanks be unto God, which always causes us to triumph in Christ, and makes manifest the savor of His knowledge by us in every place. For we are unto God a sweet savor of Christ in them that are saved, and in them that perish: to the one we are the savor of death, and to the other the savor of life, unto life. And who is sufficient for these things?" (2Co 2:14-16)

Paul concludes this historic illustration by drawing attention to the importance of keeping the Word of Christ pure and sincere, since it was the decisive factor in determining who would live forever, or die forever. This WORD is the sword of death, or scalpel of life.

Also of interest, at this point it was the custom for the emperor to ride on his White Horse. (https://books.google.com/books: *By the Emperor's Hand*. Most Americans do not like controversy and debate. They want everything to be nice, neat, and tidy. This is perfectly O.K. in terms of common blessings of life, but if we enter into the New Covenant and expect to please our "Emperor," we must "Fight the good fight of Faith" (1Ti 6:12).

While we "Rest in peace in Zion," the Hollywood hordes, the Union of Sodomite Socialist Republics in Washington, along with the bloody butchers wielding the sword of Allah, are surrounding our circled wagon train, just waiting for the chance to break through. We are being admonished to "let our guard down," and lay down our weapons of the Spirit, and the very minute we do so – WE ARE DEAD! Oh yes, the enemy has a right to live in our neighborhood; they have a right to work in our factories; they have just as much of a right to make a living in capitalistic America (if we dare mention the word capitalism) as we do, but if we compromise our Christ, compromise our Gospel, or compromise our Christian heritage, we then incur the wrath of The Lamb, and all of the wrath of the world cannot compare to The Wrath of The Lamb. It is just not worth it! How many concessions shall we make before we lay our heads on the guillotine block?

> 2. **THE RED HORSE** is war; the slaughter it causes, and the power to make it. People must live with war. The positive side of war is that more people attend the Congregation; more people pray; and some wicked people are destroyed and cannot continue their wicked ways.

SECOND SEAL (6:3)	SECOND TRUMPET (8:7)	SECOND BOWL (16:3)
The Second Seal is the Red Horse of war and the power to make war. Once again, judgment is upon the Earth. Because war is inevitable, the best we can do is to prepare for it.	The Second Trumpet is a partial judgment in which 1/3 of the creatures in the sea died and 1/3 of the ships were destroyed.	The Second Angel poured out the bowl of complete judgment in the sea and every (all) living creature died.

3. **THE BLACK HORSE** is famine and pestilence (bad economy). The balance represents the weighing out of merchandise. If we do remember God during times of plenty, maybe we will remember Him during times of depression and want. At this point, God's wrath is revealed from Heaven (Ro 1:18). The Bible says, "You did not serve the Lord your God with joy and a glad heart, for the abundance of all things" (Dt 28:47).

THIRD SEAL (6:5)	THIRD TRUMPET (8:10)	THIRD BOWL (16:4-7)
The Third Seal is the Black Horse of famine, pestilence, and bad economies. Depressions persist, and necessities are lacking. Even simple necessities, like bread, water, oil, and wine, are extremely expensive (Dt 28:48, 49), so expensive that purchase prices are inconceivable.	The Third Trumpet affects the water of the streams and drinking water. People are dying of contaminated water. Notice that 1/3 of the waters are contaminated.	The Third Angel has poured out his bowl upon the springs of water and has become blood. The Angel recognized God's right to judge the Earth because they killed His people. His judgments are just. Notice that ALL the rivers and springs flow with blood.

4. **THE PALE HORSE** is death, the funeral, and Hades. Its yellowish, black, and blue colors are those of a dead body. One fourth of the Earth is killed. Thus, a partial judgment is shown. As soon as the wicked die, they go to Hades.

FOURTH SEAL (6:7-8)	FOURTH TRUMPET (8:12)	FOURTH BOWL (16:8-9)
The Fourth Seal of the Pale Horse is 1/4 of the earth is killed. This is a partial judgment. The wicked die and await eternal hell in Hades.	The Fourth Trumpet has affected 1/3 of the constellations and the Sun, Moon, and stars.	The Fourth Bowl is poured out upon the constellations. The Sun is scorching the people with fire. This judgment affects all people. This fire will destroy the Earth.

Revelation 6:9: When he opened the fifth seal, I saw under the altar the souls of those who had been slain because of the word of God and the testimony they had maintained.

FIFTH SEAL (6:9)	FIFTH TRUMPET (9:1-12)	FIFTH BOWL (16:10-11)
The Fifth Seal is justice. Those slain by their persecutors are crying out for redemption and justice. They had been persecuted and killed. However, total vindication is yet to take place.	The Fifth Trumpet shows Satan's banishment from Heaven forever. This judgment upon Satan is partial at first. Satan is banished from accessing God's Throne. However, he still engages in covert warfare against the Body of Christ. The world is stupefied as to the intensity of this battle. The world lashes into a deathly sleep while Satan's militant host invades it with great wrath.	The Fifth Bowl is God's complete wrath upon those who persecuted the Congregation of Christ. The Beast, his kingdom, and his followers are cast into darkness where there is weeping and gnashing of teeth (Mt 8:12).

The SEVENS always come uniformly in FOURS and THREES at last. The last THREE are more severe in their distresses and harder to humanly cope with. Chapter 6:9 is a snapshot, describing what happened to Christ's martyrs in earthly time. The martyred Christians are crying out. In Revelation 6: 9-11, the Fifth Seal produces a snapshot of time in history. At the same time, within the seven seals, we consistently see parallel sections. The Fifth Seal, in linear time, refers to Nero-type bloodletting of Christians. John saw many Christians who had been killed by those who hated Christian righteousness. This martyrdom is the extreme suffering for the cause of Christ. They were killed because of the Gospel, which is the Testimony of Jesus Christ (Rev 1:2, 1:9, 6:9, 11:7, 12:11, 15:5, 19:10, and 20:4). The martyrs not only died because they were Christians, but they were *marturia*, which means they gave judicial evidence and were subpoenaed as a witness to the point of death.

There is nothing like this "testimonial-martyrdom" in the Old Testament, unless it would be the idea of "Tasaba," which is called Temple Warfare. The priests were exempt from actual physical military conflict, but they were to pray "Tsaba" for victory over the enemy. The word "Saboath" is Greek for the Hebrew "Tasaba" and means "Lord of Hosts." The word offers comfort to the fighting men and women who engage in spiritual warfare against a hostile enemy who swear allegiance to false gods. This enemy is under the control of spirits of religious and political philosophy that it is duty-bound to seriously marginalize the Lord's people, or if that fails, imprison or kill them.

David was the first to use the word "Lord of Hosts-Sabaoth" in battle when Goliath threatened to cut off his head and feed him to the birds of the air and beasts of the field (1Sa 17:45). The warfare of the New Testament is vastly different from the sword warfare of David. The New Testament sword is "The Word of God" (Eph 6:17), and it does not cut through the flesh, but splits open the body, soul, spirit, and pierces to the source of even physical life in the marrow of the bones (Heb 4:12). Even 2,000 years ago, the Bible knew that life's subsistence depended upon the marrow of the bones. To kill a man with a gun may be murder, but to slay him with the sword of the Spirit will lead to life, immortal.

The Old Testament word for testimony simply meant "record." The difference between the Old Testament record and the New Testament testimony is that God's prophets spoke the former, but in these last days, God has spoken by His Son, the *living word!* (Heb 1:2).

The written account of the New Testament on Earth is essential for proof concerning the prior probating in Heaven of the Will of Christ (Heb 9:16, 17). This Will and Testament is also confirmed on Earth for those who sacrifice to advance this New Covenant and are willing to lay down their lives for The Testimony, if necessary.

These souls are under the altar of Heaven, waiting, because the time had not yet come. It is a waiting place. The martyrs are very close to Christ in Heaven. Jesus takes us into His presence when we die (Ac 7:59). Jesus said to the thief, "This day thou shall be with Me in paradise" (Lk 23:43). The coming joy to be experienced in

Heaven will be that of redemption for those who were persecuted and suffered martyrdom at the hands of worldly men. The bravest and most noble men and women of God have been murdered by cowardly non-entities.

Revelation 6:10, 11: They called out in a loud voice, "How long, Sovereign Lord, holy and true, until you judge the inhabitants of the earth and avenge our blood?" Then each of them was given a white robe, and they were told to wait a little longer, until the number of their fellow servants and brothers who were to be killed as they had been was completed.

They cried not because they had been killed, but because they had not been vindicated. God answered them and told them they would have to wait for their vindication because others were still going to be killed. The saints called out "How long?" God does not do things in linear time according to human desires. He said, "A little longer," until the number of saints is completed (Heb 2:10). This period of vengeance would not come until the time of the Gentiles is fulfilled (Lk 21:24; Ro11:25). The Gospel is going to continue to be preached and evangelized until the last Gentile convert in God's foreknowledge is saved. During Christ's earthly ministry, only God, the Father, knew the end of time (Mt 24:36). However, in the exalted position in glory, which Christ had with the Father before the world began, Christ announces all enemies who will be subject to Him (Ac 2:34, 35). He now knows the time of the end. All things are under his feet! (Eph1: 22).

The martyrs are not complaining because they are discouraged; they simply acknowledge that God is the universal judge. God does not reprimand the martyrs for their expecting God's justice to be executed. Evil men hate justice; righteous men love it. The comforting truth concerning the saints is that they are in a perfect state because their robes are washed, and they are white. Numerous, in fact to many to fathom, Christian persecutions and purges like that of Nero have occurred since his time, including the following: the inquisitions, Hitler, Stalin, Mao, and Kim Jong Un of North Korea, and the slaughter of Christians in the Middle East, and where they can gain a foot hold in other countries, by Muslims. In addition, martyrdom suffering also occurs through cultural persecutions, boycotts, and the stifling of Christians' freedom of speech.

Revelation 6:12-17: I watched as he opened the sixth seal. There was a great earthquake. The sun turned black like sackcloth made of goat hair, the whole moon turned blood red, and the stars in the sky fell to earth, as late figs drop from a fig tree when shaken by a strong wind. The sky receded like a scroll, rolling up, and every mountain and island was removed from its place. Then the kings of the earth, the princes, the generals, the rich, the mighty, and every slave and every free man hid in caves and among the rocks of the mountains. They called to the mountains and the rocks, "fall on us and hide us from the face of Him who sits on the throne and from the wrath of the lamb! For the great day of their wrath has come, and who can stand?"

SIXTH SEAL (6:12)	SIXTH TRUMPET (9:13)	SIXTH BOWL (16:12-16)
The Sixth Seal is the countdown to judgment. The universe is affected by the Lord's judgment. The people of the Earth disperse for cover from the wrath of the Lamb, but there is no place to hide. The great day of wrath has come and none will withstand it. The end is near!	The Sixth Trumpet is God's warning pronouncing a judgment upon 1/3 of the Earth. It introduces a great war that is taking place. However, the results of the wars and the wars themselves are not enough to bring about the Earth's repentance. The wars only prevent the world from plunging deeper into spiritual ungodly insanity.	The Sixth Bowl introduces the final war between God with His Holy Ones against the Satanic forces. They have recruited demons, kings, and nations to unite themselves against God. However, they will lose. This is the great battle, which results in a condemnation of eternal hell for Satan and his followers.

By way of reiteration, we noticed the first FOUR SEALS were comparatively mild, but the FIFTH SEAL is deathly serious, even to those who love Christ. Judgment day is right around the corner. God always has the final recourse to retribution, and with the horrible thoughts of what happened to His children in Revelation 6:10, 11, we are not the slightest bit surprised to see how severe the Sixth Seal is going to be. The Sixth Seal introduces us to those cosmic events that cause the end of the world. After the Sixth Seal, only one more seal remains. This means that God's Judgment is near. Only a student of God's word can see that the Sixth Seal prepares us for the Coming Judgment.

The Sixth Seal represents man at his worst. Everything is winding down; the entire universe is ending. An earthquake is an introduction to a new scene. Christians can expect something like a literal earthquake because the final shaking of the Earth is found in non-apocalyptic writings (Heb 12:26; Mt 24:29; 2Pe 3:10-12; Lk 21:25-27). This final climatic catastrophe is not only felt in the inner spirit of humanity but also in the external senses.

Ezekiel announces the end of the Old Testament era with an earthquake. Ezekiel 38:19 is an Old Testament parallel to the end of the New Testament era and the finality of judgment. Seven climatic events or cosmic catastrophes will occur before Christ's coming and the end of the world.

A. Great earthquake (Rev 6:12)

B. Sun becomes black as sackcloth (Rev 6:12)

C. Moon becomes like blood (Rev 6:12)

D. Stars of sky fall to Earth (Rev 6:13)

E. Heaven recedes like a scroll (Rev 6:14)

F. Mountains fall (Rev 6:14)

G. Sinners will try to hide from God (Rev 6:15)

Jesus switches from this plain Scripture to apocalyptic Scripture in Revelation 6:15. He gives the following seven representations of people affected at the end time:

A. Kings

B. Princes

C. Generals

D. Rich

E. Mighty

F. Slaves

G. Free

The Lamb's wrath described in Revelation 6:16 is profound! A lamb is expected to be soft and weak, but this Lamb is also a lion. He is a lamb to those who accept Him and a lion to those who reject Him. The unexpected shock of judgment will occur when a world, which has been taught the Gospel of an effeminate Jesus, find themselves unprepared to face Him as an apocalyptic, roaring man-eating lion.

The seventh seal (8:1) announces the "Silence" that prevails prior to final judgment.

Numerous denominational teachers, false prophets, and liars deceive the nations by preaching a restoration of carnal Israel. This teaching has already been denigrated in the previous chapters; however, we must understand that the destruction of the Jewish temple in 70 A.D. ended the Old Testament. No matter how long before Christ comes again, the next significant event on God's calendar is Jesus' Second Coming. The Christians who have been martyred are not crying out for the establishment of His Kingdom and *the great tribulation*. The martyred Christians are crying out for the Second Coming of Christ and vindication of the crimes committed against them. That is why Matthew records Jesus saying, "Immediately after those days…" (24:29 – Old Testament era). He speaks of the next event, "The sun will be darkened…" (End of the New Testament era) when the Gentiles will be just as accountable for the murder of Jesus in the end, as the Jews were in 70 A.D. (Ac 2:19, 20; Joel 2:28-32; Ex 19:16-20).

Introduction to Revelation Chapter Seven

"The 144,000"

God is a Promise-Keeper. God must keep His promise. All people in the Old Testament who were looking for the Messiah's coming had to be rewarded by God (Ac 2:30; Jn 8:56; Heb 12:39, 40, 11:16). Before the visible resurrection of Christ, the best a person could hope for upon death was to go to a place called an abyss, the Pit. Both the righteous and the wicked went to this Pit. The book of Zechariah foretells of a great rejoicing that will take place when the Messiah comes.

> "Rejoice greatly, O Daughter of Zion! Shout, Daughter of Jerusalem! See, your king comes to you, righteous and having salvation, gentle and riding on a donkey, on a colt, the foal of a donkey" (Zec 9:9).

What is meant by the word Zion? *Zion* is a catchword. This word implies permanency or something that is not shifting and moving. Jesus said, "Upon this

Rock I will build my congregation" (Mt. 16:16-18). The word rock in this passage (petra-feminine) means immovable cornerstone or boulder. The word *Zionism* is used today as a political term referring to the physical Israel established by the United Nation. When Biblical Christians speak of *Zion*, it has nothing to do with Palestine. Earthly real estate is not even tenable in the light of New Testament Scripture. In this discussion, *anyone* who is focused on an earthly or worldly kingdom is in bondage (Gal 4:21). Unintentionally, anyone who thinks in terms of an earthly Zion is actually under Old Testament bondage. However, those looking to the New Jerusalem are free and living in heavenly places. There is a greater enlightenment in the New Testament concerning the meaning of Zion (Heb 12:19-28). It is the Kingdom of God, an immovable and unshakable place.

Zechariah continues:

> "I will take away the chariots from Ephraim and the war-horses from Jerusalem, and the battle bow will be broken. He will proclaim peace to the nations. His rule will extend from sea to sea and from the River to the ends of the earth. As for you, because of the blood of my covenant with you, I will free your prisoners from the waterless pit" (Zec 9:10, 11).

Now, please understand, the Prophet Zechariah is using metaphors and prophetic parables in reference to Christ's future Kingdom. The nations will learn peace from the *Prince of Peace* (vs. 10). This is a prophecy that was fulfilled by the announcement of the Angels at Christ's birth, "Peace on Earth to men of good will" (Lk 2:14 from the original Greek). This is also a New Covenant prophecy concerning the literal shedding of the Blood of the Covenant, which was shed for the remission of sins (Mt 26:28). After His crucifixion, during His three days in the tomb, Jesus descended into Hades to preach to the departed spirits and take captive into Heaven those who were formerly held captive (Eph 4:7-10; 1Pe 3:18-22). This bottomless Pit where the captives were held is Hades. Since they were not yet residents of the permanent Mt. Zion, they are called "prisoners of hope."

A description of Hades is found in the historical narrative of Luke 16, "*The Rich man and Lazarus.*"

> "And being in torment in Hades, he lifted up his eyes and saw Abraham afar off, and Lazarus in his bosom." Then he cried and said, 'Father Abraham, have mercy on me, and send Lazarus that he may dip the tip of his finger in water and cool my tongue; for I am tormented in this flame.' But Abraham said, 'Son, remember that in your lifetime you received your good things,

and likewise Lazarus evil things; but now he is comforted and you are tormented. And besides all this, between us and you there is a great gulf fixed, so that those who want to pass from here to you cannot, nor can those from there pass to us.' Then he said, 'I beg you therefore, father, that you would send him to my father's house, for I have five brothers, that he may testify to them, lest they also come to this place of torment'" (Lk 16:23-26).

Before the Cross of Calvary, both the Old Testament saints and covenant breakers were held in a waiting place. This place is described as a bottomless Pit. It is divided into three sections: Paradise, the gulf, and place of torment *Tartarus*. This entire dwelling place is known as Hades, but the bottom section, known as *Tartarus*, is the waiting place for judgment. Along with the evil angels cast out of Heaven in the pre-cosmic world, Luke 16 acknowledges that members of the human race that died outside of the Old Law (written on stone or in their conscience) also went to this horrible place.

They dwell with the evil angels cast out of heaven. The Bible says,

> "For if God did not spare the angels who sinned, but cast them down to Hades *tartarus* and delivered them into chains of darkness, to be reserved for judgment" (2Pe 2:4).

Modern scholars and Bible translators may interpret this word as "Hell" because the word describes the horrifying condition that exists in this place prepared for Satan and his angels (Rev 20:10, 14, 15). Although Hell is a good description of what it is like, Hell is not the correct understanding of the word *Hades*. Hades means, "The underground place of departed spirits" for both good and bad.[68] We read about Hades in ancient legends and mythology, but only the Bible can give accurate information on the subject because God created the place. Hades co-exists with this present world, but at the Judgment, this world will be destroyed, and Hades will be cast into a solitary existence as the Lake of Burning Fire.

As long as this world still exists, those in Hades know that the appointed Final Judgment has not taken place. The demons have not yet met their final appointed judgment (Mt 8:28, 29). Some of the disobedient angels were thrown into the bottomless pit to await judgment, while others were given dominion to roam the Earth, to torment the lost (Rev 9:5), and refine the Saints through temptation (Jas 5:6, 7; 1Pe 5:8, 9).

On the next page, the reader will see a chart of the afterlife (Created by Charles W. Doughty and edited by Professor Jeffery Wickert):

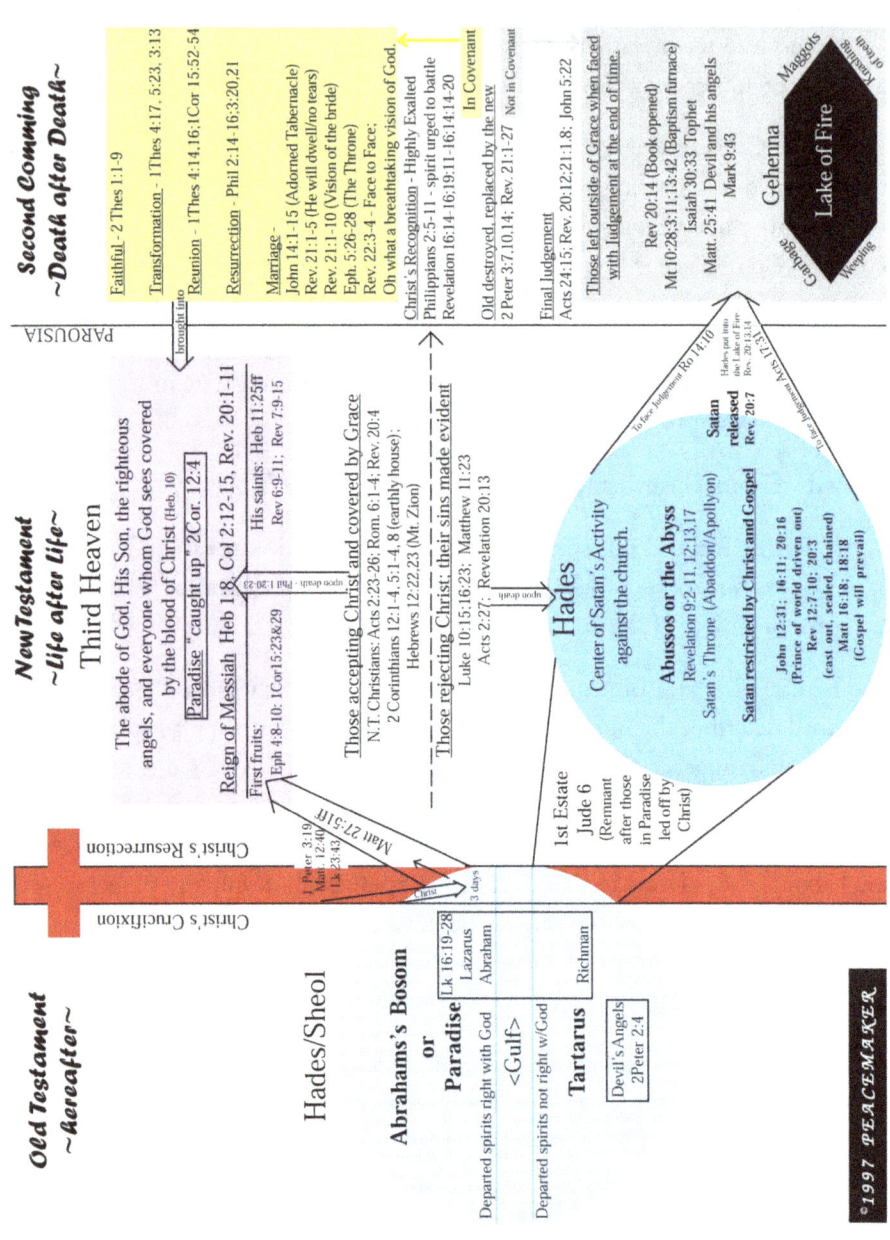

The bottomless pit is also mentioned in Isaiah 24:22, 23,

> "They will be gathered together, as prisoners are gathered in the pit, and will be shut up in the prison; after many days they will be punished. Then the moon will be disgraced and the sun ashamed; For the Lord of hosts will reign On Mount Zion and in Jerusalem and before His elders, gloriously."

The people in the bottomless pit are confined until Judgment Day. Christ reigns upon Mount Zion, forever. This is permanency. The Moon and the Sun are temporary creations, but God is forever. Isaiah is making a contrast between the finite universe and the infinite Zion. Compared to the eternal Zion, the Moon will be disgraced and the Sun ashamed (Isa 24:23). Christ gave Elders, along with evangelists, teachers, and equipped saints. He gave them these ministers to His Congregation after His ascension to the Throne and continues to give them to the present (Eph 4:11). This is similar to the teaching we saw in Revelation 4:4, concerning the 24 elders representing leadership in both Testaments.

In order for Jesus to ascend into Heaven, He was first required to go down (1Pe 3:19; Mt 27:59; Ro 10:7; 1Co 15:22). David looked forward to the appearance of his Lord when he said,

> "Therefore my heart rejoiced, and my tongue was glad; moreover my flesh also will rest in hope. For You will not leave my soul in Hades, nor will You allow Your Holy One to see corruption. You have made known to me the ways of life; You will make me full of joy in Your presence" (Ac 2:26-28).

People asked the question, "When Christ went down to the Pit, who was there in waiting?" First, we know that the generations from Adam to Noah were present (1Pe 3:18-22). Secondly, we know that the generations from Abraham to Moses were present, for the paradise mentioned in Hades is known as "Abraham's Bosom" (Lk 16:23). Thirdly, we also know that the generations from Moses to Christ were there, for Jews, such as Lazarus and the thief on Cross, were two souls who spent the least amount of time in the paradise of Hades before Christ led them up on high (Lk 16:23; Eph 4:7, 8). The Jews were definitely there. Jewish King David recounted his anticipation of Christ's coming (Ps 16:8-11; Ac 2:26-28). David's body was dead, but his soul rested in this hope. These Jews are also included in the number 144,000 of Revelation 7 and 14.

Since Jesus had not yet ascended to the Father, He had not yet made ready a place for us in His eternal abode of existence before the world began (Jn 14:2, 3; Mt 25:31-34). It is a customary teaching that John 14:3 is a reference to Christ's Second Coming; however, overwhelming evidence exists in Scripture that He was referring to His coming to the Apostles after He died, and later coming in His Holy Spirit on the Day of Pentecost. We learn that after Pentecost, all Christians go to be with Jesus when they fall asleep in death (Ac 7:59).

Jesus did not tell Stephen or Paul (Php 1:23), "You cannot come up here now! You must wait until I come again!" Jesus said, "I will come to you" after His death and Pentecost (Jn 14:18); "It will be just a little while" (14:19, 20); and "it will be in that day," Pentecost (14:20). Furthermore, Jesus even explains to His disciples that He is not speaking concerning the Second Coming, for it would come to pass on the Day of Pentecost, and "they would believe" (14:28, 29). He goes on to refer to the context of His conversation that these Disciples would remember His words after Pentecost in their persecution (Jn 16:3, 4).

Jesus also says, "in a little while," not at the Second Coming, "you will see me," after His resurrection and in the New Testament Word on the day of Pentecost (16:16). He also speaks of seeing the Disciples again after the resurrection and on the Day of Pentecost (16:22, 23). He speaks directly of the Day of Pentecost, "When they would petition the Father by the authority of Christ" (16:26). Most importantly, Jesus is not talking about the Second Coming because on the Day of Pentecost, God the Father, God the Son, and God the Holy Spirit came to them and made their abode with them (Jn 14:23-26; Ac 3:18-20).

Yes, Jesus will come again someday, but He has already come to be with Christians. We evangelists exhort sinners to come to Christ. This "come to Christ" is an acceptable expression, but we need to remind sinners also, "He came to them!"

Jesus told the thief on the cross, "Today thou shall be with me in paradise" (Lk 23:43). At the thief's death, paradise and Hades were the same place. Because Abraham's bosom was a place of comfort, the thief would not have gone there when he died. Obviously, the reason the thief is given honorable mention in Scripture is because he may have been the last person to go to Hades.

Christ descended to this place when He died.

"Now this, 'He ascended' — what does it mean but that He also first descended into the lower parts of the earth? He who descended is also the One who ascended far above all the heavens, that He might fill all things" (Eph 4:9, 10).

After His resurrection, Jesus possessed the keys over death and Hades (Rev 1:18), and those keys were used on the day of Pentecost to restore God's relationship with humanity (Mt 16:18; Ac 2:38). It is true that our prepared place with Jesus is realized the second a New Covenant Christian falls asleep, but neither they nor anyone will see God the Father until all meet together at the Second Coming (2The 1:10; Rev 21:3, 22:3, 4). At last the potential for humanity to be restored to God will have been realized.

We definitely know that *no one* went to the Third Heaven (God's Paradise, 2Co 12:2) before the New Covenant promises were given by the Apostolic executors in Acts, Chapter 2. Biblical information had yet to be revealed to account for the interim period between Christ's presenting Himself before the Father as High priest after His propitious death (Lk 23:46) and His inauguration as the anointed King (Mk 16:19). From an earthly viewpoint, some will encounter a theological difficulty because these apocalyptic events were not recognized until Peter preached on the day of Pentecost, "This same Jesus who you crucified God has made both Lord and Christ" (Ac 2:36).

Because all of us are shackled at times by the restraints of earthly time and Jesus is outside of time, we do not know exactly how many times Jesus appeared before the Father during the 40 days between His Resurrection and Ascension. Given that Jesus did take up the captives at His Ascension (Eph 4:9), two questions arise, "Did he take them up immediately on the third day, or did he take them up at His final Ascension and Coronation to the Throne?" There is one certainty, and that is the captives from Hades were with Him on Mt. Zion after His Ascension, according to Revelation 7 and 14. After Christ ascended, all New Covenant Christians had access to the glorified Christ on His Glorified Throne (2Co 5:7-9). With a proper apocalyptic understanding of the Throne and The Host who surrounded Christ's Throne, we can uncover the truth of this glorious Revelation of Christ.

Revelation Chapter Seven

Revelation 7:1-3: After this I saw four angels standing at the four corners of the earth, holding back the four winds of the earth to prevent any wind from blowing on the land or on the sea or on any tree. Then I saw another angel coming up from the east, having the seal of the living God. He called out in a loud voice to the four angels who had been given power to harm the land and the sea "Do not harm the land or the sea or the trees until we put a seal on the foreheads of the servants of our God."

We, in the 21st Century, should understand this Chapter as having already been completed. The four winds of the Earth stand for the judgment of the whole world (North, South, East, and West). This "another angel" represents God's Judgment. It is quite possible that this angel is Jesus Christ, for He has the seal of the living God (2Co 1:22; Eph 1:13, 4:30). Verse 3 describes judgment being delayed until the 144,000 (Rev 7:4) were sealed. No harm could take place until this sealing happened (Eze 9:2-11). There is a gigantic theological discrepancy in date setting when the Preterist take this "sealing" to be a reference to 70 A.D., when "sealing the 144,000" had already been done 70 years previously at Christ's Ascension.

What is this seal? It was applied to the forehead indicating that they had instant intellectual recognition of salvation and Christ of the Godhead. They did not need to be immersed in order to receive the Holy Spirit as those NOW after Christ's death (1Pe 3:21). It is strongly believed that this seal is the Holy Spirit that places us in covenant with Christ. What created angel would be given the power and authority to place this seal on the foreheads of the servants of God? The Fifth angel is infinitely different than the other four angels. He is different from the standpoint of superiority. The Fifth angel must be a reference to the Creator, or King of Angels. Certainly, this could only be Christ Jesus. (Please remember that the word "Angel" means messenger and there are ordinary created Angels, human Angels, and one divine messenger Angel, who is the Christ Jesus.) He is the one who "seals" with the Seal of the Living God. No ordinary Angel could do this.

A cross reference to Revelation 7:4 reads,

> "Then I looked, and behold, a Lamb standing on Mount Zion, and with Him one hundred and forty-four thousand, having His Father's name written on their foreheads" (Rev 14:1).

The Lamb of God is Jesus who has sealed the 144,000 with the Father's name. Christ wrote the father's name upon those "captives" with hope in Hades. The Old Testament 144,000 could not be in the Third Heaven with God before the cross for three main reasons:

1. They did not have the complete remission of Sins. God overlooked the transgressions that they had committed (Heb 10:1-18). Paul makes it clear that the Old Testament saints had *parasis*, which is a temporary suspension of sins (Ro 3:25-26). However, in the New Testament, saints have *aphesis* remission of sins, which is complete forgiveness (Ac 2:38).

2. They did not have His seal of the Spirit (Ac 2:38; Eph 1:13, 14).

3. They knew Abraham but did not know God as their "God and Father" (Jn 8:43, 20:17) nor did they know that God had a Son.

The word Father is used over 600 times in the Old Testament, but not once did an Old Testament believer understand the word "Father" in reference to creator God Yahweh. Christ was needed to reveal the Father (Mt 11:27; Jn 1:18).

In order for Christ to bring the 144,000 captives from Hades into Heaven with Him, they had to hear the same Gospel Peter preached on the Day of Pentecost (1Pe 3:18-22), to be forgiven of their sins (Jn 3:16) (the promise to the *whole* world), and to be sealed with the Spirit (Rev 7:1, 2; Eph 1:13, 4:7-10). Having received these things personally from Jesus Christ, which New Covenant Christians presently receive (1Pe 3:21), the captives now possess what all Christians have. They have the Father's name, the Son's name, and the Holy Spirit. The captives have everything they looked forward to in the Old Testament.

In the twelve-word expression: "The like figure where unto even baptism now does also save us" (1Pe 3:21), the most important word is "now." Why? It is simply because Old Testament Saints did not have to be baptized. New Testament Saints must be baptized NOW. The word "now" is in the original Greek of 1 Peter 3:21. The 144,000 were not immersed into Christ, but "now" (after Pentecost) true baptism also saves us.

The world could not be destroyed until God kept His promise (Rev 7:1). The winds could destroy the world in a minute at any time if God allowed them to blow with utmost intensity from the four global points. But like huge bulwarks, in order to prevent the global extinction of the human race before God keeps his promises, the angels are placed in proper station to prevent such a cosmic ending catastrophe. There are hundreds of promises, but I will state a few here.

1) The SEED would bruise the Serpent's head (Ge 3:15).

2) God would forgive sins completely and not, as in the past, merely "Passover" them (Ro 3:25).

3) The Captives would be taken from Sheol (Spirit world of the dead) and made secure in the Heavenly Mount Zion (Rev 14:1).

4) The Holy Spirit would seal unworthy but redeemed souls (Rev 7:4).

5) They would finally and ultimately know God intimately as "FATHER "(Jn 20:17).

6) A great miracle and mystery of God that we sometimes overlook, or forget is that God promised The Old Testament Saints (144,000) would unite with the once odious Gentiles "White Robed Throng" (Rev 7:14-17). This was a promise (Isa 9:2, 60:3, 62:2), a fulfillment (Ac 11:26), and a mystery (Eph 3:6).

So picture an angel, having at his disposal a gigantic, black twisting funnel ready to descend upon us with cosmic shattering fury from The North. Picture another angel, having in his hand a twisting funnel filling the sky in The East. Still another is threatening to wipe away human life, civilization, and everything that stands in its path to The East. Yet, another angel is in control of a monstrous twister from The South that has the potential to uplift everything in its path and to explode the world to pieces. What would happen to the planet Earth if all four of these winds came together at the same time?

Then, another Angel from The East comes. The East has a good and bad connotation in Scripture. We are warned to be on guard against the religions of The East and their impersonal gods. The Eastern Armies were a thorn in Gideon's side (Jdg 6:33). One of their images was the Crescent Star and Moon God of the Easterners[69] (Jdg 8:21, 26). But, Ezekiel prophesied the "Glory of the God of Israel" coming from The East (Eze 43:2).

Christ is THE ONE from the East who alone can save this world from extinction and its inhabitants from Hell. He has already taken the redeemed of the Old Testament to Mount Zion, and he is waiting to take the rest of us Gentiles, if we would only believe.

It is ironic that Eastern Religions have some of the weirdest, most nonsensical beliefs in the world, but it is from an Eastern Background our Lord came to us "A root out of dry ground" (Isa 53:2). Such a paradox as this crushes man's wisdom in his own conceits and glorifies the Lord in His accomplishments (1Co 1:19).

Finally, let us picture the four angels lifting up their wind barriers to prevent the winds of final judgment from blowing on the world. The world could not be destroyed until at least those six promises of God, mentioned above, were fulfilled. Now, let us consider a very serious warning. Every one of those six promises has been fulfilled! There is NOW, no such preventative measure in effect. Since the Lord's atonement, there is nothing in effect but God's grace to prevent us all from dying in the storm and going to Hell. No wonder John was absolutely astounded at this vision.

The winds of judgment will bring the world to an end. God would keep His promise of this Final Judgment, but He would gather His Old Testament Saints who were waiting for complete redemption before that happened. After Calvary, we have God's guarantee that this world can end at any time. Truly, since Pentecost, WE are living on borrowed time.

Revelation 7:4-8: Then I heard the number of those who were sealed: 144,000 from all the tribes of Israel. From the tribe of Judah 12,000 were sealed, from the tribe of Reuben 12,000, from the tribe of Gad 12,000, from the tribe of Asher 12,000, from the tribe of Naphtali 12,000, from the tribe of Manasseh 12,000, from the tribe of Simeon 12,000, from the tribe of Levi 12,000, from the tribe of Issachar 12,000, from the tribe of Zebulun 12,000, from the tribe of Joseph 12,000, from the tribe of Benjamin 12,000.

The number 144,000 cannot be a literal number, for if it were, John would have mentioned all the tribes. He left out Dan and the half tribe of Manasseh. God kept it in the range of numerology as the representative number of government, which is twelve. It is probable that Dan was not mentioned as one of the tribes because its people fell into idolatry (Jdg18: 30, 31). This is an apocalyptic number to represent all those from Moses to the thief on the cross. We can logically conclude that the 144,000 included individuals from Dan, but the evidence of Dan being left out is overwhelming proof that the number 144,000 is not literal. It is an apocalyptic, inclusive multiple of the representative number 12, which stands for government (12 times 12 represents God's overriding justice in providential government). God reveals by this number that He keeps His promises, and all who should have been saved were finally saved. Just like the number 1,000, 144,000 also manifest undetermined definiteness.

The Russellites (Jehovah's Witnesses) really got hung up on this number being literal, but we know it refers to the Jewish Tribes, not Gentiles, and God promised Abraham, "His seed would be as numerous as stars in the sky and sand on the seashore" (Ge 22:17). This certainly falls well short of a mere 144,000. No renowned Christian Scholar has ever accepted Russellism as being credible. They do with the Bible what a person suffering with dementia would do with a jigsaw puzzle.

Revelation 7:9, 10: After this I looked and there before me was a great multitude that no one could count, from every nation, tribe, people and language, standing before the throne and in front of the Lamb. They were wearing white robes and were holding palm branches in their hands. And they cried out in a loud voice: "Salvation belongs to our God, who sits on the throne, and to the Lamb."

Why would God number the representative group at 144,000, but now give a multitude that cannot be numbered? Even though 144,000 is a multiple of the number of government (12), God knows exactly how many Jews were saved even though He does not give the exact number. After 70 A.D., the exact number of pedigreed Jews (of Old Testament Pedigreed authenticity) that would have been washed in the blood of the Lamb and sealed with the Holy Spirit has been completed (Rev 14:1; Ro 11:12). On the other hand, the exact number of the white robed Gentiles is not yet complete (Ro 11:25, "Fullness of the Gentiles").

The Old Testament saints had to be saved by the same name by which Christians are saved. "There is no other name under heaven given among men by which we must be saved" (Ac 4:12). In order for the Old Testament saints to be saved and sealed, they had to hear the Gospel preached (1Pe 1:12, 3:18-22). Christ sealed them with the Holy Spirit to quicken their bodies to be glorified at Christ's return with them (Ro 8:11, 12). Christ saved them personally, but God is now adding

Christians to His Kingdom through the Apostles Doctrine (Ac 2:36-47).

In Revelation 7:10, John shows the equality of the Godhead because salvation is accredited, equally. These Old Testament saints can now call the Godhead their savior and give glory to the Lamb who sits on the Throne. They are sealed with the Spirit of Christ personally, just as He gives all of us the Spirit as a gift personally in immersion. Only a few Old Testament saints recognized The Christ and the Holy Spirit. We have difficulty (those of us who have spent a lifetime getting acquainted with Christ and His Spirit) imagining the inexpressible impact of unspeakable joy and glory the 144,000 experienced. What is a lifetime of acquaintances for us was compressed into a single moment of Revelation to them. The only way we can compare what they must have experienced is to contemplate what we will see, feel, and know at Christ's Second Coming!

Revelation 7:11, 12: All the angels were standing around the throne and around the elders and the four living creatures. They fell down on their faces before the throne and worshiped God, saying: "Amen! Praise and glory and wisdom and thanks and honor and power and strength be to our God forever and ever. Amen!"

The angels sing about redemption (Lk 15:10) for it pleases them, and they rejoice! Jesus recounts, "I say to you that likewise there will be more joy in heaven over one sinner who repents than over ninety-nine just persons who need no repentance" (Lk 15:7). Notice the complete and perfect praise to God in verse twelve. The number seven is represented again in numerology.

Revelation 7:13: Then one of the elders asked me, "These in white robes—who are they, and where did they come from?"

This may be an Old Testament Elder, and he asks this question because he is not familiar with the impact New Testament Christianity would have on Gentiles. The Elder did not ask about the 144,000 because he knew them, and they received salvation. However, as a Jew, he was shocked because of the white robed Gentile Christians. The Jews were surprised at this vast number of souls accepting their God through Jesus Christ! Some were filled with envy and indignation (Ac 13:45, 17:5), but John was pleasantly surprised.

This Jewish Elder knew prophecy. He knew the Gentiles would see the light, and nations of Gentiles would be converted (Isa 60:1-4, 62:1-4). The new name of

Christian (Ac 11:26) would be given them "written on their foreheads." Many people today know that God has bountiful blessings for all, and we expect Him to bless us. When He does, we are surprised at the execution of the super abounding blessing (Eph 3:20). This may account for the astonishment of the Elder when he saw how great and vast an impact the Gospel had on the world's Gentile nations. What was a surprise to the Elder was a shocking revelation to the carnal Israelites,

> "I say to you that many will come from the east and the west, and will take their places at the feast with Abraham, Isaac and Jacob in the kingdom of heaven. But the subjects of the kingdom will be thrown outside, into the darkness, where there will be weeping and gnashing of teeth" (Mt 8:11, 12).

Rather than this question being rhetorical in Revelation 7:13, it fits the context of an enlightened understanding of the fulfillment of Old Testament prophecy concerning the conversion of the Gentiles. The Elder did not have access to the magnitude and overwhelming results of these promises. In other words, as the following verses will reveal, he understood and answered his own question correctly.

Revelation 7:14-17: I answered, "Sir, you know." And he said, "These are they who have come out of the great tribulation; they have washed their robes and made them white in the blood of the Lamb. Therefore, 'they are before the throne of God and serve him day and night in his temple; and he who sits on the throne will spread his tent over them. Never again will they hunger; never again will they thirst. The sun will not beat upon them, nor any scorching heat. For the Lamb at the center of the throne will be their shepherd; he will lead them to springs of living water. And God will wipe away every tear from their eyes."

This is a great tribulation for the saints, *not the imaginary great tribulation* at the end of time. In this passage, the context is describing the Christian dispensation. This Revelation gave, and still gives, Christians comfort. One day soon, every child in Covenant with God will be with the Lamb they love. His presence is over them like a tent. All God wants for His people is for them to give Him honor and thanksgiving (Dt 28:27). Christians should mature in their faith to the point that they love the giver more than the gift. Christians should not be humanistic and think the prime product of salvation is the happiness of man. *This is a bi-product.* Salvation is all about the Glory of God! When Christians make the forgiveness of sins, the gift of the Holy Spirit, and eternity in Heaven all about a human commercial entrepreneurship, they remove the Glory of God.

Ever since the 2nd Century when Rome began to prostitute their church, Christianity has been faced with a powerful sinister spirit of darkness to build church membership. The numerous, unscrupulous ways used to build church membership are nothing short of satanic. These include promises of good entertainment, making people happy with promises of success with health, wealth, prosperity, and providing good music and good times. People can have all these materials blessings if they would just attend "their church."

The Bible speaks clearly that a sincere member of a Christian assembly will, "Choose rather to suffer affliction with the people of God than to enjoy the passing pleasures of sin" (Heb 11:25). Rome is correct in saying they are the first church. For the *word* church indicates only a religious building, cathedral, temple, or physical sanctuary. However, the first Ecclesia of Christ goes back to Jerusalem (Ac 2:47). There is also a dubious question in regard to Greek Orthodoxy being the first of churchanity.

THE 144,000 JOIN WITH THE WHITE ROBED THRONG IN ADORATION OF THE LAMB.

This point in eternity (Rev 7:14) addresses the relationship of the Saints with Christ, the Son. This is not the same state that is mentioned in Revelation 21:3, 4, which concerns the relationship of the Saints with God, the Father. The position expressed in Revelation 7:15, "before the Throne of God," is as close as we can be to God without seeing His face. In Revelation 21:3, 4, all of us will see His face. Thus being with the Lamb at the "Center of the Throne" may be called an interim condition (part and parcel) of eternal existence until Christ delivers up the Kingdom to God, the Father, "who will be all in all" (1Co 15: 24). They are still sharing intimate, heavenly bliss with the presence of Christ. However, they are waiting to be presented to the Father as the bride of Christ (Eph 5:27).

Stephen cried out, "Lord Jesus receive my spirit." When a Christian falls asleep in Jesus, they are in God's propinquity, but only the Bridegroom can present them to the Father at His coming. In this heavenly realm, Christians are in the presence of the Father, but they will not see His face intimately until Christ comes to present the entire Kingdom Assembly of Christ to the Father (1Co 15:24). Pre-Millennialists are unable to reach a theological completion to their scheme of things, but those who own Christ as their King can anticipate an end.

Looking at the Big Picture of the Seals

Notice that the Seventh Chapter is an interlude between the sixth and seventh seals. The seals are in multiples of 4's and 3's. The first seal is opened in Revelation 6:1 with *"come!"* The second, third, and fourth seals all open with *"come!"* However, after the fifth seal, along with the sixth and seventh, the word "come" is no more. In numerology, number *four* represents the Earth. The first four seals, as well as the first four trumpets and bowls, are preliminary warnings of God's oncoming judgment on a world that is guilty of horrible decision-making.

The first four seals underscore the insane propensities of the human race to want to bring God's Judgment upon us. God answers in the last three judgments, "You want judgment? Judgment you shall get!" (Ro 1:18, 2:5, 6). But in the interlude, God shows mercy in Christ by revealing 144,000 redeemed from Earth and her threatening woes (Rev 14:3).

The number *three* represents the Godhead. These last three seals, as well as the last three trumpets and bowls, are terrible judgments coming upon the Earth. This is the justice of the unified Godhead coming upon them.

As the seals continue and get closer to judgment, they begin to overlap and start over again. For instance, seal seven is interlinked with the first trumpet and the seventh trumpet is interlinked with the first bowl. As the cycles continue, the judgments progress in severity until the complete picture of the wrath and reward of God is revealed.

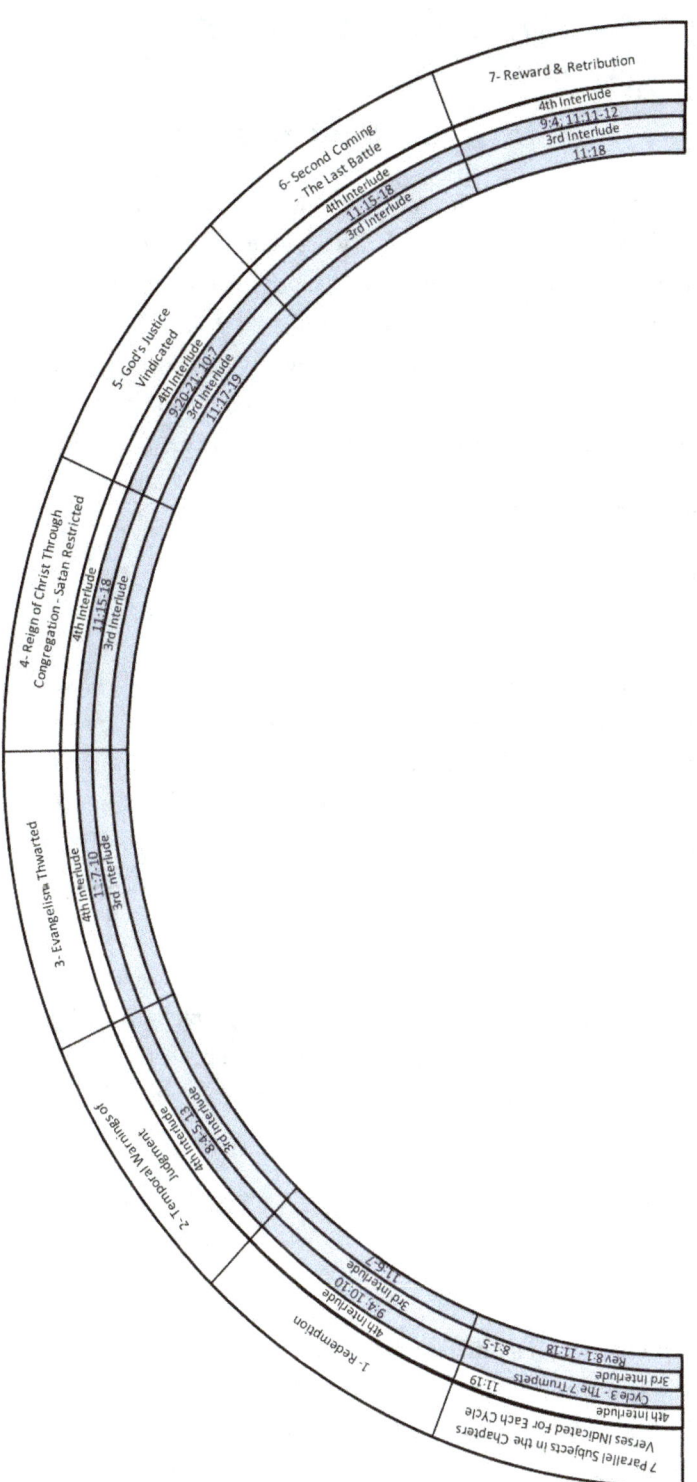

CYCLE 3 – THE SEVEN TRUMPETS

Christ in Condemnation

The Book of Revelation was written to a persecuted people who were giving their lives and the lives of their families for Christ. These truths are given to Christians to enable them to stand firm: Christ is their God; He is their advocate; and He is their Father. He is the white-robed man being served by Cherubim, standing before the Father (Eze 10:1-6). As the seventh seal is opened, it is interlinked with the first trumpet. Once again, the cycles start all over again. However, as we will see, the severity of the warnings and judgments increases.

Revelation Chapter Eight

Revelation 8:1: When he opened the seventh seal, there was silence in heaven for about half an hour.

There was silence in the presence of Heaven in anticipation of God's Judgment (Zec 2:13). Chronologically, we would expect seven to be followed with eight, but when the seventh seal is opened, it reverts to trumpet number one because Revelation repeats itself. Remember, it is cyclical time in Heaven even though it may appear to be chronological time on Earth.

Revelation 8:2: And I saw the seven angels who stand before God and to them were given seven trumpets.

These angels are in God's presence. The seven angels of Heaven are like the angels of the congregations because they bring the message of warning and judgment. Any "Evangelist (angel)" of God, who does not preach judgment alongside love, is *not* preaching truth!

Revelation 8:3: Another angel, who had a golden censer, came and stood at the altar. He was given much incense to offer, with the prayers of all the saints, on the golden altar before the throne.

There is another angel (of a different kind) with a golden censer. He is holding the prayers of the saints in his hand and offering them to God the Father. This messenger is different from all the angels *for* he has the prayers of the saints. This portrays a very important position in Heaven. This single angel has the responsibility to intercede between God and His children. Do we know who this is? He is the mediator of the New Covenant, Jesus Christ (Heb 12: 24). He is the advocate before the Father (1Jn 2:1).

Revelation 8:4-6: The smoke of the incense, together with the prayers of the saints, went up before God from the angel's hand. Then the angel took the censer, filled it with fire from the altar, and hurled it on the earth; and there came peals of thunder, rumblings, flashes of lightning and an earthquake. Then the seven angels who had the seven trumpets prepared to sound them.

This is an overlap from the seven seals to the seven trumpets. Christians are sending their prayers up to the throne. *Christ* is answering their prayers by throwing fire back on the Earth. The Christians are crying out to God because of the persecution of the world and its cultural wickedness. We need to understand this perfect example of the Revelation cycle. Ponder this question, "If there are no Revelation cycles, then what point in time did (or will) this happen?" The answer is, "This has been happening since the foundation of the Kingdom in Acts 2." This cycle has been happening for the last 2,000 years. If not, then has there only been one special limited *time* of persecution for the Congregation? If we answer "Yes," then how can one who holds this position tell the Christians who face persecutions at different times that they really are not facing persecutions? For instance, Christians in 65-90 A.D. were being tortured, murdered, and beaten in Rome and Asia Minor. Likewise, today's Christians today are being tortured, murdered, and beaten in counties like China, Afghanistan, India, Egypt, Nigeria, Syria, Pakistan, and Korea. The answer is that Christians have always been persecuted. They have always been praying to God, and He has always answered them. When Christians pray, *God is obligated to answer*. Sometimes, it might not be a desired answer, but it is the answer that is *needed*. When the prayers of the saints are presented to the Father, He responds with judgment and wrath upon the Earth.

I, like Lot in Sodom (2Pe 2:7), am vexed in heart over the sudden encroachment of Hellish moral darkness that hovers over our Country like a thick fog. Abraham interceded for Sodom, and God reduced the "quorum" of righteous souls required to save Sodom from the fiery holocaust (Ge 18:25). God afforded the mercy of a very slim minority of only ten righteous souls, but ten could not be found. In my book, *Crucified in Sodom*, we look at the background history of the city of Sodom prior to its destruction by a devastating infernal. Scripture, history, and archeology confirm that Sodom was a very fertile, productive, prosperous, tropical city, irrigated by the Jordan River. Sodom was larger than the other four cities on that Plain (Jude 1:7). We estimated Sodom's population to be about 20,000 people. If we take the 10 righteous souls requirement and compare this number to Sodom's population of 20,000, we have a possibility for 0.05% righteous people.

When we project this 0.05% onto America's population today, what would we have for a righteous quorum? If there are 320 million Americans, what would 0.05% of 320 million be? We estimate that number to be 160,000. Are there 160,000 souls in America who have been declared righteous by God? Are there presently 160,000 souls (living in homes, walking the streets, and working at various careers in this Great Country) who, according to the requirements of The New Covenant, have surrendered to the act of "imputed righteousness" (Ro 4:22-25; 2Co 5:21)? Remember, Abraham did not establish this quorum; God did.

In spite of the moral "darkness of darkness" that pervades our world, we want to believe there are 160,000 or more righteous ones, both in this Country and throughout the world. Only God knows, and Christ also knows when His angels of secret surveillance (Rev 14:15, 17) bring the final tally (at the end of this present world) of how many are left who are declared righteous by the atoning Blood of Christ. In the final harvest of human souls, His angels confirm this record with other angels of the divine, all-knowing intelligence agency.

Sodom is an example of suffering "the vengeance of eternal fire" (Jude 1:7). Just as the two angels visited Sodom (Ge 19:1), and ONE of those messengers had to be Christ (the only ONE qualified to judge the Sodomites – Ge 19:9), so God will have the absolutely, perfect records of all humanity (and human interaction) before His THRONE. God's angels of this omniscient intelligence agency will confirm the evidence and present the final reckoning and account (Rev 14:15-19). Just what they meant when the last three angels told Christ, "The world is ripe for the harvest," is an open question, but quite understandable. Obviously, the world will have been in such a deteriorated spiritual condition because "The Faith" (Lk 18:8) of Christ and His Apostles was lost. The report these angels gave to the Judge of the universe was not good. The sharp sheath was swung with the fury of divine indignation and humanity wallowed in their retributory blood. As Sodom ceased to be, so the world of humanity will breathe its last breath.

Christ being God, and God being God, He knows how many righteous souls are left in this Nation. It is not only the sin of sodomy but a whole range of sins that can overtake a nation in a short time. Not only will God judge us, but the men of Sodom will not be treated as severely by The Lord in Judgment Day as will Americans who have access to the Gospel 24 hours a day, every day of their lives (Mt 10:15, 12:42). If Sodom would have repented under the preaching of the Gospel of Christ, what does this have to say about modern-day America?

Federal judges who sponsored and exported the sin of sodomy to their circuits, precincts, and the entire nation will be held completely accountable for leading children astray. Placing a concrete block around their necks and casting them into the sea (Lk 17:2) would be an act of mercy compared to the wrath they will encounter for teaching Americans (especially children) to sin with impunity. A federal judge is guilty of soulful 1st degree murder when he or she casts their lot and decision in favor of sodomy. In addition to judges, teachers, politicians, religious leaders, counselors, and the medical community will also be held accountable.

SEPARATE THEM WITH THE SWORD OF THE SPIRIT (MT 10:34), MARK THEM WITH THE SEAL OF THE SPIRIT.

Subsequently, like Abraham and Lot, we can only intercede and grieve over these wholesale sins that can bring a nation down to the pits of Hades. Ezekiel, Chapter 9, is one of the most fascinating descriptions of how God judges a nation. I believe the white-robed appearance of the divine being in this Chapter indicates The Eternal Christ, and the six "men" correspond with the six Angels of Revelation 14.

The six "Agents of God's divine wrath toward sin" are commissioned to execute those in the city because of their detestable sins and iniquities (Eze 9:4). But when the six executors met those dear souls who wept and mourned over the sins of the city, the executors took ink from an inkpot provided by their whited-robed ruler and marked them. This mark indicated the profound agony they experienced in heart and mind because they knew their fellow countrymen and women were doomed to Hell.

This White-Robe Potentate represents our Lord, and the weeping and groaning indicates His bitter tears shed over the lost city of Jerusalem (Mt 23:37). Although people with fewer sins are just as guilty as those with many (Jas 2:10), those who weep with The Master, by the divine mercy of propitiation, are exempt from guilt and punishment. "A broken and contrite heart, the Lord will not despise" (Ps 34:18, 51:17).

Interestingly, this Apocalyptic Prophecy also refers to those of us today who are marked by The Holy Spirit, "In our heads (intellect) and hands (service)." Paul had the Ezekiel episode in mind when he wrote, "The foundation of the Lord stands firm, having this seal – for the Lord knows who are His own, and let everyone who Names the Name of The Lord depart from iniquity." The seal is of course The Holy Spirit (Eph 1:13). Those who are marked by the "ink" of the pure White-Robed Potentate weep over iniquity and depart from the advancement of the detestable sins of their city and nation.

Like the Prophet Jeremiah, we weep and grieve over the tremendous loss. The loss is not just that of a once great "Christian Nation" but also the irretrievable loss of God-sent leaders to lead our congregations, communities, and national affairs. We know there are leaders who despise our Christian Heritage and the Faith of our Godly Forefathers. They show contempt for our Founding Fathers' Constitution and National Biblical and Christian symbols. When we warn these political, Christian phonies of the consequences, they respond, in part, just as the spiritual rebels did in Jeremiah's day, "Because they did not listen, I wept in silent because of their pride. My eyes will weep bitterly and overflow with tears because the Lord's Flock is taken into captivity" (Jer 13:17). Ungodly pride is a terrible thing. I weep and pray over him, but we have in Washington, a President who cannot work with Americans who still love America: her institutions, her traditions, her Christian value system, and especially her motto, "In God (a Judeo-Christian God) We Trust."

We cannot help but wonder how the American people allowed the President from 2008-2016, during two terms of office, to tear down our bulwarks of liberty by ignoring the Constitution. What will replace the Constitution as the Founding Fathers wrote it? Would the Muslim "Moon Flag" and Sharia Law be a better fix than the God we have served the past 230 plus years? No one seems to talk about it anymore, but our President ran for his office on the Campaign Slogan "CHANGE." How many American voters thought this change also meant replacing America's Christian principles?

The axiom "Nature abhors a vacuum" is as relevant to governments as "The Law of Gravity" is to the sciences. When governments change, the people must find another type of government to govern them. As in the case of Pre-WWII Germany, Post-WWI and Post-Putin Russia, North Korea, Pre-WWII Japan and Post-WWII China (through the historical political changes in nations during the early and mid-20th Century), governments in these countries changed dramatically, for the worst.

Another axiom is "the people of a nation can only believe a lie for so long." The American people have the best record for maintaining its stability within the laws of the U.S. Constitution, but when "The bottom falls out," it takes time, often a long time, to rectify the damage caused by lies. In my book, *Crucified in Sodom*, I list *The Greatest Presidential Lies in History*, and in all fairness, we take it back to Nixon. The current President is the greatest liar of them all.

Perhaps you are reading this commentary in the year 2030. You may reside in a foreign country. You may have a President or Dictator as bad or if possible, worse than the one who is undermining the foundational truths that made the Country in which I now reside one of the greatest in the world. I may be dead by the time you read this, but the inalienable, proven, inexorable time-tested truths that govern this Apocalyptic Book apply to all nations under the sun, at all times in history. Perhaps the President and his crony appointees will repent of their insanity and nonsense and turn to Christ and be saved. I hope and pray they do. But if they do not…. If your wicked leaders in foreign countries do not, the same unchangeable truths that emerge from the pages of This Apocalypse NOW will be around long after you and I are in the grave. I do not apologize for these TRUTHS, nor do I avoid making application of these TRUTHS to men and nations. Christ REIGNS! That is final! Sin is not what Bill and Hillary Clinton say it is. Sin is what God says it is!

Like Jeremiah, we weep in secret. We think no one sees us when we cry out in grief over the national sins that are going to be reaped in judgment, especially upon our children and young adults. But God sees us. He hears our prayers and sees our tears (2Ki 20:5). We need not lose heart because "He who sees in secret will reward us openly" (Mt 6:4b).

THERE IS A DIFFERENCE BETWEEN BEING RICH AND BEING 'FILTHY-RICH.'

Many Americans think that as long as they have wealth, luxury, good times, and full sustenance, God is well pleased with them. Remember, God causes the rain and sun to bless both the just and the unjust (Mt 5:45), and that wicked Sodom was one of the most blessed metropolises in the world (Eze 16:49). Ezekiel called Sodom "Your sister" because so many of the residents would have come from Noah, through Abraham. There is some confusion as to why Ezekiel called this wicked city "Your sister." Why did not Abraham call them "Your Brother?" Could it be that Sodom was so emasculated and effeminate that a real man would be ashamed to call them "brother"?

But mere wealth has never been a test of Godliness. Creating wealth is a God-given industry, but God chooses the poor also. A person can be "filthy rich," and at the same time, "filthy poor," in character or commendation in the sight of heavenly dignitaries (1Co 1:26-28; Jas 2:5).

Dale Carpenter, Facilitator of the Shenandoah Christian Alliance (SCA), believes that children will suffer the most over the same-sex craze. Mr. Carpenter grieves with profound solemnity over the void that exists in the elementary and high school levels regarding our Godly heritage and the great faith our Founding Fathers exercised in putting together a plan and crafting valuable documents upon which this Country could grow and survive down through the decades.

Sodomy-mating is not a natural environment for raising children. The Lord intended for children to see the beauty of a divine relationship, called marriage, between one man and one woman. God will judge sexual perverts and whore-mongers (Heb 13:4).

I joined the SCA and the "grieving minority" of the Lord's Children who still groan over the commitment of the political Sin Party to the wholesale slaughter of innocent children, the rampant persecution and slaughter of Christians across the word, the legalization of sodomy, and the terrifying effects of laxity toward crime and criminal action. Our mourning is also in response to the contempt many have for law enforcement, both nationally and internationally, exercised by those who are avowed, implacable enemies of our Country and its freedoms. Most people only mourn over their own problems and common troubles, which are situations usually caused by their own selfishness. Jesus taught us to mourn over real issues that trouble Earth and Heaven, "Blessed are those who mourn", and we praise God for the epilog, "They will be comforted!" (Mt 5:4).

But lately, I have been praying, "Lord God Almighty, if they continue to crucify you spiritually in Sodom again, then pour out the fiery coals of your altar upon us now!" (Rev 8:4-6) May the Lord combine our prayers with the smoke of the fiery incense and pour it out upon the guilty nations. Thousands of Christians worldwide are being butchered, slaughtered, beheaded, raped, plundered, driven from their homes and countries, and persecuted. May the Lord intersperse our prayers with the smoke of the fiery incense from Heaven and pour it out to either convert or detain the enemies of truth and righteousness. This kind of praying is called "imprecatory" in the Psalms of David. The righteous King David would never tolerate today's sodomite perversion and abortion murder in his kingdom.

Remember, this Commentary of The Apocalypse is not just a Theological Commentary; it is a practical workbook on how to apply the truths of this Revelation to our lives. This Apocalyptic Masterpiece from the Lord, Jesus Christ, is the best information available for those who are troubled with the presence and the power of evil in today's world. The Book of Job was written to address some of these issues, but when Christ looks down from Heaven and reaches out His hands, His hands are filled with all history – good, evil, Godly, ungodly, Satanic, Angelic, wars, depression, truth, deception, hard times, good times – and just about every mix of emotions we can imagine, ranging from love to hate, hope to despair. We discover in this final Book of Divine Revelation that there is not one problem or question we can ask, that the Lord cannot answer. What a testimony to Job's integrity and trust in God...we marvel that he coped so well with the problems of evil without possessing the Book of Revelation.

Within the first four warnings, (the context of the four trumpets), God is imposing punishment in order for the wicked to repent! The reader will notice that the following judgments upon the Earth are the same judgments that were brought upon Egypt, except for the death of the first-born. John wants to convey the thought of God's sending judgments *in order for the people to repent*. What was the purpose of God's judgment upon Egypt? It was for their repentance and recognition of the one, true God (Ex 12:12; Nu 33:3, 4; Ps 149:7).

Revelation 8:7: The first angel sounded his trumpet, and there came hail and fire mixed with blood, and it was hurled down upon the earth. A third of the earth was burned up, a third of the trees were burned up, and all the green grass was burned up.

Although God afflicted Egypt with literal-historical judgments, in the apocalyptic vision, there is also the possibility of literal-historical catastrophes. But the apocalyptic events are more severe. For instance, the Egyptian plagues were removed by Moses' rebuke. In Revelation, there is no hint of removing the curse of the trumpets by prayer. The plaques of the Apocalypse are international and send more symbolic messages.

The Earth is affected, and there is blood in the sea. We can compare this with the bowls of Chapter 16. The reason the judgment of this trumpet is different from the bowls is because Chapter 8 is a partial judgment, while Chapter 16 is complete judgment. Remember, the cycles get progressively worse. These specific judgments stand for judgment upon the whole Earth. The horses of Revelation 4 are continuing to ride. There are diseases, war, lack of food, droughts, hunger, thirst, and multiple others disasters that take place.

FIRST SEAL (6:1, 2)	FIRST TRUMPET (8:7)	FIRST BOWL (16:1, 2)
The Gospel is spreading throughout the Earth. The Saints are praying. Because of the Gospel of the Saints, God is judging the Earth with His Word.	The First Trumpet is a partial judgment in which 1/3 of the Earth is affected. This includes the Earth, sea, and those that dwell on the Earth (people & animals).	The Angel is pouring the bowl out upon the Earth, which results in God's judgment. Once again, because of the Prayers of the Saints, God gives His judgment with His warning! It is now a complete judgment of God upon the Earth.

Why just partial judgments? The reason for one third of the destruction is to show that if God can destroy one third, He can destroy the whole thing. This can be a difficult teaching to accept; however, we need to understand how this is applied. If God can destroy one third of the Earth with His judgment, we should repent before He destroys the entire universe! Even if we are not personally experiencing disasters, we should sense the awe-inspiring possibility that this could happen. "Evil men hate judgment of any kind" (Pr 28:5).

Revelation 8:8, 9: The second angel sounded his trumpet, and something like a huge mountain, all ablaze, was thrown into the sea. A third of the sea turned into blood, a third of the living creatures in the sea died, and a third of the ships were destroyed.

Fire is hurled into the sea, and a third of it became blood, a third of the animals died, and third of the ships destroyed. When Tokyo, Japan was struck by an earthquake and tsunami on March 18, 2011, Governor Shintaro Ishihara said it was God's judgment. Of course, both Christians and non-Christians suffered losses, but a Christian will not make apologies for God.

Neither the Japanese, nor any other nation on Earth, could build a nuclear plant and compound to withstand a powerful tsunami, yet we hear a meteorologist on American TV state that Japan suffered a terrible blow from "a freak of nature." What an enigma! Some of the best building and construction engineers in the world work in Japan. This Pacific island nation is one of the most formidable industrial, commercial, military, and hi-tech minded, earthly powers. Then, after they were nearly wiped off the map by an act of some greater power, somewhere else in this vast universe, one of our little weather commentators, said, "It was a freak."

Can you imagine that? They blamed a "freak" for a destruction that affected the whole nation! In our nice, neat little cozy pacifistic nation that could not fight off an invasion of termites, we like to water everything down and explain everything away with euphemisms, but to blame the near annihilation of an entire nation on a dumb, purposeless, uneducated, illiterate "Freak" is ignorance epitomized. Our hedonistic and sin-glorifying mass media would rather crucify Jesus again than admit the TRUTH on any subject regarding the menace of immorality. No, I am not angry; I am a commissioned man. The Angel of the Gospel tells us, "Fear God!" (Rev 14:7). Better fear Him now! You will fear Him later!

SECOND SEAL (6:3, 4)	SECOND TRUMPET (8:8)	SECOND BOWL (16:3)
The Second Seal of the Red Horse. Once again, judgment upon the Earth. This was the power to make war and death. The world has to live with war; there is no way to avoid it.	The Second Trumpet is a partial judgment in which 1/3 of the creatures in the sea died, and 1/3 of the ships were destroyed.	The Second Angel poured out the bowl of complete judgment in the sea and every (all) living creature died.

Revelation 8:10, 11: *The third angel sounded his trumpet, and a great star, blazing like a torch, fell from the sky on a third of the rivers and on the springs of water the name of the star is Wormwood. A third of the waters turned bitter, and many people died from the waters that had become bitter.*

The third trumpet caused a third of the waters to turn bitter (wormwood). This little plant could ruin gallons of drinking water. The wormwood was a bitter plant that *no one* wanted to eat. This bitterness is not what we know as simply being sour. This is so repulsive and sickening that the human stomach cannot stand it. This bitter water was infected with diseases. Spiritually, this kind of water has caused bitterness toward God. Some people can no longer taste the living waters of Christ. They are *never* satisfied. This, by the way, is how many in Hollywood and Washington, D.C. feel about the Gospel. What is more, they have not received a good dose of bitter water yet!

From a perspective of earthly judgments, the drinking water of the rivers and the streams are affected. Many people die each year because of the bacteria in drinking water. God's justice is vindicated through judgments that are unknown to the majority of the human race. As noted, the plagues of Revelation can be closely associated with the plagues of Egypt. John uses these same emblems to convey the thought of God's judgment upon the Earth.

THIRD SEAL (6:5, 6)	**THIRD TRUMPET (8:7)**	**THIRD BOWL (16:4-7)**
The Third Seal of the Black Horse is famine, pestilence, and bad economy. There is depression and many are lacking necessities. Even the simple necessities of bread, water, oil, and wine are extremely expensive (Dt 28:48, 49). These necessities are so expensive that the purchase rate is inconceivable.	The Third Trumpet affects the water of the streams and drinking water. People are dying because the water is contaminated. Notice that 1/3 of the waters are contaminated.	The Third Angel has poured out his bowl upon the springs of water, and they became blood. The Angel recognized God's right to judge the Earth because they killed His people. His judgments are just. Notice that all the rivers and springs are flowing with blood.

Revelation 8:12, 13: The fourth angel sounded his trumpet, and a third of the sun was struck, a third of the moon, and a third of the stars, so that a third of them turned dark. A third of the day was without light, and also a third of the night. As I watched, I heard an eagle that was flying in midair call out in a loud voice: "Woe! Woe! Woe to the inhabitants of the earth, because of the trumpet blasts about to be sounded by the other three angels!"

The fourth trumpet shows the constellations are affected. A third of the sun, moon, and stars were struck. Even the days and the nights are affected. The weather and natural disasters are caused from celestial judgments. The events that take place on Earth are affected by the cosmos. Does this happen because of the natural laws or God? For people who neither know God nor understand the cycles apocalyptically, the answer is *natural laws*. Obviously, they will call such death dealing catastrophes *freaks of nature*. However, apocalyptic Christians understand that God uses the law of physics or the natural laws to bring judgment upon the Earth. If God created the laws, He can use them. Only the wise can see the partial judgments of God. The unwise can only see the immediate effects of the movement of clouds, high or low-pressure systems, and the movement of extreme air velocities in certain areas. However, they are ignorant of what the Creator said, "The wind blows where it will and no man knows where it comes from or where it goes" (Jn 3:8).

The darkening represents moral and philosophical darkness. Through this tactic, Satan wages war against the Bride of Christ in an attempt to prevent as many people as possible from accepting the Gospel. Satan's greatest passion of hatred burns against the doctrine of justice and judgment (Ge 3:4; Heb 9:27). Educators who teach utilitarianism, relativism, situation ethics, humanism, and egalitarianism, as a substitute for absolute morality and justice, usually deny the doctrine of the existence of diabolical spirits, even though many of them are so demonic depressed they cannot make it through life without some sort of "fix".

Distinction between the First Four and Last Three

As the first four seals are introduced with the word "come," notice the distinction between the first four and last three trumpets. The first four introduced warnings and natural calamities. However, the last three exclude mentioning particular warnings and judgments. Thus, in verse 13, the last three trumpets are only distinguished with three sobering declarations, "Woe! Woe! Woe!" These woes are conveying that God's complete Judgment is coming upon the Earth. Once again, God uses the partial judgments to show His power. If God is capable of destroying one third, He can destroy it all. The order of the three woes is calling for the world to repent.

The first of the last three "woes" brings us face to face with Satan and Demons (far worse than any calamity). The second woe brings fear of God as we are brought face-to-face with a war we cannot win. The third woe (11:15) brings us face to face with an angry God. Notice the progressive severity of the "woes."

FOURTH SEAL (6:5, 6)	FOURTH TRUMPET (8:12)	FOURTH BOWL (16:8)
The Fourth Seal of the Pale Horse represents 1/4 of the earth being killed. This is partial judgment. The wicked die and await eternal hell in Hades.	The Fourth Trumpet affects 1/3 of the constellations, the Sun, Moon, and stars.	The Fourth Bowl is poured out upon all of the constellations. The Sun is scorching the people with fire. All the people are affected by this judgment. This fire will destroy the whole Earth.

Revelation Chapter Nine

Revelation 9:1: The fifth angel sounded his trumpet, and I saw a star that had fallen from the sky to the earth. To Him was given the key to the shaft of the Abyss.

FIFTH SEAL (6:9)	FIFTH TRUMPET (9:1-12)	FIFTH BOWL (16:10, 11)
The Fifth Seal is justice. Those slain by their persecutors are crying out for redemption and judgment. However, this is still yet to take place. They who had been persecuted and killed are in an interim, waiting place.	The Fifth Trumpet shows Satan's banishment from Heaven, forever. This judgment upon Satan is partial at first. Satan is banished from accessing the Throne of God. However, he still engages in covert warfare against the Body of Christ, and the world is stupefied as to the intensity of this battle. The world lapses into a deathly sleep, while Satan's militant host invades them with great wrath.	The Fifth Bowl is the complete wrath of God upon those who persecuted the Congregation of Christ. The Beast, his kingdom, and his followers are cast into darkness where there is weeping and gnashing of teeth (Mt 8:12).

The star that fell is Satan. His name in Hebrew is "Abaddan" and in Greek is "Appolyon"; both mean destroyer. Even though he is a fallen star from Heaven, he still has authority to destroy and take captive the souls of men and women.

Revelation 9:1 parallels the same apocalyptic events recorded in Revelation 12:9 and 20:1-3. Satan has fallen to the Earth from Heaven where he once had access to the Throne. Those who say the language of Revelation is "literal" have a huge problem when the star is called "Him." Those insanely committed to literalism actually remove "Him" from the original text. What a travesty of Scriptural discernment!

Jesus speaks of an event that *had not* happened yet as though it had,

> "'And you, Capernaum, who are exalted to heaven, will be brought down to Hades. He who hears you hears Me, he who rejects you rejects Me, and he who rejects Me rejects Him who sent Me.' Then the seventy returned with

joy, saying, "Lord, even the demons are subject to us in Your name." And He said to them, 'I saw Satan fall like lightning from heaven'" (Lk 10:15-18). (Cross-references: Jn 12:31, 32, 19:11; 2Co 11:12-15; 2Ti 3:1-5)

After Christ's Ascension and the war with Michael and his angels, Satan can no longer act as the accuser of the Saints before God. He has not given up the fight, but *now* works through deception, delusion, wrong thinking, misery, and torment. However, he remains under Christ's power. In Matthew 8:29, we will see that with the advance of Christ on Earth, the demons are going to retreat and back off. They say, "Have you come to torture us before the time?" They know their doom. They are fearful because they realize who Jesus is. Jesus has come to take back what Satan has captured. The demons are trembling. After Calvary, Satan was cast out. He is not at war with Christ but only with the gospel-preaching congregation. The only power he has is to cloud the issue with false doctrine. Satan wants us to question the deity of Christ and the authority of Christ's Word.

Satan asked Jesus, "*if*" you are the Son of God in Matthew, Chapter 4. In the Greek, the word "*if*" can be translated three different ways.

1. If = what you may be.

2. If = what you are not.

3. If = what you are.

In this instance, Satan used the third condition. He knew who Jesus was. The demons recognized the one God (Jas 2:19), and they begged Jesus not to cast them into the Abyss (Lk 8:31).

The Abyss is also known as the *pit* or deep in the book of Genesis. If we study the word "deep", the conclusion will be the same as the Abyss. Genesis 1:1 refers to the "Darkness" on the face of the deep. An interesting question is, "Did God create the darkness or was it already present before the creation of the world?" The following Scriptures give insight to this darkness.

"He drew a circular horizon on the face of the waters, at the boundary of light and darkness" (Job 26:10).

"The dead tremble, those under the waters and those inhabiting them. Sheol is naked before Him, and destruction has no covering" (Job 26:5, 6).

"When He prepared the heavens, I was there, When He drew a circle on the face of the deep, When He established the clouds above, When He strengthened the fountains of the deep" (Pr 8:27, 28).

"For you have said in your heart: 'I will ascend into heaven, I will exalt my throne above the stars of God; I will also sit on the mount of the congregation on the farthest sides of the north; I will ascend above the heights of the clouds, I will be like the Most High.' Yet you shall be brought down to Sheol, to the lowest depths of the Pit" (Isa 14:13-15).

A Picture of Satan in the Abyss

Sometime before creation, Satan was cast out of Heaven. However, he was still allowed to present himself before the Throne and accuse the brethren (Job 1:6-12). Actually, the Book of Revelation describes Satan being cast out from Heaven in three different texts (Rev 9:1, 12:7, 8, 20:1, 2). We will understand that before Christ ascended to the Throne, Satan still had the ability to be before the Father. However, after Jesus ascended to the Throne, Christians no longer have an adversary before the Throne but an *advocate before the throne* (1Jn 2:1). The prosecuting attorney has been silenced. The defense attorney is now before our throne of Justice.

This dark pit contains different characters. As previously noted, it contains those who have perished and were *not* in covenant with God. The Scriptures record,

"Death and Hades delivered up the dead who were in them. And they were judged, each one according to his works. Then Death and Hades were cast into the lake of fire. This is the second death. And anyone not found written in the Book of Life was cast into the lake of fire" (Rev 20:13-15).

If "death" refers to the people who currently exist, but who will die a first death when Christ comes, then Hades refers to those who are already dead. Those who are dying must face the first death before entering into the second. God is going to kill them, and they will receive their resurrected bodies to enter into eternity. It is not a matter of whether or not eternity exists. No, it is a matter of *where* one will spend eternal life, in *Heaven* or H*ell*.

"Have the gates of death been revealed to you? Or have you seen the doors of the shadow of death?" (Job 38:17)

Not only is the dead spirit in the pit, but also the angels who did not keep their first estate.

> "And the angels who did not keep their proper domain, but left their own abode, He has reserved in everlasting chains under darkness for the judgment of the great day; as Sodom and Gomorrah, and the cities around them in a similar manner to these, having given themselves over to sexual immorality and gone after strange flesh, are set forth as an example, suffering the vengeance of eternal fire" (Jude 6, 7).

These angels did not keep their first state in Heaven with God. They left their own dwelling and had to accept judgment consigning them to the underworld. Their first estate is the pre-cosmic world in eternity past. When God said, "In the beginning," He is referring to time, space, and matter. The creation of this pit, however, could have been before or after the fall of the angels. In God's foreknowledge, He could have created this pit in His anger against the disobedient spirits. On the other hand, it could have been created before the fall of the angels. Logically, if the pit was created before the creation of the world that would mean the angels existed before the creation of the world.[70]

We need to understand that *Hades* is *not* the everlasting hell (Rev 20:14). It is a place of reservation for judgment, as 2 Peter 2:4 indicates.

When God created the world, Job says,

> "Where were you when I laid the foundations of the earth? Tell Me, if you have understanding. Who determined its measurements? Surely you know! Or who stretched the line upon it? To what were its foundations fastened? Or who laid its cornerstone, when the morning stars sang together, and all the sons of God shouted for joy?" (Job 38:4-7)

It is an interesting thought that the angels were present on the day the Earth was created. This would mean that God created Hades and Hell sometime between eternity past and the first day of creation.

Another time spectrum to consider in the genesis of Hell and Hades is the fall of Lucifer. Jesus confirmed the event that Isaiah described (Lk 10:18).

> "How you are fallen from heaven, O Lucifer, son of the morning! How you are cut down to the ground, you who weakened the nations! For you have

said in your heart: 'I will ascend into heaven, I will exalt my throne above the stars of God; I will also sit on the mount of the congregation. On the farthest sides of the north; I will ascend above the heights of the clouds, I will be like the Most High.' Yet you shall be brought down to Sheol, to the lowest depths of the Pit" (Isa 14:12-15).

Because Satan mocked God's justice, he was banished from God's presence, but "God is not mocked. Whatsoever is sown will also be reaped" (Gal 6:7). As "the cherub that covered," Satan stood in relationship to the angels in precisely the same way that Christ stands in relationship to the human race. The word "propitiation" or cover is the same word used of the mercy seat covering of the Ark that was later placed in the Tabernacle.

What can we make of this? It was Jesus' job to cover the guilt and sin of the human race before the eyes of God by the shedding of His blood. If we study the theology of the mercy seat, the cherubs gazed intently at the blood sprinkled on the mercy seat. Satan was guilty of gross neglect of duty in the eyes of the Holy God. Satan violated his responsibility of being the propitious covering. The awesome Holy God is both merciful and just. It is possible that since there was no sin in the world, then God's justice was unknown; there was nothing but goodness, a good God, and a good universe. However, when Satan failed to make propitiation, he uncovered the Holy-Just aspect of God's nature, and God was therefore disposed to act in justice. God cannot be mocked. It is at this very point that God expresses divine "weakness" (1Co 1:25), which is stronger than man's. Just as human beings say, "How can God allow evil in this world? Where was God when these bad things happen?" It is assumed that Satan mocked God before the angels. Humanity should be thankful to God that His Son was not negligent in His duty, when He came to shed His blood to make a covering for guilty sinners before this just and holy God. Satan failed the angels; God's Son did not.[71]

After Satan's original sin and fall, everlasting fire was prepared for him (Mt 25:41). He was not cast immediately into the Lake of Fire. Since the same word "cast down" is used of his pre-cosmic fall as is used in his post-cosmic fall into the Lake of Fire, we might say that Satan suffers this humiliating abuse at least twice. He was also cast out when Christ ascended to the Throne as the King of Kings and the Lord of Lords! (Rev 12:10). In its original context, Satan's being cast out did not prevent his accusations against the human race, especially those whom God considered saints. Satan had only one thing in common with God – he knew that even the best of saints were still sinners (Rev 12:10). So, as a political prisoner who has not repented of his crimes against the Kingdom, Satan was still able to try to exploit the weaknesses of the Kingdom.

After Christ's Ascension to the THRONE, Satan was chained, "restricted" by The Gospel. If He was cast into the Pit – Hades, he can still hold headquarters to plan for demonic attacks, but he cannot come anywhere near to doing the damage he inflicted as being a prosecutor before the THRONE of God. Does this mean Satan is no longer a terror to the Kingdom of Christ? Absolutely not! He is a roaring lion seeking whom he may devour (1Pe 5:8). Even after being cast out after the Ascension, Satan continues to seek the woman who brought forth the man-child (Rev 12:13, 14). What is comforting to Christians is the knowledge that his head is bruised, and he is bound in respect to the Gospel. We understand that Christians deal with Satan through his emissaries, demonic angels. He seeks to injure the Body of Christ through his devouring "locusts."

The greatest proof that Satan is bound is that he cannot prevent the spread of the Gospel, and he cannot afford competition with Jesus Christ. Before the Ascension, we might say from the world's perspective, that Christ and Satan were equal. Now the whole world can know that Christ is superior to Satan, and the victory is permanently on His side. Furthermore, what Satan could not be, he has now become. He wanted to be King, but Jesus is the only true King. Now, Satan is the King of the Pit (Rev 9:11). Our adversary, the Devil, was replaced with an advocate The Righteous One (1Jn 2:1).

God brought into existence the pre-cosmic abode for the incarceration of fire in Hades. The ultimate Lake of Fire was prepared for the Devil and his angels. We must remember that this doom was pronounced for the Devil and his angels, not humankind. This is why it is said, in the Judgment Day, the Beast, the false prophet, and whosoever was not written in the Lamb's Book of Life, will be joined with Satan in this fiery destiny (Rev 20:10, 15). It is a shame to the lost human race that from the beginning, God did not intend for anyone to be there except the Devil and his angels.

> "Then He will also say to those on the left hand, 'Depart from Me, you cursed, into the everlasting fire prepared for the Devil and his angels" (Mt 25:41).

Can the reader understand why the world desperately needs a savior? It does not need a savior that can only rescue them from their own insecurities and weaknesses. The world needs a savior that can rescue them from Hell. This eternal hell fire was created in God's full anger. Those who go there will experience this anger forever and ever. God says, concerning eternal hell,

> "For a fire is kindled in My anger, and shall burn to the lowest hell; It shall consume the earth with her increase, and set on fire the foundations of the mountains" (Dt 32:22).

> "Yes, for the king it is prepared. He has made it deep and large; Its pyre is fire with much wood; The breath of the Lord, like a stream of brimstone, kindles it" (Isa 30:33).

If someone suggests hell is too great a punishment for a human being, the question can also be asked, "Is hell too great a punishment for Satan?" The devil's hell is being discussed.

In all probability, the expression "circle of the deep" (Pr 8:27) refers to the crust of the Earth that God formed over the deep in Genesis 1:2. This "deep" is associated with darkness, boiling waters, steam, and mist. After Christ's Ascension, Satan was given authority to establish his throne in this place. Because of the attention drawn to this pit after the 5th angel sounded, it is obvious that even the pit is under Christ's control and authority. The world is ignorant of this. How enlightening it is for Christ's Select to know that He is in control. Even though Satan sits upon the second greatest throne in the universe, his throne is also under Christ's control. Satan is a usurper and will be found out for who he really is – a fraud. There are many usurping, undeserving leaders in the nations of this perishing world, and they have much in common with this angel of the dark underworld; not the least of which is their eternal destiny – if they do not repent!

Although Hades will be in existence until the end of time, God is trying to show us that even though Satan is a usurping coward, God is still in control. He exposes the three weak points of Satan concerning:

1) The Blood of Christ

2) The Word of God

3) The Seal of the Holy Spirit emboldens Christians (Rev 12:11)

THE APOCALYPTIC AND OCCULTIC WORLDS

The study of contrasts is a remarkable discipline. In his First Epistle, John is inspired to contrast light and darkness, love and hate, truth and error, good and evil, and those who are "of us" and those who have "gone out from us." Probably the greatest contrast in the universe is "The star falling from heaven" and then being assigned to the deepest abyss. This contrast is delineated in Isaiah 14:12 "How are you fallen from heaven Oh, Lucifer?" We read further, "Yet you shall be brought down to Hell, to the sides of the Pit" (14:15). So the reader of the Old Testament, who knew Satan fell in the past, is also an encouragement for the reader of the New Testament to understand He fell from Heaven after the ascension of Christ. Just think of it! Falling from the heights of God's Heaven to the lowest pit in the universe! What a loss. What an irreversible, irretrievable loss! In the history of contrasts, none can surpass what is found in prophecy (Ezk 28: 7, 8) and in the Apocalypse (Rev 9:1, 2, 20:1, 2). We have not mentioned it before, but, possibly, Satan wanted either authority, or perhaps in his vain mind, to be the ruler in The Eternal New Jerusalem. Like Absalom's rebellion against his Father David, Absalom attempted to gather revolutionary forces against the Throne.

Although the Apocalyptic World is hidden to the reprobate mind (Ro 1:28), it can be "revealed" to the illuminated mind (Heb 6:4, 10:32). The Lord of the Apocalypse wants to mentally transfer His world into our world (Col 3:2; 2Co 10:5; Ro 8:6; Php 4: 8).

The word "occult" means "hidden." To be sure, it is a real (not imaginary) world, but those who think they lived in the "real" world are more influenced by the occult than the real world of which they boast. Why, for instance is so much of our time filled with the gloom that comes from the mental occupation of remorse, sorrow, guilt, and unforgiving spirits? Such disparaging thinking drains our mental energy; it is not from God! This world is visibly hidden to billions of souls who have mentally migrated into its haunts. What is almost laughable is that people will pay a medium or psychic money to enter this world in our behalf, and we already live there for free.

Psychologist, psychiatrists, legal experts, law enforcement agents, and psychotherapeutic religionists are paid professionals who think they specialize in treating or countering the energy and activity of this "nether world," (1Pe 2:4), but they, themselves, are not exempt from the power of this world. Almost every politician runs on the promise that they are going to do something about heroine, methane and other drugs abuses. But NOT ONE OF THEM believes in the underworld we are describing from the Apocalypse, and most of them are afraid to even mention that which the demons of drug abuse, "pharmekia," (www.google.com: Witchcraft) fear the most – The Gospel of the Kingdom of Christ!

The word "Tartarus" – meaning "the low world" is translated "gloomy dungeons." Organized Crime Syndicates used to be called, "The Underworld," because the spirits of the underworld governed the darkened lives of those who pursued this manner of deathly existence.

THEIR FOOLISH MINDS ARE DARKENED.

(RO 1:21; EPH 4:18)

We experience different levels of darkness as we descend deeper into this occult world. We are familiar with the results of those who have gone so deeply into this world that they actually enter into the realm of demonic trances, supposed encounters with spirits of the dead, and Satan worship. The deeper we go in giving our time, talent, treasure, and tears, the more the King of The Occultist Abyss will promise us the world (Mt 4:9; Rev 9:11; Job 26:6; Pr 15:11).

We have already mentioned the deepest level – that of occulted, demon worship, but let us consider those who are occult influenced but not as dominated as others. As our spirit seeks to escape the depths of the abyss, we may number the levels necessary for us to escape the nightmare darkness of demonic imprisonment. The following steps are the occult influences in ascending order with level 1 being the worst level of existence and level 6 being the total escape from the occult world. These levels are:

1) Those who are completely possessed and obsessed with the thinking attributed to unclean spirits.

2) Those who think more logically and reasonably than average.

3) Those that have an above average self-discipline.

4) Those that have a passion for TRUE (demonstrable-observable) science.

5) Those that have family (domestic) love for spouse and children.

6) Those that have the kind of morality described in the New Testament.

Of course, those who are delivered from the kingdom of darkness into the Kingdom of Christ (Col 1:13) have escaped the occult influences (Rev 9:4). We have heard of the seal of Satan's Beast, 666, but we forget that the children of Christ are also sealed with the Holy Spirit of promise (Eph1: 13, 4:30). When we read New Covenant Scripture, we have the equivalent of a face-to-face encounter with the risen Jesus (1Co 13:12 with 2Co 3:18), for the New Testament is a mirror of the inward spirit (Jas 1:23), and this is especially true of The Book of Apocalypse. We actually see things that "are not" (1Co 1:28, 2:6; Ro 4:17; Heb 11:27).

Thus, we learn from this ascending scale that the occult world influences those who are at apparent innocent levels of occult activity (that are not as noticeable), but are still possessed by the same "devouring locust-type plagues" (Rev 9:7), to which an avowed satanist would succumb.

An example of someone who attempts to escape the dark underworld is someone who unknowingly serves a demon of good works. Of course, some self-righteous person may get angry with this evaluation, but if we have not obeyed Christ, "We are dead in our trespasses and sins in which we formerly walked according to the course of this world, according to the Prince of the power of the air, of the spirit that is now working in the sons of disobedience" (Eph 2:1, 2).

In other words, we just plain serve the Devil thorough lusts of the flesh, indulging desires of the carnal nature and mind, and by this nature, we are "children of wrath" (Eph 2:3). Thus, human nature covers evil from within by promoting benevolent works from without.

People who engage in benevolent work and give 100% to social, benevolent and humanitarian outreach, while at the same time are at war with God, are actually giving the same arguments that atheists and satanists promote to justify their refusal to make Christ the rightful Lord of their life. Perhaps the greatest argument of this attitude is when a benevolent demon enters the "Church Board," and it is convincing them that the Social Gospel outreach of benevolence is more important than The Great Commission to win lost souls. Unknowingly, by this self-righteous humanitarian spirit, "The (SON) is blotted out by the smoke of spiritual darkness" (Rev 9:2) in the same way that an "evolutionary spirit that worships father Time and Chance" tries to "Blot out The Word of God in Regard to His Creation" (Ro 1:25; Eph 4:18). The occult's influence on the soul depends upon how large a role the Word of God plays in our environment. When the Egyptians forgot their Biblical role model, Joseph (Ex 1:8; Ac 7:18, 19), they paid dearly, and many in that country are still paying the price of godless ingratitude today.

The Word of God has a powerful influence on society. Scores of examples can be given as proof of this, but one will suffice, as we have noted in Luther's and Hitler's Germany. The Word's influence varies from country to country and from time to time.

Historians once referred to certain countries as "Dark Countries," countries like the Asian nations of Burma or India, African nations, Polynesian, and Mid-Eastern, because they were influenced by Black Magic, Voodooist, Witchcraft, and certain religious exercises that delved into incantations and trances connected to very powerful spirits. People who practiced such elements of the occult testified to certain sensational results in connection with occult fantasies and emotional releases.

The Bible, in many verses, addresses such experiences with candid rebuke. God's Spirit expresses forthrightly that Satan can enter into these séances and is capable of deceiving the whole world (Rev 12:9; Jn 5:43; Mt 24:24 – referring to conditions prior to 70 A.D). The whole world lies in this darkness (1Jn 5:19) and rather than seek the light, makes apologies for the victims of the occult who dwell there, and makes excuses for the sin that drives them there.

But the apocalyptic world bursts upon the peoples in these once darken countries and now there is a Gospel revival of light in Iran, Syria, Egypt, China, North and South Korea and throughout Asia and Africa.

> "There's a call comes ringing over the restless wave
>
> Send the Light! Send the Light!
>
> There are souls to rescue, there are souls to save
>
> Send the Light! Send the Light!"
>
> "Send the Light, The precious Gospel Light

> Let is shine, from shore to shore.
>
> Send the Light, the Precious Gospel Light
>
> Let it shine, forever more!"

Russia lost 70 years of Gospel enlightenment because of its Communist Revolution, but the doors were opened to the Gospel in 1990 A.D. When our missionary team visited Russia in 1990-91, we were invited to high schools and universities to teach Biblical principles regarding citizens' responsibilities to their government and the government's responsibilities to its citizens. Now the gospel is even taught in Russian government schools (www.christianpost.com: Russia Makes Religious Education Mandatory in Schools). As a world power, can you imagine where Russia will be in the next ten years? Jesus says, "If I by Beelzebub cast out demons by whom do your sons cast them out? But if I cast out demons by the spirit of God, then the Kingdom of God has come unto you (Mt 12:28 with Lk 11:19).

The Russians know something that our American politicians fail to recognize. The Russians know that fighting Islam, among other evils, is not just economic and military, but it is spiritual warfare. If we are not fighting evil spirits with the Spirit of God, the enemy who is driven by the spirit of evil, or Satan, cannot be prevented. In secular America, the driving political force is syncretism, and the equality of all people, even our vilest and militant enemies. A political leader can be easily debunked for mentioning the Bible, the Holy Spirit, the Devil, and subsequent evil. Your children will suffer for lack of training in God's Word and Spiritual values. Jesus said that they will be your judges! History will not judge the leaders of Russia as harshly as the leaders of America, who accepted "political correctness" and missed their golden opportunity to inculcate spiritual values into the minds of their children.

Patrick Buchanan, the staunch conservative scholar, has throughout his career, steadfastly opposed Russia at almost every political twist and turn. He now has the opinion that Vladimir Putin and his government are far more righteous than the USA in virtuous convictions and morals.[72] Vladimir Putin is a political murderer, but thousands of standard moralists agree with Buchanan's assessment that not-withstanding Putin's high-handed methods to eliminate all political opposition and to strengthen the Russian state; the current Putin is a "Paleo conservative."

In just 25 years, while America is morally digressing, the Russian people are transitioning into a more moral country, like America once was. Russia, along with the once "Dark Countries," is being exposed to the "unveiling" of the Gospel light from The Throne and is no longer being exploited (as America now is) by the religious, political, and academic institutions of occulted darkness with its enticements to wholesale, widespread iniquity.

To the contrary, America, Canada, and once comparatively righteous Europe are descending rapidly into Sheol. Those nations who forget God (Ps 9:17) descend into the occult Sheol. Past righteousness exalted these countries, "They once knew God" (Ro 1:2), but then they began accepting widespread sin and iniquity. Such ungodly behavior is a shame and disgrace (Pr 14:34). In today's America, Godly people agree that our political leaders are possessed of an insane rage to glut the nation upon the lust of the flesh, which is the standard measure of how entrenched a soul may be in the occult-hadean world. For instance, the Attorney General, Governor, crony judges of the State of Virginia, and Federal Judges have even overturned the will (vote) of the majority of the people, as expressed in an Amendment to the Virginia Constitution. They have overturned traditional, God-ordained marriage in favor of Sodomite unions "redefined also as marriage." If you can believe it!

Comparing where the U.S. is today, after having had more than 200 years of freedom to practice the freedom of righteousness, to Russia's less than 20 years to practice righteousness, Patrick Buchanan's comparison of Putin and Obama is classic. Consider the following eight areas:

1) Pursuing a fierce war against terrorism,

2) Supporting other countries that fight the same terrorism that America does,

3) Recognizing that sodomy is abnormal, unnatural behavior,

4) Supporting the nation's Christians,

5) Opposing the persecution of Christians worldwide,

6) Believing that in the home and family lie the nation's strength,

7) Discouraging abortion,

8) Encouraging the birth of children and expansion of the family, and

9) Legislating Bible study in Russian schools.

If they were to grade Putin and Obama on the eight principles above, even America's liberal press would grade Putin's use of Biblical principles ahead of Obama's.

We are not indicating that Putin is an angel. I remember the Russian submarine (Kursk) explosion in the Barents Sea (August, 2000 A.D.) when 118 sailors died. Putin was blamed for a number of tactical errors in responding to this tragedy. Putin, like all of us, is implicated in many ways for less than perfect leadership. As we write on December 3, 2014, Russia completed a military move on Ukraine. This military move reminds us of Russia's invasion of Georgia under President Medvedev in 2008 A.D. The Red Horse of war is ever on notice. This horse fuels the spirits that we call "war mongers."

We need to ask ourselves, "What is the prevailing spirit that drives men to want to kill each other on the battlefield, which the spirit of the Red Horse?" Could the Red Horse sent from Christ's Throne also be the driving spirit of militant Islam's quest for human blood in spreading their religion? Can such a spirit of dilution be sent from God to those who love a lie more than they love the truth (2Th 11:12)? Putin was at war with Ukraine. Obama remains at war with us, his own countrymen. Putin's war is killing people physically. Obama's war is killing America's people spiritually.

With regard to the family, the Sochi Winter Olympics featured husband and wives pushing baby carriages in the "Opening Presentation and Welcome" to the 2014 Winter Olympic Games in Russia. Of course, America's liberal family- hating media mocked the "baby carriage routine" as amateur banality. We would expect such mocking from those "family haters" who hate the very fabric of the family that holds American society together, but God loves and blesses His families from all nations (Ge 28:14; Gal 3:16-27).

LIKE JOHN, IN OUR OWN SPIRIT, IT IS POSSIBLE FOR US TO SPIRITUALLY (APOCALYPTICALLY) ASCEND INTO HEAVEN.

We remember that people go to Heaven "affectionately" (Col 3:1-3) before they go there in glorified body. Similarly, people experience the mental torment of the Hades Occult world before they go there in soul, and the final Lake of Fire in body and soul (Mt 10:28). The word "occult" means hidden or unseen. Jesus asserted demonstratively that a lost soul must have a resurrected body to prevent incineration in Hell. On the other hand, He also taught that a Christian must have a glorified body to prevent evaporation in a foreign element outside time and space (Jn 5:28, 29).

Just as an MRI or CAT scan can determine what physical diseases or deficiencies lie beneath the surface (such as "occult diseases" hidden from the eye), we can examine our own heart, or allow someone else to apply the Scriptural test to determine what drives our thoughts – Is it the Apocalyptic of the Holy Spirit or the Occult of evil spirits? There is a deep stream within us. Just as a swollen river or the ocean in hurricane season can erupt at any time, so too our mind can flow over with rage, anger, evil surmising, jealousy, envy, covetousness, sexual immorality, fornication, adultery, sensuality, idolatry, sorcery, enmity, strife, division, dissention, jealousy, deceit, rivalry, orgies, and other sins (Gal 5:19-21).

A river also flows from Heaven (Rev 22:1; Ps 46:4), and it makes the heart glad. Although it flows down from Heaven, it can flow up out of our innermost being (Jn 7:38) and fill our heart with kindness, thanksgiving, praise, adoration, goodness, virtue, love, joy, peace, patience, and faithfulness. Heaven's river provides a good old apocalyptic feeling, like John had when he viewed the Throne of Christ (Gal 5:22-26).

DO OUR NATIONAL LEADERS WANT US TO BE GOVERNED FROM HEAVEN OR HELL?

"The (tongue) is set on fire by Hell" (Jas 3:6).

Advocates of homosexual marriage, among other things, are not really speaking from the depths of human reasoning or wisdom. They are speaking words that originate from Hell. Because homosexual marriage was totally unheard of in John's day (2,000 years ago), and for that matter not a universally accepted practiced even in the most abominable and uncultured societies preceding his day, God's chosen ambassador, James, did not address the inexplicable, absurd idea of two human beings of the same sex joining together in matrimony. It would have been acceptable if they saw two animals of the same sex trying to mate (the animals lacking the intelligence to understand no "puppies, calves, or kittens" would emerge from this union), but completely outlandish to even consider that some "god" would bless such a union in the human race. Granted, sodomy was practiced in Sodom, Greece, and Rome, but America gets a failing grade from God (Lev 18:22, 20:13) for being another nation in this abomination of national destruction by actually granting homosexuals a marriage license.

In this "Commentary on Revelation," I have spent much time focusing on the two worlds that influence human thought and philosophy. The highest is the Apocalyptic World into which John entered through the Holy Spirit (Rev 1). John's visions of the invisible world of God, the Messiah, pre-cosmic angels and demons, humanity, and nations throughout the ages have survived two millenniums of attacks by Satan. While most theologians discourage the reading of Apocalypse, the Lord encourages us to read it. Our reading the Apocalypse enables us to live blessed and holy lives under the canopy of this Apocalyptic World (Rev 1:3).

Unfortunately, most of us live in the "Occulted-Abyss" of Revelation, Chapter 9. Both the worlds of the "occult" and the "apocalypse" are unseen to the human eye. The Occult wants to remain unknown, while the Apocalyptic can be "Revealed." However, we are fools if we fail to understand that we are influenced by these two worlds, as they direct, more or less.

THREE MEN AND ONE WOMAN MANIPULATED, MANGLED, MANACLED, AND MANAGED BY THE OCCULT WORLD OF THE BOTTOMLESS PIT

Three men and their "woman" give us instructions from The Occult World.

The year 2014 A.D. was a Year of infamy in America. With President Obama's support, Virginia Governor McAuliffe, Virginia Attorney General Herring and their "henchwoman" Judge Arenda Wright Allen (all of which I pray for incessantly), overturned the will of Virginia's popular vote to preserve God's Natural Law of marriage (a union of man and woman). In doing so, they used their "Hellfire-consumed-tongues" to fight the Holy God with temporary success. By God's preserving, providential, grace, neither I nor any true Christian man or woman of God will accept such blasphemous drivel and disobedience to God's Natural Law. It is one thing for those who engage in the sin of sodomy, and thereby want justification from the "Higher Powers" to engage in their sin with impunity. It is another when we read Habakkuk 1:4, 5, and God answered this insanity with predictable and inevitable judgments on wicked leaders and their nations—one of which was having the Gospel of forgiveness of sins preached in their nations (Ac 13:38-41). All we have to do is read of Jerusalem's destruction in 70 A.D. to understand what happens to nations that rejects the Gospel (Ro 11:21; Addendums D & E).

Thus, those influenced by the "Pit" have a higher power governing them! That is Gehenna Hell that puts this occult fire in their mouths. The full realization of their unclean spirit-inspired lives will be fully known before the Godhead of Heaven who will meet us all on the other side of "The Valley of the Shadow of Death." In that fateful moment, THE JUDGE will determine who is on the RIGHT and who is on the LEFT! And we are not just talking politics.

The above three mentioned men and one woman are manipulated, mangled, manacled, and managed by the Occult World of The Bottomless Abyss. I am deeply grieved (and pray there are millions of other Americans who feel the same) and have no malice toward anyone (whether they agree or disagree), but we must in these "perilous last days" (2Ti 3:1-5) take a stand for what "The Lord hath said" in hopes of rescuing even ONE lost soul from the clutches of hell fire whose smoke defiles the very garment of their licentious flesh (Jude 23).

If we spent any time at all with other people, we discover, by the words of the tongue, the real source of their existence, whether their lives are directed from above (Jas 1:17) or below (3:14-18). James actually tells us that when there is an angry outburst, or filthy, unseemly conversation, "The tongue is set afire from Hell" (Jas 3:6). The "Hell" in this verse is actually Gehenna. How frightful it would be to me, if I knew my words were originating from a damnable destiny to which I have yet to arrive.

Just as Christ and Satan vie for supremacy in our lives, the apocalyptic or occult vies for supremacy in our world. One of the two will win out. In our own personal lives, which one do we want to win out?

THE APOCALYPTIC WORLD

Forty times in Revelation we see the THRONE of Christ on top of all things. As we identify with this Throne, we reach a higher level of existence. Just as those who are drawn into the downward spiral of the Occult World sink to different levels of existence, as mentioned previously, so those who seek the higher life in Christ identify with the Apocalyptic.

When people hear of the Apocalyptic, they are somewhat confused. People are more familiar with the Occult because most of us can and have identified with that world. People more familiar with the Occult even associate the Devil with someone who exhibits such emotional and mental traits; that someone is even called "A devil." Most scriptwriters for the modern-day pageant, the drama, or entertainment are always associated with this world. It is the common lot of sub-human life existence. It would be the best decision we have ever made, if we would quit looking down for pleasure in this world. The invitation from above is to "Come up to Jesus, and He will give us abundant, supernatural life!" (Jn 10:10). Yes, even though He ascended to Heaven on a cloud 2,000 years ago, He still invites us to come to Him today! He will then come to us! Scripture tells us repeatedly to watch for the coming of Jesus (and we should), but we may fail to realize that He will receive us when we die, "And he said, 'Lord Jesus receive my spirit!" (Acts 7:59)

Revelation 9:2: When he opened the Abyss, smoke rose from it like the smoke from a gigantic furnace. The sun and sky were darkened by the smoke from the Abyss.

This smoke represents the moral and spiritual darkness of demons.

Revelation 9:3: And out of the smoke locusts came down upon the earth and were given power like that of scorpions of the earth.

Out of this smoke comes the demonic force of Satan to bring spiritual harm and defeat to the world. The sting of false doctrine augments the penalty of sin, which is death. False doctrine causes created souls to perish. These locusts represent a very destructive force; they are demons of torment. Joel describes the power that an army of locusts can have on vegetation,

> "What the chewing locust left, the swarming locust has eaten; what the swarming locust left, the crawling locust has eaten; and what the crawling locust left, the consuming locust has eaten. Awake, you drunkards, and weep; And wail, all you drinkers of wine, Because of the new wine, for it has been cut off from your mouth. For a nation has come up against My land, Strong, and without number; His teeth are the teeth of a lion, and he has the fangs of a fierce lion. He has laid waste My vine, and ruined My fig tree; He has stripped it bare and thrown it away; Its branches are made white" (Joel 1:4-7).

THE AMERICAN SIN PARTY (AS WELL AS THOSE POLITICAL LEADERS FROM OTHER COUNTRIES WHO DEFY GOD'S NATURAL LAW) HAS PERMITTED SATAN TO RELEASE HIS LOCUSTS OF IMMORALITY.

Generally speaking, America at the turn of the 21st Century has been gridlocked by two opposing political parties, one being a "Sin Party" and the other, a "Condoning Sin Party." If there is no "righteous indignation" among the people, the encroaching victories of the "Sin Party" will plunge the country into such moral darkness as to paralyze it spiritually. This destruction represents the war against the Body of Christ. God is using Satan as His unwilling worker to test and try the saints. This constant warfare of the Congregation against the demonic forces of the world will continue until the end of time.

Satan's locusts are highly lethal and organized. These locusts understand the significance of the battle that is taking place, and they use their painful sting to cause as much damage as possible. The unfortunate casualty of this war is – Christians forget that God is in control.

Revelation 9:4: They were told not to harm the grass of the earth or any plant or tree, but only those people who did not have the seal of God on their foreheads.

The vegetation in the passage symbolizes life. As we shall see, instead of completely destroying everything, the demons were only given the ability to torture.

In this instance, these demons are only given the ability to harm the "non-Christians." However, some say demons can obsess (mentally distract) Christians, but demons do not possess them.

Revelation 9:5: They were not given power to kill them, but only to torture them for five months. And the agony they suffered was like that of the sting of a scorpion when it strikes a man.

Often, torture is much worse than death. Those who come under attack are not killed, but tormented. The five months is not an actual time of suffering, but a modified judgment has been placed on them. The interesting part about this passage of Scripture is the ability of the locusts to recognize who has the seal and who does not! They recognize the congregations of people who are the light of the world and those who are not. The suffering people who are not sealed by the

Holy Spirit are so agitated and miserable that they cause others to suffer. This is the goal of the demonic force. They want to torment a community until it reaches such a low, demoralize state that it cannot recover. Unfortunately, alcohol, sodomy, drug, and sex addiction torments every segment of the innocent population, not just the guilty.

Revelation 9:6: *During those days' men will seek death, but will not find it; they will long to die, but death will elude them.*

People who are deluded, deceived, and confused by the darkness of pseudo religion become so agitated that they want to die, but most people do not die. How often have we heard people say, "I just wish I were dead"? These people are so agitated that they would prefer death to life. Since the people who suffer make other people suffer, they become liabilities to those who are in Christ. Satan's purpose is to demoralize everyone and everything. When Satan demoralizes people, he causes them to forget that Christ is in control!

Demoralized people attempt to prevent the spread of the Gospel testimony. These locusts inspire Satan's unknowing workers to torment the Earth, so people cannot think about the Gospel, let alone allow it to spread. A wartime example of this would be when a wounded soldier becomes a liability, he may place at least three other soldiers in harm's way when they tend to him. Demons know that because of the Satanic-like love of self, tormented, "wounded" souls drag down other souls. This is part of the terrorist agenda to conquer populations through terror, fear, and shared grief that cripples the will.

The above passage is also the only Scripture to address the thought of suicide. The men seek death, and they long to die, but it eludes them." What most people are unaware of is that suicide is a way out of this world into another existence. The existence described here is not pleasant. Unless forbidden by God, Satan does have power to kill someone (Job 1:12), but in this text we see that a tormented, dysfunctional individual is of more value to Satan. There are hundreds of examples, but one alcohol or drug abuser can bring more harm to his family, community, and social network as a long term abuser than he could if he died. Why should Satan kill his victim when he can use that victim to destroy others? This way, he gets both. This is one of the greatest reasons why there is so much evil in the world. However, we must remember this world is not totally Christ-less, and Satan is not unconditionally loosed upon us all.

Revelation 9:7-12: *The locusts looked like horses prepared for battle. On their heads they wore something like crowns of gold, and their faces resembled human faces. Their hair was like women's hair, and their teeth were like lions' teeth. They had breastplates like breastplates of iron, and the sound of their wings was like the thundering of many horses and chariots rushing into battle. They had tails and stings like scorpions, and in their tails they had power to torment people for five months. They had as king over them the angel of the Abyss, whose name in Hebrew is Abaddon, and in Greek, Apollyon. The first woe is past; two other woes are yet to come.*

The demonic forces are not only highly organized, but they are ready for battle. They are wearing a "stephanos" crown of temporary worldly victory. They deceive the nations through victories of wickedness in the imitation of genuine truth; however, this victory is neither lasting nor true.

The human faces give the reader the acknowledgment of their intelligence while the sound of their wings and iron breastplates represent the loud noises that will drown out a person's serenity of a life of peace. The "teeth of a lion" is an allegory to show how Satan is a colossal pervert and thrives within the vicinity of deception.

The king and angel of the Abyss is none other than Satan himself. He is locked into a waiting place during Christ's reign until Judgment Day. Although he is chained, Satan operates from his base of operation in this place. He still has the ability to affect the world through his demonic forces that work diligently to counteract the God's plan. The binding of Satan is conditional. This binding rests upon whether or not we accept the Gospel and live by it. Satan walks around like a roaring Lion seeking to devour people (1Pe 5:8). However, he can be resisted. He can be restricted. Job, in the Old Testament, did not possess this power. Job had to endure the sufferings of Satan in misery and discomfort. Christians have power to restrict Satan's tormenting cycles. They can bind him up and remove him from the situation (Ro 16:20). The Bible says, "Resist the devil and he will flee from you" (Jas 4:7). These demonic forces do not have the authority or power to harm Christians! This fact dismisses the claim of the Historicist that the locusts are Mohammedan hordes. But a word of caution is due here. No Christian should boast of power over Satan. Christians have authority, but Christ has the power (2Co 4:7, 12:9; Eph 1:9, 6:10).

This brings an end to one woe and introduces the Euphrates battleground. The Euphrates River is so important to prophecy because it is the great dividing line. The Euphrates is important because it represents a buffer between war and peace.

From Revelation 9:15 to 11:13, we have what seems to be a lengthy break covered by these 24 modern-day verses. I am going to compare it to a half-time intermission since these verses occur in the middle of the book. This intermission falls between the sixth and seventh trumpets of the fourth cycle of our rainbow. In this long intermission, we see the following:

1) Four Angels of Death (Rev 9:15)

2) The Angel and the "Little Scroll" (10:5, 6)

3) The Measuring of the Temple (11:1, 2)

4) Two Witnesses (11:3)

This extended break begins with the second of the three woes (9:12) and ends with the Final Judgment (11:14, 15). When we review these woes, we recall the first woe proceeded the fifth trumpet (8:13); the second woe followed the opening of Satan's pit "lair" (9:12); and the third woe, of course, "came quickly" (11:14, 15) with instant, final judgment and conquest. We shall see that this third woe occurs simultaneous with the seventh and last trumpet.

THE EUPHRATES RIVER

Revelation 9:13, 14: The sixth angel sounded his trumpet, and I heard a voice coming from the horns of the golden altar that is before God. It said to the sixth angel who had the trumpet, "Release the four angels who are bound at the great river Euphrates."

As already noted, the Euphrates River separated the Kings of the East from Israel. If a person is on one side of the river, he has war; however, if one stays on the other side, the war is restrained. The enemies had to cross the Euphrates River to enter the battlefront. The Euphrates River is a natural barrier (1Ki 4: 21; Isa 8:7) and symbolizes restraint placed upon the forces of evil.

SIXTH SEAL (6:12)	SIXTH TRUMPET (9:13)	SIXTH BOWL (16:12)
The Sixth Seal is the countdown to judgment. The universe is affected by the Lord's judgment. The people of the Earth disperse for cover from the Lamb's wrath, but they have no place to hide. The great day of wrath has come and none will withstand it. The end is near.	The Sixth Trumpet is God's warning pronouncing a judgment upon 1/3 of the Earth. It introduces a great war that is taking place. However, the results of the wars are not enough to bring about the Earth's repentance.	The Sixth Bowl introduces the final war between God, with His Holy Ones, against the Satanic forces. They have recruited demons, kings, and nations to unite themselves against God; however, they will lose. This great battle results in a condemnation of eternal Hell for Satan and his followers.

The Seventh Seal is the last. It brings all opposition to the Messiah to an end (Rev 8:1, 11:15, 16:17-21). We will present a parallel diagram of The Seven Trumpets and Seven Bowls here, and read further about it in Revelation 11:15 and 16:17.

SEVENTH SEAL (8:1)	SEVENTH TRUMPET (11:15)	SEVENTH BOWL (16:17-21)
John's opening of the Seventh Seal caused fearful silence before the Final Judgment. Look for a lengthy intermission (9:15-11:3).	The Seventh Angel sounded the Seventh Trumpet, which caused awesome, frightening shouts before the Throne of God prior to the Final Judgment. This designates the expectation and elation the holy beings expressed in the desired and long awaited judgment from God because of the long history of evil and God's great grief at the death of His Son. The temple of wrath was opened.	The Seventh Angel poured out the Seventh Bowl, and at last, final judgment from heaven, "IT IS DONE!" Babylon's false religion and all anti-Christian blasphemy are judged, finally, once for all.

Revelation 9:15: And the four angels who had been kept ready for this very hour and day and month and year were released to kill a third of mankind.

These angels were ready. This war is not an unknown distant event. They knew the exact year, month, day, and hour when this would occur. We never know when the next war will come, but these four angels know exactly the very hour, day, month, and year. Heaven permits wars, and each one is a countdown to the final war. This should be a comfort to Christians, especially those who are living in the uncertain times of "cold war" or ominous events (like possible electric grid failure, wars with China and/or Russian, and continuing Islamic attacks).

We understand that there is physical war and spiritual war. In many ways, even physical war is a spiritual battle. In the spiritual realm, satanic forces have waged this war upon the Saints ever since Christ's Testimony began to be proclaimed. However, these satanic forces do not stand a chance. The satanic argumentative question is, "Why does a loving God allow evil on Earth?" To answer this question, we must remember this question goes back into the pre-cosmic eternity. Satan failed to cover (before 1/3 of His angels) the existence of evil. In his arrogance, Satan must have thought he could face the awesome challenge of correcting it. This problem still exists and is ignored by modern educators, philosophers, and politicians. Only the inspired Scriptures have an answer to why there is evil in the world and how to correct it. We are about to observe the final solution.

Revelation 9:16-19: The number of the mounted troops was two hundred million. I heard their number. The horses and riders I saw in my vision looked like this: Their breastplates were fiery red, dark blue, and yellow as sulfur. The heads of the horses resembled the heads of lions, and out of their mouths came fire, smoke and sulfur. A third of mankind was killed by the three plagues of fire, smoke and sulfur that came out of their mouths. The power of the horses was in their mouths and in their tails; for their tails were like snakes, having heads with which they inflict injury.

Symbolically, all human wars also fall under the category of the representative figure of 200 million troops. They are a universal army ready to fight at any time in history. But, this Sixth Judgment is the final call before the complete wrath of God. It is the countdown to the seventh. The four corners of the Earth are gathered together for this monumental moment. The number 200,000,000 is not a literal number with literal soldiers in a literal place. No battle has ever been fought with this many warriors. This is an apocalyptical view that these soldiers are ready to fight anywhere at any time. These warriors are decorated in the fashion of war to show their readiness and pride in fighting. Their mouths opened with fire, smoke, and brimstone to represent the false doctrine and moral darkness that is being used as spiritual warfare. Historicists say the fire and smoke are gunpowder and explosions of war, but false doctrine from the mouth of a false prophet does far more damage. Revelation teaches that evil nations have armies that are prepared to go to war at any time in history, the very hour, day, month and year (Rev 9:15), and all of these wars lead to one final battle.

Revelation 9:20, 21: The rest of mankind that were not killed by these plagues still did not repent of the work of their hands; they did not stop worshiping demons, and idols of gold, silver, bronze, stone and wood — idols that cannot see or hear or walk. Nor did they repent of their murders, their magic arts, their sexual immorality or their thefts.

They "rest of mankind" did not repent. Wars are necessary to balance the moral universe, but they do not stop rebellion against God. In the course of human nature, wars, pestilence, economic recessions, etc. are necessary to balance the moral universe in order to turn sinful man towards God, but such catastrophes do not prevent man's innate desire to return to rebellion against God. The lack of repentance is the continuous story throughout time. God continues to allow judgments to come upon the Earth so that humanity will return to a relationship with Him. God is punishing them. As God listens to the prayers of the saints, He heaps vials, trumpet blasts, and bowls of wrath upon the world. The reason why God does not destroy the world is because of His longsuffering and patience. The last woe shows the end of the world. The first four show warnings; the last three woes show judgment. Lest we be foolish enough to think we should apologize for God in these matters, let us remember that after Calvary, God owes us nothing but justice.

Revelation Chapter Ten

Revelation 10:1: Then I saw another mighty angel coming down from heaven. He was robed in a cloud, with a rainbow above his head; his face was like the sun, and his legs were like fiery pillars.

This mighty angel is the Lord Jesus Christ. Ezekiel describes this very same person (Eze 1:26) with a little portion of the book (2:9, 10), whereas in Revelation, He has a little scroll.

The Christ of Ezekiel (1:26, 27, 2:9, 8:2) is wrapped in brightness in the color of amber from His waist up and has the appearance of fire from the waist down. He is sometimes depicted as just a hand reaching down from Heaven. We should understand that the man clothed in linen noted in Ezekiel and Daniel of the Old Testament is Jesus Christ. In John's Apocalypse, Jesus comes down from Heaven and is wrapped in the robe that seems to be a cloud. This means that He is coming with judgment. He also has a rainbow covering His head, which represents His everlasting covenant. The Covenant of Christ, specifically the precepts, is now judging those who did not participate and obey. They are receiving the penalty for refusing God's offer of grace.

Revelation 10:2-4: *He was holding a little scroll, which lay open in his hand. He planted his right foot on the sea and his left foot on the land, and he gave a loud shout like the roar of a lion. When he shouted, the voices of the seven thunders spoke. And when the seven thunders spoke, I was about to write; but I heard a voice from heaven say, "Seal up what the seven thunders have said and do not write it down."*

Daniel also speaks of a man with a book or scroll in Daniel 12:1, 4. However, the little book/scroll in Revelation must be different from Daniel's account. Daniel's account was not meant for them to understand (12:8). The little book is the New Testament. It contains the "everlasting" last Covenant of Christ with the human race (Heb 10:16, 12:24, and 13:20). The little New Testament book now governs us in faith and practice (2Co 3:6). This New Testament book addresses with all authority in Heaven and Earth the plan of salvation, and it can actually "discern our thoughts and intents" (Heb 4:12). On the other hand, the Old Testament is a big book about human life, destiny, and prospect of things to come.

Everyone should understand the little book in Revelation. As Jesus holds this book, He stands on the Earth and sea to show that this message affects the whole world! This little book is quite similar to the New Testament; in fact, it is highly likely that it is the New Testament. It is little in comparison to the Old Testament. It also possesses God's hidden mysteries! No one seems to know these mysteries; however, Paul reveals the following seven mysteries in The Epistles:

1. Conversion (Jn 3:3-5)

2. Bride of Christ (Eph 5:32)

3. Resurrection in the end (1Co 15:51)

4. Marriage (Eph 5:32)

5. Conversion of the Gentiles (Ro 11:15)

6. Iniquity (2Th 2:7)

7. Incarnation (1Ti 3:16)

The seven thunders have the answers to all other Mysteries of Life. It is now possible to know the future! Revelation encourages Christians but does not give all the answers with intricate details. If Christians knew every detail of the future, such knowledge would be far too heavy a burden to carry.

Revelation 10:5-7: Then the angel I had seen standing on the sea and on the land raised his right hand to heaven. And he swore by him who lives forever and ever, who created the heavens and all that is in them, the earth and all that is in it, and the sea and all that is in it, and said, "There will be no more delay! But in the days when the seventh angel is about to sound his trumpet, the mystery of God will be accomplished, just as he announced to his servants the prophets."

The one mystery the Angel knows and has authority to announce is that there will be no more time. The time the world is governed will be no more. This is the countdown to the final hour, the final moment. This mystery of God leads to Judgment Day and the resurrection that is shortly to be fulfilled. Christians must stand firm and unequivocally on the absolute fact that God's Kingdom exists outside of time and space. Time is only a necessary concession from God for humankind, who lives in human flesh, to prepare for an infinite destiny. Christians will not be surprised when time is no more because they have already lived a timeless, deathless life in the Spirit since they were born again (Jn 3:7), through the new-birth process. When Christians are regenerated, a timeless person was formed within, and they pass from time into eternal life. Only the kingdoms of this world are governed by time and space. Remember the third woe of the seventh trumpet is yet to come!

Revelation 10:8, 9: Then the voice that I had heard from heaven spoke to me once more: "Go, take the scroll that lies open in the hand of the angel who is standing on the sea and on the land." So I went to the angel and asked him to give me the little scroll. He said to me, "Take it and eat it. It will turn your stomach sour, but in your mouth it will be as sweet as honey."

When we read the Bible, it is like a sweet tasting honey that seems palatably pleasant. The experience of faith and salvation possess no rival when it comes to the pleasure of this life. However, once the Word is digested it turns sour. After Christians accept the Covenant of Christ through immersion, the "sourness" of the Gospel sets in. The word cuts, sharpens, and convicts throughout our lifetime. It might not seem easy, but this is God's chosen program. He wants Christians to have a bittersweet relationship with the Word. He wants them to prevail in view of their gut-wrenching soul-searching experiences!

Revelation 10:10, 11: I took the little scroll from the angel's hand and ate it. It tasted as sweet as honey in my mouth, but when I had eaten it, my stomach turned sour. Then I was told, "You must prophesy again about many peoples, nations, languages and kings."

The Scripture is nice when one first receives it, but soon its responsibility becomes bitter. If Christians want the sweetness of the Word, they must be willing to endure the bitter trials and temptations. People who become bitter because they cannot handle the conviction of the Gospel often thwart evangelists. However, the Gospel's conviction is necessary for the Christian life. Probably the most common cause of this bitter condition is the world's constant pressure placed upon Christians to fulfill the lust of their flesh. Christians must embrace Biblical, moral convictions that set them apart from the world's population that does not embrace them. But the real test from God is when Christians hold these convictions, even when contradicted by spouses, family, friends, colleagues, and peers.

The Angel goes on to tell John that he must prophesy again! He could not give up! He had to press on. Under the same circumstances, Christians must experience the same victory in Scripture. Christians must be willing to rejoice in the love of God as well as His justice. They must be willing to understand, accept, and appreciate God's justice upon the lives of this Earth. A man told his friend, "I have preached for 40 years, and I am tempted to quit, but something within me will not let me go!"

The following sections, "Measuring the Temple," "The Little Scroll" and "The Testimony," are an introduction to Chapter 11.

Measuring the Temple

The Book of Daniel deals significantly with apocalyptic beastology. Assyria, Babylon, Medo-Persia, Greece, Syria, and Rome are all labeled beasts. The reason they are addressed as beasts is because of their constant conflict with Old Testament Israel. Daniel records his extreme sadness caused by the vision (10:2, 3). Daniel, like other prophets, documents his time in history to prove the validity and accuracy when penning the Word of God. As John continues, he begins to describe Jesus Christ of Revelation as Jesus was seen in apocalyptic existence (Da 10:4ff; Rev 1:9-17).

In Daniel 10:5 ff., we acknowledge that this is a distinct angel, the Son of God, for He receives worship and does not refuse it. Daniel alone saw this vision (Da 10:7), and the Lord drew close to him. Daniel falls to the ground because it is difficult for any flesh to be in the presence of divinity (10:8). After Daniel falls to the ground in a trance (10:9), the angel Gabriel comes on the scene. He also comforts Daniels and describes how the prince of Persia, who as an appointee of Satan, hindered his prayer. Satan appoints principalities and powers, or world rulers (Eph 6:11, 12), to accomplish his purpose. Gabriel tells Daniel that he is going to see another vision for the benefit of the Jewish kingdom. The prophets had visions in order to encourage and uplift the future for the Jews. This is the same function in the message of Revelation. John is writing for the encouragement of Christians. After Daniel converses with Gabriel, Jesus returns to comfort him (10:16-19). In studying the Book of Revelation, (specifically the following chapters), it will give us a significant insight into the meaning of Revelation by understanding apocalyptic Beastology. All of the beasts of Daniel are joined into one last beast in Revelation.

The Little Scroll

First, the "little scroll" or the little book (the New Testament) is in Christ's hand, the star-holding hand of the Gospel, who has authority over the land and sea. The voice of Revelation 10:8 may be that of Christ telling John to take this book. I wish preachers today would take this book. The *book* has synonymous terms. It is referred to as a book, testimony, covenant, witness, scroll, or measurement. Daniel, Peter, and John all discuss the Glory of God in the *Book*.

This prophetic word spoken of by Peter (2Pe 1:19) was given because of God's Justice. It would have been unjust if Jesus judged the world by unspoken words (Jn 12:47-50). In this passage from John, Jesus is speaking of a book and describing how He is going to judge. The book is so very important. Paul says of the book, "God will judge the secrets of men by Jesus Christ, according to my Gospel" (Ro 2:16).

The Testimony

The "first mentioned principle" (www.google.com) to testimony is recorded in John 1:7, beginning with the life of Christ, "This man came for a witness, to bear witness of the Light, that all through him might believe" (Jn 1:7). The last mentioned principle of witness is found in Revelation 20:4,

> "And I saw thrones, and they sat on them, and judgment was committed to them. Then I saw the souls of those who had been beheaded for their witness to Jesus and for the word of God."

Let us recall, the word "witness" or "testimony" comes from the word martyr. These written accounts of the testimony were made by eyewitnesses of everything that had happened. Jesus forewarned the disciples of upcoming persecution (Lk 21:13). This testimony has been unchanged for the last 2,000 years. Paul calls the testimony a codicil in Galatians 3:15. This means that it has been confirmed and could not be added to, taken from, or cancelled. This testimony was not only established forever, but it cancelled all former covenants that God had made previously (Heb 8:13). If God's people did not have the completed testimony in John's day, they could not measure the temple! It is the little book (New Testament) that measures our Congregation and life and doctrine (Ac 2:12-47).

Revelation Chapter Eleven

Revelation 11:1: I was given a reed like a measuring rod and was told, "Go and measure the temple of God and the altar, and count the worshipers there."

The true temple is the Body of Christ (Eph 2:21) and in particular, the physical bodies of each covenant believer who comprise the Body of Christ (1Co 3:16, 17).

This reed/staff is like a carpenter's measuring tape. This is the Word of God. This was the complete measuring rod used to measure the altar. Ezekiel used Old Testament terminology in describing the instruments used to measure the temple (Eze 45:3-11). Because of the dimensions, sizes, and various other items being measured, the temple described in this passage is obviously inconsistent with the modern understanding of physical architectural structures. Ezekiel is describing a supernatural temple. It is impossible for theologians to figure out the spiritual prophetic applications that Ezekiel's temple has in common with the New

Covenant invisible temple, but one truth emerges from both – God's true temple is vitally – extremely important!

In Revelation 11:1, the altar stands for worship. Worship includes doctrine, life, prayer, holiness, communion, and immersion. The temple represents the people (1Pe 2:5-7; Eph 2:20).

The Bible has 66 books, 27 of which are New Testament. The New Testament has some books that are very short such as the books of Jude, Second and Third John, and Philemon that have only one chapter. In other words, the New Testament, the "Little Book", is very small in comparison to the Old Testament. The final verdict of the Judgment Day is based upon this little book. This little book was in the hand of the angel (Rev 10:9), and we believe it was the measuring rod of Revelation 11:1. The New Covenant found in the little book is an incredible testimony to God's amazing and abundant grace. He narrowed His requirements for the human race down to such a little book that it can be carried in a vest pocket. This Word must measure everything. Remember the words of Jesus in John 12:47-50,

> "And if anyone hears My words and does not believe, I do not judge him; for I did not come to judge the world but to save the world. He who rejects Me, and does not receive My words, has that which judges him — the word that I have spoken will judge him in the last day. For I have not spoken on My own authority; but the Father who sent Me gave Me a command, what I should say and what I should speak. And I know that His command is everlasting life. Therefore, whatever I speak, just as the Father has told Me, so I speak" (Jn 12:47-50).

In describing the Judgment Day, even Revelation gives insight to how people's lives are going to be measured,

"I saw the dead, small and great, standing before God, and books were opened. And another book was opened, which is the Book of Life. And the dead were judged according to their works, by the things which were written in the books" (Rev 20:12).

The measuring of the temple means Christians must determine what is right and what is wrong. Often, we hear the phrase, "Don't judge me!" Unfortunately, the people proclaiming this message have absolutely no understanding when it comes to "judgment" in the Word of God. Paul said of the spiritual man,

"But the natural man does not receive the things of the Spirit of God, for they are foolishness to him; nor can he know them, because they are spiritually discerned. But he who is spiritual judges all things, yet he himself is rightly judged by no one. For 'who has known the mind of the Lord that he may instruct Him?' But we have the mind of Christ'" (1Co 2:14-16).

If you love me, judge me (righteously), but make sure it is by the New Testament standard. If there are three books in Revelation 20:12, one is definitely the New Testament. If one book is the Lambs Book of Life, another book could very well be a book of the record of the works of every person who ever lived, as we saw in Revelation 5:1-3.

The Human Race manifests the most absurd, empty-headed insanity when they forfeit the hope of eternal life by failing to measure life and doctrine by this Little Book, yet at the same time expect mechanics, doctors, engineers, lawyers, designers, architects, educators, musicians, navigators, and contractors to be held to the highest standards of their written codes. Such a break down in human intelligence has no equal in the world of academic integrity.

What is the Reed or Measuring Rod of Revelation 11:1?

It is an absolute mandate, a necessity for the People of the Book to determine what is true and what is false. Christians are to measure their own lives and doctrine as well as the lives and doctrine of others around them. The little Book of Revelation of 10:10 is the measuring rod of 11:1. The best place to start measuring a New Testament congregation is Acts, Chapters 1 and 2. People who doubt the New Testament was available to Christ's kingdom before 70 A.D. say that John did not write until approximately 90 A.D. John's record of being in Jerusalem contradicts this theory (Jn 5:2). How could John write of Jerusalem's currents events after the city was destroyed?

By "counting the worshippers" (Heb 10:22-26; 1Co 11:26; Ac 20:7), we see the fullness of God's people. God knows exactly who is in the New Covenant and who is not. God knows those people who are His and those who are not. Christians cannot be in the outer court and still be a part of God's inner court. They cannot be a part of His body and still be part of the world.

Revelation 11:2: but exclude the outer court; do not measure it, because it has been given to the Gentiles. They will trample on the holy city for forty-two months.

This temple is adequate, spiritual, pure, and able to accommodate Christ. Jesus commanded John to measure the temple, but *not* the outer court. We need to understand the two courts.

I. Outer Court of the Temple – *hieros*, otherwise known as the priestly hierarchy. The Gentiles (Eph 4:17) represent the visible, physical, satanic people of the world. They are not in covenant with Jesus. Through their lifestyle, they wish to push Christians off the face of the Earth. The Gentiles refer to those who are *not* a part of the spiritual Israel (Ro 9:1-4). They attempt to represent Christ on Earth, but they have no part in the Body of Christ. Both the Greek and Roman cults embraced the Babylonian, Nimrod religion (See Addendum A: number 40.).

How foolish for the Greek-Roman Church to use the *heiros* (hierarchy) to describe their priesthood. In using this word to describe their pyramid of power, they are defaming themselves and move into the arena of fulfilling a scripture of doom. The *hieros* would not submit to the measuring of the temple. Could we imagine the authorities of a hierarchy allowing an evangelist to measure their worship and their doctrine by the New Testament? It is said that Romanism is the first church, but it is actually the third church. The second church was of the Greek, called Orthodox. The first Ecclesia of Christ is found Acts 2. Just as the Romans, Turks, and Muslims have trampled the Old Testament and incorporated it into their human systems so the false churchanity is allowed to trample the true Ecclesia underfoot for 42 months, times-time-and half time, 3½ years, or 1,260 days.

II. Inner Court of the Temple – *Naos*. This is the spiritual, *invisible*, remnant, and **holiest** court. The inner court represents the true Congregation. The Gospel and the measuring rod in the hands of the New Testament witnesses measure this court constantly. The only thing measured is the true Congregation of the saints.

Jesus is using Jewish nomenclature to teach the difference between the world and the Body of Christ. When we Christians measure, Christians should only measure within the society of the Kingdom of God, *not* the world. However, we need to remember that both courts are inside of the temple *and* both courts come out of the wilderness in Revelation 12:6 and 17:3. The difference between the two is that one is a pure virgin and the other is a prostitute. After the 2nd Century, the hierarchy began to cease measuring the congregations by the "little book."

The inner court stands for the invisible, saved, white-robed Christians who are known by God. They are the spiritual temple. The visible court represents the carnal and soulish people who are not in a true relationship with Christ (1Co 2:14-3:4). The Court of the Gentiles represents all who oppose the spiritual Body of Christ. This can range from the Roman Church, the Orthodox Church, Protestant Church hierarchies, backsliding Christians, self-proclaimed Jews and anti-Christ heathens. They are the ones who bite, devour, and destroy the Congregation. The true temple of Christ can only be found when one measures with the rod, which is the New Testament Word of God. There are hundreds of Christian churches with people who wear the title, "Christian," in Name only. These *followers of God* are in fact not the true temple spoken about in Scripture (1Th 2:4; 1Co 3:16; 2Co 6:16; 1Pe 2:5; Gal 4:26).

We must investigate history for the meaning of the 42 months and 1,260 days. The 1,260 days is synonymous with the 42 months; 3 ½ years; time, times, and ½ times; and 3 ½ days. The 1,260 days represents the difficult times for the Congregation. For the 1,260 days, God protected the Congregation. This period is also known as the *Dark Ages*. In 533 A.D., one man became the head of the *Church*. This occurred when Emperor Justinian declared Pope John the head over all the Churches. The Latin word Catholic was used beginning in the 2nd Century, and these Catholics no longer called themselves Christians (2Th 2:4).

Then, in 1793, the Methodists began to call themselves Christians again. From the official departure of God's Word in 533 A.D. to the official resurrection of God's Word in 1793 A.D. is 1,260 years. Martin Luther, Seventh Day Adventists, some Mormons, Jehovah's Witnesses and other cults claim insight into this prophetic period of time. Likewise, there are some honest Historicists who attempt to interpret this period. However, in looking at the Biblical representation, the Bible uses a day to year prophecy. Scripture teaches that in prophecy one day can equal one year (Nu 14:34). The same scheme is used in Daniel 9:24 in which 70 weeks actually stands for 490 years. The view presented here does *not* contradict Scripture like the Futurist view does.

The Futurist View

The Futurists believe in a future prophetic fulfillment of the national restoration of Jews in Palestine. They base this from a promise God made to Abraham, not to the Jews. They believe the temple of Solomon will be rebuilt and reestablished as in the days of Solomon. They believe that the bloody sacrifices will be reinstituted and that Elijah and Enoch will return to the earth 3 ½ years before Christ's Second Coming. Futurists use the prophecy of Jeremiah 18:9, 10 about the return to Palestine to say that it is referring to a someday (no one knows when) future return of Jews to what was once known as the ancient land of Israel.

Jeremiah is really speaking of the physical return of the Jews to Jerusalem after the 70-year Babylonian captivity. This Futurist view grossly misconstrues prophecy when it projects the prophecy of Amos 9:11, 12 into the far-off end of the world in its alleged rebuilding of the Old Testament tabernacle. The inspired Apostle Paul settled this dispute for the last time 2,000 years ago. Under direct inspiration, he spoke of the fulfillment being the conversion of the Gentiles (Ac 13:34). In regard to Elijah's coming, Futurists miss the mark again by 2,000 years. Jesus said Elijah has already come (Mt 17:12), as a personification of John the Immerser (Mt 17:13).

The Old Testament Jewish tabernacle will never be rebuilt because a rebellious people (the Jews) cannot fulfill any of God's promises. The November 29, 1947 United Nations partition of Palestine and creation of the Nation of Israel, coupled with the response of the Jewish Peoples' Council on May 14, 1948, has nothing to do with Bible prophecy. Furthermore, all developments since then in the Middle East have nothing to do with Bible prophecy; although, we do concede to the wisdom that Israel as a nation is more governable than the Arab nations. These are all political matters that come under the predictable folly or schemes of fallible, human politicians and are not a fulfillment of divine prophecy.

The Bible says, "Not all Israel is Israel" (Ro 9:6). This tells Christians that Spiritual Israel, not physical Israel, is the true Congregation. Christians are the true fulfillment of God's promises. Yes, God has a nation but far from a physical Israel. He says His nation is a "royal priesthood" and a "holy nation" (1Pe 2:9, 10). The Futurist view has missed this! They read Romans 11:26 but not Romans 11:27.

Revelation 11:3, 4: *And I will give power to my two witnesses, and they will prophesy for 1,260 days, clothed in sackcloth. These are the two olive trees and the two lampstands that stand before the Lord of the earth.*

Once again, the 1,260 days parallel the 42 months, 3½ years, and time, times, and half time. The two witnesses represent the true Congregation witnessing during the Dark Ages and throughout history.

Instead of calling them two people, he calls them two olive trees and two lampstands. The congregations are also called candlesticks in some translations for the congregations support Evangelists as a candlestick supports the light. But while there are many congregations, there is only one lampstand that holds them up. This denotes the unity of them all into the one Bride of Christ. The word martyr is not found in the Old Testament. The Old Testament prophets were never called *marterios* witnesses. To be a martyr of Christ, we must bear the testimony concerning Jesus, even unto the point of death. The two witnesses support the truthfulness of the New Testament Testimony, since "The testimony of two is true" (Jn 8:17; Dt 17:6). The Congregation works in conjunction with the Evangelists to uphold the testimony of Jesus. Jesus always sent out disciples to preach in pairs of two. Even in the Old Testament, we will notice this Biblical approach in the Book of Zechariah, which speaks of Joshua as the high priest, and Zerubbabel, as the temple builder.

> "And he (the Angel) said to me, 'what do you see?' So I said, I am looking, and there is a lampstand of solid gold with a bowl on top of it, and on the stand seven lamps with seven pipes to the seven lamps. Two olive trees are by it, one at the right of the bowl and the other at its left. So I answered and spoke to the Angel who talked with me, saying, 'what are these, my lord?'" (Zec 4: 2-4).

> "For who has despised the day of small things? For these seven rejoice to see the plumb line in the hands of Zerubbabel. They are the eyes of the Lord, which scan to and fro throughout the whole earth" (Zec 4:10).

In this instance, God is working by His spirit. He assumes the responsibility of moving spiritual mountains and accomplishing what seems to be the impossible.

These two lampstands are accountable to the Lord of the Earth and to Him alone. The sackcloth mourning of the *Evangels* is because of the tremendous success the Roman Religion and her children had in suppressing them. They suppressed the evangel in order to control the people. As long as the role of the evangelist is suppressed, there is no restraint to prevent ambitious men from trying to bring the Body of Christ under their control and not under God's.

The "trees" of this text are not pumping the sap that comes out of the tree; they are pumping God's Holy Spirit. These witnesses are a direct flow of God's Spirit. They are bearing God's Testimony. To the world, these witnesses are nothing, but to God they are everything. They stand before His Throne and His gaze as well as that of the holy angels (1Pe 1:12; 1Ti 5:21; 2Co 5:2). They are focused upon their preaching unto the whole Earth, *for they are His*. The two olive trees represent oil, which is a figure of the Holy Spirit. From this representation, we can know that Christians are led by the Spirit of the olive tree and not by works of the law.

Revelation 11:5, 6: And if anyone wants to harm them, fire proceeds from their mouth and devours their enemies. And if anyone wants to harm them, he must be killed in this manner. These have power to shut heaven, so that no rain falls in the days of their prophecy; and they have power over waters to turn them to blood, and to strike the earth with all plagues, as often as they desire.

The fire coming out of the witness's (Rev 11:3) mouths represents the Word of God. We must realize that they (speaking of those we believe to be the first "witnesses" or the original Apostles, and those who followed them in the 1st Century A.D.) did finish their testimony. From 30 A.D. to the turn of the 1st Century, even Babylon could not hurt them at this time. In reference to this, Paul said the "mystery of iniquity is already at work, but is being restrained" (2Th 2:3-7). The word iniquity means lawlessness, not just sin in general. The lawlessness was changing the New Covenant law of the Spirit into the religious laws, customs, and seasons of men. At first, the Roman Empire and the Spirit that directed the writing of the Scriptures prevented this mysterious, Babylonish man from harming the witnesses. They had to finish their testimony before God allowed them to be in mourning and be killed by the Babylonish man of iniquity.

In the Old Testament, Moses had power to turn water into blood. In a direct parallel, through immersion into Christ's death, God sees Christ's blood. It is powerful to note that Christians possess this same power! In preaching and immersing, Christians are fulfilling this powerful testimony. This powerful testimony is, "Fire in their mouths" (Jer 5:14). Christians do not realize the power they possess in prayer. Christians are the most powerful human beings on the face of the Earth for they serve the most powerful master of the Earth, the one true God. Christians cannot be prevented from spreading the Gospel to the world, but their ministry can be greatly opposed.

Revelation 11:7: When they finish their testimony, the beast that ascends out of the bottomless pit will make war against them, overcome them, and kill them.

Notice the Holy Spirit changes its mode of speaking from prophesying (11:3) to the testimony. While the Apostles were speaking the New Testament Word, the New Testament was called a more sure Word of Prophecy (2Pe 1:19, 20). However, after the Apostles finished it, the New Testament is now also a form of written document. In finishing this Testimony, Satan has three workers whom he uses to defile the Body of Christ and oppose the spreading of the Gospel:

A. The Beast (Power of Politics) out of the abyss (later out of the sea)

B. The False Prophet

C. The False Church (Babylonian Woman with her religious offspring children)

The Beast is the Ecclesiastical Religion and can only be destroyed with prayer, soul winning, and time. The Roman Church killed Christians. They buried the Gospel beneath their creeds and dogmas. In doing this, the Bible became a dead language for 1,260 years. During this time, the cause of Christ suffered more than at any time in history. We must understand that this "beast" is not a person, but an institution. Political (Justinian) and religious (Roman Church) united to strengthen the Empire. Justinian called upon the religious world to recognize Pope John as the head of all the congregations in 533 A.D., but Boniface III was the first official Pope in 606 A.D.

The man, *anthropos,* of sin in 2 Thessalonians, Chapter 2, is similar to the woman of Revelation 17:1-7. Both are called a mystery and both are still around when Christ returns (2Th 2:8; Rev 18:20). The "Man of Sin" indicates the masculine aspect of the institution, and the Babylonian woman represents the feminine aspect of the institution. These two are of one spirit.

Two subversive acts lead to both complete suppression of truth and monarchial reign through bishops over the congregation. First, they removed completely the role of evangelist from the congregation. Following this, the *Latin Kingdom* gained power and desired to change the criteria of belief from the original Koine Greek language to Latin. This change, however subtle it may have appeared to Christian believers, was imperative to the success of Babylonian tyranny.

Jerome was commissioned by Bishop Pope Damascus to translate the Hebrew and Greek Bible into Latin in 382 A.D. It was called the *Latin Vulgate.* In the 16th

Century at the Council of Trent, the Roman Church declared that Latin would be the official language of the Bible. The Latinizing of New Testament Scriptures corrupted the ability to understand God's intended meaning. The people did not understand Latin, and as a result, could be more easily controlled. For 1,260 years, most of the world was ruled under religious Roman domination and the Congregation of Christ was boycotted. From 533 A.D. to 1793 A.D., the use of the name Christian officially disappeared. Christian was used only to describe Christendom in general but not New Testament Christianity in particular.

Revelation 11:8, 9: *And their dead bodies will lie in the street of the great city which spiritually is called Sodom and Egypt, where also our Lord was crucified. Then those from the peoples, tribes, tongues, and nations will see their dead bodies three-and-a-half days, and not allow their dead bodies to be put into graves.*

In my book, *The Crucifixion of Christ in Sodom*, I carefully document that when the sodomites surrounded the house of Lot, they had in mind the "gang rape" crucifixion of Jesus Christ (Ge 19:5-7).

According to the verse, the evangelistic lifeline of the Congregation is dead. Historians have given reliable estimates of the death of millions of Christian people at the hands of the Roman inquisitors. The dead bodies represent the evangelist and their Christian converts being slain. For 1,260 years, the world allowed the execution of God's witnesses. Although they did not completely bury or extinguish the foundational gifts of Christ (Eph 4:1-13), because, thank God, they are still with us today; yet, the Greek-Roman apostasy never allowed a resurgence of such ongoing gifts to the local assemblies of Christ.

Christ's enemies were not merely satisfied with the blood of the evangelists; for by preventing their bodies from being buried, they desired to prolong the ignominy placed on their death. This is a classic case of diabolical revisionism because they wanted to deny the very existence of their New Covenant witness. Obviously, these enemies also feared that their records and documents would survive after death because we search in vain to find historical records of Christ's pure New Covenant Congregation prior to the 3rd Century.

Revelation 11:8, 9 is difficult to interpret. When people are buried, usually dignity and honor is bestowed upon the deceased persons. However, in this Scripture passage, Christ's enemies not only wanted to deface them in life, but dishonor them in death. This is how much hatred they possessed for God's witnesses and the truth. They refused to give them honor, thus, *"they did not allow their dead bodies to be put into graves."* The rage toward New Testament witnesses continued even after they were murdered. For instance, the bones of John Wycliffe were dug up and thrown into the river. In their sight, His sin was translating the New Testament into the language of the people.[73]

If this passage is a literal 3½ days, then the whole chapter of Revelation 11, and so on, must be literal as well. The Preterist View teaches that it is the approximate days 3½ years of the Roman Jewish war prior to 70 A.D. It is true that 3½ years is a time of great testing. However, this view cannot be correct because Rome did not persecute New Testament Christians; they persecuted and killed Old Testament Jews. The Christians were not even in Jerusalem during the 70 A.D. surge.

What could these 3½ days be referring to if it is not a historical period? First, it must be a reference to the history after the completion of the prophetic Testimony. Secondly, it runs a course of great suppression to the Gospel. Thirdly, it precedes a resurrection where the witnesses stand on their feet (Rev 11:11) causing great fear to those who saw them. The Gospel that was suppressed during the great persecution is now fully expressed by the ascension of the witnesses, which causes fear in the sight of the beholders. This cannot be a reference to the end of the world and the ascension to Heaven at Christ's coming because there are still people left to fear. In history, the witnesses in their earlier career preached a great worldwide awakening of the Gospel. They preached the resurrection Gospel of New Testament Christianity.

The preaching of New Testament Christianity in Europe, followed by the French Revolution, and the restoration of New Testament Christianity in 1793 A.D. shook Roman Catholicism to her very foundation and caused her children to fear greatly. We do not have all the answers, but one thing is undeniable and that is mighty convulsions rocked the Roman *hieros* in the 18th Century through a mighty New Testament Gospel awakening. These historical facts are indelibly recorded in the archives of history. The 3½ days also correspond to Daniel's "Times, time and ½ time," another way of expressing the 1,260 days (years) of persecution at the expert hands of the hierarchical tyranny (Da 7:25, 26).

We need to recognize Biblical principles that are established in the apocalyptic vocabulary. One principle is calling preachers "witnesses" or bearers of a testimony. Witness or testimony is used throughout the New Testament, but especially in the Book of

Revelation. The apocalyptic word for preaching is testimony or witness. How sad and amazing it is that this New Covenant "preaching" almost disappeared from the Earth.

Since Christ selected the original Apostles, we recognize no religious authority or mandate proclaimed after the Apostles, including that of the Post-Apostolic Fathers. By the 2nd Century, they were already departing from the New Testament witness as taught by the original Apostles. We are told there are successors to the Apostles. We think of Rome when we use the word *successors,* but the Greeks also have successors, and we seldom think about it, but we have modern-day "divines" and self-proclaimed "apostles" in many modern-day denominations. One successor to the Apostles is one too many.

A second principle is the measuring of the temple. This goes back to Ezekiel, in which he measured in apocalyptic descriptions of physical dimensions, furniture, and terms. These passages in Revelation have an apocalyptic interpretation. This style of writing is used several times throughout Scripture. Revelation 11 refers only to measuring the faith, precepts, and doctrines by the New Testament.

The 42 months of 11:1, also referred to as 1,260 days, corresponds to Daniel's time, times, and ½ time (Da 7:25, 26). Rome would have taken longer than the longest of these periods to change times, seasons, and doctrines in corrupting the Congregation. This time period is referred to in Revelation 12:6, 14, and 13:5 using the same references. This in context is chiefly Roman persecution. This time period is referred to seven times, and 1,260 days was not enough time to evolve from Evangelist to Archbishop to Pope (See "Addendum A - Departures from the Faith.").

Revelation 11: 3 signifies two witnesses who stand for the Apostolic Evangels of the Gospel of Christ. They are exercising His work under great persecution and distress. Verse 4 shows that just as Joshua and Zerubbabel had a hard time building the city and temple (Zec 3, 4), so the witnesses have a difficult time declaring the Gospel of the Kingdom clothed in sackcloth. However, Zechariah 4:14 says that God beholds them on Earth. This vision not only addresses original Apostolic New Covenant Christianity but all who testify to this Word during the time of persecution. The Lord of Hosts will always behold those who preach His word especially during times of extreme persecution. The Lord of Hosts (Sabaoth) means that God's armies fill the Universe with ten thousand times ten thousand and thousands of thousands (1Sa 17:45 with Rev 5:11).

What is taught in Revelation 11:3 is not a one-time historical event in chronological order. The Book of Revelation, as we have seen, is written from an apocalyptic viewpoint to express the difficulties encountered by the Apostles and 1st Century witnesses who dare to continue in propagating and to finish their testimony as stated in Revelation 11:7. If history exists in these texts, it is the daring evangelistic witness as part and parcel of the overall period of war from the bottomless pit against those who preached the New Covenant on Earth. Even though the role of Evangelists-Witnesses (who followed the New Covenant doctrines of the original apostles) was suppressed, their death spoke very loudly in Heaven and among the remnant believers on Earth (Rev 18:20). Often, the death of an individual would cry out for redemption. When Cain murdered his brother, his blood spoke! (Ge 4:10). After the death of Christ, He still speaks from Heaven (Heb 12:24, 25).

Most Bible translations translate Revelation 11:8 as being bodies (plural), "the bodies" of the witnesses. They must have thought there was a mistake in the Bible, but the earliest manuscripts refer to their dead "body" that is not allowed to be buried.[74] This means that the two witnesses really speak with one voice. Jesus sent his disciples out, two by two, speaking with one voice (Mk 6:7).

Revelation 11:10: And those who dwell on the earth will rejoice over them, make merry, and send gifts to one another, because these two prophets tormented those who dwell on the earth.

They that dwell upon the Earth shall make merry. The preaching of the Gospel torments the people of the Earth. They do not want the spreading of the truth. They resist conviction, truth, and the oneness of God. Fathers and mothers have been known to curse and scream at their own sons and daughters. They bring such threats that they had never brought before when they convert from the family religion to New Testament Christianity.

Revelation 11:11: But after the three and a half days a breath of life from God entered them, and they stood on their feet, and terror struck those who saw them.

After 3½ days, the Spirit of God enters into them. Once again the 3½ is synonymous with the 1,260 days and the 42 months. It was the time of the suppression by the whore of Revelation and her children. The Gospel came back to life! Men like James O'Kelly, Thomas and Alexander Campbell, Raccoon John Smith, Rice Haggard, and Walter Scott entered the scene. They decided to call themselves

Christians only and devote their lives to restoring the New Testament only. Some of the restoration preachers struggled mightily in their attempts to come out of 1,260 years of darkness and religious confusion. It was Raccoon John Smith, one of the most honest Bible scholars of his age, who said, "I am in the dark, we are all in the dark."[75] If these 18th Century Christians made mistakes in their doctrine, we can understand this because they were coming out of darkness. Since the Protestant Reformation of the 17th Century influenced their thinking, some of the restoration fathers knew that most of Protestantism would return to their mother because they had not gone far enough in restoring the original pattern. Thus, the work of restoration must be a continuing process.

God was behind the Restoration-Remnant Movement. This was no accident. The world fears this resurrection Gospel. This is not a general resurrection from the dead. This is not a literal, historical happening but an apocalyptical presentation concerning the resurrection of the truth. Lazarus was a living demonstration of a bodily resurrection. God's anointed ones who declared the New Covenant testimony are the resurrection of the living Gospel, personified.

Revelation 11:12: *Then they heard a loud voice from heaven saying to them, "Come up here." And they went up to heaven in a cloud, while their enemies looked on.*

The Futurists say this verse refers to a "secret rapture" (or the coming of Christ), but the world saw the resurrection of the two witnesses. Those on Earth who saw the witnesses tremble in fear, but they continued to live their unbelieving lives as enemies of the Gospel. Nothing is said about them being awestricken by a spurious "secret snatch."

The witnesses died in full assurance of final redemption. The resurrection Gospel assures the resurrection of body, soul, and spirit. The adversarial enemies can only watch as souls are regenerated and resurrected, but they cannot participate in it themselves. They can only watch as they do everything in their power to prevent this action. When one of our local News Editors turned from skepticism to The Savior, his fellow editors said, "Oh no! Not you!" The man became a dynamic scholar of Scripture, went to Bible College, and remains an ardent disciple of Christ to this day. He told us that the vast majority of news editors and reporters are atheists, or at most, skeptics.

Let us review the first part of this amazing chapter:

1. The giving of "The Little Book" and the measuring of the true Temple of Christ,
2. The finishing of The Testimony (New Testament) and its impact on the world,
3. The horrible persecution to destroy and degrade the New Testament witness, and
4. A great Revival of New Testament Christianity.

We can divide Chapter 11 into five parts:

1. The Apostolic Testimony expanded (11:1-3) in the midst of powerful political-religious resistance.
2. Although successful at first (11:4-7), the world is given a completed, New Testament written testimony (11:7-10).
3. At last, the politico-religious world overcomes The Witnesses (the personification of Apostolic New Testament Christianity and its advocates with "times, time and ½ time" persecution or 1,260 days of Dark Ages - 11:8-10).
4. A resurrection Gospel revival and restoration occurred (11:11-13).
5. Babylon, in part, is identified as a fraud and judged by New Covenant Christianity.

Revelation 11:13: At that very hour there was a severe earthquake and a tenth of the city collapsed. Seven thousand people were killed in the earthquake, and the survivors were terrified and gave glory to the God of heaven.

The earthquake in this verse is not literal. It represents the punishment of skeptics. Only 1/10 part of the city was destroyed – this is temporal judgment. The apocalyptic number 7,000 who died were a sign to those who embrace the truth that God destroyed many and eventually all of their enemies. The 7,000 is also, apocalyptically used in a good way to distinguish those who do not bow to the "image" of Baal or the cultural, pagan, religious-political, and philosophical lies of their particular generations (Ro 11:4, 5). The earthquake resulted in praise to God!

Romanism was severely weakened because of the preaching of the witnesses. The power Papal Rome received from Pagan Rome was gone. This city of Romanism was severely hurt and broken into various factions. Scholars are not sure of the details of these factions; however, these factions prevented Babylon or any world religion from becoming an indestructible worldwide tyranny.

We take comfort in knowing that God prevented apostate Rome from becoming a worldwide religious tyranny through the fierce opposition of Arian-Islam. Then, He stopped apostate Islam from becoming a worldwide religious tyranny at The Battle of Tours in 732 A.D., and again, at the Battle for Vienna in 1683 A.D. What a paradox! But God can do it again and again.

No military force or power on Earth can prevent the spread of Christianity to the ends of the Earth in any age. New Covenant Christians must have powerful enemies on Earth to test their resolve and dedication to what the Lord says. But no matter how powerful these enemies may be – judges and political tyrants cannot prevail against the Lamb. On June 26, 2015 A.D., United States Supreme Court legalized homosexual agenda by ruling in favor of homosexual marriage. It is no secret to those of spiritual discretion that the whole sodomite agenda is designed to overturn the value system of the Lord Jesus Christ. Even the Supreme Court Justices admitted that the ruling is an infringement on religious liberty. Chief Justice John Roberts labeled the Supreme Court decision, "an act of will, not legal judgment." Justice Antonin Scalia's opinion states, "Today's decree says that the Ruler of 320 million Americans coast-to-coast is a majority of nine lawyers of the Supreme Court…a system of government makes the People subordinate to a committee of nine unelected lawyers does not deserve to be called a democracy… (The Court) violated a principle…more fundamental than no taxation without representation: no social transformation without representation." They rejoice presently at the aid and indulgence they receive from those they consider "The powers that be." Very soon they will tremble with terror before the presence of the real "Power that IS," the Godhead of Heaven.

Revelation 11:14, 15: The second woe has passed; the third woe is coming soon. The seventh angel sounded his trumpet, and there were loud voices in heaven, which said: "The kingdom of the world has become the kingdom of our Lord and of his Christ, and he will reign forever and ever."

This is the countdown. There are only three woes. The first woe is the warning from the bottomless pit (Rev 9:1-12). The second woe is the earth's shaking under the violence of war and organizations of satanic forces against New Testament Christianity (Rev 9:13-11:14). The final woe is God's wrath being built up and poured out upon an angry world (Rev 11:15). The kingdoms of the world have not recognized Jesus through this time of trial; they soon will. The seventh is always the last in the parallel sections.

This Concludes the Lengthy Intermission.

This intermission featured the "Four Angels" of death (9:15), the "Mighty Angel" (probably Christ Himself) with the Little Book (10:1), and the "Angel measuring the Temple" (11:1-3) for a total of six angels.

Revelation 11:16: And the twenty-four elders, who were seated on their thrones before God, fell on their faces and worshiped God,

The elders worship God. Thank God for elders! They are represented before the Lord like a heavenly Sanhedrin. The view of the apocalyptic Heaven, especially created creatures and Angels, is awe-inspiring. Responsible, caring elders of both the Old and New Covenant represent the human race before God.

Christians stand equally in awe before God that He would vest such significance in the spiritual leaders of the human race. He views them with the dignitaries of Heaven. One elder is of more infinite worth to this world than a 1,000 federal judges and one president.

Revelation 11:17: saying: "We give thanks to you, Lord God Almighty, the One who is and who was, you have taken your great power and have begun to reign.

This is a thank you to God. He reigns now. Jesus has reigned, does reign, and always will reign (Ps 110:2). However, now, He is ready at last to seize with His hand the power of His reign.

Revelation 11:18: The nations were angry; and your wrath has come. The time has come for judging the dead, and for rewarding your servants the prophets and your saints and those who reverence your name, both small and great — and for destroying those who destroy the earth."

Wrath is about to come upon the nations. They are lifting their fists to God as they always have. Although the nations succeeded in silencing the truth of the precious Blood of the Lamb, now they must confront the reality that their crime will precede no further. One of the themes running throughout the Cycles of Revelation is, "The Wicked will be judged and the righteous will be rewarded."

Revelation 11:19: Then God's temple in heaven was opened, and within his temple was seen the ark of his covenant. And there came flashes of lightning, rumblings, peels of thunder, an earthquake and a great hailstorm.

The veil in the physical temple was ripped (opened up the Holiest place) at Calvary (Mt 27:51). Peace was offered to those seeking the Ark of God's presence. Now the Ark stands for wrath and judgment. The Temple is opened; the very sight of this Ark means instant death. Revelation does not say John saw the Ark, but it "was seen." This is a symbolic picture of God's readiness to judge. The true Ark of God and the Lamb is the presence of God in Heaven. When the Ark is closed, peace and mercy exist because of the propitious covering. When the Mercy Seat is opened, wrath ensues. Exodus 25:2 explains the Judgment of the Ark of the Covenant. This wrath of the Lamb from the Ark comes because the world has murdered the innocent Lamb that is God's Bosom Son. When the world stands horrified in view of the injustices or inhuman brutality and mankind's bloody butchery, every person in this world will be brought to understand that all of the injustices of the human race cannot exact the bloody death of God's Lamb on the slopes of Mount Calvary (Mt 27:50-54). As mentioned previously, Satan failed to keep the Ark covered. Jesus succeeded masterfully, to the bitter end, in keeping it covered, but now at last, in the end, the sacred room of The Temple is opened – is the Covering of the Ark about to be opened?

Thus, this Ark has a dual purpose. Because this Ark is in Heaven, Christians have uninterrupted fellowship with Christ. The propitiation for Christians is connected to the Ark because the Mercy Seat is closed. If the sinner is willing to ask for propitiation (Lk 18:13), God will surely give it (Heb 8:12). The Ark of the Covenant is the New Testament Ark in Heaven. In the Old Testament, the Ark had two parts – the covering and the Ark itself (Lev 14:14-16.) When the Ark lid was opened, people died instantly. When the Ark lid was closed, God's wrath was propitiated.

The world will now see the invisible Reign of Christ. The carnal mind does not understand the spiritual components of the Heavenly Kingdom; however, at this coming, those of carnal mind will understand. At this Second Coming, every eye will see the Kingdom and Christ reigning as King! The carnal-minded cannot understand the spiritual nature of the Heavenly Kingdom. Those who are spiritual have no need for conclusive proof that the Heavenly Kingdom is spiritual.

The nations are angry because they do not want to see the Kingdom of God. Somehow, the eyes of their enlightenment will be opened. They will see what they should have seen all along. God will punish these rebellious enemies.

The lightning, voices, thundering, and earthquakes are intelligent representations of God's character. Listed are the following representations of God's attributes.

    A.   Lightning represents God's quickness.

    B.   Voices represent God's comfort and admonition.

    C.   Thundering represent God's Justice and Judgment.

    D.   Earthquakes represent the earth's feeling the effect of God's Judgment.

    E.   Hail represents the atmospheric pressure of God's Judgment.

We discover in this verse the world's final war against the Messianic Kingdom. This war, from beginning to end, is prophesied in Psalms 1. It is the war of the worlds. The nations are against Christ. The whole theme of Revelation is that the unrighteous rebel against God and will be punished, and the righteous will reign victorious. Question – "Will every eye look up with enlightenment and see the sacred Ark of Christ's covenant, and will the covering lid be opened or closed?" A Christian should be able to answer this question!

We have now arrived at the close of Cycle Three, with its view of the final conflict between the world of evil and the Kingdom of righteousness. We now start a new Cycle (Chapter 12). It will reveal the Congregation of Christ, which at first appeared to be very fragile in the midst of being totally dominated by the world.

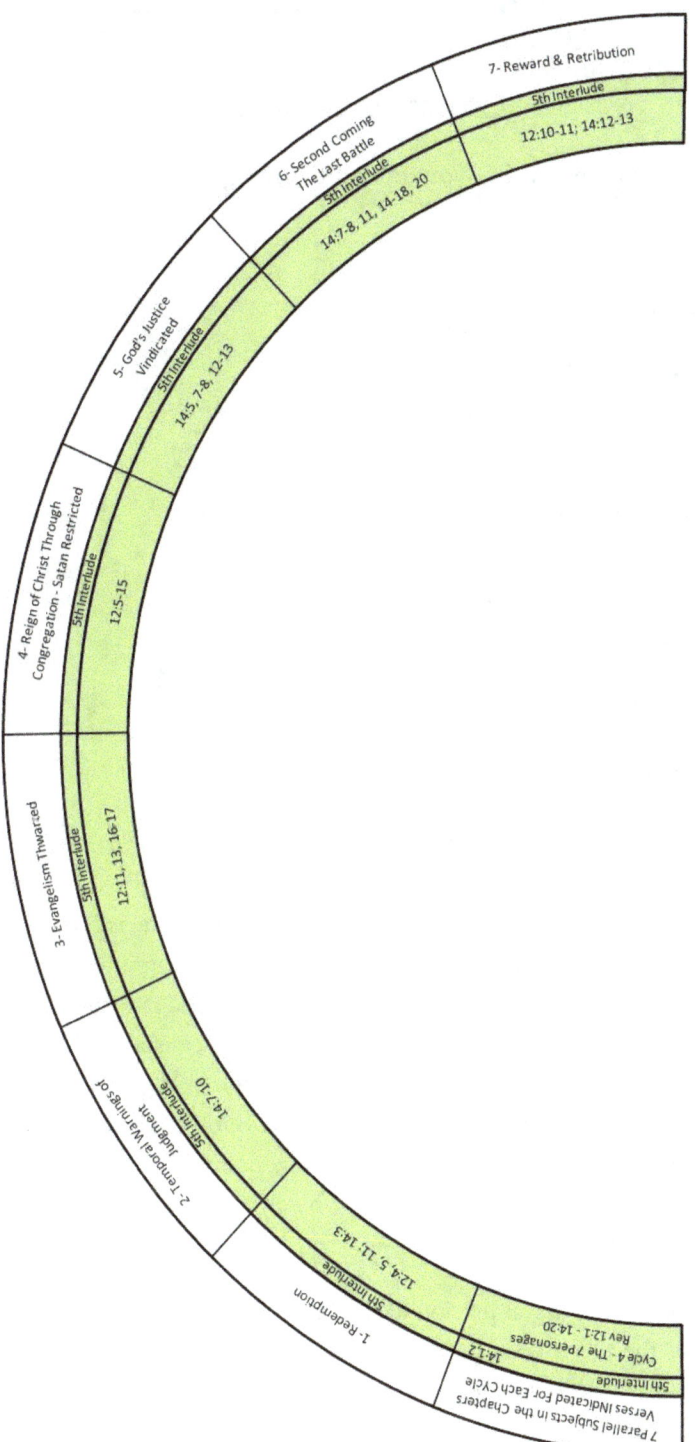

REVELATION RAINBOW | 291

CYCLE 4 – THE SEVEN PERSONAGES

Christ in Conflict

War in Heaven between the Woman and the Dragon

(Chapters 12-14)

Seven Personages

1. Radiant Woman – 12:1, 2
2. Dragon – 12:3, 4
3. Man Child – 12:5
4. Michael – 12:7
5. Great Beast – 13:1-10
6. Little beast – 13:11-18
7. Babylon (harlot) – 14:8

Chapter 12 is a panoramic view of the Congregation from Pentecost until the end of the world. The main Characters are: the Woman (Congregation), the man-child (Jesus Christ), and the dragon (Satan). The main theme is the age-old conflict between Satan and the Congregation, "Seed of the testimony." Christians, in any given historical era, are part of this conflict. A terrific struggle is manifested between Satan and the Congregation. Christians are constantly fighting Satan and his adversaries of truth. Christians must overcome! We came to the end of Cycle Three with a view of the final conflict between the wicked world and the Kingdom of Righteousness. This new cycle reveals the Congregation of Christ that initially appears very weak and fragile, barely surviving in the midst of religious, political, and worldly domination.

In God's domain, Satan was pronounced guilty before the world began. However, the Satan or the Devil was not banished from the presence of the throne until Jesus was resurrected. In condemning the Devil and his followers because of their sin, God created a place of consequence and punishment (Lk 10:18; Mt 25:41).

Christians will note that the Book of Job speaks of Satan's roaming the Earth and presenting himself before God to accuse the brethren.

Satan was the accuser in the Old Testament – and he accused the Saints.

Abraham lied (Ge 20:2).

1. Samson committed fornication (Jdg 16:1, 4).
2. David was a murderer (2Sa 12:9).
3. Joshua was clothed in filthy rags (Zec 3:1-3).
4. Satan accuses the Saints (12:10).

The Devil is an expert at accusing men before God, but now that Christians have the forgiveness of sins through Jesus Christ, Satan is silenced. Jesus now has the authority! After the Devil was cast out of Heaven, he went after the Congregation, which is the Bride of Christ. The Devil cannot hurt Christ so he goes after His Bride. Revelation 12 has nothing to do with the first casting out of Satan (Lk 10:18). Chapter 12 deals with the New Testament age when Christ ascended and banished the accuser from His domain. Having been defeated at Calvary, Satan decided to wage war against the Bride of Christ.

Romans 11:32-36 is an incredibly beautiful passage showing God's wisdom. Man put God in a difficult position by entertaining the sin of the Devil. Sin is an affront to a Holy God. Before Satan rebelled against God, no conflict existed. Perfect serenity and peace echoed throughout the foundations of Heaven.

However, Heaven was greatly troubled when Satan seduced 1/3 of the angels to sin. Then conflict came to Earth when Satan first seduced Eve to sin. We have difficulty understanding how Satan worked throughout the Old Testament after he had been thrown down to Earth (Isa 14:12 with Eze 28:12). For instance, Satan is definitely Eve's seducer (1Ti 2:14), but the "subtle" serpent is given the blame.

Some scholars say that since the serpent was cursed to crawl on the dust of the earth (Ge 3:14), the serpent could stand upright before the curse. It is obvious that Satan was attracted to the serpent since the members of the reptilian family have colorful, scaly covering instead of fur or skin like most other species of the Animal Kingdom. We also realize that Ezekiel 28:13 describes the covering of

Satan, and possibly other evil spirits – since Satan is their Prince (Mt 9:34) as jewels, crystals, or metallic-like plated designs organized as a dazzling, shining covering of their spirits. Thus, Satan is called "An angel of light" (2Co 11:14), which has to mean reflected artificial light since Satan has no inherent light of his own; he is transformed into "an angel of light."

Herod wanted to impress his subjects so he scheduled a speech for a certain day when the sun was shining directly upon his stage (Ac 12:21). He dressed in a robe of diamond or crystal studded covering and made a speech to a vast audience. The people were nearly blinded as the sun reflected from his crystal-shrouded robe. The people were so impressed that they were willing to dub him as a god of sorts. Herod was acting more the part of The Devil than he was a man, and God knew his heart. Subsequently, Herod died earlier than he should have died.

People down through the ages have worshipped the Spirit of Pythos, and even to this day, the diabolical cults have a huge fascination with serpents. Although Satan is apocalyptically called "a serpent," we know that he is totally a spirit, but Satan can possess any fleshy creature he chooses, whether man or beast. The Genesis beginning of history reveals that Satan, knowing that Eve would be fascinated with the entrancing, colorful serpent chose this among other "beasts of the field" to arrest and attract her to what he had to say.

Since Satan is given full responsibility for what was said, it is obvious that he used the serpent as an accessory to the murder of Eve's spirit in a way that a dummy can be used in pantomime. The reason this is true is that the punishment of the real serpent, "Satan," is to bruise his head (Gen 3:15; Mt 23:33; Gal 3:16, 19; Heb 2:11, 14; 1Jn 3:10), but the punishment of the accomplice to this murder (the actual serpent that Eve saw) was to be doomed to a life of "crawling in the dust of the ground."

At this juncture, especially in this 21st Century, we must realize that when we worship an animal (or any beast created by God), we are worshipping Satan. Eve and Adam, her husband, were obviously influenced more by the beast than they were by their Lord and Maker (Ro 1:23). God forbids us to abuse animals (Pro 26:17), and he says, "A righteous man cares for the life of his beast" (Pro 12:10). But men have attempted to make (or reduce) God, through satanic propaganda, to the likeness of "Four footed beast, creeping things and man" as an object of worship. This brings God's displeasure upon us (Ro 1:23)! Would not the unborn in God's eyes be of greater value than our four-footed animals? What about the bumper sticker that says, on one side of a car, "Compassionate Abortion," and on the other side, "Save the Seals"? This commentary on today's American is stated clearly in Romans 1:18-32.

Then conflict came to Earth when Satan seduced Eve to sin (Isa 14:12; Eze 28:12). These Scripture passages describe Lucifer from the standpoint of writers Isaiah and Ezekiel. In a secondary sense, they refer to the King of Tyre. These Scriptures are known in literature as "synecdoche," a literary device in which a part of something represents the whole or vice versa. These passages of Scripture have that dual reference. In Ezekiel, the actual King of Tyre is a microcosm of Satan – a majestic angel of God. The literal king of Tyre and King of Babylon resemble their father, the Devil.

The Devil proclaimed in Isaiah and Ezekiel that he would:

1. Ascend to heaven
2. Sit on the mount of assembly
3. Ascend above the clouds

Satan's spirit enters the minds of power hungry despots. This is Satan's motive. Satan wants not only to work against God's people, but he also wants his word in prophecy. Satan attracts proud people, like pagan kings, Wall Street fund managers, entertainers, sports millionaires, rich entrepreneurs, career politicians, and some TV evangelists. Satan can give them what appears to be supernatural power. Even though the chain of the Gospel binds Satan, Satan is working harder than ever. He is waging spiritual war against the invisible powers of King Jesus and His Body, the Assembly (1Pe 3:18, 19; Col 2:12-15). He also challenges the Justice of God (Rev 9:2). In our day, not since Woodrow Wilson's Administration have we witnessed such organized opposition against the Kingdom of Christ than what we are now experiencing from the Obama Administration.

This battle in the Book of Revelation 12 and 13 is much like the two camps in 1Samuel 17:1-3 where the enemies were divided into two camps, i.e., Satan and the Elect. The following are some easy ways to recognize the friends and enemies of God.

In this battle, Satan is described as an enemy of God in four different ways:

1. Dragon out of the Sea
2. Beast out of the Earth
3. Babylon "harlot"
4. Those with the mark of the beast

Likewise, God's elect is described as:

1. Those who are selected individuals.
2. The Fullness of Spiritual Israel is the elect number of men He knew would serve him.
3. The Fullness of Physical Israel is the number of people who were Covenant Jews in the Old Testament (Prior 70 A.D.).
4. The Fullness of the Gentiles is the exact number who will be saved in Covenant until the end of the world.

Revelation Chapter Twelve

Revelation 12:1, 2: *A great and wondrous sign appeared in heaven: a woman clothed with the sun, with the moon under her feet and a crown of twelve stars on her head. She was pregnant and cried out in pain as she was about to give birth.*

This apocalyptic woman is a reflection of the Light of Heaven. Jesus is called the "Sun of Righteousness" (Mal 4:2). He is as majestic to Christians as the Sun is to the Milky Way galaxy. The woman is described as being clothed with this radiance, which represents the New Testament righteousness of Christ. The moon, which is the Old Testament, is under her feet, which displays her dominion over the luminary bodies for she is the radiant woman. Restoration scholars have long proclaimed that the Patriarchal Age of the Old Testament is the Twilight Age, the Mosaic Age is the Moon Light Age, and the New Covenant is the Sunlight Age. We identify this apocalyptic woman as having 12 stars, and the stars govern her.

The 12 stars represent the 12 Apostles upon which the Congregation was built. All the woman's characteristics are radiating from her at once. Each characteristic will have occurred at different times in history. So, we are led to believe this is a deliberate, not mistaken or misplaced, anachronism placed by the Holy Spirit in this particular text for us to appreciate. She is a woman who fulfills the Old Testament prophetic utterance of Genesis 3:15. God told Eve that she would bear a child who would have victory over the satanic forces. God said that this seed would be born of a virgin and would establish an everlasting kingdom (Isa 54:1-5; Eph 4:7-12), which is the Congregation. This Everlasting Kingdom Congregation is three-fold: God planned her, Christ purchased her, and the Holy Spirit calls her. In the chart below, we notice how the man-child came at the Fullness of Time. He fulfilled the Old Law and built His kingdom upon the foundation of the Apostles and Prophets.

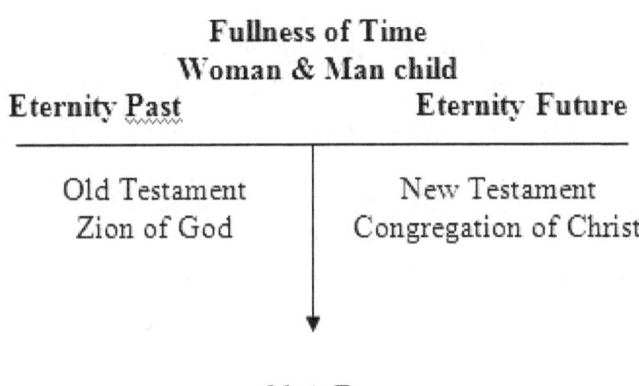

SATAN OF REVELATION, CHAPTER TWELVE

Astrological worship is forbidden in Scripture. Astronomy is one of the most fascinating scientific disciplines in the world, and we may count stars and measure their distances, but their Creator forbids their worship. If, for instance, the Moon appeared to the Apostles and the first disciples as a "Blood Sphere" (having the appearance of blood), or the Magi saw a star that moved "or stopped," we could spend the rest of our lives in astronomic research attempting to attune the Laws of Physics with Bible Prophecy. In many ways, scientific research like Biblical-scientific Apologetics is to be commended, but the apocalyptic symbols given here shine in our enlightened minds much like the light that burst from Heaven shone into the heart of Paul (Ac 22:6). We remember that Paul's companions saw the light, but only Paul understood the voice behind the light.

Thus, the symbols of this prophecy must be understood by searching other Bible Prophecy. This searching is just plain, hard hermeneutic work that most religious workers do not have the will or the heart to pursue. The symbolism in astronomy is available that allows us to deduce from the "woman," the "12 stars," the "sun," and the "moon" what cannot be found in the mere study of Astronomy. As already mentioned, Astronomy is a fabulous discipline, but it pales sorrowfully alongside Biblical Hermeneutics. As the late Henry Morris said, "Biblical Hermeneutics is The Queen of all Scientific Investigation."[76]

Further, Astronomy and Astrophysics are currently so far advanced beyond anything the Magi or wise men of biblical days could have envisioned. If we were to look at apocalyptic symbols using astronomical methods, our Godly forefathers would never have had the slightest clue as to the meaning of apocalyptic symbols until at least the 20th Century.

We once heard a Christian Astronomer lecture on the "dragon" (Draco is the dragon in the constellation of the Northern Hemisphere.). Draco is a Latin word for Dragon, and our lecturer told us that this constellation was the Dragon of Revelation 12:3, and Herod was the human representative on Earth. Of course many students "ate it up," for there is something about the bizarre and obscure that fascinates some scholars. However diabolical Herod may have been, he certainly does not deserve the recognition due the Devil himself. The dragon is definitely the Devil (Rev 20:2), and he will be around until the end (20:8, 9). As I have said many times, "Oh Hermeneutics, thou art a jewel!"

Before Christ's Ascension, Satan fought what might be called a "War of Attrition" against the Godhead. As long as there was no way of redemption by which to satisfy God's perfect Justice, Satan thought the victory could never be permanently settled on the side of good. Since Adam's sin, and throughout the history of the pre and post Flood of Noah's day, the prevailing evil of the human race had never been completely redressed. Satan thought he had a very long time to work his evil; so long in fact that Satan could easily surmise that the only way God could ever deal with the sinful human race was to make the human race extinct, and bring everlasting fiery punishment. Considering the dominate place that fatalism played in the evil serpent's nature, let us consider the following. Satan has a death wish for everything that has life and breath. Even though he would have gone down with all of us, this would have been Satan's final vengeance by wrecking God's plan to save those He loves so much.

Yes, Satan recognized his inferior position, "Prince of this world," and he knew the Godhead was the King of Heaven, but Satan was perfectly contented to exist alongside the Godhead as chief prosecutor and agent of evil. You might say he was an evil "political prisoner," and like such evil agents today, Satan would win over a great majority of sympathizers who will actually join such a notorious criminal and support him if he can "break prison."

It may have been diabolical, wishful thinking, but through the ages, Satan possibly thought that even the Holy God could make ONE mistake or accept Satan's dualistic view of good and evil. If this is not true, what did Satan have to gain by attacking the "Seed of the Woman" through the years, right down to the birth of The Seed, and later, his temptations of the Son of Man for 40 days and nights in the wilderness (Mt 4:1-11)?

Satan knew that in God's holy eyes, Satan's many sins were no worse than those of Job (or Joseph, Joshua, Jacob) and their few sins, or the fewer sins (such as Noah or Daniel) of God's other saints. Satan also knew that if God became weary of Satan's continued harassment of His saints, He just might make a preemptive strike against the original sinner, Satan (and his militant host). Satan could dare God to take him down because if the Chief of all angelic sinners went down, God MUST take the whole human race down with him. Satan knows how God feels about sin. Satan knows what sin will do to us. Oh, if we only knew how troubled God is about our sin!

Before the Cross of Christ, dualism defined the philosophy of all humanity. If one thought that evil were not equal to good, the world would call them "crazy." God Himself acquiesced to this philosophy, and the best a good man or woman could get as a reward from God in regard to an afterlife was to be confined to an underworld of spirits in Sheol. Because they were sinless, only the Godhead and Holy Angels could dwell in Heaven.

Job knew his sin separated him from God, but he had an insight that in "The latter day" (not "the last day") a redeemer would stand on this Earth (Job 19:25). Satan also knew this, and we cannot help but conjecture that he was certain that God would make one little mistake before that day came. Satan knew that "every man had sinned and fallen short of God's glory," but if he could provoke God to sin in regard to His only weakness (His love for His created man and woman), his evil would be equal to God's goodness. God's sin would have been to pardon the human race as an act of desperation without an act of atonement.

The Godhead needs to sin only one little time, and they cease to be the Godhead. Angels only need to sin one little time, and they become demons. How interesting that Satan banked ALL OF HIS STOCK on the fact that a righteous man would never be born on this Earth. In this investment, Satan was 100 percent correct. But, Satan the deceiver was greatly deceived by God's strategy to send Himself to Earth in the presence of the Second Person of the Godhead (Immanuel). Satan could have embraced the Socinian idea that Christ was a very good man. He could have embraced the Arian idea that he was a "lesser God" or even a Great Created Angel. He could have embraced the Sabbelian idea that Jesus was some kind of an appearance of One God, but not God Himself. Satan could have adopted the idea of The Smith Cult of Mormonism that Jesus was a brother to the devil even though Satan, of all the spirits, would have known better. Lastly, Satan could have adopted the Muslim idea (borrowed from the Docetists) that Jesus was just an apparition who "seemed to be" (docetic) a God and did not really die on the cross, but as a ghost (He seemed to die.). This is, of course, the Muslim belief that explains away Christ's definite will and purpose to redeem the human race through propitiation.

The last thing the Devil imagined is that the God-Man, a perfect Man, the God who became Flesh would meet Him in every conceivable battle against the lust of flesh, pride of life, and lust of eyes, and defeat him again and again (Heb 4:15). The last thing Satan ever thought is that God, in the Person of Jesus, would die (as a flesh and blood sacrifice) the horrible death of the cross (Heb 5:7) and rise from the dead. The God-Man pleased God the Father in every respect, even accepting as a substitute the guilt and punishment from God for every sin the human race has ever committed or will ever commit against Holy God.

God loved the Son, and Jesus prayed that we would love Him as the Father loved Him (Jn 17:23, 26). Oh yes, we are tempted to ask, "You mean that God laid upon His Son the iniquity of us all, and yet God loved Him?" We ask further, "You mean to tell me that God was pleased to bruise Him, and yet He loved Him?" (Isa 53:10) Well, personally I have had to spank my children with the stripes of love, and oh how it hurt. Yes, it hurt them, but it hurts the father more.

One time a father had to whip his son for sassing his Mother. He took his son into the bedroom and shut the door. He then took off his belt strap and gave it to his son. With anguish of heart he said,

> "Son, you are now almost a grown man. This may be the last whipping we will ever see in this family. I have told you over the years that 'it hurts me more than you', and you may not believe that. But I am grieved at the way you treated your mother, and I believe it must be paid for by Godly discipline so that you will never do it again. But it is going to be different this time!"

Then that Godly father took his son by the hand; they both dropped on their knees, and the father prayed his heart out. At the conclusion of the prayer, the father got up and took his shirt off. He then took his T-shirt off. He gave the belt strap to his son. He then fell down on the bed with his naked back exposed and gave order to his son,

> "Take the strap and lay it on my back with all of your might. I want you to whip me with 25 stripes, and when you get done, I want you to be able to see 25 blood red marks across my back. And if you think I am losing my mind, I just want you to know I am perfectly sane in what I am asking you to do. I want you to know how much it hurts to have to punish someone you love as much as I love you, son. I now want you to know how hard it is going to be if you ever have to administer the cords of love to your own children someday. And my dear son, after you are done, I will love you as much and even more for obeying me!"

This son was a very strong and proud young man. He would not break down and cry for anything in this world. In fact, he did not cry when his father whipped him in his earlier years, which was not very much, because through corporeal discipline early in life, he knew that Dad backed up his warning with chastisement, and he therefore listened to his Dad's wisdom. But he was not prepared for this!

Tears were streaming down his cheeks as he cried out, "Dad, I cannot do this. I refuse to do this! You surely do not expect me to do this to my loving father. I would rather die!"

The Father realized that it was futile to continue to try and persuade the son against his will, but through the remainder of their lives, they never forgot how hard it is to discipline someone you love. In fact, <u>unless there is truth and justice, there can never be true love!</u>

But this fact of family history fails to convey the truth, and pales miserably in comparison to the propitious Son under the stroke of the Father's Justice. I know we have a difficult time understanding that the Loving Father would hold the Beloved Son accountable for the punishment of the sins of the whole world. But our thoughts are more in tune with what the Devil thought, also. If the princes of this world had known what happened at Calvary, they, like their One and Only Prince of this World, would never have crucified the Lord (1Co 2:8).

Just look at Christ as He appeared alive to Mary (Mk 16:9), the Disciples (Acts 1:3), the 120 Brethren in Jerusalem (Acts 1:15), and to more than 500 Brethren in one place, probably in Galilee (Co 15: 4-9). Then imagine the expression of surprise that appeared on the dragonish face of the Serpent. Of course, Satan never expected that in the Father's Plan of Salvation, He would hold His "God-Man-Son" accountable for the world's sins, and lay upon Him the "Iniquity of us all" (Isa 53:6), including what it would be like to die and go to Hell. But Jesus loved the Father and was willing to exit Earth that way. Even after Jesus suffered both first and second deaths (Heb 2:9; 1Pe 3:18), the most severe punishment was when God forsook Him. In His Mind, God forsook Jesus that He might not forsake us. Ironically, Jesus calls upon all of us to love the Son as the Father loves Him (Jn 17:26).

Even though Christ was without sin, God reckoned, imputed, or regarded Jesus as sin (in His holy sight) so that we might be reckoned or imputed righteousness in Him (2Co 5:21). Someone ask the question, "How could God bear the wrath of Hell?" But on the cross, God reckoned, in His Mind, that Jesus would suffer as a lost sinner would suffer in Hell. By imputation, Jesus bore in His Holy Person the equivalency of whatever a lost sinner would experience in Hell. If He bore it for a fraction of a second on the cross, for the perfect Son of God, it would be equal to eternal Hell Fire for imperfect, lifetime sinners.

Satan realizes that Christ, "King of Righteousness – Melchezedec" (Ge 14:18-20), is now our Mediator. Satan realizes that we now have a Defense Attorney before the bar of God's strict justice. Satan realizes that He cannot prosecute saints any longer. Satan realizes that the blood of a man flowed from Christ's veins. It was real blood. It was the Blood of the New Covenant. Satan knows that God accepts all believers who come (Ac 2:38) and are saved by Christ's Covenant, "dispensation of grace" (Eph 3:2-4), being made as righteous as their God-Man savior is in God's sight. Our Satanic, filthy rags of self-righteousness are removed, and we are clothed with Christ (Gal 3:26-29). We are proclaimed as righteous as was our Father Abraham (Ro 4:3). Satan is baffled; Satan is cast out; God is satisfied; sinners are saved; and Satan is silenced!

Dualism, which is a belief in the equality of good and evil, is now defeated. It is no longer a valid academic philosophy. Earth's inhabitants are swallowing a false bill of goods when they accept dualism. In the end, the righteousness of Christ and true Christian goodwill prevail. Our victory is now permanently with Christ.

Satan has a "short time." Unlike the long years of the Old Testament, when Satan counted time as his ally, it is now obvious that the battle against the Godhead has been lost. Satan can no longer count on the delaying of the court appearance to give him enough time to stave off his big day in court. Yes, as far as his war with The Seed (Christ), the Serpent has lost it forever. When Christ "went up," Satan "went down." Satan's last strategy in these "last days" (Heb 1:1, 2, 9:26), in the end of the world after Pentecost, is to keep the woman (Bride of Christ) from accomplishing her work on Earth, "as it is in Heaven" (Mt 6:10). He met the husband (God) head-on and was soundly defeated; now the Devil persecutes "The Woman," the Bride of Christ, fragile, and timid as she may appear.

THE WOMAN OF REVELATION, CHAPTER TWELVE

John sees the woman in apocalyptic vision (Rev 12:1). First, we must understand that like many other apocalyptic visions in this great Revelation, this vision is not beyond our Biblical, spiritual-mental comprehension. Nevertheless, the vision defies a literal definition in time, space, and matter. No one has ever had a literal, physical view of a woman standing on the Moon whose clothing consisted of the Sun and a garland swathe of 12 planetary stars around her head.

Christians need to look for Biblical counterparts to interpret the vision. The Sun represents light (The face of Jesus "shone brighter than the sun" (Mt 17:2)). The light that blazed upon Paul from the presence of the Lord Jesus was not the Sun, but greater than the Sun (Ac 22:6, 9, 11). Since the Moon reflects the Sun, we expect the lesser Old Testament light to reflect the greater (God had the New Testament in mind even before Moses penned the Old Testament). Therefore, the woman has New Testament light from above and from below (Ge 1:16). All authority is given to Jesus in Heaven above and in Earth below (Mt 16:16-18).

Genesis 1:1, 2 says that universal light existed before the Sun was created, and John tells us that light is Christ (Jn 1:4-9). That the woman here is radiant is unmistakable, but because the Sun and Moon are given as symbols, we known that her radiance is based upon her subservience to the Creator and Maker of the Sun and Moon. She is glorified by the *One* who is superior to her, not because she possesses attributes of divinity.

We know this is true because the 12 stars obviously represent the 12 Apostles of the Lord. Since the stars cover her head (her mental equilibrium), she can only exist so long as she is focused upon apostolic authority and standard. Furthermore, she reveals an alarming vulnerability to the wiles and deceitful doctrines that poured forth from the Dragon's (Satan's) mouth, and a miraculous earthquake was required to prevent that Woman from drowning in the false doctrine. She survived until the Apostles' New Testament writings were finished (Rev 12:14-16). This compares to when the Apostles New Testament "testimony" was being finished (Rev 11:7).

Just as the 3 ½ days (Rev 11:9, 11) occurred after the New Testimony was finished, so the 1,260 days (times, time and a half time - Rev 12:6) occurred after the Woman bore the man Child, "Who was to rule all nations with a rod of iron, and was caught up to God and His throne" (Rev 12:5).

In the apocalyptic sequence, we also see the Devil cast out of Heaven after Christ's Ascension. Christ is the defense attorney who overthrows the prosecuting attorney "who accused the brethren day and night" (Rev 12:10). We will continue to see Christ's Kingdom in Heaven (12:12) and earthly citizens of that Kingdom overcome the Devil by the Blood of the Lamb, by the Apostolic Word of the Testament "Word of their testimony," and by sacrificial lives that spurn death (12:11).

The vision moves in the realm of antithetical parallelism. While the vision appears to be choppy, the vision addresses the themes of the Woman; Child;

Dragon; a Period of Dark Age persecution and suppression; "times, time, ½ times; 42 months; 3½ years; 3½ days; and 1260 days" (five different designations) which, given the Jewish 30-day month, all amount to the same time frame. We are responsible, with a spiritually enlightened mind, plus a Biblical and historical knowledge of the times in which The Revelation was given, for placing the particulars of these visions into their proper places.

The Woman flees to the wilderness (Rev 12:6) where she was able to survive throughout the Dark Ages of persecution. This fleeing is interpreted as Pagan and Papal Rome opposition under the mysterious name Babylon, the Devil's wife (Rev 17:5). When the Woman goes into the wilderness, she is as pure as the Sun, but the Devil persecutes her, and the Beast (Satan's religious-political ally (Rev 11:7)) goes to war against her. Millions of friends to Apostolic, New Testament Christianity are slaughtered for the 3½ days, a figure of the overall 1,260 days.

Both women are connected to the beast, the sea, and the Wilderness, but the first woman is radiant. The second woman is a whore.

We can reach only one conclusion concerning the Harlot of Revelation 17:1. The woman of Revelation 12:1 was crowned with the 12 apostolic stars. The head gives direction. Satan attacks at precisely this point. He eventually overcame her apostolic doctrine with the flood of false doctrine. Satan made war with her offspring (Rev 12:17) because they keep God's Commandments and the New Testament of Jesus Christ (12:17). God's Commandments are Jesus' Commandments (1Jn 2:1-5). The beast, introduced in Revelation 11:7 (as a religious-political ally of the Serpent, Dragon – Devil), came out of the apocalyptic sea of political turmoil and unrest. Now the woman is a whore on those very same waters (17:1). Once the woman was a virtuous wife; now she is a fornicator (17:2). Once she was pure; now she makes others drunk through the wine of fornication. She was persecuted as a virgin woman and chased into the wilderness where she became whore (12:14).

The Beast went to war against her in the wilderness (Rev 12:17-13:1); now she is sitting on the back of the Beast (17:3). She is not only deceived, seduced, and subject to the Beast, but she is actually on his back directing him as a rider would direct a horse. She was once a friend to the Messiah (Sun of Righteousness - Mal 4:2), now she is anti-messiah. The Blood of the Lamb once redeemed her; now she sheds the blood of saints (Rev 17:6). She is the false congregation from Rome (the city of seven mountains "elevations" (17:9)), and this causes John to wonder with great astonishment (17:6). She is called the great *mystery*, and this apostasy causes Paul to write of "The mystery that was already at work in his day" (2Th 2:7, 8). She is the whore that was judged in 1792-93 A.D. by the combined forces of Protestantism, Revolution, and Restoration. Ultimately, she will be destroyed at Christ's Second Coming (Rev 18:2, 24).

The Book of Revelation ends with the judgment of the whore (false congregation "woman"), and with the revelation of the true Bride (the Ecclesia of Christ - 21:2, 9). These two women run parallel throughout The Revelation and throughout history. The greatest *mystery* in history is how the true Ecclesia, *Bride* of Christ, could begin so pure and holy as a purchased person of Christ at Pentecost (Ac 2:36-48) and then turn around and betray the Lord with impunity. The apostates masquerade before the world as apostolic successors but are in reality the whore until the end of time. Thus, John was utterly amazed with great wonderment at the sight of such wholesale apostate profligacy being exercised by what the world thought was a Christian institution.

The 1260 Days

As we read Jamieson, Fausset and Brown, Matthew Henry, Adam Clark, Albert Barnes and other commentaries on the whole Bible (or B.W. Johnson's, *People's New Testament*, and others such as Elliot's *New Testament Commentary*, and J. Lemeul Martin's, *Voice of The Seven Thunders*, we learn that numerous Biblical scholars have attempted to work out this time frame under the day-year concept (Eze 4:6). All of these scholars may have different opinions as to when the 1,260 years began and ended. But they all agree that a day-year (taking a day to be a year) concept of trying times befell the Lord's people in history (www.wikipedia: Day-year principle). They also all agree on the following five different day-year designations: 1) 42-months, 2) 1,260 days, 3) Times, time and 1/2 time, 4) 3½ years and 5) 3½ days, are really a cryptic apocalyptic code for 1,260 years.

Alexander Campbell believed the starting date for the 1260 year was 606 A.D.; the year Pope Boniface III took power. Martin Luther also holds this date as a starting point for the very discernible and bold corruptions of the original Christian Faith ("Martin Luther's View on The First Pope" -christianity.stackexchange.com). Scholars of Christian History look for the inception of the rise of Babylonian Power to subjugate pure, primitive Christianity through the union of the empire and the apostate church. The reason they choose 606 is because of the camaraderie The Emperor Phocas had with Boniface, and the official support he rendered with his declaration, "The See of the blessed Peter the Apostle shall be the head of all the churches." The web site mentioned above conscientiously attempts to be forthright and accurate in its interpretation of religious history.

The scholars who embrace this view have different starting and ending dates. Interestingly, Emperor Justinian recognized the Pope as head of the Eastern and Western church in 533 A.D. This is why we lean toward 533 A.D. as our starting point. Then, 1,260 years later on December 25, 1793, James O'Kelly broke with the Republican Episcopal Methodist Church to accept the New Testament as the rule of faith and practice. They decided to be called Christian, only.

Christians embrace this Historic view, not because O'Kelly was 100% orthodox in understanding Scripture, but his action precipitated a worldwide movement on the part of denominational scholars to return to New Testament Christianity. It is also quite momentous that scholar Robert Fleming visited the King of England almost a century before 1793 and announced that according to prophecy (Rev 16:10), the fifth bowl of wrath would be poured out upon the Papacy.

Steve Gregg writes in his *Four Views*, p. 34

> "Sometime, around 1690, it is reported, Robert Fleming was invited before the English court of William of Orange, King William III, to lecture on Bible prophecy. The King asked when the "temporal power" of the Papacy in Europe would fall. Fleming's reply was published in his 1701 book entitled "Apocalyptic Key." Concerning the fall of the papacy as the ruling power in Europe, the prophecy scholar wrote: 'I say this judgment will begin about A.D. 1794 and expire about 1848.' This prediction was made approximately 100 years prior to the projected dates. Historicist apologists point out that in 1794 the French Revolution's "Reign of Terror" occurred, which, they say, marked the beginning of the end of the pope's temporal power in Europe. In the year 1848, the pope was temporarily driven from Rome."

Fleming used the same 1,260-year reckoning as the Remnant-Restorationist use, but Fleming determined that the French Revolution was God's method of bringing the Papacy to its knees in 1794. Fleming also predicted that Islam would begin to collapse at the turn of the 21st Century (2000 A.D.). He also predicted other events that did not fit his prophetic scheme. Being human, Fleming did not have divine revelation, and some problems exist concerning whether we should use the Jewish calendar of 30 days (360-day year), or the Julian-Gregorian calendar of 365-day years. The Gregorian 1,260 years would be about 18 years longer than the Jewish. However, we should consider that when using Old Testament prophetic dates (such as Daniel's prophecies), we have no other alternative but to use the Jewish, 360-day year. On the other hand, when using the New Testament, we may use the Julian-Gregorian dating in the application of prophecy. We can say this because John's original 3½ days were not 3½ days at all, but were to be understood as 42 months and 1,260 days; 3½ years; or time, times, and ½ time.

Obviously, we are to have the same wisdom as we were supposed to have at the close of the 13th Chapter when interpreting 666. It is not the man, but the 666 numerology of the man that we should learn. The number 666 is associated with Romulus, Lateinos, Nero, the Titan family, and the Papacy and has been proven by hundreds of scholars. All of these names are associated with Pagan and Religious Rome. When we consider the starting point to be the Papacy, some insist on 533 A.D. for *Pope* John and other scholars insist on 606 A.D. for *Pope* Boniface III. Whether we use the Jewish or Julian-Gregorian calendar, we know that religious Rome obtained both religious and political power over Rome and Europe, and exercised that power for a period of time called the "Dark Ages." Equally certain is that after a considerable period of time, Papal Rome lost dominion and temporal power. Roughly speaking, there could not be a better number to mark this deterioration of the Papacy than 1,260 years after 533 A.D. This happened when, in 1793, the Restoration of Primitive Christianity begin to sweep the Earth clean of ecclesiasticism, while at the same time a European, revolutionary outburst exploded against tyrannical Romanism. Fleming predicted the collapse of Rome would continue from 1784 to 1848, when the Pope was robbed of all his power and had to flee to Gaeta.

Mr. Fleming was more correct in his understanding that the Papacy would be shaken with retribution 1,260 years after the coronation of the Pope in 533 A.D. by Emperor Justinian or in 606 A.D. by Emperor Phocus. The establishment of the Papacy was a catastrophe that would serve as an ominous warning for her followers to flee Roman Babylon before her final judgment day, just as the Christian Jews were warned to flee Jerusalem before her desolation in 70 A.D. Due to Dark Age superstition and ignorance, especially in the realm of theology, Mr. Fleming did not have access to the understanding of the capitulatory, parallel cycles of the Apocalypse. It is true that the Papacy suffered divine, prophetic retribution from 1793 to 1848, but the fifth bowl of wrath means more than retribution on Romanism since the same judgment is a partial retribution under the fifth trumpet (Re 9:1-5) but, "The Kingdom of the beast was full of darkness" under the fifth bowl "vial of wrath" (16:10, 11). We appreciate any scholar who can sanely (and as accurately as possible) apply the judgments of The Apocalypse to certain tumultuous or very significant historical events. But while a symbol may seem to fit some particular event, it also may mean more than that and fit other events yet to come.

The Revelation teaches cyclical history through the seven parallel sections of the Book. However, Revelation also teaches chronological history, particularly in regard to the two women: The Ecclesia of Jerusalem from above and the Babylonian Whore from Rome. The Historicists commit a major blunder by attempting to continue chronological prophecy related to Egypt, Syria, Persia, Babylon, Greece, and then Rome because chronological history of certain nations stopped with the days of the Roman Empire.

The prophetic Revelation differs from the apocalyptic writings of the Old Testament. The Old Testament addresses the chronology of the seed of the woman, Israel, and the surrounding nations. But in the Apocalypse, the only concern is the chronology of the two women. The two women rise in the beginning and in the middle of the Book and stand or fall at the end. We understand that there is historical continuity between the two women from their beginning to the end of the world. We also understand that the two women represent Babylon and the true Bride of Christ. These two women represent two totally spiritually isometric, diverse systems. They are an exception to the other apocalyptic visions that should be interpreted in a parallel and cyclical context. Some scholars argue that this would place the Godhead in a restricted time frame, but the Godhead is infinitely immeasurable and ungoverned by human history or time, neither linear nor cyclical.

If Revelation teaches anything in an unmistakable and particular way, it is the fact the seven trumpets (Rev 8:2-11:15) parallel the seven bowls of wrath (Rev 15:7-16:17). The seven trumpets follow the overlapping Seventh Seal (8:1), and the seven bowls of wrath affect the same seven geographical areas (land, sea, river, sun, throne of the beast, river of Euphrates, and the air of the heavens), as do the trumpets. The fifth trumpet affects the abyss of Satan and his angels (locusts). They are stirred up to engage and accelerate a campaign to torment lost souls who are not sealed by the Holy Spirit.

Thus, I see the trumpets warning men and women in all ages of history. Likewise, I see the bowls of wrath as final judgment taking place in the same area where the warnings are issued. The same people who rejected the trumpet as a warning should not be surprised when the judgment comes. We noticed that the trumpets affect a third of the Earth, or partial judgment, while the bowls reveal total judgment.

Mr. Fleming is to be commended for his 1,260-year prophecy; but like the rest of the theologians of his post-dark age era, he had not yet discovered the idea of recapitulatory, parallel revelation writing. Fleming was an avid Historicist, who, however faulty in assigning to Revelation particular prophetic dates in known history, he was still a million times better than the next group of uninformed Biblical novices who embraced the Dispensational, Pre-Millennial, Darbyism of the rapture cult of the early 19th Century.

Whatever may be said about Robert Fleming's prophetic ideas, he deserves tremendous credit for knowing the historical and prophetic demise of the temporal power of religious Romanism. His message and writings made such an impact on the world of his day that he was invited to speak to the Court of The English King, William III of Orange, 1690 A.D., on the subject of Revelation and Bible Prophecy. What a world-changing effect for the good of America would come to pass if such an un-sectarian Bible scholar were invited to speak to The Congress of the United States today.

If we would fast and pray, open Scripture and speak to the nations as Jeremiah the Prophet (Jer 1:5) did, and then apply the truths of the apocalypse to the current events of this day and the "Rule of Christ in the affairs of His Kingdom, and in the midst of all nations who fear the Lord" (Ps 110), what a revival we could have in America. Like the government of Nineveh which God constrained to repent after hearing Jonah's preaching (Jnh 3; Mat 12:41), our national leaders would fall before the face of the Living God… Oh, what a better world we would see and know! But alas, because most preachers seem to be unable to perceive the apocalyptic content and nature of the Book of Revelation and its message to the nations of the world, they steer clear of its intended nation changing warnings and communication. The Devil has convinced them to steer clear of this treasured Heavenly Apocalypse with at least three nonsensical alibis: 1) Neither you nor your congregation will understand it. 2) The Revelation has no message for the "now times", it only applies to events in the far off future. Why worry now, the Lord will come and straighten things out later. So the world is in a mess, "Why polish brass on a sinking ship?" 3) If there is a Heavenly message from Heaven to both the congregations of Christ and also the "Nations of the world" (Re 11:18), we take the risk of making the nations angry. So the mantra has become very popular, "Do not mix religion and politics."

The Devil says, "If we stay out of politics, politics will stay out of the church". Ha, ha, go to Hades and tell this to some of the naïve pre-socialist Christians in Germany and the pre-Communist Christians in The Soviet Union and they will tell us that they forgot that Christianity is not only a purifying catalyst to any nation, it is also a powerful deterrent to the takeover of a country by Satanic empire building. There may have been Evangelists and Pastors who stood up against those like Benito Mussolini, Adolph Hitler, Hideki Tojo, Vladimir Lenin, Joseph Stalin, and Mao Zedong (www.scaruffi.com: The worst genocides of the 20th and 21st Centuries). While these dictators possessed the diabolical zeal for power and control of their countries, the Evangelists and Pastors were scorned as "Being out of touch with the times."

Watchman Nee, for instance was one of the most powerful Christian voices on Earth in his day. His Godly life (1903-1972 A.D.) almost paralleled that of the demon- possessed, "butcher of humanity" Mao (1883-1976 A.D.). Watchman Nee experienced unmerciful sufferings at the hands of the tyrants of his nation, and he spent the last 20 years of his life in a Communist prison. Mao's life was a continual success in parroting the line of social progress and liberation, stirring his followers into a frenzy of carrying his "Red Book" in one hand and a Thomson Submachine Gun in the other. Mao was born the son of a wealthy family (www.wikipedia.org: Mao Zedong) and rose to a cult hero with god-like status, while Watchman Nee (with as pure a dedication to Christ as was known in his ungodly country) languished in prison.

However, in the introduction to their book, *House Divided*, Greg Bahnsen and Kenneth Gentry mention how "Millennial Dispensationalism" was at the heart of much of the Christian evangelism done in China in the late 19th Century. There is probably no greater fanaticism in the world than a radical millennialism (pre-post-dispensational-mid, post or pretribulation). In my personal collection of

Watchman Nee books, I notice a far from radical, but slight tilt toward such millennial theology. But, I repeat it was "slight" because Nee also had a strong theological grasp of the truths respecting the sovereignty of Christ as King and the local congregations being His Kingdom fellowship on earth.

But Bahnsen and Gentry establish that had the missionaries to China taught their converts the plain New Testament message that Christ is the King of the world NOW, He reigns over the universe NOW, including China and Russia (from whence Mao got his Leninist concepts of communism), perhaps the Chinese nation would have had more spiritual resolve and courage to resist communism through prayer and a proper understanding of "The teachings and doctrines of The Kingdom" as taught by The Master in Matthew 13 and throughout the remainder of the New Testament.

Christians usually are not accustomed to speaking of "revolution" or "overthrow of a government" (Ro 13:1-5). However, we have every right to expect those who govern us to govern according to God's precepts. Christians have the inalienable right to bear arms to protect themselves and the righteous need to pray that God will obstruct those who rage against us and raise their weapons against His THRONE (Acts 4:29). Petitions to God will be heard and answered in any nation, in ways known only to God. However, if ministers or missionaries do not take this message to their people and nation, evil national leaders are emboldened to encroach more and more upon the Christian faith and liberty.

Samuel Lamb (Lin Xiangao) was considered by the Chinese Communist Party to be a traitor, "an enemy of the people" because he resisted the Communist state-controlled "Three-Self Patriotic Movement." He was imprisoned for over 20 years, and in spite of his hardship, he preached in the coal mines and labor camps. He died in 2013 A.D. at the age of 88. He violated the following restrictions: do not preach on the Second Coming of Christ, do not evangelize minors or young people, no preaching from the Book of Revelation. In all these cases, Lamb believed that if the government is evil, obedience to God supersedes the command in Romans 13 to obey government. Conversely, Christians should conform to the teachings of the Book of Acts 5. Samuel Lamb's underground house church movement grew to some 4,000 – 5,000 believers in 1979, and today, his movement has continued to increase to unknown numbers (www.wikipedia: Samuel Lamb). How interesting that the enemy did not want preaching from the Book of Revelation. Could it be that the enemy knows more about this Book than most Christians do?

Yes, bold Christian leaders have died for their faith throughout the centuries, but they were never in cowardly retreat. They took Christ's message of power and deliverance to the enemy. They never holed up inside a neat little sanctuary. They responded with the prayer of offense, "Lord, behold their threatening and slaughter, and enable your servants to speak your word with great boldness" (Read Acts 4:29-31.).

The Identity of the First Woman

Certain scholars have said that the woman cannot represent the Ecclesia from beginning to end because the Male Child is certainly Jesus Christ (the only One who rules the world with a rod of iron (Rev 2: 5)), and "The woman gave birth to the Man Child" (Rev 12:13), and not the other way around. If we were time-shackled scholars who want to place apocalyptic Scripture in the box of time and space, then this would be problematic. When scholars make the mistake of forcing time shackled ideas upon the apocalyptic text, they miss a great blessing. If only a small piece of the whole vision is interpreted with an ironclad conclusion, then we open ourselves up to being guilty of the *Black-or-White* logic fallacy. Scholars can be guilty of either not being born-again of the Spirit or not being God's workmen who compare Scripture with Scripture. But an alternative position is that we might not be praying to God for wisdom. Apocalyptic literature is not written to be understood in literal time, as the historical Book of Acts or as the history given in the Four Gospels is understood.

As already noted, the symbolism of the woman's appearance (Rev 12:1) lifts us above, beyond, and outside of time. Thus, we see things the way that Christ would see them from the Throne. One of the main themes of Revelation is "The Throne" of God and the Lamb. In this connection, 40 times the word, "throne," is found in this Book. All things are governed from this Throne. Eternity governs time, not vise-versa. What may seem so big in time is just a speck when viewed from the Throne.

People ask the question, "Could the woman be Eve?" Certainly it sounds like Eve. God told her, "The seed of the woman would bruise Satan's heel" (Ge 3:15, 16). Could the woman be Old Testament Israel? William Hendrickson in his *More Than Conquerors*[77] tells us the woman stands for the prophetic promise made to the woman who came down through Israel with much conflict, violence, and opposition,

"As a woman with child, is in pain and cries out in her pangs, when she draws near to her delivery, so have we been in your sight, O Lord" (Isa 26:17).

The Bible mentions the relationship Israel had with God. Israel was a woman who had God as her husband and redeemer and was described as a woman forsaken and grieved and a wife who married young, only to be rejected" (Isa 54:5, 6).

Jeremiah records God's analogy of the daughter of Zion (a figure of speech for God's predestined people) to a lovely and delicate woman (6:2). The idea of the daughter of Zion being in labor and laboring in birth pains is expressly given in Micah 4:9, 10. Remember, Christ came and died for the true bride of Zion (Rev 14:1).

Could the woman be Mary? Certainly, one cannot read this prophecy without thinking of the God-Man of eternity and the womb that produced the Man-Child in time. During the Christmas season, people sing, "Oh little town of Bethlehem, how still you seem tonight." However, people forget that while the babe lay in a manger, all of the Devil's Hell was being loosed to murder the child. Herod wanted the child killed immediately, and the flight to Egypt was fraught with many impending threats and hazards for the young child (Mt 2:13).

Could the woman be the Ecclesia? This is probably the most plausible explanation for the text. We conclude this because all three of the above are in the text, but they culminate with the Ecclesia being the seed of the woman, "Her offspring" (Rev 12:17), and overcoming the powerful temptations of the Whore. Later, we will see that the Whore sprang up in their midst from the very woman they considered to be pure and holy (Rev 17:3, 4). The Beast pursued the woman at first (Rev 12:13, 17) and in Revelation 17:3, she is riding on his back. In spite of the most powerful influences to seduce her into illicit idolatry by worldwide Romanism, the remnant of the true radiant woman spent her time in wilderness seclusion preparing herself for marriage to the Lamb (Rev 19:7-10).

At first, the woman seems to be a deliberate prophetic anachronism. We know it is an anachronism because the woman existed before Christ's Ascension, "He was caught up," and after "she fled into the wilderness" and she will live eternally (19:7-10). By definition, an anachronism is defined as a mistaken placement of historical events into a time sequence where they do not belong. On the other hand, what if the Scripture puts the historic woman (Bride of Christ) before Christ? This can be seen as a pre-calculated historical placing of events, because as mentioned above, the radiant woman is the woman of Biblical prophecy. So it is a deliberate prophetical anachronism for those wise enough to appreciate it.

Consider other anachronisms in Scripture. Isaiah 14:12, states, "Lucifer how are you fallen from Heaven?" Although the verse is placed in present tense, it refers to an indefinite past tense. What about Isaiah 21:9 and Revelation 18:2, "Babylon is fallen." Is this an anachronism? Further, Jesus beheld Satan "fall from Heaven" (Lk 10:18). Is the timing of Satan's fall in Scripture a prophetic anachronism? It looks like it is.

The seed of the woman encountered opposition from Cain, Nimrod, the Pharaoh, King Saul, Queen Athaliah, the Kings of Assyria, Persia, Babylon, and the evil conniver, Antiochus Epiphanes, down to King Herod's fury concerning the birth of the Man-Child. All of these combined could not do justice to the enraged fury of Pagan and Papal Rome against the true Ecclesia. What is strange is that religious Rome coined the word *ecclesia* and strained it to mean *ecclesiasticism*. The word *church* was forced upon the gullible apostates of the 3rd Century, and ecclesia was twisted to mean "ecclesiastical hierarchy." Remember the "hierarchy" is the corrupting influence of the "outer court" (hieros), but Christ did not recognize this hierarchy (Rev 11:2), even though Papal Rome and the Greeks call themselves a "Christian" Institution.

Romanism was able to maneuver the following institutions that it now had at its disposal: religion, law, philosophy, art, politics, economic sanctions, and inquisitional, military might to engage and destroy those who advocated plain, simple, pure Apostolic Christianity. Of the 17 times "witness" or "testimony" (both translated from "marturios") is found in the Book of Revelation – every time either of these words is found interchangeably – it is in the context of being persecuted, killed, or beheaded for the New Covenant Gospel of Jesus Christ. When Christians are killed because of their testimony, Christians are martyrs, regardless of whether Muslim, Buddhist, Hindu or government agents kill them.

A better description of the woman would be a prophetic allegory. Paul uses this means of communication in Galatians 4:24. An allegory is a continuous metaphor or comparison of one person or thing to another in a running narrative. An example of an allegory is the two sons of Abraham, who are Isaac, the legitimate son, and

Ishmael, the illegitimate son. The two women are the bondwoman Hagar and the free woman is Sarah. The two Covenants are the Old from Sinai (and Earthly Jerusalem) that produces bondage, and the New Covenant that originates from the New Jerusalem, which is above and produces freedom.

Notice how Paul wraps theological concepts around one person or one thing in this allegory. The ancient Greek word for this wrapping of theological concepts was "synecdoche." The prefix *"syn"* means together and *"ecdoche"* means receive. That is, if only the part is given, we also receive the whole (pars pro toto). On the other hand, if the whole is given, we also receive the part (totum pro parte). A synecdoche means to perceive the thought with "simultaneous understanding".

Thus, in this vision, the woman, giving birth to Christ is no accident, but a part of the overall contemplative Counsel of God (…the hopes and fears of all the years are born in thee tonight…from "O Little Town of Bethlehem" by Phillip Brooks). The woman was in pain, but that pain goes all the way back to the Garden of Eden. Indeed, our minds are taxed by apocalyptic visions. After being given such apocalyptic visions, Daniel was given over to cogitations" (Da 7:28). In another vision, "He fainted, was sick and was astonished at the vision" (8:26, 27) and yet later, "He saw this great vison, his strength was exhausted", and "He fell into a deep sleep" (10:8, 9). Consider the apocalyptic visions of Abraham. "Horror and great darkness" befall Abraham (Ge 15:12) and he saw a "Smoking furnace and a burning lamp" pass between the bloody pieces of Covenant flesh he offered YHWH God (15:17).

Get your Concordance and look up the word "Vision" and search for yourself. Jacob had a vison of the ladder of Christ, and we should interpret what it meant. David had visions of the THRONE of Christ, and we are to interpret what they meant. Isaiah had a vison of the THRONE, and he fell in awe before Christ's presence. Ezekiel had several visions, and we must have the Mind of the Spirit to interpret them. Zechariah's nine visions are not given to be wasted on a dust covered desk top where The Bible sits; the visions are to be interpreted. Paul's vision of Christ on the road to Damascus (left him blind, speechless and dumbfounded) is related three times in the Book of Acts and in the Book of Galatians, and there is a wealth of wisdom to be gleaned from an interpretation of the vision. The apocalyptic visions that John had on the Aisle of Patmos caused him to fall down like a dead man (Re 1:7).

It is a shame that even young children, ages three and up will spend hours, days, and weeks learning to interpret the symbols and icons of an electronic device, but both children and adults for the most part cannot interpret ONE symbol given in the Book of Revelation. This includes us pastors and teachers as well, who simply do not want to pay the price the Patriarchs, Prophets, Apostles and diligent students of The Apocalypse have paid in prayerful searching of the Apocalypse, the history of the times, the time tested meaning of apocalyptic symbols, and of course, the discipline of exegetical hermeneutics.

When is the last time we fell on the couch exhausted, our minds spinning with apocalyptic information from Heaven and we were in such prayerful meditations and ponderings that we felt like we were in a daze? The problem with students of Revelation is that they open the Book and want it to be as elementary as a Gospel story. When they face an apocalyptic truth that may requires spiritual, prayerful brainstorming, they put the book down or consult a futuristic wizard who tells him exactly the opposite of what the Word of God says. We are not so paranoid that we cannot accept a challenge or disagreement; but if we encounter a challenge, we expect the challenger to present us with a far better interpretation. This work of interpreting the Sacred Revelation is very hard work. God is to be praised. It is worth it all!

Yes, Christ's birth to the woman is in time, but Christ is the eternal Son, "In the bosom of the eternal Father" (Jn 1:16). Apocalyptically, Christ is beyond time. He came to this Earth in response to the prophetic Bride of Christ, and He ransomed her (His Bride - His ecclesia) for all eternity. Isaiah said, "Unto us a child is born" (Isa 9:6). Therefore, Christ was born unto us. In this sense, the ecclesia gave birth to Christ. Nevertheless, the same prophecy says, "Unto us a Son is given." It does not say, "The Son was born to us." Revelation says, "She gave birth to the man-child" (12:5). It does not say she gave birth to the Son. The Son existed in eternity. God gave His "only unique" Son (Jn 3:16). The Son existed eternally "as the only unique Son in the bosom of the Father," before His glory was witnessed on Earth by the Apostles (Jn 1:14). As the Man-Child, Christ was born in time, "You are My Son, and this day I have begotten Thee" (Heb 1:5). God the Father Himself placed His Son (The Word of God) in the human womb of Mary (Mt 1:18). Therefore, the woman produced the womb, and the Holy Spirit conceived the seed of the woman (Gal 3:19, 4:4). Therefore, the woman, ecclesia, gave birth to the Man-Child, Christ, because the Man-Child came to her and for her, He gave His (anthropos, human) life (Eph 5:25, 30, 32). However, as the eternal Son of God, He existed before the ecclesia was established at Pentecost 30 A.D.

How shortsighted is the Historicist who says "The man child" is Constantine, or some other Roman ruler. The same question may be asked in the expression, "Mystery Babylon." Who is Babylon? Is she Babel on the plains of Shinar? Is she the ancient nation mentioned hundreds of times in the Old Testament? Is she the nation that produced Nebuchadnezzar and Belshazzar? Is she the country that became modern-day Iraq?

We must take what the texts say to understand what they mean. In God's overall prophetic plan, Babylon has always stood for the chief enemy and rival of God's predestined program and Chosen People. Just as the last woman – who is the true Zion and Bride of Christ – fulfills all God's intentions for His glorious counsel and destiny, so the last Babylon is the epitome of all that is vile, ugly, evil, and undesirable to Holy God. When we see the glorious woman of Revelation 12, we see that which is not just central to the Book of Revelation but is central to all Bible prophecy. The seed which produces life among those human beings who seek life begins with Genesis 3:16 and ends with Revelation 21:17.

As for Satan, his false seed also begins its unholy war against the seed of the woman in Genesis 3:16. The battle is continuous and rages throughout history with the unholy trinity of Satan, i.e., the Beast of the Sea (Rev 13:1), the Beast of the Land (13:11), and Babylon, the Devil's bride (17:1-6). (But this isn't really like the Trinity because it is Satan with three others, not like God the Father with two others.) Satan's trinity come up together simultaneously with the Bride of Christ, and they go down together. Babylon (18:2-24), the Sea-Going Beast, and the Land-Going Beast together fall into the Lake of Fire (19:20). Satan, their Trinitarian Father, is also defeated and joins them in eternal misery (20:10).

So, we learn to understand the Bible in part and in whole. The Bible is an absolutely, incredibly beautiful work of God. The infallible New Testament is the greatest gift ever given to humanity after the sacrificial death of Jesus Christ for the redemption and remission of sins.

The Fullness of Time

The Bible speaks of Christ coming at the *fullness of time*. This *fullness* is described in Galatians 4:4 when God's purpose was fulfilled during the time of the Roman Empire. Christ's coming when He did was considered the fullness of time for several reasons, among which were a universal network of roads, law, order, universal language, and unity of "Pax Romana." This *fullness* promoted the establishment of Christ's Congregation. This establishment was not a last minute concoction at Pentecost, but a plan from eternity past. Some believe the Congregation is a stopgap measure (Pre-Millennialist); however, the truth is that the Law is a stopgap measure (Gal 3:24, 25). The Law held people together until the Congregation came together by faith. Peter said that the prophecy was fulfilled (1Pe 2:9 of Ex 19:5, 6) when God made his spiritual children Kings and Priests. God's Kings and Priests could only come about by the precious Blood of Jesus (Ac 20:28) with which He purchased His bride. The New Covenant Congregation is the fulfillment of Israel (Ro 11:12, 25). The end would not come until:

1. The end of sin occurred when Christ potentially redeemed the whole world through His propitiatory death. In God's mind, sin was paid for. Daniel speaks of several other "final things" – the finishing of transgressions when the Jews transgressed as far as they could by rejecting the Gospel, the atonement for iniquity on the cross, and everlasting righteousness through sanctification, which took place through the coming of the Messiah, Jesus (Da 9:24).

2. The angels looked to the "manner of time" when the preaching of the Gospel took place (1Pe 1:10-12). This has happened (Ac 3:21; Mt 19:18; Tit 3:5; Heb 9:10).

3. God said that the Jews would fill up their sins (1Th 2:16) before the abomination of desolation. This is written concerning the Jews. This has happened.

4. Fullness of the Gentiles (Ro 11:12; 25; Lk 21:24) is currently happening through the Gentiles being added to the Ecclesia, "Spiritual Israel" (Ac 2:47).

5. Fullness of Martyrs (Rev 6:10, 11). This is currently happening (Rev 6:10, 11).

The verses from Revelation 12:1, 2 are extremely important and show the advent of the King of Righteousness and the birth of the everlasting kingdom on Earth. Upon hearing the Angels sing, "Born to you THIS DAY is a Savior, Christ-Messiah-Lord" (Lk 2:11), we should emphasize two little words "THIS DAY." The angels knew something that we now understand in approximately 2015 A.D. (The meaning of A.D. stems from the Latin "anno-year" and "domini-Lord, Master or Sovereign Ruler.") The Son of God was born to rule over the world through time into eternity (Jn 18:37). But the angels were ahead of the years and got the beginning of the new calendar down to the day. Christ's birth was the first day of the world's calendar years. The "alpha" (Rev 1:8, 22:13), as the angels confirmed, was born "this day," and He who is the "omega" will bring the last day of our calendar years to an end (2Pe 3:10; 1Th 5:2; Rev 16:15). Read these texts, marvel, wonder, and believe!

Revelation 12:3: Then another sign appeared in heaven: an enormous red dragon with seven heads and ten horns and seven crowns on his heads.

Seven heads represent perfect intelligence. Each head has wisdom. Each one is very hard to kill. Even if we manage to remove one head, six remain. Mere mortals are no match for this Beast. The picture of this dragon with crowns symbolizes Satan's victory over the world. Satan prides himself on his own authority. He wants to devour the Congregation (Eph 2:2). He rules from the pits of Hades and lashes out with his satanic forces.

Revelation 12:4: His tail swept a third of the stars out of the sky and flung them to the earth. The dragon stood in front of the woman who was about to give birth, so that he might devour her child the moment it was born.

We have discussed Satan's former position as the "Cherub that covered" in other sections of this book. The Book of Jude 6 addresses this occurrence. In Satan's pride, he managed to deceive one-third of the heavenly angels into believing his lie. In rebelling against God, Satan was cast out of Heaven with his followers. Jesus speaks of this in history (Lk 10:18) when He said, "I saw Satan fall…," it is a prophetic past and future statement. Satan did not keep his first estate with God; more importantly, he lost his second position as prosecutors of the Saints with Jesus' Ascension to the Throne.

Revelation 12:5: She gave birth to a son, a male child, who will rule all the nations with an iron scepter. And her child was snatched up to God and to his throne.

When Christ sat on the Throne, the Rod of Iron Reign began. Yes, Christ still has enemies, but the enemies do not prevent his ultimate rule over them (Ps 110:2). He truly rules with an iron scepter (Ps 2:9). Jesus Christ ascended to the Throne and reigns at the right hand of God. Through His pain and suffering, Jesus defeated death because He knew no sin. God raised Him up to sit at His right hand. Jesus commissioned His Apostles to proclaim and spread His word starting in Jerusalem. The spreading of His Word established His reign so that all may recognize Him. Never underestimate the power of the Gospel (Ro 1:16). We may question the present "Rod of Iron" Reign because, at times, Christ may not seem to reign at all, but His children doubted His reign in Egypt; they despaired in Assyria and Babylon; they feared Persia, Greece and Syria; and they thought Rome was the Imperial Capital of the world, but all of these empires and rulers are gone. Very soon the dynasties that rule Korea, China, the Mid-East, and the so-called democracies of the world will be gone. Our current White House executives will all be gone. Christ chooses to rule now with grace, compassion, and long suffering, but the Rod of His Reign is still "Iron." It is, was, and always shall be.

Revelation 12:6: *The woman fled into the desert to a place prepared for her by God, where she might be taken care of for 1,260 days.*

The Revelation picks up on this again (12:13). The persecution of the Congregation began immediately. After the establishment of the testimony, the woman fled into the wilderness. The Greek-Roman Church officially removed evangelism and the Word from the Congregation, thus, instituting a time when the whole world was left in darkness.

Some ask these questions, "Was this good or not? Did she go into the wilderness relying on it for protection or just to survive? How did the woman emerge?" (Rev 17:3, 4) These Dark Ages are referenced in Fox's Book of Martyrs. Several men throughout history attempted to break from the reign of the universal church (Dragon); they failed drastically. The ecclesiastical (Roman) church removed the witnesses from the picture and then waged war against the pure New Testament Congregation. However, God protected the true Bride of Christ. He caused His Word to survive.

Remember New Covenant Christianity is not just the primitive congregation from 30 to 70 A.D. New Covenant Christianity is an invisible movement among sincere seekers of Christ until the end of time.

Revelation 12:7-10: *And there was war in heaven. Michael and his angels fought against the dragon, and the dragon and his angels fought back. But he was not strong enough, and they lost their place in heaven. The great dragon was hurled down — that ancient serpent called the devil, or Satan, who leads the whole world astray. He was hurled to the earth, and his angels with him. Then I heard a loud voice in heaven say: "Now have come the salvation and the power and the kingdom of our God, and the authority of his Christ. For the accuser of our brothers, who accuses them before our God day and night, has been hurled down.*

There is war in Heaven. This war was the most important and decisive of all conflicts throughout the ages, until the end of time. This war was God's predestined program to fight Satan. Satan was able to deceive the world (verse 9) until Christ came. Now the New Testament is a finished testimony for the entire world to read. The powerful meaning of Revelation 12:7-12 is that Satan can no longer deceive the nations! Even though deception and false doctrine continue, no man has an excuse to accept them. The Word of God is plainly written. The New Testament truth has been made manifest so that the world would believe on Christ! God created this perfect plan so that He could include the saints and exclude Satan and sinners. This perfect plan is all-inclusive and all exclusive. At one time, Satan had a place in Heaven. However, due to his sin, he was cast out. Yet, Satan could still present himself before God to accuse the brethren. When Christ came, Christ banished Satan for a second time, but this time banishment was forever. Now, the Gospel binds Satan. He can only operate from the depths of Hades. He still has power; he still has demonic forces; but they are limited by the Words of Christ. Satan is restricted from God's domain. Because of this restriction, Satan is furious! He is doing everything he can to wage war against the truth. He only has a short time before his judgment is carried out. Christians are spiritually fighting against him. They are waging a war that is not against flesh and blood but against principalities and powers (Eph 6:12). Over the course of more than 50 years, and much to our dismay, we have discovered in our intense warfare against "The Prince of Darkness" that his greatest military scheme to demoralize and break the resolve of the Lord's Armies is to capture and take back into slavery some of our most promising converts (Gal 5:4; Heb 10:29-31).

God first *declared* this war between Satan and the Godhead in Genesis 3:15. This passage corresponds with Revelation 12:1. Satan tried numerous times to attack the bloodline of Eve. This attack is the *preparation* for the battle. Satan attempted to prevent the birth of the Son of Righteousness. He wanted desperately to prevent these prophecies from coming true. The earliest clashes in the Old Testament (psychological and philosophical warfare) were between the devil, the old serpent, and the Seed of the Women. This led to deadly warfare. However, in Matthew 8:29 and Luke 10:17-20, the devil backs off and admits that Jesus is the Son of God. Next, the *invasion* took place with a tremendous offense. Christ stepped in and became the Passover Lamb for the world. In the Old Covenant, God would only *pass over* the sins of the world. The word Passover means "to suspend" (Ro 3:25). However, in the New Testament, people can receive complete (aphesis) forgiveness of sins (found in Ac 2:38). Christ not only died for people in the future, but He also died for all the sins that were *suspended* by God in the Old Testament. His blood went both ways from the cross, forward and backward. Jesus did not fight Satan as almighty God, but as a perfect man (Mt 4:4).

This *actual war* occurred when Jesus ascended to Heaven (Rev 12:5; Col 2:12; 1Pe 1:12, 3:18). Jesus confronted three questions when He went into Hades, waged war against Satan, and Michael cast Satan out after He ascended:

1. How is the accuser going to be silenced? Satan is silenced. When the prosecutor is silenced, the defense wins (Ro 8:33, 11:33; Rev 12:10). The accuser is cast down and silenced.

2. How can a Just, Holy God forgive sin? God provided a substitute in man's place, a propitiation (Ro 3:23-27; Heb 2:17, 9:5; 1Jn 2:2).

3. If a way can be found, will man accept it? Romans 8:31-39 is a masterpiece of theology. All three questions were answered when Jesus died and rose again (Rev 12:11, 12). Those on Earth overcame by the Blood of the Lamb and the Heavens rejoice.

Christ Died for Heaven (Luke 19:38)

The heavenly angels were troubled because Satan, one of their own, became an archenemy of their Creator. Of course, the good angels would rejoice at the death, burial, and Ascension of Jesus Christ just as we do. Jesus announced His *victory* (Mk 3:23; Rev 20:3; Jn 12:31, 32). He overthrew the powers and authorities everywhere (Col 2:15; Eph 4:7-9).

Peter was not exaggerating his account of the cosmological "wonders" that took place in the Heavens above and accompanying "signs on the earth" below (Ac 2:19). In God's prophetic timeframe, the next cosmic-earth upheaval after the period from Pentecost to 70 A.D. will be the Lord's return. Picture in your mind three high mountaintops and label them Pentecost (the end of the Law in close association with Mount Calvary), 70 A.D. (the end of temple worship), and the return of Jesus (end of the universe). These three mountains rise above the wrecks of all time! (Ac 2:20) Then picture the eyes of the Lord as He looks down through the ages from eternity past, and His contemplative, prophetic, foreordained, predestined counsel. He scans the top of those three highest mountain peaks. The Godhead looks down from eternity and beholds the mountaintops of providential history. He is not looking at the millions of valleys (secondary history). The Godhead is looking at the three last mountains of sacred history that leads the way to Heaven or Hell for the human race.

We know that the whole world will be convinced by the cosmological displays on the eve of the Final Judgment. We have experienced or are aware of temporary judgments that have befallen the human race (all of us) throughout history. I read somewhere that after Noah Webster finished the first edition of his monumental work, "A Dictionary of English Words," he was asked, "What is the most influential word in the vocabulary?" Without hesitation, Mr. Webster replied, "Judgment." My search for this quote has been futile. If I am unable to attribute the quote to Mr. Webster, I will take credit for it myself, and my reasoning is quite plain. Judgment in this world is proof positive, a microcosm of the plain, simple, obvious fact that every day judgments lead to ONE final, future judgment.

The Apostles and their disciples saw extraordinary signs in the sky (Ac 2:19, 20), including the Moon's having the appearance of blood. But others attended and attested to signs in Heaven that Peter did not mention, especially those associated with Christ's death on the cross (Mt 27:50-52). Some Christian astronomers seek to find evidence of these signs in the Heaven, but a sign is defined as a "Miracle with a message," and we must observe a sign first-hand to fully understand it. Jesus said that we would be given no sign, but "The sign of Jonah" (Mt 12:38ff), which would confirm that Jesus is Who He said He was and WHAT He was able to accomplish. The most significant "sign in the heavens" was the Ascension of Christ from Earth to the Throne (Ac 1:9-11; Mk 16:19, with prophecy of Isa 6:1 and Jn 12:41). Isaiah 65:17 parallels Christ's Ascension and establishes New

Heavens by virtue of His conquering the old Earth and bringing all things into submission to Himself (Rev 21:1, 2).

People in today's world are looking for physical signs and wonders. It is an amazing thought, but the systematic research of The Bible leads us to the most convincing signs and wonders imaginable. We stand amazed at the everyday judgments we witness in life, and yet see people walk away from them as though they were casual, happenstances of life. The other day I saw a man holding his young child, and he was cursing and shrieking about something in life. I ask him if there was something I could help him with. The spirit of the hour weathered his storm a little, and he finally settled down enough to communicate. After a few peaceful moments of getting acquainted and learning about his life, family, and occupation, I ask him if he wanted me to pray for some of the things that were vexing his heart and mind. He agreed. After my intercession, I patted his young child on the head and said to the Father, "You have a lot to live for, if it is just to raise this young lad for the Lord." Then thinking of my three children, whom I used to hold in my arms, I said, "Cherish the moment, Brother, you only have this little guy as a child for a little while!"

Children are a heritage and judgment for life and death. An occupation is a judgment. Friendships are constant judgments. In the Cosmic World, we are never more than a few weeks away from a sudden storm, a hurricane, a tornado, a tidal wave, a cloud burst, or a blistering hot or cold temperature. We can take all of this for granted, or we can see each judgment as a responsive decision to every day events that will wind down to the Final Judgment. While judgment is not always pleasant, judgment is necessary. It was so necessary that the Godhead agreed to direct one of His own to take our place as a substitutionary judgment and give His all that we might also make a judgment in response.

Those of us who have passed the mid-life point in life's journey will remember growing up and hearing from the pulpits across our land, "Love, Love, Love" ("All This World Needs is Love," by the Beatles). This theme song could go on until it ceases on Judgment Day. What has a one-sided philosophy of unlimited, unconditional love gotten us? Dr. Benjamin Spock who wrote on "Child Care" and sold over 50,000 books to parents who did not know the difference between the Bible and a bowl of Cream of Wheat taught a "Love Doctrine" that places no restraints on a child. Spock believed human beings know far more than our Creator.

Dr. Spock was elected "Humanist of the Year" in 1968 when the Hippie Movement's, "Make love not war," reached its peak.

Many of our families have been plagued by suicide, so it may not be a final test of generational legacies, but with all of his supposed expertise, fame, and wealth, Spock's grandson Peter, (who should have been reverently honoring the birth of God's Son) on Christmas Day, leaped from a building to commit suicide at age 22. Time-after-time, Spock would deny what critics, such as Dr. Norman Vincent Peele, said about Spock's "Instant Gratification Age" or the "Spock Generation." At no time did Spock ever acknowledge God's wisdom based on the Proverb, "Train up a child in the way he must go and when he is old he will never depart from it" (Pr 22:6).

A chasm as wide as The Grand Canyon exists between much of what Spock told mothers and fathers to do to raise children and what the Lord (who gave them to us) tells us to do. When, for instance, we see a 21st Century child whining, screaming, and throwing a tantrum (along with everything in the shopping cart) in a supermarket, and Mom (We do not know where Dad went.) just keeps picking up merchandize and keeps crying, "Please do not throw things, darling," we know that we are still suffering from the "Spock Generation." We just keep reading books by new authors who keep revising Spock's "Do your own thing" philosophy, instead of the Bible, "Spare the rod, ruin the child" (Pr 13:24, 23:13,14).

ALL THIS WORLD NEEDS IS THE PURE GOD-GIVEN LOVE THAT IS MINGLED WITH JUSTICE

The wise King said, "When crime is not punished quickly, people think it is safe to do evil" (Ecc 8:11). The Hebrew text strongly implies that when people are granted the "entitlement of permissiveness," they are emboldened to continue to disobey. If hundreds of drivers decide to drive their vehicles 70 mph in a 35 mph zone, there are not enough law enforcement officers to enforce that law. If a thousand motorcycle gang members decide to drive 100 mph, weaving in and out of traffic, driving carelessly, and passing on the emergency shoulder lane, the dispatcher may advise a State Patrolman to leave the gang alone. If thousands of people decide to protest The Court's decision to prosecute a hardened, career criminal, should The Court reverse its decision?

The story is told of two hooded, sinister looking men approaching the magnificent "pearly gates" of the Golden City of God. God's recording angel met them and said, "We have no record of your names up here." The hooded men insisted they had a right to Heaven. The angel told them to wait, and he approached the Throne of God. When the angel expressed ambiguity about admitting the men who expressed a menacing, self-assertive attitude at "The Gates," God said, "Quit being so judgmental. Don't you know in this New Age, we have become more tolerant, more passive, loving, and approving of what was once considered threatening and obnoxious behavior?"

The angel left to grant the rebels amenity and returned immediately. "What's wrong," God said. The angel said, "They're gone!" "Who's gone?" replied God. The angel said, "The hooded men," and then added, "Your pearly gates are gone too!" Quite frankly, I do not want a God like that, and furthermore, I know my God is not like that.

On the other side of the ledger, if a federal judge overturns the democratic will and intent of a majority vote, should the majority of the people accept the verdict of one judge? Dr. Spock, in his old age, began to question some of his own teachings (despite the chagrin of his many admirers) and knew that he was credited with helping parents raise children who acted more like barnyard animals than human beings. How we finish puts the asterisk on how we began. Judges express nothing but fecund hatred for society when they hand down lenient sentences to a confirmed criminal or a decision that lowers the moral standards in the country.

LOVE IS NOT INSTANT GRATIFICATION OF ON-GOING LISCENTIOUSNESS

True love is not lust. God's Word speaks in ancient Greek of "eros" lust. It also speaks of "philia" brotherly love or affection. When it speaks of God's love, the word "agape" is used, meaning love that is called out by the value of the person we love. "Eros" love says, "I love you because I want you." "Philia" love says, "I love you because we need each other." "Agape" love says, "I love you because you need me." The ultimate end of the 60s love song as expounded by the Spock Generation and his offspring is a "Codeless Love" that does not have one shred of justice. Unless Americans realize this, and demand the love of justice and integrity, we may continue to laugh, jeer, and mock our way into insanity and oblivion.

Such teaching may sound archaic, farfetched, and hopelessly old fashioned, and we have experienced in 21st Century A.D. the same "atmosphere of mockery" (Ge 19:14) that Lot did in Sodom (1600 B.C.) Lot warned his aristocratic, sodomite children of coming doom, and with a smug arrogance of worldly sophistication, "They laughed in his face." I know that when most people hear this, if they believe in Judgment at all, they think it is 1,000 years from now, but judgment will come, and when you die, judgment has come (Heb 9:27). Judgment could be ten minutes away.

Satan's presumptuous claim for Heaven's throne was thwarted, and His dynasty overthrown when Christ ascended (Ac 2:31, 32). When at Pentecost the Apostles and the 3,000 souls recognized the Ascended Lord, four inalienable truths (sometimes called "mysteries") were understood.

1. Heaven and Earth recognized Christ's Ascension and Reign (Ac 2:30-34).

2. Satan's accusations against the saints were terminated for all covenant people (Ac 2:39-42 with Lk 24:46-48).

3. Christ's New Covenant Kingdom is established on Earth (Ac 2:36-47).

4. New Covenant Christian Jews were saved from sin and destruction of the last generation of Old Covenant Judaism (Ac 2:40).

Sometimes we fail to see the intervention of The Godhead in profane history. The Israel-Jewish Religion had witnessed the destruction and desolation of their temple prior to 70 A.D. by the Babylonians and the Syrians, but they had never before witnessed a complete "desolation." The temple ruins fell under Gentile control. When the Jewish Temple was gone, authentic Israel-Judaism fell also. To understand this in modern terms, if for instance, the earthly "sacred" shrines of Mohammed were bombed into desolation, Islam as a religion would cease to exist.

This is what Jesus meant when He said, "The time will come when you will not worship in this mountain or that mountain, but they who worship me will worship in Spirit and Truth" (Jn 4:20, 21).

When their mountain-temple worship was gone (Jn 2:19-22; 1Co 3:16), the Israel-Jewish Religions disappeared forever. Cultural Judaism exists today but authentic Jews and Old Testament worship are gone. Likewise, if their sacred shrines, mosques, and holy sites were gone, Islam would disappear. As animals live by seeing through their eyes, so are they who worship at shrines. Once the shrine is gone, the worship ceases because Judaism of old has one thing in common with Islam today – they do not have the Spirit and Truth to carry on once their idol-props are removed.

The above truths may be considered mysteries to some of the world's teeming millions, but Paul in his lifetime, almost singlehandedly proclaimed the "Mystery" of the "Obedience to the Faith "in the world of his day (Ro 1:5 with 16:25, 26). Paul also revealed to us the message of the great mystery of redemption (Eph 3:9, 10), that we should take it to the world. Christians are now acting as Christ's witnesses as they go into far off countries. As this happens, Christians are continuing to fight against the powers and principalities of Satan.

Revelation 12:10: Then I heard a loud voice in heaven say: "Now have come the salvation and the power and the kingdom of our God, and the authority of his Christ. For the accuser of our brothers, who accuses them before our God day and night, has been hurled down.

This voice spoke immediately after Christ ascended. The (1) power, (2) authority, and (3) Kingdom of God with the (4) authority of Christ did come to Earth. The four aspects of the Imperial Godhead represent that they are present on the Earth (In numerology, 4 represents the Earth.). This means the Kingdom of God is here. The devil accused the brethren day and night, but now he is banished from Heaven, and Christians now have an advocate, Jesus Christ (1Jn 2:1). It is very important that we understand that Satan is forever prohibited and banished from the Throne of God. The reason why God did not stop Satan before the cross was because of the absence of redeeming blood! God could not view man in the perfection of his Son, thus, He viewed men as they were. When Jesus shed His blood and ascended on high, He cast the devil out and refused to allow him to prosecute (Rev 20:3; Mk 2:23; Jn 12:31).

Jesus did not directly cast Satan out; Jesus cast Satan out through His authoritative Word; Jesus gave that duty to Michael, the Archangel. Even though Michael cast Satan out, Satan's expulsion was really part of the Christ's predestined, redemptive work that was executed as a well-established judicial procedure still in effect today. The potentate (President/King) will not execute an anarchist criminal himself. The potentate appoints a trusted executioner to perform the execution. The King required evidence of the execution, so he would often have the executioner bring the guilty party to be slain before him (Lk 19:27). The reason that Michael was Jesus' trusted executioner is because Michael had been nursing an ongoing contention against Satan (Jude 9). But Michael was not omniscient and did not know just how Satan's accusations against the best of God's saints would ultimately be silenced forever. Now that the accuser Satan is cast out, the accuser can be accused. Michael could not accuse him before this. But with Christ's Ascension, Satan's slanderous, dragonish voice is silenced forever. We use the word "execution" in the sense that "Satan's head is bruised" as far as his long war against God is concerned. In the eyes of the Godhead, Satan is executed. Satan is the zombie God of dead people.

Revelation 12:11, 12: They overcame him by the blood of the Lamb and by the word of their testimony; they did not love their lives so much as to shrink from death. Therefore, rejoice, you heavens and you who dwell in them! But woe to the earth and the sea, because the devil has gone down to you! He is filled with fury, because he knows that his time is short."

This passage of Scripture is speaking of the Christians. They overcame Satan in three ways:

1. The Blood of the Lamb. The Lord's Supper on the first day of the week reminds Christians of Christ's Atoning Blood (Ac 20:7; 1Co 1:21-31). If we judge ourselves, we are not condemned with the world.

2. The Word of the Testimony, which is the New Testament (The Little Book).

3. They did not love their life enough to shrink back from death. The Apostles died for Christ. Not only the Apostles, but during the Dark Ages, millions of Christians died. However, today the blood of Christians stains the swords of Communism and Islam. Islam is now leading the way in Christian bloodletting. However, Islam has a long way to go to catch up with the numbers of Christians slaughtered by the Roman Inquisition. Christians must realize that this text is talking about New Testament witnesses *only*. People should be careful that their lives are not taken in vain. It is a grievous thing that some people who are or have been slaughtered may not even be Christians (1Co 13:3). Strange things play out in the name of history.

The Heavens finally rejoiced when Satan was cast out. Furthermore, the Earth was warned of his pending wrath. Satan is furious, and he is doing everything he can to persecute those Christians still on Earth. However, when Christians suffer, the whole world also suffers. Satan knows his time is short, and his appointment time is coming (Mt 8:29). Why did the Earth tremble when Satan came down? Not only does the Ecclesia suffer under the wrath of serpentine Satan, but also the whole Earth and sea trembles. If we will study history and read the ways the Body of Christ suffered at the hand of antichrist nations, we should tremble. The media ignores the slaughter of those called "Christians" in this world. (See website: voice of the martyrs.).

Revelation 12:13: When the dragon saw that he had been hurled to the earth, he pursued the woman who had given birth to the male child.

The Dragon went after the Congregation with his full fury. Satan rules the secular and religious world, but he has yet to bring the true Bride under his dominion.

Revelation 12:14-16: The woman was given the two wings of a great eagle, so that she might fly to the place prepared for her in the desert, where she would be taken care of for a time, times and half a time, out of the serpent's reach. Then from his mouth the serpent spewed water like a river, to overtake the woman and sweep her away with the torrent. But the earth helped the woman by opening its mouth and swallowing the river that the dragon had spewed out of his mouth.

For 1,260 years (times, time, and half a time), the woman is in the wilderness. Very few heard the Gospel during this time. They were called "The Remnant," which is not very many, but they exist in every generation. Although few in number in each generation, when they are gathered together in the Lord's presence, their number would swell to a multitude. In the end when they are all gathered together, they are innumerable. In our time, God is protecting those who are of the woman. He is ensuring that His truth will not be completely abolished from the Earth. The Devil is working constantly to prevent the Gospel from being spread. Christians need to be prepared to meet demonic opposition with confidence, knowing that Jesus has the victory. The Earth opened after the Apostles finished the testimony of Christ. The New Testament was completed. No matter how intense the false doctrine can get, we still have the completely perfect New Testament. The "earth opening" corresponds to the "power given the witness" (11:6) and the temporary "restraining of the man of iniquity" (2Th 2:7).

Revelation 12:17: Then the dragon was enraged at the woman and went off to make war against the rest of her offspring — those who obey God's commandments and hold to the testimony of Jesus.

Satan does not want Christians (or anyone) to keep two things:

1. God's Commandments

2. Jesus' Testimony

Obviously, the women and offspring are the Congregation of New Covenant Christians. They are the only ones who are holding on to Christ's Testimony. This encouraging chapter shows God's omnipotence in defeating Satan. Christians should be encouraged to know that no matter how severe the battle gets; Christ has the victory. If they obey His commandments, hold onto Christ's Testimony, and are bold enough to live for Jesus, they too will receive the Crown of Righteousness. The Commandments of God **AND** the Testimony of Jesus are **ONE!** (1Jn 2:3, 4, 3:22, 5:3; Jn 15:10).

New Testament Christians are not authorized to bring disciples under the Laws of Moses (Ac 2:42). Except for the Sabbath Commandment that is superseded by the Lord's "First Day of the week" (Ac 20:7), all the Laws of humanity are comprehensively wrapped up in The Ten Commandments. Imagine what a crime-free civil society we could experience if every member of the human race abided by these Commandments. However, these commands do not govern a Spirit-led Christian. For instance, the Commandment said, "Do not commit adultery," but Jesus speaks to those who after Pentecost began to walk in The Spirit and said, "Do not even look upon a woman to lust in your heart." Again, we are convinced that even the Law, "Thou shall not murder," is not sufficient, for the Spirit-led Christian is considered a murderer when he hates his brother (1Jn 3:20, 4:15).

When Jesus compared His followers to those of the political-secular world, He reminded them of how they loved to advance in order to lord it over others. The Gentiles have their lords and kings who rule over them, but he who is chief among you, "Let him be your servant" (Lk 22:25). You simply will not see a true servant of Christ seated in an ecclesial, hierarchical chair.

THE FALL OF AN EVANGELIST

We have seen the following scenario play out so many times that it is legion. A young man started out with great promise as an evangelist in the Kingdom of Christ. Although he encountered a great deal of non-essential judgmentalism in his "church," instead of patiently expounding the TRUTH of Scripture and waiting on the Lord, he allowed bitterness toward what he called "legalism" to drive him into the arms of the enemy. When bitterness toward his son-in-law, David, so filled the heart of King Saul, this bitterness created the unfortunate alternative for David to capitulate to the Philistines for sanctuary. When David had a chance to kill Saul but backed away from it, Saul "in a moment of truth" came back to his senses temporarily, and admitted that David was a man of God. In effect, David remonstrated, "Would you like to drive me into the welcoming arms of those who espouse the false gods of the Philistines?" (1Sa 26:19). Is it you, or is it the people of your congregation who could care less as to whether you join forces with the children of other Gods? Would we be so filled with jealousy and hatred toward someone doing a great work for the Lord that we would rejoice in seeing them fall under the guillotine of false doctrine?

Unknowingly, but decisively, our friend chose to go over to the opposite spectrum of false doctrine rather than suffer criticism from some of his unreasonable, judgmental brethren (Heb 11:25). Advocates of false doctrine present the façade of being non-judgmental because they believe everything and embrace nothing with any zest. Embracing nothing leads to the following the adage, "A man who stands for nothing will fall for everything."

In our library, we have workbooks on three sessions dealing with the doctrine of "Expedience." Expedience means to work through strategic processes and thereby expedite the journey from the "here" and "now" in order to arrive at the "there" and "then" (ideal state). The Greek word means "ex" (out of), "paidos" (child) "Out of care for the child." Now we know the rest of the story. An expedition is a process that moves from the current state to the ideal state, and we care for each other as a parent for a child. Mere judgmental difficulties were no excuse for our young Brother to leave New Covenant Christianity. If he wanted, God could have led him to find other New Covenant leaders.

THE NAME OF THE GAME

The name of this "New Game" is that love is lust for modern-day pleasure (1Co 13:6). Grace is license to do what makes you happy (Jude 1:4; Ro 6:1, 2). Holiness is an old fashioned, sober faced existence of absolute misery (Tit 2:12; Heb 12:14). Discipline is an old fashioned practice that no longer works (Heb 12:9; Jas 5:7; 1Co 15:58; 1Pe 5:10). Abstinence is for old fogies who are really missing out on life (1Th 4:3, 4; 1Co 6:18; 2Ti 2:22; Col 3:5) In Philippians 4:5, the word "epikeia" is mistakenly translated in K.J.V., "moderation," but means "gentleness, reasonableness, or yieldedness" (Richard Chenevix Trench).[78] Abstaining from rage and yielding to the Holy Spirit in a world that is going mad is one of the greatest tests of a child of God. Biblical expedience does not lead a person to lose their spiritual equilibrium. Biblical expedience enhances our spiritual equilibrium for the betterment and further advancement of TRUTH.

Let us return to our young evangelist. He fell under the influence of Max Lucado who changed the marquee designating his place of assembly from Oak Hills Church of Christ to Oak Hills Church because in his words, "The name church of Christ will offend some people." He went so far as to say that by dropping Christ's name he added 1,000 more people. It is a truism that many within the Church of Christ fail miserably to present the Spirit and Grace of the King in their Christian Congregation. But dropping the name of Christ from the marquee is tantamount to a "denial of His Name" (Mt 10:33). It was not "expedient" to drop the NAME of Christ for the sole purpose of opening the doors of the building to more people. If lost souls are saved simply because they attend the assembly of a congregation that had the cheek and gall to drop the NAME of the Savior, their true conversion is highly suspect. Admittedly, there is not a dime's worth of difference what human logo you attach to your organization, but as the song goes, "Jesus, Oh how Sweet the Name" (William C. Martin, 1901), the Divine Name (Mt 1:21) does makes a difference! I believe that the Lord allows us free expression of how we relate to the many NAMES and titles of Jesus. For instance, if we live long enough and God gives us a geographical base of operations for His Kingdom, we could conceive of several logos that glorify and honor our Messiah.

> "One of the many congregations who worship the King and Messiah, Jesus worships here"

"A Congregational Kingdom of our Lord and Messiah, Jesus Christ"

"A Congregation of Messiah-Christ greets you"

"One of the Assemblies in this world, over which the Lord and King Jesus Christ reigns"

"Christian Kingdom of Jesus Christ"

"The sweetest NAME of King Jesus is over us"

God the Father may have given us some creative diversity in how we use His Son's NAME. He may allow free expression as to how we word a logo or vision statement of this Divine Organization, but let us be convinced of one thing. The NAME of the King deserves preeminence over all novel and human innovative nomenclature, no matter how clever we think we are (Col 1:18).

It may sound far-fetched, but Christ is the Chief Cornerstone of His spiritual temple (Eph 2:20). If we base our spiritual conclusion on the analogy set forth in human terms, we know a building has at least four cornerstones, but the "chief" one was the first and most visible of them all. For instance, when we erected the building in Kernstown, we put the name of Jesus Christ on the cornerstone at the entrance. Every person who enters sees the NAME of Jesus Christ. Of course, the building is not the congregation, but what a visitor sees with the eye denotes what is the heart and spirit of the aggregate souls who worship the King in the place where they assemble (1Co 11:18-29). Someone may say, "Well they came together to break bread on the First Day of the Week in Acts 20:7, and in that neutral place, they could not have placed the NAME of Christ," and that is probably correct. But early Christians did not erect their own buildings. They could have placed a signpost like we do when we rent auditoriums for Gospel rallies, but unless they owned the property, they would have to obtain the management's permission. When the congregation purchases property and builds a building, it has the right of ownership to place the NAME of the Savior we love on that edifice. Jesus healed the Master of the Centurion who financed the construction of a synagogue for congregational worship (Lk 7:5).

The seriousness of dropping the name of Christ goes far beyond the mere decision to drop Christ's name from a marquee or a vision statement. Should we deny the name of Christ because other organizations, such as The Mormons, the horribly apostate, United Church of Christ, Christian Scientists (That is a real oxymoron. It is not "Christian," and it is not "science."), and various other sects use it? It makes no difference if you call an organization the The Christian Kingdom, or Christian Assembly, or as John Doughty and the Brethren in Harrisonburg-Bridge Water, Va. call it, "Ekklesia of Christ," the NAME of Christ should somehow identify the location "For there is no other NAME" (Ac 4:12). God has given Him a NAME, and highly exalted it (Php 2:9, 10). We ask, "In His NAME" (Jn 14:13). Demons are subject to His NAME (Lk 10:17). Forgiveness is preached in His NAME (Ac 10:43). Faith heals the sick in His NAME (Ac 3:16). Mighty works are done in His NAME (Mk 16:17). We call on His NAME (Ac 2:21; Ro 10:13). We are immersed into His NAME (Ac 2:38), yet we are afraid His NAME will offend someone if we put it on a sign.

We may be interested in how the Lord, "YHVH," (Yehovah) felt about His NAME being identified with a place of praise, prayer, or worship wherever His children chose to do so by erecting an altar. The place where God and man met was to bear His NAME (Ex 25:8, 29:45). The altar was a dwelling for His NAME (Dt 16:6). YHVH chooses a dwelling for His NAME (16:11); it is the place the Lord your God chooses as a dwelling for His NAME (26:2).

Interestingly, the theology of God's "NAME" found in the Old Testament came to a close in the New Testament because the name YHVH is not found anywhere in the New Testament. The Holy Spirit of New Testament writings called The Father of the Godhead, "Theos," the Greek word for God for the obvious reason that the Jews really did not care much about the NAME, YHVH, anyway. Paul said the NAME of God was blasphemed because of the insolent, ungrateful Jews (Isa 52:5; Ro 2:24). The NAME of Yashua Christos identified God to all nations.

With all due respect for Max Lucado's religious work ethic, we could continue and quote hundreds of Scripture on the Theology of the NAMES of God and Christ that lead us to think that because other people dishonor Christ (as the Jews dishonored YHVH) that they ought to choose an inferior name (simply "church") for his meeting place on Earth. But here is where the rub comes. YHVH is Hebrew for Jesus, or "Joshua" (Savior), and He dwelt, "tabernacled," among us in flesh (Jn 1:14), and we are His spiritual temple (Eph 2:22; 1Pe 2:5).

Opponents of the NAME of Christ say that names are not important, but they are insatiably zealous for the name "church" which is not even a proper translation of the word "ecclesia," which means "called out assembly." We hear our preachers mention the word "church" at least 20 times in every sermon. The word "kirk" means a building. Unconsciously, we are actually preaching "churchanity" (institutional eclecticism) instead of "Christianity." Yes, we are commanded to "come together," and there is a meeting place for the Lord's Supper (1Co 11:23-32). But when we place the emphasis on "church," we unconsciously demean the NAME Christ, which as mentioned previously, is tantamount to denying Christ's NAME.

If we argue that we are spiritual temples, and therefore the NAME of our meeting place makes no difference, then why should a woman take her husband's name? It is proper for her to do so because marriage is a spiritual as well as physical union. This tradition goes back thousands of years, all the way to Genesis 5:2, and has the imprimatur of God's authority all over it, "…God blessed them, and called THEIR NAME Adam, in the day they were created."

Some women in this new cultural age resent taking their husband's name. Even presidential contender, Hillary Clinton, wanted to be known as "Rodham" rather than "Clinton". Many of us think it makes no difference whether we call ourselves Christian or not. But in this, we make God a liar. Adam and Eve are a type of Christ and His bride (2 Co 11:2). Christ loves His bride (Eph 5:22, 23). In keeping with the Biblical tradition of marriage, the Groom presented His Bride before the Father (Eph 5:27).

The NAME of Christ will cause some to stumble (Mt 24:10), but this did not keep Paul from reverently calling the congregations by Christ's NAME (Ro 16:16). It is also true that the NAME of God the Father was connected with the congregations as we read "Congregations of God that are in Christ Jesus" (1Th 2:14 with 1Th 1:4; 2Th 2:4). The expression of congregations of Christ is an extraordinary proof that God and Christ are equal. We may think it an enigma when we read of the injunction to the Ephesian Elders, "Feed the congregation of God which He purchased with His blood" (Ac 20:28). Did not Christ shed His blood? Martin Luther said, "Leave my name alone. I pray, do not call yourselves Lutherans, but Christians. Who is Luther? Luther did not shed his blood for you. Luther was not crucified for you." Luther was right.[79]

Because God the Father and the Son are ONE (Jn 10:30), Christ's blood was considered blood offered by God. But we emphasize the NAME of Christ because God has given Him, "All authority, in heaven and on earth" (Mt 28:18). God has "given Him the NAME which is above every name." (Php 2:9).

God honors the Son (Jn 5:23), and we should love the Son as God loves Him (Jn 17:26). The Holy Spirit also honors the Son, and He is also sent in the NAME of Jesus (Jn 15:26). God the Father PLANNED the Kingdom of Christ (Eph 1:4), and Christ (the Lamb) PURCHASED the Kingdom with His blood shed as the Lamb slain from the foundation of the world (Rev 13:8). It seems reasonable to refer to those whom Christ purchased but who knew only God under the Old Testament as the Congregation of God and then to refer to the multitude of Gentiles who have come to Christ since Pentecost as the comprehensive Congregation of Christ.

If you still think we are making a big ado about nothing, please remember that all congregations are going to put a signboard at the front entrance of the parking lot of their religious meeting place. We could give hundreds of reasons why the NAME of Christ should send the first message to those who come as to who we are and what we say. Granted, the devil has stolen the name of Christ and a false prophet will use the name of Christ in an attempt to certify the message of deception (Mt 24:24). In the NAME of Christ, they will do some fairly influential things (Mt 24:24), but in the final analysis, the Lord "never knew them" (Mt 7:23).

For one to leave the "Odd Fellows Club" because of the strange behavior of the members is understandable, but for one to leave the Congregational Kingdom, or drop the NAME of the King because of wayward "church members" is unacceptable. This same thing happened when the Congregations at Ephesus (Rev 2: 3), Pergamum (2:13), Philadelphia (3:8), began to suffer "The malaise of complacency" and the numbers dwindled to just a few who continued "holding fast to His NAME." But Jesus did not tell them to "drop his NAME into the trash can of oblivion" because doing so would make their church larger. We admit the spirit and tenor of the message of Christ to the congregations means a whole lot more than just keeping His NAME visible to the public at large, but having the NAME OF CHRIST out front is important because it our honest profession of who our God and King is. He is the NAME above all names.

We know the name "Christian" was practically lost to history during the Dark Ages, and well into the 18th Century, when James O'Kelly and Rice Haggard decided, on Christmas Day (1793 A.D.), to drop the name Republican Episcopal Methodist Church and become just "Christians." Other dynamic decisions were made in accordance with Bible teachings to restore (as a remnant) the teachings of New Covenant Christianity.

Some political historians are saying we may likewise live to see the demise of our liberties from The Declaration of Independence, The Constitution with its Bill of Rights, and Congress' authority. Will we also see the demise of sound Biblical scholarship? Can we expect to see the NAME of Christ (or Christian) on the marquee, meet a lovely group of Christ-loving souls, hear the Gospel of Christ, commune around the Table of Remembrance of Christ, and be challenged to the holiness we can seek in Christ always? "How long Oh Lord?"

Isaiah was prophesying the golden age of Christianity on Earth when he said, "And they shall be called by a new NAME which the mouth of the Lord shall name" (Isa 62:2). In consideration about those who think we make too much of Christ's NAME, I wonder how proud those of the new Christian-Cultural-Churchanity-Movement are when they decide on some random name (of their own choice) and name their new institution Potter's Church, Rock Church, Living Waters Church, My Church, Victory Church, or Church of the Valley, Mountain, Plains, or Open Door, and we could go on and on. I wonder if they really think they picked the right name. If names are not important, why call it a name at all? Would Peter, James, John, or Paul be comfortable with these names?

The only reference I know where the NAME of Christ or Jesus is not directly associated with His assembly is Hebrews 12:23. But it refers to the Assembly of the First Born, whose names are written in Heaven. *Meyers Commentary* says it best. The word "panaguris" (General Assembly) designates the total gathering under the form of conception. Because of "the First Born of God," we are all born again. Ekklesia, "called-out-assembly," designates we are bound together in inner unity. The Greek Orthodox has a very worldly, carnal, annual Celebration of Panegyri. But the festivity in this verse refers not to eating and drinking but to our celebration of praise and salvation. An accurate translation reads, "The festive assembly and congregation of the first born who are enrolled in heaven." We all ought to know who The Firstborn is.

To conclude the saga of our young evangelist friend, he also cast great suspicion upon the essentiality of partaking of the Lord's Supper. He registered his new "church" in his NAME, and he called himself "The President." These are just another sign of our 21st Century's "changing times."

Revelation Chapter Thirteen

THE BEAST

(This chapter corresponds with Revelation 17, and Daniel 7 and 8.)

The witnesses of Revelation 11 and 12 were put to death because of their testimony of Christ. In the Gospels, Jesus referred to them as *witnesses* (Lk 24:48; Acts 1:8). Christ gave these apostolic witnesses a specific authority to share the things that they had experienced with the whole world (1Jn 1:1-5). He gave them this authority when he breathed on them (Jn 20:20-23). This Apostolic authority is a highly valued asset. This testimony to the authority of the Apostles continues to reside in evangelists, pastors, and teachers who continue *in* Apostolic Doctrine (Ac 2:42; Eph 4:11, 12).

If groups of men could pose as having apostolic authority, they could control the functions of the Congregation and, subsequently, the direction of the people. Although we know that the final completion of the New Testament writings occurred prior to 70 A.D., no one has been able to set the exact date. It is certain that after they were completed and the Apostles died, the *Bishops* of each congregation began to grow in their power and authority over the people. Clement of Rome referred to a collegiate of Bishops as late as A.D. 98. Shortly following 110-117 A.D., Ignatius of Antioch used the singularity of *the* Bishop over each congregation. This is when the departure from the Biblical congregational government started. The Roman Church thrives off control. It needs a monarchial Bishop to satisfy their hunger for power, but the New Testament is strictly and solely Christocentric in authority. This Chapter 13 concerns the sea-going political beast and its quest for recognition and divine authority.

The symbol of the wounded head of Pagan Rome represented Rome's destruction. At first, Satan's tactic was to destroy Christianity through physical persecution and execution. After the destruction of Political Rome, the Beast took the role of Religious Rome. Religious (Papal) Rome developed the Unholy Trinity of the Beast out of the Sea (Rev 13:1), another Beast out of the Land (13:11), and Babylon the Great (14:8). When Papal Rome supplanted Imperial (Pagan) Rome, Papal Rome enjoyed the political advantage of using philosophy, cultic religion, economic boycott, and military power in its attempt to destroy New Testament Christianity. Papal Rome loved those who sinned and went to war against the

Saints and those who supported them. Papal Rome even established the inquisition to extinguish the ecclesia who would not accept its theology.

Revelation 13:1: And I saw a beast coming out of the sea. He had ten horns and seven heads, with ten crowns on his horns, and on each head a blasphemous name.

Several different interpretations exist concerning this "beast coming out of the sea." Some Preterits believe this is Nero. The Historicists say this is Constantine. The Futurist believes this is a literal beast, and the School of Philosophy contends that it is political power in general. When we compare Daniel (Da 7:4-28) and Revelation, we acknowledge that this verse has figures representing the beast(s), nations (Babylon, Persia and Greece) down to the last beast of Rome. But after the establishment of the Kingdom of Christ, any chronological interpretation of beasts ended. The proof of this is that John's beast is a composite of all former beasts, and the only further mention is the "little horn" of Daniel's Beast that grew (Da 7:20) and John's Beast, whose wounded head is healed. (See diagram below.)

This single horn would wage war against the New Testament Saints until Judgment Day when the Kingdom "triumphant" would be given to the saints forever (Da 7:21, 22, 27). John's Beast is similar to Daniel's simply because both refer to the fall of political (Pagan) Rome and the instant rise of Papal Rome. There is a slight difference in that Daniel's horn "plucked out" three horns representing the inception of Papal Power, but John's beast had a head (instead of a horn) that was wounded and healed (also representing the inception of Papal Power – Rev 13:3,12).

Thus Daniel sees the rise of papal Rome from political Rome as a horn that displaced the Ten Kingdoms that grew out of the breakup of political Rome. John views the same prophetic scenario as the head of political Rome being wounded and then healed by religious Papal Rome.

(Rev 13:1) Then I stood on the sand of the sea. And I saw a beast rising up out of the sea, having seven heads and ten horns, and on his horns ten crowns, and on his heads a blasphemous name.   NKJV

Kingdom	Babylon	Persia	Greece	Rome	Kingdom of God
Daniel 2	Gold	Silver	Bronze	Iron	Supernatural Rock
Daniel 7	Lion	Bear	Leopard	Beast with Horns (Tyrannosaurus Rex)	Ancient of Days, Son of Man
Daniel 8		Ram	Goat		
Daniel 11			One of the Kings of North – Antiochus Epiphanies		

The beast, according to Daniel, represented political powers. In Daniel, Chapter 2, the beast represented different Kingdoms. However, the beasts of Daniel's day are in the past. The beast in Revelation is much worse than all the powers in Daniel, Chapters 2, 7, 8, and 11.

1. The Lion of Babylon: 688-539 B.C. (Daniel 7:3). Modern-day Iraq

2. The Bear of Medo-Persia: 533-330 B.C. (Three ribs to conquer were 1. Babylon 2. Egypt 3. Lydia.)

3. Leopard: Four generals (heads)' under Alexander the Great (330 B.C.).

    a. Lysimachus (Thrace, Macedonia, Asia Minor)

    b. Cassander (Macedonia, Greece)

    c. Selucius (Syria, Mesopotamia, Persia)

    d. Ptolemy (Egypt)

This beast is extremely more powerful and dangerous than any previous beast. His position of being "worthy of praise," and power means the praise due to Christ is diverted to earthly dictators.

The Seven Heads of Revelation 13: 1 are:

1. Gaius Julius (Julius Caesar): 49-44 B.C.

   Gaius was the first Roman General to seize power as the dictator of Rome. After the Roman Senate declared Gaius an enemy of Rome, he marched to an empty Rome and seized power for five years. In 44 B.C. a group of assassins, led by Marcus Junius Brutus, assassinated him on March 15. They wanted to return Rome to its former governing system as a Republic (www.historyguide.org). Instead, this assassination led to years of civil wars and then to the establishment of permanent Roman Caesars. The first permanent Caesar was Julius' adopted son, Gaius Octavius Thurinus (Augustus Caesar).

   It is said the name Caesar came from a caesarian birth of an ancestor of Gaius, Julius (Pliny the Elder). Thus, Julius Caesar and other Roman dictators adopted this name "to be cut from the womb." It was considered a godly attribute, comparable to rumors about the birth of Alexander the Great. This term has been transliterated into the following languages: German "Kaiser", Danish, Dutch, Hungarian, Japanese, Korean and Russian "Czar." The definitions of these words are "emperor incision or imperial cut." Some languages define it as "Caesar's section." The historical authenticity of this etymology is debated among historical scholars.

2. **Gaius Julius Caesar Augustus (born Gaius Octavius Thurinus):** 27 B.C. – 14 A.D. He was designated in Gaius Julius' will as his successor or heir. Although others contended for Augustus' rule, his reign began at the death of his predecessor Gaius. Not until 27 B.C. was he officially entitled Augustus, "Revered One," by the Roman Senate. His reign initiated Pax Romano or Roman peace. This was in preparation for the "fullness of Time" (See Section "Fullness of Time" – Rev 12:2.).

3. Tiberius: 14 A.D. – 37 A.D. The Caesar King of unbelieving Jews (Jn 19:15).

4. Caligula: 37 A.D. – 41 A.D.

5. Claudius: 41 A.D. – 54 A.D.

6. Nero: 54 A.D. – 68 A.D.

7. Galba: June 68 A.D. – January 69 A.D. (a "short time") He actually brought the legitimate line of Caesars to an end because the next two Caesars were imposters who reigned only for weeks. The Christian readers of Revelation would have understood the seventh Caesar in the cryptic writing of Revelation 17:10. Great turmoil rocked Rome during the brief reign (7 months) of Galba (beginning the reign of The Four). This turmoil led to Galba's decapitation assassination. Otho, who committed suicide after a three-month reign, succeeded Galba, and Vitellius, who was assassinated by Vespasian's soldiers after an eight-month reign, succeeded Otho. The soldiers of Vespasian proclaimed Vespasian emperor in 69 AD, and he began the Flavian Dynasty, which lasted 24 years from 69 to 93 AD.

In this apocalyptic prophecy, Nero was considered the sixth of the Caesarian Line. The "little while" (Rev 17:10) refers to the short reign of Galba, but probably also includes the other two aspirants for Nero's Crown (Otho and Vitellius), which all total, lasted only 18 months. With no real successor to Nero, the Caesarean Line ended with Galba. Thereafter, the Flavian Dynasty came into prominence.

Commentator Dr. Karl August Auberlen (1824-1864) believed the seven heads are actually kingdoms, not kings, namely: Egypt, Assyria, Babylon, Persia, Greece, Rome, and then the seventh being of the sixth, which is Pagan Rome becoming Papal Rome. Auberlen also believed that the eighth kingdom (out of the seventh) was an extension of the horn of Daniel into the formation of the Germanic kingdoms all the way to Napoleon (www.biblehub.com: Jamieson, Fausset, Brown Bible Commentary on Revelation 13:1).

The Ten Horns (kingdoms) assisted the leaders of Rome (political) and Roman Catholic Church (religious). The following are the kingdoms of the ten horns:

1. Vandals (Europe)

2. Visigoths

3. Suevi

4. Alans (France) Heruli

5. Burgundians

6. Franks

7. Britons or Saxons

8. Huns

9. Lombards

10. Ravenna or Ostrogoths

(NOTE: Sir Isaac Newton's list differs from other historians, but all agree to the fact that there were ten major powers that played a role in the healing of Rome's wounded head and extending the growth of the *horn of Daniel* into Europe.)

Daniel speaks of the growth of Papal Rome (Da 7:20). He sees one horn (religious, worldly, and powerful) coming up out of the ten horns and uproots three (remember, these are all kingdoms). According to Newton and Albert Barnes, the three uprooted horns are:

1. Ravenna (supported the rise of the Papacy)

2. Lombards

3. The State of Rome. The fall of the Papacy in November 1848 was designated by the departure of Pope Pius and the Papacy. They lost control of their Italian domain in 1870 and regained Vatican City in 1929 (www.wikipedia: Papal States).

Revelation 13:2-5: The beast I saw resembled a leopard, but had feet like those of a bear and a mouth like that of a lion. The dragon gave the beast his power and his throne and great authority. One of the heads of the beast seemed to have had a fatal wound, but the fatal wound had been healed. The whole world was astonished and followed the beast. Men worshiped the dragon because he had given authority to the beast, and they also worshiped the beast and asked, "Who is like the beast? Who can make war against him?" The beast was given a mouth to utter proud words and blasphemies and to exercise his authority for forty-two months.

The Beast of the Sea is one composite beast with features of the four beasts of Daniel 7:15ff. There is no horn on this head of the beast, but a fatal wound that had healed (noted previously). The healed head is the answer to Daniel's horn that grew out of the three uprooted supporters, i.e., Ravenna, Lombards, and the Papacy's State of Rome. Papal Rome healed Imperial Rome in 476 A.D. Some historians take this date to be the fall of Rome, but like many historians, they cannot see the battlefield through the fog. In reality, 476 A.D was a landmark date that ushered in the rise of Papal Rome like a sudden tempest. What was perceived to be the weakening of Imperial Rome was an absolute predisposal; it was just a matter of time before Papal Rome would take control. It was not the fall of Rome; it was the rise of Rome. When the Bishop of Pavia Epiphanius dissuaded the barbarian invader, Flavious Odoacer, from sacking the Golden City, the Papacy won their day in history.[80] They would remain in control under the power of Mystery Babylon until 1848. The Roman Church still has worldwide power, but the power of Mystery Babylon was significantly lessened after the French Revolution, starting in 1789 (www.broachweb.com: The Papacy and the French Revolution – Michael Broach) and, again, after the European Revolution of 1848 when the Pope Pius IX was forced to flee Rome (www.wikipedia: Pope Pius IX and Italy).

The healing wound was the uniting of the Roman Church (Religious) and the Roman State (Political). This beast was given 42 months, 1,260 years, or 3½ days to persecute the Congregation of Christ. From 533 A.D., when Justinian decreed a codex proclaiming John as the head of the western and eastern churches, until 1793 A.D., the most influential man in the world was the *Pope* or head of the Ecclesiastical Church.

Scripture refers to this position of power as the Man of Lawlessness (2Th 2:3-10). The Futurists take a literal understanding of this to mean one man, whereas the truth is this man is a position of power with a mindset; the Man of Lawlessness is not a specific man in history. Any person who attempts to remove Christ as the head of his Body and become the head in His place attempts to usurp Christ's earthly authority. This Man (or succession of men) fulfills the characteristics of the Man of Lawlessness. The power and blasphemies of this beast wear out the Saints during the time of the 42 months (under the day-year interpretation, a 30 day, 42-month period is 1,260 years). A careful student of history cannot deny that popes began to reign in 533 A.D. when Emperor Justinian bestowed the name of the Pope ("Pa-pa" meaning religious father) upon John, which is in direct violation of Matthew 23:9.

Revelation 13:6-10: He opened his mouth to blaspheme God, and to slander his name and his dwelling place and those who live in heaven. He was given power to make war against the saints and to conquer them. And he was given authority over every tribe, people, language and nation. All inhabitants of the earth will worship the beast—all whose names have not been written in the book of life belonging to the Lamb that was slain from the creation of the world. He who has an ear, let him hear. If anyone is to go into captivity, into captivity he will go. If anyone is to be killed   with the sword, with the sword he will be killed. This calls for patient endurance and faithfulness on the part of the saints.

The Beast has the power of the military and the government against anyone who has the New Testament. Since the secular government recognizes the power of Papal Rome, the military becomes an arm of Roman Catholicism.[81] Remember religious Rome did not have to convert the world with the truth of the "Sword of the Spirit." This Beast was more zealous to suppress the Covenant truth than all the enemies of the Old Testament combined. He wanted to annihilate the Seed of the woman to prevent the Man-Child from being born, but he could not.

The Beast (political power) united with the false prophets (religious power) tried but failed to kill the Man-Child. Now his war has shifted to that of the New Testament seed of the woman. Some might ask this question, "Why didn't the Man of Lawlessness suppress Christianity when it was first born?" If so, the Beast could have devoured Christianity in its infancy. The Man of Lawlessness with both the power of the political sea-going Beast and religious power of the land-going Beast could not stamp out Apostolic Christianity when it started for two reasons:

1. The Man of Lawlessness would not come to power until the New Testament was finished (70 A.D.). The Holy Spirit and the Spirit-inspired New Testament (2Th 2:7) restrained The Man of Lawlessness. He could not prevent the inscribing of the New Testament in history.

2. He could not sit in the worldwide temple as long as a successor of Caesar sat on Rome's throne. Nero was the sixth Roman Caesar (Rev 17:8, 10) and the one in power when John wrote The Revelation. After Nero's death, Galba assumed the role of Caesar for a short season (six months), as the last one.

The restraining of the Lawless One would be the power of the Caesars, and the Holy Spirit's working until the New Testament witness was completed. Jesus said that the Testimony would be read and completed before 70 A.D. Neither pagan nor Papal Rome could prevent the completion and the preaching of the New Testament to the world (Mt 24:14, 15). The proper time for the revealing of the Man of Lawlessness would be permitted by God "in His own time" which could be taken as both God's time and man's time. This "Man," or position, had not yet fully matured. He needed to develop certain characteristics, mindsets, and strict regulations (2 Th 2:6). In just a few verses (2Th 2:7, 8), the beginning and end are given from his rise to power in the 3rd and 4th Centuries to the coming of Christ to annihilate the Lawless One's Babylonian institution. Christ had the power to prevent the power of Satan's Trinity of evil (sea-going beast, land beast, and Babylon) from destroying the New Testament before 70 A.D., and at His Coming He has power to exterminate his infrastructure in its entirety.

Revelation 13:11-18: Then I saw another beast, coming out of the earth. He had two horns like a lamb, but he spoke like a dragon. He exercised all the authority of the first beast on his behalf, and made the earth and its inhabitants worship the first beast, whose fatal wound had been healed. And he performed great and miraculous signs, even causing fire to come down from heaven to earth in full view of men. Because of the signs he was given power to do on behalf of the first beast, he deceived the inhabitants of the earth. He ordered them to set up an image in honor of the beast who was wounded by the sword and yet lived. He was given power to give breath to the image of the first beast, so that it could speak and cause all who refused to worship the image to be killed. He also forced everyone, small and great, rich and poor, free and slave, to receive a mark on his right hand or on his forehead, so that no one could buy or sell unless he had the mark, which is the name of the beast or the number of his name. This calls for wisdom. If anyone has insight, let him calculate the number of the beast, for it is man's number. **His number is 666.**

The Beast of the Earth, (the false prophet), is correlated as a religious counterpart to Political Rome. When Rome began to Latinize the Church, they produced the mark of the beast. Pontiff Maximus, *Chief Bridge Builder*, was the Pope's claim to be the bridge between Heaven and Earth. Maxis means "chief" and pontiff means "pontoon builder." This is one of the many blasphemous antichrist titles that would be worn by the Pope "Holy Father." He attempted to remove Christ from the situation. He wanted to be viewed as a bridge to Heaven and Earth, just as Satan wanted to sit above the stars. The Pontiff could sit as the "Holy Father." While the mark of the beast signifies chiefly Papal Rome, the "mark" is upon anyone who worships anything other than Christ with their hearts, minds, and their hands. Such false worship is the sign of submission to worldly religion and philosophy! The Man of Lawlessness went through four stages of maturity. These four stages of the Papacy's growth can be classified, as follows:

1. 100 A.D. He is born. This is the time of Ignatius of Antioch.

2. 200 A.D. He is a young man. He is developing an Ecclesiastical Clergy.

3. 300-500 A.D. He is maturing during the first five ecumenical councils.

4. 533 A.D. He is full-grown by this time.

This Beast draws people to idolatry. This Beast is the Man of Lawlessness and is a system of progressions. Some skeptics say this "Man of Lawlessness" is only one carnal man who will appear sometime in the future. The Pre-Millennial doctrine parallels this description with a future "Antichrist"; however, when we place this Beast in the context of Paul's writings, the Pre-Millennial position is an unlikely possibility.

Notice the names, "Man of Lawlessness" and "Mystery of Lawlessness" in 2 Thessalonians 2:3, 7. These two names or titles are based upon the two oldest Greek manuscripts of the New Testament, where the same Greek word "anomia" (anomia) is the basis of both names, "Man of Sin" (anomia) and "mystery of iniquity" (anomia). Actually, all three names (vs. 3, 7 and 8) contain this same basic Greek word. The New American Standard (NAS) Bible translates this basic Greek word anomia in the English, "man of lawlessness" (vs. 3), "mystery of lawlessness" (vs. 7) and "that lawless one" (vs. 8).

We must consider several things in our interpretation of this "Man." Paul did not distinguish between the Man of Lawlessness and the Mystery of Lawlessness; in fact, he unified them as the same entity. The only future implication of this Man is his being revealed in destruction, not his origination. The Mystery of Lawlessness is not the only thing being restrained, but the Man of Lawlessness is also being held back. The New Testament would not be corrupted and the rise of the Papacy would not occur until after the 1st Century.

The Man of Lawlessness is *not* in the future tense, only his revealing or uncovering is in the future. The revealing of this Lawless One takes place at Christ's Coming. They assume that Christ is coming to receive His Crown and 2 Thessalonians 2:11 states this. But what does the text say? The Millenialists do not differentiate between an existing religious philosophy and a revealing of that philosophy at Christ's coming. Millennialists have the Man of Lawlessness appearing in physical life shortly before Christ's coming. However, Paul has this Man existing in his day and being revealed as "who he is" *at* the coming of Christ.

The Greek word for man is "Anthropos." This word has been used to describe a group of people, as well as one individual. Pre-Millennialists cry foul when we apply context to 2 Thessalonians. They want to use context and hypothetical language whenever they see fit; however, when it does not fit their eschatological scheme, Pre-Millennialists say it is not Biblical. This is circular reasoning, and it is unacceptable. No one would go as far as to say that the "Man of Lawlessness" represents mankind in general; however, placing Him in context proves that this man is clearly more than one carnal individual. Multiple scriptures treat this Man as being a group.

Peter describes the "will of man" in his second writing (2Pe 1:21). The use of man is in the singular with the genitive case, just like 2 Thessalonians 2. This passage is not just speaking of one man but of man throughout time. Nor is this passage speaking of one will, but the general will of man. The progressive Revelation was not brought about by any man, at any point in history, but by the Holy Spirit, as He spoke through many Godly men.

The Scriptures also say, "All Scripture is given by inspiration of God, and is profitable for doctrine, for reproof, for correction, for instruction in righteousness, that the man of God may be complete, thoroughly equipped for every good work" (2 Ti 3:16,17). The Scriptures are not just given to make Timothy, the man of God, perfect, but every man. Also note that Timothy is not the ONLY man of God, nor should Timothy be the only one to pursue Godliness (1Ti 6:11).

However, other aspects exist for understanding this verse. Paul wrote to the Romans, "Knowing this, that our old man was crucified with Him, that the body of sin might be done away with, that we should no longer be slaves of sin"

(Ro 6:6, 7). This is another general reference to man and his body. Surely, Paul is not speaking of only one man and one body. The context includes all Christians in general.

The problem with Pre-Millennial soothsayers is they cannot deal with context. In fact, their hermeneutic of the Scriptures rests upon approaching God's word like a jigsaw puzzle. This would be fine if they looked at the overall picture on the box, but they try to force the pieces together, while dismissing context. They force pieces of the puzzle into places the author never intended them to be. Their picture that emerges to the viewer is skewed.

Interestingly, John uses the exact same structure of 2 Thessalonians 2:3 in Revelation 17:5 to refer to the "Woman of Harlots." This woman is described throughout Revelation, and she definitely does not refer to one woman in the singular.

It seems acceptable that there is uniqueness concerning the description of the "Man of Lawlessness"; however, to deduct from the text that it is a single person and cannot refer to a group or succession of people is irresponsible. From context, and the previously stated facts, we conclude that this passage is not directly describing one carnal man at one point in time. This passage is describing a series of numerous carnal men of religious stature who rule one after the other and who, upon death, pass their title to his successor.

The "Man of Lawlessness" is also called the "son of perdition." This clause with the genitive is simply giving a parallel to the personification of this person. Son of perdition is simply describing a sinful person. Paul uses this phrase to describe multiple "sons of perdition" in his letter to the Ephesians (2:1-3). Even the Israelites were called this! (Isa 57:4). The writer of the Book of Hebrews even said, "But we are not of those who shrink into perdition, but of those who believe and are saved" (Heb 10:39). If Christians shrink back like Judas, they become a Son of Perdition. To take the son of perdition as literal, one might as well say the "future coming lawless one will be a man, Jew, and accountant, who is a betrayer."

Pre-Millennial doctrine promotes lackadaisical living. In their mind, they know Jesus is not going to come back because the "Man of Lawlessness is not born yet." Their doctrine teaches that "Christians" will know this man of lawlessness because he is going to sit in some Jewish temple in Jerusalem, proclaiming to be God. This is simply anti-scriptural. Is this man a person, a figure through linear time, or a system of man? For instance, the "Vicar of Christ" is considered a person. He stands in the place of God, proclaiming to be God, and is worshipped as such. Multiple popes have held this position over time, but they are one continuum.

The context clearly states that there will be a great falling away (2Th 2: 3). This is an apostasy. History shows that bishops began elevating themselves and taking the place of God (Ac 20:29) almost immediately after the Apostolic Dispensation (70 A.D.).

The Bishop also would "Oppose God and exalts himself as an object of veneration." Extensive evidence exists showing that the Hierarchy or "Bishop" of the congregation (singular, masculine) obviously departed from truth, as we shall see later in Chapter 13. This departure led a bishop to recognize himself as the Vicar of Christ (replacement or substitute for the Son of God), the Holy Father, and Holy See. He claimed to be able to remit sins, perform miracles, speak as inspired by God, and make all subject to himself rather than to Christ. We should remember that the Greek Patriarchs also made similar claims, and while they predated Roman bishops, they never received as much worldwide acclaim as the Roman clerics.

The bishop also, "sits in God's temple and sets himself up like God" (2Th 2: 4). Christians were the only temple of God during Paul's writing. The physical temple was no longer relevant to God at all. The Greek word is *naos,* used by Paul eight times. He never uses this term for the Jewish temple. After Christ's death, the Jewish temple is never again called the God's Temple. God vacated the temple. He does not dwell in buildings made with hands (Ac 17:24). Jesus told the Jews that their house is left to them desolate (Mt 23:28). He did not call it, "My Father's house," but "Your house." To indicate from this passage or any of Paul's writings that God is going to have a future temple is anti-scriptural.

Paul had already told the Thessalonian Congregation about these things while being with them. We cannot interpret this man as a physical, carnal man in the distant future. Paul says that the Mystery of Lawlessness is now being restrained.

An even greater question is, "How can someone or something (mystery of lawlessness) be restrained if it is not yet present?" In other words, how can this man be restrained if he is not in existence? He cannot. A cross reference is Romans 1:18 where Paul says that God's truth was being restrained. The truth must exist in order to be restrained. Just because ungodly men are hindering the truth does not mean the truth is not in existence. In fact, it proves the opposite.

In Paul's day, some authority restrained the Man of Sin (Man of Iniquity "lawlessness"). This was some sort of nonfigurative power. Paul said that it was a "restraining power," using the neuter form (2Th 2:6). Yet, this power was associated with a person because of the masculine form, "he who restrains" (2Th 2:7). Some associate this with the Holy Spirit. Those at the time of Paul's writing recognized this retraining power, which proves that it was present in Paul's day.

Strangely enough, the Roman Caesars themselves would also restrain the power of a worldwide monarchial bishop. This is one of many times when arrogant conceit and quest for power actually comes to the aid of God's children.

Due to the arrogance and love to control others, which leads to infighting, we have witnessed a rift in the Godless, Progressive Party in Washington. In his letters and memories, discovered after his death by The International Press (5/21/2015 A.D.), Osama bin Laden bewailed the fractious infighting within the ranks of Islamic Terror fighters that seriously weakened their resolve to destroy America and European Countries. The powerful sodomy coalition boasts of their power over media outlets and government, but the "fruit of their perverted lives" will be the most telling effect on their future. Through their own unnatural lusts and subsequent diseases, they will self-destruct in such a horrible manner that they would have preferred listening to the prophets of God over continuing on their pathway of death and self-destruction (Ro 1:32). Although we may despise them in our hearts, God's men or women who warn us of impending disasters are still our best earthly friends. Somehow, like a human body regurgitating or fighting off the death threats of invading viruses, this moral universe has a God-given way of tilting away from international evil when it threatens to destroy its righteous equilibrium, and thereby, flies out of orbit and smashes to pieces.

According to the First Law of Hermeneutics, students of God's word must side with context. Because Paul places this in an apocalyptic sense (not letting out incriminating information that the whole world would understand), only Christians know this Man of Sin. However, the whole world will know when he is uncovered and destroyed at Christ's Coming. He could not prevail while the Apostles were alive. Because the Apostles had the miraculous gift of discerning spirits, they would have rebuked the Papacy much like Paul did Elymas at Paphos (Ac 13:10). After 70 A.D., and the Apostolic Scriptures were available to the early Christians, they should have been able to test the Spirits of men and demons by the Word of Christ (their anointing - 1Jn 2: 18-20, 27, 4:1). Most early Christians failed miserably, just as they do today.

The Mystery of Lawlessness is already working. His secret power was already at work (Ac 20:29). After the Word was finished, The Mystery of Lawlessness began exercising his power. It was a mystery because it was so well hidden and covered. The term "wolf in sheep's clothing" applies here. As long as there were Caesar's in Rome, a Pope was delayed in Rome. A wolf can only be deterred by power.

The early stages of this ecclesiastical apostasy were *"already at work"* in the early Congregation. The tense in the Greek expression indicates that this movement was already working itself towards a greater goal. The child, later to become a Man, was growing in Paul's day. He was already operating but was not revealed.

Idolatry had invaded the Ecclesia of Christ (1Co 10:14). They struggled with the following: division (1Co 3:3), food (8:8), false doctrine (Gal 1:6), angel worship (Col 2:18), philosophical doctrines (Col 2:23), greed (Tit 1:11), and bad leadership (3Jn 10; Ac 20:29). This led to the official establishment of struggles for power and pre-eminence (3Jn 9).

The Ecclesiastical Church continues to blaspheme the name of Christ, generation after generation. There are hundreds of ways it blasphemes, but two primary ways are:

1. Teaching they can forgive sin.

2. Calling the Pope, a substitute for Christ.

Romanism represents the two Beasts (one of the sea and one of the land) and Babylon (These three are the Dragons or Satan's trinity.) for several of the following reasons:

1. Idolatrous institution (Jdg 2:17; 1Ch 5:25)

2. Whore – The earth was never married to Jesus (Rev 17:6)

3. Beautiful, but so corrupted that John is amazed (17:6)

4. Intoxicated with the blood of martyrs (17:6)

5. Power over Kings – Investiture staff and ring ceremony signifying temporal power[82]

6. Official colors of the Roman Catholic Church are scarlet and purple which is an attempt to take away Christ's authority as King. Over the years, Catholic apologists have been trained to resist the overwhelming evidence of Biblical prophecy pointing to their apostasy. They argue that the colors of their festive attire and worship are not scarlet and purple, but unlike those that worship in Spirit and truth, they have official colors including red and violet.[83]

7. Extreme hatred of recognizing the Word of Christ as the sole authority. Catholic doctrine is considered equal to the Biblical Scriptures (See Addendum A.).

8. Extent of the Vatican's intrusion into the secular world, not the spiritual world (17:2)

This Man of Lawlessness draws people to idolatry. This beast, "Man of Lawlessness," is a system of progression. The Greek and Roman systems progressively minimize Christ's name and authority, generation after generation.

Paul's "Man of Lawlessness" by synecdoche refers not to one man because Paul said this spirit of iniquity had already begun in his day. He also said he would continue until Christ slays him with the breath of His mouth (an obvious reference to the Second Coming). Iniquity is not the sin of breaking man's laws but of changing Christ's laws and commandments. Yet, if we allow the Bible to teach using Bible words to explain Bible doctrines, it is abundantly clear that the spirit of this Man is an idea rather than one particular person. This Man's spirit can, and has, adversely infected millions of people.

The Thessalonian Christians and others to whom Paul wrote His 1st Century letters were obviously aware that the "Man of Iniquity – Lawlessness" was a system that would arise in their day and be around until the end when Christ slays him. Paul studied at the feet of the celebrated teacher, Gamaliel, and he knew what a synecdoche was. As we have already seen, this Greek word is derived from "sun" (union or together) and "dechomai" (to receive by deliberation) and as a compound word, synecdoche means to receive together both what is said and meant.

Paul had to use a synecdoche in reference to a succession of men (or Roman Pagan and Papal Pontiffs) or the guy would be over 2,000 years old if Christ came to destroy him today. Since antichrist is a particular pre-disposition against Christ's Kingdom, and there are more antichrists in the world than just the Pagan and Papal Hierarchies, Paul does not call this Roman succession an antichrist, even though much of what is hard-core antichristian exists in the Papal religious-politic system.

The major purpose of "The Revelation Rainbow" continues to be to identify what antichrist meant to the true Prophets and Apostles of Scripture and what early Christians would have seen happening in Christ's primitive Congregation. The Roman hierarchy for instance will not deny the Deity of Christ, but it hated the prevailing theology that His congregation is independent of any earthly hierarchy, and that Christ is the only Head (The succession of Popes or Greek patriarchs are imposters.). Religious Rome is fanatically "Trinitarian," but even though they vehemently deny being anti-christ. From my experience, I have learned that most of them do not love Christ very much.

The primitive Christians would have seen this apostasy arise though the elevation of the monarchial bishops. This "lawlessness" did not originate outside the Congregation but from among them (Ac 20:29). At first, Pagan Rome restrained Papal Rome, but later Papal Rome benefitted greatly from the fall of Rome and her Caesars. God saw this Mystery of Iniquity reaching its fulfillment long before it occurred in 476 A.D. when Rome fell.

We called the "hieros" of Revelation 11:1, 2 an apocalyptic reference to the Greek-Roman apostasy. When Jesus told John to measure the temple, He called the inner "naos" the holiest part of the temple. He excluded the outer court, which is the "hieros." Paul used the word "Gentile" in a Jewish context when he said, "walk not as the Gentiles walk" (Eph 4:17). John writes of "Gentiles" here as opponents of the New Testament "Naos." The "Holy City" is the Heavenly City. When they "Trod down the city," they are at war with both New Testament Christians and Heaven. There is a true remnant or "inner" temple of New Covenant Christians who are measured by the New Testament. However, apostasy originated from the outer court. When the world looks at the "hieros" temple, they see just the outer court and think it is Christianity, but God does not want us to measure it, or recognize it because the inner court belongs to Him.

FROM AMONG YOURSELVES WILL THE WOLVES ARISE (ACTS 20:29)

Let us remember that the "little horn" of Daniel originated from this "hieros" temple (Da 7:8, 11, 20, 21). Also, the Gnostic antichrists got their beginning, "they went out from among them" (1Jn 2:17-19), from this temple, and the Man of Lawlessness sits in this temple. In other words, all of these symbols refer to an anti-Messianic spirit that would spring forth from within the ranks of the true Congregation of Christ. We would be foolish to look outside the primitive church for the origination of the anti-christ spirit. No wonder John said, "Many antichrists have entered the world" (1Jn 2:18). Similarly, at Ephesus (Acts 20:29), the Bishops worshipped Mary and started her church in 431 A.D, dedicated to the *theotokos* "birth giver of God."

The Vicarius Filii Dei – the Number of the Beast

When Christians address the Mark of the Beast, they need to possess wisdom. "If anyone has insight, let him calculate the Number of the Beast, for it is man's number." His number is 666. Three different Characteristics distinguish the beast in verse 17:

1. His Mark (Of authority)
2. His Name
3. The Number of his name (666)

The number 666 is not just a name. Revelation 19:16 states that Jesus has the name written on his vesture, "King of Kings and Lord of Lords." The same Greek word translated "name" (Strong's – word no. 3686) also appears in Revelation 13:17, 18. Hence, a number can be a title, not just a name. We require a certain understanding to discern just how this number, 666, is actually applied. Because 666 can be a title, men over the centuries have proposed several words and phrases as probable solutions to the enigma of 666.

The first man to discover the parallel between 666 and the Vicarius Filii Dei was Andreas Helwig in 1612. In his work, *Antichristus Romanus,* Helwig took 15 titles in Hebrew, Greek, and Latin and computed their numerical equivalents in those languages. He arrived at the number 666 mentioned in the Book of Revelation. He researched other numbers as well.

Greek

The numeric equivalents of Greek letters are also found in the *Encyclopedia Britannica* under "Languages of the World," Table 8. The numerical Greek alphabet is also given in the appendix of George Ricker-Berry's, *The Inter-Linear Greek-English New Testament*. He gives the Greek letter and its corresponding number. When the Papacy caught onto this wisdom, which undermined the very foundations of its structure, the Papacy stopped using *Vicarius Filii Dei* in its writings. Thus, let us examine some of the following ancient manuscripts as proof of what the Papacy used for the title of "Pope." We are greatly indebted to Michael Scheifler and his website (www.biblelight.net/666.htm) for much of the following information:

The literal meaning - Latin:

VICARIUS - substituting for, or in place of
FILII - means son
DEI - means God

V = 5	F = 0	D = 500
I = 1	I = 1	E = 0
C = 100	L = 50	I = 1
A = 0	I = 1	
R = 0	I = 1	
I = 1		
U/V = 5		
S = 0		
112	53	501

112+53+501 = 666

Greek

The ancient Greek word for "the Latin speaking man" is LATEINOS

L =	30 lambda
A =	1 alpha
T =	300 tau
E =	5 epsilon
I =	10 iota
N =	50 nu
O =	70 omicron
S =	200 sigma

666

Latin is the official language of the Roman Catholic Church. Church Documents are usually published first in Latin and then translated from Latin into other languages. Irenaeus (130 – 202 A.D.) first suggested the association of *Lateinos* with 666. He proposed, in his "Against Heresies," that 666 might be the name of the fourth kingdom in Daniel 7:7.

> "Then also Lateinos has the number 600 and 66; and it is a very probable [solution], this being the name of the last kingdom [of the four seen by Daniel]. For the Latins are they who at present bear rule: I will not, however, make any boast over this [coincidence]. (Source: *Against Heresies*, by Irenæus, Book 5, chapter 30, paragraph 3. St. Irenaeus biography online at the New Advent Catholic web site.)"

Hebrew

DUX CLERI translated means Captain of the Clergy D = 500 U = 5 X = 10 C = 100 L = 50 E = no value R = no value I = 1 ——————— 666	LUDOVICUS translated means Vicar of the Court L = 50 U = 5 D = 500 O = no value V = 5 I = 1 C = 100 U = 5 S = no value ——————— 666

The numeric equivalents of Hebrew letters can be found in the Encyclopedia Britannica under "Languages of the World", Table 50.

ROMIITH means the Roman Kingdom R = 200 resh O = 6 waw (vav) M = 40 mem I = 10 yod I = 10 yod TH = 400 taw ——————— 666	ROMITI means the Roman Man R = 200 resh O = 6 waw (vav) M = 40 mem I = 10 yod T = 400 taw I = 10 yod ——————— 666

Numerous other (to many to list) similarities exist between the Roman Kingdom and the significance of 666.

Documented Catholic Writings in using, "The Vicar of Christ (Vicarius Christi)"

> "**Vicar of Christ** . . . Title used almost exclusively of the Bishop of Rome as successor of Peter and, therefore, the one in the Church who particularly takes the place of Christ; but used also of bishops in general and even of priests. First used by the Roman Synod of A.D. 495 to refer to Pope Gelasius; more commonly in Roman curial usage to refer to the Bishop of Rome during the pontificate of Pope Eugene III (1145-1153). Pope Innocent III (1198-1216) asserted explicitly that the Pope is the Vicar of Christ; further defined at the Council of Florence in the Decree for the Greeks (1439) and Vatican Council I in Pastor Aerternus (1870). The Second Vatican Council, in "Lumen Gentium," no.27, calls bishops in general "vicars and legates of Christ." All bishops are vicars of Christ for their local churches in their ministerial functions as priest, prophet, and king, as the Pope is for the universal church; the title further denotes they exercise their authority in the Church not by delegation from any other person, but from Christ Himself." (Source: *Catholic Dictionary*, Peter M.J. Stravinskas, Editor, published by Our Sunday Visitor, Inc., Huntington, 1993, pp. 484-485.)

A Vicar General is defined in the 1994 *Catholic Almanac* on page 330 as "a priest or bishop appointed by the bishop of a diocese to serve as his deputy, with ordinary executive power, in the administration of the diocese." A vicar serves in the place of (substituting for) the bishop, and assumes his power of office for certain duties.

The Papal title of V*icar of Christ*, or in Latin "Vicarius Christi," means a *substitute for Christ*. This claim is synonymous with Antichrist because The Vicar of Christ is assuming the power of Christ on Earth, in place of God. This blasphemous claim is made repeatedly by various Popes and is the very foundation of Roman Catholicism and its Papacy.

Some Catholics, to avoid the association, may protest that the Pope represents, but is not a substitute for Jesus Christ. However, this fraudulent protest is just a play on words. Vicar of Christ and Antichrist essentially mean the same thing. This is a person that substitutes himself in God's place, on Earth.

Some Catholic Scholars claim that the term "Vicarius Filii Dei," as used by Popes, is a fabrication, a complete fake, and was never used by the Catholic Church. This claim could not be further from the truth!

Vicarius Filii Dei translates in English as Vicar of the Son of God, a phrase that has been used by Catholics in the following documents:

> "...The spirit of Protestant England its lawlessness, its pride, its contempt, and its enmity to the Church of God has made Catholics too to be cold-hearted, even when the **_Vicar of Jesus_ Christ is insulted**...There is Catholic France, and Catholic Germany, and Catholic Italy, giving up this exploded figment of the temporal power of the **Vicar of Jesus Christ**" (* St. Matt. xxvii. 42 – Pg. 140).

> "...so, because the Church seems weak, and the **Vicar of the Son of God** is renewing the Passion of his Master upon earth, therefore we are scandalized, therefore we turn our faces from him..." (* St. John xiv. 29. p. 141).

> "... Lastly, the only other point upon which I shall speak to is this. We have already seen how the powers and glories of the **Holy See** have been progressively unfolding..." (p. 230).

> "...Now I observe these powers of the **Holy See** have been always rising, always culminating. The temporal power in the hand of St. Gregory I was a fatherly and patriarchal rule over nations not as yet reduced to civil order. In the hands of St. Leo III, it became a power of building empire.... So that I may say there never was a time when the temporal power of the **Vicar of the Son of God**, though assailed as we see it, was more firmly rooted through" (p. 231).

> "...It was a dignified obedience to bow to the **Vicar of the Son of God**, and to remit the arbitration of their grieves to one whom all wills consented to obey" (p. 231).

Source: *The Temporal Power of the Vicar of Jesus Christ*, by Henry Edward Manning, D.D. (appointed Archbishop of Westminster in 1865 and Cardinal in 1875), second edition with a preface, published in 1862 in London by Burns & Lambert, 17 &18 Portman Street.

"For what is the temporal power, but the condition of peaceful independence and supreme direction over all Christians, and all Christian societies, inherent in the office of **Vicar of Christ**, and head of the Christian Church? When the Civil powers became Christian, faith and obedience restrained them from casting so much as a shadow of human sovereignty over the Vicar **of the Son of God**. They who attempt it now will do it at their peril" (*The Vatican Council And Its Definitions: Pastoral Letter to the Clergy*, By Henry Edward Manning, Archbishop of Westminster, Second Edition, New York, 1871, p. 166.)

There appears on the next page a photo copy of the official writing of Monseigneur Louis Gaston A. de Sègur that confirms in paragraph 2 their belief that the Pope is the Vicar of Christ.

(*Familiar Instructions And Evening Lectures On All The Truths of Religion*, by Monseigneur Louis Gaston A. de Sègur, translated from the French, Vol. II.; London: Burns & Oates, 1881, p. 204). This is a photo stat of the original entire page.

[p. 3] The leader of the Catholic Church is defined by the faith as the **Vicar of Jesus Christ** (and is accepted as such by believers). The Pope is considered the man on Earth who represents the Son of God, who "takes the place" of the Second Person of the omnipotent God of the Trinity.

[p. 13] The Pope is not the only one who holds this title. With regard to the Church entrusted to him, each bishop is Vicarius Christi.

The above are from: *Crossing The Threshold of Hope, by Pope John Paul II*: First Chapter: "The Pope": A Scandal and a Mystery.

Photos of a 16th century copy of the Donation are online at the Vatican Secret Archive web site. The phrase Vicarius Filii Dei appears at the end of the 5th line down of the left page of the 7th photo. The image below is enlarged by 100% and sharpened to make it readable. See also this page, #11.

are now enclosed within a church, where the stone upon which the apostle placed his head is also venerated. Not far from there, and also without the town, stands the magnificent Church of St. Paul, upon the spot where he was buried. This venerable monument, which dates from the fourth century, and which was almost entirely destroyed by fire thirty years ago, rises to-day from its ruins richer and more beautiful than ever. Even infidels and schismatics have desired to render homage to the apostle of all nations; and the great altar of malachite, given by the Emperor of Russia, is placed between four columns of alabaster sent by the Pasha of Egypt. All round the church the portraits of the Popes are represented in a long series of medallions in mosaic. Each one of these portraits is a link in the long, uninterrupted chain which unites us to the apostles of Jesus Christ. Let us glory in belonging to that ever living and immutable Church, against which the gates of hell shall never prevail.

ST. PETER'S.

WHAT Rome is to the world, St. Peter's is to Rome.

Rome is the holy city, the centre of the Catholic faith, the citadel of truth, the very sanctuary of the Catholic religion. And of all the temples that are enclosed within this one vast temple, St. Peter's is the chief; it is the central point of religious faith in Rome, and her most magnificent crown. Every one can understand why. Within these sacred walls repose the relics of the Prince of the Apostles, the first Bishop of Rome, the first of the long line of Pontiffs, the first Vicar of Jesus Christ. And close by, in an immense palace near to the church, the Pontiff lives, —the successor of St. Peter, the Vicar of the Son of God, and Sovereign Pastor of all the Christians upon the face of the whole earth.

After having preached Christianity in Rome for twenty-five years, St. Peter, with the apostle St. Paul, was arrested by the command of Nero, during the first persecution which that cruel Emperor waged against the Christians.

The sumptuous gardens and the vast circus which Nero had consecrated to the public games and races became the theatre of the first victories of Christianity. These heroes, of a type hitherto unknown, became in death triumphant.

Scanned page; Distinctio 96 Vicarius Filii Dei (Quote of Donation of Constantine) At right is the page of Gratian's Decretum printed in 1512 with the title Vicarius Filii Dei indicated by the arrow. The entire volume is online at Bayerische Staatsbibliothek, the title appears on photo 201.

AN ADDITIONAL THOUGHT ON 666

It is an intriguing fact that Hebrew, Greek and Latin are three languages that use the letters of their alphabet as a numerical scale. John 19:20 says that Pontius Pilate gave orders to place a sign over the cross of Jesus: "Jesus of Nazareth, King of Jews." It was written in Hebrew, Latin and Greek. The whole literate world could read the inscription and later when they read this Apocalypse they could figure out the name of the emperor Nero (666) who was the exact opposite of Pontius Pilate. By the third century, the number 666 could never have been associated with a modern man of any successive centuries because the Hebrew, Latin and Koine Greek ceased to be spoken languages and there were no other languages whose alphabets constituted a numerical scale.

The previous quotes, citations, and calculations undoubtedly show the rebellion and anarchy of the Catholic Church. They want power and control of the people. Their chief desire is to suppress the people, rule by a gold coin, and remove Christ as the head of the Congregation. They want to be the authority. However, as we will investigate, this Catholic uprising will be met with severe punishment from God. [84] Note how modern-day clerics seek to own so conveniently the glory of The Apostles who gave all they had to Christ until there was nothing left to give.

Revelation Chapter Fourteen

The 144,000

Revelation 14:1: Then I looked, and there before me was the Lamb, standing on Mount Zion, and with him 144,000 who had his name and his Father's name written on their foreheads.

This vision is one of the most pleasing sights in the universe. Christ is joined with the 144,000. In the Old Testament, the Chosen People did not recognize Christ on the Throne. Now, they not only recognize their true King, they are with him.

The Lamb and 144,000 with Him on Mt. Zion (2Sa 5:9) not only represent the land that David was given, but also their permanent estate in Heaven. David's kingdom was never intended to be a physical kingdom (Heb 12:22). During Christ's earthly ministry, the Disciples' chief desire was the restoration of a physical kingdom. The Disciples were focused on this concept seven days before they received the immersion of the Holy Spirit (Ac 1:6). After the Holy Spirit came and the heavenly kingdom was established on Earth, the Disciples never again inquired as to when the Kingdom of Christ would come. After the Spirit came at Pentecost, the Disciples became "witnesses" and no longer desired a carnal kingdom.

Who are the 144,000? Numerous interpretations exist concerning the 144,000. The Futurists believe this vision is of a future event. They believe a physical resurrection of 144,000 Jewish evangelists will occur. This Futurist doctrine states that the preaching by the 144,000 will bring a worldwide revival. Very few teachings contradict Scripture more than this. Scripture clearly explains that the Kingdom of God is not a physical place on this Earth, but the Kingdom is a Heavenly dwelling place from which the affairs of Earth are directed in Spirit (Mt 6:10).

The Historicists have a view that requires searching for and finding a historical parallel that corresponds with the 144,000. NONE have been found. The School of Philosophy's view is considered partially correct by recognizing that the 144,000 is symbolic, but this School has the wrong group of people. This School is mistaken because their view grasps a symbolic number of the spiritual "Ecclesia" that starts with Pentecost and continues until the end of the world. It is true that the Ecclesia reigns with Christ in the 1,000-year reign, and they are seen later in John's vision. However, these 144,000 are Jews who lived from the time of Moses through to the thief on the Cross. The 144,000 cannot contradict the 1,000 years of Revelation 20:4, 5.

The 144,000 is a symbolic number of Old Testament Jews who were not defiled; they were the first fruits, pure, and innocent. These Jews dwelt in Hades (not Hell) until Christ went down to them and "took captivity, captive" (Eph 4:8-12). This group is the same group mentioned in Revelation 7. The Jews could not have had access to the Heavenly paradise before the Cross for two reasons:

1. Their sins have not yet been completely forgiven. The word "parrasis" is used in regard to Old Testament sins (Ro 3:25). "Parrasis" means to "Passover or suspend sins." In the New Testament, sinners are completely forgiven (Ac 2:38). The word is "aphesis," which means to release, or leave off from guilt. When Christ made "propitiation," His blood reached back to satisfy God's wrath toward Old Testament saints (Ro 3:25).

2. The Jews did not have the seal of the Holy Spirit (Jn 3: 5, 7:39, 16:13; Eph 1:13). Some of the Jews had the Holy Spirit WITH them but He was not IN them (Jn 14:17). Possibly the same can be true today of those whom are convicted but not truly converted.

When scholars say, "Old Testament Saints died and went to Heaven before Jesus Christ ascended to Heaven," those scholars believe the Old Testament provided some way to the Father other than through Jesus the Son. However, these scholars cannot produce one verse of Old Testament Scripture to support the New Testament idea that a servant of God could even think that he could die and go and dwell with God, the Father, forever.

In the absolutely beautiful example of Enoch, who was "translated" (Heb 11:5), we face some difficulty. If Enoch was taken to God's eternal home in Heaven, we have a discrepancy in a person, like Elijah, who did not die what we call a "natural death." Scholars say they were "removed" from this Earth. This means they bypassed the ordinary means of removal called "death – necros, separation," and were so privileged to undergo such a "separation" by the hands and means of God Himself. This seems to be an exception to the fact that "No man comes to the Father, except through the Son" (Jn 14:6).

We may think this apparent discrepancy is resolved because Elijah appeared later on the "Mount of Transformation" with Moses (Mt 17:3). We do not believe that Moses and Elijah went to God's Heaven and then reappeared. Although Enoch is not in this scene, the same would be true of him. God indeed "took him," but Scripture does not say where God took Enoch. Paul had the most incredible privilege (so far as we know, he alone) to visit the eternal Land of Third Heaven (2Co 12:4). We can only go so far before God hides wisdom, and human beings are absolutely forbidden to visit Hades, "Have the gates of death been opened to you, or the doors of the deepest darkness?" (Job 28:17).

We believe that God took them to the same pre-ascension Paradise where He took Abraham (Lk 16:22). Even though Enoch's spirit was separated from his body, Paul tells us no Old Testament saint would receive a glorified body until all of the New Testament saints receive theirs (Heb 11:40). This understanding does not contradict the teaching of Christ that "No one comes to the Father, but through Him." The people of Noah's day were in an interim "spirit world" (1 Pe 3:16, 20), just as those after Abraham and the 144,000 were in this "waiting place," waiting for the Messiah. It is possible that those before The Flood were in the same abode of the righteous dead as those in The Bosom of Abraham after The Flood. The Earth and its works were destroyed, but the flood did not touch the underworld of spirits.

In the cases of Elijah and Enoch, God "took them" (without the experience of rigor mortis) from Earth to the same place Moses and Elijah dwelt. At the Transfiguration, Peter, James, and John saw Moses and Elijah as bodiless apparitions, and the Disciples recognized instantly whom they saw. We do not think Moses and Elijah were given glorified bodies, as that would be a contradiction of the Hebrews 11:40. Remember that Enoch is mentioned in the same context as Hebrews 11:40. Moses' and Elijah's being given glorified bodies would also contradict the fact that no final resurrection of the dead would occur until Christ returns (Jn 5:25). Whether Elijah and Enoch had a different appearance than the rest of saints in the Abode of Spirits is an open question, and what would God have done with their bodies? But it would be dangerous and a violation of Scriptural division and principle to say they went to God's Heaven (as described in Revelation 21 and 22) before the rest of the eternal Congregation of God in Christ.

When Christ's physical body was in the grave, His Spirit descended into Hades and sealed the Old Covenant Jews with the Holy Spirit (Revelation 7:3). Christ's descending to Hades was an essential redemptive act by Christ. The Holy Spirit is a seal that marks the down payment for paradise (Eph 1:13) and creates an ownership to Christ (2Co 1:22). Can we understand the importance of this process? If we do not have His spirit, we are not His! (Ro 8:9). The reason why the Father's name is written on the foreheads of the 144,000 is so that *now*, through Jesus Christ, the Jews can call Him "Father." The Jews now have the *mark of God* as Father. Of the 600 plus times that the word "Father" occurs in the Old Testament, "Father" is never used in relation to God! The Fatherhood of God was an exclusive Christian teaching that could only be taught when one understands that God has a Son. This is why the mark of God (as Father) was put in their forehead. The Jews had not previously grasped this relational concept, intellectually, or spiritually because the God-Son aspect though being referenced in the Old Testament (Isa 63:9, 10) was never understood because the indwelling of the Holy Spirit had not been given as it is in the New Testament (Jn 7:39). The Holy Spirit testifies within us, that Christ is God's only unique Son (Jn 15:26).

Revelation 14:2: And I heard a sound from heaven like the roar of rushing waters and like a loud peal of thunder. The sound I heard was like that of harpists playing their harps.

The thunder and water represent trials on Earth. These two sounds are heard, but they are one in the same. The sound is thunder to some, but music to others. So it is true of the trials of human life…they press us down or we rise above them in exhilaration. They could be considered bittersweet. Our outlook upon these contrasting experiences of life will greatly influence our divine justification and progressive sanctification. Believe it or not, even though it seems like the roar of rushing waters and loud peals of thunder, to the Covenant Children of God, it is actually like harpists playing their beautiful music. This apocalyptic poetry serves as a sedative for frazzled nerves and theological sanity in a world gone mad.

Revelation 14:3: And they sang a new song before the throne and before the four living creatures and the elders. No one could learn the song except the 144,000 who had been redeemed from the earth.

The 144,000 were redeemed from the Earth! (Ro 8:10) They have a new *Son* (Christ Jesus), new Heaven, new Earth, new Covenant, a new song, and they are new creatures. This new song is a song of the Lamb's redemption. Only repentance, suffering, loyalty, and faithfulness can bring a new song. This was a new song because the Jews had not known redemption to God. They did not have redeemed bodies, but their redeemed spirit went to be with the Lord. When the Gospel is taught, it is like hearing "The New Song." David prophesied this new song (Ps 33:3, 40:3, 144:9, 149:1). David was most certainly one of this vast Assembly presented under the 144,000 figure. Harpist figure into the apocalyptic imagery here because the "new song" in prophecy was accompanied with instrumental music (Ps 144:9).

Revelation 14:4, 5: These are those who did not defile themselves with women, for they kept themselves pure. They follow the Lamb wherever he goes. They were purchased from among men and offered as first fruits to God and the Lamb. No lie was found in their mouths; they are blameless.

This passage of Scripture is difficult to understand. Whether or not this group consisted of strictly men who did not defile themselves with women or this represents spiritual purity by adhering to the covenant in general by not practicing fornication, sodomy, adultery, etc., the Holy Spirit is assuring us that they are undoubtedly devoted to the Lamb of God. No blame could be brought against them.

The following are the two basic, contradictory views of how some Biblical scholars view the 144,000: (The Jehovah Witness doctrine of only 144,000 JW's in Heaven is so nonsensical, it is not worthy of note.)

1. Babies – This would not be hermeneutically correct because the 144,000 had a will (who kept themselves pure); they followed the Lamb; and they were purchased by the Blood of Christ. Of course, this would exclude babies.

2. Unmarried – In this reference to those who lived from Moses to the Thief on the Cross, we find it untenable to believe that all of them were men or women who never married. The fact that the text says that they were men who did not defile themselves with women aligns itself very strongly to the fact that this is a Jewish apocalyptic thought and not literal. Certainly, the 144,000 also included women. However, in Jewish thinking, the man included the woman. The man was circumcised, but the women received the benefit of the circumcision by being a part of the Abrahamic faith.

The only plausible explanation to this difficulty, "They did not defile themselves with women," is that the removal of the 144,000 from Hades to the presence of Christ bypassed the Earth and all earthly experiences including marriage.

We are living in a modern-day fascination with a "sexual revolution." Instead of a sacred, divine sexual relationship with a God-given spouse, indiscriminate sexual recreation on demand is the order of the day. The last thing on the minds of those being removed from Abraham's Bosom, in order to be present with Jesus, would have been to make plans to go on a date or to get married. As far as lying and any other temptation to sin, their spiritual voyage from Hades to Mt. Zion transcended all lust of the flesh, lust of the eyes, and pride of life. Their spiritual venture of following Jesus (just as the Disciples who left their fishing nets immediately) began the moment He entered the Hadean abode and continued as they followed Jesus into eternity (Zec 12:10).

Christ purchased those 144,000 righteous Jews in Hades and offered them as the first fruits (1Co 15:23; 1Pe 3:18-22; Mt 27:50-52; Heb 11:40). The Jews who ascended with Christ from Hades are with Christ in Spirit. They will not get perfected bodies until *Christians* get perfected bodies. All receive perfected bodies at the same time. Technically, Christ is the first "fruit" (Singular) of the Resurrection. Second are the 144,000 from Moses to the Thief on the Cross. They are the first "fruits" (plural) to Christ. The final group consists of those belonging to Christ (Christians) at His Second Coming.

People of Noah's day are not included in the 144,000 since they lived or died in the flood before the nation of Judah/Israel was established. When Jesus died and entered the prison of the spirits, He also appeared to those who died before the flood (1Pe 3:18-21). After He proclaimed, "kerusso," (Strong's no. 2784) "Good News," He ascended (3:22). We know for certain that those of the (pre-deluge) Patriarchal Age also died in hope because, one of them, Enoch, prophesied of Christ's Second Coming (Jude 14). The "Days of Noah" reach to all in the Patriarchal Age.

See the chart on the next page compiled by Gerald Wakefield on the age time lines from Adam to Moses.

Revelation 14:6: Then I saw another angel flying in midair, and he had the eternal gospel to proclaim to those who live on the earth — to every nation, tribe, language and people.

This "eternal Gospel" is the apostolic Word of Christ being proclaimed to the whole world. Christ has ascended to the right hand of the Father and has redeemed the Jews of the Old Covenant (144,000) and all of the saved who lived from Adam to Noah. He, now, has sent His disciples into all of the Earth to proclaim this Word with authority to the whole world (Ac 1:8). This angel in Revelation 14:6 is the patron angel of evangelism. Peter submitted to such an angel when he was in prison (Ac 12:7). This is probably the same angel that appeared to Peter. Christians today know that the Gospel has already come (2Th 1:3-5). Angels assist us in declaring it.

Thus, Revelation 14:6 refers to the conversion of New Covenant Christians in contrast with the Old Covenant 144,000. The Gentiles of Revelation 7:9, 10 stood in contrast to the Old Testament 144,000 (7:4-8).

Revelation 14:7: He said in a loud voice, "Fear God and give him glory, because the hour of his judgment has come. Worship him who made the heavens, the earth, the sea and the springs of water."

TABLE OF CONTEMPORARY PATRIARCHS AND LEADERS

Name (AGE)	0	100	200	300	400	500	600	700	800	900	1000	1100	1200	1300	1400	1500	1600	1700	1800	1900	2000	2100	2200	2300	2400	2500	2600	2700
MOSES (120)																									2429–2549			
AMRAM (137)																									2354–2491			
KOHATH (133)																							2264		2397			
LEVI (137)																							2234		2371			
JACOB (147)																						2164		2311				
ISAAC (180)																						2104		2284				
ABRAM (175)																					2004		2179					
TERAH (205)																			1874			2079						
NAHOR (148)																			1845		1993							
SERUG (230)																			1815				2045					
REU (239)																		1783					2022					
PELEG (239)																		1753					1992					
EBER (464)																		1723						2187				
SALAH (433)																	1693						2126					
ARPHAXAD (438)																	1658					2096						
THE FLOOD (NOAH WAS 600)																	1656											
SHEM (600)																	1558					2158						
NOAH (950)																					2006							
LAMECH (777)											874						1651											
METHUSELAH (969)								687									1656											
ENOCH (TRANSLATED AT 365)								622–987																				
JARED (962)						460									1422													
MAHALALEEL (895)					395									1290														
CAINAN (910)				325									1235															
ENOS (905)			235									1140																
SETH (912)		130									1042																	
ADAM (930)										930																		
YEARS AFTER 6TH DAY	0	100	200	300	400	500	600	700	800	900	1000	1100	1200	1300	1400	1500	1600	1700	1800	1900	2000	2100	2200	2300	2400	2500	2600	2700

NOTES:

ADAM COULD HAVE TOLD NOAH'S FATHER, LAMECH, ABOUT THE CREATION AND THE FALL FOR 56 YEARS.

ENOS, THE GRANDSON OF ADAM COULD HAVE TALKED WITH NOAH FOR 84 YEARS.

NOAH'S SON SHEM COULD HAVE SPOKE WITH HIS GRANDFATHER LAMECH FOR 93 YEARS AND AFTER THE FLOOD WITH ABRAHAM FOR 150 YEARS AND WITH ISAAC FOR 50 YEARS.

EVEN NOAH AND ABRAHAM HAD TWO YEARS TO CONVERSE WITH EACH OTHER.

MOSES, WHO WROTE THE FIRST FIVE BOOKS OF THE BIBLE, PROBABLY ALREADY KNEW BEFORE GOD DIRECTED HIM, SOME OF THE DETAILS IN GENESIS ABOUT THE CREATION, THE FALL OF MAN, AND THE FLOOD.

COMPILED BY GERALD WAKEFIELD 2010

Christians are under this angel's authority. They are told to fear God and give Him glory, for Judgment Day is approaching. However, for the Christian, Judgment Day comes every Lord's Day. The benefit to being a New Covenant Christian is that they judge themselves now so that they will not be condemned on Judgment Day! (1Co 11:31).

Revelation 14:8: A second angel followed and said, "Fallen! Fallen is Babylon the Great, which made all the nations drink the maddening wine of her adulteries."

God's Judgment has come! God is dealing with the Whore of Babylon and those who have fallen into her demonic doctrine. This verse compares to an epistolary aorist. It announces something that has not yet happened as if it already has. John, the writer of The Revelation, self-consciously puts himself in our time frame or the event being foretold. No institution of the Beast has given New Testament Christians more trouble than Babylon.

Revelation 14:9-11: A third angel followed them and said in a loud voice: "If anyone worships the beast and his image and receives his mark on the forehead or on the hand, he, too, will drink of the wine of God's fury, which has been poured full strength into the cup of his wrath. He will be tormented with burning sulfur in the presence of the holy angels and of the Lamb. And the smoke of their torment rises forever and ever. There is no rest day or night for those who worship the beast and his image, or for anyone who receives the mark of his name."

THE WINE OF GOD'S WRATH

The Hebrew connotation of this expression goes back to Numbers 28:7. The worshipper was to pour wine into the fire of the altar. The word wine can refer to freshly pressed juice from the wine press, or if it is left to the breaking down "action of purification," wine becomes old wine. The Hebrew word in this text, "ra-aph," pronounced "raw-of," is translated in some texts "wine," but according to Strong (found only one time in the Bible-7491) "ra-aph" means to drip, distill, spoiled or strong drink. The worshipper allowed the juice to become spoiled (from the root word "raw-ah" breaking down) "and then offered it in fire."

Strong drink is associated with madness and rage. The drinker can literally lose his mind to consummate madness. Once this happens, there can be no reasoning or reconciling. The worshipper realizes that the sacrificial fire is an image of the fiery wrath of God that will consume the adversary. It is a fearful and dreadful thing to fall into the hands of an angry God (Heb 10:31). Thus, we have the expression, "Wine of God's wrath." The wine of the wine press is fresh, but it is also red, representing blood. The wine is always fresh at first, and if left alone, it becomes stale. In her "Battle Hymn of the Republic," Julia Ward Howell refers to God's wrath being revealed prematurely in national affairs, "He is pressing out the vintage where The Grapes of Wrath are stored." Sometimes, the blood shed of terror, war, and criminal violence leads us to look beyond the bloodshed and gore. We are led to lift our eyes to the Throne of the universe and ask the question, "Is the God of wrath pleased with us?"

Permit me to relate an experience in the early days of my evangelistic labors. At the conclusion of the message, "Five Things in Hell I Wish Were Present in this Congregation," church attendee Charles Peterson came down the aisle to submit himself to the Acts 2:38 immersion. I said, "Remember, repentance comes before immersion. Repentance means, 'A change of mind.'...Is there anything present in your life that you really need to repent of?" Charles told me to come to his house before his immersion. Once in the kitchen, he opened the cupboard door and there on the shelves were bottles of wine, whiskey and beer. These modern-day alcoholic drinks consist of many times more "proof" in alcoholic content then the drink offered in fire (Nu 28:7). He took them one-by-one, opened the caps, and poured their contents down the drain. To me, as I witnessed this scene, it resembled a drink offering poured out into the fire. Yes, I may be stretching the point, but if I error, I am going to error on the side of God's Holiness, and not on the side of sensuality or licentiousness.

After many years, I was invited for an evangelistic campaign and returned to the congregation of my early years. Charles was in a nursing home and he contacted me. I was privileged to visit him before he was called from this world. Knowing that he was not far from the door of eternity, he thanked me for bringing him the message of repentance, salvation, and grace from God. Charles Peterson was "sold out to his savior." His wife, family, and many relatives were led to examine their souls as a result of his conversion, and they obeyed the Gospel also. He lived a sober life, in mind, spirit and body, until he died.

This Third Angel of Revelation 14:9 introduced the undiluted judgment of Christ is also introduced in Chapter 15. Until now, diluted judgment existed, but from now on, this text promises that judgment will no longer be diluted. From our standpoint, undiluted "permanent" judgment is still future or none of us would be reading this. The point our God is making is that we who may or not be experiencing one or more of the temporary "diluted" judgments in our lives must realize that these same judgments may be permanent and undiluted if we ignore God's warnings.

Those who have served satanic forces or doctrine with their mind (mark of their forehead) or their hands (mark on their hands) will receive Christ's Judgment. The Mark of the Beast is a sign of slavery, first to Pagan Rome, second to Papal Rome, and thirdly, to all the children of Babylon throughout the ages. This mark shows that one belongs to a master. However, Christians are called to release themselves from all idols (1Th 1:9), to be faithful and obedient (Ac 20:21), and to bring forth fruit (Ac 26:20).

The punishment for choosing to serve Satan was eternal hell. As noted previously, in order for an execution to take place, there has to be witnesses (Lk 19:27). The Lamb and His Holy Angels will witness this incendiary holocaust. Unlimited and unrestrained love does not always include justice. However, divine justice always includes love. *Just* persons love justice, "Love rejoices not in lawlessness, but in truth" (1Co 13:6). The holy personalities of Heaven love justice so much that they receive the benefit of witnessing eternal retribution. Those who love justice are called legalists in spite of the fact the word legalism is not in Scripture, and most people do not understand its meaning. Unjust people do not understand pure love; *just* people have the most love because they understand the real and vital needs of the human race.

The smoke arising from their torment is used as a metaphor. This apocalyptic description shows smoke as the secondary effect of the eternal *fire*. Christians do not experience the torment of the fire because they believe New Testament doctrine. Fire and smoke of everlasting punishment are metaphors. The actual experience is worse.

John contrasts the Mark of God with this Mark of the Beast. The Mark of God was a sealing of the 144,000 by the Holy Spirit, and now it is contrasted with the mark of Rome and her children that can be seen through manual and mental service. One mark is in an earthly sense visible; the other is invisible.

Revelation 14:12, 13: This calls for patient endurance on the part of the saints who obey God's commandments and remain faithful to Jesus. Then I heard a voice from heaven say, "Write: Blessed are the dead who die in the Lord from now on. "Yes," says the Spirit, "they will rest from their labor, for their deeds will follow them."

During this joyful testing time for the saints (from 33 A.D. to the end of the world), they are called to keep God's Commandments and remain faithful to Christ. The previous verses give them the hope of perseverance and comfort them concerning the future. The saints are not only blessed because they know the future events concerning judgment, but also because they go to be with the Lord, forever. There is a great contrast between verses 11 and 13. Those enslaved to the rituals of Rome and her children have no rest. Those who die after the New Covenant "from now on" will rest. This verse 13 best delineates all the difference between dying "in hope" of the Old Testament and dying "from now on" in the New Testament hope. No true and pure "rest" exists apart from "The Prince of Peace," but thousands of chemical and narcotic substitutes are available to those people dumb enough to search for a lifetime of peace that will continue to escape us.

Revelation 14:14-20: I looked, and there before me was a white cloud, and seated on the cloud was one "like a son of man" with a crown of gold on his head and a sharp sickle in his hand. Then another angel came out of the temple and called in a loud voice to him who was sitting on the cloud, "Take your sickle and reap, because the time to reap has come, for the harvest of the earth is ripe." So he who was seated on the cloud swung his sickle over the earth, and the earth was harvested. Another angel came out of the temple in heaven, and he too had a sharp sickle. Still another angel, who had charge of the fire, came from the altar and called in a loud voice to him who had the sharp sickle, "Take your sharp sickle and gather the clusters of grapes from the earth's vine, because its grapes are ripe." The angel swung his sickle on the earth, gathered its grapes and threw them into the great winepress of God's wrath. They were trampled in the winepress outside the city, and blood flowed out of the press, rising as high as the horses' bridles for a distance of 1,600 stadia.

These verses describe the end of the world because this section introduces the reader to the Sixth and Seventh angels. The Sixth and Seventh angels pave the way to a new section of the undiluted judgment of the seven angels. Six is the number of man, and this Sixth angel ends the fourth parallel section. We have seen judgment upon those that worshipped the Beast (Rev 14:11). Now judgment comes upon the whole Earth.

Christ, as King of all the angels (1Pe 3:22), is completing the judgment of the Seventh Angel (Rev 14:14-19). This passage of Scripture corresponds with Matthew 13:30-38. This scripture directly contradicts the mindset of the Futurist and their rapture conception. Christ will send His angels (1Pe 4:5; Mt 13:41, 42) and gather the *non*-Christians (tares) and throw them into everlasting fire. His angels will then gather the Christians (wheat) and place them into the abode of the Father (barn). Thus the non-Christian unbelievers, not the saints, are taken "first."

The winepress is pressed so exceedingly that the blood rises up to the bridles of the horses. The bridles symbolize the end of the world and the distance of the blood is enough to fill the whole state of Rome (1,600 Stadia = 180 square miles or about 300 kilometers). Those who have betrayed the Blood of the Lamb, because of Roman whoredom, are now being punished by God's wrath.

The fourth parallel section ends with judgment, both upon the Roman Beast and her children, as well as the whole Earth (Rev 14:18, 19). How interesting that the angels were corresponding with each other, showing the concerted effort under the authority of Christ, the King of Angels.

Outline of Christ and the Six Angels

Angel One – The gospel angel (Rev 14:6).

Angel Two – The angel who opposes false doctrine (14:8).

Angel Three – The angel announcing God's wrath against the worship of false doctrine (14:9-12).

Angel Four – The gold crowned king of angels (Christ) is in the midst with the sharp sickle of judgment (14:14). It is scarcely appropriate to call the King and Creator of angels "an angel," but here in this context, Christ humbly places Himself in the midst of His loyal, angelic regiments in such a way that He is with His fellow allies in executing judgment upon world-wide, universal adversaries. Therefore, the one in the middle is like angel number four in the middle of the perfect seven numbered angelic warriors.

Angel Five – The angel of earth intelligence announcing the end of the world (14:15).

Angel Six – The assistant angel to Angel Four confirms the forensic evidence that has been gathered as proof of how guilty humanity has been in rejecting Christ's mercy (14:17). This Angel is more than willing to participate and give consent to this execution.

Angel Seven – The angel in charge of the final Fire of Judgment gives charge to execute the first death on those alive at Christ's coming (14:18). The second death of fire is yet to come.

All totaled, these seven constitute an invincible angelic brigade.

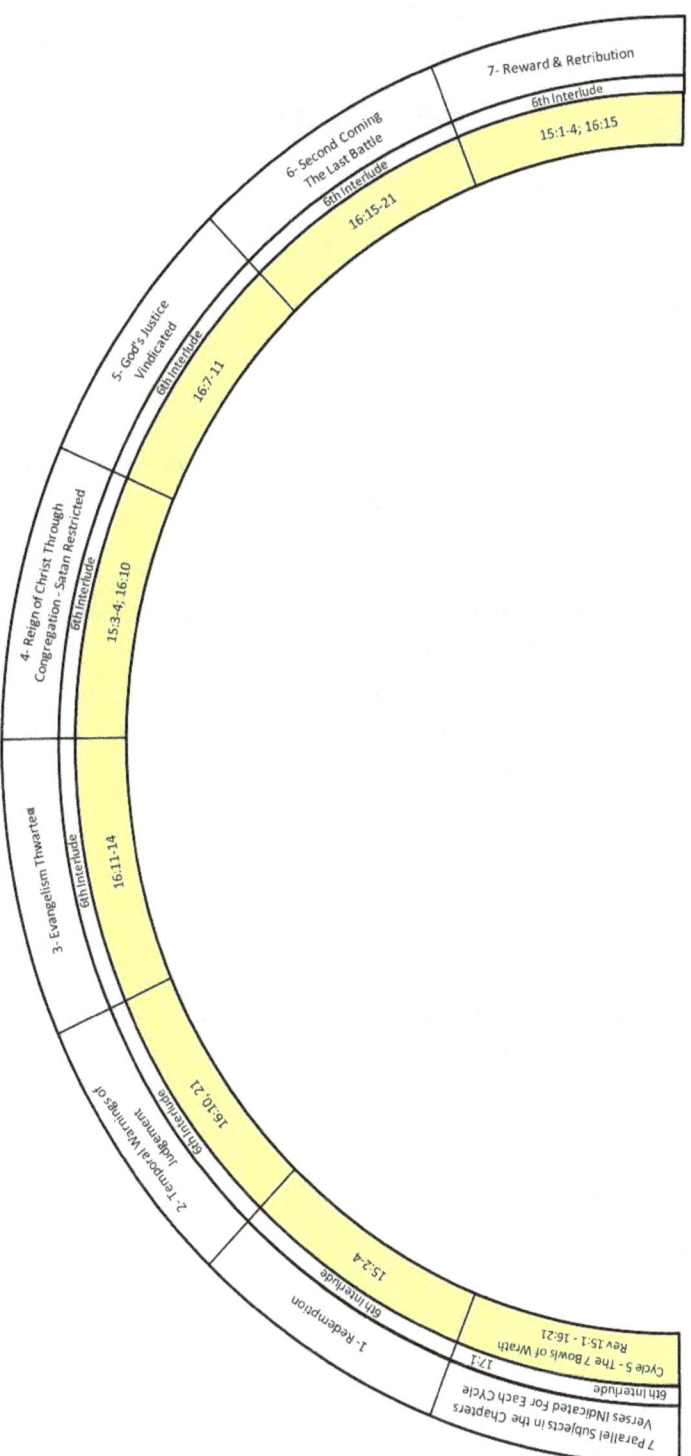

CYCLE 5 – THE SEVEN BOWLS OF WRATH

Christ in Calamity

Revelation Chapter Fifteen

Undiluted Judgment

Revelation 15:1: I saw in heaven another great and marvelous sign: seven angels with the seven last plagues—last, because with them God's wrath is completed.

The seven angels and seven plagues symbolize complete judgment. This introduces a new cycle that includes Revelation 15 and 16. John's vision from Jesus Christ seems to be breaking his thought, shifting gears, and preparing to introduce Chapter 16.

God's wrath has been completed. The word "complete" corresponds with the word "fullness." Christ came at the "fullness of time." The Jews had to kill the prophets and evangelists, in order to fill up iniquity, for the "fullness of time" to come (Mt 23:33-35; Da 9:24). At the end, Christ knows who is and who is not going to be saved. The Book of Daniel deals with the following ends in his writing:

- The End of un-forgiven sin (Da 9:24)

- The End of Old Testament visions and prophecies (1Co 13:8)

- The End of Jewish iniquity against the Messiah and his messengers (Da 9:24; 1Th 2:14-16)

- The End of Christ's life on Earth (Da 9:24)

- The End of Judaism (Da 9:27; Jn 19:30)

- The End of Sin. Potentially, Christ tasted the full wrath of God for every human being on this Earth in the completeness/fullness of transgressions (Da 9:27)

- The End of Antiochus (8:25, 26)

- The End of desolations – 70 A.D (Da 9:26, 27)

- The End of opposition to Messiah Prince's seed – 146 B.C. (Da 11:45)

- The End of the world (Da 12:5)

The End spoken of in Da 12:13.

The End of martyrdom (Rev 6:11)

- The Fullness of Gentiles (Ro 11:25)

After the destruction of the Jewish Temple in 70 A.D., Christ's divine instructions introduced the next event to take place – the fullness of the Gentiles (Ro 11:25; Luke 21:24). The Temple's destruction affected the Gentiles in significant ways. A mass conversion of Gentiles occurred after the destruction of the Temple, and Gentiles will continue to be added to the Kingdom until their fullness. Christ knows the total number of Gentiles who will accept Him forever. In His foreknowledge, God called a people who were not His people, as known in the Old Testament (Hos 2:23; Ro 9:25). Over the years of history, false prophets have erred in predicting the end of the age. Only God knows when the end will occur.

No one knows when the consummation of the age will take place; however, general attitude trends are given in 2 Timothy 3:1-9. What we can know is that Greek and Papal Rome, her children, and her worldwide cults will always exist until the end of the world. The Whore of Revelation will continue to wage war against the Bride, as they travel throughout history, partaking in the cycles of Revelation. They will continue to slay (both intellectually and physically) the Body of Christ until the last martyr is killed. The fullness of the martyrs is already filled up and completed in the mind of God. He knows who will die for Christ's testimony. We are questioned as to whether Islam is considered in this war against the true Bride of Christ. The answer is "yes" and "no." No, because Islam did not exist until approximately six centuries after John penned the Apocalypse. But, yes, Islam is a child of the Orthodox-Catholic connection because even though their fraudulent Koran teaches the ascension of Christ to Heaven, Muslims do not believe that He died on the cross. Their view is "He SEEMED to have died." Muslims obtained their low view of Christ from the Eastern Arian-Sebelius false doctrine and the western Mariolatry.[85]

Revelation 15:2: And I saw what looked like a sea of glass mixed with fire and, standing beside the sea, those who had been victorious over the beast and his image and over the number of his name. They held harps given them by God.

The Sea of Glass is transparent which represents purity, righteousness, and serenity. The Sea of Glass is mixed with fire that is God's wrath, judgment, and strength. This is peace mixed with wrath. The world is at fault, not God, if judgment is poured out upon the world. God has always dealt with humanity in this way (Ex 15:14; Ge 6; Ro1:18). It is not God's fault if people go to Hell. In fact, before the world began, God pre-determined a plan to potentially save all people. He wanted to bless and choose people in this predestined plan (Eph 1:1-7). However, because of peoples' wickedness, they chose Hell rather than God's will.

Five general classes of ungodly people are found in Scripture:

1. Very wicked people – Romans 1:29-31

2. Lovers of Themselves – 2 Timothy 3:2-4

3. Those that claim they know God, but deny Him (They may be morally upright.) – Titus 1:16

4. Disobedient and Obstinate people – Romans 10:21

5. Apostates – Hebrews 6:4-6, 10:26-31

However, in the image presented in Revelation 15:2, we acknowledge only those who are victorious over the Beast in *every way*. That is the Beast, his image, and the number of his name. The victorious ones knew what the Beast represented; they recognized his image in every civilization. Although His image resurrects in various forms everywhere, they still understood what 666 represented. It was a cryptic number; it was the number of a man, throughout the ages, and the man represented a religious system, throughout the ages.

"They held harps given them by God." God is pleased to hear songs of victory sung unto his Name. Therefore, He has rewarded them with the ability to praise Him with what would be considered an apocalyptical musical instrument in Heaven, and they sang a song unto Him. Music is a gift from God that can be used for Him or for Satan. Satan was the Chief Musician of the Mountain of God

(Isa 14:11; Eze 28:13). He was exalted to the rank that could possibly be of the same order as Michael the Archangel.

Because Satan could have been the Chief Musician of the Mountain, Satan used not only persuasive words or vain speech to persuade one third of the angels to pledge their allegiance to him, but Satan also had his musical speech; he carried them into his lie. He had instrumental onomatopoeia. He could naturally reproduce the musical sounds of instruments without engaging the use of a musical instrument. He could also change the mode of communication, naturally, from talking to singing. His voice had the built-in communication skills of vocal, instrumental, and song. Music resonates with the spirit of man. It is a very proven means for evil spirits to enter the heart of man. However, God can also use music to sooth the Spirit, and heavenly music will be heard in eternity. We make a choice now as to what kind of people, things, and music we allow to control our mind.

Revelation 15:3: and sang the song of Moses the servant of God and the song of the Lamb: "Great and marvelous are your deeds, Lord God Almighty. Just and true are your ways, King of the ages.

The Song of Moses in Exodus 15 is interpreted by New Testament Christians as the "Song of the Lamb." It is a glorious song concerning the wondrous works of God throughout the Testaments. The original Song of Moses celebrated the crossing of the Red Sea and the Hebrew deliverance from Egyptian bondage. The Song of the Lamb celebrates the covenant believer's immersion into Christ (the red blood of His death) and deliverance from the bondage of sin. The Song of Moses emphasizes the induction into Moses' leadership. The Song of the Lamb celebrates the induction into the leadership and absolute authority of Christ. Despite the world's idol worship, God gets the glory and victory. Despite the Christian's hardship and pain, God should receive the praise for He is so good. Remember the 144,000 are in this heavenly choir, and since they were redeemed from the Old Testament "earth-world," they can sing a new version of the old Song of Moses. God, through Moses, delivered them from Egyptian slavery. This "new" song celebrates Christ "the Lamb" delivering them from this "earth-world" (underworld Hades) into eternal heavenly realms.

Revelation 15:3, in the original Greek, details God as, "Thou King of Saints." This song is being sung to King Jesus for He is the King of the ages, and His ways are just and true. Even in this time of horrendous persecution and the elevation of terrible beasts and His enemies, Christ remains the King of Salem, "Melchizedek."

Similarities between the Opposition Faced by Daniel and John

Interestingly, Daniel envisions the persecution and dangers of the Jews under the Old Covenant with that of the Christians in the New Covenant. Daniel says the worst enemy of God is the Dragon (Da 7:7, 19). This force represented danger to God's people. For the Jews, the prime enemy was Antiochus Epiphanies, whereas for the saints, the prime enemy is Rome (Da 8:9, 7:29). Daniel and John both recognized that the times were tumultuous and difficult. They also both prophesied that since from the time of Daniel to the persecutions of Antiochus would be about 400 years and from the Revelation to John to Titus Vespasian a few years. In both cases, the immediate future for Israel would *not* be prosperous. However, God would be victorious in the end. The people of Daniel were experiencing slavery, whereas the people of John were suffering in tribulation and persecution. During this time, John writes about the "great and marvelous" characteristics of the Lamb. How true this is! As noted earlier, Daniel and John are facing the same issues. Both are concerned with these three events.

DANIEL 562 B.C.	JOHN 68 A.D.
Antiochus Epiphanies 146 B.C.	Pagan Rome 70 A.D.
Greek Hellenism and her offspring Papal Rome	Apostate Greek & Papal Rome and her denominational children and cults
End of Jewish World	End of Rome/World

During this time of persecution and difficulty for God's people, John was able to hear the Song of the Lamb being sung. This is true Christianity! To trust in the everlasting reign and kingdom of Jesus during visitations of tribulation is a Christian's ultimate test of character. To know the deliverance concerning the future of God's Kingdom (1Co 15:28) and trust in the co-regency of the unified Godhead (Rev 22:3) is an encouraging thought! The Song of the Lamb was a song of salvation, strength, and refreshment (Isa 11:1-10). When Jesus sits upon His Throne of justice and glory, the enemies of God will melt away with fear and dread (Ex 15:14-16). The world's view of the King is a mixed hodge-podge of patriarchs, religious emblems, clergy leaders, archbishops, ayatollahs, mullahs, maharajas, shamans, gurus, and the like. However, the question is *not*, "Who is the King of a denomination, world religion, or cult?" The true question is, "Who is the King of the Nations?" Babylon does not believe that Jesus is the King of the Nations. Nonetheless, for Christians, we know that Babylon is not the King; Caesar is not the king; Satan is not the king; and Christians are not the King. Jesus is the only King! This is the true reason for this victorious song!

Revelation 15:4: Who will not fear you, O Lord, and bring glory to your name? For you alone are holy. All nations will come and worship before you, for your righteous acts have been revealed."

Christ is adamantly anti-one-world order. We must understand that when the Hitlerian-Islamic philosophy of peace through submission, or another just as subtle, Wilsonian philosophy of peace through international passive resistance appears in human history, this must be opposed by Christians and all freedom-loving citizens. What the God of eternity sees is not what short-sighted human beings will see and that is one-world-orders are designed by Satan (for jeopardy, doom, failure, and tyranny – Isa 8:11-13). They are tyrannical and are anti-God because they are anti-freedom (Jn 8:32, 36). Christ plows through cultural barriers to prevent a one-world dictatorship possessing political, military, and religious power. The success of the Kingdom of Christ is not contingent upon compromise or alliance with any political power or any religious movement other than New Covenant Christianity. In this spiritual vision, all nations (ETHNOS-ethnic) will come and worship Him (Ro 15:9-12; Isa 11:1-7; Rev 20:3). These nations who come and worship Him are the select nations in Christ. How do we know Romans 15:9-12 fulfills Isaiah 11:1-7? The Answer: when an Apostle quotes part of the prophecy, the quotes validate the whole thing.

We must remember that in the Old Testament, the Jews were at the center of history. In the New Testament, the "Ecclesia" is the center of history. This assembly is composed of multiple ethnicities. Nationalism is a gift of God.

Revelation 15:5: After this I looked and in heaven the temple, that is, the tabernacle of the Testimony, was opened.

The New Testament Tabernacle is the new governing body of the entire universe. This is an eternal testimony! This New Testament Tabernacle has the authority of Christ. It is here and only here that we have our "Ecclesia" headquarters. As we see throughout this Apocalypse, "The Testimony" governs the whole universe. The New Covenant dynasty takes the place of the Old Covenant Ark.

Revelation 15:6: Out of the temple came the seven angels with the seven plagues. They were dressed in clean, shining linen and wore golden sashes around their chests.

These seven angels with the bowls of wrath are paralleled with the seven trumpets, and may in this verse, actually be the same seven angels given different assignments (Rev 14:18). However, the difference is that the angels with the seven bowls represent severity and finality in their judgments. The angels are holy and pure, dressed in clean and white linen. The angelic dress represents the absolute justice they possess. The golden sash or girdle represents Christ's authority and rank. Sashes were often present in military attire to signify one's possessing rank. Christ is presented as wearing this sash in the beginning of this apocalyptic writing (Rev 1:13). These sashes prove the authority of the King and His ambassadors of judgment.

Revelation 15:7: Then one of the four living creatures gave to the seven angels seven golden bowls filled with the wrath of God, who lives forever and ever.

These four creatures are the same creatures in Revelation 4:6. They are the wisest, bravest, swiftest, and most intelligent creatures of God. These creatures are giving bowls of wrath to the angels to bring about judgments upon the Earth. These creatures comprise infinite organization, which is the epitome of God's nature. Organizational skills are also a part of His gifts to the human race.

Revelation 15:8: And the temple was filled with smoke from the glory of God and from his power, and no one could enter the temple until the seven plagues of the seven angels were completed.

The smoke is God's holy compassion and longsuffering as He withholds final retribution (Ps 77:9, 10). God has always exercised these characteristics. This apocalyptic view of the temple parallels, in a way, the Temple of the Old Covenant (Ex 40:34). However, in the Old Covenant, someone always made intercession for the people. Now, no one can enter into the Holy Place. The judgment and justice of the living God cannot be restrained. Jesus was offered as the *Lamb of God* to present mercy to humanity, but now He is presented as a *Lion with wrath*. No one, not Moses, Aaron, Abraham, Daniel, Job or Noah can intercede before an angry God. After the cross, there is no hope of further propitiation.

Revelation Chapter Sixteen

The bowls of wrath

Revelation 16:1: Then I heard a loud voice from the temple saying to the seven angels, "Go, pour out the seven bowls of God's wrath on the earth."

The loud voice was probably the voice of Christ, "The Judge," in connection with the patron Angel of Fire (Rev 14:18). The loud voice sets the tone for a thundering judgment. The world did not adhere to the judgments and warnings of the trumpets. Now, this loud voice introduced God's undiluted judgment, which trembles throughout the Earth and into the deepest depths of Hades. Millions of lost souls refuse to hear the saving Gospel. They <u>WILL</u> hear this loud voice!

Revelation 16:2: The first angel went and poured out his bowl on the land, and ugly and painful sores broke out on the people who had the mark of the beast and worshiped his image.

The First Angel with the first bowl of wrath is introduced with a judgment upon the land. In this cycle of Revelation, a parallel exists between the plagues of Egypt (Ex 9:11) and the bowls. Apocalyptically, these sores are depicted as literal ulcers that are also caused by nervousness and a lack of peace. God is picking up where he left off in Egypt, but this punishment is final. This is God's undiluted Judgment, not only upon the Earth but also upon all who rejected His Son and are serving as slaves to Satan.

FIRST SEAL (6:1, 2)	FIRST TRUMPET (8:7)	FIRST BOWL (16:1, 2)
The Gospel is spreading throughout the Earth. The Saints are praying. The White Horse is carrying the gospel. Because of the prayers of the Saints, God is judging the Earth with His Word.	Partial Judgment – 1/3 of the Earth is affected. This would include the Earth, sea, and those that dwell on the Earth (people, animals).	The Angel is pouring the bowl out upon the Earth, which results in God's Judgment. Once again, because of the prayers of the saints, God gives his judgment with His warning! It is Now, it is God's complete judgment upon the Earth.

Revelation 16:3: *The second angel poured out his bowl on the sea, and it turned into blood like that of a dead man, and every living thing in the sea died.*

The Second Bowl is judgment upon the sea. All living things die from this judgment. The water turns into blood, which signifies God's complete punishment and power.

In comparing the Seven Seals, Seven Trumpets, and Seven Bowls, the Holy Spirit leads us to discern three Truths. The Seals teach us to understand the "checks and balances" God puts on the moral universe through Christ. The Trumpets teach us that God warns the moral universe through partial, percentage judgment. The Bowls of Wrath teach us that God "in Christ" is preparing the moral universe for judgment in finality and totality.

From beginning to end, humankind has experienced the seven-fold revelation of the sealed contents of "The Book"; humankind have heard the voice of the Seven Trumpets warning them; and lastly, humankind will experience the complete, final wrath of the Holy God through the Seven-fold Crucibles of Fire.

SECOND SEAL (6:3,4)	SECOND TRUMPET (8:9)	SECOND BOWL (16:3)
The Second Seal of the Red Horse – Once again, judgment upon the Earth. This was the power to make war – death. The world has to live with war, there is no way to avoid it.	The Second Trumpet is a partial judgment in which 1/3 of the creatures in the sea died, and 1/3 of the ships were destroyed.	The Second Angel poured out the bowl of complete judgment in the sea and EVERY (ALL) living creatures died.

Revelation 16:4: *The third angel poured out his bowl on the rivers and springs of water, and they became blood.*

God is distributing judgment from the land and sea to the rivers and the springs of water. Not just 1/3 but all source of life is receiving punishment.

THIRD SEAL (6:5, 6)	THIRD TRUMPET (8:10)	THIRD BOWL (16:4-7)
The Third Seal of the Black Horse is famine, pestilence (bad economy). There is depression and many are lacking necessities. Even the simple necessities of bread and water are extremely expensive.	The Third Trumpet affects the water of the streams and drinking water. People are dying because the water is contaminated. Notice that 1/3 of the waters are contaminated.	The Third Angel has poured out his bowl upon the springs of water, and they became blood. The Angel recognized God's right to judge the Earth. They had killed his people. His JUDGMENTS are just. Notice that all the rivers and springs are now blood.

Revelation 16:5-7: Then I heard the angel in charge of the waters say: "You are just in these judgments, you who are and who were, the Holy One, because you have so judged; for they have shed the blood of your saints and prophets, and you have given them blood to drink as they deserve." And I heard the altar respond: "Yes, Lord God Almighty, true and just are your judgments."

This Angel of the Water attributes righteousness to God. He proclaims that God is above reproach. This proclamation is no accident. Any intelligent being recognizes God's purpose and position. The works of Satan deserve this vengeance. The works of Satan killed the saints and shed the blood of the prophets. In addition, the religious and political world is very quick to forget the former judgments of God in the form of tornadoes, hurricanes, tsunamis, earthquakes, blizzards, and the like. We are told that an extreme Arctic cold that can paralyze a city, its transportation system, and its airport, is a "freak" of nature. Judgment Day will finally stop what some people call "the freak!"

If we view this passage from a Christian perspective, we understand God's judgments on the natural world from a different perspective than from those of a non-Christian. A Christian's view is, "We are all getting exactly what we deserve." However, to the outside world, only anger and curses cloud their minds. There is no understanding concerning God. Non-Christians do not understand why God holds the world accountable for their lifestyles. The masses of people cannot understand why God is so "just." Justice is His very nature, and He will not change His mind unless people are under His blood covenant. His judgments are just and true. Lest those saved by God's grace take this warning lightly, God tells us, "Judgment begins at the House of God" (1Pe 4:17, 18; 2Pe 2:17-22)

Revelation 16:8: *The fourth angel poured out his bowl on the sun, and the sun was given power to scorch people with fire.*

God designed the Sun with the power of photosynthetic life and the power to scorch people with fire. Fire will eventually destroy the Earth. God can create a fire and heat greater than the Sun. The fire of Hell cannot be the fire of the Sun for the fire of Hell does not produce light. It burns, but it does not consume (Dt 28: 22). This is a dark everlasting fire (Jude 6, 13). This darkness can blot out the Sun (Rev 9:2, 16:8). Is this a literal darkness? Yes. God is light and where there is no God, there is no light. This applies to both mental and physical darkness.

Revelation 16:9: *They were seared by the intense heat and they cursed the name of God, who had control over these plagues, but they refused to repent and glorify him.*

Christians are sanctified through suffering. The wicked curse God's name when they suffer (Da 9:11). Because of their hardened hearts, the wicked curse God. They have no future, no promise, and no reward. The only thing the wicked have to look forward to is the wrath and anger of God. They do not understand or know the future. They do not have a covering from this wrath because they rejected Christ's covering of their sins.

FOURTH SEAL (6:7-8)	FOURTH TRUMPET (8:10)	FOURTH BOWL (16:8)
The Fourth Seal of the pale horse equals 1/4 of the Earth is killed. This is partial judgment. The wicked die and await eternal Hell in Hades first and then Gehenna.	The Fourth Trumpet affects 1/3 of the constellations. The Sun, Moon, and stars.	The Fourth Bowl is poured out upon the constellations. The Sun is scorching the people with fire. All the people are affected by this judgment. This fire will destroy the Earth.

Revelation 16:10, 11: *The fifth angel poured out his bowl on the throne of the beast, and his kingdom was plunged into darkness. Men gnawed their tongues in agony and cursed the God of heaven because of their pains and their sores, but they refused to repent of what they had done.*

This is anarchy and anti-Christian government. Babylon and all her children gnaw their tongues and curse God because of His judgment upon them (Hab 3:12, 13). These bowls are resonating fiercely. All lost people are affected through these catastrophes; however, this particular judgment is upon Babylon and her kingdom. This is not a separate judgment but is part and parcel of the overall judgment of the moral universe. Although Satan governs all antichrist religions, we understood that his throne of authority is not in Mecca, Constantinople, Rome, Salt Lake City or any earthly headquarters. The throne of Satan's Kingdom is in Hades.

FIFTH SEAL (6:9)	FIFTH TRUMPET (9:1-12)	FIFTH BOWL (16:10, 11)
The Fifth Seal is justice. Those slain by their persecutors are crying out for redemption and judgment. However, this is yet to take place. Those slain had been persecuted and killed.	The Fifth Trumpet shows the banishment of Satan from Heaven forever. This judgment upon Satan is partial at first. Satan is banished from accessing God's Throne. However, he still engages in covert warfare against the Body of Christ, and the world is stupefied as to the intensity of this battle. The world lashes into a deathly sleep while Satan's militant host invades them with great wrath.	The Fifth Bowl is the complete wrath of God upon those who persecuted the Congregation of Christ. The Beast, his kingdom, and his followers are cast into darkness where there is weeping and gnashing of teeth (Mt 8:12).

Revelation 16:12: The sixth angel poured out his bowl on the great river Euphrates, and its water was dried up to prepare the way for the kings from the East.

Spiritually speaking, the Kings from the East and North must all cross the Euphrates River to attack spiritual Jerusalem, where God's holy ones are dwelling. Their weapons are the most powerful weapons of ideological and philosophical warfare. The Euphrates River is a dividing line, and it marks the divisions between what New Covenant Christians believe and what false prophets and the world has been trying to teach us to believe. This battle between "Truth and error" (1Jn 4:1-6) has been ongoing, but as we shall see, the apocalyptic significance of the Euphrates River marks the place where God finally brings all of His power to bear upon our enemy. We are encouraged to look into the future and know assuredly, that after the long struggle with evil and error down through the years, we know the battle between truth and error will soon be over at the Battle of the Euphrates River.

SIXTH SEAL (6:12)	SIXTH TRUMPET (9:13)	SIXTH BOWL (16:10-16)
The Sixth Seal is the countdown to judgment. The universe is affected by the Lord's Judgment. The people of the Earth disperse for cover from the wrath of the Lamb, but there is no place to hide. The great day of wrath has come and none will withstand it. The end is near.	The Sixth Trumpet warning from God pronounces a judgment upon 1/3 of the Earth. It introduces a great war that is taking place. However, the results of the wars and the wars themselves are not enough to bring about the Earth's repentance.	The Sixth Bowl introduces the final war between God and his holy ones and the Satanic forces. They have recruited demons, kings, and nations to unite themselves against God. However, they will lose. This is the great battle, which results in a condemnation of eternal hell for Satan and his followers.

Revelation 16:13: Then I saw three evil spirits that looked like frogs; they came out of the mouth of the dragon, out of the mouth of the beast and out of the mouth of the false prophet.

The three evil spirits are the unholy trinity of Satan. They are the Beast out of the Sea, the Beast from the Land, and Babylon. They look like frogs because they operate under the cover of utter darkness. They constantly croak, but never say anything. A perfect example of this is modern-day "speaking in tongues." This false "tongue speaking" is a constant rant without meaning or significance. These frogs have big mouths, but they have no comprehension concerning their words. They use their tongues to kill Christians, spiritually. One might compare the croaking of frogs to modern-day college professors in the realm of evolutionary science, philosophy, politics, logic, social studies, media commentary, and art. Of course, "secret disciples" always exist among these groups who do their job as best they can with the love of Jesus down deep in their hearts. Ungodly people of whatever group or profession make lots of noise, but eternally, it signifies nothing.

The one plague that both God and Pharaoh's magicians in Egypt preformed was the multiplication of frogs. God won the day, and He will also win the day against these frogs by proving His infinite wisdom, power, and wrath. But the senseless frogs keep on mating and croaking, completely unaware of the fact that their end is drawing neigh. A good modern-day example of false "tongue speaking" is that insane prejudice against anyone who leans, be it ever so slightly, toward publicly calling Islam what it is – a religious/political tyranny that sponsors and exports the murder of infidels (non-Muslims). We deceive ourselves when we call Islam the ridiculous and politically correct "Religion of Peace." All Muslims who read their Koran know the murderous nature of Islam, but some become so paranoid that they want to murder anyone in cold blood who reminds them of this doctrine, which is in their very own "holy" book (www.thereligionofpeace.com : What does the Religion of Peace Teach About Violence?). The aforementioned website gives 109 verses that advocate war against infidels for the sake of Islamic rule. We have difficulty believing that any rationale human being who is created by a Holy God and possessing a God-given sense of divine sensibilities could ever embrace, let alone tolerate, such a religion of hate.

Revelation 16:14: They are spirits of demons performing miraculous signs, and they go out to the kings of the whole world, to gather them for the battle on the great day of God Almighty.

These demonic spirits are causing battles between the kings (rulers) of the earth and God. These demonic spirits are also able to seduce presidents, rulers, and leaders in this great day to rebel against the Holy One. This is a great analogy that only the Lord could compare to one of His biological creations of comedy. If you want to hear "croaking frogs," just go to an evolutionary science lectures, or better yet, a liberal political rally. How about a global warming climate change lecture by Professor Gore – Nobel Peace Prize winner and holder of a Ph.D. in Frog Croaking?

Muslim clerics fanatically forbid Christian evangelism in their nations and forbid the reading of Scripture. Why? Because they know this would lead their blind disciples to undergo a universal revival and turn to the Christ of a loving, merciful God. One of the cruellest and sad episodes among nations is when political leaders enable their religious leaders to force their will upon the spiritual conscience of deceived followers by forbidding so much as praying a prayer in Christ's mighty, intercessory Name. The dreary conclusion is that if they never hear of Christ the Savior, they will only meet Him as Judge.

We are not completely certain, but it does not appear that God is trying to be funny when He compares false prophets to frogs. It is so great a disappointment to Creator God. He really has nothing else on Earth to compare with. The eternal Gospel is the most powerful message on Earth, and it is "the greatest story ever told." So our God gave us brains and ears to hear and entertain this message from Heaven, and we in turn, as His creatures, listen to the croaking of pea-brained frogs. Such "babbling-babylonish" creatures dissuade us from obedience to the Gospel of such a marvelous God and Savior. We suffer the world's greatest loss under the croaking of the world's greatest croakers of nonsense.

Revelation 16:15: "Behold, I come like a thief! Blessed is he who stays awake and keeps his clothes with him, so that he may not go naked and be shamefully exposed."

True Christians seek diligently for accuracy and honesty in academics, industry, sports, business, politics, science, and all other disciplines of life, especially religion. Christians should not permit their righteous robes to be taken away, lest they be found naked and shamefully exposed in judgment. This represents the people on Judgment Day who are not covered by the Blood of Christ. Through demonic and puffed-up speech, those who have lost their righteous robes have been deceived by Satan's frogs and have been carried away into darkness. The Body of Christ, which is His Congregation, needs to be constantly aware of false doctrine. They must not be apathetic and foolish like the five foolish virgins (Mt

25:1-9). They should always be wearing their God appointed clothes, which are their robes of righteousness. Do not be angry when a prophet like Elijah uses satire to denounce the Lord's enemy. Usually love drives the proclamation of truth, but when the enemy spurns love, the last resort is to rebuke false doctrine by any and all means. No true prophet of God ever enjoyed the proclamation of doom and judgment. It is for the good of God's enemies for them, as a last resort, to be rescued from the flames of wrath.

In the last three blocks, we reiterate the events that led up to the Seventh Seal, Trumpet, and Bowl, and then compare these events, especially the way in which the 7 Trumpets are correlated to the Seven Bowls of Wrath. The symbolic understanding of "Trumpets" is that they stand for partial judgments and temporary warnings. The understanding of the "Bowls of Wrath" is that they are final and permanent in judgment. The Seventh is always the last. It brings anti-Messiah evil opposition and the world system to an end (Rev 8:1, 11:15, 16:17).

SEVENTH SEAL (8:1,7)	SEVENTH TRUMPET (11:15)	SEVENTH BOWL (16:17)
There was silence in Heaven as opposed to the "noise of thunder" heard at the opening of the First Seal (6:1) and the great voice, "It is done!" at the pouring out of the Seventh Bowl of Wrath. After the horrible effects of opening the first six seals (the White, Red, Black and Pale Horsemen, the martyrs crying out, the Great Earthquake and the Lord's supernatural	Prior to this last Trumpet, the Kingdoms of this world have successfully defied and instigated hostility against Christ's Kingdom. Through the eons of time, the Godhead has kept this international aggression in check through intercessory prayer (8:3), fiery scorching of 1/3 of the earth (8:7), infecting 1/3 of the seas (8:9) and inland waters (8:10), cosmic	Despite Satan's fierce opposition, Christ is born and is caught up to His Throne (12:1-17). Satan diverts his vengeance toward New Testament Christianity (12:17). Thorough the sea-going beast, Satan employs Roman-type political power (13:1-10), and a union of church-state through the land-going beast "false prophet" (13:11), and the whole world goes

SEVENTH SEAL (8:1,7)	SEVENTH TRUMPET (11:15)	SEVENTH BOWL (16:17)
gathering of the Old Testament 144,000 — before the Desolation of their Nation), the whole world is NOW silent (1/2 hour, perhaps the last count between time and eternity) before the Judge of the universe. The world has experienced recurrent cosmic, moral and military judgments from the first to the last (7th) Seal. Now they are horror-struck in stunned silence as they cringe before the God they never knew (2Th 1:8).	upheaval affecting 1/3 of the luminous spheres (8:12), and invasion of evil, tormenting spirits from Satan's abyss (9:1-12), and an international offensive of terrorism and war, but the world ignored this as reason to repent (9:21). The world was about to be judged by New Covenant Christianity "little book" (10:1), but the actual time of "dooms day" was withheld, "sealed up" (10:1-4). "But in the days of the voice of this Seventh Angel" the word of judgment is settled, now and then (10:7), so no matter how bittersweet The New Testament may be, "Preach it!" (10:9-11). The New Testament measures the true temple (11:1, 2). New Testament witnesses are persecuted and murdered (11:7-11), but they will prevail (11:11), will see their enemies destroyed (11:12-14) and the Seventh Trumpet	to war against The Messiah. But light is shed from Mt. Zion as the 144,000 who looked forward to the coming Messiah, now appear with Christ on Mt. Zion as children of God the Father through Christ the Son (14:1-5). The Gospel is being preached in a dark world (14:6); Babylon is being exposed (14:8); and in lieu of Satan's trinity of evil (Sea Beast, Land Beast and the Whore of Babylon), the Saints are being blessed, are going to be with Jesus at death, and in spite of the bloody slaughter, they are faithful and patient through it all (14:12, 13). Unlike the partial judgments of the Seven Trumpets, the Bowls of Wrath are poured out in increments of six final, complete judgments that do not affect PART (1/3), but ALL of the Earth (16:2), sea (16:3), inland waters (16:4), cosmic solar

SEVENTH SEAL (8:1,7)	SEVENTH TRUMPET (11:15)	SEVENTH BOWL (16:17)
	announces that the Kingdoms of this world will come under Christ's reign (11:15), be judged (11:18), and be destroyed also by the prophets, saints, and those who fear God. God is already warming up to this final end that is very near (11:19).	system (16:8), Satan's kingdom of darkness and earthly Babylon with her children (16:10), the historic, apocalyptic River Euphrates, will "dry up" and pave the way for the final battle (16:12). Thus the Seventh Bowl is "poured out into the air" (1Th 4:17) and this Final Judgment is unlike any judgment experienced by all humanity since the beginning of time (16:17-21). "IT IS DONE!" (Rev 21:6).

Revelation 16:16-18: Then they gathered the kings together to the place that in Hebrew is called Armageddon. The seventh angel poured out his bowl into the air, and out of the temple came a loud voice from the throne, saying, "It is done!" Then there came flashes of lightning, rumblings, peals of thunder and a severe earthquake. No earthquake like it has ever occurred since man has been on earth, so tremendous was the quake.

This place, Armageddon or "Har-Megiddo," is the last great battle between truth and error. This battle is paralleled in Revelation 20:7-10. Armageddon is the battle between God and the satanic forces, between good and evil.

In the ancient days of the Old Testament, Megiddo was a prominent place for battles. Armageddon was an overlook of the Plain of Megiddo. Any competent military commander's battle plan required his taking control of this strategic area (Jdg 4, 5, 5:19, 20, 9:7; Ex 38, 39; 2Ki 9:27, 23:26-29; Zec 12:11). Megiddo, which means valley of troops, was a familiar battleground. This Hebrew word

(Strong's 4023) for Megiddo simply means "rendezvous." Strong says it is taken from "Gadad," which means to "crowd, press together, and assemble by troops." Another definition is "A band of marauding invaders, army units, troops, who raid and plunder the enemy" (Strong's 1413, 1416). "Gadad" can also mean to make an incision into the skin (Dt 14:1) or mustering invading troops (Mic 5:11). Since Megiddo is used in so many ways, we generally understand it to be a "place of troops." It was a familiar battleground.

When used apocalyptically, we must understand the historical meaning of the word and its application in Revelation. In Revelation, a great event and final conflict will occur at Megiddo. It is consummate nonsense to think of this as a human instituted nuclear war. The real war is in the hearts and minds of humanity. God is a spirit, and His war will not need the deployment of manmade weapons. Also, the apocalyptic Megiddo of Revelation is not just a geographical spot on the Earth. It is the "four corners of the earth," and the soldiers of warfare are "the sand of the sea."

For us to properly understand the context of this apocalyptic description, we must venture into the Old Testament. A key to our understanding of the present is to investigate the past. Armies naturally met and fought at Megiddo. It is known as a ground for remarkable slaughters (2Ki 23:29; Jdg 4:16, 5:19) and triumphant victories. Revelation 16:16 corresponds with Revelation 20:7, 8, which says,

> "Now when the thousand years have expired, Satan will be released from his prison and will go out to deceive the nations which are in the four corners of the earth, Gog and Magog, to gather them together to battle, whose number is as the sand of the sea. They went up on the breadth of the earth and surrounded the camp of the saints and the beloved city."

Gog and Magog were actually two people in the Old Testament. Their genealogies are found in Genesis 10:2 and 1 Chronicles 1:5. Gog is one of the descendants of Reuben (1Ch 5:4), and Magog was a descendent of Japheth (Ge 10:2; 1Ch 1:5). Magog was a grandson of Noah, and he migrated to Syria. Magog, Meshach, Tubal, and Gomer are all sons of Japheth and founders of the northern group of nations.

Old Millennial scholars were in error when they taught that Russia was "Rosh," and its capital was "Meshach." They also take Tubal in Siberia to be Tobolsk. This is fanatical phonics.[86] Dr. Roger Chambers said, "This is not phonology, but phonyology." Since Russia has fallen as a world power, Bible scholars are no longer looking to them to fulfill the Ezekiel 38 and 39 "phonyology." Rather than learn the apocalyptic truth of these matters, in their insane bend, these scholars attempt to find a modern-day country to resemble "Roch, Meshach, and Tubal." We must understand, however, that just because a word has a certain phonic sound to another word does not mean it is the same thing. This fallacy is called "fanatical phonics," and it contributes nothing to Biblical truth from a hermeneutical standpoint.

In Revelation, Gog of Magog represents and personifies all ungodly leaders who have hated God's Covenant down through the ages. Revelation is not describing one particular man, but a consummation and culmination of all antichrist evil to the end of the world. All physical battles have spiritual emphasis. Whether it is gang warfare, nuclear warfare, or just a street fight, we have to agree or disagree with our human spiritual conscience to make decisions to go to war or pull the trigger or plunge the knife. Contrary to modern psychology, it is our decisions to obey evil spirits that precipitate mass killings. Since the spirits instigate the battles, in the final analysis, it is the spirits who will suffer the loss in this battle. This, in no way means "The Devil made me do it," because the evil we choose to do is a result of our allowing the Devil and his spirits to enter our temple. Every eye will see it, and Hades will burst out of its miserable domain and partake in it. Hades is the first immediate stop on the way to eternal Hell. This great earthquake shakes the very depth of Satan's domain. He will then be brought face-to-face with his Creator and be defeated.

Revelation 16:19: The great city split into three parts, and the cities of the nations collapsed. God remembered Babylon the Great and gave her the cup filled with the wine of the fury of his wrath.

All Babylonian divisions can be categorized under three groups. There is much confusion concerning how New Testament Christianity fragmentized into thousands of spin-off sects. But Babylon, essentially, split into three parts, and we will find Roman Catholicism, Greek Orthodox, and Protestant cults until the end of time. Without personally judging all the members of these cults, we can know for sure that their hierarchal system will experience a total breakdown, complete destruction, and an end to their existence. Jesus said, "Every plant that my father has not planted will be rooted up" (Mt 15:13). We can think, "If my hierarchical system is going to be destroyed by God, I should leave it." But, such thinking is not correct because the Babylonian schisms have behind and within their systems the most powerful spirits in the world to retain their converts and believers.

The Muslims, Buddhist, Hindus, and other eastern religions say that they are not in this mix of the Babylonia trio; therefore, they think themselves exempt. However, this is not so. Believers in eastern religions should not flatter themselves; they were not even established in truth by Christ. Lest we seem prejudiced, we must remember that Christ is also not at the center of most western religious thought.

Revelation 16:20, 21: *Every island fled away and the mountains could not be found. From the sky huge hailstones of about a hundred pounds each fell upon men. And they cursed God on account of the plague of hail, because the plague was so terrible.*

This Revelation text uses the analogy of a criminal with a consuming desire to flee from justice. They flee to outbuildings, flee to the basement, hide in closets, hide in abandoned boats, or under canvass, run into dense, wooded thickets, remote areas, and climb mountains (even jump into water) to escape the wrath of an avenging God. My State Patrol man (an Elder of the Lord's Heritage) tells me a man even hid in a doghouse.

"The land has vanished," which means God's enemies have no place to regain any strength or their footing. The mountains are nowhere to be found. This symbolizes that those fleeing God have no place to hide and survive. Because they are tormented, they blasphemed God. The supernatural cause is at last made known by the enormous hailstones. Ordinary hailstones figure into God's providential arrangement in nature and judgment. Meteorologists dismiss this as simply "acts of Mother Nature."

This will not be true on the Last Day when the worldwide meteorologists from Oslo, Norway to Cape Town, South Africa; Tokyo, Japan to London, England stutter, stammer, and stand aghast at their last broadcast. Unforgiven sinners will curse God; yet they will bow their knee before the victorious Christ (Ro 14:11; Php 3:10). If our sins are not hidden beneath the Blood of Christ, there is nowhere else to hide them. The curse of the world's sin fell upon the propitious Christ. In the end, unforgiven sinners will curse God, yet bow their knees before the victorious Christ. How true is the axiom, "You can't have one without the other"! Christ is either our vicarious redeemer, who saves us, or He is our victorious conqueror, who judges us.

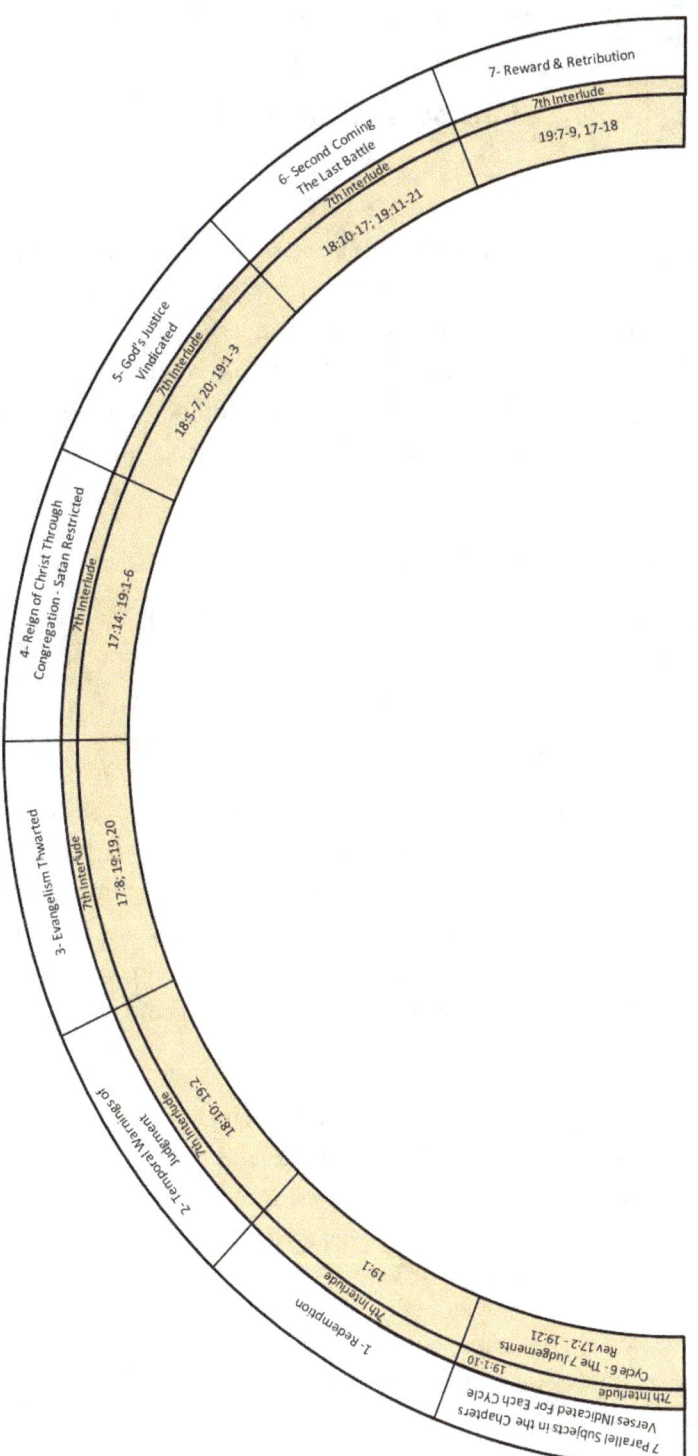

CYCLE 6 – THE SEVEN JUDGMENTS

Christ in Conquest

The Woman on the Beast

This section parallels Revelation 13. This is the sixth parallel section of our rainbow. Some scholars think there are only four cycles because the number seven is so prevalent in the seven congregations, seals, trumpets, and bowls. However, just as the Lord invites the wise to evaluate 666 (13:16), He may allow those with Godly wisdom to examine the seven themes in three other cycles. We know with certainty; however, that since Revelation 16: 21 brought us to the last cycle, a new cycle begins here.

Revelation Chapter Seventeen

Revelation 17:1, 2: One of the seven angels who had the seven bowls came and said to me, "Come, I will show you the punishment of the great prostitute, who sits on many waters. With her the kings of the earth committed adultery and the inhabitants of the earth were intoxicated with the wine of her adulteries."

John begins to describe the Woman on the Beast in more detail. She is the object of God's perfect hatred. The New Covenant Christians should hate her false doctrines and creeds (Ps 139:20-22). John describes the Woman as having power over the kingdoms of the Earth because of her religious institutions. In Chapter 12, she was a radiant bride who loved the saints; however, after persecution, the Woman is now the whore of nations who is waging war against the Holy Ones of God.

Remember, the Dragon chased the radiant Woman into the wilderness (Rev 12:13, 14), and the Dragon dispatched his political beast with ten horns of power and seven heads of authority to woo and seduce her. The Dragon succeeded beyond measure for now she is riding the Beast's back and directing the Beast that once pursued her (Rev 17:3).

At this point, we need to make some very serious observations. The same word that is translated "wilderness" in the first verse is translated "desert" in the next verse. Professor of Greek, Donald A. Nash, believed that a great hindrance in understanding the New Testament is the failure of translators to translate the same word appearing in different places as consistently as possible. Dr. Nash translated the New Testament into a work that he called a literal and consistent version of the New Testament.[87] This need for consistency is especially true as we consider our current Biblical text. Whatever the word is translated in Revelation 12:14 should be translated the same in Revelation 17:3. The *Holman CSB Bible* and some other translations translate the Greek word *eremos* as "wilderness" (Rev 12:14) and the same word "desert" (Rev 17:3). This is a tragic mistake.

Just as a forensic expert looks for clues that lead to usable evidence, so God expects us, apocalyptic readers, to look for clues and find important conclusions in apocalyptic literature. When translators alter the consistent use of a word, given by inspiration, for the purpose of their attempting to enlighten the context for us, the translators produce obfuscation, not clarity. Translators should have translated the word "desert" consistently in Revelation 12 and in Revelation 17 rather than translate the same word alternately "wilderness" in one place and "desert" in another. In doing so, the translators obscure what the text is trying to teach. By alternating words, translators can obscure truth and knowledge. We suppose that a reader with reasonable understanding of the text would compare the words "wilderness" and "desert" and see that they are both the same place, but we wonder if the translators are just "lexicographers," not theologians.

The evidence is overwhelming. We have a radiant woman in Revelation 12:1; she is clothed with the majesty of Heaven. Now, we have a woman who is called a whore. We have a woman who is chased by the Dragon into the wilderness, and now the Dragon has overtaken her in the wilderness. We have a woman who is persecuted by the Dragon in Revelation 12, and now, she is riding the Dragon's back. The vision that we saw in Revelation 12 is picked up again in Revelation 17.

The clear apocalyptic picture is given. This picture shows how clever the Dragon was in not trying to destroy the Woman, but instead, gave her a seat on his back. No greater evidence can be given of a departure from New Covenant Christianity to apostate *Christianity* than this symbolic vision. Students of God's word learn more by seeing this vision than 1,000 volumes of print on the subject. Once the Woman sponsored the apostolic teaching of "the twelve stars"; now she is exporting venomous false doctrine in conjunction with the world's political power, culture, and philosophy. No greater curse could be designed in the depths of Hades to destroy pure and primitive New Covenant Christianity than this scheme developed by the Dragon himself.

No wonder God, Himself, celebrates those who did not succumb to the Woman and the Dragon and resisted her doctrine by calling them his glorious Ecclesia (Ep 3:20, 21). The controlling theme of the Book of Ephesians may be when God could boast about His creation, His majesty, and His power over creation; He refuses to do so. God simply boasts in the glorious Ecclesia.

Revelation 17: 3, 4: Then the angel carried me away in the Spirit into a desert. There I saw a woman sitting on a scarlet beast that was covered with blasphemous names and had seven heads and ten horns. The woman was dressed in purple and scarlet, and was glittering with gold, precious stones and pearls. She held a golden cup in her hand, filled with abominable things and the filth of her adulteries.

This Dragon is composed of an unholy trinity, i.e., the Beast, the False Prophet, and the Babylonian whore. All three work for the Dragon. Upon this Whore are the blasphemous names. She is blaspheming the apostolic Christianity that she once embraced! How better to destroy God's children than this? Examples of these blasphemous names are Universal Father, Revered Holy Father, His Holiness, the Right Revered, Supreme Head of the Church, the Father of all Families, The Successor of Peter, the Prince of the Apostles, Infallible Vicar of Christ, the Ex-Cathedra, etc. She makes her clergy pass a blasphemous exam. They are subject to calling their superior the "Holy Father" and the "Substitute Son of God." (To examine an in-depth article concerning the "Steps of Departure," see Addendum A.)

Revelation 17:5, 6: This title was written on her forehead: MYSTERY BABYLON THE GREAT THE MOTHER OF PROSTITUTES AND OF THE ABOMINATIONS OF THE EARTH. I saw that the woman was drunk with the blood of the saints, the blood of those who bore testimony to Jesus. When I saw her, I was greatly astonished.

John describes two brides in the Book of Revelation. They are the Bride of Christ (Rev 19:7, 9) and the Bride (Whore) who is married to Satan. The Bride of Satan is intoxicated on the blood of Saints. This Woman and the Woman in Chapter 12 are as different as night and day. At one point, they were the same, but the devil has conquered this Woman. The woman does not kill sinners; she kills saints. She hates them because they remind her of the truth that she once embraced. Because of her reprobate mind, she can no longer embrace this truth. When people are in this condition, the only way to Heaven is to return to the truth. This is why some of the ex-brothers and sisters who have championed the love of Christ have forsaken New Covenant Christianity and have become its worst enemy. A rank and file hard-core pagan sinner will respect truth more than these ex-brothers and sisters will. The Congregation of Christ eventually buckled under persecution until only a small remnant of the faithful remained.

During this period (officially 533-1793 A.D.), the true Ecclesia of Christ went into hiding and the worldly *Universal* Church took over. Satan made an alliance with the Woman, and they are waging war against the remnant of Christ. Throughout history, the remnant is very difficult to find. The true Ecclesia is the "naos," the inner sanctuary, but the Whore is the "hieros," which is the outer court (Rev 11:1, 2). A remnant is simply a small group that always remains faithful. The following are examples of God's Remnant throughout history:

1. Those in Egypt who came out with Moses (Ps 78:42).

2. Those few who entered the Promised Land (Dt 1:36).

3. Those few who did not bow their knee to the image of Baal (1Ki 19:18; Ro 11:4).

4. Those who were left after the Babylonian captivity (Eze 2:1).

5. Those who were left after the abomination of desolation in 70 A.D. (Ro 9:27, 11:5).

6. Those who were left after the Woman's apostasy (Rev 12:17).

7. Those who preserve New Covenant Christianity and maintain the faith until the end – "When the Son of man cometh, shall he find the faith on the earth?" (Lk 18:8)

While Orthodoxies and Catholicism are surprisingly tolerant of New Testament Christianity today, Islam (by drinking the blood of those they identify as Christian infidels) is now drinking the same cup as the Whore. Of course, Muslims are almost hopelessly ignorant of the difference between a Christian (in name only), and a person governed by the New Testament dispensation. Interestingly, some of the actions and things that Muslims eschew, New Testament Christians eschew, also. For instance, in the Muslim mindset, most American women dress like a whore. Obviously, the Muslim oligarchy forces their women to cover themselves from head-to-toe because they want to control their women and not simply to exude modesty. But Christian American women are also commanded to "dress modestly," knowing that their real beauty is "the hidden man of the heart" (1Pe 3:4). The difference is that American women will dress modestly because they choose to do so.

The mother's false doctrines can be inherited by her children and become more powerful than those of their mother. Two thousand years ago, it would have been very easy, and still is, to leave Christ and go into the worldly Babylon of confusion. Interestingly, Papal Rome eventually began to lose its power after the Dark Ages. Martin Luther delivered a deathblow to Catholicism. John Calvin, John Wesley and others followed. However, the momentum shift toward the decline of Catholicism in America came when Restorationist Alexander Campbell debated Bishop John Purcell in Cincinnati, Ohio in 1820. During this Restoration Movement, the Whore was no longer the worst enemy of the true Ecclesia. In fact, many of the children she produced in denominationalism, with false doctrines inherited from her, became more powerful than their mother. Sadly, 2,000 years later as we write today (in the 21st Century), the vision statement of the Restoration, "speak where the Bible speaks," is almost forgotten. The thunder of that vision has lost its appeal under the encroaching clouds of modern-day religious culturalism.

The Apostle John's use of the term Babylon to describe Religious Rome is an exact description of that institution. The Babylon of Old is composed of confusion (Tower of Babel – Ge 11:9) and destruction. They were God's worst enemy; they destroyed the Temple and Jerusalem; and they persecuted God's people. As the mightiest empire of their day, they would carry captives of other nations into their society, including God's people. However, Babylon ended (Jer 51:37, 41, 42, 44, 47, 49, 54, and 58). Men did not destroy Babylon, God did. This city was destroyed; it will never to be rebuilt again. Christ will destroy Religious Rome and her children (2Th 2:8). After Babylon's destruction, the old Babylonian priesthood was transferred to Pergamum, and then to Rome.

John describes Babylon as the most bloodthirsty enemy of the Ecclesia. She is the author of confusion and a clear-cut picture of departure from the true Congregation. Ignorance of Scripture is a source of captivity of God's people. Religious

Rome is powerful, recognized, and persuasive on a worldwide scale. Rome has deceived the nations with its lies, and like the Old Babylon, can only be brought down by God, who will honor the truth of His apostolic messengers down through the ages. No wonder, of all Heaven's population, the Apostles are distinguished as those rejoicing at Babylon's final fall (Rev 18:20).

Religious Rome has violated the New Testament in every way, shape, and form. Rome allows its clergy to have relations with women, but not marry. Alexander Campbell and his debate with Purcell propounded this truth. He quoted Alphonsus Liguori (1696-1787) who advocated that a priest could keep a concubine, which was a venial sin, by paying a pecuniary fine. However, if he married, he committed a mortal sin. Purcell protested and denied that the standard moralist, Liguori, ever taught such a thing, at which time Campbell requested that the moderator read Liguori's writing from the *Moral Theology of Liguori,* Vol. 8, on p. 444.

> "A bishop, however poor he may be, cannot appropriate to pecuniary fines, without license of the Apostolical See. But he ought to apply them to pious uses. Much less can he apply those fines to anything else but pious uses, which the Council of Trent has laid upon non-resident clergymen, or upon those clergymen who keep concubines."

Because it took Campbell three days after the debate to find and document the Liguori quote with signed affidavits by three ministers, the Catholics wanted to proclaim Purcell the technical victor. The Devil does not fight fair, and of course, this is exactly what we would expect.

The Roman Church instituted the dogma of sprinkling at the Council of Ravenna in 1311 A.D. The Pope himself believes he has the right to change God's decrees because he believes he is the Vicarious Felii Dei, and he speaks "ex-cathedra." However, Babylon (Rome) is not married to Christ, but to the Dragon. Religious Babylon is of the world, and thus, has nullified any relationship it has with the Head of All Being (Col 2:18, 19).

Religious Babylon and its followers have managed to create a love-hate relationship with Christ in order to serve their purposes. Babylon is necessary as a fine screen to test those that are either for or against Christ. The locusts are sent from Hades to torment and turn the world against Christ. The historical thread that runs through the parallelism of Revelation is the utter contrast between the Bride of Christ and the Whore of Rome. This continuous Historical View is the view I take in Revelation as it relates to the beginning and the end of the true Bride and the Whore. Babylon had taken over what she believes to be total control of the world, but she will be proven wrong. In the end, only one woman will remain, and she is the Bride of Christ.

After Rome fell in 476 A.D., conditions developed for establishing ten separate kingdoms, all of which reluctantly derived their right to rule from Rome. The calendar was revised; there was a changing of times, seasons, and recognition of holy days. Latin became the official language of the Roman Papacy. Because Latin was not the vernacular or spoken language of the people, this led to great Babylonian confusion (2Th 2:6). The Pope does not reject blasphemous titles and in the minds of people, he willingly sits in the temple of God. He accepts homage due only to God. In fact, Benedict XIII said in 1726 A.D. that Religious Rome was the mother of all believers and the mistress of all the churches.[88]

On Christmas Day, 800 A.D., Pope Leo III conferred the title of Holy Roman Emperor on Charlemagne. This act combined the Roman and Frank realms into the Holy Roman Empire. This act showed the power and wealth of the Papacy within Europe. After Charlemagne's death, the Treaty of Verdun divided the Empire. Thus, began a ceaseless struggle between Popes and Kings for supremacy. Babylon, as represented by the Roman Church, prostituted herself among the kingdoms and flaunted her zeal for power and control.

Revelation 17: 7, 8: *then the angel said to me: "Why are you astonished? I will explain to you the mystery of the woman and of the beast she rides, which has the seven heads and ten horns. The beast, which you saw, once was, now is not, and will come up out of the Abyss and go to his destruction. The inhabitants of the earth whose names have not been written in the book of life from the creation of the world will be astonished when they see the beast, because he once was, now is not, and yet will come.*

John is greatly amazed by this Woman. He knew her appearance was a shadow of the once pure, radiant woman. She has victory, power, and control. John also seems to be intrigued at the power she possessed and the beast she rides. He is soon told of the swift punishment that will come upon her. This Beast was and is not! There is no hope for Pagan or Political Rome. She is at a total loss. Why would one remain in a religion that has no hope? This is no doubt a ponderous question. John is encapsulating both Pagan and Papal Rome as one. Like Pagan Rome, Papal Rome was an extremely powerful religious institution.

Today, Papal Rome is still powerful; however, it has received much chastisement and punishment from the witnesses and people of the Earth. The equivalent to this today would be if God brought the greatest country in the world, America, to its knees in due submission because of its own devices and evil. This is what happened to Rome. The nation of Pagan Rome existed underneath Caesars and Tyrants, but after Nero, the Empire began to diminish. Only a select few (remnant) were not surprised at its fall…those who were Christians!

John said, "The beast that you saw once was." This Beast is a composite of all former political powers leading up to Rome for she has the emblems of the lion, bear, leopard, and the dragon. What we would consider a dragon today would be called a giant lizard or dinosaur. This is going back into history. The Beast and Dragon are conjugally joined together. They have the dragonish head, which stands for Rome.

John reverses the historical order by giving a composite view of a declination from the dinosaur-dragon (Rome) to the Leopard (Greece), Bear (Medo-Persia), and the Lion (Babylon). In doing this, John brings to an end the Historical view of beastology. The phrase, "the beast was," shows the declining order. The Beast existed in history and now appears in full force, at that moment of extreme emergency, to finally devour the Seed of the Woman. However, John said, "The beast is not." Imperial, political Rome fell in 476 A.D. The devil's plot to destroy the Seed of the Woman through political power and religious, cultural, and philosophical administrations resulted in an intriguing failure. John said, "and is about to come up from the abyss."

The beginning and ongoing war strategy from the depths of the abyss is to attempt to destroy the Seed of the Woman. The religious, cultural, philosophical, and political administrations work together, in union, with the Dragon and his apostate church. The Dragon will launch his attack from the stronghold of the seven mountains upon which the Woman is seated (Rev 17:9). Astonishingly, we see that this Beast "was" in history, "fell" in history, and yet, "came back" into existence on the hills of the very city upon which this Beast fell. The damning sin was an illicit relationship to the unfaithful bride who became a harlot (Rev 17:8).

Remember, the Beast emerged from this abyss. This parallels the same Beast as an emissary of Satan, "king of the abyss" (9:11), and he emerged in the form of the Beast to go to war against New Covenant Christianity (11:7). The fact that Satan is now operating from this abyss gives final proof that after the Ascension, and the war in Heaven with Michael and His Angels, Satan was confined to the abyss until his final destiny in the "Lake of Fire" (20:10). This means he no longer operates from his heavenly advantage.

New Testament Christians now have more of an advantage over Satan than ever before. As we shall see, Satan is stripped; his works are destroyed; he is bound; and he is absolutely powerless in the face of the Resurrection Gospel. With this knowledge, we must not get "puffed up," for "The Devil is like a prowling lion, seeking whom he may devour" (1Pe 5:8). The Gospel chain is the only thing that can bind the Devil. This prevents him from the unlimited space he had to do evil in the Old Testament, by "going to and fro on the earth, and walking up and down in it" (Job 1:7 – the most literal translation). The "walking up" could mean that he once had an advantage that Christ has now taken away.

THE DRAGON IS NOT ANTICHRIST

The religious, cultural, political, philosophical administrations of the world attach themselves, in union, with the apostate "church." The Dragon will launch his attack from the stronghold of the seven mountains upon which the Woman is seated (Rev 17:9). The Dragon is neither called "Antichrist," nor is the term found anywhere in the Book of Revelation. He would never consent to the title. Satan is a subtle serpent by nature. He must be amazed when uniformed scholars call him "Antichrist." He would never dream of going to battle against Christ. He did that once and was destroyed decisively (1Jn 3:8; Heb 2:14). A coward, much like the liberal administration in Washington and the Muslim terrorists, must have the odds or "The cards stacked in his favor."

> Case in point – she is called the "Brave German." Her name is Heidi. In Martin Luther's Germany, in a supposedly Christian Church, a Muslim Imam is called to pray in an "interfaith service." Heidi is sitting in the balcony of this Memorial Church in Speyer. The acoustics are good in the Gothic constructed building. Heidi lifted up her voice,
>
> "Jesus Christ alone is Lord over Germany!"

Heidi shouted truth and wisdom,

> "Herr Christ!"

"Herr" in German means Lord or Master. Hitler compelled his lackeys to hail him, "Herr Hitler." She unfurled a German Flag that reads "Jesus Christ is Lord!" She spoke the famous words of Luther as he stood nearly 400 years ago, condemned before an inquisition tribunal,

> "Here I stand! I cannot do otherwise!"

She then shouted, "I am lifting the curse the Imam just placed on the church and on us!" People began to pull on her flag. They pushed and shoved her. The police came and escorted her out of the building.

Dale Hurd commented on this scene, "The same curse is on our Country-America." The Memorial Church in Speyer was erected in honor of Martin Luther, the brave reformer who risks his life for Christian Truth. The cowardly leaders of that city, the governors, and President of that country are betraying God, their country and all of us (entered, 11/16/2013 A.D.). The conclusion should be that there is no tolerance for the intolerance of TRUTH. There is no apology for being FREE! It appears that since 2013, Europeans are beginning to realize that Islam is not just a religion; it is a militancy that will not be content until all counties are under Islamic rule.

Thus, the colossal coward is not known as Antichrist, who cannot afford competition with Christ. A cowardly Christian will gladly enter into an "Inter-Faith-Union" with any religion in the world, just so long as there are no absolute truths except those of the Imam or Sunni cleric and "peace" is maintained. It is despicable that German "Christians" would listen to a prayer from the lips of a man, whose religion teaches,

> "Allah is God-Mohamed is His Prophet-and you are all going to Hell if you do not believe it and if you deny it we have the Sharia Law to enforce it, we will prove the authenticity of our doctrine by separating your head from your body!"

And "peace-loving," confrontation-avoiding, TRUTH-denying Americans, Canadians, Germans, and many Europeans fall over backward, like a whipped pup with their paws dangling in the air in submission.... "As for me and my house I fear God more than I do cowards who strut around like new born fawns looking for someone to patronize their clumsy attempts to walk on their own two feet." Ignorance of the eternal Christ is simply a shame and disgrace to the human race. Courage always has and always will be a Christian virtue! Winston Churchill was right when he said, "Courage is rightly esteemed the first of human qualities…because it is the quality which guarantees all others" (www.brainyquotes.com: Courage is rightly esteemed the first of human qualities)

The faith of most of the world's Christians is so weak and sickly that it would be far better to give it up, or at least quit identifying themselves as Christians. The Devil believes in Christ more than most of us. He is not at war with Christ at all. The coward lost the fight with the husband. His war is now against the Woman, "The Bride of Christ." He is not Antichrist; he is "Anti-Woman."

Once, when I debated an atheistic evolutionist, I ask him, "Why do you not just come out and deny Jesus? Call Him a liar! Call Him a fraud! Call him a deceiver?" I knew that was exactly how he felt about our Lord, but he would not come out to say it before audience in attendance. His purpose in debate was to undermine Christ. If he denied Christ publicly, he would lose the debate immediately. He was there to destroy the faith of the Bride of Christ, but he was too great a coward to denounce her husband.

Muslim debaters will not engage a New Testament Christian scholar. They debate only when the situation is "stacked in their favor." When the Imam backed out in Winchester, VA after having made a commitment to debate me on "Christianity versus Islam," we contacted a local college, and he agreed to the proposition, the debate terms, and the date so as to reserve the college auditorium. However, some "Christian" pastors and professors in the area contacted the imam and warned him to stay out of this debate. The imam backed out at the last minute. In all due respect to the man as a descendant of Father Adam, if he could have gotten a henchman to bushwhack me and render me senseless from a head blow, he just might have entered into this theological discussion that would have required extensive mental energy, from both of us.

Revelation 17: 9, 10: "This calls for a mind with wisdom. The seven heads are seven hills on which the woman sits. They are also seven kings.

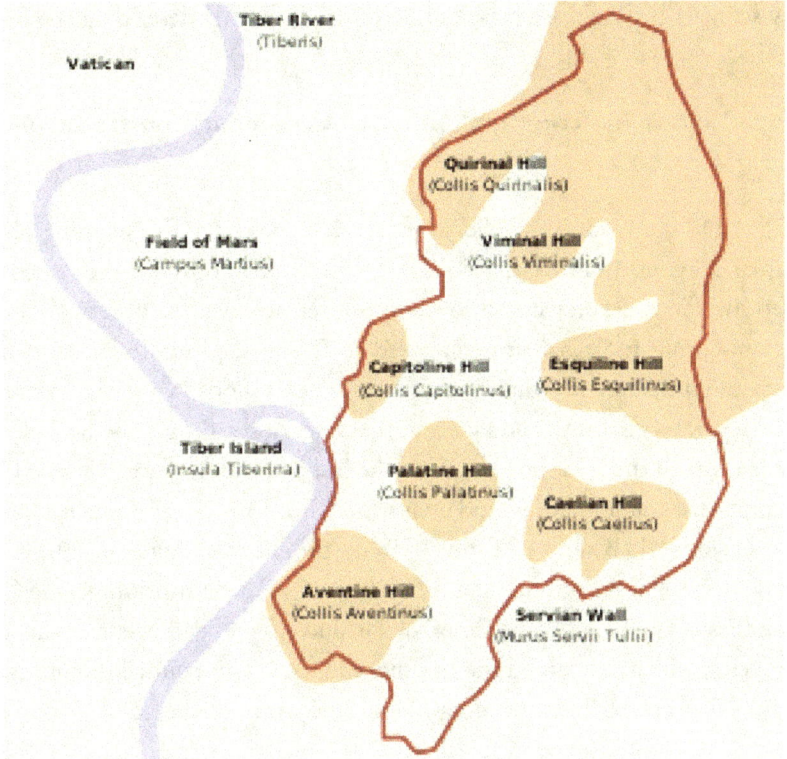

The Seven Hills (elevations) of Rome

The seven heads are upon the Seven Hills of Rome.

1. The Palatine Hill

2. Aventine Hill

3. The Caelian Hill

4. The Esquiline Hill

5. The Viminal Hill

6. The Capitoline Hill

7. The Quirinal Hill

Many scholars believe this passage of Scripture is directly describing the Roman Church.[89]

Ruling Bishops in Jerusalem, Antioch, Alexandria, Constantinople and Rome

In 325 A.D., the Council of Nicaea recognized the above five reigning bishops and their religious-political divisions.[90] These five Bishops and their successors headed five dioceses; they began to vie for supremacy over the others. Eventually this competition for papal supremacy led to Caesar-Papism. Today, students of history can understand what took place. The bishops who were vying for supremacy knew that it would take an official act of the Emperor (the Codex) to recognize one of them as the head of all the bishops and the east and west Christian empires. That emperor would be Justinian in 533 A.D., and the head bishop would be John II, Bishop of Rome.[91] Paul's prophecy in Acts 20: 29, 30 concerning the struggle of bishops and their authority came to fruition. At the Council of Ephesus in 431 A.D., the Emperor Theodosius presided over the Theotokos controversy, which concerned the "mother of God." This council, for all its blasphemy, was necessary to determine which bishop would emerge supreme.

THE POWER SHIFT TO ROME AS THE CENTER AND CROWN OF CATHOLICISM

By the time of the Council of Ephesus, 431 A.D., the monarchial bishops throughout the Roman world had authority over their separate districts. Even though Celestine I in Rome was called a pope, the bishops realized that until the Emperor decided who would be the chief bishop, they would all be merely first among equals. Theodosius became Emperor, January 19, 379 A.D., and wasted little time expressing his leaning toward Rome as the hub of religious power. In his edit (January 28, 380 A.D.), he states, "Anyone who did not follow the faith of Pope Damascus of Rome and Peter of Alexandria was a heretic" (*The Church of the Ancient Councils*, p. 104).[92] For further reading, I have found the entire content of this footnote, titled "Erroneous Petrine Primacy" to be very thought provoking. Theodosius I was extremely instrumental in leading the Catholic World toward recognizing Rome as the head of the State Church of the Roman Empire (www.wikipedia: State Church of the Roman Empire).

The so-called pope during the time of the Council of Ephesus was Celestine I. Even though he did not attend personally, he sent delegates to the First Council of Ephesus.⁹³ This First Council of Ephesus centered on the Theotokos Controversy. The Council heard archbishop of Constantinople Nestorius who argued that Christ existed as The Word before His coming to Earth and Mary was merely the womb for the Man Child, and she was not The Mother of God. Theodosius sided with Pope Celestine of Rome and Cyril of Alexandria (www.wikipedia: Theotokos). From this council their emerged a new heresy, Mariolatry, and interestingly, what may be the first actual church building built in Ephesus was called the Church of Mary.⁹⁴

THE VENERATION OF MARY

Concerning the veneration of Mary as "The Mother of God," Williston Walker writes,

> "To her, went out much of that feeling which had found expression in the worship of the mother goddesses of Egypt, Syria and Asia Minor, though in a far nobler form" (*History of the Christian Church*, Charles Scribner's, New York, p.156).

As already noted, this doctrine did not gain much popularity until the First Council of Ephesus. Let us take a break from the intensity of battle of the Council of Ephesus and learn how the True Bride of Christ was corrupted by "words." First, we must emphasize that to those who use words to build up and also to those who use words to destroy: "Words mean something!" "Words matter!" Jesus spoke wonderful, beautiful words of life. A true Disciple of Christ will use words to edify and save those who are weak or lost. The devil in our text (Revelation 12:15) uses words to destroy, "Like a flood from the Dragon's mouth."

We think of a flood "words" from the Dragon's mouth every time we hear most of our political speeches. We think of this "flood" every time we read some of the media news, or hear false teachers butcher the Bible. Such word weasels are also called "spin doctors." They can spin a word until it means exactly the opposite of its original, intended use.

Christianity has been affected by "word change agency" since the beginning of time. The word "kleros" used in Acts 1:26 means simply, "To cast lots." The Apostles used the wisdom of Proverbs and sought God's guidance to settle an issue that could have caused contention, and they "cast lots" (Pr 18:18). But a corruption of corruptions originated when the Greek-Roman apostates "spinned" this word to mean "clergy." Instead of accepting Christ's original Apostles, prophets, evangelists, pastors and teachers (Eph 4:11), the so-called clergyman or woman is given a status of power above what is called "lay men and lay women." The Chaplin of the hospital informed me that I needed a "clergy badge." I said, "No one cast lots for my appointment to this ministry." When he asked me what I meant, I told him where the word "clergy" came from. He made a special badge for me with the name "minister" on it.

We also have the name "lay person." The word "lay" comes from the Greek "laity" which simply means "people." The peculiar trait of deception is found in the way that word change agents operate. They know they are perverting the word by changing it, so we dare not ask them to define what the word really meant. Actually, "lay people" literally means "people, people." The "laity" is one of the worst departures from New Testament Faith because Peter said that ALL Christian people are "kingly priests of God" (1 Pe 2:9). No wonder we have such a hard time finding people to work for Jesus. People become what you teach them to become. If they perceive that Christ gave us a Clergy-Laity distinction, they are going to descend to the lowest level of production of such a distinction.

Word change agents also tampered with the Greek word "baptidzo," which can only mean to dip, plunge, or immerse. It can metaphorically mean to overwhelm, but it cannot, by any stretch of imagination mean to sprinkle or pour water upon a person.[95] The King James Version scholars did not translate "baptidzo"; they transliterated this word to "baptism." Although many religious sites deal with the Greek word "immerse" being transliterated instead of translated, Bob Ross, in his editorial "Black Helicopter" has as good an answer as to why the King James scholars refused to translate the word "immerse."[96] As usual, the argument against TRUTH is usually driven by ancestor worship. The translators feared that the readers of this translation in the early 17th Century would be furious at the thought that their ancestors were not taught the Bible meaning of "baptidzo." Since the method of immersion is important in God's eyes, spinning this word should not be taken lightly.

An excellent work by John C. Greider, Ph.D., *The English Bible Translation and History* (www.google.book), clearly tells why the Roman Church undermined the authority of the original Koine Greek New Testament.[97] While there is nothing wrong with Latin, any more than with any other language, Rome gravitated toward Latin as the Church's official language for a reason; that being to diminish the accuracy intended by the Greek to convey the original TRUTHS of Christ and His original apostles.

Yes, scholars of the Koine (common) Greek know that the Greek used in the New Testament had metamorphosed into Medieval Greek in the 4th Century, giving rise to modern-day Greek. New Testament Greek is a dead language, but this is good. Alexander the Great spread this Greek to the entire world. God led him to conquer the world (Da 10:20). Thus, the whole world of the Apostle's day could read the New Testament in this language. In God's providence, He allowed this ancient, original language to die so that the divine language of the New Testament could neither be tampered with nor changed to mean anything other than as originally intended.

Even Catholicism needs the original Koine Greek, like the word "ecclesia." Nothing in the Latin denotes such a word so the word "ecclesiasticism" appears in Catholic writings. The word simply means a "called out assembly." The word "church" (kirk) means an edifice (See *The Word that Changed the Word* by Andy Zelphelt.[98]).

A FLOOD 'WORDS' CAME OUT OF THE DRAGON'S MOUTH

The Catholic word change agents coined the original word, ecclesia, to mean an ecclesiastical hierarchy. They stole this word from the Lord's people in order to enhance their lordship of Christ's flock. In return, they gave the Lord's people the paltry word, "church." Today, there are millions of "churches," yet Christ is supposed to be ONE body.

Although it may not appear on the surface to be a drastic "change agency," the word "sacrament" took the place of the words "Communion" or "The Lord's Supper," but the emphasis upon the sacramental oath and who has authority to administer "The Sacrament" carries more weight for the authority of the hierarchy then do the unpretentious words "Lord's Table," "Communion," or "Lord Supper."

Even sincere Catholic people realize that "penance," "limbo," "purgatory," "infallibility," "confessional," and the revelry and bawdy behavior that accompanies their "holy celebrations," such as Mardi Gras, does not correspond to accepted behavior that we call "spiritual."

WORD CHANGE AGENCY COMES FROM THE DRAGON'S MOUTH

What does this have to do with the "Worship of Mary?" Well, word changing has plenty to do with what Mary meant to the Apostles (Remember, she was immersed into Christ for the forgiveness of her sins, Acts 1:12-14, 2:38.). In Scripture, she is never called, "The Mother of God." But if you start teaching a false syllogism to children, and later in parochial school, "Jesus is God, Mary is His mother, and, therefore, Mary is the mother of God," the child will grow to adulthood with this in mind. A valid syllogism is perhaps our best means of ensuring an argument is reliable and valid, but both its premises and the conclusion must be true; otherwise, the syllogism can be just another effective instrument of evil.

For example, Hitler's Minister of Propaganda, Joseph Goebbels, employed the motto, "Tell a lie long enough and people will believe it." Same sex marriage is as big a lie as has ever been pawned off on the mindset of supposed civilized people. But notice how the "change agents" went to work on this abomination. First, those who had sex with same sex were called "sodomites." Later they were called "perverts." Then the spin agents settled on the word "homosexual." But, in order to gain full acceptance, the word-weasels changed it to "Gay." Of course, the euphemism "gay" has nothing to do with sexual preferences.

It makes no difference if the "spin agents" are talking about an evil lifestyle or a change in government. They just keep advocating change until the people embrace it, or when they do not get their way, they get a Federal Judge to rule in their favor.

A FLOOD 'WORDS' CAME OUT OF THE DRAGON'S MOUTH

The "spin agents" have also affected the workings of the U.S. Constitution. The Constitution of our Founding Fathers included three separate, but unequal branches. The strongest branch was the Legislative, which consisted of a House of Representatives whose members are elected by and are closest to the people, and a Senate whose members are elected by the state legislature (This was unfortunately changed by the 17th Amendment for direct election by the people.) and enabled the power of the states to check or push back against the power of the Federal government. The second branch was the Executive, or president, who was to be a "vigorous Executive" to enforce the laws passed by the Legislative Branch and who was also Commander in Chief during wartime. The Judicial Branch was to adjudicate Federal legal issues and legal conflicts among the States. The Constitution did not give the Judicial Branch the power of Judicial Review. Finally, all Branches, not just the Judicial Branch, had the responsibility to ensure the Constitution's integrity. Can anyone recognize our Founder's Constitution as the Constitution that we live by today?

American leaders who hate traditional American values continue to hammer away at these values until "We the People" either finally accept their Godless agenda (and their new government camouflaged under a Constitution that the Founders could not recognize), or the politicians will fabricate a human right so as to bypass the Legislature and trust that the Supreme Court Judges rule in their favor. Just think of a "Big Lie of the 21st Century," a lie that mocks God. That big lie concerns homosexual marriage by which the Supreme Court made consummate fools of themselves by voting 5-to-4 in its favor in June 2015. Five justices redefined traditional marriage by accepting the supporting lie that homosexuals are born that way. So once again, the implication is that it is God's fault... Really?

Laws like "Universal Health Care" and "Same Sex Marriage" violate the U.S. Constitution, but this makes no difference to politicians and judges. They place their illegal positions before the public again, and again, and again; first by The Sin Party twenty years ago, and then by The Sin Party five years ago, and at lastly, by The Sin Party last year. Resistance ceased and the Bills were passed or ruled as constitutional. Diabolical persistence was the devil's ploy in the past; it is the devil's strategy today. This same wearing down works in families when children wear down parents with their and their friend's sins. It works in churches where liberal, unbiblical views are constantly harped upon at every "Bored-Meeting!"

THE BISHOP OF ROME

As previously documented, Emperor Theodosius leaned in favor of the Bishop of Rome at the Council of Ephesus. But there was nothing in Scripture to support Rome's preeminence over other cities, or to show that the Apostle Peter had a church in Rome, let alone that he was the first Roman pope. The supreme city is the City of God in Heaven (Heb 11:10, 16, 12:22). In fact, no city on Earth can house the headquarters for the Kingdom of Christ (Heb 13:14). We have not been able to identify sufficient evidence to show that Peter ever lived in Rome. While papacy leaning scholars go to great lengths to find evidence supporting their view that Peter lived and died in Rome, not one New Testament verse exist to prove his being in Rome. We do know that Peter was at Caesarea Philippi and in Jerusalem, among other cites, because the Scriptures tell us so. Rome has produced many forgeries, but none so far with an address of Peter's house in Rome. Also, while popes today cannot be married, Peter was married. There is no other way to get a mother-in-law (Mt 8:14 with 1Co 9:5; 1Ti 3:2).

THIS BLASPHEMOUS COUNCIL WAS PROPHESIED BY TWO PROPHETS

Paul was not the only prophet who foretold of the beginning of primal bishops in Ephesus (Ac 20:27-31). Jesus Himself prophesied of the rise of "nicolaitanes" in Ephesus (Rev 2:6, 15). This word is a compound, "nico" (suppress-put down) and "laity" (the common people). As stated earlier, laity had nothing to do with designating a group of Christians in contrast with the so-called "clergy."

Revelation 17:10: There are also seven kings. Five have fallen, one is, and the other has not yet come. And when he does come, he must continue for a short time.

There are Seven Kings, or Seven Kingdoms (to be discussed below) comprised of "Five fallen," "one is," and one who "has not yet come." There are actually eight Kingdoms altogether, but the "eight is of the seventh" Kingdom. History tells us of five powers that have fallen. These kingdoms preceded the Roman Kingdom.

1. Egypt
2. Assyria
3. Babylon
4. Medo-Persia
5. Greco-Macedonia
6. Rome of John the Apostle's day
7. One yet to come which is Religious Rome (Rome governed by the Roman Church, known as the Roman Catholic Church.) after the fall of Pagan Rome. The Papacy had no strength without political Rome of the Roman Empire (Imperial Rome).

8. Political Rome divided into ten kingdoms within Europe. After the fall of Imperial Rome, the kings contested for power with Religious Rome. Religious Rome had enormous political power in the temporal affairs of these kings and their subjects. Therefore, the ten kingdoms gave allegiance to Religious Rome, sometimes very reluctantly.

There are two views concerning the seven kings. One view is that the seven are the seven Caesar's of Rome; whereas, the other view is that the seven are former kingdoms.

It is inconsequential whether we view the seven as past kingdoms or Caesars; both fit the context perfectly. We can be correct in either view.

Caesars	Kingdoms
Nero "was" in John's day and committed suicide and was "not."	Imperial Rome "was" (Rev 19:11) and it existed in John's day and "is not" (Imperial Rome was destroyed.). John saw this as an already accomplished fact. Therefore, Imperial Rome "was not."
Nero's successor, Galba, only lasted for a short time. The next two (Otho and Vitellius) were imposters and only lasted a matter of months. With the reign of Vespasian begins the reign of The Flavian Dynasty.	Rome (with 10 Kingdoms) would be the eighth of the seventh. This transition happened so quickly that we do not notice a break in history. Thus the expression "the eighth is of the seventh" indicates no one could tell when the seventh left off and the eighth began. As already mentioned, some scholars believe the seven heads are actually kingdoms, not kings, namely: Egypt, Assyria, Babylon, Persia, Greece, Syria, Rome, and then the eighth being of the seventh (Pagan Rome turns into Papal Rome). Thomas Hobbes wrote, "The papacy is none other than the Ghost of the deceased Roman Empire, sitting crowned by the grave there of."[99]

This "short time" of the prophecy shows a quick transition.

The Seven Heads:

1. Gaius Julius (Julius Caesar): 100 – 44 B.C.

2. Augustus (Gaius Octavius Thurinus) (Augustus Caesar): 31 B.C. – 14 A.D. Augustus fought a three-year war with Mark Anthony for the throne.

3. Tiberius: 14 A.D. – 37 A.D.

4. Caligula: 37 A.D. – 41 A.D.

5. Claudius: 41 A.D. – 54 A.D.

6. Nero: 54 A.D. – 68 A.D.

7. Galba: June 68 A.D. – January 69 A.D. A "short time." He would have brought to an end the legitimate Caesarian line; although, the title Caesar continued until the end of the Roman Empire in 476 A.D. The next two were impostures and lasted only for weeks. Great turmoil existed during this time. The successor dynasty, the Flavians, began its reign with Vespasian.

Revelation 17:11: The beast who once was, and now is not, is an eighth king. He belongs to the seven and is going to his destruction.

Religious Rome is also called the Eighth Kingdom. Without the eighth, the seventh would not be in existence and vice versa. The eighth is of the seventh. Two bishops in the Roman sphere gained fame by intervening to prevent the sack of Rome and its vicinities. Leo I, Bishop of Rome, prevented further attacks by Attalia the Hun (452 A.D.), and Epiphanius, the Bishop of Pavia, deterred Odaccer the German Barbarian in 476 A.D. The Papacy negotiated with Rome's enemy and used it for its own benefit. Politics can be the devil's tool, whether in Religion or State. The European invaders conquered pagan Rome and religious Rome conquered them.

Revelation 17:12: "The ten horns you saw are ten kings who have not yet received a kingdom, but who for one hour will receive authority as kings along with the beast.

A man would forfeit eternal life for a moment of physical pleasure. This statement is also true of religious and political institutions. Ten Kingdoms have not yet come, but to enjoy one hour with the Beast, the ten European kingdoms will give the Beast everything he wants. These Kingdoms were contemporary with the eighth as the little horn of Daniel (Da 7:19-22, 25). They were supported by the Papacy, but none of these kingdoms existed in John's day. John's vision was remarkable. He gave such a minute, detailed prophecy of the rise of these kingdoms and their future destiny over 300 years before this occurred.

Revelation 17:13: *They have one purpose and will give their power and authority to the beast.*

They have one purpose, which is to give their power and authority to the Beast. Notice the whore is on the Beast; the Beast is not on her. She has the authority.

Revelation 17:14: *They will make war against the Lamb, but the Lamb will overcome them because he is Lord of lords and King of kings—and with him will be his called, chosen and faithful followers."*

People with short-sighted vision, who want "pleasure for an hour," are contrasted with disciplined Christians, who look at the long-range plan. These Christians are "called, chosen and faithful." Personally, we have witnessed hundreds of men and women who have forfeited a long life of marital fidelity to a faithful, loving spouse in exchange for an hour of pleasure with a harlot. What a terrible price to pay. Jesus also uses this analogy of a religious fling with the whore of Babylon. Such flings are just not worth it.

We are creatures of time. As such, we can see only what lies in our immediate path. Notice how Christ sees things as they work out in the future for "His called, chosen and faithful" followers. The Lord sees our end just as well as our beginning. This verse (17:14b) proves that those who are saved have a covenant commitment to be faithful. Christ has kept His commitment to call us through the Gospel (2Th 2:14). He kept His commitment to "choose us" (Eph 1:4). Now, we have a covenant responsibility to "Be faithful" (Lk 19:17) to Him.

We compare Christ's words here with those of John Calvin's famous "Five Points" (TULIP)....1) Total Depravity (A man dead in sin is totally incapable of responding to God.) 2) Unconditional Election (A human being is not given a choice, or condition whereby he must be saved.) 3) Limited Atonement (God alone chooses who He will atone, and by virtue of this choice, chooses also who will be damned.) 4) Irresistible Grace (Since man has no choice in the matter of salvation, God's grace overpowers his will.) 5) Perseverance of the Saints (Thus, if regardless of man's will, God gives salvation, regardless of man's will, God also gives the necessary perseverance that accompanies salvation.)

THE CALLED OF CHRIST, THE CHOSEN OF CHRIST AND THE FAITHFUL OF CHRIST

Calvinists lean heavily on John 10:28-29, "My sheep hear my voice and I know them, and they follow me, and I give them eternal life: and they shall never perish, neither shall any man pluck them out of my hand. My Father which gave them to me is greater than all: and no man is able to pluck them out of my Father's hand."

A covenant has got to have two parties, or otherwise, it is NOT a covenant. One of the most interesting and challenging aspects of Studying God's Word is the way in which He deals with the human race in covenant theology. Covenant theology is liberating theology. Take this verse above for instance. If we just emphasized the facts that 1) Jesus gives eternal life, 2) Those given life will never perish, 3) No man can pluck them out of Christ's hand, and 4) No one can pluck them out of the Father's hand. That is as much eternal security as a person can have here and hereafter. If that is the one-sided covenant of Christ, then I will give everything to get into it. Those of us who have followed Christ for many years are well aware of the eternal security and keeping power of our Lord, Savior, and Good Shepherd Jesus Christ. But we must be good Bible expositors also. We must "Search and study the scriptures" (Acts 17:11; 2 Ti 2:15). If you look closely there is a covenant relationship in the John 10:28, 29 verses. We already considered the four parts of the covenant side of Christ the son, and God the Father. But we cannot overlook the human responsibility depicted by the response of the sheep to the Good Shepherd: 1) They HEAR Christ's voice, and 2) They FOLLOW Him. Who is responsible for the HEARING of Christ Word? Hearing is a very important step in covenant salvation, "For whosoever shall call upon the Lord shall be saved" (Ro 10:13). "How shall they call upon…. How shall they believe in Him of whom they have not HEARD?" (10:14). So Faith comes by HEARING and HEARING by the Word of God (Ro 10:17).

In my debate with Calvinist, Dr. James Jordan, I quoted these versus and then ask him the question, "Who is responsible for our hearing?" Dr. Jordan thought for a second and He said, "God is. He gave us our ears." (The Debate is in transcript and on U-Tube). I have a hard time with this answer, because if God gave us ears, He also gave every other sane human being ears, or the adequacy of receiving the Gospel messages, somehow. My question is that why would he give "ears to hear and obey God's Word to some, and not give ears to obey God's Word" to others. It is obvious the Lord Jesus views this "ear problem" from a different perspective, "He who has an ear, let him hear" (Re 2:7, 11, 17; 2:29; 3:6, 13, 22). It only takes one ear to hear.

The Covenant Gospel "Plan of Salvation" of Acts, Chapter 2, is identical to the Missionary Gospel "Plan of Salvation" model in Romans, Chapter 10.

ACTS CHAPTER TWO

1) Preach Christ (Ac 2:14)

2) Hear the Word (vs. 37, 41)

3) Call on the Lord (vs. 21, 37)

4) Confess Christ's NAME (vs. 36, 37)

5) Obey what you heard (vs. 41, 42-47).

ROMANS CHAPTER TEN

1) Preach Christ (Ro 10:14, 15)

2) Hear the Word (vs. 14-17, 18)

3) Call on the Lord (vs. 13)

4) Confess Christ's NAME (vs. 9)

5) Obey what you have heard (vs. 16, 21 from a negative aspect because "They have not all obeyed the Gospel").

It should go without saying that "Obeying the Gospel" (1Th 1:8) means that the sheep continue to FOLLOW Jesus through life until the point of death (Jn 10:28; Ac 2:42; Rev 2:10).

Yes, God gave us ears to hear the shepherd and we must use them. Christ died for ALL men, so therefore He knew it was within man's heart to believe and follow the Good Shepherd. The Calvinists hate the word "conditional" and say that it is not a Bible Word, but "conditionalism" is taught through such prepositions as (if), "IF you love me, keep my commandments", (and) "He that believes AND is immersed will be saved" and (but), "I would have gathered you as a mother hen gathers her chicks, BUT you would not."

The Bible teaches clearly that God holds us in the "Hollow of His hands" (Isa 40:12, 49:14-16). Christ, the Good shepherd holds us in His arms all day long (Isa 40:11). Indeed, no one can pluck us out of his hand. But we read of another side of this covenant in Hebrews 6:6, "If they shall fall away, (It is impossible) to renew them again to repentance; seeing they crucify to THEMSELVES the Son of God afresh, and put Him to an open shame" (Heb 6:4).

Yes, no one on Earth, under the Earth, in the Heavens or in the sky OUTSIDE OF OURSELVES can PLUCK us out of the hands of our savior, but the Holy Spirit wrote we could crucify unto OURSELVES the Son of God again. The Hebrew Christians were reminded that their fathers did NOT continue in the Covenant (Heb 8:9). That covenant was very strict, with its laws, ceremonies, and regulations, but he who despised Moses' law died without mercy (Heb 10:28). Who are we to think that we can get by if we think the blood of the New Covenant is considered unholy? (Heb 10:29) Do we think that God will predestine us to eternal life if we do not respond in a simple covenant requirement such as HEARING the shepherd and FOLLOWING Him?

The fifth point of the Calvinism "Tulip Theory" is the "P." This point is supposedly representative of God's giving His saints "perseverance." The word "perseverance" is found in Ephesians 6:18, "Watching in all perseverance." In this text, perseverance is a responsible act of human will. If God gave perseverance to one, He would have given it to all; but if He did, He would not be true to His nature, for God "Has no respect of persons" (Ac 10:34). Furthermore, if God gave some the attribute of perseverance, it would not be a response from man but an act of God Himself. Whether we use the word "faithful" used by our Lord in Revelation 17:14 or the word "perseverance," it only makes sense to realize that Christ would never have commanded it if He did not expect us to exercise our will to do it.

Calvin wrote, "By predestination we mean the eternal decree of God by which he determined with himself whatever he wished to happen with regard to every man. All are not created equal, on equal terms, but some are preordained to eternal life, other to eternal damnation; and accordingly, as each has been created for one or other of these ends. We say he was predestined for life or to death" (*Institutes of The Christian Religion*, 3:21:5). (www.bereanpublishers.com : John Calvin's View of Reprobation).

Granted, the Godhead is enabling us, and without this inward work, we could not make it (Php 2:13), but faithfulness is something we should desire above all (2Ti 4:7). Faithfulness should be an end, inward desire of every Covenant Christian, and one of the ways to achieve our being faithful is by confronting the world through perseverance. In being faithful, we are "Working out our own salvation with fear and trembling" (Php 2:12). Peter told the Jews to "Save themselves from this perverse generation" (Ac 2:40).

WHAT GOD HATH JOINED TOGETHER

Notice the Lord's method of joining things together. In addressing marriage, He said, "What God has joined together." In addressing the Covenant requirements following Christian Immersion, He connected salvation with continued obedience, "They continued steadfast in the Apostles Doctrine, Fellowship, Breaking Bread, and Prayer" (Ac 2:42). He joined faith and works together (Jas 2:26). He joined salvation and being added to the Congregation (Ac 2:47). He joined love with commandments, "If you love me, keep my commands" (Jn 14:12). We are not surprised to see a powerful three-point sermon from our Lord, "Called-Chosen-Faithful," so what the Lord hath joined together, let not man put asunder!

The people whom Christ called his "called, chosen, and faithful followers" (Rev 17:14) are the same remnant we read about in Revelation 12:11, 17. In God's view, they are chosen from the beginning. The remnant is chosen, from earth's view, when they are immersed into Christ, but they must be faithful unto the end! This is what gets God's attention, "Faithfulness in the midst of such opposition." It was overwhelming for those faithful to endure religious opposition, persecution, and execution. However, lest we think that the devil has relaxed his methods today, Christians are still facing insurmountable opposition from politically-correct cultural religion, pluralism, tolerance, apathy, diversity, despair, and the infectious spiritual disease of wanting to please modern-day society. For these reasons, we need "persistence." Convenient technology and attractive pleasures have seduced the attention of Covenant breakers.

Revelation 17:15, 16: Then the angel said to me, "The waters you saw, where the prostitute sits, are peoples, multitudes, nations and languages. The beast and the ten horns you saw will hate the prostitute. They will bring her to ruin and leave her naked; they will eat her flesh and burn her with fire.

THE TEN HORNS WILL HATE THE PROSTITUTE

By 476 A.D., the European invaders conquered Pagan Rome, and Religious Rome conquered them. Then, these "Barbarian Nations" became a painful "thorn in the side" of Papal Rome when Rome discovered that the majority of the barbarians believed in the Arian (from Arius) concept of Christ. Consequently, from the 4th to the 7th Centuries, Papal Rome continued to war against many nations that comprised the Holy Roman Empire (Which Voltaire[100] said, "Was neither Roman, nor holy.").

Who is this Arius? Arius was a theorizing presbyter in 4th Century Alexandria, Egypt. He considered Jesus to be a created being, less than the Father, and therefore unworthy of the New Testament's emphasis upon accepting Him as Lord.

In the mid-2nd Century A. D, Theophillus of Antioch (115-185) originated the unscriptural word, "trinity-trias," to describe the Godhead. The newly formed Latinized Catholic church did not have Koine Greek scholars adequately trained in the Greek words that were used to describe Jesus. If the word Godhead, taken from the Greek "theosis," had been used, this controversy would probably never have developed. Theosis differs from the kindred word "theoisis" in that "theosis" refers to the eternal Godhead as family, "The fullness of Deity dwelling in Jesus Christ" (Col 1:19), whereas the later, theoisis, refers to the Godhead in nature (the Universe-Ac 17:29). Had The Catholic Priests understood the difference between these two words, it is possible there would not be Muslims, Mormons, Jehovah Witnesses, and Unitarians in today's world. All these religions originated from the very low view held by Arius and his many followers as to whom Jesus Christ is.

Even the Greek Orthodox Church based its Christological views on what some patriarch thought of Christ rather than what the Greek New Testament affirmed concerning the Logos-Christ. Since Rome masqueraded as a "Christian Institution," the pagan nations looked at her and had a very low view of Jesus Christ.

This Arian controversy divided the Catholic Church into two opposing factions. One faction believed like Theophilus (This Trinitarian view was later advocated by Athanasius and debated with Arius at the Council of Nicaea in 325 A.D., where the Theophilus-Athanasius view of Christ was accepted.), and the other faction believed like Arius. When Mohammedanism appeared in the 7th Century, most clerics along the eastern Mediterranean Sea had views similar to those of Arius' followers.[101]

When Mohamed traveled his camel trading routes, he loved to strike up conversation with so-called "Christians," so-called because they were very ignorant of "This same Jesus" (Ac 2:36, 37), "The Messiah," and "Logos" that Peter and the Apostles declared (Jn 1:1-5, 14, 15,18; 1Jn 1:1-3, 2:1-3, 2:22-28). The only Jesus these ignorant camel traders knew was that of Origen, Arius, and Sabellius. The Arabian Genie "Demon" got to Mohamed. The Demon (masquerading as the angel Gabriel) got Ali Mohamed to do something that Jesus refused to do, "Bow down to me and I will give you the kingdoms of the world!" The vast majority of Arius' disciples converted to Islam (www.shoebat.com: Muhammad Was Not the Founder of Islam-He simply continued the heresy by converting to Arianism). To this day, Arius (through his Muslim converts) still haunts Catholicism. This causes a balance of political and religious power intimidation so that neither Rome nor Islam can gain an advantage. The bad blood continues to exist. For example, self-proclaimed leader of the Islamic State (ISIS), Abu Bakr al Baghdadi, proclaimed, "Rome will be conquered next" (www.telegraph.co.uk.com).

Roman and Greek religion has suffered the threats and attacks of Arianism from the 3rd Century and Arian-Islam from the 7th Century to this day. How powerful and true are the words of The Revelation, "They shall hate the whore." Of course, Arianism leads to a low view of Christ because Rome masquerades as being Christian; and when Arian-Islam goes to war against Rome or Greek religions, they confuse the Christianity of Christ with what they see in the Roman-Greek religion.

What Catholicism could not do by argument, it finally accomplished by war. The Franks and King Clovis in the early 6th Century came to Catholicism's aid and finally conquered the Arian nations (Vandals and Visigoths) in Gaul (France).

But the Arian – Muslims renewed the war against Rome in the 7th Century; this war continues to this day.[102] Perhaps these two powers of false religion, Roman

Catholicism and Islam, are a providential "check mate from Heaven" to prevent world supremacy of one over the other. What would happen to pure Christianity if current foes Catholicism and Islam were to team up together? History has proven that supremacy from either Rome or Mecca leads to the wholesale slaughter of true Christians who refuse ecclesial tyranny of any kind.

The victory for a true understanding of Christ's nature could have been achieved without war, but by the time Papal Rome acquired the required amount of Greek scholarship at the Council of Nicaea (325 A.D.), it was too little, too late. "Too little" because the Greek word they used "homoousion" (like in substance) was better suited in the art of physics "alchemy" than in theology. "Substance" is a meteorological word, and yet this is the word Papal Rome chose to describe the relationship of God and His Word "Christ." Although this "homoousion" was the best Catholicism could offer (and it would have satisfied sincerest Christians), the Arians mocked it.

Substance is the word that appears in the Catholic Creed, "Christ is the same substance of the Father." It was also "too late" to capture the true nature of The Christ because while the Catholic Church delayed a logical New Testament approach to the controversy, the Arian "antichrist" doctrines had already infested many eastern and Germanic tribes. Once false doctrine enters the "demonic blood" of an apostate, it is too late to save these apostates.

I can only suppose that some of you have "sat at the feet" of the anti-Christ cultists (Muslim, Mormon, Jehovah Witness (Russelite), Christian Science, some Seventh Day Adventists, or other) and been subjected to a low, uneducated opinion of these who think they know whom Christ is. You also understand that restoring disciples from the cults to a true understanding of our Savior is nearly impossible. Therefore, we must teach new converts the "Real Christ of The New Testament"; otherwise, they become prey for the satanic wiles that lure them into an indoctrinating "church of human will" that inoculates them with the narcotic of controlling publications, which redefines the Biblical meaning of Christ. Jesus told the Jews, "You search the Scriptures and they are they which testifies of Me" (Jn 5:39). While the Jews were blinded to the vision of Christ in the Scriptures, modern-day anti-Christ cults are blinded more so because they are restricted from examining the Scriptures without the direction of their manmade publications, which are distributed from a central headquarters. This failure to examine the Scriptures, in totality, results in their believing in a very small, inadequate Christ as their savior. Before long, the eyes of those "little Jesus" believers roll back in their heads, and they drown in self-Gnosticism.

These churches of "self-will" (Col 2:8-22, especially vs. 23) do not teach their disciples to reach up and hold to the Head-Jesus Christ (2:19) and take away their will to bear His cross. They find ways to take the Bible out of their hearts and replace the Bible with attractive, artistic "picture book" literature. The only Scripture that the "spiritual substance dependent" reads is what the authors of the picture books put in it, and the self-Gnostics do not read the Bible for themselves.

Since the Protestant Reformation, Protestant scholars have produced hundreds of Scripture to prove the equality of God and Christ. We are amazed to think of how scripturally ignorant the Post Apostolic, "ecclesiastical fathers," and their successors really were. Arianism survived, not because their antichrist approach was scripturally correct, but because the blundering priests did not know their Bibles well enough to give an adequate defense of true "Christology" (1Pe 3:15; 2Ti 2:15). Instead of following 2Timothy 2:15, the priests were "workers who needed to be ashamed," and their shame turned to rage and fanaticism that actually led to killing Arian priests in the streets. The Arian churches fought back, and they did their share of killing also. Constantine was so frustrated with the ignorance on both sides of the controversy, he thought that, "their arguments were really just a matter of words." One historical observer said, "They were like two blind men fighting in the dark."[103]

But another problem existed that Catholic scholars confronted in this debate. In addition to being more Latin than Greek (the original language of the New Testament), the Roman Church (Catholics) lost the debate in this war with eternity at stake. Precisely at this time, early 4th Century, the apostates departed from the primitive Apostolic Faith. Ecclesiasticism was taking the place of the simple, pure ecclesia "local congregations," and the woman "Bride of Christ" was being pushed further into the wilderness. Christ was testing His ecclesia, just as He tests your congregation, your preacher, your elders and mine, today.

Consequently, Arius is not only challenging the Roman-Greek ecclesiasticism, he is ready through antichrist deception to lead millions of deluded souls into perdition. These souls were looking to the newly formed ecclesiastical hierarchy to pastor and protect them from the Arian wolves. Could these priestly lords and monarchial bishops stand up and give Biblical defense against Arianism and an account of Christ, the King? The fight against Arianism would be the final test as to whether the Greek and Roman ecclesiastical power machine would break the Arian apostasy, or would this ecclesiastical power machine break away from the Apostles Doctrine further and "fail in their defense" of New Testament TRUTH, and further apostatize themselves.

The Catholic apologists failed the Lord Jesus Christ for five reasons in these wars, and later in numerous Crusades to the Holy Land against the Muslim descendants of Arius.

1) The Catholic apologists believed in the deity of Christ for the wrong reason. The primary reason for having The Christ equal to God the Father was not because of what the apologists read in the Book of John but because they believed that The Bishops stood in Christ's place. Clement of Rome (92-101 A.D.), at a time when no clear-cut distinction existed between presbyters and bishops, was already teaching the primacy of The Bishop of Rome. The Bishop, in his mind, was to receive submission from all other bishops and their Sees throughout the Roman Empire. Clement claimed infallible authority over the consciences of over 200 million Christians in the Empire. [104]

No distinction existed between presbyters and bishops because they were actually two titles for the same man who served a local congregation (Ac 20:17 "elders," 20:18 "bishops"). The preacher "evangelist" ordained them in the local congregation (Tit 1:5). See how quickly the "Mystery of Iniquity" was developing!

The germ cell out of which the Pope would later hatch was being incubated. Vicarious Filii Dei, "God's substitute Son," was a title reserved for the Pope sometime later in the 8th or 9th Century. Already, the bishops, who were originally designated by Christ to be elders serving local flocks of believers (1Ti 3:1-7; Tit 1:6-9), were being greatly invested with power over districts, later dioceses. The bishops could not embrace the steadfast love for Christ that was required to reprove, rebuke, and exhort with longsuffering and patience. They failed to demand the work that was required to defend the integrity of the Godhead against Arian blasphemy. The bishops wanted a strong Christ because they wanted to be seen and known in His place on

Earth. If Arians were correct, then we have a weak, emasculated Christ. The reason the bishops did not want a weak Christ was because the bishop was "in the place of God."[105]

2) The Arian disciples could easily discern this ecclesiastical hypocrisy, especially when Catholics were holding up "Saints Worship," and later especially, holding Mary to a higher level and more compassionate intercessor than Christ.

3) The Catholics failed to use the Koine Greek words that were carefully chosen by the Holy Spirit (2Ti 3:16) to describe the eternal deity of Jesus Christ (1Ti 3:15). As already mentioned, the Catholic apologists never once mentioned Christ as the "Theotes" of the Godhead. They failed to turn to the Book of Colossians that is replete with Deity statements such as "The image-exact character of God" (Col 1:15), the "arche" the origin (1:15), the cause of creation (1:16), the "Primogenitor – not birth in time but cause of creation," (not in origination, but originator). In concert with the Father, Jesus is the actual creator of the known universe (1:16); He pre-existed all things, and presently "Holds the universe together" (1:17); He is the universal (catholic) head of the ecclesia; He is the "protokos" (priority) first born (not referring to a birth), but to all who rise from the dead; and that He might have preeminence in everything (1:18). It pleased God the Father that the "theotes" fullness of the Godhead should dwell in Jesus. He is the "monogenos" only unique Son in the bosom of the Father.

Because Jesus existed in the glory of eternity past (Jn 17:1-7), when He came to Earth as "Immanuel" (God in flesh), He is called the Son of God by declaration, not origination. Isaiah 9:6 said, "Unto us a child is born." It does not say, "Unto us a Son is born." Isaiah says the Son was given, and as a child, He was born. The Latin priest could not understand this one, "Whom God made Messiah" (Ac 2:36) any more than the Arians did. The hearts of Latin priests were not in the discussion. They really did not want Christ to be God any more than the Arian did, but Papal Rome needed a strong Christ to promote its role as bishops "in His place."

4) In the end, Catholicism knew it had at its disposal the political favor and military backing of the imperial crown. Catholicism would retreat to its argument by the sword when its "homoousios" (like substance) argument fell short. Their hypostatic argument was a little better (the union of God and Man as one). Because they humanized Christianity, the Holy Spirit would not bear witness to Catholicism's arguments (Jn 15:26). Obviously, both Catholicism and Arianism were in error because they possessed an insane rage to kill each other. Neither side ever read or (if they did) failed to understand Paul's admonition, "Speak the truth in love" (Eph 4:15). Our enemy may have a fine crafted and honed steel sword, but we have "The sword of the Spirit, the Word of God" (Eph 6:17; Heb 4:12). The Word of God will "cut to the heart, spirit, soul and bone marrow", but the enemy may well kill us physically. The same sword in the mouth of Christ would kill an apostate or infidel immediately (Rev 19:15).

5) In the final analysis, both the Priests and Arians resorted to violence and proved they were not filled with the Holy Spirit. Without the conviction of Spirit, even the most powerful arguments listed above will fall on deaf, dense ears. The Arians did not believe that the Holy Spirit was God, either. If the Plan of Salvation, as recorded in Acts 2:21-47 is not taught, the Holy Spirit would not have worked in the Roman Priests, and neither of the two fractions were led by God's Spirit. Without the Holy Spirit, how in the world can we fight spiritual warfare?

THE AUTHOR'S PERSONAL CONNECTION TO CATHOLICISM

I was born into a Catholic family. My mother did not have me baptized as an infant because her Catholic father and mother were more liberal in their views of Catholic dogma. I do not regret my being raised in a Catholic atmosphere. Much of my adult moral convictions are based upon what I saw in my parents and grandparents. Grandma, in addition to her own 12 children, helped raise me when my Mother had to work during World War II in the Martins Ferry, Ohio steel-manufacturing factory called "Blaw Knox." She was a Hungarian immigrant, and I had my share of "Hungarian Goulash." Later, my Catholic aunt and uncle loaned me the money to go to college. I have very fond memories of these relatives. My grandparent's 12 children (seven boys and five girls) provided me with excellent examples of how, for the most part, to adapt and adjust to the rigors of human existences. If Heaven could be earned by human virtue, they would be first in line at the Golden Gate. My dear, sweet Grandmother told me that she wanted me to stay with the New Testament and not the traditions she inherited from her fathers. By God's mercy she lived to be 93 and passed away with a Rosary in her hands.

Presently, some of the most aggressive conservatives of our time are Catholics. I have recognized their conservative principles; and in local editorials and personal conversation with others in our great Congregation of Christ, I have supported them politically.

Of the Catholic scholars whom I admire, Patrick Buchanan stands out as a "defender of the faith and soul of America." From my reading of Catholic scholarly works, I have also found that none of them agree with their "Pope's" subtle language that actually supports sodomy or same-sex-marriage. Buchanan's assessment was correct when he said that the U.S. Government is generating the conditions for a majority "Mass Civil Disobedience" (4/4/2013) by its own high-minded, arrogant support of a minority who already had a political green light to continue their sexual perversion. Buchanan will live to see whether our government continues to "cram these kinds of issues down the throats" of our Nation's best citizens. Presently, I am being counted among those "Who are leading the charge!"

This is not to say that even after providing support and voting for politicians we believe in, that we think they will not disappoint us. We know they will. We must remember that politicians are not our friend. They are sinful human beings just like we are and who have been provided the opportunity to represent us. Politicians have their price (often quite low), and they often renege on their promises after being elected. The seas, upon which the "Woman Sits" undulates back and forth, and many of those for whom we have voted become, "Undulating Politicians." This is just the nature of this political game that people play for money. I say these things because, in conservative convictions, I am in tune with conservative Catholics. Whether or not we become disappointed with our politicians, we must vote, even if it is for the least desirable person. The candidates for the general election must pass the primary election test. It is in the primaries where we have our best chance to elect candidates whom most closely emulate Biblical principles.

But we may face the facts! Paul clearly stated there would be a "Great Apostasy" or break away from Apostolic Doctrine (1Ti 4:1-5). Paul also said that Timothy would be a "good minister" if he warned his congregation of this (4:6). The apostasy (verses 1-4) is pretty much an overview of a gnostic-Greek-Roman version of what the original New Testament congregation would become in the 2nd through 4th Centuries.

The word for "apostasy" here is "husterian." Apostasy means to break away or depart from something in the immediate future. Apostasy is not talking about a "Last Day" departure. Paul also refers to the "Last Days" in 2 Timothy, Chapter 3. The word for "last" is "eschatos" from whence the word "eschatology" is derive. This word is not describing "the next to the last" or "latter days" (KJV) or "latter times" (NKJV), but the very end of time, prior to Judgment Day. I do not have to be your exegete. You can do it for yourself. Just hold the record of 2 Timothy 3:2-5 in your right hand and hold a copy of your local newspaper in your left. Read the headlines prayerfully with 2 Timothy 3:1, 2 and get down on your knees and cry out to the Lord, "How Long?" (Ps 62: 2, 3, 94:3-23, 35:1-7; Hab 1:1-4).

I must be very candid at this point. There are some conservatives who want to appear to be conservative because they play to a certain conservative audience. But there is a vast difference between a Christian conservative and a political conservative. The word conservative means "to conserve" and a Biblical conservative is interested in conserving Biblical truth. A liberal, on the other hand, is "liberal" with TRUTH. It is to our eternal peril, and we will pay a great price for being liberal with God's truth. No rational person would take the liberty to be liberal with God's Truth.

Case in point: One of my advisors called to my attention that Bill O'Reilly, a Catholic commentary of this day, criticized Kim Davis, County Clerk of Rowan County, KY, for refusing to issue marriage licenses. Because she would not issue marriage licenses to same-sex couples, she was jailed. O'Reilly's position is that she should obey man's laws. The position of Peter, James, and John is that legal justices and their supporters, like Bill O'Reilly, who rule counter to God's Word will not govern them (Ac 5:29). The proof as to the correct position in this argument is that sodomy is contrary to "natural law," or God's law, and "natural law" supersedes frail, human law that is not in accordance with God's law. Thus, even though a Catholic commentator appears to be conservative, like any leader, they cannot be trusted unless they are led of the Holy Spirit. Hopefully, someday we may look back and view Kim Davis as the Rosa Parks of a new movement for religious freedom in America.

The false doctrines of Ignatius of Antioch, Tertullian of Cartage, Clement of Rome, and Arian of Alexandria, and many others, caused the Great Apostasy. This apostasy worked its way into Arabia and Ali Mohammed's clairvoyant experience with a genie in a cave. False doctrine, with the corrupted view of whom Jesus Christ is, worked its way into the castles of the Visigoths, Ostrogoths, Burgundians, Huns, Franks, Alans, Britons, and Vandals throughout Europe. The Great Apostasy started (like all apostasies) in a small way beginning with Ignatius (turn of the 2nd Century) and grew until by the time of reformers John Huss, John Wycliffe, and Martin Luther, it had become a million times greater than the small band of New Testament Christians who had refused to surrender the Lordship of Jesus Christ throughout the ages.

While I continue to patronize the great conservative scholars who hold the faith of my early Catholic, childhood fathers, and who still embrace the heroic faith of our Constitutional Fathers whose indomitable faith can never be replicated in any age of American History, I must unequivocally and in finality hold fast to the "ONE Faith, ONCE and for ALL delivered to the saints" (Jude 3).

I am willing to work across all religious and denominational lines to humbly aid any man or woman who is willing to stop this "free fall of moral insanity" into the abyss that our President and many congressional leaders and judges are more than willing to help us plunge into, but I cannot compromise the New Testament that Christ's Spirit has taught me.

Every intelligent Greek and Roman Catholic knows what happened in the First Apostasy. They know what the original Apostles in the primitive Congregation of Christ had taught. Just as it requires eternal vigilance to be FREE, it requires eternal vigilance to be CHRISTIAN.

The apocalyptic symbol of water, the tides, and tumultuous upheaval of the waves, represents the unpredictable nature of political powers. All we have to do is read or hear the daily news to ascertain just how fragile and unpredictable political trends are. The ten horns will grow to hate the Whore. The world in general hates the Roman Religion. Before Christ comes, both Daniel and John predicted a gradual decline of the power of Religious Rome. Daniel said, "She will be consumed and destroyed to the end" (Da 7:26). The word "destroy" is pecuniary

("Chabel", Strong's 2257) which means to destroy, harm, or to hurt. This does not mean to annihilate! No better time has existed than today for converting Catholics out of Romanism (Rev 18:4).

Your author came from a Catholic background and knows how hungry for TRUTH and righteousness many of the Children of Rome can be. Many of them are also troubled with the "signs of the times" in America today. On January 22, 2015, Thousands of people gathered in Washington, D.C. for a "50th Year Remembrance of 50 Million Children" who were murdered since U.S. Supreme Court ruling (Roe v. Wade (1973)) legalized the abortion of infants. This modern-day slaughter (genocide of infants) in America is similar to King Herod's slaughter of the innocents in ancient Judea (Mt 2:18).

Dale Carpenter, with several of our Shenandoah Christian Alliance partners, reported the joy and elation that filled the Capital area to demonstrate to overturn Roe v. Wade. Carpenter said, "What was astounding was the number of youth there." A young lady from North Dakota gave a speech on the "Rights unborn children have to be born," and Mr. Carpenter said the speech by this teenage lady was so good, "I would have voted for her to be our President." The National Catholic Dioceses really got behind this rally and the license plates on the busses were Missouri, Texas, Georgia, Arkansas, and Kansas, to mention a few states. He added, "It would be a great testimony if in this kind of format to save the unborn children of America from murder could be shared by millions of Catholics and Protestants alike." We might add to this, "What kind of Christian Testimony do we have if we sit at ease in Zion and watch others sacrifice, brave the cold elements, pay the cost for travel, fund raise, and expend our time, all for the sake of one little baby who has the same right we had 'to see the light of day!'" There have been 55,772, 015 unborn children sacrificed on the altar of blood lust over the past 50 years. If we think it too late to become involved and demand an end to this murder, then we are cold, casual, and calloused to the divine right of life. Shame on us!

What is happening in our world is the reverse of Post-Millennialism! Post-Millennialism teaches that things will become progressively better before Christ comes. However, in respect to the application and diligent appreciation of moral, biblical truth, the Word teaches that things are going to get progressively worse! (2Ti 3:1-7; Lk 18:8). And they have.

Revelation 17:17, 18: For God has put it into their hearts to accomplish his purpose by agreeing to give the beast their power to rule, until God's words are fulfilled. The woman you saw is the great city that rules over the kings of the earth."

Those not deceived by the Woman's lies will rejoice when she falls. The people of the Congregation succumb to disobedience because of Babylon's ornaments and deceptions. Constantine joined what he thought was the Christian Congregation because he could not destroy her. His motives for joining are very questionable. Instead of using his influence to advance pure New Covenant Christianity, he helped create a Church-State. This Church-State led to an influx of paganism by which pagan traditions and false doctrine infiltrated the Congregation. Pagan Rome entertained a plethora of false doctrines and mystical religions. Rome was intoxicated with promiscuity. It seduced the true Congregation from its first love, with the pretentions of divine authority, pomp, and ceremony. The Ecclesia of Christ had gone into the wilderness for hiding, but she could not stay there. The Earth opened up, which represents the completed New Testament from Heaven to Earth, and swallowed up the false doctrines that did not deceive the Woman; although, these doctrines deceived the fickle world. The wilderness served as a hiding place while the Congregation of Christ passed through history. The tragedy of Revelation 17 is that the corrupt congregation, "hieros," would not enter the wilderness, but stayed in Egypt-Sodom-Babylon and perched herself on the back of the Beast. The world crept into the Ecclesia and made her a mystery of iniquity.

Revelation Chapter Eighteen

Revelation 18:1, 2: After these things I saw another angel coming down from heaven, having great authority, and the earth was illuminated with his glory. And he cried mightily with a loud voice, saying, "Babylon the great is fallen, is fallen, and has become a dwelling place of demons, a prison for every foul spirit, and a cage for every unclean and hated bird!

Like the Patron Angel of the Everlasting Gospel, This Angel is a Patron of the Authority and Light the Gospel Message Sheds on a Dark World.

This angel is a peculiar angel for he has great authority and great light. It is supposed that this may be the same angel we met in revelation 14:8, but here he is playing a much greater role in serving His King. Like the patron angel of the everlasting Gospel, this angel is a patron of the authority and light the Gospel sheds upon a dark world. Yes, even in the midst of a 1,260-year dark age, peoples of all nations were still receiving Gospel light. This light is the light of the Gospel, the Light of the World, exposing the darkness of the Whore's sins. The once great and powerful Babylon has fallen! (Isa 21:9) Religious Rome has lost their graven images, their rosaries, and their gods! She is on her way to complete and utter ruin.

A former priest of the Roman Church, Emmett McLaughlin, wrote a book, *People's Padre*. This book documents some of the self-confessed failures and evils of Religious Rome. There were 12 printings with 200,000 books selling in one year. This is only one documented resource of Babylon receiving punishment.

Revelation 18:3: For all the nations have drunk of the wine of the wrath of her fornication, the kings of the earth have committed fornication with her, and the merchants of the earth have become rich through the abundance of her luxury."

All, except the Remnant, have committed adultery with her false doctrine. Those of the world have chosen to drink her wine of agreement with inquisitional bloodshed and fornicate with her doctrine. Whether kings or nations, they have all indulged themselves in the richness of the Greek and Roman Churches. They had monetary benefits from selling idols, trinkets, rosaries, and the like. Now, they are receiving the repercussions for their lawlessness.

Revelation 18:4: And I heard another voice from heaven saying, "Come out of her, my people, lest you share in her sins, and lest you receive of her plagues.

This is the call, "Come out of her!" Notice the angel calls them, "My people." Not only did the world participate with her, but the elect as well! They shared in her sins and because they refused to repent, and as a result, they share in her plagues. The Apostate Church has no cure. We must come out of her or go with her!

Revelation 18:5, 6: For her sins have reached to heaven, and God has remembered her iniquities. Render to her just as she rendered to you, and repay her double according to her works; in the cup which she has mixed, mix double for her.

The sins of the Roman Church were so great that they reached the Heavens above the Earth. God is bringing double punishment upon her because she doubled her iniquities. This indicates that her judgment will be more than complete. God has stored up retribution toward her for her sins. An interesting sidelight is Old Babylon wanted to build a tower that reached Heaven (Ge 11:1-9). In this text, we notice that the builders finally reached Heaven. However, they did not reach Heaven with their masonry skills of architectural and engineering pride, but with their sin. If the sins of the people do not collide with the bloody slopes of Calvary, they will reach Heaven and collide with the wrath of God.

Revelation 18:7, 8: In the measure that she glorified herself and lived luxuriously, in the same measure give her torment and sorrow; for she says in her heart, 'I sit as queen, and am no widow, and will not see sorrow.' Therefore, her plagues will come in one day — death and mourning and famine. And she will be utterly burned with fire, for strong is the Lord God who judges her.

She gets double, because she is not just sinning as a damned worldly being but sinning under the masquerade of being a Christian. She led others astray! She will receive plagues, mourning, famine, and she will be overtaken by death. She thought she was strong; she thought she was everlasting; but she was wrong. Her wealth came from the benevolence of others. However, they will be amazed at how she will fall before their eyes. Her fleshly ways have caused her own death. Notice that while the apocalyptic text uses analogies of trauma and grief suffered by material loss, yet it is obvious that given the intensity of the unrelieved suffering, the misery is that after death.

Revelation 18:9, 10: "The kings of the earth who committed fornication and lived luxuriously with her will weep and lament for her, when they see the smoke of her burning, standing at a distance for fear of her torment, saying, 'Alas, alas, that great city Babylon, that mighty city! For in one hour your judgment has come.'

Those who marveled at her prestige will marvel at her destruction. They are in mourning because this subterfuge has ended. How could an institution with such great power, people, and wealth fall in such a short time? This exemplifies the fact that God is in control. Babylon is only lasting as long as God wills her to last. In this case, the people of the world are saying the same thing they said prior to Jerusalem's fall at the hands of the Romans, paraphrasing, "If this happens to those who say they are God's people, if this happens to an institution that calls itself Christian, what chances do we have?" (Ro 11:21-24)

Revelation 18:11-14: "And the merchants of the earth will weep and mourn over her, for no one buys their merchandise anymore: merchandise of gold and silver, precious stones and pearls, fine linen and purple, silk and scarlet, every kind of citron wood, every kind of object of ivory, every kind of object of most precious wood, bronze, iron, and marble; and cinnamon and incense, fragrant oil and frankincense, wine and oil, fine flour and wheat, cattle and sheep, horses and chariots, and bodies and souls of men. The fruit that your soul longed for has gone from you, and all the things which are rich and splendid have gone from you, and you shall find them no more at all.

She has had all the luxuries of life stripped from her. The merchants mourn for they no longer will benefit from the selling of their non-essential items. These imported items from all over the world made Rome the center for international trade. No merchant could compete with the Rome of that day.

Pre-Millennialists take this chapter as a literal, physical, future coming of "THE" Antichrist. However, ponder the expressions used in this specific passage. Is the merchandise listed in the text the merchandise of that day or the future? The largest gold reserve in the world, held in America, is under lock and key. It is never to be used again in the financial trade of world markets. Why are not electronics, chemical components, oil, or sophisticated metals mentioned? How absurd to apply this apocalyptic passage understood as literal merchandise of the 1st Century to an unknown 21st Century future.

Revelation 18:15-19: The merchants of these things, who became rich by her, will stand at a distance for fear of her torment, weeping and wailing, – and saying, 'Alas, alas, that great city that was clothed in fine linen, purple, and scarlet, and adorned with gold and precious stones and pearls! For in one hour such great riches came to nothing.' Every shipmaster, all who travel by ship, sailors, and as many as trade on the sea, stood at a distance and cried out when they saw the smoke of her burning, saying, 'What is like this great city?' "They threw dust on their heads and cried out, weeping and wailing, and saying, 'Alas, alas, that great city, in which all who had ships on the sea became rich by her wealth! For in one hour she is made desolate.'

There is weeping from the world because they enjoyed her. The people relied upon her to satisfy their excessive lifestyle. They are losing everything they had. The world was astounded at the fall of Imperial (Pagan) Rome after nearly seven centuries of world sway, and they will be stunned at the fall of Religious Rome who, to this day, has enjoyed 15 centuries of religious power, and at times, secular power, also.

Revelation 18:20: *Rejoice over her, O heaven, and you holy apostles and prophets, for God has avenged you on her!*

Judgment comes upon the wicked in vindication of the righteous. The righteous should rejoice for God has given her what Babylon deserved! She has become subject to the judgment she exercised upon the Christians.

How long will Babylon last? (Rev 18:19, 20). Babylon has been around for thousands of years. However, she will fall in one hour. Some scholars question whether God can destroy a worldwide institution in one hour. God could do it in one second! This is as absurd as to say that it took God four billion years to create the world! If God could create the world in six days, He could destroy it in a second. This is symbolism, but God could do it in less one hour!

The Apostles have been avenged! The New Testament has proved to be true. What happens if there is a slightest shift from the Apostles Doctrine to Babylonianism? It will all be lost. The Apostles would have lost the just cause for which they all gave their lives.

Revelation 18:21-24: *Then a mighty angel took up a stone like a great millstone and threw it into the sea, saying, "Thus with violence the great city Babylon shall be thrown down, and shall not be found anymore. The sound of harpists, musicians, flutists, and trumpeters shall not be heard in you anymore. No craftsman of any craft shall be found in you anymore, and the sound of a millstone shall not be heard in you anymore. The light of a lamp shall not shine in you anymore, and the voice of bridegroom and bride shall not be heard in you anymore. For your merchants were the great men of the earth, for by your sorcery all the nations were deceived. And in her was found the blood of prophets and saints, and of all who were slain on the earth."*

She is now in the prophetic aorist, a non-existent religious persuasion. She has lasted thousands of years only to meet her doom in the end. She will never be blessed with happiness. One can take away her purgatory, eating fish on Friday, and limbo, but no one can take away her destined misery. She will not possess profit, talent, or sympathy. She will be a city without inhabitants. Her old ways of sorcery to seduce the nations, occult rites, and pagan priests have come to an end and will never work again. Her punishment will not even be heard. She will be tossed to the bottom of the sea with a milestone around her neck, which means she will be devastated, never to be retrieved. She has taken credit for all the blood and persecution of the Body of Christ, and now she will receive her reward! Like Nadab and Abihu (Nu 3:4), no one will so much as mourn over her.

The association between the craftsmanship and industry of Pagan Rome is connected with the rise and continuing power of Religious Rome. This is given for the reader of John's day and us, who read this book, until the end. The overriding theme for both Pagan and Papal Rome is what they had in common; they both shed the blood of Prophets and Saints. This transcends history. We learn that religious Rome is here until the end of time, but this is one institution God will allow to last in order to destroy it fast.

Revelation Chapter Nineteen

Heaven Exults over Babylon

Revelation 19:1, 2: *After these things I heard a loud voice of a great multitude in heaven, saying, "Alleluia! Salvation and glory and honor and power belong to the Lord our God! For true and righteous are His judgments, because He has judged the great harlot who corrupted the earth with her fornication; and He has avenged on her the blood of His servants shed by her."*

Unbelievably, the great Satan has masterminded the building of an institution far greater than Nimrod could build on the plains of Shinar (Ge 10:9, 10). Religious Rome is the greatest institution on Earth, but the heavens recognize the source of righteousness in the Lord God. His judgments are declared true and righteous for He has pronounced punishment upon the great harlot. She has corrupted the Earth with her false doctrine and denial of Christ as the only mediating King. The conviction of corruption in this passage denotes a wasting away or moral deterioration. The word "corruption" (Strong's, no. 5351.) is "consume." Regarding the demise of religious Babylon, Daniel prophesized its "consuming" (Strong's, no. 7) and destruction (Strong's, no. 8046) (Da 7:26). "Consume" implies to waste one's status down from a higher to a lower form. Hence, we used to use the word, "consumption," for the deteriorating states of cancer. Her influence to promote sin has caused both moral and doctrinal corruption throughout the world, as well as the Congregation. God must, by necessity, avenge her destructive actions. Remember, Rome did not originate the first "Christian Church." Christ founded the first Congregation through the Holy Spirit on the Day of Pentecost 30 A. D. (Ac 2:41-47). This primitive Congregation did not reach Rome until those Christian Jews from Rome left their pilgrimage and returned there (Ac 2:10, 12:10).

Revelation 19:3, 4: Again they said, "Alleluia! Her smoke rises up forever and ever!" And the twenty-four elders and the four living creatures fell down and worshiped God who sat on the throne, saying, "Amen! Alleluia!"

In January 2014 A.D., "Pope" Francis called all of us to tolerate the abominable sin of sodomy (www.time.com: The Pope Francis Statement That Changed the Church on LGBT Issues). This doctrinal stance is diametrically opposed to the Holy Father in Heaven. This smoke is verification of eternal punishment upon her (Rev 14:11). Even the most "prominent" celestial beings in Heaven are praising God for His judgments! Remember, even Angels are interested in this Gospel we preach (1Pe 1:12).

This same "Francis" caused a lot of ruckus by his statement that even atheists will go to Heaven (www.catholic.org: Pope Francis says atheists can do good and go to heaven). The Pope and his supporters tried their best to "water down" the effect of this bold statement, but both Reuters and Huffington Post reported that Pope Francis' statement indicates his belief that because Jesus died for all humanity, even atheists will go to Heaven if they are good.

Just stop and think about this for a minute. A person saved by the covenant Grace of Christ will certainly live the life of "imputed righteousness," but knows assuredly that he could never earn salvation. The Pope believes in "infused" righteousness. How many works of goodness can we perform to earn our way to Heaven? How could a devil from Hell cheapen the effect of the blood, brutality, bigotry, agony, torment, forsakenness, mockery, the blood licking dogs, the substitutionary death, the borrowed tomb, and the bereavement of those who loved the most, if it were all done for those who do not believe and obey? This is crass universalism. Yes, Jesus died potentially for ALL universally, but not ALL of them are in blood covenant with Him, but MANY are (Mt 26:28). Like the rest of us, the Pope needs to read his Bible.

Revelation 19:5, 6: Then a voice came from the throne, saying, "Praise our God, all you His servants and those who fear Him, both small and great!" And I heard, as it were, the voice of a great multitude, as the sound of many waters and as the sound of mighty thunderings, saying, "Alleluia! For the Lord God Omnipotent reigns!

The servants of God on the Earth are joining in heavenly worship. God is omnipotent, all reigning, all-powerful, and sovereign. If all else fails, Christians should be convicted to worship God based upon the omnipotent characteristic alone! This proves His dominance over all principalities and powers.

Revelation 19:7-9: Let us be glad and rejoice and give Him glory, for the marriage of the Lamb has come, and His wife has made herself ready." And to her it was granted to be arrayed in fine linen, clean and bright, for the fine linen is the righteous acts of the saints. Then he said to me, "Write: 'Blessed are those who are called to the marriage supper of the Lamb!'" And he said to me, "These are the true sayings of God."

This marriage supper explains why Christians are in continual preparation. They have remained obedient to the Lord's commands by their own determination. Notice this Scripture says, "His wife has *made herself* ready." Christianity involves active participation as Servants of God! We must not only call ourselves Christians; we must also seek daily various ways to implement an outreach to the lost. Their pure garments prove their faithfulness, truthfulness, and diligence to the Lord. In their willful submission to Christ, imputed righteousness has been manifest (Ro 5:18-16:8).

This righteousness is not inherited for no one deserves it (Ro 3:10). It is not "infused righteousness" as if some human religious leader can bestow grace upon another. Christians have responded to the grace and mercy of God and the outcome of this Biblical response is God's imputing righteousness to His adopted children. This "imputing of righteousness" is acknowledged as the first act of God's declaring us righteous by receiving His Son through obedient faith (Mk 16:16). The soul of the obedient believer is made perfect and declared justified. In a sense, this is the Christian's down payment upon God's second act of imputed righteousness. God's second act takes place when the body of the redeemed is resurrected and declared righteous (Ro 8:11, 23; Php 3:21).

God's invitation is quite remarkable. Christians who are in the *espousal* – courtship state – are called to remain faithful and pure to Him. Paul said he was jealous of those who he espoused to Christ and then began to become unfaithful

(2Co 11:2). In this 21st Century, generally there is a very low view of sacred marriage, and the relationship is based more upon sexual union than seeing the relationship consummated after God pronounces His blessing upon it. In a Christian relationship, even the engagement courtship and the espousal relationship should involve chastity and sincere faithfulness to the prospective mate.

The next stage is the engagement and the terms of engagement. This is a solemnization of our conjugal commitment to each other in the presence of the Holy Spirit, who is the seal of our salvation. The presence of the Holy Spirit calls Christians to take up their crosses and follow Him. This involves a denial of ourselves as Christ becomes manifest in our person (Mt 10:37-39). This denial of self is the trial and testing period for Christians to decide to whom their faithful allegiance will reside.

Now, the Groom continues to perfect the Bride in His personal righteousness. God paid the price for the Bride and espoused gifts to her (Ge 34:12; Eph 4:11-3, 5:27). This is a paradox. As Christians are preparing themselves for Christ, He is preparing them for Himself. During this time, the Bride confesses to remain faithful to Christ until death. This is faithfulness to God's Word. God in Christ paid the price and engaged Himself to Christians at their baptism by immersion. The word "joined" in Romans 6:5 is the word used concerning marriage in Romans 7:3. In this moment of our immersion, God seals us with the Holy Spirit, "His diamond ring" (Eph1:13; 2Co1:22). Only steadfast faithfulness can ensure a sufficient relationship with Christ.

The diligent process described above leads to the wedding day, also known as the *processional*. This is an exciting time when Jesus returns for His Bride! Christians need to remain faithful (keep oil in their lamps of light) to be a part of this banquet, or else they will be removed (Mt 22:1-14, 25:1, 31). No one knows when this will occur. Christ can come at any time. Christians need to consult the New Covenant daily to make sure that they are ready. After Christ's return, the Bride will be presented to God the Father for the eternal wedding feast. The Hebrew marriage was consummated by the appearance of the bride and the groom, as well as the bridal party, before the groom's father. This is total redemption, hope realized, and faith made manifest. This will exceed anything anyone has ever known or experienced on Earth. The wedding feast is forever (Rev 19:9). We will never forget the honey from the honeymoon.

One of Scripture's most beautiful thoughts is that expressed to the Apostle Peter by Jesus, "When you were young, you dressed yourself and walked wherever you wanted to, but when you are old, you will stretch out your arms and another will take you where you do not want to go" (Jn 21:18). Some translate it as; "Take you where you cannot go."

My 97-year old Mother has dementia. She lived with my wife and me for years. People with this brain disease think that they are young again. Indeed, they think they are living a "second childhood." Fortunately, Mom can walk, eat, drink, sleep, and use the rest room. On the other hand, mentally she is as helpless as a three-year old child. Thus, when we think of what Jesus said, we are naturally inclined to think that Jesus predicted His old age and brain crippling dementia. Unlike Mom, He would need extensive geriatric care. But Jesus is not talking about that at all.

The clue to this is, "Jesus said this to indicate what manner of death he should die to glorify God. Then he said 'follow me'" (Jn 21:19). Jesus is not referencing an old man receiving continuous care in a nursing home. "Follow me" is a verbal encapsulation of the last moments leading up to Peter's accepting a death warrant and execution for being an Apostle of Jesus Christ. He would die for the three-fold command from John 21:15-17, "Feed my sheep, feed my lamb, and feed my flock."

Tertullian, Origen, and Eusebius wrote of Peter being crucified upside down on an X-shaped cross. This method of crucifixion would indicate that Peter was undressed of his own cloths and clothed with prison or execution type garb. He would have "stretched out his hands" in a crucifixion mode, and he would have been carried under the power of his executors to where he did not want to go.

There is also another Scriptural clue that is usually forgotten. Jesus asks Peter, James, and John if they could "drink the cup that He would drink, and be immersed with the immersion he would be immersed with." This cup represented the manner of death that He would die. Metaphorically, He would be immersed in sorrow, agony, and grief on the cross. And they answered, "Yes, we can!" (Mt 20: 22) Jesus said, "Yes, you will drink the cup I drink, and be immersed in the immersion I will be immersed with …" (20:23).

James suffered the bloody death of decapitation (Ac 12:2). Based upon ecclesiastical history, Peter suffered a very bloody death if he was crucified upside down.

Traditional history says he requested such a death because in his words, "I am not worthy to die in the same way my Lord was crucified." John's death is not recorded, but since he was one of the threesome that Jesus said would die in the bloody manner in which He died, it is a foregone conclusion that he was either beheaded or crucified.

BUT HOW WILL WE DIE?

But we might consider another beautiful story behind the manner of death that Peter died. Jesus may have been speaking to every Christian who is reading this. Allegorically speaking, when we are energetic Christians, we plan our lives; we seem to think we are in charge; and we make decisions to go places every day. Of course we walk with the Lord, but we are not always aware of His presence.

But when we mature in our Faith, along with our years, things start to change. We put more confidence in our Lord and less in ourselves. As death approaches, we extend our arms to Heaven. Stephen certainly raised his eyes and his arms to Heaven as he saw, "Jesus seated on the right hand of God the Father" (Ac 7:55). Another one has to clothe us and lift us up. That person is the ONE who comes to us. In order to be presented before the Father, we must have the absolutely pure clothing of imputed righteousness. Since flesh and blood cannot inherit eternal life, we must be clothed with something other than flesh and blood.

Before Christ went to the Cross, the angels came to carry Lazarus into Abraham's Bosom (Lk 16:22). When Christ comes down, as in the New Jerusalem, we will meet Him in the air (1Th 4:17). Just as Lazarus had angels as his pall bearers before the Cross, Christ will lead the procession of angelic "pall bearers" (Mt 25:31) when He comes to take "FIRST" those who have died, "fallen asleep in Christ," and then living Christians will be transformed and be clothed (2Co 5:2).

Those taken ("second" – by implication) have the same change of garments that the bodies of deceased Christians will have when their decomposed bodies are resurrected first. The "dead in Christ" (those who have died down through the years) are first in order because their bodies will be reunited with their Spirits, which had gone on to be with the Lord. The spirits of these Saints will accompany Christ as He returns for their bodies, "those who fell asleep (died)" (1Th 3:13, 4:14).

So Paul says that the Lord will keep His promise to resurrect the bodies of these saints before those Christians who are alive at Christ's coming get their new transformed body. Those who are alive at Christ's coming will get the "best deal" because, like Enoch, they will be translated, "in a moment, in a twinkling of an eye" (1Co 15:52). They will not die a first death.

Our allegory is complete. Christ will come for us some day in the future. THAT IS TRUE! But according to Stephen, and as with Peter, the Lord was very near to them when they died. They stretched out their arms, and we will too. They called on the Lord Jesus, and we will too. They were carried where they could not go. We will too because there is no way we can leap from Earth to the Throne of Christ and bring Him down (Ro10: 6). They were clothed with different garments. We will too. Whether we go to Heaven in spiritual form before Christ comes, or ascend in glorified bodies (resurrected from the grave or transfigured in a twinkling of an eye), our bodies will not be the same as they presently are.

Yes, Jesus will come in the future, but He may come for YOU sooner than you think. Are you ready to reach up with uplifted arms and face and cry, "Lord Jesus, receive my spirit?" The Evangelist ends his sermon and cries, "Come, ye, and receive the Lord!" But we forget that He has already come TO us with the Gospel message, and He will come FOR us at death. We need to emphasize more the coming of Christ to and for us than our coming to Him (Jn 14:18, and kindred verses in Jn 14-16).

Revelation 19:10: And I fell at his feet to worship him. But he said to me, "See that you do not do that! I am your fellow servant, and of your brethren who have the testimony of Jesus. Worship God! For the testimony of Jesus is the spirit of prophecy."

This angel of God is obviously not Christ because the angel does not accept worship. Anyone who bows to angels, prophets, evangelists, pastors, or teachers is creating an offensive crime against God's Holiness! This is the apostate tendency of man. John's worshipping the angel is a sin that is done out of fear and in ignorance. The Bible says,

> "Do not let anyone who delights in false humility and the worship of angels disqualify you for the prize. Such a person goes into great detail about what he has seen, and his unspiritual mind puffs him up with idle notions" (Col 2:18).

These angels and men, ordained by Christ, are servant leaders. They are not revered tyrants. They are to be treated as servants. This truth proves several absolutes:

1. No one has exclusive property in the Scriptures, not even angels.

2. No human being has "ex cathedra" authorization from God to be the exclusive, codified expert on what the Scriptures teach (2Pe 1:20, 21). But all covenant Christians who are filled with the Holy Spirit can be led to understand Scriptures (1Co 2:12).

3. All Christians possess the same spirit of prophecy that was in Jesus, in the angel of Revelation 19:10, and in John the Apostle. Throughout the ages, no one is superior to the written Word, other than Christ Jesus.

4. In a special way, the evangelist, as an *Angelos* in the hand of Jesus, has the spirit of prophecy when he testifies of Jesus Christ according to the New Covenant instructions.

Revelation 19:11: Now I saw heaven opened, and behold, a white horse. And He who sat on him was called Faithful and True, and in righteousness He judges and makes war.

This is one of the most exciting passages in all Scripture. The King of Kings is ready to fight! God's people have been distressed under the heavy-handed tyranny of the Beast, false prophets, and the harlot. Christ is ready to repay and punish their unrighteous actions. This White Horse is not to spread the Gospel because its presence announces eternal doom to the lost. The appearance of this Horse speaks of but one thing – Judgment and Damnation. The White Horse of Revelation 6:1 is in all probability the spread of the Gospel.

This is the coming of the Lord! The following four different terms are associated with the Jesus' coming:

1. Apocalypse – "To unveil (reveal) what is right (true) and wrong (false)." It also unveils the destinies of all nations and humanity. It unveils the destinies of Satan, demonic principalities, and the future of the universe.

2. Epiphany – "To shine upon." The brightness of His coming will be like a spotlight shining upon the whole world. This light will shine into the darkest heart and work of humanity, or shine upon the brightest uplifted faces of the saints.

3. Parousia – "To stand beside." It is His desire and will to be with His people forever. This word has a dual meaning. This presence can be a visitation like that of the destruction of Jerusalem (Mt 24:27; 2 Th 2:8; Jn 14:3). Parousia can also mean to *be beside* or a *personal presence*. This passage can be a visitation that shocks or a personal appearance and arrival to aid and comfort.

4. Erxomai – To come and bring whatever is associated with your coming. It is incomprehensible for us to know exactly what Jesus will bring to each of us and the whole world when he comes.

If we look closely at the Book of 2 Thessalonians, we see the above four words that describe Christ's coming:

1) " Apocalypse" (1:7)

2) "Parousia" (1:9)

3) "Erxomai" (1:10) Here, Paul uses "erxomai" to say, "He shall come to be glorified in His saints" as an ordinary word for come "bring, entry, see, or accompany." John uses this word at the end of His Revelation, "Even so COME Lord Jesus."

4) The word "epiphany" is used in the 2nd chapter, "The brightness and manifestation "epiphany" of His coming" (2:8).

Interestingly, we cannot use any one of these Greek words exclusively to define Christ's Coming. In one verse, Paul uses the two words, apocalypse and epiphany, to describe the Second Coming (2Th 2:8).

Revelation 19:12: His eyes were like a flame of fire, and on His head were many crowns. He had a name written that no one knew except Himself.

His eyes are like flames of fire for nothing is hid or can escape His sight (Rev 1:14, 2:18; Da 10:6). The Greek word for crown in this passage is diademata, which is the same crown mentioned in Revelation 12:3 and 13:1. This crown is a symbol of royalty and honor. This Greek word is not the other Greek word for crown, "stephanos," which also denotes royalty (Rev 6:2), but stephanos leans more toward an award as a victor at the games or a festive garland used when rejoicing (1Co 9:25). Christians neither deserve, nor should they expect a diadem, but Christ has many. Christians are honored to wear a stephanos crown, but they will even throw it down at the feet of Jesus on that day (Rev 4:10).

Upon this diadem crown is a name that will only be known at Christ's triumph. Four mysteries exist concerning Christ's return:

1. How He shall appear?

2. His new name that no one presently knows? (Rev 19:12)

3. The new name of believers?

4. The exact time of His coming?

Revelation 19:13-15: *He was clothed with a robe dipped in blood, and His name is called The Word of God. And the armies in heaven, clothed in fine linen, white and clean, followed Him on white horses. Now out of His mouth goes a sharp sword, that with it He should strike the nations. And He Himself will rule them with a rod of iron. He Himself treads the winepress of the fierceness and wrath of Almighty God.*

The robe dipped in blood most likely represents the blood of His enemies (Isa 63:2). However, ironically, when His affectionate followers see the bloody garments, they will be reminded of blood-redemption. Now, His enemies' blood will be shed. Jesus is called the Word of God because the Word is the fullest revelation of God. Even with this Word, the Godhead is incommunicable to the finite minds. This denotes Christ in His fullest glory (Jn 1:1). In Revelation 6:2, the rider had a long bow indicating "distant warfare." But here Christ has a sharp sword verdict that brings the closeness of sudden, certain death.

These armies are probably not angels, but Christian conquerors (Ro 8:37), who have gone to Him in death and will return with Him in life (Jude 14). Those with Christ are equipped and ready to follow Him into battle. How thought provoking to consider also that the rider of the White Horse in Revelation 6:2 is a conqueror. Many of them have died for Christ in the flesh; now they will see Him triumph over their enemies. They have ridden the White Horse of the Gospel ready for battle. The perception of Christ and His followers have been that of weakness, passive, meek, mild-mannered, and non-confrontational. Christians had to be this way on many occasions. However, Christ and His followers are military-minded individuals, possessing strength, and fortitude. Christ is ruling, punishing, and delivering God's wrath to all those who have not believed in Him and not obeyed the Gospel (2Th 1:8).

Revelation 19:16-19: And He has on His robe and on His thigh a name written: KING OF KINGS AND LORD OF LORDS. Then I saw an angel standing in the sun; and he cried with a loud voice, saying to all the birds that fly in the midst of heaven, "Come and gather together for the supper of the great God, that you may eat the flesh of kings, the flesh of captains, the flesh of mighty men, the flesh of horses and of those who sit on them, and the flesh of all people, free and slave, both small and great." And I saw the beast, the kings of the earth, and their armies, gathered together to make war against Him who sat on the horse and against His army.

We have seen how evangelism has been thwarted through all six cycles of this great Revelation. Now, even at the very end, Satan is making a last ditch effort to oppose the Gospel. This passage describes the great battle of the Lord. Notice He is already described as the King of Kings and the Lord of Lords. He is not a King in waiting, He is not crowned King after the spurious rapture, but He *exists* as a King. In fact, He came to this world to make that truth known (Jn 18:37). Jesus testified to the *current* truth, not the *coming* truth. He is coming to partake in the supper of the Great God (Eze 39:4, 17-20). This is a complete consummation of the enemies and their possessions.

This last battle of the New Testament is Gog and Magog. It is the end. The following enemies are represented:

1. The Beast (Kings and Kingdoms)

2. Harlot (Roman Greek Church and their many children)

3. False Prophets (Cults and religions of the world)

Some Christian teachers have taught that those who have been disobedient (but nominal believers) will enter into a waiting place to be purged of all wrong. This place was known as Purgatory. Papal Rome abolished the doctrine of purgatory at the end of the 20th century. They also teach that we can pray for dead people and buy their salvation. However, these doctrines could not be further from the truth. The Bible teaches that Christians are not redeemed with silver or gold; Christians are redeemed by the Blood of Jesus (1Pe 1:19). Once a person goes to Hades for rejecting the blood of Christ, he is destined for Hell. There can be no reprieve or stay of execution. The three abominations listed above rose together in Revelation 12 and are now going down together in Revelation 19 to everlasting punishment.

(For more information on Gog and Magog, see Chapter 20.)

Revelation 19: 20, 21: Then the beast was captured, and with him the false prophet who worked signs in his presence, by which he deceived those who received the mark of the beast and those who worshiped his image. These two were cast alive into the lake of fire burning with brimstone. And the rest were killed with the sword which proceeded from the mouth of Him who sat on the horse. And all the birds were filled with their flesh.

By observing the vultures circling the sky, the troops always knew where the battle was being fought. The final punishment for the Beast and false prophets is everlasting Hell. The others are killed with the sword (Word of God) and picked apart as the birds ate their flesh. The flesh-eating birds are divine metaphor of a thoroughgoing slaughter. Christians will enjoy the wedding feast "supper" forever (Rev 19:9), but those who refused Christ's New Covenant will become supper for the vultures (19:17, 18). The bloody metaphor given here is from ancient warfare when the enemy troops charged each other and hacked away at each other until the battlefield was bathed in the blood of the first death.

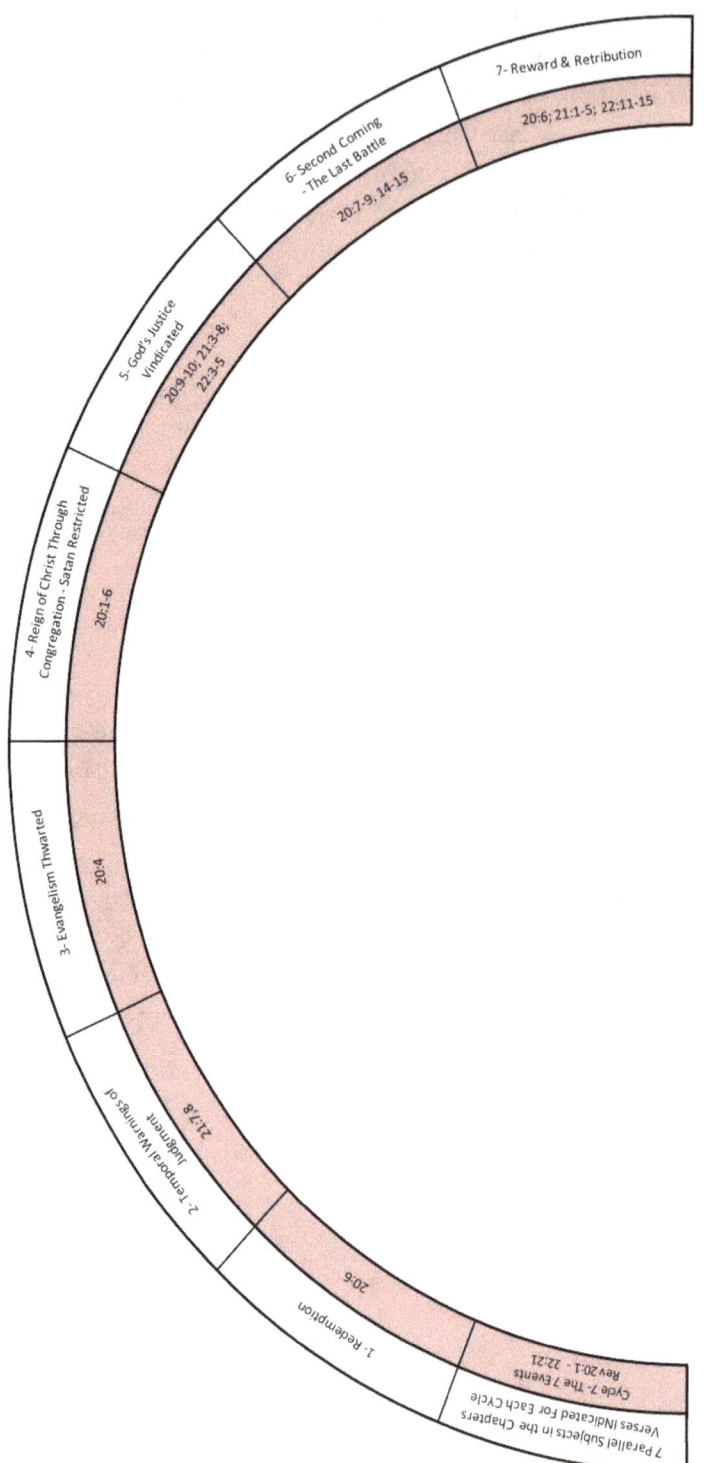

CYCLE 7 – THE SEVEN EVENTS

Christ in Consummation

There are five parallel points in Revelation 20 with Revelation 12 through 19.

Revelation 12:5-12: The birth, death, ascension, coronation, and reign of Christ bruises Satan's head. Michael defeats Satan (12:7).	Revelation 20:1-3: Satan is bound. Michael the Archangel is employed by Christ to overthrow Satan. Though this Angel is unnamed, the author highly considered his name to be Michael.
Revelation 12:13, 14: The influence of Satan is curbed.	Revelation 20:4-6: Those who refused the mark of the beast and did not worship Satan are blessed, holy, and resurrected.
Revelation 12:13-16, 13:7: The final attack against the Congregation. Satan possesses power to make war against the Bride.	Revelation 20:7-9: Satan is released and rallies allies against the Lord's small band of people.
Revelation 14:14: Christ comes on a white cloud.	Revelation 20:11: Christ is on the White Throne and reveals all.
Revelation 19:19: The end of the world.	Revelation 20:14: The end of the world.

Revelation Chapter Twenty

Revelation 20:1-3: Then I saw an angel coming down from heaven, having the key to the bottomless pit and a great chain in his hand. He laid hold of the dragon, that serpent of old, who is the Devil and Satan, and bound him for a thousand years; and he cast him into the bottomless pit, and shut him up, and set a seal on him, so that he should deceive the nations no more till the thousand years were finished. But after these things he must be released for a little while.

Christ came to institute His spiritual nation and bind Satan with the Gospel (1Pe 2:4-9; Jn 16:11ff). In one day, this nation was established with an open door to whosoever will obey (Isa 66:8, 9; Ac 2:1ff).

Christ's reign in Revelation 20:3-5 does not contradict the same reign in Acts 2:30-37. This New Testament dispensation parallels Revelation 12:5-7. Christ has taken the keys of death and Hades and shut their doors to Christians (Isa 11:1-9; Rev 1:18, 19). Christ has bound Satan and his demons with the Gospel (Jn 16:11ff; Mt 12:28, 29). Christ cast Satan into the same abyss as Revelation 11, which was created out of God's anger (Dt 32:22). This is the headquarters and operation center for all satanic activity (2Pe 2:4). This *Chilias* (Greek) reign denotes a timed period under the number 1,000. Christ is reigning with His Congregation as an eternal reign (Lk 1:31-33).

Many Pre-Millenialists deny the eternal reign of Christ because they misunderstand the use of this Greek word in this context. Revelation 20:2 is not a literal 1,000-year time period. Often, the Bible has figurative or symbolic writings to correlate spiritual truth. For instance, John 3:5 symbolizes spiritual birth, not physical. This confused Nicodemus greatly! (Jn 3:1-21) Another example is Psalm 90:4, which says, "For a thousand years in your eyes are like yesterday when it passes by, or like the hours of the night." No time restrictions can be placed upon God or His Kingdom (2Pe 3:8; Rev 22:5). If we take these 1,000 years to be a literal 360 day-to-year 1,000 years, we must also take the other symbolic numbers in Revelation literally as well. This involves the 144,000, the number 10, the 1,260 days, 3½ days literally, as well as the number 7 literally. If we read these numbers in Revelation without understanding Biblical numerology, they will appear to be discrepant and contradictory. Viewing the 1,000-years as symbolic has roots in apostolic teaching, as well as others.

Satan is bound during this time, but his demons remain at work (1Pe 5:8). The Pre-Millennials say that if Satan is bound it must be a long chain. They believe that Satan is free, and his power is unrestricted. If this is true, the Pre-Millennials must deny that Jesus is the Advocate. They must also deny that Satan has been eternally cast out of Heaven. However, in view of truth, the chain is only as long as one wants it to be. Satan's binding is only in respect to New Covenant Christian testimony. Jesus came and "bound" the strong man (Mt 12:29). The only protection from Satan is to have the Seal of the Everlasting God (Eph 1:13; Rev 7:3). Without the Seal, mere human beings are no match for satanic persuasion and doctrine. Only God in Heaven and the Congregation on Earth keep Satan bound! Each Congregation has the discretion to decide whether or not Satan will dwell in their midst or be cast out. As long as we Christians walk in the Spirit and preach the Gospel (death, burial, and resurrection) of Christ, Satan has no power over us. He will tempt, and sometimes even hinder, but he does not possess absolute power over us.

BUT THE LORD SAYS, "BUT BRING HERE THOSE ENEMIES OF MINE, HE DID NOT WANT ME TO REIGN OVER THEM, AND SLAY THEM BEFORE ME" (LK 19:27).

In the above verse, Jesus is speaking of Jerusalem's destruction, but His statement is also a reference to the propriety of a loved one who witnesses the execution of the murderer of their innocent loved one. Our pacifistic society refuses to believe human beings are evil and capable of heinous crimes because in their eyes, humans are innately good. These pacifists refuse to accept that premeditated man-slayers should be executed. In their opinion, what Jesus said is considered outlandish. While not so common today, this practice of witnessing such executions is still with us.

Could it be that we will see the greatest murderer, from the beginning to the end of the world, brought to final judgment? (Jn 8:44) Three thoughts come to mind: 1) Will the lost sinners see Satan judgment? If they do, they will suffer the same fate. "Depart from me, you cursed into everlasting fire prepared for the devil and his angels" (Mt 25:41, 46). 2) Will those who are saved see Satan? 3) How can Satan be executed if he is going to be punished for eternity? We humbly seek to answer these profound questions

Why does Satan need to be released for a little while? We do not have much Scripture to back us up, but will all the people who have ever lived see Satan in the last day? We know that the lost will see whoever personifies the political beast and the false prophet (Re 19:20). The lost will also see Satan because they will be cast into the "fire prepared for the devil and his angels" (Mt 25:41). This is the same FIRE mentioned in Revelation 19:20. The sight of Satan will certainly be by far the most horrible, revulsive, and dreadful experience ever known to humanity. It brings relief and comfort to a family when they finally realize that the murderer of their loved one has been brought to justice and judgment. We read an article about a very articulate young man who observed the execution of the man who killed his father and raped his mother (www.texasmonthly.com). He gave eloquent testimony as to what it is like to witness the execution of a murderer. Satan is also a murderer (Jn 8:44). He is a mass murderer of billions of souls.

We may be challenged with the question, "How can Satan be executed if he is going to be punished for eternity?" Death does not mean cessation of existence. Jeremy Meyers gives an exceptional treatise on the New Testament word "dead" (nekros) meaning lifeless, useless, or separated; but we agree with Mr. Meyers that death never means "nonexistent" or "annihilation" (www.redeeminggod.com). So, "eternal death" is mentioned in Scripture. Satan will not live in eternal Hell; he will die forever in eternal Hell. I trust that we will never see Satan in such eternal misery because we would share his eternal fate (Mt 5:22).

But will Christians see Satan in the Last Day? As we have already mentioned, "Satan will be loosed for a (micros) time." It has also been mentioned previously that a criminal is executed before the king (Lk 19:27). My answer is that God wants Christians to see Satan and his identity. God wants Christians to see the horrors of the last hour on Earth and the destruction of all of their enemies so they will fully appreciate their heavenly dwelling place. My argument is weak, but when Satan is released from his prison, he will go out to deceive all nations and gather his worldwide troops together to do battle against what is left of us, "The camp of saints about, and the beloved city" (Rev 20:9).

Thus, I believe that in our mind's eye, we will see the archenemy, our adversary, and the colossal antichrist, Satan, brought down and cast into the Lake of Fire. This will not just be a literal, physical type of combat with human-like grunts and groans; this will be like the eruption of a spiritual volcano charged with billion and billions of tons of nuclear explosions falling from Heaven. I must admit that I would like to be there and see, with the enlightened eyes of God's spirit, this enemy of all mankind so greatly exposed, the one who claimed to have great power over the whole world. Satan will appear weak before the King of Heaven. We know for certain that after we arrive in God's Heaven in glorified bodies, we will "see no evil, hear no evil, and do no evil" forever because all former things are passed away (Rev 21:4). But before this eternal moment of serenity and freedom from all evil that can soil our minds, thoughts, and bodies; it could be that our last view on Earth will be to see the prince of all evil, and evil in its entirety, destroyed once and for all.

Revelation 20:4-6: *And I saw thrones, and they sat on them, and judgment was committed to them. Then I saw the souls of those who had been beheaded for their witness to Jesus and for the word of God, who had not worshiped the beast or his image, and had not received his mark on their foreheads or on their hands.*

And they lived and reigned with Christ for a thousand years. But the rest of the dead did not live again until the thousand years were finished. This is the first resurrection. Blessed and holy is he who has part in the first resurrection. Over such the second shall reign with Him a thousand years.

The 1,000-year reign of Christ is not a physical reign upon this Earth. This epoch is often referred to as the *millennium*. It is interesting to know, like the word "Trinity," the Latin word *millennium* is not in Scripture anywhere. In the Revelation passages, "chillias" refers to Christ's reign and Satan's subsequent binding. The Greek word *chilias* is found two times in 2 Peter 1:8 and six times in Revelation 20:1ff. The wise men asked, "Where is He who is born King of the Jews?" (Mt 2:2) This and other questions continue to be asked and debated today. Is Christ King? Does He have a Kingdom? What and where is it?

The King's reign is rooted in Old Testament prophecy. The Jews rested their national hope and universal cosmological expectations upon The King's coming to Earth to reign. It is not surprising that even Christ's own disciples were so ignorant of kingdom prophecy that they would have taken Him by force to make Christ sit upon the materialistic throne of their self-centered ambition (Jn 6:15). Christ gave such overwhelming evidence that He was King and Messiah that those of His day faced the crisis of accepting the King or murdering Him.[106]

Antichrists *today* advocate that His Kingdom was postponed. This is the doctrine of John Nelson Darby, also known as *Darbyism*. The theory of most Pre-Millennialist presupposes that the fulfillment of the Daniel 9:25-27 prophecy was postponed when the Jews rejected Christ. Take note that the word *Christ* comes from the word *Messiah* in the Hebrew. To be anti-Christ is to be anti-Messianic-king (Lk 19:14, 20:15). Both the Pre-70 A.D. Jews and the Pre-Millennialist refuse to accept Jesus Christ as eternal King. In order for the Pre-Millennialist to prove their doctrine, they must add the following additional false doctrines to the Scripture (20:4-6):

1. The Second Coming of Christ
2. A Rapture
3. A Reign on Earth
4. A literal Throne of David

5. Jerusalem in the land of Palestine

6. Christ on Earth

When John says, "*This* is the first resurrection" in Revelation 20:5b, it is an introductory statement leading to the idea of spiritual priests and kings who reign with Christ in Revelation 20:6. The Bible exclusively points out that Christians are raised from death to life when they are immersed into Christ. This, literally, takes place in their first resurrection at their immersion. The following passages apply,

> "Or don't you know that all of us who were baptized into Christ Jesus were baptized into his death? We were therefore buried with him through baptism into death in order that, just as Christ was raised from the dead through the glory of the Father, we too may live a new life" (Ro 6: 3, 4).

> "In him you were also circumcised, in the putting off of the sinful nature, not with a circumcision done by the hands of men but with the circumcision done by Christ, having been buried with him in baptism and raised with him through your faith in the power of God, who raised him from the dead" (Col 2:11, 12).

> "Jesus said to her, 'I am the resurrection and the life. He who believes in me will live, even though he dies; and whoever lives and believes in me will never die. Do you believe this?'" (Jn 11: 25, 26)

> "Since, then, you have been raised with Christ, set your hearts on things above, where Christ is seated at the right hand of God" (Col 3:1).

> "And you He made alive, who were dead in trespasses and sins, in which you once walked according to the course of this world, according to the prince of the power of the air, the spirit who now works in the sons of disobedience" (Eph 2:1, 2).

It is obvious that John is changing the subject after he says, "The rest (remaining) of the dead (bodies) lived not until after the thousand years was finished" (20:5a). That last statement concludes the thought of the bodies of the beheaded souls coming to life after the apocalyptic 1,000- year reign.

The Saints reign with Christ, and He reigns forever (Rev 22:5). The 1,000-years are just an apocalyptic way of revealing the reign within the sphere of human time and activity in an undetermined, yet definite period of human history.

When Christ ascended to the Throne, He received an invisible, spiritual Kingdom (Lk 19:15). Note the order in this verse. Christ, the nobleman, went into a far country (Heaven), and he called servants and gave 10 of them various amounts pounds of money (19:13). However, the citizens (the Jews) hated Him and sent a message after Him, saying, "We will not have this man rule over us" (19:14). This statement was unwaveringly supported throughout His death (when they ask for Caesar to be their King). Three and a half years later, they rejected the Gospel by murdering Stephen. This rejection continued until 68 A.D. when they rejected the mighty Gospel missionary, Paul (1Th 2:16).

In the next verse (19:15), "It came to pass, that when He was returned (the Second Coming), having received the Kingdom (past tense) then He summoned those to Himself that they give an account of the stewardship of treasure." Notice, He returns after He received the Kingdom, not before. This verse blows Pre-Millennialism out of the water. Christ does not return to set up His Kingdom; He returns to call to account the citizens of His Kingdom, and the world in general.

He orders His executioners to slay His (Jewish) enemies before His presence (19:27). Christ was the Lord of the judgment that eliminated Judaism in 70 A.D. (Mt 23: 33), and He will be the Lord of their judgment when their Hadean domain belches up their spirits for the Day of Reckoning (Rev 20:13; Mt 23:39). Christ was the Prince of Daniel who had power over the little prince of Rome, "Titus."

Their crime, and that of many Gentiles, is that they would not allow Christ to reign over them. Christ's return is after He established His Kingdom. The return is after He had already received His Kingdom. There is no other way an honest reader can interpret the context of this passage. This is precisely what Daniel meant when he prophesied,

> "I saw in night visions, behold, one like the Son of man came with the clouds of heaven, and came to the ancient of days (This is prophesied also by John in Revelation 4 and 5, especially 4:7), and they brought Him (The Son), near before Him (the Father). This is The Regeneration throne scene. And there was given to Him dominion, and glory, and a Kingdom" (Da 7:13-14a.).

The Kingdom in Tribulation and Triumph

Daniel also sees the Kingdom in two stages. First, Daniel sees the spiritual Kingdom (The Covenant Kingdom of the Regeneration) that is in great persecution (Da 7:21), and he sees the Kingdom triumph in the end (7:27). However, the Kingdom is given to the saints to possess forever and ever, even forever and ever (7:19). It is an undetermined, yet definite apocalyptic 1,000 years as men and women enter it in each generation on Earth and as part and parcel of the eternal Kingdom of Heaven (Rev 22:5). But the saints leave time behind after the Second Resurrection.

A fabulous resurrection that Christians can enjoy in this world

John then, introduces the subject *"this"* is the First Resurrection (Rev 20:5b). In the Koine Greek, there are two words for *this*; the first is *tow-tace*, meaning this in the same, and the second, *hoo-tace* referring to what proceeds or follows, (after that, in this manner, as, even so, for all that, likewise, no more, on this fashion, so, in like manner, what, thus).

If John wanted the, *this*, of 20:5b to refer back to 20:5a he would have used a word more suited for this sentence construction, *tow-tace*. He would then refer the First Resurrection to "the rest of the dead" as their experience at the end of the 1,000 years.

Although the word *hoo-tace* could also refer to a previous idea, the word has 15 definitions that refer to what follows. In my research of the word, *hoo-tace*, I found it usually comes at the beginning of a sentence, whereas, *tow-tace* comes in the middle. *Tow-tace* also shows possession, and is used by John in the last chapter of Revelation as "this book" (Rev 22:9, 10, 18) and "this prophecy" (22:19).

In 1 John, the word *hoo-tace* is used at the beginning of the sentence as an introductory thought, "by this we know we love," to a conclusion "we love God and keep His commandments" (1Jn 5:2). Notice also the introduction, "this is the record," and the conclusion, "God has given us eternal life," (5:11). We can make the application for ourselves in 5:14, "This is the confidence (introduction), if we ask anything according to His will He hears us (conclusion)." Thus, John uses "this" is the First Resurrection as an introduction to the experience that blessed and holy ones experience to become Priests and Kings of God.

Remember Cardinal Hugo of Saint Cher, or Stephen Langton, added the verse numbering later. This numbering was not a part of the original text. The addition of the verse numbering is beneficial, but obviously, Revelation 20:5b really introduces the subject of 20:6. The devil does not miss things like this. He knew Millennial Maniacs would be so preoccupied with this verse that they would forget the very purpose for which Christ came and died. The devil also knew that the verse was improperly numbered.

Millennial Mythology got started over the misconstruction and placement of one little verse of Scripture. The devil believes and trembles concerning God's Word. He also believes the Word of God. Even though he misconstrues and misinterprets God's Word, the devil still believes it. He placed the italicized word "unknown" in 1 Corinthians 14:2. He started a whole denomination of "unknown" tongue talkers. The King James Version (KJV) editors inserted the word "unknown" thinking they would do people a favor. Contrarily, the KJV editors created much confusion and false doctrine.

Some say, "Bible students should not make too much of the word *this* in this passage." However, remember Jesus said, "Man shall not live by bread alone, but by *every word* that proceeds out of the mouth of God" (Mt 4: 4). We might add that the devil causes death by every word that can be misrepresented and deleted from the Scriptural Logos of God.

The case rests upon the question: "When did Christ sit on this Throne of Regeneration and provide Kingdom Living for His redeemed congregation?" When did He ascend to the Throne that was promised to David and sit on the right hand of the Majesty of Heaven? When did He receive the Kingdom from the Ancient of Days? The Heavenly Reign of Christ on the Throne, with His heavenly hierarchy surrounding Him, is portrayed in the Revelation vision. This is the Regeneration. Christ is life, and He gives life through His Apostolic Word. In the Spiritual Reign of Christ, all of the prophets spoke of the Regeneration-Restitution that took place after Heaven received Him, and His Word was spoken through Peter and the Apostles (Ac 3:19-24). The promised "restitution of all things" lasted from 30 to 70 A.D., and the history of the First Congregation in those days is the only model for all time.

In understanding this spiritual reign, we are helped when we recognize the apocalyptic symbols in Christ's reign (Ps 16:8-11, 110:1, 2; Ac 2:4, 29-37). In view of the Spiritual Reign of Christ, the Pre-Millennialists attempt to spin-doctor the word "spiritual" to make it appear as a negative word. Pre-Millennialists do this because they do not understand the apocalyptic and parabolic literature of the Old Testament prophets that describes Christ's Reign. They chose to literalize and carnalize the Reign of Christ. This jeopardizes the interpretation of Scripture, and therefore, of God.

God *is* a spirit, and they who worship God, worship Him in spirit and truth (Jn 4:24). A Spiritual God only reveals to His creation such truths through His Spirit (1Co 2:10). No man can understand the things of God without the Holy Spirit (2:11, 12). A proper understanding of Revelation, as well as the whole Bible, can occur only by comparing spiritual truths with spiritual truths. No one should be accused by a literalist for spiritualizing the Kingdom of God (Ro 14:17). The parabolic Apocalypse of Ezekiel's Temple vision can only be understood through spiritual discernment.

As King, Christ has control over the abyss (Rev 12:7; Jude 9; Jn 19:11). He brought the chain of the Word, the Testimony, and the Blood to bind Satan. These three actions do not prevent Satan from ruling the world, but they do prevent Satan from conquering the Congregation (Rev 9:11, 12:10, 11). Christ cast Satan out and ascended to a Throne that lasts forever (Lk 10:18; Jn 12:31; Heb 1:4-8).

Before the New Covenant was established, Satan could present himself before God and accuse his people (Job 1:6-12; Rev 12:10). After Christ's victorious ascension, Michael the Archangel was commissioned to bind Satan by the Gospel (Mt 12:29, 16:11, 17, 27; Mk 3:23-30; Lk 11:20, 10:17-19). This act initiated the apocalyptic 1,000-year reign. In Biblical numerology, the number 10 represents completion (10 x 10 x 10 = 1,000). John often uses numerology as a teaching technique for 1st Century Christians who were enduring persecution. The numbers seven, ten, 144,000, 1,260 days, 3½ days, and 42 months are used in an apocalyptic manner. Other passages in the Bible show this as well (Ps 50:10; Hos 8:12; Dt 5:10; Da 9:24-27; 2Pe 3:8). This 1,000-year epoch represents, in time, His undetermined, yet definite reign over His Congregation (1Co 15:25). The reign described in this passage is only part-and-partial of His eternal reign (Rev 22:4, 5).

Another apocalyptic symbol is the number 666. The mark is the number of a man. From literature written in that day, the discovery of the number Gematria matches that of both Romulus, founder of Rome, and Latainos. This is the Mark of the Beast in the heads and hands of people who embrace the false doctrine of Babylonian confusion and serve Satan with their intellect (Head-Mind) and service (Hand-Labor). Even their punishment of the Lake of Fire is described, apocalyptically, as everlasting punishment of fire and brimstone. We can be assured this is apocalyptic usage because molten lava would destroy literal flesh instantly (Rev 19:20, 20:14, 15). The pain and agony of apocalyptic description is worse than carnal torment.

To understand the rule of Christ in Revelation, we must be out of our fleshly, carnal mindset, and in the spirit. Jesus said, "My Kingdom is not of this world" (Jn 18:36). The Greek usage in this passage uses *Ek* for out of, not *Apo*, which means *from*. The Kingdom of Christ is composed of Spirit, not flesh. Jesus condemned the flesh (Jn 6:63; 1Co 1:29). When we enter the Kingdom of God, our citizenship resides in Heaven (Php 3:20). From that point forward, Christians are called to seek things above and reign in heavenly places (Col 3:1, 2; Eph 1:3). Not only is Christ reigning, but His saints are also reigning with Him (Heb 1:8f; Ac 2; 1Co 6:2, 3; 2Ti 2:12). These powerful passages convey to our mind the thrones of judgment for those who were persecuted. When Christians enter the Kingdom of God, they co-reign with Christ (for time and eternity) and prepare themselves to judge the world (1Co 4:8, 6:1-3; Rev 1:5, 3:21, 24, 4:6).

During this apocalyptic 1,000-year reign, some will not live again until the 1,000-years are finished. When they die, their bodies await the *Second* Resurrection. However, they participate spiritually in the First Resurrection. This is when one enters into the death of Christ and resurrects with Him to walk in newness of life (Ro 6:1-6). This First Resurrection takes place at the immersion into Christ. This is where the individual identifies with the death, burial, and resurrection of Jesus. In this instance, each person is united with the risen Christ, and they are blessed! Consequently, in obeying Jesus, the Second Death has no power over them. Hell and eternal punishment are no longer their end, for they are resurrected with Jesus Christ. Christians are now declared Sons of God (Gal 3:26-29) and Priests in the Kingdom (1Pe 2:9).

Notice that those who take part in the First Resurrection, render the Second Death powerless, and reign as priests co-reigning with Christ in the 1,000 apocalyptic years. This confirms Christ's axiomatic TRUTH of Matthew 16:16-18 that down through the successive ages, through the message of His Congregation, millions of souls and even circumstances that have been "loosed" or "bound" on earth (TIME) will already have been "loosed" or "bound" in Heaven (ETERNITY). Protestant scholarship on this verse has proven conclusively that Christ "rock" (feminine gender) is not Peter "Petros" (masculine gender), and therefore Peter is but a stone in the massive Rock of Christ "cut out of Heaven" (Da 2:34). There is a far cry from "Petros" being a great evangelist (Ac 1:15, 2:14) and being what Babylon called him later "Pontifex Maximus." Peter's sermon at Pentecost initiated in TIME on Earth the potential of ETERNITY in Heaven for those who obeyed His New Covenant Gospel (Ac 2:35-38).

This authenticates that the 1,000 apocalyptic year reign is in fact the New Testament dispensation that began in Ac 2:38-41 and continues for an undetermined (eternity), yet definite time, in respect to this life.

"The Rest of the Dead" (Rev 20:5)

Anthony A. Hoekema, on page 161 of Clouse's, "*The Four Views*," gives a brief synopsis of how the A-Millennialist (Menamillenialist) views the 1000- years. We use "mena" (present-abiding) to describe an apocalyptic 1000-year present reign of Christ in time, but eternally outside of time. Mr. Hoekema's commentary on the 1000-years is provided below along with mine. "My view" expounds on his position. After this overall commentary, I present his position on Revelation 20:5b, which is acceptable to many scholars. Further investigation has led me to believe that there is a more acceptable interpretation that eliminates the challenge presented by Hoekema's debating opponent.

1. Since the number 10 signifies completeness and since 1,000 is 10 to the third power, we may think of the expression,"1,000 years," as a complete period, a very long period of indeterminate length.

2. The period extends from Christ's First Coming to His Second Coming. (My view: This view is acceptable; however, we disagree with the view of many that 1,260 years extends from the First to the Second Coming.)

3. Since "the Lake of Fire" mentioned in verses 10, 14, and 15 is obviously a description of the final place of punishment, the "Abyss" mentioned in verses 1 and 3 must not be the place of final punishment. (My view: We must accept "the Abyss" to be the base of

Satan's operation. The Abyss is also a holding place for his spirit-soul prisoners until the Final Judgment.)

4. Satan was not bound in "the Abyss" in the Old Testament (Ac 17:30). In order for Jesus' commission (Mt 28:19) to be completed, Satan will not be able to deceive the nations as he has done previously (Rev 20:1-3). Satan can still do harm, even while bound, but he cannot deceive the nations in order to keep them from learning the truth. "The Gospel is not bound." (My view: On 2Ti 2:9, where the exact same word for bound is used, Satan cannot prevent the spread of the Gospel, and he cannot gather all of the enemies of Christ together to attack the church, in some world order type of scenario.)

5. Later, Satan will be loosed and do the one thing he was restrained from doing, and that is to completely deceive all nations (vs. 7-9).

6. The New Testament certainly teaches the binding of Satan by Christ. The same word used for binding the strong man (Satan) in Revelation 20 is used in Matthew 12:29. Satan's binding is evidence of God's Kingdom (Mt 12:28). Jesus personally destroyed the devil in Matthew 4. Satan is bound in order for the Gospel of the Kingdom to be preached to all nations (Mt 13:24-30).

7. Satan's fall in preliminary prospect was apocalyptically viewed by Christ in Luke 10:17, 18 and can be viewed only in connection with the Disciples' missionary activity. Preliminary prospect means that some action has not happened, but the conclusion is already known.

8. In connection with Christ being lifted up (on the cross, from the grave and Hades, and to the Throne), the Prince of the World is driven out (Jn 12:31, 32). The word "driven out" (ekballo) has the same root as is used in Revelation 20:3. Even more astonishing is the fact that with His being "lifted up," not only Jews, but also all nations will be drawn to Him. Instead of conquering them, as the nations conquered Old Israel, the Kingdom of Christ will conquer the nations.

9. The 1,000 years of verses 1-3 is the same as the 1,000 years in verses 4-6.

10. The thrones in these verses are not on Earth (as the Pre-Millennials teach) but in Heaven. Leon Morris identifies that in the Book of Revelation, the word "throne" is used 47 times and in all but three of those (2:13, 13:2, and 16:10), the throne appears to be in Heaven. When the "souls" are seen, we know the scene has shifted to Heaven. We conclude that the 1,000 years from verses 1-3 is from Earth's standpoint and that verses 4-6 depict what goes on in Heaven.

11. The authority to judge is given to these martyred saints who died *only* because of the Gospel. This is not surprising because the Book, written by an exiled Apostle "in the Kingdom and tribulation" is greatly concerned with matters of justice. (My view: The only suffering the Pre-Millennial philosophy will cause is when the fictional Christian doctrine is examined and found to be fraudulent.)

12. These persecuted and martyred saints are given judgment and authority with Christ (I call it consulter-reigning), which means the authority to make judgments, either in agreement with Christ or their own judgments about earthly matters. (My view: There would be no greater place for them to have authority over five or ten cities then in Heaven (Lk 19:17-19). In any event, reigning with Christ involves some part in Christ's judging activities (Da 7:22).)

13. The reign is with beheaded souls. (My view: Obviously, it is not on Earth with millions of Christians running around with their heads cut off). The soul (personality) that was in the body is now out of it (Rev 6:9). In vision, John could see the souls as easily as he could see the angels, but he was "in spirit" (Rev 1:10).

14. Since millions of Christians have been martyred throughout the years, Brethren and loved ones should be comforted to know that they entered into a reign of consolatory judgment of the world with Christ. "Know ye not the Saints shall judge the world?" (1Co 6:2) (My view: In a sense, all Christians, both living and dead are in this reign, but the martyrs are given due honor and recognition.)

15. Unlike the world (Rev 13:8, 15-17, 14:9-11) which cannot accept the "narrow minded" view of *one* King and *one* kingdom, who bow to the Beast (the Roman Catholic worldview of Christianity), and serve

them with their head (pluralistic intellect) and hand (menial service), the "remnant of Christ's" Covenant Church keeps His Commandments (Rev 12:17); they do not bow (15:2) or worship (13:15) with the images, rituals, cathedrals, relics, as substitutes for Apostles Doctrines. They were killed for no other reason than this. (My view: We cannot help but notice how different the world is from the remnant Christian faithful. The Christian faithful accept the singularist (narrow minded) view of ONE King and ONE Kingdom. On the other hand, the world (13:8, 15-17, 14:9-11) bows to The Beast's World View of Christianity. In light of these verses, it is really a contradiction to speak of a "Christian World View." We should speak of the view of "Christ's Kingdom in the World." A lost sinner can subscribe to a "Christian World View" but not understand the Kingdom of Christ on Earth. Everyone in the world is somehow a part of Babylon, but in Christ "We are not of the world" (Jn 15:19). The world bows to the Beast's worldview of Christianity and serves them with their head (intellect) and hand (menial service). (My View: There are some dedicated educators who use the phrase "Christian World View," but they do not know what they are doing.)

16. The Pre-Millennialists think the coming to life is a physical resurrection. This physical resurrection cannot be, however, because verses 11-13 at the end of the chapter show a physical resurrection that is distinct from verse 5. To believe this would have Christ teaching two resurrections, i.e., one resurrection at the beginning of the "millennium" and the other at the end. Plain Scripture teaches elsewhere that we will enjoy only *one* bodily resurrection for both the believer and unbeliever (Jn 5:28, 29; Ac 24:15). (My view: The resurrection is of a glorified imperishable body (1Co 15:42-50), including soul-personality and Spirit. We enter a new environment with angels, who are spirits, and the Godhead, who is Spirit. The word "apparition" fails to describe this existence. A mere physical body would become incinerated in the fiery blasts of Hell or before the flaming fire of the Holy God.)

17. Therefore, the "coming to life" is not yet in a glorified body, but the enjoyment of life with Christ after being martyred on Earth. This is a life of great joy (Php 1:23; 2Co 5:8). This consolatory reign with Christ on the Throne is a fulfillment of the promise of Revelation

3:21. What a spiritual escape and relief from the mockery and afflictions they suffered for their New Covenant beliefs. "They live and reign with Christ" (20:4) throughout His perfect reign in Heaven and Earth until they get their resurrected glorified bodies in the end. (My view: The "living again" of verse 4, 5 addresses ONLY the soul-spirit that lives in the Body. The spirit left the body, but the beheaded body remained on Earth. Those remains would be physically resurrected when Christ returns.)

This reign is in Heaven. Nothing is said about an earthly Jerusalem of Jews. This reign is not something in the future or after Christ returns to establish His kingdom; it is going on right now.

Hoekema, p.169, rightly calls the next sentence of Revelation 20:5a a parenthetical statement, and he draws attention to the fact that it is, therefore, put between parentheses in The New International Version, "The rest of the dead did not come to life until the thousand years were ended." Since the original Greek had no punctuation, Bible translators are responsible for placing punctuation correctly into the Biblical text. Bible translators have a great temptation to misapply the teaching of a verse that is not punctuated correctly, or not given its proper verse standing in order.

Hoekema correctly recognizes this problem of verse 5a being the end of the thought and verse 5b being the introduction to another thought. Pre-Millennialists form a mythological message because they do not recognize this textual problem.

Hoekema's View on Revelation 20:5b

We may see two possibilities for the text. First, Hoekema says that the rest of the dead is distinct from the believing dead previously described. Hoekema says these are the unbelieving dead who are the exact opposite of the believing dead. The unbelieving dead certainty did not live and reign with Christ during these 1,000 years. Why would the enemies of Christ share in the joy of this reign?

This does not mean that the unbelieving dead will reign with Christ at the end of the 1,000 years, or we would expect a clear statement to this effect in Revelation 20:3. Rather, what happens to the unbelieving dead after the 1,000 years is what is called in verse 6, "the second death." When it is said, "the second death has no power over" the believing dead, we imply that "the second death" does have power over the unbelieving dead. This second death is in the Lake of Fire (vs. 14).

Now, John says, "This is the first resurrection" (vs. 5b). These words depict what has happened to the believing dead whom John was describing previously at the end of verse 4, before the parenthetical statement just discussed. This "first resurrection" is not a bodily resurrection but a transition from physical death to life with Christ in Heaven. These "first resurrected" believing dead are Priests and Kings of God and reign with Him during their interim in the 1,000 years until Christ comes. When Christians "fall asleep," this terminates their participation in the time-reign of Christ on Earth, and they leave their bodies to go and be with Christ. Christ will return with them, and they will receive resurrected bodies in order to reign with Christ in an even richer way, and serve Him in glorified bodies. To be sure, Christ reigns over us while we are in bodies affected by and subject to earthly time (1,000 years), but He also did, does, and will reign over us eternally when we are released from "time shackled" earthly bodies.

This passage of scripture, particularly verse 5, has troubled many theologians for years. The differing views concerning Christ's Reign no doubt influence our interpretation of this verse.

Millennialism teaches that the First Resurrection is the rapture of the righteous, and the Last Resurrection is that of the wicked with a literal 1,000-year reign of Christ in between. In millennialism theology, 1,000 years exist in the middle of John 5:29. They also have 1,000 years between the two participles "with" His saints (1Th 4:14) and "for" His Saints (4:17).

The Author's View

Standard A-Millennialism teaches that the First Resurrection includes the righteous, and "The rest of the dead" refers to the wicked. The problem with this is it says, "They will live again" (Rev 20:5). The word "*Zoa*" is the essential, vital fullness of life. The wicked will never live, but they die forever. As we observed previously, when Revelation states that the second death has no power over the believing dead, this implies that "the second death" does have power over the unbelieving dead. This second death is in the Lake of Fire (vs. 14). The wicked are treated to this in Revelation 20:14, 15.

The New Covenant view always insists upon a spiritual resurrection, first, and then at death the rest of the Covenant installment, which is the second installment of the Resurrection of the Body. The Lamb's Book of Life is already written. Those added to the Christian Kingdom Congregation are added to Lamb's

Book (Ac 2:47), and in Covenant, Christian Kingdom Congregation names are maintained in that book (Php 4:5). Whether Covenant Christians die a martyred or natural death, they go to be with Jesus until they receive their remains (that which they left on earth). After the Second Resurrection, they will be presented to God the Father in body, soul, and spirit so God will be all in all (1Co 15:24-29). Every immersed Christian has been baptized for his dead (body).

Now, John says, "This is the first resurrection" (verse 5b). After we are immersed, we are raised with Him, mentally and affectionately. When we die on Earth, we also go up to be with Him, "absent from the body." This is not a bodily resurrection but a transition from physical death to life with Christ in Heaven. These first resurrected believing dead are Priests and Kings of God and reign with Him during the 1,000 years until Christ comes. Then, they experience a Second Resurrection and reign with Christ in an even richer way, and serve Him in glorified bodies.

It seems that verse 5b is the beginning of verse 6 as an introductory statement. Verses 5b and 6 should read as one complete thought, "This is the first resurrection, blessed and holy is he that has part in the first resurrection; on such the second death has no power, but they shall be priests of God and Christ and shall reign with Him a thousand years" (vs. 5b with vs. 6).

Pre-Millennialism does not accept that the reign is in Heaven, but on Earth. In projecting Christ's reign into an unknown future, it does not accept the argument that this reign is in the present tense (for John "saw" these things in his present, present tense, and they had meaning for people of John's day, 2,000 years ago). Pre-Millennialism does not accept the argument that there cannot be two physical resurrections. It rejects what Peter said of David's prophecy in Acts 2:25, and that God promised He would raise up Christ-Messiah-King to sit on the Throne promised to David, "He seeing this before spoke of the resurrection of Christ" (Ac 2:31).

That this was not a physical, earthly Kingdom is clearly enunciated, "Therefore, being seated on the right hand of God exalted and having received of the Father the promise of the Holy Spirit, He has shed forth this what you NOW see and hear" (Ac 2:33). Pre-Millennialism does not teach what the Apostle Peter said. It cannot accept that Christ established on Earth, through the Holy Spirit, His Kingdom. Christ's Kingdom could not be a carnal Kingdom like David reigned over. Why do Pre-Millennialist place such great importance on a physical, carnal kingdom of Christ when David already reigned over such a kingdom in the past?

This is why Peter made it clear that David's corrupted, physical body was still in the grave. A physical kingdom is of no importance. However, David looked up and saw this Kingdom of Christ through the Holy Spirit, and God assured David that of His seed (Christ, *Immanuel* after the flesh, but eternal God in spirit), He would rise up one to sit on the throne promised to David, forever.

The "Rest of the Dead" – The Remains of the Dead!

The conclusion concerning the "rest of the dead" is that they are not the unbelieving dead; they are the remains *of* the "believing dead." The "rest of the dead" refers to the *remains* or *dead bodies* of the martyred for the following reasons. These bodies are just as important to God as their souls are. Their souls are in Heaven with Jesus. Everybody has a soul-personality. The person who inhabited that body goes on living after death. If God is going to resurrect the body and reunite it with the soul, we can be sure God knows where that body died, whether on land or in the sea. We can be sure the Holy Spirit, who is a down payment on that body, knows exactly where that body resides. Certainly, the bodies of those martyred saints must be accounted for. The RESURRECTION and the LIFE said, "He that believes in ME, though he should die, yet he should live!" (Jn 11: 25). Since they died for Jesus, He is accountable to them, and He takes responsibility for their abused bodies. If this were not the case, what would the Holy Spirit do after the resurrection? His charge is to *quicken* and bring them to life again as He raised up Jesus' body. Will the Holy Spirit be put on hold in Heaven after the resurrection?

Paul answers this perplexity. He says, "The body is sown a natural body. It is raised a spiritual body" (1Co 15:44). For the body to be Spiritual, it must have the Holy Spirit. Therefore, the Holy Spirit, which now occupies the spiritual inner person at the resurrection, will move outward into the bodies as well. It may be farfetched, but perhaps the blood vessels formerly filled with blood, will then be filled with the Holy Spirit "for flesh and blood cannot inherit the Kingdom of God." Therefore, the Holy Spirit will be very active, throughout eternity, after the resurrection of Spiritual bodies that will be "forever with the Lord!" So "the rest of the dead" would be the physical remains of the person who died.

In fact, the Greek word *Loipos*, translated *rest*, is literally *remaining or remnant* (Vine, p. 971). It should be translated in effect, "That which remained of the dead," or the dead body. One can still call the corpse, the remains of the deceased, and that is precisely what this verse means. Even the ashes, or microbes of that body remain, the *remains*.

The question arises, "What is dead in the text?" It has to be the dead bodies of those who were decapitated in the preceding verses. The Apostles referred to the dead body as simply being "the dead." In 1 Corinthians 15, Paul refers to the dead and yet, from context, he is speaking of the dead body. The same truth emerges from Revelation 20: 5. The Greek word for death is *nekros*, being in this instance, that of a dead corpse; and not *thanatos*, which can refer to the act of dying. In other words, the dead body in this text had been struck down and terminated, and the soul went instantly to be with Christ. These martyred saints need to know that Christ will take care of their soul-person while they are in Heaven with Him in the 1,000 apocalyptic year reign. However, He has also made provisions for their bodies to be resurrected at the consummation of His reign when He turns the Kingdom over to the Father.

John, through the Revelation of Jesus Christ, has a knack of opening up scenes in Heaven and on Earth at the same time. The apocalyptic 1,000 years are part of Christ's eternal Reign. It is a wonder the millennial magicians do not literalize 1,000 years and simplify it further for those who try to make God's reign compatible with our 24 hour days and call it the 365,250-day reign. As we have already considered, the 1,000 years is part and parcel of the eternal, but it is also an undetermined, yet definite reign in respect to Kingdom residents on Earth who are governed physically (not spiritually) by solar time. Although living in bodies exactly like those of all men and women given time-life from God (since the beginning of time), Kingdom living is eternal in spirit.

Christians are reigning with Him on Earth in time until they die and go to be with Him. Those who have died are gone from this world in respect to the time people sojourn on Earth. There is a time span, during which the Covenant Kingdom of Christ expands its work and ministry on Earth. Each time interval includes the temporary physical life of those who are servants of the Kingdom, and the overall period of time the Kingdom militant endures on Earth. Still, all of this can be classified as a 1,000-year category within the eternal reign of the Lamb and the Father.

John even writes in Spirit of the reign of all Christians with Jesus Christ. When Christians are buried and raised with Jesus (Col 2:12), Christians become Kings to reign with Jesus (Col 3:1-3; Rev 1:6), and they are a kingly nation of priests of spiritual Israel (Ro 9:1-6, 1Pe 2:5, 2:9). How can an earthly reign in Palestine produce any better priests than described in these texts? Christians live on Earth in time, but their affections are in Heaven where eternity and the resurrected Christ are in their heart and spirit (Php 3:20).

So John envisioned the thrones in Heaven on which were seated those who had been given authority to judge. "And I saw the souls (out of body) of those who had been beheaded (referring to their former body) because of their testimony and who had not worshipped the Beast or his image and had not received his mark" (Rev 20:4). Like Stephen (Ac 7:54), they came to heavenly life (Spiritual) and reigned with Christ in the place where the Lord went at His Ascension (Jn 14:2, 3).

Some Bible scholars have told us that we will not go to this place until Jesus comes, but as we shall see in Scripture, our spirit and soul go there immediately upon falling asleep in Jesus. We know that Stephen went there the minute his spirit left his body (Ac 7:59, 60). What a comforting thought! Until Christ comes, the interim, which is actually part and parcel of the enigma of existing in both time and eternity or between our death and the coming of Jesus Christ, comes under the heading of the 1,000 apocalyptic years. This is a difficult theological concept, but this explanation is the best conceivable solution available to our finite minds.

Because Covenant Christians had not worshipped the Beast and had overcome his influence, they will receive a future resurrection body, which will make them fit (2Th 5:23: body, soul, and spirit) to stand before the God of Peace. In soul and spirit, Christians are fit to be in Christ's presence, but Christ must present us before the God of Peace in the end. Then we will be perfect in body, soul, and spirit.

We must not be confused concerning the role that Christ played by coming to redeem the world in the flesh. In eternity past, Christ enjoyed co-existence as God, with God the Father. Christ is the *monogenos* (eternal co-existing God with God the Father) in eternity, but He became God-Man in time (Php 2:1-8). If the Scriptures teach us anything, it is the divine purpose of the Godhead that Christ had to become flesh in order to redeem men in the flesh. This redemption is complete when we receive glorified bodies made fit for God's glorious presence.

Question, "How does the promise of full redemption of both body and spirit tie in with Revelation 20:5, 6?" We must understand that after Christ comes again, He will not establish His Kingdom, but present or deliver the Kingdom to God the Father (1Co 15:22-28). The redemption that Christ gave Christians is not complete until they have a perfect resurrected body (2Co 5:1-5). This is why He gave Christians the Holy Spirit as a pledge concerning their future resurrected body. No one will receive a resurrected body until all receive a resurrected body. This includes all who died in the Old Testament (Heb 11:40). Revelation 20:5, 6 answer this question! First, Christians receive heavenly life in spirit by going to be with Christ upon falling asleep (Ac 7:59). Then, at His coming, the bodies of those who have fallen asleep will be re-united with their Spirit and the bodies of living Christians will be transformed (1Th 4:13-17). This exegesis combines Scripture with Scripture, spiritual teachings with spiritual teachings (1Co 2:13). No millennial magician is capable of explaining these texts in this same manner.

Why Then Are We Immersed for the Dead? (1Co 15:24)

When Christ comes, the spirit-soul will be placed once again in the body that the dead left on Earth. The entire body of Christ will be presented before the throne of God in His glory as a community of resurrected spiritual bodies. The one thing all Christian have in common is that they have all been immersed into Christ, in time, and because all shall be both individually and collectively bodily resurrected in Him for eternity. This means that each person is immersed individually; they die and go to be with Christ individually, but simultaneously are resurrected collectively. These people were being immersed in advance for the future death of their bodies that in the end would rise above all things as an eternal community.

Do You Have an Insurance Policy on Your Body?

When we are immersed, we secure insurance on a new, everlasting body. Just as a policy is sealed or notarized, so God seals our policy with the gift of the Spirit. The Lord of Life who returns to reward His covenant faithful underwrites the policy. We are immersed for our own personal body. We are not immersed by proxy for the body of some other person who died. Many denominations and cults practice baptism on behalf of dead people. As a New Testament concept, this practice is sheer nonsense. Does the person choosing to be baptized for a deceased person choose also whether the baptism will be done by sprinkling, pouring, or by immersion?

Christians are living in a dying body that will eventually die. Paul sees the end product. Why would 1Corinthians 15: 29 allude to being immersed by proxy for the salvation of another person who died? As penitent believers, people are immersed for their dead bodies in the hope of the body's resurrection at Christ's

Coming. Paul says that Christians have died with Christ in the likeness of His death (Col 2:12; Ro 6:4, 5).

Members of the early, Primitive Congregation would have easily understood the use of the word, "dead," referring to the dead bodies. Paul uses the same expressions in 1 Corinthians 15:12-29, "...how can some among you say there is no resurrection of the dead (*body*)?" (vs.12). "But if there be no resurrection of the dead (*body*), then Christ is not risen?" (vs.13). "Yes, and we are found false witnesses of God...if in fact the dead (*bodies*) do not rise" (vs. 15). "For if the dead (*bodies*) do not rise, then Christ is not risen" (vs. 16). Otherwise, what will they do who are baptized (*immersed*) for the dead (*bodies*), if the dead (*bodies*) do not at all. Why then are they baptized for the dead" (vs. 29)? This implies those who had their bodies immersed and as a community partook of the one immersion (vs. 29).

Christians are immersed in water for the sake of their present body. By comparing Romans 6:1-5, Colossians 2:12-3:5, and Revelation 20:5, it is favorably clear that when we are immersed into Christ, we receive the promises of God. We not only get resurrected *Egiros* life with Jesus Christ in Heaven, but we who are immersed will also receive an *Anastasis* raising up of a dead body to a living one. This will take place at Christ's Second Coming. The First Resurrection occurs when one is buried and raised on Earth with Christ and affectionately raised with Him in Spirit. The Second Resurrection is when Christ comes for those who are alive on Earth to give them the second installment of their salvation, which is a transformed, incorruptible immortal, glorified body.

Clearly, "The rest of the dead" is a definite reference to the bodily remains of a Covenant Christian. Concerning those who have departed to be with Him in soul, He will return with their souls-spirits and reunite them with the same type of glorified body He received at His Ascension. Both the body of the deceased and that of the living will be changed into this glorified state. In Scripture, the dead bodies in Christ will rise to be reunited with the soul-spirit. This reunion takes place before the living bodies, of saints who are alive and present at His coming, are changed. This explanation suits the text of Revelation 20:5 perfectly and is in perfect harmony with other non-apocalyptic Scripture. Even the Old Testament teaches that after the Kingdom of God is established, one comprehensive time exists for the resurrection of all bodies (Da 12:2). How difficult the Futurists make Scripture, which is intended to be plain, clear, and simple. The remains of my dead brothers and sisters will come to life when Jesus comes. That is what Revelation 20:5, 6 says and that is what it means.[107]

Revelation 20:7-10: Now when the thousand years have expired, Satan will be released from his prison and will go out to deceive the nations which are in the four corners of the earth, Gog and Magog, to gather them together to battle, whose number is as the sand of the sea. They went up on the breadth of the earth and surrounded the camp of the saints and the beloved city. And fire came down from God out of heaven and devoured them. The devil, who deceived them, was cast into the lake of fire and brimstone where the beast and the false prophet are. And they will be tormented day and night forever and ever.

Satan is released from the prison of Hades. The prison sentence always precedes the execution. In desperation, Satan attempts to rally allies against the Bride of Christ to wage war against her (a little "camp of the saints"). At this point, Satan has no restrictions placed on him, such as his previous restrictions by the chains of the Gospel.

The Battle of Gog and Magog, or the location, Armageddon, fits perfectly into this Biblical view. In order to properly appraise this battle, we must understand its historical context. In the Old Testament, physical Israel was led to fight physical wars. These battles were fought because of a spiritual ideology that conflicted with the idolatry of the nations surrounding Israel. In the New Testament, spiritual Israel is in a spiritual warfare with false doctrine (Gal 6:16; Eph 4:1-10, 5:10-14). This battle in the New Testament Book of Revelation was written to Spiritual Israel, not physical Israel. Therefore, we must interpret the Book of Revelation and Battle of Gog and Magog through an apocalyptical view.

The historical context of Gog and Magog can be found in the Old Testament. Gog was a descendant of Reuben (1Ch 5:5). The only other time Gog is mentioned in the Old Testament is in the Book of Ezekiel 38:6. He was a leader of a confederacy of nations from the North. We can conclude from this passage that Gog is from the uttermost North (Eze 38:15). Daniel also mentions this king of the North as being one of several successive kings from the North (Da 11:13-15). This was the *Seleucia Dynasty* that descended from one of Alexander the Great's four generals, Seleucis 1 Nicator (Da 8:20-22). Alexander's Empire ultimately broke into two fractions, Kings of the North at war against the Kings of the South, whose headquarters was in Egypt. The Kings of the South were known as the Ptolemy's, who were named after a different General of Alexander's, Ptolemy (Da 11:5, 6, 9, 11, and 15).

Magog is the son of Japheth and the grandson of Noah (1Ch 1:5). In the Book of Ezekiel, Magog is known as a land rather than a man (38:2, 39:6). Neither of these men is mentioned again until Revelation 20:8, where in context, Revelation is replete with apocalyptic terms (example – "four nations," which are compass points). The Battle of Gog and Magog is associated with Armageddon (Rev 16:12, 16). Armageddon is where Judas Maccabees inflicted the final defeat upon the confederacy of armies lead by Antiochus Epiphanies.

Although it is difficult to interpret the final scene of this merger of time and eternity, this battle of Gog and Magog (Armageddon) takes place at the end of the 1,000-year apocalyptic reign. The Satanic forces surround the camp of Christians on Earth, only to be defeated by God with fire from Heaven.

There are many opinions concerning this great battle. Pre-Millennialists will often associate this battle with modern armies coming to destroy Israel. The Pre-Millennial view previously taught some world power, like Russia, will attempt to destroy physical Israel with nuclear weapons (Eze 38:1-3). However, now since the Cold War is supposedly over, Russia has been exposed as a less than formidable power. Pre-Millennialists have had to re-work their false doctrine and revamp their strategy to find a new enemy from the north. Nevertheless, alas, they must go east to choose China or south to choose the Islamic countries as some form of an enemy from the north. This Pre-Millennial doctrine does not align with the apocalyptical view. In the New Testament dispensation, God has transitioned His Covenant from the Old into the New. He no longer associates a true Jew or Israel as physical, but Spiritual (Ga 6:16; Ro 2:28, 29, 9:6-9).

Thus, Armageddon, which was the scene of a final military battle led by Judas Maccabeus against Antiochus Epiphanies, occurred in 167 B.C. This final battle was the culmination of a war that had lasted roughly seven years (160-167 B.C.). Daniel's prophecy (8:9-12 with 8:13, 14) gives the total number of days as 2,300 (mornings and evenings) that Antiochus Epiphanes profaned the Jewish religion (and Temple). The 2,300 days began with the prophecy of the "four broken horns" (Alexander the Great's four generals), and the ONE horn that grew out of the fourth (General Seleucia), namely Antiochus Epiphanes of the Seleucid Dynasty.

What in the World is Investigative Judgment?

The following may be important to thousands of people who have been taught what the Seventh Day Adventists denomination believes in regard to "the investigative temple judgment."[108] This theory began from what was called "the great disappointment." William Miller computed that the 2,300 days of Daniel's prophecy were actually 2,300 years. Instead of applying the days to the history of

Alexander the Great and the rise of Antiochus from Alexander's general Seleucus, Miller took the date of the beginning of the prophecy back to the rebuilding of the Temple in Jerusalem and according to his prophetic math, he counted forward to the year 1844. How amazing that so many people believed, and still believe, this is true.

The year 1844 passed with no sign of Christ's coming. William Miller humbly repented and admitted that his date setting was in error. Nevertheless, some kind of spirit entered into the heart of Ellen G. White (Jn 14:17). (It was not the Spirit of Truth.) She corrected Wm. Miller by saying that he misunderstood the prophecy. Her theory was that Jesus really did come in 1844, but He came invisibly. She said that Jesus' coming was not a coming to Earth at all. He just walked from one place in the Heavenly Temple to another place in the Temple, and this was invisible to us. This interpretation revived the Millerite movement and is accepted by thousands today even though Miller, himself, rejected this theory. How can we address this rationally?

Atrocious gobbledygook is the only way we can describe this twist that The Millerites, and later Ellen G. White, put on these 2,300 days. The Millerites place their beginning at the edict to rebuild the Temple (Eze, Chapter 4) in 457 B.C. and ending October 22, 1844. This latter date, of course, supposedly marks the beginning of the Seventh Day Adventist denomination. In other words, if Daniel ever expected to know that his precious sanctuary would be cleansed of Antiochus's profane abominations, he would still be alive today and a member of the Seventh Day Adventist denomination.

The Biblical fact is that the 2,300 days are also subdivided into 1,290 and 1,335 days, "From the day the daily sacrifices were abolished and the abomination set up" (Da 12:11). Thus, the blasphemous career of Antiochus is divided into the following:

1) His 2,300-day military campaign against the Jews beginning with the ONE horn that was stout and despicable (Da 8:9-14).

2) From the time Antiochus actually profaned the Temple and set up the worship of Jupiter until Judas Maccabees cleansed and rededicated the sanctuary (rekindling the sacred candlesticks) was 1,290 days.

3) The death of Antiochus Epiphanes occurred 1,335 days after the abomination of the sanctuary. Daniel said blessed is the person who lives to see it "waits for and reaches to the end" (12:11).

Thus, many Jews lived to see the end of Antiochus' blasphemous reign, who was their anti-Covenant Messiah. If you think we are being hard on the Adventist denomination, what would God and His Prophet Daniel think about someone telling us that the people whom Daniel was writing to would have had to wait until 1844 to see the fulfillment of the cleansing of their Temple prophecy? The seriousness of this is that the people who were waiting for the prophecy and who were going to be blessed by God when it was fulfilled were really not blessed. The prophecy was not fulfilled when Antiochus died in 164 B.C.[109] In fact, not one of them would have been blessed because they would have had to live 2,008 years until the fabricated blessing was to occur in 1844 A.D. In addition, after 70 A.D., there was no Jewish Temple that needed to be rededicated and cleansed! Oh my, what pretentions parade before our minds as empirical facts that would not even live up to the standard of fiction.

The Reason Scholars Have a Problem with the Apocalypse is because the Apocalypse is a Spiritual Language Requiring a Mind Filled with the Holy Spirit.

We dwell on this not so moot point because the Judas Maccabeus versus Antiochus Epiphanes is given here as an analogy with an apocalyptic overview. At the risk of appearing redundant, we emphasize again the relationship of this prophecy to what The Apocalypse calls the last battle Armageddon; therefore, we must properly understand the historical context of Old Testament Gog and Magog. The last battle between good and evil (righteousness and unrighteousness) will certainly have a physical element to it, because the people living in the last day will live in human bodies. But it is more spiritual than physical because it involves Satan, who is Spirit, and the Godhead, who is Spirit, and it involves essentially, and principally, spiritual warfare that leads to eternal defeat or victory.

The Old Testament analogy of Gog and Magog (Maccabean Covenant, YHVH versus Antiochus, Greek Gods and Hellenistic Culture) was also spiritual warfare but based mostly on human, physical, bloody conflict. Here we offer what may be conjecture. When Jesus said, "Love your enemies," we must realize that it is your enemy and not your neighbor's enemy or God's enemy. We understand perfectly that the stand we take to defend the integrity and the holiness of God may bring us into conflict with satanic enemies. They just might try to kill our families and us. God gave us government to protect us against such enemies (Ro 13:3-6). That is one of the reasons we pay taxes. But suppose our government does not or cannot protect us? By virtue of the same instructions God gave to political governments, it is incumbent upon us to protect lives and to be our brother's keeper.

Sir Winston Churchill said that Islam in a man is like rabies in a mad dog.[110] So Islam is to Christianity what the Hellenism of Antiochus was to God's people. In today's trying times, we need to pray to the King of the Universe to lead us when an overwhelming flood of trial, temptation, and hostility begins to sweep across our Nation and heed His word, "Because you have kept my command to persevere, I also will keep you from the hour of trial which will come upon the whole world to test those who dwell on earth" (Rev 3:10).

The conflict between Maccabeus and Antiochus was more than just armed warfare. Granted, while mostly armed warfare, yet the Maccabean solders were inspired by The Prophets and wise men of the day, but the final Gog of Magog will be the anti-Messiah culture of the world against the Armies of Heaven directed by King Jesus Christ, "Lord Sabaoth" (host). Gog of Magog means much more than what we see on the surface. This phrase has synergy that goes beyond how it is commonly understand. We need to also know the following:

1. There has been a struggle between God and Satan, as well as saints and sinners.

2. This struggle brings tribulation and travail to the *Seed of the woman*, which is Christ and his saints (the bruised heel).

3. This struggle forecasts victory over the *Seed of Satan*.[111]

A continuous running theme throughout the Old Testament involves the Seed of the woman verses Cain, angelic attacks through Giant men, mockers of Noah, Nimrod and the Tower of Babel, attempts upon the lives of Abraham, Isaac, and Jacob. The Seed in Judah and David were attacked along with attempts to destroy the Seed in the days of Esther. Numerous wars occurred against the Seed by Assyria, Babylon, Persia, Greece, and Rome. The last attempt to destroy the Seed and those that bore with the Covenant unto the end of the Old Testament was the war engineered by Antiochus Epiphanies as recorded in prophecy in Daniel 11:11, 15-45. We must keep this background in mind when we study the subject of Armageddon.

SECOND COMING IS LIKE A YOYO

Pre-Millennialism teaches that with the Christ's First Coming, His messianic Kingdom was postponed and the parenthetical – gap – church was established. At Christ's Second Coming, the rapture occurs and the saints are raptured. During this time, the temple of Israel is rebuilt and the Antichrist makes himself known causing seven years of tribulation. This tribulation leads to Christ's Third Coming in which He establishes His millennium, binds Satan, and Kills the Antichrist. Christ looses Satan for the Battle of Armageddon, and Christ wins. This is followed by the renovation of the Earth, as Christ comes for a Fourth Coming. Can you, the reader, see how this physical interpretation leads to an irrational conclusion?

The more rational conclusion is that after the prophets were cut off from physical Israel, God initiated 400-years of silence from Malachi to John, the Immerser. Christ's First Coming to Earth broke this silence. Through His death, burial, and resurrection, Christ purchased the Congregation (Christians) and bound Satan. This initiated an inner peace of goodwill that was previously known in Heaven as the eternal Reign of Christ and gave the opportunity for the resurrection of the soul (Jn 5:25-29).

In the Old Testament, warfare was essentially physical in nature. God's truth was accompanied by armed warfare and physical battles. In the New Testament, spiritual warfare began to be waged against principalities and powers, "Grace and truth came by Jesus Christ" (Jn 1:17). The New Testament dispensation ("the rule of the house" or administration – Strong's no. 3622) Kingdom will continue until Christ's Second Coming. Past expositors have favored the word "dispensation" over the weaker word "stewardship" (1Co 9:17; Eph 1:10, 3:2; Col 1:25).

At His Second Coming, all that is temporary in time will pass away. The spiritual Battle of Armageddon will have a physical effect only on those living at the time of Christ's appearance. This physical effect will be the first death that all must die except Covenant Christians who are living at the time when Christ comes. Christians will bypass, instantly, the first death by being transformed from mortality to immortality (1Co 15:52-55). But all who have lived since Adam have already died the first death. Their bodies will be resurrected for the purpose of damnation (Jn 5:28-30). Thus, the people living at the time of Christ's return will be slain by the sword of Jesus' mouth (Rev 14:18-20, 19:15). This thoroughgoing slaughter is referred to apocalyptically as "tramping out The Grapes of Wrath." If all the streams around Gettysburg flowed with the blood of thousands of soldiers, can you imagine the amount of blood from a first death of over seven billion people? Thus, in this regard, the Second Coming has physical ramifications.

The previous slaughter is nothing compared to the sensational overthrow of Satan and all false religions, principalities and powers throughout history and the condemnation of all opposition to the Throne of Christ. God will resurrect all to judgment where flesh and blood will be no more.

Armageddon was an extremely prominent battleground in the Old Testament. It is known as The Valley (Jezreel-Isdraelon) of Armageddon located near the Euphrates River (Rev 16:12, 16). It was known as the valley of troops and associated with expressing grief over the death of fellow comrades (Jdg 4 and 5; Zec 12:11). Armageddon possessed a strategic overlook of this valley. The following battles took place at this valley:

1. Jael vs. Sisera (Jdg 4:5-22).

2. Deborah vs. Kings of Sisera (Jdg 5:19).

3. Gideon's 300 – Amalek was as "numerous as the sand" (Rev 20:8; Jdg 6:33-7:12).

4. Jehu the Righteous vs. King Ahaziah the Evil (2Ki 9:27).

5. The anger of God kindled in Pharaoh Necco vs. Josiah (2 Kings 23:26-29).

6. Judas Maccabees vs. Antiochus Epiphanies (Da 8:9-14, 11:15-45, 12:11, 12). Daniel mentioned it would be an ongoing war from the time Antiochus Epiphanes, "a rather small horn (a formerly unknown usurper of the throne, Da 8:23), waxed exceedingly great toward.... the Beautiful Land" (Da 8:9) until Judas Maccabeus restored the worship of the temple and lit up the candelabra. The candelabra burnt miraculously for many days. His blasphemous military career lasted 2,300 days (Da 8:9-14). Ezekiel 39:1-3 also introduces the demise of Antiochus Epiphanies (See Addendum B for parallels between the

Books of Daniel and Ezekiel). As previously mentioned, the Seventh Day Adventist denomination teaches the 2,300 days' end with the beginning of their "church" in 1844. There is a far cry from 2,300 mornings and evenings to over 2,400 years from the decree of Cyrus in 536 B.C. to rebuild the temple to 1844 A.D., and a false prophetess named Ellen G. White.

7. British General Allenby defeated the Turks in World War I in 1917.

Armageddon has the following parallels in the Book of Revelation: 1:8, 3:21, 4:17, 11:15-18, 14:14-20, 16:14-21, 18:10-17, 19:11-21, and 20:7-9, 14, 15. The Old Testament battles were fought at earthly places and Armageddon was an earthly place. However, this New Testament battle will take place in the air and fire will come down from Heaven (Rev 20:8, 9). Because God and Satan are spirits who are beyond time and space, this battle must be Spiritual. As Armageddon was the final battle in the Old Testament, this will be the final battle of principalities and powers against Christ in heavenly places (Eph 6:12). When we say "spiritual," do not think that this minimizes the intensity of this fierce conflict of external life and death in the slightest degree. Even now, spiritual battles tax our souls and drain our spirits to the point of death.

Satan, the Prince of the Earth (Job 1:7), has the largest army ever assembled "from the four corners of the earth," but Satan's big problem is that his army consists only of infantry. What chance has a billion-man land maneuvering infantry against an air force that can light up the heavens with firepower? The apocalyptic paradox of this Last Conflict between good and evil compares to the prophetic prototype in Ezekiel 38:16-19 where the Earth felt the violent convulsions of God pouring out His wrath from Heaven upon the enemies of Maccabaeus (Eze 38:20-23).

Frequently, the prophetic Scriptures describe in parables both the historic, bloody, painful physical death of the soldier on the battlefield (Eze 32:10) and the apocalyptic description of his immediate descent into Sheol-Hades (32:18, 19, 21-25, 27-32). This death and descent into Sheol-Hades is an appropriate hermeneutic expression. One of the purposes of studying hermeneutics is to assist our understanding of apocalyptic literature, such as Ezekiel. When the Holy Spirit uses apocalyptic language in human literature, some scholars stumble in an attempt to explain the intended spiritual meaning. Should we be surprised then when the Holy Spirit addresses the here and the hereafter as though they were ONE event?

What a Sensational Event when Time Merges with Eternity.

We have difficulty understanding the horrors of the death of a lost person, "uncircumcised in heart," whose death consummates a long, lifetime war against God. The apocalyptic view of the soldier's last few seconds of life is given from Heaven, and the first physical death is conjoined with the immediate release of the soul into the dark dungeons of The Pit "Sheol." This soldier's death is not so much a mere *rigor mortis* of the soldier's body, but an instant removal of his spirit to the underworld prelude that leads to eternal fire and torment, far worse than just physically expiring.

One difficulty we encounter when reading apocalyptic literature is our failure to see both the invisible (to earthly, physical eyes) and the invisible activity of the Spirit of the Godhead. Throughout Revelation, we are contemplating the work of an anthropos, (Greek for "man") called John, who is in Spirit and who sees things no human eye has ever known to exist.

Thus, this War (a prototype in Ezekiel 38 and 39) and here in Revelation 20:9 involves human beings with human flesh on Earth who are about to die the first death through a divinely inflicted fiery holocaust. We understand this apocalyptic battle to be between those living on Earth against Him who rules the Heavens. This battle takes place before the Final Judgment of the billions of souls whom have existed from the creation of human kind, (who have already died the first death and have gone to Sheol-Hades). Obviously, those here in this final battle have not yet died the first death. If they must die a first death, somebody or something has to kill them physically. That "somebody" will be Christ personally, and that "something" will be the fire of His breath.

We remember this same scenario in Revelation 14:20. Those who are not in Covenant with Christ but who are alive at His coming must die a first death before they can experience the second death. The figure given in Revelation 14:20 is the shedding of human blood. The figure here is the burning of the human body with fire from Heaven. Will the Lord inflict the first death by the shedding of blood? Will He inflict death by a burning fire? The answer is both, yet neither. In the apocalyptic sense, the death the human body and soul will experience is like the sensation of being sliced open with a sword, while at the same time, being overwhelmed with a blasting fire. But neither one of these death experiences can adequately describe what it is like to be killed in "the first death," to be killed directly by our Creator before meeting Him immediately, face-to-face, in Eternal Judgment. We cringe at the very thought of it.

More than seven billion people are alive today. It is humanly impossible to kill that many people instantly. But since death is the reward for sin, and sin kills both physically and spiritually, this impossibility is fit only for the almighty Godhead. So, we see a divine punishment falling from the sky, and we see humanity physically involved in this last experience of life. That is, in this instance, only humanity, not plant and animal life, will die seconds before they stand in the Final Judgment. A problem exists with the time sequence as to the judgment of the human race and the final melt down of the universe (2Pe 3:7-17). We have searched for answers and there probably are some Bible answers to this question. On the other hand, when the Day of Judgment comes, actions will occur so quickly, it will be like the whole scenario of human history playing out in the "twinkling of an eye."

Billions of souls, from Adam to the "Last Trumpet of God," (1Th 4:16) have spent their "after life" either in the Sheol-Hades interim, or since The Cross of redemption, "With Jesus." If Christ appears now, today, the Armageddon experience will bypass Sheol-Hades and thrust our world's seven billion people into eternal judgment with either Satan or Christ. They have no interim spirit world. The righteous will be transformed and translated "in a twinkling of an eye" (as was Enoch (Ge 5:24)), and the unrighteous will experience their first and second deaths simultaneously.

Initially, as the Battle of Armageddon explodes, the world will experience the lust of the flesh, lust of the eyes, pride of life and visible, sensory matters in this world of time, matter, space, and visible objects. The invisible will also be there, at first. World leader Satan is invisibly leading this land battle against air power. Please remember that even though the battle is couched in physical terms (as the participants move from instant physical death into the realm of eternal spiritual death), we see the apocalyptic aspects of the real battle between the "good" of God and the "evil" of Satan.

How ironic then that He, who is the prince of the power of the air, must be relegated to commanding land troops. But the invisible is very prominent in this battle. For, that which motivates these enemies of Christ is the invisible spirit of culture, philosophy, and humanitarianism. The Godhead, with His angels and saints, is also invisible. But the very second the fire comes down (the blood of the sharp sickle is shed), the invisible becomes visible, and that which is unseen brings into sight that which was previously unseen (1Co 1:28, 2:6).

What a battle this will be. Wow!

We need to understand what Armageddon is conveying:

1. The lukewarm Christians are disposed (2:12, 3:16).

2. The world economy collapses instantly (6:12-17).

3. All governments fail (11:15-19).

4. The fruitless world is reaped in wrath (14:14-20).

5. The world's Kings (and rulers) are quickly disposed (16:14).

6. Babylon falls in one hour (18:17).

7. Satan falls in a short season (20:3) and fire devours his vast armies (20:8, 9).

This must be an apocalyptic battle. The prototype prophecy also included a confederacy of many people (Persia, Ethiopia, Put, Greece, Armenia) where the kings of the world will gather together, forming like a cloud covering the land (Eze 16:14). Revelation gives a similar description in that the nations of the four corners of the Earth will be as vast as the sand of seashore (Rev 20:8). This apocalyptic war is invisible to the physical eye. On the other hand, the real world consists of the Spirit of intellect, conscience, will, and emotions. This will be the mother of all wars and the father of all victories (1Co 2:29). In some strange yet revealing way, the visible and invisible will merge universally in such a sensational manner that this will happen only once, and never again.

The Pre-Millennialists literalize most of the Apocalypse and view it in the physical rather than the spiritual. Following is a comparative chart between the physical Pre-Millenialist view and the spiritual apocalyptic view.

Physical Pre-millenialist view	Spiritual Apocalyptic View
Armageddon will involve Russia or China* against physical Israel (Ezekiel 38:1-3)	Armageddon will be a war involving Christ of Spiritual Israel and Satan with his satanic forces (Gal 6:16).
Ezekiel is describing a northern nation (What do the Pre-Millenialists think it is? Russia? Greenland? Or by way of satire, (Magog Canada)?) as the opposing army (39:2) • The cloud that covers the earth is dust from Russian Horses (38:9, 15, 16). • The Russians have invented a wooden plank that is stronger than Titanium (39:7); therefore, the Jews will burn the wood of wrecked MIGS for seven years as fuel (Chick Publications). • Israel will dwell securely (38:14). So they will increase in population in the *millennium*. • They will rebuild the temple (40-42). • Animal sacrifices will be restored (39:17-20, 40:38-43, 43:18, 27). • The Levitical Priesthood will be re-established (40:46, 43:19). • Ancient ritual will be renewed (43:20-28). • There will be Levitical teaching and judging (44:23).	The Romans prevented Antiochus from conquering Egypt. These passages are describing the rage with which Antiochus left Egypt and God put it in his heart to go to Jerusalem and impose Greek culture and religion upon the Jews (Da 11:30). He conquered them easily and profaned the temple by sacrificing swine and pouring the blood on the altar. He also erected an altar to Jupiter Olympus in its place. Antiochus desolated the temple (141 B.C.). Roughly seven years later, the temple was purified (148 B.C.) and dedicated (John 10:23 – The Feast of Dedication – Hanukkah). (SEE COMPARATIVE CHART DANIEL AND EZEKIEL – Addendum B.)

Physical Pre-millenialist view	Spiritual Apocalyptic View
• The Messiah-Prince Jesus will be a part of this (45:17) as he prepares Himself a sin offering of a genuine red heifer (45:22, 23).	• The Kingdom of Christ is Eternal (Mt 16:16-19). A red heifer is useless (Heb 9:13, 14). It is blasphemy to believe a red heifer will be offered to satisfy God in the future. • The temple has already been restored (Ac 15:16-18; Amos 9:11). • Believer's body is voluntarily sacrificed (Ro 12:1, 2).
• There will be burnt and peace offerings (45:24, 25, 46:12). • Jesus will stand aside and let the priest prepare his burnt and peace offering (46:2-5). • The Sabbath will be re-instituted (46:4, 12). *Pre-millennialism is extremely fickle in its theology. It selection of nations must change as the winds of History change. Since the advent of Darbyism, various nations throughout history have been selected to fulfill the Ezekiel *Gog*. Beginning with Kaiser Wilhelm to fallen Communist Russia… Who's next?	• The Old Law was a yoke (Gal 5:1), useless circumcision (5:2), not complete truth (5:7), and destroyed grace (5:4). • Christ is superior to the Aaronic Order (Heb 5:1-10), Aaron (6:13-20), Old Temple (7:11-28), Old Pattern (8:1-5), Old Covenant (8:6-13), Old Sanctuary (9:1-10), Old Sacrifice (9:11, 28-10:1-25), and He will destroy all his enemies (10:12-14). • Christ made Christians to be both Kings and Priests (Rev 1:3-7). • Christians enjoy an eternal Sabbath (Mt 11:28; Heb 3:18, 19, 4:3, 5-9. Sabbath means "rest."). • Christians enjoy an ongoing feast (Ac 2:42ff; Ro 14:17-18; Heb 13:15).

In light of the historical text of Gog and Magog, we can conclude that these names and the Battle of Armageddon have little to do with a mere physical war and everything to do with a spiritual-physical war that engages the total person. This spiritual war (God is a spirit.) consists of Satan (Satan is a spirit.) being released to gather his forces together to wage battle against Christ and His Kingdom. The fighting place of Armageddon is a representation of the final battle of the long war against God. To apply this apocalyptic literature to physical nations at a physical battleground is not Scriptural. The real war is in the world of light versus darkness. A war of flesh and blood war compared to spiritual warfare is like a Pop-Warner football team playing against the Super Bowl Champs.

Satan has been recruiting demon-possessed soldiers for this last moral conflict throughout the ages. He will gather his armies en masse for a swift victory against Christ and his small camp of believers. Antiochus was also highly successful in gathering vast armies from many nations to battle against a small Judas Maccabean-lead camp of Covenant believers who waged a guerilla war. Antiochus thought his battle would be won easily, and he confronted them without restraint. He did not realize the power of Covenant redeeming blood that God had proposed with the coming of the Lamb of God.

Likewise, Satan has a vast number of worldly giants from Pharaoh, mighty kings, the Caesars, the dictators, Hitler, Stalin, Khrushchev, Mao, Lenin, Strauss, Thomas Paine, Kant, Rand, Tubingen, Barth, Nietzsche, Darwin, the Papacy, Marx, Engels, as well as all modern-day antichrists dedicated to destroying the Christian value system. They vastly underestimated the wrath of the Lamb!

Satan has an impressive array of mighty, diabolical, demon-possessed people. They were inspired by the strength of their numbers and the power that Satan gave them to hold sway over the masses of world's people. They believe they can actually destroy Christ and remove Him, at last, from the universe. Can you imagine what it would be like to see such powerful and numerous militant, atheistic, antagonists ready to go to battle against the Lord? (Rev 9:14-16, 16:13-15) Even as we read this book, a universal political agenda is being compiled to punish Christians for their anti-sodomy, anti-abortion viewpoints.

We find it difficult to intellectually imagine the contrast between this vast army of satanic hosts with how much time it takes for Christ to destroy them, all with the breath of Jesus' mouth! In one instant, fire punishes them all, including "the lawless one" and his successors (2 Th 2:8).

In the moment of Christ's breathing fire, God gave Satan the punishment he has always deserved. Satan had never seen God exhibit His uncontrolled wrath. There were certain things God would not do to Satan, previously, because of His Congregation. God was concerned with the collateral damage and fallout of such a holocaust, and how the damage may hurt His select ones (Mt 24:22, 31; Mk 13:20, 22). However, now that the Congregation is out of the world, God is no longer restraining His wrath. Now, not only is Satan being judged, but also all those who lived on the Earth are being judged (2Co 5:10). God's total, complete justice is administered to all who are not in Covenant with Him. They receive the same eternal fire and brimstone that the Beast and false prophet suffered (Re 19:19-21). They shall concurrently exist forever in torment and misery in the same Lake of Fire. The unholy trinity, the Sea-Going Beast (13:1), the Land-Going Beast (13:11), and the Whore (17:1) came up together; now they go down together (19:20, 20:10).

Revelation 20:11-15: Then I saw a great white throne and Him who sat on it, from whose face the earth and the heaven fled away. And there was found no place for them. And I saw the dead, small and great, standing before God, and books were opened. And another book was opened, which is *the Book* of Life. And the dead were judged according to their works, by the things which were written in the books. The sea gave up the dead who were in it, and Death and Hades delivered up the dead who were in them. And they were judged, each one according to his works. Then Death and Hades were cast into the lake of fire. This is the second death and anyone not found written in the Book of Life was cast into the lake of fire.

All things have fled from the presence of the Godhead. There is no place for the living or the dead to hide from His judgment. All who have lived and died upon the Earth are now standing before Christ to be judged by their works recorded in the book (Mal 3:16). Their actions will be compared to the words of Jesus, which are recorded in the *Books* in Heaven (Jn 12:28). Depending on their works, and whether or not they were in covenant with Jesus, will prove whether the names of the living and the dead are recorded in the Book of Life (Rev 3:5, 13:8, 21:7; Php 4:3). Each person had a choice as to whether the Lord would add him or her to His Kingdom through faith, obedience, and perseverance (Ac 2:42-47). Each person has a choice as to whether his or her name is blotted out (Ex 32:32, 33; Rev 3:5). But the Lord knows all people and all things beforehand (Ro 8:30). None of our thoughts or actions are missed by the Lord's contemplative counsel!

Also, notice that Christ makes a distinction between *Hades* and *Hell* (previously noted in Revelation 7:1ff, 14:9-20). How can He throw *Hades* into *Hell* if it is the same place? The obvious answer: They are not the same place. This proves the following important truths:

1. After Christ died, He descended into Hades and led those in Covenant with God into Heaven to be with Him (Eph 4:7ff).

2. Those who remained in Hades (Tartarus) because they were not in Covenant with God before the death of Christ are aware of their future punishment (Lk 16:19-31; 2Pe 2:4).

3. The Roman church doctrine of "Purgatory" was invented for monetary gain and power, but it is not found in Scripture. No one is purged in Hades; they are incarcerated. Only those in Christ's Congregation are exempt from this prison (Mt 16:16-18). The Papacy removed this doctrine at the end of the 20th Century.

4. Those not taken out of Hades by Christ are destined to be thrown into Hell-Gehenna (Rev 20:14).

5. The second death is eternal hell fire, also known as "Gehenna," which the Israelites knew as a garbage dump. The doctrine of annihilation is unbiblical according to this passage. What is the second death? Eternal Hell Fire. What type of punishment is eternal hell fire? It is to be tortured day and night. This is forever in eternity (Mt 24:41; Mk 9:44-48).

6. Our eternal relationship with Christ is based upon this question, "Is your name written in the Lamb's Book of Life?" Whether or not you have been added depends upon your continued obedience to the Gospel (Rev 20:12; Jn 12:28). God works in us (Php 2:13), but we work out our own salvation (Php 2:12).

How tragic, then, to think that someone would contradict Paul's statement, "to die is to gain" (Php 1:20-21). The removal of the heavenly promises after we die in Christ gives a dreadful gloom to Christians. The following is a comparative chart of eternity for Christians who die before and after Christ's return. A Millennial mythologist hardly ever talks about Heaven. Consider what Heaven is like to those who die before Christ comes, and what it will be like for those same people after Christ comes

What New Covenant Christians can expect to become, a blessed reality, when they die and depart to be with Jesus in the interim before Christ comes	The Heaven that belongs to God, after Christ comes.
The minute New Covenant Christians leave this present world, they will have perfection in Spirit along with the Old Testament Saints. (Heb 12:23, 24).	Perfection in body, soul, and spirit (1Th 5:23).
A soul apparition (Rev 20:5)	Clothed upon (2Co 5:2-4) with immortal bodies;
A spirit apparition (Ac 7:59)	A Glorified Body (Php 3:21).
Presence with Christ (2Co 5:6-9; Jn 14:6-8)	Will see God (Rev 21:3). Will see the Father Creator, and live (Rev 22:4).
The vile bodies are in the grave (Php 1:21-23).	Vile bodies are changed (Php 1:21-23).
Spirit existence in the 3rd Heaven-Paradise (2Co 12:1-3; Lk 1:32)	God will be All and Overall (1Co 15:28).
Reigning with Christ in consultation and judgment (Rev 20:5, 6)	The Throne of God and of the Lamb shall be in it (Rev 22:3). Overcomers shall reign over cities (Lk 9:17). They will judge angels and the whole world (1Co 6:2, 3).
The 3rd Heaven fills up with the spirit-souls of the covenant saints.	
Christ is authority and honor above all (Mt 28:17-19).	
Christ is recognized on the Throne on the Right Hand of God (Rev 5:6, 7, 6:1).	
1,000 years are on-going from the standpoint of eternity in Heaven and time on Earth (Rev 20:4-7)	The end comes and the rest (or remains) of the Christian or martyred dead are resurrected (Rev 20:5).
Martyred souls wonder, "How long before vengeance is executed?" (Rev 6:10)	Vengeance finally comes (2Th 1:8); Heb 10:30, 31; Rev 6:16, 17).

What New Covenant Christians can expect to become, a blessed reality, when they die and depart to be with Jesus in the interim before Christ comes	The Heaven that belongs to God, after Christ comes.
The first fruits of those who follow the Primogeniture, Jesus, "first born from the dead," who takes them to be with Him (1Co 15:23).	The harvest of the world is finished (Rev 7:11-14; Mt 13:30).
	Those who are His at His coming (1Th 3:13, 4:15, 5:23).
	The earthly house "remains" is reunited with the soul (2Co 5:1-4).
The "remains" are still in the grave (2Co 5:1, 15:42-44).	God gives all souls a house that pleases Him (2Co 5:11).
V.I.P. accommodations in one of the many abiding places of the Father's house (Jn 14:1-4).	Full reward (God Himself) "I give you Myself" (Ge 15:1; Rev 21:3).
The resurrection is yet to come (Php 3:21).	Transformation (Col 3:4).
The *Parousia* is yet to come (1Th 4:15).	Incorruption and immortality (2Ti 1:10; 1Co 15:52-54; 1Th 4:17, 5:23, 3:13).
The spirit-soul is in safe custody (Php 1:23).	A reunion of body, soul, and spirit (1Th 4:16), resurrection, and Ascension to Heaven (Php 3:20, 21).
The angels have finished their work (Heb 2:5-8, 1:14; Lk 16:22).	The marriage procession (Rev 21:1-3, 19:7-9).
We are not in Abraham's bosom, or down in Hades, nor are we gathered to the fathers (Mt 25:21-31, 16:16-18).	Dwelling with God-Jesus (Rev 21:1-10).
	A vision of the Bride (Rev 21:1-10).

What New Covenant Christians can expect to become, a blessed reality, when they die and depart to be with Jesus in the interim before Christ comes	The Heaven that belongs to God, after Christ comes.
-We are separated from the body "Fallen asleep" (2Ti 4:6) and have -made the great departure (2Pe 1:10-11) in spirit (1Pe 1:4; 2Pe 1:14).	Perfect, spotless, and presented to God the Father (Eph 5:26-28)
We are in a spiritual, espoused relationship to Christ (2Co 11:2).	Face-to-face with God our Savior (Rev 22:3, 4).
The old system is not yet destroyed.	The old is done away – the new is forever (Rev 21:1, 2; 2Pe 3:7-14).
Universal judgment is not yet final.	2Th 1:9; 2Pt. 3:10 – The Final Judgment.
Although in uncontaminated, pure holiness, and bliss, our existence is simultaneous with the unnoticed and contaminated work of the devil and his angels in the opposite realm of Hades.	God's everlasting covenant decree is at last contemplated and appreciated by creatures released from time to their timeless blessing or curse (Ac 24:15; Rev 20:12, 21:8; Jn 5:22)
The universal and eternal destinies of all peoples of all nations from all times, is yet to be revealed, but it is already determined (Rev 5: 6).	The Universe is cleansed (purged by fire) and the Earth is delivered (Ro 8:20-22). The Earth will be delivered (set free) from its own inherent death and imperfection and replaced by the New Heaven and Earth.
Universal, eternal, past evil is not yet blotted out.	The manifestation of the final apocalypse (unveiling) (Mt 25:41, 10:28, 3:11,13, 42; Isa 30:33; Mk 9:4)

This introduction to Heaven is the urgent expectation of every New Covenant Christian. A secondary motivating factor is our obedience to Christ. Study the above chart every day. The above Scripture references placed in logical order are by themselves worth the price of this book.

At Christ's ascension, He made it very clear in Mark 16:19 that He sat down at the Right Hand of God. This marks His ascension to the Throne of Glory and Majesty (Heb 1:3). This is equated with His sitting on the Throne of His glory and breaking bread with His disciples at the Lord's Supper (Mt 26:29). Christians are in a relationship with a glorious Lord in the City of the Living God, Heavenly Jerusalem, with numerous angels, for it is the same city of *Jeru*, city of *Salem*, peace (Heb 12:22). This same city has existed since eternity and existed when Melchizedek appeared to Abraham (Ge 14: 18-20) (See Addendum K: "What is Zion?"). It exists in the present tense as the mother of us all (Gal 4:26). This same eternal Jerusalem will descend, accompanied by a New Heaven and New Earth, which Abraham saw and looked upon (Heb 11:10, 12:22).

We recognize the New Jerusalem as more than a carnal city, for on that glorious day, it will appear as a Bride prepared for her Husband (Rev 21:2). So we can scarcely call it a mere city in the apocalyptic sense. We know that the New Jerusalem is the Ecclesia down through the ages because it is also the general assembly of the firstborn, whose names are written in Heaven. God, the Son, was seen in the expanse of the heavens in the Revelation of Christ, which had been given to Moses, Aaron, and the 70 Elders of Israel who had a vision of Christ's body (Ex 24:9, 10). Their vision is evidence that no one could see God the Father and live. Even during the interim of Christians in Heaven, before Christ's return, these Christians will not see His face (Php 1:21-23; Ac 7:59; 2Co 5:6-10). None of them will see God the Father until the Son presents them all to God (Rev 21:3-5, 22:3, 4). The Ecclesia's purpose is to prepare people for this breathtaking event.

Jesus gave His human gifts (Ep 4:11, 12) to the Congregation so that He might present them gloriously, first, to Himself as a Bride, and then, so that He might present them, eternally, to the Father (Eph 4:7ff, 5:27). Presently, those with Jesus are the spirits of just men made perfect (Heb 12:23). Presently, those with Jesus are in Jesus' presence as the Judge and Mediator of a New Covenant, whose Blood speaks from Heaven (Heb 12:24). After Christ comes, the whole Ecclesia (from Adam to the fullness of the last Gentile convert) will all see God the Father. They will be the spirits (and bodies) of just men declared righteous and perfect (Heb 12:23).

God's Kingdom dwells within the believers (Lk 17:26). The Greek word for "in" is εντός, which does not mean "to be in the midst of a group of people," but "to be within the believer." This word is used to describe the inside of the cup of the

Pharisees (Mt 23:26). Jesus told Pilate that His Kingdom, in the present tense, was not OF this world (Jn 18:35, 36).

The hope of the Pre-Millennial doctrine is a physical, carnal hope. However, Christian hope is in the spirit of wisdom, revelation, and knowledge of Christ. Christian hope is in the eye of understanding or being enlightened that we may know the hope of our calling (Eph 1:17-20). The hope is living in heavenly places with Christ (Col 2:12-3:1). In His body lies the Kingdom of Christ (Eph 1:21-23). This fellowship of His Body is the fellowship of the mystery. It is now revealed and is made known to the principalities and powers in heavenly places by Christ's Ecclesia (3:9, 10). However, only by the spirit of the inner man (3:16) and the Congregation (3:21ff) can we understand the riches of His glory. The Pre-Millennialist, being puffed up in a fleshly mindset, is not capable of holding to the Head (Col 2:19). However, those in the spiritual Kingdom have a new, different kind of man who is being renewed in the knowledge of the Image of Christ (3:10; Ro 8:6, 7).

The Jerusalem Above

Therefore, the whole concept of the Jerusalem, which is above, is known in the spirit of Christians living in this present world. This will fully and forcibly be made known in the consummation of all things when all those who oppose this Heavenly Kingdom are exposed. All things that oppose this Heavenly Kingdom will pass away, leaving only the New Jerusalem, and the Bride of Christ with God, forever (2Pe 3:10-13). This is the promise Christians look forward to seeing fulfilled. This is where righteousness dwells in the New Heaven and New Earth.

In Thy Seed All Nations Shall Be Blessed

We would misinterpret the Genesis, Chapter 12, prophecy if we believed that this is speaking only of the current city of Jerusalem and its surrounding areas. God concluded the blessing by saying that in Abraham's seed, all Gentile families would be blessed (Ge 12:1-3). We must distinguish between the physical land promises, which were temporary blessings promised to Abraham, and the eternal, spiritual blessings. The Bible says, "That the blessings of Abraham may come on the gentiles through Jesus Christ, that we might receive the promise of his spirit, in faith" (Gal 3:14). The real blessing at first was a promise of physical land, but in God's mind, the Seed was Christ (3:16).

The Seed that blossoms is the Word of the Kingdom of God (Mt 13:19; Lk 8:11). The promise to Abraham was actually the fulfillment of the New Covenant in Christ, the Seed (Heb 10:15-17, 11:17, 18, 32-40, 12:24), which He and the Old Testament saints did not receive in their lifetime. Pre-Millennialists want to give the cultural Jews another chance, but they were the first to be presented with the Gospel (Ro 1:16, 2:9, 10).

The Jews failed at their first chance to accept God as King (1Sa 8:1-19, 12:14-18). They had their second chance at accepting Christ as King, but they refused Him and this chance is now gone (Ac 3:13). Peter adds that Christ died (according to their initial desire) and ascended to Heaven. He spoke His covenant word from Heaven through the Apostles (Heb 12:24). With this, the Holy Spirit gave a subsequent warning,

> "See to it that you do not refuse him who speaks. If they did not escape when they refused him who warned them on earth, how much less will we, if we turn away from him who warns us from heaven? At that time his voice shook the earth, but now he has promised, 'Once more I will shake not only the earth but also the heavens'" (Heb 12:25, 26).

Therefore, in his second sermon, Peter told the Jews to repent and be converted (Ac 3:19). The translation of Acts 3:20, "that he may send Jesus," is a bad translation. The parse of the verb "send" is "aorist," active, subjunctive, third person, and singular. This verb denotes a snapshot in history whereby the subject of the sentence has performed his intentional action. Heaven received Christ at His ascension.

The restitution, restoration, or reformation (Ac 3:21) can be compared to the reformation in Hebrews 9:10, where Christ gave a greater and *more* perfect tabernacle, made without hands. Peter makes it clear in the remainder of his sermon, Acts 3:21-26, that when Christ spoke from Heaven, the listeners had better heed Him or be destroyed from the Earth (22, 23). Peter said that the promise given to Abraham was fulfilled by blessing the whole Earth and by forgiving their sins and iniquities (24-26). Daniel said the Messiah's message, among other things, would be given to them in a sealed book (Da 9:27). This is exactly what Paul said in his sermon at Lydia, "Look, you scoffers, wonder and perish, for I am going to do something in your days that you would never believe, even if someone told you" (Ac 13:41). Both the learned and unlearned could not understand the

Gospel because it was a sealed book (Isa 29:10, 11; Ro 11:8). The book was sealed because the people refused to repent and turn from their sinful ways.

They crucified the messenger of the Covenant. Jesus said, "Destroy this temple and I will raise it up again in three days" (Jn 2:19). This was a reference to the temple of His body, as well as a fulfillment of the prophecy of the destruction of David's tabernacle (Ac 15:14-18). God has already rebuilt the tabernacle of David! Pre-Millennialists are just as bad as the Jews of the 1st Century because they do not want the Gentiles to receive the promise of God. Ironically, when Gentiles embrace Pre-Millennialism, their doctrine excludes themselves! Can we acknowledge how a carnal kingdom, (conjured in the mindset of a Pre-Millennialist) destroys Scriptural truth? In making this claim, they are destroying New Testament Christianity.

Revelation Chapter Twenty-one

Revelation 21:1: Now I saw a new heaven and a new earth, for the first heaven and the first earth had passed away. Also there was no more sea.

This verse addresses the "Day of Christ" as a day in which all things will pass away (1Th 1:9, 10, 5:9).[112] Peter describes this passing away as a removal in fire (2Pe 3:10). Christ is bringing the world into judgment (Php 2:16). The lifestyle of a Christian should be lived in constant expectation of the Lord's Coming (1Th 5:2). Christians should not be ignorant concerning His delay! Christ's Coming seems so surreal; however, in the final journey from death to life, what is now the apocalyptic vision will be an undeniable reality. By faith, Christians are putting a deposit of their life in the trust and hope of Christ (2Ti 4:6, 7). This day is approaching (Heb 10:25). It is as close as our pending death. When we die, Christ has come!

This second heavenly paradise is going to be far greater than the first garden. In the context of 1 Corinthians 15:22-45, we understand that the last Adam exceeds the first Adam. The first Adam was a dying organism, whereas the last is a life-giving spirit. The rewards in Heaven from the last Adam will give man a redeemed body, soul, and spirit. This glorified body will be honorable and bear the image of the Heavenly Father (1Co 15:46-49; Co 3:4, 10).

In Koine Greek, the New Testament's original written language, two words exist for the English word *new*. The Greek word *Neos* means "new" – of the same kind, whereas, *Kainos* (2538) means "completely new" – of a different kind. The latter describes new creation, new heaven, and the new earth. Correlate Revelation 2:11 with Paul's writing to the Romans in which he says, "We were therefore buried with him through baptism into death in order that, just as Christ was raised from the dead through the glory of the Father, we too may live a new life" (new, of a different kind of life.) (Ro 6:4).

God can do what He promised to do. The New Heaven and New Earth will be that of a different kind. This New Heaven will be made manifest to all, and God's dwelling place will be known (2Co 12:2). All who have ever lived will see this heavenly Jerusalem coming down. Just as they will see Christ come down, fire come down, and Christians going up, God will have the final word concerning who and what are valuable and who and what are not valuable. The whole world will finally appropriate His value system. On the brink of Eternity, sinners will come to grips with the reality of what they missed, and what they lost. But then, it will be eternally too late.

Just as previously taught, when the wicked are taken first in full view of the Christians, Christians will recognize what might have happened if they were lost. Thus, this passage (Rev 21:1) proves the wicked will see the inexpressible reward of the joy of God's promise and city and recognize what they would have received if they were saved! This is a lamentable, irretrievable loss! Both righteous and unrighteous citizens populate this old Earth, but the New Heaven and Earth will be populated with Kingdom citizens only (2Pe 3:13). This is what Christians have been preparing themselves for! Through trial and tribulation, they are triumphing with the internal Kingdom existing in their souls (Heb 12:22, 23); however, the whole essence of just what this glorious, eternal kingdom will entail has not yet been universally manifest. The visible, first Heaven and Earth that we live in right now, consisting of time, matter, and space, will flee from the presence of the Godhead (Rev 10:6, 20:11, 21: 1) in the post-cosmos existence.

Yet, the New Heaven and Earth is being populated by those who once lived on Earth but whose affections are Heavenly-minded (Col 2:12, 3:1, 2). In this sense, the future exists now as well as hereafter. We already have eternal life in covenant with Christ (Jn 5:2; 1Jn 3:14-16), but it is within us. In Christ's presence we will have eternal life both within and without. This Earth is a proving ground. There is joy here and joy hereafter.

This new order of the New Heaven and Earth was made manifest at Pentecost. This day brought about 3,000-plus souls into the Heavenly Kingdom. They inherited the Earth by bringing heavenly values to it, and therefore gained the right to the Tree of Life in the New Heaven and Earth (Rev 22:14). Satan took the Earth by fraud and deceit when he tempted Adam and Eve. However, it was judicially returned to Christ through His Congregation.

Christians are binding on Earth what has already been bound in Heaven, including Satan himself (Mt 16:16-18). They are also loosing men and women from sin and reigning as kings (Mt 18:18; 1Co 4:8; 2Ti 2:12; 1Pe 2:8-10; Rev 1:6, 5:10, 20:4,5; Luke 19:17,12:42). This emphasizes the responsibility of evangelists, pastors, and teachers, as well as the faithful Congregation. They are all reigning in conjunction with Christ in Heaven, possessing authority over the cities in which they disciple, preach, and teach (Lk 19:17).

There may even be population centers in Heaven that are populated by millions of souls over which those of responsible stewardship oversight will reign. Departed souls also have a kind of consolatory Reign with Christ in governing particular matters on Earth (Rev 20:4-8), just as Abraham had in Sodom. It could be that Christ only consults with Christian martyrs (6:9-11) or perhaps all who are with Him. This transitional reign takes place between heavenly eternity and the eternity placed within each believer on Earth. This transition will be removed at the coming of the New Heaven and Earth. The Ecclesia at that time will take up residence there. Indeed, we who have been faithful over little will be rulers over much.

Revelation 21:2: *Then I, John, saw the holy city, New Jerusalem, coming down out of heaven from God, prepared as a bride adorned for her husband.*

Christians, by faith, can see what John saw in this vision (Heb 12:22). The real, heavenly Jerusalem can be seen in spirit (Heb 8:9, 9:23, 24). This heavenly Jerusalem is probably located in the Third Heaven. In the Old Testament, Melchizedek resided in the Heavenly Salem (Ge 14:18). If this place existed over 4,000-years ago, we can be confident that it existed before then. This heavenly Salem is a great place for many reasons; chiefly, it has the pledge that sin will be abolished.

Revelation 21:3: *And I heard a loud voice from heaven saying, "Behold, the tabernacle of God is with men, and He will dwell with them, and they shall be His people. God Himself will be with them and be their God.*

We were saved from the penalty of sin, the power of sin, and the torment of sin, but we will not be saved from the presence of sin until God's glorious day comes. Our glorified bodies will not experience the concupiscence to sin. No sin or weak flesh will exist in the New Jerusalem. Constant fellowship with God will be enjoyed forever. The Scriptures call Jesus the Tabernacle among men (Jn 1:14). Satan hated this Tabernacle and its inhabitants. Tirelessly, Satan labors to deceive the Earth with a counterfeit, earthly tabernacle. However, the Scriptures teach there is a true tabernacle to come (Heb 8:2). Christians have tasted its powers (Heb 6:5). Christ is the greater and more perfect Tabernacle (Heb 9:11). There is not a future temple, for Christ is the temple in full glory (Jn 1:14).

The following list is what God expects Christians to see when they view the Thrones:

- Behold the lamb, as one having been slain (in the center of the Throne) – He died; He shed His blood; He redeemed us, and the bloody marks are still visible (Rev 5:6).

- Behold the Lamb, before which the four highest creatures in the universe fall, and adore, crying, "Worthy is the lamb" (5:8).

- Behold the Lamb, worthy of power, wealth, wisdom, strength, honor, glory, and praise (5:12).

- Behold the Lamb, with God on the throne, and to the Lamb, praise, honor, glory and power (5:13).

- Behold the Lamb, which I watched as He opened the seals of the book of omniscient destinies (6:1).

- Behold the Lamb, from whose wrath they called upon the rocks and mountains to hide them (6:16).

- Behold the Lamb, before which the great white robed, innumerable multitude stands (7:9).

- Behold the Lamb, to which Christians cry, "Salvation belongs" (7:10).

- Behold the Lamb, in whose Blood Christians have washed their robes white (7:14).

- Behold the Lamb, who is the shepherd, in the center of the Throne (7:17).

- Behold the Lamb, by whose Blood Christians overcome, with The Word and the spurning of life (12:11).

- Behold the Lamb, slain from the foundation of the world, in whose Book of Life Christian's names are written, and Christians therefore worship not the Beast (13:8).

- Behold the Lamb, on Mount Zion, with the 144,000 (14:1), who follow the Lamb (14:4).

- Behold the Lamb, in whose presence those (who did not understand Him as such) are tormented day and night, forever and ever (14:10).

- Behold the Lamb, whose song, along with Moses' is sung (15:3).

- Behold the Lamb, against whom those who do not understand His Blood atonement righteousness go to war (17:14).

- Behold the Lamb, to whose wedding feast Christians are invited (19:7, 9).

- Behold the Lamb, in whose bright, golden, eternal city are solid foundations of the Apostles, by name (whose inspired New Covenant writing is the only information ever given once and for all from Heaven) (20:14).

- Behold the Lamb, in who, along with God, is the eternal temple (21:22).

- Behold the Lamb, who is the lamp (21:23).

- Behold the Lamb, from God's Throne, and whose throne flows the precious water of life and redemption, and there is no more curse (22:1).

- Behold the Lamb, in whose city is God's and His Throne, and they have but one name, and one face and His servants shall serve Him forever (22:3).

- Behold the Lamb's wife, for if you love the husband, you will love his Bride (21:9).

- Behold the Lamb's Book of Life, and see your name therein (21:27).

"Behold the lamb" is stated 24 times in Revelation. Six times four, numerically all humanity (6 – the number of man) times 4 (number of earth). Let all mankind on Earth look to the Lamb in Heaven, for He was potentially slain for us all.

Revelation 21:4: And God will wipe away every tear from their eyes; there shall be no more death, nor sorrow, nor crying. There shall be no more pain, for the former things have passed away.

God knows human weaknesses that result in death, tears, sorrow, and pain. Human weakness started in the Garden of Eden and will forever pass away in Eternity (1Jn 2:15-17). God is not only going to wipe away weeping and grieving, but also the inaudible sadness that is not always expressed or known. Inexpressible Tears of Joy will flow with the banishment of death and establishment of Eternal Life. True happiness will fill all in Christ. To the contrary, there will be weeping, wailing, and gnashing of teeth in the devil's Hell (Mt 22:13, 24:51, 25:30).

Revelation 21:5: Then He who sat on the throne said, "Behold, I make all things new." And He said to me, "Write, for these words are true and faithful."

The Greek word for new in the passage is also "Kainos." All things (now unfamiliar) are new of a different kind. This great achievement can be possible only in the Spirit. This spiritual testimony is faithful and true. Can we understand the impact this had on the first Congregation of Christ? This word was needed during the persecuting reign of Nero. God is validating the Bride of Christ who is a faithful and true promise.

As persecuted Christians lifted their heads from within Nero's arena, they must have certainly seen the lamp stands made to impale them as fiery human torches, the cruel cross, the dark dungeons, the racks, the whips, the wild animals, and the alienation of families. Certainly, many tears fell from the faces of these most precious, redeemed souls of Christ. Such tears continue to flow in Afghanistan, China, North Korea, Syria, Iraq, Libya, Egypt, and throughout the Middle East and South Asia.

The internet communicates scenes of religious, Muslim murder trials on a regular basis. As we write, the vision of a young lady standing by the hole dug for her grave remains fresh in our minds. Her assassins are hood covered; one is her own Father. She is accused of adultery. She asks her own father for mercy. He denied it. A trial is conducted quickly, and the men begin to throw rocks. She falls in the hole still breathing and thrashing. The man who steps up, looks down and throws the biggest rock to crush her skull is her own Father. We are ashamed, that while we enjoy desert after a sumptuous meal, much of the world is being drenched in blood and tears.[113]

Revelation 21:6: And He said to me, "It is done! I am the Alpha and the Omega, the Beginning and the End. I will give of the fountain of the water of life freely to him who thirsts.

The banishment of false doctrine ushers in completed salvation for those in Christ. Time is no more. Adam and Eve were banished from the Tree of Life and could not partake of its healing power, but there is a "water of life" given by Christ. Ponce de Leon did not find this fountain in Florida. He died. Will we die? Adam had both physical and spiritual cognizance. We will experience delights and pleasures in the eternal spirit universe of the Godhead that are unfathomable in a physical universe.

Revelation 21:7: He who overcomes shall inherit all things, and I will be his God and he shall be My son.

Only he that overcomes will inherit Eternal Life. God has offered His salvation to all who thirst. However, Christians must be overcomers in this life! This inheritance is only obtained by being adopted into God's family (Heb 2:10; Gal 3:26ff). God gives Christians the right to Christ's inheritance. People must become sons of God to accomplish the desires of their heart (Jn 3:5ff).

Revelation 21:8: But the cowardly, unbelieving, abominable, murderers, sexually immoral, sorcerers, idolaters, and all liars shall have their part in the lake which burns with fire and brimstone, which is the second death.

God has rewarded the righteous and cursed the wicked. Those who do not overcome will be thrown into the Lake of Fire, which is the second death. Christians do not partake of this second death because they partook of the First Resurrection after their Immersion into Christ (Ac 2:38; Ro 6:1-6; Rev 20:5). Not only do Jehovah Witnesses, Seventh Day Adventist, Mormons and many other cults deny the existence of the Lake of Fire for the lost, but also many Christians live as if God made some kind of mistake here. If we think we can believe in Heaven, but not the Lake of Fire – we might just as well forget about Heaven. This verse mentions "liars," if we do not believe it; we make God out to be liar.

Revelation 21:9: Then one of the seven angels who had the seven bowls filled with the seven last plagues came to me and talked with me, saying, "Come, I will show you the bride, the Lamb's wife."

This same angel, who announced the destruction of the Harlot in Revelation 17:1, now announces the invitation to see the Bride. What a contrast! For us, Heaven will be the most interesting and longed for manifestation if for only one reason – it will delineate between the true Bride and the religious Whore.

Revelation 21:10: And he carried me away in the Spirit to a great and high mountain, and showed me the great city, the holy Jerusalem, descending out of heaven from God,

This is the climatic End of the World. This is not a literal mountain. The writer is describing his *bird's eye view* of this indescribable city. This is the completely pure, Third Heaven coming to meet the Christians as an everlasting dwelling place (Eph 5:11). This Jerusalem is the mother of all Christians (Gal 4:25-28).

This city has always been there, but never seen with the physical eye. A parallel to this is the relationship between the body and spirit. The body is seen with the physical eye, yet the spirit cannot be seen with the physical eye. They both coexist, one visible and the other invisible. This same relationship exists between the Kingdom of God and His Congregation. Christians are *in* the world, but not *of* the world. As the body and spirit exist together, so the Congregation and Kingdom of God exist together. The Body without the Spirit would cease to be, so the Congregation without the Kingdom would pass away (Jas 2:26; Rev 21:1, 2).

Christ's Congregation does not need the world; the world needs the Congregation! The Spirit does not need the body, but the body needs the Spirit. Neither the world nor the body realizes this, but the Spirit does (Jas 2:26). Since the body's death is required to bring forth the full recognition of the Spirit's quality or essence (Rev 6:9, 20:4; Ac 7:59), the passing of the Old Earth (time, space, matter, force, energy, sound) is required to recognize the fullness of the New Earth. The passing of the First and Second Heavens are required to bring about the fullness of the Third (2Co 12:1-6). (Most theologians believe the First Heaven is what can be seen by the naked eye. The Second Heaven is beyond human sight and comprehension. The Third Heaven is the presence of God and His Eternal Throne as described in the Revelation.)

It would be preposterous to teach that, at the moment of Christ's return, the New Heaven and New Earth suddenly *come* into existence. To be sure, just as in the Reign *of* Christ, the Old Earth was always there since the beginning; but it took the death of the Old Heaven and Earth to bring about the full reality *of* the New Heaven and Earth.

Although Christians will get their old bodies back (in glorified state) in the Resurrection *of* the Last Day (Ac 17:31, 32), the Old Earth and Old Heavens will melt down into a liquid Lake of Fire (Rev 20: 14, 15; 2Pe 3:10-14). There will be no resurrection for this creation. In fact, the sin cursed Earth, rocking and reeling from sin's effects, has only one hope of deliverance, and that is its liquid, fiery extinction at the time when the Sons of God are completely, and totally manifest in full force and number (Ro 8: 19-22). The Old Earth must die for the New Earth to be manifest, just as the world must die in order that the Kingdom to be manifest.

What marvelous order is placed in Scripture! The next time you read, "The meek shall inherit the earth," and "the earth is eternal," remember these things! Paul speaks of the "ktisis" (the manufacturing of the entire created universe (2936, 2937)) being subject to the Children of God. Now, we are subject to the laws of physics, but after the universe is dissolved, the Children of God will be above all laws of creation. We might say in modern language, God gives them executive privileges and exemptions (Ro 8:20-22). Just think, instead of us being subject to the laws of the universe ("ktisis" should not be translated "earth"), we will ultimately see all laws of physics bow before us. Yes, we will fly!

Consequently, the overthrow of Satan's dynasty with earthly, visible effects, the birth of The Christian Nation, a change of government in Heaven, and a new purpose for the planet, Earth, all began on Pentecost and began to be recognized by the Elect (select "called-out ones") at that time.

In ways that are incomprehensible, Heaven and Earth are interchanging as Christians carry out the King's Great Commission. They cannot see The Kingdom on Earth (Lk 17:4), but like invisible, gravitational, and centrifugal forces, such forces are essential to the Earth's existence. When The Lamb seizes The Apostolic Congregation, the Earth will fly to pieces (2Pe 3:10).

Unlike many peoples' homes, the Father's Palace (prepared abiding places through Christ's redemptive work (Jn 14:2, 18, 19, 28, and 29)) is a "Forever" place.

Jesus spoke about His Father's house and gave it the following seven wonderful entities:

1. The Lamb's Wife (21: 9)
2. The Lamb's Apostles (21:14)
3. The Lamb's Temple (21: 22)
4. The Lamb's Light (21:23)
5. The Lamb's Book (2 I: 27)
6. The Lamb's Throne (22:1)
7. The Lamb's Blessing (22:3)

Are you surprised at this adding up of the entities? The number comes to the number of perfection? We wonder if John knew he was writing a book of numerology.

Revelation 21:11: having the glory of God. Her light *was* like a most precious stone, like a jasper stone, clear as crystal.

The jasper stone is similar in color to an opaque, greenish, clear crystal. Until now, the complete Glory of God has been hidden (Eph 5:11). This is the revealed Glory of God in purity. But these stones are not literal; they are representative of the glistening glory that no human eyes have ever seen.

Revelation 21:12: Also she had a great and high wall with twelve gates, and twelve angels at the gates, and names written on them, which are the names of the twelve tribes of the children of Israel:

The wall affords protection to keep out what is unwanted as well as keep in what is desired. In order for Christians to measure the temple, they must know some of the Pentateuch, as well as apocalyptic writings like Ezekiel, and various verses in Isaiah. In numerology, the number 12 represents governmental perfection. This city is perfectly structured and protected. We may forget that this city is not just for New Testament Christians, but also those of Noah's day, Abraham's children of faith, and the representative 144,000 number of Israel – Jews who looked for the long awaited Messiah to come to their abode in Sheol. The 12 tribes are inclusive of the Old Testament, in totality (Mt 19:28; Lk 22:30).

Revelation 21:13: three gates on the east, three gates on the north, three gates on the south, and three gates on the west.

Three gates on each of four sides describe a perfect cube. In numerology, the number three represents divine perfection. The Godhead consists of Father, Son, and Holy Spirit. Only through them, can we access this city.

Revelation 21:14: Now the wall of the city had twelve foundations, and on them were the names of the twelve apostles of the Lamb.

Christ's Congregation was built upon His 12 Apostles (Eph 2:20; Heb 6:1; 1Co 3:11). Christ's 12 Apostles, including Paul as a representative member of the 12, are reflected in eternity. When a man told me that he had 12 apostles in Salt Lake City, I told him I have 12 Apostles in Heaven. When he asked me, "what's the difference?" I said your apostles died and will die – my Apostles will never die.

What the Apostles began to loose on Earth (means to be loosed from guilt and sin in God's eyes) through the Apostolic Gospel (Mt 16:16-18; Jn 20:23; Ac 2:37-38) is now a reality in Heaven. Those who do not obey Apostles Doctrine (Ac 2:42) are in the sight of The Lord, bound or retained in their sins. Our foundational beliefs on Earth are based on the Apostolic New Testament. Our hope for the Heaven of our Lord, Jesus Christ, is graphically envisioned as based on an eternal Apostolic Foundation.

Revelation 21:15-17: And he who talked with me had a gold reed to measure the city, its gates, and its wall. The city is laid out as a square; its length is as great as its breadth. And he measured the city with the reed: twelve thousand furlongs. Its length, breadth, and height are equal. Then he measured its wall: one hundred *and* forty-four cubits, *according* to the measure of a man, that is, of an angel.

Heaven has absolute perfection and safety. This magnificent city is 1,500 miles long. This is not a literal number, but it describes a large city of complexity, which is far greater than numbers can describe. Ezekiel saw in a vision, a man of bronze appearance who measured the prophetic temple (40:3). But the Old Testament temple is gone. When we read Ezekiel, Chapter 40, we see the impossibility of comparing the Old Temple with the new City of God.

Revelation 21:18-20: The construction of its wall was *of* jasper; and the city *was* pure gold, like clear glass. The foundations of the wall of the city *were* adorned with all kinds of precious stones: the first foundation *was* jasper, the second sapphire, the third chalcedony, the fourth emerald, the fifth sardonyx, the sixth sardius, the seventh chrysolite, the eighth beryl, the ninth topaz, the tenth chrysoprase, the eleventh jacinth, and the twelfth amethyst.

Heaven is significantly more beautiful than the descriptive stones listed. These stones represent the beauty of God's righteousness.

Revelation 21:21: The twelve gates *were* twelve pearls: each individual gate was of one pearl. And the street of the city *was* pure gold, like transparent glass.

This is a city of unimaginable beauty and wealth (1Pe 1:17; Mt 13:43) because the eye has not seen such jewels; the ear has not heard such voices; and neither has entered into the heart of man the things God has prepared for us (1Co 2:9).

Revelation 21:22: But I saw no temple in it, for the Lord God Almighty and the Lamb are its temple.

There is no need for a structural place to worship the living God. Christians are the temple. For the Saints, the relationship between the Congregation and worship is like eating and sleeping.

Revelation 21:23: The city had no need of the sun or of the moon to shine in it, for the glory of God illuminated it. The Lamb *is* its light.

This is the Glory of Christ's light. In the beginning was light; this is Christ! (Col 2:12; 3:1). We become bored over time with the very best of delights, pleasures, inventions, and idols. But residence in the City will far exceed the best this world has to offer, and we will never grow weary or become bored with it all. A worker at Disney World told us, "I have seen it all!" To him, the once incredible place of wonder is now just a routine work place. This cannot happen in the golden city!

Revelation 21:24: And the nations of those who are saved shall walk in its light, and the kings of the earth bring their glory and honor into it.

Who are the kings? There possibly have been some great kings that have obeyed the Gospel; however, Paul is speaking about spiritual kings. These kings are the most dignified of people in God's eyes for they are in love with Jesus Christ. They are Kings and Priests of Jesus.

Revelation 21:25-27: Its gates shall not be shut at all by day (there shall be no night there). And they shall bring the glory and the honor of the nations into it. But there shall by no means enter it anything that defiles, or causes an abomination or a lie, but only those who are written in the Lamb's Book of Life.

Christ paid the price for Christians to enter into the heavenly Jerusalem. People from all nations have brought honor and glory to God throughout their lives. They are rewarded with everlasting peace. No one who is spiritually unclean, backsliding, or abominable will be there. The "gates are always open" represents complete freedom in the Kingdom of God. There is no need for the gates to be closed because all threats have vanished. There is a beautiful academic relationship between souls being added to the Ecclesia on Earth (Ac 2:41, 42, 2:47) and their names being written in the Lamb's Book of Life.

Revelation Chapter Twenty-Two

Revelation 22:1: And he showed me a river of the water of life, clear as crystal, coming from the throne of God and of the Lamb

Someone may ask, "Where is the Holy Spirit in Heaven?" Here is the answer; The Holy Spirit is "The water of life," Jn 7:38, 39. God is the essence and source of physical and spiritual life (Jn 7:37-39). This life is the true Ecclesia of God's people. This is the temple of the Spirit of God in Christians (Eze 47:1; Zec 14:8). As you will remember, the work of the Eternal Spirit in all Covenant Christians started on the Day of Pentecost.

Revelation 22:2: In the middle of its street. And on either side of the river was the tree of life, bearing twelve kinds of fruit, yielding its fruit every month; and the leaves of the tree were for the healing of the nations.

There are some who question, "How can one tree grow in three separate places and yet still be one tree?" Another alluding question to this parallel would be, "How can God exist in three Persons, and yet still be one God?" The answer to these questions can be found only in the Spirit before the Presence of God. Without a doubt, this refers primarily to the triune Godhead.

Revelation 22:3: And there shall no longer be any curse; and the throne of God and of the Lamb shall be in it, and His bondservants shall serve Him.

There is no more curse on us because Christ took on our curse (Gal 3:13). He also reversed the curse of the Earth, "cursed ground," (Ge 3:17) for Christians and banished the serpent (Gal 3:10, 11). This could be done only by the death of a God-Man. Heaven is the ultimate end of the joy of serving God (Php 3:9-12). God emptied heaven of all of His treasure that you and I may become rich (2 Cor 8:9). Our greatest treasure is Christ!

Revelation 22:4: And they shall see His face, and His name shall be on their foreheads.

Scripture states that Christians will see Jesus first (Ac 7:5; 2Co 5:1-10; Php 1:23; Col 3:1-3). No one will see God, the Father, until the time when Christ shows His Father to all (Rev 21:3, 22:3-5). When Christians see Christ as the Living Word, Christians will see the Father also, but this final encounter with God is about a face-to-face relationship with God, the Father. People cried out for the revealing of the Father (Jn 14:9). Holy men and women had heard and had read about their forefathers seeing God's face (Ge 22:30, 33:14; Ex 24:17, 33:20). However, some form of a buffer always existed to restrain the complete Glory of God. The reason for this desperate plea from the people is because of their sin. Sin separates people from God (Isa 59:2). If anyone has uncovered sin, they are not able to enter God's domain, much less, to see God's face. Only spotless Christians will be able to see Him as Christ presents them to the Father. They have God's name on their foreheads because they are in Christ (Mt 5:8). Once again, believers must be cautioned about the sin of denying Christ's name (Rev 2:13). Hundreds of Christian leaders say, "We dropped the name of Christ from our marquees but we still call it CHURCH."

Revelation 22:5: And there shall no longer be any night; and they shall not have need of the light of a lamp nor the light of the sun, because the Lord God shall illumine them; and they shall reign forever and ever.

This verse parallels Revelation 21:3. When they see God, they are looking upon the Godhead. Notice in Revelation 22:3 that both God and the Lamb are seen on the Throne. They are two separate Persons. However, verses four and five say they shall see *His* face. This is similar to one tree growing in three different places. God the Father, God the Son, and God the Holy Spirit exist as one! Heaven is also seeing the Father and the Son in unison. They are the light, the truth, and separation from evil and terror.

Revelation 22:6: And he said to me, "These words are faithful and true"; and the Lord, the God of the spirits of the prophets, sent His angel to show to His bondservants the things which must shortly take place.

God is faithful and true. In the last three chapters of the New Testament, Christians receive what they lost in the first three chapters of the Old Testament. The discovery of what we have lost will take place shortly (Rev 1:1, 3). Christians must always be at the ready! If we think this message was only for those who died 2,000 years ago, remember that all of us are dying and going out into eternity in every generation.

Genesis 1-3	Revelation 20-22
Fellowship with God lost	Fellowship restored
Eternal life lost	Eternal life restored
Paradise lost	Paradise restored
River of life lost	River of life restored
Tree of Life lost	Tree of life restored
Victory lost	Victory restored
Eternal life replaced with death	No death
Freedom from sorrow & pain lost	No Sorrow or Pain
Victory over the serpent lost	Serpent cast in fiery lake
Messiah Promised	Messiah – the light & the life
Fullness lost	Fullness restored
Fearlessness lost	Fearlessness restored
Perfection lost	Perfection restored

Revelation 22:7: "And behold, I am coming quickly. Blessed is he who heeds the words of the prophecy of this book."

Jesus will come quickly and when He is least suspected (1Th 5:2). Those who are blessed are those who heed the words of The Revelation. The word, "heed," means to keep or preserve. God rewards Covenant Keepers (2Timothy 4:7). Jesus came quickly in 70 A.D. (Mt 22:7; Lk 21:20). When anyone departs this world in death – Christ is as good as "come." (See Revelation 19:7-9 under the section of the allegory between Peter dying and our death.).

Revelation 22:8, 9: And I, John, am the one who heard and saw these things. And when I heard and saw, I fell down to worship at the feet of the angel who showed me these things. And he said to me, "Do not do that; I am a fellow servant of yours and of your brethren the prophets and of those who heed the words of this book; worship God."

Once again John is bowing down to an angel and being rebuked. This angel is just a servant. Clearly, John's heart was moved in a very deep way. Caution: Be warned about the danger of worshipping man or woman! This will ruin our spiritual life and prevent us from entering this City. No matter how inspired an individual seems, God is the only reverend one! (Ps 111:9)

Revelation 22:10: And he said to me, "Do not seal up the words of the prophecy of this book, for the time is near."

Daniel was to seal up his prophecy (Da 9:24, 12:4). This meant it would not be opened to understanding until after Christ came 600 years later. But this prophecy of The Revelation of Jesus Christ is to be made known, now. Time is at hand. Every Christian should live each day as if it were their last! Christ's Coming is the next event on *God's calendar*. There are no more significant prophecies to be fulfilled. When a person died in the Old Testament, they went down to Sheol. The afterlife was pretty uncertain. When people die now, destinies are fixed forever. In a bodiless condition, the spirit sensibilities are so amplified that a person feels they are sitting next to eternity's door.

Revelation 22:11: "Let the one who does wrong, still do wrong; and let the one who is filthy, still be filthy; and let the one who is righteous, still practice righteousness; and let the one who is holy, still keep himself holy."

All people must make the choice. They must decide whether they will be righteous or unrighteous. In God's sovereignty, He allows His creation to exercises free will as they choose which path they will take. People are not forced to do God's commands; people are not God's puppets. He desires their obedience out of free will and love, not compulsion.

Revelation 22:12: "Behold, I am coming quickly, and My reward is with Me, to render to every man according to what he has done.

When Christ appears, people will no longer be able to choose righteousness. After the Judgment, there is not time for more chances. We will either be found righteous in Christ or take our chances with our own righteousness. As any Bible student understands, human righteousness alone is not sufficient to live in God's presence. God will reward the sinner with everlasting punishment and will reward righteous with an everlasting reward. In Heaven, God's reward will exceed the most satisfying experiences ever known by humans on Earth. This is God's promised reward given in full because Christ keeps His promise (Mt 5:9). In Hades, the desire for vodka, gin, beer, brandy, whiskey, opium, cocaine, heroin, sex, lust for power and every passion and addiction imaginable will exist for man to crave, but in Hades, there is no satisfying fulfillment (Rev 22:11). According to this verse, we also realize that the dear and precious, natural Godly affections will continue still.

Revelation 22:13: "I am the Alpha and the Omega, the first and the last, the beginning and the end."

This statement is repeated to assure Christians that Christ knows the beginning before the end because He is the beginning and the end. The words "I AM" go back to Exodus 3:14. Moses saw a Christophany in the "burning bush." The "Messenger" is called an angel (3:2); but in verses 4, 5 and 6, He is called God. No man has ever seen God the Father and lived to tell about it, but Moses saw God the Son, which was accompanied with, "The best gifts of the earth and the fullness of the favor of Him who dwelled in the bush" (Dt 33:16). Moses heard the Lord's voice (Acts 7:32).

Jesus is the self-existing Third Person of the Godhead. He is the creator of all things (John 1:1-3), and He is the "arche" (Rev 3:14). According to Liddell & Scott (among the Koine Greek scholars), this word means originator or first cause.[114] It is logically implied that He who is the First Cause is also He who is the Last Cause. He who started all things in the universe will bring them also to an end. Christ knows the end, even before the beginning. Trust in His Word!

Revelation 22:14: Blessed are those who wash their robes that they may have the right to the tree of life, and may enter by the gates into the city.

Those who wash their robes are those who have placed their trust in Jesus Christ at their immersion. They now have their right to the Tree of Life and access to the City of God restored. This is the residence of obedient sons of God (Php 3:20).

Revelation 22:15: Outside are the dogs and the sorcerers and the immoral persons and the murderers and the idolaters, and everyone who loves and practices lying.

Homosexuals are called "dogs" in the Old Testament (Dt 23:13, 17, 18). The word "dog" is not used in light-hearted jest. This is a very serious, sobering fact. In our modern-day America, with less than 5% of professed homosexuals, our Progressive Sin Party has a powerful motivation to make sodomy so acceptable that it becomes the norm as it was in The Days of Sodom (See my book, *Crucified in Sodom*; Rev. 11:8).

Of course, the academic instructors, politicians, religious leaders, and social Darwinist "change agents" will not suffer until this Scripture verse judges them. When they close their eyes in death, what will augment their suffering in Hell Fire the most will be the cries of infants and young children who echo throughout the corridors of Hell, "Your chosen lifestyle of the early 21st Century has cursed us into eternity!"

The TRUTH we are not told is that children are always the worse victims and are those who suffer the greatest grief as consequences of acts of unlawful sodomy." The shame is, because we have remained silent, when this sin of sodomy reaches its fullest length of abomination in the eyes of our Holy God, the wages of this sin will be so great that no one can bear them. This will be true of both sodomites and non-sodomites who were just as guilty because they accepted and tolerated this abomination. We wish we did not even have to address this sin in writing. All we can do is speak the TRUTH, plead for mercy, and fear God in Holy reverence.

The word "outside" in this verse reveals to us that Heaven is an eternally isolated place of joy and bliss for the righteous. We are made to fear God with reverence. Heaven is an isolated place for the righteous. The righteous are separated from death, disease, torment, pain, anguish, and all the participants, thereof. Heaven is quarantined against immoral diseases.

There are the following three life choices that will either lead those of us with the "church habit" to repentance or lead us to hate a preacher of righteousness:

1) "Love of the flesh" (alcohol, drugs, food, fornication, profane living and indulgences that crave instant gratification).

2) "Lust of the eyes" (illicit sex, desiring sex outside of marriage, coveting the world's goods for the moment).

3) "Pride of life" (instead of a spiritual walk, the consuming desire to be known in the vanity fair of soulish, prideful, selfish living that seeks first place no matter what).

Over the years, an uncompromising servant of the Holy God will grow accustomed to such hostility even though He grieves greatly when He sees his beloved brothers and sisters fall into this threefold trap.

Our homosexual friend told us that because he did not think we loved him that we were responsible for his chosen lifestyle. He left us and went elsewhere where his denominational leaders told him his sexual preference was perfectly acceptable in God's eyes. Our question is, as we come to the end of Revelation, "Is this man ready to meet the Just and Holy Savior, Jesus Christ, when he comes to his end?" Another question arises, "Who really loves his soul?"

Revelation 22:16: "I, Jesus, have sent My angel to testify to you these things for the churches. I am the root and the offspring of David, the bright morning star."

This verse reiterates Revelation 1:1. Christ, "Creator and King of all Angels", has His own personal Angel "messenger and servant." He is probably Michael, the Archangel. Christ proclaims His lineage as a man of David's offspring. Jesus is the last person to validate this truthful claim. Any messiah after Him would be a false messiah for his Jewish lineage would be impossible to authenticate. However, Christ also proclaims His divinity. He is the originator or root of the Davidic line. Only a true God-Man could accomplish this physical impossibility. The lineage of Christ in Matthew's and Luke's Gospels are the only such lineage in history. If Christ is not the promised Messiah, there will never be one simply because there is no one else on planet, Earth, who has such an authentic genealogical record.

Revelation 22:17: And the Spirit and the bride say, "Come." And let the one who hears say, "Come." And let the one who is thirsty come; let the one who wishes take the water of life without cost.

The Spirit and Jesus Christ, Himself, are giving an urgent invitation for any who are thirsty to enter into a relationship with them. Anyone who hears, wishes, or is thirsty for a covenant relationship with Jesus may do so! Remember the Spirit is also called "Water of Life."

Revelation 22:18: I testify to everyone who hears the words of the prophecy of this book: if anyone adds to them, God shall add to him the plagues which are written in this book;

This Book of Revelation is complete, final, and perfect. Nothing needs to be added to this Book or any other New Testament writing. There is no need for shallow creeds, dogmas, or disciplines. If anyone wishes to add to this Book, God's punishment will be added unto him! This also includes all the rest of the New Testament, "Heaven and earth shall pass away but my words shall not pass away" (Mt 24:35). Christ's Covenant is the last covenant with the human race. Christ's Covenant was the last covenant when it was written, and it remains so today.

Revelation 22:19: and if anyone takes away from the words of the book of this prophecy, God shall take away his part from the tree of life and from the holy city, which are written in this book.

At this point, translators and readers of Scripture had better take serious heed. To be denied "the tree of life" and the "holy city" is a serious charge! The Spirit of God wanted to make sure this book remained untouched. The punishment for removing any words from this Book results in our name being removed from the Lamb's Book of Life. My conviction, as this book's author, is that God is disposed in the same manner towards his whole New Covenant. If anyone adds creeds, doctrines, dogmas, or any form of authority to the Scriptures, they are violating the precedent set in this verse. God simply will not accept "latter day" religions, prophets, or new age religions in any age.

Revelation 22:20, 21: He who testifies to these things says, "Yes, I am coming quickly." Amen. Come, Lord Jesus. The grace of the Lord Jesus be with all. Amen.

As usual, the Pre-Millennial Mythology reverses and contradicts everything Christ says:

1. Christ says the Christian dead will rise before the Christian living. Pre-Millennialism says the Christian dead will be raptured before the sinner.

2. Christ says the Kingdom is Spiritual (not of this world). Pre-Millennialism says it is physical (of the world).

3. Christ says the wicked were taken away to judgment (as the flood took sinners away) (Mt 24:37-39). Pre-Millennialism says they are taken up.

4. Christ says those "left" will be sent away or let go. Pre-Millennialism says they will be left behind for damnation. Remember the word "behind" is not in the Greek manuscripts.

There are three Biblical attitudes toward the Coming of Christ:

1. Those Secular Humanists who scoff, "Where is the promise of His coming, for since the fathers fell asleep (died) all continues just as it was (Uniformitarianism) from the beginning of creation (2Pe 4:4).

2. Those who say, "My Master is not coming for a long time, and they begin to beat their fellow servants (beat the sheep instead of feed the sheep), and eat and drink with drunkards" (Mt 24:48).

3. Those who say with the beloved Apostle, "Even so Lord, Come Lord Jesus Come quickly!" (Rev 22:20)

This is the test of Christianity. If people sincerely want Christ to come, they will testify to Christ's Coming with their lives. As they continue their lives in God's Grace, people will expectantly await His appearance and always be ready for His return. If we do not discuss Heaven, chances are that is not where we are headed!

ADDENDA

Addendum A – Steps of Departure

This addendum describes 39 Roman Catholic Church doctrines and practices that are not Biblical, and therefore, "Steps of Departure" away from the early Christian Church as established by the Apostles. These doctrines and practices introduce superstitions into Christianity and create falsehoods that divert believers away from a personal relationship with Jesus Christ.

1. The Clergy and the Laity. The Roman Catholic Church has departed from the original concept in the early Christian Church when there was no distinction between clergy and laity. How did this departure occur? The leadership of the early Christian Church established by the Apostles consisted of evangelists to spread the Gospel (Eph 4:11; 2Ti 4:5). Christ gave the Evangelist to His congregation. Timothy would have ordained Elders-Pastors, but he was not called an Elder-Pastor in the New Testament. Evangelists ordained elders to be the overseers of the flock (1Ti 5:17; Tit 1:5-7; 1Pe 5:1-4) and deacons to care for the needs of the congregation's people (Php 1:1; 1Ti 3:8-13), as practiced in Ac 6:1-5).

In the New Testament, the terms "bishop" or "overseer" (*episkopos*), "elder" or "presbyter" (*presbuteros*) and "pastor" (*poimen*) were used interchangeably (Ac 20:17, 28; Tit 1:5,7; 1Pe 5:1,2). Never did only one bishop/elder/pastor lead a church; these leaders were always plural in number (Ac 11:30, 14:23, 15:2, 4, 6, 22, 23, 16:4, 20:17,18, 21:18; Php 1:1; 1Ti 5:7; Tit 1:5; Heb 13:17; Jas 5:14), and they led as servants, by example, rather than as worldly lords (1Pe 5:1-5; cf. Mt 20:25-25; Mk 10:42-45). The use of "bishop," singular, in 1 Timothy 3:2 and Titus 1:7 does not mean that there is only one bishop in each church; it simply references the bishop as a type. The point of the office is service rather than power" (*Theological Dictionary of the New Testament, Abridged in One Volume*, by Geoffrey W. Bromily, ed., Grand Rapids, MI: William B. Eerdmans Publishing Company, 1985, reprint 1986, p. 247.) The original church structure had each Christian being treated as an equal priest unto God (Rev 1:5, 6). The Protestant Reformation resurrected this equality by the doctrine "Priesthood of all Believers."

In the New Testament, the word "clergy" comes from the Greek word *kleros*, which can mean "lot" (as in "casting lots") or "that which is assigned by lot, portion, or share." (*A Greek-English Lexicon on the New Testament and Other Early*

Christian Literature, by Ardnt & Gingrich, Chicago, IL: The University of Chicago Press, 1957, reprint 1963, p. 436). Paul wrote that God has enabled Christians "to share in the inheritance (*klerou*) of the saints in the light" (Col 1:12, *New Revised Standard Version (NRSV)*). Christians are "heirs" (*kleronomoi*) according to the promise" (Gal 3:29, *NRSV*). In this sense, all Christians constitute "the clergy" (*The Emergence of the Laity in the Early Church*, by Alexandre Faivre, trans. by David Smith, New York: Paulist Press, 1990, pp. 5, 6).

The Greek word for "laity" is *laikos*, from the term *laos*, meaning people. The New Testament never uses this term. Remarkably, we find it only once in all the Christian literature prior to the 3rd Century (Faivre, pp. 15ff.).

The Apostle's church structure began to unravel at the beginning of the 2nd Century A.D., approximately 100 A.D., when Ignatius of Antioch (Bishop of Antioch) wrote letters speaking of a single bishop (or pastor or elder), a body of elders (presbyters), and a company of deacons in each church (*Church History in Plain Language*, 2nd ed., by Bruce L. Shelley, Word Publishing: Dallas, TX, 1983, p. 70). Ignatius elevated the position of "Bishop" above the others and even contended that no one could partake of the Lord's Supper unless a presiding bishop was present. How widespread was Ignatius' view of a monarchial bishop? It was not universal. Polycarp (a contemporary of Ignatius) did not recognize even a single bishop in contrast to the presbyters (Php 5:3, 6: 1)" (*The Rise of the Clergy*, by Mark M. Mattison, http://auburn. Edu/~allenkc/openhse/clergy.html, p. 2). Ignatius did not control the whole church so his ideas initially were not implemented throughout the Church. Antioch, Constantinople, Alexander, and Rome constituted the church centers of the time, with none dominant.

Clement of Rome at the end of the 1st Century described the need for church order by appealing to Old Covenant protocol. God's "peculiar services," he writes, "are assigned to the high priest, and their own proper place is prescribed to the priests, and their own special ministrations devolve on the Levites. The layman is bound by the laws that pertain to layman" (1 Clement 40:5). But Clement did not conceive of a class of Christians not actively involved in ministry (1 Clement 41:1). The existence of a Christian "laity" was unknown to Clement. Like "laikos," the term "kleros" was not used frequently during the 2nd Century (Mattison, pp. 3, 4). It is evident that no New Testament Christian would have ever referred to a Christian leader as "Clergy man" or a brother or sister as "Lay persons" in Christ's 1st Century Congregation.

By the 3rd Century, bishops, presbyters, and deacons were recognized as the "Clerical Order" as distinguished from "the laity" (Cf. Tertullian, Monog. 11, 12). Church fathers Clement of Alexandria, his disciple Origin, and Tertullian of Carthage all recognized the distinction between clergy and laity, but differed about how much authority clergy had over laity (Mattison, pp. 3-5).

With the legalization of Christianity by Constantine within the Eastern Roman or Byzantine Empire at Constantinople in the 4th Century came a number of unhealthy developments, not the least of which was the Church's involvement in politics and its worldly pursuits. "The clergy assumed official positions of authority alongside the civil governors."[115] Bishops were given unscriptural power over churches and were also given positions in government. "Diocese" means administration. As Rome merged with Catholicism, the bishops exercised both religious and political power in politics and in their district "dioceses."

The Roman Catholic Church continued to develop into today's Catholic hierarchy. Bishops were elevated from their previous local positions to higher positions to oversee the congregations, now headed by priests. The position of the priest evolved from the prior elder or presbyter and now served the local congregations.

The question became, "Who will oversee the districts?" The answer was the creation of a term and office unknown in the Bible, that of the "archbishop" to oversee the Catholics within the province or state. Then the "cardinal" was created to oversee the Catholics in a nation. Now, as might be expected, all of these steps of departure resulted in the creation and election of the Catholic Church's highest office, the "pope," who heads the entire Catholic Church.

The title "pope" only began to be reserved for the Bishop of Rome in the 6th Century, long after its claim of primacy, because early centuries of Christian history offer abundant evidence of Rome's prominence among the churches of the western region (Bruce L. Shelley, "Church History in Plain Language," pp. 133, 134). Biblically, this entire hierarchical structure is an absolute rebellion against God's original intent and His authority. With the full development of the papacy, we have completed Roman Catholicism!

Roman Catholicism refutes New Testament authority and returns to the Old Testament, once again, by presenting the priesthood as the mediating office between God and man. In the Old Testament, the Aaronic priesthood originated with God's ordination, through Moses, of Aaron and his sons (Lev 8). The authority of the priesthood was then pasted on in priestly succession.

The Catholic Church assumes this episcopal ordination of apostolic succession by passing the Apostle's authority down through the ages to the Catholic bishops. This historically unproven method of acquiring authority has caused the Catholic clergy to become independent of their "laity" because the "clergy" claim their commission and office from God, represented by the pope, whose authority comes from the Apostle Peter. The Pope then claims to be Christ's sole representative on Earth and head of the Roman Church. Jesus never appointed Peter with "headship" of all the Apostles. Biblically, this notion is expressly forbidden (Lk 24:24-26; Eph 1:22, 23; Col 1:18; 1Co 3:11). Hence, according to Catholicism, all people submit to God by obeying a pope. This, ladies and gentlemen, is Roman Catholicism!

While Eastern Orthodoxy is less despotic than Romanism, it is just as apostate in its views of the following departures from the primitive apostolic faith. Please remember that departures from the New Testament began first in the Eastern Church and spread later to the Western Church. The first Church councils that produced much of the apostasy were held in the Eastern Roman Empire, in Byzantium (modern-day Constantinople).

2. Holy Water. This doctrine teaches that a priest may especially bless and sanctify water, thus "Holy Water." A priest creates holy water when he mixes a pinch of salt in water and blesses it. This doctrine was introduced approximately 100 A.D. and authorized in 850 A.D. This practice was borrowed from paganism. *The Catholic Encyclopedia*, III, p. 76, states, "Moreover, the use of holy water and incense (the latter originally used as a sort of disinfectant) was also no doubt suggested by the similar customs among pagans around them."

The superstitious pagan rite of holy water was supposed to give health, drive away disease, and run off the devil. The following quote states,

"The use of Holy Water among Christians must be very ancient, for the apostolic constitutions contain a formula for blessing water that it might have power 'to give health, drive away diseases, or put the devil to flight,' But there does not seem to be any evidence that it was customary for the Priest to sprinkle the people with Holy Water before the ninth century" (Catholic Dictionary, p. 403).

While the Catholic Church claims to be the only true church that teaches an infallible doctrine, I say to you that the Catholic Church admits in its own writings that it is more pagan than Christian. (www.google.com: Catholicism Against Itself by O.C. Lambert.) Lambert wrote an expanded version of this book along with a smaller paperback. The book is not merely vitriol against Catholicism; it consists of historical quotes regarding the pagan origin of Catholicism from Catholic scholars themselves, like Cardinal Newman in his *Essay on Development of the Christian Religion*. [116]

3. Doctrine of Penance. This human innovation to require church sponsored reparations to expiate sins was introduced in 157 A.D. Penance is required to expiate our "original sin." Although credited to Augustine (354-430 A.D., penance was invented by Tertullian (160-245 A.D.). All Catholics must do penance. This revealing of their innermost secrets enables the church hierarchy to control people through a glorified system of blackmail. The requirement to perform penance has been one of the Church's most effective ways of raising money used to support the clerical hierarchy. New Testament Christianity directly contracts this practice (Heb 9:22; 1Jn 1:6-8).

4. Wax Candles. These were introduced into worship approximately 320 A.D. Pagan religion always requires a fetish. Candles were even used in the Jewish worship, but when Christ came, He lit up the world (Jn 8:12; 2Co 4:3, 4).

5. Veneration of Dead Saints and Angels. This began about 375 A.D. It is a sin to worship angels (Rev.19:10, 22:9) God is not the God of the dead (Isa 26:14) but of the living (Mk 12:27). This practice was copied from the heathen religions of The East.[117] Of course, the memory of a righteous person is a healthy motivation in life, but veneration is an act of worship. Sometimes ancestor worship precludes obedience to Christ. Other times, the children imitate the unhealthy lifestyles of the parents. The Apostle Peter says that we are not to practice the "aimless conduct received by tradition from your fathers" (1Pe 1:18).

6. Mass as a Daily Celebration. This was adopted in 364 A.D. The word is an adaptation of the Latin, "Missa," meaning "go or sent." Even though "Liturgical Mass" is popular with millions of people, it is not of the Holy Spirit. Yes, the early congregations came together to break bread and receive instructions, but The Apostles never placed a universal "liturgy" upon them

in order to standardize a particular worship. Paul advised them to do things "decently and in order" (1Co 14:40), and they had the prophetic Word, Psalms, prayers, and exhortations; but an outward trapping or form of worship simply did not exist. They worshipped in SPIRIT and TRUTH (Jn 4:23). A liturgical mass requires a priest. This in a nutshell is what is wrong with it. We only have ONE priest over all of us, and He is on HIGH (Heb 4:14).

7. Worship of Mary, "Mother of God." This began about 381 A.D. and the Council of Ephesus decreed it in 431 A.D. (More on this later.)

8. Priests to Dress Differently from the "Laity." This began in 500 A.D. Outward vestments have, for human reasons, the power to attract gullible people. Outward adornment cannot beautify the saints (1Pe 3:4). If we placed as much emphasis on the reading of the WORD and intercessory prayer as we do on preparing men outwardly for religious appearances, there would be a tremendous spiritual revival in the world. This method of dressing was one more way for the clergy to show their elevated status.

9. Doctrine of Purgatory. The Council of Florence originated this doctrine in 139 A.D. This doctrine established an after-death way station between Heaven and Hell. The doctrine states that when a person dies unprepared, in sin, that person may be freed from torment and punishment by the payment of sufficient money to the priests. Pope Gregory the Great re-established this doctrine in 593 A.D., and it became a dogma at the First Council of Lyons in 1245 A.D. At The Vatican Council 11 (2011 A.D.), the church deemphasized the doctrine of purgatory. Of course, the doctrine of Limbo also has fallen out of "grace" in Catholicism. How can a baby go to Limbo when Christ said, "In Heaven their angels do always behold the face of My Father in heaven?" (Mt 18:10) Read all of Chapter 18 about the "little ones." Only the Blood of Jesus can "purge" us (Jn 5:24; Ro 8:1; 1Jn 1:7-9; Ac 22:16).

Catholic authorities admit they perverted the Scriptures in order to manufacture purgatory. *Catholic Dictionary*, p. 704, states, "We would appeal to these general principles of Scripture, rather than to particular texts often alleged in proof of Purgatory. We doubt if they contain an explicit and direct reference to it."

From *Plain Facts*, p. 125, Catholics admit, and I quote, "So we presume all Catholics who die to be in purgatory; although, it may often seem more probable for a particular soul that is in heaven or hell."

Friends, think of this. There would be no reason to pray, burn candles, and say masses for a person who is in Hell. Neither would there be any reason for the expenditure of money, a necessary part of the doctrine of purgatory, for those who are already in Heaven; therefore, Catholics just "PRESUME" that all of them will go to purgatory. How profitable for the Catholic treasury. This doctrine implies that a few people are good enough to go to Heaven and few bad enough to go to Hell; therefore, the Church just held them in purgatory until they pay up. Belatedly, in effect (while still embracing it) Catholic theologians decided to abolish purgatory. Like eating fish on Friday, purgatory is no longer a binding dogma for Catholics.

Only the blood of Christ can "PURGE" us from sin (Jn 5:24; Ro 8:1; Acts 22:16, 1Jn 1:7-9).

10. Latin Language as the Language of Prayer and Worship.[118] Pope Gregory the Great imposed this on the Church in 600 A.D. Although since Vatican II, even this is being changed. But for all the "changes," Babylon will always be the same to the end (Da 7:25-27). Alexander the Great did more than conquer the world. He gave the world the Greek Language. Alexander was chosen of God for this purpose (Da 8:21, 22, 10:22). Many sources exist to help the average student of the Bible to understand what the original koine Greek New Testament really says.

11. Kissing the Pope's Toe. This practice began in 709 A.D. *The Catholic Encyclopedia, Vol. XII*, p. 270, states, "The kissing of the pope's foot – the characteristic act of reverence by which all the faithful do honor to him as Vicar of Christ – is found as early as the eighth century." This unscriptural practice, as you observe, was begun almost 700 years after the Lord's Ecclesia began. We say this because we have forgotten two things in 700 years. First, there is only ONE Potentate, Jesus Christ (1Ti 6:15), and secondly, our human race is filled with man pleasing and man worshipping (Heb 12:28, 13:6). God's Word forbids bowing before another leader, let alone kissing his toe (Ac 10:25; Rev 19:10, 22:9). The temporal power of the pope began in 750 A.D. Jesus forbids this (Mt 4:8, 9, 20:25; Jn 18:38).

12. Worship and Veneration of Images. This began early but was decreed by the Second Council of Nice in 787 A.D. God severely condemned idolatry (Ex 20:2-6; Dt 27:15; Ps 115).

13. Veneration of St. Joseph. This began in 890 A.D.

14. Baptism of Bells. Pope John XIII began this in 965 A.D. Christ commanded us to immerse people into Christ (Mk 16:16; Mt 28:18, 19). So what is the response? We "baptize" bells; something He did not tell us to do. It may sound like a little thing, but it is the "little things," whether omitted or included, that constitute our life and response to our Master.

15. Canonization of Dead Saints. Pope John XV began this in 995 A.D. The Bible translators affixed the names to the Bible's Books (St. John, St. Jude). The expression "saint" in the New Testament is always in the plural. Even in Philippians 4:21, with "every saint," the plural is implied.

16. Fasting on Fridays and during Lent. This was imposed in 998 A.D. Some say that motive behind these fastings was to bolster a staggering fishing industry. Catholics adamantly deny this. One thing we know for sure is that there is nothing in the New Testament that teaches anything near this doctrine. These verses show the absurdity of this dogma (Mt 15:10; 1Co 10:25; 1Ti 4:1, 2; Col 2:14-17; Ro 14:1-23).

17. Doctrine of Transubstantiation. This was first taught in 1000 A.D. This doctrine leads people to believe that prayer and special powers of man mystically and literally change the fruit of the vine (wine) and the bread into the literal blood and body of Jesus Christ. What do you suppose would happen if someone prepared the loaf and wine and put deadly poison in it before giving it to a priest for "transubstantiation"? If the wine were really "transubstantiated," this act would prevent the poison's deadly effect. But would the priest have enough confidence in his theology to believe that this transubstantiation would counter the poison's effect? There is no priest who would dare attempt to drink it. The Doctrine of Transubstantiation contracts Hebrews 7:27, 9:26-28, and 10:10-14; it is a blasphemy and makes a mockery of God.

Bishop England compiled the *Roman Missal*. It states on page 9, "In the Mass, Christ is the victim; he is produced by the consecration, which by the power of

God, and the institution of the Redeemer, and the act of the priest, places the body and blood of Christ, under the appearance of blood and wine upon the alter; then the priest makes an oblation of this victim to the Eternal Father on behalf of the people, and the victim undergoes a destructive change, showing forth the death of the Redeemer, and making commemoration thereof, by the exhibition of the apparent separation of the body from the blood; the former being under the appearance of bread, and the latter under the appearance of wine, and by the consumption of both by the priest." Bishop England declares of the sacrifice, "It is not a different sacrifice from that of the cross; for the victim in each is the same."

The Roman Catechism (numbers 1374-77), states, "Not only is it the true body of Christ, to wit: all that is proper to the human body – the bones, the nerves, contained in the sacrament – but farther, Jesus Christ, whole and entire."

The Council of Trent (1545-63) decreed that, "Whoever shall affirm that a true and proper sacrifice is not offered to God in the Mass," or that it was "not a propitiatory offering," or that it "ought not to be offered for the living and the dead, for sins, punishments, satisfactions and other necessities: LET HIM BE ACCURSED."

It seems incredible that poor, mortal men, worm, and dust of the Earth would make such a mockery of the Son of God and seek to insult man's intelligence by claiming such miraculous and ridiculous powers of a priest, who himself is just another man.

1. That Jesus Christ – body and blood, flesh, bones, and nerves, the whole and entire human body, is eaten by the priest; that the identical human Body of Christ, whole and complete, is produced in a wafer of bread and glass of wine by a weak and unworthy human being called a priest. Indeed, Christ is present at the communion table, and of course, He sees His own body and blood that ultimately nailed our sins to His cross. No one is able to replicate what He sees at this table for He says, "This is My body and My blood." It is very shallow to call this memorial an emblematic ceremony.

2. That this ritual is not simply a commemoration of the sacrifice on Calvary, but a "propitiatory offering," of the Son of God afresh for the sins of the people.

3. That the bread and wine retain their "appearance," their substance being converted into the human body and blood of Christ. It is extremely important that we refer to Hebrews 9:25-28. We must note that when Christ said, "This IS MY BODY," and again, "This IS MY BLOOD," that in somebody's mind, the body and blood of Christ were seen, known, and understood. That my friends had to be IN THE MIND OF GOD. God saw His Son's blood at the Passover. God saw His Son's blood on Calvary, and when we partake of the Lord's Supper on the "first day of the week," it is God who sees the efficacy of His Son's Body and Blood, shed once for all. There is no merit in who breaks or offers The Bread. Once broken and offered, the bread need never be broken and offered again. It needs to be remembered in Covenant. Once the blood was shed (He 10:14), it need never be offered again. "The fruit of the vine" (Mt 26:29) is not fermented. The Passover Lamb requires that we "Put away the OLD leaven." We see grape juice, but God sees the blood of Christ (1Co 5:7), the Passover Lamb (Ex 12:13).

18. Doctrine of Celibacy.[119] The official ruling came from the Council of Elvira (306 A.D.) and has been revisited over time.[120] This doctrine forbids the marrying of priests. This doctrine is another departure that is a fulfillment of prophecy. Remember that Paul declared, "The spirit speaketh expressly, that in the latter times some shall fall away from the faith, giving heed to seducing spirits and doctrines of demons; through the hypocrisy of men that speak lies, branded in their own conscience as with a hot iron, forbidding marrying and commanding to abstain from meats" (1Ti 4:1-3).

Priests want people to call them "Father." We refuse to call any man on this Earth, father – except my father in the flesh. The reason is found in Christ's warning, recorded in Matthew 23:9. Hear Him, "Call no man your father who is upon the earth, for one is your Father, which is in heaven."

Ladies and Gentlemen, this doctrine brought about one of the most immoral and corrupt practices known. A priest, who takes a vow of celibacy, may live in open adultery with any number of women and still have the blessing of the church. Read the following from *Catholic Morals*, p. 149, "All celibates are not chaste: celibacy is not necessarily chastity; by a large majority. Unless something other than selfishness suggests this choice of life, the word is apt to be a misnomer for profligacy. And one who takes the vow of Celibacy does not break it by sinning against the sixth commandment; he is true to it until he weds."

According to *Catholic Encyclopedia, Vol VIII*, p. 19-20, and *D'Aubigne*, p. 372, Pope Innocent XXIII (1484-1492) had seven or eight illegitimate sons by different women. Romans gave him the name "Father."

Catholic Encyclopedia, Vol VI, p. 213, labels Pope Alexander VI (1492-1503) as the worst pope. He had eight illegitimate children by different women, including four infamous ones by one woman. All of them were brought to Rome with him when he became pope. His son, Caesar Borgia, one of the worst men in history, was made an archbishop at age 18 and promoted to a cardinal at age 19.

One may wonder about all the guarded secrets of the nunneries and other Roman Catholic institutions. When Germany required government inspection and investigation of the nunneries, the nuns were moved out of the country. Read the stories of many of the escaped nuns and ex-priests (www.google.com: Corruption in Convents and Nunneries), and you will be moved with such indignation as to ask why institutions so corrupted are permitted in civilized world. Check the site, "Abortions and Infanticide in Monasteries."

An ex-priest, B. I. Quinn, of Kalamazoo, MI, wrote the following regarding a society of priests in his book, "*Why Priests Don't Marry*," "These blessed creatures wore different insignia, sometimes a ring on the third finger, or a pair of silken mittens, etc. Both priests and women are members of this society."

Mr. Quinn continues, "At first the female may be a little timid, and somewhat surprised to learn that the priest or bishop requires this unusual, apparently wrong, mysterious right service from her, and she may object, as Mary did, in her innocent fear, when she said on hearing the unusual announcement or demand, "How can this be?" For I know not a man; but the priest, representing God's angel in his office gently soothes her mind, and quiets the fears of his future expose, by saying to her 'He who will come unto thee is not a man, but is the holy one of God, and this union is pleasing him, and if a child be born unto the fruit of this union, it will be holy and blessed; therefore, I say unto thee, as the angel said unto Mary, "Fear not" (*Why Priests Don't Marry*, pp. 4, 5).

At this point, Paul advises, "It is better to marry than to burn" (1Co 7:9). If the priest is forbidden to marry, he will definitely explore alternatives to marriage, such as homosexuality, pedophilia, or as people have heard, "marriage to a bottle of alcohol."

19. Rosary or Prayer Beads. [121] There is some controversy over who introduced prayer beads into the Catholic Church. Some say Peter the Hermit introduced this practice in 1090 A.D.[122] Others say that this practice was introduced by St. Dominic in 1214 A.D. at Prouille, France, where Dominic supposedly had a vision of Mary. This practice may have been copied from Hindus and Muslims. Christ forbade this in Matthew 6:5-13. The 54 "Hail Mary's" and five "Our Fathers" constitute the 59 prayer Beads. It is no coincidence that the Muslims have Prayer beads with 99 names of Allah. From reading Scripture, we discovered over 200 NAMES (in prophecy, in typology, and in historical descriptions) for Jesus Christ and stopped counting. But mere repetition of names without exploring the hermeneutical meanings and significance of each name is nothing but rote, indiscreet prattling. Even repeating the Name of Jesus over and over is unacceptable, repetitive babbling. We sometimes worship God in vain without knowing it. Matthew, Chapter 6, warns against vain repetitions (ostentatious praying) and the correct way of praying according to the model prayer, sometimes called the Lord's Prayer as found in John, Chapter 17.

20. Inquisition of Heretics. The Council of Verona started this religious terror in 1184 A.D. to force people to adhere to Catholic teachings and punish those who do not. The use of force to spread religion is completely unknown to the basic tenets of Christianity.

21. Doctrine of Indulgences. Indulgences originated in 1190 A.D. Catholic Church representatives sold these promises to provide some favorable action concerning the afterlife. The sale of indulgences was at the heart of the Protestant Reformation when Martin Luther was angered by the sale of indulgences to poor people. The indulgences were supposed to release their departed loved ones, who were supposedly in purgatory, so their souls would go to Heaven. The money from this particular sale of indulgences was to help build St. Peter's Basilica. Indulgences mean exactly what the word entails; it is a license purchased to have indulged in sin and then be released from it.

22. Auricular Confessions. The Lateran Council under Pope Innocent III began this practice of the laity confessing their sins to a priest in 1215 A.D. The

Gospel directs us to confess only to God (Ps 51; Isa 1:18; Lk 7:48, 15:21; 1Jn 1:8, 9). When James tells Christians to confess their faults one to another (Jas 5:16), the separate Jewish priesthood had already been abolished, and he speaks of brethren opening their hearts to other brethren in order to disciple and heal the faults that cause one to be weak in faith. No man on Earth can forgive sins. Only Jesus Christ, who gave His blood for atonement, can forgive sins, and He has established no man on Earth to reveal to Him the secrets of a man's heart. There is only one Priestly intercessor for us (1Ti 2:5), and He is Christ the Lord.

23. Adoration of the Babylonian Wafer (host). Pope Honorius instituted this in 1220 A.D. This is pure idolatry; it is contrary to John 4:24. As we shall see later, the idea of "Elevating the Host" by lifting a piece of bread toward Heaven goes back to Babylon. The Prophets rebuked this practice (Jer 7:18, 44:19). Liturgical worship requires an experiential fetish such as a priest, a ritual, an altar and a shaman.

24. Bible Forbidden to Laity. The Council of Toledo forbade the use of the Bible by laypersons and placed it on the index of forbidden books in 1229 A.D. But Scriptures state they are to be read by all (Jn 5:39; 1Ti 3:15, 16; 2Ti 2:15). Modern-day Catholics may have more access to the Bible today than in the past; however, "The Magisterium" or Teaching Authority of the (Catholic) Church states, "The task of authoritatively interpreting the word of God, whether written or handed on [Scripture or Tradition], has been entrusted exclusively to the living Magisterium of the Church, whose authority is exercised in the name of Jesus Christ."[123]

25. The Scapular. Simon Stock, an English monk, initiated the wearing of this piece of brown cloth in 1287 A.D. This cloth is supposed to contain supernatural virtue to protect those who wear it on their naked skin from all dangers. This is pure fetishism.

26. Sprinkling for Baptism. The Council of Ravenna officially adopted this practice of baptism by sprinkling in 1311 A.D. The Greek Catholic Church did not accept the practice of substituting sprinkling of water for baptism in water and does not accept it today. The Roman Catholic Church admits that the meaning of the original Greek word, "baptize," is immersion. But, of course, the Roman Church claims the Pope has the right and authority

to change and alter the Word of God, if he so desires, because he is supposed to be infallible in decrees of faith and practice.

According to the official Catholic, *The New Testament*, translated from the Latin Vulgate, publisher New Jersey: St. Anthony Guild Press, 1941, footnote to Romans 6:3, p. 415, states, "St. Paul alludes to the manner in which Baptism was ordinarily conferred in the primitive Church, by immersion. The descent into the water is suggestive of the descent of the body into the grave, and the ascent is suggestive of the resurrection to a new life. St. Paul obviously sees more than a mere symbol in the rite of Baptism. As a result of it we are incorporated into Christ's mystical body and live a new life."

The above paragraph is just the kind of statement that is made by intellectually honest Catholic theologians. O.C. Lambert, who reviewed Catholic writings in his book, *Catholicism Against Itself*, found hundreds of such references in official Catholic writings that were clear admissions that what the Catholic Church teaches as dogma is a flagrant contradiction of what the Apostles taught in the New Testament.

27. Sign of the Cross. This has its origin in the mystic "Tau" of the Babylonian Cult (to be addressed later). The sign came from the letter "T," the initial of the letter of Tammuz (Eze 8:14), but is better known as "Bracchus" (The Lamented One), who was Nimrod, son of Cush (See "Mystery Babylon," under Doctrine of Mary.).[124]

28. Orders of Monks and Nuns. The numerous orders were borrowed from the Babylonian Cult; the nuns are an imitation of the Vestal Virgins of Rome that was copied from Babylon. Pagan vestal virgins were abolished by Emperor Theodosius in 394 A.D. Although modern Catholic apologists protest, vehemently, the following interpretation of history, many historians believe that in order to accommodate the pagan traditions of pagans converting to Catholic Christianity, Papal Rome incorporated the idea of this tradition through monasteries and nunneries. The word "nun" appeared sometime before 900 A.D. and came from the Old English word "nunne," which is the feminine form of "nonnus" or monk. [125] We know one thing for certain; there were no institutions like monks and nuns in the New Testament. Paul condemned ascetical living as an erroneous practice in the New Testament (Col 2:18-23).

29. The Cup of the Lord's Supper Forbidden to the Laity. The Council of Constance instituted this practice in 1414 A.D. But we know that all covenant Christians are to partake of the New Covenant supper (Mt 26:27; 1Co 10:16-18). A Christian is to partake of both the bread and the fruit of the vine.

30. Doctrine of Seven Sacraments. These were recognized in 1439 A.D. The Catholic Church recognizes the following seven sacraments: baptism, confirmation, the Eucharist (Lord's Supper); the sacraments of healing are penance and anointing of the sick; and the sacraments of service are holy orders and matrimony. But Christ instituted only two covenant commandments, those of immersion (baptism) and the Lord's Supper (Mt 29:19, 20, 26:26-29). Paul, however, offered a third ordinance for financial support for Gospel preaching (1Co 9:14). Paul said, "We beseech you as Christ" (2 Co 5:20). Jesus said, "Teach ALL that I have COMMANDED you" (Mt 28:20). The four Gospels, plus Acts, have many commandments. The other 22 Epistles written by the Apostles (and their scribes) have many commandments. Paul calls it "The whole counsel of God" (Acts 20:27). We counted 20 commandments in The Sermon on The Mount, "ten more than the ten commandments." To reduce God's Word to seven sacred, "sacra," commandments (or as the Greek-Catholics teach "10 Mysteries") is to create Biblical illiteracy, spiritual apathy, and disobedience.

31. Ava Maria (the Hail Mary). Herbert Thurston, writing in Catholic Encyclopedia says there is little information that "Hail Marry" was used prior to the 10th Century. The idea to "Hail Mary" was initiated in 1508 A.D., and approved by Pope Sixtus V (1585-90). It is a Greek-Roman Catholic tradition to force a good verse of Scripture into a false doctrine. The angel, Gabriel, knew that God loved the woman who would provide the womb for His Spirit, and Gabriel knew it. He said, "Greetings Mary," and then blessed her with Words from God (Lk 1:28). The Angel is not worshipping Mary. The Greek Word translate "hail" merely means to greet so as to get someone's attention.

32. Equating Catholic Church Tradition to the Authority of the Bible. The Council of Trent pronounced this CRITICAL change in 1545 A.D. This human teaching, also held by the Pharisees' approach to the Old Testament, nullifies the Bible's authority (Mk 7:7-13; Col 2:8; Rev 22:18). If given a

choice between the authority of Scripture and the Magisterium, Catholics who are strict followers of Catholic dogma would turn their backs on the Bible.

33. Apocryphal Books Added to the Bible. The Council of Trent authorized these additions in 1545 A.D. These books provide excellent historical material, but they are uninspired; they are not God's Word.

34. Creed of Pope Pius IV. The Church accepted this creed as the official creed in 1560. In this lengthy Creed, Pius gives his personal views, among which is the heresy that the Catholic Church gave us the Bible. Concerning Scripture, Pius said, "Neither will I interpret them except according to the unanimous consent of the holy fathers." [126] Nothing in scripture can be clearer than the fact that God, through The Holy Spirit, gave the world The Scriptures. We frequently refer to the documented fact that the Scriptures were completed before 70 AD, almost 1,500 years before Pius was born. Pius' creed is counter to what Scripture states in Galatians 1:8.

35. The Immaculate Conception of Mary. Pope Pius IX proclaimed this doctrine in 1854. It teaches that Mary was born free of original sin. This false doctrine is a reaction to the false doctrine taught by Tertullian (2nd Century) and Augustine (4th century) that infants are born in Adam's sin. The words "original sin" are not found anywhere in scripture, unless we point out Satan as "The original sinner." Romans 5:12 does NOT teach that SIN passed onto all men. It says, DEATH passed onto all men. The false doctrine of original sin has led to many other false doctrines. Thus, when the Pope wanted a "perfect" Mary, the church had to find a way to get "original sin" off her soul. "Immaculate Conception" was the answer. If we carry this date line from Mary's life in 30 A.D. (Ac 1:14) to the Pope's decree, Mary was not officially absolved of "so called" original sin until 1,824 years later, in 1854.

On the other hand, we do believe in Immaculate Conception for adults, but that is when we are born again. As already stated from Matthew 18, it is abundantly clear that babies are not born in sin. Remember, another false doctrine of "Limbo" was concocted to cover the false doctrine of "infant damnation." But the "Birth of Water and Spirit" (Jn 3:5) is imperative for forgiveness and the reception of a regenerated life. When we "obey from the heart that form of doctrine delivered to us" (Ro 6:17 with 6:1-4), we are washed immaculately pure and clean through the redemptive blood of Christ. Mary, herself, needed a Savior, and when she was present on the Day of Pentecost (Acts 1:14), she was immersed for forgiveness of sins as stated in Acts 2:38. She was "immaculately conceived" of Christ, her Savior. The fact is, anyone can be "immaculately conceived" if they draw near to Christ with a true heart of faith, "Having their bodies washed in pure water" (Heb 10:22).

36. Papal Infallibility. Pope Pius IX declared this doctrine in 1870 A.D. This doctrine affirms that the Pope is unable to error when he speaks "Ex Cathedra." The Latin phrase implies that if he speaks "From the Chair" of his holy office, he is officially declared exempt from any error. This of course contradicts Scripture, "Let a man so speak as of the oracles of God" (1Pe 4:11) and "Study to show yourself approved of God" (2Ti 2:15). The "oracles" of God today come from the Scripture "That furnishes us unto ALL good works" (2Ti 3:17). There is nothing wrong with "speaking from a chair" as long as you are teaching the truth of God's Word.

37. Condemnation of Modernism and all Scientific Discoveries not approved by the Church. Pope Pius X (July 1907) proclaimed this condemnation just as Pius IX had done in his syllabus of 1864. Today the Catholic Church distances themselves from the ideology of these two Popes, but being "The church of the world," this institution knows how to adapt to please the popular notions of the world. Pope Francis in 2014 appeased the atheists by telling them they will go to Heaven for their good works, and sodomites will go there also whether they repent of their sins or not. For a sample of the Catholic Church's direction, see "Pope Francis sends letter praising gay children's book." [127] Catholic theology embraces evolution with a passion, and such pseudo-science is taught in their schools. What we have learned since Pius X is that on the subject of science and philosophy, Rome bends whichever way the wind blows.

38. Condemnation of Public Schools. Pius XI condemned public schools in 1930. This of course gives credence to the fact that he thought parochial schools offer a better education. As the government schools, for the most part, continue to sponsor sodomy and disrespect for the home, government, or legitimate authority, and portray pure Christianity in an unfavorable light, perhaps Pius was correct about parochial schools, but as mentioned

above, the Christ-centered Scripture is as neglected in parochial schools as it is in government schools. What a tribute to Christ's grace and power that some Christian kids still make it through school without losing their "mind of Christ." But we ponder the questions, "How much input should a parent have in their child's education in this day and age when many espouse 'it takes a village' thinking, instead of the Biblical concept of family responsibility" and "whatever happened to a parent-child education"?

39. Doctrine of Mary "Mother of God" Reaffirmed.[128] Pius XI reaffirmed this "Mother of God" doctrine in 1930. This doctrine originally came from the Council of Ephesus (431 A.D.). Pius was very firm in his resolve that perhaps the "Mother of God" emphasis was losing its appeal and needed to be highlighted in the 20th Century. Mary contradicted this doctrine in her own words in Luke 1:46-49.

Later, the Doctrine of Assumption (1950 A.D.) taught that Mary (like Jesus) was resurrected, glorified, and ascended into Heaven. Catholic churches celebrate this alleged event on August 15. The truth is, "No man has ascended up into heaven, but the Son of Man descended" (Jn 3:13), and "David is not ascended into the heavens" (Ac 2:34). It is gross presumption to prescribe to Mary a supernatural accomplishment that would cause unimaginable grief to such a humble, Godly woman.

Christ not only ascended to Heaven (Jn 20:17), but this act was due to His authority and power over demons, death, and earthly domain and came after He had descended into the Hadean world (Eph 4:8, 9). (Remember, He did not ascend until He descended first into the once indomitable, impregnable Hadean world.) Christ ascended far above the heavens (Eph 4:10). Christ is the only ascending ONE, the rest of us go up in His train. By attributing to Mary such divine actions, which rightfully belong to Jesus alone, and supernatural actions, that only Christ Her Savior could accomplish, the Catholic Church deprives Mary of privileges that are due her as a sinner saved by God's Grace. Surely, if Mary were alive today, she would be very angry with the Catholic Church!

Now, as we address this despicable doctrine of Mary's Assumption, is a good time once again to realize what a blessing for us to know that we are removed from all the sound and fury of life's imperfections and disappointment, like the guilt we may carry, and the errors of family and friends. All these are lifted from us the minute we die, "the old order of things has passed away" (Rev 21:4), and "the dead know nothing" (Ecc 9:5).

MYSTERY BABYLON

We cannot really understand how Roman Babylon rose to worldwide power and instigated such "Steps of Departure" from the original Apostolic Faith unless we study the history of ancient Mystery Babylon and see its historical applications today.

In Revelation 17:5, Babylon has a name on her forehead, "Mystery, Babylon the Great." As we have seen, three church groups exist in Scripture, and one of them is Babylon. The other two are the original congregation of Acts, Chapter Two, and the congregation of baptistic disciples of John (Acts 19:2-7). Paul called the legitimate New Testament congregation a "mystery" because she was unknown to the Old Testament Prophets (Eph 3:1-12, 5:23-32).

In this Revelation's 17:5 text, Pagan-Papal Rome is called a "mystery" for two reasons: 1) She was unknown before John wrote the Revelation of Jesus Christ, and 2) Pagan-Papal Rome operates like the Roman Mystery Religions under the guise and pretense of being a great power of God, when she is actually controlled by the Dragon (Satan). Those who follow Pagan-Papal Rome believe the "mystery" that she can give them the promise of Heaven, but inwardly the institute is devoid of Spirit breath. The only things that hold the system up are the temporary, worldly "powers that be," and they are utterly astounded when they see The Revelation. Beneath the flimsy costume, image, and façade, the system is nothing but "a cage of foul spirits" (Rev 18: 2).

Anti-Catholics are told "mystery" appeared for some time on the frontlet of the papal crown, but Pope Julius II (1503-13) removed it when he learned of the Protestant accusation of Revelation17:5 (See *Gill's Commentary* for Revelation 17:1-6. See also, books.google.com: *The New Testament in the Original Greek*, with Introductions and Notes, by Christopher Wordsworth).

Wordsworth is a very worthy scholar and the Web records his many literary works and accolades. Wordsworth writes, "The word mysterium was written on the Papal tiara whence it was removed by Julius II." Wordsworth also quotes contemporary commentators, Wolf and Poole, who wrote of Julius' decision to save his church from the embarrassment caused by Revelation 17:1-6. It is said of

Matthew Poole, "Few names will stand as high in scholarship as Matthew Poole's in Great Britain" (www.google.com). Herbert Wolf wrote, "Everyman's Bible Commentary." It is said of Dr. Wolf, "He provides helpful, concise and valuable information to the Bible student" (www.google.com). We are providing such scholarly testimony to counter any Catholic rebuttal concerning why Julius II decided to remove "mysterium" from the Papal tiara. If we are wrong, we expect those contradicting our research to exhibit scholarship to the contrary, but gross denial and mere contradiction are just not satisfactory evidence.

Romanism has always been shrouded in mystery. We think of the mystery of infant regeneration (a newborn baby being born again-Jn 3:3), the mystery of transubstantiation, the mystery of holy water, lights shining on the altar, confessions, and other rites and ceremonies that profess great things and offer zero results. All these ordinances were unknown to Christ and His Apostles.

On the subject "Check Your Brain at The Door," O.C. Lambert (whose book *Catholicism Against Itself* has the quotation, "Leave Reason at The Door," on its cover page), gives this direct quote from ("Explanation of Catholic Morals," p. 76)

> "Once he (the Catholic) does so, he has no further use for his reason. He enters the church, an edifice illuminated by superior light of revelation and faith. He can leave REASON, like a lantern at the door"

Lambert's schematic is highly justified because there is nothing that Protestants say about their corrupt establishment that the ablest Catholic scholars do not admit to being true. Even Catholic theologians admit that this description, "Mystery Babylon," fits the original, historical Rome. Cardinal Bellarmine, in his comments on Revelation, says, "St. John, in his Apocalypse, calls Rome Babylon." (See, *Commentary on the New Testament*, Daniel Denison Whedon, Rev. 17:6-7, www.books.google.com).

The French Catholic Prelate (1607-1724), Jacques Bossuet, in expositions on Revelation says, "The features are so marked that it is easy to decipher Rome under the figure of Babylon." (Wordsworth quotes Bellarmine, Baronius, and Bossuet on page 21 of his *Is the Church of Rome Babylon?* Being Catholic scholars, they are reluctant to say Babylon is Papal Rome, but admit it is political Rome. If they had just taken one more step from the wounded

'Head' of political Rome being healed and becoming Papal Rome, all three would have become Protestants.

If these theologians argue that it is just old, political Rome, their arguments make no difference. History shows us that political Rome became and remains Papal Rome.

Remember, we are tracing "The Steps of Departure" from the original, New Covenant Congregation of Christ to a Babylonian Clone, which masquerades as a Christian organization. It is important that we know something about how the past history of ancient Babylon has affected the present.

THE CULT OF ANCIENT BABYLON

Babylon is mentioned so many times in Revelation that the Lord must have expected us to know about the subject. Babylon began with Nimrod, who, as the mighty hunter, built Babylon (Ge 10:8-10). His Queen was Semiramis (www.google.com: Semiramis, Queen of Babylon.). The cults of Nimrod and Semiramis were supposed to reveal the most divine secrets. *Des Sciences Occultes*, by Eusebe Salverte, p. 259, states, "One was compelled to drink mysterious beverages, which was indispensable on the part of those who sought initiation into these mysteries." Nothing attracts the pleasure loving world to the "church" more than "Christianizing" and blessing their addictive habits.

Pre-Millennialist John F. Walvoord wrote an account of the rise of Catholic Babylon on page 196 of his, *Revelation Expounded*. I borrowed the following salient points on this subject:

Six features distinguish the Babylonian Cult worship:

1) The "mysterious beverage" of wine, honey, and flower was always intoxicating.

2) The aspirants had their understanding dimmed until they were not responsible for what they would see or hear. God's prophets understood the use of drugs in religion as "Pharmakeia" (www.google.com: witchcraft.). The word is always used in the New Testament in a negative vein.

3) The use of the "esoteric method" to convert unsuspecting disciples. The handpicked tyrannical group was given information privately and

was under steal of secrecy. The manipulators worked through a small group of people with a special knowledge and interest. This is the way Jezebel gained access to the Lord's congregation and claimed, "She taught the DEEP things of God, but Jesus said, 'She taught the so-called deep things of Satan'" (Rev 2:24). By "deep things," we learn she was merely contradicting the plain things of the Spirit of Christ, which is just plain stupid. Is there a greater ignorance than claiming we know Scripture and yet knowing nothing at all? (1Co 8:2) How very difficult for a hardworking, soul-winning evangelist to counteract the venom of a professed Christian who teaches his converts that they can continue sinning and still be justified by God's grace. This is the doctrine of Balaam, the Nicolaitans, and Jezebel (Rev 2:14, 15, 20, 24). Although we hate this doctrine, we expect it to surface in the congregation from time to time (www.goggel.com: Balaam, Nicolaitans, and Jezebel.). The bottom line of such teaching is to use the GRACE OF GOD as a cover and license for committing sin (Ro 6:1 with Jude 1:4). The propaganda of such amateur Bible students is to teach someone else's converts to sin with impudence. Since guilt should be a curtailment to sin, such teachers encourage their converts to believe that God's Grace is an encouragement for them to sin without experiencing guilt. To them, GRACE is an excuse to enjoy the maximum pleasures of the flesh rather than the JOY of the Holy Spirit.

4) Upon admission into the Babylonian cult, new members were controlled by the core group and had to confess their sins to the priest. The cultic priests gained control over them through these confessions. Modern-day followers of Jezebel actually have little "church drinking parties" in private. The Lord knows this will lead to other sins (Hab 2:14-16), but of course this Spirit of Babylon is so all pervasive that the "sin party" keeps on in their stubborn way, chanting secret slogans of their hearts, "Let us continue in sin that grace may abound" (Ro 6:1).

5) Once admitted, people were no longer Egyptians, Assyrians, or Hittites, but members of a mystical brotherhood under a supreme Pontiff. His word was final in all things concerning the brotherhood, regardless of country of origin.

6) The ostensible objects of worship were the Supreme Father, the Incarnate Female or "Queen of Heaven," and the Son. The last two were really the only objects of worship, as the Supreme Father was said not to interfere with mortal affairs. Those who do not believe in the Godhead actually use this background teaching as a basis for a false, so-called "Trinity" (a nonbiblical word). But the Father-Son relationship existed in the glory of eternity past, long before Babylon (Jn 17:1-5). The Holy Spirit of the Godhead was even present in The Creation of our present world (Gen 1:1-3). Remember, Satan was the mastermind of ancient Babylon, and the thoughts given to Nimrod and his priests would have been counterfeits for what he knew existed in eternity past. We cite hundreds of passages dealing with the unity of the Godhead in both the Old and New Testaments, but the one given here will suffice – God's messenger of the covenant "savior" is given in Isaiah 63:8, 9, and His "Holy Spirit" is given in verse 10. If anyone was aware of the three persons of the Godhead, Satan was, and he wanted to duplicate it with a false "trinity."

The reason there are existing cults who deny the "Trinity" of the Godhead is because demonic spirits, who know the truth of the Trinity, influence teachers who either deny or teach false doctrines. Of course, this book prefers the word "Godhead" to the word "Trinity" because of the tendency to pervert this doctrine.

We are addressing Mystery Babylon's power because it has great bearing on the The Apocalypse. Through His evangel, Jesus spoke to the congregation at Pergamum and said that Satan had a seat in that city (Rev 2:12). Of course, Satan is a Spirit, and he was not visibly sitting on a throne, but there is an apocalyptic meaning here that the Christians in Pergamum understood. Every seer, wise man or woman, and philosopher would have understood that when Old Babylon was destroyed, the priesthood of their cult, with its supreme potentate, was transferred from Babylon when the Babylonians fled to Pergamum to escape the invading Persians.

This Babylonian Cult was common knowledge to citizens of Pergamum when John recorded The Revelation, and if we read a book about ancient Pergamum, it will be common knowledge today. Thus, if we are to understand the history of the rise of Roman Babylon from ancient Babylon (in what is now modern-day Iraq), we need to research this subject.

The city of Pergamum was briefly the capital of the Roman Province of Asia. They were very loyal to the Roman Emperor and as a tribute to their conquerors decided to transfer the seat of the Babylonian Cult (spiritually called the "Satan's Throne") to Rome (www.google.com: F.F. Bruce, *Babylon and Rome*.).

NIMROD – MIGHTY HUNTER BEFORE THE LORD (Ge 10:9)

At first glance, the above description of Nimrod would portray him in a favorable light, but being "favorable" in the Lord's eyes is not at all what Nimrod became. Nimrod was possessed with a subversive spiritual attitude. Since evil cannot exist without God's permission, and since even the slayer and killer cannot escape God's notice (Jer 16:16), we understand that all of Nimrod's great exploits were accomplished only by God's permission. One of the things learned about Holy God is that He permits situations that He deplores, and He allows situations (in Nimrod's case – a stubborn human will) that He will later judge in uncontrollable wrath. The potter has power of good and evil over the clay. He can mold it or break it (Jer 18:4-6; Ro 9:21). The indomitable presence of evil is and has always been a test to The Righteous (1Pe 3:14, 4:1-6). Being a hunter before the Lord is not something that Nimrod could celebrate in the Lord's presence. Everything we read about the man indicates that he was evil and an enemy of YHWH God. Our consolation here is that no matter how present the evil is, and no matter how dark the environment, our worst enemies are before the Lord (under His surveillance and power). No matter how high Nimrod could have exalted himself and no matter how high the tower that he built, his work and his life were "before the Lord."

History informs us that Nimrod built great cities with walls to protect men against the wild animals that multiplied after The Flood. We know that dinosaur-like animals multiplied from the original pairs that Noah took on the Ark. We know that Job described a Brontosaurus, a Tyrannosaurus Rex, and Triceratops (Behemoth-Leviathan) in Job 40:15, 41:1ff.

We know that before the Earth began to greatly multiply, and before modern-day population centers grew and expanded, such creatures were plentiful as late as the 16th Century in Europe (See Dwayne Gish's *Dinosaurs by Design*, and *Beasts that Used to be Mythical*). There were documented sightings of dinosaurian and dragon-like creatures in Medieval Europe that are now standard fare in historical literature (www.google.com). A Japanese fishing trawler captured a giant Plesiosaur in April 1977. Several photos were taken before dropping it back into the water. It was not an ordinary sea creature. Evolutionists, who contend that the Plesiosaur lived 65-million year ago, said that it looked like a Plesiosaur, but then changed their tune and said it really was a decomposed shark. In the warmer climates, Biblical-types of dinosaurian creatures exist, like Komodo Dragons in Indonesia, Giant Gila Monsters, and of course, the common Crocodile and Alligator, which fit the description of "dino" (giant) "saurous" (lizard).

In his day, Nimrod became an ancient world celebrity by slaying animals and erecting barriers to protect people, but what caused him to be labeled the Apostate was his fleeing the post-Flood world and turning against the faith of great grandfather Noah (Ge 10:6-8). Dr. David Livingston says that since Nimrod means "rebel," his real name was Gilgamesh (www.google.com.). There are only bits and pieces of Nimrod in Scripture, and it takes a very diligent scholar to put together a fairly good profile of this mighty man.

Traditions from the earliest times bear witness that people defied God by attempting to build a tower "up to the heaven" (Ge 11:4). There were several explanations for this tower project, not the very least they wanted "to make a name for themselves." People may have wanted a place to escape another flood (even though God said He would never again destroy the world with water). It has been said that Nimrod was angry with God for destroying the world, and his building a tower was a way of "getting back" at the Lord.

Even though there was only one Biblical Tower of Babel, other towers were built, like the tower found in Ur (southern Mesopotamia, circa 2100 B.C.). The pyramid-like temple had converging stairways that ran to the top where an altar was devoted to pagan worship. These towers were similar to the ziggurats of ancient civilizations. They built the towers up to the heavens because they thought this would be the way to reach their pagan gods and goddesses.

Linguistic experts have different theories concerning where modern languages came from and how they developed, but they all agree on one thing – all modern languages came from the same source, "Behold they all have ONE language" (Ge 11:1), and that language was probably Angelic since Satan could communicate with Eve and Nimrod (1Co 13:1). Man's languages had not yet been developed. No ancient document exists that addresses authoritatively the origin of languages, other than Genesis 11:7. The evil that people can commit when they have ONE global community and ONE means of universal communication is beyond our imagination. Much more than Godly people, demons are shrewder (Lk 16:8) and highly organized under one king (Rev 9:11). Given a global opportunity to bring the world into insolent defiance of The Godhead, they would be such a threat to the Moral Universe that God would intervene personally (Rev 16:12-21).

> "For they are spirits of demons, performing signs, which go out to the kings of the earth and the whole world (global community), to gather them to the battle of the great day of God Almighty" (Rev 16:14).

While humans do not have one angelic tongue, demons (fallen angels) do, and they have ways of communicating with the spirit of man. The Babylonian System was planned by the Devil (Satan) to counteract God's truth. Incredible as it may seem, God chose Abraham from this idolatrous system to represent the true God in the midst of paganism. Read Isaiah 41 and notice the ONE raised up from the East (Isa 41:2).

Some scholars believe this is a reference to the Persian King Cyrus, but the whole tenor of the passage is the way this powerful man resisted idolatry, and this is not something for which Cyrus is credited. Read the entire chapter, and you will discover that Abraham is mentioned by name (Isa 41:8). It is through Abraham that God called all of us (anti-idolaters) from the ends of the Earth (Isa 41:9).

After the nations scattered, Babylon continued as "the seat of Satan," (www.discoverrevelation.com) until Cyrus' Army of Medes and Persians conquered it in 538/539 B.C. (See "Cyrus the Great in the Bible": www.wikipedia.com). This conquest was foretold in prophecy (Isa 44: 28, 45: 1-5, 13-14; Ezr 1: 1-2) When Cyrus took Babylon, the Babylonia priesthood was forced to move to Pergamos. When Attalus, Pontiff of Pergamos, died in 133 B.C., he bequeathed the headship of the priesthood to Rome.

Pontiff literally means "chief bridge builder" (www.wikipedia.ed: pontiff). This comes from two Latin words, "pon" meaning bridge, and "tif" meaning to build. Hence, today was say "pontoon" (www.granddesignexposed.com). "Building bridges" was, and still is a magnificent feat, but when we study it in a religious context, it implies building a bridge to Heaven (as the Babylonians tried to do). This flies in the face of Christ being THE WAY to the Father in Heaven (Jn 14:6). Jesus is The Ladder that Jacob saw (Ge 28:12), and angels descend and ascend on Him (Jn 1:51, Mk 14:62). However, in their Babylonian minds, the

Pontiff has power of life and death over the worshippers. He is more wicked than the people are, but they find no wrong in him.

Julius Caesar, the first Roman Emperor, was made Supreme Pontiff of the Babylonian order in 63 B.C., and the seat of this cult was in Pergamum (www.google.com: "Satan" on Pontiff.). This is where emperor worship began in 28 B.C. and what the Holy Spirit meant when He called the place where incense was burned to the Pontiff, "Satan's Seat!" (Rev 2:13). The emperor became heir to the rights and titles of Attalus who made Rome his heir by will in 133 B.C.

Roman Emperors held this office until 376 A.D., (www.ministrymagazine.org) when the Emperor Gratian, for Christian reasons, refused the title, Supreme Pontiff of the Babylonians, because he saw it as Babylonian idolatry. (www.google.com: *Major Cults and False World Religions and The Origin of Pontus Maximus,* p. 222 by Steve Urik.). A religious void existed during Gratian's time. People wanted a Babylonian Pontiff even though Gratian was morally honest enough to refuse it. At this time (marvel of marvels) and (hypocrisy of hypocrisies), a new Babylonian Pontiff emerged in plain sight for all to see. Who would ever have imagined that a so-called Christian would want this diabolical office? But this is exactly what happened when in 378 A.D., just two years after a pagan emperor refused it, Damascus, head bishop of the Christian Church in Rome, was elected as the Babylonian Pontiff. Damascus had been elevated to Bishop in 366 A.D. through the influence of monks at Mount Carmel, a Babylonian religious college founded by the priest of Jezebel (www.google.com: Monks of Mount Carmel, Pope Damascus, and Jezebel.). We understand that this college continues to this day.

THE CONSEQUENCES OF THE UNION OF CHRISTIAN APOSTASY AND BABYLONIAN PAGANISM

Thus from 378 A.D., the Roman Church incorporated the rites of Babylon. Christ and His Apostles did not teach these Babylonian rites because they militated against God's Word. Some of these doctrines were paramount among the former pagans who joined the Roman Church. We know, of course, that while these doctrines and rites were present within the framework of Catholicism for hundreds of years, the Popes were not so foolish as to make them official doctrines of the "church" until the false doctrines were fully developed, believed, and established in history. Remember, if a false doctrine was taught 50 years after the completion of the New Testament, it was dead wrong the first time it was taught. If it is taught for 2,000 years, it is just as dead wrong in 2015 AD as it was in 100 AD. Two hundred years of teaching a false doctrine does not make it right. There is no "Grandfather Clause" regarding God's Holy New Testament.

1) The worship or veneration of saints, especially of the Virgin Mary, greatly impacts people even today as we see cathedrals with St. Christopher, St. Augustine, St. Jude, St. Leo, and hundreds of others in many towns, large and small. The pagans were accustomed to worshipping their saints after whom their towns were named. When they "joined" Christianity, the former pagans brought their saints with them and simply renamed them with Christian names. The Apostles are so horrified at the catholic abuse of their authority (along with venerating their names) that they rejoice with the Fall of Babylon" (Rev 12:12, 18:20).

Relics and places where saints were buried were believed to have miraculous power. The worship of Mary was established in 381 A.D., 40 years before the Council of Ephesus, and just three years after Damascus became head of the Babylonian Cult. The Babylonians worshipped the Queen of Heaven. Even the apostate Jews were fascinated with her (Jer 44:17-19, 25).

We see Protestant ministers, adorned in their festive robes, take a piece of bread and hold it up to Heaven. We shall observe later how the children of the Whore are actually more antichrist than their Mother. For instance, Rome today takes a greater stand against the murder of innocent children in the womb than some Protestant ministers. Since the advent of the Social Gospel in America (1870-1920), Protestant ministers are more liberal, more anti-Bible and anti-Christian than their Catholic counterparts.

Thus, some Protestant ministers (adorned as majestically as a little Pope), hold up a piece of bread as gracefully as a "Priest at the Altar." This is a caricature of what they knowingly or unknowingly learned from Babylon. This action not only mimics the Babylonian priest who would hold up the moon shaped wafer to Heaven, but it is exactly what the reprobate Jews were doing. Like Jeremiah, Christians are hated when they expose this sort of thing. Strange as it may seem, as we read further in Jeremiah, Chapter 44, we realize the Jews knew the wafer Queen God of Heaven could not help them, and they admitted as much.

Babylonians made Mary the answer to the pagans' lust for a Magna Mater, a Diana of the Ephesians, or Matriarchal God. The original mother was Semiramis (with her nursing son), Nimrod's beautiful queen, who was a paragon of unbridled lust. Hundreds of images in many ancient civilizations can be traced back to the Babylonian concept of the Mother God and her son. (www.google.com: Mother Child images on Pinterest.).

In *Chrinicon Paschale, Vol 1*, p. 65, Semiramis is the "Mother of Gods" and the outlandish rites identify her more with Venus, the mother of impurity. Semiramis sat on the seat of idolatry and consecrated prostitution (*Hesiod Theogonia, Vol 36*, p. 453). The emblem of a harlot with a cup in hand was derived from ancient Babylon and adopted by the Greeks who realized this corresponded with Venus (*Hisoria, Book 1*, by Herodotus, cap. 199, p. 92).

In 1825, a metal was cast bearing the image of Pope Leo XII on one side and on the other was a woman, who symbolized Rome, with a cross in her left hand and a cup in her right hand. The inscription at the bottom read: "Sedet Super Universum" (The whole world is her seat.).

There is credible scholarship that the whole known religious world, except for true Apostolic Christianity, originated from Babylon. In the case of mother-god worship, we find traces of this Babylonian religious system in numerous countries (www.bible-history.com/babylonia/BabyloniaHistory_of_Babylonia: Ancient Babylonia – History of Babylonia). In Egypt, the mother and child are Isis and Osiris; in India, Isi and Iswara; in Eastern Asia, Cybele and Deoius; in Rome, Fortuna and Jupiter-puer; in Greece, Ceres or Irene with Plutus in arms. In Tibet, China, and Japan, the Jesuits were surprised to find the counterpart of the Madonna (Italian for virgin) and her child being worshipped. Shing Moo, the mother of China, is represented with a child in her arms. All this originated from Babylon. None of this is Scriptural. If we wish to document these facts, we can simply google the names of the mother gods and child given above.

2) The conclusion to all this is that whoever becomes a successor to the Babylonian Pontiffs is the Supreme Authority in matters pertaining to the Church, and it is implied, the State as well.

3) The worship of idols, while expressly forbidden in the Ten Commandments, was part of Babylonian religion. The worship of idols entered the Apostasy very early in Roman Church worship and was finally decreed by the Second Council of Nice in 787 A.D. In the 9th Century, even the emperors such as Theodosius and Gratian attempted to abolish such worship (See www.stopthereligiousright.org.). The great Iconodule-Iconoclast Controversy rocked Rome in the 9th Century. Image worshipers were call iconodules, and those opposed were iconoclasts. Icon worship is one of the reasons the Greek Orthodox Church split with Rome in 1054 A.D. This irrational controversy of warped minds on both sides engaged in futile semantics about whether a Christian violates the 2nd Commandment in Exodus 20:4 by worshipping icons (pictures) or statues. The Orthodox insisted on worshipping pictures; the Romans chose statues.

Even emperors, like the Apostate, Julian, knew that image worship was clearly a flagrant violation of Scripture, but it was so rooted in both the Eastern and Western Churches that they gave up the fight. In 869 A.D., the Synod at Constantinople officially accepted image veneration.

Other practices taken from the Babylonians included the celebration of Holy Days. Daniel said, "The Little Horn" would change times and seasons (Da 7:25). Remember, the little horn grew out of Rome just as the "Head that was wounded" (political Rome) produced a "Head that was healed" (religious Rome). When we look at the calendar, we cannot help but be impressed with the number of Holy Days associated with Roman Babylon. Christmas was copied from the day when the Babylonians honored Queen Astarte. The Chaldeans called it "Yule Day" or "Child Day." Easter derived from Ishtar, which is one of the titles of the Babylonian Queen of Heaven. The worship of Ishtar was an abomination in God's eyes (1Sa 7:3; Jer 44:18). Round cakes imprinted with the sign of "Tau," the cross, were made at this festival. (*Mosheim's History of the Church, Vol. 1*, p. 371).

The fable of the Easter egg stems from the following: "An egg of wondrous size fell from Heaven into the Euphrates River. The fishes rolled it to the bank, where the doves hatched it out, and out came Astarte, or Ishtar, the Goddess of Easter" (This fable is reported by Josephus, and the account of it appears in several websites including www.thinknot.net). This sounds a lot like Carl Sagan's desperate attempt to prove "rapid, punctuated" evolution with his fictitious lizard laying an egg and a bird hatches out. So powerful was the Babylonian word "Easter" that the King James Bible scholars translated the word "Passover" as "Easter" in Acts 12:4.

Lent is observed 40 days prior to Easter and is also derived from Babylonian mysteries. Devil worshippers in Kurdistan accepted Lent from Babylon and observe it to this day (www.google.com: Babylon on the subject of Lent.). The scholar Humboldt found Lent early in Mexico (See "Easter-Restoration" www.google.come), and Wilkinson informs us that Lent was a custom in ancient Egypt. (www.google.com: Celebration of Lent in Ancient Egypt and Is Lent a Christian Holiday?).

Both Easter and Lent were introduced into the Roman Church in 519 A.D. Johannes Cassianus, a 5th Century scholar, said, "The observance of Lent has no existence so long as the Church remained inviolate." Cassianus is making an amazing reference to something we of The Restoration take very seriously. We must remember that these deviating, essentially blasphemous, holidays are not observed by those who retain the purity and unbroken perfection of Christ's original congregation (First Conference Abbot Theonas, Ch. 30, www.bibletools.com).

The celebration of the "Rape of Proserpine" was a pagan celebration used to counter the Roman Lent (www.google.com: Rape of Proserpine and Is lent a Christian Holiday?). This was a celebration of 40 day of unbridled lust after 40 days of fast. Roman Babylon reversed this and offered the Mardi Gras, a time of debauchery and gay festivals, that ended on Shrove Tuesday, the day before Ash Wednesday. No wonder God calls the church, "Whore." (Rev 17: 1, 5, 15, 16; 19:2).

In our attempt to be as reasonable as possible and without violating our Scriptural conscience, we have determined that, except for Mardi Gras and Lent (forbidden by 1Ti 4:1-4), it is best to accept Christmas and Easter (without the imposter Santa, Easter eggs and bunnies) because of the expedience Christians are told to exhibit in Romans 14:5-7.

There is so much that New Covenant Christians believe that absolutely contradicts everything the other religions believe. When Christians stand aloof from the world's holy days, they place a greater burden upon the heathen, like your author was prior to his coming to freedom in Christ. Incredibly, when I was a young 19 years old, Christmas was when I began to enquire about who Jesus really is. The whole Christmas season led me to investigate the "reason for the season." Also, I took advantage of the seasons by opening the Scripture and addressing the timely themes that surround our Savior during these festive times. Finally, I strongly believe that Christmas and Easter are more for the world than the Church, for we sing the powerful and moving hymn, "Joy to the world, the Lord has come. Let earth, receive her King!" In a farfetched way, these two great holy days' amount to an unsophisticated apology to God the Father for crucifying His Son.

Ladies and Gentlemen, the previous paragraphs describe briefly the development of the doctrines and practices of the Roman Catholic Church. The Eastern Orthodox apostasy is similar, and although little known, the Orthodox Branch was the first apostasy from the original Congregation of Christ. It is "little known" not because church history neglects it but because Rome overshadows it. The Eastern Orthodox claim to "Orthodoxy" is the most ludicrous idea in history. The Orthodox split from Rome in 1054 A.D. by rejecting the Pope's sovereign jurisdiction, and other issues concerning rituals and the shaving of priests' heads. Orthodox priests can marry, but the bishops cannot. The Orthodox worship icons, but they do not worship statues. This icon worship is so embedded in the Orthodox mind that an ex-Soviet Communist, Victor Nikitina (now a Christian missionary) told Missionary John Doughty that Braille icons are even made for the blind. Neither Catholicism nor Orthodoxy has any intention of practicing pure New Testament Christianity. These two institutions stand as vanguards in the western and eastern worlds to prevent poor, lost, deluded souls from seeing the pure light of New Testament truth.

SO SHALL WE SAY THAT ALL IS WELL IN THE PROTESTANT WORLD?

Having addressed Catholicism and Orthodoxy, what can we say about Protestantism? We must remember that the Catholic Church has a name on her forehead, 'THE MOTHER OF HARLOTS,' (Rev 17:5). Initially, Rome killed many of her protesting dissenters. From the 12th Century to the Reformation, the blood of saints (Petrobrusians, Cathari, Albigenses, Waldenses, Brethren, Lollards, Bohemian Brethren, and Huguenots) was unmercifully shed. After the Reformation, hundreds of brands (denominations) of Protestant Christianity emerged. After more than 300 years of freedom, the remaining Protestant branches (denominations) have returned, to a greater or lesser extent depending upon the denomination, back so close to their MOTHER that there is little difference between a modern-day denomination and Babylonian Catholic, Hindu, Buddhist, or New Ager.

The Roman Catholic Church also has on her forehead, "THE MOTHER OF THE ABOMINATIONS OF THE EARTH (Rev 17:5). Abomination means anything detestable and hateful in the eyes of Holy God. The greatest abominations are anti-Scriptural, doctrinal persuasions. As we have seen, we cannot just call Catholicism, "Babylon," because doctrines and practices exist in Protestant Christendom that are as loathsome as those of Rome, but Catholicism is the MOTHER. All Christian "cults" and Protestant sects have their creeds. Writers of creeds try to convince us that their creeds are based on Scripture. But creeds produce different "sects" of Christianity because each creed is used to justify why a Protestant sect should break away from another Protestant sect. These different Protestant sects rope in Christ's children, place them in different folds, stamp their name brand on them, and produce mass religious confusion, just like "Babylon." Their name tag instantly sends a signal to the unchristian world that one denomination is different in worship and government from other Protestant sects. Like their Mother, most Protestants believe in Original Sin, sprinkling innocent babies, practicing "confirmation," and even while some will not admit it, making their Creed (and the writings of their Divine's) more authoritative than God's Word.

Probably the most heinous affront to King Jesus is when the leaders of a schism decide to form a hierarchy similar to that of Mother (pagan or papal) Rome. If we read reputable "church" history scholars, they will affirm that the 1st Century congregations were all local, independent organizations with Elders and Deacons (Php 1:1). Some Baptist churches claim independence and have deacons, but most of them do not have elders. Clearly, Christ (along with the foundational personnel of Apostles and Prophets) gave (and continues to give) on-going evangelists and pastors (same as elders) to His Congregation. Deacons are not mentioned as being part of the "people gifts" to the Congregation because they were chosen by the Congregation to serve widows and the weak or unfortunate members of The Body, after Christ's Ascension (Ac 6:3).

Thirty-four different congregations are mentioned in the New Testament, none of which were governed by "outside authority." Mosheim writes,

> "The overseers of the church were either called presbyters or bishops, that two titles are in the New Testament, undoubtedly applied to the same order of men (Ac 20:17-18; Php 1:1), (*Mosheim's Ecclesiastical History*, Vol. 1, p. 99).

Mosheim did not understand how these Elders, "Presbyters," were appointed. He said, "Each church was a kind of a small independent republic, governing itself by its own laws, enacted or at least sanctioned by the people. But in process of time it became customary for all Christian churches within the same province to unite and form a larger society or commonwealth" (*Mosheim's Ecclesiastical History*, Vol. 1, p 116).

The missing link in Mosheim's History, and for that matter most writings of early church history, is the ministry of The Evangelist. The Great Apostasy would probably never have taken place without "The Death of The Evangelist." The work of evangelists was, and always has been, behind closed bars on "death row." Paul tells us exactly how the elders were appointed in the local congregations, "For this cause, I left you in Crete that you might ordain Elders in every city" (Tit 1:5).

Albert Barnes wrote about Ephesians 4:11, "What was the precise office of evangelist in the primitive church, it is now impossible to determine," but what seems difficult for church historians to comprehend is easy to understand. Evangels were simply men who declared the Gospel through evangelism and won souls to Christ. This was their main focus and duty; this is what congregations expected them to do so. If there is one ministry that the devil does not want to see practiced in the congregation, it is the evangelistic outreach to lost and dying, hell-hound souls. Should we really be surprised that this is the one ministry the devil sought to kill in the early Church and seeks to kill so as to prevent resurrection today?

Another ministry the devil tries to kill is the Christ gift of TEACHERS TO THE CONGREGATION. A Bible teacher is as much a gift of Christ to the congregation as any of the other ministries. Paul said, "You ought to be teachers" (Heb 5:12), and due to the lack of teachers with strong Bible knowledge, the congregation is filled with a milk-fed congregation of infants (1 Co 3:2).

A great indicator of how Ephesians 4:11 can be corrupted is the modern-day idea that "Teachers" are not even a gift from Christ. This corruption came from the idea promoted by some commentators that "Pastors and Teachers ought to be hyphenated as 'Pastors-teachers'." This idea reduces Christ's gifts from two to one. That is, there is only one gift "The Pastors," and they are also "teachers."

This interpretation is based on the Granville Sharp rule that the conjunction "and" connects two equals (www.google.com: Granville Sharp rule.). Sharp's rule was used effectively against The Socinian Heresy that denied the divinity of Jesus Christ, but Sharp's rule breaks down when the conjunction connects two plural words. Even the casual reader would say there is something wrong with the grammatical use of pastors-teachers. I have heard some very illustrious speakers address this text and say the ministry of teachers is not in this text. We beg to differ. Just because Granville Sharp's original thesis was correct when it was based upon the expressions of God being "Lord and Christ," and Christ being "Lord and God," this does not justify the use of Sharp's rule for treating pastors and teachers in the same manner.

There are many arguments given eliminating the ministry of teachers from Ephesians 4:11, but the clincher to this polemic is in Acts 13:1, which says, "Now in the congregation of Antioch there were Prophets and Teachers." No one can get prophets-teachers out of this text any more than they can get pastors-teachers out of Ephesians 4:11 (www.google.com: Granville Sharp, Pastor-Teacher Controversy, Grace Theological Journal 4, Gordon College Faculty).

There may be exceptions, but the Ecclesiastical System has never been celebrated as a system that emphasizes the dogmatic, systematic, theological teaching of God's Word. It makes no difference if it is a little, elderly Christian lady sitting with children in Lord's Day Bible Class, or a woman "Teaching Women" the duties of marriage and home, (Tit 2:4), or a man who specializes in teaching Bible school or Home Congregations. All these, plus others, are ministers of Christ who need to know that they are as much a gift of Christ to His Assembly as the man in the pulpit.

This sin of establishing man-made hierarchies is perhaps the worst sin. The gullible flock accepted this sin because most of us accept being governed by our fellow man. The hardheaded Israelites bucked God's will by refusing to have the powerful (yet merciful) YHWH God lead them. They became like modern-day

American apostates, "We do not want to have such a slogan as, 'In God We Trust'." (1Sa 8:19, 20). Yes, God allowed them to have a King, but this was not His true model of government, and the nation paid dearly for this crime of insolent, irreverent contempt for God.

This contempt for God happened in the Old Testament, but the New Testament has Christ as the HEAD of His Body, which is the Congregation (Col 1:18; Eph 5:23). When Protestants set up doctrinal decision-making synods, consistories, parliaments, and national (regional, or district) conferences, they are more like Babylon (in her contempt of the King of Heaven) then they would like to admit.

Caesar has a secular government, and we, as Christians, will be held accountable for our failure to vote in regard to the moral issues that appear on our ballots. Every congregation should have men (like Jerry Begley and Gerald Wakefield) whose Christian duty is to inform us as to where political candidates stand on moral, economic, and political issues.

But the Kingdom of Christ is a spiritual institution. Christ is King, but He allows each of His congregations to have evangelists and elders as servant leaders of The Flock (Ac 20: 17-28). They are to "feed the flock" and protect them against the "wolves of hierarchy." In a discussion on the local autonomy of Christ's Congregation, Jerry Begley said, "It would be wonderful if our government would allow more local autonomy to govern this nation." Jerry sees the government's increasing encroachment upon local state and community government as an unscrupulous attempt to gain a more despotic government. In other words, the dictatorial attempt to gain control of state and local government corresponds to the tyrannical corruption that occurred in church history during the 3rd and 4th Centuries.

Church authorities of various hierarches tell us that because of state, national, and international hierarchies, many people have been converted. We disagree! In the 1st Century, men and women went everywhere spreading the Word, and the whole world was "turned upside down" (Ac 17:6). They did this without human hierarchies. We also suspect that the hierarchies that were formed by Roman and Her children do not attract people with the Gospel of the Kingdom of Christ, but through vanity and pride. In other words, the whole world was not filled with wonder and reverence for Jesus Christ, but "The whole world wondered at the beast" (Rev 13:3, 17:8).

Although 21st Century Protestantism is now experiencing serious death throes (most young people do not even know what the word "Protestant" means), Protestant divisions are again surfacing as many 21st Century, independent "churchanity groups" are being established in store fronts, abandoned houses, offices, schools, and new "church" plants across The Nation. This religious cultural movement is often based on the early 20th Century theology of the "Social Gospel," which has made a comeback in the early 21st Century. It appeals to "selfie" religious people. "This movement applied Christian ethics to social problems, especially issues of social justice such as economic inequality, poverty, alcoholism, crime, racial tensions, slums, unclean environment, child labor, inadequate labor unions, poor schools, (illegal drug use), and the danger of war" (www.wikipedia.com: Social Gospel).

Some believe the "The "Social Gospel" resulted from the late 19th Century concept of "Social Darwinism," which was a social offshoot of Charles Darwin's evolutionary theories. "Social Darwinism claims to apply biological concepts of natural and survival of the fittest to sociology and politics. Economically, social Darwinists argue that the strong should see their wealth and power increase while the weak should see their wealth and power decrease." (www.wikipedia.com: Social Darwinism). It is understandable how some people with an incomplete understanding of Christianity could believe that they have a Christian duty to help those on the wrong end of the Social Darwinist economic ladder. The Social Gospel sprang from the desire to make people more equal economically. This Social Gospel, reinforced by Marxism's concepts of class warfare and economic equality, has caused Social Gospel adherents to push for economic redistribution. This is a completely incorrect reading of Scripture. Apostolic Covenant Christianity espouses helping those real victims who cannot help themselves, but there is no doctrine of redistribution within the New Testament.

Another misguided philosophy confronting modern-day religion is "Humanism." This is founded on the idea the "Man is the Measure of All Things." Christian Humanism follows this design very well. A so-called Christian (not God's Word on the subject) is one who controls the flow of Christian thought. Christian thought is subservient to what the Christian Humanist thinks it is. As Hillary Clinton said in reference to Christians still believing that Sodomy is a sin, "You've got to change your religious beliefs" (www.glenbeck.com). See also www.google.com: Saint Hillary Seeks to Save Christians against Christianity). Christians WILL change their doctrine to fit the "Hitler-type" of political and media pressure, but they cannot find it in THE BIBLE because it is not there.

The final word will not be uttered by some compromising priest or pastor, but by the King in power and vengeance (Heb 10:30).

Thus, Protestantism is fast giving way to a 21st Century Social Churchanity. Protestantism was never founded upon the context of New Covenant, Apostolic Christianity. It is doomed in the light of our Lord's prophecy, "Every plant my Father has not planted will be rooted up" (Mt 15:13). This is happening today! Mainline Protestant denominations are disintegrating. The reason is because the Protestant Reformation did not go back to the 1st Century Apostolic Faith. By trying to Reform Catholicism, they forgot to RESTORE the New Covenant Faith, and in doing so, Catholicism actually reattached itself to its former nemesis under a different trademark.

Just as the Jews of the 1st Century required the blood of the prophets (Mt 23:29-34; Rev 18:24), so Rome and her children have required the blood of the more famous Huss (burned at stake), Hippolytus (allegedly pulled apart by horses, but none the less greatly hated by the Roman hierarchy), Wycliffe (died of a stroke), and Luther (died of natural causes). Thus, some were murdered and others survived the persecution. The Protestants were not much better than the Catholic Hierarchy in their hatred of heretics. Zwingli (died among soldiers in battle), Latimer and Ridley (burned at the stake), New Covenant Theologian, Pilgrim Marpeck, and millions of other Anabaptists were persecuted and slaughtered. Various claims were made to justify the Catholic Inquisition and Protestant scourges of Anabaptists, but the main reason is that the accused refused to align with the accuser's doctrine. Catholicism, paved the way historically, but in matters of persecution, the murders committed by both Catholics and Protestants mostly during the 16th and 17th Centuries differed little from the Islamic butchers of today.

THE GREAT WHORE

One of the seven angels in Revelation said, "I will show you the judgment of the whore!" This whore sits on many waters. We know that Revelation is not to be taken in a strict literal sense because even God said the waters are a metaphor for peoples, multitudes, nations, and tongues (Rev 17:15). The seven heads of the apocalyptic beast are allegorical of the elevated pinnacles upon which the city of Rome sits (Rev 17:9). Ancient coins unearthed in Rome have a tribute to Rome's annual Septimonium Feast and a background graphic of the seven hills. "Septi" means seven, and "montani" means hills or peaks (www.google.com).

A student of apocalyptic verse understands such visions clearly, i.e., the vision of the restless waters of the Mediterranean Sea into which the peninsula of ancient Rome extends (Rev 17:1). Water surrounds Rome, and those waters also touched the many nations and peoples of the known world.

The "fornication of the whore" (17:2) refers to the superstitious pagan ceremonies and religious license used to bring followers into illicit promiscuity. This term is not just physical but refers also to spiritual harlotry (Jer 3:6-9; Eze 16:32; Hos 1:2; Rev 2:22), and doctrinal heresy is the worst form of fornication.

She is that great city (Rev 17:18). No city in the history of the world has been greater than Rome. But Rome is also a system. Washington, D.C. is at the center of the nation, United States of America; Moscow of Russia; but Rome is the center of the allegiance of peoples throughout the Earth and has been for over 2,000 years. The Czars of Russia used the Russian "Czar" for Caesar. The Holy Roman Empire thought they were the "First Reich." Hitler and the German Fascists thought they were the "Third Reich." Catholicism, as a "Religious Reich," will be around till the end (2Th 2:8). No one can take her place. She accomplished her rise to power first as Pagan and later, continues to the end as Papal Rome.

> "The church of God (Roman), therefore is an empire within an empire, and the governors and princes of this world are jealous for that reason. The Pope is in himself a personal sovereign, and can be subject to none…a divine authority overall all other powers…the whole world is in his hands…to enforce obedience to the faith…to judge nations and their princes" (*The Temporal Power of the Vicar of Jesus Christ*, by Cardinal Manning, pp. 48-50, 124-126, and 155-156).

The whore was arrayed in purple and scarlet (Rev 17:4). Scarlet is the color of pontiffs and cardinals. The inner surface of the popish cloak is scarlet; his carriage is scarlet; and the carpet upon which he treads is scarlet. The hats, cloaks, and stockings of cardinals are scarlet. Five of the various items of attire a pope wears when he is installed are scarlet. "And decked with gold and precious stones" (Rev 17:4). At his coronation, a pope wears a vest covered with peals, and a miter adorned with gold and precious stones.

The whore is drunk with the blood of saints. Walvoord says, "Two million people have been slain because they would not conform to her (Catholic Church) system of religion and yield to the supremacy of the pope" (*Revelation Expounded*, p. 209).

The Roman Catholic Church is not literally Old Babylon; Papal Rome is Mystery Babylon. The reason that Catholicism has been able to conceal herself so easily for so long is because she pretends to hold Christ's teachings. As long as she professes to hold to the Christian truths, she is able to masquerade behind the cover of being a legitimate institution. Under similar pretenses, Old Babylon seduced and lured God's people away from Him.

Writing on Revelation, Chapter 17, B.W. Johnson, in his *Peoples New Testament* puts Babylon into two categories, 1) Old Babylon and 2) new Babylon.

Old Babylon was 1) a master of confusion, 2) an impenitent enemy of God, 3) corrupted the worship of God, 4) led God's people into 70 years of captivity, 5) was a mighty empire, and 6) destroyed by God, not man. Xerxes, a man, destroyed Babylon as an instrument of God. God acts through men. Xerxes conquest was prophesied in Isaiah 13:17, 18.

New Babylon is 1) confusion of doctrines, 2) apostate doctrine with a clear departure from the Apostolic Church of the 2nd Century, 3) corrupted the doctrines of Apostolic Scripture, 4) took away Scripture and led God's people into 1,260 years of bandage 5) has been the richest, mightiest empire, and longest ruling since 533 A.D. and 6) as with Belshazzar, "mene-mene- tekel-upharsin" (Da 5:25), only Christ can destroy her.

Until Christ comes, Papal Rome will continue to appear to be a Christian religion. Only on that final day will she, her Greek companion, and children be exposed. The false bride must be exposed before the true Bride is revealed. Catholicism can only exist as she tricks the world into believing that she is the Christian Church. The true Christian Church existed hundreds of years before the first pope, but the academic, secular, and religious world is ignorant of this. Satan could not have deceived the world as he has if he did not incorporate Christian truth into the Babylon's fabric. Paul knew this would happen, when he told the elders, "For I know this, that after my departing, shall grievous wolves enter in among you (elders), not sparing the flock (of Christ)" (Ac 20:29).

It was imperative for the devil to establish Babylon from within the oversight of the true flock (Christian Church). Remember, "Paul said the wolves will enter among you." Professor Donald Nash, Ph.D., used to quote the Restoration Forefathers, "The Pope is simply an Elder who got too big for his britches." As New Testament evangelists, we can sit down with a priest, or debate a bishop, and hear that everything we have learned from the New Testament remains in the Catholic Church, but in corrupted form.

Catholic doctrines must compromise Scripture without denying Christ. Such compromise serves the devil's purposes much better than going on an outright tangent of contradiction or war against Christianity. The deadly virus of apostasy was spawned within the ranks of the first eldership. That Elder was Ignatius of Antioch, Syria who died a martyr in 117 A.D. and who called himself "The Bishop." Less than 60 years after Paul, an Elder was already calling himself, "The Bishop." Just in case you think I am picking only on Catholics, the Protestants also have their "the Bishops."

The reason I still have some sincere Christ-loving Catholic friends is because Catholicism still has enough of Christ in it to produce a love for Him. The problem does not lie with the Catholic faithful; the problem lies with the hierarchy. God commands, "Come out of her, my people" (Rev 18:4). I do not want any of my Babylonian friends to receive her plagues. I love them. The fact that they are people of Christ means that they can potentially receive TRUTH, as I did as a young man. I do not know whether these are people who entered into Catholicism without realizing what they were doing, or if they potentially belong to Christ, and He knows that they will ultimately obey Him. Some Catholic scholars from the past, as previously explained in the Various Views of Eschatology (www.wikipedia.com: Lacunza and Ribera), saw in Revelation the rise of antichrist popes and priests in the future, but Christ calls the church members "His people" and bids them "come out" NOW! (Rev. 18:4)

At Wittenberg, Germany, when Martin Luther's supporters urged violence against the Roman Church, Luther said, "Remember that antichrist according to Daniel will be broken without man's hand. Violence will only make him stronger" *(Here I Stand: A Life of Martin Luther by* Mentor Books, 1950, p. 159).

Concerning Catholicism, its teachings and practices have influenced practically all denominations. Many doctrines and practices of so-called "Protestant denominations" are nothing but polished reproductions of Roman Catholicism with women added. May God help us to return to the Bible and be satisfied with its divine teaching and examples about how we should worship.

The temptation for clergy to win disciples to themselves and to assimilate within their ranks a system of temple worship appears to be irresistible. The culture of temple worship and ceremony will replace the worship of God in Spirit and Truth and will remain with us to the end. We might add that the modern-day "Worship of Self" with religious music, bands, ear piercing sounds, and high-pitched enthusiasm (which in itself may have value) can very easily replace good, solid exposition of God's Word and its application to holiness in a wicked world.

The sole difference between Orthodox, Roman, and Protestant ritual worship and Millennialism is that these children of Babylon already have the outward, impressive liturgy down pat, but the Red Heifer is missing from the Mass. The Millennialist is looking steadfastly for a return to outward, ceremonial temple rituals, and is getting the Red Heifer ready for an offering. AS FAR AS THIS NONSENSICAL MILLENNIAL BLASPHEMY IS CONCERNED, THERE WILL NEVER BE ANOTHER RED HEIFER; THE WHOLE IDEA IS A RED HERRING! (*Trashing the Bible* by Charles W. Doughty, pp. 382-399)

Addendum B – Twenty-four Similarities between Daniel and Ezekiel

Revelation 20:8 uses the expression Gog of Magog. We must remember that while such an expression many not mean much to the average 21st Century reader, it would have had a ton of meaning to the reader of the 1st Century. The Bible has been around for a long time and down through the centuries, millions of people have read it, and I believe that most Biblical readers understood the Bible better than the average read today. Since great gains have been made in scientific and technical knowledge, people spend more time working with gadgets and are less interested in history. This is especially true of ancient history and religion. Therefore, we will attempt to interpret this vastly misunderstood expression, "Gog of Magog," in light of what the people living at the time of Daniel's and Ezekiel's writings would have understood when they read prophecies of historical events that have worldwide implications.

We know that Daniel, Ezekiel, and Jeremiah were contemporaries who would have read each other's prophesies. We assume that each wrote their own prophecy independent of the others. There is overwhelming evidence that both Daniel and Ezekiel had Antiochus IV Epiphanes, King of the Seleucid Empire, in mind when they wrote about the crucial historical events occurring during the 400-year period of silence (Am 8:11) when no prophet appeared from God to speak to the apostate Israel and Judah. Although the 400 years were silent, Daniel, Ezekiel, and Jeremiah uttered long range prophecies of the unfolding, historical struggles and battles that would occur between God's people and their many enemies. So before we can appreciate the beginning of the New Testament, it seemed that God's program was in great jeopardy as the Old Testament was winding down to a historical halt. Ezekiel and Daniel focus on the last conflict (176-164 B.C.) between the nations (Satan's Seed) and the Prophetic Seed of the Woman (nation of Israel), an Israel that was barely viable and very close to being destroyed.

The historical events we are about to examine in prophecy are not concurrent with God's prophets who spoke of these events. Because Daniel, Ezekiel, and others were prophesying 600 B.C. and the events they foresaw were in the 160 B.C. era, they were prophesying approximately 480 years before the events occurred. We are studying this history for the following reasons:

1) During the 400-year period between the Old and New Testaments, God's people were made hungry for prophetic utterances. So, to satisfy this hunger, they read the prophetic books, and paid special attention to Ezekiel, Daniel, and Jeremiah.

2) Ezekiel and Daniel prophesied of the dominating influence of Greek rule (Hellenism) during this intertestamental period, which began with Alexander the Great (Da 7:4, 10:13) and the division of Alexander's Kingdom into four kingdoms (Da 7:6, 8: 9-12). This division led to the rise of the Seleucid Empire (the most powerful of the four) that initiated the last large-scale conflict against the Seed of the Woman. We can argue that this prophecy did not end until Christ came.

3) Clearly, this last, all-out war, between those Jews who were still just barely clinging to the Old Covenant, and their Seleucid enemies led by King Antiochus the Great, "enlightened one," is a microcosm of the true, Apostolic New Covenant faith at the end of the world, as expressed in The Revelation. Jesus said, "When the son of man comes will He find THE faith on earth?" (Lk 18:18). Just as God's covenant people in the Old Testament dwindled down to a small fraction, so will Christ's Covenant people be like a "little camp" when Christ comes. Therefore, in Ezekiel's prophecy, Gog and Magog play an important role by signifying the kind of opposition we can expect and in leading the world's ungodly opposition against The Messiah. It is certain, from reading Daniel's prophecy, that while we will see that Daniel did not mention Gog or Magog by name, his prophetic writing does mention Antiochus as the fourth descendant from Alexander's general Seleucus 1 Nicanor.

Let us examine the similarities between the prophesies of Daniel and Ezekiel.

Both Daniel and Ezekiel Mention Gog and Magog

Daniel calls Gog "The King of the North" (Da 11:36, 40). Ezekiel also speaks of Gog from the northern Caspian Sea countries settled by Noah's offspring Rosh, Tubal, and Meshech (Eze 38:2), which to Jerusalem's inhabitants would have been "the remotest parts of the north" (Eze 39:2) in history.

Magog is identified with Syria in Pliny's historical writing (Pliny 5:28). 78 The ancient names of these countries have changed, and they no doubt formed an alliance with Antiochus since Alexander the Great's former Empire had been converted to Hellenistic Greek pluralism. Herodotus writes of nations who banded together as "a horde of northern Asiatics," probably including Moschi and Tibareni "Meshech...Tubal," and undertook an expedition against Egypt in Ezekiel's time (*Herodotus 1*, pp.103-106). Of course, if we want to identify these people or nations by their ancient names on a modern-day map, we will be disappointed. History records that the nations surrounding the Caucasus region were called by the names that Ezekiel labeled them. Jamieson, Fausset, and Brown state,

> "(Gog), the chief prince of Rosh or (Rhos-LXX), The Scythian Tauri in the Crimea were so called. The Arazes also were called Rhos." (Eze 38:1).

Commenting further, the illustrious authors Jamieson, Fausset, and Brown admit that some scholars may want to associate "Rhos" with Russia, and Moscow and the Siberian "Tobalsk," but the proper ancient names for these ancient areas of modern Russia were "Slavi" and "Wends." The word for modern Russia comes from the Viking word "rus."

In his well-written book, *End Times Fiction*, pp. 6, 7, Gary DeMar debunks the idea that any nation called Rosh ever existed. He gives good evidence that the word "rosh" simply means "beginning or chief." This is why the *New American Standard Bible* (NASB) has a marginal note on Ezekiel 39:1 that reads, "Chief Prince of Meshech and Tubal." DeMar Lamar quotes Edwin M. Yamauchi, Professor of History at Miami University, Oxford, OH, on page 7 of "End Times Fiction,"

> "There is no evidence from the ancient Near East that a country name Rosh ever existed. Some would understand Rosh as modern Russia. Proponents of this view usually appeal to etymology based on similar sounds (to the hearing between two words). Such an etymological procedure is not linguistically sound nor is etymology alone a sound hermeneutical basis on which to interpret a word. The word 'Russia' is a late eleventh-century A.D. term. Therefore the data does (sic) not seem to support an interpretation of Rosh as a proper name of a geographical region or country."

DeMar is correct to write that the modern name Russia stems from the name "Rus," which was brought into the region of Kiev by the Vikings during the

Middle Ages. Thus, the evidence shows that while Rosh could remotely be a nickname for the Scythian and Araxes peoples, it has nothing to do with any nation in particular, but simply means "chief or beginning," as Rosh Hodesh is the celebration of the beginning of the year on the Jewish calendar. However, one thing we know for certain is that that name, Rosh, has nothing to do with modern Russia.

Dr. Roger Chambers accuses modern-day Millennialists of being defiantly ignorant of ancient history. In his book, *The Plain Truth about Armstrongism*, (Baker Book House), 79 he has a chapter, "Phonology or Phonyology?" in which he examines Herbert W. Armstrong's British-Israeli claims that the British are the lost tribes of Israel. Armstrong used to love to sell snake oil to his credulous disciples by telling them that the word "Saxon" really came from the expression "Sons of Isaac." Like the naïve Mormons, who go to any length to prove their spurious claims that the American Indians are descendants of Israel, so the self-deceived Armstrongites went to their graves believing the above "phonyology."

Armstrong came up with several other outlandish "phonyisms," and we might just as well believe that the Jujitsu Tribe descended from Judah. The Mormons might just as well believe Cree Indians built a ship and sailed to Canada from the Island of Crete. Remember, Mormons are taught that American Indians descended from the Lost Tribes of Israel, and this deceitful lie is the very basis of their blind faith. When this lie is fully exposed, the whole delicate fabric of Mormonism will unravel.

THE ECCENTRICS WHO BASE THEIR HOPE OF ETERNAL LIFE ON MADE-UP VISIONS RATHER THAN REVELATION

There is historical evidence tracing the American Indian population back to the Mongolian descendants of Noah's son, Ham. Ham's descendants traversed the land and ice bridge from Siberia to Alaska and as the Hopi and Eskimo, along with other tribes, dispersed into what is now California and Western North America (www.wikipedia: The settlement of the Americas). Not one shred of historical truth exists that ancient Israel heard of a land we now call America (www.christiananswers.net) Jesus did not visit the Nephites (3 Nephi). Mormons would be astonished if we were to ask them, "Where in America was Nephi located?"

Unlike modern-day cults like Mormonism, the reason, throughout the ages, intelligent people have accepted the accuracy of Biblical history is because when history was recorded, The Holy Spirit left nothing to blind faith. For example, let us consider the very important doctrine that is essential to our eternal salvation, that of the historicity of The Ascension of Jesus Christ. Jesus ascended to His Throne from the historical site called in Scripture, "The Mount of Olives" (Ac 1: 9-12). Further historical details are provided to silence the skeptics. The historic site was a Sabbath day's journey from Jerusalem, by way of Bethany (Ac 1:9-12). Additional evidence is given in prophecy some 600 years before Christ was born (Zec 14:4).

After Christ ascended, He sat on The Throne and remains there until all enemies are vanquished (Heb 1:3; Ps 110:1 with Heb 8:1). Mormons insult a rational person's intelligence by not only fabricating a supposed visit of Christ to American, but also, producing mythological art work of Jesus standing in an imagined ancient city square standing among alleged Nephite citizens dressed in what is supposed to be Indian garb. No such Nephite people have ever been documented in history. No such city has ever been found. And we just as well might believe in the City of Oz and an animated citizenry walking around in a fairy fiction.

Jesus ascended and sat down on the right hand of God (Mk 16:14). He will sit in glory and majesty until all His enemies become a footstool (1Co 15: 25). God highly exalted Christ above all (Php 2:9-11), and Paul declared the "Whole counsel of God" (Ac 20: 27). This Faith "persuasion" was "once for all delivered to the Saints" and is revealed in New Testament Scripture (Jude 1:3). This New Covenant is the Last Dispensation of Christ, "Of the fullness of time that He might gather together in one all things in Christ, both which as in heaven, and which are on earth: even in Him" (Eph 1:10). This "Dispensation of the fullness of time" does not allow for a further dispensation in the 2nd Century, 5th Century, or 18th Century. The New Covenant, written in the "Fullness of Time" (The days of the Roman Empire), is greatly contradicted and offended at the outlandish suggestion that Christ came to America after His Ascension and visited the Indians, and He or His angel left a "Manuscript Lost," or "Manuscript Found" (Golden Book) in a Mormon Hill call Cumorah. No such site as Cumorah has ever been found in America (www.wikipedia: Historical Authenticity of the Book of Mormon).

We can be sure that in the final judgment, the sin of this doctrine will identify those who advocate such mendacity. There is only ONE Second Coming of Christ (Heb 9: 28). If He came to Earth in a no one knows place in America, at a no one knows time in history, then His Second Coming will be an unbiblical Third Coming.

Apart from His intercession for all saints, the only direct activity with a man in the flesh, in which Christ engaged from His Throne, was to instruct Paul for three years in Arabia by direct revelation (Gal 1:17-2:2), and his Apostolic instructions were exactly the same as those that Christ personally gave to the other Apostles (Gal 1:7, 8 with 2:7-9).

The dwellers of Pontius, Cappadocia, Parthia, Media, and Elam (Ac 2:9) would have taken the Resurrection Gospel of New Covenant King Jesus to the descendants of Ham in the Eastern world. Christ told them to take the Gospel into all the world (Mk 16:16), and they did. If the Mongols, Chinese, Japanese, and other Easterners rejected the Gospel, then they were without excuse. Christ's work was done 2,000 years ago. He became our High Priest (Heb 3:1, 2, 4:6), entered into His rest, and ceased from His works (Heb 4:10).

Christ will give us no other revelation but the New Covenant, and He will give us no other book but the New Covenant; to believe otherwise is to bring upon ourselves not a blessing, but a curse. If there is a fictitious account of Christ making a special appearance to the American Indians, and the leaders are possessed of an above average clairvoyance and sinister motives to deceive feeble religious minds, then we congratulate any and all who purposely betrayed gullible souls into basing their eternal life on such nonsense, but no such appearance can be found in Holy Scripture.

A man named Solomon Spaulding used his lively imagination to write a fictitious novel about Christ's visiting America. His novel *Manuscript Found* evolved from a figment of Spaulding's fertile imagination to become the divining document and foundation upon which approximately 15 million Mormons place their hope for everlasting salvation. Mormon history is built on a flimsy house of cards, and their self-serving historians go to great lengths to disprove the Spaulding connection to the *Book of Mormon*. If we are foolish enough to believe that Smith actually wrote the novel with his "peep stone" (urim and thummim) trick, then all they have to do is compare Mormon theology with the New Covenant record, and they will see the flimsy, straw bridge that they are trying to cross into eternity. If a person is so foolish as to believe that Joseph Smith, with the help of an angel, Moroni, was led to discover ancient tablets or "Golden Plates" by which he was able to translate the book named after the angel, and that he took the plates to an Egyptologist for verification (www.wikipedia.ed: Anton Transcript.) and everything was exactly confirmed by empirical historical facts, then all we can do is consign that person to the fate of Second Thessalonians 2: 11,12.

Instead of "glass looking" or "crystal ball gazing," Smith used a seer stone and a hat (held over his face) to distract those who were his hand-picked "scribes" from actually looking at a piece of paper that he held in his hand (www.mrm.com: A Seer Stone and a Hat by Aaron Shafovaloff at.). In his effort to be historically objective to a fault while attempting to refrain from outrage at such deliberative and obvious Smithite deceptions, Shafovaloff never the less provides us information with historical accuracy. It is one thing to read of God's miracles and mighty works in the Bible; it is quite another, however, and a far cry from the way that God worked Biblical miracles, to read of the amateurish and childish methods used by Smith to cast his spell over would be believers.

We can expect the Mormon kind of heresy because the New Testament provides warnings such as, "entering houses and leading silly women captive" (2Ti 3:8); "old wives fables" (1Ti 4: 7), and deceitful spirits and doctrines of demons (1Ti 4:1).

The spirit of Mormonism and the spirit of Millennialism have one thing in common: both are greatly intimidated by accurate history. History can be kind or cruel. I know that of all Christ's actions which are now embedded in my spirit, I learned from history. All my successes and failures stem from either my knowledge or wisdom in accordance with the facts of history or my ignorance and disrespect for those facts. Failure to confront historical facts and Scripture, while embracing visions, will lead to the great fall of Mormonism and Millennialism (Mt 8:27), and the consequences will be eternally unbearable.

So Gog was a title given to the Northern King of Syria, Antiochus IV Epiphanes.

4) Daniel states that Antiochus desired "universal" worship. He wished to substitute the worship of Yahweh with Zeus, and he knew other religions would not oppose him except those of a singular Covenant persuasion (Da 11:28-31). Ezekiel records how God deserves the glory for His subduing the Covenant people's enemy (Eze 38:17-19, 39:5, 14, 22). Christians are puzzled when they read Daniel's factual, historical narrative of the great exploits of Antiochus. It appears as if

God is unmoved as He, with longsuffering and endurance, bears with Antiochus throughout the entire ordeal of his infamous crusade against truth and righteousness. Unlike Daniel, Ezekiel looks at the entire matter from an apocalyptic viewpoint, and his record presents an altogether different matter. We see God's anger against the apocalyptic "Gog," who is Antiochus, and God's wrath is smoldering and burning throughout the whole narrative.

5) Daniel says Gog was from the North, but went south to conquer (Da 8:9). Jamieson, Fausset, and Brown write that during the wars between the Seleucian and Ptolemy dynasties (Da 11:16), Jerusalem and Palestine were always in the way (the arena of conflict) between the North (Seleucian) and South (Ptolemy). So Ezekiel credits God with putting a hook in Antiochus' mouth and yanking him like an animal, south, to the mountains of the Holy Place (Eze 38:4, 15, 39:2).

6) Daniel says Antiochus had pretensions of being the greatest star of Heaven and even greater than "The God of gods" (Da 11:36). Antiochus tottered the stars (God's leaders in Israel) to the ground and trampled them (Da 8:9, 10).

7) Daniel says Antiochus was of fierce countenance and wily, and took the throne by craftiness, but only by God's permission (Da 8:23-25). He would be a profane man who profaned holy things. So Ezekiel says, "I will not let My Holy Name be profaned anymore "(Eze 39:7). At least three or more times, Antiochus had previously profaned the temple. Ezekiel is writing of an event that will follow a repeated act of profanation on the part of one man. That man is none other than Antiochus Epiphanes, an apocalyptic Gog of Magog.

8) Daniel say Antiochus even fought against the "Prince of Peace," Jesus Christ, God's own Prince. This fight is definitive of the whole Biblical scenario involving Daniel, Chapters 8, 11, 12, with Ezekiel, Chapters 38, 39. Daniel 8:25 is a key verse in this context. Satan is trying to prevent the seed (Messiah) from coming to Earth as the God-Man. The spirit of modern-day Millennial madness wants us to think of a modern-day antichrist when we read these Old Testament verses. But

Antiochus was an Old Testament antichrist only in the sense that Satan wanted Antiochus to prevent the birth of the Man-Child.

All interpreters of Scripture should ask themselves the same questions that editors, lawyers, or managers would ask, "Who-What-When-Where-Why- and possibly How?" The modern-day Millennial cult of the Futurist School almost always ignores the question, "When?" The "When?" being addressed here is when God still has an Old Covenant people from whom the Messiah will come as the Son of Man; the end of the Old Covenant is approaching; and Satan is desperate. Satan must use Antiochus to not just destroy Old Covenant Judaism; Satan must annihilate them…totally liquidate them. Strangely enough, the total annihilation of Old Testament Judaism is one thing that God and Satan had in common. Judaism would be annihilated, all right, but neither by Satan nor by Antiochus (for the time of their transgression had not yet come completely to its fullest (Da 8:23 with Mt 23:32-37) but by Christ (Lk 19:41-44, 20:16, 18, 21:22; Mt 22:7).

So Ezekiel celebrates the knowledge of the one God that would spread from sea to sea after Antiochus' disgraceful death. His death would pave the way for the exact opposite of what Satan wanted from Antiochus, which was the destruction and end of the Messianic seed. At first, Antiochus and his Generals Apollonius and Demetrius expected a quick and easy victory so they did not take the Maccabean guerrillas seriously. Conversely, Ezekiel records a horrible slaughter of the armies of Appollonius. After this defeat of Satan's agent of world domination, we no longer hear of any organized opposition against the Seed of the Woman until Christ is born, and then all hell broke loose, once again. But even then, God said, "When I bring them back from the peoples" (Eze 39:27) and reestablish them until my Son is born, and then, on The Day of Pentecost, I will pour out my Spirit and all nations will constitute Christ's Kingdom, Spiritual Israel on Earth (Eze 39:29).

THE RELATIONSHIP BETWEEN GOD'S GREAT NUMBER SEVEN AND ANTIOCHUS

Christians make the following observation about the use of the apocalyptic number "seven." The desolation of the Jews began in 141 B.C. From then date until 148 B.C., a period of six years and four months (approximately 2,300 days, if we accept 365 days in the Seleucian year), we have roughly 2,300 days, as stated in Daniel 8:14, when the general, overall profanations, were performed in the Holy

Temple. However, within these 2,300 days, Antiochus instituted a more concentrated effort to profane the temple for 1,290 days and then an even greater effort to profane the Temple for 335 days, until Antiochus died in 149 B.C. This period ended with the final blessed relief from all these profanations and the rededication of the Temple (Da 12:11 with Maccabees 4:52).

The Jews had rest from Antiochus and celebrated Encaenia "Hanukah" (Jn 10:22). The whole period of 2,300 days in round numbers is seven years. Thus, the entire period is more than the evil number 6 and shy of the perfect number 7. Unless some unknown numerological scholar has done additional investigative research on the number 2,300, we can only say that the number is unusual compared to other apocalyptic numbers. Is it possible that while evil appeared to conquer during this time of Antiochus' profanations, God's underlying goodness was right on course numerically and would emerge triumphant in the end? Of course, whether it was 230 days or 2,300 days, those who read Daniel's prophecy could trust that there would be peace at the end of those days. Some people may think it would be great if the Lord would give us a day-rendering number of how long we have to confront the moral darkness and uncertainties of live. This is true of us, both as individuals and as a Nation. But, we who have the first fruits of the Holy Spirit of God have something those in the Old Testament did not have, so asking God to give us a number of how long our grief will last is not in keeping with the New Testament idea of "Living in Faith."

God's concept of underlying goodness is also expressed in other numbers, like the 153 fish the disciples caught miraculously (Jn 21:11). The catch was miraculous so that the number of fish would have had a miraculous connection, since Divinity is consistent with Divinity in operational time (time elapsing consistently with the will of the Infinite God), good numbers, and eternity. At first glance, the number 153 appears to be accidental. However, after performing serious research, we are astonished to learn that this rare number is one of the most thought-provoking in divine mathematics. (See levendwater.org: Bullinger's, *Biblical Numerology*, under the number.). 153

MATTATHIAS, JUDAS, SIMON, AND JONATHON MACCABEUS:

A VERY BRAVE FAMILY

As an aside, Mattathias was the Jewish patriotic leader, and his son, Judas, was the military general who defeated the Syrians. Judas retook Jerusalem and dedicated the Temple. Judas' brothers, Simon and Jonathan, succeeded him. I supposed their nickname was Maccabeus, which means "hammerer"; although, they hailed from Hasmonean ancestry. Some may surely need hammers for righteousness and truth in these days. Jewish independence was secured and the crown was vested in the Hasmonean Dynasty until the first non-Jew, Herod the Great; he was half Jew. Only full-blooded Jews could carry the Messianic line, and after Herod, it made no difference.

Christ, the Messiah, was born, and after Matthew, Chapter 1, and Luke, Chapter 3, religious genealogies became foolish in God's eyes, and no longer mattered. (Tit 3:9). Being Jewish or Gentile (Roman or Greek) did not amount "to a hill of beans" for we must be born again of the Spirit of Christ (Jn 1:13; Mt 16:17).

9) Daniel says that as a punishment for the Jews' transgressions, God allowed Antiochus (Da 8:24) to prosper and succeed against His Covenant people (Da 11:28-36). Ezekiel says this punishment was prophesied of old, long before it happened (Eze 38:17), and this punishment was due to their transgressions (Eze 39:22-24).

10) Daniel says the vision of the history of Antiochus refers "to the time of the end (or toward the end of the Old Testament) (Da 8:17). Ezekiel says the history of Antiochus would happen in "the latter years" (Eze 38:8).

11) Daniel says Antiochus would destroy many Jews while they were at ease (Da 8:25). Ezekiel uses the same Hebrew word for ease (secure), "when My people Israel are living securely" (Eze 38:11, 14). Antiochus used the malaise of the people to his fullest advantage, just as the Islamic terrorists wait for the United States to let its guard down.

12) Daniel, as "a prophet of old," was astonished at the vision about Antiochus (Da 8:27). He wrote of nations and rulers of whom he had not heard. Ezekiel refers to Daniel and other "prophets of old" (Eze 38:17; Joel 3:1). Isaiah 27:1 speaks of Antiochus as the dinosaur dragon, (for such creatures roamed the Earth at that time and could be compared to Antiochus). Zechariah, another "prophet of old," speaks of the refining process of fire that the children of Israel must pass through before the Day of Pentecost comes and some of the Jews (the remnant) are added to the Christian Kingdom, and the others, "half of the city," (Zec 14:2) shall be cut off.

The Lord Jesus Christ will fight with "The Sword of the Spirit" (New Covenant Christianity) against the nations who gather "to fight against Jerusalem" (Zec 14:3). He shall stand on the Mount of Olives, from whence He ascended to Heaven after giving the Great Commission, and the Gospel went East and West, North and South (Zec 14:3), and "Living Waters," the refreshing ministry of the Holy Spirit (Ac 2:1-4, 3:19) flowed out of Jerusalem (Zec 14:8) for the first time to the East and West "all the world" (Mt 28:17-20). Prior to the spread of the Resurrection Gospel as commenced by the glorious Ascension from Mount Olivet, God's Old Testament message went only North and South. It is not hard to interpret Old Testament apocalyptic writings when we can find the corresponding symbols in the New Testament. However, how confusing apocalyptic writings can be when people play leapfrog with Scriptures, when they leap over Pentecost and The New Testament divine writings, and try to foist an unknown futuristic interpretation upon the text.

13) Daniel says that many nations will join with Antiochus, "and forces for him will arise" (Da 11:31). Even Gabriel admitted that the whole world order was against Israel; and except for the angel Michael, Israel's prince, no other Principalities in the invisible world would defend Israel against the universal enemy. Today, Christians have a much greater arsenal of weapons in New Covenant Christianity, but still, the innumerable militant host from the occult world of darkness continues to oppose them (Eph 6:12; 2Co 10:3-5).

Hence, our battle against the occult is not only literal (as the nations line up against God's people in physical array and military splendor) but also apocalyptic because the battle is viewed and aided by the invisible eyes and powers of the spirit world. So Ezekiel concurs with this thought by referencing Persia, Ethiopia, Put, Beth-Togarmah, Gomer (Greece, land of Antiochus' affection), Sheba, and Dedan (Eze 38:5, 6,13), or those "who do wickedly against the covenant," (Da 11:32).

As I follow the modern-day academic agenda (high school and college), I am aware of the same powerful spirit that possessed Antiochus. This spirit also permeates the thinking of many in our news media and especially the pretenders in the entertainment industry. This spirit is clearly an anti-New Covenant force in the Revelation 20:8 parallel. The leaders of the philosophical and political world were encouraged by their academic professors and are extremely confident of their ability to overthrow the exclusive, prophetic process that leads to the New Covenant of Christ. To those who are wise, this political, pluralistic logic made no more sense than the "croaking of frogs" (Rev 11:18, 16:13, 14). Every time I see one of those "anti-covenant" personalities on TV, or hear them speak, the sound in my ears is like the "croaking of frogs." Who can blame us when some historical TV personality comes to mind? In the 21st Century, Christians are being blamed for the world's ills and woes. For instance, President Obama calls himself a "Christian," yet does not so much as raise his little finger to prevent the rape, plundering, imprisonment, torturing, and murder of Christians around the world. President Obama, like most political leaders, does not have a clue as to what a New Covenant Christian is, as described in the New Testament.

Let us must remember that the lying spirit who had entered the teacher or professor does not identify the reason for his presence. The spirit does not come out and say,

> "I am with you in your study and in the class room to help you undermine New Covenant Christianity. My job is to work in you and go before you to get educational grants and financial assistance from governmental agencies and institutions. It is very easy to hoodwink such depraved souls to give millions to our cause. They are the minions who share my spirit."

The deceived professors of anti-covenant philosophy think their ideas are their own. To associate such ideas as being blunders cultivated by an evil spirit (as empty and hollow as the croaking of frogs) would cause great damage to the excessive pride that drives them. So they foist upon their students the most blundering nonsense in the area of religion and philosophy, while vainly imagining that their nonsense passes for intelligence. This is just fine with the evil spirit because pride is what he and his father, the devil, thrive upon.

For example, even as I type this manuscript (January 24, 2007 A.D.), I glance over at the TV screen and see the caption, "ARE MUSLIMS BEING POR-

TRAYED AS VIOLENT PEOPLE IN MOVIES?" The answer to this question is twofold, and political and entertainment leaders know the trusting "easy to fleece" American public who watches TV can be easily suckered into their way of thinking. First of all, they know the dupes of their viewing audience will say, "YES, THE POOR MUSLIMS ARE UNFAIRLY BEING LABELED AS VIOLENT RELIGIONISTS." The second answer to the question is implied by those who have had no training in logic (Dense people think they have to accept your premise, and therefore, automatically accept your conclusion.) and, therefore, conclude, "NO, NOT ALL MUSLIMS ARE VIOLENT RELIGIONISTS; THEREFORE, WE ARE UNJUSTIFIED IN PORTRAYING THEM AS SUCH!" But politicians and entertainers are not only ignorant of New Testament Christianity, they are also ignorant of the Koran that teaches Muslims to terrorize, plunder, intimidate, kill, and strike fear into the hearts of all infidels (Islam non-believers) who refuse to embrace Islam favorably. In a public poll taken, approximately, late September 2015, 51% of Muslims interviewed said they want Sharia law to replace the Constitution (www.google.com: Shock Poll.). In the same poll, 25% of those Muslims said they agree with the Koran's teachings about killing infidels. Yes, these, so-called American citizens, who work alongside us, live among us, attend our educational institutions, conduct commerce, and enjoy entertainment, would plunge a dagger into our heart or shoot us in an instant if they were told "It is Allah's will." To accept this is not to accept "Religious Pluralism"; this is accepting insanity.

THE DOCTRINE OF PLURALISM HAS A SHARP EDGE THAT IS INTENDED TO DIAMETRICALLY CUT THE HEART OUT OF CHRISTIANITY

What pluralists mean by "Pluralism" is not just accepting all religions as equal; it means accepting all religions as equal except exclusive "Covenant Christianity." Paradoxically, pluralists want us to embrace and love Islam as an equal world religious view, and yet, all leading Islamic religious leaders believe that all non-Muslims are going to Hell, and the sooner Muslims kill the non-believers and get them there, the better.

Pluralists are cowards. They wilt like an inflamed marshmallow when terrorists threaten to cut off their heads with a carving knife. Pluralists will renounce their ideology, pedigree, and tradition for just one minute of reprieve from their murders.

Things have not changed since the Black Muslim met me on the street in Youngstown, OH, handed me Muslim literature, and said,

> "Excuse me, Sir, but it is my duty to inform you that if you are not a Muslim, you are going to Hell."

And I promptly replied,

> "Yes, Sir, and it is my duty to inform you that if you do not know Jesus Christ, the Way, the Truth, and the Life, that you will perish in your sins! But it is my duty also to present to you the Gospel that God so loved the world that He gave His Only Begotten Son, that whosoever believes in Him should not perish but have everlasting life."

My Muslim acquaintance ceased being my friend. He and his hierarchy of Islamic tyrants are so paranoid about what they believe. They refuse to entertain any who question their faith, and they refuse to entertain the truth of New Covenant Christianity. Islamic countries imprison and kill evangelists and missionaries who broadcast the Christian Gospel in their countries, and yet they are absolutely free to spread their religion of terror in America. And, to add insult to indignity, our political leaders, from Hillary Clinton down to the "Mouse of the House" give "The Nation of Islam" in America the red carpet treatment. Hillary is paying dearly, but not nearly enough, for her lies and political hypocrisy after the Bengasi debacle occurred under her watch as Secretary of State.

The trifecta of political, entertainment, and academic "frogs" have persuaded many influential people to forsake Jesus Christ and undermine America's Christian value, but as much as their hatred is in their depraved hearts, and as much as they would love to come out and simply shout, "To Hell with Christianity in America!" they are still afraid to show their true colors. Hypocritical actors still need the money of ignorant Christians. Hypocritical political leaders still need Christian votes. The time is net yet ripe to throw exclusive Covenant Christianity to the lions, but it is near! The time is nearer than we think. The sodomite agenda by many politicians, religious leaders, and certain corporations like Frito Lay, Instagram, Jet Blue, Master Card, Face Book, Orbitz, Marc Jacobs, Ben & Jerry's, EBay, Google, Huffington Post, Johnson & Johnson, Safeway, AT&T, American Express, Levi's, Ford Motor, Old Navy, Penny's, Macy's, Pepsi, Buitoni, Garofila, Betrolis, Citi, Walgreens, Microsoft, Tylenol, and Starbucks are on some kind of bandwagon to get everyone from the eldest to the youngest to not only buy their products but to also buy into sodomy as it was practiced in Sodom of old (Ge 19:1-11). It is difficult to find a company to conduct business with that continues to observe Biblical values. I just dropped my "gay bank," Wells Fargo, and am looking for ways to connect with "Traditional Marriage Friendly" corporations with which to do business.

14) Daniel kept calling the scene of the horrible desecrations, bloodshed, terror, and abominations, "The Glory Land" (Da 11:16, 41). The word in the Hebrews means pleasant or glorious. Ezekiel called the land by the exact same Hebrew word in Ezekiel, Chapters 20, 6, 15.

15) Daniel knew that during the Seleucian-Ptolemy era, the Jews, by their own human effort and through their own political stratagems and cunning, attempted to restore Judah's power rather than trust Divine interposition. This Jewish effort failed so God sent Antiochus, thus, "no one could withstand him – the Antiochian Dynasty" (Da 11:16, 33, 36). Ezekiel draws even greater attention to Antiochus' war not being just like any ordinary war between two or more equally wicked nations. No, it is war against God, and to God, Antiochus must give account (Eze 38:19, 21-23, 39:3-8), "and it is coming thus says the Lord God, and it will come!"

The attitude that we can solve everything by ourselves permeates the academic and political philosophies in today's America. The current tendency is to attribute everything that happens, i.e., crime, war, catastrophes, and phony interpretation of Meteorology called "Global Warming" or "Climate Change," to some cause that man is capable of solving. This is "political" science at its best because solving these humanly unsolvable problems requires extracting extra taxes for the purposes of enlarging government and political control. The essence of "Climate Change" is that man can affect the weather in a big way. People who are pushing this must try to "Play God" with their interpretations of the universe. Fact is, the globe is cold or hot depending on its tilt, winds, oceanic temperatures, rainfall, and sunspot activity. I have no confidence in any man or woman who extricates the sovereign Lord and Creator, the Great Meteorologist, from the discussion of climate. All human effort in the world cannot counteract Divine interposition if God decides it will not rain on Earth for 3 ½ years (Jas 5:17).

16) Daniel says this last conflict with Antiochus would tend to purify the remnant (Da 11: 32, 12:1). Ezekiel says, "God will be sanctified through you (Antiochus), through their (the Jewish) eyes" (Eze 38:16).

17) Daniel says that the Maccabean revolt would get "little help," (Da 11:34). Ezekiel draws the picture of the "little camp" of believers dwelling in peace in unwalled cities with their cattle and goods as "sitting ducks" for the slaughter (Eze 38:10-15). Although Judas Maccabees is not mentioned in Daniel's or Ezekiel's account, it is obvious from both that while God gives the apocalyptic version of the battle from His standpoint of angels and demons, the battle was fought on Earth with real flesh and blood soldiers of truth and justice. If the name "Maccabees" was given in prophecy and Antiochus read it, he would have been alert and made provision to liquidate the Maccabean family.

As we have seen (Da 7:6, 10:20), the exploits of Alexander the Great were predicted in the Book of Daniel with details of his conquering Persia. When Alexander approached Jerusalem to conquer the city, Jaddus, the high priest, and a company of white robed citizens met him. Jaddus read the Book of Daniel to Alexander. When Alexander heard the prophecies of his great successes, he gave the God of Heaven glory and worshipped Him (www.livius.org: Alexander the Great visits Jerusalem.). Antiochus would never have done what Alexander did. The difference between Antiochus and Alexander is that the former worshipped the God Mars (and fortresses) believing in no other god except himself, while Alexander's spirit sought oracles. In the end, Alexander worshipped Zeus, but also lured his followers to worship he, himself.

We can easily relate the scene of the "little camp" referenced above to the New Covenant prophecy of Christ's Second Coming (Rev 21:8, 9), where we see the remnant of true New Covenant Christians reduced to a little "camp and the beloved city of the saints," which is the spiritual city of Jerusalem composed of saints on Earth and in Heaven (Heb 12:22). The Gog of Magog of worldwide pluralism seeks to destroy the saints by the sheer strength of worldwide numbers, and it appears for the moment that they will succeed.

Allow me to interject at this point a personal experience concerning an individual's conflict with pluralism. Since Antiochus' day, I know of no historical period when pluralism has been so widespread as it is today. There are, however, certain groups of people who react strongly against pluralism. Before our senior evangelist, Doug Hartman, spoke to our congregation on August 14, 2005, a young Canadian man visiting the congregation with his fiancée ask to speak with me. I prayed with him in my office, and then he related his purpose for his being there. He said,

> "I have some serious questions to ask you, Preacher "D". I hope you can answer them because I am a deeply disturbed man. I have read of the philosophies and religions of the world. I prided myself in being a very broadminded man. I have always looked down on the few people who actually believe that there is a truth to believe in this world. Like Pilate of old, I have repeated the statement with sarcasm, "What is truth?"

And then, with tears beginning to form in his eyes, he continued,

> "But lately I have become a father to a baby who is now nine months old. I am beginning to experience guilt and remorse because of my sins. Pluralism and world philosophy or religion is not satisfying my hungering soul. I know I am not prepared for the journey of life. For certain, I am not prepared to die and meet the ONE you call in your sermons, 'God, Creator and Maker.' My fiancée is a wonderful Christian girl, and she is praying for me. Life is getting harder and harder. You know Preacher "D", I have come to the conclusion that there just still may be The Truth in the world and that the solution to my problem is that I ought to be narrower-minded."

G.P.S. God's Providential System

First, I told him he came to the right person for I am so narrow-minded that I could look through a keyhole with both eyeballs. Secondly, I agree that the only way out of the maze of confusion in this world is to have a little G.P.S. I told him that the G.P.S. is the Apostles Doctrine of the New Covenant (Ac 2:42), and that if he followed it, he would definitely find his way out of the labyrinth of religious, political, and philosophical pluralism. While I agreed with him that worldwide pluralism was as vast as the 100,000,000 acres on the Earth's surface, I assured him that with a good G.P.S., he could find his way to any spot on Earth. And then, I placed the New Testament before him and said,

"Brother, if you follow this G.P.S., you will find your way through 100,000,000 acres of confusion and cut your course through 100,000,000 demons of pluralistic, false doctrine, even if by the millions, 'they shall depart from THE Faith teaching DOCTRINES of demons'" (1Ti 4:1, 2).

The next week this young man obeyed Acts 2:38. He was delivered from a life of confusion, despair, and madness and took on the life of Christ as his own. He moved into a steadfast covenant life in Acts 2:42, and if you knew him before his acceptance of Christ, you would not think this happy, radiant young man was the same man you used to know.

I have one word for Roman and religious-cultural pluralism in general. If you are reading this, and you are a pluralist and cannot stand confrontation with THE THRUTH, then consider the following, your ultimate destiny:

"Fire came down from God in Heaven, and devoured them" (Rev 21:9).

THE NEW TESTAMENT GOG OF MAGOG IS NOT JUST A PERSON. GOG OF MAGOG IS PLURALISM EPITOMIZED. IT STANDS FOR A WORLD VIEW THAT ACCEPTS ANY PHILOSOPHY THAT A DEMON POSSESSED PERSON COULD PUT TOGETHER JUST SO LONG AS IT IS NOT NEW COVENANT CHRISTIANITY.

18) Daniel says that Antiochus IV Epiphanes would covet gold, silver, costly stones, and treasurers (Da 11:38). In fact, Antiochus' final downfall was because of his cupidity to steal treasures from the Temple of Diana in Elymais. Polybius and Deodorus write of the avarice that consumed the heart and mind of Antiochus IV. Robbing the temple of Diana, who was worshipped in many cities, was a crime that his own father, Antiochus III, "The Great," committed and for which he was killed. The son, Antiochus IV Epiphanes, was guilty of the same crime. A temple guard apprehended Antiochus IV, and the whole town of Elymais rose up in one accord and almost killed him. Having failed to fetch his treasure there, Antiochus IV was moved by indignation to steal from the wealthy Jews.

Ezekiel makes this point quite clear. Gog (Antiochus IV) wanted both to exterminate Judaism, and with the help of his united nations, he could easily have done so. He had an intense covetousness of their independent riches and treasures (Eze 38:12, 13). God had allowed Antiochus IV to steal from His people for so long that Antiochus neither feared God nor respected anyone.

19) Daniel says, "He will enter the beautiful pleasant land of glory," and many countries will fall into his hands, and many will join him in alliance against Israel, namely Edom, Moab and Ammon (Da 11:41). After plundering the "hidden things" of Egypt (no doubt the "hidden treasures" of the mysterious Sphinx and Pyramids), he had the Libyans and Ethiopians vying with each other to cash in on the loot from Egypt and the wealth they anticipated by crushing the Jews again. Ezekiel said, "They all came to capture spoil" (Eze 38:13). To my way of thinking, the Bible is the only ancient document that exposes the real culprit who pilfered the astronomical wealth of Egypt (It was not Indiana Jones.). Like a child given antique valuables, Antiochus had no regard or appreciation for the treasures and artifacts of Egypt's pyramids and other ancient institutions that in today's estimation would be worth billions and billions of dollars.

20) Daniel says Antiochus anticipated an easy crushing of Jerusalem, "The King shall do according to his will" (Da 11:36). Several times, Antiochus had taken liberty from his worldwide campaigns to assault, massacre, plunder, rape, and seize the treasures of Jerusalem and the Temple without the slightest fear of reprisal or retribution. Judea, to Antiochus' way of thinking, was like a raw, novice fighter entering the ring against a professional, champion boxer. Even the pleas of a tenderhearted girl could not dissuade him from his lust for power and treasure (Da 11:36-38).

Ezekiel records the exact words from God's mouth, "(Antiochus) has come to a land that is restored from the sword (They had been slaughtered many times previously.), and "which has been a continual waste" (Eze 38:8). Several of the Seleucian rulers had slaughtered the people of Judah and plundered the City of Jerusalem previously. God puts His hand in Antiochus' face and says, "NO MORE!"

21) Daniel speaks of the tremendous power that God allowed Antiochus to enjoy for a time. Even after Antiochus had to split his army into

sections in order to exterminate the many uprisings that he faced along his empire's border, he continued to go forth in great wrath to destroy and annihilate (Da 11:44).

Ezekiel provides insight at this point. God says, "My holy name will be made known in the midst of My people, Israel" (Eze 39:7). From the apocalyptic viewpoint of Ezekiel's vision, God appears to do all the fighting. God brings an earthquake (Eze 38:19); the sea and humankind are shaken (vs. 20); the mountains and walls collapse (vs. 20); and God calls for the Maccabean sword. Matthew Henry's *Commentary on The Whole Bible* (one of the most widely read commentaries in history) comments, "The great men of Syria shall undermine and overthrow one another, shall accuse one another, shall fight duels with one another" (Eze 38:21). With pestilence and blood shall God enter into judgment with Antiochus (vs. 22), and it was of pestilential disease, not the sword, that Antiochus died. God fought them with torrential rain, hail, fire, and brimstone (vs. 22).

What we learn from this is that Antiochus really never reached Jerusalem. Antiochus attempted to rejoin General Lysais for he had sent Antiochus the alarming news that Judas Maccabees was winning the war. Miraculous prodigies befell Antiochus and his vast armies long before they reached Lysais, and then there were the guerrilla forces of the Maccabees. Of course, when we read apocalyptic language like this, we agree with some commentators that this is a "prophetical parable." However, this is in no way lessons the effect of God's intervention without whose concurring aid the small band of Maccabean guerrilla soldiers could not have prevailed. Jonathon Maccabees defeated General Apollonius and buried 8,000 soldiers alive (1Maccabees 82). In the first battle with Lysais, Judas slew 5,000 of Antiochus' soldiers.

Cringing before the sword and spear of the Maccabees, Lysais and Antiochus saw more than just one defeat after the other…they saw more than we can see with physical eyes. In the eyes of their departing spirits, they saw the sword of God bathed in blood descend from Heaven (Isa 35:5). They saw the artillery of Heaven raining down fire, hail, lightening, and torrential rain that would make Hurricanes Hugo and Katrina look like a garden hose. These events were probably not unlike the infernal fire and a horrible tempest seen in Sodom (Ps 11:6).

When a soldier is dying and going to Hades, his eyes cease to see the instruments of death that struck the mortal blow. He begins to see the judgments of God that accompany rigor mortis. Everything becomes apocalyptic bereavement.

WHY THESE PROPHECIES WERE NOT WRITTEN FOR SOME POST 21ST CENTURY AUDIENCE TO SEE THEIR FULFILLMENT

Daniel and Ezekiel were not only giving a history of the last major conflict between God's Covenant people and the Devil's World Order; they were also giving a historical countdown to the Great Year of Christ's birth and the "Alpha" beginning of a New World.

Even pagan writers, especially those from Chaldea-Babylon, who knew Daniel's prophecy of a new world precipitated by the Messiah's coming, expected something ominous to happen in "the fullness of time" when God chose to send His Son to redeem the Earth. Indeed, the year, 1 A.D., was a New Year and the beginning of eternity.

I appreciated reading *Times Arrows* by Dr. Richard Morris, who is a theoretical physicist. While he and I are certainly do not share the same Biblical mindset, his commitment to academic honesty is commendable. Dr. Morris would be of great assistance to God in using his discipline and wisdom to address the theme of "time" in connection with Bible Chronology. This theme of "time" would be especially helpful in our knowing what Chaldean astronomers knew about Daniel's prophesies, and what influence these prophesies had on the Chaldean kings who were so compelled, by either Astronomy or Biblical prophecy, to travel hundreds of miles across desert sands to meet Jesus Christ, the Messiah, in the Great Year of His birth.

Dr. Morris writes,

> "Sometime around 290-270 B.C., according to the ancient writers, the Babylonian priest, Berossos, migrated to the Island of Cos, where he lectured on Babylonian Philosophy. According to the Roman Philosopher, Seneca, who lived approximately 300 years later, Berossos expounded a doctrine concerning the great year when the world would be destroyed and

then created at periodical intervals when all the stars come together in the constellation of the Crab."

"However, it is very likely that the Chaldeans believed in some sort of great year. References to the idea appeared after in the writings of the Greeks of the classical era, and it is possible that the Greek took the idea from the Chaldeans, who were the source of much of their astronomical knowledge." 80

Even though the Babylonian wise men were pagan astrologers, they were led to understand that prodigious signs from the heavens would precede the coming of the Christ-Messiah to the world. A study of Matthew, the ex-publican, in his (Mt 1:18-2:23), and Dr. Luke's accounts (Lk 2:1-20) of Christ's birth provide significant insight into the impressive signs of Heaven that attest to the Birth of the God-Man on Earth. The wise men believed that there would be astronomical heavenly signs of His coming to the world; hence, "they followed his star" (Mt 2: 1-7).

The Babylonian wise men also believed that in the past, heavenly, cosmological intervention as the "Windows of Heaven opened" and a constant global downpour for 40 days and nights destroyed all mankind and the Earth's existing surface. These wise men did not owe it to the constellation of the Crab (of the unscientific, erroneous Zodiac) but to the instructions from God's Word that they obtained from Daniel's writings while he was in Babylon. Just as a new year and a new Earth began after The Flood of Genesis, Chapter 6, so a new year and a new world began with the Babylonian Magi's Star Search for the birth of Christ-Messiah.

THUS, THE WHOLE WORLD EXPERIENCED A NEWBIRTH AT THE BIRTH OF CHRIST

These prophesies from Daniel and Ezekiel were written for those who lived before and after 146 B.C., and also for all of us who have lived from the birth of Christ up to the present. Far from being a future war that has yet to be fought, this ancient conflict between Antiochus' forces of atheistic cultural pluralism and the Maccabean force of a small, remnant band of exclusive covenant keepers should provide edification and encouragement to any person living in this last New Covenant age. In fact, can we find reference to this war in God's Hall of Faith (Fame) in Hebrews, Chapter 11: 34-39? Just as the Israelite encounters with

Pharaoh were an example to us...just as their warfare in the wilderness was an example for us, so too is the Maccabees band an uplifting inspiration to all New Covenant persons who dare to stand against worldwide, atheistic pluralism.

> "...they are written for our admonition, upon whom the ends of the world have come" (1Co 10:11).

This is a lesson we will not learn from any modern-day interpretation of Daniel and Ezekiel.

God will be glorified in mercy or in justice. If man does not glorify God, He will glorify himself (Jn 13: 32). The end of the enemies of the New Testament Church will come exactly like the end of the enemies of the Old Testament people. God will rain down fire upon the impenitent, implacable foes of the New Covenant Church (Rev 20:9, 10). The foes will be baptized in a Lake of Fire and Brimstone, and after their physical eyes have beheld a literal first death, their spiritual eyes will be opened to such a ghastly second death that even apocalyptic vocabulary cannot describe it (Rev 20: 15, 20).

In keeping with the prior thought, Antiochus finally decided that he would not just destroy the Jews; he would annihilate them. This annihilation was for a purpose, as already mentioned, because Satan put it in Antiochus' heart to wipe out the chosen seed through which Christ would come. Satan knew wiping out the chosen seed would be a huge task, but Satan knew that he could accomplish this end if he could cause the Jewish high priesthood and governorship to cease to exist. This act would kill the prophecy of Genesis 49:10 and God the Father would have to cancel His predestined counsel to bring His Son, "Shiloh," to the world to gather the people of all nations unto Him. Ezekiel sees the same seriousness surrounding the battle. God says of Antiochus, "You will come against MY people!" (Eze 38:16) He repeats the thought, "When Gog comes against the land of Israel" (Eze 38:18). And God continues, "And I shall call for a sword against him on all of MY mountains" (Eze 38:21).

Never was such an army routed as Antiochus.' Five of every six soldiers (83%) died (Eze 39:2), "I will leave but a sixth part of thee." His armies could not find a mountain pass to escape the slaughter. Antiochus, as Gog, the leader of the world order, was really at war with God, and now and then fools like him come along.

22) Daniel says Antiochus would die on the "beautiful-glorious, pleasant" mountain (Da 11:45). Antiochus died alone with no one to help him. He did not have the honor of dying on the battlefield. We know Antiochus had a change of heart before his death, and he wrote a letter to the Jews promising them that if he lived, he would redecorate the beautiful Temple and become a Jew himself (www.usccb.org: 2Maccabees 9:16-28.). Perhaps he wanted to die where the holy man of God, Moses, had died. Yet, Antiochus' death was so disgraceful that even his medical attendants turned their heads. Ezekiel says he will die of pestilence and blood (Eze 38:22). Ezekiel speaks of Gog as a personification of all his armies and troops who would die horrible deaths and be fed upon by birds and wild animals and take seven months to bury them (Eze 39:3-12). Here we see the apocalyptic, parabolic nature of Ezekiel's prophecy. Daniel is more factual, but he also sees the battle from its hyperbolic-parabolic nature. The number seven adds to the apocalyptic numeric attractiveness of the narrative.

WILL THE BOW AND ARROW AND SWORD RETURN TO WARFARE IN THE 21ST CENTURY?

The spirit of Millennialism is greatly embarrassed by the conclusion of Ezekiel, Chapter 39. When Millennialists insist upon a futurist interpretation, they make a Battle of Gog of Magog a Nuclear War or, at least, a war that employs modern-day weapons. Since they think this battle will be fought in the future, it will certainly differ from the Maccabean and Syrian war strategies in how and the means by which it is fought. The Battle of Gog versus the Maccabees in February 164 B.C. was fought essentially the same as the Hundred Years War between England and France as late as 1337 – 1453 A.D. when the long bow ruled supreme. So how can The Battle of Gog of Magog be a modern war when "the bow is struck out of their left hand (most men hold their bows with the left hand), and their arrows out of their right hand (most men hold their arrows with the right hand) (Eze 39:3).

My question for those with the Millennial spirit is, "Why on Earth would anyone in the 21st Century even want to fight a battle with bows and arrows?" Furthermore, "Why would anyone in the 21st Century even want to fight a battle with shields, bucklers, hand staves, and spears?" (Eze 38:9). One more question, "Why would anyone in the 21st Century want to fight a battle with horses and chariots?" (Eze 39:20). I mean, get serious. If Israel is going to be invaded, and according to prophecy, they needed bows and arrows and swords to fight back, we would think by now that they would be building some military sword and bow and arrow factories.

Another thing the Futurists overlook is the method of burial that took seven years. If our hypothetical spin doctor, Dr. Larry Literalist, literalizes Ezekiel, then in the aftermath of this bloodbath, a few million people are going to dig a grave with a pick and shovel?" We may say, "I agree with that…We would dig them with a backhoe or a mass grave with a bull dozer!" But did Daniel and Ezekiel or Antiochus own bulldozers?

The fact is that Ezekiel is wording his prophecy in words that exactly correspond to the weapons that the Syrians and Jews used in 146 B.C. Although Ezekiel's vision is hyperbolic in its description of the blood, gore, and corruption of dead bodies, along with the accompanying birds and beasts that gorge themselves on the flesh of the bodies, the figure would still correspond to what the ancient armies would have experienced in 146 B.C. The apocalyptic figure of the vile, corrupted body being devoured by the lower creatures of the Earth is all the more augmented because Antiochus and his princes, and arrogant soldiers were possessed of the idolatrous Greek mentality that worshipped the body, and the powerfully build bodies of their war-gods Mars, and other gods like Zeus and Jupiter. Many people are impressed with the physical stature of Greek soldiers depicted in ancient art.

> 23) The gravity of Daniel's writings express the "moment of truth," the "life and death" circumstances encountered by the Jewish Nation. These unimaginable circumstances tested the faith, resolve, and courage of God's people who had to fight against a raging madman, bent on destroying them. How they responded determined on Earth whose names will be written in the Book of Life (Da 12:1; Ps 56:8, 69:28; Lk 10:20; Rev 20:15, 21:27; Ne 7:5; Mal 3:16). The nearest thing we can think of in the 21th Century is when Muslim terrorists ask us if we are Christian. When the final battle is over, God will be known among all the nations (Da 39:21-23). A great revival and restoration among Covenant people will occur (Da 39:27, 28). For all the confusion over which religion or denomination is right or wrong, the Bible is very clear about which group is going to Heaven. Quite simply, the

Heaven-bound are those whose names are written in the Book of Life, also known as the Lamb's Book. Old Testament people would not have understood the Messiah as the Lamb of God, slain from eternity past. Just as God identifies those who are in that Book, as the Old Testament history drew to a close, so He is identifying those in the Lamb's Book of Life as New Testament history and the world draw to a close (Rev 20:12-15, 21:27). The Book of one's life, The New Testament, and the Lamb's Book are opened, and those people whose names are in the Lamb's Book are in the right (Heaven-bound) group. They entered into the Book by participating in the first resurrection (Rev 20: 5b, 6) which is the new birth (Jn 3:5 with Col 2:12), became kings and priests of God, and reigned with Christ in the apocalyptic "chiloi" (Greek word for 1,000) (Rev 20:6) and did not worship the beast of Romanism, pluralism, and false doctrines, and were willing to suffer for the New Testament Word (Rev 20:4). These people comprise the true Ecclesia. If you want to know those in the wrong (not Heaven-bound) group, they are simply those whose names are not written in the Lamb's Book (Rev 20:15), and their destiny is spelled out in three words – "Lake of Fire" (Rev 20:15). Just as Antiochus tempted the true Covenant people of the Old Testament, and God was using this temptation to test who was in the Book of Life, or not, so the same is true as this present New Testament age surely draws to an end. The Maccabean revolt was primarily against Hellenistic culture that threatened to remove the religion and way of life mandated by God. The way we confront any culture that opposes our Christian conviction is a determining factor as to whether our names are written in Heaven's Book of Life. The Old Testament "Book of Life" and "The Lamb's Book of Life" are surely the same because Jesus descended into Sheol to save the Old Testament Saints after offering His redemptive blood as "The Lamb of God" and took them to the same Heaven that we are going to.

After this crucial, Old Testament battle, Christ's coming in the incarnation will be the next prophetic event. He will arrive when the first non-Jew is seated upon the throne of Judah. Amazingly, God kept a descendant of Judah (Ge 49:10) on the throne (Shilo – to gather His people) until the Star of Jacob (Nu 26: 17) appeared 900 years later during the reign of Herod (Mt 2: 7). And all this takes place, notwithstanding the opposition of every one of the myriad thousands of demons who opposed this succession of the "seed of the woman," and Judean rulers down through the years of Egyptian, Assyrian, Babylonian, Grecian, and yes, at last, Syrian resistance before the "fullness of time." The Christ would gather together all of spiritual Israel on the great day of Pentecost, and then "God would hide His face from them no longer" (Eze 39:29). When those converted at Pentecost were added to Christ's Congregation (Ac 2:38-42, 47), God added them to the Book. So the real reason this Antiochus-Maccabean War was fought is to keep a Jewish descendant on the throne until Messiah came to Earth the first time.

The Millennialists have this battle afterthought at the end of the world preceding Christ's Second Coming. I have heard people being called "screwballs," but it takes a mixed up mind to confuse events so badly that they think a war fought before the First Coming is yet to be fought before the Second Coming. No wonder the world has so many Bible skeptics! Some preachers just love to "Trash the Bible!"

24) In the final analysis, Daniel says that Antiochus was destroyed by God, not man, "for there was (neither) no man to help him" (Da 11:45) nor was there any man to hurt him. He died of pestilential disease. Daniel did not see it, but God in His providence appointed it for the end time (Da 12:9). Ezekiel starts at the beginning with "God is against you Gog" (Eze 38:3). We should be thankful to know at the beginning, NOT THE END that God is against our enemies, no matter how powerful and successful they appear to be.

THE DIFFERENCE BETWEEN PARABLES AND HISTORICAL ACCOUNTS WITH METAPHORS, AND ALLEGORICAL INTERPRETATIONS

We compared the prophetic accounts of Gog and Magog to what we read in The Revelation, Chapters 19-20, regarding the end and destruction of humanity and the whole world, as we know it. As we have referred to the physical and spiritual aspects of life, death, judgment and eternity, we will never really know where the physical leaves off completely and the eternal begins completely until God brings us to that place, sooner or later.

Other apocalyptic references also exist that bring the physical awareness and an acute spiritual awareness of time and eternity together. There are apocalyptic messages of profound meaning for the spiritual mind in Revelation, Chapters 9, 11, and 16. Instead of comparing the apocalyptic message of physical lives being tested and wearing down almost beyond human endurance through the constant mental, emotional, and spiritual bombardment like that experienced by Antiochus IV, we also have the historical episodes of the Egyptian armies under Pharaoh.

In Egypt, Israel experienced spiritual harassment, national censorship, torture, threats, and painful deaths much like the Jews did in 164 B.C. In our Commentary on Revelation, we see that those ancient experiences in history also had apocalyptic ramifications that involved survival in life, death, demons, spiritual endurance, and applications of life that overshadowed mere physical living. Yes, the Old Testament, more than the New Testament, addressed physical aspects of life, but there was an underlying theme of something going on in the spiritual world that transcended the physical world. It is this very thing that we readers of The Apocalypse must not miss!

Exodus 10:12ff – This verse portrays locusts in plain Scripture. The locusts are physical, actual, and literal. Their destruction of the land is an actual occurrence.

Revelation 9 – There are apocalyptic uses of a physical locust plague. Descriptions such as LIKE locusts and AS the scorpions of the Earth are used for apocalyptic uses. Just as the locusts in Exodus are under the permissive will of God, apocalyptic descriptions are also under the God's permissive will because "they are told" (vs. 4), which means they are under the control of the higher power. The locusts cannot kill (they are power restricted), and they do not hurt anything that is green. This is the exact opposite of what the locusts in Exodus did. The locusts destroyed crops in Egypt and may have caused hunger, but they did not directly attack the Egyptians. However, in Revelation, Chapter 9, the locusts are attacking the emotional and mental state of humans.

Revelation 9:6 – This is not a physical occurrence because to be so would be absurd. The apocalyptic language employs allegory. This is an allegory, "like that of Hagar and Sarah" (Gal 5). An allegory is a continuous running of similes.

Revelation 11:8 – Nothing can describe Apocalyptic writing better than this chapter. What is spiritual (Apocalyptic) literature? 1 Corinthians 2:9-15 addresses the spiritual man who discerns the things God. Spiritual man is a direct contrast to the carnal understanding of humanity. The spiritual and carnal are opposites. The spiritual man cannot be judged (1Co 1:15).

To understand spiritual literature, we must have the important prerequisite of a regenerated mind, a regenerated spirit, or the hidden man of the heart. Having one of these prerequisites is extremely important. The un-Godly man understands by fleshy rather than spiritual discernment (1Co 2:9, 10). We ask the question, "Who is the Son of Man?" Flesh and blood have not revealed this answer to us, but God will (Mt 16:18, 19). God's answer will come by His revelation. So, we should compare the spiritual with the spiritual (1Co 2:13-15). Therefore, Christians understand spiritual language because they are spiritual. The Book of Revelation describes historical events in spiritual vocabulary.

This is why the locusts are spiritual (Rev 9) whereas the locusts in Exodus 10 are physical. The Revelation locusts are worse because they are damaging the Spirit. Can allegorical statements involve actual characters? Yes! For instance, we see Hagar, Sarah, and Abraham in Galatians 4:22-31.

Revelation 16 speaks of the Seven Bowls.

Revelation 16:4 – The third angel is pouring out his bowl. In Exodus 7:17, the water undergoes a physical change into blood. This Exodus change is the second plague in Egypt, whereas in Revelation, the second angel is pouring out his bowl into the sea. This pouring is a reference back to God's physical judgment in Egypt, which is given as a background for the spiritual language of Revelation.

In Exodus 9:11, the magicians gave up when the boils came upon them. They could not continue. But this is where God starts in Revelation 16:2. This first plague depicts a spiritual, not a physical boil. What was the sixth plague in Egypt is the first plague of the bowls of wrath. God starts where the Egyptians quit. This is more severe. In this regard, it is the instantaneous death and judgment of many (Rev 16:7). In the plague of Egypt, the plague was a warning. From man's viewpoint, the plague was an actual occurrence in Egypt, but the boils in Revelation are more a spiritual occurrence from Heaven's view.

Now, when Christ said I give you the keys to the Kingdom, and whatsoever you bind on Earth will (already has been) bound in Heaven, and whatsoever you loose on Earth will (already has been) loosed in Heaven, the eternal Christ is portraying our earthly existence in historical time and space. But the spiritual man sees this work for what it really is in Heaven – part and parcel of eternity. God's judgments in Egypt were both physical and spiritual, but the over powering physical aspects tormented the heathen Pharaoh. The Holy Spirit had not yet been given (Jn 7: 39) to convict a sinner's spirit, but even if He had, Pharaoh would probably still have hardened his own heart. Today, the message Christ proclaims is even more powerful to the heathen in this moral universe. The Holy Spirit of Judgment backs our message, and on the Judgment Day, the very breath "Spirit" of the Messiah's Word will reinforce Christ's message.

Heaven is above time, space, and history. However, a Kingdom Thinker thinks in terms of infinity governing time and eternity governing space. Therefore, in apocalyptic literature, the historical narrative is turned around. Instead of looking at the historical narrative in terms of physical elements and people in physical context that requires a miracle in time, the historical is turned around, and we go up into Heaven, which is outside of time and space and man. This whole scenario is viewed from God's view in Heaven. Satan and Michael are actual beings, and the abyss is an actual place. But Satan and Michael are spirits and the abyss is the place for confinement, like a death row of spirits, before the abyss is eventually cast into the "Lake of Fire."

Divorcing the physical from the spiritual and debunking the spiritual as being inferior to the physical is sheer nonsense. Such thinking is a one-way trip to Hell. When we address the spirit world, whether it be Heaven, above, or the occult, below, we are taking a trip from here to eternity. God will allow us to go there in mind before we enter there in body, soul, and spirit. Such an eternal abode that exists for both the saved and the lost is so far beyond our flimsy manmade concept of what we think religion is. The world that exists beyond our finite comprehension would make the most grandiose achievements of our religious inventions appear to be as a drop of water compared to the Pacific Ocean. So, when we talk about the Kingdom of Christ, it is like the Pacific Ocean, and the maharaja surrounded by an armed guard is like a drop of water. It is not a mosque in Mecca waiting to be evacuated. It is not a Salt Lake City or Vatican City temple that will melt in the near future. This is the Kingdom of God, not Solomon's temple, for One greater than Solomon is here.

When we talk about the occultic abyss, we are not talking about a reformatory, like the Bastille, or Alcatraz. We are talking about the agonizing torment of body, soul, and spirit that exceeds the very worst torments that we can imagine suffering.

Jesus said the flesh profited nothing (Jn 6:63) for no flesh can glory in God's presence. The dogmatic statement – that which is flesh is flesh and that which is spirit is spirit – cannot be refuted in any age. This is the Kingdom of God.

Addendum C – Fulfilled prophecies of 70 A.D.

The fulfillment of the prophecies of the Lord and prophet Jesus Christ, as seen in Bible and secular history prior to 70 A.D.

Prophecy	*Fulfillment*
Matthew 24:5 - false Christs	**Acts 5:34-38, 8:9** -Josephus mentions several false Christ's -Judas, son of Ezekias, Theudus -Simon Athronges and Dositheus
Matthew 24:6 - wars, rumors of wars	-Josephus says there were 10,000 tumults and 18 wars during this period. Antiquities of Jews, Bk.17, Chapter. 10, Tacitus writes of wars in Germany, Africa, Thrace, Gaul, Parthian, Britain and Armenia.
Matthew 24:8 - "beginning of sorrows"	**Acts 11:28**. -Josephus mentioned famines as a by-product of the 18 wars. -Suetonius tells of 30,000 deaths from pestilences. -Tacitus says that 12 highly-populated Asian cities falling to earthquakes. -Seneca said, "Whole cities of Asia fell in 'one fatal shock.'" Syria, Macedonia, Cyprus, and Paphos experienced earthquake. In 60 A.D., Hieerapous, Colosse, and Ladicea fell. Later, earthquakes hit Crete, Miletus, and Judea.
Matthew 24:9 - "persecution"	**Acts 4-8, 16:21-22, 24** -All Apostles but John were murdered. -Stephen is stoned. -James is beheaded. -The church is scattered (Acts 8:1). -Paul is stoned and beaten to death. Jesus said they would have no need to worry about what to say beforehand (Ac 4:8, 31-"filled with the Spirit and spoke boldly"). "They could not resist Stephen's wisdom" (Ac 6:10).

Prophecy	Fulfillment
Matthew 24:11-13 - "many false prophets"	2 Peter 2:1-22; 1 John 4:1; Titus 1:10, 11
Matthew 24:12 - "love grows cold"	Josephus writes of Jews killing one another, fighting among themselves, poisoning each other's water, and burning their grain bins. History records that during this political upheaval, the Jews did not sow crops.
Matthew 24:13 - "endure to the end"	The Christian Jews endured and were spared the Abomination of Desolation.
Matthew 24:14 - "Gospel to the world"	Acts 2:5, 8:1; Colossians 1:6, 23; Romans 1:5,8, 10,18
Matthew 24:18 - "Seeing the Abomination	Luke 21:15-21 -When they saw Titus throw up embankments around the city, thousands fell by the sword. - The temple was abominated (Da 9:26-27). The word abomination is used of detestable idols (1Ki 11:5-7; 2Ki 23:13; Jer 4:1, 7:30; Eze 5:11). It is a day of vengeance for Judaism (Da 9:26 with Lk 21:22-24). It is war with Jerusalem (Lk 21:20). The enemy stands in the holy place, where it ought not to be (Mk 13:14). The enemy's presence is a sign to flee to the mountains of Judea. The Jews prayed it would not be a Sabbath because Jewish authorities would have prevented their flight. Josephus says the Romans brought their ensigns into the temple and set them against the Eastern Gate. There the Romans offered sacrifices to their ensigns and proclaimed Titus IMPERATOR with greatest acclamations of Joy. Remember when the Jews wanted no King but Caesar. Now they got him. The armies made Jerusalem desolate. Daniel 9:26 did not say the desolation took place at the end of the 70 weeks but that the desolation-ruin was determined (Mt 23:38).

Prophecy	Fulfillment
Matthew 24:19+ - "Pray concerning your flight".	*Josephus, War, Book 2, Chapter 19, Section 6-7* - "Had Cestius continued the siege a little longer, he could have taken the city, but it was, I suppose, owing to the aversion God had already at the city and the sanctuary, that he was hindered from putting an end to the war that very day. It then happened that Cestius was not conscious either how the besieged despaired of success, nor how courageous the people were for him, and so recalled his soldiers from the place, and by despairing of any expectation of taking it, without having reviewed any disgrace, he retired from the city, without any reason in the world. That when the robbers perceived this unexpected retreat of his, they resumed their courage, and ran after the hinder parts of his army, and destroyed a considerable number of both their horsemen and footmen, and now Cestius lay all night at the camp, which was at Scopus, and as he went off further the next day, he thereby invited the enemy to follow him, who still fell upon the hindmost, and destroyed them. They also fell upon the flank on each side of the army and threw darts upon them obliquely. And this was the reason the Romans suffered greatly, without being able to revenge themselves upon their enemies, so they were galled all the way. Those put out of rank were slain, among whom were Priscus the commander of the sixth legion and Longinus the tribune, and Emilius Secundus, the commander of a troop of horsemen. With great difficulty they made it to Galbao, their former camp, and that not without a loss of a great part of their baggage. There it was that Cestius stayed two days, and it was in great distress that he wonders what he should do in these circumstances, but when on the third day, he saw a still greater number of the enemy, and all parts around him filled with Jews, he understood that his delay was to his detriment, and if he stayed any longer there he would have even more enemies upon him."

Prophecy	Fulfillment
Matthew 24:21 - "Great Tribulation"	*Josephus, Wars Book 6, Chap. 9, Sec. 4* -"97,000 Jews taken captive. 1,100,000 perished. A vast amount, perhaps 2,700,000 were collected in the city. The ENTIRE NATION was shut up by fate as in a prison, and the Roman Army encompassed the city when it was crowded with citizens. The actual siege lasted from April 14, 70 A.D. to September 8, five months. Some were tortured and crucified, in fact 500 were crucified daily. There was not enough wood in the forests for the crosses."
Matthew 24:23-26 - "False Christ's"	*Josephus, War Book 6, Chap. 5, Sec. 2-3* -"The soldiers came to the cloisters that were in the outer court of the temple, whither the women and children, and a mixed multitude fled in number about six thousand. The soldiers were in such a rage they set the cloisters on fire destroying some of the multitude. The Jews, throwing themselves down headlong. Some were burnt in the cloisters themselves. Nor did any of them escape with the FALSE PROPHET who was the occasion of these people's destruction, who had made proclamation in the city that very day, that God commanded them to get up on the temple, and that they should receive miraculous signs and deliverance. Now, there were then a great number of false prophets who told them to wait for the deliverance of God and this kept them from deserting."

Prophecy	Fulfillment
Matthew 24:28 - "The carcass and eagles"	*-Deuteronomy 28:49*: "The Lord shall bring a nation against thee from afar, from the end of the earth, as the eagle flieth, a nation whose tongue thou shalt not understand." Conscripts in the Roman army came from as far as Britain and France. *-Hosea 8:1*: "Set the trumpet to thy mouth. He shall come as an eagle against the house of the Lord, because they have transgressed my covenant and trespassed my Law." *-Habakkuk 1:8:* "Their horses also are swifter than the leopards and are more fierce than the evening wolves, and their horsemen shall spread themselves, and their horsemen shall come from far, they shall fly as the eagle hastens to eat." (The Roman emblem-the eagle.)

1 Josephus' editor added this footnote. "There may be another very important, and very providential reason here assigned for this strange and foolish retreat of Cestius, which if Josephus were now a Christian he might probably have taken notice of also, and that is, the affording the Jewish Christians in the city the opportunity of calling to mind the prediction and caution given them by Christ about 36½ years before, that when they should see the abomination of desolation (the idolatrous Roman armies, with the images of their idols in their ensigns, ready to lay Jerusalem desolate), they should then flee to the mountains. By complying with which, those Jewish Christians fled to the mountains of Perea and escaped this destruction." (See Lit. Accompl. Of Prophets, Pages 69, 70) There was, perhaps, no one instance of a more impolitic, but more providential conduct than this retreat of Cestius.

Addendum D – Chronological Order of the Destruction of Jerusalem by Dan Dyke

Dan Dyke, Professor of Hebrew and Theology at Cincinnati Christian University

68-73 A.D. – Jewish-Roman War

68 A.D. – Caesarea (on the Mediterranean Sea). The Jews petitioned Rome. "Do Jews have equal religious standing in the Empire?" Caesars reply was "No!" When the Gentiles sensed that Imperial Rome had disdain for Judaism they went to a synagogue and killed birds on the steps. This was a symbolic act and sign that the Jewish nation had the leprosy stigmatism, for the offering of a bird was to be made by the leper. This greatly offended the Jews.

The Romans moved to kill 20,000 Jews in one hour. The Jews retaliated and slaughtered a great many Romans in Jerusalem. This action became an international debacle when it was learned later that the Romans had surrendered.

A Civil War erupts. On one of the earliest days of the war 2,500 Jews were killed. On another day, 2,300 were killed. The Sect of Pharisees now becomes rebel, Zealots. The Priests no longer made sacrifice to Caesar. This was an official declaration of War.

The Governor of Syria and his twelve legions, called the "Thundering Hoard" go to the temple, stop for some reason and then flee. But the Jews ambushed them at Beth Horon and slaughtered the Syrian troops. The Jews felt vindicated and supposed that God was with them now because the troops of Judas Maccabees had won against the Greeks at this same location.

67 A.D. – Vespasian destroyed Galilee, Judea and Idumea. The Edomites joined the Jews and together they fight the Romans. The Edomites were famous for immorality. This was a very unattractive coalition.

68 A.D. – Vespasian attacks Jerusalem. God always wanted to protect Jerusalem, but now things are different. However, the Jews are nauseatingly ignorant that God has abandoned them. But, as if providence is mocking them, they take it as an omen when Nero dies and his son was called home to Rome.

69 A.D. – In June, Vespasian returns. He simultaneously destroys all of the existing cities of Judah except for these four, Herodian, Macaras, Jerusalem and Masada.

70 A.D. – In April, Vespasian returned to Rome. His son, Titus stayed at Jerusalem. He had four legions and 80,000 troops. He surrounded Jerusalem at Passover time. There were maybe, 2.6 million people in town. Since all other towns were destroyed, they assumed this was the safe place to be. Nothing could be more untrue!

> May 25 – They destroyed the third wall of the city
>
> May 30 – They destroyed the second wall
>
> June 16 – They took the preeminent tower of Antonia.
>
> July – The Romans built their own wall to prevent the Jews from escaping. This also was a means of cutting off all supplies and starving them to death.
>
> August 6 – They took the temple
>
> August 15 – They burned the porticos.
>
> August 28 – They burned down the temple and leveled it.

Josephus says that 1.1. Million died, 2000 committed suicide and the Jews thought it was the end of the world. Ninety-seven thousand Jews were dispersed. In 70 A.D., there were 250 Synagogues. By September, it was all over for Jerusalem, but minor strife continues until 73 A.D. and the final massacre at Masada.

Addendum E – George Peter Holford's "Destruction of Jerusalem"

Before discussing the End of Judaism, consider an excellent work by George Peter Holford describing the City of Jerusalem (1805) edited by Debbie Cousins and Charles Walter Doughty:[129]

> *Jerusalem was built on two mountains. Three celebrated walls surrounded the city on every side, except that which was deemed inaccessible, and there it was defended by one wall only. The most ancient of these walls was remarkable for its great strength, and was, moreover, erected on a hanging rock, and fortified by sixty towers. On the middle wall, there were fourteen towers only; but on the third, which was also distinguished by the extraordinary merit of its architecture, there were no less than ninety. The celebrated tower of Psephinos, before which Titus at first encamped, was erected on this latter wall, and even excelled it in the superior style of its architecture: it was seventy cubits high and had eight angles, each of which commanded most extensive and beautiful prospects.*
>
> *In clear weather, the spectator had from them a view of the Mediterranean Sea, of Arabia, and of the whole extent of the Jewish dominions. Besides this there were three other towers of great magnitude, named Hippocos, Phasael, and Mariamne. The two former, famed for their strength and grandeur, were nearly ninety cubits high; the latter, for its valuable curiosities, beauty and elegance, was about fifty-five cubits. They were all built of white marble; and so exquisite was the workmanship, that each of them appeared as if it had been hewn out of an immense single block of it. Notwithstanding their great elevation, they yet must have appeared, from the surrounding country, far loftier than they really were. The old wall, it has just been remarked, was built upon a high rock: but these towers were erected upon the top of a hill, the summit of which was itself thirty cubits above the top of the old wall! Such edifices, so situated, it is easy to conceive, must have given to the city a very great degree of grandeur and magnificence. Not far distant from these towers stood the royal palace, of singular beauty and elegance. Its pillars, its porticoes, its galleries, its apartments, were all incredibly costly, splendid and superb; while the groves, gardens, walks, fountains, and aqueducts, with which it was encompassed, formed the richest and most delightful scenery that can possibly be imagined.*

The situation of these structures was on the north side of Jerusalem. Its celebrated temple, and the strong fort of Antonia, was on the east side, and directly opposite to the Mount of Olives. This fort was built on a rock fifty cubits in height, and as steep as to be inaccessible on every side; and to render it still more so, it was faced with thin slabs of marble, which, being slippery, proved at once a defense and an ornament. In the midst of the fort stood the castle *of Antonia, the interior parts of which, for grandeur, state, and convenience, resembled more a palace than a fortress. Viewed from a distance it had the appearance of a tower, encompassed by four other towers, situated at the four angles of a square. Of these latter, three were fifty cubits high, and the fourth seventy cubits.*

The tower last mentioned commanded an excellent view of the whole temple, the riches grandeur, and elegance of which it is not in the power of language to describe. Whether we consider its architecture, its dimensions, its magnificence, its splendor, or the sacred purposes to which it was dedicated, it must equally be regarded as the most astonishing fabric that was ever constructed. It was erected partly on a solid rock, which was originally steep on every side. The foundations of what was called the lower temple were 300 cubits in depth, and the stones of which they were composed, more than sixty feet in length, while the superstructure contained, of the whitest marble, stones nearly sixty-eight feet long, more than seven feet high, and nine broad. The circuit of the whole building was four furlongs; its height one hundred cubits; one hundred and sixty pillars, each twenty-seven feet high, ornamented and sustained the immense and ponderous edifice. In the front, spacious and lofty galleries, wainscoted with cedar, were supported by columns of white marble, in uniform rows.

In short, says Josephus, nothing could surpass even the exterior of this temple, for its elegant and curious workmanship. It was adorned with solid plates of gold that rivaled the beauty of the rising sun, and were scarcely less dazzling to the eye than the beams of that luminary. Of those parts of the building which were not gilt; when viewed from a distance, some, says he, appeared like pillars of snow, and some, like mountains of white marble. The splendor of the interior parts of the temple corresponded with its external magnificence. It was decorated and enriched by everything that was costly, elegant and superb. Religious donations and offerings had poured into this wonderful repository of precious stores from every part of the world, during many successive ages. In the lower temple were placed those sacred curiosities, the seven branched candlestick of pure gold, the table for the showbread, and the altar of incense; the two latter of which were covered with plates of the same metal. In the sanctuary were several doors fifty-five cubits high and sixteen in breadth which were all likewise of gold and before these doors hung a veil of the most beautiful Babylonian tapestry, composed of scarlet, blue, and purple, exquisitely interwoven, and wrought up to the highest degree of art. From the top of the ceiling were branches and leaves of vines with large clusters of grapes hanging down five or six feet, all of gold and of most admirable workmanship. In addition to these proofs of the splendor and riches of the temple, may be noticed its eastern gate of pure Corinthian brass more esteemed even than the precious metals — the golden folding doors of the chambers — the beautiful carved work, gilding, and painting of the galleries, golden vessels—the sacerdotal vestments of scarlet, violet, and purple —the vast wealth of the treasury—abundance of precious stones, and immense quantities of all kinds of costly spices and perfumes. In short, the most valuable and sumptuous of whatever nature, or art, or opulence, could supply was enclosed within the consecrated walls of this magnificent and venerable edifice.

So much concerning this celebrated city, and its still more celebrated temple. We shall now consider our LORD's prophecies relating to their destruction.

On the second day of the week, immediately preceding his crucifixion, our blessed SAVIOUR made his public and triumphal entry into Jerusalem, amidst the acclamations of a very great multitude of his disciples, who hailed him KING OF SION, and with palm branches, the emblems of victory, in their hands, rejoiced and gave praises to GOD for all the mighty works they had seen, singing "Hosanna! Blessed be the KING that cometh in the name of the LORD! Peace in heaven, and glory in the highest!" But while the people exulted and triumphantly congratulated the MESSIAH, He struggling with the deepest emotions of pity and compassion for Jerusalem, beheld the city and wept over it, saying, "If thou hadst known, even thou, at least in this thy day, the things that belong unto thy peace! but now they are hid from thine eyes; for the days shall come upon thee, that thine enemies shall cast a trench about thee, and compass thee around, and keep thee in on every side; And shall lay thee even with the ground, and thy children within thee and they shall, not leave in thee one stone upon another; because thou knewest not the time of thy visitation." (Luke 19:41-44)

On the 4th day of the week following, being only two days before his death, he went for the last time into the temple to teach the people. While He was thus *employed, the High Priests and the Elders, the Herodians, the Sadducees, and Pharisees, successively came to him, and questioned him subtly, being desirous to "entangle him in his talk; " to whom, with his accustomed dignity and wisdom, he returned answers which carried conviction to their hearts, and at once silenced and astonished them. Then, turning to his disciples, and the whole multitude, he addressed to them a discourse of very uncommon energy, in which, with most exquisite keenness of reproof, he exposed and condemned the cruelty and pride, the hypocrisy and sensuality of the Pharisees and Scribes. Having next foretold the barbarous treatment which his Apostles would receive at their hands be proceeded to denounce against Jerusalem the dire and heavy vengeance, that had for ages been accumulating in the vials of divine displeasure, expressly declaring that it, should be poured out upon the then existing generation, adding that inimitably tender and pathetic apostrophe to this devoted city, "0 Jerusalem, Jerusalem, thou that killest the prophets, and stonest them- which are sent unto thee, how often would I have gathered thy children together, even as a hen gathereth her chickens under her wings,, and ye would not! Behold! Your HOUSE is left unto you desolate; for I say unto you, ye shall not see me henceforth, till you shall say, blessed is he that cometh in the name of the Lord!" (Matthew 23:37-39)*

Nero, having been informed of the defeat of Cestius, immediately appointed Vespasian, a man of tried valor to prosecute the war against the Jews, who, assisted by his son Titus, soon collected at Ptolemais an. army of sixty thousand men. From hence, in the spring of 67 A. D. he marched into Judea, everywhere spreading the most cruel havoc and devastation; the Roman soldiers, on various occasions, sparing neither infants nor the aged. For fifteen months Vespasian proceeded in this sanguinary career, during which period he reduced all the strong towns of Galilee, and the chief of those in Judea, destroying at least one hundred and fifty thousand of the inhabitants. Among the terrible calamities which at this time happened to the Jews, those which befell them at Joppa, which had been rebuilt, deserve particular notice. Their frequent piracies had provoked the vengeance of Vespasian. The Jews fled before his army to their ships; but a tempest immediately arose, pursued such as stood out to sea, and overset them, while the rest were dashed vessel against vessel, and against the rocks, in the most tremendous manner. In this perplexity many were drowned, some were crushed by the broken ships; others killed themselves, and such as reached the shore were slain by the merciless Romans. The sea for a long space was stained with blood; four thousand two hundred dead bodies were strewed along the coast, and, dreadful to relate, not an individual survived to report this great calamity at Jerusalem.

(Big Chance Number 1)

Vespasian, after proceeding as far as Jericho, returned to Caesarea, in order to make preparation for his grand attempt against Jerusalem. While he was thus employed, he received intelligence of the death of Nero; whereupon, not knowing what the will of the future emperor might be, he prudently resolved to suspend, for the present, the execution of his design. Thus the Almighty gave the Jews a second respite, which continued nearly two years; but they repented not of their crimes, neither were they in the least degree reclaimed, but rather proceeded to acts of still greater enormity.

The flame of civil dissension again burst out and with more dreadful fury. In the heart of Jerusalem two factions contended for the sovereignty and raged against each other with rancorous and destructive animosity. A division of one of these factions having been excluded from the city (Vide page 26) forcibly entered it during the night. A thirst for blood, and inflamed by revenge, they spared neither age, sex, nor infancy; and the morning beheld eight thousand five hundred dead bodies lying in the streets of the holy city.

They plundered every house, and having found the chief priests Anais and Jesus, not only slew them, but also, insulting their bodies, cast them forth unburied. They slaughtered the common people as unfeelingly as if they had been a herd of the vilest beasts. The nobles they first imprisoned then scourged, and when they could not by these means attach them to their party, they bestowed death upon them as a favor. Of the higher classes twelve thousand perished in this manner; nor did any one dare to shed a tear, or utter a groan, openly, through fear of a similar fate. Death, indeed, was the penalty of the lightest and heaviest accusations, nor did any escape through the meanness of their birth, or their poverty. Such as fled were intercepted and slain. Their carcasses lay in heaps on all the public roads. Every symptom of pity seemed utterly extinguished, and with it, all respect for authority, both human and divine.

While Jerusalem was a prey to these ferocious and devouring factions, every part of Judea was scourged and laid waste by bands of robbers and murderers, who plundered the towns; and, in case of resistance, slew the inhabitants, not sparing either women or children. Simon, son of Gioras, the commander of one of these bands, at the head of forty thousand banditti, having with some difficulty entered Jerusalem, gave birth to a third faction, and the flame of civil discord blazed out again, with still more destructive fury. The three factions, rendered frantic by drunkenness, rage, and desperation, trampling on heaps of slain, fought against each other with brutal savageness and madness. Even such as brought sacrifices to the temple were murdered. The dead bodies of priests and worshippers, both natives and foreigners were heaped together, and a lake of blood stagnated in the sacred courts. John of Gischala, who headed one of the factions, burnt storehouses full of provisions; and Simon, his great antagonist, who headed another of them, soon afterwards followed his example.

Thus, they cut the very sinews of their own strength. At this critical and alarming conjuncture, intelligence arrived that the Roman Army was approaching the city. The Jews were petrified with astonishment and fear; there was no time for counsel, no hope of pacification, and no means of flight. All was wild disorder and perplexity. Nothing was to be heard but "the confused noise of the warrior," "nothing to be seen but garments rolled in blood," and nothing to be expected from the Romans but signal and exemplary vengeance (Isaiah 9:5). A ceaseless cry of combatants was heard day and night, and yet the lamentations of mourners were still more dreadful. The consternation and terror which now prevailed induced many inhabitants to desire that a foreign foe might come, and effect their deliverance. Such was the horrible condition of the place when Titus and his army presented themselves, and encamped before Jerusalem."

Take another look at an excerpt from Holford

"These armies, we do not hesitate to affirm were those of the Romans, who now infested the city. From the time of the Babylonian captivity, the Jews had held idolatry as an abomination. This national aversion was manifested even against the images of their gods and emperors, which the Roman armies carried in their standards; so that, in a time of peace, Pilate, and afterwards Vitellius, at the request of some eminent Jews, on this account avoided marching their forces through Judea. Of the desolating disposition which now governed the Roman army, the history of the Jewish war, and especially of the final demolition of the holy city, presents an awful and signal example. Jerusalem was not captured merely, but with its celebrated temple, laid in ruins. Lest, however, the army of Titus should not be sufficiently designated by this expression, our LORD adds,

"Wheresoever the carcass is, there will the eagles be gathered together." Matt. xxiv. 28. The Jewish state, indeed, at this time, was fitly compared to a carcass (editor's note – this city was filled with thousands of dead people before Titus began his siege due to the Civil war!).

The scepter of Judah, i.e. its civil and political authority, the life of its religion, and the glory of its temple, were departed. It was, in short, morally and judicially dead. The eagle, whose ruling instinct is rapine and murder, as fitly represented the fierce and sanguinary temper of the Romans, and, perhaps, might be intended to refer also to the principal figure on their ensigns, which, however obnoxious to the Jews, were at length planted in the midst of the holy city, and finally on the temple itself.

(Big Chance Number 2)

The day on which Titus encompassed Jerusalem, was the feast of the Passover; and it is deserving of the very particular attention of the reader, that this was the anniversary of that memorable period in which the Jews crucified their Messiah! At this season multitudes came up from all the surrounding country, and from distant parts, to keep the festival. How suitable and how kind, then, was the prophetic admonition of our LORD, and how clearly he into futurity when he said "Let not them that are in the countries entering into Jerusalem." Luke xxi. 21

Nevertheless, the city was at this time crowded with Jewish strangers, and foreigners from all parts, so that the whole nation may be considered as having been shut up in one prison, preparatory to the execution of the Divine vengeance; and, according to Josephus this event took place suddenly; thus, not only fulfilling the predictions of our LORD, that these calamities should come, like the swift-darting lightning" that cometh out of the east and shineth even unto the West," and " as a snare on all of them (the Jews) who dwelt upon the face of the whole earth" (Matt. xxiv. 27, and Luke xxi 35), but justifying, also, his friendly direction, that those who fled from the place should use the utmost possible expedition.

The beginning destruction of Jerusalem.

(Big chance number 3)

On the appearance of the Roman army, the factious Jews united, and, rushing furiously out of the city repulsed the tenth legion, which was with difficulty preserved. This event caused a short suspension of hostilities, and, by opening the gates, gave an opportunity to such as were so disposed to make their escape; which before this they could not have attempted without interruption, from the suspicion that they wished to revolt to the Romans. This success inspired the Jews with confidence, and they resolved to defend their city to the very uttermost; but it did not prevent the renewal of their civil broils.

The faction under Eleazer having dispersed, and arranged themselves under the two other leaders John and Simon, there ensued a scene of the most dreadful contention, plunder, and conflagration: the middle space of the city being burnt, and the wretched inhabitants made the prize of the contending parties. The Romans at length gained possession of two of the three walls which defended the city, and fear once more united the factions. This pause, to their fury had, however, scarcely begun when famine made its ghastly appearance in the Jewish army. It had for some time been silently approaching, and many of the peaceful and the poor had already perished for want of necessaries. With this new calamity, strange to relate, the madness of the factions returned, and the city presented a new picture of wretchedness. Impelled by the cravings of hunger, they snatched the staff of life out of each other's hands, and many devoured the grain unprepared.

Tortures were inflicted for the discovery of a handful of meal; women forced food from their husbands, and children from their fathers, and even mothers from their infants, and while sucking children were wasting away in their arms, they scrupled not to take away the vital drops which sustained them! So justly did our LORD pronounce a woe on "them that should give suck in those days?" (Matt. xxiv. 19) This dreadful scourge at length drove multitudes of the Jews out of the city into the enemy's camp, where the Romans crucified them in such numbers, that, as Josephus relates, space was wanted for the crosses, and crosses for the captives; and it having been discovered that some of them had swallowed gold, the Arabs and Syrians, who were incorporated in the Roman army, impelled by avarice, with unexampled cruelty ripped open two thousand of the deserters in one night Titus, touched by these calamities, in person entreated the Jews to surrender, but they answered him with reviling.

Exasperated by their obstinacy and insolence, he now resolved to surround the city by a circumvallation, (a trench of 39 furlongs in circuit and strengthened with 13 towers,) which with astonishing activity was effected by the soldiers in three days. Thus was fulfilled another of our LORD's predictions, for he had said, while addressing this devoted city," Thine enemies shall cast a trench about thee, and compass thee roundabout, and keep thee in on every side." Luke xix, 43. As no supplies whatever could now enter the walls, the famine rapidly extend, itself, and, increasing in horror, devoured whole families.

The tops of houses, and the recesses of the city, were covered with the carcasses of women, children, and aged men. The young men appeared like specters in the places of public resort, and fell down lifeless in the streets. The dead were too numerous to be interred, and many expired in the performance of this office. — The public calamity was too great for lamentation. Silence, and, as it were, a black and deadly night, overspread the city. — But even such a scene could not awe the robbers; they spoiled the tombs, and stripped the dead of their graveclothes, with an unfeeling and wild laughter. They tried the edges of their swords on their carcasses, and even on some that were yet breathing; while Simon Goras chose this melancholy and awful period to manifest the deep malignity and cruelty of his nature in the execution of the High Priest Matthias, and his three sons, whom he caused to be condemned as favorers of the Romans. The father, in consideration of his having opened the city gates to Simon, begged that he Might be executed previously to his children; but the unfeeling tyrant gave orders that he should be dispatched in the last place, and in his expiring moments insultingly asked him, whether the Romans could then relieve him.

(Big Chance Number 4)

While the city was in this dismal situation, a Jew named Mannaeus fled to Titus, and informed him, that from the beginning of the siege (4th mo. 14th) to the 1st of 7th mo. following, one hundred and fifteen thousand eight hundred and eighty dead bodies had been carried through one gate only, which he had guarded. This man had been appointed to pay the public allowance for carrying the bodies out, and was therefore obliged to register them. Soon after, several respectable individuals deserted to the Romans, and assured Titus that the whole number of the poor who had been cast out at the different gates was not less than six hundred thousand. The report of these calamities excited pity in the Romans, and in a particular manner affected Titus, who, while surveying the immense number of dead bodies which were piled up, raised his hands towards heaven, and, appealing to the almighty, solemnly protested that he had not been the cause of these deplorable calamities; which, indeed, the Jews, by their unexampled wickedness rebellion, and obstinacy, had brought down upon their own heads.

After this, Josephus, in the name of Titus, earnestly exhorted John and his adherents to surrender; but the insolent rebel returned nothing but reproaches and imprecations, declaring his firm persuasion that Jerusalem, as it was GOD'S own city, could never be taken: thus literally fulfilling the declaration of Micah, that the Jews, in their extremity, notwithstanding their crimes, would presumptuously "lean upon the LORD, and say, 'Is not the LORD among us? No evil can come upon us." (Micah iii. 11)

Meanwhile the horrors of famine grew still more melancholy and afflictive. The Jews, for lack of food were at length compelled to eat their belts, their sandals, the skins of their shields, dried grass, and even the ordure of oxen. In the depth or this horrible extremity, a Jewess of noble family urged by the intolerable cravings of hunger, slew her infant child, and prepared it for a meal; and had actually eaten one half thereof, when the soldiers, allured by the smell of food, threatened her with instant death if she refused to discover it. 'Intimidated by this menace, she immediately produced the remains of her son, which petrified them with horror. At the recital of this melancholy and affecting occurrence, the whole city stood aghast, and poured forth their congratulations on those whom death had hurried away from such heartrending scenes. Indeed, humanity at once shudders and sickens at the narration, nor can any one of the least sensibility reflect upon the pitiable condition to which the female part of the inhabitants of Jerusalem must at this time have been reduced, without experiencing the tenderness emotion of sympathy, or refrain from tears while he reads our savior's pathetic address to the women who " bewailed him" as he was led to Calvary, wherein he evidently refers to these very calamities: "Daughters of Jerusalem, weep not for me, but for yourselves and for your children; for behold, the days are coming in which they shall say, 'Blessed are the barren, and the wombs that never bare, and the breasts that never gave suck." Luke xxiii. 29.

The above melancholy fact was also literally foretold by Moses: "The tender and delicate women among you (said be addressing Israel) who would not adventure to set the sole of her foot upon the ground for delicateness and tenderness, her eye shall be evil . . . toward her young one . . . which she shall bear," and "eat for want of all things, secretly, in the siege and straightness wherewith, thine enemy shall distress thee in thy gates." (Deut. xxviii. 56, 57) This prediction was partially fulfilled, when Samaria the capital of the revolted tribes, was, besieged by Benhadad; and afterwards at Jerusalem, previously to its capture by Nebuchadnezzar; but its exact and literal accomplishment in relation to a lady of rank, delicately and voluptuously educated, was reserved for the period of which we are now speaking. It deserves particular regard, as a circumstance which vary greatly enhances the importance of this prophecy that the history of the world does not record that a parallel instance of unnatural barbarity ever occurred during the siege of any other place, in any other age or nation whatsoever. Indeed, Josephus himself declares that, if there had not been many credible witnesses of the fact, he would not have recorded it," because," as he remarks," such a shocking, violation of never having been perpetuated by any Greek or barbarian," the insertion of it might have diminished the credibility of his history.

While famine continued thus to spread its destructive rage through the city, the Romans, after many ineffectual attempts, at length succeeded in demolishing part of the inner wall, possessed themselves of the great tower of Antonia, and advanced towards the Temple, which Titus, in a council of war had determined to preserve as an ornament to the empire, and as a monument of his success; but the Almighty had determined otherwise; for now, in the revolution of ages, was arrived that fatal day, (the 10th of 8th mo.) emphatically called " a day of vengeance," (Luke xxi. 21) on which the Temple had formerly been destroyed by the king of Babylon. A Roman soldier, urged, as he declared, by a divine impulse, regardless of the command of Titus climbed on the shoulders of another, and threw a flaming brand into the golden window of the Temple, which instantly set the building on fire. The Jews, anxious above all things to save that sacred edifice, in which they superstitiously trusted for security, with a dreadful outcry, rushed in to extinguish the flames. Titus also, being extinguish the conflagration, hastened to the spot in his chariot, attended by his principal officers and legions; but in vain he waved his hand and raised his voice, commanding his soldiers to extinguish the fire; so great was the uproar and confusion, that no attention was paid even to him. The Romans, willfully deaf instead of extinguishing the flames, spread them wider and wider. Actuated by the fiercest impulses rancor and revenge against the Jews, they rushed furiously upon them, slaying some with the sword, trampling others under their feet, or crushing them to death against the walls. Many, falling amongst the smoking ruins of the porches and galleries, were suffocated. The unarmed poor, and even sick persons, were slaughtered without mercy. Of these unhappy people numbers were left weltering in their gore. Multitudes of the dead and dying were heaped round about the altar, to which they had formerly filed for protection, while the steps that led from it into the outer court were literally deluged with their blood.

(Big Chance Number 5)

Finding it impossible to restrain the impetuosity and cruelty of his soldiers, the Commander in chief proceeded, with some of his superior officers, to take a survey of those parts of the edifice which were still uninjured by the conflagration. It had not, at this time, reached the inner Temple, which Titus entered, and viewed with silent admiration. Struck with the magnificence of its architecture, and the beauty of its decorations, which even surpassed the report of fame concerning them; and perceiving that the sanctuary had not yet caught fire, he redoubled his efforts to stop the progress of the flames. He condescended even to entreat his soldiers to exert all their strength and activity for this purpose, and appointed a centurion of the guards to punish them if they again disregarded him: but all was in vain.

The delirious rage of the soldiery knew no bounds. Eager for plunder and for slaughter, they alike condemned the solicitations and menaces of their General. Even while he was thus intent upon the preservation of the sanctuary, one of the soldiers was actually employed in setting fire to the door-posts, which caused the conflagration to become general. Titus and his officers were now compelled to retire, and none remained to check the fury of the soldiers or the flames. The Romans, exasperated to the highest pitch against the Jews, seized every person whom they could find, and, without the least regard to sex, age or quality, first plundered and then slew them. The old and the young, the common people and the priests, those who surrendered and those who resisted, were equally involved in this horrible and indiscriminate carnage. Meanwhile the Temple continued burning, until at length, vast as was its size, the flames completely enveloped the, whole building; which, from the extent of the conflagration, impressed the distant spectator with an idea that the whole city was now on fire.

The tumult and disorder which ensued upon this event, it is impossible (says Josephus) for language to describe. The Roman legions made the most horrid outcries; the rebels, finding themselves exposed to the fury of both fire and sword, screamed dreadfully; while the unhappy people who were pent up between the enemy and the flames, deplored their situation in the most pitiable complaints. Those on the hill and those in the city seemed mutually to return the groans of each other. Such as were expiring through famine, were revived by this hideous scene, and seemed to acquire new spirits to deplore their misfortunes.

The lamentations from the city were re-echoed from the adjacent mountains, and places beyond Jordan. The flames which enveloped the Temple were so violent and impetuous, that the lofty hill on which it stood appeared, even from its deep foundations, as one large body of fire. The blood of the sufferers flowed in proportion to the rage of this destructive element; and the number of the slain exceeded all calculation. The ground could not be seen for the dead bodies, over which the Romans trampled in pursuit of the fugitives; while the crackling noise of the devouring flames mingled with the clamor of arms, the groans of the dying and the shrieks of despair, augmented the tremendous horror of a scene, to which the pages of history can furnish no parallel.

Amongst the tragically events which at this time occurred, the following is more particularly deserving of notice: a false prophet, pretending to a divine commission, affirmed that, if the people would repair the Temple, they should behold signs of their speedy deliverance. Accordingly, about six thousand persons, chiefly women and children, assembled in a gallery that was yet standing, on the outside of the building. Whilst they waited in anxious expectation of the promised miracle, the Romans with the most wanton barbarity, set fire to the gallery; from which, multitudes; rendered frantic by their horrible situation, precipitated themselves on the ruins below, and were killed by the fall: while, awful to relate, the rest, without a single exception, perished in the flames. So necessary was our Lord's second premonition not to give credit to "false prophets," who should pretend "to show great signs and wonders." In this last caution, as the connection of the prophecy demonstrates, he evidently refers to the period of the siege, but in the former to the interval immediately preceding the Jewish war. (Vide Matt. xxiv. Compare 5, and 23, 24, 25, 26, verses) The Temple now presented little more than a heap of ruins; and the Roman army as in triumph on the event, came and reared their ensigns against a fragment of the eastern gate, and, with sacrifices of thanksgiving, proclaimed the imperial majesty of Titus, with every possible demonstration of joy. Thus terminated the glory and existence of this sacred and venerable Edifice, which from its stupendous size, its massy solidity, and astonishing strength, seemed formed to resist the most violent operations of human force, and to stand, like the pyramids, amid the shocks of successive ages, until the final dissolution of the globe.

(Big Chance Number 6)

For five days after the destruction of the temple, the priests who had escaped, sat, pining with hunger, on the top of one of its broken walls; at length, they came down, and humbly asked the pardon of Titus, which, however, he refused to grant them, saying, that," as the temple, for the sake of which he would have spared them, was destroyed, it was but fit that its priests should perish also:" - whereupon he commanded that they should be put to death.

The leaders of the factions being now pressed on all sides begged a conference with Titus, who offered to spare their lives, if they would lay down their arms. With this reasonable condition, however, they refused to comply; upon which Titus, exasperated by their obstinacy, resolved that he would hereafter grant, no pardon to the insurgents, and ordered a proclamation to be made to this effect. The Romans had now full license to ravage and destroy. Early the following morning they set fire to the castle, the register-office, the council- chamber, and the palace of the queen Helena; and then spread themselves throughout the city, slaughtering wherever they came, and burning the dead bodies which were scattered over every street, and on the floors of almost every house. In the royal palace, where immense treasures were deposited, the seditious Jews murdered eight thousand four hundred of their own nation, and afterwards plundered their property.

Prodigious numbers of deserters, also, who escaped from the tyrants, and fled into enemy's camp, were slain. The soldiers, however, at length, weary of killing, and satiated with the blood which they had spilt, laid down their swords and sought to gratify avarice. For this purpose, they took the Jews, together with their wives and families, and publicly sold them, like cattle in a market, but though very multitudes were exposed to sale, while the purchasers were few in number. Now were fulfilled the words of Moses: "And ye shall be sold for bond-men and bond-women, and no man shall buy you." (Deut. xxviii 68)

The Romans having become masters of the lower city set it on fire. The Jews now fled to the higher, from whence, their pride and insolence yet unabated, they continued to exasperate their enemies and even appeared to view the burning of the town below them with tokens of pleasure. In a short time, however, the walls of the higher city were demolished by the Roman engines and the Jews, lately so-haughty and presumptuous now, trembling and panic-struck, fell on their faces, and deplored their own infatuation. Such as were in the towers, deemed impregnable to human force, beyond measure affrighted, strangely forsook them, and sought refuge in caverns and subterraneous passages; in which dismal retreats no less than two thousand dead bodies were afterwards found. Thus, as our Lord had predicted, did these miserable creatures, in effect, say "to the mountains, 'Fall on us;' and to the rocks, 'Cover us.' " (Luke xxiii. 20) The walls of the city being now completely in possession of the Romans, they hoisted their colors upon the towers, and burst forth into triumphant acclamations.

After this, all annoyance from the Jews being at an end, the soldiers gave an unbridled license to their fury against the inhabitants. They first plundered, and then set fire to the houses. They ranged through the streets with drawn swords in their hands, murdering every Jew whom they met, without distinction; till at length, the bodies of the dead choked up all the alleys and narrow passes while their blood literally flowed down the channels of the city in streams. As it drew towards evening, the soldiers exchanged the sword for the torch, and, amidst the darkness of this awful night, set fire to the remaining divisions of the place. The vial of divine wrath, which had been so long pouring out upon this devoted city was now emptying, and JERUSALEM, once "a praise in all the earth," and the subject of a thousand prophecies, deprived of the staff of life, wrapped in flames, and bleeding on every side sunk into utter ruin and desolation. This memorable siege terminated on the eighth day of the ninth month, (A. D. 70). Its duration was nearly five months, the Romans having infested the city on the fourteenth day of the fourth month preceding.

Before their final demolition, however, Titus took, a. survey of the city and its fortifications; and, while contemplating their impregnable strength, could not help ascribing his success to the peculiar interposition of the ALMIGHTY HIMSELF. "Had not God himself (exclaimed he) aided operations, and driven the Jews from their fortresses, it would have been absolutely impossible to have taken them; for what could men, and the force of engines, have done against such towers as these?" After this he commanded that the city should be razed to its foundations, excepting only the three lofty towers Hippocos, Phasael, and Mariamne, which he suffered to remain as evidences of its strength, and as trophies of his victory.

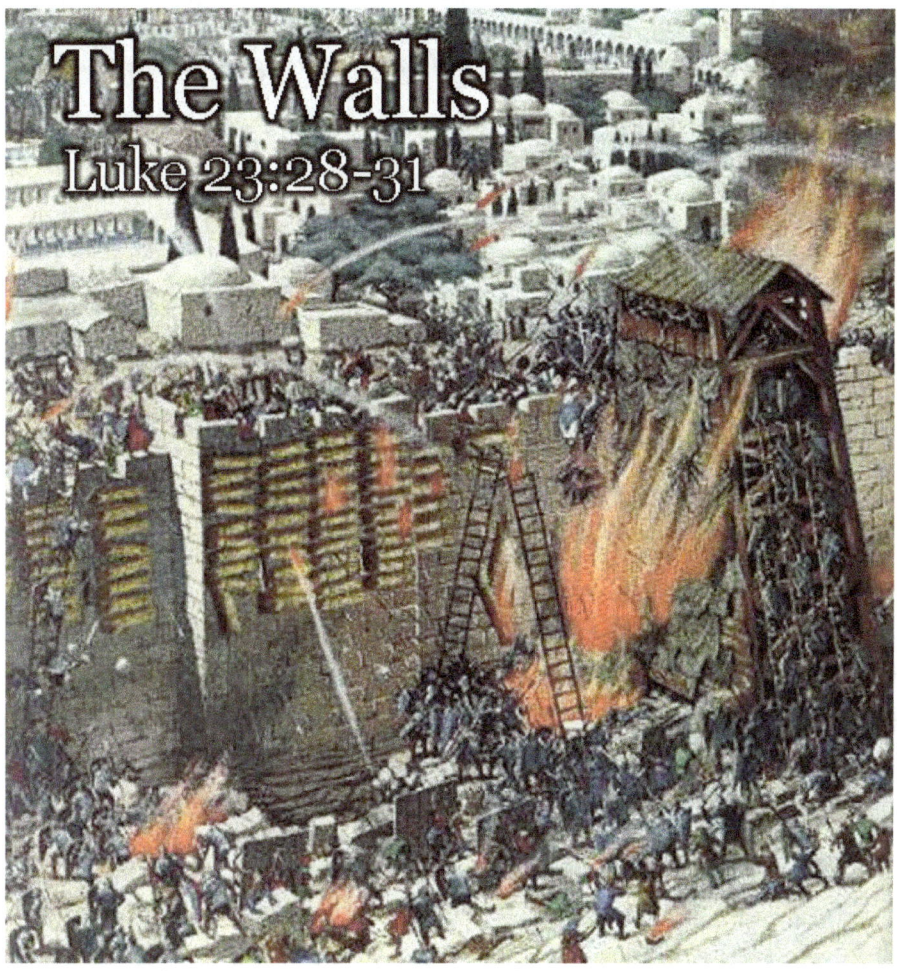

The Walls
Luke 23:28-31

There was left standing, also, a small part of the western wall; as a rampart for a garrison, to keep the surrounding country in subjection. Titus now gave orders that those Jews only who resisted should be slain; but the soldiers, equally void of pity and remorse, slew even the sick and the aged. The robbers and seditious were all punished with death: the tallest and most beautiful youths, together with several of the Jewish nobles were reserved by Titus to grace his triumphal entry into Rome. After this selection, all above the age of seventeen were sent in chains into Egypt, to be employed there as slaves, or distributed throughout the empire to be sacrificed as gladiators in the amphitheaters; whilst those who were under this age, were exposed to sale. During the time that these things were transacted, eleven thousand Jews, guarded by one of the generals, named Fronto, were literally starved to death. This melancholy occurrence happened partly through the scarcity of provisions, and partly through their own obstinacy, and the negligence of the Romans.

Of the Jews destroyed during the siege, Josephus reckons not less than one million and one hundred thousand, to which must be added, above two-hundred and thirty-seven thousand who perished in other places, and innumerable multitudes who were swept away by famine, and pestilence, and of which no calculation could be made. Not less than two thousand laid violent hands upon themselves. Of the captives the whole was about ninety-seven thousand. Of the Two great leaders of the Jews, who had both been made prisoners, John was doomed to a dungeon for life; while Simon, together with John, in triumph at Rome was scourged, and put to death as a malefactor.

In executing the command of Titus, relative to the demolition of Jerusalem, the Roman soldiers not only threw down the buildings, but even dug up their foundations, and so completely leveled the whole circuit of the city that a stranger would scarcely have known that it had ever been inhabited by human beings. Thus was this great City, which only five months before, had been crowded with nearly two millions of people, who gloried in its impregnable strength, entirely depopulated, and leveled with the ground. And thus, also was our LORD'S prediction, that her enemies should "lay her even with the ground," and "should not leave in her one stone upon another," (Luke xix. 44) most strikingly and fully accomplished! — This fact is confirmed by Eusebius, who asserts that he himself saw the city lying in ruins; and Josephus introduces Eleazer as exclaiming "Where is our great city, which, it was believed, GOD inhabited? It is altogether rooted and torn up from its foundations; and the only monument of it that remains, is the camp of its destroyers pitched amidst its relics!"

Concerning the Temple, our LORD had foretold, particularly, that, notwithstanding their wonderful dimensions, there should "not be left one stone upon another that should not be thrown down;" and, accordingly, it is recorded, in the Talmud, and by Maimonides, that Terentius Rufus, captain of the army of Titus, absolutely ploughed up the foundations of the Temple with a ploughshare. Now, also, was literally fulfilled that prophecy of Micah- "Therefore shall Zion, for your sakes (i.e. for your wickedness,) be ploughed as a field, and Jerusalem shall become heaps, and the mountain of the LORD's house as the high places of the forest." (Micah iii. 12)

Thus awfully complete were the calamities which befell the Jewish nation, and especially the city of Jerusalem. With what truth, then, did our LORD declare, that there should "be great tribulation, such as was not since the beginning of the world, no, nor ever shall be!" (Matt. xxiv. 21) Such was the prediction: the language in which Josephus declares its fulfillment is an exact counterpart to it: "If the misfortunes," says he," of all nations, from the beginning of the world, were compared with those which befell the Jews, they would appear far less in comparison;" and again, "No other city ever suffered such thing's, as no other generation, from the beginning of the world, was ever more fruitful in wickedness." These were, indeed, "the days of vengeance," that all things which are written (especially by Moses, Joel, and Daniel,) might be fulfilled." Luke xxi. 22. Nor were the calamities of this ill-fated nation even now ended; for there were still other places to subdue; and our LORD had thus predicted, "wheresoever the carcass is, there will the eagles be gathered together." (Matt. xxiv. 28)

After the destruction of Jerusalem seventeen hundred Jews who surrendered at Macherus were slain, and of fugitives not less than three thousand in the wood of Jardes. Titus having marched his army to Caesarea, he there, with great splendor, celebrated the birthday of his brother Domitian; and according to the barbarous manner of those times, punished many Jews in honor of it. The number who were burnt, and who fell by fighting with wild beasts, and in mutual combats, exceeded two thousand five hundred. At the siege of Massada, Eleazer, the commander, instigated the garrison to burn their stores, and to destroy first the women and children, and then themselves

Dreadful as it is to relate, this horrid design was executed. They were in number nine hundred and sixty. Ten were chosen to perform the bloody work: the rest sat 'on the ground,' and embracing their wives and children stretched out their necks to the sword: one was afterwards appointed to destroy the remaining nine, and then himself. The survivor, when he had looked round to see that all were slain, set fire to the place, and plugged his sword into his own bosom. Nevertheless, two women and five children successfully concealed themselves, and witnessed the whole transaction. When the Romans advanced to the attack in the morning, one of the women gave them a distinct account of this melancholy affair, and struck them with amazement at the contempt of death which had been displayed by the Jews. After this event, if we accept the transitory insurrection of the Sicarii, under Jonathan, all opposition on the part of the Jews everywhere ceased. It was the submission of impotence and despair. The peace that ensued was the effect of the direst necessity. The rich territory of Judea was converted into a desolate waste. Everywhere ruin and desolation presented itself to the solitary passenger, and a melancholy and death-like silence reigned over the whole region.

The mournful and desolate condition of Judea, at this time, is exactly described by the prophet Isaiah, in the following of his prophecy: "The cities were without inhabitant, and the houses without a man, and the land was utterly desolate, and the LORD had removed men far away, and there was a great forsaking in the midst of the land." (Isa. vi. 11, 12)

The Catastrophe which has now been reviewed, cannot but be deemed one of the most extraordinary that has happened since the foundation of the world; and as it has pleased the Almighty to make it the subject of a very large proportion of the prophecies both of the Jewish and Christian Scriptures, so he has ordained that the particular events which accomplished them should be recorded, with very remarkable precision, and by a man most singularly preserved, qualified, and circumstanced for this purpose.

But with respect to this latter point, he shall speak for himself: "At first," says Josephus," I fought against the Romans, but was afterwards forced to be present in the Roman camp. At the time I surrendered, Vespasian and Titus kept me in bonds, but obliged me to attend them continually. Afterwards I was set at liberty, and accompanied Titus when he came from Alexandria to the siege of Jerusalem. During this time nothing was done that escaped my knowledge. What happened in the Roman camp I saw, and wrote down carefully as to the information the deserters brought out of the city, I was the only man that understood it. Afterwards I got leisure at Rome; and when all my materials were prepared, I procured the help of one to assist me in writing Greek. — Thus I composed the history of those transactions, and I appealed both to Titus and Vespasian for the truth of it; to which also Julius Archelaus, Herod, and king Agrippa, bore their testimony."

All remark here is needless; but it should not be forgotten, that Josephus was a Jew, obstinately attached to his religion; and that, although he has circumstantially related every remarkable event of that period, he seems studiously to have avoided such as had any reference to JESUS CHRIST, whose history, and even the genuineness of this is disputed, he sums up in about twelve lines. No one, *therefore, can reasonably entertain a. suspicion, that the service he has rendered to Christianity, by his narrative of the transactions of the Jewish war, was at all the effect of design. The fidelity of Josephus, as an historian, is, indeed, universally admitted; and Scaliger even affirms, that, not only in the affairs of the Jews, but in those of foreign nations also, he deserves more credit than all the Greek and Roman writers put together. (13)*

Nor is the peculiar character of Titus, the chief commander in this war, unworthy of our particular regard. Vespasian, his father, had risen out of obscurity and was elected emperor, contrary to his avowed inclination, about the commencement of the conflict; and thus the chief command devolved upon Titus, the most unlikely man throughout the Roman armies to become a scourge to Jerusalem. He was eminently distinguished for his great tenderness and humanity, which he displayed in a variety, of instances during the siege. He repeatedly made pacific overtures to the Jews, and deeply lamented the infatuation that rejected them. In short, he did everything which a military commander could do, to spare them, and to preserve their city and temple, but without effect. Thus was the will of God accomplished by the agency, although contrary to the wish, of Titus; and his predicted interposition, to punish his rebellious and apostate people, in this way rendered more conspicuously evident.

The history of the Jews, subsequently to the time of Josephus (13) still further corroborates the truth of our SAVIOUR'S prophecies concerning that oppressed and persecuted people. Into this inquiry, however, the limits of the present essay will not allow us to enter particularly. Our LORD foretold, generally, that they should "fall by the edge of the-sword, and be led away captive into all nations; and that Jerusalem should be trodden down of the Gentiles, until the times of the Gentiles should be fulfilled" (Luke xxi. 24) and these predictions may be regarded as a faithful epitome of the circumstances of the Jews and also of their city, from the period in which it was delivered, down even to our own times.

In order to demonstrate the accomplishment of these predictions, we appeal, therefore, to universal history, and to every country under heaven.

"In the reign of Adrian," say Bishop Newton," nine hundred and eighty-five of their best towns were sacked and demolished, five hundred and eighty thousand men fell by the sword, in battle, besides an infinite multitude who perished by, famine, and sickness, and fire; so that Judea was depopulated, and an almost

incredible number of every age and of each sex, were sold like horses and dispersed over the face of the earth-" (Newton,, vol. I, page xviii) The war which gave rise to these calamities happened about forty-four years after the destruction of Jerusalem; during which time the Jews had greatly multiplied in Judea. About fifty years after the latter event, Ælius Adrian built a new city on Mount Calvary, and called it Ælia, after his own name; but no Jew was suffered to come near it. He placed in it a heathen colony, and erected a temple to Jupiter Capitolinus, on the ruins of the temple of JEHOVAH. — This event contributed greatly to provoke the sanguinary war to which we have just alluded.

The Jews afterwards burnt the new city; which Adrian, however, rebuilt, and re-established the colony. In contempt of the Jews, he ordered a marble statue of a sow to be placed over its principal gate, prohibited them entering the city under pain of death, and forbad them even to look at it from a distance. He also ordered fairs to be held annually for the sale of captive Jews, and banished such as dwelt in Canaan into Egypt. Constantine greatly improved the city, and restored to it the name of Jerusalem, but still he did not permit the Jews to dwell there. To punish an attempt to recover the possession of their capital, he ordered their ears to be cut off, their bodies to be marked as rebels, and dispersed them through all the provinces of the empire as vagabonds and slaves.

Jovian having revived the severe edicts of Adrian, which Julian had suspended, the wretched Jews even bribed the soldiers with money, for the privilege only of beholding the sacred ruins of their city and temple, and weeping over them, which they were peculiarly solicitous to do on the anniversary of that memorable day, on which they were taken and destroyed by the Romans. In short, during every successive age and in all nations, this ill-fated people have been constantly persecuted, enslaved, contemned, harassed, and oppressed; banished from one country to another, and abused in all; while countless multitudes have, at different periods, been barbarously massacred, particularly in Persia, Syria, Palestine, and Egypt; and in Germany, Hungary,, France, and Spain.

The undisputed facts are, that Jerusalem has not since been in possession of the Jews, but has been successively occupied by the Romans, Arabic Saracens, Franks, and lastly by the Turks (George Peter Holford wrote this in 1805), who now possess it. It has never regained its former distinction and prosperity. It has always been trodden down. The eagles of idolatrous Rome, the crescent of Mahomet, and' the banner of Popery, have by turns been displayed amidst the ruins of the sanctuary; and a Mahomedan mosque, to the extent of a mile in circumference, now covers the spot where the Temple formerly stood. — The territory of Judea, then one of the most fertile countries on the globe, has for more than seventeen hundred years continued a desolate waste."

Addendum F – Extra Evidential Resources

What Were the Signs of Jerusalem's Destruction,

and What are the Signs of Christ's Second Coming?

While there are hard eschatological questions, the above questions are easy to answer. Jesus was perfectly clear that many signs would be given before 70 A.D.

Long before the 70 A.D. slaughter, thousands of people were reading the circulated books that would become the New Testament Scriptures. If we deny this fact, we might just as well deny that Caesar ever issued a decree that the whole Roman world should be registered for a census. We might as well also deny that Joseph and Mary ever went to Bethlehem to be registered and conclude that Christ was never born. It is paramount to this discussion for us to believe that circulating documents in the Roman World could be done as effectively, although more slowly, as circulating a document over the World Wide Web today. The New Testament documents were circulated throughout the Roman Empire with the same speed as a decree that Caesar Augustus sent out for the entire Roman world to be registered (Lk 2:1). We must not underestimate the scientific advancements of that time.

The New Testament documents had to be completed before 70 A.D. in order for those early Christian disciples living in Jerusalem to read and then heed the Scriptural warnings during the Roman siege. When believing disciples read Matthew 24, they would have been expecting the abomination of desolation when they heard of false christs (Mt 24:5), wars (vs. 6), famines and earthquakes (vs. 7), martyrdom and hatred for the Apostles and disciples (vs. 9), apostasy (vs. 10), deception (vs. 11), and spiritual coldness (vs. 12), but the Gospel is preached to the whole world (vs. 14 with Col 1:6). If we believe it took as long as 300 years to get the Gospel to the world, then we are placing more faith in Caesar Augustus than in Christ and His Spirit.

The question is asked, "How can some future abomination of desolation be expected when the disciples of Jesus Christ already saw it?" When the disciples *saw* the abomination of Roman idolaters profaning the sacred things of God and erecting images of Jupiter in defiance of God, they remembered the words of Christ! They saw the desolation that Rome was placing upon everything the Jews built. *Indeed, they had to read about it before they saw it happen.* How could they read it if the Roman religion had not canonized it until 325 A.D. at the Council of Nicaea? It is practically atheism to conclude that the Bible was not completed until the 4th Century. It is also amateurish to conclude that the Bible was not completed until 96 A.D. because this date lacks evidence. Believing the 96 A.D. date is to believe hearsay unsupported by evidence, as we have already shown in this Commentary's introduction.

The circulation of the New Testament books was done when Peter was alive. Peter refers to all Paul's writings (2Pe 3: 15,16), as well as to the rest of Scripture. Jude says remember what the Apostles of Jesus Christ foretold (Jude 17). The New Testament provides us more evidence that the early Christians possessed the original manuscripts of Apostolic writings at least 10 years before Jerusalem's destruction. The supposed canonization at Nicaea in 325 A.D. was really nothing more than recognition of New Testament books that had been circulating among the Christians since the days of the Apostles.

The disciples did flee to the mountains of Judea (Mt 24:16). Those who dwelt in the shade of the housetop ran down into the main storage rooms of the house to gather up what belongings they could take with them (vs. 17). They pitied the pregnant mothers and those who nursed babies because they would have a hard time in making haste (vs. 19). They prayed that the flight was not in winter (It was not.) and not on a Sabbath because the locked gates would have barred their escape (Ne 13: 19). Jewish authorities would have prevented their escape. Such an escape would also have violated the distance a person could travel on a Sabbath (Mt 24: 20) without violating the Jewish religious law.

As Christian, Jews looked back on the holocaust in Jerusalem, just as Lot did upon the smoke of Sodom, and as they hurried toward the safety of Pella, these Christians trembled at the greatest tribulation they had ever seen or heard. Although their escape would be the greatest *escape plot* in history, it was as understandable and expeditious as a person following a road map today. There were signs at every corner. If Christians did not escape the slaughter and destruction of the Roman armies, it was because they did not read their Bibles, or take its warnings seriously. Eusebius, as is recorded elsewhere in this book, documents that not one Christian Jew perished in the Desolation. They not only read Matthew's account of 70 A.D.; they also read Luke's account! They possessed copies of New Testament writings during this time. When Jesus spoke, they did not have copies of the New Testament. However, by 70 A.D., they had all of the apostolic writings.

Luke's insight into Jesus' prophecy is even clearer. He told the disciples that the end would not come immediately upon the arrival of false christs (Lk 21:9). There will be earthquakes, wars and famines, terrors and signs in the heavens (vs. 10, 11 with Ac 2:19), and Apostolic persecution (vs. 12). There was apostolic infallibility in preaching (vs.12-15), betrayal of family members (vs. 16, 17), divine protection (vs. 18), perseverance (vs. 19), and the *sight* of Jerusalem surrounded by armies.

Jesus adds this break in the discourse: "Then recognize that the abomination of desolation is within reach" (vs. 20); they who were in the area fled to the mountains; those in the city ran out of it; and those in the countryside did not enter it (vs. 21) because the things they escaped were the days of God's vengeance for murdering His Son and rejecting the Gospel of mercy and pardon. Luke follows Matthew's order closely in Luke 21: 24 where he adds, in effect,

"They would fall by the sword (over a million of them according to the combined estimates of Josephus and Eusebius) and will be led captive into all nations (hundreds of thousands were taken as slaves to other nations, Egypt in particular), and Jerusalem will be trampled underfoot of the Gentiles (Rome, and now Islam have placed their

feet of authority on the Old Jerusalem grounds right to the present) and will continue to do so until the last Gentile is saved."

The completely delicate fabric of Pre-Millennialism rests upon the flimsy proposition that Judaism has always existed since the formation of the tribe of Judah. It is imperative for Pre-Millenialists to judicially prove the proposition that there has been a continuous, successive line of descendants. They need to prove just as they did in Ezra (Ezr 8:1-14, 9:1-4, 9: 7, 8, 12, 14, 10: 2, 10:10, 16, 17) that they are pure blood descendants of Judah. It will not do for some man or woman to step out in 2020 A.D. and say, "I am a Jew." Men or women are expected to have legal documents in keeping with the genealogies that were kept by the Old Testament scribes in such a fastidious manner. It will not do, as Warner said in The Doughty – Warner Debate, "When Christ comes He will create a Jewish race."[130]

It will not do for them to trace the genealogy back a few years on one side of the family. They must trace it back beyond 70 A.D., back beyond the Diaspora, all the way to Genesis 38:6 and 49:10. Furthermore, the record must be as authentic and accurate as the most famous seed of Judah, whose genealogy is recorded in Matthew 1:1-17 and Luke 3:23-38. In addition, the genealogy must not be merely a record of one person, or one family, it must be the genealogies of every member of the entire nation of Judaism.

These are not rules made up arbitrarily; they are predicated upon and expected requirements set forth in the Old Testament, in various Scriptures such as Ezra, Chapters 9 and 10). If such a nation could not be found after the dispersion, and certainly not after the Romans destroyed the temple administration and records in 70 A.D., how on Earth are they to be found in 2020 A.D.? If such legal, notarized documents cannot be found, than the whole millennial scheme collapses under its own weight. The millennial expectation of a restoration of physical, genealogical Judaism in the "no one knows when future" is a do-or-die prerequisite to whether this system is truth or a lie.

Millennialism teaches that because the Jewish nation did not except the Lord Jesus Christ as King, the Lord postponed the Kingdom until His Second Coming when Jews will be converted to Him, end-masse. If this is a false doctrine, Millennialism, in its totality, will collapse. In the Doughty-Warner Debate at James Madison University, April 2011, Tim Warner admitted that since 70 A.D., no individual could claim Jewish ancestry. Rather than give up his Pre-Millennialism because there would be no authentic Jews alive when Christ comes, Warner believes that Christ will create a Jewish nation to worship Him when He comes (See *www.google.com*: Doughty-Warner Debate.).

The Jewish holocaust in Germany is one of the saddest examples of human genocide in history. But a good historian is neither governed by religious information that teaches that currently there is an authentic Jewish nation descended from the tribe of Judah nor by emotion. The beautiful race of Chazars or Khazars "call themselves Jews," but they are actually Caucasians not of "Shem" (See Arthur Koestler's *The Thirteenth Tribe*.). Hitler's main reason for ordering the Jewish genocide was his insane jealousy of their industrious spirit to be able to control and drive the German economy through their amazing corporate and industrial skills. (See Topyas.com: 10 Reasons Why Hitler Hated the Jews. Three of the reasons concerned Jewish economic determinism and control.) Rational souls, and especially Christians, have a profound love for those "who call themselves Jews" today, but it is not because they are a biblically prophesied people…it is because Christ laid down His life for them.

We readers of Matthew, Chapter 24; Luke, Chapter 21; and Mark, Chapter 13, should have no difficulty differentiating between references to the end of Judaism in 70 A.D. and references to the end of the known world. Matthew 24:18 records how easy it is to understand *the abomination of desolation* (24:4-28) that took place in "those days" (24:39). "Signs" accompanied the abomination (24:24). It was called "these days," days of vengeance, in which "*all things*" written (Dt 28-31) were fulfilled (Lk 21:22). Luke 21:23-24 does not say they will fall by machine gun bullets, missiles, and bombs, but by the sword. He does not say, "Pray that your flight not be during the Super Bowl or Mardi Gras." The abomination entailed a Jewish national Sabbath holiday.

Christ's coming is called "that day" (Mt 24:36) and "the sign" (24:30). When it took place, it was "as it was in the days of Noah" (24: 26-37), with "no signs." Christ's statements are spoken in prospect of His Second Coming as if it had already taken place. This type of statement is called a "prolepsis" because it is anticipating and answering in advance. Just as nothing was left of the Noachian world after the flood, so nothing was left of the Jewish Nation after 70 A.D., and nothing will be left of today's world after Christ's Coming. All that was left for the Jew was condemnation to Hell (Mt 23:33), and the next event of final judgment for them will be to see with eyes of bodies resurrected unto damnation (Mt 23: 39). On bended knees, they will cry, "Blessed is He who comes in the name of the Lord." Inadvertently, my debating opponent, Tim Warner, was correct in a far-fetched sense. Christ will re-create the nation of Jews that cursed and hated Him 2,000 year ago by resurrecting them from Hades and along with all nations and peoples of all time to be judged by Him who had been their savior. In addition to those who will bow reverently before Him, those who cursed Him will also bow, saying, "Blessed is He who comes in the Name of the Lord." So Paul says, "Every knee will bow and every tongue will confess" (Php 2:10, 11), but it will be too late; none of them will escape the Gehenna Fire (Mt 23:33).

Most of what God directed Paul to write in Romans 1 and 2 are serious indictments against the Jews. These charges are so serious that the only verdict the Judge of the Universe could render is capital punishment. Another verdict to be rendered for that final day is how Muslims and Islamic Arabs can hate a race of people that were "desolate" from 70 A.D. to the present? God knows they really hate Caucasians who call themselves Jews (Rev 3:9). If Muslims really understood what happened in 70 A.D., they would bow down and worship the Christ whose blood was on Jewish hands for 40-years of longsuffering and patient preaching of the Gospel before Jerusalem's destruction.

There is a hypothesis that states that "Allah" is a derivative of the Hebrew, uni-plural "Elohim" which is literally translated "Gods," as in "In the beginning Gods created the heavens and the earth" (Ge 1:1) (www.plim.org/1Allah: Is the Word Allah Similar to Elohim?, www.wikipedia.org: Allah). There is another hyposthesis stating that the Meccans had a heathen worship including the worship of their god, Allah, centuries before Mohammed was born. It is possible that both hypotheses are correct.

The first hypothesis shows that sometime in history, the word Allah became a corrupted derivation of the name Elohim. The second hypothesis reveals that name Allah was being used both in Mecca and the Middle East long before Mohammed was born (www.bible.com/islam-allah-pre-islamic-origin.com: The pre-Islamic origin of Allah).

There are many ways in which the true God can be supplanted in our minds through the conception of a false god in our hearts. One of the ways in which the worship can be corrupted when we worship a false god in place of the true God is by corrupting His name, such as Isis, Vishnu, Bacchus, etc. We cannot help but think of God's Word, "Although they knew God, they did not glorify Him as God nor were thankful, but became futile in their thoughts, and their foolish hearts darkened" (Ro 1:21). No discrepancy exists between the use of the uniplural Elohim since God existed as a Godhead unity, as in "He spoke the WORD – Jesus (Jn 1:1), and the "Spirit moved on the face of the deep" (Ge 1:2).

God is much greater than the NAMES we call Him, for He "Appeared to Abraham, to Isaac, and to Jacob as God almighty, but by My Name the Lord (YHWH-Yaweh) I did not make myself fully known to them" (Ex 6:3). The word YHWH means "Yah-Saves." The Godhead gave Jesus this name (Mt 1:21).

The Godhead exists as one and is greater than any name that can be given in human literature. Much fuss is made about the name, "Allah," but it is actually a corruption of the original word Elohim. Jehovah is also a corruption of Yaweh. (Concerning the use of the Tetragammaton, YHWH (Yaweh), in Scripture, most Bible translations have an explanation of how they translate the word in their preface.) This issue of how God is named is critical to certain religious groups, for instance, the Jehovah's Witnesses (JW).

When I was teaching two disciples at their home in Warren County, VA, two JW doorknockers interrupted our Bible session. They held a small book that explained how they are to convert, "the ignorant Gentiles." In the course of our discussion, the lead JW laid the book down on a chair. I glanced down at a paragraph, which I paraphrase, "If the people you are teaching are ignorant of the fact that Yaweh rather than Jehovah is the accurate interpretation of YHWH then you should speak of the authority of Jehovah. But if the listeners understand that Yaweh is the most excellent rendering of YHWH, then do not bring the subject up." I picked up the book and the JW told me, in no uncertain words, "Give the book back." I said I would after I read what I have just written. The host family was appalled that JWs have such a callous disregard for truth; they ask them to leave.

If we understood the meaning of the names of God, we will find unity in worship of the uniplural Being that exists behind the names (Jn 17:3, 20, 21). If the Apostles' writings direct the flow of our theology, we would all be caught up in the current of unity.

In the first two chapters of the Holy Scripture, in connection with the creation of the universe, God is first called Elohim (Ge 1:1-2:3). But God is also call Yaweh-Elohim (consistently translated, "Lord God") in connection with His being a potential savior of the human race (Ge 2:4-3:23).

If Muslims would realize that modern-day Pre-Millennials, which abuse Scripture by teaching Jewish supremacy, is actually a false doctrine, they might reevaluate their thinking and realize that Christ had as much love for the Arabs who are ignorant of the Lamb of God as He did for the Jews who clamored for the crucifixion of the Lamb of God. A huge obstacle to converting Muslims is the false idea that some Christians have about the Jews continuing to be God's chosen nation and favored people. Once this false theology is exposed, and Christians cease to preach it, the door to Christ's loving arms for all nations would be opened wide. They would heed the Gospel of Christ and start loving others as fellow Christians. There would be a huge worldwide revival!

Addendum G – The Biggest Fear of a Pre-Millennialist

What causes a soothsayer to cringe in fear? The answer is simple. After he interprets a verse, ask him to read the context of the Scripture before and after his proof text. Also, search for the meaning of the words in the Greek language.

We can illustrate this by using Matthew 24:36-42. Jesus said, "But of the day and hour (of the Son of Man's coming) no one knows, not even the angels of heaven, but My Father only. But as the days of Noah were, so also will the coming of the Son of Man be. For as in the days before the flood, they were eating and drinking, marrying and giving in marriage, until the day that Noah entered the ark, and did not know until the flood came and took them all away, so also will the coming of the Son of Man be. Then two men will be in the field: one will be *taken* and the other *left*. Two women will be grinding at the mill: one will be *taken* and the other *left*. Watch therefore, for you do not know what hour your Lord is coming."

Read the context of this Scripture and compare it with the Pre-Millennial secret rapture. Nothing can be as clear as the following facts found in this context.

1. Jesus is comparing His Second (and only) Coming to Noah's flood, which came unexpectedly.

2. Noah's flood ended the world of that day. The Christ's Coming will bring our present world to an end.

3. There were two groups when the world of Noah's day ended, those in the Ark that Noah had built in covenant with God and those outside the Ark. There will be two groups at Christ's Coming; they were those in His Congregation of His Covenant and those outside His Congregation. Remember, He is coming for His Bride!

4. The lost people of Noah's day were taken away (perished), and the righteous Noah and his family were saved (left).

5. The Great Separation of Christ's coming (Mt 25) has been described by the separation of the following two groups: wheat and tares (Mt

13: 24-30), and sheep and goats (Mt 25: 31-46), those virgins prepared for the Bridegroom's coming and those who are not (Mt 25: 1-13). For each of these pairs, one will be taken and the other left (The word "behind" is not even implied in Matthew 24:42.).

The key to understanding Matthew 24:36-42, which Millennialism has so badly mutilated and muddied, is to first define the Greek words para*lambiano* (taken) and *aphesis* (left). Then, perceive how they are used in this context and in scriptural context elsewhere.

One shall be "Taken"

Strong (2983) defined the root word *lambano* as "to take or get hold of." But the word In Matthew 24:40, 41 is a compound, "paralambano." Moulton's *Lexicon* renders it "To carry off." This is as opposed to another Greek word, *dechomai*, which means, "to accept or receive." On page 44 of his Concordance under the Greek Dictionary, section (Thomas Nelson Pub. -1965), Strong gives three words for *taken*, two of which ("airo" and "paralambano") are in the Matthew 24:39, 40 contexts. The three words are:

1. *Lambano*, which means, "to get hold of," is used in an active sense. This word is used when Jesus takes hold of children, or when Christians take hold of the cup to drink the Covenant Supper. The control is maintained by the one taking possession. When "para" is placed before lambano as a prefix it means to take to oneself, take charge, take possession, to acknowledge or carry off.

2. *Dechomai* (1209) is rather subjective or passive, as something is offered to someone.

3. *Airo* (138) is more violent than the other two, "to seize or take by force". This is the word used of the removal of the wicked in Noah's Flood (Mt 24:39). We remember that Jesus compares the taking of the wicked at His coming to the taking of the wicked in the days of Noah. This word is similar to the word "paralambano." Jesus looks at the taking of the wicked in Noah's flood "airo" and by using "paralambano," He compares it to the taking possession of Jewish captives, their city, temple, and nation. The Jewish Sanhedrin actually prophesied this last and final event of their long history when they

expressed fear that the Romans would take away their place and nation (Jn 11:48). They used the word "airo" to describe the "taking away" by force, captivity, and slaughter that occurred in 70 A.D. With amazing accuracy, Jesus employs the two words, "airo" and "paralambano" in the context of 1) Noah's Flood, 2) The Abomination of Desolation in 70 A.D., and 3) The end of the world.

Airo is used to describe those wicked people being taken away violently by the flood of destruction. This was their horrible judgment. Jesus then proceeds to explain in this contextual analogy that those taken away para*lambano* will deserve the same fate as those taken away in the days of Noah.

While Noah's Flood was a universal catastrophe of death and destruction, or if you prefer, "a clean break," the Destruction of Jerusalem (a national catastrophe) and the end of the world are pictured as thoroughgoing, bloody slaughters (Mt 24:28; Lk 17:37 with Rev: 14 18-20, 19:15, 17, 18).

Jesus employs a gruesome sight that is usually witnessed by ground troops in battle. The dreadful burial or removal of the dead soldiers leaves an unforgettable impression upon those who remove the cadavers. The horrific sight becomes even more horrid when they are required to place masks over their faces to partially block the stench of decaying flesh, and fight off the flesh-eating vultures that are attracted to the stench, "Where the eagles are there will the corpses be." The word in the Greek "aetos" means wind like flight (Strong's 105), and is translated "eagle" (King James Version (KJV)). Although it could certainly mean other flesh eating birds such as hawks, vultures, buzzard's, raptors or osprey, we choose to agree with the KJV scholars because aside from eating both dead and living flesh, the eagle was the prominent symbol and emblem of Empirical Rome.

Josephus tells us that the Romans not only slew the citizens of Jerusalem; they also robbed both the helpless dead and the dying of any valuables they possessed. We also remember that the Roman siege of Jerusalem lasted about six months, from April 14 to September 8, 70 A.D. Jesus said the enemy would erect an embankment around the entire city (Lk 19:43). Remember, both the Romans and Jewish zealous suffered not the bodies of the dead to be buried, but to putrefy in the sun (Book 4, Chap. 5, Sec. 3, Josephus (*Wars of The Jews*). The number, 1,000,000, is used in the historical accounts of how many people were killed in the events leading up to and during the 70 A.D slaughter. That is a lot of dead bodies!

Jesus uses the depiction of the "eagle and the carcasses" at the conclusion of the Abomination of Desolation – 70 A.D. accounts in both Matthew 24:28 and in Luke 17:37. Jesus compares His coming "Parousia" visitation in 70 A.D. as judgment upon the Jew first (Ro 2:9) and as a microcosm of His final visitation of judgment of the Greek (the whole world) in the Last Judgment (Mt 24:27). We know the word "Greek" is a figure for all humankind because it is used of world judgment in Romans 2:9, and of the salvation of glory, honor, and peace upon the Greek in Romans 2:10. Dr. Alford Marshall (*Interlinear Greek New Testament*) attempts to save us from the textual difficulty of why Paul used the word "Greek" for all humankind except Jews by translating the word "Greek" as "Gentiles." But the original word is the word "Greek" and in those days, since Alexander the Great had conquered the world and spread the Greek language and customs everywhere, the whole non-Jewish world was called "Greek."

Thus, the last vision the lost Jewish nation would have had on Earth was either the eagles gathering to devour flesh, or the image of an eagle on the helmet, spear, sword, or shield of the Roman soldier who was about to thrust a missile through their wounded Jewish bodies. The eagles would have swooped down upon the bodies of the Jews first in 70 AD., and if we Gentiles reject Christ, apocalyptically speaking, there will be something like, but far worse happening to us when, "I saw an angel standing in the sun; and he cried with a loud voice, saying to all the fowls that fly in the midst of heaven, 'Come and gather yourselves together unto the supper of the great God!'" (Re 19:17).

The historical image of how Jesus describes the end of the world, past and future, and the end of Judaism is not a very pretty scene, but this is THE JUDGMENT OF ALMIGHTY GOD. It is called "the cup of the wine of His wrath" and "fury undiluted." This means God mixes absolutely no MERCY in with the totality of His WRATH. We must not forget that while we know God NOW as unlimited in His love and mercy toward us through Jesus Christ, we must also remember that the same BOOK that teaches His MERCY teaches His unlimited WRATH toward those who reject HIS PROPITIOUS CHRIST, and carelessly come before Him in judgment despising His love, mercy, and longsuffering (Ro 1:18, 32, 2:3-9).

We have noticed that while Jesus answers the questions of His disciples regarding the 1) End of the Temple (Mt 24:1, 2), 2) The sign of Christ's coming at the end of the world (24:3, 29-31), and 3) The end of the age, "aiownos," (mistakenly translated "world" in Matthew 24:3).

The Old Testament Age passed away with the end "desolation" (Mt 23:38) of the Jewish generation that managed to survive until 70 A.D. (Mt 23:36 with Mt 24:14, 34). As we can see, there is a difference between the end of the world "cosmos" (1Jn 2:17) and the end "completion" of the Jewish generation or Old Testament Age. When we exegete a verse we must look up the words of the context. For instance the words "end of the world" are used in Hebrews 9:26 (KJV), but the actual Greek word is "aionown," which refers to the end of the Old Testament ages (The Old Testament also included the Patriarchal Age (He 1:1-3).). Jesus emphasized that the "generation" (genea) of Jews living in His day was the last of the age of legitimate Jews to exist on Earth. At the Doughty-Warner Debate (James Madison University), Warner used a common argument of Millennial theology that "generation" is a race of people. The rebuttal to this argument was given from New Testament Scripture in which the word, "generation," is used approximately 20 times in reference to the generation of Jews living in Jesus' day (See Mt 23: 36; Mk 13: 28-30.).

Let us read for ourselves the not so flattering descriptions divinely given to describe that generation (Mt 3:7, 12:34, 39, 41, 42, 45, 16:4, 17:17, 23:33, 36, 24:34; Mk 8:12, 38, 9:19, 13:30; Lk 9:41, 11: 29, 11:31, 32, 11:50:51, 16:8, 17:25, 21:32; Acts 2:40). Notice the words "vipers," "perverse," "faithless," "adulterous," "sinful," and, "untoward" used in the above texts to describe the generation of Jews who despised God and His Son. The worst judgment ever pronounced up to that time was, "All of the innocent blood ever shed since the beginning of the world was required of THIS GENERATION" (Lk 11:50).

Thus, Jesus' disciples knew that something terrible would befall the END of The Jewish Age of their day. It was the END of their world. But it was the beginning of the New Testament Dispensation of Grace (Ep 3:2). We like the word DISPENSATION because it means "the Rule of the House of Christ" (He 3:1-6). This rule is the "dispensation of the Gospel" (1Co 9:17), "dispensation of the fullness of time" (Ep 1:10), or "Dispensation of God" (Col 1:25). The word is actually "oikonomia" (the administration, dispensation of a household).

Consequently, just as The Patriarchal Age came to a violent end (in a worldwide deluge), so the Jewish age would come to a violent end "Where the eagles (carrion flesh eating birds are gathered), so shall the carcasses be." This is plain enough for even the amateur reader to understand. This means that being taken was bad for those of Noah's day; it was bad for those taken by the Romans; and being *taken* is likewise going to be bad for those at Christ's Coming. This contextual logic should be easy to follow. But such a contextual interpretation terrorizes the soothsayer.

Had Christ wanted His reader to interpret being *taken* in a favorable light in reference to those who, in the words of End Time Fiction, will be secretly *snatched up,* He would have used the more gentle expression *dechomai,* or taking those who offer themselves. This is why the translation "receive" is better than the word *dechoma.* However, those *taken* in Matthew 24:40 and Luke 17:35 are actively seized without a choice.

As mentioned previously, the actual word used in both Matthew 24:40, 41 and Luke 17:35, 36 is *paralambano. The root word is lambano,* and Vine adds this note on page 938 of his *Expository Dictionary,*

> "There is a certain distinction between *lambano* and *dechomai* (more pronounced in the earlier classical use), in that in many instances *lambano* indicates a self-prompted taking, whereas *dechomai* more frequently indicates "a welcoming or an appropriate reception." Vine cites the illustrious Grimm and Thayer as his references.

If the Savior wanted to convey the thought that "being *taken*" was a welcoming and appropriate response to His secret coming to take away souls that are just waiting to receive Him, why did He not use the proper grammatical word *dechomai*? This word would fit perfectly the context of a neat, tidy, secret rapture.

It is true that *paralambiano* can be used for Christ's coming to receive His disciples (Jn 14:3). But Christ is not referring to rapture. Christ came in the Holy Spirit on the Day of Pentecost (14:17), and The Holy Spirit entered them (Ac 2:38). We should study the context of John 14:19, 20, and 28 to see how Christ comes to us both now, and then will come to us in the end. *Paralambiano* is also used to describe Joseph's taking Mary due to a divine command from God (Mt 1:20). However, the context in this passage does not justify the usage given above. Mary, for instance, was told by the angel to place herself at the disposal of her future husband, Joseph.

The context of Matthew 24: 39, 40 is that the *"ones taken"* are in contrast to the *"one's left."* We shall study the meaning of the word "left" and the way it is used in context later. Our correct understanding is that whoever is taking these lost people (perhaps the righteous angels) is taking them under absolute control, not as a welcoming reception. Just because scholars teach and assume that Christ was secretly taking the whole church in this context does not make it true for the following reasons:

1. The text does not say the *congregation is taken* and the lost are left. It says *one* shall be taken. When the enemy takes prisoners to the slaughter, they take them one by one.

2. The text does not say it will be a *secret coming*. The ones taken away knew perfectly well what happened to Noah and his household. There was nothing secret about it. The foolish virgins of the next chapter (Mt 25) knew what happened to the other five virgins. They even ask, "Give us of your oil for our lamps have gone out" (25:8).

3. In that fatal, final day, the virgins even conversed among each other while the final hour of world history was in process, "The wise answered, 'not so, lest there not be enough for us and you.'" (25:9)

4. The foolish virgins banged on the door, just as, no doubt the people of Noah's day, crying, "Lord, open to us," but He answered and said, "Truly I say to you, I know you not!" (25:11,12)

Nothing in this context suggests that this is Christ's next to last coming, His secret coming before a tribulation, a coming before He comes to reign on Earth for 1,000 years, a next to His last coming, or a third and final coming. Christ's coming was no secret to those who were "taken"; neither was it a secret to those who were "left."

Why are soothsayers terrorized when held to contextual accountability? It is like pronouncing a death sentence to their theological interpretations of end-time mania. They will either be driven to wisdom or justified by their reasoning, or they will be driven mad.

Although we have been vigorously defending the integrity of the word "paralambano," we need to analyze the root word "lambano" again. *Analytical Greek Lexicon*, by Zondervan Pub, p. 246, gives the various ways this word "lambano" is used, "To take hold, take up; take in hand, to seize, to catch, to take a wife (such as Joseph took Mary), and to take counsel. It is used in a good sense, to be reconciled (Ro 5:11) and in a bad sense, to be condemned or punished (Mk 12:40)."

Dr. Harold K. Moulton's excellent work gives the actual Greek compound word "paralambano" on page 304, and it translates the word "taken" in Matthew 24:40, and Luke 17:34 as meaning, "to be carried off." Dr. Moulton cites Luke 17:34, 35, and 36 where the Lord says of those in bed, "One shall be carried off" and those grinding together, "and one shall be carried off," and those in the field, "and one shall be carried off." This makes sense in the context of the question His disciples ask, "Where Lord?" (Lk 17: 37). The context dictates that the question concerns not those who are "left," but those who are "paralambano" or "taken away." The word "para" means "from the vicinity or proximity" and "lambano" means "to take." The Disciples wanted to know where the ones who were carried off would be taken. The Lord's answer confirms this thought, "Wherever the body (carcass) is, there will the eagles be gathered together!" (Mt 24: 28)

The *koine* Greek, the language of the New Testament, is celebrated for how it depicts "word pictures." It is possible that the picture behind the word can depict in context the taking of a person who is pleased with being brought under the control of the apprehender. But the "taking" at Christ's Coming is not the taking of a willing accomplice. The horrible fact is that there is nothing good about "being taken." We have listened to modern-day religious leaders speaks of this "being taken" as the rapture. But no *rapture* can be found in the Matthew and Luke texts. There is only a taking away to death and eternal destruction and a release from such for those who are left. No one in their right mind would welcome being taken by force, slaughtered, and left in a field to be eaten by buzzards.

Because of the gross unfamiliarity with the subjects of history, context, and syntax, we must revisit some of the thoughts that emerged from Christ's stern warnings to His Disciples in frequent lectures regarding the end of the Jewish Age and of the World, and especially the Olivet Discourse (Matthew, Chapter 24; Mark, Chapter 13; and Luke, Chapter 21). As mentioned previously, the figure of the eagle is a symbol of the insignia of the Roman armies who executed upon the Jews their final desolation in 70 A.D. Those who were taken by the Romans were literally slaughtered. Their bodies and blood presented a spectacle for the carrion vultures or eagles. This same illustration is presented in the end of the Gentile world where the apocalyptic announcement is made to the birds of prey figuratively, "Come and gather yourselves together for the supper of the great God, that you may eat the flesh of kings..." (Rev 19:17, 18).

A Comparison of the End of the Jewish and Gentile World

We should expect Jesus to compare the end of the Jew and Gentile worlds with the reference to the eagles of prey when He is answering His disciples because they had asked Him previously to explain the end of the Jewish Temple and the end of the world (Mt 24:1-4 with Lk 21:7)

Vine addresses the word lambano, *"taken,"* (to lay hold of) on page 1127 of his *Expository Dictionary*. He says it is used metaphorically for fear, as in taking hold of people. It is used when a sinful occasion requires taking hold of a corruptible source of action (Ro 7:8, 11), when the power of temptation takes hold (1Co 10:13), and when taking peace from the Earth (Rev 6:4). Vine has *apolambano* as to "shut up," *epilambano* "to take in hold," and *katalambano,* "to lay hold." He cites Matthew 27:27 as the *paralambano* taking of Christ by the officers for scourging and to crucifixion (Jn 19:16). In addition, *proslambano*, (to take to oneself), can be used for good purposes (Ac 18:26) or bad purposes (17:5).

One thing is known for sure, the compound word "paralambano" in our text "one shall be taken" is not *apolambano*, which means "to take up." If Christ intended the word to have a favorable meaning of saints being taken up in a secret snatch, He would have used good grammar. If Jesus wanted us to think that those "taken" are taken up in a future so-called "rapture," the proper grammatical word would be *analambano,* not the word in Matthew 24: 40-41, *paralambano* (to take under control).

Yes, we are belaboring this point because week after week a soothsayer, predicting a future "rapture" is rubbing an unbiblical foreign element in our faces. But in the immediate context of Jesus and His Disciples, they were expecting those "taken" to be taken somewhere in the immediate future, not 2,000 years or so later. The Disciples said, "Where Lord?" (Lk 17: 37). The Disciples expected those who did not heed Christ's warnings to be "taken" into the custody of damnation, and their judgment would correspond to the Abomination of Desolation in their country of Judaea (Mt 24:16), when people lived on housetops for summertime coolness (24: 17), when people did field work (24:18), when women breastfed children (24:19), when people were immobilized by winter weather (24:20), when those days were shortened (24:22); and Jesus told them before it happened (24:25).

If the above scholars are not sufficient to make the case, let us introduce another, George Ricker Berry. The first four definitions of paralambano given by Berry are:

> "To take as in the hand (Mt 14:19), to claim (Lk 19:12), to take by force-seize (Mt 21:35), to take away by violence or fraud (Mt 5:40)" (*Interlinear Greek New Testament* by George Ricker Berry, p. 59)

Contrary to the way in which modern soothsayers use "paralambano" to describe the saved "being taken" in a secret so called *rapture*, this word is frequently used to describe bad things happening to those being taken. For instance, it is used when Christ is being taken to judgment. Pilate said, "Take Him!" (*Lambano* – Jn 18:31), and they took Him (*sunlambano*), with swords and staves (Mt 26:55), to crucify him (Jn 19:16). Their behavior is not surprising because they had sought full authority to take Jesus under their power to execute their carnal wrath upon Him a few years earlier in John 7:3-32. The word "take" in this connection means to arrest. They *took* (*paralambano*) Jesus into the Judgment Court (Mt 27:27).

The 'under rower' Slaves took Him Away

Another interesting word, *huperetes*, is used for the officers who took Christ to His execution site (Mt 26:58; Mk 14:65). These officers "Buffeted him and smote him with the palms of their hand." The word means "under rower slaves" and refers to slaves who were the worst convicts. They were given the worst assignments with three tiers of oarsmen on the bottom tier of Roman galley ships, where the oars were the shortest and pulled the hardest.

Later, the word *under rower* became associated with the unpleasant task of torturing without mercy and bringing the condemned prisoner to judgment. The word referred to the harshest and brutal officials of the Jewish and Roman law enforcement. They showed no mercy on those unfortunate enough to be arrested by them. Only the insensitive and unsophisticated would desire such an assignment. They had authority to torture their prisoners as they saw fit. When Pilate said, "Take Him," he was releasing his prisoner to the authority, fury, and evil judgment of the *under rowers*.

Christians also are called upon to be *under rowers*. They are not seen, and they do not consider suffering for the betterment of the Ship of Zion to be beneath their dignity. Mark was called an *under rower* minister to Paul and Barnabas, which meant that he was in charge of some very difficult assignments. This may be why he left Paul and Barnabas in the middle of the missionary journey. Later, he was restored (Ac 13:5 with 2Ti 4:11).

The 'under rowers' of the Lord

Strangely enough, this word *huperetes* is used to describe the holy angels who are sent to reap the world of all unbelievers. Jesus said, "If my Kingdom were of this world, then my "hupretes," *under rowers,* "hupo" (under) "eresso" (oarsmen) would fight that I should not be delivered to the Jews" (Jn 18:36).

The Roman and Jewish *under rowers* were about to beat Jesus to a bloody pulp. In His heart, Jesus knew that He had *under rowers* who would serve Him and fight for Him as well. These *under rowers* are no doubt the angels, for Jesus said He could have called twelve legions of angels to His rescue (Mt 26: 53). The angels are called *under rowers* in their ministry of executing God's justice upon the Earth.

> "The Son of Man shall send forth His angels, and they shall gather out of His Kingdom all things that offend, and them who do Iniquity, and shall cast them into the furnace of fire..." (Mt 13:41, 42)

The order is given in Matthew 13:30, "first gather the (wicked) tares," and in 13:43, "and then (after the tares), the righteous shall shine forth as the sun in the Kingdom of their Father."

This order of first, the "tares," and then, "the righteous," compares exactly to the understanding of the wicked being taken away first in Noah's Day (Mt 24:39), with the wicked field worker taken first (24:40). Those instructed to take them are the angels; Christ's *under rowers* take the wicked tares first. They will "gather out" all who offend God's moral universe because they were offensive to His Kingdom. The similarity between "gather out" and "taken" is not coincidental. Like "*under rower*" slaves, the Holy Angels will participate in the most demanding and rigorous work ever known since Calvary. They will assist in the execution of God's wrath upon the world. No one has a reason to believe that those who will take the wicked away are not God's angels.

As a propitious offering for the sin of the world, Christ was subject to the wrath of the evillest men (slavish, undisciplined, and unscrupulous, under rowing vassals to the will of evil rulers), and they loved to abuse the power given them. In His undying and unyielding mercy, Christ sought to save all from the similar wrath of the good angels, for had He experienced such wrath and knew what it was like.

Christ knew of the coming wrath upon humanity. He also knew of the future power of the Holy Angels as they would execute God's wrath upon them. Christ is also the only one who ever experienced the full fury of God's wrath this side of Hell, and He dreaded what that would be like as He set His face, like flint, to the cross. When the time of that wrath would arrive, He cried out in pathetic anguish, "My God, My God why have your forsaken me?" In His divine grace, Christ desires all to escape God's wrath and His *under rower* angels. Nevertheless, the angels "will take" all who spurned Christ's grace and mercy, and rejected His New Covenant. Just as the Flood took the wicked away in Noah's Day, just as the wicked Roman soldiers took the Jewish nation away in bloody wrath, so the angels will first take away "gather out the tares of the wicked One" (Mt 13:41) those who spurned the New Covenant of Christ. Let us emphasize that the wicked "tares" are gathered FIRST (Mt 13:30).

The Other Left

The Greek word for the English phrase, "the other left," is *aphiemi*. This Greek word has several definitions, but not one lexicon authority translates it, "left behind." If the Holy Spirit intended "left behind" to be used, He would have employed the word *enkataleipo*, "leave behind," or *kataleipo*, "leave down or leave behind" (Vine's *Expository Dictionary*, p. 666). On the contrary, the word used is *aphiemi (Strongs 863)*. Several Greek scholars have commented on the use of this word.

Zondervan's *Analytical Greek Lexicon*, p. 62, reveals that *aphiemi*, which means to send away, dismiss, suffer to depart, to emit, send forth, to let alone, remit, pardon, relax, suffer to be less intense, dismiss, deliverance, is a passive form of the word for "forgiveness." Strong's *Lexicon* (863) defines aphiemi "to go or send forth." We are not surprised that the word "aphesis" (Strong's 859) is derived from aphiemi and means freedom, pardon, deliverance liberty, remission or complete forgiveness of sins. Christ used the word "aphesis" to connect the inauguration of

His New Covenant Kingdom and remission of sins at Pentecost (Lk 24:47). Most interestingly, this word "aphesis," is used in the first mention of forgiveness through the name of Christ in Acts 2:38. *Aphesis* is distinguished from *parasis* in Romans 3:25, 26 because "aphesis" promised full pardon and remission of sins. This full pardon differs from the Old Covenant in which God simply "passed over and overlooked sin temporarily."

Aphesis is the New Covenant word used on the association of the Cup of Communion Covenant with forgiveness in Matthew 26:28. The Old Testament could not give the believer *total forgiveness* of sins, so Romans 3:23 says that their sins were suspended, or passed over (Ro 3:25). This incomplete forgiveness was because Christ had not died yet.

Vine (p. 462) explains *aphesis* as –

> "Primarily to send forth, send away, and denotes besides its other meaning to forgive or remit (debts) Mt 6:12, 18:27 (completely cancelled), (sins) Matthew 9:2, 5, Acts 8:22 'the thoughts of your heart'."

What a triumph Christians enjoy in Christ Jesus. If they understand *aphesis* in its full context, then when they are immersed by Christ's mighty authority, (Ac 2:38), they will be *aphesis* forgiven, and receive the Holy Spirit as in the beginning of Christ's Kingdom at Pentecost (Ac 2:42-47). If Christ's followers are like the wise virgins, aphesis-forgiven and full of the oil of the Holy Spirit when He comes, they shall be *apheimi*, "released from punishment," in the end. Remember, the Greek words "apheimi" and "aphesis" are essentially the same. The difference is that *apheimi* means "to send forth, release or go", whereas *aphesis* means "To forgive or pardon from guilt."

Thus, in context those who were aphesis-forgiven in the beginning of their journey, at immersion, will be *aphemi* "left off" from the judgment of the world in the end. They will be left, or sent away from the judgment of those who were taken. Like Noah, the forgiven will hear the unforgiven knocking on the door and screaming. Like the wise virgins, the unforgiven will hear the Lord say to the foolish, "I do not know you" (Mt 7:23).

The Bible uses the word "know" as a Covenant term. If we are not in Christ, we do not have a covenant with Him. According to Acts 2: 36-42, we can determine easily those who are in Covenant, and those who is not. There is nothing secret about it. There will be nothing secret about those knocking on the door begging Christ to let them in on Judgment Day. If Christians are going to help those begging to be let in, Christians must teach them the Gospel of the Kingdom of Christ, now! Teaching a secret *rapture* and encouraging the false security of a second chance that is un-Biblical, creates false hope, and cannot be successful because the *rapture* is a big lie. The context of these End Times passages makes that perfectly clear.

However, the Devil hates context. He quoted Scripture out of context when he tempted the Lord, and he quotes Scripture out of context even today. Remember, a soothsayer is terrorized when we insist upon maintaining scriptural context. When Jesus told Satan, "It is written," he left Jesus alone. This is as true for Christians today as it was then.

Thus, the *left* in Matthew 24 are those who will escape judgment. How blessed are those New Covenant Christians who will not be ashamed at Christ's coming (2Ti 2:15; 1Jn 2:28). They will see those who are *taken*, incarcerated, and thrown into the furnace. God does not want those in paradise to forget what would have happened to them. It will be a fearful and awesome sight for all who foreknew that God's Grace and justice advertised this deserved fate. We do not know exactly how the Covenant Ones will react when they see the tares cast into the furnace, but when the door closes on this hostile, godless world, the door to the Golden City will also open, and all things will then become NEW!

Titus and the Romans "took away" the Jewish nation (Jn 11:48). But the Christians escaped this slaughter and desolation because they fled Jerusalem.

The context is very clear. The flood took away the wicked. The righteous Noah and his family were left. The angels will take away the wicked. The righteous will escape the terrifying eternity that every lost person faces without Christ. The righteous will then shine as the Sun in Christ's eternal Kingdom. The righteous will never forget what could have been; they will always remember what it cost Christ to save them and from what they were saved.

There is one additional thought that has a very important bearing upon this subject. Have we ever thought that we are actually saved twice? First, we consider how important REDEMPTION is to our salvation and Christian life. The word "redemption" means to purchase by paying a price. We have no problem believing that when we are washed in the blood (Ac 22:16), the blood of the Lamb purchases us. This payment had been made in behalf of our debt of guilt and sin (1Pe 1:18). We usually understand this marvelous thought, but there is another aspect to redemption that we seldom think about. When we are born again of the water and spirit (Jn 3:5), we also receive the Holy Spirit, which is the earnest of our inheritance (Eph 1:14). The word "earnest" means down payment (2Co 1: 22, 5:5). When we study the Olivet Discourse, we discover that Jesus reminded us of the universal catastrophe of The Flood for which people had 120 years of preparation from Noah's preaching. Jesus then took us to the events leading up to 70 A.D., and how, in anguish and grief, He warned the Jews of the impending disaster, "Oh Jerusalem, how often I would have gathered you under my wings as a mother hen would gather her chicks, but you would not." Then at last, He warns the whole world of the next global catastrophe at the end of time, and reminds those of us who accept His warning, "And when these things begin to come to pass, then lift up your heads, for your redemption draws nigh" (Lk 21:28).

What does this mean? Paul answers this question. As we have seen in our verse-by-verse Commentary of Revelation, we are not only immersed for our spiritual life, we are also immersed for our body (Ro 6:1-5; 1Co: 15:29). Even though we will die and go to be with Jesus, our bodies will not be resurrected until Christ comes for us. Thus, the first installment is the gift of the Holy Spirit, and the second installment is the redemption of our body (Ro 8:23). How exciting to know that even though the world will be in a panic, seeking to die a death of suicide (by rocks falling on them), rather than face the Lamb of God in judgment, yet we will lift up our faces to scan the heavens and see Him come for His Bride and know that in a few seconds our full redemption of "body, soul, and spirit" will be experienced at His coming (1Th 5:23).

Addendum H – THE END!

"Where is our great city, which, it was believed, GOD inhabited? It is altogether rooted and torn up from its foundations; and the only monument of it that remains, is the camp of its destroyers pitched amidst its relics!" (Eleazar, son of the High Priest in Jerusalem).[131]

It is a disservice to a Bible student to improperly prepare and invade a mind with a presupposition of eschatology. The most atrocious approach to a lost soul is to teach a person concerning *the end* without giving proper context. Unfortunately, many modern-day *Bible scholars* and *theological professors* attempt to captivate the world with a fairy tale ending in order to seduce our minds with a fairy tale beginning. We must study plain Scripture and understand parabolic writings before attempting to interpret the apocalyptic Scripture of Revelation.

Which end is being discussed?

When Bible scholars talk about *the end*, we must understand what end of which prophecy is being discussed. Is it the end of Israel in B.C. 722? Is it the temporary end of Judah in 586? Is it the in-between-the Testaments history of Greece and the Old Testament ending (Da 8:19-21)? Is it the end of the Old Testament Law (Ro 10:4)? Is it the last days of the Old Testament (Ac 2:17)? Is it the end of the Jewish world (Heb 9:26)? Is it an end to all things that pertained to the Old Economy (1Pe 4:7)?

When reading history, we should not be surprised to hear about the end of the Jewish world from both Daniel and Jesus. There are hundreds of Scripture references to the *end* of the completely Gentile world that shall pass away with all of its lusts of eyes, flesh, and pride of life. However, the end of the Jewish world has already come. The various designated Biblical ends are unfortunately confused with one another.

Daniel understood the end of Judaism some 500 years before it happened. Gabriel told him he would gain insight and understanding (Da 9:22). He further assured Daniel that he would give heed to the message and gain understanding of the vision. How foolish and absurd it is to abuse these prophetic verses and exhort us to look for the restoration of a Jewish dynasty on Earth in these modern days.

Daniel, in those far away years in Babylon, could easily foretell and understand the end of the earthly Jewish nation.

The end comes after Christ-Messiah is "cut off," not before.

Daniel speaks of the one Covenant-making Messiah, Jesus Christ, making a Covenant through His atoning death. This is Christ being "cut off" (Da 9:26). This refers to His death on the cross. After Christ's being "cut off," "the people of the prince" would come. Any reader of history knows this happened in 70 A.D., 40 years after Christ was "cut off." In contrast with the Messiah Prince …with a capital "P," (which is the Son of the Lord God the King) in 9:25, the translators put a small "p" on the prince of 9:26. This is Vespasian, the Caesar King, and his prince-son, Titus. Yet, all the people of this earthly prince were under the control of Christ. Thus, Titus is inconsequential to this day of Heaven's vengeance (Lk 21:22). The little prince (son of Caesar) was in the hand of the big Prince (Son of God). Truly, at this time, the Jews had no King but Caesar Vespasian, and no Prince but his son, Titus. They received their desires to have "no king but Caesar" in full as the Roman Armies, under Caesar's direction, wrecked their nation and devastated their religion.

Judaism was wiped from the earth as in a flood.

The city of Jerusalem and the sanctuary (temple) were standing in 70 A.D. and were destroyed quickly (Da 9:26). The bringing of a city to an end is compared to an overpowering flood in Isaiah 28:2. In reference to the end of Nineveh (Na 1:1), the Prophet wrote, *"But with an overflowing flood, He will make a complete end of it!" (1:8).*

Just as the flood took the world away in the days of Noah, so the Romans took Judaism away in 70 A.D. (Jn 11:48). The destroying flood was not simply a disaster that did some damage to the Jews; it was the end, "And its end will come with a flood even to the end" (Da 9:26). Rome was at war with Judaism, and "desolations (utter ruining) shall be determined" (9:26). Remember, the abomination of desolation did not happen during the last week (from Christ's immersion in 26 A.D. to Stephens's death in 33 A.D.). However, it was "determined" through Christ's prophetic messages during his 3½ year ministry prior to His death in 30 A.D.

God stood steadfastly with Judaism in great patience and long-suffering. Although He promised the Jewish people, repeatedly, that He would not destroy them, yet He also foretold of their complete destruction. Paul had Isaiah 10:21-23 in mind when he wrote Romans 11:5, *"Even so, there is at this present time a remnant according to God's gracious choice."*

Both Jesus and Paul saw the last "remnant" of true Jews. They were circumcised in heart by the "operation of faith" in Christian immersion (Col 2:12), prior to Jerusalem's destruction. Paul uses the term "at this present time" because they were the authentic Jews, including Paul himself, who were converted from 30 to 70 A.D.

> *"A remnant will return, the remnant of Jacob to almighty God, for though*
>
> *Your people, O Israel may be as the sand of the sea, only a remnant within them will return: destruction is determined, overflowing with righteousness. For a complete destruction, one that is decreed, the Lord God of hosts will execute in the midst of the whole land" (Isa 10:21-23).*

Isaiah knew that destruction from Assyria befell Israel in B.C. 722 (10:24). He also knew that destruction from Babylon would befall Judah in B.C. 586. Always, there would be a remnant that kept the faith and returned to Jerusalem after the destruction. However, Paul lived to see the "fullness" of Israel (Ro 11:12). This refers to the full number of Jews converted while the Old Testament temple was still standing. Paul told the Gentiles to have compassion upon the Christian Jews. They were a small number (a remnant) in comparison to the multitude of converted Gentiles. They were the last generation of Godly Jews who escaped the entire generation that Christ sentenced to Hell:

> *"You generation of vipers, how shall you escape the sentence of Hell?" (Mt 23:33).* (Read thoroughly the context of 2 Chronicles 7:19-22).

Concerning all of the culminating woes and curses God had pronounced upon the Jews from the time that they had built the first temple (and God knew they would be faithless and obdurate even then), until the time they cried for His crucifixion and claimed no King but Caesar, EVERY ONE OF THEM CULMINATED TOGETHER INTO ONE CURSE IN 70 A.D.!

> *"Truly I say to you, ALL THESE THINGS shall come upon this generation" (Mt 23:36).*

In this light, Paul, who understood prophecy better than any man in the world, held up the Jewish remnant of that present time as being special. They went against the tide of unbelief; they listened to Jesus, the Prophets, and Apostles. They converted to Christ-Messiah and obeyed the Gospel of the New Covenant (Ro 11: 26, 27). They later fled from Jerusalem to Pella for safety when Commander Cestius withdrew his troops from Jerusalem because they heeded the words of their Savior-

> *"And unless those days had been cut short (Cestius could have ordered the destruction immediately upon entering the city the first time, but in God's providence, he retired from the city to give the Christian Jews a chance to escape), no life would have been saved; but for the sake of the select (Christian Jews) those days shall be cut short" (Mt 24:22).*

The "remnant" Jews as contrasted with Jews "fitted for destruction"

In addition to the Gentile Christians, Paul addressed two classes of Jews in the Roman congregation. The Christian Jews existed at the "present time" in Rome, and elsewhere as a remnant. On the other hand, Paul knew the disobedient Jews were "Vessels fitted for destruction," (Ro 9:22) who existed alongside the remnant. God had protected the disobedient Jews for thousands of years. Therefore, He admonished the Gentiles to bear with them until the complete destruction that was fitted to befall them:

> *"From the standpoint of the Gospel they are enemies for your sake but from the standpoint of God's choice they are beloved for the sake of the fathers." (Ro 11: 28).*

In other words, Paul is saying,

> *"Give them a break. They are going to be destroyed. They are going to fall hard. Don't forget how hard it is for a Jew to be a 1st Century Christian. Keep preaching to them before their day comes. But don't get conceited when you see them get the full fury of punishment for their sin."*

Remember, Gentile, your day is coming next! The fullness of the Gentiles will arrive someday (Lk 21:24). Paul knew the last generation of Jews, "Fitted for destruction," were on Earth at that *present time*. A day will come very soon when the last generation of Gentiles on Earth will be called in the end of the world and that time will be called "at this present time." It will come sooner than expected if people today, who are Gentiles, die in unbelief. The day of reckoning for the Jews has already come. The day of reckoning for the Gentile is right around the corner.

The non-New Covenant Jews of the 1st Century will be resurrected from their Hadean Spirit world when Christ comes. They have been there from 70 A.D. to the present. They will be resurrected with all the Jews who have lived since Judah's sons (Ge 46:12). These Jews lived and died during the last generation of Jews in Jesus and Paul's day. They will also be resurrected with the Jews, who since they no longer had a nation or a Temple, were dispersed after 70 A.D. They will be resurrected with those of Turkish (Khazars), Spanish, Russian, German, and Asian descent that produced population centers of cultural and unauthentic Jews after the collapse of authentic Judaism in 70 A.D. They will also be resurrected with those of dispersed Israel who were scattered and lost their identity in the Gentile world. The entire multitude will bow before the King as one man, and all will exclaim in anguish and grief, "Blessed is he who comes in the name of the lord!" (Mt 23:39)

Yes, the Jew was warned repeatedly. God pined away and grieved over the rudeness of His people. He brought chastisements upon them from the Book of Judges to the Book of Malachi, but to no avail. Last of all, He sent His Son and they said,

"WE DO NOT WANT THIS MAN TO REIGN OVER US!"

It broke God's resolute, determinate promise to not make a final end of them. They had gotten by with covenant breaking for thousands of years; now the Covenant would break them entirely.

Imagine the soldiers of Titus and Cestius trotting and splashing through the streets of Jewish blood. God said the end of the Jew would come with a flood, and as one can see in Nahum 1:8, God likens the utter destruction of a nation to the devastating, catastrophic ruin of a flood. However, according to the accounts of Josephus and Eusebius, the Romans literally sloshed through streets flooded with Jewish blood. The solders desecrated the sacred altar and Ark of God. They hoisted the images of Jupiter-Capitolinus high above the desecrated altar of YHVH,

> *"Even until a complete destruction, one that is decreed is poured out upon the desolate" (Da 9: 27).*

The translators vary in the sentence construction of this verse. Some have it "poured out upon the desolate" (speaking of desolated Judaism), others have it "poured out on the one who makes desolate" (or the Jews who brought this divine judgment upon themselves).

DID THE JEWS THEMSELVES DESECRATE THE TEMPLE?

Not only did the Roman Gentiles make the Temple an abominable-desolation, but also history substantiates that the Jews themselves abominated the most holy precincts of the Temple by rushing inordinately into the most holy places and setting them on fire. The Jews were robbing each other, killing each other, and because of the extreme cruelty and debauchery, those with the Spirit of God should not describe in detail what lewd and indecent acts the Jews forced upon their fellow men, women, and children (Eph 5:12). Complete destruction was poured out upon the one who makes desolate (Da 9:27). So the Romans did not cause the desolation; the Jews themselves caused their own desolation. The Jews were desolated and also underwent desolation because of their abomination of the Temple. Yes, they brought God's wrath down on themselves.

Truly, God had decreed in prophecy, and Christ had confirmed the decree and sentence in his earthly ministry that the generation of Jews that lived from the time of Jesus and the apostles until the abomination of desolation would be the last generation of authentic Jews to ever live on planet Earth.

Many resources are available that document the events of 70 A.D. It is not just a matter of entertaining research. Jesus exclaimed,

> *"Let him who reads (of this final destruction of Judaism) understand what he is reading" (Mt 24:15).*

Jesus expects Christians to read this account of history with understanding. There is no way we can claim love and reverence for the Messiah (Prophet, Priest, and King) and not read His prophecy. A Christian should diligently search history to find the fulfillment of every word Jesus spoke. (See Addendum "E" for a description of Jerusalem by George Holford.)

It is not outlandish to say that all who do not understand the context of Jesus' prophecies, as recorded in Matthew, Chapters 23 and 24; Mark, Chapter 13; and Luke, Chapter 21, and their connection with the events of A.D. 70, disqualify themselves as reliable expositors of prophetic Scripture.

When we look at "The End," the context of the end of Judaism cannot be applied entirely to the context of the end of the world. The link between the two is in comparing God's vengeance upon the Jews in 70 A.D. and Gentiles at the end of the world. In order to properly understand the end of the world and the book of Revelation, we must understand the end of Judaism. This investigative study will begin with a verse-by-verse commentary of Matthew 23:37 through Matthew, Chapter 25.

Matthew 23:37-39: "O Jerusalem, Jerusalem, the one who kills the prophets and stones those who are sent to her! How often I wanted to gather your children together, as a hen gathers her chicks under her wings, but you were not willing! 38 See! Your house is left to you desolate; 39 for I say to you, you shall see me no more till you say, 'Blessed is He who comes in the name of the Lord!'"

Jesus begins his discourse by showing His remorse and lamenting over Jerusalem! The nation chosen to bring the messiah to the world rejected Him from their foundation until their annihilation! Let the reader understand this treacherous beginning written in 1 Samuel 8:7, 8,

> "And the Lord said to Samuel, 'Heed the voice of the people in all that they say to you; for they have not rejected you, but they have rejected me, that I should not reign over them. According to all the works which they have done since the day that I brought them up out of Egypt, even to this day — with which they have forsaken Me and served other gods — so they are doing to you also'" (NKJV).

The Godhead wanted to have a relationship with Israel and Judah. He took care of them even when they worshipped other idols. He protected them; He bought them back; and He loved them. This would be the same as children hating and rejecting their parents for loving them. What a sad story! However, God's anger has now turned to wrath, and His judgment upon the House of Israel is soon at hand. "Your house is left to you desolate!"

The next time they see Jesus will be at the judgment. They will recount their rejection of their Messiah, fall to their knees, and exclaim, "blessed is He who comes in the name of the Lord!'"

Matthew 24:1, 2: Then Jesus went out and departed from the temple, and His disciples came up to show Him the buildings of the temple. 2 And Jesus said to them, "Do you not see all these things? Assuredly, I say to you, not one stone shall be left here upon another, that shall not be thrown down."

We cannot imagine what was going through the minds of the Disciples. The Jews were ignorant and puffed up. Even though they had been taken into captivity and enslaved on five major occasions (Egyptians, Assyrians, Babylonians, Greeks, and currently, Romans), the Jews could not admit that they had been or ever were placed into captivity. When Jesus spoke to the Jews about the spiritual, they tried to carnalize His words into the physical. They sought physical food, physical blessings, physical warfare, a physical nation, and a physical King. In the Book of John, Chapter 8:31-33, the Jews gave a comical response concerning freedom,

> "Then Jesus said to those Jews who believed Him, 'If you abide in my word, you are my disciples indeed. And you shall know the truth, and the truth shall make you free.' They answered Him, 'We are Abraham's descendants, and have never been in bondage to anyone. How can you say, 'You will be made free'?"

Jesus is speaking of a spiritual truth regarding spiritual freedom, and they truly believed they had never been in physical bondage! Apparently, they had not considered their history of God's bringing them out of bondage. They never recognized that He did this because of His love and mercy. The mindset of the Jews was, "We are Abraham's descendants and have never been in bondage to anyone."

Fast forward: Just as the Jews before them, even the Apostles were still thinking of a physical kingdom. Prior to His ascension, they posed a question in Acts 1:6,

> "So when they met together, they asked him, 'Lord, are you at this time going to restore the kingdom to Israel?'"

We can only ponder what thoughts were going through their minds when Jesus said, "All of these stones will be thrown down" (Mt 24:2). We can understand the amazement and beauty of the temple when considering these parallel passages of Scripture in Mark and Luke.

> Mark 13:1, 2: then as He went out of the temple, one of His disciples said to Him, 'Teacher, see what manner of stones and what buildings are here!' And Jesus answered and said to him, "Do you see these great buildings? Not one stone shall be left upon another that shall not be thrown down."

> Luke 21:5, 6: some of his disciples were remarking about how the temple was adorned with beautiful stones and with gifts dedicated to God. But Jesus said, 'As for what you see here, the time will come when not one stone will be left on another; every one of them will be thrown down.'

The Jews thought that they and their Temple were invincible. They could not fathom the wonder, magnitude, splendor of the Temple and City of Jerusalem could be destroyed. How could such a beautiful and powerful city ever fall under the power of God? The answer is simple. Jesus said, "Your house is left to you desolate!" God no longer dwelt within the Temple, and He no longer supported Judaism. In fact, God's wrath and vengeance was getting ready to be poured out upon this City and religion like the world has not seen before, nor will ever see again until the end of the world.

They thought it could not happen to them.

They thought they would have peace, even though they walked in the dictates of their own heart (Dt 29:19). When the neighboring nations and enemies see what happens to them because their nation is turned to fire and brimstone, and their fields become a desert, the nations will say, "Why has the Lord done this to them?

And you will give the answer, 'they broke covenant'" (29:35). The Gamara, which is a section of the Talmud, cites the Roman engineer Turnus Rufus plowing the entire city so that where once the beautiful city and temple stood, nothing was left standing, not even a stone. All that was visible of the original city was a part of the wall surrounding the city.

God said twice that He would bring plague after plague until He destroyed them (Dt 28:45-48). King Jesus would slay them before His own eyes because they would not permit Him to rule over them. God told them they would utterly perish (30:18) and not prolong their stay in Palestine.

God knew all along that they would forsake His covenant.

God told Moses, that after his death, the people would play the harlot, and they would break the covenant. God's anger would be aroused, and He would forsake them, hide His face from them, and devour them (Dt 31:16, 17). God knew the inclination of their perverse behavior (31:21). Moses knew that in the latter day (A.D. 70), an evil would befall them on that day (31:29).

Jesus, the prophet, gives accurate commentary upon Moses' prophecy. Matthew, Chapter 23, should have struck terror in the hearts of the Jewish leaders because of the indictments Jesus levied against them!

1) Their false works branded them unworthy of leadership (23:4).

2) They thought their long flowing robes made them holy (23:4).

3) They loved to be seen (23:6).

4) They loved religious titles (23:7-10).

5) Precisely as the Pre-Millennialists do today, they shut up the Kingdom of Heaven to lost sinners (23:13).

6) They took religious donations from poor widows (23:14), "Devouring their houses."

7) They convert people to a philosophy that condemns them to Hell (23:15), and like the Pre-Millennial philosophy, it was a Jew first, (Jewish supremacy); all others last, philosophy.

8) They swore by the gold of the Temple. Instead of a sacred Temple the place became a bank. The Romans were surprised to find hidden gold in the temple, and for this reason, they leveled it to fetch every piece (23:16, 17). They forsook their parents by saying and paying "Corban."

9) They taught that a person could swear by the sacred altar but not by the gift they so greedily coveted (23:18, 19).

10) They placed an emphasis on tithing and trivialized the idea of showing judgment, mercy, and faith (23:23).

11) They were immaculately clean in house and body, but inwardly they were filthy (23:24, 25).

12) They appeared righteous outwardly, but inward they were dead and deathly (23:26, 27).

13) They gave lip service to the greatness of the Old Testament prophets, but if they were to return to Earth, these leaders would have them put to death (23:29-31).

14) Now, says Jesus in effect, "You are going to kill me!" In doing so you are going to fill up, finish, and exceed the transgression measure of your fathers (Da 9:24 with 1Th 2:15, 16).

15) That generation of vipers could not escape the damnation of Hell (Mt 23:33).

16) Even after they killed Christ, He would send His Loving Apostles, compassionate evangelists, and ministers of the New Testament. They also killed, imprisoned, scourged, and persecuted them. It would take a little while for them to *fill up* the measure of such ungodly iniquity, but Christ said they would fill it to the full and finish transgressing against God Most High and His Lamb. In fact, it would be the climax to all of the blood that was shed from Abel, to the last holy man they murdered, Zacharias. They actually murdered him within the holy precincts of the Temple. Since they sinned to the maximum degree by murdering God's Son and by rejecting the mercy He extended to them when they murdered the executors and ministers of the Holy

New Covenant, they brought upon their own heads the guilt of all the holy blood their father's drank down throughout the ages (23:35). There could be no mistake. Jesus assured them that this was the terminal, last generation of Jews for all God's judgments would descend upon that generation of Jews to whom Jesus was speaking (Mt 23:36).

17) Jesus still loved them, even unto the end (23:37), but they would not accept God's way. What was formerly God's house, and later, Jesus called it, "My house," has now become "your house"; and it is about to become desolate, "nothing" (23:38).

18) Unlike Pharaoh, who said, "I will not see the face of Moses again" (Ex 10:28, 29), this would not be the end of the Jews' seeing Jesus. The last generation of the Tribe of Judah would become desolate, dispersed, and die disinherited deaths and go to Hades. They would be incarcerated in that spirit world until Jesus returns. And when they look upon Him whom they pierced, they will recognize Him as the same holy, righteous child of God whom He was when He stood before them on that fateful day in Anno Domini 30, and with the last sermon of Matthew, Chapter 23, still fresh in their minds, they will cry the lamentable, woeful refrain that they should have verbalized then, "Blessed is He that comes in the Name of the Lord!" (23:39). The Jewish leaders refused to bless the King when they were alive (Lk 19:37-39). However, they will bless Him at the end of the world, and even the stones will cry out (Lk 19:40).

After saying this Prophecy, Jesus and His Disciples left the Temple and withdrew to the Mountain of Olives for a more in depth understanding of the catastrophic events that would happen. Jesus' departure from the Temple marks the departure of God's Spirit and Glory. "Ichabod," the glory is gone!

Matthew 24:3: Jesus was sitting on the Mount of Olives; the disciples came to him privately. "Tell us," they said, "When will this happen, and what will be the sign of your coming and of the end of the age?"

Parallel passages:

Mark 13:3, 4: Now as He sat on the Mount of Olives opposite the temple, Peter, James, John, and Andrew asked Him privately, 4 "Tell us, when these things will be? And what will be the sign when all these things will be fulfilled?" (NKJV)

Luke 21:7: So they asked Him, saying, "Teacher, but when these things will be? And what sign will there be when these things are about to take place?" (NKJV)

There has been great debate over whether the Disciples were asking two or three questions. Matthew's account records three questions.

1) **WHEN WILL THIS HAPPEN?**

It will come after the Messiah shall be cut off (Da 9:26).

2) **WHAT WILL BE THE SIGN OF YOUR COMING?**

This question could be two-fold. What signs will be given before Jesus executes Judgment upon Judah, *or* they could be asking what signs are going to be given for Christ's Second Coming.

3) **AND OF THE END OF THE AGE?**

Some take this question to be the end of the Jewish age and *not* the end of the world. One question to consider, "Why would Jesus discuss the end of Judaism and in the same context the end of the world if His Disciples didn't inquire about both events?" When the reader considers the whole context, Matthew 23:37 – 24:39, we must conclude that there are two main questions, "When is the end of Judaism, and when is the end of the world?"

Jesus is speaking about the destruction of Jerusalem with His immediate response. He was not talking about the end of the world when He pointed to the stones and prophesied that they would all come down. Thus, it would be the greatest disservice to Scripture and blatant rejection of the law of Hermeneutics to believe Jesus is speaking about the end of the world in his immediate answer. However, in the context of this passage, He includes answers to their question concerning the end of the world. As we will discover, Jesus does not address the three events in sequential order. He addresses the events interspersed in reference to one, such as the end of Judaism, "this generation," and then back to the creation of the world. He also parallels the end of the world in the days of Noah with the end of the world. He changes the discourse back to Christian Jews who should be watching for the immediate end, before going forward to Christians who should be looking toward the final end of the world. One phrase can refer to a retroactive event and then fast-forward to a future event. This can be acknowledged in so much as one verse of Scripture that proceeded from His mouth. The Holy Spirit must educate us because the Disciples had an advantage over us by seeing the body language, eye contact, demeanor, and tone of voice when Jesus addressed these three events.

The Greek word used for *end* or *completion* in the verse (Mt 24:3) is *sunteleias*. Vine's definition signifies, "a bringing to completion together," (sun with, teleo, to complete), marking the completion or consummation of the various parts of a scheme.

Matthew 24:4-6: "And Jesus answered and said to them: 'Take heed that no one deceives you. For many will come in my name, saying, 'I am the Christ,' and will deceive many.'"

Parallel Passages:

> Luke 21:8, 9: And He said: "Take heed that you not be deceived. For many will come in my name, saying, 'I am He,' and, 'The time has drawn near.' Therefore, do not go after them."

> Mark 13:5, 6: And Jesus, answering them, began to say: "Take heed that no one deceives you. For many will come in my name, saying, 'I am He,' and will deceive many."

Immediately after Christ resurrected from the dead, He sent his Apostles into the entire world to preach the Gospel. False christs begun to arise and started claiming to be somebody.

> Acts 5:34-39: "Then one in the council stood up, a Pharisee named Gamaliel, a teacher of the law held in respect by all the people, and commanded them to put the apostles outside for a little while. And he said to them: 'men of Israel, take heed to yourselves what you intend to do regarding these men. For some time ago, Theudas rose up, claiming to be somebody. A number of men, about four hundred, joined him. He was slain, and all who obeyed him were scattered and came to nothing. After this man, Judas of Galilee rose up in the days of the census, and drew

away many people after him. He also perished, and all who obeyed him were dispersed. And now I say to you, keep away from these men and let them alone; for if this plan or this work is of men, it will come to nothing; but if it is of God, you cannot overthrow it — lest you even be found to fight against God'."

Acts 8:9, 10: But there was a certain man called Simon, who previously practiced sorcery in the city and astonished the people of Samaria, claiming that he was someone great, to whom they all gave heed, from the least to the greatest, saying, 'This man is the great power of God'."

Also, within one year of the Lord's resurrection, **Dositheus the Samaritan** and **Simon Magus** arose to claim to be the Son of God or Power of God.

"It has been proclaimed to the entire world that Jesus Christ is the only Son of God who visited the human race: for those who, like Celsus, have supposed that (the acts of Jesus) were a series of prodigies, and who for that reason wished to perform acts of the same kind, that they, too, might gain a similar mastery over the minds of men, were convicted of being utter nonentities. Such were Simon, the Magus of Samaria, and Dositheus, who was a native of the same place; since the former gave out that he was the power of God that is called great, and the latter that he was the Son of God" (*Ante-Nicene Fathers*, Origen: Against Celsus: Book 6: Chapter 11/Chapter 57/).

Theudas: A false prophet.

"Judas of Galilee also, as Luke relates in the Acts of the Apostles, wished to call himself some great personage, as did Theudas before him; but as their doctrine was not of God, they were destroyed, and all who obeyed them were immediately dispersed" (*Ante-Nicene Fathers*, Origen: Against Celsus: Book 6: Chapter 11/Chapter 57.)

Many other false christs came and persuaded many people to follow them. Pilate, Cuspius Fadus, Felix, and Porcius Festus all dealt with and defeated false christs and their followers. It may be objected that none of these imposters other than Dositheus proclaimed to be the Messiah. However, the Jews were merely looking for someone to deliver them from the Roman yoke and restore the kingdom to Jerusalem. They were not concerned with the more than 1,000 Old Testament prophecies concerning the Messiah. If a man claimed to be something and resisted the Roman government, he was an acceptable candidate to be the Messiah! Jesus said truthfully,

> John 5:43: "I have come in My Father's name, and you do not receive me; if another comes in his own name, him you will receive."
>
> Matthew 24:7: for nation will rise against nation, and kingdom against kingdom.
>
> Parallel Passages:
>
> Mark 13:7, 8: But when you hear of wars and rumors of wars, do not be troubled; for such things must happen, but the end is not yet. For nation will rise against nation, and kingdom against kingdom.
>
> Luke 21:9, 10: But when you hear of wars and commotions, do not be terrified; for these things must come to pass first, but the end will not come immediately." Then He said to them, "Nation will rise against nation, and kingdom against kingdom.

Jesus was not a congressional representative who knew the *ins and outs of the government*. Jesus is not the President of the United States or the Head of the Federal Bureau of Investigation (FBI). He did not belong to the Central Intelligence Agency (CIA) or Homeland Security. Jesus was a carpenter! For Christ, a carpenter, to know what was getting ready to take place, not only with the Jews, but also with the end of the world, is overwhelming proof that He was a true prophet!

Wars and Rumors of wars

To prove how wars affected the Jewish nation, we need only to read Josephus to understand how the years 30 - 70 A.D. were stained with blood. Josephus says there were 10,000 tumults and 18 wars during this period (*Antiquities of Jews*, Book 17, Chapter 10).

Tacitus, the Roman historian, writes of wars in Germany, Africa, Thrace, Gaul, Parthian, Britain, and Armenia. About three years after the death of Christ, a war erupted between Herod and Aretas (King of Arabia Petraea) in which Herod's army was cut off. Approximately, during this time, the Emperor Caligula ordered that a statue to be placed in the temple of Jerusalem. This caused the whole nation of Judah to verge on the brink of war. During this period, a great pestilence raged in Babylon, which caused many Jews to flee to Seleucia where the Greeks and Syrians rose against them and killed over 50,000. Five years later, a conflict arose between the Jews at Perea and the Philadelphians within the city limits of Mia in which many Jews were killed. Four years later under Cumanus, 10,000 Jews were slaughtered because of a Roman Soldier's disgracing the Temple. Merely four years later, the Jews made war against the people of Samaria and ravaged their country for the murder of a Galilean who was going up to Jerusalem to keep the Passover.

The Jews found their most bloodstained battle against the Syrians at Caesarea, where 20,000 Jews were slain. Wars erupted in Damascus, Tyre, Ascalon, Gadara, and Scythopolis, where 13,000 Jews perished in one night. At the first three, previously mentioned cities, 10,000 Jews were slain in one hour! At Alexandria, the Romans slew 50,000 Jews, Jotapa (40,000), Japha (15,000), Joppa (4,200), and at Idumea (10,000 +). During these wars with the Jews (of which the prophecy "wars and rumors of war" was mainly concerned) the western parts of the Romans Empire were in fierce contentions with Galba, Otho, and Vertellis. And finally, the whole nation of the Jews took up arms against the Romans in 70 A.D. Over 1,357, 660 Jews perished, along with the Temple and Holy City. Thus, such death and destruction made it impossible to practice Judaism and impossible to be a Temple-worshipping Jew. So, what does it take to be a Jew?

If there is no genealogy, there is no Jew.

Unlike the nations that surrounded them, and unlike all of the Gentile nations today, God wanted the Old Covenant Jew to remain separate and distinct. The Jew thought it was because of His superiority, but from God's perspective, it was for a very different reason. The reason God wanted genealogical purity was in order that the promised seed, His Son in eternity, might be born on Earth according to a bloodline that went back to the woman, Eve, to whom the promise had been made. After Christ was born, there was no further need of genealogical record keeping. It no longer makes any difference as to what nationality a person is; there is no religious benefit in genealogical record keeping.

Without a genealogy, Judaism could not have existed upon the Earth. As far back as Ezra, claimants to Jewish genealogy sought their register among those that were reckoned by genealogy, but since they could not find it, they were expelled from the priesthood as being polluted (Ezr 2:61, 62; Ne 7:63, 64).

> Ezra 2:61, 62: "and of the sons of the priests: the sons of Habaiah, the sons of Hakkoz, and the sons of Barzillai, who took a wife of the daughters of Barzillai the Gileadite, and was called by their name. These sought their listing among those who were registered by genealogy, but they were not found; therefore, they were excluded from the priesthood as defiled."

> Nehemiah 7:5: "Then my God put it into my heart to gather the nobles, the rulers, and the people, that they might be registered by genealogy. And I found a register of the genealogy of those who had come up in the first return, and found written in it:"

> 7:63-65: "and of the priests: the sons of Habaiah, the sons of Hakkoz, the sons of Barzillai, who took a wife of the daughters of Barzillai the Gileadite, and was called by their name. These sought their listing among those who were registered by genealogy, but it was not found; therefore, they were excluded from the priesthood as defiled. And the governor said to them that they should not eat of the most holy things till a priest could consult with the Urim and Thummim."

It is a very dangerous thing to call ourselves Biblical Jews today. God says that all liars will have their place in the lake that burns with fire and brimstone (Rev 21:8). If Ezra and Nehemiah had problems finding official records to support a person's claim to call himself a Jew 2,500 years ago, it would be absurd to make that claim today. God made it easy for the so-called Jewish converts of the first Congregation of Christ. He called them "Christians" (Ac 11:26). What on earth is wrong with the name "Christian? William H. Griffin Thomas,[132] in his *Commentary on Acts*, referencing Acts 11:26 writes,

> "The word 'called' in the text comes from chrematidzo, a Divine oracle, or divinely called."

During the siege of 70 A.D., the Temple was defiled and *abominated* by the Jews themselves. They used the temple yard as a fortress and set fire to the outer cloisters. The Temple itself was set on fire by one of the soldiers, contrary to the orders of Titus, and all that was combustible was destroyed (Josephus, *War* vi 3, 1:4, 5: cf, 5:1:9,2). No shred of genealogical documentary evidence would have remained to support the authenticity of the few surviving Jews. Even if some Jews had escaped the famine, sword, disease, and fire left in the wake of the Roman armies, these Jews could no longer be classified as covenant-keeping Jews.

The conquerors, afterwards, threw down the walls (Josephus, *War* vii 1:1). Skeptics arose and questioned the authenticity of Jesus' prophecy, "Not one stone will be left upon another." They point to the modern day *Wailing Wall,* as if Jesus lied. This is such a flimsy argument that it seems unnecessary to even address it. The *Wailing Wall* was not part of Herod's original Temple.

On the original Temple site, Emperor Hadrian dedicated a temple to Jupiter Capitolinus in 136 A.D. or earlier. In 363 A.D., Emperor Julian, in order to defeat Christ's prophecy (Mt 24:1, 2), undertook to rebuild the Temple. However, flames burst forth from the foundation and frustrated his plan. In 691 A.D., 'Abd-al-Malik' built the Dome of the Rock (wrongly called the Mosque of Omar) on the site of the Temple of Solomon. (See John D. Davis, *Westminster Dictionary of Bible*, p. 597)

Steve Bayne in *Understanding Jewish History*, page 87, quotes a Spanish traveler, Benjamin of Tudela "*70 A.D. was the end of our history.*" He states further that in 140 A.D., Judah was renamed, "Palestine."

Cultural Jews? Yes. Authentic Jews? No.

The modern cultural Jew does not truly worship through the Bible; he worships through the Talmud. He does not speak Hebrew, but Yiddish. He is not descended from Israel but from the dwellers of the eastern Mediterranean. This is vividly illustrated by H. G. Wells in his *Outline of History*.[133]

> "The Jewish idea was and is a curious combination of theological breadth and intense racial patriotism. The Jews looked for a special savior, a Messiah, who was to redeem mankind by the agreeable process of restoring the fabulous glories of David and Solomon, and bringing the whole world at last under the benevolent but firm Jewish heel. As the political power of the Semitic peoples declined and Carthage followed Tyre in the darkness and Spain became a Roman province, this dream grew and spread. There can be little doubt that the scattered Phoenicians in Spain and Africa and throughout the Mediterranean, speaking as they did a language closely akin to Hebrew and being deprived of their authentic political rights, became proselytes to Judaism. Phases of vigorous proselytism alternated with phases of exclusive jealousy in Jewish history."

> "On one occasion the Idumeans, being conquered by John Hyracunus, were all forcibly made Jews. There were Arab tribes who were Jews in the time of Muhammad, and a Turkish people who were mainly Jews in South Russia in the ninth century. Judaism is indeed the reconstructed political ideal of many shattered peoples—mainly Semitic. It is to the Phoenician contingent and to Aramean accessions in Babylon that the financial and commercial tradition of the Jews is to be ascribed. As a result of these coalescences and assimilations, almost everywhere in the towns through the Roman Empire, and far beyond it in the east, Jewish communities traded and flourished. They were kept in touch through the Bible and a religious and educational organization. The main part of Jewry never was in Judea and had never come out of Judea."

The Turkish people whom Wells mentions were the Khazars, who built an empire in south Russia in the 9th Century A.D. This Chazar or Khazar Empire was infiltrated by large numbers of Byzantine Jews. By process of intermarriage and conversion, these Chazars became identified as Jews, and in all Jewish histories and encyclopedias, the words "Chazar" and "Jew" are used interchangeably. In the 10th Century, a succession of invasions destroyed the Chazar Empire and large numbers of these Chazar-Jews settled in what is now Poland. Others found their way to Western Europe and Spain, where they mingled with the already ethnically diverse conglomeration.

One of the most analytical histories of the rise of unauthentic Judaism after 70 A.D. is the excellent research documentary of the celebrated writer and author, Arthur Koestler. His work, *The Thirteenth Tribe (1976)*, is a classic. He quotes from 85 historical scholars who debunk the idea of modern Jewry being a Semitic, chosen race.

> Page 16 – In the 1973 edition of the *Encyclopedia Judaica*, the article, 'Khazzars' is signed by Dunlop, but there is a separate section dealing with 'Chazar Jews after the Fall of the Kingdom,' signed by the editors, and written with the obvious intent to avoid upsetting believers in the dogma of the Chosen Race:

The Turkish-speaking Karaites [a fundamentalist Jewish sect] of the Crimea, Poland, and elsewhere have affirmed a connection with the Khazars, which is perhaps also confirmed by evidence from folklore and anthropology, as well as language.

Page 17 – "If so, this would mean that their ancestors came not from the Jordan but from the Volga, not from Canaan but from the Caucasus, once believed to be the cradle of the Aryan race; and that genetically they are more closely related to the Hun, Uigur, and Magyar tribes than to the seed of Abraham, Isaac, and Jacob. Should this turn out to be the case, then the term 'anti-Semitism' would become void of meaning, based on a misapprehension shared by both the killers and their victims. The story of the Chazar Empire, as it slowly emerges from the past, begins to look like the cruelest hoax that history has ever perpetrated."

To quote Bury once more:

Page 59 – "There can be no question that the ruler was actuated by political motives in adopting Judaism. To embrace Mohammedanism would have made him the spiritual dependent of the Caliphs, who attempted to press their faith on the Khazzars, and in Christianity, lay the danger of his becoming an ecclesiastical vassal of the Roman Empire. Judaism was a reputable religion with sacred books, which both Christian and Mohammedan respected; it elevated him above the heathen barbarians, and secured him against the interference of Caliph or Emperor."

Page 169 – "On the evidence quoted in previous chapters, one can easily understand why Polish historians – who are, after all, closet to the sources – are in agreement that 'in earlier times, the main bulk of the Jewish population originated from the Khazzars country.'"

Page 172 – "Further evidence against the supposedly Franco-Rhenish origin of Eastern Jewry is provided by the structure of Yiddish, the popular language of the Jewish masses, spoken by millions before the holocaust, and still surviving among traditionalist minorities in the Soviet Union and the United States."

Yiddish is a curious amalgam of Hebrew, medieval German, Slavonic, and other elements, written in Hebrew characters.

Page 180 – "The numerical ratio of the Khazzars to the Semitic and other contributions is impossible to establish."

Page 181 – "The Jews of the times fall into two main divisions: Sephardim and Ashkenazim."

The Sephardim are interracial Jews who, since antiquity, had lived in Spain. The word "Sephardim" is taken from the Hebrew word "Sephard" (Obadiah 1:20). After they were expelled at the end of the 15th Century from the Iberian Pennisula, the Sephardim settled in the countries bordering on the Mediterranean, the Balkans, and to a lesser extent in Western Europe. They spoke a Spanish, Hebrew dialect knows as Ladino (see VII, 3), and preserved their own traditions and religious rites. In the 1960s, the Sephardim were estimated to be 500,000.

For the sake of piquantly, it should be mentioned that the Ashkenaz of the Bible refers to a people living somewhere in the vicinity of Mount Ararat and Armenia. The name occurs in Genesis 10:3 and 1 Chronicles 1:6 as one of the sons of Gomer, who was a son of Japheth. Ashkenaz is also a brother of Togarmah (and a nephew of Magog) whom the Khazzars, according to King Joseph (Jewish name adopted by this gentile King) claimed as their ancestor.

Summing up a very old and bitter controversy in a laconic paragraph, Koestler continues by quoting Raphael Patai:

> Page 182 – "The findings of physical anthropology show that, contrary to popular view, there is no Jewish race. Anthropometric measurements of Jewish groups in many parts of the world indicate that they differ greatly from one another with respect to all the important physical characteristics – stature, weight, skin color, cephalic index, facial index, blood groups, etc."

The author, Professor Juan Comas, draws the following conclusion from the statistical material:

> Page 183 – "Thus despite the view usually held, the Jewish people is racially heterogeneous; its constant migrations and its relations – voluntary or otherwise- with the widest variety of nations and peoples have brought about such a degree of crossbreeding that the so-called people of Israel can produce examples of traits typical of every people. For proof it will suffice to compare the rubicund, sturdy, heavily built Rotterdam Jew with his coreligionist, say in Salonika with gleaming eyes in a sickly face and skinny, high-strung physique. Hence, so far as our knowledge goes, we can assert that Jews as a whole display as great a degree of morphological disparity among themselves as could be found between members of two or more different races."

> Page 189 – "The old Jewish families of England (who arrived here long before the nineteenth-twentieth century influx from the east). The Montefiores, Lousadas, Montagues, Avigdors, Sutros, Sassoons, etc., all came out of the Iberian mixing bowl, and can claim no purer racial origin than the Ashkenazi's – or the Jews named Davis, Harris, Phillips or Hart."

One distressingly recurrent type of event was miscegenation by rape. That too has a long history starting in Palestine. It is said, for example, that a certain Judah ben Ezekial opposed his son marrying a woman who was not of 'the seed of Abraham,' whereupon his friend Ulla remarked: 'How do we know for certain that we ourselves are not descended from the heathens who violated the maidens of Zion at the siege of Jerusalem?'

> Page 223 – "I am aware of the danger that it may be maliciously misinterpreted as a denial of the State of Israel's right to exist. But that right is not based on the hypothetical origins of the Jewish people, nor on the mythological covenant of Abraham with God; it is based on international law –i.e., on the United Nations' decision in 1947 to partition Palestine, once a Turkish province, then a British Mandated Territory, into an Arab and a Jewish State. Whatever the Israeli citizens' racial origins, and whatever illusions they entertain about them, their State exists de jure and de facto, and cannot be undone, except by genocide."

> Page 225 – "To sum up, the Jews of our day have no cultural tradition in common, merely certain habits and behavior-patterns, derived by social inheritance from the traumatic experience of the ghetto, and from a religion which the majority does not practice or believe in but which nevertheless confers on them a pseudo-national status."

When asked why he attends the Synagogue, the man said, "It is not to worship a God; it is to fraternize with my Jewish friends."

God has but one chosen race today, *"But you are a chosen generation, a royal priesthood, a holy nation, His own special people, that you may proclaim the praises of Him who called you out of darkness into His marvelous light;"* (1Pe 2:9). Before this chosen race of people could be chosen, the kingdom had to be taken from the Jews (Mt 21:43).

What does it take to become a Jew?

> "Behold, I will make them of the synagogue of Satan who call themselves Jews and they are not; but they do lie" (Rev 3:9).

During the Israel-Arab hostilities at the turn of the 21st Century, newspaper articles appeared asking what constituted whether a person was a Jew. The conclusion reached was that if a person claimed their grandmother was a Jew, then they could prove Jewish citizenship. For some reason, yet to be determined, the modern-day proof of Jewishness is through the maternal side of the family. This stands in direct contradiction to the Biblical method of genealogical tracking, which was paternal, from the father's side. Thus, the Jews loved to refer to themselves as "children of Abraham," a claim that was rightly debunked by the Lord in John 8:36-42, 53-59.

John the Immerser referred to the stubborn resistance of the Jews to the truth, while at the same time they claimed to be physical children of Abraham (Lk 3:8). According to God's reckoning, a true Jew was no longer a matter of physical genealogy (Ro 9:6-8). Note that spiritual circumcision was by no means a New Testament idea only. The prophet Jeremiah uses cynicism in admonishing the Jews to circumcise not the foreskin, but the heart (Jer 4:4). In this way only, a physically circumcised Jew could please God. In this way only, an uncircumcised Gentile could please God. A Jew was a person circumcised of heart and not flesh (Ro 2:28, 29 with Col 2:12). God was clear; there is no longer a chosen, physical nation. Now, all Christians regardless of national background (Gal 3:27-29) can be His chosen people, a royal "priestly" Kingdom (1Pe 2:9; Rev 1:6).

Just a cursory reading of the above verses will lead the honest observer to the conclusion that the pedigree that ties a man or woman to God is not genealogical but regeneration. The name Jew was given of old as a type of thing to come in the New Testament when all nations would learn to praise God through Jesus Christ. The word Jew, "Yehuddiah," simply means, *"praise,"* and the word, "Israel," simply means, "Prince of God." When God gave these words, He always had in mind a people who would later be regenerated through new birth (Jn 3:5) and not those who would follow physically as the offspring of Abraham or Jacob (Jn 1:13).

All nations will ultimately fall at the feet of the King of Regeneration (Heb 1:13, 2:13; Ge 14:22). Those who claim to be Jews are attempting to place themselves on the same genealogical plane as the one and only Christ whose genealogy is impeccably recorded in Matthew, Chapter 1, and Luke 3:23-38. These Jew-claimers will fall down before Him. Jesus Christ will command all praise, for He is the only legitimate, genealogical descendant of the seed of the woman and Abraham. As paradoxical as it may seem, both the ancient authentic Jew and the modern unauthentic, cultural Jew will fall down before those of all nations who became spiritual Israel and remained steadfast in New Covenant obedience,

> *"Behold, I will make them (who call themselves Jews and are not) come and worship before thy feet and come to know that I have loved thee!" (Rev 3:9)*

Messiah Christ has great love for the world's individuals. Throughout the New Testament age, people can love and embrace the God of Abraham, Judah, and David more than their original, biological pedigreed seed. Jesus said the "first would be last." These are the people to whom the Lord referred when He remembered, "They said they would do the will of God," and did not. The Gentiles said, "They would not do the will of God," and they did. Truly, Hell's fire swallowed the last generation of authentic Jews when they tumbled from the Desolation of 70 A.D. (and in the ensuing tumults that followed) into the damnation of Hell (Mt 23:33). "Weeping and gnashing of teeth" is an expression the Lord used when describing eternal Hell. The Lord employed this phrase because many of His followers underestimated the wrath of Hell and even thought it was instant oblivion. Far from being a state of nothingness, the Lord made it clear that "weeping, wailing, and gnashing of teeth," indicate a state of acute awareness. We must remember that torment is as much a state of perception as comfort and bliss are. If people can experience "weeping, wailing, and gnashing of teeth" the minute they die, they can also experience it an hour or a million years after they die.

The physical descendants of Abraham had a Hell to experience that no other lineage of people could experience. What would that experience be? Hell is separation, cruelly inflicted stripes, separation, isolation, darkness, fire, loneliness, accusation, falling, cursing, and hopelessness (to mention a few of the torments); but there is one torment the ancient pedigree of genealogical Jews experienced that no Gentile will ever face. What is it?

Jesus in Luke's account,

> *"There shall be weeping and gnashing of teeth when you shall see Abraham, Isaac and Jacob; and all the prophets in the Kingdom of God, and you yourselves*

thrust out. And they (The Gentiles) shall come from the east and from the west and from the north, and from the south; and shall sit down in the Kingdom of God. And behold there are last (Gentiles) that shall be first (to accept New Covenant Christianity) and there are first (Jews) who shall be last" (to hear and reject New Covenant Christianity) (Lk 23: 28-30).

The world to the east, west, north, and south of Judah was the Gentile world. In this Scripture, Jesus prophesied three things. First, there would be a great rejection and blasphemy of the New Covenant Gospel (given by the Holy Spirit) by a majority of the Jewish world. Next, of this last generation, there could be no escape from the just fire of Hell. It is a fitting punishment for blasphemers of the Spirit and haters of God's Son. Finally, with the blasphemous rejection of the last descendants of Abraham, there was a subsequent turning to God's Messiah-Christ by the Gentile masses. Those who should have accepted the Messiah of Abraham, Isaac, and Jacob experienced Desolation in 70 A.D.

However, those whom one would not expect to accept Him fell upon the 70 A.D. rock. That same rock crushed the Jews into fine powder. Since the Jew did not understand when Christ spoke to them, they certainly understood full well after the Desolation swept them into eternity. They wept uncontrollably and gnashed their teeth in pain but to no avail. Their hatred and jealousy of Gentiles was augmented by the fact that these despised "pagans" possessed a more loving and compassionate love for God's Messiah-Christ than they did. The fact that these Gentile *pigs* would sit with their venerated Fathers, Abraham, Isaac, and Jacob in the New Covenant Kingdom would drive them eternally mad.

Are these anti-Semitic words? No, it is mere New Testament Scripture. Is it a doctrine of hate? Yes, it is a doctrine that teaches how much the Jews hated God, the Gentiles, and an even greater hatred of the Messiah who laid down His life for them. Do we hate Jews? No. After 70 A.D., no Jews remain. But we still love those who call themselves Jews because the Messiah died for them, too.

The Kingdom of God is "Near."

Luke 21:31, "Even so, when you see these things happening, you know that the kingdom of God is *near*," appears to be addressing the destruction of Jerusalem. This word, eggnus, "near," is used for worldwide events like the fall of Judaism and the conversion of millions of Gentiles to God's Kingdom. Interestingly, "eggnus" is used in Hebrews 8:13 concerning the disappearance of the Old

Covenant economy. The actual Greek describes this disappearance in the following words of the Nestles text, "It is near vanishing away." The Hebrews writer records, "In that He says, 'A new covenant,' He has made the first obsolete. Now what is becoming obsolete and growing old is ready to vanish away" (Heb 8:13). Notice, the word eggnus, "is nearly," is used to mean to vanish away within a short time after Paul's writing.

The New Covenant Kingdom of God would achieve a great advancement by doing away with the Old Covenant dispensation. Unquestionably, the evidence is incontrovertible that the advancement of the New Testament Kingdom of God must be predicated upon the annulment of the Old Testament Kingdom on Earth. What barred the Gentiles from a mass conversion to Yahweh was the obstruction that they encountered through Old Testament temple worship. That obstruction, having been removed through the Abomination of Desolation, would no longer prohibit the Gentiles' entering into God's Kingdom. The only obstruction for the Gentiles would be their own foolish will. A like obstruction would be the frenzied tendency to build temples, mosques, cathedrals, and other architectural worship centers to replace Solomon's or Herod's temple.

How profoundly humbling to know that Christ feels this way about the Gentile Christians in His Congregations, like those Christians in Philadelphia who knew that Christ had the Key of David to open and shut Hades or Heaven (Rev 3:7), and whose names were written in the New Jerusalem (3:12) and cared less about the theological or Biblical significance of the Old Jerusalem. Physical pedigree means something to some people, but with God, Kingdom pedigree means everything here and in the hereafter. The citizens of His spiritual Israelite Kingdom are the *apple of His eye*. Christ wants to honor them for their humble submission and service, and He will! It certainly is not a human prerequisite for a born again Christian to gloat over those who call themselves Jews and worship Christ at their feet (Rev 3:9). However, this experience is yet to be revealed.

Qualifying for Jewish citizenship in the Old Testament required proof.

Why is it so easy today to be called Jewish simply by claiming the Jewish-ness of a mother or grandmother? Most people would not bother themselves to either read the ancient book where the word, *Jew,* first appeared, or even attempt an intellectual discussion about the propriety of being called by the title.

The Scriptures contain the following three passages on this subject:

1. The Levites had to set the Old Testament Tabernacle in order.

    These priests had to be direct descendants of Levi. Detail is given to their numbering in Exodus 38:21, "According to the commandment of Moses, for the service of the Levites." In the New Testament, all Christians are priests. Does this mean that Christians have to trace their priestly ancestry back to Levi? Or would it be more logical for New Testament readers to trace their priestly ancestry back to their High Priest after the rank of Melchezedec (Heb 7:1-22), who pre-dated the law and temple?

    "For it is evident that our Lord arose from Judah (not Levi,) of which tribe Moses spoke nothing concerning priesthood" (7:14).

2. Not only the Priesthood of Levi, but all of Israel and Judah had to be reckoned by genealogy –

    "And behold they were written in the books of the Kings of Israel" (1 Ch 9:1).

3. Ezra, Chapter 2, is a long, detailed list of Jews who returned to Jerusalem and Judah from captivity in Babylon. Literally thousands of self-styled Jews were excluded from the right to claim Israel-Jewish pedigree because they had no record to prove their ancestors.

    "But they could not show their father's house (not mother's house) and their seed, whether they were of Israel" (2:59).

    "These sought their register among those that were reckoned by genealogy, but they were not found; therefore were they as polluted, put from the priesthood" (3:62).

The only way these people could have access to the priestly worship in the Temple was when the Governor of Judah told them they could receive a variance when a priest with the Urim and Thummim stood up on their behalf (3:63).

Matthew 24:7b, 8: "And there will be famines, pestilences, and earthquakes in various places. All these are the beginning of sorrows."

Parallel Passages

Mark 13:8b: "And there will be earthquakes in various places, and famines. These are the beginning of birth pains" (NIV).

Luke 21:11: "There will be great earthquakes, famines and pestilences in various places, and fearful events and great signs from heaven" (NIV).

Famines

"The prophecy of Agabus respecting the famine in the world, and the liberal relief sent to the brethren in Jerusalem" (*Ante-Nicean Fathers*, Volume Six: Pamphilus: An exposition of the Acts of the Apostles).

Of the prophetic famines, the most prominent was that which Agabus foretold would happen in the days of Emperor Claudius, as related in the Book of Acts of the Apostles. It begun in the fourth year of his reign and was of long duration. This famine spread throughout Greece, parts of Italy, and most certainly to Judea, prominently in Jerusalem. Many families perished for want of bread. Josephus also recorded this famine, and relates, "An assaron of corn was sold for five drachmae" (*Antiquities Book 3*: Chapter 15: Section 3:320, 321). Eusebius and Orosius confirmed this famine. Dion Cassius also speaks of a famine that prevailed in Rome and other parts of Italy in the first year of Claudius' reign. In the *eleventh* year of the same emperor, Eusebius mentioned another famine.

Pestilences

"Pestilence" closely parallels "famine." These pestilences accompanied the previously noted famines. Because of these famines, raging diseases and plagues produced deaths numbering in the thousands. There are documented instances of historical pestilences. Tacitus, Suetonius, and Josephus recorded pestilences occurring in Babylon (40 A.D.), Italy (66 A.D.) and Rome (65 A.D.). The greatest pestilence took place in the City of Jerusalem when Prince Titus surrounded the city with his armies.

Earthquakes

During Claudius' reign, earthquakes shook Rome, Aramea, and Syria (both mentioned by Tacitus). Philostratus mentioned another earthquake taking place in Crete in "*Life of Apollonius*." This also states that others occurred at Smyma, Miletus, Chios, and Samos. During Nero's reign, an earthquake occurred at Laodicea (Tacitus). Other earthquakes happened at Hieropolis and Colossae (Eusebius/Orosius) and Campania (Tacitus/Seneca), and also later in Rome during the Galba's reign (Suetonius).

Fearful events and signs from heaven

Luke adds Christ saying, "...fearful events and great signs from heaven." Listed below are some astounding quotes from Josephus:

> "Thus were the miserable people persuaded by these deceivers, and such as belied God himself; while they did not attend, nor give credit, to the signs that were so evident and did so plainly foretell their future desolation; but, like men infatuated, without either eyes to see, or minds to consider, did not regard the denunciations that God made to them. (289) Thus there was a star resembling a sword, which stood over the city, and a comet, that continued a whole year." Josephus, Flavius; Whiston, William: *The Works of Josephus: Complete and Unabridged*. Peabody: Hendrickson, 1996, c1987, S. Wars 6.288-289)

> "Thus also, before the Jews' rebellion, and before those commotions which preceded the war, when the people were come in great crowds to the feast of unleavened bread, on the eighth day of the month Xanthicus e [Nisan], and at the ninth hour of the night, so great a light shone round the altar and the holy house, that it appeared to be bright day time; which light lasted for half an hour" (Josephus, Flavius; Whiston, William: *The Works of Josephus : Complete and Unabridged*. Peabody: Hendrickson, 1996, c1987, S. Wars 6.290).

> At the same festival also, a heifer, as she was led by the high priest to be sacrificed, brought forth a lamb in the midst of the temple" (Josephus, Flavius; Whiston, William: *The Works of Josephus: Complete and Unabridged*. Peabody: Hendrickson, 1996, c1987, S. Wars 6.292).

> Moreover, the eastern gate of the inner [court of the] temple, which was of brass, and vastly heavy, and had been with difficulty shut by twenty men, and rested upon a basis armed with iron, and had bolts fastened very deep into the firm floor, which was there made of one entire stone, was seen to be opened of its own accord about the sixth hour of the night. (294) Now,

those that kept watch in the temple came hereupon running to the captain of the temple, and told him of it: who then came up thither, and not without great difficulty, was able to shut the gate again (295). This also appeared to the vulgar to be a very happy prodigy, as if God did thereby open them the gate of happiness. But the men of learning understood it, that the security of their holy house was dissolved of its own accord, and that the gate was opened for the advantage of their enemies. (296) so these publicly declared, that this signal foreshowed the desolation that was coming upon them" (Josephus, Flavius; Whiston, William: *The Works of Josephus: Complete and Unabridged*. Peabody: Hendrickson, 1996, c1987, S. Wars 6.293-296).

Besides these, a few days after that feast, on the twenty-first day of the month Artemisia's [Jyar], (297) a certain prodigious and incredible phenomenon appeared; I suppose the account of it would seem to be a fable, were it not related by those that saw it, (298) and were not the events that followed it of so considerable a nature as to deserve such signals; for, before sun setting, chariots and troops of soldiers in their armor were seen (299) running about among the clouds, and surrounding of cities" (Josephus, Flavius ; Whiston, William: *The Works of Josephus : Complete and Unabridged*. Peabody: Hendrickson, 1996, c1987, S. Wars 6.296-299)

Moreover, at that feast which called Pentecost, as the priests were going by night into the inner [court of the] temple, as their custom was, to perform their sacred ministrations, they said that, in the first place, they felt a quaking, and heard a great noise, (300) and after that they heard a sound as of a great multitude, saying, "Let us remove hence" (Josephus, Flavius; Whiston, William: *The Works of Josephus : Complete and Unabridged*. Peabody: Hendrickson, 1996, c1987, S. Wars 6.299, 300).

But, what is still more terrible there was one Jesus, the son of Ananus, a plebeian and a husbandman, who, four years before the war began, and at a time when the city was in very great peace and prosperity, came to that feast whereon it is our custom for everyone to make tabernacles to God in the temple, (301) began on a sudden cry aloud, "A voice from the east, a voice from the west, a voice from the four winds, a voice against Jerusalem and the holy house, a voice against the bridegrooms and the brides, and a voice against this whole people!" This was his cry, as he went about by day and by night, in all the lanes of the city. (302) However, certain of the most eminent among the populace had great indignation at this dire cry of his, and took up the man, and gave him a great number of severe stripes; yet did not he either say anything for himself, or anything peculiar to those that chastised him, but still he went on with the same words which he cried before. (303) Hereupon our rulers supposing, as the case proved to be, that this was a sort of divine fury in the man, brought him to the Roman procurator; (304) where he was whipped till his bones were laid bare; yet did he not make any supplication for himself, nor shed any tears, but turning his voice to the most lamentable tone possible, at every stroke of the whip his answer was, "Woe, woe to Jerusalem!" (305). (Josephus, Flavius; Whiston, William: *The Works of Josephus: Complete and Unabridged*. Peabody: Hendrickson, 1996, c1987, S. Wars 6.300- 305).

And when Albinus (for he was then our procurator) asked him who he was, and whence he came, and why he uttered such words; he made no manner of reply to what he said, but still did not leave off his melancholy ditty, till Albinus took him to be a madman, and dismissed him. (306) Now, during all the time that passed before the war began, this man did not go near any of the citizens, nor was seen by them while he said so; but he every day uttered these lamentable words, as if it were his premeditated vow, "Woe, woe, to Jerusalem!" (307) Nor did he give ill words to any of those that beat him every day, nor good words to those that gave him food; but this was his reply to all men, and indeed no other than a melancholy presage of what was to come. (308) This cry of his was the loudest at the festivals; and he continued this ditty for seven years and five months, without growing hoarse, or being tired therewith, until the very time that he saw his presage in earnest fulfilled in our siege, when it ceased; (309) for as he was going round upon the wall, he cried out with his utmost force, "Woe, woe, to the city again, and to the people, and to the holy house!" And just as he added at the last, — "Woe, woe, to myself also!" there came a stone out of one of the engines, and smote him, and killed him immediately; and as he was uttering the very same presages, he gave up the ghost" (Josephus, Flavius; Whiston, William: *The Works of Josephus: Complete and Unabridged*. Peabody: Hendrickson, 1996, c1987, S. Wars 6.305-309)

All the above occurrences were the beginning of sorrows! What a terrifying thought. Wars, diseases, famines, and fearful signs in Heaven were just the beginning. The worst was yet to come.

Matthew 24:9-13: "Then they will deliver you up to tribulation and kill you, and you will be hated by all nations for my name's sake. At that time many will turn away from the faith and will betray and hate each other, and many false prophets will appear and deceive many people. Because of the increase of wickedness, the love of most will grow cold, but he who stands firm to the end will be saved."

Parallel Passages

> Mark 13:9: "You must be on your guard. You will be handed over to the local councils and flogged in the synagogues. On account of me you will stand before governors and kings as witnesses to them.
>
> Luke 21:12, 13: "But before all this, they will lay hands on you and persecute you. They will deliver you to synagogues and prisons, and you will be brought before kings and governors, and all on account of my name. This will result in your being witnesses to them.

What a troublesome time for the disciples and future followers of Jesus. He predicted their mocking, beatings, imprisonments, and death. However, their mountainous faith was displayed in the written word. They were,

1. Delivered to councils, by Peter and John, Acts 4:5.

2. Brought before rulers and kings, by Paul before Gallio, Acts 18:12; before Felix, Acts, Chapter 24; before Festus and Agrippa, Acts Chapter 25.

3. Imprisoned, with Peter and John, Acts 4:3.

4. Beaten, both Paul and Silas, Acts 16:23.

5. Put to death, as Stephen, Acts 7:59; and James, the brother of John, Acts 12:9.

After the Book of Acts, more horrible blood persecutions occurred during Nero's reign. Numerous Christians were slaughtered, placed in fighting rings, threatened with death, and tortured. Tertullian records that a war was waged against the very name of Christ. To bear the name of Christ meant instant death! This is probably the most compelling proof that The Revelation was completed during Nero's reign and that all New Testament inspired writings were completed before 70 A.D.

Matthew 24:14: "And this gospel of the kingdom will be preached in the whole world as a testimony to all nations, and then the end will come."

Mark then interludes with a greater insight into Christ's discourse. He adds,

> Mark 13: 10, 11: "And the gospel must first be preached to all nations. Whenever you are arrested and brought to trial, do not worry beforehand about what to say. Just say whatever is given you at the time, for it is not you speaking, but the Holy Spirit."

> Luke 21:14-16: "But make up your mind not to worry beforehand how you will defend yourselves. For I will give you words and wisdom that none of your adversaries will be able to resist or contradict. You will be betrayed even by parents, brothers, relatives, and friends, and they will put some of you to death."

This Gospel was delivered unto all nations before 70 A.D. The Apostle Paul wrote his Epistles to Christians at Rome, Corinth, Galatia, Ephesus, Philippi, Colossae, and Thessalonica. Peter wrote to Christians who resided in Pontus, Cappadocia, and Bithynia. Paul encouraged the Church in Rome,

> Romans 1:8, 9: "First, I thank my God through Jesus Christ for you all, that your faith is spoken of throughout the whole world. For God is my witness, whom I serve with my spirit in the gospel of His Son, that without ceasing I make mention of you always in my prayers,"

Paul also wrote to the Colossians,

> Colossians 1:23: "if indeed you continue in the faith, grounded and steadfast, and are not moved away from the hope of the gospel which you heard, which was preached to every creature under heaven, of which I, Paul, became a minister."

Eusebius says,

> And they also, being illustrious disciples of such great men, built up the foundations of the congregations which had been laid by the apostles in every place, and preached the Gospel more and more widely and scattered the saving seeds of the kingdom of heaven far and near throughout the

whole world. (*Nicene and Post-Nicene Fathers*: Series 2: Volume 1: Eusebius: Section 1).

Clement, Bishop Newton, and Tacitus all record that the Gospel was spread throughout the world. From Church History, we can know where the other Apostles may have gone and preached the Good News of the Kingdom of God. However, we cannot say for sure where the other eight Apostles went and proclaimed the Gospel. As these men proclaimed the truth of Christ, they were inspired directly by the Holy Spirit. What an exciting thought! No doubt, as these Apostles and Prophets went into the world proclaiming the one, true God, they were hated, despised, and killed.

Consider that the Gospel went throughout the whole world but was rejected. When the missionary evangelist preached the Gospel of one God and one way, those who believed in multi-religions and pluralistic religious cultures killed the messengers. The Revelation 5:9 and 7:9 describes people from all nations, tribes, and languages and proves the biblical confirmation that the Gospel was spread worldwide. Thus, God settles the dispute when He says that all nations had access to the Gospel.

Evidences of what appear to be corrupted aspects of Christianity exist in the religious practices of western hemisphere Indians. These corruptions are blood covenants among members of their community, blood sacrifices to appease the one supreme god, and blood offering of the most celebrated champion of all young men to appease their god. Their cultures recognize the theology of an afterlife. Of course, the Apostles could also have related to the strong legends that existed throughout the world, like a worldwide catastrophic flood. They could have shared with the nations that they evangelized the true Biblical account of Noah's flood.

The Mormon version of the Indians being the lost tribe of Israel is profound gobbledygook. This fable rests upon a fictitious novel written by Solomon Spaulding and not upon empirical science. For more information concerning this subject, see *Who Really Wrote the Book of Mormon?* by Wayne L. Cowdrey, Howard A. David, and Arthur Vanick.

We know for certain that the Gospel was corrupted in the 2nd Century through Gnosticism, Judaism, and Roman paganism. The Gospel was corrupted by

Persian folklore when it went east and by a strong movement on the part of the easterners to develop a Papal system like that which developed in Rome. They promoted a Dali Lama-type mediator to take the place of Jesus Christ. Consequently, two things occurred that prevented the clear understanding of the worldwide spread of the Gospel. First, the corruptions of Christianity substituted a human ecclesiastical system in place of the Apostles' structure, as described in the New Testament. Secondly, almost all-historical information was lost during the 1,260 years of dark ages.

Through idol worship, like that which had occurred on Old Testament Israel, other cultures would have polluted Christianity with the worship of their imaginary deities. Jesus proclaimed that this Gospel would be preached to the known civilized world before 70 A.D. In the Great Commission he said, "Go into all the world." We are compelled to believe that this would include the Gentile missionary activity to all nations as far away as the British Isles after 70 A.D. Obviously, the Gospel had to go into the world in two stages. The first stage was to supplant the obsolete Old Testament religion, which occurred in 70 A.D., and secondly, to spread the Gospel to the whole world by presenting the Kingdom of God to the Gentiles.

God allows the Christian (Apostolic faith) to be corrupted wherever and whenever it goes to the whole world. We have learned that Christ's Apostolic New Testament is the touchstone test as to whom Christ will accept or reject. Thus, rejection can be just as much a critical proof for us as acceptance.

The Books of Mark and Luke record a chilling truth about what was going to happen to the Apostles as they preached the Gospel and to the nation of Jerusalem as the Old Testament was abolished.

> Mark 13:12, 13: "Brother will betray brother to death and a father his child. Children will rebel against their parents and have them put to death. All men will hate you because of me, but he who stands firm to the end will be saved" (NIV).

> Luke 21:16-19: "You will be betrayed even by parents, brothers, relatives and friends, and they will put some of you to death. All men will hate you because of me. But not a hair of your head will perish. By standing firm, you will gain life."

The last days of the real terminal generation

James pinpointed the heaping up of Jewish treasure in the "last days" (Jas 5:3). Peter declared the fulfillment of Joel's prophecy concerning the "last days" (Ac 2:17) as being what happened in Jerusalem in 30 A.D., nearly 2,000 years ago. These were the last days of the Old Testament Heaven and Earth. The chapter content of Isaiah 34, 51, 65, and 66 explains that the demise of Judaism would be accompanied with both signs in Heaven and on Earth. Hebrews says, "In these last days has spoken to us by His Son" (Heb 1:2). Paul says in 1 Corinthians 10:11 that the Old Testament things were "Written for us, upon whom the end of the ages has come." God now speaks only through the Apostolic Word, only through the Apostles who lived during the end of the Jewish world.

In addition, those who live after 70 A.D. have no other Biblical age to look forward to, for Christ once offered Himself for sin. Christ's next and final Coming is not to die for sin but to bring promised, full eternal redemption (Heb 9:26-28).

The Lord of Armies

The Lord of Sabbath armies listened to the cries of the swindled laborers, and He sent the vengeance-minded armies of Titus, from as far away as Britain and Germany. Titus was waiting for the Lord's command to strike Jerusalem (Jas 5:4). The greedy Jews were appalled when they heard that the Romans would pulverize the temple stones in order to find and melt down the gold that they had hidden among the stones. The Jews then swallowed their gold, hoping to recover it later in their excretion. After the Roman soldiers discovered this, they disemboweled the Jews, ripping their intestines to get to the gold. What a day of slaughter!

James 5:7: "Therefore, be patient unto the coming of the Lord."

James 5:7 has to refer to this slaughter, as well as referring to Christ's Coming in visitation to the Jews who called for His blood to be upon them, two generations, or 40 years after Christ's atoning death in A.D. 30 (Mt 27:25).

When James speaks of "The coming of the Lord at hand" (Jas 5: 8), and "Behold the Judge is standing at the door!" (5:9), he is not speaking of the unknown future that has yet to come after these two chiliads of time to the present. In addition, when John the Immerser used the same terminology, saying "The Kingdom of Heaven is at hand "(Mt 3:2, 4:17), he also was not speaking of some unknown future to come, from these two chiliads of time to the present. No, "At hand" means almost within your grasp. Consider the following, amazing facts.

The Coming of Christ in 70 A.D. Judgment

The Bible in Matthew 24:34 very definitely takes aim on the coming judgment through the avenging armies of Titus upon the Christ-rejecting Jews when he said, "This generation will not pass away until all these things be fulfilled." The Jews told Pilate in 30 A.D., *"Let His blood be on us and on our children"* (Mt 27:25). If we consider the 40 years from when the Jews asked for the vengeance of Christ's blood to be upon them, it would certainly have included those living at the time of the crucifixion and their children, both of whom will be living in 70 A.D. Those Jews living when Jesus spoke this prophecy would have experienced this vengeance first hand. This is what Luke meant when He called 70 A.D., *"The days of vengeance, that all things that are written might be fulfilled"* (21:22). Who was the judge presiding over the 70 A.D. desolation? It was not Titus. It was the Lord,

> *"Unless The Lord had shortened those days, no flesh would have been saved, but for the select's sake, which He chose (Ac 2:39, 40). He shortened the days" (Mk 13:20).*

This is a prophecy of either Cestius' relaxing of the siege when he retreated or Titus' recall to Rome. In both instances, Eusebius and Josephus said the Christians, forewarned by Christ in this prophecy, escaped to the town of Pella. This was a definite visitation of Christ in judgment upon Old Testament Israel by bringing it to an end, just as He will to the whole world at His Second Coming.

History of the events that lead to the destruction of Jerusalem

There was utter chaos in the streets of Jerusalem. They were rebelling against the Roman yoke. Sadduc, the Pharisee, had taught the Jews that submission to the Romans meant slavery. This resulted in a Jewish rebellious spirit. The son of the High Priest, Eleazer, persuaded those who officiated in the temple to reject the sacrifices of foreigners and to no longer offer up prayers for them. Their rejection of Caesar's sacrifice produced the slaughter of thousands of Jews. Cestius Gallus gave the Jews their *first big chance* to understand what Christ had foretold about fleeing the oncoming wrath. Their chance came when Cestius' officers convinced him to withdraw from conquering Jerusalem and to flee the city. However, the

Jews pursued him to Antipatis and slew his army (nearly 6,000 men). After this disaster, many Christians heeded Matthew 24:15 and fled, taking refuge in Pella, a place beyond the Jordan River in mountainous country.

Matthew 24:15: "So when you see standing in the holy place 'the abomination that causes desolation,' spoken of through the prophet Daniel — let the reader understand."

Parallel Passages

> Mark 13:14: "When you see 'the abomination that causes desolation' standing where it does not belong — let the reader understand.
>
> Luke 21:20: "When you see Jerusalem being surrounded by armies, you will know that its desolation is near."

These verses have been the most misrepresented and misinterpreted verses in this context. What is the abomination of desolation? Has it happened yet? This prophecy was predicted by the Prophet Daniel and repeated by Christ. How absurd to apply this verse to the far distant future? Jesus points out that when this Abomination takes place, it would be read as they saw it happening, "Let the reader understand." It is comforting to know that the New Testament was recorded and completed before 70 A.D. The "understanding" of what was happening does not apply to what Christ was saying to His disciples. The "understanding" is associated with "when" they saw it happen, and what they read in the New Testament when it began to happen.

They saw Titus throw up embankments around the city, and thousands fell by the sword. The temple was abominated (Da 9:26, 27). The word "abomination" is used to describe detestable idols (1Ki 11:5-7; 2Ki 23:13; Jer 4:1, 7:30; Eze 5:11). It is a day of vengeance for Judaism (Da 9:26 with Lk 21:22-24). It is war with Jerusalem (Lk 21:20). The enemy stands in the holy place, where it ought not to be (Mk 13:14). This is a sign to flee to the mountains of Judea, praying it would not be a Sabbath, because the Jewish authorities would have prevented their flight. Josephus says the Romans brought their ensigns into the temple and set them against the Eastern Gate. There they offered sacrifices and proclaimed Titus *imperator* with great acclamations of joy. The Jews wanted no King but Caesar; now they got him. The armies made Jerusalem desolate. Daniel 9:26 did not say the desolation took place at the end of the 70 weeks, but that the desolation-ruin would be "determined" at that time (Mt 23:38).

Daniel 9:24: "Seventy weeks are determined for your people and for your holy city, To finish the transgression, To make an end of sins, To make reconciliation for iniquity, To bring in everlasting righteousness, To seal up vision and prophecy, And to anoint the Most Holy."

A Simple Explanation Given in one Verse

In every way, Jesus fulfilled this six-fold prophecy.

"To finish the transgression"

Most theologians agree that this points to the Jewish rejection of Jesus Christ. Jesus said, "Fill up the measure of the sins of your fathers" (Mt 23:32). Even Daniel previously said, "All of Israel have transgressed thy law" (Da 9:11). They filled the very height of their transgressions at Golgotha Hill; they rejected the Gospel; and they continued to fill up their sins. But, their greatest sin was not just the murder of Christ, but rejecting His gospel (1Th 2:14).

"To make an end of sins"

Jesus was pierced for the world's transgressions, crushed for their iniquities, and by his being scourged, the world is healed (Isa 53:5). In fact, the Hebrew writer proclaimed that Christ made "one sacrifice for sins for all time" (Heb 10:12).

"To make reconciliation for iniquity"

According to the Futurist School, Christ died in vain because it placed the fulfillment of this prophecy into the future. This act nullifies Christ's sacrifice for sins. Jesus Christ came not only to atone for sin, but also to reconcile man to God the Father (Eph 2:16). This was needed because man is not only a sinner; he is also an enemy of God (Ro 5:8). Only Satan wants us to think that the Anointed One did not accomplish all these prophesies.

"To bring in everlasting righteousness"

One of Christ's main designs for His coming to Earth was to bring everlasting Righteousness. The Futurist School casts all this into the blessings of the future millennium age, but "the kingdom of God is righteousness" (Ro 14:17).

"To seal up the vision and Prophecy"

The word "sealed" used in Isaiah 29:10, 11, is the same word used in Daniel 9:24. Paul warned the Jews that they fulfilled prophecy by refusing to believe… (Ac 13:40, 41), and this fulfills Isaiah 29:14. Something that is sealed should be opened at a later time, but instead of opening it in the New Testament covenant as the Gentiles did, the Jews kept the prophecy as a closed, "sealed" book. Interestingly, the Book of Revelation is not to be a "sealed Prophecy" (Rev 22:10).

I mentioned this previously, but allow me to mention it again. Rejecting the Gospel is just as marvelous and incredible as accepting it. How is this possible? This is what God said, "I will proceed to do a marvelous work among this people, even a marvelous work and a wonder: for the wisdom of their wise men will perish and the wisdom of their prudent men will be hid" (Isa 29:14). God is using sarcasm. In effect, what He is saying, in a modern-day clique is, "If you are such a fool as to reject the ultimate wisdom of Heaven, you are a marvelous fool, so marvelous that it is a wonder that a human being could descend to such consummate idiocy." This was the prophecy that Paul was thinking of when he spoke in Antioch of Pisidia, and he was so astounded at the rejection of the works that God was doing in the mist of the Jews that he used this same sarcasm, paraphrased, "Behold you despisers and wonder and perish" (Ac 13:41).

"To anoint the Most Holy One, (or Place).

(Heb 1:9) ("Therefore God, Thy God, hath anointed Thee with the oil of gladness above Thy companions" (Ac 10:38). "God anointed Jesus of Nazareth with the Holy Spirit and with power" (Lk 4:18). God anointed Jesus to preach the Gospel (His ministry).

In his *Revelation and the End of all Things*, author Craig R. Koester very successfully sites the indictments against the foolishness of Dispensationalism. It would be foolishness to apply Daniel's Prophecy to an unknown future time period. Dispensationalists, and others, have a complete misunderstanding concerning this Prophecy. Dispensationalists attempt to harmonize Daniel's vision with that in the Revelation, but these two visions are simply not the same. Dispensationalists attempt to create a chapter division between Daniel 9:26 and 9:27 when Daniel saw a continuous vision, with no separation or indication of a different time. Dispensationalists interpret Daniel's prophecy from an English translation, like King James Version, rather than from the original language. It fails to admit that neither Daniel's nor Revelation's vision refers to the secret rapture. It fails to recognize that Revelation describes Christians going through persecution and tribulation on Earth, not converted Christians during the "Great Tribulation."

Dispensationalists confuse the literal and symbolic writings of Revelation and Daniel, as well as contradicting their own view. For instance, if we were to take a literal view of Daniel, Chapter 9, it would be a farce to force a stopgap of thousands of years between verses 26 and 27. On the other hand, Dispensationalists claim that the temple found in Revelation 11 is a literal temple and not symbolic, while holding the lamp stands (11:4) are symbolic. They conclude that the Beast of Revelation, Chapter 13, is the computerized economy, yet they do not assume that the Beast will have seven literal heads with 10 literal horns. They assume that the wars in Revelation are describing modern-day nations, yet believe the uses of the weapons "bows and arrows" represent nuclear warfare (Eze 39:3). And finally, Dispensationalists fail to understand the spiritual significance of "Spiritual Israel." Paul describes how the Gentiles have been grafted into God's covenant as a continuation of the story of Israel. This is based on faith and not the works of the law (Ro 11:13-24; Eph 2:11-22). The term "Israel" includes all who has placed their faith in Christ through obedience (Gal 3:26-29).[134] The Good News Bible deliberately omitted "Israel" from Gal. 6:16.

> Daniel 9:25, 26: "Know therefore and discern, that from the going forth of the commandment to restore and to build Jerusalem unto the Messiah, The Prince, shall be seven weeks, and threescore and two weeks: it shall be built again, with street and moat, even in troublous times. And after the threescore and two weeks shall the anointed one be cut off, and shall have nothing: and the people of the prince that shall come shall destroy the city and the sanctuary; and the end thereof shall be with a flood, and even unto the end shall be war; desolations are determined." (Note "desolations are determined "after the Messiah is "cut off" at the end of the final week of Daniel).

Christ's ministry lasted only 3½ years before He died, but the total ministry of Christ through his Apostles continued for 3½ years. Christ spoke from Heaven through these ordained men. In the middle of this week, Jesus was crucified. The next event after Daniel's final week would be the abomination of desolation accomplished through Titus, the prince (small "p"), who came to destroy the city of Jerusalem and the Temple. The Dispensationalists are woefully ignorant of who came to conquer these Jews (Da 9:26). After Messiah, the Prince (big "P") died;

another prince (small "p") came who is Titus. Titus was working for Jesus Christ. This sign of Christ's coming, *Parousia*, in the abomination of desolation (Mt 24:3) was unseen with physical eyes. Titus himself admitted that God destroyed the Jews, and he refused to receive the glory for the victory.[135]

> Daniel 9:27: "… and he shall make a firm covenant with many for one week: and in the midst of the week he shall cause the sacrifice and the oblation to cease; and upon the wing of abominations [shall come] one that maketh desolate; and even unto the full end, and that determined, shall [wrath] be poured out upon the desolate.

The final week begins in 26 A.D. when Jesus was immersed. He died in 30 A.D. and then in 33 A.D., Stephen was put to death. Jesus died in the middle of the week (30 A.D.). In the middle of this week, He put an end to sacrifice with His once for all blood sacrifice on the cross (Heb 7:27, 9:12, 10:10). Even though Jesus died, the Jews continued to sacrifice animals. However, when Jesus died, sacrifices stopped in the mind of God. Historically, the sacrifices stopped in 70 A.D. with Jerusalem's destruction. Thus, it says that the act of the abomination made Judaism desolate. Titus entered the city, and both the Romans and the Jews profaned the temple. When the Romans offered swine on the altar, they abominated it. Abomination is defiling; desolation is destruction.

A contradiction of Daniel's prophesies that brings untold grief to the God of Heaven.

A doctrine of the *seven years of tribulation* is simply not found in God's Holy Word. Incorrectly, in Daniel 9:27, the doctrine is inferred by reading seven years of future *tribulation* into the final week of Daniel's 70-week prophecy.

From the time people attended denominational Sunday school up to the present time, they have believed what they have been told and have allowed a powerful spirit to misled them into growing comfortable with reading this obscure *seven-year tribulation* into Daniel 9:27. This is not at all what it meant to the Apostles and New Testament evangelists. The *seven years* has nothing at all to do with a future *tribulation* that has happened. The Spirit-lead reader will acknowledge the *seven years* as a direct prediction of the 3½ years before Christ died and the 3½ years afterward, during which the Gospel was preached first to the Jews. This time period is not a one-time period called *The Tribulation*.

Because the Pre-Millennialists are wrong in their interpretation, they have committed great violence against the Counsel of God Almighty. Their futuristic interpretation of *seven years,* that they say has not yet happened, not only lifts the *seven years* out of its proper context, but also robs both Jesus Christ and the Apostolic Ministry to the Jews of their designated historical significance in the predestined prophecy. This is a very serious indictment indeed! The Millenarians and their listeners have grown comfortable with accepting it as fact. Their listeners do not search the Scripture for themselves. They do not question their preachers. They simply believed them because the preachers said it was in the verse.

The Tares the Enemy Has Sown

The following quotes are from publications by Tim LaHaye.

> "The tribulation is generally considered to be seven years in length, based on Daniel's prophetic vision of 9:24-27. In this vision the prophet was told that "70 weeks" (or heptads, meaning 70 times seven weeks of years, for a total of 490 years) were 'determined for your people (the Jews) and for your holy city.' He then lists three periods of time, beginning with seven weeks (49 years) 'from the going forth of the command to restore and rebuild Jerusalem' (which is described in the book of Ezra and Nehemiah as the time when the walls and the temple were rebuilt). The second period was two weeks (434 years) until 'Messiah shall be cut off, but not for Himself.' (This is an obvious reference to the period from the rededication of the temple to the crucifixion of Jesus the messiah). This is usually called the "time of Jacobs' trouble" which is described in Jeremiah 30:3-11. It is also described by the Lord in the Olivet Discourse and in the book of Revelation, where it is called 'the tribulation'." (*Understanding Bible Prophecy for Yourself* by Tim LaHaye, Harvest House Pub, p. 53)

> "Only 69 heptads (weeks of years) have been fulfilled so far. One heptad of seven years has never been fulfilled" (*Ibid.* paragraph 2, p. 53)

> "Notice instead that Daniel 9:26b points out that "the prince who is to come" which can only be (capitals used for emphasis by your author) the Antichrist, will be a Roman, for it says that his people (the Romans of 70 A.D.) shall destroy the city and the sanctuary"(*Ibid.* paragraph 2, p. 53).

"So in the midst of talking about the rebuilding of the temple and the holy city (during 49 years), Daniel predicted that it would be used for 434 years, then 'the Messiah shall be cut off.' Isaiah 53 describes this 'cutting off,'" or the crucifixion, as the details of Isaiah 53 match the descriptions of Christ's death as given in the Gospels. Then after an unspecified period of time the temple would be destroyed. Historically that took 40 years. After another undesignated period of time (the church age, which really began at Pentecost and has gone on for more than 1,900 years) there would be a period in which "there will be war: desolations are determined." A quick glance at those 1,900-plus years of church history will reveal that it has been a continuous period of wars…'" (*Ibid*. paragraph 3, p. 53).

"Then Daniel 9:27 says, "He (the prince who is to come) shall confirm a covenant with many for one week, but in the middle of the week he shall bring an end to sacrifice and offering". This is an obviously a future event and because it parallels prophetic teachings in 2 Thessalonians 2 and the book of Revelation, most prophecy teachers believe that the Antichrist will be the one who officially begins the tribulation period by signing a covenant with Israel for seven years (that unfulfilled seven years in Daniel 9). He will then break that covenant in three-and-a-half years (or 42 months as Revelation 13 says), after which the end (the 'consummation') comes: the physical return of Christ to this earth to set up His Kingdom." (Ibid. p. 55)

The Great Contradictor

There is a powerful Spirit that, like an opiate, overcomes and possesses the heart and mind of those committed to Pre-Millennialism. Once overpowered by this Spirit, we lose our ability to reason in the Scripture hermeneutically. We find ourselves possessed with an insatiable desire to contradict God's Word. This consuming, energizing Spirit of contradiction is unmistakably evidenced in the writings of Tim LaHaye. To verify my charges, I included the above quotes, word for word, from Tim LaHaye's book.

Tim Lahaye's Contradictions of God's word

Contradiction number one: "The tribulation is generally considered to be seven years in length."

God's word – Jesus speaks of the Abomination of Desolation in 70 A.D. When referring to the end of the world, He says, "Immediately after the tribulation of those days" (Mt 24:29). As a Prophet, Jesus does not look at events in a linear or chronological manner. He looks down on events, as God would see them from his eternal, sovereign Throne in Heaven. The Matthew, Chapter 24, context begins with a question regarding the end of the temple, Jesus' Coming, and the end of the age (24:3). Jesus is concerned with answering these questions. Thus, He addresses the end of the temple in 70 A.D., and the next important event is the end of the age. The end of the age is called "that day" (24:36); the events of 70 A.D. are called "those days"(24:22, 29, 36). Jesus foretold "Those days" so that the people of that generation could experience them (24:15) and see them come to pass (24:25), for the generation of those days passed away in the desolation of Jerusalem (24:34), and not before then.

There is No Seven Years Tribulation Here.

The Apostles experienced tribulation and death (24:9). The people of Judea (24:16), those on top of their houses (literally upon the flat surfaced roofs: 24:17), those farming the soil as they did in 70 A.D. (24:18), all pregnant women who breast fed babies (24:19), and those who were stranded by cold winter weather or snow, or forbidden to travel on the national Sabbath went through a great tribulation, such as has never occurred before or since (24:21). Tim LaHaye can read the newspaper, but it is as obvious to a contextual Bible student as it would be to an English professor that he is violating and contradicting all the known rules of interpreting literature, not withstanding, furthermore, a deplorable disregard for the most fundamental elements of Biblical hermeneutics. The tribulation, "those days" (Mt 24:29) of 70 A.D., was generally 3 ½ years long (from the invasion of Titus in the spring of 67 A.D. to the end in 70 A.D.), and specifically "A short work" (Ro 9:22-28).

Contradiction number two: The *tribulation* is generally called "Jacob's Trouble" and is referred to in the Olivet Discourse (Mt. Chapter 24; Mk, Chapter 13; Lk, Chapter 21) and the Book of Revelation.

Only a Bible scholar whose mind is already made up, and given over to fanciful delusions of being a modern-day prophet, could be capable of trying to scramble God's Divine Word to fit into his personal scheme of things. There is nothing in

Jeremiah's prophecy to indicate a so-called Great Tribulation of the post-crucifixion era, or some yet to be determined future events.

Jacob's trouble – One of the first advocates of Hermeneutics was Alexander Campbell. Campbell held the opinion that people who are not skillfully trained in Hermeneutics are incapable of teaching the Bible. We may not want to call it a law of Hermeneutics, but a common sense approach to this section of Scripture is to determine the historical background and reason for the prophecy. Jeremiah predicted the 70 years Babylonian Captivity. He gave comfort to those who were under the yoke of that captivity. The background theme of Chapter 30:1-24 is the restoration of the Jews from Babylon and the raising up of the Messiah.

This prophecy is quite simple. Jeremiah's Prophecy, in Jeremiah 30: 3, said they would return to Jerusalem, which they did upon Cyrus' decree. The Jews had experienced a wide range of emotions, especially the terror they had experienced after being subjugated by Babylon and Cyrus' Media-Persian Armies had overwhelmed them in Babylon. Their joy of returning to Jerusalem was mingled with their former sorrow, like a woman being in travail with child. They were the seed of Jacob, and Jacob had made lots of mistakes and, subsequently, had experienced lots of sorrow for his choices. Thus, by synecdoche, when the Jews made wrong choices, Jacob's children from the "captivity generation" found themselves experiencing troubles similar to father Jacob's (Jer 30: 3-7).

Jacob had plenty of trouble and so did his children, but how, pray tell, does this have anything to do with a great tribulation? Just as God saved Jacob from tribulation by His grace, so shall the Jews be saved from physical captivity. The spirit of Millennialism perverts "Jacob's Trouble" by refusing to focus on the true meaning of this Prophecy. Verses 8 through 9 present terrific insights into the coming of the Messianic King, Jesus Christ. As a descendant of Jacob, Jesus the Messiah-King would be a star out of Jacob (Nu 24:17) and rule over the House of Jacob, forever (Lk 1:33), not for a mere 1,000 earthly years. The 1,000 years refers only to the time that the citizens of His Kingdom sojourn in it from generation to generation. The "forever" refers to the eternal dominion that is inherent to Christ-Messiah. Verse 9 refers to the Day of Pentecost, when the Son of God ascended to the throne promised to David (Lk 1:32 with Ac 2:30, 13:23). God is only someone's King when they are subject to Christ, for Christ is equal to God and deserving of equal allegiance (Ac 2:36-38).

The word *tribulation* is not found in the 24 verses of Jeremiah, Chapter 30. The Apostles and Evangelists of the New Covenant knew what these verses meant. The return from Babylonian Captivity was just a temporary reprieve. On the day of Pentecost, they knew the true meaning of freedom. Three thousand from the House of Israel were saved (Ac 2:35-38) so God did not put a final end to the Jews (and the remnant of Israel who returned with them), because they were in Jerusalem to hear the first Gospel sermon. God broke the yoke from the neck of Jacob (His seed-vs. 8). The wound of physical Israel was incurable (vs. 15). God would punish their subjugators (Babylon and Persia), and the descendants of Jacob would once again set up their "tents" (not modern-day condominiums) "and ye shall be my people (vs. 22)." No Apostle or Evangelist could ever understand this prophecy in any way other than its being a twofold fulfillment. First, the historical restoration of the Jews back to the city and palace (which was laying in heaps at the time of this prophecy), and then the coming of the Davidic King, Jesus Christ-Messiah, to bring both Jew and Gentile into one fold as His people and God's people-

"...And I will be their God, and they shall be my people," (2 Co 6:16).

When any Apostolic writer of the New Testament comments on an Old Covenant prophecy, it settles it! Those awaiting a future tribulation and the Antichrist are playing the part of antichrist themselves. They do this when they bypass the New Covenant understanding of Christ' sitting on the Throne promised to David and ruling over the House of Jacob. Their doctrine causes them to deny the Christ Messiah and His rightful place on the Heavenly Throne. This is the promise that Peter said was granted to Him at His ascension (Ac 2:31-36). When a New Covenant Apostle comments on an Old Covenant prophecy, it settles the question of fulfillment.

It is mind-boggling how LaHaye, a Pre-Millennialist, can find *the great tribulation* in any verse of the Thessalonians Scripture. This doctrine teaches that every verse of Scripture is *the great tribulation and the rapture*. In doing so, it kills the Scripture's real meaning. The word *tribulation(s)* occurs in I Thessalonians three times.

"For, in fact, we told you before when we were with you that we would suffer tribulation, just as it happened, and you know." (1 Th 3:4).

This passage states nothing about *the great tribulation*. Paul simply told them they would suffer tribulation, and when it happened, they remembered what Paul said. What was true then has been equally true for all Christians throughout history.

> "...since it is a righteous thing with God to repay with tribulation those who trouble you" (2Th 1:6).

The reader can be sure LaHaye and Pre-Millennialists would read *the great tribulation* into this passage if they could, but it simply is not there. What has happened to the persecuted Thessalonian Christians of that day has happened to all true New Covenant Christians throughout the ages, and God brought tribulation on antichrists as well.

The same truth is reiterated in verse 4 where Paul uses the plural, "tribulations." No rational person would attempt to find *the great future tribulation* from this passage.

In Revelation, John calls himself a companion to all Christians in tribulation (1:9). Jesus told the New Covenant Christians at Smyrna, "I know thy works, and tribulation and poverty" (2:9). There is nothing more extraordinary about their tribulation in this verse than their poverty. "Tribulation" is used in an apocalyptic sense in 2:10, in which tribulation lasts ten days, in which the Christians of Smyrna took to mean a complete sentence and jail time imposed by Christ's enemies upon the poor Christians who dared to defy the laws enacted against Christianity.

The context of Revelation 7:14 is not addressing a future event. It is contrasting the Gentile Christians of 7:9-17 to a representative, apocalyptic number of 144,000. This number is the totality of Israel who were taken from Hades to Heaven, for they are found in the recapitulation of Revelation 14:1 with the Savior, the Lamb of God, on the eternal apex of Mount Zion. They would be some of the many souls of Old Covenant saints whom John saw already with Christ, for they do not yet have resurrected bodies,

> "God having provided some better thing for us (the New Covenant doctrine of the resurrection made good by Christ's resurrection example), that they (the Old Covenant saints) without us, should not be made perfect (in body, soul and spirit)" (Heb 11:40).

Later, John sees the souls of New Covenant saints. This would be the "fullness of the Gentiles" called "a great multitude that no man could number of all Gentiles (nations)…" (7:9). The 144,000 of Israel, "fullness of Israel," could be numbered because after the Abomination of Desolation of 70 A.D., no true descendants of Israel (Jacob) were left to number, but the "fullness of the Gentiles" is still coming and continues until the last Gentile to be saved, is saved. Granted, the number is already filled up in God's mind, for He knows all things, but God has not finished dealing with spiritual Israel, as He finished with physical Israel. Both groups, the 144,000 of the past (now with the true Lamb, and not the bloody lambs of the old tabernacle), and the multitudes of the Gentile nations are all authentic, spiritual Israel.

> "These are they which have come out of great tribulation, and have washed their robes (a reference to Christian immersion), and made them white in the blood of the lamb" (7:14).

The first-mentioned principle of obeying the Gospel was given first to the Jew (Ac 2:38) and later to the Gentile (Ac 10:47) "a far off" (Eph 2:17). This principle continued for both Jew and Gentile as spiritual Israel until 70 A.D. After this, it references the fullness of the Gentiles only. In some way, all Israel has and is being saved from and through great tribulation (Ac 14:22; 2Co 1:4, 7:4).

There is no *future tribulation* in any of these verses. In fact, the only other place that a *great tribulation* is found in Revelation will give absolutely no comfort to LaHaye and his millenarian cause. The verse, Rev 2:22, refers to Jezebel and her paramours, who will be cast no doubt into the tribulation in Hell. This is the same tribulation of 2 Thessalonians 1:6, an experience that is amplified by the flaming fire of 1:8.

The other reference LaHaye gives to his alleged *great tribulation* is taken from Matthew 24:21, the Olivet Discourse. However, a third grade Sunday school student could conclude that this refers to Jerusalem's destruction by the Roman armies in 70 A.D. There are no Gentiles in this context, only Jews from Judea.

Contradiction number three: LaHaye says that one heptad of seven years (Da 9:27) has never been fulfilled.

In other words, LaHaye makes a liar out of both the angel Gabriel and Daniel himself. Gabriel said, "I have come to give you skill and understanding" (9:22), and "...Therefore understand the matter and consider the vision." The vision has a commencement, "the going forth to restore and rebuild Jerusalem" (9:25), and it has a consummation "…. and the end thereof shall be like a flood, and unto the end of the war, desolations are determined" (9:26), "...even unto the consummation, and that determined shall be poured upon the desolate" (9:27).

There was nothing difficult about this prophecy. At first, Daniel was greatly agitated in mind and troubled. However, after Gabriel explained it, Daniel could see clearly. The prophecy began after the desolations of the Babylonian captivity (9:17). It began with the restoration of the Temple and ended with the abomination of the Temple (not one stone left upon the other), the destruction of Jerusalem, and the desolation of Judaism. In other words, it was a completed prophecy; it had a beginning; and it had an end. If LaHaye is correct, that only the first part of this prophecy was fulfilled when Christ was cut off, "crucified," then the New Covenant is an incomplete book. This would also mean that none of the Apostles, Prophets, and Evangelists ever understood what God was trying to say. This left Daniel, who remained in Heaven, scratching his head and wondering when this prophecy would be fulfilled. Notice that LaHaye purposefully shuns the old-line Dispensational twaddle of a *postponement* of prophetic fulfillment which teaches that this prophecy did not reach its logical conclusion because God postponed it when the Jews rejected the Kingdom and His son, Jesus Christ-Messiah. The critics of this nonsensical interpretation were so vocal that the rapture cultists had to change their tune. They accused the Millenialists of worshipping a weak God whose eternal counsel was subject to a wicked nation. They also asserted that if God changed His mind on the last week of Daniel's prophecy, He could change His mind on anything He had said in Scripture. God could not be trusted if the likes of LaHaye are correct. The spirit of *millennial madness* backed off. They dropped the postponement theory. However, they retain this same idea in their theology. They change the truth of God into a lie (Ro 1:25).

Historians document that the New Covenant was being completed (before 70 A.D.). The early Christians widely used the Book of Daniel when evangelizing the lost. They understood this Book and the above-mentioned prophecy. LaHaye thinks early Christians did not understand it, and no one understands it to this day. It all boils down to the question, "Are God, Gabriel, Daniel and Jesus right or is Tim LaHaye?" If the Lord tarries until 2050 A.D., Lahaye will be dead; his books will not be worth a penny because they were proven false. Nevertheless, there will be another prophet, possessed of the spirit of millennial madness, who will be preaching, and teaching, and writing this same nonsense. Unfortunately, some will believe it. God has given them "a strong delusion that they should believe a lie" (2Th 2:11).

Contradiction number four: The prince who is to come can only be *the Antichrist*.

LaHaye adds that the antichrist will be Roman because the Romans destroyed Jerusalem in A.D.70. The only Romans ever mentioned today are Roman Catholics! Of course, there are ethnic groups of people who call themselves Italians, and they originated from the nation that once had the illustrious Rome as the capital of the known world. However, those days are gone. Rome was revived through Roman Catholicism as previously noted. The reason people do not refer to themselves as Romans today is that every ethnologist knows there is no longer such a thing as a pure race of people on planet Earth.

LaHaye puts the label of Antichrist upon Christ Himself. Instead of rendering the prince who is to come as Titus who was employed by Christ to fight His enemies, LaHaye believes it will be some future person who will call himself a "Roman." He does this even though he admits that some 40 years after the crucifixion, the Roman General, Titus, destroyed Jerusalem. What is sad, tragic, and shocking is that LaHaye also calls the "He who shall confirm the Covenant with many for one week" (9:27) the same Roman antichrist as the prince of the people in verse 26. As we will come to understand, the Prince of the Covenant (vs. 27) is none other than Jesus, the Christ-Messiah. The covenant He confirms with many is the New Covenant, and LaHaye, along with other millennial cultists, call Him *the antichrist*. The blessed Lord and Savior, Jesus Christ, God's only unique Son and Covenant Maker is called *the antichrist* according to a gross, abhorrent misconstruing of a prophecy concerning what Gabriel said, "I will give you skill and understanding."

Contradiction number five: LaHaye says this Antichrist will make a covenant with Israel for a week (seven years) and then break the covenant in the middle of the week (three 1/2 years).

Where in this text do we read about anyone breaking a covenant? After the year, 70 A.D., where can we find authentic Israelites (descendants from Jacob) who will make a covenant with the Antichrist? Matthew Henry, in his exposition of

9:27, indicates that after 70 A.D., there were no authentic temple-certified Jews left. If there were no authentic Israelites at that time, nearly 2,000 years ago, certainly there were no Israelites to challenge Matthew Henry's statement made 200 years ago. The exact quote is,

> "'The end of it shall be with a flood'. It shall be a deluge of destruction like that which swept away the old world; and which there will be no making head against. Hereby the sacrifices and oblation shall be made to cease. And it shall be made to cease when the family of the priests was so extirpated, and the genealogies of it were so confounded, that (they say) there is no man in the world that can prove himself of the seed of Aaron."

Matthew Henry is a brilliant theologian. He goes on record to affirm the universal consensus of historical scholarship (not that of fanatics), which is that after 70 A.D., there can be no seed of the High Priest Aaron. There can be no genealogical, Levitical priesthood, and never again will there be a Jewish Temple in which to restore such clerical offices. In fact, the Apostle Paul called, "foolish," any attempt to try to prove that there was a genealogical descendant of Aaron or Levi fit for such a holy office.

"Do not give heed to fables and endless genealogies" (1 Ti 1:4).

"But avoid foolish genealogies, and questions and contentions and strivings about the law, for they are unprofitable and vain" (Tit 3:9).

What is Paul talking about? He is not talking about personally tracing your lineage back to your ancestors to try and determine whom your great, great grandma or grandpa may be. In both verses, he is talking about the Old Law and not the New Covenant faith. The Old Law required genealogies, for without them the Law and Temple Worship would fail,

"For all these were reckoned by genealogies…" (1Ch 5:17)

"They were reckoned in all by their genealogies…. ", (7:5, 7, 9:1, 5:1, 7, and 7:9, 40, 9:22).

"The sons of Aaron…. the Levites…. to all that were reckoned by genealogies (2Ch 31:19, 16, 17, and 18)

"Those that were reckoned by genealogy…." (Ezr 2:62)

"These are now the chief of their fathers, and this is the genealogy of them that went up with me from Babylon...." (8:1, 3; Ne 7:5)

"And I found a register of the genealogy of them that came up first (from Babylon)" (Ne 7:5, 64).

In reading the painstaking efforts these holy scribes took to preserve the priestly genealogies, we realize how important it was at the time. In reading the genealogy of Messiah, Jesus Christ, we also realize that the efforts of Ezra, Nehemiah, Haggai, and Zechariah were not in vain. If there are no restored genealogical records of these prophets and scribes, then there would not be any absolute proof that Christ descended from the seed of the woman, according to the flesh (Ge 3:15, 16). Christ's genealogy would signify nothing if the old chronicles of Ezra and Nehemiah had not been recorded historically.

Paul's words are meaningful in regard to this whole mess of Jew first, restoration of Judaism theology, and exercise unto "vain jangling-desiring to be teachers of the Law, understanding neither what they say, nor whatever they teach," (1Ti 1:6b, 7). Even though the Law was good, it was necessary for the Old Law to be changed to the New Covenant Law of Spirit and life (Heb 7:12). The Old Law was disannulled, "put away," for it made nothing perfect (7:18, 19). We now have a *better covenant* (7:22, 9:6-13).

Therefore, what are we to conclude from the efforts of the proponents of Millennial Mania? Pre-Millennialists will not put it in these exact words, but they want an End Time restoration of Old Law Temple worship and a reestablishment of the very things that Paul said of witchcraft, foolishness, and slavery. Do they expect God to respond to this nonsense? Do they expect God to dig out of the ruins of ancient Jerusalem the molecular residue of genealogical records that were consumed by fire? Do they, then, create a new nation of physical, genealogical descendants of Abraham, Aaron, and Levi so that they can qualify for service in the New Temple? Do they expect God to contradict the Spirit inspired writings of Paul and the Apostles? If He did, God would be a Devil!

Paul said that any attempt to track genealogical records according to the Law was foolish. Therefore, after Christ died, any attempt on the part of a person to do so would render him a fool in God's sight, "For Christ is the end of the law" (Ro 10:4). Christ is the END of the temple for He "was able to destroy the temple"(Mt 26:61) because it was faulty, "made with hands" (Mk 14:58). Christ raised it up in three days (Jn 2:19). Obviously then, it was not a physical temple, and if not, then what other kind of temple could there be? The Millennial Cultist has not yet figured that out. Paul said, "You are the temple of God" (1Co 3:16). Christ's Congregation "grows into a holy temple unto the Lord," (Eph 2:21). God the Father and the Lamb, Messiah-Christ, are eternally the Temple of the City of God (Rev 21:22).

We need to issue a serious warning and caution to those insisting that non-authentic, non-certified modern-day *Israel* will rebuild a temple in physical Jerusalem. It does not matter if it is prior to or after the bogus *rapture* to restore sacrifices and offer *a red heifer*. The questions that should be asked are, "Who has bewitched you that you should not obey the truth?" (Gal 3:1). "This only would I learn of you, received you the spirit by the works of the law, or the (*pletheo*) obedient hearing of faith?" (3:3). "How turn you again to the weak and beggarly elements (of the Law) wherein you desire again to be in bondage?" (4:9b.) "I am afraid of you; lest I have bestowed upon you labor in vain!" (4:11) LaHaye and a consenting tribe of anti-present-messiahs have done much harm to the Counsel of God.

Contradiction number six: LaHaye says that Antichrist will make a Covenant with Israel in the last week of Daniel (7 years) and in the middle of the week (3½), he will break the Covenant.

The question is asked again, where does the text of 9:27 even remotely indicate that a Covenant is broken? Verse 27 says simply," He will cause the sacrifices and oblations to cease." Consequently, the covenant-maker will make sacrifices and oblations (obviously from the former Covenant) to cease. LaHaye has some very serious troubles with God in this interpretation. First, the He who causes sacrifices to cease has to be King, Messiah-Christ. He has to be the same as the Messiah, the Prince of verse 25. How could Daniel, who was given to understand this Prophecy, introduce the Messiah in verse 25 and speak of that same Messiah-Christ being cut off in the middle of the week (3 1/2 years after His immersion in the Jordan River), only to discontinue the subject of this same Messiah in verse 27? How could it not be the subject of the Messiah confirming the (*new*) Covenant through His death, nailing the Old Law to the Cross, ending it, and thus causing sacrifices and oblations to cease? How could Daniel, who understood this Prophecy, write down the vision in such a disjoined literary style that he would need Tim LaHaye to explain to his gullible disciples that the Prophecy suddenly broke into two parts between verses 26 and 27? And these two parts now stand 1994 years apart in history? To make matters worse, the second part of the disjoined Prophecy is not only yet unfulfilled, but no one on Earth or in Heaven can know or give special revelation as to when in the devil-only-knows future, it ever will be fulfilled! What an insult to the Prophet Daniel.

It must be re-iterated that the whole Millennial scheme falls apart if a modern, genealogical, authentic nation of Aaronites and Levites cannot be found.

Parable of the Wicked Vinedresser

Remember, it was not Titus who destroyed Judaism. It was Jesus Christ the Son and God the Father. Jesus made this as lucid as possible in the Parable of the Wicked Husbandmen (or Wicked Tenants). I will abbreviate this parable (Lk 20:9-18). God planted a vineyard (Old Covenant economy), and He expected the vinedressers to honor Him by faith. God sent Moses and the Law to encourage the vinedressers to bear fruit, but they spurned God's operation. God then sent the Prophets, and the vinedressers wounded them and killed them. Lastly, God sent His Son, thinking they would revere His Only Son, but they treated him shamefully and murdered Him with the hope that they would receive His inheritance after His death. Then Jesus, who is the main protagonist in this Parable, asked the poignant question, "What therefore shall the Lord of the vineyard do to them?" (20:15b) Since the Lord of the vineyard is God, the Father, it shows that "He shall come and destroy these husbandmen!" Jesus identifies the destroyer, and *when* He would destroy,

> "Whoever shall fall upon that stone *Jesus Christ* shall be broken (pierced in heart and crying unto the Lord for Salvation-Ac 2:37-38); but on whosoever it shall fall, it will grind him powder" (the stones of the temple and city falling upon the frightened inhabitants and Rufus Turnus, the chief engineer of Titus, grinding the dead bodies intermingled with the rubbish and wreckage with a plow) (20:18).

Turnus thought he was preventing the spread of pestilential disease by turning under dead bodies, but he was unconsciously fulfilling prophecy. This Prophecy of Jesus had its fulfillment, first in preaching to the Jews before 70 A.D. (Ac 4:11) and then in the Abomination of Desolation itself, "When the Kingdom was taken from you and given to another nation (Christian Covenant Kingdom of Kings and Priests, a Holy Nation) who would bear fruit," (Mt 21:43). It is difficult to determine whether this parable depicts God, the Father, or God, the Son, coming in the 70 A.D. judgment, and it was probably intended to read that way, because both Persons of the Godhead are involved in another Parable,

> *"But bring here those enemies if mine (the Jews), who do not want to reign over them (70 A.D.), and (Titus) slay them before me" (Lk 19:27).*

Christ's enemies, the Jews, are contrasted with the Jewish enemies, the Romans, in Luke 19:43-44 (author's emphasis),

> *"For days will come upon you (70 A.D.) when your enemies will build an embankment around you (the siege works and escape prevention mounds build around the city by Engineer, Rufus Turnus), surround you and close you in all every side, and level you and your children within you (the pregnant women referred to in Matthew 24:19), to the ground (grinding their dead bodies along with the debris and stones into powder); and they will leave in you one stone upon another, because you did not know the time of your visitation (when the Lord came to you)."*

This visitation compares to the coming (*Parousia*) of Matthew 24:3. This is the remarkable presence of God in his glory, for good or evil (Da 9:24; 1Pe 2:12; Lk 1:68, 78.)

The Jews were the enemies of Christ's Kingdom. The Romans were the enemies of the Jewish Kingdom. The armies that encompassed Jerusalem (Lk 21:20) were actually the armies of Jesus Christ,

> *"But when the King heard about this, he was furious. And he sent out his armies, destroyed those murderers, and burned up their city" (Mt 22:7).*

Both God the Father and the Son

This concludes the first part of the Parable of the Marriage Feast (the arrangements for Christ to marry His Bride, the Congregational New Covenant Kingdom, as prophesied in Hosea), which is very similar to the Parable of the Husbandmen in the vineyard. This Parable of The Marriage Feast places more emphasis upon the Son as the King of this New Covenant Kingdom. The Husbandmen Parable seems to show God's patience through the dark, dismal years of the Old Covenant until the time was providentially ripe for the King, His Son, to come.

This Husbandmen Parable (Lk 20: 9-19) appears to emphasize the pre-70 A.D. preaching of the Kingdom of God for the 40-years, from the Crucifixion to the Desolation. However, even a casual reading of the Parables reveals the shocking fact that it was not Titus, but both God the Father and God the Son who destroyed Judaism. Even though those like Tim LaHaye just do not seem to get it, Titus surely did. Titus was smarter than all those adhering to today's Millennial-rapture cult. Titus refused the victors crown bestowed by the Roman Senate because he knew that it was God who destroyed the Jews.

LaHaye is dead wrong. Christians are not to look for a future antichrist to make a covenant with a false Israel and later break it. No, Christ made a firm Covenant with many, and those are the people who break bread with Him in His Kingdom, every first day of the week (Ac 20:7), as stated below,

> *"For this is my blood of the New covenant which is shed for many (as Daniel predicted) for the remission of sins (same word as Ac 2:38): but I say unto you that I will not drink henceforth of this fruit of the vine (not alcoholic beverage), until that day (of Pentecost, 30 A.D) when I drink it NEW (Covenant) with you in my Father's Kingdom (Blood Covenant Congregation)" (Mt 28:26-29 with Hebrews 9:22; Mk 14:24; Lk 22:18).*

We should observe that all these passages regarding the Lord's Supper being taken in the Kingdom of God (Jesus Christ) are connected with the eventual taking away of the sacrifices and oblations in the Abomination of Desolation of 70 A.D. When the Temple fell, the sacrifices and oblations fell with it. Christ took the physical Temple away in order to establish a Spiritual Kingdom. *Christians* make a huge mistake when they look for a future antichrist to do what the real, Messiah-Christ-King has already done.

Contradiction number eight: LaHaye thinks that after the end, the "consummation," then Christ will come to set up His Kingdom.

LaHaye miss's prophecy by 2,000 years. He thinks the Temple is yet to be rebuilt. On the other hand, Jesus Christ built it three days after His death 2,000 years ago. LaHaye thinks the blood of a red Heifer is needed to appease God. Yet, Christ's blood made propitiation 2,000 years ago. LaHaye thinks a Covenant has yet to be made. However, Christ cut a Covenant with many 2,000 years ago. LaHaye thinks a covenant will yet be made and broken. Nevertheless, Christ will never break His New Covenant of 2,000 years with those of Acts 2:42. LaHaye thinks that the Ark of the Covenant still needs to be found; yet it was found in Heaven 2,000 years ago (Rev 11:19). LaHaye thinks Christ still has to establish a Kingdom. Yet, Christ established a firm Covenant Kingdom with many 2,000 years ago, and every first day of the week (in God's eyes) someone, somewhere on Earth is eating His flesh and drinking His blood at the Covenant Table, and has been doing so for 2,000 years. LaHaye is looking for a big antichrist to come someday. Yet, John said there were many antichrists in the world, 2,000 years ago (1Jn 2:18). LaHaye is looking for *the great tribulation* to come someday, and yet, Jesus said of the Abomination of Desolation, 70 A.D, "For then shall be great tribulation, such as was not from the beginning of the world to this time (the 70A.D. which they seen-Mt 24:15), no, nor ever shall be," (Mt 24:21), and this about 2,000 years ago. Jesus said, 2,000 years ago, "Behold I have told you before" (24: 25). If it did not come to pass in that generation 2,000 years ago, then Jesus was a liar. Tim LaHaye, and anyone who teaches this demonic doctrine, should be ashamed. The duty and commission of the evangelist like it or not is to reprove, rebuke, and exhort with long suffering and doctrine those who depart from the Faith (2Ti 4:1-3). A man does not have spiritually, discerning eyesight that consistently misses the mark by 2,000 years.

A Comprehensive Analysis of the Coming of Christ-Messiah and His Redemptive Work (Da 9:24-27)

This is a more in-depth expunction of the six-fold prophecy and fulfillment.

First – "To finish transgression." Jesus' commentary in Matthew 23:29-39 should settle this question completely. Daniel was crying out because the Jews were perpetual transgressors (Da 9:11), and "all Israel had transgressed the Law." The supreme heights of their transgressions poured out along with God's wrath at Golgotha Hill, as they crucified the Lord, and made possible a savior for those who crucified Him.

Second – "To make an end of sins." Although Jesus was numbered with the transgressors, He was also stricken for the transgressions of His people as addressed in the Book of Isaiah, Chapter 53. He was cut off in the middle of the seven years. He offered one sacrifice for sins forever (Heb 10:12). Obviously, the Jews were ignorant of what they were doing, and Jesus said, "Forgive them for they know not what they are doing." After Stephen preached to them 3½ years later, they knew exactly what they were doing. They resisted the truth by being stiff-necked and committing blasphemy against the Holy Spirit (Ac 7:50 ff.) In God's Holy Sight, however, Christ put an end to sin by His perfect atonement and satisfactory *propitiation* for the sins of the whole world. By Himself alone, He purged the world's sins, and not for Himself, but for all (Heb 1:3). His next to last statement on the cross, "It is finished," may apply to both the first and second proposition of Daniel's prophecy, "He finished transgression and made an end to sins."

Third – "To make reconciliation for iniquity." Tim LaHaye, or any other lesser prophet, shall not be allowed to take this complete prophetic panorama and postpone it or break it into two pieces; one piece occurred more than 2,000 years ago, and he is still waiting for the second piece to occur. This nullifies Christ's sacrifice for sins. Christ not only came to atone for sins, but He also reconciled the world to God. God demanded reconciliation because all in sin are His enemies (Ro 5:8-10). While being enemies, God reconciled potentially the whole world by the death of His Son. Whether or not we become reconciled to God depends upon our obedience to Him. The Bible stresses, in Colossians 1:12-22, the reconciling work of Christ that causes people to become members of His Kingdom and to receive peace through His *once* shed blood. If this prediction of Daniel is still in the future, Satan would lead us to believe that none of this has been accomplished by the Christ-Messiah-King.

Fourth – "To bring in everlasting righteousness." When did Christ bring everlasting righteousness? According to the Millennial Cult, He has yet to deliver the goods. The whole thing has been postponed. George H. Clement said, "The futurist school casts all of this into the 'blessing of the future millennium age'."

Jesus has become, to the Christian, His righteousness (1Co 1:30). "The Kingdom of God is.... righteousness, and peace and joy in the Holy Spirit" (Ro 14:17). Isaiah foretold of this righteousness that would last forever (Isa 51:8). Jeremiah pointed to Christ as "The Lord our righteousness" (Jer 23:5, 6). Paul stresses again and again that God *imputes* this righteousness to Christians for Christ's sake. Those people in Covenant with Christ are counted, reckoned, and imputed to be as blameless, righteous, and faultless as Christ Himself. When people are immersed into Covenant with Him, becoming Christians, they receive His righteous merit and are clothed with His righteousness (Gal 3:25-27). Notice how the sequence of Colossians 1:21, 22 fits the sequence of Daniel's prophetic utterance. Christians are reconciled in verse 21 and presented before Christ and the Holy

God in Covenant with Christ. This covenant is through His fleshy, bloody sacrifice. In His body, the Congregation Kingdom is holy, unblameable, and irreprovable *in His sight*. Paul uses this same vein of thought (Eph 1:4). Daniel was prophetically correct! The Messiah did make a covenant with us in the middle of the week.

Fifth – "To seal up the vision and prophecy." Isaiah 29:10-14 describes that God hid this prophecy from the Jews and sealed it up because they were so ignorant and blind from keeping their eyes closed.

> *"For the Lord has poured out on you the spirit of deep sleep, And has closed your eyes, namely the prophets; And He has covered your heads, namely, the seers. The whole vision has become to you like the words of a book that is sealed, which men deliver to one that is literate, saying, "Read this, please." And he says, "I am not literate." Therefore, the Lord said: "inasmuch as these people draw near with their mouths and honor Me with their lips, but have removed their hearts far from Me, and their fear toward Me is taught by the commandment of men, Therefore, behold, I will again do a marvelous work Among this people, a marvelous work and a wonder; For the wisdom of their wise men shall perish, And the understanding of their prudent men shall be hidden."*

Paul quoted this prophecy when he preached at Antioch of Pisidia in Acts 13:14. Paul's sermon covers verses 15 through 39. Paul gave an overview of Jewish history and the Davidic prophecies of Christ, the seed of David who would sit on the promised spiritual Throne. He preached the perfect life, sacrificial death, and resurrection of Jesus Christ. And then he warned them of what Isaiah predicted could happen to them,

> *"Behold you despisers, Marvel and perish! For I work a work in your days, A work which you by no means believe, though one were to declare it to you" (Ac 13:41).*

There is nothing within the Universe of Time and Space Even Close to a 7-year Tribulation in Scripture, but there is the last 7-years of Christ's Life on Earth.

It is not a tribulation, but the last seven years of Christ's total ministry consisting of His 3½ years and the Apostles 3½ years. This whole prophetic scenario has a lot to do with Daniel. Daniel understood that 490 years after the decree to rebuild the temple, Christ would come. He understood that He would be murdered and cut off violently in the middle of the last seven years of the prophecy. He understood that this one final sacrifice would not be that of an animal, but of a *God-Man*, who would cause all temple sacrifices and oblations to cease. For the most part, the Jews had never had their heart in these practices anyway. However, God remained with them, patiently, and with much longsuffering. He understood that most of the Jews would reject this final offer of pardon and the cessation of the temple sacrifice through the death of Christ Jesus in 30 A.D. However, the physical Earth (and cosmos) recognized and recoiled because of the instantaneous overthrow of the powerful bulwarks of Judea, 40 years after the death of Christ. No nation in history, past or present, has ever been destroyed so completely, suddenly, and consummately as was Judaism in 70 A.D. This is an inexplicable phenomenon of the might and power of God. God forgave them, literally "70 times 70" for 490 years before His long suffering turned into eternal wrath.

Daniel may not have understood the 40-year period from Christ's death to 70 A.D., but he understood that it would be just a short time. It would only be 3½ years after Christ's being "cut off" that almost all hope for converting Judaism to Christ would be lost. This is true because God, in His mercy, gave them 36½ more years to repent. During that time the Apostles, prophets, evangelists, deacons, disciples, and every man and woman, as God's priests and priestesses, went forth, house to house, warning and admonishing the Jew first (later the Greek-Gentile) of Daniel's prophecy and those of other prophets with whom the Jews were familiar. Thousands of souls were swept into the Kingdom of Christ through 1st Century apostolic preaching. At first, after the Apostles performed many miracles, signs, and wonders (Ac 2:43 with Heb 2:1-4), there was great joy and favor with God and the people. The Gospel would penetrate the immediate vicinities of Jerusalem, Judea, and Samaria as Zechariah 12-14, and Ezekiel 47, 48 had prophesied, apocalyptically. The apocalyptic parables of the Kingdom would continue, even in the ministry of the Great Prophet, Messiah-Christ, until Pentecost, 30 A.D. After the Kingdom was established, parabolic kingdom preaching would cease because the Apostles clearly understood the spiritual kingdom.

THE INCREDIBLE PARABOLIC-PROPHECY OF LUKE 13:6-8

This brief parable can be divided into seven parts. Three main players constitute the vital message this parable is conveying. God is the owner of the vineyard.

Jesus, "The Man," is the only designated manager of the vineyard. Attention is drawn to a lone "fig tree" in this vineyard, which represents the Jews.

Part 1) "The Man," Christ (vs. 6), represents God's expectation of His people accepting with great joy, the arrival of His Son (Son of Man) on Earth.

Part 2) Attention is drawn to a very great and disturbing problem encountering God's eternal, contemplative counsel for the salvation of all people. The problem is the fruitless "fig tree," or the Jews (physical, not spiritual Israel).

Part 3) "Looking for fruit" represents the life and entire ministry of Jesus Christ.

Part 4) "Not finding any (fruit)" represents the Jewish complacent apathy toward being a people chosen who will bear the name of YHVH before the world.

Part 5) "He" (God the Father), said to "The Man," (God the Son), who cared for the vineyard, "For three years I have been looking for fruit AND I FOUND NONE!" This fulfills the first three years of Daniel's final seven-year week, "in the middle of the week" (Da 9:27). During His 3½ year ministry, He sought salvation, first for the Jew (Mt 15:24). He came to His own, and His own received Him NOT! (Jn 1:11).

Part 6) God told "The Man," "THEN CUT IT DOWN!" Here we have the greatest example of how The Godhead always works in concert. At the most critical juncture of this apocalyptic parable, we are brought face to face with the most critical juncture in the history of the human universe. God told the Son to "CUT IT DOWN!" If The Son had obeyed, He would never have gone to the cross, and neither the Jews nor Gentiles would have a Savior from sin. He could have....and would have called 10,000 legions of angels to wipe the Jewish nation (and for that matter all nations) from the face of the planet Earth. Would the Jews get what they deserved? Would you and I get what we deserved? Owing to His equality within The Godhead, would He dare say, "Forgive them Father for they know not what they do!" The whole of the human universe is hanging in balance.

Part 7) In keeping with His role of intercessor between man and God, "The Man" (1Ti 2:5) said, "Let's dig around and fertilize it" (vs. 8). Indisputably, the second part of this parabolic parable is a prophecy of Christ's prayer, "Forgive them for they know not what they are doing" (murdering God's Son), and "dung or fertilize" the Christ-killing Jewish nation with the Gospel of New Testament prophets,

Apostles, and evangelists (Mt 23:34) to remind them of what they really did at the Cross of Calvary (Ac 2:23). Would they, like the broken hearted people in Acts 2:36-37, be "cut to the heart" with true repentance, or would they be like the obstinate ones who hardened their hearts, "being cut to the heart," with anger and rage (Ac 5:33)? Would The Jews who heard the Apostles and disciples preach cry out, "What must we do to be saved?" Or would they seethe with rage and complain, "You intend to bring this man's blood on us!"? (Ac 5:28)

It is not that God did not know they would murder His Son (and the Gentiles are equally guilty), for God (in His contemplative counsel) already saw this (Ac 3:14, 15). But the amazing fact we discover from this short apocalyptic parable is that it was not because of the bloody atrocity committed at Calvary that the Jews would be "Cut down" and "destroyed from among the people" (Ac 3:23); it was because they rejected the New Testament Apostolic Doctrine. This is why we are led to believe, among other things, the Blasphemy of the Holy Spirit is rejecting and speaking against New Covenant doctrine.

This second 3½ years of Daniel's prophecy lasted until the Jews murdered another New Testament saint, Stephen, in 33 A.D. (Ac 7:58-60). From Jesus' immersion in 26 A.D. to His death in 30 A.D. are roughly 3½ years. From Christ's death until Stephen's are 3½ years. When He died, Jesus cried, "Father, they know not what they do!" A great change takes place 3½ years later. The text describing Stephen's death, "They cupped their hands over their ears" to shut out the TRUTH of the Gospel, tells us ONE thing; they knew exactly what they were doing. So why did not Christ "CUT THEM DOWN"? Because of ONE little prayer, "Lord, lay not this sin to their charge!" And it was ONE little man who was forgiven because of it and that man was The Apostle of the Gentiles, Saul, whose name was changed to Paul!

While Stephen's prayer led to Paul's salvation, it also gave the Jews another reprieve. It bought them some time while Paul preached to them. If anyone could win them, Paul could because of his Jewish background and pedigree (Php 3:5). His prayer for them was heard, and God gave them another reprieve (even though they could care less about bargaining for time (Ro 10:1)). But the Jews were "vessels fitted for destruction" (Ro 9:22), and they despised God's longsuffering and patience, in spite of intercession by Stephen and Paul. Daniel knew their reprieve would last 40 Years.

Daniel had prophesied their destruction and "sealed it up" until its delivery through the Apostolic Gospel (Da 9:24). Their doom could not and would not be changed. Thus, it was not until 40 years after the crucifixion in 70 A.D. that THE TREE (Lk 3:7-9) was finally CUT DOWN!

Now you know, as He bowed over with a splintered piece of timber crushing the ragged skin of His aching back and stumbling through the street called "Via Delorosa," what Jesus meant when through parched, cracked lips, he uttered,

> "For if they (the Romans) do these things to the green wood (Jesus), what will be done (by the Romans) to the dry (wood)?" (Lk 23:31).

Yes, John the Baptist, you were right; the dry wood was finally CUT DOWN!

> "Oh, the depths of the riches both of the wisdom and knowledge of God! How unsearchable are His judgments and His ways past finding out!" (Ro 11:33).

From Christ's sacrifice until Stephen's brutal murder 3½ years later, God was working apostolic signs and wonders in the midst of the stiff-necked Jews. This New Covenant Gospel Ministry lasted another 36½ years until 70 A.D. Then, they would be unable to recognize God's work. Paul said, '*Behold, you despiser, Marvel and perish!*" (Ac 13:41a) It has been said that Paul was not great with words, at least not as eloquent as Apollos, but he versed the reaction of the Jews in one condensed statement, "*Oh you despisers. Look at what is going on here in 1st Century Christianity and wonder.... And perish in hell.*" This encapsulated statement fits perfectly alongside Jesus' statement in Matthew 23:33, "Serpents, brood of vipers! How can you escape the damnation of Hell?" That was the last generation of genuine, authentic Jewry on Earth. It passed away in its entirety.

Rather than wonder with awe and appreciation at God's work, that generation honored God with lips only. The Bible says, "But when the Jews saw the multitudes (of mostly Gentiles hearing New Covenant Christianity), they were moved with envy" (Ac 13:45a). They contradicted and blasphemed Paul and Barnabas. Paul then quoted Isaiah 49:6b, "I will also give You as a light to the Gentiles, That You shall be My salvation to the ends of the earth." Paul then began to turn to evangelize the Gentiles. This was a sealed book to the Jews because they were dull of its understanding.

It was as sealed as the lion's den (Da 6:17), and the sepulcher after Christ's burial (Mt 27:66). The Jews refused to hear and were blind to Moses and the Prophets, just as the millennial cult has much of the same spirit today (2Co 3:14, 15). The fulfillment of this prophecy is not for the eons of future history; it is found in the history of the first Congregation of Christ.

If a book is sealed, it can also be unsealed to the spiritual mind. This is exactly what happened to millions of souls in the 1st Century who walked through the open door of Christ's Kingdom for their soul's salvation. His Kingdom remains in the world today, and Peter used the keys to that Kingdom on Pentecost, 30 A.D. (Ac 2:36-47). Those keys (New Testament doctrine) are still available.

Sixth – "**To anoint the most holy One (or place).** What can this mean? 1) Some scholars think it means that Christ appeared in the Heavenly sanctuary after His ascension (Heb 9:23, 24). 2) Others think it took place on the day of Pentecost, when the Holy Spirit came to anoint the first Congregation of Christ. This Congregational Kingdom became the real "temple of the living God" (2Co 1:21 with 6:16). 3) Some scholars think it is the giving of the Apostolic Word to equip Christians, "…. for this anointing teaches you…" (1Jn 2:20, 27). 4) The respectable Bible expositor, George H. Clement, thinks this refers to the anointing of Jesus Christ at His baptism. Clement says,

> "He surely is 'The Holy One of Israel!' (Lk 1:35; Isa 60:9, 14), and when the Holy Spirit descended in bodily shape as a dove, Christ was then anointed for the work before Him. He likely referred to that occasion when He said, 'The Spirit of the Lord is upon me because He has anointed me to preach the Gospel' (Lk 4:18). The historian, Luke, recorded, 'God anointed Jesus of Nazareth with the Holy Spirit and power.'[136]

However, the anointing may be a combination of all four of these marvelous New Covenant viewpoints. Clement's idea of Christ's immersion can be considered because that occurred about 26 A.D, exactly 3½ years before the Messiah-Christ was cut off in the middle of the seven-year week. This would be the sign that Daniel's prophecy was winding down to completion. In any event, Christ's immersion was followed by His wilderness temptation (Lk 4) and His first public appearance coupled with His first sermon (4:18). All three of these events refer to His Spirit anointing, 1) "Being full of the Holy Spirit" and "Led by the Spirit

(4:1), 2) "Jesus returned in the power of the Spirit into Galilee" (4:14), and 3) "The Spirit is upon me because He has anointed me to preach" (4:18).

A fifth anointing is the capstone of this sixth prophetic point of Daniel's prophecy. His Spirit-inaugurated ministry concluded with His Kingly ascension to the Throne and God said, "You have loved righteousness and hated lawlessness; Therefore, God, Your God, has anointed You with the oil of gladness more than Your companions" (Heb 1:9).

The period from the beginning of Christ's ministry at his immersion to the anointing by God at His enthronement can be taken together in the fulfillment of Daniel's prophecy, "To anoint the Most Holy." This can mean no other than Jesus Christ. The word for Christ is from the Hebrew, "Messiah," and means the same, or "Anointed." The expression "above your companions" refers to those who were associates, partners, or fellow partakers of God's anointing. From the anointing of Samuel, the first of the line of Prophets, to the anointing of Aaron, the first of a line of Priests, to the anointing of Saul and David, the first in a line of Kings, Christ is anointed Prophet, Priest, and King above all. Later, the Apostle Peter recognized Jesus-Messiah as being God's Holy One (Ac 2:28). My personal opinion is that of the five proofs of the anointed Holy Christ, the last is the most comprehensive because it validates the prophecy of Christ's being the Messiah.

Daniel's 70 weeks or 490 years saw the accomplishment of all five of the above predictions. There is no future seventeenth week. Cyrus Scofield's *Bible* teaches the *gap theory*, or the *dispensational break* in two pieces of Daniel's prophecy. It separates the last half from the first half with an indefinite period of time. Like their Father, the Devil, who induces evolutionists to worship Father Time, so the millennial cult worships at the shrine of Father Time. In every generation, they publish and peddle hundreds of books parroting the same old theme, "If given enough time, the last half of Daniel's prophecy may come to pass." Regarding this, George Clement said,

> "Instead of being united in their gratitude to God for sending the Redeemer to accomplish these promises prophesied so remarkably by Daniel, the dispensational school scoffs at the only true and scriptural interpretation of Daniel 9:24, and places all who thus understand this verse in the class of heretics!"[137]

It is a wondrous thing to behold how God terminated the Old Covenant and established the New. The New Covenant is a completed book. One can read the New Covenant and study the historical record of the times in which Christianity was born and be in absolutely amazement and fear before God. It happened exactly as Daniel said it would. This Book which is sealed to some has been opened to others.

The Two Princes of Daniel's Prophecy

Daniel 9:25 lays the foundation for the prophecy of the Messiah, the Prince. In 9:26 is a reference to the people of the prince. The King James Version and other Bible translations mention this prince with a small "p".

To determine the two princes of the prophecy, the reader needs to return to Daniel's previous visions. Our reading all of Daniel, Chapter 2, leads us to the understanding that the Kingdom of God replaced the last of the world empires (Rome).

> *"The stone that struck the image became a great mountain (Heb 12:22-New Covenant spiritual Jerusalem) and filled the whole earth" (Da 2:35c).*

Matthew 21:42-44 is a definite reference to the Abomination of Desolation. The Temple stone which is the head of the corner (which in God's mind referred to the typology of Christ Messiah) was rejected by Judaism. That stone then fell and obliterated them. But the Congregation of Christ is built upon that stone and those who fall upon it in penitent, obedience of faith are not crushed. Daniel continues, -

> *"And in the days of these kings (a composite of all Kingdoms and Kings that lead up to the Roman Kingdom) the God of heaven will set up a kingdom which shall never be destroyed; it shall break in pieces and consume all these kingdoms, and it shall stand forever" (Da 2:44).*

This Kingdom is cut out of the mountain without hands. This is an obvious reference to the spiritual nature of the Kingdom of Heaven that God established on Earth.

Daniel says earlier that the Kingdom would be conferred. This is when he installed His Kingly Son on the Holy Mountain (Psalms 2 and 110). This glorious kingship rests upon one "like unto the Son of man," which is a direct reference to His God-Man character.

Then in Daniel 7, Daniel addresses the rise of a lion (Babylon), the rise of a bear (Media-Persia), the rise of a leopard (Greece with Alexander and his four generals), the rise of an iron-toothed dinosaur (Rome),

> *"I was watching in the night visions, and behold, One like the Son of Man, Coming with the clouds of heaven! (the ascension) He came to the Ancient of Days, And they brought Him near before Him (God the Father with a book in His hands (Rev 5:1))" (Da 7:13).*

In light of this, should we not naturally look to Daniel for further information about receiving the Kingdom from The Father (taking the book with the seven seals from God the Father – Revelation 5) and using His authority to establish the Messianic Kingdom on Earth? Only the dispensational Millennialists would have the insolence and gall to introduce some foreign element into the latter part of Daniel's easy to understand prophecy.

The progression of kingdoms is the same in all of Daniel's visions. He starts with Babylon, progresses to Persia, proceeds to Greece (which was very important in God's counsel in order to establish the Greek of the New Testament writings), and then to the last Kingdom, Rome. The Kingdom of Christ is to be established in the days of Augustus Caesar. The next prophetical event is the end, with eternal judgment and the world's recognition that *only* Christ is the King of Kings. Only a false prophet would seek to disrupt this historical harmony of prophetic Scripture. In approaching Daniel 9:24-27, we should not expect a postponement of that Kingdom. One should not look for a foreign element such as a time void into the no-one-knows-when-future. One should not look for a parenthetical, stopgap period of time, when God stops His prophetic time clock and then kick-starts it again in 1948 A.D.

George Clement refers to the spiritual and physical use of the word "stone." Jesus said the stone would fall upon them (Jews) and grind them to pieces. "Not one stone would be left upon another." When John the Immerser began His ministry, he discounted the fleshy line of Abraham crying, "God is able to raise up children to Abraham from these stones" (Mt 3:9b). We must remember the "these *stones*" reference when we study the Abomination of Desolation.

The Messiah, the Prince

Christ is not only called The King, but He is also called the PRINCE. A PRINCE is the son of a King. The Kingdom of God can be established only upon the redemptive work of the Son of God, called "one like unto the Son of man." Peter warned his listening audience about what really happened when they crucified the Son of man, "And killed the prince of life!" (Ac 3:15) He repeated this truth in Acts 5:31, "He has God exalted ... to be a prince and Savior." Again, "It became Him ... to make the captain (prince) of their salvation perfect through sufferings" (Heb 2:10). The Hebrew writer continues, "Looking unto Jesus the author (prince) and finisher of our faith...." (12:2). This Prince began and finished the Christian Faith; there is no postponement or stopgap in these verses.

In light of this, how could Daniel be referring to some future antichrist, prince? The Christ-Messiah is the main character in the last four verses of Daniel, Chapter 9. Christ confirmed the New Covenant (9:27), not some future antichrist. There is not even a hint of a Second Coming of Christ in Daniel 9:24-26. Yet, dispensational Millennialists drive a spike into the text and split it into two opposite sections. In their doctrine, the true Messiah Christ is "cut off at the cross," so they say, and will start a new age millennium when He comes again. Daniel equates the Messiah-Christ death with the stopping of sacrifices in the temple. Jesus did this when He died, and the veil in the temple was rent from top to bottom. He nailed the Law to the Cross. This event took place in the middle of the last week (9:27). How can Millennialist read into this a future antichrist-messiah? Will the real antichrist please stand up?

The obvious meaning of Christ confirming the Covenant with many for one week is in the definition of two words. First, "confirm," which comes from the Hebrew word meaning, "to be strong, to prevail insolently, and to exceed, greatly, mightily, valiantly." The seven-day week of Daniel begins with Christ's immersion in the Jordan River (26 A.D.), and His ministry prevailed: "a Man attested by God to you by miracles, wonders, and signs which God did through Him in the midst, as you..." (Ac 2:22). Matthew refers to His mighty works (11:20, 21, 23, 13:54, 58) as being exclusive and irresistible. Mark 6:2 reveals how His mighty works confirmed His Messiah-ship (6:2, 5, 14). Luke 19:37 explains that no greater works of might and power need to be added to His confirmation. In 24:19, He records the assessment of Jesus' Disciples, who accepted Him as Messiah even though they thought He was dead.

The *seven-year week* ends with Stephen's death, and Stephen concluded his last message to a blasphemous generation with a statement regarding the mighty Covenant Maker. Read the following excerpts from Stephen's sermon.

> *"…. Moses said to the children of Israel 'The Lord your God will raise up for you a Prophet like me from your brethren. HIM YOU SHALL HEAR.'" (Ac 7:37).*

> *"But he (Stephen), being filled with the Holy Spirit, gazed into heaven and saw the glory of God, and Jesus standing on the right hand of God, and said, 'Look! I see the heavens opened and the Son of Man standing at the right hand of God'!" (Ac 7:55, 56)*

And they stoned Stephen to death.

The Old Covenant gave way to the New Covenant (Jer 31:31 with Heb 8:7, 8:8-13). If we read the Book of Hebrews, Chapters 9 through 12, and still doubt that Daniel 9:27 did not happen in the last 3½ years of Christ's life and the first 3½ years of Apostolic preaching, we have received professional help from someone other than the Holy Spirit. Such conniving, manipulation of Scripture will never altar the fact that,

> *"And for this reason He is the Mediator of the new covenant, by means of death (being cut off in the middle of the week), for the redemption of the transgressions under the first covenant, that those who are called (by the Gospel) may receive the promise of eternal inheritance" (Heb 9:15).*

The Messiah-Christ died that *all* might potentially be saved. But, when *all* consider the claims of His eternal Son-ship and divinity, they are reduced to *many* who will receive Him. Nothing on Earth serves as a better reminder of His Covenant than when Christians partake of His supper each first day of the week (Ac 20:7). When they "come together" (1Co 11:25-28) and lift the cup of the fruit of the vine to their lips, they are reminded, "This cup is the new covenant in My blood. This do, as often as you drink it, in remembrance of Me" (11:25). Jesus Himself put it this way,

> *"Then He took the cup, and gave thanks, and gave it to them, saying 'Drink from it, all of you. For this is my blood of the new covenant, which is shed out for MANY for the remission of sins'" (Mt 26:27, 28).*

There is no doubt concerning the *covenant* and the *many* who are having an acceptance ceremony of that Covenant, along with a celebration of "preaching" His death until He comes (1Co 11:26). No foreign element of a stopgap or a postponement time period exists between His death and His Coming.

In describing who the real sons of Abraham are, Paul writes,

> "*For as MANY of you were baptized (immersed) into Christ have put on (the righteousness of) Christ*" (Gal 3:27).

Under the classification of *many* are people of all nations (Rev 7:9-14), and Paul again explains this, thusly,

> "*(...much more those who receive the abundance of grace and the gift of righteousness will reign in life (have salvation) through the One, Jesus Christ.)*" (Ro 5:17b).

> "*For as by one man's disobedience many were made sinners, so also by one Man's obedience many were made righteous*" (5:19).

Because so much of New Covenant writings involve celebrating the strong, valiant, mighty Covenant Maker, it is pointless for us to belabor the subject. *Many* have and *many* will continue to come under the Covenant Reign of King Jesus and continue in it. This would be impossible if He never confirmed ("made strong and mighty to save" – Psalms 24:8) His Covenant with *many*. For us to deny that Christ ever made a Covenant according to Daniel 9:27, and that, to the ugly contrary, an antichrist will someday come and make the covenant that Christ was supposed to make, is a false doctrinal blasphemy of Spirit-inspired Scripture. Unless repented of, this is unforgivable! Christ accomplished the entire, necessary Covenant-making activity and paid for it with His Blood in the middle of the final, 70th week. To teach the world anything more or less is a stupendous error. There is no future 70th week. If Millennialists are still held by a spirit that leads them to believe otherwise, let it be known to all that this spirit is not from God. It is not the Holy Spirit. A disciple of Christ does not need to know the volume of Scriptural teaching on this subject. Admittedly, it demands mental energy and spiritual discernment. But, a disciple who follows superficial understanding is certainly placing their soul in the hand of a thief and robber (Jn 10:1).

The Second Prince, with a Little "p" in Daniel 9:27

The people of this prince would destroy the city and its sanctuary. Christians possess a complete prophecy because it begins with the edict of Cyrus to rebuild the Temple and Jerusalem (2Ch 36:22, 23; Ezr 1:1, 2; Isa 44:28, 45:21 when God stirs up this Persian King), and ends with another king, Vespasian, and his son (Lk 21:20). Consequently, the next historical figure that had anything to do with the Temple just happened to be Prince Titus. As the Roman Commander of the 10th Legion, Titus came against the city and the temple of Jerusalem in 70 A.D. Also, how interesting that this was exactly two generations, or 40 years, after Christ's death in 30 A.D. Because people learn the history in which they have a personal interest, Jesus expected His followers to study the history of Titus's siege and invasion. Titus was as much an agent of Christ as were Nebuchadnezzar and Cyrus. A majority of this history is recorded in the books of Josephus. The people who followed the prince, Titus, were the Romans who came to take the Jewish nation away (Jn 11:48). What a profound truth that the words of the unbeliever Caiaphas were fulfilled.

> *"If we (the chief priests and Pharisees) let Him alone like this, everyone will believe in Him, and the Romans will come and take away both our place (Jerusalem temple) and our nation (Judah)" (Jn 11:48).*

Silence fell upon the Sanhedrin bosses! "And one of them, Caiaphas, being high priest that year, said to them...." (Jn 11:49).

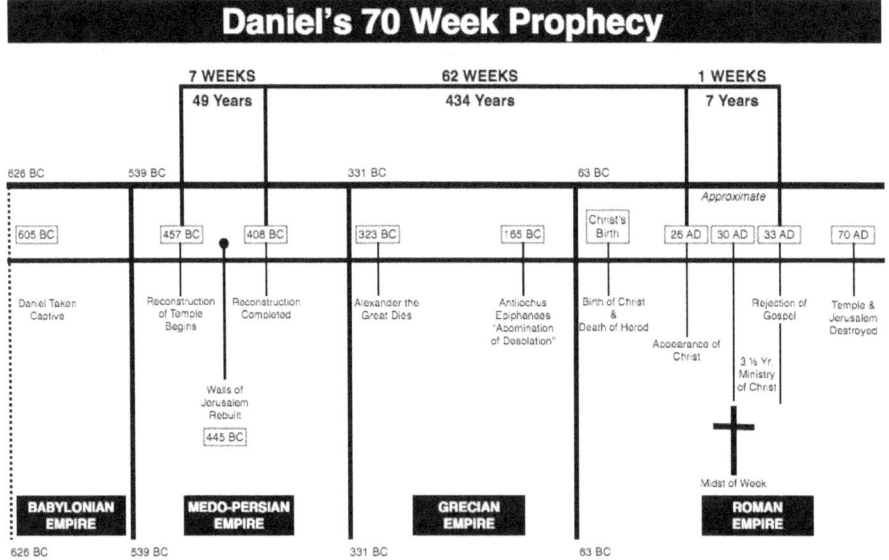

(By Kenneth Hylton)

Abomination of Desolation

Christians are taught the fear of God in Deuteronomy 28-31. Blessings and curses are plainly set before God's people. Chapter 28:15-58 gives the plaintive information from God's lips. If Israel turns from God's Covenant, they will be cursed as a country; their produce, domestic tranquility, and security will be cursed. They will be cursed with different types of diseases. They will experience hunger, thirst, famine, and pestilence. They will be terrorized and defeated by their military enemies. Others will take their harvest. They will be an indebted nation. They will shrink from being a world power to a fifth-world country. All this degradation and destruction would come about because they did not thank God and glorify Him when things were going well.

At last Israel will be destroyed by a nation from afar (Dt 28:49); Rome will lay siege to Jerusalem, and all the high and fortified gates and walls will come down (28:52). Jesus spoke of the siege works that the Romans would erect around Jerusalem. At least four other main communities had fallen prior to this final destruction of the Capital, Jerusalem. In fact, the inhabitants of other cities fled to Jerusalem thinking the "holy" city would be safe. This proved to be the worst thing they could have done.

Women would be so famished from hunger during the siege that they would eat the flesh of their own babies (28:56-57), and as God rejoiced to do good to the Jews, He would rejoice to destroy them and bring them to nothing. He would pluck them off the land (28:63). Jesus said their house would become *desolate*. Josephus wrote of how the Romans sent them back to Egypt in ships as slaves. However, the Egyptians would not buy them because no one wanted them (28:68).

Jesus continues to explain,

> Matthew 24:16-22: "then let those who are in Judea flee to the mountains. Let him who is on the housetop not go down to take anything out of the house. And let him who is in the field not go back to get his clothes. But woe to those who are pregnant and to those who are nursing babies in those days! And pray that your flight may not be in winter or on the Sabbath. For then there will be great tribulation, since has not been since the beginning

of the world until this time, no, nor ever shall be. And unless those days were shortened, no flesh would be saved; but for the elect's those days will be shortened."

Mark 13:14-21: "...then let those who are in Judea flee to the mountains. Let no one on the roof of his house go down or enter the house to take anything out. Let no one in the field go back to get his cloak. How dreadful it will be in those days for pregnant women and nursing mothers! Pray that this will not take place in winter, because those will be days of distress unequaled from the beginning, when God created the world, until now — and never to be equaled again. If the Lord had not cut short those days, no one would survive. But for the sake of the elect, whom he has chosen, he has shortened them."

Luke 21:20-24a: "When you see Jerusalem being surrounded by armies, you will know that its desolation is near. Then let those who are in Judea flee to the mountains, let those in the city get out, and let those in the country not enter the city. For this is the time of punishment in fulfillment of all that has been written. How dreadful it will be in those days for pregnant women and nursing mothers! There will be great distress in the land and wrath against this people. They will fall by the sword and will be taken as prisoners to all the nations."

Consider the following questions: "If this whole passage is speaking about a Second Coming of Christ, how will fleeing to the mountains help? What does it matter if people are on top of their houses or inside their houses? Why would people take their clothes if this were Christ's Second Coming? Why are women who are nursing children at a disadvantage when Jesus comes on the clouds of heaven? Why should there be perturbation if His Second Coming is in winter?" The final question is this: "Does Christ's Second Coming occur over multiple days (Mt 24:22; Mk 13:17; Lk 21:23) or on one day?" Take a look at this discourse between *those* days and *that* day.

Notice the change of expression from those days, these days and that day.

The following expressions come from Matthew 24 and concern the 70 A.D. End:

"But woe to those who are pregnant and to those who are nursing babies in THOSE DAYS (vs.19)." And unless THOSE DAYS were shortened, no flesh would be saved; but for the elect's sake THOSE DAYS will be shortened" (vs. 22).

The following expressions from Matthew of the end of the world –

"Immediately after the tribulation of THOSE DAYS the sun will be darkened, and the moon will not give its light" (vs. 29).

"But of THAT DAY and hour no one knows," (vs. 36).

The following expressions come from Mark 13 concerning the 70 A.D. end.

"But woe to those who… are nursing babies in THOSE DAYS" (vs. 17).

"For in THOSE DAYS shall be tribulation," (vs. 19).

"Except the Lord had shortened the (THOSE) days" (vs. 20).

The following expression from Mark of the end of the world –

"But in THOSE DAYS, *after* THAT tribulation," (vs. 24).

The word "meta or after" means "amidst-or in association with." This emphasizes the truth that the two events of 70 A.D. and the End of the world are closely linked together.

"But of THAT DAY and hour no one knows," (vs. 32).

The following expression of 70 A.D. comes from Luke, Chapter 21,

"But woe to those who are pregnant and to those who are nursing babies in THOSE DAYS" (vs. 23).

The following expression from Luke regarding the end of the world,

"But take heed to yourselves, lest your hearts be weighed down with carousing, drunkenness, and cares of this life, and THAT DAY come on you unexpectedly" (vs. 34).

Matthew 24:23-28: "…at that time if anyone says to you, 'look, here is the Christ!' or, 'There he is!' do not believe it. For false Christs and false prophets will appear and perform great signs and miracles to deceive even the elect — if that were possible. See, I have told you ahead of time. "So if anyone tells you, 'There he is, out in the desert,' do not go out; or, 'Here he is, in the inner rooms,' do not believe it. For as lightning that comes from the east is visible even in the west, so will be the coming of the Son of Man. Wherever there is a carcass, there the vultures will gather.

Mark 13:21-23: "At that time if anyone says to you, 'Look, here is the Christ!' or, 'Look, there he is!' do not believe it. For false Christ's and false prophets will appear and perform signs and miracles to deceive the elect — if that were possible. So be on your guard; I have told you everything ahead of time."

Christ would come to them with vengeance and furry. His Second Coming will be as quick as lightening from the east just as the siege upon Jerusalem was quick and magnificent. (www.preteristarchive.com: Jewish Wars Time Line). General Titus (with 60,000 soldiers of the 10th Roman Legion) arrived in Jerusalem in April 70 A.D. and approximately four months later, the ninth day of the Jewish Month of Av, 70 A.D., Jerusalem fell and all resistance ceased.

The Prophecy of Ezekiel 21:27 was fulfilled: "A ruin! A Ruin! I will make it a ruin! -It shall be no more until the one comes who has the right to be King, then I will give that right to Him." Some scholars believe this prophecy is from Titus who conquered and destroyed Jerusalem. Others believe it is a prophecy of Christ who fulfilled the Genesis 49:10 prophecy, "The scepter shall not depart from Judah until The Messiah comes." Herod was the first non-Jew to reign over Jerusalem and Judea. It was in Herod's reign that Christ was born. Christ had been on the Throne of His Spiritual Kingdom for 40 human years, since 30 A.D., so it may seem incongruent to say that after Jerusalem's destruction, He is given the right to reign after the Jewish line of Kings came to its bitter end. However, I am of the opinion that after the Kingdom of Judah came to its ultimate end and desolation, thousands of Gentiles were converted to Christ as a result of it.

Remember, the Jews ask that the "Blood of Christ be upon them and their children" (Mt 27:25). This was a culmination of all of the blood that was shed from Able to the Patriarchs, Prophets to the Apostles, and Stephen to Antipas. Pontius

Pilate, with all The Gentiles (including these Romans), knew that what happened to Jesus on the Cross was instigated by Jewish leaders (Jn 19:6). We also recall, Titus refused the victors crown because he believed that God had given him the victory (www.wikipedia.org: Titus).

As the Temple and the city of Jerusalem lay in ruins, it was obvious that Moses and the Law would never be King. The whole world should have known that the only King who possessed the right to be King was the King of Kings. Jesus said, "As the lightening shines out of the east and is visible in the west, so shall the coming of the Son of Man be" (Mt 24:27). This verse implies that just as the sun comes up and shines suddenly, so will Christ's Coming be sudden, just like Titus made very short work (less than four months) of destroying a city many thought to be impregnable after he conquered several other Galilean towns. The effectiveness and efficiency of the Roman Army to destroy its enemies inside and outside of fortifications in relatively short time periods is legendary. In our modern day, we have probably not seen such rapid advancement and destructiveness since Hitler's German Blitzkrieg method of invading other nations, which was successful for a while.

The context of Romans 9:22 is poignant with God's grief over Jerusalem. He calls them "vessels of wrath prepared (fitted) for destruction" (NKJV). After Paul expresses how God has been merciful and longsuffering to His people, and how prior to 70 A.D., even the Gentiles were commanded to reach out to them with the Gospel hope, Paul realized that the end was coming for Jerusalem because "For the Lord will carry out his sentence on earth with speed and finality" (Ro 9:28). This, by no means compares to the sudden appearance of Christ's coming in Judgment in the last day, but the quickness of the destruction and desolation of the Galilean towns and Jerusalem reveals to us that we must always be alert. "No one knows about the day or hour (when Jesus will return), not even the angels in heaven nor the Son (Jesus), but only the Father. Be on guard! Be alert! You do not know when the time will come" (Mk 13:32, 33).

The Roman Army was known for strength and fierceness. The eagle was embedded upon the brass shields, ensigns, and ensign-staves. Roman's armies were like eagles that were awaiting and devouring every person in sight. For a deeper insight to this viciousness, read *Josephus: Wars of the Jews* (Chapter 9).

The context of this subject is critical to our determining whether Christ is speaking of 70 A.D., the end of the world, or correlating both events.

> Matthew 24:29-31: "Immediately after the distress of those days" 'the sun will be darkened, and the moon will not give its light; the stars will fall from the sky, and the heavenly bodies will be shaken.' At that time the sign of the Son of Man will appear in the sky, and all the nations of the earth will mourn. They will see the Son of Man coming on the clouds of the sky, with power and great glory. And he will send his angels with a loud trumpet call, and they will gather his elect from the four winds, from one end of the heavens to the other."

> Luke 21:25-28: "There will be signs in the sun, moon and stars. On the earth, nations will be in anguish and perplexity at the roaring and tossing of the sea. Men will faint from terror, apprehensive of what is coming on the world, for the heavenly bodies will be shaken. At that time, they will see the Son of Man coming in a cloud with power and great glory. When these things begin to take place, stand up and lift up your heads, because your redemption is drawing near."

> Mark 13:24-27: "But in those days, following that distress, 'the sun will be darkened, and the moon will not give its light; the stars will fall from the sky, and the heavenly bodies will be shaken.' At that time men will see the Son of Man coming in clouds with great power and glory. 27 And he will send his angels and gather his elect from the four winds, from the ends of the earth to the ends of the heavens.

70 A.D. or The End?

Is this speaking of 70 A.D.? Is this speaking of the End of the world? Over the years, many Biblical scholars have disputed the events that Christ is describing in these passages of Scripture. The Preterists want these passages of Scripture to be fulfilled before 70 A.D. Their interpretation is that the sign of the Son of Man in the sky was seen by the Jews and was never meant to be the end of the world. They hold that the signs in the sky were figurative. They refer the Son of Man coming in a cloud with great power to Daniel 7:13. Also, they interpret the angels gathering the elect from the four winds as the nation of Israel, not the world. In addition, the loud trumpet that all will hear did not actually happen; it was a figurative proclamation of the Gospel.

No doubt the Scriptures (Mt 24:32-35) address Jerusalem's destruction, for Jesus said, "This generation will certainly not pass away until all these things have happened." However, 21st Century minds think differently from those of the 1st Century. Also, as mentioned previously, people today were not there with Jesus to see His body language and expressions in moving from topic to topic. We must understand this to be a prophetic Scripture that is given from an apocalyptic mind. We do not always follow strict chronological order when answering these questions. This apocalyptic approach does not necessarily address historical chronology but the overall view of history from Heaven. Such an apocalyptic viewpoint is essential in order to properly understand the Book of Revelation and other Scriptural apocalyptic utterances.

The Preterits, in many particulars, have a flawed understanding of these Scriptural passages. They force the meaning of all "End of the World" prophecies to conform to 70 A.D. They fail to connect the prophecy of the horrible judgment inflicted by God in the bloody slaughter of thousands of Jews with a prophetic apocalypse of the last judgment in the bloody slaughter of non-covenant inhabitants of the Earth (Rev 19:10).

Consequently, after dealing with the destruction of Jerusalem, Jesus said "immediately after those days." As previously noted, a comparison to "those days" and "that day" has already been established. "Those days" are the many days (three years) of Titus' siege on Jerusalem. On the other hand, "that day" is the single day of Christ's return. Jesus says "that day" will come like a thief in the night; of "that day," no man knows; and of "that day," the heavenly bodies will be shaken and the Earth's atmosphere will be changed drastically. Preterism teaches that this passage (Lk 21:26) must be speaking of 70 A.D. because it states "immediately" and does not refer to some distant event. We must understand that Christ is addressing historical events in the light of God's view of the world and of Scripture. From the speaker's standpoint, the next event on God's calendar is the Second Coming of Christ. Apocalyptically, the next event "immediately" follows the first event.

If God created the world in 4004 B.C., this means it took God 4,000 years to bring His Son into the world. From the death of His Son (30 A.D.) to the destruction of Jerusalem (70 A.D.) is 40 years. From the destruction of Jerusalem to the present period is roughly 2,000 years. Four thousand years and 2,000 years might seem like a long time, but in God's mind, it is short (Ps 90:4; 2Pe 3:8). With the Bible's "one day is a 1,000-years" philosophy of God's timetable, it has been only six days since the world began. We must understand that God's next event on His calendar is the Second Coming of Christ, and since a "day is a thousand years" (2Pt 3:8), it has been only two days! In God's mind, Christ's coming will occur immediately. The destruction of Jerusalem was only a short time. In Paul's Epistle written to the Romans, he said that Jerusalem would be destroyed by God's power. They are "vessels fitted for destruction" (Ro 9:23). The Roman victory would be a thorough and quick slaughter. The Bible records, "For the Lord God of hosts will make a determined end in the midst of all the land" (Isa 10:23). It also says, "For He will finish the work and cut it short in righteousness, because the Lord will make a short work upon the earth" (Ro 9:28). This represents the short time required for Titus to overthrow, destroy, and desolate Israel's capital city, Jerusalem.

Jesus continues, "The Son of Man will appear in the Sky and all nations will mourn because of him." The Preterists interpret this Scripture to mean that all tribes of the land in the nation of Israel will mourn when they see Jesus. However, the Son of Man appearing in the sky cannot be associated with Daniel 7:13. This Scripture in Daniel speaks of Christ *going to the father on the clouds,* otherwise known as the Ancient of Days (God the Father). In Matthew's account, Jesus is *coming* to the world on the clouds of Heaven. Daniel's account cannot be speaking of Christ's destroying Jerusalem with Titus' army as He *goes* to the Ancient of Days. Daniel also says that when Jesus presented Himself, God gave Him, "Authority, Glory, and Sovereign Power." The Bible documents the time when Christ received all authority of power in Heaven and on Earth (Mt 28:19, 20). This cannot be a future millennium or 70 A.D. Daniel also says, "All peoples, nations, and men of every language will worship Him and His kingdom will be forever and not be destroyed" (Da 7:14). We already know from reading previous Scripture in Matthew that the Gospel went out to the entire known world, and all people worshipped Him. It would be a far stretch and a bending of the Scripture to apply Daniel 7:13 to this passage of in Matthew 24:30.

In fact, such "stretching and bending" would violate hermeneutics. The Bible says the Son of Man's appearing in the sky with power and great glory will appear to "*all*" of the tribes of the "*land,*" not just the Jews, as the Preterists teach. If the Preterists are correct, this would mean that only *two*, at most, tribes would be present during this time, Judah and Benjamin. The other tribes of Israel had joined Judah when they returned from Babylonian Captivity. It is absurd to state all the tribes of the land if there are only two tribes.

Also, Christ is said to return exactly how He left!

> Acts 1: 7-11: "He said to them: 'It is not for you to know the times or dates the Father has set by his own authority. But you will receive power when the Holy Spirit comes on you; and you will be my witnesses in Jerusalem, and in all Judea and Samaria, and to the ends of the earth.' After he said this, he was taken up before their very eyes, and a cloud hid him from their sight. They were looking intently up into the sky as he was going, when suddenly two men dressed in white stood beside them. 'Men of Galilee,' they said, 'why do you stand here looking into the sky? This same Jesus, who has been taken from you into heaven, will come back in the same way you have seen him go into heaven'."

Thus, we cannot accept the position that the tribes of the land are referring to only two Jewish tribes. The Greek word for land is *ge* with the definition "of earth, world, and land." This word has multiple meanings throughout Scripture, and it is up to the hermeneutical interpreter to provide the correct definition.

Preterists take the angels in the passage to mean messengers of the Gospel. It is true that "angel" means messenger. However, it makes no sense for angels to mean messengers in this context. A question for this interpretation is, "How can the messengers of God actually gather the elect from the land if there were no elect to be gathered?" The Christians *fled*! In the historical documentation, not one author says that any Christians perished in the destruction of Jerusalem. Why would Jesus send out His messengers to gather the elect from the four corners of the land if it was just the land of Israel? Also, His messengers had already gone out to the four corners of the land and preached the Gospel even further into the world. The Gospel went to the Jews, Romans, Egyptians, Greeks, Indians, Africans, and many other places! The Angels gathering the elect from the four corners of the Earth (North, South, East, and West) are the exact same Angels of Matthew 13:27-30. They will be sent out to gather the wheat (*elect*) from the Earth. They will come with a loud trumpet call (1Co 15:52; 1Th 4:16).

Who are those that will see the Son of Man coming on the clouds?

Luke's account given below seals the deal concerning this Scripture passage's reference to a post-70 A.D. Luke says, "At that time *they* will see the Son of Man coming on a cloud with great power and glory" (Lk 21:27). Who are the "they" to whom Luke is referring in his account? Unlike verse 28, Luke is not referring directly to the disciples. Jesus indicates that the "they" are those alive on Earth during His Second Coming.

Luke continues to write in 21:28, "When these things begin to take place, stand up and lift up your heads, because your redemption is drawing near." If this passage of Scripture is referring to the disciples 70 A.D., then we have some contradictions. Some questions need to be answered regarding this interpretation. Were Christ's Apostles still alive in 70 A.D.? No! Were they in Jerusalem when "Christ came?" No! Did they receive redemption at that time? NO! How could the Apostles see these things, lift up their heads, and be "Redeemed?" This cannot be a reference to 70 A.D.

The "redemption that drew near" was the final installment of the salvation promise—the redemption and glorification of our bodies. The Bible says that when Christ returns, the atmosphere will undergo a quick, drastic change. The Bible says that Christ will come in the twinkling of an eye (1Co 15:52). This is a beautiful passage of Scripture. At His Second Coming, Paul says the dead in Christ will arise first (1Th 4:16; 1Co15: 54). The events of Luke 21:25-28 do not have local, geographical application to Jerusalem. They have universal significance in keeping with the cosmic convulsions that accompany Christ's Coming and the subsequent havoc that will terrify the human race at that time. This section of Scripture also applies to that remnant of New Covenant Christians who will be living on Earth at that time. They will see the resurrection of the unjust and the just and then also receive their resurrected bodies. These generations of Christians living at the time of Christ's coming are those referred to in 1 Thessalonians 5:23, who will not die a physical "first death" but be preserved in spirit, body, and soul, blameless at Christ's Coming." This is the last installment of the pledge of their total redemption.

This is a good hermeneutic. Remember, Jesus is addressing the end of the Jewish world *and* the end of the present age. He moves into Luke 21:34-36 with His final warning for all Christians to be ready for His coming. Jesus included the Apostles in this direct context. The Apostles would have concluded that the Second Coming of Christ would occur in their lifetime. Even though it did not, they were still supposed to watch for it. The whole thrust of Christ's return is that it can happen at any time in any generation. After the Apostles died, they would go to be with Jesus. They would return with Him; their dead bodies would rise.

Jesus spoke to the Apostles in the context of their readiness. In looking back into history, Christians can know that the Apostles are not included in this context because the Second Coming of Christ did not happen in their age. However, the Apostles did not know this at that time. They were to always live as good stewards and ready servants for their Master's return (Mt 25:1-13). Paul wrote numerous times that Christians should live in an obedient state, for Christ could come as a thief in the night. Christians now know the Apostles currently reside in Heaven and will return with Him at His Second Coming (Rev 18:20, 24, 21:14).

Those living on Earth at His coming will look up because they know that soon their bodies will be changed into an incorruptible existence. This is the last installment of their redemption (Eph 1:7; 2Co 5:2-5). They will lift up their heads in anticipation. When they see the cosmological destruction of the universe, and the dead in Christ rise, as well as the wicked rise, they will know that they are next!

The phrase, "Lifting up your heads" can refer to two different states. The first is that it would be the posture the disciples would have had if they were living during His coming. The second is the posture all living Christians will have at His Second Coming. If Jesus had said, "In the far-off future, when my second coming takes place, *they* will look up and lift up *their* heads, because *their* redemption is drawing near" (21:27, 28), this would have dismissed the readiness of the first congregation. In the context of the passage, Jesus is speaking as if His return meant something to every generation in each age. Christ had to include the first generation in the readiness for His coming. If He did not include them, they would have become lazy stewards and lived as if their Master would not return. This would have contradicted Paul's writings of his anticipation of Christ's coming. It follows that "lift up your heads" is a synecdoche of an all-encompassing, uplifting posture of hope for the generation of Christians living when Christ comes.

If we can properly understand the resurrection, then we will understand this verse Biblically. We noted earlier that those not in Christ will be taken for incarceration and hell *first* (Mt 13:30), then, *secondly*, those will be taken who have died in Christ, and finally those who are alive in Christ when He comes. One day, a group of Christians will see Christ coming on the clouds of glory; they will hear the loud trumpet and will *feel* their bodies being transformed into the imperishable body that Christ will give them. This will make them ready to be presented to God in glory. Whether or not this passage of Scripture can be applied to the present generation is yet to be known, for Christ has not yet come.

It is interesting that this verse will affect one generation of Christians living in the last day, and it will also answer Paul's presently unanswered prayer, "Now may the God of peace Himself sanctify you completely; and may your whole spirit, soul, and body be preserved blameless at the coming of our Lord Jesus Christ" (1Th 5:23).

> Matthew 24:32-35: "Now learn this lesson from the fig tree: As soon as its twigs get tender and its leaves come out, you know that summer is near. Even so, when you see all these things, you know that it is near, right at the door. I tell you the truth; this generation will certainly not pass away until all these things have happened. Heaven and earth will pass away, but my words will never pass away."

> Mark 13:28-31: "Now learn this lesson from the fig tree: As soon as its twigs get tender and its leaves come out, you know that summer is near. Even so, when you see these things happening, you know that it is near, right at the door. I tell you the truth; this generation will certainly not pass away until all these things have happened. Heaven and earth will pass away, but my words will never pass away."

> Luke 21:29-33: "He told them this parable: 'Look at the fig tree and all the trees. When they sprout leaves, you can see for yourselves and know that summer is near. Even so, when you see these things happening, you know that the kingdom of God is near. I tell you the truth; this generation will certainly not pass away until all these things have happened. Heaven and earth will pass away, but my words will never pass away'."

Remember, Christ does not give answers in chronological order. He correlates between the end of the world and the destruction of Jerusalem several times. Review the table below and see the comparison between "those days" (destruction of Jerusalem) and "that day" (end of the world).

Those days – the Destruction of Jerusalem	**That Day** – The End of the World
Mathew 24:4-28, 29 – The destruction of Jerusalem	Mathew 24:29-31
Mathew 24:32-35	Mathew 24:36-51
Mark 13:1-23, 24	Mark 13:24-37
Luke 21:5-24	Luke 21:25-28
Luke 21:29-33	Luke 21:34-36
Luke 17:20-25, 37	Mathew 26:29; Mark 13:32; Luke 10:12, 17:1, 2, 24-36

Jesus speaks of the destruction of Jerusalem in Matthew 24:10-28 and then the end of the world in Matthew 24:29-31. He then returns to 70 A.D. in Matthew 24:32-35. Next, He speaks about *the day* that no one knows about in Matthew 24:36-41. In Luke's account, Jesus speaks about the destruction of Jerusalem in 21:5-24 and the end of the world in verses 25-28. Then, He interprets the destruction of Jerusalem in verses 29-36. Jesus is not obligated to interpret in accordance with 21st Century chronological readers. The important aspect is that the Disciples understood perfectly what He was saying, for all who read His account in the documents that were circulated in the 1st Century and heeded them escaped Jerusalem and its slaughter. Likewise, we should understand His prophetic utterances well enough to escape the judgment and slaughter at the end of the present world. In any event, Christ's return will certainly arrest the attention for the last use of those who have orbs of sight called "eyes." The last sight of the eyes of the human race will be the sight and sign of our Lord's majestic, spectacular coming. After this, the earthly eyes of the covenant-saved will be changed and made fit to behold the King and His glory. The eyes of the non-covenant damned will be blinded with eternal darkness. The last thing the eyes of a lost man and woman will see is the majestic view of the conquering King (Rev 1-7).

Christ says, "Be always on watch, and pray that you may be able to escape all that is about to happen, and that you may be able to stand before the Son of Man." Jesus is basically saying, "*Pray that you escape the judgment of Israel* (Destruction of Jerusalem in 70 A.D.) *and that you can stand before the Son of Man* (End of the World)." There were no Christians in this city during the slaughter of 70 A.D.

He said in Matthew 25:31, "When the Son of Man comes in his glory, and all the angels with him, he will sit on this throne in heavenly glory. All the nations will be *gathered* before him, and he will separate the people from each other as a shepherd separates the sheep from the goats." Jesus has already told them of this event in Matthew 24: 29-31. He is now explaining it in more detail. As proved earlier, Jesus does not answer the questions in the chronological order of the western, analytical mind. What He does for sure is answer all the questions, and it is our responsibility to devise the Word of God properly.

Of utmost importance is our understanding of the destruction of Jerusalem in order to understand the Book of Revelation. We must go into great detail to explain the prophecies concerning Jerusalem's destruction. Teaching the history of the destruction of Jerusalem helps us understand what Revelation says, and, as importantly, what it does not say.

Some scholars teach that Paul did not address the events of the 70 A.D. abomination of desolation. In order to determine whether these scholars are correct, let us consider the indictments he made against the Jewish nation in Romans, Chapter 2. Clearly, the final thrust of Paul's judicial arguments, after nearly 1,500 years of provocation against God's holiness, was the death penalty.

God's Divine Judicial Indictments against the Jews

An Evaluation of Romans, Chapter 2

An Omniscient Judgment from an Omnipresent Judge

Nothing in modem jurisprudence could be more skillful than the mode of argument Paul advances on the Jews.

> The guilty Jew was without justification in judging Gentiles because they practiced the same crimes (Ro 2:1).
>
> God's judgment against the Jews **is** according to truth (2:2).
>
> God's capital punishment of the Jewish Nation is inescapable (2:3).
>
> The Jew despised God's longsuffering and patience (2:4).
>
> God's wrath will be held back no longer. Judah must be executed in approximately six years (64 to 70 A.D.). The verdict is given (64 A.D.). The Jew

was judged first (70 A.D.) and then the Greek (all cultures) at the end of the world (2:9, 10).

There is now no comfort or security in being a Jew (2:6). Judgment is according to deeds and not nationality. Judgment is based on performance, not position.

By their own law, the Jews were cursed, condemned to Hell, and on the verge of extinction (2:6-11). Paul does not discuss the Gospel till later in Chapter 3. Under the Law, Gentiles fared better than the Jews, and under the Law, Jews perished according to God's true judgment (vs. 2), its inevitability (vs. 3), and its basis of good works (vs. 6), chivalry, and equitability (vs. 7, 11).

The Jews were condemned before an impartial God (vs. 11), thus ruling out such flimsy criminal defenses as 1) being descents of Abraham, 2) circumcision, 3) observers of the only legal, divine law, or 4) God would be partial. We should note that some commentators have a problem with an order of judgment, "Jew first", so let us interpret it as "first" in distinction. However, most commentators do not understand or accept that what happened in 70 A.D. when the Jewish nation suffered is a prototype for what the whole world will suffer in the end.

Jews were lost to eternal life. The profound folly of annihilation never entered Paul's mind. The revenge was steeped in the view of eternal punishment and eternal reward (2Th 1:6-9). Jew were lost under the law, and lost even after the Gospel was preached.

By the law, God can acquit no one who has broken it. Lawbreakers must have sought redemption through some means of divine mercy, which for both Jews and Gentiles, was Christ. Under the Old Covenant, Jews did not want this proffered mercy, and in the initial, 40 years of preaching from Pentecost to 70 A.D., they would not accept the New Covenant mercy of the Gospel (Ro 2:12-15). Although a small number of Jews were saved, the Book of Hebrews tells us that among those who were saved, many fell back into apostasy (Hebrews, Chapters 6 and 10), and Paul quotes the attitude of the Jews in Romans 10:21, "All day long I have stretched out my hand to a disobedient and naysaying people" (Ro 10:21). The Jews said to the Gentile, Pilate, "Let His blood be on our hands." God held them to that vow. Pilate revealed the want of mercy more than the Christ-murdering Jews.

God arraigned the Jews in public court. According to common justice, we should see how He stands on specific indictments (2:17-24).

    A.   The Jew knew God's prophetic will.

    B.   He knew the good, excellent things.

    C.   He was instructed in the Law.

    D.   He was to be a guide to the blind.

    E.   He was a light for darkness.

    F.   He was a corrector of the foolish.

    G.   He was a teacher of babes.

    H.   He was like an artificial globe is to the world. They had the form, (shadow and type likeness) of Christ, the truth; they were just one step from the real thing.

But

    A.   They were thieves.

    B.   Adulterers.

    C.   Loved temple riches (Until 70 A.D., theirs and other temple cathedrals still stood.).

    D.   Lawbreakers.

    E.   Invited blasphemy of God (Ex 36:20; Isa 55; 2Sa 12:13). Even today, hostile sects profess Christianity, yet because they are ignorant of truth, they invite blasphemy into Christianity.

    F.   If men do not live up to circumcision, they are no better than the uncircumcised. If we do not live up to baptism, we are as un-baptized. Remember Esau despised his birthright (2:24-28; Co 2:11-13).

Jews boasted about giving the world a crucified savior.

In other words, even though their unrighteousness abounds to God's glory, but they are still going to pay (Ro 3:5). The Jews said that God's truth was magnified all the more because of Paul's blasphemy. They also said God's cause was advanced because they murdered God's son. They said they were justified in doing so and should be held innocent. On the other hand, it is Paul who should be punished. The Jews thought that since both they and Paul were guilty of the same crime and false philosophy, they should not be punished. Paul said, "Why am I condemned?" (3:7). The Jews would not accept the mercy offered in Christ. However, Paul did.

God's warning through the Apostles (Ro 9-11; Jas 5:6, 8, 10). "When James wrote his Epistle, the coming of the Lord to punish the wicked Jews was then very neigh" (Matthew Henry). They refused every offer of mercy (Mt 22:8, 9, 21:41-43; Lk 14:2). This is also valid evidence that the Book of James is one of the last books of the New Testament written, not The Revelation.

Abomination of Desolation (Lk 19:42-44, 23:28-31). Jewish Jerusalem was so desolated and stripped that Rufus Turnus ploughed up the ground after everything was leveled, (Mic 3:12; Jer 36:18). "Let us weep with Jesus." The Jews heard The Gospel before the desolation (Mt 23:14, 24:1-3; Ro 10:10; Jn 11:48; Col 1:6-23; Heb 1:1-4; Lk 21:20; Da 11:31, 12:11; Jas 4: 1-3).

All New Covenant Christians escaped (Lk 21:20, 21). The vessels of wrath and destruction perished (Ro 9:22).

See Addendum "D" for a chronological history chart of events leading up to the destruction of Jerusalem by Dan Dyke.

See Addendum "F" for extra biblical resources concerning the destruction of Jerusalem.

Addendum I – Satan's Powerful Persuasive

"Ye shall be as Gods, knowing good and evil" (Ge 3:5). Eve thought the serpent was talking, but in reality, Satan was doing the talking. He was actually preaching his favorite sermon, "The Equality of Evil with Good, That Leads to the Superiority of Evil over Good!" What a powerful sermon! He continues to preach this today.

"AM I GAY?"

It still works. Just ask the parents of the boy who put him in a Christian School. The Principal ask the boy's parents why they had the boy in government school one day and pulled him out the next. They replied, "He came home from a lecture in school with a troubled heart." When the parents ask him what was wrong, he cried, "Am I Gay?" His parents taught him that sodomy was evil. His government schoolteacher taught him it was, "O.K. to be Gay."

Notice the word "gay" which is the end result of "Word Smith Change Agency." W.S.C.A. results from the communication of supernatural evil in the imagination of workers of iniquity. Society would never accept a drastic change from the word "strange" (describing the sexual acts of men with men and women with women), so it would be too great a leap from "strange" to "gay." But if the predetermined works of an evil spirit can calculate how long it takes the gullible mind of Adam's descendants to absorb acceptance of evil under the label of a friendlier euphemism, then the process moves from strange, to homosexual, to "same sex," to gay.

Ten years ago, people were taught "Global Warming," and this was intended to justify the exorbitant costs of cleaning up the ozone. When people caught on to the futility of such an effort, and the time and waste of money poured into it, the W.S.C.A. changed the names to "Climate Change." Knowing that even dumb people "wise up" over time, the W.S.C.A. is already contemplating something like The Air Purification Act to keep reaping tax dollars from the "numskulls" in the future. By the way, sodomy has never been a gay way of life in history. If you were to ask these poor souls who have been deceived by their nation and their educators, and have thus entered into such a death pact with another human being, "What does "GAY" mean?" In a sincere, honest moment of truth, they just might reply, "Got Aids Yet?"

ATTENTION: THE EDITORIAL CONTENT OF MUCH OF THE FOLLOWING AND OTHER LIKE PUBLISHED MATERIAL IN THIS BOOK MAY BE TIME DATED.

HOWEVER, THE ISSUES OF THE DARK WORLD EXISTING IN AMERICA DURING THE PRESIDENCY OF BARAK OBAMA (AT THE TIME OF THIS WRITING) CAN EXIST IN ANY COUNTRY AND AT ANY TIME IN HISTORY.

EXCEPT, FOR THE CHRONOLOGICAL ENDURANCE OF THE 'CHURCH' FROM GREECE OR ROME, AND THE PARALLEL CHRONOLOGY OF THE 'CONGREGATION' FROM JERUSALEM (THE BOOK OF ACTS, CHAPTERS ONE AND TWO), THE REVELATION DEALS WITH CYCLICAL TIME, AT ANY TIME IN HISTORY. THEREFORE, THE READER WILL SEE CONDITIONS SUCH AS OCCURRED IN AMERICA IN 2014-16 A.D. OCCUR AGAIN (FROM TIME TO TIME) IN THE HISTORY OF OTHER COUNTRIES.

THE THEME OF THE BOOK OF REVELATION IS THE CONTINUED 'TESTIMONY' OF NEW TESTAMENT CHRISTIANITY FROM PENTECOST 30 A.D. TO THE END OF THE WORLD (MT 28:20). WHAT GERMANY, CHINA, N. KOREA, MODERN-DAY ISRAEL, AND THE ARABIAN COUNTRIES HAVE DONE TO PREVENT THE SPREAD OF THE 'TESTIMONY OF CHRIST' IS WHAT ANCIENT ROME TRIED TO DO. WHAT RUSSIA DID TO THE TESTIMONY OF CHRIST FROM 1919-1990 A.D. IS WHAT AMERICA IS TRYING TO DO IN 2014 A.D.

ALTHOUGH CHRISTIAN PERSECUTION CAN TAKE DIFFERENT TURNS, SUBTLETIES, AND METHODS, DEPENDING UPON THE COUNTRY (SUCH AS EUROPEAN NATIONS THAT THINK NEW TESTAMENT CHRISTIANITY IS NOT SOPHISTICATED ENOUGH TO SUIT THEIR SOULISH WHIMS), YET THE SPIRITUAL READER CAN SEE THE ANTI-NEW TESTAMENT SPIRIT OF THE POLITICAL BEAST AND FALSE PROPHET AS CLEAR AS DAY.

IN SPITE OF THE MACHINATIONS OF POLITICAL AND RELIGIOUS PERSECUTION, ALONG WITH THE ARMS OF THE STATE TO MURDER CHRISTIANS OR TO TAKE THEIR LIVELIHOOD, NEW TESTAMENT CHRISTIANS (OF ALL COUNTRIES) KNOW THAT CHRIST IS ON THE THRONE, AND THE ENEMY CAN GO ONLY AS FAR AS CHRIST PERMITS-AND NO FURTHER!

CONSEQUENTLY, (IF THE EARTH REMAINS), ALL THAT FUTURE READERS OF THIS BOOK HAVE TO DO IS TO INSERT THE NAME OF SOME NEW FUTURE MAN OR WOMAN WHO DESIRES TO TAKE POLITICAL OR RELIGIOUS LEADERSHIP IN ORDER TO PURGE AND DESTROY THE INFLUENCE OF THE MOST PRECIOUS, SAINTLY CITIZENS WHO HAVE EVER LIVED. WHY WOULD SUCH LEADERS DO THIS? BECAUSE THAT MAN OR WOMAN WILL BE FULFILLING THE REQUIREMENTS OF WHAT SOME TRANSLATIONS OF THE APOCALYPSE CALLS "BEASTS."

We mention "Obama's" name, and in Scripture we are told to pray for him, but we are not to worship or bow before his "image" (which is his human philosophy); neither are we to bow before the "image" of any person.

HEDONISTIC EDUCATION WILL NEVER

PRODUCE A SUPERIOR HUMAN PRODUCT

When education is divorced from morality, it cannot produce an enlightened, intelligent mind. In our association with the intellectual giants and contributors to the betterment of government and society, we have never met one great leader with a reprobate mind. The purpose of education is not only to inform but, also, to transform a person into a creature of moral splendor and beauty.

If people desire to study the works of Hegel (atheistic realism-1870s), Kant (atheistic rationalism-1800s), Renan (French infidel -1845), Nietzsche, who in 1882 said, "God is dead," (less than 8 years later "Nietzsche is dead") or the critical method of Bible research established by the Tubingen German School of Rationalism in the Pre-Hitler era, that is their choice. However, we have studied their questionable quest toward "Higher Criticism" and have compared their arrogant ideas with Scripture. We find them wanting of truth (Ro 3:4). Nietzsche said

"God is Dead" in 1882, and seven years later (January 1, 1889 A.D. Nietzsche's spirit died. The caption that announces his death explains that he existed in demented darkness until his death in the flesh - 8/25/1900 A.D.)

Wellhausen and Freud both believed the Bible was a myth. Wellhausen's "Elohim-YHVH, Two-God-Theory" is debunked in one verse where both names (identifying ONE God) are found together in Genesis 31:49-50. How strange for self-styled intellectuals to celebrate Wellhausen and Freud, who were both Biblical illiterates. John Doughty said, "Wellhausen's antiquated theories were still being taught at Milligan College as late as 1985 A.D.". If we are going to write against God's Word, we must know what God says in His Word. Freud was supposed to be a pioneer expert in the field of psychology. The word "psychology" stems from the Biblical word, psychos, meaning "soul." In the beginning, God created man "a living soul." Granted, we learn about the soul throughout human history and experience, but to omit the teaching of God's Word in treating "psychotic" disorders is to court disaster. There is no disputing that we who have an understanding of God's Word have a better understanding of ourselves and of the world in which we move.

In 1918 Hitler said, "People laughed at me when I said I would one day govern Germany." Why were we surprised? The Germans were saturated with so-called "rationalism," the denial of God's existence, and the veracity of His Word. If Hitler had encountered the philosophy of Martin Luther's Germany, Hitler could not have stood up to this TRUTH for one minute. But Germany forgot their history and Christian stimulus.

Hitler's atheistic Germany was 180 degrees opposite The Germany that led the way to freedom on Halloween Day of 1517 A.D. This is the day when Luther posted his 95 Thesis on the door of Wittenberg Church. The Luther-Melanchthon connection so inspired the Germans, from the Peasantry to the Castle, that they revolutionized the world of their day. Philip Melanchthon (Melanchthon was Greek for Schwartzerdt) was the founder of public schools. Like the schools in early American history, the Bible, Greek and Latin were taught along with other scientific disciplines. Spiritual training of children in the home and school lies at the very heart and soul of great countries.

But the Germany of Luther-Melanchthon (of whom it is said unwittingly sparked economic freedom and advancement-see "Martin Luther" www.google.com and

The Pheasant's Revolution) was not the Germany of Hitler-Himmler, in the early 20th Century. It is said that even though Luther had mixed emotions about The Pheasant's Rebellion of 1525, it is conceded by historians that it was Luther's defiance of Religious dictatorship that led thousands of Pheasants to strive for economic freedom and equality. Sometimes called the first economic revolution against social inequality in history, this revolution would never have happened without the influences of The Protestant Reformation (See Luther's influence on culture and politics, www.newworldenclycopedia.org). Jesus said, "You shall know the TRUTH and the TRUTH will set you free!" It is conceded by those of us who love Biblical TRUTH that sometimes the knowledge of the TRUTH creates an atmosphere of mixed emotions. The revolution caused by Biblical TRUTH led to certain acts of revolution that would certainly be questionable in a New Testament context. But, unlike Islamic Koranic verses, Christ never told us to kill someone to advance His TRUTH. But the power of His TRUTH to stir masses of people to action is undeniable.

However, if we consider the reforms prompted by Luther's introduction of Biblical TRUTH in 16th Century Germany to be radical, how could we compare it with Hitler's bloody regime that was not based on Biblical principles of justice and love, but racial arrogance, hatred of those who disagree and blood shed without a tinge of remorse. When Hitler brought his menacing shadow from Austria, his sleuth loomed over Germany like a dark cloud of despair and spiritual disavowal. The Germans now lacked the Holy Spirit's incentive (that once sparked a worldwide Christian revival) to successfully resist this human-demon.

The University of Tubingen (founded 1477 A.D., now Eberhard Karls University) offered Germany a "two-edged sword," one edge, representing true science and medicine cut like a healing scalpel for health and improvement, and the other edge, representing theology (taught by God-hating fools) brought spiritual despair, immorality, infidelity, and lack of discretion. Ignorance, coupled with doubt of what the overall message of God's Word teaches, leaves a nation to its own wits and invention. God would not reverse the scientific ingenuity He freely gave the German scientists, but He CERTAINLY DID REVERSE THEIR BLESSINGS WHEN THEY GLORIFIED THEMSELVES INSTEAD OF GOD! Such, arrogant, self-righteous philosophies create a vacuum in the soul of a nation. No matter how strong the people feel or think they are, when they encounter the demons that drove the likes of Hitler, they are no match without a unifying slogan, "In God We Trust."

Because many Germans and Americans possess the same arrogant attitude of intolerance toward Godly instruction and citizenship, the German and American leadership of today are not much better than Hitler's. The National Review reports,

> "Homeschooling is verboten in Germany, a ban dating back to that country's totalitarian past, and German authorities have gone so far as to construct a new wall to enforce it. The Wunderlich family has lost custody of its children and is being held hostage in Germany by authorities who refuse, in the face of German law, to let the family relocate to France, where homeschooling is legal. Another family, the Romeikes, sought, and were granted asylum in the United States, but the Obama Administration revoked asylum status and now seeks to deport them. The Romeikes, like the Wunderlichs, are evangelical Christians who are at the very bottom of the Democrat Party's social totem pole. To reject the Romeikes in America and the Wunderlichs in Germany, while rolling out the red carpet for millions of illegals, is grotesque (and may we add, 'Discrimination, unmatched in history')." (National Review 2/10/14 A.D., p. 10)

A one-sided, humanistic, practicing atheistic approach to the existence of God will lead to fatalism and Hitler-type government. We have spent a considerable part of our days praying for The Romeike family and their six beautiful children. Gestapo-like, German police officers broke into the Wunderlich's home and seized their four children (9/30/2013 A.D.) In today's Germany, they face exactly the same persecution that existed in the days of The Third Reich. Either capitulate to The State or lose your children. The gods of Government Education are on the lookout for ONE family that may have neglected to Home School a child according to the acceptable norms of Government mandated educational curriculum, such as teaching their child that "Same Sex" and being GAY is a wonderful and normal alternative lifestyle.

Do we propose a law, that if ONE child is found to be a little deficit in the Government Standard Achievement test, he is to be enrolled immediately in a "government" school or taken from the parents and given to The State? How incredible can we get? Thousands of students fail the Standard Achievement Tests in Government Schools. This "flunking" does not stigmatize the thousands of good teachers, who really care about students and their aptitude for learning; but do we call the schools and insist they pull the students out because they are lagging behind miserably in academic achievement? Where are we going to find a Home School family to fill the gap the government schools cannot fill in attempting to educate America's millions of young people?

The chasm between the public schools envisioned by Melanchthon and the schools of Hitler (400 years later) is as vast as the Grand Canyon. Melanchthon, who by the way, was called upon on many occasions to lecture at Tubingen in 1534 A.D., envisioned a spiritual and ethical education for German students. Whereas, Hitler seized children and made them wards of the State, not just to kill those considered mentally or physically crippled, but all children were required to attend Germany's academic institutions, where education was mandated and manipulated to suit the State's totalitarian doctrine.

Hitler and Mussolini ordered Fascists to take control of government schools and the textbooks were rewritten to glorify Fascism. (See "The Rise of Fascism in public schools, movies, history books and media - www.google.com). Mussolini actually invented the idea of using the Latin word "fasces", which was a bundle of rods tied together as a whip, with an iron ax head slightly extended from the end of it. In a lictor's hand such a whip would tear human flesh to pieces. The word stood for ONE political party and ONE administration to control the entire country. Not one word of dissent from an opposing person or party would be tolerated in the least.

Today's version of German education, while rejecting Fascism, embraces with a vice-like hold the totalitarian dogma of absolute humanism. This humanism does not sound old-fashioned in 21st Century Germany or America, does it? And how long, may we ask, before both countries, and those of like persuasion throughout the world, are brought down into the abject slavery that comes from reaping what we sow. Even if we are not Christian and actually despise Christian life, Christian thinking, and Christian ways, history proves that how a nation treats its Christian population is how Eternal God will treat that nation (Psalms 8:8, 17, 20, 50:22).

> "Oh ye humanist who despise God
>
> Devise traps and snares to cover sod
>
> Wherever His children trod

> Your treatment of the Lords heritage is surely odd"
>
> "Due to your Makers long suffering and patience
>
> Life for you is good through God's forbearance
>
> But the one thing you may know for certain
>
> Is that you will die, and God will close the curtain"
>
> "Then, those poor children you treated as dregs
>
> Will stand on the right hand of Him who will appraise
>
> And standing on the right hand, will to you say,
>
> 'If only you had prepared for this judgment day!'"

Mussolini was fanatically given over to the polemic rather than the pragmatic. Google in the speech Mussolini made in 1940 in which he gave God (if there be a God) five minutes to strike him dead. Speaking from a balcony, the dictator looked at his watch and counted off the minutes. There was a breath taking hush that settled over his vast audience. As the minutes dwindled down to seconds, and the last second arrived, Mussolini proclaimed victoriously, there is no God. But five years later, April 28, 1945, in the little Italian town of Guilini, the lifeless body of Mussolini and his mistress were hanging upside down, riddled with machine gun bullets. One of the most dynamic speakers of evangelistic outreach in The Restoration Movement was Ed Bousman. He cited Mussolini's boast of a God who could not kill him in five minutes with the following disclaimer, "God obliged him with five more years".

It is an ironic piece of history that while Mussolini's body was being desecrated, Adolph Hitler, his mistress Eva Braun and some of his high intelligence officers were in an underground bunker in Berlin. Within hours of Mussolini's death Hitler received the news from one of his aids. Hitler was like a mad animal (www.dailymail.co.uk on "Hitler's Last 24 Hours"), and when he heard of Mussolini's ignominious death he was mortified. When we swell up with pride and loudly proclaim the exploits and benefits of rank, atheist humanism we are more like Hitler, Mussolini, Stalin and Mao than we think. They just carried our humanistic ways to excess. One of the most frightening thoughts in scripture is inculcated in this praise, "And the end thereof is a death. (Pr 14:12; 16:25). In the Beginning we find God. In the end, we find God!

THERE IS A DIFFERENCE BETWEEN LEX REX AND REX LEX!

Samuel Rutherford was a Scottish clergyman who confronted the Church of England and King Charles I and II for Presbyterian religious freedom in the mid-1600s. His book, "Lex, Rex, (literally "Law King" or "The Law is King") or The Law and the Prince," argued against the political theory that kings can rule as they please under the guise of having "The Divine Right of Kings." The Kings favored "Rex Lex" ("King Law" or "The King is Law"). Rutherford turned "Rex Lex" to "Lex Rex" to mean that temporary kings or rulers, just like all human beings, are subject to God's Laws.

The President, Federal Legislators and Judges, and state Governors, Representatives, Judges, and in fact all people possessing power over others will live short earthly lives, and then die. They will give an account to the Laws of God. They have never seen God face to face, but they have been exposed to His Laws (in the moral and natural universe), from the time they were born and began breathing God's air. Meanwhile, the Lord lives and reigns from Heaven through the Laws of the moral and spiritual universe.

Modern-day leaders are not given the RIGHT to Rule, they are given permission to govern, "For all government (whether good or evil rulers) are of God (Ro 13:1, 2). According to God's Laws (the Laws of human nature and the New Testament Law of the Spirit), modern-day leaders will give account both here and hereafter. Evil rulers may deny the truth, but they cannot change it. The President is NOT the Law. The Law governs the President. The President does not rule. The President works for the people, and is under the control of God's Law. It is not Lex Rex; it is Rex Lex.

America is the first and only nation to be founded (from the Mayflower Compact, the Declaration of Independence, and the Constitution of The U.S.A.) ..., as ONE Nation under GOD not under MAN. We are paying for our ignorance of history. George Santayana said,

> "Those who cannot remember the past are condemned to repeat it."

"LEX REX" OR "REX LEX"? IT IS OUR CHOISE TO MAKE!

Of course, the emperors, kings, dictators, tyrants, Nazis, Communists, Fascists, New World Order fanatics, and so-called modern-day Progressives are still seeking world control. They disagree with Rutherford and all who still believe that ultimately, here and now, we are accountable to God our Creator and the Giver of all inalienable rights. Would you believe that Rutherford was persecuted for writing this? After the throne was restored to King Charles II, all copies of "Lex, Rex" were confiscated, the Scottish Parliament in Edinburgh ordered Rutherford to appear before the Parliament on high treason. Rutherford died from poor health before he traveled to appear before the Parliament. Would you believe something like this could happen today? Come now!

COME AND LET US REASON TOGETHER

Why are we putting all of this political stuff in a Commentary on Revelation? There is a very good and valid reason. John the Apostle was encountering the evil Nero. Nero had hatred with a vengeance toward the Christian Ecclesia. We all know that he did not just cause a traffic jam on a bridge in New Jersey to wreak havoc upon his political adversaries. We know he did not just run a political and editorial smear campaign against Christians. Nero's actions went much a further than that. He rounded them up like a herd of cattle and forced them into the amphitheater to be mauled and torn to shreds by wild beasts. He stripped them naked and made a public spectacle of them. He imprisoned them and allowed them to languish in the dungeon for weeks until they died of hunger. He tortured them until they mocked or blasphemed their Savior, or until they offered incense to Caesar and called him Lord "Herr-Caesar."

When he wearied from all of the pleasure and orgy of humiliating Christians in the worst ways, he hung them up like butchered animals on meat hooks, and lit their tar covered bodies with fire making them human torches. He enjoyed his evenings by watching the light glowing on his beautiful gardens as their bodies melted down in his outdoor patio. When Nero thought that his political fortunes were floundering under the speculation of public opinion, he created a stir in Rome by hiring arsonists to set Rome on fire. He played his lyre while Rome burned. Accounts vary concerning who and how the fire actually started, but it burned for six to seven days and destroyed at least 70 percent of the city. That Nero blamed the fire on Christians is indisputable. The best way to salve one's evil conscience is "KILL A CHRISTIAN AND SEE IF HE OR SHE IS ACCURATE IN THE WAY THEY DIE!"

> STUDENTS ARE DESPERATE FOR BIBLICAL KNOWLEDGE AND INSTRUCTION, BUT MANY OF THE TEMPORARY "LEADERS THAT BE" THINK STUDENTS ARE "SOULLESS ANIMALS" AND STEAL FROM THEM THE ONLY REMEDY GOD HAS PROVIDED FOR EMPTY SOULS AND HUNGERING SPIRITS.

> THESE SELF RIGHTEOUS LEADERS HAVE NOTHING BETTER TO DO (IN ORDER TO BOLSTER THEIR INFLATED EGOS) THAN RUN FOR SOME OFFICE IN ORDER TO POSSESS CONTROL OVER OTHERS. THEY DELIGHT IN TAKING FROM PARENTS THE MOST VALUABLE POSSESSION THEY HAVE – THEIRS AND THE ETERNAL SOUL OF THEIR CHILD!

After students heard the debates between Christianity versus Communism (or Evolution) at the universities in Moscow, St. Petersburg, Kharkov and Kiev, we ask them for feedback. They gave almost unanimous acclaim to the TRUTH of the Bible and Christianity. The majority of these students would hang around for hours afterward. They were appalled at how their professors in the Science, History, Political, and Philosophy Departments had lied to them, again and again. Human beings are so fickle; they can be easily duped into the same kind of atheistic subversion in America as has occurred in France, Germany, Russia, North Korea, the Muslim Countries, and China.

Christ said only, "The TRUTH will make you free!" (Jn 8:32). In modern-day America, the same thing that happened in these former atheistic countries is happening again. The difference is that the atheistic nations of the past were straight forward in their denial of The God of the Scripture, the Deity of Christ, and the Holy Spirit's work in the hearts of men and women. Now, a host of American leaders have found a way to deceive us without coming right out and denying the Lord who made them. If they have a God at all, their god is so weak that the god or goddess is as great a sinner as those who worship them.

Hitler said, "Take the kids from their parents and give them to Germany's government schools as a "Ward of The State." Government schools can do whatever they want with our kids. They have them at least 40 hours a week and as many as 60 hours if you consider the after-school projects. Yes, of course, there are some

Christian schoolteachers, and yes, many of our Christian children made it through, but this is the 21st Century, Mom and Dad. This is the Century that follows the death of God's Word and Prayer in school. This is the Century that follows the Sodomy and Same Sex rulings that are mandated by Law to be supported and upheld by government schools. Yes, the same philosophy propagated by the Serpent to one woman and man in The Garden is the propaganda of millions of educators in government schools across this nation and the world. The government school owns the world. Satan said, "Bow down to me and I will give you the Kingdoms of the World"! Pray for Christian schoolteachers. I repeat - It is imperative, "Pray for Christian Schoolteachers!"

Satan will never rest until he has every teacher, parent, and child bowing down to him. If we do not believe this, dare to read the curriculum taught under the subjects of Art, Earth Science, Social Studies, Parenting, and Sex Education. The reason that great scholars and orators of Scripture are no longer invited to the "Holiday" festivals (once called Christmas, Thanksgiving, and Easter), Baccalaureate, and Commencement services is because many of the school officials and administrators are in such psychological darkness that they cannot stand the "light of Scripture" (Jn 9:1-41, 3:18-20; Ps 4:6, 18:28, 36:9). Darkness hates light (Jn 3:20; 1Jn 2:9). True Biblical wisdom removes the hypocritical "cloak of sin" (Jn 15:20; 1Pe 2:16).

YOU ARE A CITY ON A HILL THAT CANNOT BE HIDDEN

In the early 17th Century, John Winthrop wrote, "A City on a Hill Cannot be Hidden." It was based upon the words of Jesus, "You are a city" (Mt 5:14). Jesus was speaking primarily of His Covenant Children, Jesus was talking about how His Kingdom of believers would conquer the world and because of their reflection of New Testament Gospel Light, they would be seen the world over. Winthrop applied this thought to the Massachusetts Bay Colony. As governor, his desire was that through covenant encouragement, hard work, discipline, and cooperation The Massachusetts Bay Colony would lead the way in building on the North American Continent a powerful nation that could be seen the world over. Winthrop's dream came true.

Winthrop was a very wealthy man, but possessing wealth is not a sin in the eyes of God. It is the way priority is place on wealth and how it is handled. The greatest capitalistic statements in history was uttered by our Lord in Matthew 13:12,

"For whoever has, to him more will be given, and he will have abundance; but whoever does not have, even what he has will be taken away from Him. Matthew 25:21 says, "His lord said to him, 'Well done good and faithful servant: you were faithful over a few things, I will make you ruler over many things...'" This is a far cry from Barak Obama's view, "Take from the producer of wealth and give to those who have no desire or will to produce." Our Lord taught the exact reverse, "Take from him who has one and give to him who has ten talents" (Mt 25:28). Before we jump to conclusions, let us also remember that the historian Luke, in his Book of Acts, wrapped up the whole ministry of Jesus, "Remember the poor" (Ac 24:17). But we cannot help the poor if we are discouraged from investing capital in order to harvest capital. The basic difference between Communism and Socialism is quite simple. Communism is a system whereby everyone puts their money in a pot and the government tells us how to spend it. Socialism puts everyone's money in the pot and the Government votes on how to spend it. Obama's reasoning defies human sense and fits right into the counter philosophy that Margaret Thatcher warned against, "Socialism is great until you run out of other people's money."

Obama's image of "caring for others" is that of a classic thief. When he takes money from people and gives that money to others, it is grand larceny. The Christian model is Benevolent Capitalism. The Holy Spirit taught this exactly when He said, "Let those who have, share with those who have not" (Eph 4:28). This "sharing" requires a voluntary action. The redistribution promoted by Obama's government Socialism fails the Christian test above because it is not voluntary giving to the less fortunate; such Socialism only takes place through government coercion. This is anything but Christian. The biggest beneficiaries of government Socialism are government workers, and often, those who do not want to work. It does not take one long to figure out that Obama wants to gain support and notoriety for supporting those who are busybodies, who do not want to work, and yet live off the fat of Washington. Obama's is the exact opposite of that part of the Christian model found in (2Th 3:10, 11), where the Apostle Paul says, "For even when we were with you, we commanded you this: If anyone will not work, neither shall he eat. For we hear that there are some who walk among you in a disorderly manner not working at all, but are busybodies." Government postal workers are some of the hardest working Americans and we see many others who serve faithfully in government, but the larger the bureaucratic network grows, the greater the opportunity exists to control Communist-type masses.

If everyone worked for or with government, people would be starving. When we spread the Gospel in the old Soviet Union, food crises and shortage was widespread. Even as late as August 2014, a panic occurred in Russia over a sausage shortage. Russia specializes in meat products, and there was much irritation over this meat crisis. If the private, capitalist sector does not work, there can be no tax returns. If there are no tax returns, you can be sure Obama and his family will not starve. They can take their "pay backs," political profits, and retirement benefits and head for Hawaii or Arabia. But the next generation of politicians could not reap the wealth of taxpayers. Socialism would "eat up" capitalism, and if there is no wealth, there can be no charity for the poor people or for the rich politicians. Even the Law of Christianity would collapse, for if we are unmercifully punished by government, we conclude there is no benefit going through the grueling effort of working, and we do not "Give to the poor" because we have nothing to give.

This Law of Christianity is based on voluntary giving. The Law of socialism is based on theft and "forced giving" through the extortion of taxes. When a person chooses to give, Christ gets the glory, "Even if it is a cup of water in His Name (Mt: 10:42). Voluntary giving gives glory to God. Forced giving gives glory to The State and The Emperor. It is a wonder that Obama is not posting his picture in every public place in America.

The reason people have things is because of capitalism. The reason they share things with the poor is because they have things to share. We might summarize Robin Hood's interpretation of Ephesians 4:28 as follows, "Let him who steals, continue to steal so that like Robin Hood he can give it to the poor." (See several sites on Obama's strategy of taking from the rich and giving to the poor. (www.google.com).

There is a dark philosophy of Satan. It is calculated to keep people in poverty. His philosophy is to convince the abled bodied, depressed folks (yet of sound minds) of the world into thinking that someone, other than themselves is responsible for their depression. Politicians who prey on this weakness of human nature realize that this is the easiest way to get votes. What those of sound minds, and able bodies (with depressed minds) do not realize is that no one in this world can give them enough money, and material things to create within their spirit the incentive to work their way to success. They do not realize that, in fact, the political leader they vote for is actually beating them down with goodies rather than lifting them up to the heights of their ability by encouraging the capitalistic enterprises of their communities to create a vast work force and subsequent training to be what we ought to be by the grace of God. The reason that people have things (unless they inherited them) is (by the Grace of God) they have been enabled and worked for everything they have. This is capitalism, the grand old philosophy of labor, investment and return, called by the old economists, simply, "Consumer demand, production and supply." You may shuffle the order of the three, but this has always been the foundation of the advancement of corporate America, or of civilization worldwide.

If the wealthy want to share and this country has been built largely by the contributions of wealthy industrialists, then it MUST BE an act of their own free will and not through the THEFT of Big Government. If there are no people capable of producing wealth, there can be no wealth. Monetary wealth should be a reflection of our production and its contribution to society. People or industries which produce what others want (not government) create wealth and jobs. That is not to say they were wealthy when they started, but they had a mental wealth of dreams, incentive, and industry. It is government's purpose to encourage this production, not only for the sake of The Investor, but also for the sake of their employees, and all of us. To discourage such thrift, economy, and private enterprise is tragic and will only work to the future peril of this great country.

The five-talented-man (Mt 25:16-20) did not increase his wealth to ten talents by sleeping in every morning and expecting a government handout. Obama's program will backfire like socialism in Europe because, before long the Capitalistic financial feeder market will shrink. Denmark and Sweden are the most socialist nations in Europe, and there is great alarm that the greater percentages of people in these nations will not be working at all. (See "European Socialism, Why America Does Not Want It" - www.forbes.com). The economy in Socialist Greece is in shambles (See www.cnbc.com, "The collapse of Greece is all about socialism").

Karl Marx wrote a satirical, smear of capitalism, "Das Kapital". "Das" means "That", and Kapital is German for the English "capital" which in this case simply means money. You can just see the sneer on Marx's face, as he concocts a powerful scheme prepared for him from the depths of Hades. With a disgusting contempt for anyone who has the ambition to get up and go out and make some money he scoffs "That Money!" It is actually a cuss word for capitalism. From the outset, the very name of the book is a joke. Mr. Marx would have needed money to buy food. He would have needed money to buy cloths. He would need money for transportation, books, education and travel. So his dad gave him money. His wealthy wife gave him money. His Uncle, of all things, a banker gave him money. His friend, Frederick Engels gave him money. See www.quora.com: Who Financed Karl Marx? This Marx guy had some nerve. He wrote a complete disaster of an economic theory, and yet, never held a real job.

Communism does not work. Communism falls hard. Socialism takes a little longer to fall, but it falls hard too. It did not work in Russia, N. Korea and China. The Russian government saw the fall coming. Gorbachev and Yeltsin started to talk about "Privatization", a replacement word for that dreaded word, "Capitalism". Even the Chinese economists are already envisioning this problem, and although it is a clumsy effort, they are trying to rectify this huge problem with their own version of private enterprise. In fact, they are learning capital competition so well they may surpass America. Some of our readers may say, "They already have!"

Before long, there will be no capitalistic entrepreneurship left in our Nation. Before long there will be no net, capital increases. Quite frankly, those who succeed Obama will find out that he has drained the well dry. Ten years from now, while he is in retirement in Arabia (helping to finance the erection of mosques with his American, financial stipends), he can look back at this country and laugh. What his weak religion could not do by destroying America militarily, he will accomplish economically, by destroying entrepreneurialism.

Winthrop had his faults, but he was not greedy. His biggest fault was his failure to distinguish between Law and Grace. Like most of the pioneer American Theologians, he could not understand the New Testament congregation established by Christ and build upon The Apostles Doctrine, not the Law of Moses (Eph 2:19-22). This problem still exists today through The Dominion Theory and Calvinist Reconstructionist who are correct in wanting Christian leaders to govern America, but greatly in error when they think it can be done through the application of the Commandments of the Law of Moses. It is The Apostles who sit on the thrones, not Moses (Mt 19:28).

Winthrop shared his wealth voluntarily, and when he moved to Boston to help the colonists build the city, he actually gave up much of his former wealth. To whom did He bequeath his blessings? It was to the men and women who invested much and got much in return. John Winthrop governed The Massachusetts Bay Colony for nearly 20 years.

It is as conclusive as "The light of the rising sun," that from Winthrop to Ronald Reagan, this country has been a "City on a hill that cannot be hidden." It is just as conclusive, on the other hand, that Barack Obama has "covered the lamp of Christ with a tar papered bushel basket," and pulled the shades down in America. This once Great Nation, "Under God," can no longer be seen because of gross darkness. His sins, and those of his cronies against such a great Nation, are very great in the eyes of The Almighty, and out of fear for their souls (for there is no fear of the Lord before their own eyes: Dt 25:18; Ps 36:1; Ro 3:18), we can only pray for them.

We are not talking about Canada, European, or Asian Countries. Their founding fathers did not call their nations, "A City on a hill." Would they have known that this verse (Mt 5:14) was even in The Bible? While the Lord, by this statement meant much more than just the U.S.A. or any nation, and we are probably violating the Law of Hermeneutics when we apply this statement to a nation, but I have a lot of respect for a government leader who thinks of his nation in terms of "A city on a hill". In the first place, our Lord is addressing the Kingdom of Christ as "The city on a Hill."

Thus, no nation can take the place of the Kingdom of Christ. But what a tribute to Winthrop, and others who picked up on his application that The United States of America would have enough citizens who were in the Kingdom of Christ that they could make this nation be seen, known and respected as "A City on A Hill". We cannot deny that God has held America to a greater standard than any other Nation on Earth. Who knows? Perhaps some other country (even of all countries, the former communist Russia) whose majority leadership decides to adopt the Godly principles of our forefathers, and they rise up in unison and proclaim, "We want to be like that city on a hill that cannot be hidden!"

We take one step further. The reason that millions of Christians did not vote in the 2013 A.D. Virginia election was because many of them believe that Christians should not be involved in politics in any manner. They argue that since Christians did not vote in the days of the Apostles, we should not vote today. This is a totally unscriptural conclusion. The reason we do not read of their voting or being involved in the electoral process is because Rome, the nation that governed them, was not a voting democracy.

However, we do read of the apostolic command to "Pray for them-Government leaders" (1Ti 2:1, 2), "Be obedient" (6:1-2). You can be sure if Rome was a "Voting

Republic," the Christians would have known where their political leaders stood on "the right to work," government handouts to delinquents and poltroons, abortion on demand, same sex marriage, and among many other things, the encouragement of industry and thrift which are classic Christian values. You can be sure that if they could have voted, they would have, and they would have all voted for the same person because they had a "common faith and spirit."

It is just this shameful way of thinking that allowed a pro-sodomy Governor McAuliffe and a pro-sodomy Attorney General Herring to take office in 2014 A.D. and use their influence to overturn every principle of the Christian Value system. Candidate Mike Obenshain's stand on moral issues rose above Herring's as the Himalaya Mountains rise above a dollhouse. It is well known to most Christians how much the righteousness of Ken Cuccinelli exceeded that of McAuliffe yet McAuliffe got his nose across the finish line by less than 1% of the vote. Herring made it with less than 1%, estimated at about 120 votes. Just think- if a hundred or so Christians had been warned (given the ungodly standards McAuliffe and Herring embrace) that their vote would determine the outcome of whether their State is governed by God-fearing, praying leaders, or those who possess the mindset of a Sodomite State that God had to destroy.

We are convinced that more Christians voting would have made a difference. Hireling, conviction-less ministers convinced Christians their vote does not count. The fact is, the professional clergy for the most part does not really care about sin and the darkness of evil. They would never rebuke Herod for his fornication with his brother's wife. They would never rebuke the soldiers for extorting money. They would never tell Zacchaeus to make restitution for stealing from his clients. They would never tell those who rape the children's mind with the suggestion that sodomy is a natural choice, and tell them that "It would be better that a mill stone was hung about their necks and they were cast into the sea." In the future many of our children will go to Hell because we remained silent when the Lord wanted us to speak out. We stayed home when the Lord wanted us to cast our vote against The Devil. Think about it!

> "If a minister of Christ is tempted to error on the side of caution,
> or to error on the side of virtue, which choice should he make?

Christ, being our judge, and our Christian conscience, being our guide – that is a good question today. We know hundreds who take the former stand. Do we know any that take the latter?

EVEN THOUGH OUR HOLY GOD HATES SIN AND CANNOT SIN HIMSELF (JAMES 1:13), YET HE PERMITS FREE WILL, FREE SPEECH, AND THE CHOICE OF EVERY HUMAN BEING TO SIN.

"God is a Spirit," but when God became a man in Christ, Christ was tempted in every way conceivable to reveal to us that God did not sin even when He became flesh and was tempted, as no man was ever tempted.

What we forget in this "spiritual warfare" is the bottom line. What is at stake for us is the "Freedom of Speech." There are two things about freedom of speech that come into play as America faces a very critical crossroads at the advent of the 21st Century. First, those who cherish freedom of speech know full well that giving expression to one's thoughts about sodomy, same sex marriage, or fornication of any kind of evil does not automatically stop the acts of evil or sinful behavior. Things that are prohibited by God still fall under the category of the "Permissive Will of God." God commanded Eve to not eat of the tree of the knowledge of good and evil, but He did not prevent her from doing so. Her husband Adam, in the same manner followed suit. The first freedom in the Bill of Rights, even before freedom of speech is freedom of religion, because freedom of religion includes freedom of conscious. Without freedom of conscious, there can be no other freedoms, including freedom of speech.

OBAMA'S HEDONISTIC GOVERNMENT BELIEVES NEITHER IN THE FREEDOM OF SPEECH NOR OF THE CHOICE NOT TO SIN BECAUSE THE JUDICIAL SYSTEM HAS ORDAINED IT.

Secondly, when the federal government sponsors wholesale sin, unlike God, it eventually enacts laws that prohibit the freedom of speech because a righteous citizen has to rebuke or expose wholesale sin for what it is. In this, the government not only PLAYS GOD, it goes beyond God by discriminating in reverse. While God "permits" the full exercise thereof of a person to sin "glut themselves on the fruit of the tree of evil," the GOD-PLAYING STATE forbids the freedom a righteous person has by simply saying, "Hey, that is wrong!"

When the Federal Government makes laws to justify homosexuality, the next step is to find ways and laws to prevent normal parents, normal children, normal citizens and normal employers-employees from saying that in the eyes of Holy God, this is just as evil as murder (Ro 1:27, "homosexuality," Ro 1:29 "murder"). Such laws will not only curtail the God-given freedom of speech; it will also bring moral retribution upon all other God-given freedoms of speech. The REX LEX, "The ruler is law," can make any law he deems necessary to suppress any expression of speech with which he disagrees.

Thus, government rewards those who engage in and give wholehearted support to a "man with man" and "woman with woman" homosexual union, and those who oppose such perversions are frowned upon. Let us remember that while this downward political spiral into wholesale acceptance of Sodomy is in the initial stages of becoming the predominate philosophy of the country, Obama and his minions will scream to high heaven, "Oh no, this law will not infringe upon the right of speech and choice in the general population of America!" But, Obama has proven to be both a hypothetical and pathological liar (See "Crucified in Sodom" by your author.). We, who have made a serious effort to listen to what Obama says in connection with what he does and really believes, must, as a matter of fact, conclude that, "He does not know how to consistently tell the truth." To reinforce the pathetic state of affairs in which Obama finds himself, we know that Obama surrounds himself with self-appointed liars who, while maybe not being quite as bad as he is, counsel him on what is best for him politically and for his socialist agenda. The TRUTH be damned!

THE CONSEQUENCES OF SIN WILL BE FELT IN THE NEXT GENERATION.

God told us two things about sin being reaped in the next generations of family offspring. First, the consequences of sin will be felt deeply by the children (Ex 20:2, 5-7. 34:6-7; Dt 5:9; 2Ki 4:6). The father and mother can lead their children astray. The Obama's have two children. Judge Arenda Wright Allen has two children. Gov. McAuliffe has six children. Attorney General Herring has a wife, but we have found no information about his children, if he has any. A pro-sodomy father and mother are going to have adverse effects upon their children's choice of mates. If the children of these parents bring their same-sex-mate or spouse to spend the night in their homes, the pro-sodomy parents cannot voice a word of dissent or exhibit any unusual or queasy feeling about this intimate union. If we accept sodomy as a norm for all Americans, then it is the norm for our children.

IS THE PHRASE 'ALL MEN ARE CREATED EQUAL' IN THE CONSTITUTION OF THE UNITED STATES OF AMERICA?

In giving her opinion in favor of Sodomy Marriage, Judge Wright quoted the, "All men are created equal," phrase and actually wrote in her "Brief" (the main argument of her supporting evidence) that this phrase came from The Constitution of The United States. Manifesting less intelligence than a first year, grade school History student, Judge Wright attributed the phrase to The Constitution. The Judge was "dead wrong." This phrase was borrowed from "The Declaration of Independence."

In addition to being grossly ignorant of the source of her quote, we can be sure that Judge Wright does not believe the very phrase she used to justify her conclusions. First, the phrase uses the word "Created." If Judge Wright were to rule on a "Creation-Evolution" debate, she would have to favor the "Ameba-Monkey-Man" conclusion in order to curry favor with the President who appointed her. You can be sure; Judge Wright does not believe what is written, "In the Beginning, God Created." Secondly, by appealing to the wrong document for her information, Judge Wright seals her own doom. Kerry L. Morgan writes,

> "The essential American legal principles of equality, rights and government by consent, are derived from the laws of God, articulated in the Declaration of Independence under the general appellation of "The Laws of Nature, and of Natures God," and incorporated into the various state constitutions and the federal constitution."

The reason the use of Judge Wright's appeal to five words, "All men are created equal," is such a flagrant violation of what the writers intended it to mean is because it undermines the very intention the phrase meant in context. The pioneer leaders of this greater country wanted God to bless America. They considered Him their Creator. They believed He Created all (humankind) equally, and ENDOWED them with certain unalienable rights. By rights, they meant those that came from the CREATOR. By rights, they meant the right to act according to "Natural Law." They knew that all mankind had a "conscience" (or at least should have one), and they realized that a God-given conscience would ultimately agree with what was right or wrong, but they may have not envisioned this 21st Century, when even the conscience of our elected officials becomes defiled (Ti 1:15).

Judge Wright does not know the difference between "Natural Law" and a "Conscience seared by a hot iron" (1Ti 4:2). The word picture is that of an animal who has been branded by the mark of its master. The seared flesh no longer has feelings. The only explanation to the Obama care mandate that men must purchase maternal insurance benefits is simply – The asylum in Washington is being run by inmates.

The facts are indisputable; "Natural Law" as understood by those men and women who pioneered the "Modus Operandi" of the way normal human beings should interact in this country is based on God's instructions in Romans 1:26, 27, 31 2:14. Although the violation of "natural law" addresses many other sins, even the cursory reader can detect that homosexuality is its most flagrant violation.

Judge Wright "seals her own doom" because she dared touch the forbidden Ark of Sanctification in her insolent assault on God's holiness. Unless she repents, her defiance of Her Creator, by using a phrase to justify abominable behavior that was used by our Founding Fathers and Mothers to condemn such acts, is completely reprehensible. She falls under the category of "The natural man who does not receive the things of God's Spirit" (1Co 2:14). I realize I must pray for her soul (and I do), and there may be certain of us who think I am overstepping my bounds. I am not a successor to Prophets from Moses to John the Immerser, but I do know that the prophets antiquate The Judges, and I have "The Spirit of prophecy, which is the Testimony of Jesus" (Rev 19:10). Judge Wright listens to the wrong people, and her Obama cronyism may be to her eternal peril.

"The guy was so open minded in regard to morality that when he encountered Divine Truth with such force his head tilted to the right and his brains gushed out" (C.W.D.).

THE SON SHALL NOT BEAR THE INIQUITY OF THE FATEHR

The second thing that God said "Is the son should not bear the iniquity of the father" (Eze 18:20). God will not hold the child responsible for his father's sin, but the child shall bear the consequences of his own sin. If you read the entire text of Ezekiel, Chapter 18, we see that the children were complaining about their father's sins, "The Father ate sour grapes and the children's teeth are set on edge." Children who were complaining that they were sinning because their fathers were sinning used this riddle. Their fathers ate the sour fruit, but the children were experiencing the bitter taste.

The greater percentage of "Sodomite-Children" has no sense of identity as to who they are, where they are going, and where they came from. Presently, Obama, McAuliffe, Herron, Wright and other sodomite-politicians are just as giddy as chimps, nonchalant as busy gadflies, laughing and mocking at the sin that got them elected, and mocking God, as if, "Their sin has not found them out!" (Gal 6:7).

Nevertheless, God's laws, like a millstone, grinds very slowly but exceeding fine. Remember, you do not have to be a Sodomite to be guilty. All you have to do is support, condone, and remain silent about their sin.

In a few years, America will feel the impact of this sodomite obsession with a fury. Laws are going to be changed to suit their dictatorial regulations further and further. Homosexuals will try and might succeed in having people who are not favorable to homosexuality declared mentally incompetent by the psychiatric community. The Courts are going to be burdened further with sodomite lawsuits. Sacred marriages are going to suffer. Children and grandchildren are going to suffer the most. There will be much strife and internal dissension to be borne with sodomite lawsuits. The cost of Sodomite Unions is going to increase the cost of health insurance and marriage benefits. The medical costs of treating sodomy-related diseases are going to be astronomical. The Government Police will have to prosecute (for alleged civil disobedience) their best friends and best citizens of America. The burden this will place upon the taxpayers is going to turn more people away from the work force to the welfare rolls. You can be sure at present (Judge Wright's ruling was 2/14/2014 A.D.) that the heathen who rage against The Throne of God and His Messiah (Ps 2) are contemplating ways to penalizes religions that do not accept sodomy, and they know full well that only Bible Believing Christians are going to fall under the category of adamantly opposing sodomite behavior in all its forms. But what these political and religious leaders do not know and soon will discover in the afterlife following the Judgment Day is that true Christians were the best friends they had.

Even the children of the richest Americans will suffer. May God have pity upon them? They will not go to hell for the sins of their parents, but "They will feel the bitter taste in their teeth." Worse yet, what if a God of longsuffering and patience "Rises up in His Holy Temple?" (Ps 11:4, 97:2. Isa. 6:1)

"And I beheld, smoke filled the Lord's Temple!" (Rev 15:7, 8)

What if, because the politicians refuse to listen, God's people bring their prayers before The Throne of God in unison and those prayers mix with the hot coals of the holy altar, and The Lord removes the coals of fire, "And they are poured out upon the earth?" (Rev 8:4). First, let us speak to the God-appointed politicians; they deserve to hear us. Then, at last let us pray to God that the coals of fire will fall with accuracy on their God-intended targets. Wicked leaders deserve this also if they foolishly refuse to receive the Words of the Prophets, the Apostles, and the modern-day evangelists.

Read again the Apocalyptic Chapters of the Seven Seals, the Seven Trumpets, and the Seven Vials of wrath, and see how God's children respond to all this.

What happened when the authorities "powers that be" in the days of the Apostles forbid them the right to freely speak The Gospel? (Ac 4:18) Peter and the Apostles answered them,

> "Judge for yourselves whether it is right in God's sight to obey you rather than God. For we cannot help but speak the things we have seen and heard!" (4:19, 20).

And this is precisely what columnist Patrick Buchanan meant when he said that if The Government continues to encroach upon the "Freedom of Speech," just as the witless, numbskulls, who opposed Christ in Apostolic days,

> "They are creating the environment for Civil Disobedience."

God called America to the highest standard of moral responsibility. By far, the most damnable thing the government could do is to make laws that prohibit freedom of speech that calls sin by its first name. In England, during the mid-17th Century, King Charles and his Cavaliers, by dint of immorality, led England to the brink of total disaster.

> "Cavalier was a term of reproach and contempt. It refers to several sorts of malignant men, who were about the King (Charles) some known by the name 'Cavalier,' without any respect for the laws of the land, or any fear of God and man.
>
> We petition your majesty to remove these men of violence and outrage. That your Majesty would be pleased to dismiss your guards, named cavaliers, since they have little affection for the public good. Their language and behavior speaks of nothing but division and war." (Oxford Dictionary, under "Cavalier")

It is no secret that God always has the last word. It makes no difference if it is immoral Egypt, Babylon, Persia, Greece, Syria, Rome, France, Germany, England, Russia or China, and now The U.S.A., God always rises up a Prophet like Moses, Joseph, Daniel, Judas Maccabeus, Charles Martell, Oliver Cromwell, Winston Churchill, George Washington, or Ronald Reagan.

Oliver Cromwell ran King Charles and his Cavaliers into the sea. Their evil kingdom was overthrown; Charles was beheaded and England was saved from the wrath of God. King Charles was petitioned and warned, but he refused to heed the call to cease from insanity and turn to God.

Cromwell was called a "Religious Dictator," and chose at times the sword rather than the Word of God to enforce his beliefs, but in comparison to Charles and the Cavaliers, "He was an Angel of illumination."

We have cited some of the major factors of political involvement in the affairs of both ancient and modern history and have interpreted these events in the light of God's sovereignty as revealed from the pre-cosmic angelic world to the history of earth's parade of nations to the present. We have not interpreted these events as happenchance in the world of naturalism and humanism (the false philosophy that man is the sum of all things). We have taken the rare School of Philosophy approach that the Apocalyptic Universe of God governs all history (good or evil). Let us explain why that we have taken the liberty to address the evils of the United States of America in this book on The Apocalypse. The simple reason we have dwelled on the political scene in America (2015 – 16 A.D.) is because giving the horrendous moral free fall into the cesspool of iniquity in so short a time period, the America in which we presently live is the worst example of wicked government and evil leadership in our Nation's history. This is the message we send to readers in the future until our Lord comes again. You, the beloved reader, are what the Apocalypse is all about. You can read this amazing Revelation from our Lord and see some of the same things happening in our Country's history 100 years from now.

We are studying The Apocalypse of Jesus. We are also studying history. What is history? It is "His Story." I do not know how He continues to do it, nor do I understand some of the men and woman Christ chooses to be "players in the history of good and evil," but I do know that The Apocalypse teaches that Christ is on the Throne of the Universe. He is in control. It is "His Story!"

Addendum J – The Eccentrics Who Base Their Hope of Eternal Life on Made-Up Visions Rather than Divine Revelation

We ask the question, "What did Ali Mohammed really see in that cave?" Did he see a genie as he originally confessed? After being persuaded by family members, he acquiesced to their suggestion that he saw the angel Gabriel (www.bigfaithministries: Encounter With A Demon in Cave Hira). We believe the entire vision was nothing but the figment of his fertile imagination that was calculated as a power play to deceive others. You can decipher for yourself why Muslims placed a million-dollar ransom on the life of Salmon Rushdie concerning his novel, *Satanic Verses*, published in 1988. Iranian Muslim clerics decreed a fatwa against Rushdie, causing him to flee for his life. He is now in the United States. How diabolically strange that a religious person could be so paranoid that the slightest innuendo against their "straw-man prophet," like a spark, ignites them into murderous flames of hatred. All Rushdie did was to connect the vision of genies or demonic spirits with the compilation and writings of Islamic writings about Muhammad, especially those of Ibn Ishaq (www.wikipedia: Satanic Verses Controversy). To this day, to our knowledge, Rushdie has not retracted what he wrote (www.wikipedia: Salmon Rushie).

Another question, "Did Joseph Smith see Peter, James, and John (or Jesus according to what version of Mormon history we read) along the banks of the Susquehanna River, near Harmony, PA, or was he just an American version of Mohammed with an active fertile imagination? In order to conceal their polluted and deceitful religious origin, the Mormon spiritual mafia floods the Internet with denials of any and all who threatened them with truth. In addition to all their others outrageous claims and visions, Mormons claim in their writings that Peter, James, and John appeared to Joseph Smith sometime before June 14, 1829 (www.lightplanet.com: Restoration of the Melchizedek Priesthood).

The entire foundation of Mormonism is not based upon Biblical revelation. Rather, it is predicated upon the totally unproven theory that the American Indians are descendants of the lost tribes of Israel. There is historical evidence tracing the American Indian population back to the Mongolian descendants of Noah's son Ham. Ham's descendants traversed the land and ice bridge from Siberia to

Alaska and as the Hopi and Eskimo, along with other tribes, dispersed into what is now California and Western North America (www.wikipedia.org: The settlement of the Americas.). Not one shred of historical truth exists that ancient Israel heard of a land we now call America (www.christiananswers.net.). Jesus did not visit Nephites (3 Nephi). Mormons would be astonished if we were to ask them, "Where in America was Nephi located?"

Unlike modern-day cults, such as Mormonism, the reason, throughout the ages, intelligent people have accepted the accuracy of Bible history is because when history was recorded, The Holy Spirit left nothing to blind faith. For example, let us consider the very important doctrine that is essential to our eternal salvation, that of the historicity of The Ascension of Jesus Christ. Jesus ascended to His Throne from the historical site called in Scripture, "The Mount of Olives" (Ac 1: 9-12). Further historical details are provided to silence the skeptics. The historic site was a Sabbath Day's journey from Jerusalem, by way of Bethany (Ac 1:9-12). Additional evidence is given in prophecy some 600 years before Christ was born (Zec 14:4).

After Christ ascended, He sat on the Throne and remains there until all enemies are vanquished (Heb 1:3; Ps 110:1 with Heb 8:1). Mormons insult a rational person's intelligence by not only fabricating a supposed visit of Christ to American, but also, producing mythological art work of Jesus standing in an imagined ancient city square standing among alleged Nephite citizens dressed in what is supposed to be Indian garb. No Nephite people have ever been documented in history. No such city has ever been found. And we just as well might believe in the City of Oz and an animated citizenry walking around in a fairy fiction.

Jesus ascended and sat down on the right hand of God (Mk 16:14). He will sit in glory and majesty until all of His enemies become a footstool (1Co 15: 25). God highly exalted Christ above all (Php 2:9-11), and Paul declared the "Whole counsel of God" (Ac 20: 27). This Faith doctrine was "once for all delivered to the Saints" and is revealed in New Testament Scripture (Jude 3). This New Covenant is the Last Dispensation of Christ, "Of the fullness of time that He might gather together in one all things in Christ, both which as in heaven, and which are on earth: even in Him" (Eph 1:10). This "Dispensation of the fullness of time" does not allow for a further dispensation in the 2nd Century, 5th Century, or 18th Century. The New Covenant, written in the "Fullness of Time" (The days of the Roman World) is greatly contradicted and offended at the outlandish suggestion that Christ came to America after His Ascension and visited the Indians, and He or His angel left a "Manuscript Lost," or "Manuscript Found" (Golden Book) in a Mormon Hill call Cumorah. No such site as Cumorah has ever been found in America (www.wikipedia: Historical Authenticity of the Book of Mormon.).

We can be sure that in the final judgment, the sin of this doctrine will identify those who advocate such mendacity. There is only ONE Second Coming of Christ (Heb 9: 28). If He came to Earth in a no-one-knows place in America, at a no one knows time in history, then His Second Coming will be an un-Biblical Third Coming.

Apart from His intercession for all saints, the only direct activity with a man in the flesh, in which Christ engaged from His Throne, was to instruct Paul for three years in Arabia by direct revelation (Gal 1:17-2:2), and his Apostolic instructions were exactly the same as those that Christ personally gave to the other Apostles (Gal 1:7, 8 with 2:7-9).

The dwellers of Pontius, Cappadocia, Parthia, Media, and Elam (Ac 2:9) would have taken the Resurrection Gospel of New Covenant King Jesus to the descendants of Ham in the Eastern world. Christ told them to take the Gospel into all the world (Mk 16:16), and they did. If the Mongols, Chinese, Japanese, and other Easterners rejected the Gospel, then they were without excuse. Christ's work was done 2,000 years ago. He became our High Priest (Heb 3:1, 2, 4:6), entered into His rest and ceased from His works (Heb 4:10).

Christ will give us no other revelation but the New Covenant, and He will give us no other book but the New Covenant; to believe otherwise is to bring upon ourselves not a blessing, but a curse. If there is a fictitious account of Christ making a special appearance to the American Indians, and the leaders are possessed of an above average clairvoyance and sinister motives to deceive feeble religious minds, then we congratulate any and all who purposely betrayed gullible souls into basing their eternal life on such nonsense, but no such appearance is found in Holy Scripture.

But a man named Solomon Spaulding used his lively imagination to write a fictitious novel about Christ visiting America. His novel, *Manuscript Found,* evolved from a figment of Spaulding's fertile imagination to become the divining document and foundation upon which approximately 15 million Mormons placed their hope for everlasting salvation. Mormon history is built on a flimsy house of cards, and their self-serving historians go to great lengths to disprove the Spaulding connection to the Book of Mormon. If we are foolish enough to believe that Smith actually wrote the novel with his "peep stone" (urim and thummim) trick, then all they have to do is compare Mormon theology with the New Covenant record, and they will see the flimsy, straw bridge that they are trying to cross into eternity. If a person is foolish enough to believe that Joseph Smith, with the help of an angel, Moroni, was led to discover ancient tablets or "Golden Plates" by which he was able to translate the book named after the angel, and that he took the plates to an Egyptologist for verification (www.wikipedia: Anton Transcript.), and everything was exactly confirmed by empirical facts of history, then all we can do is consign that person to the fate of Second Thessalonians 2: 11,12.

Instead of "glass looking" or "crystal ball gazing," Smith used a seer stone and a hat (held over his face) to distract those who were his hand-picked "scribes" from actually looking at a piece of paper that he held in his hand (www.mrm.com: *A Seer Stone and a Hat*, Aaron Shafovaloff at.). In his effort to be historically objective to a fault while attempting to refrain from showing his outrage at such deliberative and obvious Smithite deceptions, Shafovaloff, never the less, provides us information with historical accuracy. It is one thing to read of God's miracles and mighty works in the Bible; it is quite another, however, and a far cry from the way that God worked Biblical miracles, to read of the amateurish and childish methods used by Smith to cast his spell over fellow human beings.

We can expect the Mormon's kind of heresy because the New Testament warns repeatedly of such allusions as, "entering houses and leading silly women captive" (2Ti 3:8); "old wives fables" (1Ti 4: 7), and deceitful spirits and doctrines of demons (1Ti 4:1).

The spirit of Mormonism, Mohammadanism, and the spirit of Millennialism have one thing in common: both are greatly intimidated by accurate history. History can be either kind or cruel. All I know, even of Christ's person now embedded in my spirit, I learned from history. I could not have known Christ who dwells in us if I had not read of the Christ who dwelt in history. All our successes and failures stem from either our knowledge or wisdom in accordance with the facts of history or our ignorance and disrespect for those facts. Failure to confront historical facts and Scripture, while embracing visions, will lead to the great fall of the Mormonism, Mohammadanism, and Millennialism (Mt 8:27). The consequences will be eternally unbearable!

Addendum K – "WHAT IS ZION?"

The idea of "Zion" can be confusing to Bible readers. I doubt if it is fully understood by many Biblical scholars. It is said that songs of Zion (such as "Zion Eternal") are sung in churches across the world and perhaps the preacher may be the only one who really knows what the Biblical word "Zion" means. Zion is often presented in a heavenly sense in the Bible, and then again, in an earthly, political sense, some apply the word to the attempt by the Jews to establish a modern-day Israel. Let us examine Zion by asking and answering the following questions: 1) What is Zion Eternal? 2) What was Zion in the Old Testament? 3) Was Old Testament Israel taken to Heaven? 4) Is Spiritual Zion on Earth? 5) What is the Zion "Heavenly Jerusalem" in Heaven? 6) What is secular, political Zion? Answers to these questions should better enable us to understand "Zion" and how it relates to other Biblical and earthly actions and activities.

1)   WHAT IS ZION ETERNAL?

God has a city; that city is Zion or the Heavenly Jerusalem. He has an eternal High Priest (Heb 7:17) over the House of God (Heb10: 21). Unlike the temporary tents of Abraham and the early dwellers, God's city has foundations (above time, space, matter, and distance), and God Himself is the architect and builder of that city (Heb 11:10, 12:22; Rev 21:10). God's city existed (eternally, past, present and future) before the worlds were created (Heb 1:2). Since God existed in eternity past, the Godhead dwelt in what Christ called "My Father's House" (Jn 14: 2), which was a place of uplifted glory and majesty (Jn 17: 5). Before our world was created, God's eternal counsel existed. It is not just something we understand in the here and now or in the future, but such a contemplative counsel existed in the pre-cosmic universe before our world began (2Ti 1:9; Tit 1:2; Pr 8:23). The Apostle Paul tells us that we have not come to an earthly mountain, but "To Mount Zion and to the city of the living God, the Heavenly Jerusalem" (Heb 12:22).

Zion is also equated with the earthly city of Jerusalem, the City of Peace. Melchizedec appeared to Father Abraham (Ge 14:18), and the Bible's divine writings tell us that He was the King of Righteousness and King of Salem, which means peace. Salem was an early name for Jerusalem (www.wikipedia: Names of Jerusalem). Melchizedec was the Priest of El Elyon, or "God Most High." Some translations say this mysterious visitor who appeared to Abraham was "made like unto the Son of God" (Heb 7:3). The Greek translation for "made like unto" is "aphomoio" and means "to assimilate closely" (Strong's Greek Dictionary – 1st definition, 871). This word, aphomoio, without the prefix is found in Acts 14:11. In the vocabulary of Lycaonia, even the heathen priests of Jupiter had a word for "assimilation," and they thought Paul and Barnabas were gods who had come down in the assimilation of men. The priests were wrong, but they knew that somehow, one of their gods (the unknown God) could become a man. The word is used in reverse of the Son of God assimilating "homoios" unto The Son of Man (Rev 1:13). It is true this word can be applied to impersonal objects such as "Like unto fire," or "like jasper, sardine stone," or "Like unto an emerald" (Rev 4:3), but the likeness connects one as equal in comparison to the other. George R. Berry's *Greek-English New Testament* translates it, "But assimilated to the Son of God, abides as a priest in perpetuity."

A simple definition of "to assimilate" means to absorb into the system. The word "osmosis" can only be defined with its companion word, "assimilate," and means, "To assimilate or pass through a semipermeable." Certain molecules or ions can pass through a membrane by diffusion and be assimilated into the organism. In biology, assimilation occurs in every cell of the body in order to nourish and build new cells. This is an incredible scientific analogy of Christ's assimilating from His glorious status and place in the eternal Godhead to what, in Father Abraham's wondrous eyes, was The Son of God standing before him in time, on Earth. God our Father could not have used a better analogy of how involved He would be in trying to save lost humanity than to identify the Second Person of the Godhead, Jesus as His WORD (Jn1: 1, 2) and send Him to this cruel, lost world as His SON (Jn 3:16).

While Abraham, 2,500 years ago may have not comprehended such a process, as we do today, we do know that Abraham (comparing Joshua 24:2 with Isaiah 41:2) was a former idolater (www.brettburrows@wordpress.com: Transformed into His Image) who became monotheistic and worshipped only ONE God. But when Abraham met Melchezedec, Abraham actually bowed and worshipped Melchezedec by giving him tithes was an act of worship (Heb 7:4). Melchizedec also provided a feast of bread and wine to share with Abraham, which corresponds to our Lord's Supper Communion with the Body and Blood of Jesus (Ge 14:18).

Paul said that Jesus was perfect, "And He became the author of eternal salvation unto all them that obey Him" (Heb 5:9). Then Paul said (The Jesus of verse 9) was "called of God a High Priest after the order of Melchizedec" (Heb 5:9, 10). The word for call is not just a casual, nonchalant "Hi, how do you do?" The word denotes that God saluted or hailed Him. Of the billions of people who have lived, when did God pick out this ONE individual and "Hail or salute" Him as the High Priest after the order of Melchizedec? The answer is as plain as day. It was when Jesus sat on the right hand of the THRONE as recorded in Psalms 110:1, and the Lord God the Father turned to Him and said, "Sit Thou at my right hand until I make all of your enemies Thy footstool." This was about 600 years before the Savior was born. And then God swore a divine vow and will not repent (change His mind), "Thou are a Priest forever after the order of Melchizedec."

Just think about this awesome fact. "A Priest Forever" means forever, past, present, and future. Jesus was of the rank of Melchizedec in eternity past. He was of the rank of Melchizedec when He assimilated closely unto the Son of God in Abraham's sight. He was of the rank of Melchizedec in the days of David (who wrote most of the Psalms), and He was of the rank of Melchizedec when He ascended back to His Heavenly THRONE. How interesting to discern that God the Father called God the Son "The Priest after the Rank of Melchizedec" one time in Heaven (Ps 110:10). Paul then declared this truth to Hebrew Christians, and those of us who read it on Earth. Christ was on the THRONE when God "hailed or saluted" The Messiah as The Priest of the rank of Melchizedec, and Christ was on the THRONE of Majesty "On the right hand of God" (Mk 16:19) when Paul declared this same truth.

The same Hebrew Christians who were reading Paul's writings had in the past heard the New Testament Gospel of Peter and the Apostles and were told what King David said in Psalms 110:1, "The Lord (Father) said to My Lord (the son) sit THOU on my right Hand, until I make Thy enemies Thy footstool" (Acts 2:34, 35). Peter declared further," God has made this same Jesus, whom you have crucified, "both LORD and MESSIAH" (2:36). In their hearts the Jews knew they had "Crucified this same Jesus!" Now we must not miss what follows. The Jews were "Pierced in their hearts" by the truths they heard from the inspired Apostles. The Jews whom Paul was writing to in Hebrews recognized that Jesus was LORD and MESSIAH, but now, about 38 years after Peter's sermon on Pentecost, they are growing deaf and dumb or "slow of hearing" this precious Gospel, and Paul discerns they are having a problem understanding this Melchizedec of whom we are writing (Heb 5:10-11). My guess is that Paul is not making the case for the Christ-Melchizedec connection a dogmatic explanation but an enigmatic proposition for them to figure out in their minds. In other words, if they reject the Risen Christ, the Messiah of Peter's preaching at Pentecost, God is giving them one more chance to renew their understanding of Christ in their spiritual minds by looking to Christ as the Melchizedec of their Old Testament.

Even though Paul "had many things to say" (Heb 5:11) about Melchizedec, he had to drop the subject because they were sitting there with drooping eyes and slouching posture. This is evidence that Paul both wrote and taught the Book of Hebrews. Paul drops the subject of Melchizedec, launches into how impossible it is for Christians to be renewed to repentance if they "fall away" (6:4-8), encourages them to press on to the hope beyond The Veil (6:9-19), and then picks up the subject again in Hebrews 7.

Paul's divine strategy was very remarkable. He knew they accepted the Christ that Peter preached in the past, but now that they are on the verge of "falling away," would they accept the Melchizedec that Paul is declaring? If they accepted the Risen Lord whom they once crucified, and then begin to "fall away," would they reject Him again when He is presented to them as the same rank as Melchizedec? Paul said they (and we "Christians" as well) could "Crucify to themselves the Son of God again" (6:6). A crucifixion to oneself is an inner crucifixion that indicates that the crucifixion is under our control. We become so used to hearing of the crucifixion that we actually become immune to it. We are no longer moved by the cruel travail and bereavement of the propitious cross. Believe me; these Hebrew Christians were well aware of the death of our Lord. Since we estimate it was less than 38 years ago, and some of them were there on the Day of Pentecost, they were not far removed from the spectacle and upheaval that surrounded the death and resurrection of our Lord. The first time they heard "This same Jesus whom you have crucified," they were "Pricked in their hearts" and obeyed the Gospel (Ac 2:36-42). Now, Paul is trying to reach them with the "Priest of the rank of Melchizedec." Would they "Crucify Him Again?" What about you and me?

> "Oh the blessed hands of Jesus
>
> Ministering blessings to all men.
>
> Once, oh once I crucified them
>
> Shall I crucify again?"

There are many reasons we believe Melchezedec and Jesus Christ is the same person. Read and diligently study Hebrews 7 and discover the following truths that will reaffirm your faith in The Messiah. Melchezedec is also correctly spelled Melchizedec in the King James Version.

1) Melchizedec is King of Righteousness; Jesus Christ is King of Kings.

2) Melchizedec is King of Peace; Jesus is King of Kings. As God's Son, He is "Prince of Peace." A Prince is the Son of a King. However, Abraham recognized Him as King because the Old Testament world did not recognize God as a Father. After Jesus taught that His Father was God, we could then pray, "Our Father Who is in Heaven." Jesus is the King of His Kingdom, but He is also The Prince of God.

3) Melchiezdec is without earthly father. Jesus was born of the Holy Spirit.

4) Melchizedec had no maternal mother. Jesus was conceived of the Holy Spirit.

5) Melchizedec had no descendants. Christ never married nor did He have biological offspring. He does have spiritual offspring.

6) Melchizedec did not have beginning of days. Jesus is the eternal WORD.

7) Melchizedec did not have an end of life. Jesus' body did not undergo decay or corruption in the tomb. He has an indestructible life.

8) Melchizedec remained a priest FOREVER. God called Jesus God (Heb 1:8), and David called both God the Father and the Son "LORD" (Ps 110:1). The "LORD" of Psalms 110:4 is the same LORD of (110:1) and The LORD God swore and would not change His mind, "You are a Priest FOREVER after the order of Melchizedec!" The word "order" is used of earthly priests (Lk 1:8). This is not the same word as a command, decree, or giving an order. The word is "taxis" (Strong's-5010) meaning a succession of rank or character. Someone may say, "Oh, then there was a succession of hundreds of Melchizedecs in history." Not at all. Jesus did not succeed a Melchezedec who lived 1,900 years earlier. Melchezedec of the Old

Testament had no beginning in time or ending in time, and Jesus is eternal (immortal life), so how could Christ succeed Him in time? Both the Melchizedec of the Old Testament and The Christ of the New Testament have the same rank and, therefore, are the same person.

9) Both GOD (The Father) Most High and Melchizedec blessed Abraham.

10) There is only one Priesthood greater than Aaron's Priesthood and that is The High Priesthood of Jesus Christ.

11) Melchizedec had the power of endless life. Christ is THE LIFE.

12) God the Father swore that He was of the Order (rank) of Melchizedec, and by the same token, Jesus is made the "surety" (pledge, guarantee) of a better Testament.

13) Old Testament priests died off with each generation, but the Priest of the Order (rank) of Melchezedec has an unchangeable priesthood; it is unaffected by death or sickness.

14) Melchizedec saved Abraham our father in a spectacular way. This same Melchizedec "Prince of Peace" and "King of Righteousness" is able to save us also, to the uttermost.

The divine Biblical number is seven. Should we be surprised that the expression, "Order of Melchizedec," occurs seven times in the following Hebrews verses: 5:6; 5:10; 6:20; 7:11; 7:11; 7:17 and 7:21? Christ's appearance to Abraham as Melchizedec is an Old Testament microcosm of His divine appearance to His disciples approximately 1,900 years later (Mt 17:1, 2). Most translations use the word "transfigure" to describe how Christ assimilated quickly from the human to the divine. But the Greek word is "metamorpha" (metamorphous), which means there was an instant assimilation from His humanity to His divinity.

WHY WE USE THE EXPRESSION "GODHEAD" RATHER THAN "TRINITY."

In the past 20 years, I have never used the word "Trinity" except with an explanation. I always translate "Theotes" (Ac 17:29; Col 2:9) as Godhead. Some translate it

"Divinity" and it differs from "Thoites," which is a weaker word for "God's nature or divine attributes" (Ro 1:20). As any of us can see, the prefix (GOD-THEOS) is in both words; the only difference is the "iota" (i) is not in the first word. The first word looks at the Godhead as a person; the other looks at the Godhead as appearing in nature.

When Melchizedek assimilated unto the Son of God in Abraham's presence, He took on His nature as The Son of the Godhead. When Christ was transformed "metamorphed," He appeared as the son of the Godhead in Matthew 17:2. Even though Berry's *Interlinear Greek-English New Testament* translates Christ being "transfigured," in the lexicon addendum of his work, page 64, he defines "metamorphao" (The word he translated "transfigured.") as changing form and "metaschema" as to change the figure, which is to assume the appearance of anyone (2Co 11:13, 14, 15). Although we may define transfigure and transform as being one and the same, the words in the Greek are entirely opposites.

I have never seen such blatant bias on the part of the so-called scholars who do not understand the difference between the two words, "morphe" and "skema" as they occur in Philippians 2. Christ knew who He was, and He knew where He came from (Php 2:6). He knew that His claim to equality was not taking something that did not belong to Him (rapine-robbery). Christ's "form" of God was something that was eternally, internalized, and it was His true eternal nature both in and out of a physical body (Php 2:7), whether in eternity past, in His time on Earth when "He morphed as a man," and eternity future. In "skema" (outward figure), He humbled Himself and agreed to be "found as a man" on Earth for the purpose of redeeming us from sin (Php 2:7, 8).

Anti-Trinitarian views may be based on the fact that the word, "Trinity," does not appear in the New Testament. Theophilus of Antioch,[138] writing in the late 2nd Century, simply used the word "trias" in describing the three persons of The Godhead such as in 1John 5:7. Even though I do not use the word "trinity," I recognize the tri-unity of the Godhead, and I realize that Anti-Trinitarians are really just a carry-over from the old Gnostic anti-Christs of the 1st Century.

Antichrists do not want Christ to be equal to God. They do not believe in the absolute TRUTHS of His Word. They are the religious counter-parts to those in philosophy and politics who do not believe in absolute TRUTH. But, this is a lie because they want Absolute Truth in the kind of car they buy, or they sue the dealership. They want Absolute Truth when they are on the operating table, and if there is just one little slip of the scalpel to the left or right they will sue the surgeon for all they can get. They want Absolute Truth on the part of their airline pilot and the airplane manufactures and mechanics that service the plane they chose for their flight or they will sue for any minor flaw that may have led to the injury or death. The only time those Gnostic, humanistic liberals seem to hate Absolute Truth is when it is taught in religion, politics, and morality. In the three preceding areas that govern life, TRUTH is not recognized as RELEVANT! These humanistic, liberal fools do not recognize TRUTH as RELEVANT; however, they are being destroyed by their own philosophy. One example, they say that there is no such thing as evil, but evil consumes them in our society just like it is destroying society for the rest of us.

Concerning the Deity of the Son of God, in the eyes of such modern-day Gnostics, He is not "THE WAY, and THE TRUTH, and THE LIGHT, and no man comes to the Father except through ME" (Jn 14:6). In their corrupt versions of New Testament TRUTH, Christ becomes "The REVELANT way, the RELEVANT truth, and the RELEVANT life." In the 21st Century, Christ has become so RELEVANT to what anyone thinks or wishes HIM to be that He has become in their own Gnostic, pleasure-loving-only minds, subservient to their own definitions of whomever they want Him to be.

On the other hand, Paul says that such people have a God who can "transfigure" Himself (2Co 11:14). Yes, you read it correctly. Those who are anti-Christ Gnostics (Mormons, Jehovah Witnesses, Muslims, Christian Scientists, Christadelphians, and some Seventh Day Adventists who believe Christ came again in 1844, and many other "Christian" leaders who deny the Virgin Birth.) actually believe in a transfigured God. Some of them say they serve Christ in faith, but in doctrine they serve the devil. How can this be? (See Addendum J: Eccentrics Who Base Their Hopes on Visions Rather than on Divine Revelation)

Well, Paul says there is built within the very infrastructure of antichrist-professed "Christian Leaders," an ability to transfigure themselves into authoritarian figures just as the original Apostles were to the First Christians (2Co 11:14, 15). We must remember that even though some translators render the change that took place in these deceitful workers a "transformation," the word is "metaskema" (transfigured) which comes from the Greek word "schema" (figure) which means to scheme, plot, plan, or contrive. I am sorry that many readers do not know that

Christ's shining brighter than the sun in Matthew 17:13 was not a "Transfiguration," but a "Transformation."

If Paul said they "transformed" themselves they would be in the same company as Christ, and worthy of worship (2Pe 1:16-18). Thus, when we worship this coming Saturday, Sunday, or any day in a temple, mosque, church building or cathedral, we just may be worshipping those who have "transfigured" themselves into deceitful workers. Does this cause you to marvel as though it were some strange thing? Paul said, "Marvel not, for Satan himself is transfigured into an angel of light, therefore it is not a great thing if his ministers also be transfigured into ministers of righteousness, whose end will be according to their works" (2Co 11:14, 15).

Even the heathen priests of Jupiter thought that "the gods are come down to us in the likeness of men," after they saw the miracle done by Paul and Barnabas and heard Paul speak (Ac 14:11, 12). It is amazing to find that these ancient heathen scholars were more correct than some modern scholars in their understanding that a God could "assimilate" (homoioo mistakenly translated "likeness") into a man (Ac 14:11).

Paul said even Satan has power to metaskema himself. This means to change the figure or appearance. That is, he appeared in an external nature that contradicted who He was internally. Christ "morphed" into an external nature that did not contradict who He was internally. That is the basic difference in the two words. Probably Vine's "Greek New Testament Dictionary" (www.gospelhall.org/bible/bible) has a good explanation of the two words. It says "morphoo" refers not to the external and transient but to the inward and real, and "schema" refers to the external, outward fashion.

H.D. Spence has the best definition I have ever read on the difference between the two words. On page 25 of His book, *Confronting Contemporary Christian Music-A Plain Account of its History*, Spence writes,

> "The word transfigure, comes from "meta" (come across) and "schema" (outward expression). But the Greek word "morphe" is (an inner expression). But the difference is, "schema" (outward) does not correlate to the inner nature of things. Satan knows how the true nature should act and falsifies it (1Co 11:13-15). On the other hand, in "morphe" the outward expression does correlate with the inner nature. When Christ was transformed, His glorious outer

nature was compatible to His inner nature" (www.books.google.com/books).

Brother Spence addresses the problem that some contemporary music can be more designed to appeal to the "outer man" rather than the "inner man." It is possible for this to happen with the "Old Hymns of The Faith" as well, but today's society has numerous ways to make singing and playing music more outwardly attractive.

Those claiming to be lexicographers but who do not believe in the Son of God steal from The Lord what He considered His very own legacy and inheritance (Php 2:6, 7). There is a big difference between schema and morphe, and there is a big difference between the Devil and Christ, and those who follow the lying wiles of the Devil and the pure, eternal pristine light of the Son of God. God expects us to pay the price of seeking, investigating, and finding the TRUTH of His Son, who is THE TRUTH. We have cheapened Christianity so much that we have put the Divine son of God on the same level as an imposter and cheapened His value in such a way as to reduce him to equal the likes of a Buddha, a Mohammedan fanatic, a Pontiff Maximus, a shaman, or a dead man on a dead cross.

God will not intervene until The End. He wants it this way. He allows us to live our lives under the providence of His mercy and love. This is the test of our lives. The question is, "Who do men say that I the Son of Man am?" (Mt 16:13) Our answer to that question is the different between life, death, eternal quench of life's thirst or fire, and Heaven and Hell. We had better get it right. It is the final question on life's exam. It is the final exam. It is the entrance exam into God's presence.

Just as the vision of Melchizedec caused Abraham to lift up his hand in solemn promise to the Lord, the Most-High God (Ge 14:22), Disciples Peter, James, and John were awe-struck by the vision of the Transformed Christ (Mt 17:1-3). They never forgot it. This confirmed to them that the New Testament words given to them from Christ were infallibly authentic, a very sure, divine revelation from the Godhead (2Pe 1:16-19). Paul concurs with this idea that Christ looked like a man "skema" (in external fashion or figure (Php 2:7), but the real Christ was "In the form (morphe) of God," and therefore, "equal to God" (Php 2:7). "Skema" refers to an outward appearance. "Morphe" refers to the inner quality of the God-Man, Christ.

In this light, we wonder if Muslims, Mormons, and Jehovah Witnesses know why Jesus died on the cross. Our interest is aroused to sublime heights when we read of the discussion that the "metamorphic" Christ had with Moses and Elijah in their "after death," out of body appearance to Peter, James, and John on the Mount of Transformation. Although Matthew's account is silent about this particular subject, we are curious as to what they discussed? We are beholden to Luke's Gospel account of this historic event for our answer, "And behold, there talked with Him two men, which were Moses and Elijah, who appeared in glory, and spoke of His decease which He should accomplish in Jerusalem" (Lk 9:30, 31). The glorious vision that these three Disciples had of the transformed Christ is exactly the same as Abraham saw of Christ, "Melchizedec," about 1,900 years B.C.

Christ was not "Made into the Son of God" for He WAS The Son of God before He appeared to Abraham. Even the King James Version (KJV) says He was made UNTO the Son of God, not made INTO The Son of God. Consequently, this mistranslation has caused a lot of bad theology concerning Christ's appearances in the Old Testament. Christ in the present tense "Abides as a Priest in perpetuity, or forever" (Heb 7:3). How could an eternal priest be "Made" at a certain point in history? (See our *Commentary on Hebrews* for an in-depth treatment of Melchiezdec.)

If Melchizedec were an earthly man, how could He still be living "a priest forever'" (Heb 7: 17) when Paul wrote in (probably 68 A.D.)? Jesus appeared as an earthly man. He called Himself "The Son of Man" about 78 times, and the Gospel writers called Him "Son of Man" about four times. Scholars tell us that in the Book of Ezekiel, Ezekiel is called "Son of Man" about 90 times. The difference is that God called Ezekiel "Son of Man," but Jesus called Himself "THE Son of Man." In Ezekiel's case, God saw him as a fragile man born of man striving to be a Godly person. In the case of The Lord Jesus Christ, God saw a God-Man born of the seed of woman who was God in man's flesh.

God called His Son "Lord" in Psalms 110:1, called Him "God" in Hebrews 1:8, and called Him Melchizedec in Psalms 110:4. If He could "assimilate" (passing from His eternal status as King of Salem unto what Abraham perceived Him to be as the Son of God on Earth), we should have no problem believing that He could assimilate in the same way from Heaven to Earth through the womb of Mary and "Unto us a Son is given, unto us a child is born" (Isa 9:6). This prophecy settles forever the question of Melchizedec's being Christ.

But, notice that Melchizedec was King of Salem (King of Peace), i.e. King of Jerusalem or Zion, and He appeared before Abraham in such a manner that Abraham recognized His divinity, paid homage, and gave a tithe of all of the battlefield spoils to Him. So while we know that the true Jerusalem (City of Peace) or Zion is in Heaven "above" (Heb 12: 22) and is the Mother of all the faithful (Gal 4: 26), we also understand that there was an earthly Salem or Jerusalem or Zion where the earthly Jerusalem exists today.

Melchizedec, "God Most High," (Ge 14: 22) was actually the transformed Christ who met Abraham. But Christ also has a heavenly Zion. Since Christ, as the Second Person of the Trinity, has always existed, it is clear that Jerusalem-Zion existed before the world began. Zion eternal is the heavenly city occupied by the Godhead and His uplifted host (See the "Song of Zion", Psalms 46, with other Psalms such as 48, 76, 84, 87, and 122).

2) WHAT WAS ZION IN THE OLD TESTAMENT?

The etymology and meaning of "Zion" are obscure. It appears to have been a pre-Israelite Canaanite name for the hill upon which Jerusalem was built. The name "mountain of Zion" is common. The Bible uses "Mount Zion" to often mean the city rather than the hill itself. Zion appears 152 times in the Old Testament, including 46 times in the Book of Isaiah and 38 times in the Psalms. (www.britannica.com/place/Zion-hill-Jerusalem).

The first mention of the word "Zion" as having religious significance is in 2 Samuel 5:7 (www.gotquestion.org/Zion) where it is also named Jerusalem or "the City of David" because David captured the city from the Jebusites. Previously, while making no mention of Zion, Jerusalem is mentioned in Joshua 15:8 as "the Jebusite city (which is Jerusalem)," 18:16 as "the Jebusite city," and in 18: 28 as "Jebus (which is Jerusalem)." Judges 19:10 takes this a step further and names this Jebusite city, "Jebus (that is, Jerusalem)."

Prior to the naming of the earthly city of Jerusalem, the only mention of anything even close to the name Jerusalem was the name given to Abraham's mysterious visitor, Melchizedec, Mel "King" of "Tzedec" Righteousness. The divine narrative goes on to call Him, "King of Salem "Peace" (Ge 14:18). As we have already established, there has, and always will be a Heavenly place where Christ is King of Salem. The prefix "Jerus" is not in the divine text. The emphasis is on the words "King," "Righteousness," and "Salem." So the idea of a heavenly city, (far beyond this Earth that will be burned up), where The King, righteousness, and peace abound, compels us "According to His promise, to look for new heavens, and a new earth, wherein dwells RIGHTEOUSNESS" (2Pe 3:14).

Thus, we conjecture that as Abraham reminisced on his mysterious visitor from Heaven, "The King of Peace," he did disclose to the King of Sodom what he saw and heard, and the heavenly name "King of Salem" was spoken among the other Kings (Ge 14:2), and it became a popular expression. Of course, King David would have known about Melchizedec and when he captured the idolatrous, pagan city of Jebus, the prefix "Jerus" (city) could have been placed before "Salem." It would have been an honor to call this earthly city after the "Salem" of heaven. It is thought provoking to realize that David may have written more prophecies about King Messiah than any of the Prophets.

The word "Jebus" is difficult to define, but it is definitely an elevated city on hard, dry rock that indicates natural strength. David accomplished a magnificent feat in conquering this city, which was later appropriately called, "The City of David." Zion, as mentioned in 2 Samuel 5:7 and other Bible verses seems to indicate "highness," or to "set up," and by all practical Biblical observations, it seems to refer to permanency, or a dwelling of the Lord in the highest (Isa 2:2, 40:9). The highest point became the site of Solomon's Temple (www.wikipedia.com: Mt. Zion). It was such a solid, permanent rock that Christ must have had in mind when He said to Peter "petros-a stone," "upon this ROCK 'petra-a massive boulder' (cut out of Heaven's mountain – Da 2:34), I will build MY congregation" (Mt 16:18). Old Testament Zion relates primarily to an earthly Jerusalem.

3) IS THE WORD "ZION" FOUND IN PROPHECY?

"Rejoice greatly, O daughters of Zion! Shout, O daughter of Jerusalem! Behold your King is coming to you; He is just and having salvation, lowly and riding on a donkey" (Zec 9:9). This is a definite prophecy of Christ entering Jerusalem the week before His crucifixion. But, the Prophecy continues, "As for you also, because of the blood of your covenant, I will set your prisoners free from the waterless pit. Return to the stronghold, you prisoners of hope, even today I declare double to you" (Zec 9:11, 12).

The daughters of Zion are mentioned in the first verse because they would be given a status of salvation that they never knew under the male-dominated Old Testament ("For there is now no longer Jew or Greek (Gentile), or male and female in Christ" (Gal 3:28), and the prisoners in the pit are those men who died (usually in battle) but would go to an interim abode to await the King who entered the City of Jerusalem on the young donkey (Zec.9: 9) to die and enter their abode of spirits and set them free from such captivity (Eph 4:10). So, yes, the word "Zion" is mentioned in prophecy in The Old Testament. This prophecy was required so Christ would ultimately be crucified and be raised from the dead so we could have the opportunity for everlasting life.

4) DOES THE ZIONIST MOVEMENT, OR "ZIONISM," HAVE ANY RELATIONSHIP TO OLD TESTAMENT SAINTS?

What does this mean? Is it possible that The Zionist Movement has already taken place once and for eternity? If we place a ping pong ball, the size of a pin head in the center of the Pacific Ocean, what would its total mass be compared to the largest ocean on Earth? We human beings forget that we are bobbing in an eternal sea much like a ping pong ball. The sphere of life that we see is confined to a very small area. God loved Abraham because he looked up and saw the stars that could not be numbered, and he sought a city whose builder and maker is God (Heb 11:10). Abraham had faith to see the invisible and the eternal. He lived in tents, he was a nomad, and he knew "Here we do not have a permanent city, but we seek one to come" (Heb 13:14).

Earthly Jerusalem, in time is like every city in time, and it is like our own lives in time, "a ping pong ball in the middle of a sea of eternity." The continuing city is the Jerusalem of eternity, the Mt Zion above us. This is why we see the 144,000 as the "Sealed" ones (Rev 7:2-4) who are the same 144,000 as those with Christ on "Mount Zion" with The Father's name written in their foreheads (Rev 14:1, 2). We know these were Old Testament saints because they are distinguished from the multitude of New Testament saints who are adorned in white robes (Rev 7:9-14) and from those of every nation, kindred, and tongue who heard the New Testament Gospel (Rev 14:6). This number 144,000 is like other numbers in Revelation. This number is a representative number (12 multiplied by 12), which represents the total number saved under the Old Testament. After Christ descended, He also made a Messianic announcement to those in the Old Testament prison of spirits (from Noah's Days) (1Pe 3:18-21). Obviously, Christ's appearance to those of "Noah's Days" was in the same sequence as His appearance to the 1440,000 (from Abraham to the thief on the cross).

Noah lived 950 years (Ge 9:29) and the word "day" (without a night) is a synecdoche. The water of the flood brought "Noah's Days" to an end, but in reading the genealogies of the First Ten Patriarchs (Ge 5:3-32), "Noah's days" reaches back into an uncertain but an extensive period of Bible history. The chart by Gerald Wakefield gives the number of years the first ten Patriarchs lived, and how their lives overlapped. (See under Revelation 14:6). Because they all lived well over 600 years, the people proceeding Noah would have spanned ten generations back to Adam. For instance, Adam lived 930 years (Gen 5:5). Thus, if we are correct in the estimate that it was 2,000 years from Adam to Noah's Flood (when Noah was 600 years old – Ge 7:6) then THE world was only 470 years old the day Noah was born. What we have said is that the "Days of Noah" go all the way back to Adam, who was the first patriarch; Noah was the last patriarch.

Some Bible students believe The 144,000 included those of "Noah's Days." We are sure that those who called upon YHWH, "The Lord Jesus," would have known about Christ Jesus' coming into the world at some future time, and Jude quotes Enoch (of the seventh patriarchal genealogy from Adam), "The Lord comes with 10,000 of His saints" (Jude 14). This tells us that as Enoch "walked with God" (Ge 5:22), the Lord would certainly have revealed to him about the glorious future victory of the 144,000 when they were taken to Mt Zion. Enoch knew he could leave this little time capsule called Earth (likened to our allegorical ping pong ball) because there came a time when he simply disappeared from Earth, "The Lord took Him" (Ge. 5:24). (See the author's work, *The Greatest Mystery Story in The World*.)

We doubt that the 144,000 includes those of Noah's Day, but we do know, as in the case of Enoch, they are as much "With the Lord" as The 144,000 of The 12 Tribes who were taken up with Christ as His "First Fruits" (1Co 15:20, 23). The 144,000 received two things that they could not have received from the Old Testament: 1) The Father's Name in their forehead because it was not conclusively revealed to them that God had a Son, and 2) The seal of the Holy Spirit, which (instead of Old Testament circumcision) is the "Seal of the New Testament" (2Co 1:22; Eph 1:13).

We do not think that one Old Testament scholar or prophet could have known that the Earth would not be destroyed (or Jewish desolation in 70 A.D.) until God kept His promise to the faithful in "Noah's Days," and also, the 144,000 from Abraham's Bosom to the last Jewish convert before Christ ascended. The godly scribes and prophets of the Old Testament "Enquired and searched diligently, who prophesied of the grace that should come unto you, searching for the manner and time, the spirit of Christ which was in them did signify, when it testified beforehand the sufferings of Christ, and the glory that should follow" (1 Pe 1:10, 11). Peter adds that these prophets knew they were writing things for those who are now under the New Testament, things that even angels desire to look into (1:12). "Many of these prophets and righteous men have desired to see those things which you see, and have not seen them, and to hear those things which you heard and have not heard them" (Mt 13:17).

But The Angels of World Judgment could not let "The Winds of Destruction" blow on Earth until Christ had gathered all of these saints to Mount Zion (Rev 7:1). The "winds of destruction" could possibly refer to 70 A.D.

How awesome and fearful a thought to consider that after "The Zionist Movement" of Christ from Hades to Heaven there is really nothing to prevent "The Angels of World Destruction" from releasing a hurricane blast of worldly demolition. God's promise to redeem, seal, and give the 144,000 His Name through His Son's reconciliation, and His obligation to make propitiation, and redeem the sins of past generations (Ro 3:25-26) from Adam to Noah's Day has been fulfilled through Christ's vicarious death and glorious ascension into The Heavenly reward. Additionally, all of His saints from Abraham to the thief on the cross have gone to be with Jesus on Mt Zion. Glory Hallelujah!

But alas, we of the "White Robe Throng" (Rev 7:9), who have heard the everlasting Gospel (The Old Testament did not have The Gospel – 14:6), have been living on borrowed time. Yes, we are amazed that we have been spared "The Winds of Judgment" for nearly 2,000 years, but this is because how we mortals view time. With God, 1,000 years is a day. With God, it has only been two days. Soon He will shout to the Four Angels, and cry, "Let the four winds blow!"

5) THE ZIONISTS MOVEMENT FOR NEW TESTAMENT SAINTS

It is quite clear that the True Zion, Israel of God (Gal 6:16) is the New Testament Congregation of Christ. The true Israel of God is not physical; it is Spiritual Israel (Ro 9:6, 7). We cannot be scripturally correct in defining Israel as a physical earthly nation, for we who are children of God in Christ and have been immersed into Christ, are all Abraham's seed (Gal 3:16, 29). Yes, "All Israel shall be saved"

(Ro 11:26). This includes those of physical Israel who converted to New Covenant Christianity before 70 AD, which we take to mean the full number of Jews (the fullness of Physical Israel) who were saved in the pre-70 A.D. Apostolic Day (Ro 11:12), and also "Spiritual Israel" (all New Covenant Christians) according to Romans 9:6-9. Romans 11:26 includes all Gentiles potentially saved in New Covenant in every generation until the end of time, "Fullness of the Gentiles," which indicates the last Gentile saved before Christ's appearance to reward His saints.

The "full number" of authentic, pedigreed Jews-Israel has already been saved? For it is written (Isa 59:20), "There shall come out of ZION the Deliverer and shall turn godliness away from Jacob. For this is my COVENANT unto them, when I shall take away their sins." The bottom line is this; along with a multitude of Gentiles, a remnant of Jews would refuse to worship at the altar of Old Testament Law and would accept New Covenant Christianity before 70 A.D. After 70 AD, there was no Old Testament Temple of Moses or Herod to compete with New Testament Christianity. The COVENANT of Romans 11:27 is the NEW COVENANT. There is no other Christianity other than NEW COVENANT CHRISTIANITY!

The congregation of the First Born is the Congregation of Christ. They have already come to Mount Zion in spirit, and they will soon be there in resurrected bodies (Heb 12:22). Zion in this passage is called the Heavenly Jerusalem. The "General Ecclesia-ASSEMBLY" is the festive assembly whose names are written in Heaven. They assemble on Earth and are incorporated into the universal Body of Christ with those in Heaven; they are the Spirits of just men made perfect" (Heb 12:23). This Zionist Movement is so near and real, both in earthly understanding and eternal destiny that it seems we are already there!

"Oh Zion, Zion- I long thy gates to see!

Oh Zion, Zion, soon I shall dwell in thee"

6) WHAT IS SECULAR OR POLITICAL ZION?

There are two peoples vying for control of what was once earthly Zion. This life and death struggle goes back to two sons, Isaac and Ishmael. Certain aspects of Ishmael's character were described to his mother Hagar before he was born. God said, "I will multiply thy seed" (Ishmaelite descendants' number over a billion today). Behold, you shall bear a child, Ishmael (God shall hear); he will be a wild man; his hand will be against every man and every man's hand against him; and he will dwell in the presence of all of his brethren" (Ge 16:10-12).

We are told there are about 300 million or so Arabic descendants of Ishmael (not all Arabs are Muslim) from the Middle East to North Africa. About 7 million people call themselves Jews (but not descended from Judah). This disparity is found in prophecy, (Ge 16:10-12). Those of physical Isaac number in the thousands, but those of Ishmael number in the millions.

There are five supernatural births (birth origins) in Scripture: 1) Adam, 2) Eve 3) Isaac 4) Christ and 5) all who are "born again." We can understand that Isaac was an extremely important part of God's plan for the Jewish people, and subsequently, for all of us.

As we have already acknowledged, Abraham and his spiritual descendants sought a heavenly city (Heb 11:10, 16), so there was no real emphasis placed on early Jerusalem. It was through Isaac (not Ishmael Ge 21:12) that God reckons the seed of Christ-Messiah (Ro 9:7). (Is this paragraph supposed to belong to the next?)

In my debate with a Pre-Millennialist at James Madison University (See Doughty-Warner debate, U-Tube, or order the printed debate from genesisjd@gmail.com.), I spent considerable time on the subject of "Land Promises," and when we study God's Old Testament promises to Abraham, we discover that those promises that were temporary and earthly were all fulfilled in the Old Testament. Jews who clung to Jerusalem as their permanent hope would lose their Temple, city, and nation in 70 A.D.

Nothing of this magnitude has ever befallen the children of Ishmael. Strangely enough, if it were a choice of land promises, Isaac would have allowed Ishmael to take all the land he wanted because Isaac had a spiritual value system. When Isaac would dig a well, the Philistines would swoop down and steal his wells. He called one well, "contention," and the other, "hatred," because this is the attitude expressed by his neighbors, the Philistines (Ge 26:18-25). Isaac's name means "laughter" and he must have laughed in the face of adversity. But his seed is blessed to this day through Jesus Christ.

God allowed Ishmael's progeny to "dwell on the face of the land," and they still do. Throughout the numerous conflicts down through the centuries, Ishmaelites, through Esau, have maintained control over their land. In spite of attempts to extirpate or subdue them, this progeny has maintained their independence.

In his book, *A History of The Jews*, Paul Johnson writes about the heterogeneous Jews after 70 A.D. On page 140, he refers to the "Philostratus Vita Apollonii" which includes Titus' refusal of the conqueror's wreath because, "The people were abandoned by their own God." Johnson also gives sketchy details of the Jews of the Diaspora and how in 135 A.D. Simon Bar Kokhba, called himself the messiah and raised up further resistance to Rome which led to the deaths of 580,000. Johnson on page 157 adds that the Torah, Talmud, and Mishna were written in the 2nd Century for the purpose of legal jurisdiction. Thus, the era of modern, religious cultural Judaism began. Johnson also writes that by 245 A.D. the Jew was heterodox, "The physical traces of Jewish history were not impressive."

On page 87 of *Understanding Jewish History*, author Steve Bayne quotes a Spanish traveler, Benjamin of Tudela, "70 A.D. was the end of our history." He states further that in 140 A.D. Judah was renamed "Palestine." As we shall see later, Arthur Koestler, (www.google.com: The Thirteenth Tribe) calls these post-70 A.D. Jews, Kazar Jews, who have no genealogical connection to the Tribe of Judah.

The Catholic Crusades (started in 1054 A.D. by an appeal from Byzantium Emperor Alexius I to Pope Urban II) were not so much an attempt to restore Jerusalem to the Jews but to acquire access to the lucrative "Holy Land," as a catholic shrine or tourist attraction and to empower the Papacy as a world power. Pope Urban II ordered the first crusade (Nov 17, 1095) to reclaim the Holy Land so Christians could continue their pilgrimages (www.google.com: Pope Urban II's Crusade).

PRAY FOR THE PEACE OF JERUSALEM (PSALM 122:6)

One way to study the Sacred Scripture is called "Hermeneutics." The word comes from the Greek word "Hermenuein," which means "interpretation." (See the author's book, *Hermeneutics*.) The starting points of this science of interpretation are to determine who was writing, when it was written, to whom it was written, why it was written, and what is the writer attempting to convey within the context of other Scripture on the same subject.

David wrote Psalms 122 approximately 3,000 years ago. B.C.? This psalm is a comparatively easy chapter to "exegete" (to draw out the intended meaning). First, we identify a play on words, "Pray for the "salem" PEACE of "Jeru" CITY of PEACE. People were entering its gates (122:1). There are no such gates today. The feet of David and others were standing in the gates of the City (122:2). The Tribes of Israel went up to the City (122:4). There are a representative number of souls, i.e., 144,000 souls from the 12 Tribes of Israel, but these tribes do not exist on Earth today. The Statutes of the Law of Moses existed then and were a basis for a National Government (122:4, 5). Today, after Jesus fulfilled The Law with His perfect life (Mt 5:17, 18), The Law of Moses passed away (Heb 4:14-5:10, 6:19; 8:1-3; 10:1-18). King David requested that his subjects "Pray for the peace of Jerusalem" in the context of its being the national capital, with high walls and citadels. King David, at this time, was anxious that peace would prevail in his city.

We forget that David died; and because of the disobedience of future generations (Dt 28:45-50), the Lord allowed His city to be destroyed and abominated by the Babylonians, and later Hellenistic Syria and Rome. After David's earthly death, David's soul went to Hades, "Sheol," and rested in the hope (Ps 62:5) that someday the King of PEACE would come and sit on the eternal throne promised to David (Ac 2:26). As Prince of Peace, Melchizedec (King of Righteousness and Peace) Jesus Christ sat on the THRONE of Zion-Jerusalem in the Heavens (Mk 16:19; Mt 19:28; Rev 4:1-11, 5:1-8; 11-14). Since Peter proclaimed the heart changing, convicting TRUTH of the risen-ascended Christ sitting on the THRONE promised to David (Acts 2:35-37), this overriding TRUTH was and continues to be the greatest declaration of The Gospel.

Why is it called The Gospel of Peace?" (Eph 6:15) Why did the tumultuous crowd cry, "Blessed is the King who comes in the Name of the Lord, Peace in heaven, and glory in the highest?" (Lk 19:38) Is it not because King Jesus brought "Peace to Heaven" by satisfying the demands of Heaven that hitherto had not been satisfied? Peace to Heaven came because Satan was cast out after Jesus ascended to Heaven (Jesus brought PEACE to Heaven, and He also brought PEACE to Earth "AMONG" (Greek word 'en') men of good will" (Lk 2:14). Christ became our PEACE, "He (PERSONALLY) is our PEACE!" (Eph 2:14)

Why did some of the Pharisees tell Jesus to rebuke the disciples for declaring Him to be "The King of the Lord, PEACE in Heaven," which is tantamount to calling Jesus, Melchizedec, "King of PEACE" (Lk 19:38-39)? Why, in the aftermath of this sensational occasion, did the chief priests, scribes, and political leaders try to kill Jesus? (19:47-48) Were they not like the modern-day United Nations which will not even so much as mention Jesus' Name within its four walls. Even "Pope" Francis refused to make one single reference to Jesus Christ in his speech before the U.N. Assembly (9/25/2015 A.D.) (www.thewildvoice.org). The underlying anti-Christ attitude in The U.N. is all over the website, but people do not want to believe it. The truth as to why the U.N. cannot foster world peace is found in the simple truth, "Satan cannot cast out Satan." We are told in the website mentioned below that the Lucis Trust organization prints U.N. material. Established in 1922 as the Lucifer Trust by Alice Bailey and her husband Foster Bailey, the name was changed to Lucis Trust because of the haunting, creepy association with the name Lucifer (www.jesus-is-saviour.com). This trust became the spiritual foundation of the United Nations.

What sardonic mockery parades in the midst of men and women who are arrogant in their search for international PEACE; yet, they lounge inside a building that purports to foster international PEACE while the real The Prince of Peace is locked outside its doors. Such action is sarcastic irony, calculated to deceive and dismantle reason, incarnated in the hearts and minds of most self-serving world leaders who in each succeeding generation keep saying "Peace! Peace! ... and there is no peace" (Jer 6:14; 8:11, Ezk 13:10).

As mentioned above, the Jews were abominated, desolated, and dispersed, but a vast majority of Arabs remained in The Middle East according to the prophecy (Ge 16: 10-12). Arthur James Balfour is credited with producing the Balfour Declaration (11/9/1917/A.D.). There was probably no better time for the success of Earthly, Political Zionism then after the fall of the Muslim Ottoman Empire (10/28/1918). In regard to those who were "Cultural Jews," The Balfour Declaration confirmed support from the British government for the establishment in Palestine of a "national homeland" for the Jewish people. The League of Nations accepted The Balfour Declaration (6/24/1922).

In the opinion of Winchester Star Editor Adrian O'Connor, President Woodrow Wilson was a microcosm of today's Progressive-Liberal-Democrat Party. Wilson was also one of the first "Social Darwinist" who was driven by his evolutionary faith in progressive politics to create a social world utopia. Wilson also denied God's creation and sovereignty because he believed "that faith is more important than doctrinal details" (www.pbs.org: "God in The White House"). Rather than

Paul's definition of faith (that comes "from hearing the Word of God" – Ro 10:17), Wilson had faith in the evolution of man to solve the problems of his world. Paul told Timothy to "watch his life and doctrine closely" (1Ti 4:16). He also told Timothy that "Some would depart from the Faith, giving heed to doctrines of demons" (1Ti 4:1). Creation is a doctrine, and faith is a companion to doctrine (He. 11:1-2). Good faith "adorns the doctrine of God" (Tit 2:10). We are to encourage others by sound doctrine and refute those who oppose it (Tit 1:9).

When a leader, like Wilson, is ignorant of a sovereign, personal Creator God, Wilson's theory of evolution was able to permeate his frame of reference and decision-making by placing his blind faith in "time" and "chance." No matter how much he may have said about his religion, Wilson's commitment to evolution is no different than the Muslim idea of "Fatalism." While Germany was gearing up for war, Wilson's faith caused him to believe that man could solve the world's problems by an idealistic, utopian faith in human determinism. We should have known The League of Nations was designed for failure from the get-go. This united coalition of nations was abolished after World War II (4/20/1946), but unfortunately, replaced by the United Nations.

Wilson ignored the fact that in God's sovereign will, He gave national leaders the authority to pursue wars against aggressive coalitions (whether religious or political) if necessary to prevent further bloodshed. Wilson's cowardly hesitation to respond to Germany's wartime threats parallels President Barak Obama's response to his Isis Brethren at the time of this writing. Theodore Roosevelt scolded Wilson for thinking that negations with unreasonable human beings can bring peace. Wilson could not stand a man with the strength and conviction of Theodore Roosevelt because Roosevelt was a courageous military leader and unafraid to fight the enemy in order to eliminate them totally (www.loc.gov: Theodore Roosevelt). Wilson did not want man like Theodore Roosevelt in command during World War I. If Wilson had such men, he may have saved thousands of American soldiers.

Living at the time when Wilson was President was a very brave and influential America man who was not a politician. He was Elbert Hubbard, an editor for The New York Times. I admire Hubbard because he possessed the same appreciation of apocalyptic imagery and was able to apply it to the time when he lived. An example of one of his editorial captions read like this, "Kaiser lifted the lid of hell," and the implication was that hordes of German soldiers came forth on earth. This is, of course, a reference to Revelation, 9:2, 3. Kaiser Wilhelm was not the least bit appreciative of this bit of apocalyptic sarcasm. Hubbard was of German ancestry, but he still wrote several other articles that denigrated the German Kaiser. Wilhelm thought Hubbard ought to be on Germany's side.

Wilson, on the other hand, was a spineless excuse for a world leader during those international crises that led up to and brought the world into such a horrendous plight of international homicide. While Obama compares favorably to Antiochus Epiphanes, he also has the same spirit of Wilson, and simply put, does not have the righteous fortitude to go to war against his Muslim Brethren no matter how vile and evil they are. Obama is like the whipped bully who runs across the street and declares war against an imaginary foe, acting as though climate change as a greater threat than his Muslim, Koran-poisoned Brethren who think they please their God by killing infidels. As a master of subterfuge, Obama diverts our attention, from those who will relentlessly murder innocent Americans, to his modern version of Chicken Little, "The Sky is Falling," and flees to Washington's bureaucracies for condolence.

How strange for these Muslim fanatics to call themselves "The NATION of Islam" when there is not a free, governable NATION of Islam on Earth. With a little common sense, we would realize that in the deranged minds of the murderous thugs who form their oligarchs, they think they can bring down ALL NATIONS, and the NATION of Islam would become a conglomerate of YOURS and MY NATION, or any other NATION on Earth.

Secretary to President Obama, Valerie Jarret, in her own words said,

> "I am Iranian by birth and of my Islamic Faith. I am also an American citizen and seek to help change America to be a more Islamic Country. My faith guides me and I feel like it is going well in the transition of using freedom of religion in America against itself". (www.overpassesforamerica.com).
>
> Valerie Jarrett Stanford U., 1977

But in this book you are reading, it is my desire to point you to the THRONE and to be aware that all earthly affairs are governed by The King of Kings or to a lesser extent by the permissive will of The Messiah and Satan, who is Prince of the World (Jn 14:30). Christ has authority in Heaven, and brings "Peace on earth to men of good will." We may live to see the weakening and demise of Islam just we saw the weakening and demise of other religions and philosophies which misjudged the stamina of nations that are butressed in Christ. Satan reigns in the hearts of foolish men and women who allow him such liberty on Earth.

Now, let us consider the real event that turned the weak hand of President Wilson and forced him into a war that turned the tide against Kaiser Frederick Wilhelm II. It was a six-worded title of a small booklet, "Kaiser Lifted the Lid of Hell." The man who wrote this title was none other than Elbert Hubbard, the American editor and publisher. There is no doubt in my mind; Hubbard's book referenced Revelation 9:2, 3, "He opened the abyss." Most commentators believe the "Fallen Star" (Rev 9:1) is Satan, and he opened the pit of Hades Fire. Hubbard said, "Kaiser lifted the lid of Hell," and by implication, he accused Kaiser of releasing the German hordes of death like locusts on the face of the Earth. Hubbard also called Kaiser a "mastoid degenerate" with dripping ears. Some writers say that Wilhelm was burning with the wrath of Hell toward Hubbard.

Anyway, after getting in trouble with the post office for allegedly distributing obscene literature, Hubbard was eventually pardoned by President Wilson and permitted to go to Berlin to interview, of all people, Kaiser Frederick Wilhelm. Many writers believe (www.amazon.com: Who Lifted The Lid of Hell?) that Kaiser did not want the interview to happen, and he directed his U-Boat Commander to target Hubbard's ship, The Lusitania. After the second torpedo struck its fatal blow to the luxury liner, Hubbard insisted on going down with the ship, embracing his wife Alice in a gallant death of two very brave people.

What is interesting is that it was the German U-Boats striking non-military American and British ships that finally turned the weak hand of Wilson and that led to America's Declaration of War against Germany. No ship sinking had such an impact on American public opinion than did that of the Lusitania. Thus, it was a writer who won the day for millions in Western Europe, Great Britain, America, and much of the "civilized" world when he wrote a little pamphlet, with six little words, "Who Lifted the Lid of Hell?"

While visiting a nursing home in 1973, I met with a very old man (nearly 90 years old) who was of such sound mind and judgment. We discoursed for some time. The Lusitania went down and Hubbard and his wife perished in the Atlantic Ocean, May 7, 1915. My friend was born about 1883 and would have been about 32 years old when this sensational event took place. Eighteen months later, April 6, 1917, America finally entered the war. The Germans sank thousands of ships with millions of tons of shipping cargo which they thought was being shipped to their enemies, the British, French, and Russians.

This old gentleman told me it was common knowledge among students of history in those days that if Hubbard had not had the courage to write a work of such strong editorial substance, the British liner Lusitania would not have been sunk, and those Americans like Wilson who wanted to remain neutral would not have entered the war. Without America's entrance into the war, there was a high probability that Germany would have conquered and controlled the European continent.

To this day, I will never forget the stolid look of affirmation on the old man's face as he related the nursery rhyme of the power of little things called, "The Want of a Nail."

> "For want of a nail a shoe was lost,
>
> For want of a shoe, a horse was lost,
>
> For want of a horse a King was lost,
>
> For want of a King, a Kingdom was lost"

German U-Boats terrorized innocent people on the seas in those days. Modern-day religious terrorist think they will terrorize civilized people into submission. The nail that brought down the German terrorists was an editorial heading that introduced the world to the pending curse of failing to resist an enemy that cannot be appeased, and the ominous curse of indecision when a country's fate and tranquility are threatened by implacable evil from the pit of Hell. Yes, Hubbard was far from being an angel, and there was much to be desired of virtue in his life; but as a writer, he upheld the morality of resisting an evil force, and he made the supreme sacrifice for what he believed to be the TRUTH. Throughout history, God has always blessed us by providing a "Want of a Nail" to the war horses of religious and political demons disguised as humans; and whether we live to see it or not, God will bring wicked leaders and nations down ...It is Apocalyptic. "The Kingdom of the world has become the Kingdom of the Lord and His Christ (Messiah), and He shall reign forever and ever" (Apocalypse or Rev 11:15).

Thus, Wilson and Obama had reason to act wimpy and aloof when the country needed strong, decisive leadership; and as Adrian O'Connor put it so aptly, Wilson was the icon of modern-day, progressive liberalism. War is a terrible thing, but in The Apocalypse, it is impossible to avoid the Red Horse of war "empowered to take the peace from the earth" (Rev 6:4). When Jesus said there would "be wars and rumors of wars" (Mt 24:6), He was addressing the Pre-70 A.D. Desolation; but He was also addressing the evils of men and women who have war in their hearts. A standing army and a well-equipped and financed military are indispensable in curtailing the hatred and animosity that leads a nation to desire the extermination of another and its people. Wilson's evolutionary faith led him to put on "the rose colored glasses" of a utopian society and believe that the world had evolved to the place of peace and goodwill.

Progressive liberals even hate liberals who are not liberal enough to suit their bigoted taste. Adrian J. O'Connor writes:

> "Isn't it rich that not until the latest outcropping of the campus grievance culture casts its sights on a progressive Icon-Woodrow Wilson-did the media finally take notice and umbrage? That is, none of the lugubriously outrage rose to defend Condi Rice when Rutgers students trashed the choice of the former Secretary of State as graduation speaker in 2014. But let the relentlessly aggrieved at Princeton hint at scrubbing Wilson's name from Ol' Nassau because of benighted views on race, and the lamentations start flowing.
>
> We're no fans of the priggish Mr. Wilson, not by a long shot, but Princeton President Christopher Eisgruber was wrong to spinelessly accede to this hue-and-cry" (Winchester Star 11/24/2015 A.D.).

Again, O'Connor addresses the new academic mindset of destroying the historical values of this nation under the title, "History as Micro-Aggression." O'Connor asks the question,

> "Do you find certain segments of history offensive, not to your liking? Ah, go ahead and erase them. In the parlance of the day, it's almost as if the past, or at least parts of it, should be registered as a "micro-aggression." Think we're immune in the Northern Valley? It happened here this summer, in the manufactured controversy over the Winchester city seal. Frankly, it's happening all over, most distressingly on college campuses such as Princeton

where, as we noted earlier, not even progressive icon (and one-time university president) Woodrow Wilson escapes vilification because of his views on race, exhibited a century ago, do not measure up to modern sensitivities. Again, we hold no truck with Mr. Wilson, but this eradicate-history movement does not bode well for a nation founded on freedom – and allegedly enlightened" (The Winchester Star 11/27/2015 A.D.).

Then, O'Connor cites another incident of tearing down valued bulwarks, and defacing ancient landmarks (Pr 23:10),

"Thomas Jefferson requested that but three accomplishments be placed on his gravestone. The stone still reads: 'Here was buried Thomas Jefferson – Author of the Declaration of American Independence, of the Statute of Virginia for religious freedom, and Father of the university of Virginia.' This legacy is apparently all but forgotten, at least at Mr. Jefferson's alma mater, the College of William and Mary, where students plastered his bronze likeness with sticky notes calling him, among other things, a "racists", a "rapist" and a "pedophile." Yes, Thomas Jefferson, whose words – and the ideas behind them – helped forge a nation unparalleled, is the latest victim of campus craziness.

Mr. Jefferson, as one writer said, would not likely take umbrage at such displays of protest emblematic of a free people, but would look askance at folks reluctant, or even fearful, to challenge them. No such reluctance here."

May we ask two questions at this point? Are these students being taught the satanic philosophy of Islam that embraces the annihilation of all infidels or any who do not agree with their distorted views? This is the paranoid philosophy that led Muslim Taliban to dynamite into smithereens a 1,700 years old, 175-foot high statue of Buddha in Afghanistan, and Isis bulldozing into powder the Old Testament city of Nimrud in ancient Assyria.

It is very interesting to note that Paul spoke of how Christians should not profane another religion, no matter how erroneous or ridiculous it may be. Paul mentioned the sin of robbing temples and committing sacrilege (profaning or desecrating) the religious shrines of others (Ro 2:22). The City Clerk of Ephesus had enough sense to defend Aristarchus and Gaius against the charges of their enemies, "These men have not committed sacrilege, nor blasphemed your goddesses" (Ac 19:37). The Muslim tragedy is to destroy completely the ancient history, the traditional landmarks, and all that their conquered foes held to be sacrosanct in their own eyes, right or wrong.

A second question is, if the professors of these institutions delight in raping the minds of their students by demeaning our Country's Forefathers as rapists, adulterers, pedophiles, and racists (caring less for any good they may have done to build a historical national comfort zone for them to park their lazy carcasses); I wonder what they say about Ali Mohammed who was a murderer, a ruthless savage, a child rapists, married to Aisha (a six year old girl), a military seeker of blood lust, an illiterate man possessed of a jinn (genie), the world's worst racist, a tyrant and suppresser of women's rights, and so much so that President Obama's secretary and adviser, Valerie Jarret (who boasts of her Muslim faith) would be a second class citizen if she returned to Iran. If she chose to be one of five wives to a Muslim man, he could beat her or behead her if she displeased him in the least, or committed adultery. If these students are products of the kind of education they receive at Princeton, Rutgers, and Mary Washington institutions of learning, it would appear that "The inmates are running the asylum."

Europe used to be governed at least in part by the Judea-Christian Philosophy, which is through the freedom of expression and democratic government. After the French revolution, atheism began to reign in France and Europe. Atheism always creates a vacuum. It may seem like an over simplification, but now through immigration, Islam sees the opportunity to infiltrate and change the history, culture, and value systems of the European countries. There appears to be a momentary lull as whether there can or will be any resistance from Western Europeans to this establishment of Islamic tyranny and the establishment of Sharia Law. Except for Russia and Eastern Europe, Islam is waiting for the opportunity to see France, Germany, Great Britain, and other Western European nations become satellites of The Nation of Islam. Mohammed's example is, when Islam is weak, it makes truces with infidel nations; but when Islam senses itself to be stronger, Islam breaks the truces and annihilates the infidel.

Some professors think they can appeal to their students by being academic rebels. In doing so, they think that nations they label as having been "imperialistic" should now be anathematized. What we fail to realize is that even though human rights have been violated by imperialist invasion, the conquered people, over the years integrate into the society, and depending upon the conqueror, may fare much better under benevolent conquerors. But Mohammedanism presents us with a dark and ghastly contrast. Under Sharia Law, the conquered people are usually slaughtered if they fail to convert to Islam or pay the dhimmi tax required of all non-Muslims who are treated as fifth rate citizens. This is true, not only of the conquered people but also of their pedigree, legacy and children born in the next generations. Mohammedism is a far cry from imperialism; it is annihilationism.

The ancient Roman armies advanced upon opposing armies with the slogan, Venimus, Videmus, Vincimus - "We Come, We See, We Conquer." But if Latin language could describe modern day Islam, it would be Venimus, Videmus, Annihilare – "We Come, We See, We Annihilate."

Modern Islamic Murderers love to hit "soft targets." They are descendants of the hated Esau (Ro 9:13). Esau formed an alliance with the profane Ishmaelite's through marriage (Ge 28:9). The Amalekites were descendants of Esau, the man who despised his spiritual, YHWH birthright (Heb 12:16-17). The marauding bands of Amalekite cowards would not face the enemy; and Almighty God Himself did not forget their defiance of natural, human, and moral law when they came out against the Children of God who were progressing toward the Promised Land. Although unprovoked, the Amalekites fell upon the Israelites as they were travelling innocently on the road. The Israelites were leaving hard bondage in Egypt; their spirits were broken; they were not used to war; and the Amalekites attacked the faint, weary, young and old who lagged behind. The Amalekites slaughtered the Israelites with the edge of the sword. They took advantage of the weak and weary and massacred the people who had not in the least injured them. God did not forget this cold-blooded and dastardly atrocity (Ex 17:8-14 with Dt 25:17).

Now, it must be known, that this kind of aggression is justified in The Koran (Qur'an) and advocated by Mohammed in his wars with the Jews, the citizens of Mecca, and surrounding communities. We must also understand that these descendants of Ishmael, Esau, and Amalek can still be converted to the love of Christ with the indwelling of the Holy Spirit to a peaceful, God-fearing, and holy life.

But there is a difference in how the Kingdom of Christ operates and how the kingdoms of national governments operate. The Christ's Kingdom fights with the Sword of the Spirit (which is reason and revelation), but God gives the sword of vengeance to national governments to slay those who undermine authority and commit evil (Ro 13:3-5). Unfortunately, America's national government does what it can to prevent the spread of the Gospel of Christ, and actually discourage the efforts to convert those of Islamic vengeance to the love of Christ.

So, what will happen if, God Forbid, "Trojan Horse" tactics of infiltration and manipulation of the democratic vote getting system are used to destroy America and her allies from within? They know that in just a day or so, many of them can receive, along with an assault rifle purchased On Line, free food, housing, healthcare, access to leadership and tax sponsored favors to all, including the most implacable, dreaded enemies. Then these Christ-hating Progressive, liberal, Democrat socialists will also find themselves in the chains of Islamic academic restraints under such a LAW and will regret to their dying day that they ever taught such a waste product of academic insanity, unfit for sane, mental consumption.

The best illustration of Islamic or Sharia Law insanity is the way in which about 150 French, God-given lives were snuffed out by Satanic Muslim murderers in the Bataclan Theater in Paris (11/15/2015 A.D.). But what we fail to realize is that the last vision these dear souls had before going out into eternal judgment was that of their Rock Stars, the "Eagles of Death." Although forgiven of my sins by the Blood of the Lamb, I am still a frail human being who continues to suffer physically for my past sins, and I have no right to be judgmental; however, I do know that the last words that rang in the ears of nearly 150 spirits before they entered into the twilight of eternity was the marquee song of "The Eagles of Death" –

Kiss the Devil

> "Who'll love the Devil? Who'll sing his song?
>
> I'll love the Devil. I'll sing his song.
>
> Who'll love the devil? Who'll kiss his tongue?
>
> I'll love the devil. I'll kiss his tongue.
>
> Who'll love the Devil? I will love the Devil and sing his song".

When we realize the shortness of life and breath and as Shakespeare said,

> "And all our yesterdays have lighted fools
>
> The way to dusty death. Out! Out, brief candle!
>
> Life's but a walking shadow, a poor player
>
> That struts and frets his hour upon the stage
>
> and then is heard no more:
>
> It is a tale told by an idiot, full of sound and fury,
>
> Signifying NOTHING!" (The Tragedy of Macbeth – 22380)

How arrogant fools we mortal human beings can be. It was probably true, that worldwide, John Lennon's "Beatles" were more popular than Jesus, or when challenged, Lennon changed it to "Bigger than Jesus" (www.wikipedia: More Popular than Jesus); but after strutting and fretting his hour upon the stage, where is he singing and playing now? Shot to death by one of his fans (12/8/1980) according to the Ancient Book, Lennon would either be with His Savior Jesus Christ in Paradise (2Co 12:4) seeing the Lord of Glory and hearing the sweetest sounds of eternity that are forbidden to human ears or he is with His accuser and King Satan (Apollyon- "Destroyer") in the abyss of smoke, fire, and torment (Rev 9:11).

If we were to compare the world's most popular musician of all time, Satan the Luciferian "shining star" of all time would win this popularity test hands down. God, of all potentates, gives His vote to the Great Slanderer,

> "The workmanship of thy tabrets and of thy pipes was prepared in thee the day that thou wast created" (Eze 28:13).

A created being, Satan had "tabrets" (small drum like instruments used for praise and intercession, like a tambourine) (www.worshipexpressions.net) and "pipes" (tubes or wind instruments used to produce music by blowing air through them) built into his very being. When we see a young man apply himself to music, we hear the expression, "He has music in his blood," and this is especially true of Satan whom by far was the most influential musician ever known, "The one who was on The Mountain of God, walking on stones of fire" (Eze 28:14).

Some scholars have difficulty with this verse. Some translators (such as the New International Version) leave "tabrets" and "pipes" out of the text altogether. Granted, the Hebrew word for "pipes" is somewhat obscure, but in the context, it fits the other musical instrument, which is definitely a drum-type of instrument (tofe-Strongs 8596 with 8608). The word is definitely used of music in Genesis 31:27 and 1 Samuel 10:5 where Laban refers to joyful singing to the music of tabrets and harps. Several other Scriptures mention the tabret as a musical instrument (1Sa 10:5, 18:16; Job 17:6; Isa 5:12, 24:8). The word "pipe" is a bezel or metal beaten into a ring (5345); and while we think only of a bezel as a ring on the finger, a pipe is also a ring. Pipes used as wind instruments are also found throughout Scripture (1Sa 10:5; Isa 5:12, 30:29; 1Ki 1:40; Jer 48:36) Pipes are called flutes in the New Testament (Mt 11:17; 1Cor 14:7). Satan's tabrets and pipes were prepared in him. As a verb, prepared means "firmly established" (3559). God fitted or provided Satan with this musical paraphernalia.

I hesitate to label Satan the pre-original sin music director of the Heavenly Choir because when we think of earthly music, we think not only of the human voice but also of man-made stringed instruments, organs, pianos and wind instruments. But even though we have harps or trumpets and heavenly singing in the apocalyptic world, there is no music or voice on earth that compares to the music of Heaven. For certain, we know that the apocalyptic harps or trumpets are not constructed of chemical, molten metal, or wood, and we get into trouble when we force apocalyptic expressions into our world of chemistry. Throughout our Commentary of the Apocalypse, we caution scholars about carrying a literal interpretation of this Book of Revelation so far that we "crash land" the invisible world of the Godhead onto Earth. Heaven's music was a billion times more perfect in glory and satisfaction then the best earthly music. God is a Spirit, and they who worship Him worship in spirit and truth; the best songs are worshipful, spiritual songs.

Yes, Heaven communicated with earth through angelic singing and most importantly during the visitation of the eternal Christ, but the sounds of angelic voices and the sounds of what we call human musical instruments that resonated from the inner being of Satan or angels were beyond human description. In other words, Satan did not play an instrument, but through a method such as divine onomatopoeia, he could communicate music that sounded like any, or all human instruments, that constitute a symphony orchestra. He was created with music built into his very communication scheme. Yes, "The

Eagles of Death" encouraged their hearers to "Sing the devil's song," and maybe they know more about the Devil than we give them credit for.

Another Satan worshipper by the name of Anton LaVey founded the First Satanic Church, which greatly influenced the formation of KISS and other Rock Groups (Google-Anton LaVey and Rock Groups). The group KISS (Knights in Satan's Service) would leap on stage .... puking fake blood (www.jesusissavior.com). LaVey died (10/19/1997A.D.) and according to many testimonies, he begged God to help him repent. A secret Satanic Service funeral was conducted (www.google.com: Anton LaVeys Death Bed Cry for God's Mercy). See also, www.jesusissavior.com on Rock and Roll Hall of Shame. Just as music plays a part in the worship of the True God, so music plays a very prominent place in Satan worship.

At times, the Bible is a very complex book, and especially when attempting to understand the creation of Angels, good and bad, like Satan and evil angels who fell from Heaven after rebelling against God. I confess that it takes a lot of prayer, Bible forensics, and soul searching to arrive at conclusions. Hermeneutics is the science of proper Biblical study and application, and there are two words, "personification and "parallelism," that bear on this subject in Ezekiel 28:11-19.[139] Yes, the King of Tyre is mentioned but because he was never the model of perfection, he was covered with human flesh (not a spirit covered with metallic stones); he was never in Heaven (The Mount of God); he was never a "propitious cherub"; he did not walk on stones of fire and was never in Eden; he was never driven out from the Mount of God, then he is a "personification" of His Father, The Devil. When talking of a very evil person, we still use the expression "He is a devil."

Regarding the parallelism in this Scripture passage (See my *Book on Hermeneutics*), the deeds and performances of the King of Tyre on Earth parallel the attitudes and acts of Satan. We apply the same rules of Hermeneutics to Isaiah 14:12 because it is obvious that Isaiah speaks of the King of Babylon in the same manner as Ezekiel speaks of The King of Tyre. In apocalyptic literature, we have discovered that the prophet speaks of things in the unseen Heaven and their counterparts on Earth as if they were one subject.

Remember that the word "Lucifer" comes from the Hebrew "Heylel" (brightness- to shine-1966), and is derived from the root word "Halal" (to shine with clarity

– 1984). When Jerome translated *The Bible* he used the two Latin words "Lux" (light) and "Ferre" (bringing or bearing) and composed them into Luxferre "Lucifer." It is a nickname for the Devil "son of the morning" (Isa 14:12), the Angel of Light (2Co 11:14). Since angels are like stars (both exist in space and angels can accomplish the incredible act of interplanetary flight – Job 28:7; Da 10:12-14), it appears that Luxferre fell from Heaven because he challenged the true "Morning Star," Lord Jesus Christ (Re 22:16). Some scholars think the planet Venus (seen both in the morning and twilight) is the cosmic image of the subject of Christ, "The true Light" (Jn1:9; 1Jn 2:8), in contrast to Satan who is the pretentious and false light. Literally, we can translate it, "Shining light bearer, Son of the morning, why are you fallen from heaven?" (Isa 14:11)

In this context, it is interesting to note that the root word "Halal" is the prefix of the most famous word in the world, "Hallelujah." It means that we worship and celebrate the brightness and glory "Heyel" of "Yaweh" Jesus. How Luxferre, "Lucifer," and Hell's foundations must tremble when he hears shouts of praise "Hallelujah" on Earth. It makes sense that if Satan were in Heaven with His creator Jesus, and he apostatized, given his extraordinary blessings and benefits, he could use them to draw people away from Jesus.

EARTHLY SUPERSTARS MAY THINK OF THEMSELVES AS BEING MORE POPULAR THAN MELCHEZEDEC, THE PRINCE OF HEAVEN, BUT IN THE EYES OF BILLIONS AND BILLIONS OF CELESTIAL BEINGS IN GOD'S ETERNAL CITY OF SALEM "ABOVE THE STARS", THERE IS ONLY ONE SONG THAT DRIVES THEIR UPLIFTED PRAISE- "WORTHY IS THE LAMB!" (RE. 5:12).

Thus, Lennon's words, "We are more popular than Jesus," goes back into the pre-cosmic world. Satan said in his heart (remember that the King of Babylon is paralleled to Satan just as the King of Tyre in Ezekiel 28:11-19), "I will raise my throne above the stars of God" (Isa 14:13, 14). Above the stars of God (more than just astronomical stars) means that Satan wanted to have the fame of the ONLY Rock Star. It makes sense that if Lucifer were allowed to retain his inbred gifts and talents of music, he could use them (among other miraculous endowments) to lead other angels astray and "yes," to lead an anthropos astray, especially young impressionable human beings. Music was originally given to uplift, edify, and bring glory to God; it is now used to glorify anti-Christ ideas and draw attention to the ideology and things Lucifer espouses. It has a very destructive effect upon a God-given soul.

Your academic liberal, progressive members of the Sin Party are getting your vote, and they tell you are a fool for believing in The Devil. But, the Devil was around long before you were born and will be there long after you die. The Devil has the power of death (Heb 2:14). Some people have the Devil as their Father, "and he is a murderer from the beginning" (Jn 8:44).

Jesus destroyed the works of the Devil (1Jn 3:8), but he did not destroy the Devil himself. The progressive, evolutionary simpleton thinks we have evolved far beyond belief in the Devil, and the Devil thinks this is just fine. Satan cannot afford open confrontation with Jesus Christ so he fares much better under the guise of denial and obscurity. Satan is also a terrorist; he intimidates through a lifetime of our fear and power of death. It is a good name for him because he indeed is an "Eagle of Death." Satan is a spirit creature, and every man and woman has a spirit. There is far more in this cosmic universe than just what we see with our eyes. Most animals live by seeing with their eyes and so do demon-possessed individuals who are blinded by the Prince of this World (2Co 4:4). They are blinded to the Gospel of deliverance. They despise the Gospel; they despise the Holy Spirit; and they despise the God who made them.

Nearly 150 souls went out into eternity while the "Eagles of Death" fled to the safety of their dressing rooms. Bodies were strewn on the blood stained floor of the rock concert theater. They went to the theater to have a good time; and before nightfall, they went to meet their eternal fate and destiny. We should all "Prepare to Meet Thy God" at all times (Am 4:11-14). So much for Sharia Law, the tragedy of Muslim passion for Massacre, and their choice of a rock concert to commit a cowardly manslaughter; these Islamic devils executed a dastardly unforgiven crime that paid them the wages of the wrath of Hell.

After Dr. Pitirim Sorokim fled the brutal darkness of Russian Communism and came to "Christian" America, we would think that he would have blamed the collapse of Russian morality on the anti-Christian Communist doctrine, but Sorokim (who founded the Department of Sociology at Harvard University in 1930) would have said, "The word altruism is now used in place of Christian love" (www.thecrimson.com). In the book, *Research on Altruism and Love* (www.templetongpres.org), the first topics we are introduced to in the flyleaf of the book are major studies in Psychology, Sociology, and Evolutionary Biology, and at the end of the list is Theology.

So the search goes on and on as the lost world looks for love apart from God, "Who is LOVE" (1Jn 4:16), and refuses to appreciate the width, length, height and depth of CHRIST'S LOVE, and know such love that surpasses all human knowledge in psychology, sociology, evolutionary theory, and theology (Ep 3:18, 19).

The United Nations replaced the League of Nations and was established (10/24/1945). Since then there have been over 140 wars (www.ign.com: wars after the U.N.) with millions of deaths. This figure is as of 5/12/2010 A.D. This is probably not too bad a human achievement when we realize it occurred without one prayer to Christ, "The King of Peace," from within their vain, self-righteous assembly halls. Just two years later (11/29/47), the United Nations Partition Plan for Palestine went into effect. This plan revoked the old Balfour Declaration, called for the withdrawal of British forces from Palestine, and created boundaries between the new State of Israel and the adjacent, independent Arab States.

When the state of Israel was established, theological millennial mania began to run wild and was hardly challenged by theologians who should have understood that God's Israel-Zion is not a physical parcel of land in what used to be called Canaan-Israel. After 70 A.D., a final Jewish revolt under Simon Bar Kokhba was crushed by the Romans (133 A.D.), and their land, formerly called "Israel," was changed to "Palestine" (www.jewishvirtuallibrary: Palestine). With the defeat of Kokhba's Army, any idea of a political, nationalistic Zionism was also crushed.

We ask, "How in 1947 could a holy nation be formed by such an unholy organization as the U.N.?" Forty years later, in 1988, Edgar G. Whisenant wrote, *88 Reasons Why Christ Will Return in 1988*. Scores of other Millennialists, including John Hagee, said that according to Daniel's prophecy, Christ would return after "A 40-year tribulation" even though nothing in Scripture expresses anything about a "40-year Tribulation." Did God permit the U.N., which was administered by many anti-Christians and atheists, to make a declaration that divided a nation that they called "Israel" from other states called "Arab"? Was it God's choice that this "new" nation be more secular than religious? Was the U.N. decision (11/29/47) found somewhere in Divine Prophecy? Has this U.N. Declaration brought Peace to the Middle East?

Let our Lord help us with these questions. The Holy Speaks through Scripture, "For in Christ Jesus, neither circumcision nor uncircumcision avails. And as many as walk according to this rule, PEACE be upon them, and mercy and upon the Israel of God" (Gal 6:15, 16). "The Israel of God" is not the United Nation's Israel. The Israel of God is neither a circumcised Jew nor uncircumcised Gentile. PEACE and mercy rests upon both the cultural Jew and the Palestinian, or Arabian Gentile if they choose to cease glorying in their race, national distinction, man-made religions, or pedigree and come to the foot of the Cross and behold "The Lamb Slain from the foundations of the world" (Rev 13:8) and glory in what that "Old Rugged Cross" really stands for (Gal 6:14). When that happens, we will cease from the glory of the perishing flesh and begin to glory in why Christ came to Earth, and why He died for all mankind.... Jew, Greek, Gentile, Arab, African, European, Asian, North and South American and all who have ever lived on planet Earth.

We can, by no means, justify terrorism. No reasonable person would ever support a religion like Islam or Mohammedanism that is so paranoid and so useless that it must be spread with autocratic law enforcement, the sword of violence, and murder. Jesus said, "Love your enemies," and I love my enemies. But I do not love YOUR enemies. I do not love God's enemies. I do not love the "Enemies of State," and that is why God gave us government and "the sword" in order to protect us against these enemies (Ro 13:3, 4). In a speech at Hillsdale College (9/15/2015 A.D.), U.S. Senator Tom Cotton (AR-R) addressed the growing threat of how a President thinks he can circumvent Congress and obligate the U.S. to nuclear-power-seeking ayatollahs by a mere executive agreement. Cotton invoked the weight and authority of The Constitution declaring that,

> "Only congress can raise and support armies: only Congress may declare war and invoke the legal obligations and protections that this state of international relations confers; only Congress regulates foreign commerce, and with it control over important levers of influence with foreign nations in order to build better relations, exact costs, and prevent war." (*Imprimis*, "Foreign Policy and the Constitution," presented by U.S. Senator Tom Cotton to Hillsdale College, Vol. 44, No. 10, (10/2015 A.D.)

There is a time for humble, gut wrenching expedience and negotiation with threatening enemies, but there also comes the time when we as "Our brother's keeper" must unsheathe the sword to prevent the further slaughter of the innocent. After having their fill of King George III's tyrannical rule and disregard for his own subjects, God provided our Founding Fathers the wisdom to keep ONE President from damning the country through unilateral decisions, which today is "rule by executive orders." The results of executive rule (by a partisan minority) without Congressional approval (and ignoring sovereign States Rights) can lead to the tyrannical rule exercised by those like Napoleon, Joseph Stalin, Adolph Hitler, Xi Jinping, Mao Zedong, Deng Xiaoping, Castro, and Kim Jung Il, who killed millions of people. But there is another way we kill millions of people.

Sometimes we fail to realize that democratic tyranny can lead to a socialist state that will eventually, if left unchecked, lead to an impoverished nation. We must be alert to would be earthly political saviors who end up creating a system that causes people to damn themselves. Medgar Evers said, "You can kill a man, but you can't kill an idea." May we add, "What is worse, to kill a man or try to kill an idea?" Thus, we wonder how many ideas have been killed by Eugene Debs and modern-day counterparts Bernie Sanders and the 30% of Americans who believe socialism is a good political system.

Our Founding Fathers were well aware of the threat posed, even by religious groups (Catholic and Protestant), who resorted to the spread of their religion in Europe through the use of weaponry. Most of us have forgotten, but Islam is not the first religious nation that has tried to conquer the U.S. Joseph Smith was fascinated with Mohammedanism, and he and Sydney Rigdon concocted a clone religion very similar to Mohammedanism in doctrine and practice (www.google.com: Danites, Mormon Secret Police).

The attitude in Washington at the time the Mormon leaders were advocating armed rebellion and anarchy (and that should exist now) was that any religion has the right to exist in this country, but no religion has the right to establish a foreign nation within this nation and sponsor an armed assault against our government. President Obama's Secretary, Valerie Jarrett is wrong, dead wrong when she said as a member of the Islamic Faith she will help "Change America to be a more Islamic Country." She is wrong because while numbskull Americans have allowed, through democratic tomfoolery, a tyrant to CHANGE the country for the worse; Muslims would face the most ferocious battle and bloody holocaust since the days of Charles Martell if they try to bring freedom loving Americans under Sharia Law.

In my book, *Sydney Rigdon University*, I reference historical sources existing at the time of the Mormon Rebellion. We can safely say that Joseph Smith had designs of being an American King, and our apostate brother from the Restoration Movement, Sydney Rigdon, would be his Vice President. Of course, their thinking that they could take over America by force of arms was less than wishful thinking (www.google.com: The Mormon War of 1838 and Did Joseph Smith Commit Treason?).

How anyone who lives in a sandcastle on the shores of the ocean of eternity can be filled with the insane obsession to think he or she (in a speck of time compared to eternity) can rule over the affairs of their nation or world, is unquestionably the nincompoop in time and the consummate loser in eternity.

If what we believe is such a weak, unsubstantial concoction of disconnected human ranting and raving that we would kill people who investigate and are too intelligent to embrace what we believe, then no matter how fanatically we feel about our religion, it fails God's tests of TRUTH and logic. We should denounce it immediately!

> YES, THOSE WHO CALL THEMSELVES JEWS, AND MUSLIMS HAVE MUCH POTENTIAL TO CONVERT TO CHRIST IF THEY HEAR THE GOSPEL.

Pure, New Testament Christianity instructs us in the Last Will and Covenant of our Lord Jesus Christ with the human race, and it includes ALL just men made perfect by the Covenant Blood (Heb 12:22-24). This includes even those we may consider political enemies in the Middle East. The will and testament of Jesus is for all mankind to receive His inheritance. Six times the word "WILL" is used (Heb 8:6-13) of the Testimonial "WILL" of Christ's "New Covenant" (Heb 8:8), His "Law in their hearts and minds" (vs. 10), His desire "To be their God and they be His people" (vs. 10), His mercy toward "their unrighteousness" (vs.12), and His willingness to forget their sins and iniquities (vs.12).

My hope is that we agree with President Ronald Reagan's very wise and noble gesture to those who were our enemies in the Middle East when he said,

> "Iranian Parliament Speaker Hashemi Rafsanjani on Wednesday showed reporters the Bible he said was sent by President Reagan and said the U.S. leader is courageous but old, weak, in bad health and undercut by political rivals. Rafsanjani displayed the leather-bound (*Open Book Bible-Expanded Edition*) at a news conference, holding it open to the title page bearing Reagan's name and a handwritten New Testament verse: "And the Scripture, foreseeing that God would justify the Gentiles by faith, preached the gospel

beforehand to Abraham saying, 'All nations shall be blessed in you' (Galatians 3:8" (signed) Ronald Reagan, Oct. 3, 1986." Jan. 29, 1987 (From *New York Times Wire services*)

PRESIDENT REAGAN WAS MORE COURAGEOUS THAN MANY OF US CHRISTIANS.

Observant Muslims hate us Christians because they think we still think that God has ONLY ONE NATION and that is the Jewish State of Israel (even though there is not an authentic Jew on Earth). Even though their tyrannical rulers forbid us to preach the Gospel of worldwide redemption to them, the stark and tragic TRUTH is that most Christians are not much interested in preaching it to them. When the world looks at Christianity, they see Catholic "Christians," Greek "Christians," Coptic "Christians," Russian, Armenian, and Protestant Christians. The stark, tragic truth is that since the time from the death of the original Apostles to the writing of the Nicaean Creed by the "ecclesiastical over lords," billions of people from all parts of the world have never had the privilege of seeing many New Covenant Christians.

While we admit that the nation of Cultural Jews-Israel is a democracy more governable than nearly all Muslim Nations, we are not excused from our responsibility to make the Gospel known, even though modern-day Israel may tolerate our "bearing of the Saving Gospel" as a nuisance; and Muslim nations may treat this as a capital offense. But we must preach the Gospel to ALL because then AND ONLY THEN, will there be PEACE on Earth and good will among men of good will; and PEACE, MERCY, and GRACE will exist presently in the spiritual minds of those whose affections are in the New Jerusalem-Zion (Col 3:1-5). This is what we think of when we "Pray for the PEACE of Jerusalem" (www.puritanboard).

ZIONISM, IN A NUTSHELL, REPRESENTS FIRST AND FORMOST THE JERUSALEM WHICH IS ABOVE.

As New Covenant Christians who represent a minority of the Christian community, we seek to understand the international struggles and calamities in the Middle East and the world in the light of The New Testament and not in the eyes of human religions. For us, the solution to the age old controversy of earthly Jerusalem lies in the Apostle Paul's inspired writings of "The allegory of Sarah (the wife of Abraham) and Hagar (the Mother of Mohammedanism)." This is the final word on our subject of Jerusalem's place in history when Paul wrote and now.

Paul begins the allegory with Abraham's two sons, one to bondmaid Hagar and the other by his wife, freewoman Sarah (Ga 4:22). The child of the bondwoman (Ishmael, Father of Mohammedanism) was of the flesh, but the child of the free woman, Isaac (miraculously born in a 90 year old womb) was the child of promise (4:23). In Paul's allegorical comparison, Hagar stands for Mt. Sinai in Arabia (where the Old Covenant was given), and answers or "responds" to the Jerusalem of both Paul's day, "now is," and in our modern-day. But the characteristic of those who are affectionately tied to this old city (considering it a sacred spot or shrine) is that they and their children "are in bondage" (4:24, 25).

Anyone who worships a sacred shrine on Earth is in bondage. They are in bondage to sin, self, Satan, and harsh servitude. The Jews killed Stephen after he told them the absolute, candid, unvarnished TRUTH, "Howbeit, the God Most High does not dwell in temples made with human hands" (Ac 7:48). It makes no difference if it is a Turkish Minaret, Arabian Mosque, a Greek or Roman Catholic Cathedral, Protestant megachurch, a "Holy" shrine in Medina, Mecca, Rome, Salt Lake City or Moscow. The fact is that the God of The Bible does not dwell in these man-made shrines. Christ's Kingdom is "made without human hands" (Da 2:34). The Kingdom of Christ is from above (Col 3:1-3). The earthly Jerusalem is "Trodden under the feet of Gentiles" (Lk 11:2). The "gentiles" who have been there since 70 A.D. includes Gentiles who call themselves Jews. The trodding (pressing down the feet upon something) of Jerusalem means to control the city. We measure the true temple with the New Testament (Rev 11:1), and it will stand forever. God said, leave the Outer Court alone (The false temple from Jerusalem and Rome), which is being trodden down of the Gentiles (not of true spiritual Israel) (Rev 11:2). Hagar is in bondage with her billions of children, and they are prone to persecute the children of the promise (Gal 4:29). They will even persecute those of their own people if they convert to The Messiah, who came of the promise through Isaac.

Paul said, "The Jerusalem which is above is free, and is the mother of us all" (4:26). This is the Jerusalem that is populated with millions of Children of the Messiah at present, and will in the end be seen by all who have ever lived, "I, John, saw the holy city, New Jerusalem, coming down from God out of heaven, prepared as a bride adorned for her husband" (Rev 21:2). The foolish notion that this eternal, spiritual abode of glorified bodies "spirits made perfect" (Heb 12:22, 23) is going to rematerialize (just like the Old Jerusalem on Earth) is pure, crass nonsense. The New Heaven (singular), and New Jerusalem will be revealed after the Old Heavens and Old Earth, and oceanic seas have passed away (Rev 21:1). There is no rendezvous of Christ and His bride on Earth. The City shall come down, "The Lord shall descend," and we shall go up and the meeting will be in the air (1Ti 4:16).

In the meantime, what do those cultural Jews, who want to live in Old Jerusalem, do today? First, the political, religious leaders of Jerusalem got it right. They have accepted the fact that the governments of Israel and Jerusalem are just governments of temporary existence on planet Earth. This attitude exists in spite of the fanatical zeal of evangelical Christian Zionism that still stubbornly adheres to the Old Testament idea that God has a favored, Jewish people in the world. Of course, many in Jewish leadership bow to the enormous amounts of "Israel First" propaganda and egregious financial support they get from "The Rapture Cult" and evangelical, Christian Zionism movements across America and from other countries.

A Christian Missionary friend of mine went to Israel to preach. He knew they would not let him through security if he told them of his real intentions, so he registered as a social, benevolent worker from America, and they allowed him to go through customs, although not without a lot of tense questioning. He related that while the Israeli Government compliments the huge donation of funds and religious support shown them by the evangelical, Christian Zionist Millennial Movement, he said that inwardly, most of the Government Officials think the application made by such Zionists to Bible prophecy is frivolous and silly. "The nation," he said, "Is mostly secular and practically atheist, and if in America most of them would all vote for Democrats or any politician of exclusive Social Causes." (There are many web sites that deal fairly accurately with Christen Zionism and what the Bible really says about Israel, such as, www.patheos.com: Standing with Israel, www.jesus-is-savior.com: Worshipping Israel, www.religion.blogs.cnn.com: Evangelical Christians give Millions to Israel, www.realjewnews.com: Christian, not Jews are God's Chosen.)

Now, lest the reader misunderstand the Biblical thrust of our thesis, we must clearly delineate our position as American Citizens, as well as Citizens of Heaven. We do not have the space or time to address it here, but the New Testament Scriptures clearly expound the idea that in a voting republic, it is sinful for Christians to stay away from the voting polls and refuse to cast a ballot. This is especially true when we vote for or against an elected official who is faced with the responsibility of making decisions that affect the moral destiny and Christian principles of the nation.

When I quote Scripture, I can do it with the authority and backing of Heaven (Mt 28:18-19). But, like all other mortal human beings, I do not have authoritative answers regarding the international crises and problems facing our nation politically. Far from being a Middle East expert, I can make judgments only as I learn them from what I know to be the biased, American Media because I do not have anywhere else to turn, except through intercessory prayer to the unbiased Father in Heaven. I am not anti-Palestinian, anti-Arabian or anti-anti-Semitic; I am FOR God's Creation of every human being created of ONE blood, by ONE God. When I read of conflict in the Middle East, I try to determine what the mind set or schematic is that creates the driving forces behind the skirmish or war between two opposing fractions.

I have no qualms about dismissing my first conclusion. If one fraction is killing another because it considers the other faction to be infidels, then that is wrong, dead wrong and MUST be opposed with all reason and might. If the problem is created because of unfair treatment of one fraction toward another, that is equally wrong. However, if it boils down to one faction simply wanting to take land, property, and wealth from another, then I tend to stand on the side of the resisting faction. Thus, if modern-day, secular Israel seeks to exist as a nation, then I think we should support them, but it has nothing to do with Bible prophecy or that God favors one nation over another.

The idea of the resurrection of Jewish world dominance, as it was in the days of Solomon (Ac 1:6) is a very carnal theology which appeals to carnal-minded Christians. The disciples of Jesus had this same "Zionistic" theology in mind, and Jesus did not argue with them. Neither should we argue with Jewish Supremacist. Like the disciples, it is under God's power to know the times and the seasons, not ours. We learn from our Master that it is best to simply teach the Scripture and let the Holy Spirit convict us in regard to this subject, "But you shall receive power, after the Holy Spirit is come upon you, and you shall be my witnesses (and notice the four places this New Testament witness will penetrate – 1) Jerusalem, 2) Judaea, 3) Samaria (modern-day "West Bank"), and 4) the uttermost parts of the Earth (Ac 1:8). We realize we cannot cram the Kingdom of Christ down the throats of cultural Jews, Arabs, Muslims, apostate Christians and millions of adherents of other world religions, but Jesus said for us to "witness" (Rev 11:3-8) and to allow the Holy Spirit to do His job. When people are born of the Holy Spirit, (Jn 3:5) the Kingdom of Christ means everything to them.

Physical Israel has a right to defend their democracy and to try to live as peacefully as possible with their neighbors, but God will never favor a people (Jewish, Muslim, or other) who fights fanatically to defend an earthly holy shrine. The Muslim oligarchies in The Middle East constitute some of the last Kingdoms on earth that still believe in a theocratic government. However, after Christ ascended to The THRONE, God will not accept an earthly theocracy. Even though some Muslim leaders fanatically desire a theocratic government, it will never come from God, but from Satan, who is the "Prince of this World" (2Co 4:4). Yes, demon-inspired men will attempt to establish such theocracies, and Christ will not (at least at this present time) interfere with the devastating, counter force of His Kingdom of Heaven. Jesus recognizes that some people want Satan as their Prince (Jn 13:40), and they can set up their frail kingdoms, but only at their own peril, problems, and misfortunes, because their kingdom and their life is like a "Vapor that appears for a while, then vanishes away" (Jas 4:14).

With our Lord, the only permanent citizenship we have, is in Heaven (Php 3:20). After our foolish Supreme Court, and complicit government legislators, ruled in favor of "Same-Sex" homosexual marriage, and many religious leaders compromised what the Lord taught us about "Divine Marriage" because they thought they might lose tax exemptions; our elders were questioned on what they intended to do. We were not surprised when they decided, "We will obey God, not man" (Ac 5:29); we will oppose it with all of the resources given us by God's Grace, and if the government takes away our property, we will go underground.

We will never compromise! The 30 acres of property we own used to belong to the Shawnee Indians. Later, it fell into the hands of colonial developers. It passed back and forth into the hands of various Virginia farmers. During the Civil War, it was occupied for a while by the Southern Armies (The Kerns Town Battlefield is a mile away from our congregation), and then for a while by the Northern Armies. But we do not own it; we just borrow it for a while. We do not own anything. After we die, someone else will govern our property, and when they die, someone else will step in. The only thing we own permanently is our right, given by Jesus Christ, to have property in Heaven, forever (Jn 14:1-6).

Abraham, known to Muslims as Ibrahim, is considered by some to be the common father to modern-day Jews and Muslims, and in the verse selected by President Reagan, God told Abraham that "Through His seed all the families of the earth would be blessed" (Ge 26:4), and that SEED is Christ (Gal 3:16) "The Word of God" (Jn 1:1, 2; Lk 8:11). One of the greatest days in history will dawn on this dark planet Earth when our cultural Jewish and Arabian brothers want to go to the Heavenly Jerusalem as much as the rest of us.

Let us conclude at the same place we began in this Addendum. The King of the Heavenly Jerusalem is Jesus, King of Salem, or Melchezidec "King of Righteousness." When the people of this Earth look up to the King who has ALL authority in Heaven and Earth (Mt 28:18), there will be peace among those of good will, and they will beat their swords into plowshares and learn war no more (Isa 2:4; Mic 4:3).

WORKS READ

A Dictionary of the Bible Dealing With Its Language, Literature, and Contents
Edited by James Hastings, M.A., and D.D. with the assistance of John A. Selbie, M.A. Volume II Feign—Kingsman
New York, Charles Scribner's Sons
Edinburgh: T. & T. Clark Copyright 1899

A History of Christianity
By Kenneth Scott LaTourette
Harper & Row, Publishers, New York, Evanston, and London
Copyright 1953

A History of the Christian Church
By Williston Walker
Charles Scribner's Sons, New York
Copyright 1959 Charles Scribner's Sons
Copyright 1918 Charles Scribner's Sons; renewal copyright 1946 Amelia Walker Cushing and Elizabeth Walker

Amillennialism Today
By William E. Cox
Presbyterian and Reformed Publishing Co.
Phillipsburg, New Jersey Copyright 1966

An Exposition of the Old and New Testament
By Matthew Henry
Fleming H. Revell Company, New York, Chicago, Toronto

Word Pictures in the New Testament
By Archibald Thomas Robertson
Harper & Brothers Publishers, New York and London
Copyright 1930

Ante-Nicene Fathers of the Christian Church. 9 vols. Roberts, Alexander, James Donaldson, and Cleveland A. Coxe, Eds. Edinburgh: Christian Literature Publishing, 1885.

Antichrist Two Thousand Years of the Human Fascination with Evil
By Bernard McGinn
Harper San Francisco
A Division of Harper Collins Publishers

Christians Only
By James DeForest Murch
Standard Publishing, Cincinnati, Ohio 2766
Copyright MCMLXII the Standard Publishing Copy, Cincinnati, Ohio

Cobbin's Commentary on the Bible for Young and Old
By Rev. Ingram Cobbin, of England Volume II.
New York: Selmar Hess, Publisher Entered, according to Act of Congress, in the year 1876

Compton's Pictured Encyclopedia and Fact-Index Volume 14
Published by F.E. Compton & Company – Chicago
Copyright 1922 – 1951

Concise Commentary on the Holy Bible: Being a Companion to the New Translation of The Old and New Covenants. Young, Robert. 1865. Edinburgh: George Adam Young & Co.

Daniel
By Paul T. Butler
College Press, Joplin, Missouri
Copyright 1970

Davis Dictionary of the Bible – Fourth Revised Edition
By John D. Davis
Fleming H. Revell Company – Old Tappan, New Jersey Twenty-third printing March 1977

Dictionary of the Bible Volume IV
Edited by James Hastings, M.A., and D.D. with the assistance of John A. Selbie, M.A., and D.D.
New York, Charles Scribner's Sons, Edinburgh: T. & T. Clark 1902
Copyright 1902

Discovering Our Roots: The Ancestry of Churches of Christ
By C. Leonard Allen/Richard T. Hughes Copyright 1988
ACU Press, Abilene Christian University, Abilene, Texas

End Times Fiction
By Gary DeMar
Thomas Nelson Publishers – Nashville = A Division of Thomas Nelson, Inc.
Copyright 2001

Exposition of Genesis
By H.C. Leupold, D.D.
Volume I Chapters 1-19
Baker Book House, Grand Rapids, Michigan 1963
Copyright 1942 the Wartburg Press

Greek and English Lexicon of the New Testament
By Edward Robinson, D.D. LL. D.
Boston and New York:
Houghton, Mifflin And Company. The Riverside Press, Cambridge 1887.
Copyright, 1878

Handbook of Denominations in the United States
Second Revised Edition
By Frank S. Mead
Abingdon Press, New York - Nashville Copyright 1961, 1951, 1956

House Divided: The Break Up of Dispensational Theology.
Bahnsen, Greg L. Tyler,
Texas Institute For Christian Economics, 1989.

Interlinear Greek-English New Testament with a Greek English Lexicon and New Testament Synonyms by George Ricker Berry
King James Version Baker Book House
Grand Rapids, Michigan Copyright 1897 by Hinds & Nobel
ISBN: O-8010-0700-3   Fifteenth printing, August 1993

Iranian Christian
By Nasser Lotfi
Word Books Publisher, Waco Texas
Copyright 1980

Israel and the Bible
By William Hendriksen
Baker Book House, Grand Rapids, Michigan Copyright 1968

New Testament Times
By H. E. Dana
Central Seminary Press, Kansas City, Kansas 1946
Copyright 1938

Nicene and Post-Nicene Fathers of the Christian Church, series 2.
Philip Schaff, and Henry Wace, Ed.
Edinburgh: Christian Literature Publishing, 1890.

Omega
By Lewis R. Walton
Review and Herald Publishing Association, Washington, D.C.
Copyright 1981

Revelation and the End of All things. Koester, Craig R.
Grand Rapids: Wm. B. Eerdmans Publishing Co, 2001.

Revelation, Four Views, a Parallel Commentary. By Steve Gregg,
Thomas Nelson, 1997. Nashville

The ABC's of the Prophetical Scriptures
By George H. Clement
Broadman Press – Nashville, Tennessee
Copyright 1970

The Analytical Greek Lexicon Zondervan Publishing House, Grand Rapids, Michigan, Fifth Zondervan printing January 1970, Sixth printing December 1970, Seventh printing 1972, Catalog Number 6257

The Bible Code
By Michael Drosnin
Simon & Schuster, Rockefeller Center, New York, NY
Copyright 1997

The Christian Restoration Assoc., Cincinnati, Ohio.

The Columbia – Viking Desk Encyclopedia A – K Volume One
Compiled and edited at Columbia University
Published By the Viking Press – New York
Copyright 1953

The Coming King
By James Edson White
Review And Herald Publishing Co., Battle Creek, Mich., Chicago, Ill, Atlanta, GA 1900Copyrighted 1898, 1900

The End of the Age
By James H. McConkey
1928 Silver Publishing Society, Pittsburgh, Pa.
Copyright 1918

The End Times Controversy
By Tim LaHaye & Thomas Ice
Harvest House Publishers, Eugene, Oregon
Copyright 2003

The Great Cover up. Mac Pherson, Dave.
New Lebanon: Omega Publishing, 1975.

The Kingdom of God. Bright, John. Nashville: Abingdon Press, 1980.

The Mustard Seed Conspiracy
By Tom Sine
Word Books Publisher, Waco, Texas
Copyright 1981 by Word, Inc., Waco, Texas 76796

The New Testament, an Expanded Translation
By Kenneth S. Wuest
William B. Eerdmans Publishing Company
Grand Rapids, Michigan
Copyright Wm. B. Erdmans Publishing Co. 1961

The Plain Truth about Armstrongism
By Roger R. Chambers
Baker Book House – Direction Books

The Rapture
By Tim LaHaye
Harvest House Publishers, Eugene, Oregon

The Revelation of St. John
By Albertus Pieters, D.D.
Wm. B. Eerdmans Publishing Company, Grand Rapids, Michigan
Copyright 1943

The Scofield Reference Bible. Scofield, Charles.
New York: Oxford University Press, 1945.

The Thirteenth Tribe
By Arthur Koestler
Copyright 1976 Published in the United States by Random House, Inc., New York. Originally published in Great Britain by Hutchinson & Co (Publishers) Ltd., London,

The Thompson Chain-Reference Bible, New International Version
Compiled and Edited by Frank Charles Thompson, D.D., and Ph.D.
B.B. Kirkbride Bible Co., Inc., Indianapolis, Indiana

The Westminster Dictionary of the Bible
By John D. Davis, PH.D., D.D., LL.D.
Revised and Rewritten by Henry Snyder Gehman, Ph. D., and S.T.D.
The Westminster Press, Philadelphia Copyright, 1944,
A Dictionary of the Bible Copyright, 1898, 1903, 1911, 1924

The Works of Flavius Josephus Translated by William Whiston, A.M.
William P. Nimmo, London, 14 King William Street, Strand; and Edinburgh

Theological Dictionary of the New Testament
Abridged In One Volume
By Geoffrey W. Bromiley
William B. Eerdmans Publishing Company
Copyright 1985

Understanding Bible Prophecy for Yourself
By Tim LaHaye
Harvest House Publishers, Eugene, Oregon
Copyright 1998, 2001

Unger's Bible Dictionary
By Merrill F. Unger
Moody Press, Chicago
Copyright 1957

Vine's Complete Expository Dictionary with topical index. Vine,
W.E. Edited by Merrill F. Unger and William White, Jr.
Nashville: Thomas Nelson, 1996.

Vines Expository Dictionary of New Testament Words – Unabridged Edition
W. E. Vine, M.A. Riverside Book and Bible House, Iowa Falls, Iowa 50126

Webster's Unified Dictionary and Encyclopedia Lewis Mulford Adams, C. Ralph
Taylor, A.M., Edward N. Teall, A.M. D'Arcy G. Van Bokkelen 1955
H.S. Stuttman Co., Publishers
New York, N.Y. Copyright 1955

Who Really Wrote The Book Of Mormon?
The Spalding Enigma
Wayne L. Cowdrey – Howard A. Davis – Arthur Vanick
Concordia Publishing House, Saint Louis
Copyright 2005

Word Pictures in the New Testament
By Archibald Thomas Robertson
Harper & Brothers Publishers, New York and London
Copyright 1930

Word Studies in the New Testament
By Marvin R. Vincent, D.D.
Volume III, The Epistles of Paul

New York, Charles Scribner's Sons, 1904
Copyright 1890
Zondervan Bible Publishers
Grand Rapids, Michigan
Copyright 1978

IMPORTANT NOTICE IN REGARD TO WIKIPEDIA

The so called scholarly attacks on Wikipedia by acolyte students who are warned by their class room professors that Wikipedia is not a very good clearing house for knowledge, is completely unwarranted and here is why. It is possible this attitude toward the free market in the exchange of ideas (offered by Wikipedia to any and all who seek it) is generally motivated more by a professional jealousy of pseudo scholars who want to carve out a "coin on the market", then by the facts of science offered by the grand and generous hearts of those who work behind the Wikipedia scenes.

Yes, scholars want to lecture, write books and gain a huge amount of respect and financial remuneration from their works and research, and justly so. On the other hand, there is nothing to gain by a dishonest censorship of properly given knowledge, with respect for equal balance in its presentation and due recognition for each successive author; just because it is free.

We cite Wikipedia frequently, simply because it is so accessible for the average reader and scholar. In our investigation of the wisdom in using Wikipedia we discovered that a "cite" is also a "reference" to where we derived our sources of information for some of the quotes in this book. Sometimes the citation in given with an End Note number, or within the paragraph itself. The reader can click on our

End Note paragraph reference (or End Note number) and check the site itself with all of the additional references the Wikipedia Site gives. We make no apologies for using Wikipedia. It introduces the material of our designated Author of interest, and if we reference a certain historical subject, Wikipedia gives a brief general history and background of the subject of interest to the reader. Wikipedia then gives additional, special, very detailed and scholarly references that can be brought up with a right click of the cursor. We are amazed that Wikipedia can continue to give us such free information. We need to pause and thank God for such earthly grace and give a donation as we may be led to do so. Wikipedia is a human reproduction of God's grace exhibited on this earth.

INDEX

Abomination Of Desolation, 4, 26-27, 37-38, 40, 66, 78-79, 82, 154, 156, 158, 319, 407, 601, 604, 630, 632, 634, 640-641, 646, 654, 658, 680, 692, 695, 699, 703, 709, 711-712, 721-722, 727, 740, 743, 840, 851

Adoration of Wafer, 534, 538, 553-554

Aesculapius, 136

Alexander the Great, 130, 146, 149, 343-344, 419, 482-484, 532, 569-570, 584, 641, 722

Alfred, Dean, 88

Allah, 157, 206, 413, 537, 581, 635-636

Altruism, 807

Am I Gay?, 744

A-millennial, 70, 74, 470, 475

Anachronism, 6, 297, 314-315

Ancient Of Days, 93, 183-185, 193-195, 343, 465, 467, 722, 734

Angel of Fire, 389

Angel of the Water, 391

Angels, 5, 22, 24, 62, 66, 71, 96, 109-111, 145, 149, 169, 178, 186, 189, 191, 197, 201, 214-215, 220, 222-223, 225, 230, 231-233, 241, 244, 246-248, 258, 264, 266, 279, 288, 293, 299-300, 309, 319-320, 322-323, 373, 375, 377-379, 382, 385, 388-389, 404, 412, 447, 451-453, 455, 461, 472-473, 492, 498-501, 511, 513, 522, 530-531, 551, 563, 584, 638, 644, 648-649, 651, 716, 731-732, 735, 740, 788, 804-806

Annulling the Old Law, 35, 680, 707

Antichrist, 41, 50, 52-53, 56-57, 73, 86, 94, 349, 350, 357-358, 362, 393, 401, 412-414, 432-433, 444, 462-463, 487, 495, 553, 566, 575-576, 697-698, 701-702, 705, 708, 711-712, 723, 725, 779-780

Anti-Semitism, 132, 674

Aphesis, 221, 323, 368, 639, 649-650

Apocalypse, xi, xv, xvii-xviii, xxvi, 3, 11-14, 18, 29, 31, 45, 57, 75, 123, 189, 197, 204, 235, 237-238, 250-252, 258, 268, 309-311, 317, 366, 383, 388, 453-454, 468, 485, 492, 500, 545, 548, 596, 733, 746, 768, 797, 804

Apocryphal Books, 541

Apostolic Collegium, 39, 123

Apostolic Father, 45, 112, 283, 839-840

Apostolic Succession, 35, 113-114, 127, 529

Arche, 158, 435, 520

Arethas, 45, 844

Arian-Sebelius, 300, 383, 430-436, 439,

Arius, 430-431, 433-434

Ark of the Covenant, 289, 712

Armageddon, 4, 52, 399, 482-483, 485-489, 491-494

Assimilate, 566, 774-775, 778-779, 781, 783

Astrological Worship, 297

Athanasius, 431

Attalus, 150, 551-552

Auberlen, Karl August, 345

Auricular Confessions, 537

Ava Maria, 540

Babylonian Religion, 136, 555
Bacon, Francis, 139
Bahnsen, Greg L., 64, 311-312
Balaam, 135, 140, 547
Baptidzo, 418
Barnes, Albert, 306, 346, 559
Bayne, Steve, 672, 791
Beastology, 47, 73, 183, 270-271, 411
Behold the Lamb, 3, 507-509
Berry, George Ricker, 359, 647
Bishop Damascus, 280, 416, 552-553, 670, 853
Bosom of Abraham, 214, 217-218, 369, 372, 451, 499, 787
Bossuet, Jacques, 545
Bowing Down to an Angel, 519
Broach, Michael, 347
Bruce, F.F., 549
Buchanan, Patrick, 254-255, 437, 767, 847
Caesar Worship, 31, 130-131, 136, 139, 143
Caesar, Julius, 44, 130, 344, 424, 552
Calvin, John, 80, 118, 138, 160, 408, 425-429, 759
Campbell, Alexander, iii, xxiv, 48, 55, 284, 306, 408-409
Cassianus, Johannes, 556
Catholic Dictionary, 362, 529, 531
Catholic Encyclopedia, 529, 532, 536, 540
Catholicism, 47, 57-58, 74, 117, 123, 282, 348, 362, 401, 407-408, 416, 419, 431-432, 436, 528-531, 539, 545, 552, 557-558, 563-566, 705
Celestine of Rome, 416-417
Celibacy, 535-536
Chambers, Richard C., xiv, xxv
Chambers, Roger, 401, 571
Cherub that Covered, 247, 320
Chief Musician, 384-385

Chilias, 460, 463
Christ Ascended, 93, 97, 100, 102, 104, 107, 167-168, 175, 194, 200, 218-219, 245, 247, 260, 293, 321, 323, 328-329, 369, 372-373, 465, 468, 503, 543, 572, 579, 700, 770, 775, 787, 792, 816
Christ Died for Heaven, 323
Christian Humanism, 562
Christian Kingdom College, xiii, xviii, xxii, 27, 186, 846-847
Christian Zionism, 814
Church of Mary, 126, 417
Churchill, WInston, 414, 486, 768
Clement Of Rome, 340, 434, 436, 439, 527
Clergy, 54, 83, 123, 125-127, 350, 361, 364, 387, 406, 409, 418, 422, 526-529, 531, 566, 752, 761, 845
Cleros, 126
Clinton, Hillary, 235, 337, 562, 582
Coad, F. Roy, 55
Comas, Juan, 675
Completion Of New Testament Scripture81
Conditional, 263, 428
Coniah, 166, 168
Constantine, 318, 341, 366, 433, 441, 528, 628, 840
Cotton, Tom, 809
Council Of Ephesus, 122-123, 126-127, 416-417, 421, 531, 543, 553
Council Of Ephesus 431 AD, 122-123, 126-127, 358, 416-417, 531, 543
Council of Nice, 533, 555
Council of Trent, 281, 409, 534, 540-541
Covenant Broken, 52, 708, 711
Cowdery, Davis and Vanick, 55
Cromwell, Oliver, 768
Crossing the Threshold of Hope, 364

Crowns, 133-134, 175, 177, 179, 202, 263, 320, 341, 454
Crucified in Sodom, 763, 838, 847
Cultural Jews, 503, 672, 793, 812, 814-815
Cumorah, 572, 771
Cyrus, 118, 145, 149, 489, 551, 700, 726, 845
Dale, L. Edsil, 127-128
Daniel's "Little Horn", 68-69, 185, 341, 358, 425, 555
Danites, 810
Darby, John N., 51, 54, 56, 59-61, 310, 463, 494
Das Kapital, 758
Dating Of Book Of Revelation, 34, 46-47
David's Throne, 49, 166, 171
Davis, Kim, 438-439
Day of Christ, 504, 733
Deaconate, 40, 81-82
Deity of Christ, 244, 357, 434, 754
DeMar, Gary, 570
Depths Of Satan, 144
Desecrate the Temple, 657-658
Diadem, 180, 203, 454-455
Diana, 122, 554, 586
Diocese, 124, 362, 416, 434, 440, 528
Dispensational, xxiii, xxiv, 51-52, 56-57, 60, 74, 310-311, 694-695, 704, 720, 722-723
Domitius Nero, 42
Doughty Warner Debate, 633-635, 642, 790
Doughty, John, xiv, 187, 336, 557, 747, 847
Dualism, 299, 303
Dyke, Dan, 27, 605, 743
Eagles of Death, 802, 805, 807
Eberhard Karls University, 748
Egyptologist, 574, 772

Element, 16, 54, 96, 257, 485, 620, 722, 725
Elijah, 121, 189, 277, 369-370, 397, 783, 830
Elliot, Vaughn, xxiv, 64
Elohim, 132, 156-7, 635-637, 747
Emperor Justinian, 116, 138, 276, 280, 307-308, 347, 416, 844
Enoch, 277, 369-370, 373, 452, 491, 787
Epiphanes, Antiochus, 139, 315, 483-485, 488, 568, 574-575, 586, 795
Epiphanies, 44, 343, 386, 483, 486, 488
Epiphanius, 347, 424
Epiphany, 55, 454
Erxomai, 454
Eschatology, xxvi, 5, 47, 58, 64, 69, 72, 438, 566, 653
Eternal Gospel, 373, 396
Eumenes II, 150
Euphrates River, 264, 394, 488, 556
Ex Cathedra, 406, 409, 453, 542
Exact Character, 435
Expedience, xiii, 333-334, 556, 809
Faivre, Alexander, 527
First Day Of The Week, 13, 88, 91, 98, 162, 330, 332, 335, 535, 711-712, 724
First Pope, 128, 306, 565
First Resurrection, 52, 463-464, 466, 469, 475-476, 481, 510, 594
Firstborn, 119, 159, 162, 339, 501
Flavian Dynasty, 44, 345, 423-424
Fleming, Robert, 307, 310
French Revolution, 128, 282, 307, 347, 800
Froom, Leroy E., 55
Fullness of Time, 177, 297, 319, 344, 382, 572, 589, 595, 642, 770
Futurist, xxii, 33, 46, 48-52, 57-58, 68-69, 75, 173, 175, 276-277,

285, 317, 341, 347, 368, 379, 481, 576, 579, 592-593, 693, 697, 713,
Galba, 44, 345, 348, 423-424, 670, 683
Gehenna, 259, 392, 497, 635
Genealogy, 633, 670-671, 677-678, 681, 706-707, 787
General Allenby, 489
Gideon, 222, 488
Gill's Commentary, 544, 848
Gish, Dwayne, 549
Glorified Body, 94, 96, 99, 102, 105-106, 256-257, 369, 473, 481, 498, 504
Gnostics, 85, 107, 433, 780
God Exist in Three, 516
God Made Messiah, 435
Godhead, ii-iii, xvii, 13, 16, 38, 93, 96, 106, 119, 130-131, 175-177, 184-185, 197, 220, 225, 228, 259, 287, 298-300, 303, 309, 322, 324-325, 328-330, 336, 386, 397, 429-430, 434-435, 455, 473, 479, 485, 490-492, 496, 505, 510, 514, 516-517, 520, 548, 551, 636, 659, 710, 716, 773-774, 778-779, 782, 784, 804, 832, 836, 846
Gog and Magog, 400, 456-457, 482-483, 485, 494, 569, 595
Grassie, William, 138
Great Tribulationists, 52
Gregg, Steve, 42, 307
Greider, John C., 418
Hades, 94, 108, 166, 188, 204, 207, 214-215, 217-219, 221, 233, 242-243, 245-246, 248-249, 256, 311, 320, 322-323, 368-370, 372, 385, 389, 392-393, 401, 406, 409, 457, 460, 471, 482, 489-491, 496-497, 499-500, 520, 589, 635, 665, 680, 702, 758, 760, 788, 792, 796
Hardman, Doug, xiii, xvi, xxii, 832, 844

Healed Head, 69, 347
Heavenly Jerusalem, 30, 95, 501, 505-506, 516, 773, 789, 817
Helwig, Andreas, 358
Hendrickson, William, 21, 71, 88, 313
Hermeneutical, xxvi, 3, 31, 49, 65, 75, 372, 401, 537, 570, 698, 735, 853
Herodotus, 146, 554, 570, 845
Herring, Mark, 258, 761, 763
Hieros and Naos, 275, 282, 315, 353, 357-358, 407, 441
Hippolytus, 184, 563, 845-846
Historicism, xxvii, 71, 133
Hitchcock, G.S., 57
Hobbes, Thomas, 423
Hoekema, Anthony A., 470, 474
Hold Fast, 137, 144, 148, 439
Holford, George Peter, 27, 607, 612, 628, 658, 851
Holy Spirit in Heaven, 516
Homoousion, 432, 436
Homosexuals, 257-258, 287, 420-421, 521-522, 537, 744, 762-763, 765-766, 816, 831,-832, 838-839
Huperetes, 647-648
Hurd, Dale, 413
Hylton, Kenneth, xvi, 727
Hypostatic, 436
I AM, 520
Ignatius Of Antioch, 35, 91, 114-117, 340, 350, 439, 527, 566
Imam in Winchester, 414
Immaculate Conception, 541
Immanuel, 300, 435, 477, 852-853
Immersed for the Dead, 480-481
Incense, 131, 200, 205, 230-231, 237, 444, 529, 552, 608, 753
Interludes, 12-13, 16, 173
Irenaeus Of Lyons, 32, 41-42, 360, 839

Irving, Edward, 53-56, 58-61
Ishihara, Shintaro, 239
Israel, xvi, xxiii, 30, 43, 48-49, 73-74, 78, 90, 97, 105-106, 120, 132, 135, 140, 144-156, 162-164, 167-168, 171, 176-177, 199, 213-214, 222-223, 226, 264, 271, 275, 277, 296, 309, 313-314, 319, 328, 352, 373, 386, 471, 479, 482-483, 487, 493, 497, 501, 513, 541, 568, 571, 575-576, 578-579, 587-588, 591, 593, 595-596, 617, 653, 655, 657, 659, 661, 667, 672, 675-678, 680-681, 688-689, 691, 693, 695, 698, 701-703, 705-706, 708, 711-712, 716, 719, 724, 727, 732, 734-735, 739, 745, 769, 773, 784, 788-789, 792, 808-809, 812-816
Jamieson, Fausset, Brown, 306, 345, 570, 575
Japheth, 400, 482, 675
Jarrett, Valerie, 795, 810
Jehovah Witness, 85, 158, 372, 430, 432, 510, 780, 783
Jehu, 488
Jerusalem's Destruction, 259, 461, 630-631, 635, 655, 696, 703, 730, 733, 740
Jesus First, 517
Jewish Temple, 43-44, 66, 213, 328, 352-353, 383, 485, 646, 706
Jezebel, 142-144, 180-181, 547, 552, 830
John II Bishop of Rome, 116, 416
Johnson, Paul, 791
Josephus, 43, 154, 556, 600-604, 606, 608, 613, 615-617, 619, 624-627, 632, 640, 657, 669, 671-672, 682-685, 691-692, 726-727, 731
Julian, 43, 308, 555, 628, 672
Kainos, 505, 509
Kelly, William, 59

Khazar, 155, 634, 657, 673
King Clovis, 431
Kingdom Of God, ii, 48, 51, 71, 84, 86, 103-104, 107, 162, 170, 196, 214, 254, 275, 290, 329, 343, 368, 468-469, 477, 481, 503, 511, 516, 598-599, 678-680, 688-689, 693, 711, 713, 721, 723, 738
Kirk, 337, 419
Koestler, Arthur, 155, 634, 673, 675, 791
Koine Greek, 61, 280, 366, 418-419, 430, 435, 466, 504, 520, 532, 645
Kokhba, 791, 808
Koran (Qur'an), 383, 395, 581, 748, 795, 801
Kromminga, D. H., 54
Lacunza, Manuel, 56
LaHaye, Tim, 29, 58, 697-699, 701-705, 708, 711-713
Laity, 115, 125, 127, 418, 422, 526-529, 531, 537-538, 540
Lake of Fire, 134, 245, 247-248, 256, 318, 412, 457, 462, 469-470, 474-475, 482, 496, 510, 512, 591, 594, 598
Lamb, Samuel, 312
Lambert, O. C., 363, 530, 539, 545
Lamb's Book of Life, 149, 191-193, 248, 475, 497, 508, 516, 523, 594
Lamp Stands, 92, 119-120, 509, 695
Langton, Stephen, 11, 18, 467
Lateinos, 308, 360
Latinize, 349, 430
Lavey, Anton, 805
Left Behind, xxiv, 61-64, 524, 649
Lennon, John, 803, 806
Lent, 533, 556
Lex Rex, 752-753
Livingston, David, 550
Logos, 80, 430-431, 467
Loipos, 477

Lord's Day, x, xxiii, 31, 87-88, 91, 375, 560, 843
Lucado, Max, 334, 336
Lucifer, 246, 250, 295, 315, 793, 803, 805-806, 853
Luther, Martin, 276, 306, 337, 408, 412-413, 439, 537, 566, 747
Lycaonia, 774
Lysimachus, 130, 343
Maccabean Revolt, 584, 594
Maccabeus, Judas, 483-485, 488, 495, 584, 588, 605, 768
MacDonald, Margaret, 51, 59-61
MacPherson, Dave, 52-53, 56, 59-61
Man of Lawlessness, 347-352, 356, 358
Mariolatry, 383, 417
Mark of God, 370, 377
Martyr, 39-40, 69, 71, 79, 116, 188-189, 208-211, 213, 272, 278, 315, 319, 321, 331, 355, 383, 397, 472-473, 476-478, 498, 506, 566, 845
Martyr, Justin, 32, 91, 846
Mattathias, 577
Mattison, Matt M., 527-528
McAuliffe, Terry, 258, 761, 763, 766
Mclaughlin, Emmett, 442
Measuring the Temple, 270, 288
Melchezidek, 386, 501, 506, 769, 773-779, 782-785, 792, 851
Menamillennialist, 470
Meyers, Jeremy, 462
Michael And His Angels, 244, 322, 412
Millennial Reign, 50
Millennium, xxiv, 50-52, 54, 56, 64, 70, 258, 463, 473, 487, 493, 693, 713, 723, 734
Miller, William, 483-484
Milligan, Robert, 71
Milligan, William, 11, 21

Mohammad, Ali, 439, 769, 800
Mommsen, Theodore, 139
Monogenos, 435, 479
Morris, Leon, 11, 472
Morris, Richard, 589,
Moses, 35, 88-89, 93, 105-106, 121, 154, 194, 199, 217, 224, 238, 279, 304, 332, 368-370, 372-373, 385, 388, 407, 428, 501, 508, 520, 528, 592, 617, 621, 625, 663, 665, 681, 709, 719, 724, 731, 759, 765, 768, 783, 789, 792
Mosheim's History of the Church, 556, 559
Mother of God, 122, 126, 416-417, 420, 531, 543, 554
Mother of Harlots, 557
Moulton, Harold K., 82, 639, 645
Mount Carmel, 552
Muratorian Canon, 45
Murray, Iain H., 56
Muslims, 85, 93, 156, 188, 210, 275, 383, 395, 402, 407, 430-431, 537, 580-581, 635, 637, 769, 780, 783, 801, 810-812, 815, 817
Mysteries, 8, 196, 268-269, 328-329, 455, 540, 546, 556
Mysterium, 544-545
Mystery Babylon, 318, 347, 406, 539, 544-545, 548, 565
Nash, Donald, xxiii, 12, 14, 173, 565
Neatby, William B., 54-55
Nee, Watchman, 311-312
Nero's Persecution, 41-42
New Earth, 371, 501-502, 504-505, 511-512, 590, 785
New Heaven, 64, 371, 500-502, 504-506, 512, 785, 813
Newton, Isaac, 128, 139, 346
Nikitin, Victor, 187, 557
Nimrod, 275, 315, 446, 486, 539, 546, 548-550, 554

95 A.D. Late Date, 33, 39, 41-43, 533
Noah's Day, 298, 369, 373, 513, 638, 643-644, 648-649, 786-788
Norton, Robert, 59
Numerology, 7, 13, 43, 47, 84, 112, 133, 173, 180, 201-202, 223, 225, 228, 308, 329, 460, 468, 513-514, 577
O' Kelly, James, 126, 128, 139, 284, 307, 338
Occultic Abyss, 598
O'Conner, Adrian, 793, 798-799
Odoacer, Flavious, 347
Olivet Discourse, 41, 43, 66, 645, 652, 697, 699, 703
144,000, 24, 213, 217, 220-225, 227-228, 367-373, 377, 385, 399, 460, 469, 508, 513, 702, 703, 786-788, 792,
One Shall Be Taken, 62, 644, 646
1,260 Days, 49, 120, 128, 138, 275-277, 280-286, 304-308, 310, 321, 331, 347, 442, 460, 468, 470, 565, 689
Order of Melchizedec, 775, 777-778
Orthodoxism, 47
Otho, 44, 345, 423, 670
Papal Infallibility, 542
Parousia, 55, 454, 499, 641, 696, 710
Patai, Raphael, 675
Payne, Barton J., 54
Pergamum, 21, 135-136, 139-140, 142, 150, 203, 338, 408, 548-549, 552
Petrine Primacy, 416
Pharmakeia, 546
Philosophical Darkness, 241
Philosophical School Of History, 70
Pieters, Albertus, 11, 88
Pisteuo, 160
Plaisted, David A., 69

Pontiff, 349-350, 356, 547, 551-552, 555, 564, 782
Poole, Matthew, 544-545
Pope Francis, 447, 542, 793
Pope Julius II, 544, 848
Pope Leo XII, 410, 554
Pope Urban II, 791
Post-Millennial, xxiv, 48, 59, 64, 73, 440
Preeminence, 34, 335, 421, 435
Pre-Existed, 435
Pre-Millennial, xxiii, xxiv, xxvii, 28, 33, 49, 51, 59, 61-65, 74, 107, 133, 162-163, 166-167, 169, 171, 174, 184, 194, 227, 310, 319, 350-352, 444, 460, 463, 465, 468, 472-474, 476, 483, 487, 492, 494, 502-504, 523-524, 546, 633-634, 637-638, 663, 697-698, 701-702, 707, 790
Preterism, xxiii, xxvii, 12, 64-66, 68-70, 73, 133, 220, 282, 732-735
Primogenitor, 435
Prophetic Allegory, 315
Protokos, 85, 159, 435
Ptolemy, 343, 482, 575, 583
Purgatory, 419, 445, 457, 497, 531-532, 537
Putin, Vladimir, 188, 254-256
Queen of Heaven, 548, 553, 555
Quinn, B. L., 536
Rafsanjani, Hashemi, 811
Rape of Proserpine, 556
Recapitulationist, 12
Remnant Restoration, 72-73, 307
Rest of the Dead, 3, 463, 466, 470, 474-475, 477, 481
Restitution, 4, 467, 503, 761
Restoration Movement, xxiv, 117, 126, 138, 408, 751, 810
Resurrection Gospel, 82, 282, 285-286, 412, 573, 579, 771

Ribera, Francisco, 57
Rigdon, Sydney, 55-56, 810
Roberts, John (Chief Justice), 287
Roman Missal, 533
Romulus, 184, 308, 469
Rosary, 437, 537
Ross, Bob, 418
Rowdon, Harold H., 55
Rushdie, Salman, 769
Russia - religious education, 254
Sabbath Day, 88-90, 572, 770
Sacrament, 419, 534, 540
Salverte, Eusebe, 546
Same Sex Marriage, 420-421, 437, 761-762, 831, 834
Sandeen, Ernest, 59-60
Satan Bound, 52, 70, 248, 412, 459-460, 471, 487
Satan Cast Out, 244-245, 247-248, 254, 293, 303-304, 320, 322, 330-331, 460, 792-793
Satan Loosed, 262, 462, 471
Satan's Locusts, 70, 248, 260-263, 309, 409, 596-597, 796
Satan's Seat, 136-137, 139, 551-552
Scapular, 538
Scofield, Cyrus, 51, 61, 720
Seal up the Prophecy, 268, 519, 693-694, 714
Secret Rapture, 51-53, 56, 59-60, 86, 285, 638, 651, 695
Selah, 12, 173
Seleucid, 483, 568-569
Semiramis, 546, 554
Seneca, 589, 600, 683
Seven Angels, 230-231, 378, 382, 388-389, 404, 511, 563
Seven Heads, 320, 341, 344-345, 404, 406, 410, 414-415, 423-424, 563
Seven Hills, 414-415, 563, 848
Seven Sacraments, 540

7-Year Tribulation, 714
70 A.D., xxiii, 4, 26-28, 34-41, 43, 45-47, 51, 64-69, 73-74, 77, 79-83, 154-155, 158, 195, 213, 220, 224, 259, 274, 282, 296, 308, 321, 324, 328, 340, 348-349, 353-354, 383, 386, 407, 463, 465, 467, 485, 519, 600, 603, 606, 630-631, 633-635, 640-642, 645, 652, 654-655, 657-659, 669-673, 678-679, 686-687, 689-692, 696-697, 699, 703-706, 709-711, 715, 718, 726, 728-736, 739- 742, 787-791, 798, 808, 813, 840-841
Sharia Law, 234, 413, 581, 800-802, 807, 810
Sharp, Granville, 560
Shelley, Bruce L., 527-528
Sheol, 222, 244-245, 247, 255, 299, 489-491, 514, 519, 594, 792
Short Time, 303, 345, 424
Sign of the Cross, 539
Signs Of His Coming, 65, 590
Sin Party, 236, 261, 421, 521, 547, 807, 836
Sisera, 488
Skema/schema, 779-782
Slay them Before Me, 461, 710
Smith, Joseph, 55, 573, 769, 772, 810-811
Sochi, 188, 256
Social Gospel, 252, 553, 562, 833
Sodom, 193, 231-233, 236, 246, 258, 281, 327, 441, 506, 521, 583, 589, 631, 763, 785, 838, 847
Song of Moses and the Lamb, 385
Song of the Lamb, 371, 385-386
Sorokim, Pitirim, 807
Soulish Man, 96
Spaulding, Solomon, 573, 688, 771-772
Spence, H.P., 781-782

Spin Agents, 420
Spiritual Israel, 49, 120, 275, 277, 296, 319, 479, 482, 493, 576, 595, 678, 680, 695, 703, 716, 788-789, 813
Spock, Benjamin, 325-327
Stanton, Gerald B., 54
Stephanos, 177, 179, 202-203, 263, 455
Supper Of The Great God, 161, 456, 641, 646
Supper Of The Lamb, 161, 448
Synecdoche, iii, 6, 295, 316, 356, 700, 737, 787, 847
Tanner, Paul J., 12
Tartarus, 215, 251, 497
Tasaba, 209
10 Righteous, 232
Tertullian, 32, 44, 86, 439, 450, 528, 530, 541, 686, 840
Testimony, 27-28, 37, 39-40, 46, 78-83, 86, 100-111, 116-117, 159, 208-209, 262, 266, 270-273, 278-280, 282, 284-286, 292, 304, 315, 321-322, 330-332, 340, 349, 383, 387, 406, 440, 452, 460-461, 468-469, 509, 687, 745, 765, 830, 833
That Which Is Perfect, 35
Thayer, Joseph, 77, 643
The Accuser of the Brethren, 244, 293, 322-323, 329-330, 563, 803
The Bowls of Wrath, 9, 20, 23, 183, 228, 238, 265, 267, 309-310, 382, 388-390, 393, 397-398, 404, 511, 597
The Dragon, 22, 292, 296, 298, 304-305, 320-322, 330-332, 346, 349, 355, 386, 394, 404-406, 409, 411-412, 417, 419-420, 459, 544
The END, xxii, xxiv, 9, 11, 28-29, 48, 50, 61-62, 65-66, 70-71, 73, 78-79, 88, 177, 185, 189, 191, 210-212, 226, 232, 249, 261, 265, 267, 282, 292, 296, 298, 303, 306, 309, 319, 321-322, 324, 356, 368, 378-379, 383, 394, 401, 407, 446, 456, 459, 461, 466, 473-474, 498, 532, 564, 567, 569, 591, 595, 606, 640-643, 646, 650, 652-653, 656, 659, 661, 665-666, 669, 690, 694, 699, 711, 722, 729, 732, 738-739, 741, 745, 782, 789, 813, 841, 851
The Evangelist, 45, 74, 84, 108, 118, 123, 180, 278, 311, 333, 452-453, 526, 559, 844
The Flood, 10-11, 37, 63, 66, 298, 369, 373, 549-550, 590, 634, 638-640, 649, 651-652, 654, 688, 787
The Frogs, 394-396, 580, 582
The Great Tribulation, 50, 52, 86, 132, 213, 226, 701-702, 712
The Great Whore, 563
The Harlot, 71, 305, 453, 511
The Lamb's Wife, 508, 511, 513
The Land has Vanished, 402
The Little Book, xvii, 24, 268, 271-272, 273-275, 286, 288, 330, 398
The Lord of Armies, 690
The Mark of the Beast, 88, 296, 349-350, 358, 377, 389, 457, 459, 469
The Messiah the Prince, 695, 708, 721, 723
The Millennium, xxiv, 50-52, 54, 56, 64, 70, 258, 463, 473, 487, 493, 693, 713, 723, 734
The Other Left, 62, 66, 638-639, 649
The Prince Of Daniel, 465
The Rapture, 50-54, 56, 59-62, 64-65, 86, 175, 285, 310, 379, 456, 463, 475, 487, 524, 638, 643, 645-647, 651, 695, 701, 704, 708, 711, 814
The Seal, 9, 12, 20-21, 24, 45, 72, 183, 185-186, 189-190, 193, 195,

197, 200, 202-204, 206, 208-213, 220-225, 228, 230-231, 233-234, 238-243, 249, 252, 261, 265, 295, 309, 389-394, 397-399, 404, 460, 722, 767, 787

The True Ecclesia, 275, 306, 315, 407-408, 516, 594

The Trumpets, 204, 238, 309-310, 389, 390

The Whore, 6, 57, 69, 71-75, 136, 185, 284, 305-306, 309, 314, 355, 375, 383, 398, 404-408, 410, 425, 431, 439, 442, 496, 511, 553, 556, 563-564, 848

The Wilderness, 26, 125, 127-128, 275, 299, 305, 314, 321, 331, 404-405, 433, 441, 591, 719

The Woman of Revelation Chapter 12 280, 303, 305, 318

Theodosius, 126, 416-417, 421, 539, 555

Theoisis, 430

Theophilus of Antioch, 431, 779, 840

Theosis, 430

Theotokos Controversy, 126, 358, 416-417

This is the First Resurrection, 52, 463-464, 466, 469, 475-476, 481, 510, 594

Those Days, 78, 213, 615, 634, 656, 691, 699, 727-729, 732-733, 738-739

3 1/2 Years, 708

Three Uprooted Horns, 346-347

Thrones in Heaven, 70, 479

Time Merges With Eternity, 490

Titus, 37, 77, 195, 386, 465, 601, 606-607, 610, 612-613, 615-628, 651, 654, 657, 671, 682, 690-692, 695-696, 699, 705, 709-711, 726, 730-731, 733-734, 791

Topyas.com, 634

Transubstantiation, 533, 545

Tregelles, Samuel P., 53, 58

Tribulation Before The Rapture, 52

Tulip, 425, 428

24 Elders, 175-177, 197, 217

Two Witnesses, 24, 119-121, 264, 277-278, 283-285, 847

Two Women, 66, 306, 309, 316, 625, 638

Tyconius, 11

Undiluted Judgment, 20, 376, 378, 382, 389

Unholy Trinity of Satan, 318, 340, 395, 406, 496

United Nations, 277, 676, 793-794, 808

Urik, Steve, 552

Veneration Of Mary, 122, 417

Venus, 554, 806

Vicarius Filii Dei, 358-359, 362-364, 366

Vitellius, 345, 423, 612

W.E. Vine (Dictionary), 63, 79, 83, 118, 477, 643, 646, 649-650, 667, 781

Walker, Williston, 417

Wars and Rumors of War, 669-670, 798

Wellhausen, Julius, 747

Wells, H.G., 672

What Heaven is Like, 497

Whatever You Loose, 196-197

Whisenant, Edgar G., 808

White, Ellen G., 55, 109, 484, 489

Wilcock, Michael, xxvi, 1112

Wine of God's Wrath, 375-376

Winthrop, John, 755, 759-760

Witness, 26, 28, 79-82, 84-85, 116-117, 157-159, 200, 209, 271-272, 278, 281-283, 286, 315, 330-331, 340, 349, 368, 462, 815

Wolf, Herbert, 545

Wordsworth, Christopher, 544
Wright, Arenda, 258, 763
Yahweh, 132, 157, 221, 574, 680
Year of Infamy in America, 258
Yehudah, 132
YHVH, 336, 485, 657, 716, 747
Zachariah, 186
Zionism, 30, 154-155, 214, 786, 793, 812, 814
Zondervan's Analytical Greek, 82, 644, 649

ENDNOTES

1. THE REASON FOR SUCH A LENGTHLY DEDICATION OF THIS BOOK

I have never been conventional in my approach to the ministry. I make no apologies for this. The Prophets and Apostles were not smooth-talking, people-pleasing conventional members of what Billy Sunday used to call the "Hail brothers well met society." The Disciples compared Jesus to Elijah, Jeremiah, and John the Immerser (Mt 16:14). Yes, these ministers were loving servants, but they loved enough to tell the TRUTH. John told the TRUTH and died for the testimony of Jesus. Jeremiah got in trouble with the government and served time in prison. Queen Jezebel put a price tag on Elijah's neck. What we know of these three men was the certainty of their love of God, country, and lost souls.

Yes, it is very unconventional to refer back to The Dedication Page at the end of a book. But I do this for at least two reasons. First, because I believe that every Christian who lives in a voting republic, pays taxes, is an American Citizen, and has the right to vote, has a Christian duty to vote and to speak out on the convictions that leads to his voting choice, especially those that relate to Biblical principles or values. The Book of Revelation is about politics. The Revelation was the politics of Nero that got John in trouble with The Rome Empire. John could not vote because Rome was a governing dictatorship, but John did speak out and Nero and Roman plutocrats knew exactly where he stood on issues. But I saved my political remarks, which will follow, for the end of this Revelation because it is my hope that after considering why we reached these Biblical "Now Time Apocalyptic Conclusions," we will be more compatible with and have the spiritual heart to share these convictions.

Actually, by revisiting my Dedication Page with this salvo against the 21st Century "Moral Meltdown" in America, I am following the Apostle Paul's strategy. Paul started the subject of "Tongues and supernatural gifts" with the introduction, "I would not have you ignorant, brethren" (1Co 12:1). Three Chapters later he said, "If any man is ignorant, let him be ignorant" (1Co 14:38). Paul knew, and I know that if someone bumps, casually into our conclusions without first investigating our premise and process, they may have sufficient personal prejudices to prevent them from pursuing the TRUTH altogether. It is far better for the us (whoever we may be) to evaluate this Commentary on the 21 Chapters of the last book of The Bible, and then learn of the author's God-given convictions on the way this country is mismanaging the same sex marriage fiasco, abortion, and other moral issues. Then, if the reader thinks I am hopelessly lost to both Earth and Heaven because of my convictions, then so be it.

Paul was convinced that his argument against supernatural gifts would "cease, vanish away, fail" (1Co 13:8, 9) was sufficient enough that if a man was "contentious or doubtful," no further information would convince him. I offer this information as an addendum to the Dedication of this book to my darling wife because we both believe that America is only as strong as her marriages and homes. If I made this information known at the outset, you, a reader, would have missed the blessing of my indefatigable labor in The Book of Revelation because of animosity toward me as the author, based on the Biblical conviction concerning the evil of homosexuality.

Secondly, it is considered an absolute, divine necessity to share the spiritual, moral convictions in regard to the sins that rise to the Heavens and bring God's displeasure on a people and a Nation. I am personally sick and tired of being treated as a member of a 21st Century fraternal society of American libertines. I am an individual, and I appreciate other individuals who are rare, rugged, independent thinkers.

A PERSON IS A CONSUMATE DISGRACE WHO SPEAKS THE TRUTH OF HIS CONVICTIONS AND THEN A DAY LATER CAPITULATES TO THE VIEW DIAMETRICALLY OPPOSED TO HIS PREVIOUSLY STATED PHILOSOPHICAL, MORAL, POLITICAL, OR RELIGIOUS STANCE, AND BOWS LIKE A PUPPY DOG BEFORE POLITICAL OR LIBERAL, SOCIALISTIC, MEDIA PRESSURE BY TELLING THEM EXACTLY WHAT THEY WANT TO HEAR.

Just because the paragraph stated above seems to describe every spineless aspirant for fame, fortune, or public office does not mean it has to happen; it is not a requirement for public office. For instance, Jeb Bush got elected on his record as a man who wanted to serve his State and Country. I am sick and tired of seeing elected officials make promises, break promises, and serve the political machine rather than the people. Governor Bush got elected, in part because he took a stand against same-sex marriage and stated his conviction that same-sex couples should not raise children. We know what Jeb Bush has stated about same-sex issues, but what will he finally do? Is he going to miss Heaven's blessing and back down?

AN EXAMPLE OF THE TOUGH LOVE IT TAKES TO EXERCISE BIBLICAL, MORAL CONVICTIONS

When we heard that two men were given legal permission by the City Attorney to adopt a baby boy, an Elder of the congregation, Evangelist Doug Hardman, and me went to the Office of the Attorney. We told the Attorney that we would announce on our television show that his actions were a disgrace to God and man. He was enraged. He approached me with the force of a defensive lineman. His face was blood red, and he shaped his lips to shout, "I will sue." But his professional sense caught up with his emotions, and he backed off. I then said, "Go your way and sue me if you wish. I would love to meet you in court. Win or lose I know that God will get the glory!" We walked out of the attorney's office, but as we passed his secretary's desk, we were met with her obvious, broad smile of approval. As soon as I arrived home, the Mayor called me and said that the homosexual men would be denied the right of having this child. A few months later, I met one of the homosexual men in a department store. I did not know who he was. He blurted out, "You are the man who ruined my life!"

Regardless of whether it is:

1) "the love of the flesh" (alcohol, drugs, food, fornication, profane living and indulgences that crave religious justification),

2) " the lust of the eyes" (illicit sex, desiring sex outside of the marriage bond, coveting the world's goods for a moment), or

3) "the pride of life" (instead of a spiritual walk, the consuming desire to be known for the vanity fair of soulish, prideful, selfish living that seeks first place no matter what), a person with a "church habit" will either repent or hate the preacher when he hears the three preceding subjects.

Over the years, an uncompromising servant of The Holy Godhead gets used to this when he teaches heavenly things that bring us into conflict with worldly passions. This homosexual who wanted to adopt the boy then told me that I was responsible for taking the "Love of their life" from him and his sexual partner. I replied that it was the best thing that ever happened, and may well lead them to some serious adjustments in life and salvation in Heaven.

The man said, "I am now an Atheist!" He explained that he joined some Denominational Church (celebrated for every social gospel tirade except declaring the Word of God and His holiness) and was given the leadership of the Youth Department (There is a reason it always happens this way, whether Boy Scouts, or Youth Counseling, but I will not go there just now.). This denomination's church board further instructed him that his sexual preference was no problem, and it would support him. Thus he was confident when he approached his Church Board in regard to this problem with my church, and later "City Hall," his denomination would rise up and fight us. He said, "You should have seen the look on their faces … You would think they were headed to an execution." They fled the battle instantly.

The man told The Board, "So it is all a lie! You said you would back me, but when it comes to a showdown with a Biblical Congregation, you are cowards!" He then hung his head and said, "I am now an atheist." Actually, he always was an atheist. Yes, when a professed Christian remains silent on the sodomy issue, that person is a practicing "Christian Atheist." But what is really interesting is when he ask me, "Do you think I am going to Hell?" After I taught him from Scripture he said, "I know it is wrong, but I hate you. But on the other hand, I have more respect for you and your congregation than any church in town."

GET UP, AND GO PREACH BECAUSE I HAVE MANY PEOPLE IN THIS CITY (Ac 14:19, 18:10)

After the uproar in the suburbs of Corinth, Paul was stoned outside of Lystra so severely that his assassins thought he was dead. Paul may have thought the whole world was against him and the New Covenant TRUTH he taught, but the Lord told him to go into both cities. The Lord knew that morally and potentially, "He had many people in these cities" (Ac 18:10). We should be motivated more by those "many people" than any other encouragement in Heaven and Earth. Christ had enough faith in the human race to lay down His life. We stagger at the thought that the whole world was potentially saved by His propitious act. Christ knows there are millions of souls who will love Him and will overcome by His Blood, the New Testament testimony, and the hatred and disdain of a life in this dark world (Rev 10:12). Because of the potential of eternal life that millions of souls had when they learned of Christ's Death and Ascension (2000-years ago), Heaven rejoiced. When we also realize the same potential of millions of our fellow inhabitants on planet Earth, we rejoice with them 2000 years later.

We have facts that provide us with great energy and fortitude. They are 1) Fervent, diligent intercessory PRAYER, 2) a PATIENCE that follows, which allows patience to have its perfect work in us, because it takes work to be patient, 3) PROVIDENTIAL PROTECTION because the Lord promises that He is with us; He will never forsake or leave us; and He will provide the resources from Heaven even when it seems nothing is happening or ever will happen, and 4) PERSISTENCE because for if it is Biblical, as Persistence is, it is right, and if it is right, we keep on preaching it, and eventually, The Lord will vindicate His TRUTH.

No matter what the people of this world think of us or do to us, the above four facts do not lie. The world may despise us, rebuke us, belittle us, defame us, and treat us as if we are dead men and women, but we will rise up and keep on "keeping on" because the Lord has many people in this city. He has many people in this State. He has many people in this Country. He has many people in this world. Keep on preaching New Covenant Christianity. The world is wicked, but Jesus has overcome the world. Read the whole of Colossians and Ephesians, Chapter One, and let us accentuate in our minds, "He has risen above all things."

THERE ARE MANY VISIBLE SOULS IN OUR CITY

Just a few years ago, in 2005; 58% of the people in my State voted against Same Sex Marriage. Many of those people are still alive. I do not know at this point how much they understand, but in the understanding of divine marriage, "They are the Lord's people!" They are on the Lord's side. The Lord has many people in my city.

THERE ARE MANY INVISIBLE SPIRITS FILLING THE HEAVEN

In fact, The Lord told Elisha to tell his fearful, intimidated servant, "Don't be afraid for there are more with us than with them" (2Kg 6:16; 2Ch 32:7). Indeed, we look at the monolithic media and the campaign from the White House in Washington to the little Clerk's House in our town to sponsor wholesale slaughter of infants, promote immorality, and waste of human resources, sponsor sodomy, and destroy Christianity, and we think we are hopelessly outmanned, outnumbered and outgunned, and we howl, bow, and flee like "a whipped pup." But the Lord looks down from His Heavenly Throne and sees what we do not see (though we look down from His Heavenly Throne and see what we do not see (though we should see, Heb 11:3, 27), and He commands us, "Get up and go!" The battle is the Lords! The enemy is hopelessly outnumbered! They don't stand a chance!"

WHERE IS THE MAN OR WOMAN WHO REALIZES THEY DO NOT HAVE TO "BACK DOWN" TO "GO UP"?

Millions of Americans voted in the mid-term election (11-4-14 A.D.) to "clean house" of this filthy, man pleasing, political back-scratching mentality that serves political protocol instead of the millions in this Country who still believe in Heaven-sent morality. Millions of Americans believe that sodomy, abortion, and pork barrel waste is absolutely, un-Godly and wrong. There is only one way to escape the "Just go along with the crowd (belt-way) mentality," and that is take a STAND as an individual; rise up, and be counted as ONE person. State your convictions, stick to them, and tell the American people, "This is just the way it is! … And if you do not like it, vote for more misery!" I believe America is ready for a man or woman of God who will take the hand of our Savior with one hand, reach out to the rest of us with the other, and pray fervently, "Lead us through!"

The City Attorney did not take me to court, but another day may be coming. I am not weathering or melting down in old age. I could still wind up in court, prison, on an island like John's exile, or even in the execution chamber. But at last, our extremity is the Lord's opportunity. I would love to see what He will do as God, when I can do nothing more as a man.

WHEN THE ONCE GREAT STATE OF FLORIDA HAD THE CHANCE TO SET AN EXAMPLE OF RIGHTEOUS GOVERNING, IT "WHIMPED OUT" LIKE THE REST OF THEM

So as I approach completion of this fifty-year project, I am in the State of Florida (1/14/2015 A.D.) doing some final editing. Like the cowardly, politico-religious judges, and other immoral, worldly significants of weak leadership from formerly Godly states, this Great State has finally succumbed to the tyranny of anti-Messiah, hi-tech media machinery that is hell bent on destroying Judaic-Christian values in our Country. From morning to evening every mass media connection, from newsrooms to newspapers, is filled with a diabolical spirit to celebrate the decision of a Federal Judge to join the ranks of other states whose Judges overrode and contradicted the democratic majority votes to sustain traditional marriage, thus making a decision that will ultimately bring the wrath of God from Heaven (Ro 1:18).

The next step is for the politic-media to continue their daily news briefs on the "Glory of Sodomy" in advance of a forced recognition of Sodomy as a national legal marriage union by the "Fawns of The Press" judges on The Supreme Court. Obviously, the judges read what The Press says more than what history, or their own moral conscience, says on such subjects. Since the Court has justified in June 2015, this anti-Christian act of immorality, millions of Christians will choose to obey God rather than man.

Because The Court made a decision that no disciple of Christ can accept (Mt 19:11; Ac 4:19, 5:29), the Court's decision will lead to persecution, imprisonment, and even death of many true Christians who are undeniably the best citizens of their land. The Court shows contempt for the Godhead, and overstep the boundaries of moral authority by making a fool-hearted choice to undermine the Lord's definition of marriage (man and woman) and redefine what a few immoral judges (and prodigious senior news editors) want for this country, "men with men, or (woman and woman) working that which is unnatural" (Ro 1:27). Because we slept while the enemy sowed poisonous weeds (Mt 13:25), we who have a loving devotion to our Savior may now have to choose "silence over freedom of speech," or even "Liberty or Death" at the hands of our own fellow countrymen and women whom we voted into office.

The Supreme Court is guilty of a manifest absurdity. They ruled in favor of sodomy when there was a national calm existing concerning the hopeless divide between pro-sodomy and anti-sodomy. However, this national ruling would embolden those whom we call the "Sin Party" (whose singular agenda is to destroy Christian morality and witness) to wage a political and legislative war against God's children "to death." Such a decision by those who are supposed to be our God-appointed judges led to the colossal blunder of creating further national unrest and like the old Supreme Court (the Sanhedrin), bring the grief and blood of the children of Christ down upon their own heads (Ac 5:28, 29). Of course, when political might is used to hurt or kill Christians, Christ said they are in reality "persecuting Me" (Ac 9:4, 22:7).

May we say candidly, that even if our Supreme Courts, or other supreme courts from other countries, prosecute Christians and have read the quintessence of what I have written here, their indictment of persecuting Christ would probably not faze them in the least. Only the Holy Spirit can convict of sin (Jn 16:8). Because we are "mere men" called upon to reprove, rebuke, and exhort (2Ti 3:16, 17), we can only rely upon The Holy Spirit of judgment to convict earthly judges. Unfortunately, these so-called judges may even be humored, as if it were buffoonery. I do not believe like the Egyptians, that their hieroglyphics lived on into eternity, but I do believe that if a person who is filled with the Spirit of God writes a TRUTH of God, that TRUTH will go on and be met in judgment.

EVOLUTION FROM A PRIMORTAL EXPLOSION TO AMEBA TO APE TO MAN TO SAME-SEX MATING

I wrote letters to political leaders in my state, Virginia, and I asked them for a sane explanation as to why this exercise in sexual insanity (called in God's Word "perversion") can be legally justified by those given leadership to uphold God's moral laws (Ro 13:1-3). Senator Tim Kaine replied with an answer, which in effect is probably the greatest excuse men and women give who want to be "Christian Atheists." That answer is, "We have evolved to a more compassionate view of the sin of sodomy." What this really means is that we have "evolved" into self-made gods, and we know more than God does about this subject.

Intellectual idiots call rapid evolution, "punctuated evolution," (see Comparative Views on Origins.com) where "The Hopeful Monster is Born" through a reptile laying an egg and a bird hatches out rapidly. I guess you might say they are right since we are evolving into "Hell" faster than we have in past history (Ps 9:17, 55:15). Yes, Senator Kaine wants to call himself a believer in Jesus Christ, but he wants to "call the shots" and dictate to Christ what does or does not constitute morality.

Just two years ago, Sodomy was illegal, now most Federal Judges want to make it as legally acceptable as having a date with your spouse. Senator Kaine said this is a product of evolution. Since grade school, we have been taught the little ditty that it took millions of years for the ameba-man-ape evolutionary process. Now, Stephen J. Gould (Wikipedia) speaks from the grave to those who read his trashy science books, "Evolution can be punctuated in a reptile laying an egg and a bird hatches." That is really "rapid evolution". However, Tim Kaine comes in second to Gould. Kaine's evolution from normal, natural sex to perverted sex only took but two years.

I appreciate Tim Kaine's courtesy and candor in responding to my enquiry. He provided us with the criterion upon which all "Christian atheist" base their conclusion to profess Christ as savior but refuse to believe a thing He says. That misguided criterion is that the human race has evolved beyond what the Lord said in Holy Scripture. What a showdown faces these lost souls when they face the final judgment, and the ONE and ONLY JUDGE of America and the universe (past, present, future-Ac 17:31), has the FINAL WORD on this subject.

What precipitated a response from Richmond and Washington was the mailing of our book "Crucified in Sodom" to many of our political leaders. The book outlines and details the steps that led to the sodomizing of Sodom and the final, just judgment from God in Heaven. These leaders know exactly what the Bible says on the subject, and they know exactly what they are doing. The ONLY hope these leaders have for the eternal future and ONLY consoling benefit for the present is that somehow, GOD IS DEAD!

"REAFFIRMATION OF TRADITIONAL MARRIAGE"

In brotherhood with thousands of congregations across America, we are contemplating a "Reaffirmation of Traditional Marriage" celebration of those who are, or are planning on BEING HAPPILY MARRIED TO THEIR LOVING WIFE OR HUSBAND OF THE OPPOSITE SEX. Recent statistics reveal that from 3 to 6 % of Americans are homosexuals. Thousands of "normal" marriages are performed across the nation. They are usually well-planned, well-attended, and elegant in beauty and style. The Media does not pay a whit of attention to traditional marriages, except in the "society pages." On the other hand, as a lead front-page story or the leading subject on news or talk shows, we are supposed to sit silently and shake our head in absolute approval of homosexual marriages.

Homosexual marriages are nothing more than an "officiating mating" stance in the public square, and some Bible denying so-called "minister" stands in front of a circle of five or ten people and two same-sexed human beings kiss each other (while the attendees turn their heads to watch cars on the street or people walk up the concrete steps where the marriage is officiated), and we are forced to endure this ad nauseam.

The Devil gives them a little celebrity status, and some effeminate guy (womanish man or mannish woman), announces, "I am coming out!" He may be a one-out-of-a-million football player, but he becomes famous for his sexual preference, and his teammates should bow down to him. Some female actress says she is attracted to "Miss Piggy." As the media would have it, the rest of the world should bow down in adoration of two female same-sex-inmates. It is a media game the perverts who run the show love to play with peoples' minds, and it is a deadly game that will always end in loss, ruin, disease and Eternal Judgment.

So they are "Coming Out." Truth-be-told, they always were "Out." They have practiced this perverted sexual lifestyle for years and no one, not even God would stop them. "Coming out" for them simply means the rest of the world must accept it, approve it, tolerate it, and celebrate it, without speaking a word against it. That just might sound sort of "Judgmental," but it looks as if the way they force the philosophy of this perversion on the rest of us; it is being judgmental in reverse. Those who approve of sodomy are actually judging their God and Creator. They think they are wiser than God. So they think He just does not know what He is talking about.

Yes, over 90% of Americans are NOT avowed homosexuals. Can you imagine how great an impact it would make on this nation if just ten percent of them met in various cities and participated in a "MARRIAGE REAFFIRMATION" DECLARATION OF FAITH IN TRADITONAL MARRIAGES AND THE BENEFITS OF BEING IN WEDLOCK WITH A GOD GIVEN SPOUCE?

Thus, when I dedicate this book to my darling wife, Dotty, it is my way of making an unequivocal statement that I am "Coming Out," and I want the whole word to know that I am hopelessly, "head over heels" in love with the woman God gave me, and now have more than 50 more years of reasons why I will love her then when I first met her in 1960 A.D.

2. (www.creationconcept@wordpress.com : The Number Seven in Scripture)

3. W.E. Vine, Vine's Complete Expository Dictionary with topic index. (Ed. Merrill F. Unger and William White, Jr.; Nashville: Thomas Nelson, 1996). 531.

4. Roberts, Alexander et al., eds.," Ante-Nicene Fathers: Dialogue with Trypho," in Ante-Nicene Apostolic Fathers with Justin and Irenaeus (volo. 1 of Ante-Nicene Fathers of the Christian Church. Christian Literature Publishing, 1885), 31.

5. Roberts, "Against heresies," in Ante-Nicene Apostolic Fathers with Justin and Irenaeus, 4:20:11.

6. Roberts, "Anti-Marcaion, or writings against heresy," in Ante-Nicene Apostolic Fathers, Latin Christianity: Its Founder, Tertullian. (Trans. P. Holmes; vol.3 of Ante0Nicene Fathers of the Christian Church> Christian Literature Publishing, 1885), 3:14, 24.

7. Roberts, Alexander et al. eds., "Who is the Rich Man that shall be saved," in Fathers of the Second Century: Hermas, Tatian, Athenagoras, Theophilus, and Clement of Alexandria. (trans. W. Wilson; vol. 2 of Ante-Nicene Fathers of the Christian Church. Christian Literature Publishing, 1885), p. 42.

8. Schaff, Philip and Henry Wace, eds., "The Apocalypse of John," in Eusebius: Church History and life of Constantine (vol. 2 of Nicene and Post Nicene fathers of the Christian Church, Series, 2. Christian literature Publishing, 1890), 7:25.

9. Roberts, "The writings of Papias," in Eusebius: The Church History of Eusebius (vol. 2 of Nicene and Post Nicene fathers of the Christian Church, Series 2. Christian literature Publishing, 1890), 3:39:7.

10. https://en.wikipedia.org/wiki/Cerinthus

11. We do not know exactly who invented the word the "Anti-Christ" or "Antichrist" in the singular, but it seems that this attention getting expression appears early in church history. This is either due to the fact that advocates of the modern day "Anti-Christ" fanaticism have made an attempt to fasten the term to the Post-Apostolic era, or such a bogie man theological scare tactic was already being advocated by false prophets who John said, "You have heard that THE antichrist is coming" (1Jn 2:18). Almost all translations have a footnote, "The word (THE) is not found in the NU-Text." The N stands for the Nestle-Aland Greek N.T. and the U stands for the United Bible Societies' fourth edition. John does not call anyone THE ANTICHRIST, but he said, "You have heard." In other words, the news of some particular Antichrist was nothing but hearsay. Comparing Scripture with Scripture, we learn two things. First, Jesus said that before the Destruction of Jerusalem "Abomination of Desolation" there would come many who would say, "I am the Christ." Jesus warned those of pre-70 A.D., "Many will say to you, 'Look, here is The Christ!'" (Mt 24:5). Further He states, "For false Christ and false prophets will arise and show great signs and wonders,

to deceive if possible, even the elect" (24:23-24). The key to this passage which parallels with what John said about hearing of a coming Antichrist is what Jesus said in Matthew 24:25, "See I told you beforehand." It is clear that John's disciples knew what Jesus said about a false Christ coming before 70 A.D. 70 A.D. was not far from John's writing during the reign of Nero, thus the Apostle says, "Little Children, it is the last hour" (1Jn 2:18a.) He continues, "As you have heard." The question is, "Who did they hear and what did they hear?" Obviously they heard what Jesus said in Matthew 24, 5 and 23-25. They heard that false christs would come, and they would understand what Jesus meant in 70 A.D. when it happened because He "Told them beforehand." Thus John said, "This is the last hour." It was not the end of the world, but it was the last hour for the Jewish world. John gave proof to the veracity of what Jesus said, " EVEN NOW many antichrists (plural) have come, this is how we know it is the last hour" (I1Jn 2:18). Indeed, the Christian world prior to 70 A.D. was filled with false christs. It may be acceptable to call false Christ's as antichrists, but John made it perfectly clear that they were not looking for ONE particular Antichrist. Somehow they misinterpreted what Jesus said about "false Christ's" in the plural, and misconstrued it to be ONE big, bad antichrist. It would be just as unscriptural to do such a thing today as it was then. I personally wish there was only ONE antichrist; it sure would make my warfare on false doctrine a whole lot easier. True, "The man of sin" has the nature of antichrist, but he does not profess to be Antichrist, and he also is one of many who vie with Christ for dominion, power, and authority. The indisputable fact is that John connected an antichrist attitude with the Fourth Kingdom, Rome. We can affix numerically the number of the name of several Roman antichrists, and their successors in both the political and religious realms.

12. Robert Young, 1865, p. 179.

13. Steve Gregg, 1997, p. 18. Four Views of Revelation

14. Gregg, 1997, p. 18.

15. http://bibleworld.com/domper.pdf

16. Antiquities 18:2, 10, 19:1-11 Suetonius, "Lives of 12 Caesars," Dio Cassius Rom. Hist. 5.

17. Roberts, Alexander et al., eds., "Clement of Alexandria: Miscellanies (Stro-

mateis)," in Ante-Nicene Apostolic Fathers of the Second Century (vol. 2 of Ante-Nicene Fathers of the Second Century. Edinburgh: Christian Literature Publishing, 1885), 7:17.

18. Heresies 51:12, 33.

19. Greg Bahnsen, 1989, 259.

20. Ibid. 260.

21. Ibid. 260.

22. Charles Scofield, 1945, pp. 976-977.

23. John Bright, 1980, 7. Steve Gregg op.cit.

24. The Incredible Cover-Up, Dave MacPherson, Omega Pub. –Amazon.

25. Ibid. 10.

26. Ibid. 11.

27. Ibid. 14.

28. Ibid 116.

29. Ibid. 18.

30. Ibid. 18.

31. Ibid. 20-21.

32. Ibid. 22.

33. G.S. Hitchcock "The Beasts and the Little Horn", Present Truth Magazine, Art. 6, Vol. 4

34. Dave MacPherson, 1975, pp. 30-31.

35. Ibid. 32.

36. Ibid. 37.

37. Ibid. 39.

38. Ibid. 53.

39. Ibid. 57.

40. Ibid 75.

41. Ibid. 85.

42. House Divided: The Breakup of Dispensational Theology- Greg L. Bahnsen, Kenneth L. Gentry, Amazon (see introduction to the book).

43. http://www.cs.unc.edu/~plaisted/estimates.html

44. Tertullian, Prescription against Heretics Chap. 36 "Apostolic Churches-The Voice of the Apostles".

45. (Precept Austin) Henry Dean Alford, Commentary on Entire New Testament "The New Testament for the English Reader", p. 947.

46. More Than Conquerors, William Hendrickson, Baker Books, 1940, Grand Rapids, p.70. Excellent, additional comments p. 263, "Only a confirmed futurist, unschooled in the original languages, will attempt to do this (embrace the notion that John was transported in spirit to the day of the Lord's second coming) which is silly". See also W. Scotts, "The Lord's Day". New Testament Studies, Vol. 12, 1965, pp. 74-75. Also Ignatius' Letter to the Magnesian's, and The Didache, p. 14 www.earlychristianwritings.com.

47. Studies in The Revelation of St. John, Albertus Pieters, Wm. B. Eerdmans Pub. Co., Grand Rapids, MI, pp. 86-87.

48. Clement, I Corinthian Letter, ch. 42 "Order of Ministers", New Advent.org

49. Polycarp's Epistle to the Philippians, chs. 5,6, A translation by Rick Brahnan, www.supakoo.com

50. Ignatius to the Smyrnaeans, translated by Charles Hoole, ch. 8:2 www.earlychristian writings.com

51. Epistle to the Magnesian's, translated by Lightfoot & Hammer, 1891, www.earlychristianwirtings.com

52. Epistle to the Smyrnaeans, Chap. 9 op. cit.

53. Epistles to Magnesian's, Chap. 7 op. cit.

54. Ignatius, Letter to the Trallians, Chap. 3, translated by Lightfoot and Hammer, www.earlychristianwritings.com

55. Ignatius, Letter to the Trallians, Chap.3 ibid

56. From the Codex of Emperor Justinian, March 533 A.D. Written to Arch Bishop John of Rome, www.moellerhaus.com

57. According to the Codex Alexandrinus (A), Codex Vaticanus, Codex Ephraemi (C), as well as Arethas, the original Greek text of the oldest manuscripts uses singular "body" instead of "bodies", plural, then switches to the plural "bodies" in verse 9. This plural versus singular ambiguity is reinforced in Rev 11:5 where the oldest Greek manuscripts uses the term "mouth" in the singular instead of "mouths" plural. Assuming that there was a mistake in the original manuscripts, modern translators are almost unanimous in translating it "bodies" in the plural. We have no problem that these witnesses (Gospel evangelists) had ONE voice and died ONE common death. We have no problem with the fact that the husband and wife are ONE flesh. Do we think the oldest manuscripts are in error? Or do we understand the apocalyptic message of the evangelistic witnesses? Although they may both die as two individuals, yet they are one in their lifetime of preaching One Body, One Spirit, One hope of the calling, One Lord, One faith, One immersion, One God and Father (Eph 4:4-6). There is a seven-fold perfection of ONENESS here. Some Bible translations have "Their dead body" in the footnotes or reference columns.

58. http://archive.constantcontact.com/fs086/1103027403968/archive/110536 1364045.html

59. See Front Page story by Sharon Dale Schantz, The restoration Herald, Jan 2010 edition. See also Jeff Wickert "Authorized Congregational Polity", Dean Mills "Unity on the Kings Highway", Mike Pemberton articles on the "Role of the Evangelist", and lately George Faul and Jack Cottrell who have embraced the role the evangelist has as a Christ gift to the congregation. More and more of today's Restoration leaders are seeing why Christ gave evangelists to His congregation (Eph 4:11). Doug Hardman lectures frequently, and accurately on this subject.

60. The October Horse: A Novel of Caesar and Cleopatra, Colleen McCullough on Caesar's Godhead, Simon and Schuster

61. William Grassie "Hermeneutics and Science" (edited by j. Wentzel Van Huyssteen (Maximillian 2003).

62. See Speculum Cambridge Journals, Medieval Academy of America, Wikipedia.

63. http://www.worldcat.org/title/rice-haggard-the-american-frontier-evangelist-who-revived-the-name-christian/oclc/3452982

64. See Wikipedia.org. Solon's travels finally brought him to Sardis, capital of Lydia. According to Herodotus and Plutarch, he met with Croesus and gave the Lydian king advice, which however Croesus failed to appreciate until it was too late. Croesus had considered himself to be the happiest man alive and Solon had advised him, "Count no man happy until he be dead." The reasoning was that at any minute, fortune might turn on even the happiest man and make his life miserable. It was only after he had lost his kingdom to the Persian king Cyrus, while awaiting execution, that Croesus acknowledged the wisdom of Solon's advice.[26][27]

65. See Wikipedia "Hippolytus", pp. 170-235. History records his death as a martyr (perhaps by his body, tied to two horses, being pulled asunder). His career began as a Presbyter (Elder). Ironically it was not until 1300 years later that he was identified as a Bishop and saint by Pious 1V (Giovanna Medici). As noted through my book, I refer again and again to the hatred the church had toward the Christ given work, and death of the New Testament evangelist, and local elders-presbyters. It is hard to trace in history just when this death occurred and who may have been some of the last, well known evangelists. Catholic historians obscure the subject so badly, that when they finish muddying the water it is almost impossible to find where the work of the evangelist left off, (2 Ti 4:5) and the dictatorial bishop took over in the local church and later the ecclesial hierarchy. I am led to believe that Hippolytus just may have been one of those Christ loving evangels (or preaching elder – 1Ti 5:17) who was so hated by the Roman Church, that like Roger Williams, he was persecuted and banished at first, and then made a celebrity later. So, the words of Jesus to the Jewish Clergy come to mind, "You erect monuments to the prophets, and it is your ancestors who killed them" (Lk 11:47), and He did not consider it to rash to accuse them of the same

thing. Convictions held by Hippolytus early in his career incurred the hatred of Rome, these being he was anti-pope, anti-ecclesiastical and was far from being what the catholic theology would love to consider as being a "BISHOP". In their zeal to form an unbroken hierarchy from Peter down through the ages, both the Roman and Greek denominations desire to claim men like Justin Martyr, Hegesippus and Hippolytus as part of their fraternizing line. Hippolytus certainly was not a "Presiding Elder", as would be, say Diotrephes (3Jn 9-11), but he was a dynamic Bible Scholar (especially of prophecy), and a great teacher of Christ. Hippolytus especially loved the prophecies of Daniel. If these men were alive today and preached the way they did in their former lives, both the Roman and Greek Catholic would kill them again.

66. www.teknia.com

67. An excellent exegesis of the word "luo" is given by Timothy Rowe – "To break what is compacted together, dissolve, sever, demolish as Christ 'Loosed us from the works of the Devil'." The Magnificent Goodness of God and How it Will Transform Your Life", p. 303, books.google.com

68. https://en.wikipedia.org/wiki/Hades

69. https://en.wikipedia.org/wiki/Star_and_crescent and http://islam.about.com/od/history/a/crescent_moon.htm

70. See syllabus by your author, "Angels, Demons and Satan", published by Christian Kingdom College. Throughout this work the author contends that before the Godhead created our present cosmological universe a pre-cosmic world existed in eternity past. It is believed that the Genesis record of the BEGINNING comprises the sudden, abrupt appearance of the visible universe of time, space and matter. This involved the inception of time and matter but because of the disorder of sin, it led to dissipation, entropy, the Second Law and death. All things were created whole with light bearing celestial stars and fruitful maturity and constant, inherent life giving terrestrial properties. But as the Angels sinned and brought death to the pre-cosmic angelic universe, so Adam sinned and brought death to the cosmic universe of human kind and nations. It is a Scriptural deduction and more than logical to conclude that in the spiritual "or apocalyptic universe" prior to the creation of this visible universe that the eternal Godhead existed along with especially created creatures (cherubim, seraphim and myriad angelic beings) in spiritual form outside of time and modern day laws governing physics.

71. See syllabus by your author, "Pneumatology", ibid. See also, a collaborative effort by John and Charles Doughty on the extreme importance of having at least an elementary understanding of the meaning of BIBLICAL PROPITIATION. John Doughty has published a small booklet on this subject. See, John Doughty, Bridgewater Va. Your author addresses the significance of PROPITIATION in connection with God's hatred of sodomy. See "Crucified in Sodom", Christian Kingdom College.

72. In an article, "Why Patrick Buchanan Loves Vladimir Putin" (The Daily Beast, Dec. 2013 AD) Caitlin Dickson reports that Buchanan considers Putin a "Paleoconservative".

73. John Wycliffe's Translation of the Bible was condemned and banned at The Council of Constance, May 4, 1415 A.D. On July 6 (same year) Wycliffe's companion, in the Restoration of Biblical teachings, John Huss was burned at the stake. The Roman Apostasy could not capture Wycliffe in his life, but in 1428, Pope Martin V exercised a very brave course of action. He commanded a posthumous exhuming of Wycliffe's corpse, burned it to ashes and threw them into the River Swift that flows through Lutterworth, England. This was not an isolated act of some mad man; this was an official decree of the Roman Denomination.

74. In their work on this verse, The Jameson, Fausset and Brown Commentary cites the earliest manuscripts along with the Syriac and Coptic Versions as the Two Witnesses having ONE body in death and burial. Almost all of our modern translations gloss over the "ONE BODY" understanding as if the earlier translations were in error or a copyist mistake. J F & B indicate that it is like a synecdoche … that is, the enemies were not just killing bodies but the TRUTH of the message both were declaring.

75. http://www.therestorationmovement.com/_states/kentucky/smith,john.htm

76. Genesis Flood, Baker Book House, Grand Rapids MI, CW. 1976

77. William Hendriksen, "More Than Conquerors", Baker Book House, Grand rapids, MI. p. 164

78. "Synonyms of the New Testament," Richard C. Trench, Amazon, (See "Moderation").

79. Life OF Luther by Michelt, p. 262, See Google.

80. http://biblehub.com/library/neander/light_in_the_dark_places/epiphanius_of_pavia.htm

81. http://www.fsmitha.com/h3/islam02.htm

82. http://www.catholic.org/encyclopedia/view.php?id=6158

83. http://www.catholic.org/clife/lcolors.php

84. See biblelight.net, Vicarius Filii Dei, 666

85. http://1400years.org/MassoudAnsari/PshychologyOfMohammad.pdf , pp. 13-15-It is quite obvious that Mohammed learned by word of mouth from those who had a very low view of the eternal Christ.

86. "The Plain Truth about Armstrongism", see Chapter on "Phonology", Baker Book House, www.amazon.com.

87. http://bibles.wikidot.com/nash

88. Benedict X111 in his indiction for a Jubilee, 1725 A.D. Book of Rev., www.adishakti.org. Also, on Revelation 17:5 "Gill's Commentary on the Entire Bible". Joseph Scaliger (late 16th. Century) affirms that he saw in Rome, on the Pope's MITRE the inscription "MYSTERY". Gill argues that Pope Julius had the inscription removed when Protestants used this as an argument. See Gill's Commentary under Revelation 17:5. See Pope Julius 111 under "Removing The Name MYSTERY from his MITRE".

89. Dante equated the Papacy (and simony) with the whore on the seven hills "elevations", see en.wikipedia.org "Whore of Babylon". Chrysostom (349-407) in his "Homily on 2 Thess. 2:6-9", writes, "The Pope who calls himself 'King', and 'Pontific Maximus' is Caesar's successor", Adolph Harnack, "What is Christianity?" pp. 269-270. See: https://theantipaschronicles.wordpress.com. We see in Dante and Chrysostom a residue of the evangelistic spirit to "reprove, rebuke and exhort, with longsuffering and doctrine. When we ask, "Whatever happened to the New Testament Evangelist?" It is a far cry from the Timothy-Titus evangelistic epistles, but perhaps Dante and Chrysostom come close.

90. http://www.friesian.com/popes.htm

91. http://moellerhaus.com/studies/JUS533.HTM

92. www.reformation.org.

93. https://en.wikipedia.org/wiki/Pope_Celestine_I

94. See Church of Mary in www.google.com.

95. See www.aconquoringfaith.net, on the meaning of the word, baptism.

96. See www.earthage.org, for why the word baptidzo was not translated.

97. See booksgoogle.com, "The English Bible Translation History," by Dr. John C. Grieder

98. www.therealchurch.com

99. See Hobbes from Leviathan, "The Comparison of the Catholic Church and The Kingdom of The Fairies", www.m14m.net

100. Holy Roman Empire, en.wikipedia.org under Voltaire

101. https://en.wikipedia.org/wiki/Arian_controversy

102. http://stottilien.com/2012/05/12/heretic-docetism-and-christian-views-of-jesus/

103. Arianism, www.newworldencyclopadia.org and Emperor Constantine 325.

104. http://www.ccel.org/a/schaff/history/2_ch13.htm

105. https://en.wikipedia.org/wiki/Vicar_of_Christ

106. See "What the Bible Says About End Times" by Russell Boatman http://www.barnesandnoble.com/c/russell-boatman

107. See an excellent commentary on 1st and 2nd Thessalonians by Wilber Fields (1st Thess. Chapter 4) http://www.barnesandnoble.com/c/wilbur-fields

108. https://en.wikipedia.org/wiki/Investigative_judgment

109. https://en.wikipedia.org/wiki/Antiochus_IV_Epiphanes

110. http://www.azquotes.com/quote/880343

111. Russell Boatman ibid

112. http://doctrine.org/the-day-of-christ/

113. Voice of the Martyrs http://www.persecution.com/

114. https://en.wiktionary.org/wiki/%E1%BC%80%CF%81%CF%87%CE%AE

115. https://en.wikipedia.org/wiki/Diocese#History

116. http://forums.catholic.com/showthread.php?t=977645

117. https://en.wikipedia.org/wiki/Veneration_of_the_dead

118. http://christianity.stackexchange.com/questions/18053/what-is-the-reasoning-for-latin-being-the-official-language-of-catholic-mass

119. http://w2.vatican.va/content/paul-vi/en/encyclicals/documents/hf_p-vi_enc_24061967_sacerdotalis.html

120. https://en.wikipedia.org/wiki/Clerical_celibacy#Background

121. https://en.wikipedia.org/wiki/Rosary

122. http://classroom.synonym.com/difference-between-rosary-islamic-prayer-beads-5660.html

123. http://www.ewtn.com/faith/teachings/chura4.htm

124. http://babylonmysteryreligion.com/motherandchild.htm

125. http://origin-dictionary.reference.com/browse/Nun

126. http://www.catholictradition.org/Tradition/tridentine-creed.htm

127. http://www.theguardian.com/world/2015/aug/28/pope-francis-sends-letter-praising-gay-childrens-book

128. https://en.wikipedia.org/wiki/Roman_Catholic_Mariology

129. George Peter Holford believed that these prophecies made by The Lord were the greatest proof that Jesus Christ was the divine Son of God. Messiah means "Anointed", and Prophets, Priests and Kings were the anointed ones. As Melchizedek, "Prince of Peace-Salem", Christ is forever a High Priest. As the only King immortal, King of Kings and Lord of Lords, Christ is above all. But we somehow forget that He was also The Prophet that we should hear, and if we fail to hear Him we shall be cut off from life and people. Looking at the long term prophecies of the Destruction of Jerusalem as given by the Prophet Daniel, and later confirmed unto us by The Prophet Jesus (just forty years before fulfillment) proves beyond all shadow of doubt that Jesus Christ is the very Son of the living God. The Prophet Daniel said the Messiah would come in the middle of the last week and make atonement on the altar, thus make the sacrifice to end all sacrifice. After that, Daniel said "The end would come like a flood", with "abomination" profanation of the sacred religion and afterwards, a complete end "desolation". Thus, it was given to the Son of God to prophecy in minute, accurate, detail this Abomination of Desolation that shook the world in 70 A.D. Once more, the Lord Jesus Christ will shake the world directly, again.

130. Send requests to church of Christ at Mountain View, or order from genesis.jd@gmail.com

(See www.plim.org/1Allah: "Is the Word Allah Similar to Elohim?" www.wikipedia.org/wiki/Allah: Allah; www.bible.ca/islam/islam-allah-pre-islamic-origin: The pagan origin of the word, "Allah". Islam is paganism...; www.christriananswers.net/q-eden/allah: "Allah"?; www.ukapologetics.net/el: Where Does Elohim Come From?.)

131. The Columbian Class Book-Geographical-Historical Data, book.google.com, Subject "Jerusalem", paragraph 43, p. 225, Abraham T. Lowe

132. William G. Thomas, en.wikipedia.org

133. "Outline of History" en.wikipedia.org

134. Craig R. Ioster, 2001, p. 24-26 "Revelation and the End of all Things" William B. Erdmans Pub Co.

135. "Titus reportedly, refused to accept from The Senate a wreath of victory, as he realized he had not won the victory on his own, but had been the vehicle through which their God had manifest His wrath against His people". See Titus, under "Siege of Jerusalem" en.wikipedia.org. Also "Philostratus-The Life of Apollonius of Tyma", 6.29

136. "The A.B.C.s of Prophetical Scripture, George H. Clement, Broadman Press, Nashville Tenn., p. 44

137. Ibid, p. 45

138. https://en.wikipedia.org/wiki/Theophilus_of_Antioch

139. Another use of Biblical parallelism, personification (as well as a dual prophecy) is found in Isaiah 7:11-14). Through the word of Isaiah, God challenged the wicked King Ahaz to ask him for a sign. Obviously, because he did not want such an intimate relationship with His God, Ahaz begged the issue and lied, "I will not ask, neither will I tempt the Lord" (7:12). God knew Ahaz was acting the part of a wimpy coward who did not desire the kind of courage that comes from being intimate with a mighty God, and he asks, "It is a small thing for you to weary men (wear them out by foolhardy arguments), but will you weary my God also?" (7:13).

At this point, the very famous prophecy is given in Isaiah 7:14,

> "Therefore, the Lord himself shall give you a sign; Behold a virgin shall conceive, and bear a son, shall call His name Immanuel 'God with us!'"

Here we see that a virgin shall conceive. The word is "almah", (meaning a lassie, kept out of sight or concealed-5959). This prophecy was fulfilled shortly in the birth of Isaiah's son (8:1-3). Isaiah's son was not born to a virgin, but the birth of his son was a not a very pleasant SIGN to the unbelieving Ahaz. The boy's name "mahershalalhashbaz" (longest Bible word) meant "Speedy is the prey" which prophecy was fulfilled by the King of Assyria (in whom Ahaz trusted) who sent his armies to invade the surrounding countries and overflow Judea (8:7-9).

Thus the SIGN of Isaiah 7:14 was fulfilled in the near future through the natural birth of Mahershalalalhashbaz. It is a dual prophecy, because it was fulfilled also in the distant future through the supernatural birth of our Lord, Jesus Christ (Mt.1:22-23). (www.jesuswalk.com "Dual Prophecies").

So we return to the three Hermeneutical principles in this text (Isa 7:11-17: 8:1-11) that compare to the King of Babylon and Lucifer (Is 14:4;12-22). 1) Personification- by exhibiting the evil qualities of the Spirit of Lucifer in human form, the King of Babylon personifies Lucifer. Likewise, Mahershalalhashbaz as a very young child (7:15-16; 8:4) personifies and exhibits the innocent qualities of the sinless Son of God. 2) Parallelism- The fall of Lucifer into apostasy parallels the fall of the King of Babylon into apostasy, and the birth of Mahershalalhashbaz parallels the apostasy and fall of Israel and Judah. But the birth of Immanuel is a SIGN that even when times (like those of Lucifer, the King of Babylon or Ahaz) appear to be evil, "Immanuel" (8:8) still means that "God is with us" (8:10). 3) Dual prophecy-Both the King of Babylon and Satan were overthrown and suffered great loss. Thus, the natural birth of Mahershalalhashbaz announced the quick overthrow of surrounding nations Damascus and Samaria (and a great threat to wicked King Ahaz), and the Virgin Birth of Immanuel announced to the world that the King, Jesus Christ will rule forever, and His reign is a threat to the rule of Satan and portends the complete overthrow of his evil empire.

www.ingramcontent.com/pod-product-compliance
Lightning Source LLC
Chambersburg PA
CBHW071112080526
44587CB00013B/1314